Mobil 1999
TRAVEL GUIDE®

Southeast

ALABAMA • FLORIDA • GEORGIA • KENTUCKY MISSISSIPPI • TENNESSEE

Fodor's Travel Publications, Inc.

Guide Staff
General Manager: Diane E. Connolly
Editorial/Inspection Coordinator: Doug Weinstein
Inspection Assistant: Brenda Piszczek
Editorial Assistants: Sheila Connolly, Susanne Ochs, Julie Raio, Kathleen Rose,
   Elizabeth Schwar
Creative Director: Fabrizio La Rocca
Cover Design: Chermayeff & Geismar Inc.
Cover Photograph: Fred Hirschmann

917.3
M687se
1999

Acknowledgments

We gratefully acknowledge the help of our more than 100 field representatives for their efficient and perceptive inspection of every lodging and dining establishment listed; the establishments' proprietors for their cooperation in showing their facilities and providing information about them; the many users of previous editions of the *Mobil Travel Guide* who have taken the time to share their experiences; and for their time and information, the thousands of chambers of commerce, convention and visitors bureaus, city, state, and provincial tourism offices, and government agencies who assisted in our research.

Published in 1999 by Fodor's Travel Publications, Inc.
201 E. 50th St.
New York, NY 10022

Southeast
ISBN 0-679-00199-9
ISSN 1040-1067

Printed in the United States of America
10 9 8 7 6 5 4 3 2 1

Contents

Southeast

Maps

Larger, more detailed maps are available at many Mobil service stations

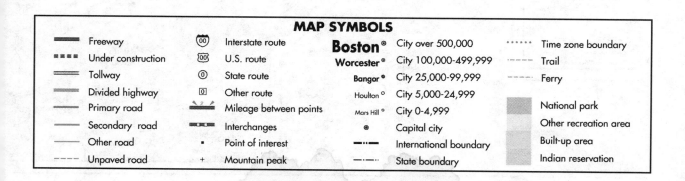

MAP SYMBOLS

Freeway	Interstate route	**Boston** ⊛ City over 500,000	Time zone boundary
Under construction	U.S. route	**Worcester** ⦾ City 100,000-499,999	Trail
Tollway	State route	**Bangor** ● City 25,000-99,999	Ferry
Divided highway	Other route	Houlton ○ City 5,000-24,999	
Primary road	Mileage between points	Mars Hill ○ City 0-4,999	National park
Secondary road	Interchanges	⊛ Capital city	Other recreation area
Other road	Point of interest	International boundary	Built-up area
Unpaved road	+ Mountain peak	State boundary	Indian reservation

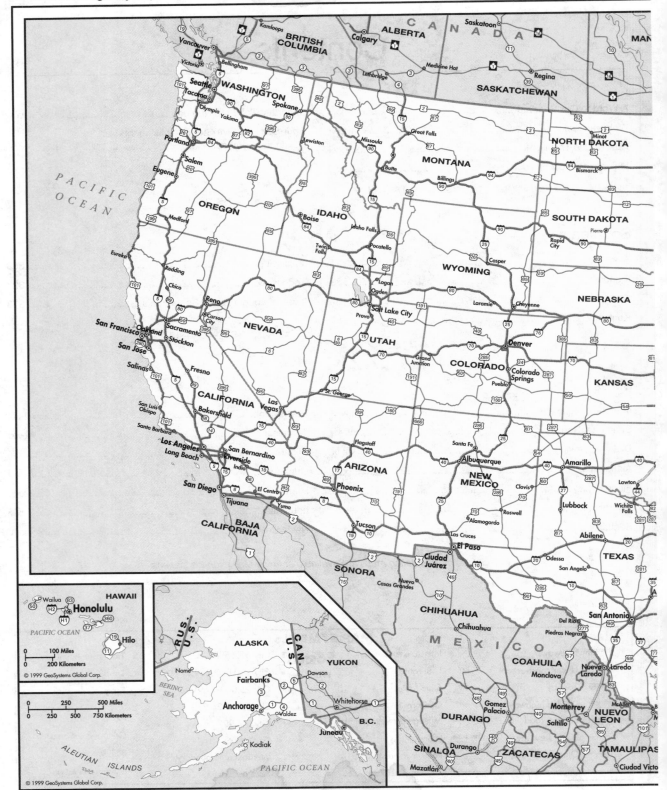

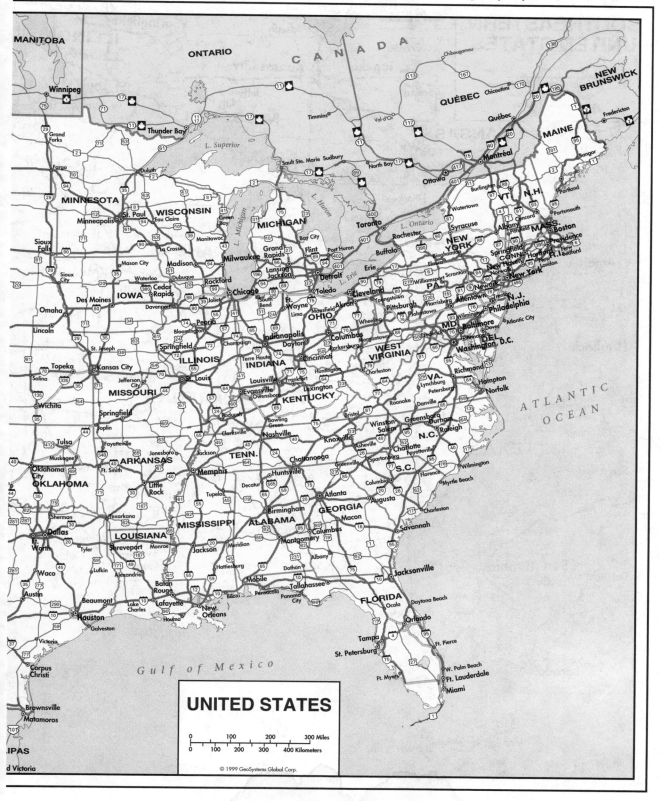

UNITED STATES

0 100 200 300 Miles

0 100 200 300 400 Kilometers

© 1999 GeoSystems Global Corp.

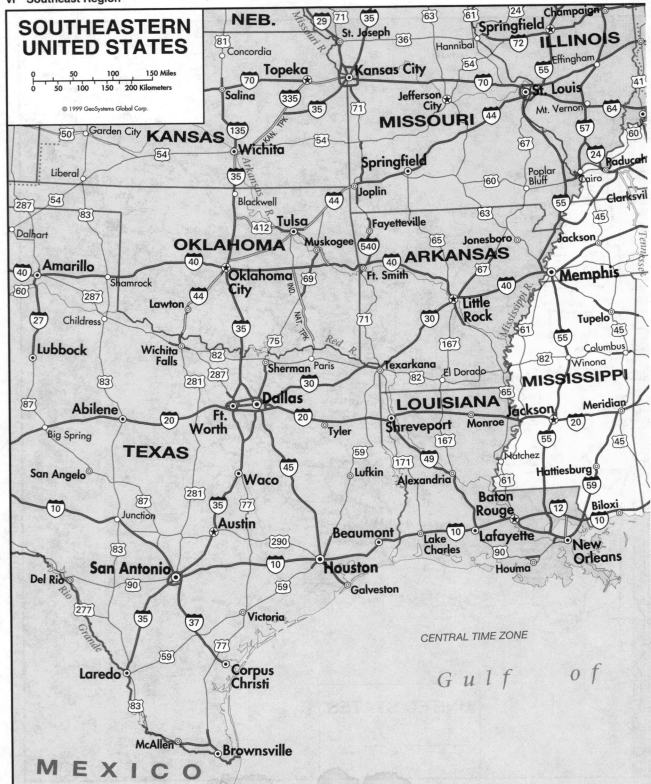

SOUTHEASTERN UNITED STATES

0   50   100   150 Miles
0 50 100 150 200 Kilometers

© 1999 GeoSystems Global Corp.

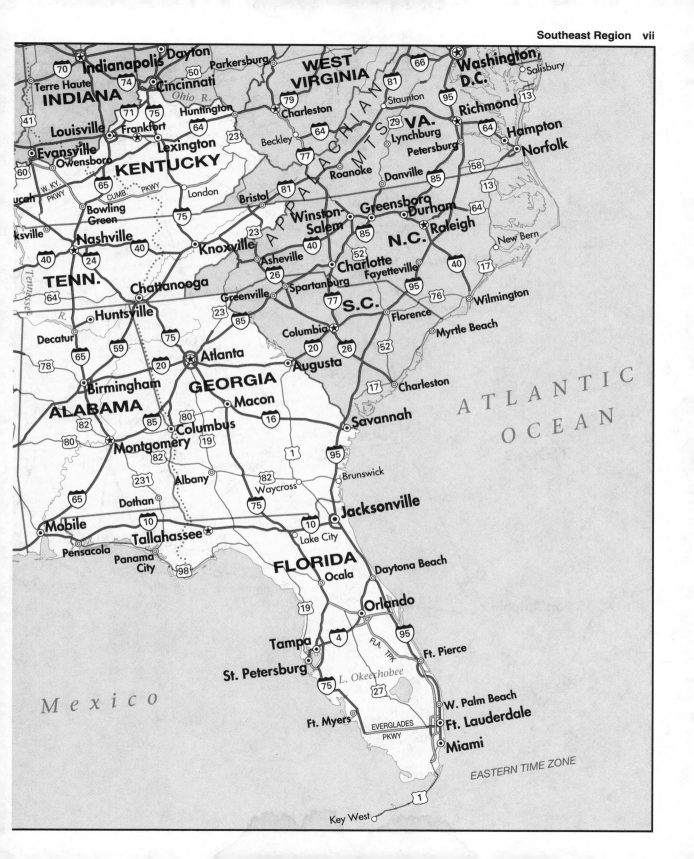

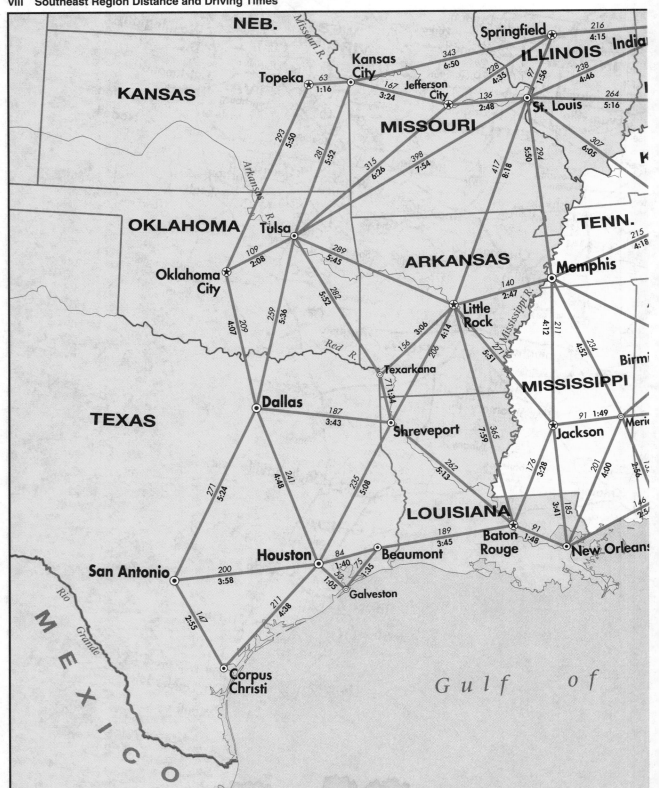

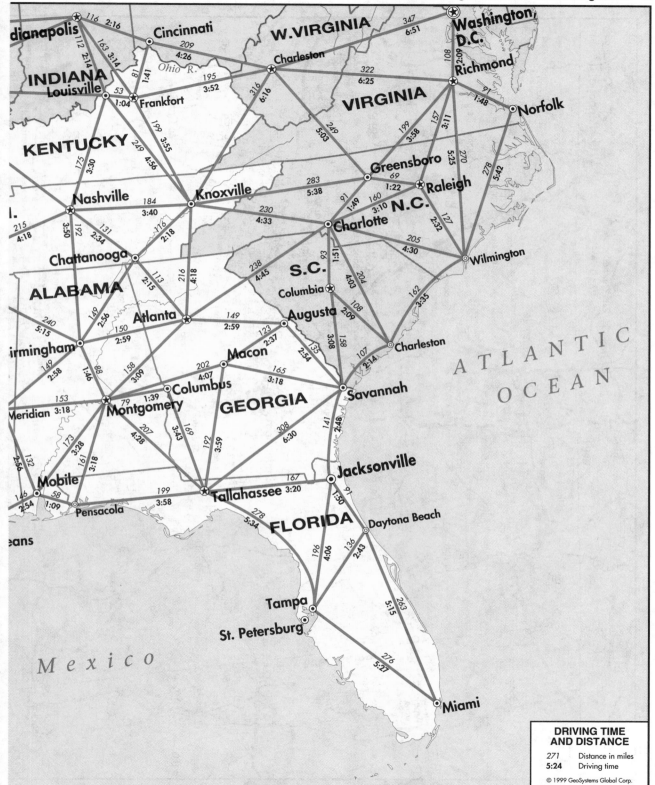

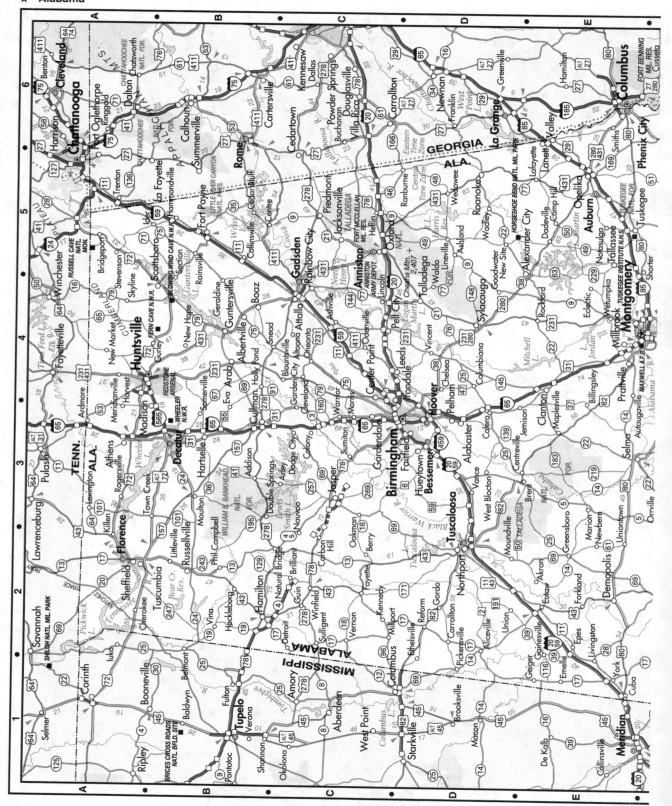

ALABAMA

© 1999 GeoSystems Global Corp.

Scale:
0 10 20 30 40 50 Miles
0 10 20 30 40 50 60 70 Kilometers

GA.
FLA.
FLORIDA
ALABAMA
GULF OF MEXICO

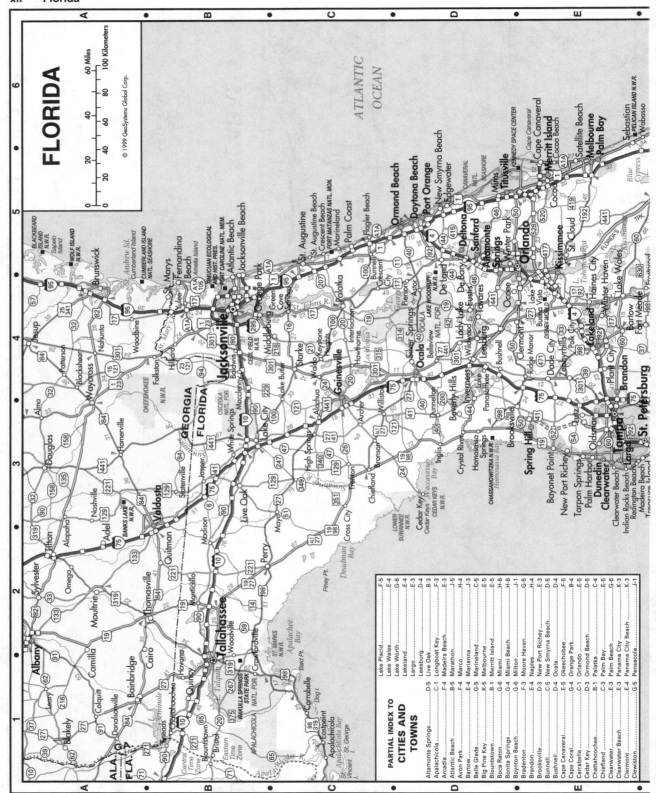

FLORIDA

© 1999 GeoSystems Global Corp.

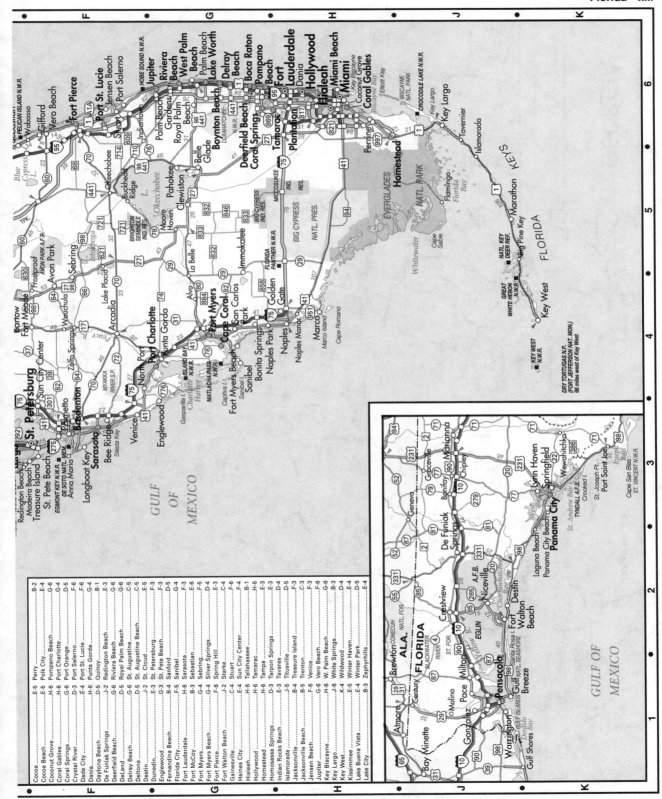

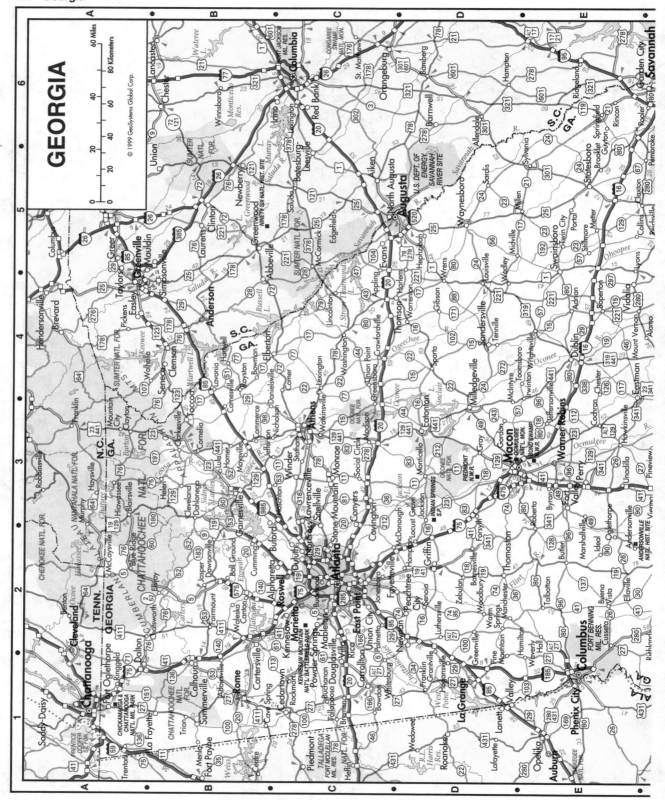

GEORGIA

© 1999 GeoSystems Global Corp.

60 Miles
80 Kilometers

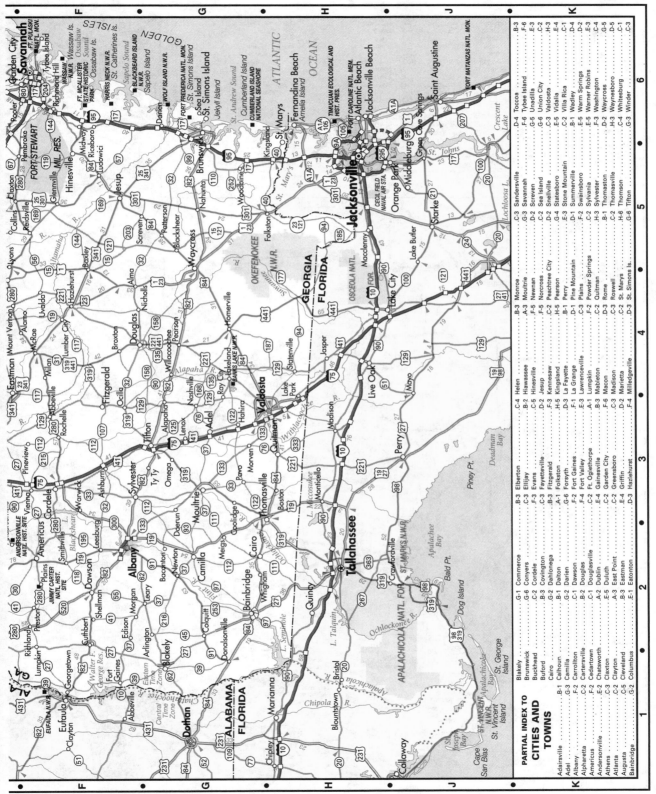

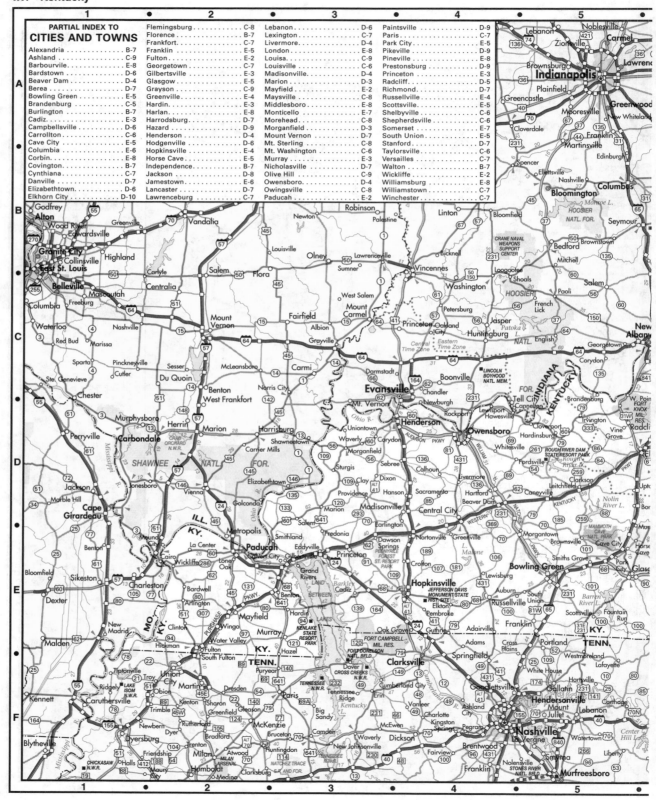

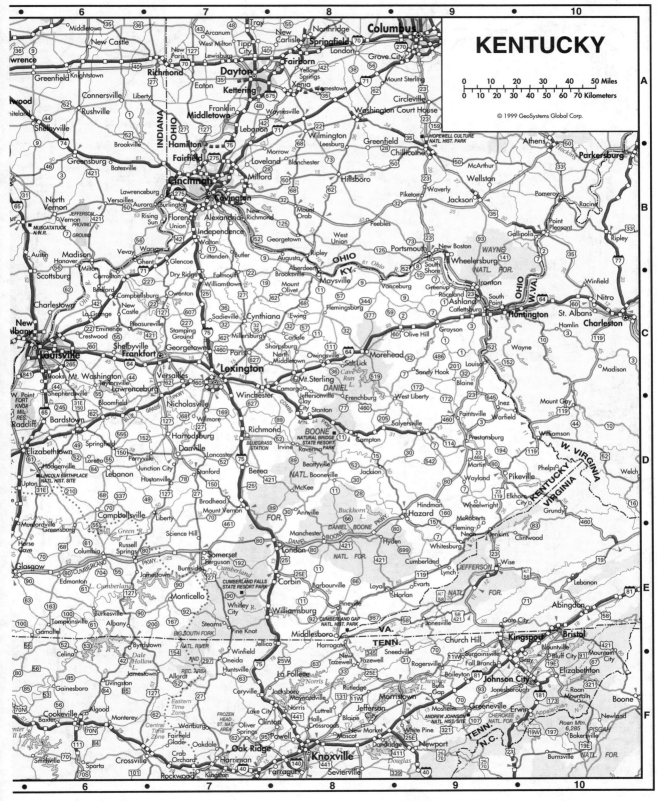

KENTUCKY

0   10   20   30   40   50 Miles

0 10 20 30 40 50 60 70 Kilometers

© 1999 GeoSystems Global Corp.

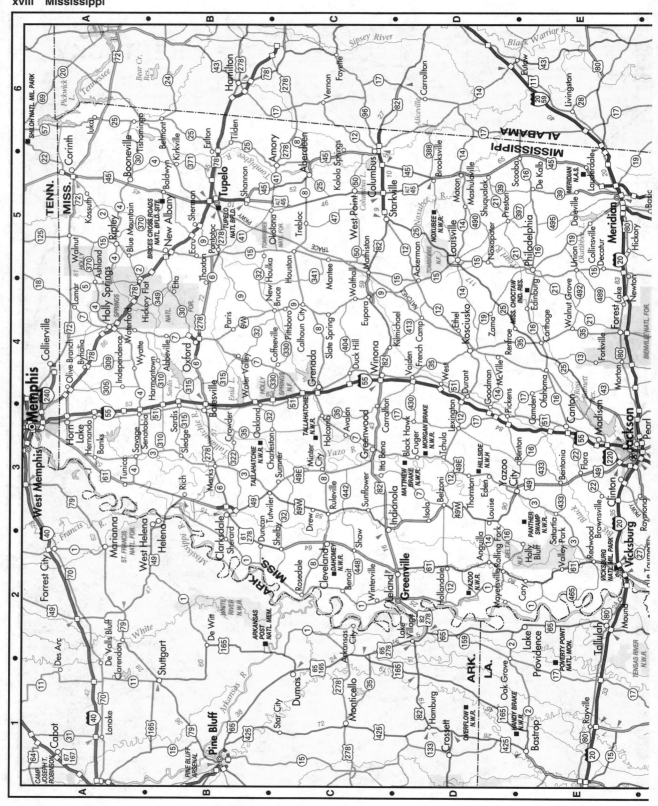

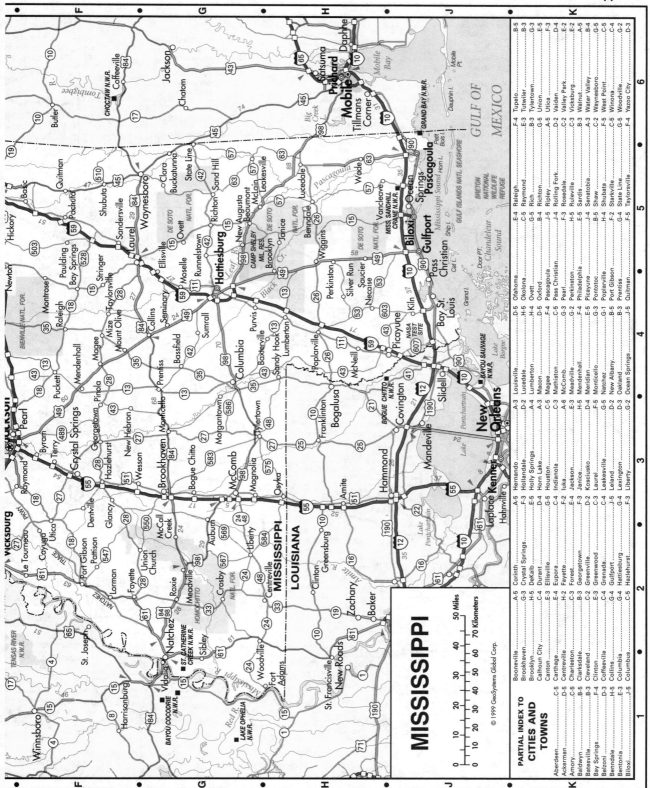

PARTIAL INDEX TO CITIES AND TOWNS

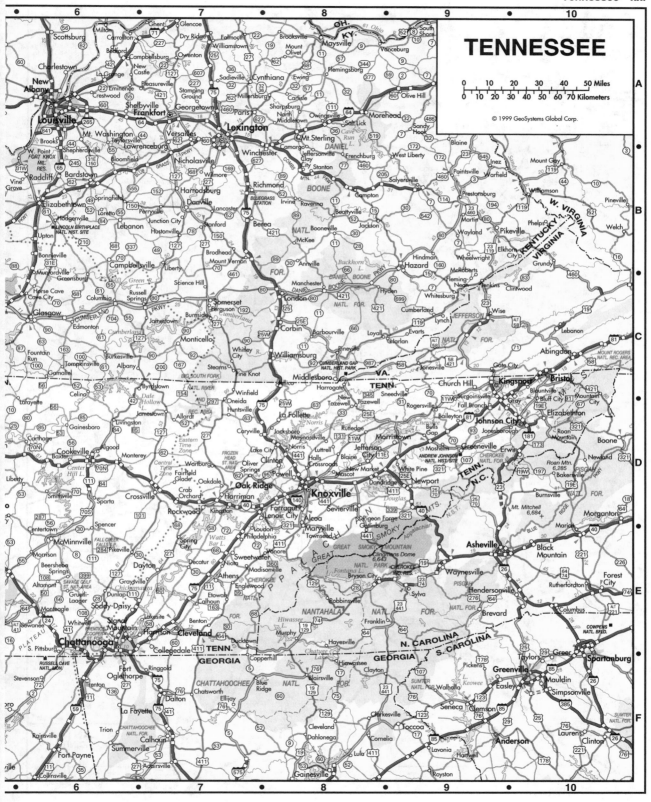

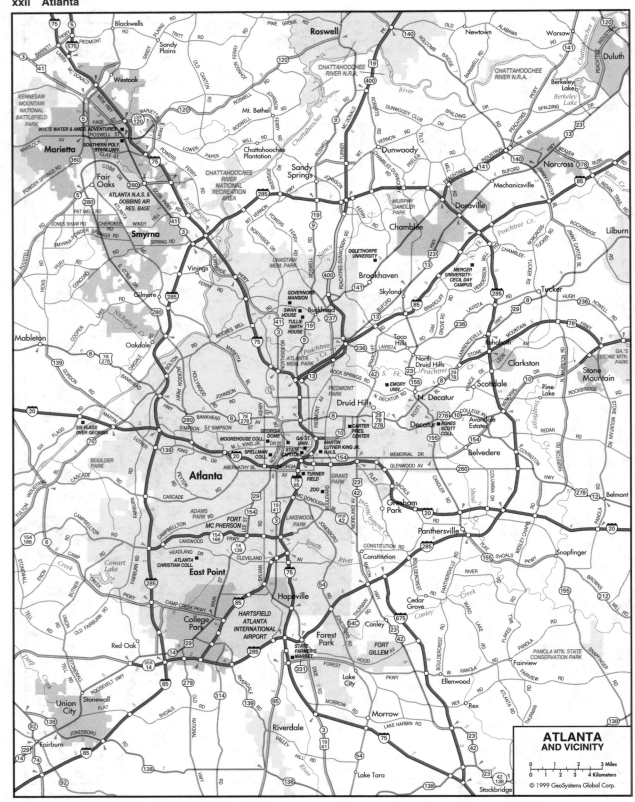

ATLANTA
AND VICINITY

© 1999 GeoSystems Global Corp.

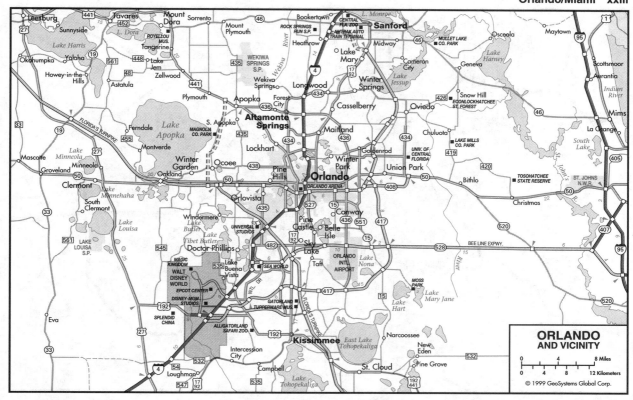

ORLANDO
AND VICINITY

0   4   8 Miles
0 4   8   12 Kilometers

© 1999 GeoSystems Global Corp.

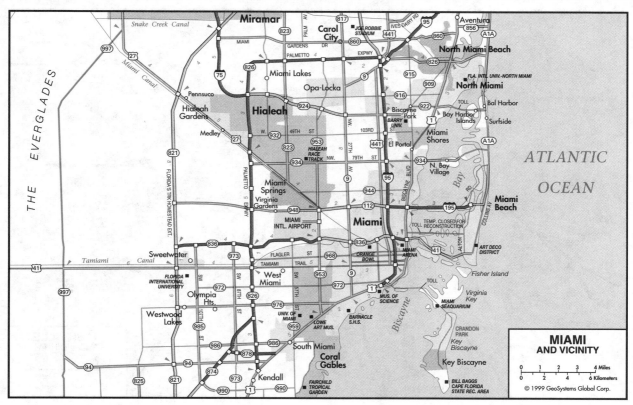

MIAMI
AND VICINITY

0   1   2   3   4 Miles
0   2   4   6 Kilometers

© 1999 GeoSystems Global Corp.

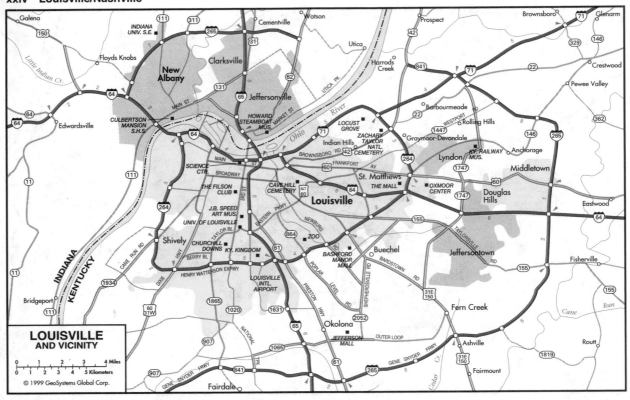

LOUISVILLE
AND VICINITY

0 1 2 3 4 Miles
0 1 2 3 4 5 Kilometers
© 1999 GeoSystems Global Corp.

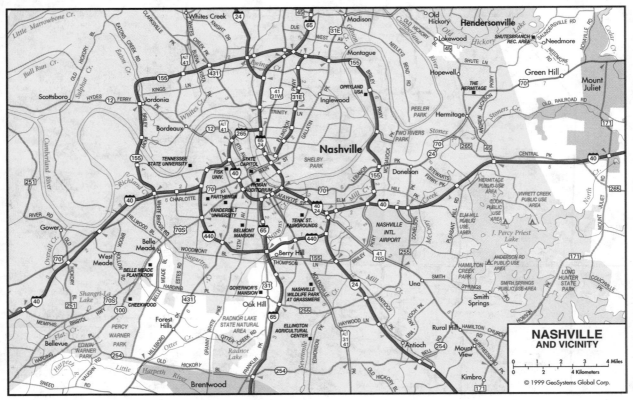

NASHVILLE
AND VICINITY

0   1   2   3   4 Miles
0   2   4 Kilometers
© 1999 GeoSystems Global Corp.

Travel first class.

Before a long trip,
it's always smart to stop at Mobil.

On its ten-year, billion-mile mission, the International Space Station won't make pit stops, and its air system can't ever break down. So the grease for its fans and motors isn't a detail. It had to pass nearly as many tests as astronauts do, and in the end a Mobil synthetic won the job. What excites us is that we didn't create this grease for outer space. You can buy the same stuff (Mobilith SHC® 220) for your bicycle, bus or paper mill. Which, to us, shows the value of how we do research, trying to make things better than necessary. Nobody asked us to develop synthetic lubes, but we pursued it because that's how real innovation works. You aim to exceed present-day expectations so that when the future arrives, you're already there. To learn more, visit www.mobil.com.

Mobil® The energy to make a difference.™

A Word to Our Readers

Whether you're going on an extended family vacation, a weekend getaway, or a business trip, you need good, solid information on where to stay and eat and what to see and do. It would be nice if you could take a corps of well-seasoned travelers with you to suggest lodgings and activities, or ask a local restaurant critic for advice on dining spots, but since these options are rarely practical, the *Mobil Travel Guide* is the next best thing. It puts a huge database of information at your disposal and provides the value judgments and advice you need to use that information to its fullest.

Published by Fodor's Travel Publications, Inc., in collaboration with Mobil Corporation, the sponsor since 1958, these books contain the most comprehensive, up-to-date information possible on each region. In fact, listings are revised and ratings reviewed annually, based on inspection reports from our field representatives, evaluation by senior staff, and comments from more than 100,000 readers. These incredible data are then used to develop the *Mobil Travel Guide*'s impartial quality ratings, indicated by stars, which Americans have trusted for decades.

Space limitations make it impossible for us to include every fine hotel and restaurant, so we have picked a representative group, all above-average for their type. There's no charge to any establishment for inclusion, and only places that meet our standards are chosen. Because travelers' needs differ, we make every effort to select a variety of establishments and provide the information to decide what's right for you. If you're looking for a lodging at a certain price or location, or even one that offers 24-hour room service, you'll find the answers you need at your fingertips. Take a minute to read the next section, How to Use This Book; it'll make finding the information you want a breeze.

Also look at Making the Most of Your Trip, the section that follows. It's full of tips from savvy travelers that can help you save money, stay safe, and get around more easily—the keys to making any trip a success.

Of course, the passage of time means that some establishments will close, change hands, remodel, improve, or go downhill. Though every effort has been made to ensure the accuracy of all information when it was printed, change is inevitable. Always call and confirm that a place is open and that it has the features you want. Whatever your experiences at any of the establishments we list—and we hope they're terrific—or if you have general comments about our guide, we'd love to hear from you. Use the convenient card near the end of this book, or drop us a line at the *Mobil Travel Guide*, 3225 Gallows Rd., Suite 7D 0407, Fairfax, VA 22037 or www.mobil.com/travel.

So pack this book in your suitcase or toss it next to you on the front seat. If it gets dog-eared, so much the better. We here at the *Mobil Travel Guide* wish you a safe and successful trip.

Bon voyage and happy driving,

THE EDITORS

Welcome

For over 40 years, the *Mobil Travel Guide* has provided travelers in North America with reliable advice on finding good value, quality service, and the attractions that give a destination its special character. During this time, our teams of culinary and hospitality experts have worked hard to develop objective and exacting standards. In so doing, they seek to fully meet the desires and expectations of a broad range of customers.

At Mobil, we demonstrate the energy to make a difference through a commitment to excellence that allows us to bring the best service and products to the people we serve. We believe that the ability to respond to and anticipate customers' needs is what distinguishes good companies from truly great ones.

It is our hope, whether your travels are for business or leisure, over a long distance or a short one, that this book will be your companion, dependably guiding you to quality and value in lodging and dining.

Finally, I ask that you help us improve the guides. Please take the time to fill out the customer feedback form at the back of this book or contact us on the Internet at www.mobil.com/travel.

Lucio Noto

Lucio A. Noto
Chairman and
Chief Executive Officer
Mobil Corporation

How to Use This Book

The *Mobil Travel Guide* is easy to use. Each state chapter begins with a general introduction that both provides a general geographical and historical orientation to the state and covers basic statewide tourist information, from state recreation areas to seat-belt laws. The balance of each chapter is devoted to the travel destinations within the state—cities and towns, state and national parks, and tourist regions—which, like the states themselves, are arranged alphabetically.

What follows is an explanation of the wealth of information you'll find within those travel destinations—information on the area, on things to see and do there, and on where to stay and eat.

Maps and Map Coordinates

The first thing you'll notice is that next to each destination is a set of map coordinates. These refer to the appropriate state map in the front of this book. In addition, there are maps of selected larger cities in the front section as well as maps of key neighborhoods within the sections on the cities themselves.

Destination Information

Because many travel destinations are so close to other cities and towns where visitors might find additional attractions, accommodations, and restaurants, cross-references to those places are included whenever possible. Also listed are addresses and phone numbers for travel-information resources—usually the local chamber of commerce or office of tourism—as well as pertinent vital statistics and a brief introduction to the area.

What to See and Do

More than 11,000 museums, art galleries, amusement parks, universities, historic sites and houses, plantations, churches, state parks, ski areas, and other attractions are described in the *Mobil Travel Guide*. A white star on a black background ★ signals that the attraction is one of the best in the state. Since municipal parks, public tennis courts, swimming pools, and small educational institutions are common to most towns, they are generally excluded.

Following the attraction's description are the months and days it's open, address/location and phone number, and admission costs (see the inside front cover for an explanation of the cost symbols). Note that directions are given from the center of the town under which the attraction is listed, which may not necessarily be the town in which the attraction is located. Zip codes are listed only if they differ from those given for the town.

Events

Events—categorized as annual, seasonal, or special—are highlighted. An annual event is one that's held every year for a period of usually no longer than a week to 10 days; festivals and fairs are typical entries. A seasonal event is one that may or may not be annual and that is held for a number of weeks or months in the year, such as horse racing, summer theater, concert or opera festivals, and professional sports. Special event listings occur infrequently and mark a certain date or event, such as a centennial or other commemorative celebration.

Major Cities

Additional information on airports and transportation, suburbs, and neighborhoods, including a list of restaurants by neighborhood, may be included for large cities.

Lodging and Restaurant Listings

ORGANIZATION

For both lodgings and restaurants, when a property is in a town that does not have its own heading, the listing appears under the town nearest its location with the address and town in parentheses immediately after the establishment name. In large cities, lodgings located within 5 miles of major, commercial airports are listed under a separate "Airport" heading, following the city listings.

LODGING CLASSIFICATIONS

Each property is classified by type according to the characteristics below. Because the following features and services are found at most motels, lodges, motor hotels, and hotels, they are not shown in those listings:

- Year-round operation with a single rate structure unless otherwise quoted
- European plan (meals not included in room rate)
- Bathroom with tub and/or shower in each room
- Air-conditioned/heated, often with individual room control
- Cots
- Daily maid service
- Phones in rooms
- Elevators

Motels and Lodges. Accommodations are in low-rise structures with rooms easily accessible to parking (usually free). Properties have outdoor room entry and small, functional lobbies. Service is often limited, and dining may not be offered in lower-rated motels and lodges. Shops and businesses are found only in higher-rated properties, as are bellhops, room service, and restaurants serving three meals daily.

Lodges differ from motels primarily in their emphasis on outdoor recreational activities and in location. They are often found in resort and rural areas rather than in major cities or along highways.

Motor Hotels. Offering the convenience of motels along with many of the features of hotels, motor hotels range from low-rise structures offering limited services to multistory buildings with a wide range of services and facilities. Multiple building entrances, elevators, inside hallways, and parking areas (generally free) near access doors are some of the features of a motor hotel. Lobbies offer sitting areas and 24-hour desk and switchboard services. Often bellhop and valet services as well as restaurants serving three meals a day are found. Expanded recreational facilities and more than one restaurant are available in higher-rated properties.

The distinction between motor hotels and hotels in metropolitan areas is minor.

Hotels. To be categorized as a hotel, an establishment must have most of the following facilities and services: multiple floors, a restaurant and/or coffee shop, elevators, room service, bellhops, a spacious lobby, and recreational facilities. In addition, the following features and services not shown in listings are also found:

- Valet service (one-day laundry/cleaning service)
- Room service during hours restaurant is open
- Bellhops
- Some oversize beds

Resorts. These specialize in stays of three days or more and usually offer American Plan and/or housekeeping accommodations. Their emphasis is on recreational facilities, and a social director is often available. Food services are of primary importance, and guests must be able to eat three meals a day on the premises, either in restaurants or by having access to an on-site grocery store and preparing their own meals.

Inns. Frequently thought of as a small hotel, an inn is a place of homelike comfort and warm hospitality. It is often a structure of historic significance, with an equally interesting setting. Meals are a special occasion, and refreshments are frequently served in late afternoon. Rooms are usually individually decorated, often with antiques or furnishings representative of the locale. Phones, bathrooms, and TVs may not be available in every room.

Guest Ranches. Like resorts, guest ranches specialize in stays of three days or more. Guest ranches also offer meal plans and extensive outdoor activities. Horseback riding is usually a feature; there are stables and trails on the ranch property, and trail rides and daily instruction are part of the program. Many guest ranches are working ranches, ranging from casual to rustic, and guests are encouraged to participate in ranch life. Eating is often family-style and may also include cookouts. Western saddles are assumed; phone ahead to inquire about English saddle availability.

Cottage Colonies. These are housekeeping cottages and cabins that are usually found in recreational areas. Any dining or recreational facilities are noted in our listing.

DINING CLASSIFICATIONS

Restaurants. Most dining establishments fall into this category. All have a full kitchen and offer table service and a complete menu. Parking on or near the premises, in a lot or garage, is assumed. When a property offers valet or other special parking features, or when only street parking is available, it is noted in the listing.

Unrated Dining Spots. These places, listed after Restaurants in many cities, are chosen for their unique atmosphere, specialized menu, or local flavor. They include delis, ice-cream parlors, cafeterias, tearooms, and pizzerias. Because they may not have a full kitchen or table service, they are not given a *Mobil Travel Guide* rating. Often they offer extraordinary value and quick service.

QUALITY RATINGS

The *Mobil Travel Guide* has been rating lodgings and restaurants on a national basis since the first edition was published in 1958. For years the guide was the only source of such ratings, and it remains among the few guidebooks to rate restaurants across the country.

All listed establishments were inspected by experienced field representatives or evaluated by a senior staff member. Ratings are based upon their detailed inspection reports of the individual properties, on written evaluations of staff members who stay and dine anonymously, and on an extensive review of comments from our readers.

You'll find a key to the rating categories, ★ through ★★★★★, on the inside front cover. All establishments in the book are recommended. Even a ★ place is above average, usually providing a basic, informal experience. Rating categories reflect both the features the property offers and its quality in relation to similar establishments.

For example, lodging ratings take into account the number and quality of facilities and services, the luxury of appointments, and the attitude and professionalism of staff and management. A ★ establishment provides a comfortable night's lodging. A ★★ property offers more than a facility that rates one star, and the decor is well planned and integrated. Establishments that rate ★★★ are professionally managed and staffed and often beautifully appointed; the lodging experience is truly excellent and the range of facilities is extensive. Properties that have been given ★★★★ not only offer many services but also have their own style and personality; they are luxurious, creatively decorated, and superbly maintained. The ★★★★★ properties are among the best in North America, superb in every respect and entirely memorable, year in and year out.

Restaurant evaluations reflect the quality of the food and the ingredients, preparation, and presentation as well as service levels and the property's decor and ambience. A restaurant that has fairly simple goals for menu and decor but that achieves those goals superbly might receive the same number of stars as a restaurant with somewhat loftier ambitions but whose execution falls somewhat short of the mark. In general, ★ indicates a restaurant that's a good choice in its area, usually fairly simple and perhaps catering to a clientele of locals and families; ★★ denotes restaurants that are more highly recommended in their area; ★★★ restaurants are of national caliber, with professional and attentive service and a skilled chef in the kitchen; ★★★★ reflects superb dining choices, where remarkable food is served in equally remarkable surroundings; and ★★★★★ represents that rarefied group of the best restaurants in the country, where in addition to near perfection in every detail, there's that special something extra that makes for an unforgettable dining experience.

A list of the four-star and five-star establishments in this region is located just before the state listings.

Each rating is reviewed annually and each establishment must work to maintain its rating (or improve it). Every effort is made to assure that ratings are fair and accurate; the designated ratings are published purely as an aid to travelers.

In general, properties that are very new or have recently undergone major management changes are considered difficult to assess fairly and are often listed without ratings.

Good Value Check Mark. In all locales, you'll find a wide range of lodging and dining establishments with a ✔ in front of a star rating. This indicates an unusually good value at economical prices as follows:

In Major Cities and Resort Areas

Lodging: average $105–$125 per night for singles; average $115–$140 per night for doubles

Restaurants: average $25 for a complete lunch; average $40 for a complete dinner, exclusive of beverages and gratuities

Local Area Listings

Lodging: average $50–$60 per night for singles; average $60–$75 per night for doubles

Restaurants: average $12 for a complete lunch; average $20 for a complete dinner, exclusive of beverages and gratuities

LODGINGS

Each listing gives the name, address, directions (when there is no street address), neighborhood and/or directions from downtown (in major cities), phone number (local and 800), fax number, number and type of rooms available, room rates, and seasons open (if not year-round). Also included are details on recreational and dining facilities on property or nearby, the presence of a luxury level, and credit-card information. A key to the symbols at the end of each listing is on the inside front cover. (Note that Mobil Corporation credit cards cannot be used for payment of meals and room charges.)

All prices quoted in the *Mobil Travel Guide* publications are expected to be in effect at the time of publication and during the entire year; however, prices cannot be guaranteed. In some localities there may be short-term price variations because of special events or holidays. Whenever possible, these price changes are noted. Certain resorts have complicated rate structures that vary with the time of year; always confirm listed rates when you make your plans.

RESTAURANTS

Each listing gives the name, address, directions (when there is no street address), neighborhood and/or directions from downtown (in major cities), phone number, hours and days of operation (if not open daily year-round), reservation policy, cuisine (if other than American), price range for each meal served, children's meals (if offered), specialties, and credit card information. Additionally, special features such as chef ownership, ambience, and entertainment are noted. By carefully reading the detailed restaurant information and comparing prices, you can easily determine whether the restaurant is formal and elegant or informal and comfortable for families.

TERMS AND ABBREVIATIONS IN LISTINGS

The following terms and abbreviations are used consistently throughout the listings:

A la carte entrees With a price, refers to the cost of entrees/main dishes only that are not accompanied by side dishes.

AP American plan (lodging plus all meals).

Bar Liquor, wine, and beer are served in a bar or cocktail lounge and usually with meals unless otherwise indicated (e.g., "wine, beer").

Business center The property has a designated area accessible to all guests with business services.

Business servs avail The property can perform/arrange at least two of the following services for a guest: audiovisual equipment rental, binding, computer rental, faxing, messenger services, modem availability, notary service, obtaining office supplies, photocopying, shipping, and typing.

Cable Standard cable service; "premium" indicates that HBO, Disney, Showtime, or similar services are available.

Ck-in, ck-out Check-in time, check-out time.

Coin lndry Self-service laundry.

Complete meal Soup and/or salad, entree, and dessert, plus nonalcoholic beverage.

Continental bkfst Usually coffee and a roll or doughnut.

Cr cds: A, American Express; C, Carte Blanche; D, Diners Club; DS, Discover; ER, en Route; JCB, Japanese Credit Bureau; MC, MasterCard; V, Visa.

D Followed by a price, indicates room rate for a "double"—two people in one room in one or two beds (the charge may be higher for two double beds).

Downhill/x-country ski Downhill and/or cross-country skiing within 20 miles of property.

Each addl Extra charge for each additional person beyond the stated number of persons at a reduced price.

Early-bird dinner A meal served at specified hours, typically around 4:30–6:30 pm.

Exc Except.

Exercise equipt Two or more pieces of exercise equipment on the premises.

Exercise rm Both exercise equipment and room, with an instructor on the premises.

Fax Facsimile machines available to all guests.

Golf privileges Privileges at a course within 10 miles

Hols Holidays

In-rm modem link Every guest room has a connection for a modem that's separate from the phone line.

Kit. or kits. A kitchen or kitchenette that contains stove or microwave, sink, and refrigerator and that is either part of the room or a separate room. If the kitchen is not fully equipped, the listing will indicate "no equipt" or "some equipt".

Luxury level A special section of a lodging, covering at least an entire floor, that offers increased luxury accommodations. Management must provide no less than three of these four services: separate check-in and check-out, concierge, private lounge, and private elevator service (key access). Complimentary breakfast and snacks are commonly offered.

MAP Modified American plan (lodging plus two meals).

Movies Prerecorded videos are available for rental.

No cr cds accepted No credit cards are accepted.

No elvtr In hotels with more than two stories, it's assumed there are elevators; only their absence is noted.

No phones Phones, too, are assumed; only their absence is noted.

Parking There is a parking lot on the premises.

Private club A cocktail lounge or bar available to members and their guests. In motels and hotels where these clubs exist, registered guests can usually use the club as guests of the management; the same is frequently true of restaurants.

Prix fixe A full meal for a stated price; usually one price is quoted.

Res Reservations.

S Followed by a price, indicates room rate for a "single," i.e., one person.

Semi-a la carte Meals include vegetable, salad, soup, appetizer, or other accompaniments to the main dish.

Serv bar A service bar, where drinks are prepared for dining patrons only.

Serv charge Service charge is the amount added to the restaurant check in lieu of a tip.

Table d'hôte A full meal for a stated price, dependent upon entree selection; no a la carte options are available.

Tennis privileges Privileges at tennis courts within 5 miles.

TV Indicates color television.

Under certain age free Children under that age are not charged for if staying in room with a parent.

Valet parking An attendant is available to park and retrieve a car.

VCR VCRs in all guest rooms.

VCR avail VCRs are available for hookup in guest rooms.

Special Information for Travelers with Disabilities

The *Mobil Travel Guide* symbol D shown in accommodation and restaurant listings indicates establishments that are at least partially accessible to people with mobility problems.

The *Mobil Travel Guide* criteria for accessibility are unique to our publication. Please do not confuse them with the universal symbol for wheelchair accessibility. When the D symbol appears following a listing, the establishment is equipped with facilities to accommodate people using wheelchairs or crutches or otherwise needing easy access to doorways and rest rooms. Travelers with severe mobility problems or with hearing or visual impairments may or may not find facilities they need. Always phone ahead to make sure that an establishment can meet your needs.

All lodgings bearing our D symbol have the following facilities:

- ISA-designated parking near access ramps
- Level or ramped entryways to building
- Swinging building entryway doors minimum 3'0"
- Public rest rooms on main level with space to operate a wheelchair; handrails at commode areas
- Elevators equipped with grab bars and lowered control buttons
- Restaurants with accessible doorways; rest rooms with space to operate wheelchair; handrails at commode areas
- Minimum 3'0" width entryway to guest rooms

- Low-pile carpet in rooms
- Telephone at bedside and in bathroom
- Bed placed at wheelchair height
- Minimum 3′0″ width doorway to bathroom
- Bath with open sink—no cabinet; room to operate wheelchair
- Handrails at commode areas; tub handrails
- Wheelchair accessible peephole in room entry door
- Wheelchair accessible closet rods and shelves

All restaurants bearing our D symbol offer the following facilities:

- ISA-designated parking beside access ramps
- Level or ramped front entryways to building
- Tables to accommodate wheelchairs
- Main-floor rest rooms; minimum 3′0″ width entryway

- Rest rooms with space to operate wheelchair; handrails at commode areas

In general, the newest properties are apt to impose the fewest barriers.

To get the kind of service you need and have a right to expect, do not hesitate when making a reservation to question the management in detail about the availability of accessible rooms, parking, entrances, restaurants, lounges, or any other facilities that are important to you, and confirm what is meant by "accessible." Some guests with mobility impairments report that lodging establishments' housekeeping and maintenance departments are most helpful in describing barriers. Also inquire about any special equipment, transportation, or services you may need.

Making the Most of Your Trip

A few diehard souls might fondly remember the trip where the car broke down and they were stranded for a week, or the vacation that cost twice what it was supposed to. For most travelers, though, the best trips are those that are safe, smooth, and within their budget. To help you make your trip the best it can be, we've assembled a few tips and resources.

Saving Money

ON LODGING

After you've seen the published rates, it's time to look for discounts. Many hotels and motels offer them—for senior citizens, business travelers, families, you name it. It never hurts to ask—politely, that is. Sometimes, especially in late afternoon, desk clerks are instructed to fill beds, and you might be offered a lower rate, or a nicer room, to entice you to stay. Look for bargains on stays over multiple nights, in the off-season, and on weekdays or weekends (depending on location). Many hotels in major metropolitan areas, for example, have special weekend package plans, which offer considerable savings on rooms and may include breakfast, cocktails, and meal discounts. Prices change frequently throughout the year, so phone ahead.

Another way to save money is to choose accommodations that give you more than just a standard room. Rooms with kitchen facilities enable you to cook some meals for yourself, reducing restaurant costs. A suite might save money for two couples traveling together. Even hotel luxury levels can provide good value, as many include breakfast or cocktails in the price of the room.

State and city sales taxes as well as special room taxes can increase your room rates as much as 25% per day. We are unable to bring this specific information into the listings, but we strongly urge that you ask about these taxes when placing reservations in order to understand the total price to you.

Watch out for telephone-usage charges that hotels frequently impose on long-distance calls, credit-card calls, and other phone calls—even those that go unanswered. Before phoning from your room, read the information given to you at check-in, and then be sure to read your bill carefully before checking out. You won't be expected to pay for charges that weren't spelled out. (On the other hand, it's not unusual for a hotel to bill you for your calls after you return home.) Consider using public telephones in hotel lobbies; the savings may outweigh the inconvenience.

ON DINING

There are several ways to get a less-expensive meal at a more-expensive restaurant. Early-bird dinners are popular in many parts of the country and offer considerable savings. If you're interested in sampling a ★★★★ or ★★★★★ establishment, consider going at lunchtime. While the prices then are probably relatively high, they may be half of those at dinner and come with the same ambience, service, and cuisine.

PARK PASSES

While many national parks, monuments, seashores, historic sites, and recreation areas may be used free of charge, others charge an entrance fee (ranging from $1 to $5 per person to $5 to $15 per carload) and/or a "use fee" for special services and facilities. If you plan to make several visits to federal recreation areas, consider one of the following National Park Service money-saving programs:

Park Pass. This is an annual entrance permit to a specific unit in the National Park Service system that normally charges an entrance fee. The pass admits the permit holder and any accompanying passengers in a private noncommercial vehicle or, in the case of walk-in facilities, the holder's spouse, children, and parents. It is valid for entrance fees only. A Park Pass may be purchased in person or by mail from the National Park Service unit at which the pass will be honored. The cost is $15 to $20, depending upon the area.

Golden Eagle Passport. This pass, available to people who are between 17 and 61, entitles the purchaser and accompanying passengers in a private noncommercial vehicle to enter any outdoor NPS unit that charges an entrance fee and admits the purchaser and family to most walk-in fee-charging areas. Like the Park Pass, it is good for one year and does not cover use fees. It may be purchased from the National Park Service, Office of Public Inquiries, Room 1013, US Department of the Interior, 18th and C Sts NW, Washington, DC 20240, phone 202/208–4747; at any of the 10 regional offices throughout the country; and at any NPS area that charges a fee. The cost is $50.

Golden Age Passport. Available to citizens and permanent residents of the United States 62 years or older, this is a lifetime entrance permit to fee-charging recreation areas. The fee exemption extends to those accompanying the permit holder in a private noncommercial vehicle or, in the case of walk-in facilities, to the holder's spouse and children. The passport also entitles the holder to a 50% discount on use fees charged in park areas but not to fees charged by concessionaires. Golden Age Passports must be obtained in person. The applicant must show proof of age, i.e., a driver's license, birth certificate, or signed affidavit attesting to age (Medicare cards are not acceptable proof). Passports are available at most park service units where they're used, at National Park Service headquarters (see above), at park system regional offices, at National Forest Supervisors' offices, and at most Ranger Station offices. The cost is $10.

Golden Access Passport. Issued to citizens and permanent residents of the United States who are physically disabled or visually impaired, this passport is a free lifetime entrance permit to fee-charging recreation areas. The fee exemption extends to those accompanying the permit holder in a private noncommercial vehicle or, in the case of walk-in facilities, to the holder's spouse and children. The passport also entitles the holder to a 50% discount on use fees charged in park areas but not to fees charged by concessionaires. Golden Access Passports must be obtained in person. Proof of eligibility to receive federal benefits is required (under programs such as Disability Retirement, Compensation for Military Service-Connected Disability, Coal Mine Safety and Health Act, etc.), or an affidavit must be signed attesting to eligibility. These passports are available at the same outlets as Golden Age Passports.

FOR SENIOR CITIZENS

Look for the senior-citizen discount symbol in the lodging and restaurant listings. Always call ahead to confirm that the discount is being offered, and be sure to carry proof of age. At places not listed in the book, it never hurts to ask if a senior-citizen discount is offered. Additional information for mature travelers is available from: the American Association of Retired Persons (AARP), 601 E St NW, Washington, DC 20049, phone 202/434–2277.

Tipping

Tipping is an expression of appreciation for good service, and often service workers rely on tips as a significant part of their income. However, you never need to tip if service is poor.

IN HOTELS

Doormen in major city hotels are usually given $1 for getting you a cab. Bellhops expect $1 per bag, usually $2 if you have only one bag. Concierges are tipped according to the service they perform. It's not mandatory to tip when you've asked for suggestions on sightseeing or restaurants or help in making reservations for dining. However, when a concierge books you a table at a restaurant known to be difficult to get into, a gratuity of $5 is appropriate. For obtaining theater or sporting event tickets, $5–$10 is expected. Maids, often overlooked by guests, may be tipped $1–$2 per day of stay.

AT RESTAURANTS

Coffee shop and counter service wait staff are usually given 8%–10% of the bill. In full-service restaurants, tip 15% of the bill, before sales tax. In fine restaurants, where the staff is large and shares the gratuity, 18%–20% for the waiter is appropriate. In most cases, tip the maitre d' only if service has been extraordinary and only on the way out; $20 is the minimum in upscale properties in major metropolitan areas. If there is a wine steward, tip him or her at least $5 a bottle, more if the wine was decanted or if the bottle was very expensive. If your busboy has been unusually attentive, $2 pressed into his hand on departure is a nice gesture. An increasing number of restaurants automatically add a service charge to the bill in lieu of a gratuity. Before tipping, carefully review your check.

AT AIRPORTS

Curbside luggage handlers expect $1 per bag. Car-rental shuttle drivers who help with your luggage appreciate a $1 or $2 tip.

Staying Safe

The best way to deal with emergencies is to be prepared enough to avoid them. However, unforeseen situations do happen, and you can prepare for them.

IN YOUR CAR

Before your trip, make sure your car has been serviced and is in good working order. Change the oil, check the battery and belts, and make sure tires are inflated properly (this can also improve gas mileage). Other inspections recommended by the car's manufacturer should be made, too.

Next, be sure you have the tools and equipment to deal with a routine breakdown: jack, spare tire, lug wrench, repair kit, emergency tools, jumper cables, spare fan belt, auto fuses, flares and/or reflectors, flashlights, first-aid kit, and, in winter, a windshield scraper and shovel.

Bring all appropriate and up-to-date documentation—licenses, registration, and insurance cards—and know what's covered by your insurance. Also bring an extra set of keys, just in case.

En route, always buckle up!

If your car does break down, get out of traffic as soon as possible—pull well off the road. Raise the hood and turn on your emergency flashers or tie a white cloth to the roadside door handle or antenna. Stay near your car. Use flares or reflectors to keep your car from being hit.

IN YOUR LODGING

Chances are slim that you will encounter a hotel or motel fire. The ⬛ in a listing indicates that there were smoke detectors and/or sprinkler systems in the rooms we inspected. Once you've checked in, make sure that any smoke detector in your room is working properly. Ascertain the locations of fire extinguishers and at least two fire exits. Never use an elevator in a fire.

For personal security, use the peephole in your room's door.

PROTECTING AGAINST THEFT

To guard against theft wherever you go, don't bring any more of value than you need. If you do bring valuables, leave them at your hotel rather than in your car, and if you have something very expensive, lock it in a safe. Many hotels have one in each room; others will store your valuables in the hotel's safe. And of course, don't carry more money than you need; use traveler's checks and credit cards, or visit cash machines.

For Travelers with Disabilities

A number of publications can provide assistance. Fodor's *Great American Vacations for Travelers with Disabilities* ($19.50) covers 38 top U.S. travel destinations, including parks, cities, and popular tourist regions. It's available from bookstores or by calling 800/533–6478. The most complete listing of published material for travelers with disabilities is available from *The Disability Bookshop,* Twin Peaks Press, Box 129, Vancouver, WA 98666, phone 360/694–2462. A comprehensive guidebook to the national parks is *Easy Access to National Parks: The Sierra Club Guide for People with Disabilities* ($16), distributed by Random House.

The Reference Section of the National Library Service for the Blind and Physically Handicapped (Library of Congress, Washington, DC 20542, phone 202/707–9275 or 202/707–5100) provides information and resources for persons with mobility problems and hearing and vision impairments, as well as information about the NLS talking-book program (or visit your local library).

Important Toll-Free Numbers
and On-Line Information

HOTELS AND MOTELS

Adam's Mark 800/444–2326
Web www.adamsmark.com
Best Western .... 800/528–1234, TDD 800/528–2222
Web www.bestwestern.com
Budgetel Inns 800/428–3438
Web www.budgetel.com
Budget Host 800/283–4678
Clarion 800/252–7466
Web www.clarioninn.com
Comfort 800/228–5150
Web www.comfortinn.com
Courtyard by Marriott 800/321–2211
Web www.courtyard.com
Days Inn 800/325–2525
Web www.travelweb.com/daysinn.html
Doubletree 800/528–0444
Web www.doubletreehotels.com
Drury Inns 800/325–8300
Web www.drury-inn.com
Econo Lodge 800/446–6900
Web www.hotelchoice.com
Embassy Suites 800/362–2779
Web www.embassy-suites.com
Exel Inns of America 800/356–8013
Fairfield Inn by Marriott 800/228–2800
Web www.marriott.com
Fairmont Hotels 800/527–4727
Forte 800/225–5843
Four Seasons 800/332–3442
Web www.fourseasons.com
Friendship Inns 800/453–4511
Web www.hotelchoice.com
Hampton Inn 800/426–7866
Web www.hampton-inn.com
Hilton .... 800/445–8667, TDD 800/368–1133
Web www.hilton.com
Holiday Inn .... 800/465–4329, TDD 800/238–5544
Web www.holiday-inn.com
Howard Johnson .... 800/654–4656, TDD 800/654–8442
Web www.hojo.com
Hyatt & Resorts 800/233–1234
Web www.hyatt.com
Inns of America 800/826–0778
Inter-Continental 800/327–0200
Web www.interconti.com
La Quinta .... 800/531–5900, TDD 800/426–3101
Web www.laquinta.com
Loews 800/235–6397
Web www.loewshotels.com
Marriott 800/228–9290
Web www.marriott.com
Master Hosts Inns 800/251–1962

Meridien 800/225–5843
Motel 6 .... 800/466–8356
Nikko International 800/645–5687
Web www.hotelnikko.com
Omni 800/843–6664
Web www.omnirosen.com
Quality Inn 800/228–5151
Web www.qualityinn.com
Radisson 800/333–3333
Web www.radisson.com
Ramada .... 800/228–2828, TDD 800/228–3232
Web www.ramada.com/ramada.html
Red Carpet/Scottish Inns 800/251–1962
Red Lion 800/547–8010
Web www.travelweb.com/travelweb/rl/common/redlion.html
Red Roof Inn 800/843–7663
Web www.redroof.com
Renaissance 800/468–3571
Web www.niagara.com/nf.renaissance
Residence Inn by Marriott 800/331–3131
Web www.marriott.com
Ritz-Carlton 800/241–3333
Web www.ritzcarlton.com
Rodeway 800/228–2000
Web www.rodeway.com
Sheraton 800/325–3535
Web www.sheraton.com
Shilo Inn 800/222–2244
Signature Inns 800/822–5252
Web www.signature-inns.com
Sleep Inn 800/221–2222
Web www.sleepinn.com
Super 8 .... 800/848–8888
Web www.super8motels.com/super8.html
Susse Chalet 800/258–1980
Web www.sussechalet.com
Travelodge/Viscount 800/255–3050
Web www.travelodge.com
Vagabond 800/522–1555
Westin Hotels & Resorts 800/937-8461
Web www.westin.com
Wyndham Hotels & Resorts 800/996-3426
Web www.travelweb.com

AIRLINES

Air Canada 800/776–3000
Web www.aircanada.ca
Alaska 800/426–0333
Web www.alaska-air.com/home.html
American 800/433–7300
Web www.americanair.com/aahome/aahome.html
America West 800/235–9292
Web www.americawest.com

British Airways 800/247–9297
Web www.british-airways.com
Canadian 800/426–7000
Web www.cdair.ca
Continental 800/525–0280
Web www.flycontinental.com
Delta 800/221–1212
Web www.delta-air.com
IslandAir 800/323–3345
Mesa 800/637–2247
Northwest 800/225–2525
Web www.nwa.com
SkyWest 800/453–9417
Southwest 800/435–9792
Web www.iflyswa.com
TWA 800/221–2000
Web www.twa.com
United 800/241–6522
Web www.ual.com
USAir 800/428–4322
Web www.usair.com

TRAINS

Amtrak 800/872–7245
Web www.amtrak.com

BUSES

Greyhound 800/231–2222
Web www.greyhound.com

CAR RENTALS

Advantage 800/777–5500
Alamo 800/327–9633
Web www.goalamo.com
Allstate 800/634–6186
Avis 800/331–1212
Web www.avis.com
Budget 800/527–0700
Web www.budgetrentacar.com
Dollar 800/800–4000
Web www.dollarcar.com
Enterprise 800/325–8007
Web www.pickenterprise.com
Hertz 800/654–3131
Web www.hertz.com
National 800/328–4567
Web www.nationalcar.com
Payless 800/237–2804
Rent-A-Wreck 800/535–1391
Web www.rent-a-wreck.com
Sears 800/527–0770
Thrifty 800/367–2277
Web www.thrifty.com

Four-Star and Five-Star Establishments

in the Southeast

FLORIDA

★★★★★ Lodgings

The Breakers, *Palm Beach*
The Four Seasons, *Palm Beach*
The Ritz-Carlton, Naples, *Naples*

★★★★ Lodgings

Biltmore Westin, *Coral Gables*
Boca Raton Resort & Club, *Boca Raton*
Chesterfield Hotel, *Palm Beach*
Disney's Grand Floridian Resort & Spa
Walt Disney World
Disney's Yacht Club Resort, *Walt Disney World*
Grand Bay, *Miami*
Hyatt Regency Grand Cypress, *Walt Disney World*
Hyatt Regency Westshore, *Tampa*
Little Palm Island, *Key West*
The Lodge and Club at Ponte Vedra Beach, *Jacksonville Beach*
Mayfair House, *Miami*
Peabody Orlando, *Orlando*
Ponte Vedra Inn & Club, *Jacksonville Beach*
Renaissance Vinoy Resort, *St Petersburg*

The Resort at Longboat Key Club, *Longboat Key (& Lido Beach)*
The Ritz-Carlton, Amelia Island, *Amelia Island*
The Ritz-Carlton, Palm Beach, *Palm Beach*
Saddlebrook Resort, *Tampa*
Turnberry Isle Resort & Club, *Miami*
Villas of Grand Cypress, *Walt Disney World*

★★★★ Restaurants

Chef Allen's, *Miami*
Dux (Peabody Orlando), *Orlando*
The Grill (The Ritz-Carlton, Amelia Island), *Amelia Island*
La Vieille Maison, *Boca Raton*
Pacific Time, *Miami Beach*
The Restaurant at Four Seasons (The Four Seasons), *Palm Beach*
The Restaurant (The Ritz-Carlton, Palm Beach), *Palm Beach*

GEORGIA

★★★★★ Restaurant

The Dining Room (The Ritz-Carlton, Buckhead), *Atlanta*

★★★★ Lodgings

1842 Inn, *Macon*

The Cloister, *Sea Island*
Four Seasons, *Atlanta*
Inn at Chateau Elan, *Buford*
The Kehoe House, *Savannah*
The Ritz-Carlton, *Atlanta*
The Ritz-Carlton, Buckhead, *Atlanta*

★★★★ Restaurants

Canoe, *Atlanta*
Elizabeth on 37th, *Savannah*
Hedgerose, *Atlanta*
The Restaurant (The Ritz-Carlton), *Atlanta*
Seeger's, *Atlanta*

KENTUCKY

★★★★ Lodgings

The Camberley Brown, *Louisville*
Marriott's Griffin Gate Resort, *Lexington*
Seelbach Hilton, *Louisville*

★★★★ Restaurants

Lilly's, *Louisville*
Vincenzo's, *Louisville*

TENNESSEE

★★★★ Lodgings

Blackberry Farm, *Marysville*
Peabody, *Memphis*

Alabama

Population: 4,040,587
Land area: 51,998 square miles
Elevation: 0-2,407 feet
Highest point: Cheaha Mountain (Cleburne County)
Entered Union: December 14, 1819 (22nd state)
Capital: Montgomery
Motto: We Dare Defend Our Rights
Nickname: Heart of Dixie
State flower: Camellia
State bird: Yellowhammer
State tree: Southern pine
State fair: 10 days mid-October, 1999, in Birmingham
Time zone: Central
Web: www.touralabama.org

From the Confederacy's first capital at Montgomery to America's first "space capital" at Huntsville, Alabama has successfully spanned a century that began in sectional conflict but is ending in a dedication to man's quest to bridge the universe. The drive from the business center of Birmingham to the heart of the Cotton Kingdom surrounding Montgomery and Selma is less than 100 miles, but these miles mark one of the transitions between the 19th and 20th centuries.

Harnessing the Tennessee River made it possible to control floods and turn the eroded soil into bountiful crop land. The river became the South's most important waterway, and giant Tennessee Valley Authority (TVA) dams brought electric power and industrialization to once-bypassed cities. They also gave northern Alabama nationally renowned water recreation areas.

Cotton, the traditional wealth of Alabama's rich Black Belt, fed the busy port of Mobile until the 1870s, when Birmingham grew into an industrial center. TVA brought the other great shift in the 1930s, culminating in new hydroelectric and steam-plant power production in the 1960s.

Cotton and river waterways were the combination on which the Old South was built. Alabama, the Cotton State supreme by the 1850s, built river towns like Selma, the old capital of "Cahawba," and Montgomery, the new capital and "cradle of the Confederacy." The red iron ore in the northern mountains was neglected, except for isolated forges operated by individuals, until just before the Civil War.

On January 11, 1861, Alabama became the fourth state to secede from the Union. Jefferson Davis was inaugurated as president of the Confederacy in Montgomery the following month and on April 12, he ordered General P.G.T. Beauregard to fire on Fort Sumter. The Confederate capital was moved to Richmond on May 21, 1861.

Alabama's troops fought with every active Southern force, the state contributing between 65,000 and 100,000 men from a white population of 500,000. At least 2,500 white soldiers and 10,000 black soldiers went north to support the Union. When Huntsville, Decatur and Tuscumbia fell to Union forces in 1862, every male from 16 to 60 was ordered to the state's defense. Little fighting took place on Alabama's soil and water again until Admiral Farragut's Union fleet won the Battle of Mobile Bay in 1864, though the city of Mobile did not fall. Full-scale invasions by Wilson's Raiders occupied several important cities in the spring of 1865.

Reconstruction days were made bitter by carpetbaggers who supported the Republican Party. The state refused to ratify the Fourteenth Amendment, and military law was reinstated. But by the 1880s, recovery was beginning. Birmingham had weathered the national panic of 1873 successfully and was producing steel in earnest.

Historic attractions are plentiful. There is the birthplace of Helen Keller at Tuscumbia (see SHEFFIELD); the unusual Ave Maria Grotto in Cullman (see), an inspiring work of faith by one Benedictine monk who built scores of miniature religious buildings; and the museum and laboratory of the great black educator and scientist George Washington Carver at the Tuskegee Institute (see TUSKEGEE).

For golf enthusiasts, the Robert Trent Jones Golf Trail has 18 championship golf courses offering a total of 324 holes, located at the following 7 sites: Anniston/Gadsden, Auburn/Opelika, Birmingham, Dothan, Greenville, Huntsville and Mobile (phone 800/949-4444 for more information).

On Alabama's Gulf Coast, the port city of Mobile makes a splendid entry to the whole Gulf strip between Florida and New Orleans. Mobile is famous for the Bellingrath Gardens and Home, the annual Azalea Trail and Festival and its own Mardi Gras celebration.

When to Go/Climate

Alabama's climate is mild almost year round, although the extreme northern part of the state can experience cold weather and even some snow in winter. The southern part of the state can be extremely hot, beginning as early as March. Fall is usually comfortable throughout the state and is generally a good time to visit.

AVERAGE HIGH/LOW TEMPERATURES (°F)

BIRMINGHAM

Jan 52/31	**May** 81/58	**Sept** 84/63
Feb 57/35	**June** 87/65	**Oct** 75/50
Mar 66/42	**July** 90/70	**Nov** 65/42
Apr 75/49	**Aug** 89/69	**Dec** 56/35

MOBILE

Jan 60/40	**May** 85/64	**Sept** 87/69
Feb 64/43	**June** 90/71	**Oct** 80/57
Mar 71/50	**July** 91/73	**Nov** 70/49
Apr 79/57	**Aug** 91/73	**Dec** 63/43

Parks and Recreation Finder

Directions to and information about the parks and recreation areas below are given under their respective town/city sections. Please refer to those sections for details.

NATIONAL PARK AND RECREATION AREAS

Key to abbreviations: I.H.S. = International Historic Site; I.P.M. = International Peace Memorial; N.B. = National Battlefield; N.B.P. = National Battlefield Park; N.B.C. = National Battlefield & Cemetery; N.C. = National Conservation Area; N.E.M. = National Expansion Memorial; N.F. = National Forest; N.G. = National Grassland; N.H. = National Historical Park; N.H.C. = National Heritage Corridor; N.H.S. = National Historic Site; N.L. = National Lakeshore; N.M. = National Monument; N.M.P. = National Military Park; N.Mem. = National Memorial; N.P. = National Park; N.Pres. = National Preserve; N.R. = National Recreational Area; N.R.R. = National Recreational River; N.Riv. = National River; N.S. = National Seashore; N.S.R. = National Scenic Riverway; N.S.T. = National Scenic Trail; N.Sc. = National Scientific Reserve; N.V.M. = National Volcanic Monument.

Place Name	Listed Under
Bankhead N.F.	CULLMAN
Conecuh N.F.	EVERGREEN
Horseshoe Bend N.M.P.	same
Russell Cave N. M.	same
Talladega N.F.	TALLADEGA
Tuskegee Institute N.H.S.	same
Tuskegee N.F.	TUSKEGEE

STATE PARK AND RECREATION AREAS

Key to abbreviations: I.P. = Interstate Park; S.A.P. = State Archaeological Park; S.B. = State Beach; S.C. = State Conservation Area; S.C.P. = State Conservation Park; S.Cp. = State Campground; S.F. = State Forest; S.G. = State Garden; S.H.A. = State Historic Area; S.H.P. = State Historic Park; S.H.S. = State Historic Site; S.M.P. = State Marine Park; S.N.A. = State Natural Area; S.P. = State Park; S.P.C. = State Public Campground; S.R. = State Reserve; S.R.A. = State Recreation Area; S.Res. = State Reservoir; S.Res.P. = State Resort Park; S.R.P = State Rustic Park.

Place Name	Listed Under
Blue Springs S.P.	OZARK
Buck's Pocket and Lake Guntersville S.P.	GUNTERSVILLE
Cheaha S.P.	TALLADEGA
Chewacla S.P.	AUBURN
Claude D. Kelley S.P.	ATMORE
DeSoto S.P.	FORT PAYNE
Gulf S.P.	GULF SHORES
Joe Wheeler S.P. (Elk River, First Creek and Wheeler Dam units)	FLORENCE
Lake Lurleen S.P.	TUSCALOOSA
Lakepoint Resort S.P.	EUFAULA
Monte Sano S.P.	HUNTSVILLE
Oak Mountain and Rickwood Caverns S.P.	BIRMINGHAM
Paul M. Grist S.P.	SELMA
Tannehill Historical S.P.	BESSEMER
Wind Creek S.P.	ALEXANDER CITY

Water-related activities, hiking, riding, various sports, picnicking, camping and visitor centers are available in many of these areas. Nominal entrance fees are collected at some parks. The state parks accept telephone reservations for motel rooms, cabins and improved campsites; primitive campsites are on a no-reservation basis. Fees for improved campsites are $8-$25/site/night. No pets at motels and cabins; pets on leash only at campgrounds. There are many state park fishing lakes and 12 parks that offer boat rentals and water-recreational equipment. Bait, tackle and freshwater fishing permits are $2/day; under 13, 75¢/day. Contact the Alabama Department of Conservation and Natural Resources, Alabama State Parks Division, 64 N Union St, Montgomery 36130; 334/242-3334 for details. For reservations phone 800/252-7275 or 334/242-3333.

SKI AREA

Place Name	Listed Under
Cloudmont Ski Resort	FORT PAYNE

FISHING & HUNTING

More than 50,000 small ponds and lakes, including 22 public lakes and more than one-half million acres of public impounded waters, provide ample freshwater fishing. Crappie, striped and white bass, bluegill and redear sunfish can be caught statewide. State and national forests and state parks cater to anglers. White sandy beaches of the Gulf Coast are good for surf casting; trolling farther out in Gulf waters can net tarpon, snapper, king mackerel and other game fish. Largemouth bass abound from the Tennessee River to Mobile Bay. The Lewis Smith and Martin reservoirs have both largemouth and spotted bass; the Wilson and Wheeler Dam tailwaters have smallmouth bass; the East Central Alabama

CALENDAR HIGHLIGHTS

MARCH

Historic Mobile Tours (Mobile). Houses, buildings open to visitors. Phone 800/566-2453.

MAY

Alabama Jubilee (Decatur). Point Mallard Park. Highlight of festivities are the hot-air balloon races. Phone 800/524-6181.

JUNE

City Stages (Birmingham). Music festival of national artists. Food, dancing, children's activities and regional craftsmen. Phone 205/251-1272.

SEPTEMBER

Big Spring Jam (Huntsville). Music festival, including pop, rock, jazz, country and other genres. Foods from local restaurants, shows for kids. Phone 256/551-2223.

OCTOBER

Greater Gulf State Fair (Mobile). Commercial, industrial, military and educational exhibits; entertainment. Phone 334/344-4573.

State Fair (Birmingham). Contact Alabama State Fair Authority. Phone 205/786-8100.

Alabama Renaissance Faire (Florence). Renaissance-era arts and crafts, music, food, entertainment. Fair workers in period costumes. Phone 205/760-9648.

DECEMBER

Blue-Gray Football Classic (Montgomery). Contact Lion's Club/Blue-Gray Association, 334/265-1266.

streams have redeye bass. Alabama has no closed season on freshwater game fish. Sport fishing licenses, nonresident: annual, $31; 7-day, $11 (includes issuance fee). The fees for reciprocal licenses for the residents of adjoining states and Louisiana vary.

Waterfowl, small game, turkey and deer are found in the state, with state-managed and national forest wildlife areas providing hunting in season. Deer and turkey hunting require an all-game hunting license for nonresidents. Federal and State Waterfowl Stamps are required in addition to a regular hunting license, when hunting waterfowl. Because nearly all lands in Alabama are under private ownership and state law requires written permission from the owner prior to hunting, persons desiring to hunt should make arrangements accordingly. Hunting licenses, nonresident: annual all-game, $200; annual small game, $40; 7-day all-game, $75; 7-day small game, $25. Management Area Deer and Turkey licenses ($4) are required in the management areas in addition to the regular hunting license. A reciprocal agreement among Alabama and the state of Florida may alter the license fees charged residents of Florida. License costs for nonresident hunting licenses include a $2 issuance fee. For detailed information on seasons and other regulations, contact Alabama Dept of Conservation and Natural Resources, Game and Fish Division, 64 N Union St, Montgomery 36130; 334/242-3467. For information on fishing and hunting licenses, phone 334/242-3829.

Driving Information

All passengers in front seat must wear a safety belt. Children under 6 years must be in an approved passenger restraint anywhere in vehicle; ages 4 and 5 may use a regulation safety belt or child seat; age 3 and under must use a federally-approved safety seat. For further information phone 334/242-4445.

INTERSTATE HIGHWAY SYSTEM

The following alphabetical listing of Alabama towns in *Mobil Travel Guide* shows that these cities are within 10 miles of the indicated Interstate highways. A highway map should, however, be checked for the nearest exit.

Highway Number	Cities/Towns within 10 miles
Interstate 10	Mobile.
Interstate 20	Anniston, Bessemer, Birmingham, Tuscaloosa.
Interstate 59	Bessemer, Birmingham, Fort Payne, Gadsden, Tuscaloosa.
Interstate 65	Athens, Atmore, Birmingham, Clanton, Cullman, Decatur, Evergreen, Greenville, Mobile, Montgomery.
Interstate 85	Auburn, Montgomery, Opelika, Tuskegee.

Additional Visitor Information

Travel and vacation information is offered toll free, phone 800/ALABAMA (Mon-Fri, 8 am-5 pm). Travelers also may contact the Alabama Bureau of Tourism & Travel, 401 Adams Ave, PO Box 4927, Montgomery 36103-4927; 334/242-4169 or 800/ALABAMA for additional information.

There are eight welcome centers in Alabama; there visitors will find information and brochures that will help plan stops at points of interest: Alabama (I-59S), Ardmore (I-65S), Baldwin (I-10W), Grand Bay (I-10E), Hardy (I-20W, near Heflin), Houston (US 231N), Lanett (I-85S) and Sumter (I-59N/20E); inquire locally for further information on these centers.

Alexander City (E-5)

(See also Sylacauga)

Settled 1836 **Pop** 14,917 **Elev** 707 ft **Area code** 256 **Zip** 35010 **E-mail** coc@lakemartin.net **Web** www.alexandercity.com
Information Chamber of Commerce, 120 Tallapoosa St, Box 926, 35011; 256/234-3461.

Martin Dam at Cherokee Bluffs not only supplies power, but also creates Lake Martin on the Tallapoosa River. Lake Martin, with a 760-mile shoreline, was the largest of its kind when it was formed in 1926. Today, it is one of the South's finest inland recreation areas.

What to See and Do

Horseshoe Bend National Military Park (see). 13 mi NE on AL 22 to New Site, then S on AL 49.

Wind Creek State Park. A 1,445-acre wooded park on Lake Martin. Swimming beach, bathhouses, waterskiing; fishing; boating (marina, ramps). Hiking, bicycling. Picnic area, concessions. Improved campsites. Observation tower. Standard fees. (Daily) 7 mi SE off AL 63. Phone 256/329-0845.

Motels

✔★ **HORSESHOE INN.** *US 280 at AL 22. 205/234-6311; FAX 205/234-6314.* 90 rms. S $39-$44; D $39-$54; each addl $5. TV; cable. Pool. Restaurant opp open 24 hrs. Bar 4-10 pm, closed Sun. Ck-out 11 am. Meeting rms. Business servs avail. Cr cds: A, C, D, DS, MC, V.

D ≈ ⚲ 🐾 SC

★★ **JAMESON INN.** *4335 US 280. 205/234-7099; FAX 205/234-9807; res: 800/541-3268.* 60 rms, 2 story. S, D $48; each addl $5; suites $53-$58; under 13 free. Crib free. Pet accepted, some restrictions. TV; cable. Pool. Complimentary continental bkfst. Restaurant nearby. Ck-out 11 am. Meeting rms. Exercise equipt. Some refrigerators. Cr cds: A, C, D, DS, MC, V.

D 🐾 ≈ 🏋 ⚲ 🐾 SC

★ **SUPER 8.** *4000 US 280 Bypass. 256/329-8858.* 44 units, 3 story. No elvtr. S, D $41.95-$48.95; each addl $5; under 12 free; wkly rates. Crib free. TV; cable (premium). Complimentary coffee in lobby. Restaurant adj 6 am-10 pm. Ck-out 11 am. Business servs avail. Cr cds: A, C, D, DS, MC, V.

D ⚲ 🐾 SC

Restaurant

★ **CECIL'S PUBLIC HOUSE.** *243 Green St. 256/329-0732.* Hrs: 11 am-2 pm, 5-9 pm; Sat from 5 pm. Closed Sun; most major hols. Bar 5 pm-midnight. Semi-a la carte: lunch $5.50-$6.95, dinner $5.50-$14.95. Child's meals. Specializes in seafood, steak. Old house (1902); antique plate collection; stained-glass windows. Cr cds: A, MC, V.

D

Anniston (C-5)

(See also Gadsden, Talladega)

Settled 1872 **Pop** 26,623 **Elev** 710 ft **Area code** 205 **Zip** 36202 **Web** carolm@calhounchamber.org
Information Convention & Visitors Bureau, 14th St & Quintard Ave, PO Box 1087, 36202; 205/237-3536 or 800/489-1087.

Anniston was founded by Samuel Noble, an Englishman who headed the ironworks in Rome, Georgia, and Daniel Tyler, a Connecticut capitalist. They established textile mills and blast furnaces designed to help launch the South into the industrial revolution after the devastation of the Civil War. In 1879, the owners hired accomplished Eastern architects, including the renowned Stanford White, to design and build a modern company town. The town was named after Mrs. Anne Scott Taylor (Annie's Town), wife of one of the local iron magnates. Anniston remained a private company town until 1883 when it was opened to the public. Today, Anniston retains many historic structures and much of its original character.

What to See and Do

Anniston Museum of Natural History. Museum featuring Regar-Werner bird exhibit with 600 specimens including many endangered and extinct birds; reconstruction of pteranodon, a 30-ft flying dinosaur; large African animal exhibit featuring large bull elephant; Egyptian mummies; North American mammals; live reptiles; giant termite mound; replica of an Alabama cave; and changing exhibition gallery. Situated in 187-acre John B. Lagarde Environmental Interpretive Center; nature trails, picnic facilities. (Daily exc Mon; closed some major hols) 800 Museum Dr, Lagarde Park. Phone 205/237-6766. ¢¢

Berman Museum. Collection of unique artifacts amassed by a real spy on his worldly missions. Treasures from the American West and World War II era are featured including a Royal Persian Scimitar encrusted with 1,295 rose-cut diamonds, 60 carats of rubies and a single 40 carat emerald set in three pounds of gold. (Daily exc Mon; closed major hols) 840 Museum Dr, Lagarde Park. Phone 205/237-6261.

Coldwater Covered Bridge. Built prior to 1850; one of 13 restored covered bridges in Alabama. 3 mi S via US 431, 5 mi W on US 78 in Coldwater at Oxford Lake and Civic Center.

Dr J.C. Francis Medical Museum and Apothecary (1850). Unusual one-story Greek-revival building served as doctor's office until 1888; medical artifacts, period furnishings. Tours by appt only. 310 Church Ave SE, 12 mi N, off AL 21 in Jacksonville. Phone 205/435-5091. **Free.**

Fort McClellan. Established in 1917, the fort houses the US Army Chemical School, US Army Military Police School and DOD Polygraph Institute. It also serves as a center for basic combat training. Includes three museums (Mon-Fri; wkends by appt; closed hols). On AL 21, 6 mi N of I-20 exit 185. US Army Chemical Corps Museum, phone 205/848-3355; US Army Military Police Corps Musuem, phone 205/848-3522. **Free.**

The Church of St Michael and All Angels (Episcopal) (1888). Gothic church, parish house, assembly room and bell tower of native stone are connected by cloisters. Twelve-foot Carrara marble altar with alabaster reredos surmounted by seven statues of angels. Stained-glass memorial windows. Lithographs of Christian history are in assembly room. (Daily) W 18th St & Cobb Ave. Phone 205/237-4011.

Motels

✔★ ★ **BEST WESTERN RIVERSIDE INN.** *(11900 US 78, Pell City 35125)* I-20 exit 162 & US 78. 205/338-3381; FAX 205/338-3183. 70 rms, 2 story. S $35-$40; D $45-$55; each addl $6; under 12 free; race wkends 4-day min. Crib $2. Pet accepted, some restrictions. TV. Pool; wading pool. Restaurant 6 am-2 pm, 5-9 pm. Ck-out 11 am. Coin lndry. Meeting rms. Boating; waterskiing. Pier. On Logan-Martin Lake. Cr cds: A, C, D, DS, MC, V.

★ ★ **HAMPTON INN.** *(1600 AL 21 S, Oxford 36203)* 2 mi S via AL 21 S. 205/835-1492; FAX 205/835-0636. 129 rms, 2 story. S $47-$57.50; D $55-$65.50; under 18 free; 3-day min Talladega Races. Crib free. TV; cable (premium), VCR avail. Pool. Complimentary continental bkfst buffet. Restaurant opp open 24 hrs. Ck-out noon. Meeting rms. Business servs avail. In-rm modem link. Cr cds: A, C, D, DS, MC, V.

D ≈ ⚊ 🐾 🏊 SC

★ ★ ★ **HOLIDAY INN.** *(Jct US 78 & AL 21, Oxford 36203)* near Municipal Airport. 205/831-3410; FAX 205/831-9560. 194 rms, 2 story. S, D $68; each addl $6; suites $109; under 18 free. Crib free. TV; cable. Pool; whirlpool. Playground. Coffee in rms. Restaurant 6 am-11 am. Rm serv. Bar 11 am-11 pm. Ck-out noon. Coin lndry. Meeting rms. Business servs avail. In-rm modem link. Bellhops. Refrigerators avail. Picnic tables, grills. Cr cds: A, C, D, DS, JCB, MC, V.

D ≈ ⚊ 🐾 🏊 SC

Inn

★ ★ ★ **VICTORIA.** 1604 Quintard Ave (36201). 256/236-0503; FAX 256/236-1138; res: 800/260-8781. E-mail victoria@thevictoria.com; web www.thevictoria.com. 60 units, 4 bldgs, 3 story. S $69; D $79; each addl $10; suites $129-$219; under 12 free. Crib $10. TV; cable (premium), VCR avail. Pool. Restaurant (see THE VICTORIA). Rm serv. Ck-out noon, ck-in 3 pm. Business servs avail. Health club privileges. Built in 1888. Cr cds: A, C, D, DS, MC, V.

D ≈ ⚊ 🐾 🏊 SC

Restaurants

★ **BETTY'S BAR-B-Q.** 401 S Quintard (36201). 256/237-1411. Hrs: 10:30 am-8:30 pm; Fri, Sat to 9 pm. Closed Sun; major hols, also wk of July 4. Beer. Semi-a la carte: lunch $2.95-$5.15, dinner $5.15-$9.75. Child's meals. Specializes in barbecue, catfish, fried chicken. Antique farm implements. Family-owned. Cr cds: A, DS, MC, V.

D SC

✔★ **TOP O' THE RIVER.** 3220 McClellan Blvd (36201). 205/238-0097. Hrs: 5-9 pm; Thurs to 9:30 pm; Fri to 10 pm; Sat 4:30-10 pm; Sun noon-9 pm. Closed some major hols. Res accepted Sun-Thurs. Bar. Complete meals: lunch, dinner $7.95-$14.95. Child's meals. Specializes in catfish, seafood. Historic photos on display. Nautical decor. Cr cds: A, C, D, DS, MC, V.

D SC ⬛

★ ★ **THE VICTORIA.** *(See Victoria Inn)* 205/236-0503. Hrs: 6-9 pm; Fri, Sat to 10 pm. Closed Sun; most major hols. Res accepted. Bar. Semi-a la carte: dinner $13.95-$18.95. Specializes in pasta, game, fish. Pianist Fri, Sat. Outdoor dining. Romantic dining experience in Victorian house. Cr cds: A, D, DS, MC, V.

D

Athens (A-3)

(See also Decatur, Huntsville)

Founded 1818 **Pop** 16,901 **Elev** 720 ft **Area code** 256 **Zip** 35611 **E-mail** alcc@companet.net **Web** companet.net/cc/athenscc.html
Information Athens-Limestone County Chamber of Commerce, PO Box 150, 35612; 256/232-2600 or 232-2609.

The quiet, tree-lined streets and Greek-revival houses lend an air of the old antebellum South to Athens. This was the first major Alabama town to be occupied by Union troops in the Civil War (1862).

It was also the first Alabama city to get electricity (1934) from the Tennessee Valley Authority. Electrification soon spread to the surrounding area, aiding in the development of light manufacturing.

What to See and Do

Athens State College (1822). (2,600 students) On campus is Founders Hall (1843), as well as many examples of Greek-revival architecture. On the second floor of Founders Hall is the Pi Tau Chi Chapel, housing a hand-carved altar depicting scenes from New Testament. Tours of campus (academic yr, Mon-Fri). Beaty & Pryor Sts. Phone 256/233-8100.

Houston Memorial Library and Museum. Built in 1835, this house was once owned by George S. Houston, governor of Alabama and US senator. It is now maintained by the city of Athens. Meeting rooms display Houston coat of arms, family portraits and drawing-room furniture. (Mon-Fri, also Sat mornings; closed most hols) Market & Houston Sts. Phone 256/233-8770. **Free.**

Annual Events

Musical Explosion. Athens Bible School. Mostly country music, some contemporary. Phone 256/232-3525. Two wkends late Mar.

Homespun. Craft show featuring woodworking, quilting, basketmaking; also buggy rides. Phone 256/232-3525. Early May.

Tennessee Valley Old Time Fiddler's Convention. Athens State College. A weekend of traditional American music. Fiddle, mandolin, guitar, banjo and old-time singing; also buck dancing. National and international musicians perform; ends with the naming of the Tennessee Valley Fiddle King. Phone 256/233-8100. Fri, Sat of 1st full wkend Oct.

Motels

★ **BEST WESTERN.** *PO Box 816, 2 mi E via I-65, at US 72 exit 351. 205/233-4030; FAX 205/233-4551.* 88 rms, 2 story. S $36; D $44; each addl $4; under 12 free. Crib free. Pet accepted, some restrictions. TV; cable (premium). Pool. Complimentary continental bkfst. Restaurant opp 6 am-midnight. Ck-out noon. Picnic tables. Cr cds: A, C, D, DS, MC, V.

[D] [symbols] [SC]

✓★ **BOMAR INN.** *1101 US 31 S, 1 mi S on US 31 at jct US 72. 205/232-6944; FAX 205/232-8019; res: 800/824-6834.* 80 rms, 1-2 story. S $38-$39; D $44-$45; each addl $5; under 12 free. Crib free. Pet accepted. TV; cable (premium). Pool. Restaurant 6 am-9 pm; Sun to 2 pm. Rm serv. Ck-out noon. Meeting rms. Valet serv. Sundries. Cr cds: A, C, D, DS, JCB, MC, V.

[D] [symbols] [SC]

★ **HAMPTON INN.** *1488 Thrasher Blvd, I-65 exit 351. 205/232-0030; FAX 205/233-7006.* 56 rms, 2 story. S $49.95-$59.95; D $54.95-$64.95; each addl $5; whirlpool rms $69.95; under 18 free; higher rates special events. Crib free. TV; cable (premium), VCR. Heated pool; whirlpool. Complimentary continental bkfst. Restaurant opp 6 am-10 pm. Ck-out 11 am. Meeting rm. Business servs avail. In-rm modem link. Health club privileges. Refrigerators. Cr cds: A, C, D, DS, MC, V.

[D] [symbols] [SC]

★ **TRAVELODGE.** *1325 US 72E, 1 mi E of jct US 72 & I-65 exit 351. 205/233-1446; FAX 205/233-1454; res: 800/578-7878.* 60 rms, most rms with shower only, 2 story. S $33-$38; D $43-$48; each addl $5; suites, kit. units $50; under 15 free. TV; cable, VCR avail (movies). Complimentary continental bkfst. Complimentary coffee in rms. Restaurant opp open 24 hrs. Ck-out 11 am. Coin lndry. Business servs avail. In-rm modem link. Some refrigerators. Cr cds: A, C, D, DS, JCB, MC, V.

[D] [symbols] [SC]

Atmore (H-2)

(See also Mobile)

Pop 8,046 **Elev** 287 ft **Area code** 334 **Zip** 36502 **E-mail** chamber@atmore.frontiernet.net **Web** www.atmore.frontiernet.net/~chamber/
Information Chamber of Commerce, 501 S Pensacola Ave; 334-368-3305.

What to See and Do

Claude D. Kelley State Park. A 25-acre lake is located beneath the towering pines of this 960-acre park. Swimming; fishing; boating (ramps, rentals). Picnicking. Primitive camping, RV hookups, cabins. Standard fees. 12 mi N of I-65, on AL 21 at Atmore exit. Contact Rte 2, Box 77; 334/862-2511.

Auburn (E-5)

(See also Opelika, Tuskegee; also see Columbus, GA)

Settled 1836 **Pop** 33,830 **Elev** 709 ft **Area code** 334 **Zip** 36831 **E-mail** mail@auburn-opelika.com **Web** www.auburn-opelika.com
Information Auburn/Opelika Convention & Visitors Bureau, 714 E Glenn Ave, PO Box 2216; 334/887-8747 or 800/321-8880.

Auburn took its name from the opening line in Oliver Goldsmith's poem, "The Deserted Village," that reads "Sweet Auburn, the loveliest village of the plain . . ." Located on the southeastern slope of the Piedmont plateau, this trading and university community is graced with Greek-revival, Victorian and early 20th-century architecture. The Tiger Trail of Auburn, granite plaques bearing the names of athletes and coaches that have brought recognition to Auburn, can be found in uptown Auburn along College St and Magnolia Ave.

What to See and Do

Auburn University (1856). (22,000 students) One of the nation's earliest land-grant colleges and the first 4-yr educational institution in Alabama to admit women on an equal basis with men. A golden eagle, the university mascot, is housed on campus. Tours of campus. SW section of town off I-85, US 29, AL 14, 147. Phone 334/844-4000. Adj is

The Tiger Trail of Auburn. Granite plaques bearing the names of athletes and coaches that have brought recognition to Auburn. Uptown Auburn along College St and Magnolia Ave.

Chewacla State Park. This 696-acre park, on the fall line separating the Piedmont plateau from the coastal plain, includes a 26-acre lake. Swimming; bathhouse; fishing; boating (rentals). Hiking, nature and mountain bike trails. Picnicking, playground, concession. Improved camping, cabins. Standard fees. 4 mi S off US 29; 2 mi off I-85 exit 51. Phone 334/887-5621 or 800/252-7275.

Motel

✓★ ★ **QUALITY INN.** *1577 S College St (36830), I-85 exit 51. 334/821-7001; res: 800/282-8763.* 122 rms, 3 story. S, D $42-$69; each addl $5; suites $64-$84; under 18 free; higher rates Auburn Univ football games (2-day min). Crib free. Pet accepted. TV; cable (premium). Pool. Complimentary continental bkfst. Restaurant hrs vary. Bar 4 pm-1 am. Ck-out 11 am. Meeting rms. Business servs avail. In-rm modem link. Sundries. Exercise equipt. Refrigerators in suites. Cr cds: A, C, D, DS, JCB, MC, V.

[D] [symbols] [SC]

Hotel

★ ★ ★ **AUBURN UNIVERSITY HOTEL & CONFERENCE CENTER.** *241 S College St (36830). 334/821-8200; FAX 334/826-8755; res: 800/228-2876.* E-mail auhotel@mail.auburn.edu; web www.auhcc.com. 248 rms, 6 story. S, D $59-$125; each addl $10; suites $165-$250; under 18 free; higher rates football games. Crib free. Pet accepted. TV; cable. Pool. Restaurants 6:30 am-11 pm. Bar 11:30 am-11 pm. Ck-out noon. Business servs avail. In-rm modem link. Convention facilities. Gift shop. Exercise equipt. Health club privileges. Located on eastern edge of campus opp Samford Hall. Cr cds: A, C, D, DS, MC, V.

Inn

★ ★ **CRENSHAW GUEST HOUSE.** *371 N College St (36830), I-85 exit 51. 334/821-1131; FAX 334/826-8123; res: 800/950-1131.* E-mail crenshaw-gh@mindspring.com; web www.auburnalabama.com. 6 rms, 2 story, 2 suites. S $48-$55; D $58-$75; suites $65-$75; higher rates football games. TV; cable, VCR. Complimentary continental bkfst in rms. Coffee in lobby. Restaurant nearby. Ck-out 11 am, ck-in 2 pm. Meeting rm. In-rm modem link. Health club privileges. Refrigerators. Picnic tables. Restored house built in 1890; antiques. Cr cds: A, MC, V.

Restaurant

★ ★ **NOODLE'S ITALIAN EATERY & GRILL.** *103 N College St (36830). 334/821-0349.* Hrs: 5-10 pm. Closed Sun; Thanksgiving, Dec 24, 25. Res accepted. Italian, Amer menu. Bar. Semi-a la carte: dinner $5-$15. Specializes in seafood, steak. Own pasta. Outdoor dining. Cr cds: A, C, D, DS, MC, V.

Bessemer (D-3)

(See also Birmingham, Tuscaloosa)

Founded 1887 **Pop** 33,497 **Elev** 513 ft **Area code** 205
Information Bessemer Area Chamber of Commerce, PO Box 648, 35021; 205/425-3253 or 888/423-7736.

The city of Bessemer was founded on April 12, 1887 by Henry F. De-Bardeleben. It was, however, named after Sir Henry Bessemer, inventor of the steel-making process that bears his name. As additional furnaces were built in Bessemer, the population grew. By the 1930s, the town ranked second only to Birmingham as a state center for heavy industry. The factories turned out iron and steel, cast-iron pipe, steel railway cars, explosives, fertilizer and building materials. Today a variety of industries dominate Bessemer's economy; the medical community is among the city's largest employers.

What to See and Do

Hall of History Museum. Displays of pioneer life in Jefferson County, Mound Indians, prehistoric life, the Civil War and Bessemer city history. (Tues-Sat; closed hols) In Southern Railway Depot, 1905 Alabama Ave. Phone 205/426-1633. **Donation.**

Tannehill State Historical Park. Restored ironworks that once produced 20 tons of pig iron a day for the Confederacy. Iron & Steel Museum (daily). Park features bathhouses; fishing. Nature trails. Picnicking, concession. Camping (hookups, dump station; fee); bathhouses. Park (daily). 12 mi SW off I-59, exit 100 at Bucksville . Phone 205/477-5711. Day use ¢

Annual Event

Christmas Parade & Tour. Usually 2nd Sat Dec.

Motel

★ **RAMADA INN.** *1121 9th Ave SW (35020), on US 11 at jct I-20, I-59. 205/424-9780.* 156 rms, 2 story. S $46-$51; D $52-$57; each addl $6; under 12 free. Crib free. TV; cable. Pool; wading pool. Restaurant 6-10 am, 6-9 pm. Bar 3 pm-2 am; entertainment exc Sun. Ck-out noon. Coin lndry. Meeting rms. Business servs avail. Some refrigerators. Cr cds: A, D, DS, MC, V.

Restaurants

★ ★ **BRIGHT STAR.** *304 19th St N. 205/424-9444.* Hrs: 11 am-10 pm. Closed major hols. Res accepted. Greek, Amer menu. Bar. Semi-a la carte: lunch $4-$7, dinner $9.95-$21.95. Child's meals. Specialty: Greek broiled red snapper. Cr cds: A, C, D, DS, MC, V.

✔ ★ **FURNACE MASTERS.** *(22851 Eastern Valley Rd, Mc Calla 35111) at Tannehill State Park. 205/477-6102.* Hrs: 11 am-9 pm; Sat, Sun from 7 am. Closed Mon; major hols. Semi-a la carte: bkfst $3.25-$5.95, lunch $4-$7, dinner $5-$13. Buffet: bkfst (Sat, Sun) $5.99, dinner (Fri, Sat) $12.95. Child's meals. Specialties: Bessemer fried chicken, country ham steak. Rustic setting. No cr cds accepted.

Unrated Dining Spot

BOB SYKES BAR-B-QUE. *1724 9th Ave (35020). 205/426-1400.* E-mail oink2@aol.com; web www.bobsykes.com. Hrs: 10 am-10 pm; Fri, Sat to 11 pm. Closed Sun; Jan 1, Thanksgiving, Dec 25. Semi-a la carte: lunch, dinner $2.50-$8. Specializes in open pit barbecued pork, homemade pies. Family-owned. Cr cds: A, DS, MC, V.

Birmingham (D-3)

(See also Bessemer, Cullman)

Founded 1871 **Pop** 265,968 **Elev** 601 ft **Area code** 205 **Web** www.birminghamal.org
Information Convention & Visitors Bureau, 2200 9th Ave N, 35203; 205/458-8000 or 800/458-8085.

A city of great industrial strength, Birmingham once proudly called itself the "Pittsburgh of the South." Today, Birmingham is equally proud of its reputation as an international medical center. Advances in medical science through research at the University of Alabama medical complex attract patients worldwide.

At the turn of the 19th century, Native Americans who painted their faces and weapons red were known by early settlers as "Red Sticks." Even when the red paint was found to be hematite iron ore, it was still considered worthless, and many years passed before Red Mountain ore became the foundation for Birmingham's steel industry. The Confederacy's lack of iron in 1863 led to the building of a small blast furnace, which produced cannonballs and rifles until Wilson's Raiders destroyed it in 1865.

Birmingham was born in 1871 when two railroads intersected. A year later, the Elyton Land Company had sold most of its 4,150 acres at fabulous prices. (It had bought the land for $25 an acre.) But, in 1873 a double disaster struck. First, cholera drove hundreds from the new city; then, the nationwide financial panic nearly doomed Birmingham to extinction. Refusing to give in, Charles Linn, a former Civil War blockade runner who had opened a small bank in 1871, built a grand three-story brick bank for the huge (at that time) sum of $36,000. He then sent out 500 invitations to a "Calico Ball," as he called it, to celebrate its opening. Guests came from all over the state; women in ball gowns and men in formal dress all cut from calico. "Linn's folly" paid off—Birmingham was saved.

Today, Birmingham is a modern, progressive city—one of culture as well as steel, and of education as well as the social life that began with the Calico Ball. To visitors, it offers much in recreational and sightseeing opportunities. Birmingham Green, a major renaissance of the downtown area, added walkways, plantings, benches and the DART trolley. The Five Points South area, featuring clubs with many styles of quality entertainment, plays a major role in Birmingham's nightlife. This is indeed the heart of the New South.

Transportation

Birmingham International Airport: Information 205/599-0500; lost and found 205/458-8002; weather 205/945-7000.

Car Rental Agencies: See IMPORTANT TOLL-FREE NUMBERS.

Public Transportation: Buses (Birmingham/Jefferson County Transit Authority), phone 205/521-0101.

Rail Passenger Service: Amtrak 800/872-7245.

What to See and Do

Alabama Sports Hall of Fame Museum. Showcase for memorabilia of Alabama sports figures; sound-sensored displays; theater. (Mon-Sat, also Sun afternoons; closed some major hols) Civic Center Blvd & 22nd St N. Phone 205/323-6665. ¢¢

Arlington (ca 1850). Birmingham's last remaining antebellum house in the Greek-revival style features a diverse collection of 19th-century American decorative art. Located on a sloping hill in Elyton, the house is surrounded by shady lawns, oak and magnolia trees and seasonal plantings. (Daily exc Mon; closed major hols) 331 Cotton Ave SW. Phone 205/780-5656. ¢¢

Birmingham Botanical Gardens. Includes orchids, lilies, dogwood, wildflowers, azaleas; 26-ft floral clock, conservatory and arboretum of rare plants, shrubs and trees. (Daily) Restaurant on grounds. 2612 Lane Park Rd. Phone 205/879-1227. **Free.** Includes

Japanese Gardens. Gardens landscaped with Oriental plants, waterfalls. Also here is a bonsai complex, Oriental statuary and a Zen garden. Gravel paths. (Daily) **Free.**

Birmingham Civil Rights Institute. Exhibits portray struggle for civil rights in Birmingham and across the nation from the 1920s to the present; multimedia presentations. (Daily exc Mon; closed some major hols) 520 16th St N. Phone 205/328-9696. ¢¢

Birmingham Museum of Art. Features collections of Renaissance, Asian and American art, including Remington bronzes; 20th-century collection; 17th-19th-century American and European paintings and decorative arts. Also featured are pre-Columbian art and artifacts, art of the Native American and the largest collection of Wedgwood outside of England. Changing exhibits. Multi-level sculpture garden with 2 reflecting pools and a waterfall. (Daily exc Mon; closed major hols) 2000 8th Ave N, across from Linn Park. Phone 205/254-2565. **Free.**

Birmingham-Jefferson Convention Complex. The entire complex covers 7 sq blks. The center contains 220,000 sq ft of exhibition space; 3,000-seat concert hall; 1,100-seat theater; 18,000-seat coliseum. Between 9th & 11th Aves N, 19th & 21st Sts. For event information phone 205/458-8400.

Birmingham-Southern College (1856). (1,900 students) A 200-acre campus on wooded rolling hills. Here is the state's first planetarium (for schedule, reservations, phone 205/226-4771; fee). Tours of campus. Arkadelphia Rd. Phone 205/226-4600.

Birmingham Zoo. Nearly 1,000 animals on display. Highlights include sea lions, Siberian tiger and the predator building. (Daily) 2630 Cahaba Rd. Phone 205/879-0409. ¢¢

DeSoto Caverns Park. (See SYLACAUGA) Approx 38 mi SE via AL 280 to AL 76.

Miles College (1905). (700 students) Extensive collection of African-American literature; exhibits of African art forms. Two historic landmark buildings. Tours. 5500 Myron Massey Blvd in Fairfield. Phone 205/923-2771.

Oak Mountain State Park. Peavine Falls and Gorge and two lakes sit amidst 9,940 acres of the state's most rugged mountains. Swimming; fishing; boating (marina, ramp, rentals). Hiking, backpacking, bridle trails; golf (18 holes; fee), tennis. Picnicking (shelters, barbecue pits, fireplaces), concession. Camping, cabins. Demonstration farm. Standard fees. 15 mi S on I-65, exit 246, near Pelham. Phone 205/620-2524.

Red Mountain Museum and Road Cut. Natural history museum located on slopes of Red Mountain. Extensive collection of fossils includes a 14-ft mosasaur (extinct marine lizard); geologic history displays and exhibits; hands-on exhibits. Walkway carved into the face of the mountain above expressway. More than 150 million yrs of geologic history are exposed for one-third of a mile. Picnicking. (Daily; closed hols) 1421 22nd St S. Phone 205/933-4153. ¢

Rickwood Caverns State Park. This 380-acre park offers swimming pools; hiking; carpet golf; miniature train ride. Picnicking, concession, gift shop. Primitive and improved camping (standard fees). One-hr tours of cave with 260 million-yr-old limestone formations (Memorial Day-Labor Day, daily; rest of Sept-Oct & Mar-May, wkends). Park (all yr); pool (seasonal). Fee for some activities. 20 mi N on I-65 to exit 284 (just N of Warrior) then 4 mi W on Skyline Dr to Rickwood Rd, follow state signs. Phone 205/647-9692. Park entrance ¢; Cave tour ¢¢¢

Ruffner Mountain Nature Center. 538 acres of the last undeveloped section of this area's Appalachian Mountains. Displays focus on Ruffner Mountain's biology, geology and history. Wildlife refuge with nature trails. (Daily exc Mon; closed most major hols, also Dec 24) Fee for special programs. 1214 81st St S. Phone 205/833-8112. **Free.**

Samford University (1841). (4,600 students) A 172-acre campus with brick Georgian-colonial buildings. The Samford Murals on view in Rotunda, Dwight and Lucille Beeson Center for the Healing Arts. Beeson Divinity Hall Chapel is topped by a copper-clad dome that has a detailed ceiling mural on the interior (tours avail). Tours of campus. 800 Lakeshore Dr in Shades Mt section. Phone 205/870-2011 or 205/870-2921.

Sloss Furnaces National Historic Landmark. An industrial museum and site for concerts and downtown festivals. (Daily exc Mon) 20 32nd St N.For event and further information phone 205/324-1911. **Free.**

University of Alabama at Birmingham. (16,500 students) 70-sq-blk area on S edge of downtown. **Reynolds Historical Library** in the Lister Hill Library of the Health Sciences, 1700 University Blvd, 6 blks W of US 31 and US 280, has collections of ivory anatomical manikins, original manuscripts and rare medical and scientific books; **Alabama Museum of Health Sciences** has memorabilia of Alabama doctors, surgeons, optometrists and other medical practitioners; reproductions of doctor and dentist turn-of-the-century offices (Mon-Fri). Phone 205/934-4475.

Vulcan (1904). The figure of Vulcan, designed for the Louisiana Purchase Exposition in St Louis, is one of the largest iron figures ever cast, standing 55 ft tall and weighing 60 tons. It surveys the city from a pedestal 124 ft high. Made of Birmingham iron and cast locally, Vulcan, Roman god of fire and forge, legendary inventor of smithing and metalworking, stands as a monument to the city's iron industry atop Red Mountain since 1939 holding a lighted torch aloft over the city. A glass-enclosed elevator takes passengers to observation deck. Vulcan's torch shines a bright red when there's been a traffic fatality in the city in the previous 24 hrs. Park (daily; closed Thanksgiving, Dec 25). On Valley Ave off US 31 at top of Red Mountain in Vulcan Park. Phone 205/328-6198 or -2863. ¢

Annual Events

Festival of Arts. Different country featured each yr. Mid-Apr.

City Stages. Music festival, street vendors and regional crafstmen. Mid-June.

State Fair. Alabama State Fairgrounds. Contact Alabama State Fair Authority, PO Box 3800-B, 2331 Bessemer Rd, 35208; 205/786-8100. 10 days mid-Oct.

Additional Visitor Information

Contact the Greater Birmingham Convention & Visitors Bureau, 2200 9th Ave N, 35203, phone 205/458-8000; or the Birmingham/Jefferson Visitor Information Center, 1201 University Blvd, 35233, phone 205/458-8001.

City Neighborhoods

Many of the restaurants, unrated dining establishments and some lodgings listed under Birmingham include neighborhoods as well as exact street addresses. Geographic descriptions of the Downtown and Five Points are given, followed by a table of restaurants arranged by neighborhood.

Downtown: South of 10th Ave N, west of 26th St, north of L & N Railroad tracks and east of 15th Street N. **North of Downtown:** North of US 20/US 59. **South of Downtown:** South of First Ave. **East of Downtown:** East of 26th St.

Five Points: Area at the intersection of 20th St S and Highland Ave.

BIRMINGHAM RESTAURANTS BY NEIGHBORHOOD AREAS

(For full description, see alphabetical listings under Restaurants)

DOWNTOWN
La Paree. 2013 5th Ave N

NORTH OF DOWNTOWN
Niki's West. 233 Finley Ave W

SOUTH OF DOWNTOWN
Bombay Cafe. 2839 7th Ave S
Connie Kanakis' Cafe. 3423 Colonade Pkwy
Golden City. 4647K US 280
Grady's American Grill. 3470 Galleria Circle
Winston's (Wynfrey At Riverchase Galleria Hotel). 1000 Riverchase Galleria

FIVE POINTS
Bottega. 2240 Highland Ave
Cobb Lane. 1 Cobb Lane
Highlands. 2011 11th Ave S
Merritt House. 2220 Highland Ave

Note: When a listing is located in a town that does not have its own city heading, it will appear under the city nearest to its location. In these cases, the address and town appear in parenthesis immediately following the name of the establishment.

Motels

✔★ **BAYMONT INN.** 513 Cahaba Park Circle (35242), I-459 and US 280, south of downtown. 205/995-9990; FAX 205/995-0563. 102 rms, 3 story. S $41.95; D $47.95; each addl $7; suites $55.95-$62.95; under 18 free. Crib free. Pet accepted, some restrictions. TV; cable (premium). Complimentary continental bkfst. Ck-out noon. Meeting rm. Business servs avail. In-rm modem link. Cr cds: A, C, D, DS, MC, V.

D ⟨⟩ ≋ ⇗ ⟨⟩ SC

★★ **COMFORT INN.** 195 Oxmore Rd (35209), south of downtown. 205/941-0990; FAX 205/941-1527. 155 rms, 2 story. S $60; D $69; each addl $8; under 18 free. Crib free. TV; cable (premium). Pool. Complimentary continental bkfst. Restaurant adj open 24 hrs. Ck-out 11 am. Meeting rms. Business center. Valet serv. Exercise equipt. Cr cds: A, C, D, DS, JCB, MC, V.

D ≋ ⟨⟩ ⇗ ⟨⟩ SC ⟨⟩

★★★ **COURTYARD BY MARRIOTT.** (500 Shades Creek Pkwy, Homewood 35209) S via I-65. 205/879-0400; FAX 205/879-6324. 140 rms, 1-3 story, 14 suites. S $86; D $98; suites $95-$110; wkend rates. Crib free. TV; cable. Pool; whirlpool. Restaurant 6:30 am-11 am; Sat, Sun from 7 am. Bar 5-11 pm. Meeting rms. Business servs avail. In-rm modem link. Guest lndry. Valet serv. Exercise equipt. Private patios, balconies. Cr cds: A, C, D, DS, MC, V.

D ≋ ⟨⟩ ⇗ ⟨⟩ SC

★★ **DAYS INN AIRPORT.** 5101 Airport Blvd (35212), I-20/I-59 Airport exit, near Municipal Airport, east of downtown. 205/592-6110; res: 800/329-7466; FAX 205/591-5623. 138 rms, 5 story. S $48-$55; D $53-$61; each addl $5; under 18 free. TV; cable. Pool. Playground. Ck-out noon. Business servs avail. Airport transportation. Exercise equipt. Cr cds: A, C, D, DS, MC, V.

D ≋ ⟨⟩ ⇗ ⟨⟩ SC

✔★ **FAIRFIELD INN BY MARRIOTT.** (155 Vulcan Rd, Homewood 35209) 3 mi S on I-65 exit 256. 205/945-9600; FAX 205/945-9600. 132 rms, 3 story. S $54.95; D $65.95-$70.95; under 18 free. Crib free. TV; cable. Complimentary continental bkfst. Ck-out noon. Business servs avail. In-rm modem link. Cr cds: A, C, D, DS, MC, V.

D ⟨⟩ ⟨⟩ SC

✔★★ **HAMPTON INN.** 3910 Kilgore Memorial Dr (35210), east of downtown. 205/956-4100; FAX 205/956-0906. 70 rms, 2 story. S $65-$69; D $69-$73; under 18 free; higher rates special events. Crib free. TV; cable (premium). Pool. Complimentary continental bkfst. Restaurant nearby. Ck-out noon. Meeting rms. Business servs avail. Health club privileges. Cr cds: A, C, D, DS, MC, V.

D ≋ ⟨⟩ ⟨⟩ SC

★★ **HAMPTON INN.** (2731 US 280, Mountain Brook 35223) S on I-65, NE on Oxmoor Rd to US 280. 205/870-7822; FAX 205/871-7610. 131 rms, 5 story. S $62; D $62-$67; under 18 free. Crib free. Pet accepted, some restrictions. TV; cable. Pool. Complimentary continental bkfst. Restaurant adj 6 am-11 pm. Ck-out noon. Meeting rm. Business servs avail. In-rm modem link. Cr cds: A, C, D, DS, MC, V.

D ⟨⟩ ≋ ⟨⟩ ⟨⟩ SC

★★ **LA QUINTA MOTOR INN.** 905 11th Court W (35204), near jct I-20, US 78, north of downtown. 205/324-4510; FAX 205/252-7972. 106 rms, 3 story. S, D $57-$77; each addl $10; under 18 free. Crib free. Pet accepted, some restrictions. TV; cable. Pool. Complimentary continental bkfst. Restaurant adj open 24 hrs. Ck-out noon. Meeting rms. Cr cds: A, C, D, DS, MC, V.

D ⟨⟩ ≋ ⟨⟩ ⟨⟩ SC

★★ **MOTEL BIRMINGHAM.** 7905 Crestwood Blvd (35210), I-20 Montevallo Rd exit, east of downtown. 205/956-4440; FAX 205/956-3011; res: 800/338-9275. 242 rms, 1-2 story, 18 kits. (no equipt). S $48-$63; D, kit. units $58-$68; suites $95-$250; under 16 free. Crib free. Pet accepted, some restrictions; $15. TV; cable (premium). Pool. Playground. Complimentary continental bkfst. Restaurant adj open 24 hrs. Ck-out noon. Meeting rms. Business center. In-rm modem link. Valet serv. Health club privileges. Cr cds: A, C, D, DS, MC, V.

D ⟨⟩ ≋ ⟨⟩ ⟨⟩ SC ⟨⟩

★★ **RESIDENCE INN BY MARRIOTT.** 3 Greenhill Pkwy (35242), at US 280, south of downtown. 205/991-8686; FAX 205/991-8729. 128 kit. suites, 2 story. Kit. suites $104-$129; wkly, monthly rates. Crib free. Pet accepted; $165-$215. TV; cable. Pool; whirlpool. Complimentary continental bkfst. Ck-out noon. Coin lndry. Meeting rms. Business servs avail. Valet serv. Health club privileges. Sport court. Gas grills. Cr cds: A, C, D, DS, JCB, MC, V.

D ⟨⟩ ≋ ⟨⟩ ⟨⟩ SC

Motor Hotels

★★ **CLARION-AIRPORT.** 5216 Airport Hwy (35212), I-20/I-59, Airport exit, near Municipal Airport, east of downtown. 205/591-7900; FAX 205/592-6476. 193 rms, 4 story. S, D $69-$75; each addl $8; suites $100-$140. Crib free. Pet accepted, some restrictions; $25. TV; cable (premium). Pool. Coffee in rms. Restaurant 6 am-10 pm; Sat, Sun from 7 am. Rm serv from 7 am. Bar 2 pm-2 am; entertainment. Ck-out noon. Meeting rms. Business servs avail. In-rm modem link. Bellhops. Valet serv. Free airport transportation. Exercise equipt. Cr cds: A, C, D, DS, JCB, MC, V.

D ⟨⟩ ≋ ⟨⟩ ⟨⟩ ⟨⟩ SC

★ ★ **HAMPTON INN-COLONNADE.** 3400 Colonnade Pkwy (35243), south of downtown. 205/967-0002; FAX 205/969-0901. 133 rms, 5 story. S $72-$88; D $81-$97; under 18 free; higher rates sports events. Crib free. TV; cable (premium). Pool. Complimentary continental bkfst. Coffee in rms. Restaurant nearby. Ck-out noon. Meeting rms. Business servs avail. In-rm modem link. Health club privileges. Cr cds: A, C, D, DS, MC, V.

D ⇌ ⋈ 🔥 SC

★ ★ ★ **HAWTHORN SUITES.** 5320 Beacon Dr (35210), I-20, exit 133, east of downtown. 205/951-1200; FAX 205/951-1692; res: 800/772-7463. 290 suites, 3 story. 1-bedrm $75; 2-bedrm $125; each addl $10; under 12 free; wkend, wkly, monthly rates. Crib free. TV; cable. Pool. Complimentary continental bkfst. Restaurant 6:30-9:30 am, 11 am-1:30 pm, 5-10 pm; wkends hrs vary. Rm serv. Bar 5-11 pm. Ck-out noon. Meeting rms. Business servs avail. Valet serv. Airport transportation. Tennis privileges. Private patios, balconies. Cr cds: A, C, D, DS, MC, V.

D 🏃 ⇌ 🎿 ⛷ 🔥 SC

★ ★ **HOLIDAY INN AIRPORT.** 5000 10th Ave N (35212), near Municipal Airport, east of downtown. 205/591-6900; FAX 205/591-2093. 224 rms, 9 story. S, D $69. Crib free. TV; cable (premium). Pool. Restaurant 6 am-2 pm, 5-10 pm. Rm serv. Bar; entertainment exc Sun. Ck-out noon. Meeting rms. Business servs avail. In-rm modem link. Bellhops. Free airport transportation. Cr cds: A, C, D, DS, MC, V.

D ⇌ ✈ ⋈ 🔥 SC

★ ★ **HOLIDAY INN-GALLERIA SOUTH.** 1548 Montgomery Hwy (35216), south of downtown. 205/822-4350; FAX 205/822-0350. 166 rms, 3 story. S, D $78; each addl $10; suites $135-$145; under 19 free; higher rates special events. Crib free. TV; cable, VCR avail. Pool; whirlpool. Playground. Restaurant 6:30 am-1:30 pm, 5-10 pm. Rm serv. Bar 3 pm-2 am. Ck-out noon. Coin lndry. Meeting rms. Business servs avail. In-rm modem link. Bellhops. Valet serv. Health club privileges. Picnic tables, grills. On 4½-acre stocked lake. Cr cds: A, C, D, DS, MC, V.

D 🐾 ⇌ ⛷ 🔥 SC

Hotels

★ ★ ★ **EMBASSY SUITES.** 2300 Woodcrest Place (35209), south of downtown. 205/879-7400; FAX 205/870-4523. Web www.embassysuites.com. 243 units, 8 story. S, D $100-$150; each addl $10; under 12 free; wkend rates. Crib free. TV; cable, VCR (movies $6). Indoor pool; whirlpool. Complimentary full bkfst. Restaurant 11 am-10 pm. Bar to midnight. Ck-out noon. Meeting rms. Business servs avail. In-rm modem link. Gift shop. Free airport transportation. Sauna. Health club privileges. Refrigerators. Cr cds: A, C, D, DS, MC, V.

D ⇌ ⋈ 🔥 SC

★ ★ **HOLIDAY INN REDMONT-CITY CENTRE.** 2101 5th Ave N (35203), downtown. 205/324-2101; FAX 205/324-0610. 112 rms, 12 story. S, D $99-$109; each addl $12; suites $124-$169; under 18 free. Crib free. TV; cable (premium), VCR avail. Restaurant 6:30 am-2 pm, 5-10 pm. Bar from 4 pm. Ck-out noon. Meeting rms. Business servs avail. In-rm modem link. Concierge. Free airport transportation. Health club privileges. Refrigerators. Cr cds: A, C, D, DS, JCB, MC, V.

D ⋈ 🔥 SC

★ ★ ★ **MOUNTAIN BROOK INN.** 2800 US 280S (35223), south of downtown. 205/870-3100; FAX 205/414-2128; res: 800/523-7771. E-mail mountainbrookinn@mindspring.com; web www.mountainbrookinn.com. 162 rms, 8 story. S $115; D $125; each addl $10; suites $199; under 18 free; wkend rates. Crib free. Pet accepted. TV; cable (premium). Pool. Restaurant 6:30 am-10 pm. Bar noon-2 am; entertainment. Ck-out noon. Meeting rms. Business servs avail. In-rm modem link. Free airport transportation. Health club privileges. Bathrm phones; wet bar in some suites. Cr cds: A, C, D, DS, MC, V.

D 🐾 ⇌ ⋈ 🔥 SC

★ ★ ★ **PICKWICK.** 1023 20th St S (35205), downtown. 205/933-9555; FAX 205/933-6918; res: 800/255-7304. 63 rms, 8 story, 28 suites. S, D $86-$89; each addl $10; suites $109; under 12 free; wkend rates. Crib free. Pet accepted, some restrictions; $50. TV. Complimentary continental bkfst. Ck-out noon. Business servs avail. In-rm modem link. Shopping arcade. Barber, beauty shop. Free covered parking. Health club privileges. Some refrigerators. In historical area. Art-deco decor. Cr cds: A, C, D, MC, V.

D 🐾 ⋈ 🔥 SC

★ ★ **RADISSON.** 808 S 20th St (35205), at University Blvd, opp Medical Center, south of downtown. 205/933-9000; FAX 205/933-0920. Web www.radisson.com. 287 rms, 14 story. S, D $109-$119; each addl $10; suites $150-$500; family rates; some wkend rates. TV; cable. Pool. Sauna. Restaurant 6:30 am-10 pm. Bars 4 pm-midnight. Ck-out noon. Convention facilities. Business servs avail. In-rm modem link. Barber, beauty shop. Free covered parking. Airport transportation. Health club privileges. Cr cds: A, C, D, DS, ER, MC, V.

D ⇌ ⋈ 🔥 SC

★ ★ ★ **SHERATON.** 2101 Civic Center Blvd (35203), downtown. 205/324-5000; res: 205/307-3000; FAX 205/307-3045. Web www.sheraton.com/birmingham. 770 rms, 17 story. S, D $140; each addl $15; suites $215; under 16 free; wkend rates. Crib $15. TV; cable. Indoor pool; whirlpool. Complimentary coffee in rms. Restaurant 6 am-11 pm. Bar 11-2 am; entertainment. Ck-out noon. Convention facilities. Business center. In-rm modem link. Concierge. Gift shop. Valet parking. Exercise equipt; sauna, steam rm. Balconies. Cr cds: A, C, D, DS, JCB, MC, V.

D ⇌ 🍴 ⋈ 🔥 SC 🏃

★ ★ ★ **SHERATON-PERIMETER PARK SOUTH.** 8 Perimeter Dr (35243), south of downtown. 205/967-2700; FAX 205/972-8603. 202 rms, 8 story. S, D $120-$140; each addl $10; under 18 free; wkend rates. Crib free. TV; cable (premium). Pool. Complimentary coffee in rms. Restaurant 6:30 am-10 pm. Bar 10-1 am. Rm serv. Ck-out noon. Meeting rms. Business center. In-rm modem link. Gift shop. Free airport, RR station transportation. Exercise equipt. Cr cds: A, C, D, DS, MC, V.

D ⇌ 🍴 ⋈ 🔥 🏃

★ ★ ★ **TUTWILER.** Park Place at 21st St N (35203), downtown. 205/322-2100; FAX 205/325-1183; res: 800/845-1787 (exc AL). 147 rms, 8 story, 52 suites. S, D $134-$154; suites $151-$178; under 12 free; wkend rates. Crib free. TV; cable (premium), VCR avail (free movies). Restaurant 6-10 am, 11 am-2 pm, 5-10 pm. Rm serv 24 hrs. Bar 11 am-midnight. Ck-out noon. Meeting rms. Business servs avail. In-rm modem link. Concierge. Free valet parking. Free airport, RR station, bus depot transportation. Some bathrm phones; refrigerators avail. Balconies. Luxury level. Cr cds: A, D, DS, MC, V.

D ⋈ 🔥 SC

★ ★ ★ **WYNFREY AT RIVERCHASE GALLERIA.** 1000 Riverchase Galleria (35244), south of downtown. 205/987-1600; FAX 205/988-4597; res: 800/996-3739. 329 rms, 16 story. S, D $115-$219; suites $250-$825; under 12 free; wkend rates. Crib free. Valet parking $6. TV; cable (premium), VCR avail. Pool; poolside serv. Restaurant 6 am-midnight (also see WINSTON'S). Rm serv 24 hrs. Piano bar. Ck-out 11 am. Convention facilities. Business center. Concierge. Airport transportation. Golf privileges. Exercise equipt; steam rm. Health club privileges. Bathrm phone, refrigerator in suites. Luxury level. Elegant decor features marble, brass and Chippendale and French Regency furnishings. Cr cds: A, C, D, DS, MC, V.

D 🍴 ⇌ 🍴 ⋈ 🔥 SC 🏃

Restaurants

★ ★ **ARMAN'S.** (2117 Cahaba Rd, Mountain Brook 35223) S on I-65, NE on Oxmoor Rd to US 280. 205/871-5551. Hrs: 5-10 pm; Fri, Sat to 11 pm. Closed Sun; most major hols. Res accepted; required Fri, Sat. Italian, Amer menu. Bar. Wine list. Semi-a la carte: dinner $13.95-$24.95. Specializes in seafood, pasta. Valet parking. Bldg once a grocery store. Antique bar. Cr cds: A, C, D, DS, MC, V.

D

★ ★ **BOMBAY CAFE.** *2839 7th Ave S (35222), south of downtown.* 205/322-1930. Hrs: 6-9:30 pm; Fri, Sat to 10:30 pm. Closed Sun; major hols. Res accepted. Bar. Semi-a la carte: dinner $14.95-$22.95. Child's meals. Specializes in seafood, veal, lamb. Valet parking. Modern decor; marble fireplace, artwork. Cr cds: A, MC, V.

D ♥

★ ★ **BOTTEGA.** *2240 Highland Ave, at Five Points.* 205/939-1000. Hrs: 11 am-11 pm; Sat from noon. Closed some major hols. Italian, Amer menu. Bar. Complete meals: lunch $3.50-$10. Semi-a la carte: dinner $5-$20. Child's meals. Specializes in veal, homemade ravioli, seafood. Valet parking. Outdoor dining. Lunch in casual cafe-style surroundings; dinner in more formal atmosphere. Cr cds: A, MC, V.

D

✔★ ★ **COBB LANE.** *1 Cobb Lane, at Five Points.* 205/933-0462. Hrs: 11 am-2:30 pm; Fri, Sat also 6-10 pm. Res accepted. Bar. A la carte entrees: lunch $6.95-$13.95, dinner $13.95-$17.95. Specializes in she-crab soup, Southern cuisine, chocolate roulage. Outdoor dining. In historic district. Cr cds: A, DS, MC, V.

★ ★ **CONNIE KANAKIS' CAFE.** *3423 Colonade Pkwy (35243), in shopping center, south of downtown.* 205/967-5775. Hrs: 11 am-2:30 pm, 5-10 pm; Fri to 11 pm; Sat 5-11 pm. Closed Sun; major hols. Res accepted. Bar. Semi-a la carte: lunch $4-$9.50, dinner $7.95-$27.95. Child's meals. Specializes in seafood, steak. Cr cds: A, C, D, DS, MC, V.

D

★ **FORMOSA.** *(2109 Lorna Ridge Lane, Hoover 35216) S on I-65 to Hoover exit, then 1 mi W to Lorna Ridge Lane.* 205/979-6684. Hrs: 11 am-2:30 pm, 5-10 pm; Fri, Sat to 11 pm. Closed July 4, Thanksgiving, Dec 25. Res accepted. Chinese menu. Bar. Semi-a la carte: lunch $5-$6, dinner $6.25-$25. Specializes in egg rolls, Mongolian beef, sesame chicken. Chinese decor. View of flower garden. Cr cds: A, DS, MC, V.

D

★ **GOLDEN CITY.** *4647K US 280 (35242), in Riverhills Shopping Center, south of downtown.* 205/991-3197. Hrs: 11 am-2:30 pm, 5-10 pm. Closed most major hols. Res accepted. Chinese menu. Bar. A la carte entrees: lunch $3.99-$5.46, dinner $6.40-$18. Specializes in Mongolian beef, chicken with vegetables. Oriental decor. Cr cds: A, MC, V.

D

✔★ ★ **GRADY'S AMERICAN GRILL.** *3470 Galleria Circle, adj to Galleria Mall, south of downtown.* 205/985-4663. Hrs: 11 am-11 pm; Fri, Sat to midnight. Closed Thanksgiving, Dec 25. Bar. Semi-a la carte: lunch, dinner $5-$15. Child's meals. Specializes in prime rib, seafood, mesquite-grilled chicken. Cr cds: A, D, DS, MC, V.

D ♥

★ ★ **HIGHLANDS.** *2011 11th Ave S, at Five Points.* 205/939-1400. Hrs: 6-10 pm. Closed Sun, Mon; major hols. Res accepted. Bar to 1 am. Wine list. A la carte entrees: dinner $17-$22. Specializes in seafood, grain-fed beef. Own pastries, desserts, ice cream. Valet parking. Cr cds: A, MC, V.

D

★ **LA PAREE.** *2013 5th Ave N (35203), near civic center, downtown.* 205/251-5936. Hrs: 6:45-10 am, 11 am-2:30 pm. Closed Sat, Sun; major hols. Serv bar. Semi-a la carte: bkfst $2.75-$6.95, lunch $4.95-$7.25. Child's meals. Specializes in fresh gulf seafood, steak, lamb. Family-owned. Cr cds: MC, V.

★ ★ **MERRITT HOUSE.** *2220 Highland Ave, at Five Points.* 205/933-1200. Hrs: 11 am-2 pm, 5-10 pm; Sat from 5 pm. Closed Sun; some hols. Res accepted. Continental menu. Bar 11 am-10 pm. Wine cellar. A la carte entrees: lunch $6.50-$12, dinner $16.95-$22. Specializes in seafood, lamb, beef. Own baking, pasta. Valet parking. Located in restored mansion (1909); 6 dining areas. Cr cds: A, D, DS, MC, V.

D ♥

✔★ ★ **NIKI'S WEST.** *233 Finley Ave W (35204), north of downtown.* 205/252-5751. Hrs: 6 am-10 pm. Closed Sun; some major hols. Res accepted. Serv bar. Semi-a la carte: bkfst $4-$8.25, lunch $4.75-$9, dinner $7.25-$13.50. Cafeteria dining area: avg ck (lunch) $6.50. Specializes in fish, chicken. Nautical decor. Family-owned. Cr cds: A, DS, MC, V.

D

★ ★ **ROSSI'S.** *(2737 US 280, Mountain Brook 35216) E on US 280.* 205/879-2111. Hrs: 11 am-10 pm; Fri to 11 pm; Sat 4:30-11 pm. Closed Sun; some major hols. Res accepted. Bar. Complete meals: lunch $4.95-$9.95, dinner $7.95-$22.95. Child's meals. Specializes in seafood, steak, Italian dishes. Outdoor dining. Cr cds: A, C, D, DS, MC, V.

D ♥

★ ★ **WINSTON'S.** *(See Wynfrey At Riverchase Galleria Hotel)* 205/987-1600. Web www.wynfrey.com. Hrs: 6-10 pm. Closed Sun. Continental menu. Bar. Wine list. A la carte entrees: dinner $17-$28. Specializes in seafood, steak. Own baking. Valet parking. English decor. Cr cds: A, C, D, DS, MC, V.

D

Clanton (E-4)

(See also Montgomery)

Founded 1873 **Pop** 7,669 **Elev** 599 ft **Area code** 205 **Zip** 35045 **E-mail** cccoc@scott.net
Information Chamber of Commerce, PO Box 66; 205/755-2400 or 800/553-0493.

A peach and truck farming area, Clanton also caters to fishermen along the Coosa River and its tributaries. Lay and Mitchell dams, to the north and east respectively, are backed by lakes and furnish power to the region. Clanton is the seat of Chilton County.

What to See and Do

Confederate Memorial Park. Two Confederate cemeteries are located on 100 acres that once were the grounds of the Confederate Soldiers Home of Alabama. Museum contains mementos of Alabama's role in the Civil War as well as artifacts, records, documents and photographs. Also hiking trails, picnicking (shelters). (Daily; closed Jan 1, Dec 25) 10 mi S via US 31 in Marbury. Phone 205/755-1990. **Free.**

Lay Dam. Hydroelectric generating plant offers 30-min guided tours (Sat & Sun, also Mon-Fri afternoons). Plant (daily). 12 mi NE via AL 145, County 55. For reservations phone 205/755-4520. **Free.**

Motels

★ ★ **HOLIDAY INN.** *2000 Holiday Inn Dr, 3 mi SE at jct US 31, AL 22 & I-65.* 205/755-0510; FAX 205/755-0510, ext. 116. 100 rms, 2 story. S, D $45-$56; each addl $5; under 19 free. Crib free. Pet accepted. TV. Pool; wading pool. Restaurant 6 am-2 pm, 5-10 pm. Rm serv. Bar 4-11 pm, closed Sun. Ck-out noon. Meeting rms. Business servs avail. In-rm modem link. Valet serv. Free airport transportation. Cr cds: A, C, D, DS, MC, V.

⊞ ✦ ⊠ ⚹ SC

✔★ **KEY WEST INN.** *2045 7th St S, I-65 exit 205.* 205/755-8500; FAX 205/280-0044; res: 800/833-0555. 43 rms, 2 story. S $42; D $46; each addl $5; under 18 free; higher rates fishing tournaments. Crib free. Pet accepted. TV; cable. Complimentary coffee in lobby. Restaurant nearby. Ck-out noon. Coin lndry. Business servs avail. In-rm modem link. Totally nonsmoking. Cr cds: A, C, D, DS, MC, V.

D ✦ ⊠ ⚹ SC

Cullman (B-3)

(See also Birmingham, Decatur)

Founded 1873 **Pop** 13,367 **Elev** 799 ft **Area code** 256
Information Cullman Area Chamber of Commerce, 211 Second Ave NE, PO Box 1104, 35056; 205/734-0454.

Cullman was founded by Colonel John G. Cullmann, an immigrant whose dream was to build a self-sustaining colony of other German refugees and immigrants. In 1873, 5 German families settled on the 5,400 square miles of land he purchased from the Louisville & Nashville Railroad. He also laid out the town. Cullman's residents still enjoy the 100-foot-wide streets. In 1880 there were 6,300 people, many of them Germans, in the county that had already been named for Cullmann by the legislature. Located on the Cumberland Plateau, the area is rich in timber and coal. Today, Cullman is one of the main centers for agriculture and poultry production.

What to See and Do

🟦 **Ave Maria Grotto.** Brother Joseph Zoettl, a Benedictine monk, spent nearly 50 yrs building some 150 miniature replicas of famous churches, buildings and shrines, including Bethlehem, Nazareth, Jerusalem, the Basilica of St Peter's and the California missions. He built them using such materials as cement, stone, bits of jewelry and marble. The miniatures cover four acres of a terraced, landscaped garden. Free picnic grounds adj to parking lot. (Daily; closed Dec 25) I-65 exit 308. Phone 256/734-4110. ¢¢

Clarkson Covered Bridge (1904). One of the largest covered bridges in Alabama, the truss-styled Clarkson is 270 ft long and 50 ft high. Also here are a dogtrot cabin and gristmill. Nature trail. Picnic facilities. 9 mi W via US 278W. Phone 256/739-3530. **Free.**

Cullman County Museum. Large, eight-room museum features items related to the origin and history of Cullman. (Daily exc Sat; closed some major hols) 211 2nd Ave NE. Phone 256/739-1258. ¢

Hurricane Creek Park. Gorge with observation platform; trail over swinging bridge; unusual rock formations, earthquake fault and waterfalls. Picnic tables. (Daily) 6 mi N on US 31, near Vinemont. Phone 256/734-2125. ¢¢

Sportsman Lake Park. Stocked with bream, bass, catfish and other fish. Miniature golf; kiddie rides. Picnicking, concession. Camping. (Apr-Sept, daily) Fee for some activities. N off US 31. Phone 256/734-3052. **Free.**

William B. Bankhead National Forest. This 180,684-acre forest includes the Sipsey Wilderness Area, which contains the last remaining stand of old-growth hardwood in the state. Swimming; fishing (bass, bream), hunting (deer, turkey, squirrel); boating. Hiking, horseback riding. Fee for some activities. 25 mi W on US 278. Contact District Ranger, PO Box 278, Double Springs 35553; 256/489-5111.

Motels

✔★ **DAYS INN.** *1841 4th St SW (35055), jct I-65 & US 278.* 205/739-3800; FAX 205/739-3123. 117 rms, 2 story. S, D $41-$52; each addl $5; family, wkly rates. Crib free. Pet accepted; $3. TV; cable (premium). Pool. Playground. Complimentary full bkfst. Restaurant 6 am-8 pm. Ck-out noon. Meeting rms. Business servs avail. In-rm modem link. Sundries. Picnic tables. Cr cds: A, C, D, DS, MC, V.

🈁 🈁 🈁 🈁 **SC**

★★ **RAMADA INN.** *PO Box 1204 (35056), I-65 & AL 69W, ¹/₄ mi E of I-65 Cullman-Good Hope exit.* 205/734-8484; FAX 205/739-4126. 126 rms, 1-2 story. S, D $40-$60; each addl $5; under 18 free. Crib free. Pet accepted. TV; cable (premium). Indoor pool; whirlpool. Restaurant 6 am-2 pm, 5-10 pm. Rm serv. Ck-out noon. Coin lndry. Meeting rms. In-rm modem link. Cr cds: A, C, D, DS, JCB, MC, V.

D 🈁 🈁 🈁 🈁 **SC**

Restaurant

★★ **ALL STEAK.** *314 2nd Ave SW (35055).* 256/734-4322. Hrs: 6 am-9 pm; Thurs-Sat to 10 pm; Sun to 3 pm. Closed major hols. Semi-a la carte: bkfst $2.50-$4.50, lunch $3.98-$5.50, dinner $5-$26. Child's meals. Specializes in steak, seafood. Own baking. No cr cds accepted.

D

Dauphin Island (J-2)

(See also Mobile)

Pop 824 **Elev** 10 ft **Area code** 334 **Zip** 36528

Dauphin Island is rich in history. Spaniards visited and mapped it in the 16th century. Pierre Le Moyne, Sieur d'Iberville, used the island as his base for a short time in 1699. Native Americans left a bit of their past with the "Shell Mound," an ancient monument. Today, the island is part of Mobile County and a playground for Mobile's citizens. It is also a haven for birds; a 60-acre sanctuary is home to many local and migratory species.

The Battle of Mobile Bay began on the island on August 5, 1864. Admiral David G. Farragut assembled a fleet of Union warships near the mouth of the bay and faced cross-fire from Fort Morgan to his east and Fort Gaines, on Dauphin Island, to his west. He proved successful; both forts were captured, and the port of Mobile was blocked.

Dauphin Island is reached from the north on AL 193, via a four-mile-long, high-rise bridge and causeway, which crosses Grants Pass. The island also has a 3,000-foot paved airstrip. A ferry service to Fort Morgan operates year round.

What to See and Do

Fort Gaines. This five-sided fort was begun in 1821 and completed in the 1850s. It was manned by Confederate forces from 1861 until its capture by Union land troops on Aug 23, 1864. Museum. (Daily; closed Thanksgiving, Dec 25) At E end of island. Phone 334/861-6992. ¢¢ Nearby is

Dauphin Island Campground. Private path to secluded Gulf beaches; fishing piers; boat launches. Hiking trail to Audubon Bird Sanctuary. Recreation areas. Camping; tent & trailer sites. For fee information phone 334/861-2742.

Decatur (B-3)

(See also Athens, Cullman, Huntsville)

Founded 1820 **Pop** 48,761 **Elev** 590 ft **Area code** 256 **E-mail** Info@Decaturcvb.org **Web** www.decaturcvb.org
Information Convention & Visitors Bureau, 719 6th Ave SE, PO Box 2349, 35602; 256/350-2028 or 800/524-6181.

Decatur, center of north Alabama's mountain lakes recreation area, is a thriving manufacturing and market city with historic districts and sprawling public parks.

The town site was selected by President Monroe in 1820. The Surveyor General was instructed to reserve the area near an old Tennessee River crossing. The place was already a settlement called Rhodes Ferry, named for pioneer Dr. Henry Rhodes' ferry business. The new town was named for Commodore Stephen Decatur.

The Civil War placed Decatur in a constant seesaw between invasion and resistance. It was continually attacked and abandoned; in fact, only five buildings were left standing at war's end.

The TVA brought industry to Decatur by creating a nine-foot channel in the Tennessee River, making it a port for vessels from as far away as Minneapolis. Wheeler Lake, formed by the TVA's Wheeler Dam (see FLORENCE) downstream, offers fishing, boating and other recreational activities.

What to See and Do

Cook's Natural Science Museum. Extensive collection of insects; rocks, minerals, coral, sea shells. Mounted wildlife. (Daily; closed Jan 1, Thanksgiving, Dec 24, 25) 412 13th St SE. Phone 256/350-9347. **Free.**

Mooresville. State's oldest incorporated town is preserved as a living record of 19th-century life. Features the house of Andrew Johnson, who was a tailor's apprentice here; community brick church (ca 1840); frame Church of Christ (1854) in which James Garfield is said to have preached during the Civil War; antebellum houses (private); also the oldest stage coach tavern in the state (1825). Details at Mooresville Post Office, which has original wooden call boxes (1830), mail hand-stamped. (Daily exc Sun; closed hols) 6 mi E on AL 20. Phone 256/350-2431. **Free.**

Old Decatur & Albany historic districts. Walking tour of Victorian neighborhood begins at restored Old Bank on historic Bank Street; includes 3 antebellum and 194 Victorian structures. Contact Convention & Visitors Bureau.

Point Mallard Park. A 749-acre park on the Tennessee River. Includes swimming pool, wave pool, water slide, beach (mid-May-Labor Day). Hiking, bicycle trails; 18-hole golf course, tennis courts. Outdoor ice rink (mid-Nov-mid-Mar). Camping (hookups), recreation center. Fee for activities. 1800 Point Mallard Dr SE. Phone 256/350-3000 or 800/669-9283.

Princess Theatre. Renovated art deco-style theater featuring children's theatre, dramatic and singing groups. 112 2nd Ave NE. Phone 256/350-1745.

Wheeler National Wildlife Refuge. Alabama's oldest and largest (34,500 acres) wildlife refuge. Wintering ground for waterfowl and home to numerous species of animal and plant life. Fishing, hunting (limited, permit required for hunting); boating. Picnicking. Bird study and photography. Wildlife Visitor Center and Waterfowl Observation Building. (Mar-Oct, Wed-Sun; rest of yr, daily) 2 mi E via AL 67. Phone 256/350-6639. **Free.**

Annual Events

Alabama Jubilee. Point Mallard Park (see). Highlight of festivities are the hot-air balloon races. Phone 800/524-6181. Memorial Day wkend.

Spirit of America Festival. Point Mallard Park (see). Games, contests, beauty pageant, concerts, exhibits, fireworks. July 3, 4.

Civil War Reenactment/September Skirmish. Point Mallard Park (see). Re-creates camp life of soldiers; features skirmishes led by General "Fighting Joe" Wheeler. Labor Day wkend.

Racking Horse World Celebration. Southeastern Sports Arena. Well-known event features gaited horses. Last full wk Sept.

Southern Wildlife Festival. Competition and exhibits of wildlife carvings, art work, photography and duck calling. 3rd wkend Oct.

Motor Hotel

★ ★ ★ **AMBERLEY SUITE.** *807 Bank St NE (35601), 4 blks W of jct AL 72, US 31.* 205/355-6800; FAX 205/350-0965; res: 800/288-7332. 110 kit. suites, 3 story. S $49-$64; D $60-$75; each addl $10; under 18 free; wkly, wkend rates. Crib free. TV; cable (premium). Pool; whirlpool. Complimentary coffee in rms. Restaurant 6 am-11 pm; Sat, Sun 7 am-noon. Bar 4-11 pm. Ck-out noon. Coin lndry. Meeting rms. Business servs avail. Free airport transportation. Exercise equipt; sauna. Grills. Cr cds: A, C, D, DS, MC, V.

D ⇌ 🏌 🎿 🐾 SC

Restaurant

★ ★ **SIMP McGHEE'S.** *725 Bank St (35601).* 256/353-6284. Hrs: 5-9 pm; Fri, Sat to 9:30 pm. Closed Sun; major hols. Bar. Semi-a la carte: dinner $13.95-$19.95. Child's meals. Specializes in seafood, grilled

prime rib, Cajun dishes. In 1890s dry goods bldg; many antiques. Cr cds: A, C, D, DS, MC, V.

D 🐾

Demopolis (E-2)

Founded 1817 **Pop** 7,512 **Elev** 125 ft **Area code** 334 **Zip** 36732 **E-mail** dacc@westal.net **Web** www.chamber.demopolis.al.us

Information Demopolis Area Chamber of Commerce, 102 E Washington, PO Box 667; 334/289-0270.

Visions of French-made wines and olive oil prompted the first European settlements in this region. The name, meaning "city of the people," is all that remains of the first settlers, a group of French exiles who were, for the most part, habituées of the French court and officers of Napoleon's armies. In July 1817, they were granted four townships by Congress as the "French Emigrants for the Cultivation of the Vine and Olive." In the end, the colonists failed to cope with the wilderness; and by the mid-1820s, they had scattered.

Americans came afterward to settle on the banks of the Tombigbee River. They established flourishing cotton plantations in this Black Belt area, and many of their fine Greek-revival mansions still can be seen. Agriculture, beef and dairy cattle, as well as a diversified industry support Demopolis today.

What to See and Do

Bluff Hall (1832). Restored antebellum mansion built by the slaves of Allen Glover, a planter and merchant, as a wedding gift for his daughter. The interior has Corinthian columns in drawing room, period furniture, many marble mantels. Also clothing museum and craft shop. (Daily exc Mon; closed major hols) 405 N Commissioners St. Phone 334/289-1666. ¢¢

Forkland Park. This park is on 10,000-acre Lake Demopolis, which was formed by a 40-ft-high dam on the Tombigbee River. Waterskiing; fishing; boating (ramp). Camping (hookups, dump station; fees). (Mid-Mar-mid-Dec, daily) 12 mi N on US 43, 1 mi W of Forkland on River Rd. Phone 334/289-3540 or -5530.

Foscue Creek Park. On Lake Demopolis. Boating (ramps). Trails. Picnic area, pavilion, playground, ballfields. Camping (hookups, dump station; fees). (Daily) 2 mi W via US 80W, exit Maria St, on Lock & Dam Rd. Phone 334/289-3540 or -5535.

Gaineswood (1860). Restored 20-rm Greek-revival mansion furnished with many original pieces. (Daily; closed hols) 805 S Cedar St. Phone 334/289-4846. ¢¢

Magnolia Grove (1840). Built for wealthy planter, Col. Isaac Croom, Magnolia Grove was also the home of the builder's nephew, Richmond Pearson Hobson, congressman and admiral who was responsible for sinking the *Merrimac* and for blockading the Spanish fleet in Santiago Harbor in June 1898. Greek-revival house features an unsupported winding stairway; original furnishings. (Daily exc Mon) 2 mi S on US 43, then 3 mi E on US 80, then 15 mi NE on AL 69; at 1002 Hobson St in Greensboro. Phone 334/624-8618. ¢¢

Annual Event

Christmas on the River. Children's parade, evening river boat parade, fireworks, arts & crafts. 1st Sat Dec.

Motels

★ **BEST WESTERN-MINT SUNRISE.** *1034 US 80 SE.* 334/289-5772; FAX 334/289-5772, ext. 100. 70 rms. S $45.95; D $49.95; each addl $2; under 12 free; wkly rates. Crib free. Pet accepted. TV; cable, VCR avail (movies $6). Pool. Complimentary continental bkfst. Ck-out 11 am. Meeting rms. Business center. In-rm modem link. Exercise equipt. Health club privileges. Refrigerators. Cr cds: A, C, D, DS, ER, JCB, MC, V.

★ **DAYS INN.** *1005 US 80 E.* 334/289-2500. 42 rms, 2 story. S $37; D $40; each addl $5; under 12 free; higher rates special events. Crib $1. TV; cable (premium). Pool. Complimentary continental bkfst. Complimentary coffee in rms. Restaurant nearby. Ck-out 11 am. Coin lndry. Business servs avail. In-rm modem link. Refrigerators. Cr cds: A, C, D, DS, JCB, MC, V.

D ≈ ⤢ ⛱ SC

✔★ **WINDWOOD INN.** *628 US 80 E.* 334/289-1760; FAX 334/289-1768; res: 800/233-0841. 90 units, 2 kits. S $29-$32; D $31-$35; each addl $5; kit. units $34-$43; under 12 free. Crib free. Pet accepted. TV; cable (premium). Pool. Restaurant adj 5 am-10 pm. Ck-out 11 am. Meeting rm. Business servs avail. Some refrigerators. Cr cds: A, C, D, DS, MC, V.

⤢ ≈ ⤢ ⛱ SC

Restaurant

★ **ELLIS V.** *708 US 80 E.* 334/289-3446. Hrs: 10 am-10 pm; Sun to 9 pm. Closed some major hols. Bar to 2 am. Semi-a la carte: lunch $4.95-$7.25, dinner $6.95-$15.95. Specializes in steak, catfish. Salad bar. Cr cds: A, C, D, DS, MC, V.

Dothan (G-5)

(See also Ozark)

Settled 1858 **Pop** 53,589 **Elev** 326 ft **Area code** 334 **E-mail** dothancvb@gnn.com **Web** www.dothanalcvb.com

Information Dothan Area Convention & Visitors Bureau, 3311 Ross Clark Circle NW, PO Box 8765, 36304; 334/794-6622.

This marketing center in the "wiregrass" section of Alabama's southeastern corner is the seat of Houston County. Local agricultural products include peanuts, soybeans, corn and cattle. Dothan is also a retail center.

The town had a lusty start. It was a rough pioneer settlement full of lumberjacks and turpentine workers in 1889 when the first railroad reached it. As the railroads developed, Dothan's population grew rapidly. The city owes a large part of its growth to its strategic location—almost equidistant from Atlanta, Birmingham, Jacksonville and Mobile.

What to See and Do

Adventureland Theme Park. Park includes two 10-hole miniature golf courses, a go-cart track, bumper boats and a game room. Snack bar. (Daily) 3738 W Main St. Phone 334/793-9100. Charge for each separate activity ¢¢

Landmark Park. This 60-acre park features an 1890s living-history farm, natural science and history center, planetarium; nature trails; picnic area. (Daily; closed Jan 1, Dec 25) US 431N. Phone 334/794-3452. ¢

Opera House (1915). Refurbished historical theater; 590 seats. (Daily) Appt recommended. 115 N St Andrews St. Phone 334/793-0127. **Free.**

Westgate Park. Recreation facility includes Water World, with child's pool, wave pool and giant slide (early May-Labor Day, daily; fee); recreation center with indoor pool, tennis, racquetball, basketball courts and ball-fields. (Daily; fee for various activities) Choctaw St & Westgate Pkwy off Ross Clark Circle. Phone 334/793-0221 or -0297.

Annual Events

Azalea Dogwood Festival. Marked route through residential areas at peak of bloom. Late Mar or early Apr.

National Peanut Festival. Houston County Farm Center. Livestock exhibits, sports events, arts & crafts, midway, beauty pageants, parade. Phone 334/793-4323. Late Oct-early Nov.

Motels

★ ★ **BEST WESTERN-DOTHAN INN.** *3285 Montgomery Hwy (36303).* 334/793-4376; FAX 334/793-7720. 150 rms, 2 story. S, D $55-$60; each addl $5; suites $75-$95; under 12 free. Crib free. TV; cable. Pool. Complimentary continental bkfst. Coffee in rms. Restaurant adj open 24 hrs. Ck-out 11 am. In-rm modem link. Free airport transportation. Health club privileges. Some refrigerators, microwaves. Cr cds: A, C, D, DS, JCB, MC, V.

D ≈ ⤢ ⛱ SC

★ ★ ★ **COMFORT INN.** *3593 Ross Clark Circle NW (36304).* 334/793-9090; FAX 334/793-4367. 122 rms, 5 story. S $62-$93; D $67-$98; each addl $5; suites $76-$98; under 18 free. Crib free. Pet accepted. TV; cable (premium). VCR avail (movies). Pool. Continental bkfst. Restaurant open 24 hrs. Ck-out 1 pm. Meeting rm. Business servs avail. In-rm modem link. Exercise equipt. Health club privileges. Many refrigerators. Near shopping centers. Cr cds: A, C, D, DS, ER, JCB, MC, V.

D ⤢ ≈ ⛱ ⤢ SC

✔★ ★ **DAYS INN.** *2841 Ross Clark Circle SW (36301).* 334/793-2550; FAX 334/793-7962. 120 units, 2 story. S $31-$38; D $36-$48; each addl $5; family rates; some wknd rates. Crib free. Pet accepted; $5. TV; cable (premium). Pool. Coffee in rms. Restaurant adj open 24 hrs. Ck-out noon. Business servs avail. In-rm modem link. Cr cds: A, D, DS, MC, V.

D ⤢ ≈ ⤢ ⛱ SC

★ ★ **HOLIDAY INN-SOUTH.** *2195 Ross Clark Circle SE (36301).* 334/794-8711; FAX 334/671-3781. 144 rms, 2 story. S $50-$56; D $56-$62; each addl $6; under 18 free; suites $64-$74. Pet accepted. TV; cable. Pool. Complimentary full bkfst. Complimentary coffee in lobby. Restaurant 6 am-9:30 pm; Sun from 7 am. Rm serv (limited hrs). Bar 2:30 pm-2 am. Ck-out noon. Meeting rms. Business servs avail. In-rm modem link. Cr cds: A, C, D, DS, JCB, MC, V.

D ⤢ ≈ ⤢ ⛱ SC

★ ★ **HOLIDAY INN-WEST.** *3053 Ross Clark Circle (36301).* 334/794-6601; FAX 334/794-9032. 102 rms, 2 story, 44 suites. S, D $57-$62; suites $66-$71; under 18 free; wknd rates. Crib free. Pet accepted. TV; cable (premium). Pool; wading pool. Restaurant 6 am-9 pm. Rm serv. Bar 5 pm-1 am. Ck-out noon. Meeting rms. Business center. In-rm modem link. Bellhops. Valet serv. Refrigerators avail. Cr cds: A, C, D, DS, MC, V.

D ⤢ ≈ ⤢ ⛱ SC ⤢

✔★ **MOTEL 6.** *2907 Ross Clark Circle SW (36301).* 334/793-6013; FAX 334/793-2377. 102 rms, 2 story. S, D $28.99-$34.99; each addl $5-$6; under 17 free. Crib free. Pet accepted. TV; cable. Pool. Coffee in lobby. Ck-out noon. In-rm modem link. Cr cds: A, C, D, DS, MC, V.

D ⤢ ≈ ⤢ ⛱

★ ★ ★ **RAMADA INN.** *3011 Ross Clark Circle SW (36301).* 334/792-0031; FAX 334/794-3134. 159 rms, 2 story. S $50; D $56; each addl $6; suites $75-$105; under 18 free; wkly rates; some wkend rates. Crib free. Pet accepted. TV; cable (premium), VCR avail (movies). Pool; wading pool. Complimentary bkfst. Restaurant 6 am-9 pm. Rm serv. Bar; entertainment. Ck-out noon. Meeting rms. Business center. Valet serv. Free airport transportation. Cr cds: A, C, D, DS, JCB, MC, V.

D ⤢ ≈ ⤢ ⛱ SC ⤢

Restaurant

✔★ **AUGUST MOON.** *3530 Montgomery Hwy (36031).* 334/677-6035. Hrs: 11 am-2 pm, 5-9 pm. Closed Thanksgiving, Dec 25.

Chinese menu. Private club. Buffet: lunch $3.99, dinner $5.95. Cr cds: A, DS, MC, V.

[D]

Eufaula (F-6)

Settled 1823 **Pop** 13,220 **Elev** 257 ft **Area code** 334 **Zip** 36027
Information Chamber of Commerce, 102 N Orange St, PO Box 697, 36072-0697; 334/687-6664 or -6665.

This city stands on a bluff rising 200 feet above Lake Eufaula, a 45,000-acre impoundment of the Chattahoochee River known throughout the area for its excellent bass fishing.

What to See and Do

Eufaula National Wildlife Refuge. Partially located in Georgia and superimposed on the Walter F. George Reservoir, the refuge was established to provide a feeding and resting area for waterfowl migrating between the Tennessee Valley and the Gulf Coast. Ducks, geese, egrets and herons are among the 281 species of birds found at the refuge; beaver, fox, bobcat and deer are among the 16 species of mammals. Observation tower, nature trail; hunting; photography. (Daily) 10 mi N on US 431, AL 165. Contact Refuge Manager, 509 Old Hwy 165; 334/687-4065. **Free.**

Hart House (ca 1850). Single-story, Greek-revival white frame structure with fluted Doric columns on porch serves as headquarters for the Historic Chattahoochee Commission and Visitor Information Center for the Chattahoochee Trace of Alabama and Georgia. (Mon-Fri) 211 N Eufaula Ave. Phone 334/687-9755 or -6631. **Free.**

Lakepoint Resort State Park. A 1,220-acre picturesque park on the shores of the 45,200-acre Lake Eufaula. Swimming; fishing; boating (marina). Hiking; 18-hole golf (fee); tennis. Picnicking, concession, restaurant, resort inn. Camping, cottages. Standard fees. 7 mi N off US 431. Phone 334/687-6676 or -8011.

Shorter Mansion. Neoclassical mansion built in 1906; two floors contain antique furnishings, Confederate relics and memorabilia of six state governors from Barbour County. (Daily; closed major hols) Mini-tour by appt (fee). 340 N Eufaula Ave. Phone 334/687-3793. **¢¢** Mansion is headquarters for the Eufaula Heritage Association and is part of

Seth Lore and Irwinton Historic District. Second-largest historic district in Alabama, with approx 582 registered landmarks. Mixture of Greek-revival, Italianate and Victorian houses, churches and commercial structures built between 1834 and 1911. Many are private. Obtain driving tour brochure from the Chamber of Commerce or Eufaula Heritage Association, PO Box 486.

Annual Events

Eufaula Pilgrimage. Daytime and candlelight tours of antebellum houses and churches, antique show and sales, historic reenactments and Civil War displays. Phone 334/687-3793. 1st or 2nd wkend Apr.

Indian Summer Days. Festival including arts & crafts, music, food, children's activities. Phone 334/687-6664. 1st or 2nd wkend Oct.

Motels

✔★ **BEST WESTERN INN.** *1337 S Eufala Ave, On Dothan Hwy (US 431S).* 334/687-3900; FAX 334/687-6870. 42 rms, 2 story. S $38-$42; D $42-$48; each addl $4; under 12 free; higher rates: Eufaula Pilgrimage, wkend of July 4. Crib free. TV; cable, VCR avail (movies). Pool. Complimentary continental bkfst. Restaurant opp 10 am-10 pm. Ck-out 11

am. Business servs avail. In-rm modem link. Some refrigerators. Cr cds: A, D, DS, MC, V.

[D] [≈] [✕] [🏍] [SC]

★★ **HOLIDAY INN.** *Riverside Dr, at US 82.* 334/687-2021. 96 rms, 2 story. S $44.50-$55; D $49.50-$66.50; each addl $5; suites $61.50-$65.50; under 18 free; golf plans. Crib free. Pet accepted. TV; cable (premium). Pool. Restaurant 6 am-10 pm. Rm serv. Bar 4 pm-midnight. Ck-out noon. Meeting rms. Business servs avail. In-rm modem link. Bellhops. On lake. Cr cds: A, C, D, DS, JCB, MC, V.

[D] [🐾] [≈] [✕] [🏍] [SC]

★★ **LAKEPOINT STATE PARK RESORT.** *US 431 N (36072), 7 mi N on US 431.* 334/687-8011; FAX 334/687-3273; res: 800/544-5253. 101 rms in lodge, 29 kit. cottages. Mar-Oct: S $44-$49; D $49-$58; each addl $5; cottages $68-$125; under 12 free; golf plan; lower rates rest of yr. Crib $5. TV; cable, VCR avail. Pool; lifeguard in season. Playground. Restaurant 7 am-9 pm. Bar 4 pm-midnight. Ck-out 11 am. Coin lndry. Meeting rms. Business center. In-rm modem link. Lighted tennis. 18-hole golf, greens fee $14, pro, putting green, driving range. Boats, waterskiing. Game rm. Lawn games. On Lake Eufaula; swimming beach. Operated by state park. Cr cds: A, MC, V.

[D] [🐾] [🏃] [⛷] [≈] [✕] [🏍] [SC] [⛵]

Evergreen (G-3)

Pop 3,911 **Elev** 367 ft **Area code** 334 **Zip** 36401 **E-mail** everclif@net1inc.net **Web** evergreen@alabama-net.com
Information Chamber of Commerce, 100 Depot Square; 334/578-1707.

The seat of Conecuh County, this town is appropriately named for its abundance of evergreens. Each year carloads of Christmas trees and other evergreen products for use as decoration are shipped from the town.

What to See and Do

Conecuh National Forest. This 84,400-acre forest, mostly of southern pine, offers swimming (at Blue Pond, fee per vehicle); fishing, hunting; boating. Hiking includes 20 mi of the Conecuh Trail. Campsites at Open Pond only (fee for overnight). 25 mi E on US 84, then 11 mi S on US 29. Contact District Ranger, US Forest Service, Rte 5, Box 157, Andalusia 36420; 334/222-2555 or Supervisor, 2946 Chestnut St, Montgomery 36107; 334/832-4470.

Motels

✔★★ **COMFORT INN.** *1 blk W on AL 83 Business, I-65 exit 96.* 334/578-4701; FAX 334/578-3180. 58 rms, 2 story. S $38; D $50; each addl $5. Crib $5. Pet accepted; $5. TV; cable (premium). Pool. Restaurant adj open 24 hrs. Ck-out 11 am. Business servs avail. In-rm modem link. Cr cds: A, C, D, DS, JCB, MC, V.

[D] [🐾] [≈] [✕] [🏍] [SC]

★ **DAYS INN.** *Rte 2, Box 38, I-65 & US 83, exit 96.* 334/578-2100. 40 rms, 2 story, 4 suites. Mid-June-Labor Day: S, D $48; each addl $5; suites $55-$60; under 12 free; lower rates rest of yr. Crib free. Pet accepted, some restrictions; $5. TV; cable (premium). Complimentary continental bkfst. Ck-out 11 am. Cr cds: A, DS, MC, V.

[D] [🐾] [🏍] [SC]

Florence (A-2)

(See also Russellville)

Settled 1779 **Pop** 36,426 **Elev** 541 ft **Area code** 205 **Zip** 35630 **E-mail** dwilson@floweb.com **Web** www.flo-tour.org

Information Florence/Lauderdale Tourism, One Hightower Place; 205/740-4141 or 888/356-8687.

First settled as a trading post, Florence is still the trading center of a large area. Florence, with Sheffield, Tuscumbia and Muscle Shoals, lies along the Tennessee River's famous shoals area near Wilson Dam. Inexpensive TVA power helped to bring a number of industries to the town.

What to See and Do

Indian Mound and Museum. Largest ceremonial mound in the Tennessee Valley. Museum has large collection of Native American artifacts. (Tues-Sat; closed major hols) S Court St. Phone 205/760-6427. ¢

Joe Wheeler State Park. Named for Confederate General Joseph Wheeler of the Army of Tennessee, the 2,550-acre park is divided into three parts.

Wheeler Dam. Swimming; fishing (daily); boat liveries and harbor. Tennis. Picnic facilities. 18 mi E on US 72, then 4 mi S on AL 101. Cabins (reservations through Park Manager, phone 205/685-3306).

First Creek. Beachfront swimming; boating (marina). Nature and hiking trails; 18-hole golf, tennis. Picnicking. Resort lodge overlooking the Tennessee River (see RESORT). Camping (primitive & improved). 2 mi W of Rogersville via US 72. Phone 205/247-5466 (office), 205/247-1184 (campground).

Elk River. Fishing; boating (launch). Picnic facilities, playground, concession. Group lodge. (Daily) Standard fees. 15 mi W of Athens (see). Phone 205/729-8228.

Pope's Tavern (1830). General Andrew Jackson stayed in this stage stop, which served as a hospital for both Union and Confederate soldiers during the Civil War. (Tues-Sat; closed major hols) 203 Hermitage Dr. Phone 205/760-6439. ¢

Renaissance Tower. One of the tallest structures in the state; offers magnificent view of the Tennessee River and Wilson Dam. Aquarium with more than 60 exhibits (fee). Restaurant. (Daily; closed Jan 1, Dec 25) 1 Hightower Place. Phone 205/764-5900. ¢

University of North Alabama (1830). (5,600 students) Tours. University Art Gallery (Mon-Fri), Planetarium-Observatory (open by appt, phone 205/760-4284). Wesleyan Ave.

W.C. Handy Home, Museum and Library. Restored birthplace of famous composer and "father of the blues" contains hand-written sheet music, personal papers, trumpet and piano on which he composed "St Louis Blues." (Tues-Sat; closed major hols) 620 W College St. Phone 205/760-6434. ¢

Wheeler Dam. Part of the Muscle Shoals complex, this is a multipurpose TVA dam chiefly built for navigation. It is 72 ft high and 6,342 ft long, impounding a lake 74 mi long. Lobby (daily). 18 mi E on US 72 to Elgin, then 4 mi S on AL 101.   **Free.**

Wilson Dam. This dam is the foundation stone of the Tennessee Valley Authority. For many years, the Muscle Shoals area of the Tennessee River had been discussed as a source of power, and in 1918, the War Department began construction of Wilson Dam as a source of power for making munitions. The dam was completed in 1924, but little use was made of its generating capacity until the TVA took over in 1933. Today, it has the largest generating capacity (630,000 kilowatts) of any TVA dam; its main lock (completed Nov 1959) is 110 ft by 600 ft and lifts vessels 100 ft, one of the world's highest single lift locks. The treacherous Muscle Shoals are no longer a bottleneck to shipping. The dam, 4,541 ft long and 137 ft high, is one of the many TVA dams that prevents floods, provides 650 mi of navigable channel and produces electricity for the area's residents, farms and industry. 5 mi E on US 72, then 2 mi S on AL 133.   **Free.**

Wilson Lake extends more than 15 mi upstream to Wheeler Dam. Swimming; fishing; boating.

Annual Events

Tennessee River Fiddler's Convention. McFarland Park. Traditional fiddlers and bluegrass competition. 1st wkend May.

W.C. Handy Music Festival. Wk-long celebration of the musical contribution of the "father of the blues." Jazz, blues, gospel concerts, street celebration, running events, bike rides. Phone 205/766-7642 or -9719. 1st full wk Aug.

Festival of the Singing River. McFarland Park. Honors the history and culture of Native Americans. Traditional dance competition, arts and crafts. Phone 888/356-8687. 4th wkend Sept.

Alabama Renaissance Faire. Renaissance-era arts & crafts, music, food, entertainment. Fair workers in period costumes. Phone 205/760-9648. 4th wkend Oct.

Motels

✔★ **BEST WESTERN EXECUTIVE INN.** *504 S Court St.* 205/766-2331; FAX 205/766-3567. 120 rms, 2 story. S, D $51-$56; each addl $5; under 12 free. Crib free. Pet accepted, some restrictions. TV; cable (premium), VCR avail (movies). Pool; poolside serv. Restaurant 6 am-10 pm; Sat, Sun from 7 am. Rm serv. Bar 4 pm-1 am; closed Sun. Ck-out noon. Coin lndry. Meeting rms. Business servs avail. Cr cds: A, C, D, DS, MC, V.

🐾 ≈ ⊠ 🏃 SC

★ **DAYS INN.** *(2700 Woodward Ave, Muscle Shoals 35661)* S on US 43, then E on AL 133. 256/383-3000. 77 rms, 2 story. S $44; D $50; each addl $5; under 12 free; wkly rates. TV; cable (premium). Pool. Complimentary continental bkfst. Coffee in rms. Restaurant opp 6-1 am. Bar 11-2 am. Ck-out noon. Cr cds: A, C, D, DS, MC, V.

D ≈ ⊠ 🏃 SC

★ **HOWARD JOHNSON.** *400 S Court St.* 205/760-8888; FAX 205/766-1681. 88 rms, 5 story. S $44-$49; D $49-$54; each addl $5; suites $98; under 18 free. Crib free. TV; cable (premium). Complimentary continental bkfst. Ck-out 11 am. Meeting rms. In-rm modem link. Refrigerator in suites. Cr cds: A, DS, MC, V.

⊠ 🏃 SC

Resort

★ ★ **JOE WHEELER STATE RESORT LODGE.** *(PO Drawer K, Rogersville 35652)* 20 mi E on US 72, then 4 mi S. 205/247-5461; FAX 205/247-5471; res: 800/544-5639. 75 rms, 3 story. S $58-$61; D $63-$68; each addl $5; suites $78-$119; under 12 free; golf plans. Crib free. TV; VCR avail. Pool; wading pool. Playground. Dining rm 7 am-9 pm. Ck-out 11 am, ck-in 3 pm. Coin lndry. Meeting rms. Business servs avail. Sundries. Lighted tennis. 18-hole golf, greens fee, pro, putting green, driving range. Private beach, marina, boat rentals. Hiking trails. Some refrigerators; wet bar in suites. Private patios, balconies. Picnic tables, grills. State-owned; facilities of park avail. Cr cds: A, MC, V.

D 🐾 🕴 🧗 ≈ ⊠ 🏃 SC

Fort Payne (B-5)

(See also Gadsden)

Pop 11,838 **Elev** 899 ft **Area code** 256 **Zip** 35968 **E-mail** pattyt@peop.tdsnet.com **Web** www.hsr.tis.net/~dekbtour
Information DeKalb County Tourist Assoc, 2201-J Gault Ave N, PO Box 681165; 256/845-3957.

The county seat and market town of DeKalb County, Fort Payne is in an area famed for natural wonders and Native American history. Sequoyah, who invented the Cherokee alphabet, lived in Will's Town, a Cherokee settlement located near Fort Payne.

What to See and Do

Cloudmont Ski Resort. Two pony lifts; patrol, school, rentals; 100% snowmaking; concession area, snack bar. Chalets. Longest run 1,000 ft; vertical drop 150 ft. (Mid-Dec-early-Mar, daily) Summer activities include swimming; fishing;.hiking; 9-hole golf. 5 mi NE via I-59, exit 231 off AL 117 on County Rd 89. Phone 256/634-4344. ¢¢¢¢¢

DeSoto State Park. The 5,067-acre park includes Lookout Mountain, Little River Canyon and DeSoto Falls and Lake. The area, rich in Cherokee lore, was a base of military operations prior to the Trail of Tears. The park is noted for its variety of plant life, including spring-blooming rhododendrons, wild azaleas and mountain laurel. Songbirds abound. A scenic drive skirts the canyon, and 20 mi of hiking trail crosses the mountain top. Swimming pool, bathhouse; fishing. Hiking trail; tennis. Picnicking, playground, restaurant, country store, resort inn. Nature center. Camping (all yr), cabins (res required for both). Standard fees. 8 mi NE on County 89. Phone 256/845-5380 (cabins) or -5075 (campground).

Fort Payne Opera House (1889). Alabama's oldest opera house still in use today. Restored and reopened in 1970 as a cultural arts center. Tours of theater include historic murals (by appt). 510 Gault Ave N. Phone 256/845-2741. **Donation.**

Landmarks of DeKalb Museum (1891). The museum, Richardsonian Romanesque in style, features Native American artifacts from several different tribes; turn-of-the-century house and farm items; railroad memorabilia; photographs and art work of local historical significance. Special rotating exhibits. (Mon, Wed & Fri, also Sun afternoons; closed hols) 105 Fifth St NE. Phone 256/845-5714. **Free.**

Sequoyah Caverns. Thousands of formations, reflecting lakes and rainbow falls with indirect lighting; level walkways. Cave temperature 60° F all year. Rainbow trout pools, deer, buffalo. Swimming pool. Picnic area. Camping. Guided tours. (Mar-Nov, daily; rest of yr, wknds) 16 mi N off US 11, I-59. Phone 256/635-0024. ¢¢¢

Annual Event

DeKalb County VFW Agricultural Fair. VFW Fairgrounds, 18th St NW. Phone 256/845-4752. Early Oct.

Motels

✔★ **BEST WESTERN FORT PAYNE.** *1828 Gault Ave N (35967), 1¹/₂ mi S of jct I-59, US 11.* 253/845-0481; FAX 253/845-6152. 68 rms, 1-2 story. S $35-$45; D $45-$55; under 18 free. Crib $6. Pet accepted. TV; cable (premium), VCR avail. Pool. Restaurant 5 am-9 pm. Rm serv. Ck-out noon. Meeting rms. Business servs avail. Free airport transportation. Downhill ski 10 mi. Cr cds: A, C, D, DS, ER, MC, V.

D ✸ ✍ ⚓ ⚒ ⚒ SC

★★ **QUALITY INN.** *1412 Glenn Blvd SW (35967).* 205/845-4013; FAX 205/845-2344. 79 rms, 2 story. S $38-$42; D $42-$45; each addl $5; under 16 free; higher rates hols. Crib free. Pet accepted, some restrictions. TV; cable (premium), VCR avail. Pool; wading pool. Compli-

mentary coffee in lobby. Ck-out 11 am. Coin lndry. Meeting rms. Business servs avail. Cr cds: A, C, D, DS, ER, MC, V.

D ✸ ✍ ⚓ ⚒ ⚒ SC

Gadsden (C-4)

(See also Anniston, Fort Payne, Guntersville)

Founded 1840 **Pop** 42,523 **Elev** 554 ft **Area code** 205 **Web** cybrtyme.com/tourism
Information Gadsden-Etowah Tourism Board, PO Box 8267, 35902; 205/549-0351.

The town was named for James Gadsden, the man who negotiated the purchase of Arizona and New Mexico in 1853. Today, it is one of the largest industrial centers in the state. Iron, manganese, coal and limestone are found nearby. Steel, rubber, fabricated metal, electrical equipment and electronic devices are among its chief products. It is the seat of Etowah County, a diversified agricultural area.

Union troops sacked Gadsden in 1863 and rode on toward Rome, Georgia. Two heroes were born of this action. Fifteen-year-old Emma Sansom bravely guided General Nathan Bedford Forrest and his men across a ford on Black Creek after the bridge was destroyed. John Wisdom made a night ride of 67 miles to warn the defenders of Rome that the Yankees were coming, a ride the people of Alabama celebrate more than Paul Revere's.

In 1887, electricity came to Gadsden when William P. Lay built an electrical plant. It was the result of years of effort to interest investors in the industrial future of the region. In 1902 it was replaced with a hydroelectric plant on Big Wills Creek. Eventually, Lay's dream of developing the water resources of the Coosa-Alabama river system led to the organization of the Alabama Power Company in 1906.

What to See and Do

Center for Cultural Arts. Center features wide variety of cultural and artistic traveling exhibits from the US and Europe; children's museum with "hands on" exhibits features a miniature "walk-through" city. (Daily; closed major hols) 501 Broad St. Phone 205/543-2787. ¢¢

Gadsden Museum of Fine Arts. Features works by local, national and international artists. Antique china and crystal collection, historical memorabilia. (Daily exc Sat; closed hols) 2829 W Meighan Blvd. Phone 205/546-7365. **Free.**

Horton Mill Covered Bridge. This 220-ft-long structure is the highest covered bridge in the US, 70 ft above the Black Warrior River. Trails. (Daily) 18 mi W on US 278, then 11 mi S on AL 75. **Free.**

Noccalula Falls Park. Black Creek drops 90 ft over a limestone ledge on Lookout Mountain; according to legend, these falls were named for an Indian chief's daughter who leaped to her death after being disappointed in love. A 65-mi trail ending at DeSoto Falls in DeSoto State Park in Fort Payne (see) includes four waterfalls and many Native American sites. Also originating in the park is the Lookout Mountain Parkway, a scenic drive extending 100 mi to Chattanooga, TN. Swimming pool, bathhouse. Nature and hiking trails; miniature golf. Picnic area, playground. Camping, hookups (fee). Pioneer homestead and museum; train. Botanical gardens. (Daily) Noccalula Rd. Phone 205/549-4663 (office) or 205/543-7412 (campground). Fee for each activity. Admission ¢-¢¢

Weiss Dam and Lake. An Alabama Power Company project impounds a 30,200-acre lake. Swimming; fishing; boating (daily). Picnicking. Tours of power plant (daily, by appt). 18 mi NE off US 411. Phone 205/526-8467.

Motel

★ **KEY WEST INN.** *(410 E Mill Ave, Boaz 35957) 20 mi N on US 431.* 205/593-0800; FAX 205/593-9100. 41 rms, 2 story. Oct-Dec: S, D $46.50-$51.50; each addl $5; under 18 free; lower rates rest of yr. Crib free. Pet accepted, some restrictions; $5. TV; cable (premium). Complimentary continental bkfst. Restaurant opp 11 am-4 pm. Ck-out 11 am. Meeting rm. Some refrigerators. Cr cds: A, C, D, DS, MC, V.

D ⚑ ≋ ⊠ 🔥 SC

Greenville (F-4)

(See also Montgomery)

Settled 1819 **Pop** 7,492 **Elev** 422 ft **Area code** 334 **Zip** 36037

What to See and Do

Hank Williams, Sr Boyhood Home & Museum. Restored house where Hank Williams, Sr, country music legend, lived as a young boy. Large collection of memorabilia including recordings, posters and sheet music. (Mon-Sat, Sun afternoons) Approx 20 mi S on US 31, at 127 Rose St in Georgiana. Phone 334/376-2396. ¢¢

Motel

★ ★ **HOLIDAY INN.** *941 Fort Dale Rd, jct AL 185, I-65, E off Greenville exit 130, on Fort Dale Rd.* 334/382-2651. 96 rms, 2 story. S, D $57; each addl $6; under 18 free. Crib free. Pet accepted; $5. TV; cable. Pool. Coffee in rms. Restaurant 6 am-2 pm, 5-9 pm. Rm serv. Bar 4:30-9 pm. Ck-out noon. Meeting rms. Business servs avail. In-rm modem link. Cr cds: A, C, D, DS, MC, V.

D ⚑ ≋ ⊠ 🔥 SC

Gulf Shores (J-2)

(See also Mobile; also see Pensacola, FL)

Pop 3,261 **Elev** 6 ft **Area code** 334 **Zip** 36542 **E-mail** info@gulfshores.com **Web** www.gulfshores.com
Information Alabama Gulf Coast Convention & Visitors Bureau, 3150 Gulf Shores Pkwy, PO Box 457, 36547; 334/968-7511 or 800/745-SAND.

Located on Pleasure Island, southeast of Mobile, Gulf Shores is separated from the mainland by the Intracoastal Waterway. Between Alabama Point on the east and Mobile Point on the west is a 32-mile stretch of white sand beach that includes Orange Beach. Swimming and fishing in the Gulf are excellent, and charter boats are available. The island also has a number of freshwater lakes. At the eastern end, a bridge across Perdido Bay connects Orange Beach with Pensacola, Florida.

What to See and Do

Bon Secour National Wildlife Refuge. Consists of 6,000 acres of coastal lands ranging from sand dunes to woodlands; native and migratory birds, small mammals and reptiles including the endangered loggerhead sea turtle. Swimming; fishing (fresh and salt water). Foot trails, hiking. Visitor center (daily; closed major hols). AL 180 W. Phone 334/540-7720. **Free.**

Fort Morgan Park. This area on the western tip of Mobile Point was explored by the Spanish in 1519. Between that time and 1813, Spain, France, England and finally, the United States held this strategic point. It was the site of two engagements during the War of 1812. Fishing pier. Picnicking, concessions. 22 mi W on AL 180 (Fort Morgan Pkwy). ¢ Park admission includes

Fort Morgan. This star-shaped, brick fort was begun in 1819 and replaced a sand and log fort that figured in two battles during the War of 1812. Fort Morgan's most famous moment occurred during the Battle of Mobile Bay (Aug 1864). The Confederates' use of mines, then known as torpedoes, was the source of Union Admiral Farragut's legendary com-

mand, "Damn the torpedoes, full speed ahead!" Following the battle, the fort withstood a two-week siege before surrendering to Union forces. The fort was in active use during the Spanish-American War and World Wars I and II. (Daily; closed Jan 1, Thanksgiving, Dec 25) Phone 334/540-7125 or -7127. ¢

Fort Morgan Museum (1967). Patterned after the 10-sided citadel damaged in 1864, the museum displays military artifacts from the War of 1812 through World War II; local history. (Daily; closed Jan 1, Thanksgiving, Dec 25) **Free.**

Gulf State Park. The 6,000-acre park includes more than 2 mi of white sand beaches on the Gulf and freshwater lakes. Swimming, bathhouse, waterskiing, surfing; fishing in Gulf of Mexico (825-ft pier) and in lakes; marina, boathouse, rentals. Hiking, bicycling; tennis, 18-hole golf (fee). Picnic area, pavilion, grills, restaurant, resort inn (see MOTELS). Cabins (for reservations contact Cabin Reservations, 20115 State Hwy 135, phone 334/948-7275). Camping (14-day max in season). 2 mi E on AL 182 from jct AL 59. Phone 334/948-6353 for reservations (Mon-Fri). (Daily) Standard fees. For park information phone 334/948-7275.

Zooland Animal Park. A 15-acre park with native and exotic animals; petting zoo; concession. (Daily; closed Thanksgiving, Dec 25) AL 59 S to 12th Ave. Phone 334/968-5731. ¢¢¢

Annual Events

Mardi Gras Celebration. Late Feb.

Pleasure Island Festival of Art. Early Mar.

National Shrimp Festival. 2nd wkend Oct.

Motels

★ ★ **BEST WESTERN ON THE BEACH.** *337 AL 182E.* 334/948-2711; res: 800/788-4557; FAX 334/948-7338. Web www.bestwestern-onthebeach.com. 111 units, 6 story, 50 kits. May-Sept: S, D $99-$225; under 12 free; wkly rates; lower rates rest of yr. Crib $5. TV; cable, VCR (movies). 2 pools; whirlpools. Restaurant 6 am-11 pm. Ck-out 11 am. Meeting rms. Business servs avail. Refrigerators. On Gulf beach. Cr cds: A, C, D, DS, MC, V.

D ⚑ ≋ ⊠ 🔥 SC

★ **DAYS INN.** *(1517 S McKenzie St, Foley 36535)* 8 mi N on AL 59. 334/943-3297; res: 888/282-3297; FAX 334/943-7548. 90 rms, 2 story. May-Aug: S, D $69-79; suites $99-109; under 12 free; lower rates rest of yr. TV; cable (premium). Pool. Complimentary continental bkfst. Ck-out 11 am. Meeting rms. Business servs avail. Exercise equipt. Game rm. Cr cds: A, C, D, DS, MC, V.

D ≋ 🍴 ⊠ 🔥 SC

★ ★ **HAMPTON INN.** *(22988 E Beach Hwy, Orange Beach 36561)* AL 59 to AL 182 E/Beach Blvd. 334/974-1598; res: 800/981-6242; FAX 334/974-1599. 65 rms, 3 story. May-Labor Day: S, D $99-$159; each addl $10; under 12 free; higher rates special events; lower rates rest of yr. Crib free. TV; cable (premium). Complimentary continental bkfst. Complimentary coffee in rms. Restaurant nearby. Ck-out 11 am. Meeting rms. Business servs avail. In-rm modem link. Pool. Refrigerators, microwaves. Some balconies. On beach. Cr cds: A, C, D, DS, MC, V.

D ≋ ⊠ 🔥 SC

★ **LIGHTHOUSE.** *455 E Beach Blvd (36547).* 334/948-6188. 219 rms, 1-5 story, 136 kits. May-Labor Day: S, D $73-$120; kit. units $86-$160; wkly rates; lower rates rest of yr. Crib $3. TV; cable (premium). 3 pools, 2 heated, 1 indoor; whirlpool. Restaurants nearby. Ck-out 11 am. Business servs avail. Refrigerators. Private patios, balconies. On Gulf beach. Cr cds: A, D, DS, MC, V.

D ⚑ ≋ 🔥

Motor Hotels

★ ★ ★ **HILTON GARDEN INN-ORANGE BEACH.** *(23092 Perdido Beach Blvd, Orange Beach 36561)* AL 59 to AL 182E/Beach Blvd.

334/974-1600; res: 888/644-5866; FAX 334/974-1012. 137 rms, 6 story. May-Labor Day: S, D $129-$189; suites $265; hols (2-day min); lower rates rest of yr. Crib free. TV; cable (premium). Complimentary coffee in rms. Restaurant 6 am-9 pm. Rm serv 5-9 pm. Bar. Ck-out noon. Meeting rms. Business center. In-rm modem link. Coin lndry. Indoor/outdoor pool; whirlpool. Refrigerators, microwaves. Balconies. On beach. Cr cds: A, C, D, DS, JCB, MC, V.

D ⇌ ✕ 🏃 SC 🚶

✔ ★ ★ ★ **HOLIDAY INN.** 365 E Beach Blvd, on AL 182. 334/948-6191; FAX 334/948-8240. 149 rms, 4-6 story. May-Sept: S, D $143-$248; each addl $12; under 19 free; lower rates rest of yr. Crib free. TV; cable (premium). Pool; wading pool, whirlpool, poolside serv. Complimentary coffee in rms. Restaurant 6-11 am, 5-10 pm. Rm serv. Bar from 11 am (in season); entertainment. Ck-out 11 am. Coin lndry. Meeting rms. Business servs avail. In-rm modem link. Sundries. Exercise equipt. Patios, balconies. On beach. Cr cds: A, C, D, DS, JCB, MC, V.

D ➤ ⇌ ✕ ✕ 🏃 SC

★ **HOLIDAY INN EXPRESS.** (24700 Perdido Beach Blvd, Orange Beach 36561) AL 59 to AL 182 E/Beach Blvd. 334/974-1634; res: 888/974-7444; FAX 334/974-1185. Web www.gulf coastrooms.com. 119 rms, 6 story. May-Labor Day: S, D $109-$159; each addl $10; under 21 free; lower rates rest of yr. Crib free. TV; cable (premium). Complimentary continental bkfst. Restaurant opp 10 am-10 pm. Ck-out noon. Meeting rms. Business servs avail. In-rm modem link. Pool. Some refrigerators, microwaves. Balconies. On beach. Cr cds: A, C, D, DS, JCB, MC, V.

D ⇌ ✕ 🏃 SC

★ ★ **QUALITY INN BEACHSIDE.** 931 W Beach Blvd. 334/948-6874; FAX 334/948-5232; res: 800/844-6913. 158 units, 6 story, 72 kits. May-Labor Day: S, D $112-$152; each addl $6; suites, kits. $162-$265; under 18 free; wkly rates; lower rates rest of yr. Crib $6. TV; cable. 2 pools, 1 indoor; poolside serv. Playground. Restaurant 7-10 am, 5-10 pm. Rm serv. Bar 5-11 pm. Ck-out 11 am. Coin lndry. Meeting rms. Business servs avail. Sundries. Some refrigerators. Patios, balconies. On beach. Cr cds: A, C, D, DS, ER, MC, V.

D ➤ ⇌ 🏃 SC

Hotel

★ ★ ★ **PERDIDO BEACH RESORT.** (27200 Perdido Beach Blvd, Orange Beach 36561) 8 mi E of AL 59, on AL 182. 334/981-9811; FAX 334/981-5672; res: 800/634-8001. 345 units, 10 story. May-Labor Day: S, D $135-$155; each addl $10; suites, studio rms $197-$297; package plans; lower rates rest of yr. Crib free. TV; cable (premium), VCR avail (movies). Indoor/outdoor pool; whirlpool, poolside serv. Supervised child's activities (Apr-Oct); ages 5-11. Restaurant 6 am-11 pm. Bar; entertainment Tues-Sat. Ck-out noon. Convention facilities. Business servs avail. In-rm modem link. Concierge. Shopping arcade. Some covered parking. Lighted tennis. 18-hole golf privileges, greens fee $35-$55; pro. Exercise equipt; sauna. Game rm. Some refrigerators. Balconies. On beach. Cr cds: A, C, D, DS, ER, MC, V.

D ➤ 🏃 🏂 ⇌ ✕ 🏃 SC

Restaurants

★ **BOUDANZ.** 632 AL 59 S (36547). 334/948-4349. Hrs: 11 am-10 pm; Fri, Sat to 11 pm; Sun 3-11 pm. Closed Thanksgiving, Dec 24, 25. Creole menu. Bar. Semi-a la carte: lunch $4.99-$8.99, dinner $12.50-$17.25. Child's meals. Specialties: gumbo, jambalaya, etouffee. Entertainment wkends. Parking. Outdoor dining. Nautical decor. Cr cds: A, MC, V.

D ⇌

✔ ★ **GIFT HORSE.** (209 W Laurel, Foley 32535) on US 98. 334/943-3663. Hrs: 11 am-9 pm. Closed Dec 25. Buffet: lunch $8.50, dinner $11.50. Sun brunch $11.50. Child's meals. Specialties: apple

cheese casserole, fried biscuits, blueberry muffins. Own desserts. Restored building (1912); antique tables. Cr cds: MC, V.

D

★ **HAZEL'S.** (AL 182, Orange Beach) 6 mi E of AL 59, on AL 182. 334/981-4628. Hrs: 6:30 am-9:30 pm; Apr-Oct 6 am-10 pm; Sat, Sun brunch 11 am-4 pm. Serv bar. Semi-a la carte: bkfst $2.99-$6.25, lunch $2.29-$5.99, dinner $5.95-$18.95. Sat, Sun brunch $7.95. Child's meals. Parking. Cr cds: A, D, DS, MC, V.

D SC ⇌

★ **KIRK KIRKLAND'S HITCHIN' POST.** 3401 Gulf Shores Pkwy, AL 59, N of Intracoastal Bridge. 334/968-5041. Hrs: 11 am-10 pm; Fri, Sat to 10:30 pm. Closed some major hols. Serv bar. Semi-a la carte: lunch $3.95-$9.99, dinner $6.99-$16.99. Specializes in baby-back ribs, steak, mesquite-grilled fish. Casual dining; open country-style kitchen for viewing. Cr cds: A, DS, MC, V.

D SC

✔ ★ **MIKEE'S.** 1st St N & 2nd Ave E (36547). 334/948-6452. Hrs: 11 am-11 pm. Bar. Semi-a la carte: lunch $3-$12, dinner $4-$15. Child's meals. Nautical decor. Parking. Cr cds: A, C, D, DS, MC, V.

★ **ORIGINAL OYSTER HOUSE.** AL 59 at Bayou Village. 334/948-2445. Hrs: 11 am-10 pm; Fri, Sat to 11 pm. Closed Dec 24, 25. Bar. Semi-a la carte: lunch $5-$9.95, dinner $5-$19. Child's meals. Specializes in seafood. Salad bar. Parking. Nautical decor. On Bayou. Cr cds: A, C, D, DS, MC, V.

D

★ ★ **PERDIDO PASS.** (27501 Perdido Beach Blvd, Orange Beach 36561) 8 mi E of AL 59, on AL 182, at Alabama Point Bridge. 334/981-6312. Hrs: 11 am-9 pm. Bar. A la carte entrees: lunch $4.99-$7.99, dinner $11.99-$19.99. Child's meals. Specializes in seafood, grilled steak. Parking. Overlooks Gulf of Mexico. Cr cds: A, D, DS, MC, V.

D ⇌ ♥

✔ ★ **SEA-N-SUDS.** 405 E Beach Blvd. 334/948-7894. Hrs: 11 am-8 pm; Apr-Aug to 9 pm. Closed Sun off-season; Thanksgiving; also Dec. Bar. Semi-a la carte: lunch, dinner $3.95-$11.95. Specializes in fried seafood. Salad bar. Parking. On pier, overlooking gulf. Totally nonsmoking. Cr cds: A, MC, V.

★ ★ **THE VIEW.** 1832 W Beach Blvd, on ninth floor of Gulf Shores Surf and Racquet Club. 334/948-8888. Hrs: 5:30-9 pm; Fri, Sat to 10 pm. Closed Sun; Dec 25. Res accepted. Continental menu. Bar. Wine list. Semi-a la carte: dinner $14-$24. Specializes in seafood, veal, lamb. Parking. Formal dining with views of the Gulf of Mexico. Cr cds: A, DS, MC, V.

D SC

✔ ★ ★ **ZEKE'S LANDING.** (26619 Perdido Beach Blvd, Orange Beach 36561) 7 mi E on AL 182. 334/981-4001. Hrs: 4-9 pm; Fri, Sat to 10 pm; Fri, Sat to 11 pm; Sun brunch 10:30 am-3 pm; Apr-Oct hrs vary. Bar. Semi-a la carte: dinner $12.95-$34.95. Sun brunch $14.95. Child's meals. Specializes in seafood, prime rib. Parking. Overlooking harbor. Cr cds: A, C, D, DS, MC, V.

D

Guntersville (B-4)

(See also Gadsden, Huntsville)

Pop 7,038 **Elev** 800 ft **Area code** 256 **Zip** 35976 **E-mail** gcc@lakeguntersville.org **Web** www.lakeguntersville.org
Information Chamber of Commerce, 200 Gunter Ave, PO Box 577; 205/582-3612 or 800/869-5253.

A thriving port and power-producing center of the Tennessee Valley Authority, this town was once the site of a Cherokee village. In the 1820s, steamboats plying the river turned Guntersville into a boomtown; still the Cherokees and settlers continued to live alongside each other peacefully. "Boat Day," it was said, was a great occasion for the settlers and Cherokees alike.

The Cumberland River Trail, the route Andrew Jackson took on his way to the Creek War in 1813, passed through Guntersville, and Cherokees from this area joined and fought bravely with Jackson's troops against the Creeks. But, in 1837, just 24 years later, General Winfield Scott, under the direction of Andrew Jackson, rounded up the area's Cherokees and moved them westward.

Today, Guntersville receives and distributes river freight. South of town is the plateau of Sand Mountain, one of the great food-producing sections of the state. Part of the growing resort area of north Alabama's TVA lake country, Guntersville's municipal parks have numerous boat docks and launches.

What to See and Do

Buck's Pocket State Park. Natural pocket of the Appalachian mountain chain on 2,000 acres. Fishing; boat launch. Hiking trails. Picnic facilities, playground, concession. Primitive and improved camping. Visitor center. 16 mi N & E via AL 227, County 50 to Groveoak. Phone 256/659-2000.

Guntersville Dam and Lake (1939). Fifth of the nine TVA dams on the Tennessee River, it impounds a 67,900-acre lake that is 76 mi long. It is a favorite recreation area for swimming, fishing and boating. Lobby (daily). 12 mi W and N via AL 69 & County 240, 50. **Free.**

Lake Guntersville State Park. A 5,909-acre park with ridge tops and meadows. Swimming beach, waterskiing; fishing center; boating. Hiking, bicycling; golf (18 holes, fee); tennis. Nature programs. Picnicking, play-ground, concession, restaurant, chalets, lakeside cottages, resort inn on Taylor Mountain (see RESORT). Camping (hookups). 6 mi NE off AL 227 on Guntersville Reservoir. Phone 256/571-5444 or 800/548-4553.

Motels

✔★★ BEST WESTERN BOAZ OUTLET CENTER. (751 US 431S, Boaz 35957) Jct US 431 & AL 168. 205/593-8410; FAX 205/593-8410, ext. 300. 116 rms, 2 story. S $39-$46; D $48-$60; each addl $5; under 12 free. Crib free. Pet accepted. TV; cable. Pool; wading pool. Ck-out 11 am. Business servs avail. Cr cds: A, C, D, DS, MC, V.

★★ HOLIDAY INN. 2140 Gunter Ave. 256/582-2220; FAX 256/582-2059. 100 rms, 2-3 story, 20 kits. S, D $55-$75; each addl $6; kits. $65-$75; under 19 free. Crib free. TV; cable (premium). Pool. Coffee in rms. Restaurant 6 am-9 pm; Fri, Sat to 10 pm; Sun to 8 pm. Rm serv. Bar; entertainment exc Sun. Ck-out 11 am. Meeting rms. Business servs avail. Health club privileges. Refrigerators. View of lake. Cr cds: A, C, D, DS, JCB, MC, V.

★ MAC'S LANDING. 7001 Val-Monte Dr. 205/582-1000; FAX 205/582-1385. 53 units, 2 story. Apr-Oct: S, D $47-$56; each addl $5; suites, kit. units $78-$93; under 19 free; lower rates rest of yr. Crib $5. Pet accepted. TV; cable (premium). Pool. Complimentary continental bkfst. Restaurant adj 11 am-10 pm. Bar 3:30 pm-1 am; Thurs-Sat noon-2 am. Ck-out 11 am. Coin lndry. Meeting rms. Business servs avail. Gift shop. Balconies. Picnic tables, grills. On lake; swimming. Cr cds: A, C, D, DS, MC, V.

Resort

★★ LAKE GUNTERSVILLE LODGE. 1155 Lodge Dr, 6 mi NE on AL 227. 205/571-5440; FAX 205/571-5459; res: 800/548-4553. 100 rms in lodge, 2 story, 15 cottages, 20 chalets. Mar-Oct: lodge: S $55-$59; D $57-$61; each addl $5; suites $98; kit. cottages for 4 (2-day min) $99; chalet for 1-6, $99; under 12 free; golf plans; lower rates rest of yr. Maid serv daily in lodge, alternate days in cottages. Crib $5. TV. Pool; wading

pool, sauna. Playground. Dining rm 7 am-10 pm; Sun from 11:30 am. Box lunches. Ck-out 11 am, ck-in 2 pm. Coin lndry. Meeting rms. Grocery 2 mi. Sports dir. Lighted tennis. 18-hole golf, greens fee $15, pro, putting green. Private beach, waterskiing, launch ramps. Seaplane docking. Rec rm. Hiking, fitness, nature trails. Some fireplaces. Private patios, balconies. Heliport. Native American artifact "gold mine." Cr cds: A, MC, V.

Hamilton (B-2)

(See also Russellville)

Pop 5,787 **Elev** 498 ft **Area code** 205 **Zip** 35570

What to See and Do

Natural Bridge of Alabama. Two spans of sandstone, longest is 148 ft, created by natural erosion of a tributary stream more than 200 million yrs ago. Picnicking. (Daily) 1 mi W of AL 5 on US 278. Phone 205/486-5330. ¢¢

Motel

★★ BEST WESTERN OF HAMILTON. 2031 Military Street S, 1 mi S on US 43S, near US 78E, 278W. 205/921-7831; FAX 205/921-7831, ext. 361. 80 rms, 2 story. S $49-$54; D $53-$58; each addl $5; under 19 free. Crib free. TV; cable. Pool. Restaurant 6 am-2 pm, 5-10 pm. Rm serv. Ck-out noon. Coin lndry. Meeting rms. Business servs avail. In-rm modem link. Golf privileges. Cr cds: A, C, D, DS, JCB, MC, V.

Horseshoe Bend National Military Park (D-5)

(See also Alexander City)

(12 mi N of Dadeville on AL 49)

Early Spanish explorations, led by DeSoto, found the Creeks in Alabama and Georgia living in a settled communal-agricultural society governed by complex rituals and customs. Following the American Revolution, a horde of settlers moved south and west of the Appalachians. Despite territorial guarantees in the Treaty of 1790, the United States repeatedly forced land and road concessions from the Creeks. The Creek Indian Agency was ordered to oversee trade and to reestablish the Native Americans' prehis-toric agricultural economy.

The Lower Creeks of Georgia adjusted to life with the settlers. The Upper Creeks living in Alabama did not and vowed to defend their land and their customs after heeding the preachings of Tecumseh in 1811. When a few Upper Creeks, called Red Sticks, killed settlers near the Tennessee border, the Indian Agency ordered the Lower Creeks to execute the attending warriors. The order produced civil war within the Creek Nation by the spring of 1813. By summer, the settlers became involved in the fray, attacking an Upper Creek munitions convoy at Burnt Corn Creek, fearing the Creeks' intentions. The Upper Creeks retaliated on August 30, 1813, attacking Fort Mims and killing an estimated 250 people. Soon after, the militias of Georgia, Tennessee and the Mississippi Territory were brought in to combat the uprising of the "Red Sticks." The Georgia troops defeated the Creeks in two battles at Autosee and Calabee Creek, but the Tennes-see Militia, under Andrew Jackson, was the most effective force; battles were fought by Jackson's army at Talladega, Emuckfaw and Enitachopco. In March of 1814, they struck and routed the Creeks at the Horseshoe

Bend of the Tallapoosa River, the bloodiest battle of the Creek War. The peace treaty that followed soon after this battle cost the Creeks more than 20 million acres of land, opening a vast and rich domain to settlement, and eventually lead to the statehood of Alabama in 1819.

For Jackson, Horseshoe Bend was the beginning; for the Creek Nation, the beginning of the end. In the 1830s, during Jackson's presidency, they were forced to leave Alabama and move to "Indian Territory" (Oklahoma).

A museum at the visitor center depicts the battle with a slide presentation and an electric map exhibit. The park contains 2,040 acres of forested hills and is situated on the banks of the Tallapoosa River. A three-mile loop road tour with interpretive markers traverses the battle area. There are nature trails, picnic areas and a boat ramp. (Daily; closed Dec 25) Contact 11288 Horseshoe Bend Rd, Daviston 36256-9751; 256/234-7111. **Free.**

Huntsville (A-4)

(See also Athens, Decatur)

Settled 1805 **Pop** 159,789 **Elev** 641 ft **Area code** 256 **E-mail** info@huntsville.org **Web** www.huntsville.org

Information Convention & Visitors Bureau, 700 Monroe St, 35801; 256/551-2230 or 800/772-2348.

In Huntsville, the old and the new in Alabama meet. Now the seat of Madison County, the constitutional convention of Alabama Territory met here in 1819 and set up the state legislature. Many stately houses of that era may be seen. Today, Huntsville is deeply involved in space exploration. The NASA-Marshall Space Flight Center is NASA's rocketry headquarters and where the space station is being built.

Situated in a curving valley, Huntsville was an early textile town processing cotton raised in the surrounding country. Six Alabama governors called it home; so did the Confederate Secretary of War. The University of Alabama-Huntsville is located here.

What to See and Do

Alabama Constitution Village. Re-created complex of buildings commemorating Alabama's entry into the Union at the 1819 Constitutional Convention; period craft demonstrations and activities; guides in period dress. (Daily exc Sun; closed Dec 24-Jan) 404 Madison St. Phone 256/535-6565. ¢¢¢

Big Spring International Park. The town's water supply, this natural spring produces 24 million gallons daily. The first homesteader was John Hunt, and it was this spring around which the town's nucleus grew. Spragins St, W of Courthouse Square.

Burritt Museum & Park. Unusual 11-rm house built in shape of a cross. Exhibitions on gems and minerals, archaeology, antiques, historical items. On the grounds of this 167-acre park are 4 authentically furnished cabins, a blacksmith shop, a smokehouse and a church. Nature trails, gardens. Picnicking. Panoramic view of city. Museum (Mar-late Dec, Tues-Sat, Sun afternoons). Grounds (daily). 3101 Burritt Dr, just off Monte Sano Blvd. Phone 256/536-2882. ¢¢

Huntsville Depot Museum. Opened in 1860 as "passenger house" and eastern division headquarters for the Memphis & Charleston RR Co, the Huntsville depot was captured by Union troops and used as a prison; Civil War graffiti survives. Street car trips (addl fee); transportation exhibits. (Mar-Dec, daily exc Sun; closed some major hols) 320 Church St. Phone 256/539-1860 or 800/678-1819. ¢¢¢

Huntsville Museum of Art. Five galleries featuring traditional and contemporary work by regional and national artists; permanent collection and changing exhibits. Tours, lectures, concerts, films. (Daily exc Mon; closed major hols) Downtown, 300 Church St. Phone 256/535-4350. **Free.**

Madison County Nature Trail. Original house on first homestead. Chapel; covered bridge; 16-acre lake; waterfall; wooded hiking trails.

Braille trail. (Daily) 12 mi SE on S Shawdee Rd, Green Mountain. Phone 256/883-9501.

Monte Sano State Park. A 2,140-acre scenic recreation area on top of 1,800-ft Monte Sano ("Mountain of Health"). Hiking trails. Picnicking (tables, shelters, barbecue pits, fireplaces), playground, concession. Camping, cabins. Amphitheater. Park open all yr. Standard fees. 4 mi E, off US 431. Phone 256/534-3757 or -6589.

Twickenham Historic District. A living museum of antebellum architecture, the district contains Alabama's largest concentration of antebellum houses. Several of the houses are occupied by descendants of original builders/owners. Tours can be self-guided; guided tours avail for groups. Downtown, S and E of the Courthouse Sq. Contact the Convention and Visitors Bureau, 256/551-2230.

⚔ US Space and Rocket Center. Space exhibits include Apollo capsule and space shuttle objects returned from orbit. Rocket Park displays development of Apollo-Saturn V moon rocket and life-size space shuttle model. Omnimax Theater with tilt dome screen seats 280 and shows 45-min space shuttle and science films photographed by astronauts. NASA bus tours are escorted 1- or 2-hr bus trips through Marshall Space Flight Center featuring mission control, space station construction and tank where astronauts simulate weightlessness. US Space Camp offers 1-wk programs for children grade 4 and up. Campground. (Daily; closed Thanksgiving, Dec 25) 5 mi W on AL 20 just off I-565 at exit 15. Phone 256/837-3400 or 800/63-SPACE. ¢¢¢¢

Von Braun Center. Largest multi-purpose complex in northern Alabama, named for noted space pioneer, Dr Wernher von Braun. Center has 9,000-seat arena, 2,171-seat concert hall, 502-seat theater-playhouse; 100,000 sq ft exhibit space, 25,000 sq ft meeting rooms; the city Tourist Info Center (24-hr phone 256/533-5723). Downtown, 700 Monroe St. Phone 256/533-1953.

Annual Events

Panoply of the Arts Festival. Big Spring International Park. Last wkend Apr.

Big Spring Jam. Big Spring International Park. Music Festival. Late Sept.

Motels

★ ★ **BAYMONT INN.** *4890 University Dr NW (35816).* 205/830-8999; FAX 205/837-5720. 102 rms, 3 story. S $41.95; D $49.95-$54.95; each addl $5; under 16 free. Crib free. Pet accepted. TV. Pool. Complimentary continental bkfst. Restaurant adj open 24 hrs. Ck-out noon. Meeting rm. Business servs avail. In-rm modem link. Cr cds: A, C, D, DS, MC, V.

D ✦ ☒ ☒ ☒

✔★ ★ **COMFORT INN.** *3788 University Dr (35816).* 205/533-3291; FAX 205/536-7389. 67 rms, 2 story, 8 suites. S $44; D $48; suites $49; under 16 free. Crib $4. TV; cable (premium). Pool. Complimentary continental bkfst. Restaurant opp open 24 hrs. Ck-out 11 am. Meeting rms. Business servs avail. Health club privileges. Refrigerators. Cr cds: A, D, DS, MC, V.

☒ ☒ ☒ ⚑ SC

★ ★ **COURTYARD BY MARRIOTT.** *4804 University Dr (35816).* 205/837-1400; FAX 205/837-3582. 149 rms, 3 story. S $66; each addl (after 1st person) $10; suites $76; under 12 free; wkend rates. Crib free. TV; cable (premium). Pool; whirlpool. Restaurant 6-10:30 am. Bar 4-11 pm. Coin lndry. Meeting rms. In-rm modem link. Valet serv. Exercise equipt. Refrigerator in suites. Cr cds: A, C, D, DS, MC, V.

D ✦ ☒ ✗ ☒ ⚑ SC

✔★ **ECONO LODGE.** *3772 University Dr NW (35816).* 205/534-7061. 82 rms, 2 story. S $27-$49; D $30-$49; suites $39-$59; under 18 free. Crib free. Pet accepted, some restrictions; $12.50. TV; cable (premium), VCR avail (movies). Pool. Complimentary coffee in lobby.

Restaurant nearby. Ck-out 11 am. Refrigerator in suites. Cr cds: A, C, D, DS, JCB, MC, V.

`D` `⛵` `≈` `⛱` `🔥` `SC`

★ ★ **HAMPTON INN.** *4815 University Dr (35816). 205/830-9400; FAX 205/830-0978.* 164 rms, 3 story. S, D $50-$60; under 18 free. Crib free. TV; cable (premium). Heated pool; whirlpool. Complimentary continental bkfst. Ck-out noon. Business servs avail. In-rm modem link. Health club privileges. Cr cds: A, C, D, DS, MC, V.

`D` `≈` `⛱` `🔥` `SC`

★ ★ **HOLIDAY INN-SPACE CENTER.** *3810 University Dr (35816), W on US 72 at jct AL 53. 256/837-1171; res: 800/345-7720; FAX 256/837-9257.* E-mail HI@worldnet.att.net. 112 rms, 2 story. S, D $69; under 12 free; some wkend rates. Crib free. Pet accepted, some restrictions; $50 refundable. TV; cable (premium). Pool. Coffee in rms. Restaurant 6:30 am-2 pm, 5:30-10 pm. Rm serv. Bar 4 pm-2 am. Ck-out noon. Coin lndry. Meeting rms. Business servs avail. In-rm modem link. Bellhops. Valet serv. Sundries. Free airport transportation. Health club privileges. Cr cds: A, C, D, DS, ER, JCB, MC, V.

`⛵` `≈` `⛱` `🔥` `SC`

★ ★ **HOLIDAY INN-WEST.** *9035 US 72A (35824), 3 mi S, near Intl Airport. 256/772-7170; FAX 256/464-0762.* 173 rms, 2 story. S, D $82; suites $125; under 18 free. Crib free. TV; cable (premium), VCR avail. Pool; whirlpool. Complimentary coffee in rms. Restaurant 6 am-10 pm. Rm serv. Bar 11 am-11 pm. Ck-out 11 am. Meeting rms. Business servs avail. In-rm modem link. Valet serv. Free airport transportation. Health club privileges. Cr cds: A, C, D, DS, JCB, MC, V.

`D` `≈` `✈` `⛱` `🔥` `SC`

★ ★ **LA QUINTA.** *3141 University Dr NW (35816). 205/533-0756; FAX 205/539-5414.* 130 rms, 2 story. S $52; D $58; each addl $6; under 18 free. Crib free. Pet accepted, some restrictions. TV; cable. Pool. Complimentary continental bkfst. Restaurant adj open 24 hrs. Ck-out noon. Meeting rms. Business servs avail. In-rm modem link. Refrigerators avail. Health club privileges. Cr cds: A, C, D, DS, MC, V.

`D` `⛵` `≈` `⛱` `🔥` `SC`

★ ★ **RESIDENCE INN BY MARRIOTT.** *4020 Independence Dr (35816). 205/837-8907; FAX 205/837-5435.* 112 kit. suites, 1-2 story. Suites $75-$105; some wkend rates. Crib free. Pet accepted, some restrictions; $50. TV; cable (premium), VCR avail. Pool; whirlpool. Complimentary continental bkfst. Ck-out noon. Business servs avail. Valet serv Mon-Fri. Airport transportation. Sports court. Health club privileges. Fireplaces. Private patios, balconies. Picnic tables. Cr cds: A, C, D, DS, MC, V.

`D` `⛵` `≈` `⛱` `🔥` `SC`

Hotels

★ ★ ★ **FOUR POINTS BY SHERATON-HUNTSVILLE AIRPORT.** *1000 Glen Hearn Blvd (35824), at Huntsville Intl Airport. 205/772-9661; FAX 205/464-9116.* 148 rms, 6 story. S, D $79-$89; suites $89-$109; under 18 free. Crib free. TV; cable (premium). Pool. Restaurant 6 am-10 pm. Rm serv from 7 am. Bar 11 am-10:30 pm. Ck-out noon. Meeting rms. Business center. Lighted tennis. 18-hole golf, pro. Exercise equipt; sauna. Bathrm phone in suites. In air terminal. Luxury level. Cr cds: A, C, D, DS, JCB, MC, V.

`D` `🏋` `⛱` `✈` `⛱` `SC` `🚶`

★ ★ ★ **HILTON.** *401 Williams Ave (35801), at Freedom Plaza. 256/533-1400; FAX 256/534-7787.* 279 rms, 4 story. S $95-$103; D $105-$113; each addl $10; suites $130-$295. Crib free. Pet accepted. TV; cable. Pool; whirlpool, poolside serv. Restaurant 6 am-10 pm. Bars 11 am-midnight; entertainment exc Sun. Ck-out noon. Convention facilities. Business center. In-rm modem link. Free airport transportation. Exercise equipt. Health club privileges. Wet bar in suites. Civic Center, city park opp. Luxury level. Cr cds: A, C, D, DS, ER, MC, V.

`D` `⛵` `≈` `✈` `⛱` `🔥` `SC` `🚶`

★ ★ ★ **HOLIDAY INN RESEARCH PARK.** *5903 University Dr (35816), at Madison Square Mall. 256/830-0600; FAX 256/830-9576.* 200 rms, 5 story. S, D $70-$86; each addl $8; suites $125-$145; under 19 free; wkend rates. Crib $6. TV; cable. Indoor/outdoor pool; whirlpool. Restaurant 6 am-2 pm, 5-10 pm. Bar 4:30 pm-2 am; entertainment Tues-Sat. Ck-out noon. Meeting rms. Business servs avail. In-rm modem link. Guest lndry. Airport transportation. Exercise equipt; sauna. Cr cds: A, C, D, DS, JCB, MC, V.

`D` `≈` `✈` `⛱` `🔥` `SC`

★ ★ ★ **MARRIOTT.** *5 Tranquility Base (35805), at Space Center. 205/830-2222; FAX 205/895-0904.* 290 rms, 7 story. S, D $69-$120; suites $275; under 18 free; wkend rates. Crib free. Pet accepted, some restrictions. TV; cable (premium). Indoor/outdoor pool; whirlpool, poolside serv. Restaurants 7 am-10 pm. Bar 5 pm-2 am. Ck-out noon. Convention facilities. Business center. In-rm modem link. Concierge. Airport transportation. Exercise equipt; sauna. Game rm. Space & Rocket Museum adj. Cr cds: A, C, D, DS, JCB, MC, V.

`D` `⛵` `≈` `✈` `⛱` `🔥` `SC` `🚶`

★ ★ ★ **RADISSON SUITES.** *6000 S Memorial Pkwy (35802), at Gate 1 NASA Space Flight Center. 205/882-9400; FAX 205/882-9684.* 153 suites, 3 story. May-Oct: S $68-$78; D $73-$83; each addl $5-$10; kit. units $78-$199; under 17 free; wkly rates; lower rates rest of yr. Crib free. TV; cable (premium). Pool; whirlpool. Complimentary coffee in rms. Restaurant 6 am-2 pm, 5-10 pm. Bar 11 am-midnight. Ck-out noon. Free lndry facilities. Meeting rms. Business center. In-rm modem link. Free airport, RR station, bus depot transportation. Exercise equipt. Refrigerators, wet bars. Picnic tables. Cr cds: A, C, D, DS, JCB, MC, V.

`D` `≈` `✈` `⛱` `🔥` `SC` `🚶`

Restaurants

★ ★ **FOGCUTTER.** *3805 University Dr NW. 205/539-2121.* Hrs: 11 am-2 pm, 5-10:30 pm. Closed major hols. Res accepted. Bar to midnight. Semi-a la carte: lunch $3.95-$7.95, dinner $9.95-$18.95. Specializes in steak, seafood. Entertainment. Nautical decor; antiques. Cr cds: A, C, D, MC, V.

`D`

✔ ★ ★ **OL' HEIDELBERG.** *6125 University Dr NW, Unit E-14. 205/922-0556.* Hrs: 11 am-9 pm; Fri, Sat to 10 pm. Closed some hols. German, Amer menu. Semi-a la carte: lunch $3.75-$6.75, dinner $5.50-$14.50. Specializes in Wienerschnitzel, sauerbraten. Bavarian decor. Family-owned. Cr cds: A, MC, V.

`D` `🍽`

Jasper (C-3)

(See also Birmingham, Cullman)

Settled 1815 **Pop** 13,553 **Elev** 339 ft **Area code** 205 **Zip** 35501

Motels

★ **DAYS INN.** *101 6th Ave N. 205/221-7800.* 44 rms, 2 story. June-July: S $55; D $60; each addl $5; under 12 free; lower rates rest of yr. Crib free. TV; cable (premium). Pool. Complimentary continental bkfst. Restaurant adj 9 am-10 pm. Ck-out 11 am. Coin lndry. Business servs avail. Valet serv. Many refrigerators. Cr cds: A, C, D, DS, MC, V.

`D` `≈` `⛱` `🔥` `SC`

✔ ★ **TRAVEL-RITE INN.** *200 Mallway Dr (35504), opp mall. 205/221-1161.* 60 rms, 2 story. S $31-$34; D $40; each addl $3; under 12 free. Crib $4. Pet accepted. TV. Restaurant adj 6 am-11 pm. Ck-out 11 am. Meeting rm. Cr cds: A, C, D, DS, MC, V.

`D` `⛵` `≈` `🔥`

Motor Hotel

★ **JASPER INN.** *1400 US 78W Bypass. 205/221-3050; res: 800/554-0238.* 153 rms, 2-4 story. S $34; D $42; each addl $6; under 12 free. Crib free. TV, VCR avail (movies $3). Pool; wading pool. Restaurant 6 am-2 pm, 5-9 pm. Ck-out noon. Meeting rms. Business servs avail. Valet serv. Cr cds: A, C, D, DS, MC, V.

D ≈ ⊁ ⊀ SC

Mobile (H-2)

(See also Dauphin Island, Gulf Shores)

Founded 1702 **Pop** 196,278 **Elev** 7 ft **Area code** 334 **E-mail** info@mobile.org **Web** www.mobile.org
Information Convention & Visitors Corporation, PO Box 204, 36601; 334/208-2000 or 800/566-2453.

Mobile, Alabama's largest port city, blends old Southern grace with new Southern enterprise. The city was begun in 1702 when Jean Baptiste LeMoyne, Sieur de Bienville, moved his colony from Twenty-Seven Mile Bluff to the present site of Mobile.

Shipping, shipbuilding and a variety of manufacturers make Mobile a great industrial center. Today many millions of tons of cargo annually clear this international port. Paper, petroleum products, textiles, food processing and woodworking are among the principal industries.

While remaining very much the vibrant industrial seaport, Mobile has still managed to retain its air of antebellum graciousness and preserve its past in the Church Street, DeTonti Square, Oakleigh Garden and Old Dauphinway historical districts. These areas are famous for azaleas, oak-lined streets and an extraordinary variety of architectural styles.

What to See and Do

Alabama State Docks. Berths for 35 ocean-going vessels of up to 45-ft draft; 1,000-ft-wide turning basin. (Mon-Fri; closed some hols) Port of Mobile. Phone 334/441-7001.

Battleship Memorial Park, USS *Alabama*. Visitors may tour 35,000-ton USS *Alabama*, which serves as a memorial to the state's men and women who served in World War II, the Korean conflict, Vietnam and Desert Storm. Also, submarine USS *Drum*, World War II aircraft, a B-52 bomber and an A-12 Blackbird spy plane. (Daily; closed Dec 25) Parking fee. 1 mi E via Bankhead and Wallace Tunnels on Battleship Pkwy, US 90. Phone 334/433-2703. ¢¢¢

Bellingrath Gardens and Home. This 905-acre estate comprises natural woodland and some 65 acres of planted gardens on the Isle-aux-Oies (Fowl) River. It is also a bird sanctuary. Many varieties of native and other trees are background for the innumerable flowers and flowering plants that are in bloom all year. Each season has its own special flowers but many bloom for more than one. There are approximately 250,000 azalea plants of 200 varieties, camellias, roses, water lilies, dogwood and hydrangeas. Travels to world-famed gardens abroad inspired the Bellingraths to create their gardens in the 1920s. Visitors receive a pictorial map showing gardens' walks and principal features. Included in the gardens' admission is the world's largest public display of Boehm porcelain. There is a restaurant, a video display at the entrance and a free "pet motel" near the exit. The Bellingrath house, in the center of the gardens, is furnished with antiques, fine china and rare porcelain; it is open to a few people at a time (daily tours). Since the home is located within the gardens, it is not possible to visit the house without visiting the gardens. The riverboat *Southern Belle* provides 45-min cruises along the Fowl River. House, gardens and river cruise (daily). 20 mi SW via US 90 or I-10 and Bellingrath Hwy, near Theodore. Phone 334/973-2217 or 800/247-8420. Gardens ¢¢¢; house & gardens ¢¢¢¢; river cruise ¢¢¢¢; gardens, house and river cruise ¢¢¢¢¢

Bragg-Mitchell Mansion (1855). Greek-revival, 20-rm mansion sits amidst 12 acres of landscaped grounds. Restored interior includes extensive faux-

grained woodwork and stenciled moldings; period furnishings. (Daily exc Sat; closed major hols) 1906 Springhill Ave. Phone 334/471-6364. ¢¢

Carlen House Museum (1842). "Creole cottage" furnished in period style. Guided tours by appt. (Tues-Sat, also Sun afternoons; closed hols) 54 Carlen St at Willcox St. Phone 334/470-7768. **Free.**

Cathedral of the Immaculate Conception (1835). Greek-revival minor basilica with German art glass windows, bronze canopy over altar and hand-carved stations of the cross. (Daily; limited hrs Mon-Fri) Dauphin & Claiborne Sts. Phone 334/434-1565.

Condé-Charlotte Museum House (1822-24). Originally a jail, the museum house is now furnished with period antiques and artifacts; period kitchen and Spanish garden. (Tues-Sat; closed hols) 104 Theatre St, adj to Fort Condé. Phone 334/432-4722. ¢¢

Eichold-Heustis Medical Museum. At the University of South Alabama's USA Springhill campus. Named in honor of Dr. James Heustis and Dr. Samuel Eichold, this museum is the largest of its kind in the southeast. It contains displays of medical artifacts and photographs. (Mon-Fri) 1504 Springhill Ave. Phone 334/434-5055. **Free.**

Exploreum Museum of Science. Hands-on investigative science and health museum. More than 80 life science, earth science, physical science and "imagination" exhibits and displays. (Tues-Sat; closed hols) 1906 Spring Hill Ave. Phone 334/476-6873. ¢¢

Fort Condé Mobile Visitor Welcome Center. Reconstructed 1724-1735 French fort features workable reproductions of 1740s naval cannon, muskets and other arms. Staffed by soldiers dressed in period French uniforms. (Daily; closed Mardi Gras & Dec 25) 150 S Royal St at Church St. Phone 334/434-7304. **Free.**

Gray Line City tours. 210 S Washington Ave. For information and reservations phone 334/432-2228.

Greyhound racing. Mobile Greyhound Park. Parimutuel wagering; restaurant. Minimum age 18. (Nightly Mon & Wed-Sat, matinees Mon, Wed, Fri, Sat; closed mid-late Dec) W via I-10, Theodore-Dawes exit (#13). For reservations phone 334/653-5000.

Malbis Greek Orthodox Church (1965). Impressive Byzantine church, copied from a similar one in Athens, Greece. Pentelic marble is from same quarries that supplied the Parthenon; skilled artists from Greece created the authentic paintings; hand-carved figures and ornaments were brought from Greece. Stained-glass windows, dome with murals, icons and many works of art depicting life of Christ. Guided tours by appt. (Daily exc Dec 25) 13 mi E off I-10 exit 38 or US 90. Phone 334/626-3050. **Free.**

Mobile Museum of Art. Permanent collection includes furniture, decorative arts; American and European 19th-century paintings and prints; contemporary arts & crafts; changing exhibits. (Daily exc Mon; closed major hols) 4850 Museum Dr on S shore of lake in Langan Park. Phone 334/343-2667. **Free.**

Museum of Mobile. Paintings, documents and artifacts of Mobile's French, British, Spanish and Confederate periods; Mobile's maritime history, ship models, antique carriages, arms collection, Mardi Gras and other costumes. World's second-largest collection of Edward Marshall Boehm porcelains. Guided tours by appt. (Tues-Sat, also Sun afternoons; closed hols) 355 Government St in Bernstein-Bush House (1872), an Italianate town house. Phone 334/434-7569. **Free.**

Oakleigh. This 1833 antebellum house stands on the highest point of Simon Favre's old Spanish land grant, surrounded by azaleas and the live oaks for which it was named. Bricks for the first story were made on the site; the main upper portion is of hand-hewn timber. The Historic Mobile Preservation Society has furnished the house in the pre-1850 period; 1850s Cox-Deasy Creole cottage included in tour. Museum collection of local items. (Daily; closed major hols; also day of Mardi Gras & Christmas wk) 350 Oakleigh Place. Phone 334/432-1281. ¢¢

Phoenix Fire Museum. Fire-fighting equipment; memorabilia dating from first Mobile volunteer company (1819); steam fire engines; collection of silver trumpets and helmets. Housed in restored fire station (1859). Guided tours by appt. (Tues-Sat, also Sun afternoons; closed hols) 203 S Claiborne St. Phone 334/434-7554. **Free.**

Richards-DAR House (ca 1860). Restored Italianate town house features elaborate ironwork, curved suspended staircase, period furniture. (Tues-

Sun, also Sun afternoons; closed Thanksgiving, late Dec) 256 N Joachim St. Phone 334/434-7320. ¢¢

University of South Alabama (1964). (12,000 students). Theater productions presented during school year at USA/Wright Auditorium (phone 334/460-6305) and at Saenger Theatre (phone 334/438-5686). Of architectural interest on campus are Seaman's Bethel Theater (1860); the Plantation Creole House (1828), a reconstructed Creole cottage; and Mobile town house (1870), a federal-style building showing Italianate and Greek-revival influences that also houses the USA campus art gallery. Tours of campus. 307 University Blvd. Phone 334/460-6141 or -6211.

Annual Events

Senior Bowl Football Game. Ladd Stadium. 3rd Sat Jan.

Historic Mobile Tours. Houses, buildings open to visitors. 2nd wkend Mar.

Blessing of the Fleet. Bayou la Batre, 25 mi SW. Phone 334/824-2415. 4th Sun June.

Bay Fest. Various musical performers provide entertainment on five stages. Downtown, in the historic district. Phone 334/470-7730. 1st wkend Oct.

Greater Gulf State Fair. Commercial, industrial, military and educational exhibits; entertainment. Phone 334/344-4573. Mid-Oct.

Seasonal Event

Azalea Trail Festival. During the period when the azaleas are usually at full bloom, many events are scheduled to entertain visitors in the city. A 35-mi-long driving tour winds through the floral streets in and around Mobile; printed guides available. Azaleas were first introduced to Mobile in the early 18th century, and today they grow throughout the city. The Convention & Visitors Corporation has further details and has maps for self-guided tours of Azalea Trail route and local historic sites. Phone 800/566-2453. Mar-early Apr.

Motels

★ ★ **DRURY INN.** 824 S Beltline Hwy (36609). 334/344-7700. 110 rms, 4 story. S $55-$63; D $63-$71; each addl $8; under 18 free. Crib free. Pet accepted, some restrictions. TV; cable. Pool. Complimentary continental bkfst; afternoon refreshments. Restaurant adj open 24 hrs. Business servs avail. In-rm modem link. Ck-out noon. Meeting rms. Valet serv. Cr cds: A, C, D, DS, MC, V.

D ⚡ ≋ ⋈ 🐾 SC

✔★ ★ **HAMPTON INN.** 930 S Beltline Hwy (36609). 334/344-4942; FAX 334/341-4520. 118 units, 2 story. S $46; D $56; each addl $5; under 18 free. Crib free. TV; cable (premium). Pool. Complimentary continental bkfst. Ck-out 11 am. Business servs avail. In-rm modem link. Cr cds: A, C, D, DS, MC, V.

D ≋ ⋈ 🐾 SC

★ ★ **LA QUINTA.** 816 S Beltline Hwy (36609). 334/343-4051; FAX 334/343-2897. 122 units, 2 story. S, D $59-$79; each addl $8; under 18 free. Crib free. Pet accepted, some restrictions. TV; cable (premium). Pool. Complimentary continental bkfst. Coffee in rms. Restaurant adj open 24 hrs. Ck-out noon. Business servs avail. In-rm modem link. Cr cds: A, C, D, DS, MC, V.

D ⚡ ≋ ⋈ 🐾 SC

✔★ **RED ROOF INN.** 5450 Coca Cola Rd (36619). 334/666-1044; FAX 334/666-1032. 108 rms, 2 story. S $36-$60; D $48.49-$56.99; each addl $8; under 18 free. Crib free. Pet accepted, some restrictions. TV; cable. Complimentary coffee in lobby. Restaurant nearby. Ck-out noon. Business servs avail. Cr cds: A, C, D, DS, MC, V.

D ⚡ ≋ 🐾 SC

★ **SHONEY'S INN.** 5472-A Inn Rd Tillman's Corner Pkwy (36619), at I-10 exit 15B. 334/660-1520; FAX 334/666-4240; res: 800/222-2222. 118 rms, 3 story, 15 suites. S $50; D $54; each addl $6; suites $62; under 18 free; golf plan. Crib free. Pet accepted; $5. TV; cable. Pool. Complimentary coffee in lobby. Restaurant adj 6 am-midnight. Ck-out noon. Business servs avail. Some refrigerators. Cr cds: A, C, D, DS, MC, V.

D ⚡ ≋ ⋈ 🐾 SC

Motor Hotels

★ ★ **HOLIDAY INN.** 5465 AL 90W (36619), AL 90 & I-10 exit 15B. 334/666-5600; FAX 334/666-2773. 160 units, 5 story. S, D $69-$89; suites $81-$95; under 18 free. Crib free. TV; cable. Pool; whirlpool. Restaurant 6 am-2 pm, 5-10 pm. Rm serv. Bar 5 pm-2 am. Ck-out noon. Coin lndry. Meeting rms. Bellhops. Valet serv. Free airport transportation. Luxury level. Cr cds: A, C, D, DS, JCB, MC, V.

D ≋ ⋈ 🐾 SC

★ ★ ★ **RAMADA PLAZA HOTEL.** 600 S Beltline Hwy (36608), jct I-65 & Airport Blvd. 334/344-8030; FAX 334/344-8055. 236 rms, 4 story. S $79-$99; D $89-109; each addl $10; under 18 free. Crib $10. TV; cable (premium). 2 pools, 1 indoor; wading pool, whirlpool. Restaurant 6 am-1 pm, 5-10 pm. Rm serv. Bar; entertainment. Ck-out 1 pm. Meeting rms. Business servs avail. In-rm modem link. Bellhops. Sundries. Free airport transportation. Lighted tennis. Putting green. Exercise equipt. Cr cds: A, C, D, DS, JCB, MC, V.

D ⚡ 🏃 ≋ ⋈ 🎾 🐾 SC

Hotels

★ ★ ★ **ADAM'S MARK AT RIVERVIEW PLAZA.** 64 South Water (36602). 334/438-4000; FAX 334/415-3060; res: 800/444-2326. 375 units, 28 story. S, D $150-$170; each addl $12; suites $215-$315; under 18 free; wkend rates. Crib free. Covered parking $6.50. TV; cable. Pool. Restaurant 6:30 am-2 pm, 5:30-11 pm. Rm serv 24 hrs. Bar 11 am-midnight; entertainment. Ck-out noon. Convention facilities. Business center. In-rm modem link. Concierge. Shopping arcade. Luxury level. Cr cds: A, C, D, DS, MC, V.

D ≋ ⋈ 🐾 SC 🏂

★ ★ **CLARION.** 3101 Airport Blvd (36606), I-65 Airport Blvd exit. 334/476-6400; FAX 334/476-9360. 250 rms, 20 story. S, D $69-$89; each addl $10; suites $150-$200; under 18 free. Crib free. Pet accepted, some restrictions. TV; cable (premium), VCR avail. Pool; whirlpool. Restaurant 6:30-2 am. Bar. Ck-out noon. Convention facilities. Business servs avail. In-rm modem link. Some refrigerators. Some balconies. Cr cds: A, C, D, DS, MC, V.

D ⚡ ≋ ⋈ 🐾 SC

★ ★ ★ **RADISSON ADMIRAL SEMMES.** 251 Government St (36602). 334/432-8000; FAX 334/405-5942. 170 rms, 12 story. S, D $94-$114; each addl $10; suites $138-$350; studios $105; under 17 free; wkend rates. Crib free. Parking $4. TV; cable (premium). Heated pool; whirlpool, poolside serv. Restaurant 5:45 am-10 pm. Rm serv 6-2 am. Bar; entertainment Fri, Sat. Ck-out 11 am. Meeting rms. Business center. In-rm modem link. Health club privileges. Some refrigerators. Restored landmark hotel in heart of historical district; antiques, artwork. Cr cds: A, C, D, DS, MC, V.

D ≋ ⋈ 🐾 SC 🏂

Inn

★ **MALAGA INN.** 359 Church St (36602). 334/438-4701; FAX 334/438-4701, ext. 123; res: 800/235-1586. 39 rms, 2-3 story. S $62-$72; D $69-$79; each addl $5; suites $135. TV. Pool. Complimentary coffee. Dining rm 6 am-10 pm; closed Sun. Rm serv. Bar. Ck-out 11 am, ck-in noon-1 pm. Meeting rms. Business servs avail. Luggage handling. Private patios, balconies. Twin restored antebellum town houses built 1862; many original antique furnishings. Garden courtyard, fountain. Cr cds: A, C, DS, MC, V.

≋ ⋈ 🐾

Resort

★ ★ ★ **MARRIOTT'S GRAND HOTEL & GOLF CLUB.** *(1 Grand Blvd, Point Clear 36564) 23 mi SE of Mobile on US 98 Scenic.* 334/928-9201; FAX 334/928-1149. 306 hotel rms, 2-4 story, 8 multi-unit cottages (2 & 4 bedrm). Mar-Nov: S, D $169-$229; cottage units $199; under 18 free; MAP avail; lower rates rest of yr. Crib free. TV; cable (premium). Pool; whirlpool, poolside serv. Playground. Supervised child's activities (Memorial Day-Labor Day & special wkends); ages 5-12. Dining rm 7-10:30 am, noon-2 pm, 6:30-9:30 pm (also see BAY VIEW). Rm serv. Box lunches, snack bar, picnics. Bars 11 am-midnight. Ck-out noon, ck-in 4 pm. Meeting rms. Business center. In-rm modem link. Concierge. Grocery, package store 1 mi. Airport transportation; 24-hr notice. Tennis, pro. 36-hole golf, pro. Luxury yacht, sailboats, paddleboats, windsurfing. Bicycles. Lawn games. Game rm. Exercise equipt. Fishing guides; fish clean & store. Refrigerators avail. Some private patios, balconies. Picnic tables. Historic Civil War cemetery on site. 550 landscaped acres on Mobile Bay. Cr cds: A, C, D, DS, ER, JCB, MC, V.

Restaurants

★ ★ ★ **BAY VIEW.** *(See Marriott's Grand Hotel & Golf Club Resort)* 334/928-9201. Hrs: 6:30-9:30 pm. Closed Sun, Mon. Res accepted. Bar. Semi-a la carte: dinner $10.95-$21.50. Child's meals. Own baking. Parking. Overlooks Mobile Bay. Cr cds: A, C, D, DS, ER, JCB, MC, V.

★ **PIER 4.** *(Battleship Pkwy, Daphne 36526)* 334/626-6710. Hrs: 11 am-10 pm; Fri, Sat to 11 pm. Closed Thanksgiving, Dec 25. Continental menu. Semi-a la carte: lunch $4.50-$8.50, dinner $8.95-$19.25. Child's meals. Specialties: shrimp Dijon, snapper Ponchartrain. Own desserts. Parking. View of bay. Cr cds: A, C, D, DS, MC, V.

★ ★ **THE PILLARS.** *1757 Government St (36604).* 334/478-6341. Hrs: 5-10 pm. Closed Sun; major hols. Res accepted. Continental menu. Serv bar. Wine cellar. Semi-a la carte: dinner $14.95-$19.50. Complete meals: dinner $18-$24. Child's meals. Specializes in fresh gulf seafood, veal, Angus beef. Own baking. Restored plantation house. Cr cds: A, C, D, DS, MC, V.

★ ★ **ROUSSOS SEAFOOD.** *166 S Royal St (36602), I-10 Water St exit to Fort Condé Welcome Center.* 334/433-3322. Hrs: 11 am-10 pm. Closed Sun; most major hols. Res accepted. Bar. Semi-a la carte: lunch, dinner $4.95-$21.95. Child's meals. Specializes in fresh seafood, steak, chicken. Parking. Nautical decor. Family-owned. Cr cds: A, C, D, DS, MC, V.

★ ★ ★ **RUTH'S CHRIS STEAK HOUSE.** *271 Glenwood St (36606).* 334/476-0516. Hrs: 5-10 pm; Sun to 9 pm; also Thurs 11:30-2 am. Closed Thanksgiving, Dec 25. Res accepted. Bar. A la carte entrees: dinner $30 and up. Parking. Cr cds: A, C, D, DS, JCB, MC, V.

Montgomery (E-4)

Settled 1819 **Pop** 187,106 **Elev** 287 ft **Area code** 334 **E-mail** tourism@montgomerychamber.org **Web** www.montgomery.al.us

Information Montgomery Area Chamber of Commerce Visitors Center, 401 Madison Ave, 36104; 334/262-0013.

Between tall, stately columns on the portico of the state capitol, a bronze star marks the spot where Jefferson Davis was inaugurated president of the Confederate States of America on February 18, 1861. At that moment, Montgomery became the Confederacy's first capital. From this city went the telegram "Fire on Fort Sumter" that began the Civil War. Approximately 100 years later, Montgomery became embroiled in another kind of "war," the battle for civil rights.

Today, Montgomery is home to the nation's first Civil Rights Memorial. The memorial chronicles key events and lists the names of approximately 40 people who died in the struggle for racial equality from 1955-1968.

Montgomery is a city of considerable distinction, with many historic houses and buildings. Although Montgomery's most important business is government, it is also a livestock market and a center of manufacturing. As an educational center it offers many cultural activities.

What to See and Do

Alabama Shakespeare Festival. Professional repertory company performs classic and contemporary comedy and drama. Musical performances as well. Two theaters: 750-seat Festival Stage and 225-seat Octagon. (Nov-Sept, Wed-Sun; wkend matinees) Hotel/play packages available. #1 Festival Dr. Inquire about facilities for the disabled and hearing impaired; phone 800/841-4273 (box office).

Alabama State University (1874). (5,500 students) Authorized by the legislature in 1873 as the Lincoln Normal School, this university was moved from Marion to Montgomery in 1887. On campus are an art gallery, African-American collection and Tullibody Fine Arts Center (daily during academic yr; closed hols). Tours. S Union & I-85. Phone 334/229-4100.

★ **Civil Rights Memorial.** Designed by Vietnam Veterans Memorial artist Maya Lin. Washington Ave & Hull St at the Southern Poverty Law Center.

★ **Dexter Avenue King Memorial Baptist Church** (1877). The Rev. Dr. Martin Luther King, Jr, was a pastor from 1954 to 1960; from the church he directed the Montgomery bus boycott, which sparked the modern civil rights movement; mural and original painting "The Beginning of a Dream." (Daily exc Sun, by appt; closed hols) 454 Dexter Ave. Phone 334/263-3970.

F. Scott and Zelda Fitzgerald Museum. The famous author and his wife lived in this house from 1931-1932. Museum contains personal artifacts detailing the couple's public and private lives. Paintings by Zelda, letters and photographs; 25-min video presentation. (Wed-Fri, Sat & Sun afternoons; closed most major hols) 919 Felder Ave. Phone 334/264-4222. **Free.**

Fort Toulouse/Jackson Park National Historic Landmark. At the confluence of the Coosa and Tallapoosa rivers, Fort Toulouse was opened by Bienville in 1717 to establish trade in the heart of Creek territory. Abandoned in 1763, Andrew Jackson built a fort on the same site in 1814 after the Battle of Horseshoe Bend. Fort Toulouse has been reconstructed, and Fort Jackson has been partially reconstructed. This is also the site of mounds dating from approximately A.D. 1100. The park features a boat ramp, nature walks, picnicking, improved camping and a museum. A living history program can be seen the 3rd wkend of each month. (Daily; closed Jan 1, Dec 25) 12 mi NE, 3 mi W off US 231 near Wetumpka. Phone 334/567-3002. ¢

Greyhound racing. VictoryLand Track. Clubhouse, restaurant. Over 19 yrs only. (Nightly exc Sun; Mon, Wed, Fri & Sat afternoons; closed early Jan, Thanksgiving, late Dec) 20 mi E via I-85, exit 22, in Shorter. Phone 334/269-6087. ¢

Hank Williams' grave. Gravesite memorial to country music legend. Hank Williams Memorial, Oakwood Cemetery. 1305 Upper Wetumpka Rd.

Huntingdon College (1854). (800 students) Founded in Tuskegee to provide higher education for women, the liberal arts school became coeducational after World War II; 58-acre campus of woods and hills; Gothic buildings. Tours (by appt). 1500 Fairview Ave, 2 mi SE. Phone 334/265-0511.

Jasmine Hill Gardens. Extensive 17-acre garden, flowering year round. Designed as setting for statues, fountains and other works of art, including an exact copy of the ruins of the Temple of Hera in Olympia, Greece. Features a series of pools and avenues of flowering cherries and azaleas and of longleaf pine; 1830s cottage. Gardens (daily exc Mon). 8 mi N on

US 231, then right on Jasmine Hill Rd, follow signs for 2 mi, near Wetumpka. Phone 334/567-6463.   ¢¢

Lower Commerce Street Historic District. Wholesale and railroad district along the Alabama River. Buildings, primarily Victorian in style, date from the 1880s to turn of the century. Riverfront tunnel to Riverfront Park dates to cotton days. 100 blk of Commerce St.

Maxwell AFB. This has been an airfield since 1910, when Wilbur Wright began the world's first flying school on this site. Orville Wright made his first flight in Montgomery on Mar 26, 1910, four years before the Aviation Section of the Signal Corps was created. Maxwell Field was named Nov 8, 1922, for Lieutenant William C. Maxwell of Atmore, AL, killed while serving with Third Aero Squadron in the Philippines. It is now the site of Air University. Tours by appt. (Daily; closed hols) 2 mi S, off I-65. Phone 334/953-1110 or -2014 (tour information).   **Free.**

Montgomery Museum of Fine Arts. Collections of 19th- and 20th-century American art; European works on paper; regional and decorative arts. Hands-on children's exhibits. Lectures, concerts. (Daily exc Mon; closed Jan 1, July 4, Thanksgiving, Dec 25) 1 Museum Dr. Phone 334/244-5700. **Free.**

Montgomery Zoo. An 8-acre zoo housing 147 species; 600 mammals, birds and reptiles in geographical groupings. (Daily; closed Jan 1, Dec 25) 329 Vandiver Blvd off North Blvd. Phone 334/240-4900.   ¢¢

Murphy House (1851). Fine example of Greek-revival architecture with fluted Corinthian columns and wrought-iron balcony is now headquarters of the Montgomery Water Works. (Mon-Fri; closed hols) Bibb & Coosa Sts. Phone 334/206-1600.

Old Alabama Town. Includes the Ordeman-Shaw House, an Italianate town house (ca 1850) with period furnishings; service buildings with household items; reconstructed 1840 barn; carriage house; 1820s log cabin depicting pioneer life; shotgun cottage depicting black urban life; urban church (ca 1890); country doctor's office; drugstore museum and cotton gin museum; corner grocery from the late 1890s; one-rm schoolhouse; exhibition (Grange) hall. Taped driving tour of historic Montgomery also available. Films, tours, information center. (Daily; closed Jan 1, Easter, Thanksgiving, Dec 25) 301 Columbus St. Phone 334/240-4500 or -4501. ¢¢¢

St John's Episcopal Church (1855). Stained-glass windows, Gothic pipe organ, Jefferson Davis's pew. (Daily exc Sat) 113 Madison Ave & N Perry St. Phone 334/262-1937.

State Capitol (1851). Seat of Alabama's government for more than 100 yrs. Bainbridge at Dexter Ave. Phone 334/242-3935.Opp the capitol are

> **First White House of the Confederacy** (1835). This two-story, white frame house was the residence of Jefferson Davis and his family while Montgomery was the Confederate capital. Moved from its original location at Bibb and Lee streets in 1921, it is now a Confederate museum containing period furnishings, personal belongings and paintings of the Davis family and Confederate mementos. (Mon-Fri; closed major hols) 644 Washington Ave. Phone 334/242-1861.   **Free.**

> **Alabama Department of Archives and History.** Houses historical museum and genealogical research facilities. Artifact collections include exhibits on the 19th century, the military and early Alabama Native Americans. Also an interactive children's gallery. (Daily exc Sun; closed hols) 624 Washington Ave. Phone 334/242-4363.   **Free.**

Annual Events

Southern Livestock Exposition and World Championship Rodeo. Garrett Coliseum. NE on Federal Dr. Late Mar-early Apr.

Jubilee City Fest. Downtown. Memorial Day wkend.

Alabama National Fair. Garrett Coliseum. NE on Federal Dr. Early Oct.

Blue-Gray Football Classic. Cramton Bowl. Dec 25.

Motels

✔★ **BAYMONT INN.** 5225 Carmichael Rd (36106). 334/277-6000; FAX 334/279-8207. 102 rms, 3 story. S, D $42.95-$52.95; each addl $7; under 18 free. Crib free. TV; cable. Pool. Continental bkfst in rms.

Ck-out noon. Meeting rm. Business center. In-rm modem link. Cr cds: A, C, D, DS, MC, V.

D ≋ ⋈ ⋈ ⤢

★★ **BEST WESTERN-STATEHOUSE INN.** 924 Madison Ave (36104). 334/265-0741; FAX 334/834-6126; res: 800/552-7099. 162 rms, 6 story. S $44-$60; D $52-$58; each addl $6; suites $85; under 12 free. Crib free. TV; cable. Pool; wading pool. Restaurant 6 am-10 pm. Rm serv. Bar from 3 pm. Ck-out noon. Meeting rms. Business services avail. Cr cds: A, C, D, DS, MC, V.

D ≋ ⋈ ⋈ **SC**

★★ **COURTYARD BY MARRIOTT.** 5555 Carmichael Rd (36117). 334/272-5533; res: 800/321-2211; FAX 334/279-0853. 146 rms, 3 story. S $89; D $99; each addl $10; suites $99-$109; under 18 free; wkend rates. Crib free. TV; cable. Pool; whirlpool. Bar 4-11 pm. Ck-out noon. Guest lndry. Meeting rms. Business servs avail. In-rm modem link. Exercise equipt. Health club privileges. Refrigerators avail. Some private patios, balconies. Cr cds: A, C, D, DS, MC, V.

D ≋ ⋔ ⋈ ⋈ **SC**

✔★ **DAYS INN.** 2625 Zelda Rd (36107), I-85 exit 3. 334/269-9611; res: 800/325-2525; FAX 334/262-7393. 120 rms, 2 story. S, D $55-$60; each addl $5; under 12 free. Crib free. Pet accepted; $5. TV; cable. Pool. Complimentary continental bkfst. Coin lndry. Ck-out noon. Business servs avail. In-rm modem link. Health club privileges. Cr cds: A, C, D, DS, MC, V.

✔ ≋ ⋈ ⋈ **SC**

✔★ **ECONO LODGE.** 1040 W South Blvd (36105), near Montgomery Airport. 334/286-6100. 35 rms, 2 story. S $40-$50; D $45-$55; each addl $4; under 18 free. Crib free. TV; cable (premium). Complimentary continental bkfst. Restaurant adj open 24 hrs. Ck-out 11 am. Cr cds: A, C, D, DS, MC, V.

D ⋈ ⋈ **SC**

★ **FAIRFIELD INN BY MARRIOTT.** 5601 Carmichael Rd (36117), I-85 exit 6 at East Blvd. 334/270-0007. 133 rms, 3 story. S $51.95; D $53-$59; each addl $6; under 18 free. Crib free. TV; cable. Pool. Complimentary continental bkfst. Restaurant adj 6 am-11 pm. Ck-out noon. Business servs avail. In-rm modem link. Valet serv Mon-Fri. Cr cds: A, C, D, DS, MC, V.

D ≋ ⋈ ⋈ **SC**

★ **HAMPTON INN.** 1401 East Blvd (36117). 334/277-2400; FAX 334/277-6546. 105 units, 2 story. S $61-$65; D $65-$69; under 18 free. Crib free. TV; cable (premium). Pool. Complimentary continental bkfst. Coffee in rms. Restaurant adj. Ck-out noon. Business servs avail. In-rm modem link. Cr cds: A, C, D, DS, MC, V.

D ≋ ⋈ ⋈ **SC**

★★★ **HOLIDAY INN-EAST.** 1185 Eastern Bypass (36117). 334/272-0370; FAX 334/270-0339. 213 rms, 2 story. S, D $71.95-$79.95; each addl $10; suites $160; under 16 free; golf plan. Crib free. Pet accepted. TV. Indoor pool; whirlpool. Restaurant 6:30-9:30 am, 5:30-9:30 pm. Rm serv. Bar 4 pm-1 am. Ck-out noon. Meeting rms. Business servs avail. In-rm modem link. Bellhops. Valet serv. Sundries. Putting green. Exercise equipt; sauna. Game rm. Rec rm. Cr cds: A, C, D, DS, JCB, MC, V.

D ⤢ ≋ ⋔ ⋈ ⋈ **SC**

✔★★ **LA QUINTA.** 1280 Eastern Blvd (36117). 334/271-1620; FAX 334/244-7919. 130 rms, 2 story. S $50.40; D $60; each addl $6; under 18 free. Crib free. Pet accepted. TV; cable (premium), VCR avail (movies). Pool. Complimentary continental bkfst. Restaurant adj 6 am-10 pm; Fri, Sat to 11 pm. Ck-out noon. Meeting rms. Business servs avail. In-rm modem link. Cr cds: A, C, D, DS, MC, V.

D ⤢ ≋ ⋈ ⋈ **SC**

★★ **RAMADA INN-EAST.** 1355 Eastern Bypass (36117). 334/277-2200; FAX 334/270-3338. Web www.ramada.com. 152 rms, 2 story. S $54-$57; D $55-$57; each addl $8. Crib free. TV; cable. Pool.

Complimentary continental bkfst. Bar from 4 pm; entertainment. Ck-out noon. Meeting rms. Business servs avail. In-rm modem link. Cr cds: A, C, D, DS, JCB, MC, V.

D ≈ ⇥ ⋒ SC

✔★ **WYNFIELD INN.** *1110 East Blvd (36117), SE at jct I-85, Eastern Bypass exit.* 334/272-8880. 64 rms, 2 story. S $35-$42; D $45-$60; each addl $6; under 18 free. Crib free. TV; cable. Pool. Complimentary continental bkfst. Ck-out 11 am. Coin lndry. Meeting rms. Business servs avail. In-rm modem link. Private patios, balconies. Cr cds: A, C, D, DS, JCB, MC, V.

D ≈ ⇥ ⋒ SC

Motor Hotels

★★ **COMFORT SUITES.** *5924 Monticello Dr (36117), I-85 exit 6.* 334/272-1013; FAX 334/260-0425. 49 suites, 3 story. Suites $69.95-$125; wkend rates. Crib free. TV; cable (premium). Pool. Complimentary continental bkfst. Coffee in rms. Ck-out noon. Business servs avail. In-rm modem link. Cr cds: A, C, D, DS, MC, V.

D ≈ ⇥ ⋒ SC

★★ **GOVERNOR'S HOUSE.** *2705 E South Blvd (36116).* 334/288-2800; FAX 334/288-6472; res: 800/334-8459. 194 rms, 2 story. S $59-$66; D $65-$72; each addl $5; under 18 free. Crib free. TV; cable (premium). Pool. Restaurant 6:30 am-10 pm. Rm serv. Bar from 4 pm. Ck-out noon. Meeting rms. Business servs avail. Bellhops. Valet serv. Some bathrm phones. Cr cds: A, C, D, DS, MC, V.

D ≈ ⇥ ⋒ SC

★★ **HOLIDAY INN SOUTH/AIRPORT.** *1100 W South Blvd (36105), I-65 exit 168.* 334/281-1660. 150 rms, 4 story. S, D $51-$56; suites $67-$72; under 10 free. Crib free. Pet accepted, some restrictions. TV; cable (premium). Pool. Restaurant 6 am-10 pm. Rm serv. Bar 4-11 pm. Ck-out noon. Coin lndry. Meeting rms. Business servs avail. In-rm modem link. Bellhops. Free airport transportation. Cr cds: A, C, D, DS, ER, MC, V.

D ⇤ ≈ ⇥ ⋒ SC

Hotel

★★ **HOLIDAY INN.** *120 Madison Ave (36104).* 334/264-2231; FAX 334/263-3179. 172 rms, 6 story. S $69; D $75; suites $79-$89. Crib free. TV. Pool. Restaurant 6 am-10 pm. Bar 11 am-midnight. Ck-out noon. Meeting rms. Business center. In-rm modem link. Free covered parking. Free airport transportation. Cr cds: A, C, D, DS, ER, JCB, MC, V.

D ≈ ⇥ ⋒ SC ☆

Restaurants

★★ **SAHARA.** *511 E Edgemont Ave.* 334/262-1215. Hrs: 11 am-10 pm. Closed Sun; most major hols. Bar. Semi-a la carte: lunch $5.95-$9.95, dinner $9.95-$18.95. Specializes in fresh seafood, steak. Cr cds: A, C, D, DS, MC, V.

D

★★ **VINTAGE YEAR.** *405 Cloverdale Rd.* 334/264-8463. Hrs: 6-10 pm. Closed Sun, Mon; major hols. Bar 4:30 pm-midnight. Wine list. A la carte entrees: dinner $14-$19. Specializes in chicken, seafood. Cr cds: A, MC, V.

D

Natural Bridge
(see Hamilton)

Opelika (E-5)

(See also Auburn, Tuskegee; also see Columbus, GA)

Settled 1836 **Pop** 22,122 **Elev** 822 ft **Area code** 334 **Zip** 36801

Motels

★★ **BEST WESTERN MARINER INN.** *1002 Columbus Pkwy, jct I-85 & US 280.* 334/749-1461; FAX 334/749-1468. 95 rms, 2 story. S $29-$34; D $36-$46; each addl $7; under 12 free; wkly rates. Crib $7. Pet accepted. TV; cable. Indoor pool; whirlpool. Complimentary coffee in lobby. Restaurant nearby. Bar 3 pm-2 am, Sat to midnight. Business center. In-rm modem link. Cr cds: A, C, D, DS, MC, V.

D ⇤ ≈ ⇥ ⋒ SC

★★ **DAYS INN.** *1014 Anand Ave.* 334/749-5080. 43 rms, 2 story. S $38-$45; D $42-$50; each addl $5; suites $65-$80; under 12 free; higher rates special events. Crib free. Pet accepted; $5. TV; cable (premium). Indoor pool; wading pool, whirlpool. Complimentary continental bkfst. Restaurant opp open 24 hrs. Ck-out 11 am. Refrigerators. Cr cds: A, C, D, DS, MC, V.

D ⇤ ≈ ⇥ ⋒ SC

★★ **HOLIDAY INN.** *1102 Columbus Pkwy, 2 mi SE on US 280 at jct I-85 exit 62.* 334/745-6331; FAX 334/749-3933. 120 rms, 2 story. S $47-$80; D $52-$85; each addl $5; under 18 free; football wkends (2-day min). Crib free. TV; cable, VCR avail. Pool. Restaurant 6 am-2 pm, 5-10 pm. Rm serv. Bar 3 pm-midnight. Ck-out noon. Meeting rms. Business center. In-rm modem link. Exercise equipt. Cr cds: A, C, D, DS, JCB, MC, V.

D ≈ ⋔ ⇥ ⋒ SC

Restaurant

✔★ **PROVINO'S.** *3903-B Pepperell Pkwy.* 334/742-0340. Hrs: 4:30-10 pm; Fri, Sat to 11 pm; Sun 11 am-9 pm; early-bird dinner Sun-Thurs 4:30-6:30 pm. Closed major hols. Italian menu. Wine, beer. Semi-a la carte: dinner $7.95-$12.95. Italian atmosphere. Cr cds: A, C, D, DS, MC, V.

Ozark (G-5)

(See also Dothan, Troy)

Pop 12,922 **Elev** 409 ft **Area code** 334 **Zip** 36360 **Web** www.snowhill.com/ozark
Information Ozark Area Chamber of Commerce, 308 Painter Ave; 334/774-9321 or 800/582-8497.

What to See and Do

Blue Springs State Park. This 103-acre park features a spring-fed pool, swimming pool, bathhouse. Tennis. Picnic facilities, playground, softball field. Primitive and improved campsites. Standard fees. 20 mi NE via AL 105, County 33, AL 10. Phone 334/397-4875.

Russell Cave National Monument (A-5)

(See also Scottsboro; also see Chattanooga, TN)

(8 mi W of Bridgeport off US 72 via County 91, then County 98)

This cave shelter is located on the edge of the Tennessee River Valley. Stone Age man made his home here in a giant room 210 feet long, 107 feet wide and averaging 26 feet in height. Excavation of refuse and debris deposited in the cave has been dated to approximately 7000 B.C. Archaeological exploration has revealed a record of almost continuous habitation to A.D. 1650. Paleo, Archaic, Woodland and Mississippian cultures are represented. The 310-acre site, given to the US by the National Geographic Society, is administered by the National Park Service and is preserved in its natural state.

The visitor center has displays detailing the daily life of the cave's prehistoric occupants including exhibitions of weapons, tools and cooking processes. Audiovisual programs; slide programs. Area and visitor center (daily; closed Jan. 1, Thanksgiving, Dec 25). Contact 3729 County Rd 98, Bridgeport 35740; 256/495-2672. **Free.**

Russellville (B-2)

(See also Florence, Sheffield)

Pop 7,812 **Elev** 764 ft **Area code** 256 **Zip** 35653 **E-mail** fklcoc@getaway.net. **Web** www.getaway.net/fklcoc
Information Franklin County Area Chamber of Commerce, PO Box 44; 256/332-1760.

What to See and Do

Reservoirs. Bear Creek Development Authority has built four dams in the area and, with the assistance of the TVA, has developed recreational facilities at several of the resulting reservoirs. For information and camping fees contact PO Box 670; 256/332-4392. Four-reservoir user permit per day ¢

Cedar Creek. A 4,300-acre reservoir with 5 recreation areas. Swimming, bathhouses (Slick Rock Ford); boat launches (at dam, Slick Rock Ford, Lost Creek, Hellums Mill, Britton Bridge). Picnicking. Camping, hookups (Slick Rock Ford). 10 mi W via AL 24 & County 41. Phone 256/332-9809.

Little Bear Creek. A 1,560-acre reservoir. Boat launch (Williams Hollow, Elliott Branch, McAfee Springs). Picnicking. Camping; tables, grills, electricity (Willams Hollow, Elliott Branch). 12 mi W via AL 24. Phone 256/332-9804.

Upper Bear Creek. A 1,850-acre reservoir. Boat launch (Twin Forks, Quarter Creek, Batestown, Mon Dye). Picnicking. Camping; tables, grills (Twin Forks). Float stream 28 mi below dam. 16 mi S via US 43 near Phil Campbell.

Bear Creek. A 670-acre reservoir that runs through a deep narrow canyon. Swimming, bathhouse (Piney Point); fishing, pier; boat launch (Piney Point, Horseshoe Bend, Scott's Ford). Picnicking. Camping, electricity (Piney Point, Horseshoe Bend). 30 mi SW via US 43 & AL 172.

Restaurant

★ **SPEEDY PIG.** *13670 US 43 SE. 256/332-3380.* E-mail stevej@speedypig.com; web www.speedypig.com. Hrs: 10:30 am-8:30 pm; Sun 11 am-2 pm. Closed Easter, Dec 25. Semi-a la carte: lunch, dinner $4-$7. Child's meals. Specializes in barbecue ribs, sandwiches. Cr cds: A, DS, MC, V.

D SC ⊟

Scottsboro (B-4)

(See also Huntsville)

Pop 13,786 **Elev** 653 ft **Area code** 205 **Zip** 35768

Motels

★ **DAYS INN.** *1106 John T. Reid Pkwy. 205/574-1212; FAX 205/574-1212, ext. 253.* 84 rms, 2 story. S $39-$60; D $42-$60; each addl $5; suite $60; under 18 free; higher rates June Jam. Crib free. Pet accepted. TV; cable (premium). Pool. Complimentary continental bkfst, coffee. Restaurant adj 11 am-9 pm. Ck-out 11 am. Business servs avail. In-rm modem link. Cr cds: A, C, D, DS, MC, V.

D ⊷ ≈ ⊁ ⋏ SC

★ ★ **HAMPTON INN.** *46 Micah Way, jct US 72 & AL 35. 205/259-4300; FAX 205/259-0919.* 50 rms, 2 story. S $46-$65; D $52-$75; each addl $6; under 19 free; higher rates 2nd wkend June. Crib free. TV; cable (premium). Heated pool. Complimentary continental bkfst. Restaurant adj 11 am-10 pm. Ck-out 11 am. Business servs avail. In-rm modem link. Refrigerators. Cr cds: A, C, D, DS, MC, V.

D ≈ ⊁ ⋏ SC

Selma (E-3)

(See also Montgomery)

Settled 1815 **Pop** 23,755 **Elev** 139 ft **Area code** 334 **Zip** 36701 **Web** www.olcg.com/selma/
Information Chamber of Commerce, 513 Lauderdale St, PO Drawer D, 36702; 334/875-7241 or 800/457-3562.

High on a bluff above the Alabama River, Selma is a marketing, agricultural and manufacturing center. William Rufus King, vice president under Franklin Pierce, named the town after a poem by the Gaelic poet Ossian. The classic lines of Greek-revival and elegance of Georgian-colonial architecture blend with early-American cottages, Victorian mansions and modern houses to lend the city an air of the antebellum South. Once an arsenal of the Confederacy—second only to Richmond—Selma was a leading target for Union armies in 1865.

Selma fell on April 2, 1865 when 2,000 troops were captured, ending the city's role as the Confederacy's supply depot. The naval foundry (where the warships *Tennessee, Huntsville, Tuscaloosa* and others were built), a rolling mill, powder works and an arsenal were all destroyed. With defeat came an end to the era of wealthy plantation owners and a leisurely living where horse racing and cockfighting were gentlemanly diversions.

Selma was also the scene of civil rights activity in the mid-1960s with a march on the Edmund Pettus bridge. Spiritual leadership was provided by Dr Martin Luther King, Jr and Andrew Young at the Brown Chapel A.M.E. Church.

County farmers raise cattle, pecan trees, cotton, soybeans, hay, corn and grain. Selma is also the headquarters of a number of industries. The town became an inland port city in 1969 when a nine-foot-deep channel on the Alabama River was completed.

What to See and Do

Black Heritage Tour. Selma was a leading city in the march towards civil rights. Visit Brown Chapel A.M.E. Church (also a part of the Martin Luther King, Jr self-guided Street Walking Tour), the Edmund Pettus Bridge, the National Voting Rights Museum, Selma University, the Dallas County Courthouse and the Wilson Building. Contact Chamber of Commerce.

Cahawba. Alabama's first permanent capitol was a flourishing town from 1820 to 1860. By 1822, 184 town lots were sold for $120,000. Nearly swept away by floods in 1825, the capital was moved to Tuscaloosa in 1826; Cahawba was close to being abandoned by 1828 but rose again. By 1830, it had become the most important shipping point on the Alabama River. Despite another flood in 1833 and subsequent rebuilding in 1836, the city reached a peak population of approximately 5,000 by 1850. However, the Civil War and a third flood finally finished the town. Today, only a few of the original buildings remain intact. Ruins include the brick columns of a mansion on the river, old cemeteries and walls enclosing artesian wells. Site currently under development as an historical park; in-progress archeological projects may be viewed by visitors. Welcome center. (Daily; closed Thanksgiving, Dec 25) 9 mi W on AL 22, then 4 mi S on county road. Phone 334/872-8058. **Free.**

Joseph T. Smitherman Historic Building (1847). The building has been restored and furnished with artifacts and antiques; art pavilion. (Tues-Sat, also by appt; closed hols) 109 Union St. Phone 334/874-2174. ¢¢

Old Depot Museum (1891). Interpretive history museum with artifacts of Selma and Alabama's "black belt" region. (Daily exc Sun; other times by appt; closed major hols) Water Ave at Martin Luther King, Jr St. Phone 334/874-2197. ¢¢

Old Town Historic District. District includes over 1,200 structures. Museums, specialty shops, restaurants. Self-guided tours (cassette, deposit required). 513 Lauderdale St. Contact Chamber of Commerce.

Paul M. Grist State Park. This 1,080-acre park has a 100-acre lake. Swimming, bathhouse; fishing; boating (launch rentals). Hiking. Picnic facilities (grills, shelters), playground. Primitive camping. Standard fees. 15 mi N on County 37. Phone 334/872-5846.

Sturdivant Hall (1853). Fine example of Greek-revival architecture designed by Thomas Helm Lee, cousin of Robert E. Lee, features massive Corinthian columns, original wrought iron on balconies and belvedere on roof. Fully restored with period furnishings; kitchen with slave quarters above; smokehouse; wine cellar; carriage house; garden. Guided tour (1 hr). (Daily exc Mon; closed major hols) 713 Mabry St. Phone 334/872-5626. ¢¢

Annual Events

Historic Selma Pilgrimage. Guides conduct daylight and candlelight tours of historic houses; antique show. Contact Chamber of Commerce. Mid-Mar.

Reenactment of the Battle of Selma. Battlefield Park. Late Apr.

Cahawba Festival. Bluegrass & country music, arts & crafts show; flea market; greased pole climbing contests; games; regional food; walking tours of the old town. Phone 334/872-8058. 2nd Sat May.

Tale Telling Festival. Early Oct.

Motel

✔★★ **HOLIDAY INN.** *US 80W, 3 mi W on US 80. 334/872-0461.* 165 rms, 2 story. S $50-$53; D $55-$60; each addl $5; under 19 free. Crib free. Pet accepted. TV; cable. Pool; wading pool. Restaurant 6 am-2 pm, 5-10 pm. Rm serv. Bar 5 pm-1 am. Ck-out noon. Meeting rms. Business servs avail. In-rm modem link. Valet serv. Cr cds: A, C, D, DS, JCB, MC, V.

D ✔ ≈ ✗ 🔥 SC

Inn

★★ **GRACE HALL BED & BREAKFAST.** *506 Lauderdale St. 334/875-5744; FAX 334/875-9967.* E-mail coy@the-link.net; web www.olcg.com/selma/gracehal.html. 6 rms, 2 story. S $70-$90; D $77-$107; each addl $15; higher rates special events. Pet accepted. TV; cable (premium), VCR. Complimentary full bkfst. Ck-out 11 am, ck-in 4 pm. Business servs avail. Health club privileges. Antiques. Library/sitting rm. Restored antebellum mansion (1857); some original furnishings. Cr cds: A, DS, MC, V.

D ✔ ✗ 🔥 SC

Restaurants

★★ **MAJOR GRUMBLES.** *1 Grumbles Alley. 334/872-2006.* Hrs: 11 am-11 pm. Closed Sun; most major hols. Res accepted Mon-Fri. Bar. Semi-a la carte: lunch $5.95-$13.95, dinner $7-$20. Specializes in char-broiled chicken & steak, seafood. Located on river in former cotton warehouse (1850). Cr cds: A, D, MC, V.

★★ **TALLY-HO.** *507 Mangum Ave. 334/872-1390.* Hrs: 5-10 pm. Closed Sun; major hols. Res accepted. Bar to midnight; Fri, Sat to 2 am. Semi-a la carte: dinner $8-$15.50. Child's meals. Specializes in seafood, steak. Own baking. Entrance & waiting area in old log cabin. Cr cds: A, C, D, DS, MC, V.

SC

Sheffield (A-2)

(See also Florence, Russellville)

Settled 1815 **Pop** 10,380 **Elev** 502 ft **Area code** 256 **Zip** 35660
Information Colbert County Tourism and Convention Bureau, PO Box 440, Tuscumbia 35674; 256/383-0783.

One of the Quad-Cities, along with Florence (see), Tuscumbia and Muscle Shoals, Sheffield was named for the industrial city in England. Andrew Jackson is said to be the first white man to foresee the potential of this stretch of the river. Deposits of iron ore spurred the building of five huge iron-making furnaces by 1888, giving Sheffield its start as a part of the major industrial center of the South.

What to See and Do

Alabama Music Hall of Fame. Honors the contributions made to music by Alabamians. Exhibits on accomplishments of a variety of performers such as Hank Williams, Nat King Cole and Lionel Richie. Recording stars of Rock, Rhythm & Blues, Gospel, Contemporary and Country music are all included. A recording studio is available to record personal cassettes or videos. (Mon-Sat, Sun afternoons) 5 mi S on US 43, W on US 72, in Tuscumbia. Phone 256/381-4417. ¢¢¢

★ **Ivy Green** (1820). Birthplace and early home of Helen Keller. Anne Sullivan, of Boston's Perkins Institute, was hired to come to Tuscumbia and help Helen Keller, who after an illness was left blind and deaf at the age of 19 months. Miss Sullivan and Helen lived together in a small cottage, which had once been the plantation office. The cottage area includes the pump at which Helen learned her first word, "water"; the Whistle Path between the house and outdoor kitchen; and many personal items. (Daily; closed major hols) (See ANNUAL EVENT and SEASONAL EVENT) 300 W North Commons in Tuscumbia. Phone 256/383-4066. ¢¢

Annual Event

Helen Keller Festival. Ivy Green (see). Late June.

Seasonal Event

The Miracle Worker. Ivy Green (see). Outdoor performance of William Gibson's prize-winning play based on Helen Keller's life. Limited number of tickets available at gate; advance purchase recommended. Price includes tour of Ivy Green preceding play. Phone 256/383-4066. Mid-June-July, Fri, Sat.

Motel

★ **KEY WEST INN.** *(1800 US 72W, Tuscumbia 35674) 3 mi S. 256/383-0700.* 41 rms, 2 story. S $43-$60; D $48-$60; each addl $5; under 18 free. Crib free. Pet accepted, some restrictions; $5. TV; cable (premium). Complimentary continental bkfst. Restaurant nearby. Ck-out noon. Coin lndry. Meeting rm. Business servs avail. Some refrigerators. Cr cds: A, C, D, DS, MC, V.

D ⟲ ⤳ ⟐ SC

Motor Hotels

★ ★ ★ **HOLIDAY INN.** *4900 Hatch Blvd. 256/381-4710; FAX 256/381-4710, ext. 403.* 204 units, 3 story. S, D $69-$83; each addl $6; suites $203-$281; under 18 free. Crib free. Pet accepted, some restrictions. TV; cable. Pool; whirlpool. Coffee in rms. Restaurant 6:30 am-2 pm, 5:30-10 pm. Rm serv. Bar 4 pm-2 am; entertainment exc Sun. Ck-out noon. Coin lndry. Meeting rms. Business servs avail. In-rm modem link. Bellhops. Free airport transportation. Tennis privileges. Golf privileges. Exercise equipt. Some refrigerators. Cr cds: A, C, D, DS, JCB, MC, V.

D ⟲ ⤳ ⚘ ⟐ ✕ ⟐ ⟐ SC

✔★ **RAMADA INN.** *4205 Hatch Blvd. 256/381-3743; FAX 256/381-2838.* 150 rms, 2 story. S $42-$57; D $42-$64; each addl $7; suites from $125; under 18 free. Crib free. Pet accepted; $10. TV; cable (premium). Pool; whirlpool, poolside serv. Coffee in rms. Restaurant 6 am-10 pm. Rm serv. Bar 4 pm-1 am; entertainment. Ck-out noon. Meeting rms. Business servs avail. Free airport transportation. Golf privileges. Some in-rm whirlpools, refrigerators. Cr cds: A, C, D, DS, JCB, MC, V.

D ⟲ ⚘ ⟐ ✕ ⟐ SC

Restaurants

★ ★ **GEORGE'S STEAK PIT.** *1206 Jackson Hwy. 256/381-1531.* Hrs: 4:30-10:30 pm. Closed Sun, Mon; hols. Bar. Semi-a la carte: dinner $11-$25.50. Specializes in steak, fresh seafood. Cr cds: A, C, D, DS, MC, V.

D

★ **THE SOUTHLAND.** *1309 Jackson Hwy. 256/383-8236.* Hrs: 10 am-9 pm; Sun 11 am-8 pm. Closed Mon. Semi-a la carte: lunch $4.50-$6.95, dinner $4.50-$11.95. Specializes in barbecued chicken & pork, catfish, homemade pies. Family-owned. No cr cds accepted.

Sylacauga (D-4)

(See also Alexander City, Talladega)

Pop 12,520 **Elev** 600 ft **Area code** 256 **Zip** 35150 **E-mail** sylacaug@mindspring.com **Web** www.mindspring.com/~sylacaug
Information Sylacauga Chamber of Commerce, 17 W Ft Williams St, PO Box 185; 256/249-0308.

The city's fortune is literally its foundation—a bed of prized translucent white marble estimated to be 32 miles long, 1.5 miles wide and about 400 feet deep. The bed is, in many places, only 12 feet below ground level. Marble from Sylacauga (said to mean "meeting place of the Chalaka Indians") has been used in the United States Supreme Court Building and many other famous buildings in the US and abroad. Sylacauga stone is also crushed and ground for use in products such as paint, putty, plastics, asphalt tile and rubber.

What to See and Do

DeSoto Caverns Park. Scenic 80-acre wooded park, famous for its historic mammoth, onyx caverns. Visited by Hernando DeSoto in 1540, the onyx caverns are the historic birthplace of the Creek Nation and one of the first officially recorded caves in the United States—reported to President Washington in 1796. On display in the caverns is a 2,000-yr-old "Copena" burial ground, Civil War gunpowder mining center and a moonshine still from prohibition days when the caverns were known as "the bloody bucket." The main cavern, the Great Onyx Cathedral, is larger than a football field and higher than a 12-story building; a sound, laser and water show is presented here. Featured at the park is DeSoto's Lost Trail, a 3/4-acre maze (fee). Also, visitors may view a water-powered rock cutting saw in operation, pan for gold and gemstones or visit the Bow and Arrow Arcade. Other facilities include picnic areas; shipboard playground; RV campground and tepee island. Guided tours of the caverns. Park (daily). Fee for activities. 12 mi NW via AL 21 & County 36; on AL 76, 5 mi E of jct US 280. For information phone 256/378-7252.

Isabel Anderson Comer Museum & Arts Center. Permanent exhibits of local and Native American artifacts; special visiting exhibitions. (Tues-Fri; or by appt) 711 N Broadway Ave. Phone 256/245-4016. **Free.**

Talladega (D-4)

(See also Anniston, Birmingham, Sylacauga)

Founded 1834 **Pop** 18,175 **Elev** 555 ft **Area code** 256 **Zip** 35161 **E-mail** chamber@coosavalley.net **Web** www.talladega.com
Information Chamber of Commerce, 210 East St S, PO Drawer A; 256/362-9075.

Andrew Jackson defeated the Creeks in this area on November 9, 1813; it was the first of the battles by which he defeated the Creek Confederacy. Today, Talladega is both a center of diverse manufacturing and a center of preservation with many fine old buildings. It is the home of Talladega College, founded by two former slaves, and the Alabama Institute for the Deaf and Blind. Logan Martin Lake, to the northwest, offers excellent water and outdoor recreation activities, and a large section of the Talladega National Forest is to the east. A Ranger District office is located in Talladega as well.

What to See and Do

Cheaha State Park. This park includes Mt Cheaha (2,407 ft), the state's highest point with an observation tower on top, and 2,719 acres of rugged forest country in the surrounding foothills. The area is mentioned in Hernando DeSoto's journal of his 1540 expedition. (During the expedition the Spanish introduced hogs and horses to local Native Americans.) Swimming in Lake Cheaha, sand beach, wading area, swimming pool, bathhouse; fishing; boating. Hiking. Picnicking, motel, restaurant. Park (daily). Camping, cabins. Standard fees. 7 mi NE on AL 21, then 15 mi E on County 398. Phone 256/488-5111.

Historic areas. Silk Stocking District. District includes much of East Street South, Court Street South and South Street East; many antebellum and turn-of-the-century houses along tree-lined streets. **Talladega Square** (1834), in the heart of town, includes renovated Talladega County Courthouse, the oldest courthouse in continuous use in the state.

Talladega National Forest. This 364,428-acre forest offers high ridges with spectacular views of valleys heavily wooded with Southern pine and hardwood. Divided into two sections, the park includes the Talladega and the beautiful Oakmulgee, southwest of Birmingham. The Talladega division has lake swimming (fee); fishing. Hiking trails, including the 100-mi Pinhoti National Recreation Trail, National byway extending from AL 78 to Cheaha State Park. Camping (no electric hookup; fee). SE on AL 77. Contact District Ranger, phone 256/362-2909; or Forest Supervisor, 2946 Chestnut, Montgomery 36107, phone 334/832-4470.

Talladega Superspeedway. Said to be one of the world's fastest speedways, with 33-degree banks in the turns. Stock car races include the Winston "500" NASCAR Winston Cup Race, the Sears DieHard 500 NASCAR Winston Cup Race, the Birmingham Automobile Dealers 500K and the NASCAR Busch Grand National Series Race. 10 mi N on AL 77, then 6 mi E on I-20. Also here is

International Motorsports Hall of Fame. Official hall of fame of motor sports, with memorabilia and displays of over 100 vehicles. Race car simulator. Gift shop. (Daily) Annual hall of fame induction ceremony (late Apr). Speedway Blvd. Phone 256/362-5002. **¢¢¢**

Talledega-Texaco Walk of Fame. An outdoor tribute to stock car racers including a memorial for Davey Allison. Downtown.

Theodore
(see Mobile)

Troy (F-5)

(See also Montgomery, Ozark)

Settled 1824 **Pop** 13,051 **Elev** 543 ft **Area code** 334 **Zip** 36081 **E-mail** pikeccoc@p-c-net.net **Web** www.pikecounty.com

Information Pike County Chamber of Commerce, 246 US 231 North; 334/566-2294.

What to See and Do

Pike Pioneer Museum. Antique farm and household implements; reconstructed log house, country store and other buildings re-create 19th-century life. (Mon-Sat, also Sun afternoons; closed Easter, Thanksgiving, Dec 25) 2 mi N on US 231. Phone 334/566-3597. ¢¢

Troy State University (1887). (4,700 students) Guided tours of campus. Home of the National Hall of Fame of Distinguished Band Conductors and the Malone Art Gallery. University Ave, 1½ mi SE. Phone 334/670-3000 or -3196.

Motel

✔★ **ECONO LODGE.** *1013 US 231.* 334/566-4960; FAX 334/566-5858. 69 rms, 2 story. S $38-$43; D $43-$51; each addl $5; under 18 free; higher rates football wkends. Crib free. Pet accepted. TV; cable (premium). Pool. Complimentary continental bkfst. Ck-out 11 am. Business servs avail. Cr cds: A, C, D, DS, MC, V.

D 🐾 ⚓ ✕ 🐾 SC

Restaurant

✔★ **MOSSY GROVE SCHOOLHOUSE.** *AL 87S.* 334/566-4921. Hrs: 5-9 pm. Closed Sun, Mon; some major hols. Res accepted. Southern menu. Complete meals: dinner $4.95-$14.95. Child's meals. Specializes in ribeye steak, char-broiled shrimp, seafood. Restored schoolhouse (1857); original fireplace, blackboard; antiques. Cr cds: MC, V.

D

Tuscaloosa (D-2)

(See also Bessemer)

Founded 1818 **Pop** 77,759 **Elev** 227 ft **Area code** 205 **E-mail** tuscacvb@dbtech.net **Web** www.tcvb.org

Information Convention & Visitors Bureau, PO Box 3167, 35403; 205/391-9200 or 800/538-8696.

Located on the Black Warrior River, Tuscaloosa (Choctaw for "Black Warrior") was the capital of Alabama from 1826 to 1846. It was an exciting capital; cotton was a highly profitable crop, and the planters gave extravagant parties. But an increase in cotton production toppled prices, and the capital was moved to Montgomery. While the Civil War ravaged the university and most of the town, some antebellum houses do remain. After the war, industry and farm trading grew, making Tuscaloosa the busy, pleasant metropolis it is today. It is also the home of the University of Alabama.

What to See and Do

Battle-Friedman House (ca 1835). This house was built by Alfred Battle and was acquired by the Friedman family in 1875. It contains fine antiques; period gardens occupy ½ blk. (Tues-Sat, also Sun afternoons) 1010 Greensboro Ave. Phone 205/758-6138. ¢¢

Children's Hands-on Museum. Participatory exhibits for children include a Choctaw Indian Village, a bank and general store as well as a hospital and TV studio. Also available is a computer and science lab resource center. (Tues-Fri, also Sat afternoons) 2213 University Blvd. Phone 205/349-4235. ¢¢

Lake Lurleen State Park. This 1,625-acre park has a 250-acre lake. Swimming, bathhouses; fishing (piers), bait & tackle shop; boating (ramps, rentals). Hiking. Picnic shelters, playgrounds, concession. Camping. Standard fees. 12 mi NW off US 82. Phone 205/339-1558.

Moundville Archaeological Park. Group of more than 20 Native American ceremonial mounds (A.D. 1000-1450); reconstructed village and temple with displays depicting Native American lifestyles and activities. The Archaeological Museum traces prehistory of southeastern Native Americans and exhibits products of this aboriginal culture. Nature trails along river. Picnic facilities. Tent & trailer sites (fee). (Daily; closed Jan 1, Thanksgiving, Dec 24, 25, 31) 16 mi S on AL 69 in Moundville, part of the Alabama Museum of Natural History. Phone 205/371-2572. ¢¢

National Headquarters of Gulf States Paper Corporation. Four Oriental buildings house an outstanding collection of sculpture and art, including primitive artifacts from Africa and the South Pacific; Oriental art; large collection of paintings including works by Georgia O'Keeffe, Mary Cassatt and James A.M. Whistler. Guided tours. (Mon-Fri evenings, Sat, Sun afternoons) 1400 River Rd. Phone 205/553-6200. **Free.**

Old Tavern (1827). Frequented by Governor Gayle (1831-1835) and members of the Alabama legislature when Tuscaloosa was capital. (Daily; closed Jan 1, Thanksgiving, Dec 25) University Blvd & 28th Ave, on Historic Capitol Park. Phone 205/758-2238. **Free.**

University of Alabama (1831). (21,000 students) Tours of the 850-acre campus may be arranged in Rose Administration Building, Rm 151 (daily exc Sun). The information desk is located in Ferguson Student Union. University Blvd (US 11) between Thomas St and 5th Ave E. Phone 205/348-6010. On the campus is an art gallery in Garland Hall with changing exhibits, a museum of natural history, a 60-acre arboretum on Loop Road and the Paul W. Bryant Museum. The Frank Moody Music Building holds concerts and is home of the largest pipe organ in the Southeast. Four antebellum buildings remain, the only ones on campus spared from burning by Union troops. Other buildings on campus are

Gorgas House (1829). A three-story brick structure named for General Josiah Gorgas, former university president. One of the school's original structures, Gorgas now houses a museum with historical exhibits; Spanish-colonial silver display. (Daily; closed all university hols) 9th Ave & Capstone Dr. **Free.**

The Old Observatory (1844). The only pre-Civil War classroom building still standing.

Little Round House (Sentry Box ca 1860). Once used by students on guard duty, it was fired on but not destroyed by Union troops. Adj Gorgas Library.

Denny Chimes. A 115-ft-high tower erected in honor of former university president Dr. George H. Denny. On the quarter-hour the Westminster Chimes are struck, and selections are played each afternoon on the campanile carillon. University Blvd, opp President's Mansion.

Will T. Murphy African American Museum (ca 1925). House features two rooms with changing exhibits relating to culture and heritage of African Americans; antique doll collection; rare books; some period furnishings. (By appt only) 2601 Paul Bryant Dr. Phone 205/758-2861. ¢¢

Annual Event

Moundville Native American Festival. Moundville Archaeological Park (see). Celebrates the culture of the Southeastern Native Americans with craft demonstrations, songs, dances and folktales. Final day (Sat) is Indian Market Day where artisans exhibit their wares. Phone 205/371-2572. Late Sept.

Motels

★ ★ **BEST WESTERN-PARK PLAZA.** *3801 McFarland Blvd (35405), at jct US 82 Bypass, I-20, I-59.* 205/556-9690. Web www.bestwestern.com/best.html. 120 rms, 2 story. S $56.95-$62.95; D $60.95-$66.95; each addl $5. Crib free. TV; cable (premium). Pool; whirlpool. Complimentary bkfst. Restaurant adj 11 am-10 pm. Ck-out noon. Business servs avail. In-rm modem link. Cr cds: A, C, D, DS, MC, V.

D ≈ ⚓ 🔥 SC

★ ★ **HAMPTON INN.** *600 Harper Lee Dr (35404).* 205/553-9800; FAX 205/553-0082. 102 rms, 3 story. S $66; D $72; under 18 free; higher rates special events. Crib free. TV; cable (premium). Pool. Complimentary continental bkfst. Complimentary coffee in rms. Ck-out noon. Business servs avail. In-rm modem link. Valet serv. Gift shop. Health club privileges. Cr cds: A, C, D, DS, MC, V.

D ≈ ⚓ 🔥 SC

✓★ ★ **RAMADA INN.** *631 Skyland Blvd E (35405).* 205/759-4431; FAX 205/758-9655. 108 rms, 2 story. S $39-$63; D $47-$85; each addl $5; under 18 free. Crib free. Pet accepted. TV; cable. Pool. Restaurant 6 am-2 pm, 5-10 pm. Rm serv. Bar 5 pm-1 am; Fri, Sat to 2 am; entertainment exc Sun. Ck-out noon. Meeting rms. Business servs avail. Valet serv. Cr cds: A, C, D, DS, JCB, MC, V.

D 🐾 ≈ ⚓ 🔥 SC

✓★ **SLEEP INN.** *4300 Skyland Blvd E (35405), I-59/I-20 exit 76.* 205/556-5696. 73 rms, shower only, 2 story, 20 suites. S, D $37-$42; suites $52; each addl $5; under 17 free. Crib free. TV; cable (premium), VCR (movies avail $3). Pool. Complimentary continental bkfst. Complimentary coffee in rms. Restaurant adj open 24 hrs. Ck-out noon. Meeting rm. Business servs avail. In-rm modem link. Exercise equipt. Cr cds: A, C, D, DS, JCB, MC, V.

D ≈ 🏃 ⚓ 🔥 SC

★ **SUPER 8.** *4125 McFarland Blvd E (35405), I-20 exit 73.* 205/758-8878; FAX 205/758-2602. 62 rms, 3 story. No elvtr. S $35.99; D $38.99; each addl $5; under 12 free. Crib free. TV; cable (premium). Complimentary coffee. Ck-out 11 am. Cr cds: A, C, D, DS, MC, V.

D ≈ 🔥 SC

★ ★ **TRAVELODGE.** *3920 E McFarland Blvd (35405), 3½ mi S at jct US 82, I-20, I-59.* 205/553-1550; res: 800/322-3489. 166 rms, 2 story. S, D $50-$70; each addl $5; under 19 free. Crib free. TV; cable. Pool. Playground. Complimentary continental bkfst. Complimentary coffee in rms. Bar 5-10 pm. Ck-out noon. Meeting rms. Business servs avail. Valet serv. Sundries. Cr cds: A, C, D, DS, JCB, MC, V.

D ≈ ⚓ 🔥 SC

Motor Hotel

★ ★ ★ **FOUR POINTS BY SHERATON CAPSTONE.** *320 Paul Bryant Dr (35401).* 205/752-3200; FAX 205/759-9314. 152 units, 3 story. S, D $93-$99; each addl $10; suites $189-$269; under 17 free. Crib free. TV; cable (premium), VCR avail (movies). Pool; poolside serv. Restaurant 6:30 am-11 pm. Rm serv. Bar 4-11 pm. Ck-out noon. Meeting rms. Business servs avail. In-rm modem link. Bellhops. Free airport, RR station transportation. Tennis. Refrigerator in suites. Cr cds: A, D, DS, MC, V.

D 🏃 ≈ ⚓ 🔥 SC

Restaurants

★ ★ **HENSON'S CYPRESS INN.** *501 Rice Mine Rd N.* 205/345-6963. Hrs: 11 am-2 pm, 5:30-9:30 pm. Closed some major hols. Bar from 4:30 pm. Semi-a la carte: lunch $5.95-$8.95, dinner $10.95-$16.95. Child's meals. Specializes in catfish, steak, chicken. Own desserts. Riverfront view. Cr cds: A, DS, MC, V.

D

✓★ ★ **O'CHARLEY'S.** *3799 McFarland Blvd.* 205/556-5143. Hrs: 10:30-1 am; Fri, Sat to 2 am; Sat, Sun brunch 10 am-3 pm. Closed Dec 25. Bar. Semi-a la carte: lunch $4.99-$6.99, dinner $6.19-$12.99. Sat, Sun brunch $4.99-$12.99. Child's meals. Specializes in seafood, prime rib. Cr cds: A, C, D, DS, MC, V.

D SC ♥

✓★ **TREY YUEN.** *4200 McFarland Blvd E (35405), in Delchamp Plaza South.* 205/752-0088. Hrs: 11 am-2:30 pm, 4:30-10 pm. Closed some major hols. Chinese menu. Bar. Semi-a la carte: lunch $4-$10, dinner $5-$12. Specialty: Mongolian beef. Chinese decor. Cr cds: A, DS, MC, V.

Tuskegee (E-5)

(See also Auburn, Montgomery)

Settled ca 1763 **Pop** 12,257 **Elev** 468 ft **Area code** 334 **Zip** 36083
Information Office of the Mayor, City Hall, 101 Fonville St; 334/727-2180.

An important part of Tuskegee's history lies in the story of Tuskegee Institute and two well-known men in African Amerian history, Booker T. Washington and George Washington Carver. But it was Lewis Adams, a former slave, who was largely responsible for gathering financial support from northern and southern whites to launch Tuskegee Normal and Industrial Institute. It began on July 4, 1881, with 30 students housed in an old frame building; Booker T. Washington was its president. Tuskegee also has a number of antebellum houses and a Ranger District office of the Tuskegee National Forest.

What to See and Do

✪ **Tuskegee Institute National Historic Site** (1881). Booker T. Washington is generally given credit for having founded Tuskegee Institute. In 1965 the college was designated a National Historical Landmark in recognition of the outstanding role it has played in the educational, economic and social advancement of African Americans in our nation's history. In 1974, Congress established Tuskegee Institute National Historic Site to include "The Oaks," home of Booker T. Washington, the George Washington Carver Museum and the Historic Campus District. The 5,000-acre campus consists of more than 160 buildings. (Daily; closed Jan 1, Thanksgiving, Dec 25) Phone 334/727-6390 for site information. **Free.**

Booker T. Washington Monument. Larger than life bronze figure of the man who advocated "lifting the veil of ignorance" from the heads of freed slaves.

Chapel (1969). Paul Rudolph designed this unusual structure with saw-toothed ceilings and deep beams. Adjacent are the graves of George Washington Carver and Booker T. Washington.

George Washington Carver Museum. The museum includes Dr Carver's original laboratory, his extensive collection of native plants, minerals, needlework, paintings, drawings, personal belongings and the array of products he developed including the peanut and sweet potato. (Daily; closed Jan 1, Thanksgiving, Dec 25) Phone 334/727-3200. **Free.**

Tuskegee National Forest. An 11,077-acre forest with fishing; hunting; hiking on Bartram National Recreation Trail. Atasi and Taska picnic sites. Primitive camping. Tsinia Wildlife Viewing Area. E via US 80. Contact District Ranger, 125 National Forest Rd 949; 334/727-2652 or Supervisor, 2946 Chestnut, Montgomery 36107; 334/832-4470.

Hotel

★ ★ ★ **KELLOGG EXECUTIVE CONFERENCE CENTER.** *(E Campus Dr, Tuskegee Institute 36088) at Tuskegee University.* 334/727-3000; FAX 334/727-5119; res: 800/949-6161. 110 rms, 4 story, 10 suites. Feb-Mar: S, D $120; each addl $10; suites $170-$415; under 19 free; higher rates special university events; lower rates rest of yr. Crib free. TV; cable (premium). Indoor pool; lifeguard. Restaurant 6:30-10 am, 11 am-2 pm, 5:30-9 pm. Bar noon-10 pm. Ck-out noon. Meeting rms. Business center. In-rm modem link. Concierge. Gift shop. Airport transportation. Exercise equipt. Minibars. Cr cds: A, C, D, DS, MC, V.

D ⌇ ⊀ ⊁ ⚠ SC 🚶

Florida

Population: 12,937,926
Land area: 58,560 square miles
Elevation: 0-345 feet
Highest point: Near Lakewood (Walton County)
Entered Union: March 3, 1845 (27th state)
Capital: Tallahassee
Motto: In God We Trust
Nickname: Sunshine State
State flower: Orange blossom
State bird: Mockingbird
State tree: Sabal palm
State fair: February 5-16, 1999, in Tampa
Time zone: Eastern and Central

Florida is the nation's tropical area, surrounded by balmy waters. The state's first tourist, Ponce de Leon, didn't find the fountain of youth he was searching for in 1513, but modern-day tourists, at the rate of nearly 47 million a year, still are trying. At poolside, on the beach, at a jai alai fronton, in a nightclub or on a park bench, today's visitors look for rejuvenation.

To winter-weary northerners, Florida is a magnetic Eden. The pull of this land of beaches, palms and springs is so mighty that those who cannot come in winter flock here in ever-increasing numbers in summer. More people migrate to Florida to retire than to any other state. Those not yet ready to retire come here seeking a happier balance between work and relaxation. Florida is one of the top 10 states in population, rising dramatically from the early part of the century. Among 12 southeastern states, Florida has moved from last place in 1940 to first place today.

An almost 450-mile-long peninsula, rarely more than 150 miles wide and only a few feet high in many places, Florida has 8,426 miles of tidal coastline including that of the panhandle. The gentle Gulf Stream flows through the Florida straits between Florida and Cuba and north up the Atlantic coast, bestowing a tropical caress on the land. The pines near the Georgia border give way to palms and sea grape, then to bougainvillea and hibiscus, and finally to saw grass and mangrove down in the Everglades. Florida from north to south prides itself on being green and clean.

Florida's east coast has glamour and gloss; the west, a more earthy mood of informality. Between the two is a vast flatland with a spine of shallow ridges—a land that produces approximately $5.8 billion worth of agricultural products a year. Florida leads the nation in citrus fruits and is second only to California in winter vegetables. Cattle ranches and dairy farms prosper in great numbers; forests continue to provide lumber, naval stores and pulp at a seemingly inexhaustible rate; and from the sea, Florida harvests millions of pounds of fish and shellfish each year.

Nevertheless, tourism remains the major industry, providing annual taxable sales of approximately $41 billion. Facilities for the tourist trade include 724 hotels, 4,000 motels and more than 45,000 restaurants. Kennedy Space Center, selected in 1961 as the launch facility for the Apollo Moon Mission, is visited by more than three million visitors each year, and Walt Disney World, the gossamer fantasyland of central Florida, has welcomed untold millions since its opening in 1971.

That day in 1513 when Ponce de Leon stepped ashore near St Augustine began Florida's long history. The explorer mapped the coast but failed to find his fountain of youth or to establish a colony. After him, Hernando De Soto traversed the tropical land, beginning his march in 1539 from what is now the Tampa Bay area, to discover the Mississippi River and stake Spain's claim to the Southwest. Spanish settlements became rooted at St Augustine and Pensacola in the 17th century. In the 18th century Florida was taken as a British province. Spanish rule resumed following the British defeat in the American Revolution, but in 1812 a group of Americans took over and declared the peninsula an independent republic. Finally, in 1819 the United States took formal possession of Florida through a treaty of purchase. During the Civil War, Tallahassee was the only Confederate capital east of the Mississippi not captured by Union forces.

Henry Morrison Flagler, a colorful tycoon with a passion for railroads and hotels, was the major figure in the transformation of Florida from a remote and swampy outpost to its present day status. Flagler pushed his Florida East Coast Railroad from Jacksonville to Key West, opening one area after another along the coast to tourist and commercial development. On the west coast, Henry Plant, another millionaire railroader, competed with Flagler on a somewhat more modest scale.

Florida's stock climbed in the 1920s like one of its present-day rockets. A real estate boom unrivaled in history gripped the east coast. Dream cities sprouted everywhere as the voice of the real estate salesperson was heeded. Property values increased from hour to hour and thousands of persons bought uninspected acres, many of them under water. A double disaster—a hurricane and the stock market crash of 1929—burst the bubble. The lure of Florida, however, had by now been implanted in the American soul, and the state's progress since has been at an ever-accelerating pace.

When to Go/Climate

Most parts of Florida are warm and sunny year round. Evenings can get chilly in winter, so bring a sweater or jacket if you're visiting then. You may want to avoid the summer months in the extreme south, which can be very hot and humid. Hurricane season runs from June through October and is carefully monitored by the National Hurricane Center in Miami.

AVERAGE HIGH/LOW TEMPERATURES (°F)

JACKSONVILLE

Jan 64/41	May 85/62	Sept 87/69
Feb 67/43	June 89/69	Oct 80/59
Mar 73/49	July 91/72	Nov 74/50
Apr 79/55	Aug 91/72	Dec 67/43

MIAMI

Jan 75/59	May 85/72	Sept 88/76
Feb 77/60	June 88/75	Oct 85/72
Mar 79/64	July 89/76	Nov 80/67
Apr 82/68	Aug 89/77	Dec 77/62

Parks and Recreation Finder

Directions to and information about the parks and recreation areas below are given under their respective town/city sections. Please refer to those sections for details.

NATIONAL PARK AND RECREATION AREAS

Key to abbreviations: I.H.S. = International Historic Site; I.P.M. = International Peace Memorial; N.B. = National Battlefield; N.B.P. National Battlefield Park; N.B.C. = National Battlefield & Cemetery; N.C. = National Conservation Area; N.E.M. = National Expansion Memorial; N.F. = National Forest; N.G. = National Grassland; N.H. = National Historical Park; N.H.C. = National Heritage Corridor; N.H.S. National Historic Site; N.L. = National Lakeshore; N.M. = National Monument; N.M.P. National Military Park; N.Mem. = National Memorial; N.P. = National Park; N.Pres. = National Preserve; N.R. = National Recreational Area; N.R.R. = National Recreational River; N.Riv. = National River; N.S. = National Seashore; N.S.R. = National Scenic Riverway; N.S.T. = National Scenic Trail; N.Sc. = National Scientific Reserve; N.V.M. = National Volcanic Monument..

Place Name	Listed Under
Apalachicola N.F.	APALACHICOLA
Big Cypress N.Pres.	MIAMI
Canaveral N.S.	TITUSVILLE
Castillo de San Marcos N.M.	ST AUGUSTINE
De Soto N.Mem.	BRADENTON
Dry Tortugas N.P.	same
Everglades N.P.	same
Fort Caroline N.Mem.	same
Fort Matanzas N.M.	same
Gulf Islands N.S.	PENSACOLA
Ocala N.F.	OCALA
Osceola N.F.	LAKE CITY

STATE PARK AND RECREATION AREAS

Key to abbreviations: I.P. = Interstate Park; S.A.P. = State Archaeological Park; S.B. = State Beach; S.C. = State Conservation Area; S.C.P. = State Conservation Park; S.Cp. = State Campground; S.F. = State Forest; S.G. = State Garden; S.H.A. = State Historic Area; S.H.P. = State Historic Park; S.H.S. = State Historic Site; S.M.P. = State Marine Park; S.N.A. = State Natural Area; S.P. = State Park; S.P.C. = State Public Campground; S.R. = State Reserve; S.R.A. = State Recreation Area; S.Res. = State Reservoir; S.Res.P. = State Resort Park; S.R.P. = State Rustic Park.

CALENDAR HIGHLIGHTS

JANUARY

Florida Citrus Bowl (Orlando). Battle of the number-two college teams in the Southeastern and Big Ten conferences. Phone 407/849-2500; for tickets 407/849-2020.

FEBRUARY

Florida State Fair (Tampa). Florida State Fairgrounds. County exhibits, livestock shows, orchid show, industrial exposition, amusement rides and entertainment. Phone 813/621-7821.

Auto races (Daytona Beach). Speed weeks with Rolex 24 and Daytona 500, Feb; Daytona 200 (AMA motorcycle races), early Mar; Pepsi 400 stock car race, early July; several other races. Contact Daytona International Speedway; phone 904/253-RACE (tickets) or 904/254-2700.

Doral Ryder Open PGA Golf Tournament (Miami). Held on the famed Blue Monster course of the Doral Resort and Country Club. Phone 305/477-4653.

MARCH

Players Championship (Jacksonville Beach). PGA event. Tournament Players Club at Ponte Vedra. Phone 904/285-7888.

Lipton Championship (Key Biscayne). Major two-week tournament attracting top-ranked players. Phone 305/442-3367.

JULY

Fourth of July (Walt Disney World). Pyrotechnical tour de force over the Seven Seas Lagoon in the Magic Kingdom; also at Disney-MGM Studios and Epcot. Phone 407/824-4321.

SEPTEMBER

Sarasota Sailing Squadron Labor Day Regatta (Sarasota). Largest one-design regatta held on the Florida suncoast. Two days of racing. Phone 941/388-2355.

OCTOBER

Jazz Holiday (Clearwater). Coachman Park. One of the Southeasts largest free jazz festivals, held in Coachman Park. Phone 813/461-5200.

NOVEMBER

Blue Angels Air Show (Pensacola). US Navys world-renowned precision flights demonstration team performs; also parachuting and static displays of military and civilian aircraft. Phone 800/874-1234.

DECEMBER

Winterfest (Fort Lauderdale). Month-long festival including a boat parade and downtown New Years Eve celebration. Phone 954/767-0686.

Gator Bowl Festival (Jacksonville). Major college football bowl game. Phone 904/353-1188.

Orange Bowl Festival (Miami). Pro Player Stadium. Orange Bowl Football Game (Jan 1) and King Orange Jamboree Parade (Dec 31). Two weeks of activities also include tennis tournament, 10K footrace, regatta series and more. Phone 305/371-4600.

Place Name	Listed Under
Alfred B. Maclay State Gardens and Edward Ball Wakulla Springs S.P.	TALLAHASSEE
Anastasia S.R.A.	ST AUGUSTINE
Bahia Honda S.P.	BIG PINE KEY
Bill Baggs Cape Florida S.R.A.	KEY BISCAYNE
Blue Spring S.P., DeLeon Springs S.R.A. and Hontoon Island S.P.	DELAND

Caladesi Island S.P. and Honeymoon Island S.R.A.	DUNEDIN
Collier-Seminole S.P.	MARCO ISLAND
Florida Caverns S.P., Three Rivers and Falling Waters S.R.A.s	MARIANNA
Fort Clinch S.P.	FERNANDINA BEACH
Fort Pierce Inlet S.R.A.	FORT PIERCE
Gamble Rogers Memorial S.R.A. at Flagler Beach and Tomoka S.P.	ORMOND BEACH
Grayton Beach S.R.A.	DESTIN
Highlands Hammock S.P.	SEBRING
Hillsborough River S.P.	ZEPHYRHILLS
Hugh Taylor Birch S.R.A.	FORT LAUDERDALE
John Pennekamp Coral Reef S.P.	KEY LARGO
John U. Lloyd Beach S.R.A.	DANIA
Jonathan Dickinson S.P.	JUPITER
Lake Griffin S.R.A.	LEESBURG
Lake Kissimmee S.P.	LAKE WALES
Little Talbot Island S.P.	JACKSONVILLE
Long Key S.R.A.	ISLAMORADA
Manatee Springs S.P.	CHIEFLAND
Mike Roess Gold Head Branch S.P.	STARKE
Myakka River S.P.	SARASOTA
O'Leno, Ichetucknee Springs and Paynes Prairie Preserve S.P.	GAINESVILLE
Oscar Scherer S.R.A.	VENICE
Ponce de Leon Springs State Recreation Area	DE FUNIAK SPRINGS
Sebastian Inlet State Recreation Area	VERO BEACH
St Andrews S.R.A.	PANAMA CITY BEACH
St George Island and T.H. Stone Memorial St Joseph Peninsula S.P.	APALACHICOLA
Suwannee River S.P.	LIVE OAK
Three Rivers S.R.A.	MARIANNA
Torreya S.P.	BLOUNTSTOWN
Wekiwa Springs S.P.	ALTAMONTE SPRINGS

Water-related activities, hiking, riding, various other sports, picnicking and visitor centers, as well as camping, are available in many of these areas. Approximately half of the state recreation areas have camping facilities: $10-$20/site/night; $2/day extra for waterfront sites. Stay is limited to two weeks; no pets overnight. Most campsites are available on a first-come, first-serve basis only; however, in 24 parks (26 in summer) reservations are taken by telephone only, no more than 60 days in advance. Electricity fee is $2/night. Camping groups over 4 people (limit 8) will be charged $1 for each additional person. Notification is advised for parties arriving after closing hours. Some parks have vacation cabins, $25-$125/night. Boat ramp use costs $2-$4. Basic state park entrance fee per vehicle is $3.25; additional passenger fee (after 8th person) is $1. Several parks charge additional fees for tours, etc. All parks are open daily, 8 am-sundown. Some parks with camping open wkends preceding holidays and are open until 10 pm; other parks open to 10 pm during busy season. For further information and a free color brochure, *Florida State Parks Guide,* contact the Department of Environmental Protection's Division of Recreation and Parks, MS 535, 3900 Commonwealth Blvd, Tallahassee 32399; 850/488-9872.

FISHING & HUNTING

Florida has approximately 600 varieties of fish in its offshore waters and freshwater fish in more than 10,000 lakes. Freshwater fishing is most productive in the spring; sport fishing is good all year. Annual nonresidents saltwater fishing license is $30, residents $12; nonresidents 7-day license is $15; residents 10-day license is $10. Licenses also are required to sell saltwater catch. Annual nonresidents freshwater license is $31.50, residents $13.50; nonresidents 7-day license is $16.50; there is no short-term residents license. Anglers should obtain the proper license, freshwater or saltwater, that covers the species of fish they intend to keep.

Because of the climate and large forest areas, Florida has an abundance of wildlife, including white-tailed deer, small game and game birds. Open seasons are established annually but usually fall between late September and mid-April. Nonresidents (exc AL) annual license is $151.50; annual hunting license for Alabama residents is $101.50; residents annual license is $12.50; nonresidents 10-day license is $26.50. An annual residents combination hunting/fishing license is $23.50. Additional stamps required: archery or muzzleloaders, $5; turkey, $5; state waterfowl, $3. There is a $25 fee for both residents and nonresidents hunting in state management areas.

Hunting and fishing licenses are not required for persons younger than 16. Residents older than 65 do not need to purchase a hunting or freshwater fishing license, but they must obtain a special permit (free). An additional charge of up to $3 may be added to the price of all hunting and fishing licenses and stamps. For further information on saltwater fishing contact the Florida Department of Environmental Protection, 3900 Commonwealth Blvd, Tallahassee 32399; 850/488-5757. For information on hunting or freshwater fishing contact the Game and Fresh Water Fish Commission, 620 S Meridian St, Tallahassee 32399-1600; 850/488-4676.

Driving Information

Safety belts are mandatory for all persons in front seat of vehicle. Children under 6 years must be in an approved passenger restraint anywhere in vehicle: ages 4 and 5 may use a regulation safety belt; age 3 and under must use an approved safety seat. For further information phone 850/488-5370.

INTERSTATE HIGHWAY SYSTEM

The following alphabetical listing of Florida towns in *Mobil Travel Guide* shows that these cities are within 10 miles of the indicated interstate highways. A highway map, however, should be checked for the nearest exit.

Highway Number	Cities/ Towns within 10 miles
Interstate 4	Altamonte Springs, Daytona Beach, DeLand, Haines City, Kissimmee, Lakeland, Orlando, St Pete Beach, Sanford, Tampa, Winter Haven, Winter Park.
Interstate 10	De Funiak Springs, Jacksonville, Lake City, Live Oak, Marianna, Pensacola, Tallahassee.
Interstate 75	Arcadia, Bonita Springs, Bradenton, Brooksville, Cape Coral, Dade City, Englewood, Fort Myers, Fort Myers Beach, Gainesville, Lake City, Lakeland, Leesburg, Live Oak, Naples, Ocala, Port Charlotte, Punta Gorda, St Petersburg, St Pete Beach, Sanibel, Sarasota, Siesta Key, Tampa, Venice, White Springs, Zephyrhills.
Interstate 95	Atlantic Beach, Boca Raton, Boynton Beach, Cocoa, Cocoa Beach, Coral Gables, Dania, Daytona Beach, Deerfield Beach, Delray Beach, Fort Lauderdale, Fort Pierce, Hialeah, Hollywood, Homestead, Jacksonville, Lake Worth, Marineland, Melbourne, Miami, Miami Beach, New Smyrna Beach, Ormond Beach, Palm Beach, Pompano Beach, St Augustine, St Augustine Beach, Stuart, Titusville, Vero Beach, West Palm Beach.

Additional Visitor Information

Details on accommodations and resort facilities throughout the state may be obtained by writing to the Florida Hotel and Motel Association, Box 1529, Tallahassee 32302-1529; 850/224-2888. For general information contact VISIT FLORIDA, 661 E Jefferson St, PO Box 1100, Tallahassee 32301; 888/735-2872. Another source of information is *Florida Living*, monthly, 102 NE 10th Ave, Suite 6, Gainesville 32601; 352/372-8865.

There are several official state welcome stations in Florida; visitors who stop by will find information and brochures most helpful in planning stops at points of interest. Their locations are as follows: at the north central edge of the state, 3 miles north of Campbellton on US 231; in the northeastern part of Florida, 4 miles north of Jennings on I-75, and 3 miles north of Yulee on I-95S; in the northwestern section, 18 miles west of Pensacola on I-10; and in Tallahassee at the Capital Welcome Station. (Daily, 8 am-5 pm)

Altamonte Springs (D-5)

(See also Orlando, Sanford, Winter Park)

Pop 34,879 **Elev** 87 ft **Area code** 407
Information Greater Seminole County Chamber of Commerce, 4590 S US 17/92, Casselberry 32707; 407/834-4404.

What to See and Do

Greyhound racing. Sanford-Orlando Kennel Club. (Nov-early May, nightly exc Sun; matinees Mon, Wed & Sat) No minors. 6 mi N on US 17/92, at 301 Dog Track Rd in Longwood. Phone 407/831-1600. ¢

Jai-Alai. Parimutuels. (Wed-Sat evenings, matinees Thurs, Sat & Sun) Fronton, 1 mi E on US 17/92, in Fern Park. Phone 407/339-6221. ¢

Wekiwa Springs State Park. A 7,000-acre park with springs that flow through limestone caverns beneath Florida's central ridge. Swimming; fishing; canoeing (rentals). Nature trails. Picnicking, concession. Camping (dump station). Standard hrs, fees. 5 mi NW on FL 436, I-4. Phone 407/884-2009.

Motels

✔★★ **CROSBY'S MOTOR INN.** *(1440 W Orange Blossom Trail, Apopka 32712) 12 mi W on Orange Blossom Trail (FL 441).* 407/886-3220; res: 800/821-6685. 61 rms, 2 story, 14 kit. units. S $49-$89; D $59-$109; suites $99-$125; kit. units $15 addl. Crib $6. Pet accepted. TV; cable (premium). Pool. Complimentary coffee in lobby. Ck-out 11 am. Coin lndry. Some refrigerators. Picnic tables. Cr cds: A, DS, MC, V.

★★ **HAMPTON INN.** *151 N Douglas Ave (32714), I-4 exit 48.* 407/869-9000; FAX 407/788-6746. 210 rms, 2 story. S, D $79-$99; under 18 free; wkend rates; higher rates special events. Crib free. Pet accepted, some restrictions; $60. TV; cable (premium). Heated pool; whirlpool. Complimentary continental bkfst. Restaurant nearby. Ck-out noon. Coin lndry. Meeting rms. Business center. Valet serv. Exercise equipt. Refrigerators. Cr cds: A, C, D, DS, MC, V.

★★★ **HOLIDAY INN.** *230 W FL 436 (32714), just W of I-4, exit 48.* 407/862-4455; FAX 407/682-5982. 202 rms, 4 story. Jan-Mar: S, D $129; each addl $10; suites $170; under 18 free; higher rates special events; lower rates rest of yr. Crib free. TV; cable (premium). Pool. Restaurants 6 am-2 pm, 5-9 pm. Rm serv. Bar 4 pm-2 am; entertainment. Ck-out noon. Coin lndry. Meeting rms. Business servs avail. In-rm modem link. Exercise equipt. Microwaves. Cr cds: A, C, D, DS, JCB, MC, V.

✔★★ **LA QUINTA.** *150 S Westmonte Dr (32714), 3 blks W of I-4 exit 48.* 407/788-1411; FAX 407/788-6472. 115 rms, 2 story, 11 suites. S, D $84-$94; each addl $10; suites $24 addl; under 18 free. Crib free. Pet accepted. TV; cable (premium). Complimentary continental bkfst. Coffee in rms. Restaurant nearby. Ck-out noon. Meeting rms. Business servs avail. Valet serv. Health club privileges. Cr cds: A, C, D, DS, JCB, MC, V.

✔★★★ **RAMADA INN-NORTH.** *(2025 W FL 434, Longwood 32779) On FL 434 at jct I-4, exit 49 (Longwood exit).* 407/862-4000; FAX 407/862-3530. 200 rms, 2 story. Feb-Easter: S $58; D $72; each addl $6; under 18 free; higher rates special events; lower rates rest of yr. Crib free. TV; cable (premium). Pool. Restaurant 6:30 am-10 pm; Sun to 2 pm. Bar 11-1 am; entertainment. Ck-out noon. Coin lndry. Meeting rms. Business servs avail. Valet serv. Airport, RR station, bus depot transportation. Cr cds: A, C, D, DS, ER, JCB, MC, V.

★★★ **RESIDENCE INN BY MARRIOTT.** *270 Douglas Ave (32714), I-4 exit 48W.* 407/788-7991; FAX 407/869-5468. 128 kit. suites, 1-2 bedrm, 2 story. Suites $124-$200; wkly rates. Crib free. Pet accepted; $150 deposit & $5/day. TV; cable (premium). Heated pool; whirlpools. Complimentary continental bkfst; afternoon refreshments. Ck-out noon. Business servs avail. Coin lndry. Meeting rm. Valet serv. Health club privileges. Microwaves, fireplaces. Private patios, balconies. Grills. Cr cds: A, C, D, DS, MC, V.

Hotels

★★★ **EMBASSY SUITES.** *225 E Altamonte Dr (32701), I-4 exit 48E.* 407/834-2400; FAX 407/834-2117. Web www.orlando.com. 277 suites, 7 story. S, D $134-$159; each addl $15; under 18 free; wkend rates; higher rates special events. Crib free. TV; cable (premium), VCR avail. Indoor pool; whirlpool. Complimentary full bkfst. Restaurant 11 am-11 pm. Bar 4 pm-midnight. Ck-out noon. Meeting rms. Business servs avail. Gift shop. Airport transportation. Golf privileges. Exercise equipt; steam rm. Microwaves, refrigerators. Some private patios, balconies. Cr cds: A, C, D, DS, ER, JCB, MC, V.

★★★ **ORLANDO HILTON-NORTH.** *350 S North Lake Blvd (32701).* 407/830-1985; FAX 407/331-2911. 322 rms, 8 story. S, D $115-$150; each addl $10; family, wkend rates. Crib free. TV; cable (premium). Heated pool; whirlpool, poolside serv. Complimentary coffee in rms. Restaurant 6:30 am-10 pm. Bars 11-2 am; entertainment. Ck-out noon. Convention facilities. Business servs avail. Concierge. Gift shop. Exercise equipt. Health club privileges. Opp Altamonte Mall. Luxury level. Cr cds: A, C, D, DS, ER, JCB, MC, V.

★★★ **SHERATON-ORLANDO NORTH.** *(Maitland Blvd, Orlando 32853) I-4, exit 47.* 407/660-9000; FAX 407/660-2563. E-mail sales@sheratonorlandonorth.com; web www.sheratonorlandonorth.com. 400 rms, 6 story. Jan-Apr: S, D $140-$155; each addl $10; under 18 free; wkend rates; lower rates rest of yr. TV; cable (premium). Heated pool; poolside serv. Restaurant 6:30 am-2 pm, 5-11 pm. Bar. Ck-out noon. Convention facilities. Business center. In-rm modem link. Concierge. Shopping arcade. Beauty shop. Valet parking. Lighted tennis. Golf privileges. Exercise rm. Balconies. Fountains in lobby. Luxury level. Cr cds: A, C, D, DS, ER, JCB, MC, V.

Restaurants

★★★ **ENZO'S.** *(1130 S US 17/92, Longwood 32750) ¼ mi S of FL 434.* 407/834-9872. Web www.enzos.com. Hrs: 11:30 am-2:30 pm, 6-11 pm; Sat from 6 pm. Closed Sun exc Mother's Day; also Jan 1, Dec 25. Res accepted. Central Italian menu. Bar. Semi-a la carte: lunch $6-

$15, dinner $17.75-$35. Child's meals. Specialties: bucatini alla Enzo, zuppa di pesce. Own baking. Restored lakeside house. Family-owned. Cr cds: A, C, D, DS, MC, V.

[D] [⊐]

★ ★ KOBÉ JAPANESE STEAK HOUSE. 468 W Semoran Blvd (32714), 1 mi W of I-4 exit 48. 407/862-2888. Hrs: 5-10:30 pm. Closed Thanksgiving. Res accepted. Japanese menu. Bar. Complete meals: dinner $10.95-$29.95. Child's meals. Specializes in steak & shrimp, filet mignon & lobster tail. Sushi bar. Parking. Meals prepared by Kobé chef on a teppanyaki table. Japanese-style architecture. Partitioned dining areas. Cr cds: A, D, DS, MC, V.

[D] [⊐]

★ ★ ★ LA SCALA. 205 Lorraine Dr (32714). 407/862-3257. Hrs: 11:30 am-2 pm, 5:30-10:30 pm; Fri to 11 pm; Sat 5:30-11 pm. Closed Sun; hols. Res accepted. Italian menu. Bar. Wine cellar. A la carte entrees: lunch $10.50-$12.50, dinner $16-$32. Specializes in veal, seafood. Pianist in season. Parking. Elegant decor; crystal chandeliers. Cr cds: A, C, D, MC, V.

[D] [⊐]

✔★ MACARONI GRILL. 884 W FL 436 (32714). 407/682-2577. Hrs: 11 am-10 pm; Fri, Sat to 11 pm. Closed Thanksgiving, Dec 25. Northern Italian menu. Bar. Semi-a la carte: lunch $4.95-$8.95, dinner $6.95-$16.99. Specializes in pizza, pasta. Parking. Italian wine cellar decor. Cr cds: A, C, D, DS, MC, V.

[D] [⊐]

★ ★ ★ MAISON & JARDIN. 430 S Wymore Rd (32714), 1/2 mi S of jct FL 436, I-4 exit 48. 407/862-4410. Web www.maison-jardin.com. Hrs: 6-10 pm; Sun (Oct-mid-June) 11 am-2 pm (brunch), 6-9 pm. Closed some major hols. Res accepted. French, continental menu. Bar. Wine list. Semi-a la carte: dinner $19.50-$30. Sun brunch $21.50. Specializes in rack of lamb, fresh fish. Own baking. Mediterranean decor. Antiques. Cr cds: A, C, D, DS, MC, V.

[D] [⊐]

★ ★ ★ PETER SCOTT'S. (1811 W FL 434, Longwood 32750) approx 2 mi E on FL 434. 407/834-4477. Hrs: 6-11 pm; Fri, Sat to midnight. Closed Sun. Res accepted. Continental menu. Bar 5 pm-2 am. Wine list. A la carte entrees: dinner $19.95-$32.95. Child's meals. Specialties: rack of lamb, Dover sole. Entertainment. Parking. Atmosphere of 1940s supper club. Totally nonsmoking. Cr cds: A, D, DS, MC, V.

[D]

★ ★ ★ RUTH'S CHRIS STEAK HOUSE. 999 Douglas Ave (32714). 407/682-6444. Hrs: 5 pm-closing. Closed Thanksgiving, Dec 25. Res accepted. Bar. A la carte entrees: dinner $18.25-$29.95. Specializes in steak. Bi-level dining. Cr cds: A, C, D, MC, V.

[D] [⊐]

★ ★ STRAUB'S. 512 E Altamonte Dr (32701), I-4 exit 48E. 407/831-2250. Hrs: 4:30-10 pm; Fri, Sat to 11 pm; early-bird dinner 4:30-6 pm. Closed Thanksgiving, Dec 25. Res accepted. Bar. Semi-a la carte: dinner $11-$21. Child's meals. Specialties: mesquite-grilled yellowfin tuna, grilled shrimp. Parking. Florida tropical decor. Cr cds: A, C, D, DS, ER, MC, V.

[D]

Amelia Island (B-4)

(See also Atlantic Beach, Fernandina Beach, Jacksonville)

Pop 7,250 (est) **Elev** 10 ft **Area code** 904 **Zip** 32035 **Web** www.ameliaisland.org
Information Amelia Island-Fernandina Beach-Yulee Chamber of Commerce, 102 Centre St, PO Box 472, Fernandina Beach 32034; 904/277-0717 or 800/226-3542.

Amelia Island is separated from the mainland by the St Mary's River on the north, the Amelia River Intracoastal Waterway on the west and Nassau Sound on the south. Cumberland Island and the Georgia coast can be seen from the north shore.

Motel

✔★ BEACHSIDE MOTEL INN. (3172 S Fletcher Ave, Fernandina Beach 32034) 904/261-4236. 20 rms, 2 story, 10 kit. units. Mar-Sept: S, D $68-$103; each addl $5; kits. $94-$139; wkly rates; higher rates: major hols, special events; lower rates rest of yr. Crib $2. TV; cable. Pool. Complimentary continental bkfst. Ck-out 11 am. On ocean; beach. Cr cds: A, MC, V.

[⊠] [≋] [♨]

Motor Hotel

★ ★ AMELIA SURF & RACQUET CLUB. 4800 Amelia Island Pkwy (32034). 904/261-0511; FAX 904/261-0512; res: 800/323-2001. 64 kit. villas, 7 story. Mar-Sept: S, D $145-$265; wkly, monthly rates; lower rates rest of yr. Maid serv avail (fee). TV; cable. 2 pools; wading pools. Restaurant nearby. Ck-out 11 am. Business servs avail. In-rm modem link. Lighted tennis, pro. Microwaves avail. Balconies. Extensive oceanfront grounds. Cr cds: A, MC, V.

[⊼] [≋] [⊠] [♨]

Inns

★ 1735 HOUSE. 584 S Fletcher (32034). 904/261-4148; FAX 904/261-9200; res: 800/872-8531. Web www.ameliaisland.com. 6 suites, shower only, 2 story. No rm phones. S, D $131-$160. TV. Complimentary continental bkfst in rms. Ck-out 11 am, ck-in 4 pm. Refrigerators, microwaves. Picnic tables. In 1928 ocean-front building; named for the year island was discovered. Cr cds: A, DS, MC, V.

[⊠] [⊠] [♨]

★ ★ ★ THE AMELIA ISLAND WILLIAMS HOUSE. (103 S 9th St, Fernandina Beach 32034) 904/277-2328; res: 800/414-9257; FAX 904/321-1325. Web www.williamhouse.com. 8 rms, 3 with shower only, 2 story. S, D, suites $135-$195; each addl $20; 2-day min wknds, special events. Children over 12 yrs only. TV; cable, VCR (movies). Complimentary full bkfst; afternoon refreshments. Restaurant nearby. Ck-out 11 am, ck-in 3 pm. Luggage handling. Concierge serv. Balconies. Built in 1856, mansion has elegant decor with many antiques. Cr cds: MC, V.

[D] [⊠] [♨]

★ ★ ★ BAILEY HOUSE. (28 S 7th St, Fernandina Beach 32034) 904/261-5390; res: 800/251-5390; FAX 904/321-0103. Web www.bailey-house.com. 9 rms, 2 story. S, D $95-$140; each addl $20; wkly rates; hols (2-day min). Children over 8 yrs only. TV. Complimentary full bkfst. Ck-out 11 am, ck-in 3 pm. Business servs avail. Bicycles. Queen Anne-style house (1895) with bays, turrets, gables; antiques. Totally nonsmoking. Cr cds: A, MC, V.

[D] [⊠] [♨]

★ ★ ★ ELIZABETH POINTE LODGE. (98 S Fletcher Ave, Fernandina Beach 32034) 904/277-4851; FAX 904/277-6500; res: 800/772-

3359. E-mail Eliz.Pt@worldnet.att.net. 25 rms, 3 story. S $110-$180; D $125-$215; each addl $20; under 5 free. Crib $10. TV; cable (premium), VCR avail. Complimentary full bkfst; afternoon refreshments. Dining rm. Rm serv. Ck-out 11 am, ck-in 3 pm. Business servs avail. In-rm modem link. Bellhops. Valet serv. Concierge. Airport transportation. 1890s Nantucket shingle-style inn (1992). On ocean; beach. Totally nonsmoking. Cr cds: A, DS, MC, V.

★ ★ ★ **THE FAIRBANKS HOUSE.** *227 S 7th St (32034). 904/277-0500; FAX 904/277-3103; res: 800/261-4838.* Web www.net-netmajic.net/fairbank-index.htm. 12 rms, 3 story, 3 suites, 3 cottages. D $125-$225; suites $195-$225; cottages $175. TV; cable. Pool. Complimentary full bkfst; afternoon refreshments. Restaurant nearby. Ck-out 11 am, ck-in 3 pm. Some kits; microwaves avail. Balconies. Italianate villa (1885) with courtyard; antiques. Flower gardens. Cr cds: A, DS, MC, V.

↙★ ★ ★ **FLORIDA HOUSE.** *22 South 3rd St (32034). 904/261-3300; FAX 904/277-3831; res: 800/258-3301.* E-mail Innkeepers@Floridahouse.com; web www.floridahouse.com. 14 rms, 3 story. S, D $70-$140; each addl $10; under 6 free. TV; cable. Complimentary full bkfst. Dining rm 11 am-2:30 pm, 5:30-9 pm; Mon to 2:30 pm; Sun brunch to 2 pm. Bar. Ck-out 11 am, ck-in 2 pm. Business servs avail. Valet serv. Balconies. Old hotel building (1857); wrap-around veranda with rocking chairs. Totally nonsmoking. Cr cds: A, MC, V.

★ ★ **GOODBREAD.** *(209 Osborne St, St Marys 31558) approx 8 mi N on I-95, exit 2, 9 mi E.* 912/882-7490. 5 rms, 2 story. S, D $65. Children over 12 yrs only. TV; cable. Complimentary full bkfst. Complimentary coffee in library. Restaurant nearby. Ck-out 11 am, ck-in 2 pm. 18-hole golf privileges, pro. Balconies. Built in 1870. Antiques. No cr cds accepted.

★ ★ ★ **HOYT HOUSE.** *(804 Atlantic Ave, Fernandina Beach 32034)* 904/277-4300; FAX 904/277-9626; res: 800/432-2085. 9 rms, 7 with shower only, 2 story. S, D $104-$144. TV; cable, VCR avail (free movies). Complimentary full bkfst; afternoon refreshments. Restaurant nearby. Ck-out 11 am, ck-in 2 pm. Queen Anne-style house built 1905 by local merchant. Many antique furnishings. Totally nonsmoking. Cr cds: A, DS, MC, V.

★ ★ **SPENCER HOUSE.** *(200 Osborne, St Marys 31558) approx 15 mi N on I-95, 9 mi E on GA 40.* 912/882-1872; FAX 912/882-9427. E-mail spencer@eagnet.com; web www.spencerhouseinn.com. 14 rms, 4 with shower only, 3 story, 1 suite. S, D $65-$95; each addl $15; suite $112; under 2 free; hols (2-day min). Crib free. TV; cable (premium). Complimentary full bkfst. Restaurant nearby. Ck-out 11 am, ck-in 3 pm. Concierge serv. Balconies. Built in 1872 as a hotel. Totally nonsmoking. Cr cds: A, DS, MC, V.

Resorts

★ ★ ★ **AMELIA ISLAND PLANTATION.** *3000 First Coast Hwy, on FL A1A, 18 mi SE of I-95 Fernandina Beach-Callahan exit.* 904/261-6161; FAX 904/277-5159; res: 800/874-6878 (exc FL). E-mail aip052@net-majic.net; web www.amelianow.com. 685 units, 435 kit. apts in 1-6 story villas. Mid-Feb-mid-Apr: S $245; D $278; villas, 1-bedrm: S $245-$546; D $278-$546; 2-3 bedrm for 4-6 persons $278-$710; daily, wkly, package plans; EP, AP, MAP avail; hol wkends (3-day min); serv charge $11/day; lower rates rest of yr. Crib $10. TV; cable (premium), VCR avail (movies $4). 25 indoor/outdoor pools; wading pools, whirlpool. Supervised child's activities; ages 3-17. Complimentary coffee in rms. Dining rms 7 am-9:30 pm (public by res on Sun only, brunch at Inn). Rm serv to midnight. Ck-out 11 am, ck-in 4 pm. Convention facilities. Business center. In-rm modem link. Valet serv. Grocery, package store. Barber, beauty shop. Airport transportation. Sports dir. 25 tennis courts, 3 lighted, pro. 54-hole golf, greens fee $85-$125, putting green, driving range. Beach;

lifeguards. Paddleboats. Bicycles; trails; electric cars. Boardwalks through sunken forest (lighted), marshland. Soc dir; entertainment. Game rm. Rec rms. Exercise rm; sauna. Massage. Refrigerators, microwaves; dishwasher, washer, dryer in apts; indoor pool in some. Private patios, balconies. Picnic tables. Attractive resort on 1,300 acres. Cr cds: A, D, DS, MC, V.

★ ★ ★ ★ **THE RITZ-CARLTON, AMELIA ISLAND.** *4750 Amelia Island Pkwy (32034), I-95 exit 129E.* 904/277-1100; FAX 904/261-9063. Along with stylish elegance, superb comfort and excellent service comes one of the prettiest and most pristine beaches on Florida's east coast. All rooms have ocean views. 449 units, 8 story, 45 suites. Mar-May: S, D $255-$305; suites $269-$1,500; under 18 free; package plans; lower rates rest of yr. Crib free. Garage parking, valet $13. TV; cable (premium), VCR avail. 2 pools, 1 indoor; whirlpool, poolside serv. Supervised child's activities; ages 5-14. Restaurants 6:30 am-11 pm (also see THE GRILL). Rm serv 24 hrs. Bar 11-1 am; entertainment. Ck-out noon, ck-in 3 pm. Convention facilities. Business center. In-rm modem link. Bellhops. Valet serv. Concierge. Shopping arcade. Beauty shop. Airport transportation. Lighted tennis, pro. 18-hole golf, pro, putting green, driving range. Exercise rm; sauna, steam rm. Bathrm phones, refrigerators, minibars, wet bars. Balconies. Luxury level. Cr cds: A, C, D, DS, JCB, MC, V.

Restaurants

★ **BAMBOO HOUSE.** *(614 Center St, Fernandina Beach 32034)* 904/261-0508. Hrs: 11:30 am-10 pm; Sat from noon. Closed Sun; Jan 1, Thanksgiving, Dec 25. Res accepted. Chinese menu. Bar. Semi-a la carte: lunch $5.95-$6.95, dinner $6.50-$16.50. Buffet: lunch $5.95. Child's meals. Specialties: beef Szechuan, Bamboo House steak, scallops with peppercorn sauce. Jazz wkends. Chinese decor, artwork. Cr cds: A, DS, MC, V.

★ ★ ★ **BEECH STREET GRILL.** *(801 Beech St, Fernandina Beach 32034)* 904/277-3662. Hrs: 5:30-10 pm. Closed Jan 1, Thanksgiving, Dec 25; also Super Bowl Sun. Res accepted. Serv bar. Wine list. Semi-a la carte: dinner $16.95-$24.95. Child's meals. Specializes in seafood, poultry, veal. Pianist Fri, Sat. Restored house built in 1889 contains many intimate dining areas; cast iron fireplaces. Cr cds: A, D, DS, MC, V.

★ ★ **BRETT'S WATERWAY CAFE.** *1 S Front St (32034), Harbour Marina.* 904/261-2660. Hrs: 11:30 am-2:30 pm, 5:30-9:30 pm; Sun from 5:30 pm. Closed most major hols. Bar. Semi-a la carte: lunch $5.95-$10.95, dinner $14.95-$24.95. Child's meals. Specializes in steak, seafood. Parking. Outdoor dining. Player piano in center of restaurant; view of river. Cr cds: A, MC, V.

★ ★ ★ ★ **THE GRILL.** *(See The Ritz-Carlton, Amelia Island Resort)* 904/277-1100. All of the usual elegance of a Ritz-Carlton dining room is combined with superior cuisine, dedicated service and a relaxed ambience, plus piano music to help create a romantic evening. If you're seated at one of the floor-to-ceiling windows, the Atlantic Ocean is just over your shoulder. Specializes in meat & game, fresh Florida seafood. Hrs: 6-10 pm; Sun brunch 11 am-3 pm. Res accepted. Bar to midnight. Wine cellar. A la carte entrees: dinner from $35. Prix fixe: dinner from $65. Sun brunch $38. Pianist. Valet parking. Jacket. Cr cds: A, C, D, DS, JCB, MC, V.

★ ★ **HORIZONS.** *802 Ash St (32034).* 904/321-2430. Hrs: 6-11 pm. Closed Sun; most major hols. Res accepted. Continental menu. Bar. Semi-a la carte: dinner $13.50-$18.95. Child's meals. Specialties: salmon Napoleon, roasted rack of lamb. Own baking. Cr cds: A, D, MC, V.

Apalachicola (C-1)

(See also Panama City)

Founded 1821 **Pop** 2,602 **Elev** 16 ft **Area code** 850 **Zip** 32320 **E-mail** Chamber1@digitalexp.com **Web** www.homtown.com/apalachicola
Information Chamber of Commerce, 99 Market St, Ste 100, 32320-1776; 850/653-9419.

Once known as West Point, the town took the name of Apalachicola (Native American for "people on the other side") soon after it was incorporated. At one time a leading cotton-shipping port, the town now turns to the sea for its major crop—nearly 90 percent of Florida's oysters are harvested from nearby St George Sound. Local history goes back to 1528, when the Spanish conquistador Narváez stopped to build boats to sail to Mexico. Trinity Church (1839) on Gorrie Square was brought in sections on a schooner from New York; the original bell was melted down to make a Confederate cannon.

What to See and Do

Apalachicola National Estuarine Research Reserve. This 193,758-acre area, the largest in the US reserve system, preserves the Apalachicola Bay and a large portion of the Apalachicola River, adjoining floodplains, sounds and three barrier islands. Fresh and saltwater marshes, swamp forests, open water and beaches serve as field laboratory; programs, tours. Fishing, boating, hiking. (Daily; building Mon-Fri) Headquarters located at 261 7th St. Contact Reserve Manager, 261 7th St; 850/653-8063.

Fort Gadsden State Historic Site. In 1814 the British built a fort on this 75-acre area as a base for recruitment during the War of 1812. The fort was later destroyed by US forces, but in 1818, Andrew Jackson ordered another built as a supply base. Occupied by Confederate forces from 1862-1863, some earthworks remain visible. Open-sided kiosk has miniature replica of Fort Gadsden, interpretive exhibits. Fishing. Hiking trails. Picnicking. (Fri-Mon & Wed) E on US 98/319, then 17 mi N on FL 65, just N of Bucks Siding. Phone 850/670-8616.   **Free.**

John Gorrie State Museum. Memorial to Dr. John Gorrie, who built the first ice-making machine (1845) to cool the rooms of yellow fever victims; replica of first ice machine, scenes of early local history. (Thurs-Mon; closed Jan 1, Thanksgiving, Dec 25) Ave D & 6th St. Phone 850/653-9347. ¢

St George Island. Swimming beaches; surf fishing. 7 mi E on US 98/319 to Eastpoint, then S on causeway (FL G1A). Also here is

St George Island State Park. More than 1,800 acres with miles of undeveloped beaches, dunes, forest and marshes. Swimming; saltwater fishing. Hiking. Picnicking. Backwoods & improved camping (hookups). Vehicles prohibited in dune areas. Standard hrs, fees. Phone 850/927-2111.

Annual Event

Florida Seafood Festival. Parade, oyster eating and shucking contests, blessing of the fleet, entertainment. 1st Sat Nov.

Inn

✔★ ★ **GIBSON INN.** *51 Ave C. 850/653-2191.* 30 rms, 3 story. S, D $70-$85; suite $115; higher rates hols. Crib $5.30. Pet accepted; $5.30. TV; cable. Restaurant 7:30 am-3 pm, 6-9 pm. Ck-out 11 am, ck-in 3 pm. Luggage handling. Built in 1907; served as an officer's club in WW II. Cr cds: A, MC, V.

⊞ ⊠ ⊠ SC

Arcadia (F-4)

(See also Port Charlotte)

Founded 1886 **Pop** 6,488 **Elev** 57 ft **Area code** 941 **Zip** 34266 **E-mail** dccdoc@desoto.net **Web** desoto.net/desotocounty
Information De Soto County Chamber of Commerce, 16 S Volusia Ave; 941/494-4033.

The seat of De Soto County, Arcadia is a marketplace for cattle and a local government and retail center. It is a predominantly rural community, surrounded by ranches and citrus groves of the Peace River Valley.

Annual Events

De Soto County Fair. Fairgrounds, S on Brevard Ave, US 17. Mar.

All-Florida Championship Rodeo. Fenton Arena, Heard St. Professional rodeo circuit; parade, mock shoot-out, barbecue. 1 wkend Mar & 1 wkend July.

Watermelon Festival. De Soto Park. Memorial Day wkend.

Motel

✔★ **BEST WESTERN ARCADIA INN.** *504 S Brevard Ave, on US 17S. 941/494-4884; FAX 941/494-2006.* 33 rms. Jan-June: S $50; D $60; each addl $5; under 12 free; lower rates rest of yr. Crib $5. Pet accepted, some restrictions; $10. TV; cable. Pool. Complimentary continental bkfst. Ck-out 10 am. Business servs avail. Gift shop. Cr cds: A, C, D, DS, MC, V.

 ⊞ ⊠ ⊠ ⊠ SC

Restaurant

★ **PARADISE.** *903 N Brevard Ave (US 17N). 941/494-2061.* Hrs: 7 am-9 pm; Fri to 10 pm; Sun to 3 pm. Closed Dec 25; also Mon June-Oct. Bar. Semi-a la carte: bkfst $2.50-$6.95, lunch $4.95-$7.95, dinner $4.95-$16.95. Child's meals. Specializes in steak, seafood, chicken. Salad bar. Cr cds: A, DS, MC, V.

⊞ ⊡

Atlantic Beach (B-5)

(See also Amelia Island, Jacksonville, Jacksonville Beach)

Pop 11,636 **Elev** 17 ft **Area code** 904 **Zip** 32233 **E-mail** jaxflcvb@jax-inter.net **Web** www.jaxcvb.com
Information Jacksonville and the Beaches Convention & Visitors Bureau, 201 E Adams St, Jacksonville 32202; 904/798-9111or 800/733-2668.

What to See and Do

Hanna Park. This 450-acre recreation area includes 2 plazas overlooking the ocean. Salt- and freshwater fishing. Nature, bicycle trails. Picnicking. Camping (hookups; fees). (Daily; closed Jan 1, Thanksgiving, Dec 25) Mayport Rd & Wonderwood Dr. Phone 904/249-4700. Park ¢

Mayport Naval Station. Home port of more than 15 vessels, including an aircraft carrier, cruisers, destroyers and frigates. Guided tours of ships (Sat, Sun). No skirts, high heels; identification required. N on Mayport Rd in Mayport. Phone 904/270-NAVY.   **Free.**

Motel

✔★ ★ **COMFORT INN MAYPORT.** 2401 Mayport Rd. 904/249-0313; FAX 904/241-2155. E-mail comfortinn@mayport.com. 108 rms, 3 story. No elvtr. S, D $49-$109; each addl $10; under 18 free. Crib free. TV; cable (premium). Pool. Complimentary continental bkfst. Restaurant adj open 24 hrs. Ck-out noon. Coin lndry. Business servs avail. Sundries. Refrigerators, microwaves. Cr cds: A, C, D, DS, JCB, MC, V.

Motor Hotel

★ **SEA TURTLE INN.** 1 Ocean Blvd. 904/249-7402; FAX 904/247-1517; res: 800/874-6000. 194 rms, 8 story. Mar-Labor Day: S, D (up to 4) $119-$199; lower rates rest of yr. TV; cable (premium), VCR. Pool; poolside serv (in season). Rm serv. Bar. Ck-out noon. Coin lndry. Meeting rms. Business servs avail. Bellhops. Gift shop. Airport transportation. Tennis privileges. Golf privileges. Health club privileges. Some balconies. On ocean, swimming beach. Cr cds: A, D, DS, MC, V.

Restaurants

★ **PAPA JOE'S GRILL & BAR.** (100 First St, Neptune Beach 32266) FL A1A, end of Atlantic Blvd at 1st St. 904/246-6406. Hrs: 5-10 pm. Closed Sun; Dec 25. Res accepted. Bar to 2 am. Semi-a la carte: dinner $5.99-$13.99. Child's meals. Specializes in ribs, seafood, steak. View of ocean. Cr cds: A, D, DS, MC, V.

★ ★ **PLANTAINS AT THE SEA TURTLE.** (See Sea Turtle Inn Motor Hotel) 904/249-7402. Web www.seaturtle.com. Hrs: 6:30 am-10 pm; Sun to 9:30 pm; Sun brunch 11 am-2:30 pm; early-bird dinner Mon-Thurs 5-7 pm. Res accepted. Bar. Semi-a la carte: lunch $5.95-$9.95, dinner $10.95-$21.95. Sun brunch $15.95. Child's meals. Specializes in chicken, seafood, steak. Entertainment Fri-Sun, seasonal. Outdoor dining. Cr cds: A, D, DS, MC, V.

★ ★ **RAGTIME.** 207 Atlantic Blvd. 904/241-7877. Hrs: 11 am-10:30 pm; Fri, Sat to 11 pm. Closed Thanksgiving, Dec 24, 25. Bar. Semi-a la carte: lunch $5.95-$8.95, dinner $9.50-$22.95. Child's meals. Specializes in seafood, bouillabaisse. Jazz, blues Thurs-Sun. Own beer. Cr cds: A, C, D, DS, MC, V.

✔★ ★ **SERGIO'S.** 1021 Atlantic Blvd. 904/249-0101. Hrs: 5:30-10 pm; Fri, Sat to 10:30 pm. Closed Mon; some major hols. Res accepted. Italian menu. Bar. Semi-a la carte: dinner $9.50-$17.95. Specializes in pasta, seafood, veal. Atmosphere of Italian courtyard. Casual dining. Cr cds: A, C, D, DS, MC, V.

Bartow (E-4)

(See also Haines City, Lake Wales, Winter Haven)

Settled 1851 **Pop** 14,716 **Elev** 125 ft **Area code** 941 **Zip** 33830
Information Chamber of Commerce, 510 N Broadway Ave, PO Box 956; 941/533-7125.

Bartow, named for a Confederate Army general, is the seat of Polk County. It is noted for the nearby mines, which annually produce more than 70 percent of the country's phosphate, a major ingredient in chemical fertilizers. Citrus and cattle also add to Bartow's economy.

What to See and Do

Polk County Historical and Genealogical Library. Extensive collection relating to southeastern US. (Tues-Sat; closed first Tues & Wed of month; also county hols) 100 E Main St, in Old Courthouse. Phone 941/534-4380. **Free.**

Annual Event

Bloomin' Arts Festival & Flower Show. Downtown. Juried art show, flower show, quilt show, entertainment, concessions. Early Apr.

Motel

✔★ **DAVIS BROS.** 1035 N Broadway Ave. 941/533-0711; FAX 941/533-0924; res: 800/424-0711. 102 rms, 2 story. Jan-mid-Apr: S $45; D $50-$55; each addl $5; under 16 free; lower rates rest of yr. Crib $5. Pet accepted. TV; cable. Pool; wading pool. Restaurant adj open 24 hrs. Ck-out noon. Meeting rm. Coin lndry. Cr cds: A, C, D, DS, MC, V.

Restaurant

✔★ ★ **JOHN'S.** 1395 E Main St. 941/533-3471. Hrs: 6 am-11 pm. Bar 10-2 am. Semi-a la carte: bkfst $1-$2.25, lunch $2.25-$5.95, dinner $4.95-$11.95. Child's meals. Specializes in seafood, steak. Salad bar. Entertainment Fri, Sat. Greek decor. Family-owned. Cr cds: A, C, D, DS, MC, V.

Belle Glade (G-5)

(See also Okeechobee, West Palm Beach)

Founded 1928 **Pop** 16,177 **Elev** 20 ft **Area code** 561 **Zip** 33430
Information Chamber of Commerce, 540 S Main St; 561/996-2745.

With Lake Okeechobee's floods tamed by a network of dikes and canals, the incredibly rich Everglades' "black gold" muckland turns out a variety of winter vegetables. Approximately 550,000 acres of sugar cane are processed by 7 mills in the area. The sod and rice industries also are important.

What to See and Do

Belle Glade Marina. Fishing; dock, boat slips, ramps. Picnicking. Camping. 3 mi W on FL 717, on Lake Okeechobee. Phone 561/996-6322. Camping/site/night ¢¢¢¢-¢¢¢¢¢

Lake Okeechobee. Covering 730 sq mi, Okeechobee is the second largest freshwater lake completely within the boundaries of the US. Shallow, only 22 ft at its deepest, with many grassy spots and shoals, the lake is renowned for its bass, crappie, bream and speckled perch; more than one million pounds of fish are caught in the lake annually by commercial and sport fishermen. The Herbert Hoover Dike provides an unobstructed view of the lake. Picnicking; pavilions with cookers. 3 mi from town.

Lawrence E. Will Museum. Artifacts of Calusa Indians, one of the oldest and least known cultures that ever existed in this country; pioneer and Seminole exhibits; sugar cane display. (Daily exc Sun; closed hols; also Fri after Thanksgiving) 530 S Main St, in library. Phone 561/996-3453. **Free.**

Annual Event

Black Gold Jubilee Celebration. Sports tournaments, parade, arts & crafts, beauty contest, concessions. Usually late Apr.

Big Pine Key (K-5)

(See also Key West, Marathon)

Pop 4,206 **Elev** 8 ft **Area code** 305 **Zip** 33043 **E-mail** LKChamber@aol.com **Web** florida-keys.fl.us/lowerkeys.htm
Information Lower Keys Chamber of Commerce, PO Drawer 430511; 305/872-2411 or 800/872-3722.

Largest of all the lower keys, Big Pine consists of 7,700 acres thick with silver palmetto, Caribbean pines and unusual growths of cacti. Rare white herons and the elusive, tiny Key deer, long thought extinct, live on the island and are favorite subjects for photographers. Drivers should be alert to Key deer crossing roadways.

What to See and Do

Bahia Honda State Park. More than 635 acres of beach, dunes, coastal strand hammocks and mangroves cover the skeleton of an ancient coral reef. Swimming, skin and scuba diving, snorkeling trips, rentals; fishing for grouper, mangrove snapper and grunt; boating (ramps, docks, basin). Nature trails. Picnicking, concession. Camping (dump station). Standard hrs, fees. mi marker 31, US 1. Phone 305/872-2353.

National Key Deer Refuge. Approximately two-thirds of the present population of Key deer, smallest of all white-tailed deer, inhabit this refuge. The deer can most likely be seen in early morning, late afternoon and evening. A nature walk is located 1.5 mi N of Key Deer and Watson Blvds; nearby is Blue Hole, an old rock quarry that is home to several alligators. (Daily; headquarters Mon-Fri) **Note:** Feeding Key deer and alligators is prohibited by state law; be alert for Key deer crossing roadways. N of US 1 on Key Deer Blvd (FL 940); refuge headquarters on Key Deer Blvd in Big Pine Shopping Center. Contact Refuge Manager, PO Box 430510; 305/872-2239. **Free.**

Blountstown (B-1)

(See also Marianna, Panama City)

Founded 1823 **Pop** 2,404 **Elev** 69 ft **Area code** 850 **Zip** 32424
Information Calhoun County Chamber of Commerce, 340 E Central Ave; 850/674-4519.

Blountstown is named for John Blount, the Seminole chief who acted as a guide for Andrew Jackson in his campaign against the Creek Indians in 1818. The town sits on a bluff overlooking the Apalachicola River. The Apalachicola National Forest (see APALACHICOLA) is south of here; a ranger district office is located in Bristol.

What to See and Do

Torreya State Park. Park, more than 1,000 acres overlooking the Apalachicola River, is named for a tree native only to a 20-sq-mi area at this site. In the park is the antebellum Gregory House of typical plantation architecture (guided tours daily). Confederate gun pits, pylons of old riverboat landing. Nature trails (7 mi). Picnicking. Camping (dump station). Standard hrs, fees. 4 mi E on FL 20, then NW off FL 12, 7 mi N on county rd 1641, near Rock Bluff. Phone 850/643-2674.

Boca Raton (G-6)

(See also Delray Beach, Fort Lauderdale, Pompano Beach)

Founded 1897 **Pop** 61,492 **Elev** 16 ft **Area code** 561
Information Greater Boca Raton Chamber of Commerce, 1800 N Dixie Hwy, 33432-1892; 561/395-4433.

Florida architect Addison Mizner bought several thousand acres of farmland on which to build his dream city, Boca Raton, only to be foiled by the bust that followed the Florida land boom of the 1920s. For three decades, Boca Raton was a small resort town with little more than the architecture of Mizner's Boca Raton Resort and Club to commend it. In recent years, however, the town has been in the forefront of Palm Beach County's explosive growth. Throughout this period, Boca Raton has retained its resort atmosphere while becoming an educational, technical and cultural center.

What to See and Do

Boca Raton Museum of Art. Exhibits include paintings, photography, sculpture and glass. Lectures, tours. (Mon-Fri, also Sat & Sun afternoons; closed Jan 1, Thanksgiving, Dec 25) 801 W Palmetto Park Rd. Phone 561/392-2500. **Donation.**

Children's Museum. Learning experiences in a historical setting; creative exhibits and hands-on activities; nature path. (Tues-Sat; closed Jan 1, Thanksgiving, Dec 25) 498 Crawford Blvd. Phone 561/368-6875. ¢-¢¢

Florida Atlantic University (1964). (16,000 students) On 850-acre campus are concerts, dance, theater (Nov-mid-Apr); art gallery (Sept-Apr); library. Center of town, 3 mi from ocean. Phone 561/367-3000.

Gumbo Limbo Nature Center. The center lets children view four 20-ft-diameter saltwater sea tanks, stroll a 1,628-ft boardwalk through a dense tropical forest, and climb a 40-ft tower to overlook the tree canopy. The forest is a coastal hammock, with tropical species growing north of the tropics. One tree species you're sure to see—the gumbo-limbo, with its red peeling bark—is often called "the tourist tree." The center's staff leads guided turtle walks ($3) to the beach to see nesting females come ashore and lay their eggs. (Daily) 1801 N Ocean Blvd. Phone 561/338-1473. **Donation.**

★ **International Museum of Cartoon Art.** Showcases exhibits that cover 200 yrs of cartoon history. Contains samples of many different art forms such as comic strips, animation, editorial cartoons, greeting cards and computer-generated cartoons. Museum has permanent and changing exhibition galleries, an education orientation center, classrooms, library and video center. (Daily exc Mon) 201 Plaza Real, in Mizner Park. Phone 561/391-2200. ¢¢¢

Mizner Park. A 30-acre shopping village with gardenlike spaces that make for distinctive shopping. There are some three dozen retail stores to choose among, restaurants with sidewalk cafes, and movie screens. Federal Hwy between Palmetto Park Rd & Glades Rd.

Annual Event

KidsFest. At Children's Museum (see).Entertainment, museum booths and theater performances. Apr.

Seasonal Event

Royal Palm Polo. Games played at the Royal Palm Polo Sports Club, considered by many the winter polo capital of the world. Special events. Phone 561/994-1876. Sun, Jan-Apr.

Motels

✔★ ★ **BEST WESTERN UNIVERSITY INN.** *2700 N Federal Hwy (US 1) (33431). 561/395-5225; FAX 561/338-9180.* 90 rms, 2 story. Mid-Dec-Apr: S, D $79-$109; each addl $8; under 12 free; lower rates rest of yr. Crib free. TV; cable (premium). Heated pool; whirlpool. Complimentary continental bkfst. Restaurant 4-11 pm. Bar. Ck-out 11 am. Coin lndry. Meeting rm. Business servs avail. In-rm modem link. Valet serv. Sundries. Free airport transportation. Exercise equipt. Refrigerators, microwaves. Cr cds: A, C, D, DS, ER, JCB, MC, V.

D 🏊 ✕ 🛇 🖂 SC

★ **HOLIDAY INN-WEST BOCA.** *8144 Glades Rd (33434). 561/482-7070; FAX 561/482-6076.* 97 rms, 4 story. Dec-Apr: S $89-$139; D $95-$149; each addl $10; under 18 free; lower rates rest of yr. Crib free. TV; cable (premium). Pool. Coffee in rms. Restaurant (see PETE ROSE BALLPARK CAFE, Unrated Dining). Rm serv. Bar noon-2 am. Ck-out noon. Business servs avail. In-rm modem link. Health club privileges. Private patios, balconies. Cr cds: A, C, D, DS, ER, JCB, MC, V.

D 🏊 🖂 SC

★★ **RESIDENCE INN BY MARRIOTT.** *525 NW 77th St (33487). 561/994-3222; FAX 561/994-3339.* 120 kit. suites, 2 story. Early Dec-mid-Apr: suites $175-$225; lower rates rest of yr. Crib free. Pet accepted, some restrictions; $100-$150. Heated pool. TV; cable, VCR avail (movies $6). Complimentary bkfst buffet. Complimentary coffee in rms. Ck-out noon. Coin lndry. Meeting rms. Business servs avail. In-rm modem link. Valet serv. Tennis privileges, pro. 18-hole golf privileges, pro, putting green, driving range. Health club privileges. Microwaves. Balconies. Picnic tables, grills. Cr cds: A, C, D, DS, JCB, MC, V.

D 🏌 🏋 🏊 🖂 SC

✔★ **SHORE EDGE.** *425 N Ocean Blvd (33432). 561/395-4491; FAX 567/347-8759.* E-mail shoreedge@prodigy.net; web www.safari.com. 16 units, 9 kits. Mid-Dec-May: S, D $55-$75; kit. units $75-$95; wkly, monthly rates; lower rates rest of yr. TV; cable. Heated pool. Ck-out noon. Coin lndry. Beach opp. Cr cds: MC, V.

🏊 🛇

Motor Hotels

★★ **DOUBLETREE GUEST SUITES.** *701 NW 53rd St (33487), in Arvida Park of Commerce. 561/997-9500; FAX 561/994-3565.* 182 suites, 4 story. Mid-Dec-Apr: suites $159-$209; under 12 free; monthly rates; lower rates rest of yr. Crib free. Pet accepted, some restrictions; $50. TV; cable (premium). Heated pool; whirlpool. Complimentary coffee in rms. Restaurant 6 am-10 pm. Rm serv. Ck-out noon. Coin lndry. Meeting rms. Business servs avail. In-rm modem link. Bellhops. Sundries. Health club privileges. Refrigerators, microwaves. Cr cds: A, C, D, DS, ER, MC, V.

D 🏋 🏊 🖂 SC

★ **HOLIDAY INN I-95 & GLADES.** *1950 Glades Rd (33431). 561/368-5200; FAX 561/395-4783.* 184 rms, 5 story. Jan-Apr: S $109-$185; D $119-$195; each addl $10; suites $135-$235; under 16 free; lower rates rest of yr. Crib free. Heated pool; wading pool; whirlpool. Coffee in rms. Restaurant 6:30-11 am, 5-10 pm. Rm serv 5-10 pm. Bar 11 am-10 pm. Ck-out noon. Meeting rms. Business servs avail. Bellhops. Golf privileges. Health club privileges. Balconies. Cr cds: A, C, D, DS, JCB, MC, V.

D 🏌 🏊 🖂 SC

Hotels

★★ **EMBASSY SUITES.** *661 NW 53rd St (33487), at I-95 & Yamato Rd, in Arvida Park of Commerce. 561/994-8200; FAX 561/994-9518.* E-mail tpriley@aol.com. 263 suites, 7 story. Dec-Apr: S, D $159-$235; lower rates rest of yr. Crib free. TV. Heated pool; whirlpool. Complimentary full bkfst. Coffee in rms. Restaurant 7 am-10 pm. Bar noon-midnight. Ck-out noon. Convention facilities. Business servs avail. In-rm modem link. Gift shop. Concierge. Valet parking. Tennis privileges. Golf privileges. Exercise equipt; sauna. Refrigerators, microwaves. Balconies. On small lake. Atrium with garden pools, glass-enclosed elvtrs. Cr cds: A, C, D, DS, JCB, MC, V.

D 🏌 🏋 🏊 ✕ 🖂 SC

★★ **MARRIOTT.** *5150 Town Center Circle (33486), at I-95 exit 39. 561/392-4600; FAX 561/395-8258.* 256 rms, 12 story. Jan-Apr: S, D

$179-$219; each addl $10; suites $250-$400; under 18 free; lower rates rest of yr. Crib free. TV; cable (premium), VCR avail. Heated pool; whirlpool, poolside serv. Restaurant 6:30 am-10 pm. Bar 11:30 am-midnight; entertainment. Ck-out noon. Convention facilities. In-rm modem link. Gift shop. Valet parking. Tennis privileges. 18-hole golf privileges. Exercise equipt; sauna. Health club privileges. Minibars. Balconies. Luxury level. Cr cds: A, C, D, DS, ER, JCB, MC, V.

D 🏌 🏋 🏊 ✕ 🖂 SC

★★★ **RADISSON BRIDGE RESORT.** *999 E Camino Real (33432). 561/368-9500; FAX 561/362-0492.* 121 rms, 11 story. Mid-Dec-Apr: S, D $199-$239; each addl $10; suites $295-$375; under 18 free; lower rates rest of yr. Crib free. TV; cable (premium). Heated pool; poolside serv. Complimentary continental bkfst. Coffee in rms. Restaurant 7 am-11 pm; dining rm (see CARMEN'S). Bar 11 am-11 pm; entertainment. Ck-out noon. Meeting rms. Business servs avail. Tennis privileges. Golf privileges. Exercise equipt; sauna. Some refrigerators. Balconies. Cr cds: A, C, D, DS, MC, V.

🏌 🏋 🏊 ✕ 🖂

★★ **RADISSON SUITE.** *7920 Glades Rd (33434), at Arvida Pkwy Ctr. 561/483-3600; FAX 561/479-2280.* 200 suites, 7 story. Dec-Apr: S, D $185-$399; each addl $10; lower rates rest of yr. Crib free. Pet accepted, some restrictions; $100. TV; cable (premium), VCR avail (movies $5). Heated pool; whirlpool. Complimentary full bkfst. Coffee in rms. Restaurants 11:30 am-10:30 pm. Bars. Ck-out noon. Coin lndry. Meeting rms. Business servs avail. In-rm modem link. Gift shop. Exercise equipt. Health club privileges. Refrigerators, microwaves, minibars. Private patios, balconies. Lake adj. Cr cds: A, C, D, DS, ER, JCB, MC, V.

D 🏊 ✕ 🖂 SC

★ **RAMADA INN.** *2901 Federal Hwy (33431). 561/395-6850; FAX 561/368-7964.* 97 rms, 4 story, 32 suites. Mid-Dec-mid-Apr: S, D $105-$120; each addl $10; suites $120-$135; family, wkly rates; lower rates rest of yr. Crib free. TV; cable. Pool; whirlpool. Complimentary continental bkfst. Complimentary coffee in rms. Restaurant 5-10 pm. Bar. Ck-out noon. Meeting rms. Business servs avail. In-rm modem link. Refrigerators, microwaves avail. Balconies. Cr cds: A, C, D, DS, ER, MC, V.

D 🏊 🖂 SC

★ **SHERATON.** *2000 NW 19th St (33431), I-95 at Glades Rd. 561/368-5252; FAX 561/750-5437.* E-mail ittboca@ix.netcom.com; web bocaraton.com/sheraton/. 193 units, 5 story. Jan-Mar: S, D $119-$169; each addl $10; suites $259; under 17 free; lower rates rest of yr. Crib free. TV; cable (premium). Heated pool; poolside serv. Complimentary continental bkfst. Coffee in rms. Restaurant 6:30 am-10 pm. Bar 11 am-midnight. Ck-out noon. Meeting rms. Business servs avail. In-rm modem link. Sundries. Golf privileges. Exercise equipt. Health club privileges. Some refrigerators. Cr cds: A, C, D, DS, MC, V.

D 🏌 🏊 ✕ 🖂 SC

Resort

★★★ **BOCA RATON RESORT & CLUB.** *501 E Camino Real (33432), 2 blks E of US 1. 561/395-3000; FAX 561/391-3183; res: 800/327-0101.* This historic, long-time dazzling resort on 351 land-scaped acres has almost everything a vacationer would desire; the tennis and golf facilities are world-renowned. The main buildings and beach club (reachable by car, bus or yacht) are a mecca for convention-eers, and the almost-constant hustle and bustle are fun if you like lots of company. 963 units in 4 bldgs, 242 rms in 27-story tower, several villa apts with kit., 214 rms in beach club, 327 cloister rms. Mid-Dec-Apr: S, D $230-$430; suites $460-$5,500; MAP avail; lower rates rest of yr. Maid and bellman serv charge $9/day. Dining facilities: 18% food & beverage serv charge at all dining outlets. Crib free. TV; cable. 4 pools; poolside serv, lifeguard. Supervised child's activities. Dining rm 7 am-midnight. Box lunches, snack bar. Rm serv 24 hrs. Bar 11-2 am. Ck-out noon, ck-in 3 pm. Convention facilities. Business center. Barber, beauty shop. Shopping arcade. Airport transportation. Sports dir. 34 tennis courts, 9 lighted, pro. 36-hole golf, 2 putting greens, driving range. Private beach; cabanas. Charter boats. 23 yacht slips. Bicycles. Lawn games. Soc dir. Exercise rm; sauna. Massage. Some balconies. Luxury level. Cr cds: A, C, D, DS, ER, JCB, MC, V.

D ⚡ 🏌 🏊 🎾 🏃 🚭 🔥 SC 🚶

Restaurants

★ ★ ★ **ARTURO'S RISTORANTE.** *6750 N Federal Hwy (US 1) (33483).* *561/997-7373.* Hrs: 11:30 am-3 pm, 6-10 pm; Sat, Sun from 6 pm. Closed July 4, Thanksgiving, Dec 25. Res required. Northern Italian menu. Bar. Wine cellar. A la carte entrees: lunch $12-$16.50, dinner $16-$35. Complete meals: dinner $35. Specialties: osso buco, veal chop Modenese, zuppa di pesce. Own baking, pasta. Valet parking. Jacket. Outdoor dining. Cr cds: A, C, D, MC, V.

D

★ ★ **AUBERGE LE GRILLON.** *6900 N Federal Hwy (US 1) (33487).* *561/997-6888.* Hrs: 6-9:30 pm. Res accepted. Continental menu. Wine list. Semi-a la carte: dinner $16-$30. Specialties: Dover sole with lobster and mousseline sauce, roast duckling with apricot and Grand Marnier sauce. Own baking. Valet parking. Outdoor dining. Intimate dining rm with original art and fireplace. Cr cds: A, C, D, MC, V.

D

★ ★ **BASIL GARDEN.** *5837 N Federal Hwy (33487).* *561/994-2554.* Hrs: 5:30-9:30 pm; wkends to 10 pm. Closed Jan 1, Thanksgiving, Dec 25. Res accepted. Italian menu. Bar. A la carte entrees: dinner $11.95-$22.95. Specializes in veal, pasta, fresh seafood. Own pasta, desserts. Parking. Intimate, trattoria-style dining. Totally nonsmoking. Cr cds: A, MC, V.

★ **BISTRO ZENITH.** *3011 Yamato Rd (33434), in Regency Court.* *561/997-2570.* Web restaurantsonline.com/bistrozenith. Hrs: 11:30 am-2:30 pm, 5:30-10 pm; Fri to 11 pm; Sat 5:30-11 pm; Sun 5:30-10 pm. Res accepted. Bar. Semi-a la carte: lunch $4-$10, dinner $9-$22. Child's meals. Specialties: veal meatloaf, pistachio-crusted salmon, chicken savoy. Outdoor dining. Contemporary decor in celestial theme. Cr cds: A, DS, MC, V.

D

★ ★ **BREWZZI.** *2222 Glades Rd (33431).* *561/392-2739.* E-mail brewzzi@aol.com. Hrs: 11:30-1 am; Fri, Sat to 2 am; Sun to midnight. Closed Dec 25. Italian, Amer menu. Semi-a la carte: lunch $5.95-$10, dinner $8.95-$25. Child's meals. Specialties: pizza, grilled chicken sandwich, chicken scarpariello. Valet parking. Outdoor dining. Microbrewery. Cr cds: A, MC, V.

D 🚬

★ ★ **CARMEN'S.** *(See Radisson Bridge Resort Hotel)* *561/750-8354.* Hrs: 5:30-10 pm; Fri, Sat to 11 pm; Sun brunch 11 am-3 pm. Closed Mon. Res accepted. Continental menu. Bar. Semi-a la carte: dinner $15.95-$35. Sun brunch $19.95. Specializes in veal, lobster, pasta. Entertainment Tues-Sun. Valet parking. Panoramic view of Intracoastal Waterway and ocean. Cr cds: A, D, DS, ER, JCB, MC, V.

D 🚬

★ ★ **CHEF RETO'S.** *41 E Palmetto Park Rd (33432).* *561/395-0633.* Hrs: 6-11 pm; Fri, Sat to midnight. Res accepted. Continental menu. A la carte entrees: dinner $19.50-$34.50. Specialties: whole roasted yellowtail snapper, Dover sole in vegetable broth, clams with walnut and garlic. Parking. Cr cds: A, DS, MC, V.

D

★ ★ **FIREHOUSE PUB & EATERY.** *6751 N Federal Hwy (US 1) (33487).* *561/997-6006.* Hrs: 5-10 pm. Closed Dec 25. Bar. A la carte entrees: dinner $8.95-$28.95. Specializes in beef, steak, fresh seafood. Entertainment. Parking. Firehouse decor, memorabilia throughout. Cr cds: A, D, MC, V.

D

★ ★ ★ **GAZEBO CAFE.** *4199 N Federal Hwy (US 1) (33431).* *561/395-6033.* Hrs: 11:30 am-3 pm, 5:30-10 pm; Sat from 5:30 pm; Sun

from 5 pm (exc mid-May-Dec). Res accepted. French, continental menu. Serv bar. Wine list. A la carte entrees: lunch $8.95-$16, dinner $18.95-$33.95. Specialty: Dover sole. Open kitchen. Outdoor dining. Jacket (dinner). Cr cds: A, C, D, DS, MC, V.

D

★ ★ **GIGI'S.** *346 Plaza Real (33432), at Mizner Park.* *561/368-4488.* Hrs: 11:30 am-11 pm; Fri, Sat to midnight; Sun brunch 10:30 am-3:30 pm. Res accepted. French menu. Semi-a la carte: lunch $4.95-$15.95, dinner $13.95-$21.95. Sun brunch $3.95-$10.95. Child's meals. Specialties: pork choucroute, duck a l'orange. Oyster bar. Entertainment Tues-Thurs. Valet parking. Outdoor dining. Cr cds: A, C, D, DS, MC, V.

D 🚬

★ ★ ★ **LA FINESTRA.** *171 E Palmetto Park Rd (33432).* *561/392-1838.* Hrs: 6 pm-2 am. Closed Sun May-Sept. Res accepted. Northern Italian menu. Bar. Semi-a la carte: dinner $12.95-$28.95. Specialties: veal chops, yellowtail snapper, Norwegian salmon. Own baking. Guitarist, jazz band. Parking. Continental art prints, chandeliers. Chef-owned. Cr cds: A, D, MC, V.

D

★ ★ **LA PETITE MAISON.** *366 Palmetto Park Rd (33432).* *561/750-7483.* Hrs: 11:30 am-2 pm, 5:30-9:30 pm; Sat-Mon from 5:30 pm; early-bird dinner 5:30-6:30 pm. Closed Dec 25. Res accepted wkends. French, Mediterranean menu. A la carte entrees: lunch $6.50-$13.50, dinner $18.50-$25. Specialties: broiled lobster tails with aioli, rack of lamb with herb stuffing, shrimp with curry and chutney. Bistro decor. Cr cds: A, JCB, MC, V.

D

★ ★ ★ **LA VIEILLE MAISON.** *770 E Palmetto Park Rd (33432).* *561/391-6701.* This country French oasis just off the beach has many tastefully decorated rooms for quiet dining. Chef Richard Ruiz presents an extensive selection of contemporary French Provencale delicacies; there's a four-course "grand menu" and, every night except Saturday, a three-course "temptation menu" in addition to a la carte choices. French menu. Specialties: shrimp Pernod, medallions of lamb and beef, fresh Dover sole. Own baking. Hrs: May-Oct 6:30-9:30 pm; Nov-Apr 6-10 pm. Res accepted; required in season. Bar. Wine list. A la carte entrees: dinner $18-$40. Prix fixe: dinner $60 excluding beverage. "Temptation" menu (May-Nov 1, Sun-Fri) $40. Treetop balcony dining. Outdoor courtyard. Patio & private dining area. Valet parking. Jacket. Cr cds: A, C, D, DS, MC, V.

D 🚬

★ ★ **LA VILLETTA.** *4351 N Federal Hwy (33431).* *561/362-8403.* Hrs: 5:30-10:30 pm. Closed Jan 1, Dec 25. Res accepted. Italian menu. Wine, beer. Semi-a la carte: dinner $13.25-$24.95. Specialties: grilled Maine lobster, veal chop, yellowtail with lemon and white wine sauce. Parking. Cr cds: A, MC, V.

D ♥

★ ★ ★ **MARCEL'S.** *1 S Ocean Blvd (33432), in shopping center.* *561/362-9911.* Hrs: 11:30 am-2:30 pm, 5-11 pm. Res accepted. French menu. Semi-a la carte: lunch $6.95-$12.95, dinner $15.95-$29.50. Specialties: lobster, Dover sole, rack of lamb. Own baking. Parking. Bistro atmosphere. Limoges china, paintings. Cr cds: A, DS, MC, V.

D

✔★ ★ **MAX'S COFFEE SHOP.** *404 Plaza Real (33432).* *561/392-0454.* Hrs: 11 am-10:30 pm; Fri to midnight; Sat 11:30 am-11 pm; Sun 10 am-10 pm. Bar. Semi-a la carte: lunch, dinner $5-$16.95. Child's meals. Specialties: maple glazed salmon, turkey dinner. Valet parking. Outdoor dining. Diner atmosphere. Cr cds: A, C, D, DS, MC, V.

D 🚬

★ ★ ★ **MAX'S GRILLE.** *404 Plaza Real (33432), in Meyner Park shopping area.* *561/368-0080.* Hrs: 11:30 am-3 pm, 5:30-10:30 pm; Fri, Sat to 11 pm. Sun brunch to 3 pm. Bar. Semi-a la carte: lunch $5.95-$15.95, dinner $6.95-$26.95. Sun brunch $6.95-$14.95. Specialties: herb marinated pork chops, sesame seared tuna, filet mignon. Valet parking.

Outdoor dining. Menu changes daily. Open kitchen. Contemporary setting. Cr cds: A, D, MC, V.

★ ★ ★ **MAXALUNA.** *5050 Town Center Circle #245 (33486), in Boca Center.* 561/391-7177. Hrs: 11:30 am-2:30 pm, 6-10:30 pm; Fri to 11 pm; Sat 6-11 pm; Sun 6-10 pm. Closed Thanksgiving. Res accepted. Italian menu. Bar. A la carte entrees: lunch $8-$15, dinner $13-$32.50. Specializes in veal chops. Own pasta. Valet parking. Covered outdoor dining. Cr cds: A, C, D, DS, MC, V.

★ ★ ★ **NICK'S ITALIAN FISHERY & CHOPHOUSE.** *1 Boca Place (33431), on Glades Rd, 1 blk W of I-95.* 561/994-2201. Hrs: 11:30 am-2:30 pm, 5-11 pm; Sun brunch to 2:30 pm. Res accepted. Italian, seafood menu. Bar. A la carte entrees: lunch $7.95-$10.95, dinner $15.95-$36.95. Sun brunch $19.95. Specialties: seafood Fra Diavolo, blue claw crab feast, prime beef. Entertainment Fri, Sat. Valet parking. Glass-enclosed atrium dining; 1,200-gallon fish tank. Cr cds: A, D, DS, MC, V.

✔★ ★ **PADRINO'S.** *20455 State Rd Seven (33498).* 561/451-1070. Hrs: 11:30 am-10 pm; Fri to 10:30 pm; Sat noon-10:30 pm; Sun noon to 10 pm. Closed Mon; most major hols. Cuban menu. A la carte entrees: lunch $4.95-$11.95, dinner $6.95-$11.95. Child's meals. Specialties: bistek de pollo, lechon asado. Guitar Sun eves. Parking. Totally nonsmoking. Cr cds: A, D, DS, MC, V.

★ ★ ★ **PETE'S BOCA RATON.** *7940 Glades Rd (33434).* 561/487-1600. E-mail f.quitko@petesbocaraton; web www.petesbocaraton.com. Hrs: 11:30 am-3 pm, 4:30-10 pm; wkends 4:30-11 pm. Res accepted. Bar 11:30-3 am. Wine cellar. Semi-a la carte: lunch $4.95-$13.95, dinner $15.95-$30. Specialties: Cajun blackened swordfish, prime rib, seafood Valencia. Entertainment. Valet parking. Outdoor dining. Casual waterfront dining in elegant setting. Cr cds: A, D, MC, V.

★ ★ **TAVERN IN THE GREENERY.** *301 Yamato Rd (33431), in the Northern Trust Plaza.* 561/241-9214. Hrs: 11:30 am-2:30 pm, 5:30-9:30 pm; early-bird dinner 5-6 pm. Res accepted. Continental menu. Bar. A la carte entrees: lunch $5.95-$9.95, dinner $14.95-$29.95. Sun brunch $14.95. Specialties: cedar plank baked salmon, pan-roasted duck breast, Dover sole. Own pastries. Entertainment. Parking. Formal dining rm & casual eating area. Tropical atrium garden. Cr cds: A, MC, V.

✔★ ★ **UNCLE TAI'S.** *5250 Town Center Circle (33486), in shopping center.* 561/368-8806. Hrs: 11:30 am-2:30 pm, 5-10 pm; wkends 5-10:30 pm; early-bird dinner 5-6:30 pm. Res accepted Fri-Sun. Chinese menu. Serv bar. A la carte entrees: lunch $6.95-$13.25, dinner $9.75-$23.95. Specialties: Hunan-style crispy beef, Uncle Tai's jumbo shrimp. Parking. Outdoor dining. Elegant Oriental decor. Cr cds: A, C, D, MC, V.

✔★ **WILT CHAMBERLAIN'S.** *8903 W Glades Rd (33434).* 561/488-8881. Hrs: 11:30 am-11:30 pm; Fri, Sat to 12:30 am. Varied menu. Bar. A la carte entrees: lunch, dinner $4.99-$15.99. Child's meals. Specialties: designer pizza, oak-grilled chops, Wilt's clubhouse sandwich. Own desserts. Magician Sat evenings. Parking. Many TVs throughout rm; large arcade area. Cr cds: A, C, D, DS, MC, V.

Unrated Dining Spot

PETE ROSE BALLPARK CAFE. *(See Holiday Inn-West Boca Motel)* 561/488-7383. Hrs: 7-10 am, 11:30 am-1 am. Bar. Buffet: bkfst $3.95-$5.95. A la carte entrees: lunch $3.95-$7.95, dinner $8.95-

$16.95. Child's meals. Specializes in fajitas, ribs, hamburgers. Sports memorabilia; video arcade. Cr cds: A, C, D, DS, MC, V.

Bonita Springs (G-4)

(See also Naples)

Pop 13,600 **Elev** 10 ft **Area code** 941 **E-mail** info@bonitaspringschamber.com **Web** www.bonitasprings.com
Information Chamber of Commerce, 25071 Chamber of Commerce Dr, 34135; 941/992-2943 or 800/226-2943.

Located directly on the Gulf of Mexico, with the Imperial River flowing through the city, Bonita Springs has several popular boat and nature tours.

What to See and Do

Everglades Wonder Gardens. Native reptiles, birds and animals in Everglades setting. Natural history museum. Guided tours. (Daily) On US 41 Business. Phone 941/992-2591. ¢¢¢

Greyhound racing. (Wed-Sat evenings; matinees Wed, Sat, Sun) Naples-Fort Myers Greyhound Track, on Old US 41. Phone 941/992-2411. General admission ¢

Motel

★ ★ **COMFORT INN.** *9800 Bonita Beach Rd (34135).* 941/992-5001; FAX 941/992-9283. 69 rms, 3 story. Jan-Apr: S, D $93-$98; each addl $5; under 18 free; lower rates rest of yr. Crib free. TV; cable (premium). Heated pool; whirlpool, poolside serv. Coffee in rms. Restaurant 7 am-2 pm, 5-9 pm. Ck-out 11 am. Coin lndry. Business servs avail. Health club privileges. Wet bars, refrigerators. Balconies. Cr cds: A, C, D, DS, ER, JCB, MC, V.

Restaurants

★ ★ **CAFE MARGAUX.** *3405 Pelican Landing Pkwy #1 (33923).* 941/992-6588. Hrs: 11:30 am-2 pm, 5-9 pm; Fri, Sat to 9:30 pm; early-bird dinner 5-6 pm; hours vary off season. Closed July 4, Dec. 25. Res accepted. Contemporary French menu. Bar. Semi-a la carte: lunch $6-$9, dinner $9-$36. Child's meals. Specialties: snapper francaise, prime aged beef, blue crab cakes. Outdoor dining. European atmosphere. Cr cds: A, DS, MC, V.

✔★ **JADE ISLAND.** *8951 Bonita Beach Rd #625 (34135), in Springs Plaza.* 941/992-8881. Hrs: 11 am-10 pm; Sun noon-9 pm. Chinese, Amer menu. Bar. Semi-a la carte: lunch, dinner $3.95-$14.95. Child's meals. Specializes in Cantonese and Szechwan dishes. Two dining rms; Oriental motif. Cr cds: A, DS, MC, V.

★ **ROOFTOP.** *25999 Hickory Blvd (34134), in Casa Bonita Plaza.* 941/992-0033. Hrs: 11:30 am-2:30 pm, 5-10 pm; Sat from 5 pm; Sun brunch 10:30 am-2 pm; hours vary off season. Closed Mon May-Nov. Res accepted. Continental menu. Bar. Semi-a la carte: lunch $4.95-$14.95, dinner $11.95-$21.95. Sun brunch $14.95. Child's meals. Specializes in fresh seafood, lamb, beef. Entertainment; piano bar. Nautical decor. Scenic view of inlet. Cr cds: A, D, MC, V.

Boynton Beach (G-6)

(See also Boca Raton, Delray Beach, Palm Beach, Pompano Beach, West Palm Beach)

Pop 46,194 **Elev** 16 ft **Area code** 561 **E-mail** chamber@boyntonbeach.org **Web** www.boyntonbeach.org
Information Greater Boynton Beach Chamber of Commerce, 639 E Ocean Ave, Suite 108, 33435; 561/732-9501.

Fishing docks and two marinas make Boynton Beach a gateway to Sailfish Alley, five minutes away in the Gulf Stream, and Kingfish Circle, another Gulf Stream spot where king mackerels are found. Boynton Beach Inlet connects the Intracoastal Waterway and Lake Worth with the Atlantic Ocean.

What to See and Do

Arthur R. Marshall Loxahatchee National Wildlife Refuge. More than 145,000 acres of freshwater marsh in the Everglades. Fishing. Nature trails. Visitor center (daily; Wed-Sun in summer). No pets. (Daily) Golden Eagle, Golden Age, Golden Access passports accepted (see MAKING THE MOST OF YOUR TRIP). 10 mi W via FL 804 to US 441, then 2 mi S. Contact 10216 Lee Rd, 33437; 561/734-8303. Per vehicle ¢¢; Per pedestrian ¢¢

Fishing, boating. Pioneer Canal Park at NW 13th Ave & 8th St; drift boat fishing at Sea Mist Marina on E Ocean Ave at Intracoastal Bridge; fishing at Boynton Inlet; launching ramps, fishing pier and picnicking at Boat Club Park, N of town, off US 1 at Oak St.

Annual Event

Boynton's GALA. Downtown, Ocean Ave. Selected arts & crafts by area artists. Usually mid-Mar.

Motels

★ ANN MARIE. *911 S Federal Hwy (US 1) (33435).* 561/732-9283; *FAX* 561/7329283; *res:* 800/258-8548. E-mail jerry-scott@ msn.com; web www.annmariemotel.com. 15 rms, 4 kits. Mid-Dec-mid-Apr: S, D $62-$65; each addl $3; lower rates rest of yr. Crib free. Pet accepted, some restrictions; $35. TV; cable, VCR (movies $5). Heated pool. Complimentary continental bkfst. Ck-out 11 am. Business servs avail. Refrigerators. Picnic tables, grill. Cr cds: A, C, D, DS, MC, V.

D ⇆ ≈ 🌊

✔★ COMFORT LODGE. *2607 S Federal Hwy (US 1) (33435).* 561/732-4446; *FAX* 561/731-0325. 21 units, 10 kits. Mid-Dec-mid-Apr: S, D $59-$84; each addl $8; varied lower rates rest of yr. TV; cable (premium). Heated pool. Restaurant adj 6 am-3 pm. Ck-out 11 am. Lawn games. Refrigerators. Private patios. Grills. Cr cds: A, D, DS, MC, V.

≈ 🌊

✔★ SUPER 8. *(1255 Hypoluxo Rd, Lantana 33462) N on I-95 exit 45.* 561/585-3970; *FAX* 561/586-3028. 129 units, 13 kits. Jan-Apr: S $50-$57; D $52-$59; each addl $3; kits. $62-$75; under 18 free; lower rates rest of yr. Crib free. Pet accepted. TV; cable (premium). Pool. Complimentary continental bkfst. Restaurant adj 6 am-11 pm; wkends to 1 am. Ck-out noon. Business servs avail. Cr cds: A, C, D, DS, ER, MC, V.

⇆ ≈ ⋈ 🌊 **SC**

Motor Hotel

★ ★ ★ HOLIDAY INN CATALINA. *1601 N Congress Ave (33426).* 561/737-4600; *FAX* 561/734-6523. 152 rms, 4 story. Dec-Apr: S, D $105-$140; each addl $10; under 19 free; lower rates rest of yr. Crib free. TV; cable. Heated pool; whirlpool. Restaurant 7-10:30 am, 11:30-1 am.

Rm serv. Ck-out noon. Meeting rms. Business servs avail. In-rm modem link. Exercise equipt. Balconies. Cr cds: A, C, D, DS, ER, JCB, MC, V.

D ≈ 🏋 🍴 ⋈ 🌊 **SC**

Restaurants

★ ★ BANANA BOAT. *739 E Ocean Ave (33435).* 561/732-9400. Hrs: 11-2 am; Sun from 9 am. Bar. Semi-a la carte: bkfst $4-$9, lunch $5-$14, dinner $7-$25. Specialties: conch chowder, shrimp scampi. Reggae band Sun. Outdoor dining. Nautical artifacts; on Intracoastal Waterway. Cr cds: A, D, MC, V.

D ⇆

★ ★ ★ BENVENUTO. *1730 N Federal Hwy (US 1) (33435).* 561/364-0600. Hrs: 5-9 pm. Italian, Amer menu. Res accepted. Bar. Wine list. Semi-a la carte: dinner $9-$17 Complete meals: dinner $15-$23. Specializes in seafood, veal, beef. Own baking. Valet parking. Spanish architecture; lighted tropical garden viewed through large picture windows. Totally nonsmoking. Cr cds: A, DS, MC, V.

D

★ ★ LUCILLE & OTLEY'S. *1021 S Federal Hwy (US 1) (33435).* 561/732-5930. Hrs: 5-9 pm; Sun noon-8 pm. Closed Mon; also Aug-mid Sept. Bar. Semi-a la carte: dinner $8.95-$18.95. Specialties: chicken, shortcake, lemon meringue pie. Child's meals. Family-owned since 1935; original artwork. Cr cds: A, DS, MC, V.

D ♥

✔★ TWO GEORGES HARBOR HUT. *728 Casa Loma Blvd (33435), on Intracoastal Waterway at E Ocean Ave drawbridge, Boynton Marina.* 561/736-2717. Hrs: 11 am-10 pm. Closed Dec 25. No A/C. Bar. A la carte entrees: lunch $3.95-$8, dinner $8-$38. Semi-a la carte: dinner $7.95-$13.95. Specializes in fresh seafood. Outdoor dining. Open waterside building with woven thatched roof. Cr cds: A, DS, MC, V.

D

Bradenton (F-3)

(See also St Petersburg, Sarasota)

Settled 1878 **Pop** 43,779 **Elev** 23 ft **Area code** 941 **E-mail** gulfisl@bhip.infi.net **Web** www.floridaislandbeaches.org
Information Bradenton Area Convention and Visitors Bureau, One Haben Blvd, Palmetto 34221; 941/729-9177 or 800/462-6283.

Located on the Manatee River, Bradenton provides access to river, bay and Gulf fishing, as well as 20 miles of white sand beach. The city took the name of Dr. Joseph Braden, whose nearby fort-like house was a refuge for early settlers during Native American attacks.

What to See and Do

De Soto National Memorial. At a spot believed to be somewhere near this memorial, Don Hernando De Soto landed on May 30, 1539, with 600 conquistadores to begin the first European expedition into the interior of what is now the southeastern United States. In a 4,000-mi, 4-yr wilderness odyssey, De Soto and his army explored beyond the Mississippi, staking out claims to a vast empire for Spain. Visitor center has weapons and armor of the De Soto era, movie depicting the De Soto expedition; living history area depicts aspects of 16th-century Spanish life (Dec-mid-Apr, call for schedule); self-guided nature trail along beach and through mangrove swamp. (Daily) 2 mi N off FL 64, at end of 75th St W; on Tampa Bay. Phone 941/792-0458 or -5094. **Free.**

Gamble Plantation State Historic Site. Confederate memorial and the only antebellum house surviving in south Florida. Major Robert Gamble ran a 3,500-acre sugar plantation and refinery here with 190 slaves. In May 1865, Judah P. Benjamin, Secretary of State of the Confederacy, fled to the plantation to hide from Union troops. Avoiding a surprise raid by Union forces, Benjamin escaped to Bimini and then to Nassau and England. Restored mansion furnished with period pieces. Picnicking. Visitor center with displays. Tours of mansion. (Thurs-Mon; closed Jan 1, Thanksgiving, Dec 25) 1 mi N, then 2 mi E on US 301 in Ellenton. Phone 941/723-4536. ¢¢

Manatee Village Historical Park. Park contains renovated historic buildings: First Court House (1800s); old church (1887); Wiggins Store Museum (1903); one-rm schoolhouse (1908); potter barn; smokehouse; sugar mill; Fogarty's Boat Works; and the Stephens House (1912), built in a style known as Cracker Gothic, and an excellent example of a Florida rural farm house in the period between the 1870s and World War I. Tour guides avail in winter. (Sept-June, daily exc Sat; rest of yr, Mon-Fri; closed hols) 6th Ave E and 15th St E. Phone 941/749-7165.   **Free.**

South Florida Museum & Bishop Planetarium. Native American and natural history exhibits; Spanish plaza; historical dioramas; dental and medical exhibits; manatee education and research facility. Planetarium shows. (Daily exc Mon; Jan, daily; closed Jan 1, Thanksgiving, Dec 25). 201 10th St W. Phone 941/746-4132 or -STAR (planetarium).   ¢¢¢

Seasonal Event

Spring training. McKechnie Field, on 9th St at 17th Ave W.Pittsburgh Pirates baseball spring training; exhibition games. Phone 941/747-3031. Early Mar-early Apr.

Motels

★★ **BEST WESTERN INN-ELLENTON.** (5218 17th St E, Ellenton 34222) Off I-75 exit 43. 941/729-8505; res: 800/581-3953; FAX 941/729-1110. 73 rms, 2 story, 11 kits. Feb-Apr: S, D $60-$100; each addl $5; kits. $110-$150; under 12 free; lower rates rest of yr. Crib free. Pet accepted, some restrictions; $10. TV; cable (premium). Heated pool; whirlpool. Complimentary continental bkfst. Restaurant nearby. Ck-out 11 am. Coin lndry. Meeting rm. Business servs avail. Cr cds: A, C, D, DS, MC, V.

D ⟋ ≋ ⤢ 🔥 SC

★ **CATALINA BEACH RESORT.** (1325 Gulf Dr N, Bradenton Beach 34217) W via FL 64, S on FL 789, on Anna Maria Island. 941/778-6611; FAX 941/778-6748. 35 units, 2 story, 27 kits. Feb-Apr: S, D $81-$115; each addl $6; 1-bedrm apts $112; 2-bedrm apts $125-$184; wkly rates; lower rates rest of yr. Crib $6. TV; cable. Heated pool. Ck-out 11 am. Coin lndry. Lawn games. Boat rentals. Picnic tables, grills. Private Gulf beach opp; dock. Cr cds: A, C, D, DS, MC, V.

D ⟋ ≋ 🔥

✔★ **HOWARD JOHNSON EXPRESS.** 6511 14th St W (US 41) (34207), near Sarasota-Bradenton Airport. 941/756-8399; FAX 941/755-1387. 49 units, 2 story, 12 kits. Jan-Apr: S $65; D $85; kits. $75-$95; under 18 free; wkly rates in summer; lower rates rest of yr. Crib free. Pet accepted; $5. TV; cable (premium). Heated pool. Complimentary continental bkfst. Restaurant nearby. Ck-out 11 am. Coin lndry. Some refrigerators. Cr cds: A, C, D, DS, MC, V.

D ⟋ ≋ ⤢ 🔥 SC

★★ **PARK INN CLUB & BREAKFAST.** 4450 47th St W (34210). 941/795-4633; FAX 941/795-0808. 130 rms, 3 story, 28 suites. Mid-Jan-Easter: S, D $104-$134; each addl $8; suites $134-$154; under 18 free; lower rates rest of yr. Crib free. Pet accepted, some restrictions; $25. TV; cable. Heated pool; whirlpool. Complimentary continental bkfst. Restaurant adj open 24 hrs. Ck-out noon. Meeting rms. Business servs avail. Health club privileges. Bathrm phones. Cr cds: A, C, D, DS, ER, JCB, MC, V.

D ⟋ ≋ ⤢ 🔥 SC

★★ **SHONEY'S INN.** (4915 17th St E, Ellenton 34222) 941/729-0600; res: 800/222-2222; FAX 941/722-5908. Web www.shoneysinn.com. 63 rms, 3 with shower only, 2 story, 6 suites. Feb-mid-Apr: S, D $80-$100; each addl $5; suites $85-$125; under 18 free; family, wkly rates; higher rates special events; lower rates rest of yr. Crib free. Pet accepted,

some restrictions; $10. TV; cable (premium). Complimentary continental bkfst. Restaurant adj 6 am-midnight. Ck-out 11 am. Business servs avail. In-rm modem link. Pool; whirlpool. Some bathrm phones; in-rm whirlpool, refrigerator, microwave in suites. On lake. Cr cds: A, C, D, DS, MC, V.

D ⟋ ⟋ ≋ ⤢ 🔥 SC

✔★ **SILVER SURF.** (1301 Gulf Dr N, Bradenton Beach 34217) 10 mi W on FL 684. 941/778-6626; FAX 941/778-4308; res: 800/441-7873. E-mail silversandsurf@mail.pcsonline.com; web www.manatee-online.com/silver. 49 units, 3 story, 10 kits. Feb-Apr: S, D $84-$86; each addl $9; kits. $89-$108; wkly rates; lower rates rest of yr. Crib $3. TV; cable. Heated pool. Ck-out 11 am. Lawn games. Refrigerators; many wet bars; some microwaves. Picnic tables. Opp Gulf; private beach. Cr cds: A, D, DS, MC, V.

D ≋ ⤢ 🔥 SC

Motor Hotel

★★★ **HOLIDAY INN-RIVERFRONT.** 100 Riverfront Dr W (34205). 941/747-3727; FAX 941/746-4289. Web www.riverfronthotel.com. 153 rms, 5 story, 57 suites. Jan-Apr: S $109-$119; D $119-$129; each addl $10; suites $129-$149; under 18 free; wkend packages off-season; lower rates rest of yr. Crib free. TV; cable (premium). Heated pool; whirlpool, poolside serv. Restaurant 6:30 am-11 pm. Rm serv. Bar 11-2 am. Ck-out noon. Meeting rms. Business servs avail. In-rm modem link. Bellhops. Sundries. Gift shop. Exercise equipt. Balconies. Picnic tables. On Manatee River. Cr cds: A, C, D, DS, JCB, MC, V.

D ≋ ⚒ ⤢ 🔥 SC

Inns

✔★ **FIVE OAKS.** (1102 Riverside Dr, Palmetto 34221) N off US 41 Business. 941/723-1236; res: 800/658-4167. 4 rms, 2 story. S, D $75-$110; wkly, monthly rates. Adults only. TV rm. Complimentary continental bkfst. Ck-out 11 am, ck-in 4 pm. Patio, grill. Library. Built 1912 from plans out of Sears Roebuck catalog. Opp river. Cr cds: A, DS, MC, V.

⟋ ⤢ 🔥

★★ **HARRINGTON HOUSE.** (5626 Gulf Dr, Holmes Beach 34217) 5 mi W on Gulf Dr. 941/778-5444; FAX 941/778-0527. E-mail harhousebb@mail.pcsonline.com; web www.harhousebb.com. 13 rms, 3 story, 1 guest house. Mid-Dec-Apr: S $170-$206; D $189-$229; guest house $206-$229; package plans; wkends, hols (3-day min); lower rates rest of yr. Closed mid-Dec. Children over 12 yrs only. TV; VCR avail (movies). Complimentary full bkfst. Restaurant nearby. Ck-out 11 am, ck-in 3 pm. Luggage handling. Pool. Refrigerators. Grills. On beach. Built in 1925. Elegant decor; antiques. Totally nonsmoking. Cr cds: MC, V.

≋ ⤢ 🔥

Restaurants

★★★ **BEACH BISTRO.** (6600 Gulf Dr, Holmes Beach 34217) 941/778-6444. Hrs: 5:30-10 pm. Closed some major hols. Res accepted. Continental menu. Bar. Wine list. Semi-a la carte: dinner $25-$40. Specialties: rack of lamb, bouillabaisse. Parking. View of beach, gulf. Totally nonsmoking. Cr cds: A, D, DS, MC, V.

D

✔★ **CHINA PALACE.** 5131 14th St W (US 41) (34207). 941/755-3758. Hrs: 11:30 am-9:30 pm; Fri, Sat to 10 pm. Closed Thanksgiving. Res accepted. Chinese menu. Bar. Semi-a la carte: lunch $3.95-$5.50, dinner $6.50-$12.95. Buffet: lunch, dinner $5.50-$8.50. Specializes in Szechwan, Cantonese dishes. Parking. Authentic Chinese decor. Cr cds: A, D, DS, MC, V.

D ⟋

✔★ **GULF DRIVE CAFE.** (900 Gulf Dr N, Bradenton Beach 34207) 10 mi W on FL 684 (Cortez Rd) to Gulf Dr. 941/778-1919. Web www.dinefind.com. Hrs: 7 am-9:30 pm. Closed Dec 25. Semi-a la carte:

bkfst $2.50-$5.50, lunch $4.25-$5.95, dinner $6.95-$10.95. Child's meals. Specializes in waffles, fresh fish, pasta. Parking. Outdoor dining with ocean view. Cr cds: DS, MC, V.

★ ★ **LEE'S CRAB TRAP II.** *(4815 Memphis Rd, Ellenton 34222) Off I-75 exit 43. 941/729-7777.* Hrs: 11:30 am-9 pm; Fri, Sat to 10 pm. Closed Thanksgiving, Dec 25. Bar. Semi-a la carte: lunch $7.25-$11, dinner $11-$25. Child's meals. Specializes in crab dishes, Florida seafood. Parking. Nautical decor; overlooks water. Cr cds: DS, MC, V.

✔ ★ **MILLER'S DUTCH KITCH'N.** *3401 14th St W (US 41) (34205). 941/746-8253.* Hrs: 11 am-8 pm. Closed Sun; some major hols. Amish menu. Semi-a la carte: lunch $4.75-$10.75, dinner $5.95-$12.95. Salad bar. Child's meals. Specialties: Dutch casserole, beef tips & noodles. Own pies. Parking. Totally nonsmoking. Cr cds: MC, V.

★ ★ **SANDBAR.** *(100 Spring Ave, Anna Maria 34216) 941/778-0444.* Hrs: 11:30 am-10 pm; early-bird dinner 4-6 pm. Bar. Semi-a la carte: lunch $5.95-$11.95, dinner $11.95-$18.95. Child's meals. Specializes in fresh seafood. Parking. Outdoor dining overlooking gulf. Original local artwork. Cr cds: A, D, DS, MC, V.

★ ★ **SEAFOOD SHACK.** *(4110 127th St W, Cortez 34215) 10 mi W on FL 648 (Cortez Rd), east side of bridge. 941/794-1235.* Hrs: 11:30 am-9 pm; Fri, Sat to 10 pm. Closed Thanksgiving, Dec 25. Bar. Semi-a la carte: lunch $4.50-$12.95, dinner $9.95-$39.95. Specializes in seafood, beef. Parking. On waterfront, paddlewheel boat rides avail. Cr cds: A, DS, MC, V.

Brooksville (D-3)

Pop 7,440 Elev 230 ft Area code 352 Web www.hernandochamber.com
Information Greater Hernando County Chambers of Commerce, 101 E Fort Dade Ave, Brooksville 34601; 352/796-0697 or 800/601-4580.

Amid hilly countryside unusual to Florida lies Brooksville, a center for limestone quarrying, cement production, and forest and dairy products.

What to See and Do

Buccaneer Bay. Natural spring water park features 140-ft sand beach, 4 water flumes, Fantasy Island for children, rope swings, game arcades, 2 volleyball courts; picnicking; concessions. (Apr-early June, Thurs-Sun; early June-Sept, daily) 12 mi W on FL 50, at jct US 19, adj to Weeki Wachee Spring. Phone 352/596-2062 or 800/678-9335. ¢¢¢¢

★ **Weeki Wachee Spring, the City of Mermaids.** Underwater amphitheater combines nature and engineering to showcase underwater mermaid shows. The spring, which produces more than 168 million gallons of water daily, has a measured depth of 250 ft, but goes deeper. After a former Navy frogman developed underwater breathing techniques at Weeki Wachee, he recognized the commercial possibilities and, in 1947, had an auditorium built 6 ft below the surface. The first underwater show was so successful that a second, million-dollar auditorium seating 500 was built 16 ft below the surface. Today's visitors watch underwater performances through 19 plate-glass windows nearly 3 inches thick. Each performance lasts approximately 30 min, with 3 performances daily. Other attractions include Wilderness River Cruise, down the Weeki Wachee River to Pelican Orphanage. Various 30-min shows include a live performance of *Pocahontas Meets the Little Mermaid;* Free-Flying Exotic Birds, with macaws and cockatoos performing tricks; and Birds of Prey Show with free-flying eagles, hawks, vultures and owls performing within close view. Also Animal Forest Petting Zoo.

(Daily) 12 mi W on FL 50 at jct US 19. Phone 352/596-2062 or 800/678-9335. ¢¢¢¢¢

Annual Events

Brooksville Raid Festival. Civil War reenactment of the July 1864 Union attack on Brooksville; more than 700 participants, blue/gray ball, barbecue, museum display. Phone chamber of commerce for more information. Late Jan.

Hernando County Fair. Phone 352/796-4552. 1 wk late Mar-early Apr.

Motels

★ ★ **HOLIDAY INN.** *30307 Cortez (34602). 352/796-9481; FAX 352/799-7595.* 122 rms, 2 story. S, D $70-$75; each addl $5; under 18 free. Crib free. Pet accepted, some restrictions; $25. TV; cable (premium), VCR avail. Pool; wading pool. Playground. Complimentary bkfst buffet. Restaurant 6:30 am-9:30 pm. Rm serv. Bar 4-11 pm. Ck-out noon. Coin lndry. Meeting rms. Business servs avail. Valet serv. Lighted tennis. Game rm. Some refrigerators. Picnic tables. Cr cds: A, D, DS, JCB, MC, V.

★ ★ **HOLIDAY INN.** *(6172 Commercial Way, Weeki Wachee 34606) 12 mi W on FL 50. 352/596-2007; FAX 352/596-0667.* 122 rms, 2 story. Late Dec-May: S, D $79-$89; each addl $6; under 18 free; lower rates rest of yr. Crib free. Pet accepted, some restrictions. TV; cable (premium). Pool; wading pool. Complimentary coffee in lobby. Restaurant 6:30 am-10 pm. Rm serv. Bar noon-1 am. Ck-out 11 am. Meeting rms. Business servs avail. Lawn games. Picnic tables. Cr cds: A, C, D, DS, JCB, MC, V.

Cape Coral (G-4)

(See also Bonita Springs, Fort Myers, Sanibel & Captiva Islands)

Pop 74,991 Elev 10 ft Area code 941 Zip 33904 E-mail info@capecoralfl.com Web www.capecoralfl.com
Information Chamber of Commerce, 2051 Cape Coral Pkwy, PO Box 747; 941/549-6900.

Settled only since 1958 and incorporated since 1970, Cape Coral is rapidly growing and has the second largest area of Florida's cities. Water-related activities on the Caloosahatchee River and golfing are popular.

Motels

✔ ★ ★ **CASA LOMA.** *3608 Del Prado Blvd. 941/549-6000; FAX 941/549-4877.* 49 kit. units in 2 bldgs, 2 story. Feb-Mar: S, D $70-$80; each addl $5; wkly rates lower rates rest of yr. Crib $5. TV; cable. Pool. Restaurant nearby. Ck-out 11 am. Coin lndry. Business servs avail. Microwaves avail. Private patios, balconies. Picnic tables. On canal. Cr cds: A, DS, MC, V.

★ **QUALITY INN.** *1538 Cape Coral Pkwy. 941/542-2121; FAX 941/542-6319.* 144 rms, 5 story. Feb-Apr: S, D $80-$110; each addl $10; under 18 free; lower rates rest of yr. Crib free. Pet accepted; $5-$10/day. TV; cable. Pool; poolside serv. Restaurant adj open 24 hrs. Ck-out 11 am. Coin lndry. Meeting rm. Business servs avail. Health club privileges. Cr cds: A, C, D, DS, ER, JCB, MC, V.

Resort

★ ★ **CAPE CORAL GOLF & TENNIS RESORT.** *4003 Palm Tree Blvd. 941/542-3191; FAX 941/542-4694; res: 800/648-1475.* 100 rms, 2 story. Late Jan-Easter: S, D $119-$152; each addl $15; under 17 free; package plans; lower rates rest of yr. Crib free. TV; cable (premium). Heated pool; poolside serv. Restaurant 7 am-9 pm. Rm serv. Bar; entertainment. Ck-out noon. Meeting rms. Business servs avail. 8 lighted tennis courts, pro. 18-hole golf, greens fee $25-$70 (incl half-cart), pro, putting green, lighted driving range. Cr cds: A, C, D, DS, MC, V.

Restaurants

✔★ ★ **ARIANI.** *1529 SE 15th Terrace (33990), in Del Prado Mall. 941/772-8000.* Web www.fibd.com/ariani. Hrs: 5-10 pm. Closed Sun; Easter, Thanksgiving, Dec 25. Res accepted. Northern Italian menu. Bar. Semi-a la carte: dinner $11.95-$24.95. Child's meals. Specialties: veal & chicken scallopini, eggplant rolatine parmigiana. Intimate dining. Cr cds: A, DS, MC, V.

✔★ **JIMBO'S.** *1604 SE 46th St. 941/540-9533.* Hrs: 7 am-9 pm. Closed Jan 1, Thanksgiving, Dec 25. Semi-a la carte: bkfst $1.79-$6.75, lunch $2.75-$6.20, dinner $5.95-$9.99. Specialties: chicken & steak teriyaki, steak & fried shrimp, barbecued ribs. Cr cds: MC, V.

★ ★ **MR. C'S.** *850 Lafayette St. 941/542-2001.* Hrs: 4-10 pm; Sun to 9 pm; early-bird dinner to 6 pm. Closed Mon; Dec 25. Res accepted. Bar. Semi-a la carte: dinner $8.95-$17.95. Child's meals. Specializes in fresh seafood, steak, beef. Cr cds: A, DS, MC, V.

★ **VENEZIA.** *1515 SE 47th Terr. 941/542-0027.* Hrs: 5-9 pm; wkends to 9:30 pm. Closed Mon; also Dec 25. Northern Italian menu. Serv bar. Semi-a la carte: dinner $6.75-$14.95. Specializes in veal, seafood, chicken. Salad bar. Casual dining in small, intimate cafe setting. Cr cds: A, DS, MC, V.

Captiva Island
(see Sanibel & Captiva Islands)

Cedar Key (D-3)

Pop 668 **Elev** 5 ft **Area code** 352 **Zip** 32625 **Web** cedarkey.org
Information Cedar Key Area Chamber of Commerce, 480 2nd St, PO Box 610; 352/543-5600.

All that remains of the cedars that once lined the shores of this key is the name. Cedar Key, once one of the busiest seaports in the state, is today a quiet island-city with extensive fishing, crabbing, clam farming and oystering.

What to See and Do

Cedar Key Historical Society Museum. Early photos, maps, records of Cedar Key; old pencil mill exhibit; self-guided tour. (Daily) Corner of 2nd St & FL 24. Phone 352/543-5549. ¢

Cedar Key State Museum. Dioramas and exhibits illustrate history of Cedar Key; shell collection. (Thurs-Mon; closed Thanksgiving, Dec 25) W of town, on Museum Dr, overlooking Gulf of Mexico. Phone 352/543-5350. ¢

Annual Events

Fine Art & Crafts Festival. 3rd wkend Apr.

Seafood Festival. 3rd wkend Oct.

Motel

★ ★ **ISLAND PLACE.** *Box 687, 1st & C Street. 352/543-5307; FAX 352/543-9141; res: 800/780-6522.* E-mail islandplace@aol.com; web crestcomm.com/islandplace/. 30 kit. condos, 2 story. Kit. condo $75-$140; each addl $5; under 5 free; higher rates: hols, special events. TV; cable. Pool; whirlpool. Sauna. Restaurant nearby. Ck-out 11 am. Refrigerators. Balconies. Washer, dryer, dishwasher in all units. Cr cds: A, DS, MC, V.

Inn

★ ★ **ISLAND HOTEL.** *2nd & B Streets. 352/543-5111; FAX 352/543-6949.* 10 rms, 6 with bath, 2 story. No rm phones. S, D $80-$100; each addl $10; children over 12 wkend only; wkly, wkend rates; higher rates special events. Complimentary full bkfst. Restaurant (see ISLAND HOTEL). Bar 5-11 pm, closed Tues. Ck-out 11 am, ck-in 2 pm. Built 1859; 11-inch tabby exterior walls. Traditional ambience; some feather beds, claw foot tubs. Totally nonsmoking. Cr cds: A, DS, MC, V.

Restaurants

★ **THE CAPTAIN'S TABLE.** *222 Dock St, at west end of Pier. 352/543-5441.* Hrs: 11 am-10 pm. Res accepted. Semi-a la carte: lunch $3.95-$7.95, dinner $8.95-$26.95. Child's meals. Specializes in fresh seafood. Entertainment Fri-Sun. Outdoor dining. Family-owned. Cr cds: A, DS, MC, V.

★ ★ **ISLAND HOTEL.** *(See Island Hotel Inn) 352/543-5111.* E-mail ishotel@islandhotel-cedarkey.com; web islandhotel-cedarkey.com. Hrs: 8-10 am, 6-9 pm; Sat, Sun to 8-11 am, 6-9 pm. Res accepted. Continental menu. Bar. Semi-a la carte: bkfst $8-$12, dinner $15-$26. Child's meals. Specializes in salad, meat, seafood. Parking. Outdoor dining. Totally nonsmoking. Cr cds: DS, MC, V.

Chiefland (C-3)

(See also Cedar Key, Gainesville)

Founded 1845 **Pop** 1,917 **Elev** 31 ft **Area code** 352 **Zip** 32644
Information Chamber of Commerce, 17 N Main St, PO Box 1397, 32644; 352/493-1849.

The town name honors the Native American farmers who once lived in the area. Peanuts, watermelons, tobacco, timber and corn are processed in and marketed from Chiefland.

What to See and Do

Manatee Springs State Park. The major attraction of this 2,075-acre park is a natural spring that produces 117 million gallons of water daily. Swimming, skin and scuba diving, bathhouse, wading pool; fishing; boat dock (canoe rentals). Nature trails, boardwalk. Picnicking, concession. Camping (dump station). Standard hrs, fees. 1 mi N on US 19/98, then 6 mi W on FL 320. Phone 352/493-6072.

Annual Event

Watermelon Festival. Watermelon-eating & seed-spitting contests, parade, beauty contest, watermelon auction. 3rd Sat June.

Clearwater (E-3)

(See also Clearwater Beach, Dunedin, St Petersburg, Tampa, Tarpon Springs)

Settled 1842 **Pop** 98,784 **Elev** 24 ft **Area code** 813 **Zip** 33767 **Web** www.clearwaterflorida.org
Information Greater Clearwater Chamber of Commerce, 1130 Cleveland St, PO Box 2457, 33757, phone 813/461-0011; or the St Petersburg/Clearwater Area Convention & Visitors Bureau, 14450 46th St N, 34622, phone 800/951-1111.

Clearwater is a tourist city that has retained its quiet ways under pressure of rapid population growth. The town is the seat of Pinellas County and has numerous light industries.

What to See and Do

Boatyard Village. Shops and restaurants in 1890s-style fishing village. (Daily) 16100 Fairchild Dr. Phone 813/535-4678.

Florida Gulf Coast Art Center. Regional and national exhibits; school. (Daily; may be closed between shows) 222 Ponce de Leon Blvd in Belleair. Phone 813/584-8634. **Free.**

Florida Orchestra concerts. Classical and pops performances. (Sept-May) Ruth Eckerd Hall & Tampa Bay Performing Arts Center. Phone 800/662-7286 or 813/286-2403 (Tampa).

Heritage Park. Historical museum and 21-acre village with 22 historic structures. Changing displays; seasonal craft demonstrations. (Tues-Sat, also Sun afternoons; closed some major hols) S via US 19, then 5 mi W via FL 688 at 11909 125th St N in Largo. Phone 813/582-2123. **Donation.**

Moccasin Lake Nature Park. An environmental and energy education center consisting of 50-acre wilderness preserve; nature trails and boardwalks (1 1/4 mi); native wildlife and plant exhibits; alternative energy displays. Guided tours (by appt; fee). Special programs (fee). (Daily exc Mon; closed Jan 1, July 4, Thanksgiving, Dec 25) 2750 Park Trail Lane. Phone 813/462-6024. **¢**

Sightseeing.

Clearwater Ferry Service. Water taxi to Clearwater Beach, Caladesi Island; special tours to Tarpon Springs (Tues-Sat; res required); dolphin encounter cruises avail. (Daily exc Mon) W end of Drew St and Clearwater Marina. Phone 813/442-7433. Taxi to beach **¢**;   Tarpon Springs tour (includes lunch) **¢¢¢¢¢**;   other tours **¢¢¢-¢¢¢¢¢**

Gray Line bus tours. Contact PO Box 145, St Pettersburg 33731; 813/535-0208.

Annual Events

Fun 'n Sun Festival. Pageant, parade, city-wide festivities mark end of winter season. 10 days Apr-May.

Jazz Holiday. Coachman Park. One of the Southeast's largest free jazz festivals. 3rd wkend Oct.

Seasonal Event

Spring training. Jack Russell Memorial Stadium, 800 Phillies Dr. Philadelphia Phillies baseball spring training, exhibition games. Phone 813/441-8638. Early Mar-early Apr.

Motels

★★ **BAY QUEEN.** *1925 Edgewater Dr (33755).* 727/441-3295. 18 units, 16 kits. Mid-Dec-late Apr: S, D $58-$70; each addl $5; kit. units $370-$395/wk; lower rates rest of yr. Crib free. TV. Pool. Restaurant nearby. Ck-out 11 am. Lawn games. Refrigerators. Overlooks Clearwater Bay. Cr cds: MC, V.

★★ **BEST WESTERN-CLEARWATER CENTRAL.** *21338 US 19N (33765),* 1 blk N of FL 60. 727/799-1565; FAX 727/797-6801. 150 rms, 2 story. Feb-mid-Apr: S, D $75-$85; each addl $5; under 12 free; lower rates rest of yr. Crib free. TV; cable (premium). Heated pool; whirlpool. Coffee in rms. Restaurant nearby. Ck-out noon. Coin lndry. Meeting rm. Business servs avail. Tennis. Lawn games. Some refrigerators. Cr cds: A, C, D, DS, MC, V.

★★ **COURTYARD BY MARRIOTT.** *3131 Executive Dr (33762),* off FL 688. 727/572-8484; FAX 727/572-6991. Web www.marriott.com. 149 rms, 3 story. Jan-June: S, D $125-$145; under 18 free; wkend rates; lower rates rest of yr. Crib free. TV; cable (premium). Heated pool; whirlpool. Complimentary coffee in rms. Restaurant nearby. Ck-out noon. Coin lndry. Meeting rms. Business servs avail. In-rm modem link. Valet serv (Mon-Fri). Exercise equipt. Health club privileges. Some refrigerators; microwaves avail. Cr cds: A, C, D, DS, MC, V.

✔★ **EDGEWATER DRIVE.** *1919 Edgewater Dr (33755).* 727/446-7858. 22 rms, 1-2 story, 12 kits. Jan-Apr: S, D $58-$75; each addl $5; kit. units $385-$425/wk; some wkend rates; lower rates rest of yr. Crib $5. TV. Pool. Restaurant 7 am-12:30 pm. Ck-out 11 am (kit. units 10 am). Refrigerators; microwaves avail. Private fishing dock. On Clearwater Bay. Cr cds: MC, V.

✔★ **HAMPTON INN.** *3655 Hospitality Lane (33762),* at Ulmerton Rd (FL 688), 2 mi E of US 19. 727/577-9200; FAX 727/572-8931. Web clwatmindspring.com. 18 rms, 2 story. S, D $65-$85; under 18 free. Crib free. TV; cable (premium). Pool; whirlpool. Complimentary continental bkfst. Restaurant nearby. Ck-out noon. Coin lndry. Meeting rm. Business servs avail. In-rm modem link. Lighted tennis. Exercise equipt; sauna. Health club privileges. Cr cds: A, C, D, DS, MC, V.

✔★ **HAMPTON INN.** *21030 US 19 N (33765).* 727/797-8173; FAX 727/791-7759. 158 rms, 2 story, 22 kit. units. Feb-Apr: S $80-$95; D $86-$101; each addl $6; kit. units $95-$101; under 18 free; lower rates rest of yr. Crib free. TV; cable (premium), VCR avail. Complimentary continental bkfst. Complimentary coffee in rms. Restaurant nearby. Ck-out noon. Meeting rms. Business center. Sundries. Gift shop. Coin lndry. Exercise equipt; sauna. Pool; wading pool, whirlpool. Wet bar in kit. units. Many balconies. Cr cds: A, C, D, DS, JCB, MC, V.

★★ **HOLIDAY INN BAYSIDE.** *20967 US 19N (33765).* 727/799-1181; FAX 727/712-8404. 148 rms, 3 with shower only, 3 story, 91 suites. Jan-Apr: S, D $83.95-$94.95; suites $119.95; under 18 free; lower rates rest of yr. Crib free. TV; cable (premium). Heated pool; whirlpool, wading pool, poolside serv. Playground. Complimentary coffee in rms. Restaurant 6:30 am-2 pm, 5-10 pm. Rm serv. Bar 4 pm-1 am; entertainment Fri, Sat. Ck-out noon. Coin lndry. Meeting rms. Business servs avail. In-rm modem link. Valet serv. Gift shop. Exercise equipt; sauna. Health club privileges. Refrigerator, microwave in suites. Some balconies. Cr cds: A, C, D, DS, JCB, MC, V.

★★ **HOLIDAY INN EXPRESS.** *13625 ICOT Blvd (33760),* in ICOT Ctr. 727/536-7275; FAX 727/530-3053. E-mail holidayexpress@travelbase.com. 127 rms, 3 story, 26 suites. S, D $95-$100; each addl $5; suites $100-$110; under 18 free. Crib free. Pet accepted, some restrictions. TV; cable (premium), VCR avail. Heated pool; whirlpool. Complimentary continental bkfst. Restaurant opp 11 am-11 pm. Ck-out noon. Meeting rms. Business servs avail. In-rm modem link. Health club privileges. Bathrm phones. Cr cds: A, C, D, DS, ER, JCB, MC, V.

★ **KNIGHTS INN.** *(34106 US 19N, Palm Harbor 34684)* N on US 19, 1 blk S of Nebraska Ave. 727/789-2002; FAX 727/784-6206. 114 rms. Jan-Apr: S, D $69.95-$79.97; under 18 free; wkly rates; lower rates rest of yr. Crib avail. Pet accepted, some restrictions; $5/day. TV; cable (premium). Heated pool. Coffee in rm. Restaurant adj 7 am-8 pm. Ck-out 11 am. Lndry facilities. Meeting rm. Business servs avail. Cr cds: A, C, D, DS, MC, V.

⊡ ⊬ ≋ ⊠ ⊼ SC

★ ★ **LA QUINTA.** 3301 Ulmerton Rd (33762), off I-275 at FL 688 exit, near St Petersburg/Clearwater Intl Airport. 727/572-7222; FAX 727/572-0076. Web www.laquinta.com. 115 units. Jan-May: S, D $99; suites $105; under 18 free; lower rates rest of yr. Crib free. Pet accepted, some restrictions. Heated pool; whirlpool. Coffee in rms. Restaurant adj 6 am-10 pm. Ck-out noon. Coin lndry. Meeting rms. Business servs avail. In-rm modem link. Valet serv Mon-Fri. Free airport transportation. Exercise equipt; sauna. Refrigerators; microwaves avail. Cr cds: A, C, D, DS, MC, V.

⊡ ⊬ ≋ ⊼ ✈ ⊠ ⊼ SC

★ ★ ★ **RESIDENCE INN BY MARRIOTT.** 5050 Ulmerton Rd (33760), at 49th St, 1 mi E of US 19 on FL 688. 727/573-4444; FAX 727/572-4446. Web www.marriott.com. 88 kit. suites, 2 story. Kit. suites $129-$189; under 18 free. Pet accepted, some restrictions; $125 & $250 deposit. TV; cable (premium). Heated pool; whirlpool. Complimentary continental bkfst. Ck-out noon. Coin lndry. Meeting rm. Business servs avail. In-rm modem link. Valet serv. Health club privileges. Lawn games. Microwaves, fireplaces. Some private patios, balconies. Grill. Cr cds: A, C, D, DS, JCB, MC, V.

⊡ ⊬ ≋ ⊠ ⊼ SC

Motor Hotels

★ ★ **COMFORT INN.** 3580 Ulmerton Rd (34622), near St Petersburg/Clearwater Intl Airport. 727/573-1171; FAX 727/572-8736. 120 rms, 3 story. Mid-Jan-Apr: S, D $89-$109; suites $99-$119; under 18 free; wkly rates; higher rates special events; lower rates rest of yr. Crib free. TV; cable. Heated pool; whirlpool. Complimentary continental bkfst. Restaurant adj 11-1 am. Ck-out noon. Guest lndry. Meeting rm. In-rm modem link. Bellhops. Sundries. Free airport transportation. Health club privileges. Refrigerators, microwaves avail. Cr cds: A, C, D, DS, JCB, MC, V.

⊡ ≋ ✈ ⊠ ⊼ SC

★ ★ ★ **HOLIDAY INN SELECT.** 3535 Ulmerton Rd (33762), on FL 688 (Ulmerton Rd), near St Petersburg/Clearwater Intl Airport. 727/577-9100; FAX 727/573-5022. E-mail clwap2@aol.com; web www.hiselect.com/fla/clwapt. 174 rms, 5 story. S, D $99-$130; each addl $10; under 18 free; some wkend rates. Crib free. TV; cable (premium), VCR avail. Pool; whirlpool. Restaurant 6 am-11 pm. Rm serv. Bar 2 pm-1:30 am; entertainment Tues-Sat. Ck-out noon. Coin lndry. Meeting rms. Business center. In-rm modem link. Bellhops. Gift shop. Free airport transportation. Lighted tennis. Exercise equipt. Health club privileges. Refrigerators, microwaves avail. Luxury level. Cr cds: A, C, D, DS, ER, JCB, MC, V.

⊡ ⊬ ≋ ⊼ ✈ ⊠ ⊼ SC ⊼

★ ★ **RAMADA INN COUNTRYSIDE.** 26508 US 19N (33761), opp Countryside Mall. 727/796-1234; FAX 727/796-0452. 125 rms, 5 story. Feb-mid-Apr: S, D $89-$99; each addl $10; kit. units, suites $109; under 18 free; wkend rates; lower rates rest of yr. Crib free. TV; cable (premium). Pool; whirlpool. Coffee in rms. Restaurant 6:30 am-2 pm, 5-10 pm. Bar 5 pm-midnight. Ck-out noon. Coin lndry. Meeting rm. Business servs avail. In-rm modem link. Valet serv. Lighted tennis. Health club privileges. In-rm whirlpools; microwaves avail. Some private patios, balconies. Cr cds: A, C, D, DS, ER, JCB, MC, V.

⊡ ⊬ ≋ ⊠ ⊼ SC

Resorts

★ ★ ★ **BELLEVIEW BILTMORE RESORT & SPA.** 25 Belleview Blvd (33756). 727/442-6171; res: 800/237-8947; FAX 727/441-4173. Web www.belleviewbiltmore.com. 292 rms, 4 story. Mid-Jan-Apr: S, D $190-$260; each addl $20; suites $260-$450; MAP $45 addl per person; lower rates rest of yr. Crib free. TV; cable. Heated pools; whirlpool, poolside serv. Playground. Dining rm 7 am-10 pm. Bars 11-1 am; Sun 1 pm-midnight;

entertainment Fri, Sat (seasonal). Ck-out noon. Convention facilities. Business center. In-rm modem link. Valet serv. Specialty shops. 4 clay tennis courts, pro. 18-hole golf, pro, putting greens. Bicycles avail. Lawn games. Exercise rm; sauna, steam rm. Massage. Minibars; some refrigerators. Dock, 4 boat slips. Cr cds: A, C, D, DS, JCB, MC, V.

⊡ ⊬ ⊳ ⊼ ≋ ⊼ ⊠ ⊼ SC ⊼

★ ★ ★ **SAFETY HARBOR RESORT AND SPA.** (105 N Bayshore Dr, Safety Harbor 34695) 2 mi N of FL 60. 727/726-1161; FAX 727/726-4268. E-mail safety.harbor@ssrc.com; web www.southsea.com. 192 rms, 3-6 story. Feb-mid-Apr: S, D $139-$189; each addl $20; AP avail; under 13 free; special rates hols; lower rates rest of yr. Crib free. Pet accepted, some restrictions. TV; cable (premium). 3 heated pools; 2 whirlpools. Complimentary continental bkfst. Dining rm 7-10 am, 11:30 am-10 pm; Sun brunch 10:30 am-3 pm. Rm serv. Bar. Guest lndry. Meeting rms. Business center. Valet serv. Bellhops. Concierge. Shopping arcade. Barber, beauty shops. Tennis, pro. 18-hole golf, pro. Bicycles. Lawn games. 300-seat theater. Exercise rm. Spa. Four mineral springs. Cr cds: A, C, D, DS, ER, JCB, MC, V.

⊡ ⊬ ⊳ ⊼ ≋ ⊼ ⊠ ⊼ ⊼

Restaurants

★ ★ ★ **ALFANO'S.** 1702 Clearwater/Largo Rd (33756). 727/584-2125. Hrs: 11:30 am-3 pm, 5-10 pm; Fri, Sat 5-11 pm; Sun 4-9:30 pm; early-bird dinner 5-6 pm. Closed most major hols. Res accepted. Italian menu. Bar. Extensive wine list. Complete meals: lunch $6.75-$9.95, dinner $8.95-$21.95. Child's meals. Specialties: Caesar salad, veal sacco, roast duckling amaretto. Pianist Mon-Wed, Fri-Sat; jazz Wed. Outdoor dining. Mediterranean formal atmosphere. Cr cds: A, C, D, DS, MC, V.

⊡ ⊐

★ ★ **E & E STAKEOUT GRILL.** (100 N Indian Rocks Rd, Belleair Bluffs 33770) in Plaza 100 Shopping Center. 727/585-6399. Hrs: 11:30 am-10 pm; Fri to 10:30 pm; Sat 4-10:30 pm; Sun 4-10 pm. Res accepted. Southwestern menu. Bar. Complete meals: lunch $4-$17.50, dinner $5.50-$24.75. Child's meals. Specialties: rack of lamb, rodeo steak. Southwestern decor. Cr cds: A, C, D, DS, MC, V.

⊡ ⊐

★ ★ **FORBIDDEN CITY.** 25778 US 19N (33763). 727/797-8989. Hrs: 11:30 am-10 pm; Fri to 11 pm; Sat 4-11 pm; early-bird dinner 3:30-6 pm. Res accepted. Chinese menu. Bar. A la carte entrees: lunch $4.95-$6.35, dinner $8.95-$25. Buffet: lunch $5.95. Specialties: Peking duck, cashew chicken, pan-fried dumpling. Pianist Fri-Sat. Parking. Large imported Chinese wood carving. Cr cds: A, D, DS, MC, V.

⊡ ⊐

★ ★ **GRILL AT FEATHER SOUND.** 2325 Ulmerton Rd (33762). 727/571-3400. Web www.thegrillatfeathersound.com. Hrs: 11:30 am-10 pm; Fri to 11 pm; Sat 5:30-11 pm. Closed Sun; most major hols. Res accepted. Bar. Semi-a la carte: lunch $6.95-$11.95, dinner $18.95-$28.95. Child's meals. Specializes in steak, fresh seafood. Valet parking. Outdoor dining. Contemporary decor. Cr cds: A, C, D, DS, MC, V.

⊡ ⊐

★ ★ **KEY WEST GRILL.** 2660 Gulf-to-Bay Blvd (FL 60) (33759). 727/797-1988. Hrs: 11:30 am-10 pm; Fri, Sat to 11 pm. Closed Thanksgiving, Dec 25. Semi-a la carte: lunch $4.99-$6.29, dinner $5.99-$26.99. Child's meals. Specializes in barbecued ribs, fresh fish, stone crab (in season). Parking. Outdoor dining. Key West atmosphere. Cr cds: A, D, DS, MC, V.

⊡

★ **LA TOUR EIFFEL.** (796 Indian Rocks Rd, Belleair Bluffs 33770) FL Alt 19S to West Bay Dr, then right on Indian Rocks Rd. 727/581-6530. Hrs: 11 am-2 pm, 5-9 pm; Sat, Sun brunch 9 am-2 pm. Closed Mon; most major hols. Res accepted. French menu. Wine, beer. A la carte entrees: lunch $3.75-$6.25, dinner $10.95-$15.95. Sun brunch $4.45-$7.45. Specialties: crêpes, filet au poivre, coquilles St-Jacques. Parking. Romantic Parisian atmosphere. Cr cds: DS, MC, V.

⊡ ♥

★ ★ ★ **MARCO POLO.** *2516 McMullen Booth Rd (33761), in Northwoods Shopping Plaza. 727/791-7979.* Hrs: 11 am-10 pm; Sun noon-9 pm. Closed Memorial Day. Res accepted. International menu. Bar. Wine list. Semi-a la carte: lunch $3.95-$7.95, dinner $5.95-$16.95. Child's meals. Specializes in black Angus steak, fresh seafood. Entertainment Wed. Elegant dining rms. Cr cds: A, C, D, DS, ER, JCB, MC, V.

[D] [⌐]

✔ ★ **PANDA.** *1201 Cleveland St (33755), in Cleveland Plaza Shopping Ctr. 727/447-3830.* Hrs: 11:30 am-10 pm; Fri, Sat to 11 pm; Sun from 5 pm. Closed Thanksgiving, Dec 25. Res accepted. Chinese menu. Bar. A la carte entrees: lunch $3.35-$4.50, dinner $3.75-$12.50. Specializes in Szechuan and Mandarin dishes. Carved entrance archway of Chinese cypress. Cr cds: A, DS, MC, V.

[D] [⌐]

★ **PEKING PALACE.** *1608 Gulf-to-Bay Blvd (FL 60) (33755). 727/461-4414.* Hrs: 11:30 am-10 pm; Fri to 11 pm; Sat 4:30-11 pm; Sun from noon; early-bird dinner 3-6 pm. Closed Thanksgiving. Res accepted. Chinese menu. Bar. A la carte entrees: lunch $4.25-$4.99, dinner $6.25-$19.95. Specialties: Peking duck, orange chicken. Parking. Cr cds: A, D, DS, MC, V.

[D] [⌐]

★ ★ **PEPPER MILL.** *1575 S Fort Harrison Ave (33756). 727/449-2988.* Hrs: 11:30 am-2:30 pm, 4:30-10 pm; Sun 4-9 pm. Closed Jan 1. Res accepted. Bar. Complete meals: lunch $3.75-$8, dinner $8.95-$21. Child's meals. Specialties: Maryland crab cakes, Pepper Mill NY steak. Parking. Garden rm dining. High wood-beamed ceiling; panoramic view. Cr cds: A, D, MC, V.

[D] [⌐]

★ ★ **SUKHOTHAI.** *2569 Countryside Blvd (33761). 727/724-2995.* Hrs: 11 am-10 pm; Sat, Sun from 5 pm. Closed Memorial Day, Thanksgiving, Dec 25. Res accepted. Thai menu. Wine list. Semi-a la carte: lunch $4.95-$6.95. A la carte entrees: dinner $5.95-$19.95. Specialties: pad Thai, Sukhothai duck, lobster nam dang. Thai decor. Cr cds: A, C, D, DS, MC, V.

[D] [SC]

Clearwater Beach (E-3)

(See also Clearwater, Dunedin, St Petersburg, Tampa, Tarpon Springs)

Elev 24 ft **Area code** 813 **Zip** 33767 **Web** www.clearwaterflorida.org

Information Greater Clearwater Chamber of Commerce, 1130 Cleveland St, PO Box 2457, Clearwater 33757, phone 813/461-0011; or the St Petersburg/Clearwater Area Convention & Visitors Bureau, 14450 46th St N, Clearwater, 34622, phone 800/951-1111.

This four-mile-long island of white sand beaches is connected to the mainland by Memorial Causeway. The beach extends the full length of the island and is between 350 and 1,700 feet wide. There is a fishing pier, and the marina has slips, docks, boat rentals, sailing and a sport fishing fleet. Skin diving and shelling are also popular activities.

What to See and Do

Clearwater Marine Aquarium. One of two facilities on Florida's west coast equipped for the rescue and treatment of marine mammals and sea turtles. Visitors watch progress and feeding of recuperating sea turtles. Research laboratories and educational programs. (Daily; closed major hols) 249 Windward Passage, off Memorial Causeway. Phone 813/441-1790. ¢¢

Sightseeing Cruises.

Starlight Majesty Dinner Boat. Triple-deck, 100-ft, 400-passenger cruiser provides luncheon/sightseeing and dinner/dance cruises. Two departures (daily exc Mon). Clearwater Beach Marina. Phone 813/462-2628 or 800/444-4814. ¢¢¢-¢¢¢¢¢

Captain Memo's Pirate Ship Cruise. Pirate ship sails through the Intracoastal Waterway into the Gulf of Mexico on two-hr cruises. Free refreshments. Three departures (daily). Clearwater Beach Marina. Phone 813/446-2587. ¢¢¢¢¢

Sunsets at Pier 60. Artists, performers and musicians celebrate the setting of the sun two hrs before and after sunset. Pier 60 Park. **Free.**

Motels

✔ ★ **AEGEAN SANDS.** *421 S Gulfview Blvd, on Clearwater Beach. 727/447-3464; FAX 727/446-7169; res: 800/942-3432.* E-mail info@travelbase.com; web www.travelbase.com/aegean. 68 rms, 4 story, 57 kits. Feb-Apr: S, D $60-$145; each addl $10; kit. units $70-$145; lower rates rest of yr. Crib $7. Pet accepted, some restrictions; $25. TV. Heated pool. Ck-out noon. Coin lndry. Business servs avail. Gift shop. Sundries. Lawn games. Refrigerators. Many balconies. Beach opp. Cr cds: A, D, DS, MC, V.

[🐾] [≈] [🔥] [SC]

★ **BEACH PLACE.** *301 S Gulfview. 727/442-6714; FAX 727/446-8944; res: 800/393-2978.* E-mail andrea@gate.net. 18 kit. units, 3 with shower only, 2 story, 6 suites. Feb-mid-Apr: kit. units $69-$82; suites $89-$109; lower rates rest of yr. Crib $5. TV; cable. Pool. Complimentary coffee in rms. Restaurant nearby. Ck-out 11 am. Meeting rm. Business servs avail. Refrigerators, microwaves. Picnic tables. Opp beach. Cr cds: MC, V.

[≈] [🔥] [SC]

★ ★ **THE BEACHOUSE.** *421 Hamden Dr. 727/461-4862; FAX 727/442-4494.* 6 rms, 2 with shower only, 5 kit. suites. Jan-Apr 15: S, D, kit. suites $85-$185; 3-day min wkends, hols; lower rates rest of yr. TV; cable. Pool; whirlpool. Restaurant adj 7 am-10 pm. Ck-out 10 am. Refrigerators, microwaves. Modern decor; view of bay. Totally nonsmoking. Cr cds: MC, V.

[≈] [🏊] [🔥]

★ **BELLEAIR BEACH RESORT.** *(2040 Gulf Blvd, Belleair Beach 33786) N on Gulf Blvd. 727/595-1696; FAX 727/593-5433; res: 800/780-1696.* E-mail belleair@gte.net; web www.belleairbeachresort.com. 43 rms, 2 story, 29 kits. Mid-Jan-Apr: S, D $69-$77; each addl $5; kits. $84-$115; under 5 free; lower rates rest of yr. Crib free. TV; cable. Heated pool. Complimentary coffee in lobby. Ck-out 11 am. Coin lndry. Lawn games. Refrigerators. On beach. Cr cds: A, DS, MC, V.

[🐦] [≈]

★ ★ **BEST WESTERN SEASTONE RESORT.** *445 Hamden Dr, at S Gulfview Blvd. 727/441-1722; FAX 727/461-1680.* Web www.bestwestern.com. 106 rms, 5-6 story. Mid-Feb-Apr: S, D $99-$129; each addl $10; kit. suites $179-$199; under 18 free; lower rates rest of yr. Crib free. TV; cable, VCR avail. Heated pool; whirlpool. Supervised child's activities (mid-June-mid-Aug); ages 5-12. Coffee in rms. Restaurant 7-11 am. Ck-out noon. Coin lndry. Meeting rms. Business servs avail. In-rm modem link. Beauty shop. Refrigerators. Microwave in suites. Opp beach, marina. Sun deck. Cr cds: A, C, D, DS, JCB, MC, V.

[D] [🐦] [≈] [🔥] [SC]

★ **CLEARWATER BEACH RESORT.** *678 S Gulfview Blvd. 727/441-3767; FAX 727/449-2701; res: 800/334-3767.* 42 kit. units, 3 story. No elvtr. Mid-Feb-Apr: kit. units $105-$155; wkly, monthly rates; lower rates rest of yr. Crib free. TV; cable (premium). Heated pool; whirlpool. Complimentary coffee in lobby. Restaurant adj 7 am-11 pm. Ck-out 11 am. Free lndry facilities. Business servs avail. Lighted tennis. Lawn games. Covered parking. Microwaves. Balconies. Picnic tables, grills. Cr cds: A, C, D, DS, MC, V.

[🎿] [≈] [🔥] [SC]

★ ★ **EAST SHORE RESORT.** *473 E Shore Dr. 727/442-3636; FAX 727/449-8302.* E-mail clrwmotel@aol.com; web www.simplicity.new/business/eastshore. 12 kit. units, 1 with shower only, 2 story. Mid-Dec-Apr: kit. units $75-$108; each addl $10; wkly rates; lower rates rest of yr. Crib free. TV; cable, VCR avail. Restaurant nearby. Ck-out 10 am.

Business servs avail. Guest lndry. Pool. Refrigerators. Many bathrm phones. Picnic tables, grills. Some balconies. Opp beach. Cr cds: DS, MC, V.

[D] [⟶] [≈] [⚲]

★ ★ **ECONO LODGE.** *625 S Gulfview Blvd. 727/446-3400; FAX 727/446-4615.* E-mail GJasmin826@aol.com; web www.clearwater beachecono.com. 64 kit. units, 5 story. Feb-Apr: $100-$159; under 18 free; lower rates rest of yr. Crib free. TV; cable. Heated pool; whirlpool. Complimentary coffee in lobby. Ck-out 11 am. Business servs avail. In-rm modem link. Guest lndry. Balconies. Picnic tables, grill. On beach. Cr cds: A, C, D, DS, JCB, MC, V.

[D] [≈] [≈] [⚲] [SC]

✔ ★ **FALCON.** *415 Coronado Dr. 727/447-8714; FAX 727/461-3735; res: 800/411-1977.* E-mail edzia@gate.net. 19 rms, 4 with shower only, 2 story, 7 suites, 16 kit. units. Early Feb-Mar: S, D $60-$82; each addl $8; suites, kit. units $66-$82; under 10 free; lower rates rest of yr. Crib free. TV; cable, VCR avail. Pool. Playground. Restaurant opp 7-2 am. Ck-out 10 am. Lawn games. Refrigerators; microwaves avail. Balconies. Cr cds: A, DS, MC, V.

[≈] [⚲] [⚲]

★ ★ **HOWARD JOHNSON EXPRESS INN.** *656 Bayway Blvd. 727/442-6606; FAX 727/461-0809.* 40 units, 2 story. Feb-Apr: S, D $79-$99; each addl $10; under 18 free; lower rates rest of yr. Crib free. TV; cable. Heated pool. Complimentary continental bkfst. Ck-out 11 am. Coin lndry. Some refrigerators, microwaves. Cr cds: A, C, D, DS, MC, V.

[⟶] [≈] [≈] [⚲] [SC]

✔ ★ **NEW YORKER.** *332 Hamden Dr, at Brightwater Dr. 727/446-2437; FAX 727/446-5818.* E-mail mijaae@aol.com; web www.internet-ad.com/newyorker. 15 kit. units, 2 story. Feb-Apr: S, D $75-$87; each addl $6; lower rates rest of yr. TV; cable. Heated pool. Restaurant nearby. Ck-out 10 am. Lndry facilities. Refrigerators, microwaves. Grills. Cr cds: A, DS, MC, V.

[≈] [⚲] [SC]

★ ★ **SEA CAPTAIN RESORT.** *40 Devon Dr. 727/446-7550; FAX 727/298-0100; res: 800/444-7488.* Web www.internet.com/pages/seacaptain. 27 rms, 2 story, 23 kits. Mid-Feb-Apr: S, D $68-$77; each addl $8; kit. units $84-$95; 1-bedrm apts $105-$125; under 13 free; lower rates rest of yr. Crib free. TV; cable. Heated pool. Complimentary coffee. Restaurant nearby. Ck-out 11 am. Business servs avail. Lawn games. Microwaves. Picnic tables, grills. On bay; dockage, fishing dock. Totally nonsmoking. Cr cds: A, DS, MC, V.

[⟶] [≈] [⚲] [⚲]

✔ ★ ★ **TROPICAL BREEZE.** *333 Hamden Dr. 727/442-6865; res: 888/530-1088; FAX 727/443-4371.* Web www.tropicalbreeze.clearwater beach.com. 20 units, 2 story, 16 kits. Feb-late Apr: S, D $73-$85; each addl $8; wkly rates; lower rates rest of yr. Crib free. TV; cable. Heated pool. Restaurant nearby. Ck-out 10 am. Coin lndry. Business servs avail. Sundries. Lawn games. Refrigerators, microwaves. On bay. Cr cds: A, DS, MC, V.

[⟶] [≈] [⚲] [SC]

★ **VIKING.** *124 Brightwater Dr. 727/441-3001; FAX 727/441-3001.* 7 kit. units. No rm phones. Feb-Apr: S, D $48-$90; each addl $8; wkly rates. Crib free. TV. Restaurant nearby. Ck-out 10 am. Shuffleboard. Whirlpool. Microwaves. Picnic tables. On waterfront. Totally nonsmoking. Cr cds: MC, V.

[⟶] [⚲] [≈]

Motor Hotels

★ ★ **BEST WESTERN SEA WAKE INN.** *691 S Gulfview Blvd. 727/443-7652; res: 888/329-8910; FAX 727/461-2836.* Web www.bestwestern.com. 110 rms, 6 story, 50 kits. Mid Feb-Apr: S, D $130-$275; each addl $10; kit. units $140-$235; under 18 free; lower rates rest of yr. Crib

free. TV; cable (premium). Heated pool. Playground. Free supervised child's activities (mid-June-mid-Aug); ages 5-12. Coffee in rms. Restaurant 7 am-8 pm. Rm serv. Bar noon-11 pm; Sun 1-10 pm. Ck-out noon. Meeting rm. Business servs avail. Balconies. On beach. Cr cds: A, C, D, DS, JCB, MC, V.

[D] [≈] [⚲] [⚲] [SC]

★ ★ ★ **CLEARWATER BEACH HOTEL.** *500 Mandalay Ave. 727/441-2425; FAX 727/449-2083; res: 800/292-2295.* Web www.clearwaterbeachhotel.com. 180 rms, 2-6 story, 42 suites, 99 kits. Feb-Apr: S, D, kit. units $145-$180; suites $189-$240; lower rates rest of yr. Crib free. TV; cable; VCR avail. Heated pool; poolside serv. Restaurant 7 am-10:30 pm. Rm serv. Bar 10-2 am; entertainment. Ck-out noon. Meeting rms. Business servs avail. Bellhops. Valet serv. Sundries. Free covered parking; valet. Lighted tennis privileges. 36-hole golf privileges, pro. Health club privileges. Lawn games. Refrigerators. Balconies. On gulf; beach. Cr cds: A, C, D, MC, V.

[D] [🏃] [⟶] [≈] [⚲]

★ ★ **QUALITY INN BEACH RESORT.** *655 S Gulfview Blvd. 727/442-7171; res: 800/228-5151; FAX 727/446-7177.* Web www.qualityinn/hotel/fl815. 91 rms, 5 story. Early Feb-Apr: S, D $145-$175; each addl $10-$20; under 17 free; lower rates rest of yr. Crib free. TV; cable (premium). Heated pool. Complimentary coffee in rms. Restaurant open 24 hrs. Bar 11 am-midnight; Sun from 1 pm. Ck-out 11 am. Coin lndry. Valet serv. Business servs avail. In-rm modem link. Health club privileges. Refrigerators, microwaves. Private patios, balconies. Private beach. Cr cds: A, C, D, DS, MC, V.

[D] [≈] [⚲] [⚲] [SC]

★ ★ ★ **RAMADA INN GULFVIEW.** *521 S Gulfview Blvd. 727/447-6461; res: 800/770-6461; FAX 727/443-5888.* Web www.ramada.com. 289 rms, 7-9 story. Mid-Feb-May: S, D $129.50-$179.50; each addl $10; under 18 free; lower rates rest of yr. Crib free. TV; cable. Heated pool; wading pool. Restaurant open 24 hrs. Rm serv. Bar noon-1:30 am; entertainment. Ck-out 11 am. Meeting rms. Business servs avail. In-rm modem link. Bellhops. Valet serv. Sundries. Barber, beauty shop. Game rm. Balconies. On Gulf. Cr cds: A, C, D, DS, ER, JCB, MC, V.

[D] [≈] [⚲] [⚲] [SC]

★ **SPYGLASS.** *215 S Gulfview Blvd. 727/446-8317; res: 800/942-3432; FAX 727/446-7169.* Web www.travelbase.com/aegean. 91 rms, 9 story, 12 suites, 79 kit. units. Feb-mid-Apr: S, D $70; each addl $7; suites $80-$90; kit. units $105-$145; under 18 free; wkly rates; hols (3-day min); lower rates rest of yr. Crib $7. Pet accepted; $25. TV; cable. Restaurant adj 8 am-10 pm. Ck-out noon. In-rm modem link. Sundries. Gift shop. Coin lndry. Pools. Microwaves avail. Many balconies. On beach. Cr cds: A, C, D, DS, MC, V.

[⟶] [≈] [⚲] [SC]

Hotels

★ ★ **ADAM'S MARK RESORT.** *430 S Gulfview Blvd. 727/443-5714; FAX 727/442-8389; res: 800/444-2326.* Web www.adamsmark.com. 207 rms, 6 suites, 14 story. Feb-Apr: S, D $139-$209; suites $195-$400; under 18 free; lower rates rest of yr. Crib free. Covered parking (fee). TV; cable, VCR avail. Heated pool; wading pool, whirlpool, poolside serv. Restaurant 7 am-10 pm. Bar 11-2 am; entertainment. Ck-out 11 am. Coin lndry. Meeting rms. Business servs avail. Gift shop. Golf privileges. Health club privileges. Private patios, balconies. On Gulf. Cr cds: A, C, D, DS, MC, V.

[D] [🏃] [≈] [⚲] [⚲] [SC]

★ ★ ★ **HILTON.** *400 Mandalay Ave, at jct FL 60. 727/461-3222; FAX 727/461-0610.* Web www.hilton.com. 426 rms, 9 story. Jan-Apr: S, D $119-$220; each addl $10; suites $350-$525; under 18 free; lower rates rest of yr. Crib free. TV; cable. 2 heated pools. Supervised child's activities. Coffee in rms. Restaurants 6:30 am-10 pm. Bars 11-2 am; entertainment. Ck-out 11 am. Coin lndry. Convention facilities. Business center. In-rm modem link. Concierge. Shopping arcade. Game rm. Exercise equipt.

Microwaves avail. Balconies. Cabanas. On 10½-acre beach. Cr cds: A, C, D, DS, ER, JCB, MC, V.

⊡ 🏊 ✕ 🏋 🎿 SC 🚶

★ ★ ★ **HOLIDAY INN SUNSPREE.** *715 S Gulfview Blvd.* *727/447-9566; FAX 727/446-4978.* 205 rms, 2-9 story. Mid-Feb-Apr: S, D $129-$179; each addl $10; suites $310-$425; under 19 free; lower rates rest of yr. Crib free. TV; cable (premium). Heated pool; wading pool, poolside serv. Playground. Supervised child's activities; ages 4-12. Coffee in rms. Restaurant 6:30 am-1 pm, 5-10 pm. Bars 11 am-midnight; Sun from 1 pm. Ck-out 11 am. Meeting rms. Business servs avail. In-rm modem link. Concierge. Gift shop. Golf privileges. Exercise rm. Game rm. Lawn games. Refrigerators. Some balconies. Private beach. Cr cds: A, C, D, DS, ER, MC, V.

🏋 🏊 ✕ 🏋 🎿 SC

★ ★ ★ **RADISSON SUITE RESORT ON SAND KEY.** *1201 Gulf Blvd.* *727/596-1100; FAX 727/595-4292.* Web www.internet-ad.com/ radisson. 220 suites, 10 story. Feb-Apr: S, D $189-$269; under 18 free; wkly rates; lower rates rest of yr. Crib avail. TV; cable (premium), VCR avail. Pool; whirlpool, poolside serv. Playground. Supervised child's activities; ages 4-12. Complimentary coffee, tea in rms. Restaurants 6:30 am-11 pm. Bars 11-1 am; entertainment Tues-Sat. Ck-out noon. Coin lndry. Meeting rms. Business servs avail. In-rm modem link. Concierge. Shopping arcade. Barber, beauty shop. Free valet parking. Tennis privileges. Golf privileges. Exercise equipt; sauna. Massage. Health club privileges. Rec rm. Refrigerators, microwaves, wet bars. On bay. Cr cds: A, C, D, DS, ER, JCB, MC, V.

⊡ 🏋 🎿 🏊 ✕ 🏋 🎿 SC

★ ★ ★ **SHERATON-SAND KEY RESORT.** *1160 Gulf Blvd.* *727/595-1611; FAX 727/596-8488.* 390 rms, 8 story. Feb-Apr: S, D $150-$200; each addl $10; suites $250-$425; under 18 free; lower rates rest of yr. Crib $5. TV; cable (premium). Heated pool; wading pool, whirlpool, poolside serv. Supervised child's activities (June-Aug); ages 4-12. Restaurants 7 am-11 pm. Bar 11-2 am. Ck-out 11 am. Coin lndry. Convention facilities. Business servs avail. In-rm modem link. Gift shop. Lighted tennis, pro. Golf privileges. Exercise rm. Balconies. On Gulf; private beach. Cr cds: A, C, D, DS, ER, JCB, MC, V.

⊡ 🏋 🎿 🏊 🚶 🏋 🎿 SC

Restaurants

★ ★ ★ **BOB HEILMAN'S BEACHCOMBER.** *447 Mandalay Ave.* *727/442-4144.* Hrs: 11:30 am-midnight; Sun noon-10 pm. Res accepted. Bar. Wine list. Semi-a la carte: lunch $4.50-$12.95, dinner $9.95-$23.95. Child's meals. Specializes in fresh seafood, aged prime beef, chicken. Own baking. Pianist. Valet parking. Beachcomber murals. Waterfall. Family-owned. Cr cds: A, C, D, DS, MC, V.

⊡ 🍴

★ ★ **THE GALLERY.** *1370 Gulf Blvd, ¾ mi S of Sand Key Bridge.* *727/596-5657.* Hrs: 11:30 am-11:30 pm; Sun 4-10 pm; early-bird dinner 4-6:30 pm. Res accepted. Continental menu. Bar. Semi-a la carte: lunch $3.95-$9.95, dinner $7.95-$35. Child's meals. Specializes in fresh seafood, steaks, duckling. Classical pianist. Old World atmosphere. Overlooks Gulf. Cr cds: A, D, DS, MC, V.

⊡ 🍴

✔★ **JULIE'S SEAFOOD AND SUNSETS.** *351 S Gulfview Blvd.* *727/441-2548.* Hrs: 11 am-10 pm. Wine, beer. Semi-a la carte: lunch, dinner $2.95-$24.94. Child's meals. Specializes in fresh seafood, charbroiled dishes. Outdoor dining. Scenic sunset view. Cr cds: A, MC, V.

⊡ 🍴

Clermont (E-4)

(See also Orlando, Tavares)

Pop 6,910 **Elev** 112 ft **Area code** 352 **Zip** 34711 **Web** www.lakecountyonline.com/slcc
Information South Lake Chamber of Commerce, 691 W Montrose St; 352/394-4191.

Claiming the highest average elevation of any town in Florida, Clermont has 100 lakes at its doorstep, 17 within the city limits, providing easy access to fishing and waterskiing. The town is named for Clermont, France, the birthplace of its founder.

What to See and Do

Lakeridge Winery & Vineyards. Tours and tasting of Florida wines; audiovisual presentation; art gallery. (Daily; closed Jan 1, Thanksgiving, Dec 25) 19239 US 27N, 6 mi N. Phone 352/394-8627. **Free.**

Motels

★ ★ **RAMADA INN ORLANDO WESTGATE.** *9200 Irlo Bronson Memorial Hwy, on US 192 E of US 27.* *941/424-2621; FAX 941/424-4630.* 198 rms, 2 story. Feb-Apr, June-Aug, most major hols: S, D $65-$95; under 17 free; lower rates rest of yr. Crib free. TV; cable, VCR avail (movies). Heated pool. Restaurant 7-11 am, 6-10 pm. Bar 5 pm-midnight. Ck-out noon. Coin lndry. Business servs avail. Valet serv. Sundries. Gift shop. Game rm. Refrigerators; microwaves avail. Cr cds: A, C, D, DS, JCB, MC, V.

⊡ 🏊 🎿 🎿 SC

✔★ **VACATION VILLAGE.** *US 27 (34712), 4 mi S on US 27.* *352/394-4091; FAX 352/394-4093; res: 800/962-9969.* Web www.usvac. com. 90 kit. units, villas & lofts. Mid-June-Aug, mid-Dec-Mar: villas (up to 6 persons) $77; lofts to 8, $83; wkly rates; lower rates rest of yr. Crib free. TV; cable. Pool; wading pool. Playground. Ck-out 10 am. Coin lndry. Meeting rm. Sundries. Lighted tennis. Lawn games. Microwaves. Private patios, balconies. Picnic tables, grills. On Lake Louise. Cr cds: MC, V.

🎿 🎿 🏊 🎿 🔥

Cocoa (E-5)

(See also Cocoa Beach, Melbourne, Titusville)

Settled 1860 **Pop** 17,722 **Elev** 25 ft **Area code** 407 **E-mail** chamber1@iu.net **Web** www.iu.net/cocoa.beach/chamber
Information Cocoa Beach Area Chamber of Commerce, 400 Fortenberry Rd, Merritt Island 32952; 407/459-2200.

When the name "Indian River City" was rejected in 1882 by the US postal authorities because it was too long for a postmark, the boys in the general store chose the town's present name from a box of Baker's cocoa. The city was swept into the space age due to its proximity to both Cape Canaveral and Kennedy Space Center.

What to See and Do

Brevard Museum of History and Natural Science. Exhibits include native artifacts, memorabilia of early residents Grace and Albert Taylor, hands-on Discovery Room, mollusk collection, nature center and 22 acres of nature trails through 3 different ecosystems. (Tues-Sat; closed Jan 1, Dec 25) 2201 Michigan Ave. Phone 407/632-1830. ¢¢

Historic Cocoa Village. Self-guided, tour of four-block historic area, including Cocoa Village Playhouse (1924), Porcher House (1916), Gothic church (1886) and eleven other sites. Also unique shops, restaurants. (Advance res required) 430 Delannoy Ave. Phone 407/631-9075.

Kennedy Space Center (see). 2 mi E on FL 520, then N on FL 3.

Motels

✔★ ★ **BEST WESTERN-COCOA INN.** 4225 W King St (32926), I-95 exit 75. 407/632-1065; FAX 407/631-3302. Web www.bestwestern. com/thisco/bw/1050/10150-b.hmt. 120 rms, 2 story. Jan-Apr: S, D $59-$79; under 18 free; higher rates: special events, hols; lower rates rest of yr. Crib $4. Pet accepted; $4. TV; cable. Heated pool. Complimentary coffee in lobby. Bar 4 pm-midnight. Ck-out 11:30 am. Coin lndry. Meeting rms. Game rm. Picnic tables, grills. Cr cds: A, C, D, DS, MC, V.

D ✦ 🏊 ⊠ 🔥 SC

★ **DAYS INN.** 5600 FL 524 (32926), at I-95 exit 76. 407/636-6500; FAX 407/631-0513. 115 rms, 2 story. Jan-Mar: S, D $49-$100; each addl $10; under 12 free off-season; wkly rates; higher rates special events; lower rates rest of yr. Crib free. Pet accepted; $5. TV; cable (premium). Pool. Complimentary coffee in lobby. Ck-out 11 am. Some refrigerators; microwaves avail. Cr cds: A, D, DS, MC, V.

✦ 🏊 ⊠ 🔥 SC

★ ★ **HOLIDAY INN-MERRITT ISLAND.** (260 E Merritt Island Causeway, Merritt Island 32952) E on FL 520. 407/452-7711; FAX 407/452-9462. 128 rms, 2 story. Jan-Apr: S, D $75-$125; under 18 free; higher rates special events; lower rates rest of yr. Crib free. TV; cable. Pool. Coffee in rms. Restaurant 7-10 am, 3-10 pm; wkends to 11 pm. Rm serv. Bar 3 pm-2 am; entertainment. Ck-out noon. Meeting rms. Tennis. Cr cds: A, C, D, DS, ER, JCB, MC, V.

D 🏂 🏊 ⊠ 🔥 SC

★ ★ **RAMADA INN.** 900 Friday Rd (32926), I-95 exit 76. 407/631-1210; res: 800/860-7557; FAX 407/636-8661. E-mail ramada@ iu.net; web www.iu.net/ramada/. 98 rms, 2 story. Early Jan-Apr: S, D $59-$79; each addl $7; package plans; higher rates special events; lower rates rest of yr. Crib free. Pet accepted; $25 deposit. TV; cable (premium). Heated pool. Restaurant 6-10:30 am, 4-10 pm. Rm serv. Bar 4 pm-2 am. Ck-out 11 am. Coin lndry. Meeting rms. Lawn games. Microwaves. Private lake. Cr cds: A, C, D, DS, ER, JCB, MC, V.

D ✦ ✦ 🏊 🏂 ⊠ 🔥 SC

Restaurants

★ ★ **BLACK TULIP.** 207 Brevard Ave (32922), FL 520, Historic Cocoa village. 407/631-1133. E-mail hietpas@yourlink.net; web www.blacktulip.com. Hrs: 11:30 am-2 pm, 5:30-10 pm. Closed Sun; most major hols. Res accepted. Continental menu. Wine, beer. A la carte entrees: lunch $3.95-$12, dinner $10.95-$19.95. Specialties: roasted duckling with apples and cashews, fresh fish baked with bananas and citrus sauce. Own desserts. Pianist Tues-Sat. Totally nonsmoking. Cr cds: A, D, MC, V.

★ ★ **CAFE MARGAUX.** 222 Brevard Ave (32922), FL 520 Historic Cocoa Village. 407/639-8343. Web www.margaux.com. Hrs: 11 am-9:30 pm. Closed Tues. Res accepted. Continental menu. Semi-a la carte: lunch $4-$10, dinner $13-$20. Specializes in beef, seafood, French cuisine. Outdoor dining. Courtyard entry. Art deco decor. Cr cds: A, C, D, DS, MC, V.

D ⊐

Cocoa Beach (E-5)

(See also Cocoa, Melbourne, Titusville)

Settled 1925 **Pop** 12,123 **Elev** 12 ft **Area code** 407 **Zip** 32931 **E-mail** chamber1@iu.net **Web** www.iu.net/cocoa.beach/chamber

Information Cocoa Beach Area Chamber of Commerce, 400 Fortenberry Rd, Merritt Island, 32952; 407/459-2200.

Inaccessible except by boat until 1923, when a bridge was built to Merritt Island, Cocoa Beach remained a sparsely populated hamlet until about 1940. Located south of the city is Patrick Air Force Base. This facility includes the Logistical and Administrative Center of the Air Force Eastern Test Range. North of the city are Cape Canaveral and the Kennedy Space Center (see).

What to See and Do

Kennedy Space Center (see). N on FL A1A, W on FL 520, N on FL 3.

Missile and space vehicle watching. Cocoa Beach offers a good view; missile launches can be seen from almost any point.

Port Canaveral. Deep-sea port, connected to the Intracoastal Waterway via Barge Canal and Canaveral Lock, serves downrange missile ships and nuclear submarines, as well as shrimp fleet and major cruise ships. Also avail are three public parks, campground, fishing charters, boat rentals, boat tours and partial day gaming. N on FL A1A, 401.

The Cocoa Beach Pier. An 800-ft pier, with restaurants, shops, fishing and beach rentals, extends into the ocean. 401 Meade Ave. Phone 407/783-7549.

Annual Events

Port Canaveral Seafood Festival. Port Canaveral. Last wkend Mar.

National Surfing Tourneys. Easter wkend.

Space Coast Art Festival. 3 days following Thanksgiving.

Motels

✔★ ★ **BEST WESTERN-OCEAN INN.** 5500 N Atlantic Ave (FL A1A), near ocean pier. 407/784-2550; FAX 407/868-7124. E-mail north corp@northcorp.w1.com; web www.northcorp.w1.com/bestwestern. 103 rms, 2 story. S $60-$75; D $78-$90; each addl $10; kit. units $89-$109; under 18 free. Crib free. Pet accepted, some restrictions. TV; cable. Pool. Complimentary coffee in lobby. Restaurant adj. Ck-out 11 am. Coin lndry. In-rm modem link. Exercise equipt. Refrigerators avail. Cr cds: A, C, D, DS, ER, JCB, MC, V.

D ✦ 🏊 🏂 ⊠ 🔥 SC

★ **DAYS INN OCEANFRONT.** 5600 N Atlantic Ave (FL A1A), near ocean pier. 407/783-7621; FAX 407/799-4576. 180 rms, 2 & 7 story. S $75-$125; D $85-$135; each addl $10; kit. units $109-$119; under 18 free. Crib free. TV; cable. Pool. Playground. Complimentary coffee in lobby. Restaurant opp. Ck-out 11 am. Coin lndry. In-rm modem link. Exercise equipt. Beach access. Cr cds: A, C, D, DS, ER, JCB, MC, V.

D 🏊 🏂 ⊠ 🔥 SC

✔ ★ ★ **LUNA SEA.** 3185 N Atlantic Ave (A1A). 407/783-0500; res: 800/586-2732; FAX 407/784-6515. 43 rms, 2 story. Jan-June: S, D $56.95-$65.95; each addl $5; suites, kit. units $65.95-$85.95; under 13 free; higher rates special events; lower rates rest of yr. TV; cable. Complimentary continental bkfst. Restaurant nearby. Ck-out 11 am. Coin lndry. Pool. Many refrigerators, microwaves. Picnic tables, grills. Cr cds: A, D, DS, MC, V.

🏊 ⊠ 🔥 SC

★ **SEA ESTA VILLAS.** 686 S Atlantic Ave, FL A1A S of FL 520. 407/783-1739; FAX 407/783-4969; res: 800/872-9444. 8 kit. suites, 2 story. S $150-$200; D $175-$225; each addl $25; wkly rates; higher rates shuttle launches. TV; cable (premium), VCR avail. Pool; whirlpool. Ck-out 11 am. Coin Indry. Concierge. In-rm modem link. Exercise equipt. Microwaves. Some balconies. Cr cds: A, C, D, DS, MC, V.

★ **SURF STUDIO.** *1801 S Atlantic Ave (FL A1A), FL A1A S of FL520.* 407/783-7100; FAX 407/783-2695. 11 rms, 9 with kit. Mid-Jan-Apr: S, D $70-$75; each addl $12; kit. units $95-$145; under 10 free; wkly rates; min stay hols; lower rates rest of yr. Crib free. Pet accepted; $10. TV; cable (premium), VCR avail. Pool. Ck-out 11 am. Coin Indry. Refrigerators, microwaves. On beach. Cr cds: A, C, D, DS, MC, V.

★ **WAKULLA.** *3550 N Atlantic Ave (FL A1A), FL A1A S of FL 520.* 407/783-2230; FAX 407/783-0980; res: 800/992-5852. E-mail Wakulla@travelbase.com. 116 kit. suites, 2 story. Feb-Apr: S, D $96-$106; each addl $6; under 5 free; lower rates rest of yr. Crib free. TV; cable (premium). Heated pool; wading pool. Restaurant nearby. Ck-out 11 am. Coin Indry. Valet serv. Sundries. Lawn games. Microwaves. Balconies. Grills. On beach. Cr cds: A, C, D, DS, MC, V.

Motor Hotels

★ ★ **COMFORT INN AND SUITE RESORT.** *3901 N Atlantic Ave (FL A1A), FL A1A S of FL 520.* 407/783-2221; FAX 407/783-0461. 144 rms, 6 story, 40 kit. units. Jan-Apr: S, D $65-$115; each addl $8; suites $105-$165; kit. units $75-$125; higher rates special events; lower rates rest of yr. Crib $7. TV; cable. Pool; poolside serv. Playground. Restaurant 8 am-3 pm. Bar noon-2 am. Ck-out 11 am. Coin Indry. Meeting rms. Valet serv. Sundries. Exercise equipt. Rec rm. Lawn games. Some refrigerators. Picnic tables, grill. Cr cds: A, C, D, DS, ER, JCB, MC, V.

★ ★ **OCEAN SUITE.** *5500 Ocean Beach Blvd, FL A1A near ocean pier.* 407/784-4343; FAX 407/783-6514; res: 800/367-1223. 50 suites, 5 story. Feb-Apr, July-Aug: suites $89-$119; each addl $10; under 12 free; package plans off-season; lower rates rest of yr. Crib free. TV; cable (premium), VCR avail (movies). Heated pool. Restaurant 6:30-10:30 am. Ck-out 11 am. Meeting rms. Business servs avail. Valet serv. 18-hole golf privileges, greens fee. Microwaves. Balconies. Ocean view. Cr cds: A, C, D, DS, ER, MC, V.

✔ ★ ★ **OCEANSIDE INN.** *1 Hendry Ave, FL A1A near ocean pier.* 407/784-3126; FAX 407/799-0883; res: 800/874-7958. Web www.cocoa beach.oceanside.com. 74 rms, 6 story. S, D $59-$109; each addl $10; under 18 free; higher rates special events. Crib $10. TV; cable. Heated pool; poolside serv. Restaurant 7 am-11 pm. Bar 4 pm-midnight. Ck-out 11 am. Balconies. On beach. Cr cds: A, C, D, DS, MC, V.

★ ★ **RADISSON RESORT.** *(8701 Astronaut Blvd, Cape Canaveral 32920) N on FL A1A, 1 mi S of Cape Canaveral.* 407/784-0000; FAX 407/784-3737. 200 rms, 2 story. S, D $89-$140; under 18 free. Crib free. TV; cable. Heated pool; wading pool, whirlpool. Restaurant 6:30 am-10 pm. Rm serv. Bar. Ck-out noon. Coin Indry. Meeting rms. Business servs avail. In-rm modem link. Bellhops. Gift shop. Airport transportation. Lighted tennis. Exercise equipt. Cr cds: A, C, D, DS, ER, JCB, MC, V.

Hotels

★ ★ **DOUBLETREE-OCEANFRONT.** *2080 N Atlantic Ave (FL A1A).* 407/783-9222; res: 800/552-3224; FAX 407/799-3234. 148 rms, 16 story. Mid-Feb-Apr, mid-June-mid-Aug: S $110-$125; D $125-$165; suites $150-$265; under 18 free; 2-day min (hols); higher rates special events; lower rates rest of yr. Crib free. TV; cable. Complimentary coffee in rms. Restaurant 6:30 am-10 pm. Bar 5 pm-midnight. Ck-out 11 am. Meeting

rms. Business center. In-rm modem link. Gift shop. Coin Indry. Exercise equipt. Pool; wading pool, poolside serv. Some bathrm phones, refrigerators, microwaves; wet bar in suites. On beach. Cr cds: A, C, D, DS, MC, V.

★ ★ **HILTON.** *1550 N Atlantic Ave (FL A1A).* 407/799-0003; FAX 407/799-0344. E-mail cbhsales@aol.com; web www.cocoabeach. hilton.com. 300 rms, 7 story. S $99-$149; D $109-$159; each addl $15; suites $155-$175; under 18 free; lower rates rest of yr. Crib free. TV; cable (premium). Heated pool; poolside serv. Restaurant 6:30 am-10 pm. Bar 11-1 am. Ck-out 11 am. Convention facilities. Business servs avail. Concierge. Gift shop. Free valet parking. Exercise equipt. Sun deck. On ocean. Luxury level. Cr cds: A, C, D, DS, ER, MC, V.

Restaurants

★ ★ ★ **HEIDELBERG.** *7 N Orlando Ave, FL A1A S.* 407/783-6806. Hrs: 10 am-10 pm; Sun from 5 pm. Closed Mon; Thanksgiving, Dec 25. Res accepted. German menu. Bar. Semi-a la carte: lunch $4.95-$11.95, dinner $13-$18.95. Child's meals. Specialties: gulasch, sauerbraten, beef stroganoff. Bavarian decor. Family-owned. Cr cds: A, MC, V.

★ ★ **JACK BAKER'S LOBSTER SHANTY.** *2200 S Orlando Ave, FL A1A at ocean pier.* 407/783-1350. Web www.sunet.net/lobster shanty. Hrs: 11:30 am-9:30 pm; early-bird dinner Mon-Sat 3-6 pm; Sun 11:30 am-6 pm; Sun 11:30 am-6 pm. Closed Thanksgiving. Res accepted. Bar. Semi-a la carte: lunch $4.50-$9, dinner $12.99-$24.95. Child's meals. Specializes in seafood. Salad bar. Outdoor dining. Multi-level dining overlooking Banana River; dock. Cr cds: A, C, D, MC, V.

★ ★ **MANGO TREE.** *118 N Atlantic Ave (FL A1A), FL A1A S of FL 520.* 407/799-0513. Web members.aol.com/mangotreer/page1. Hrs: 6-9:30 pm. Closed Mon. Res accepted. Continental menu. Bar. Wine list. A la carte entrees: dinner $12.95-$38.95. Specialties: grouper Margarette, veal Française, filet mignon Béarnaise. Own baking. Pianist. Indoor fish pond. Orchid greenhouse and butterfly collection. Gazebo. One of the first cottages in Cocoa Beach. Cr cds: A, MC, V.

★ **PIER.** *401 Meade Ave, FL A1A at Ocean Pier.* 407/783-7549. Hrs: 11 am-midnight; Sun brunch 10 am-2 pm. Res accepted. Bar 10-2 am. Semi-a la carte: lunch $4.95-$13.95, dinner $8.95-$29.95. Sun brunch $12.95. Child's meals. Specializes in seafood, steak. Multi-level dining area on ocean pier. Nautical decor. Family-owned. Cr cds: A, C, D, DS, MC, V.

Coconut Grove
(see Miami)

Coral Gables (H-6)

(See also Hialeah, Homestead, Miami, Miami Intl Airport Area, Miami Beach)

Established 1925 **Pop** 40,091 **Elev** 10 ft **Area code** 305 **E-mail** development@coralgables.net **Web** www.coralgables.net

Information City of Coral Gables, 1 Alhambra Plaza, suite 1110, 33134, phone 305/460-5311.

Coral Gables, one of the 29 separate municipalities that make up Metropolitan Miami-Dade County, was designed by George Merrick, the son of a Massachusetts minister. Merrick laid out the entire city as the "American Riviera" and a "new Venice," but relied on slightly sensational techniques to populate it. To lure prospective buyers from the north, Merrick offered steamship and bus service to Coral Gables, with transportation expense reimbursed for anyone who purchased land. He hired William Jennings Bryan to lecture on the merits of Coral Gables investments and engaged Paul Whiteman and the chorus of Earl Carroll's *Vanities* to entertain buyers. Houses were designed in Mediterranean-Florida style, with sections in French, Italian, Dutch South African and Chinese styles to provide contrast. Today, Coral Gables requires that every new building be approved by its board of architects. The city includes eight planned entrances, two with arched gateways constructed of carved native rock, and fourteen planned plazas.

What to See and Do

Coral Gables Merrick House (1899). "Coral-rock" plantation house, boyhood home of the city's founder, George Merrick, was built of oolitic limerock and Dade County pine; reflects the New England roots of the family while adapting to southern climate; original furnishings, historic pieces; gardens. (Wed afternoons or by appt) 907 Coral Way. Phone 305/460-5361. ¢-¢¢

Fairchild Tropical Garden. An 83-acre tropical botanical garden featuring rain forest, sunken garden, vine pergola, rare plant house. Hourly tram tour. 10901 Old Cutler Rd. (Daily; closed Dec 25) Phone 305/667-1651. ¢¢¢

University of Miami (1925). (13,100 students) Largest independent university in the Southeast; campuses cover 287 acres and contain more than 153 buildings. Gusman Concert Hall and Jerry Herman Ring Theatre present various programs throughout the year. Phone 305/284-3355. On the main campus is

Lowe Art Museum. Permanent collections of fine arts, Asian, pre-Colombian, Native American and African art; Samuel H. Kress Collection of Renaissance and Baroque art; American Art of the 19th & 20th centuries; special exhibitions. (Daily exc Mon; closed Jan 1, July 4, Dec 25) 1301 Stanford Dr. Phone 305/284-3536. ¢¢

Venetian Pool. Much of the coral used to build homes in the city came from a quarry, which afterward was converted into this elaborate swimming pool. It is edged with shady porticos, vine-covered loggias and Spanish towers; palm trees, 2 waterfalls, an island, swim-through caves and a stone and wrought iron bridge complete the landscaping. (Daily exc Mon; closed Jan 1, Thanksgiving & Fri after, Dec 24 & 25) 2701 De Soto Blvd. Phone 305/460-5356. ¢¢

Annual Event

Junior Orange Bowl Festival. Events include 5K run, prestigious juniors' golf, gymnastics & tennis tournaments, cheerleading, soccer, queen's pageant and ball, gala evening parade and much more. Phone 305/662-1210. Nov-Jan.

Motor Hotel

★ ★ ★ **HOTEL PLACE ST MICHEL.** *162 Alcazar Ave (33134).* 305/444-1666; res: 800/848-4683; FAX 305/529-0077. Web www.place stmichel.com. 27 rms, 3 story, 3 suites. Nov-Apr: S, D $165; suites $200; under 12 free; lower rates rest of yr. Crib free. Garage parking $7. TV; cable (premium). Complimentary continental bkfst. Restaurant (see RESTAURANT ST MICHEL). Bar 4 pm-midnight; entertainment. Ck-out noon. Meeting rms. Business servs avail. Health club privileges. Cr cds: A, D, MC, V.

D ⊠ ⋒

Hotels

★ ★ ★ ★ **BILTMORE WESTIN.** *1200 Anastasia Ave (33134).* 305/445-1926; FAX 305/913-3159. E-mail reservations@biltmorehotel. com; web www.biltmorehotel.com/guest.html. The ornately carved tower of this Spanish Colonial hotel has dominated the Coral Gables skyline since 1926. Recreational opportunities abound here; the Biltmore has a complete fitness center and spa, a championship golf course and, at 22,000-square-feet, the largest swimming pool of its kind in the country. 280 rms, 15 story. Late Jan-Mar: S $268-$289; D $289-$309; each addl $20; suites $469-$589; under 18 free; wkend rates; golf, tennis plans; lower rates rest of yr. Crib free. Garage parking $12, valet. TV; cable (premium). Pool; whirlpool. Restaurants 6:30 am-10 pm (also see COURTYARD CAFE). Rm serv 24 hrs. Ck-out noon. Meeting rms. Business center. In-rm modem link. Concierge. Barber, beauty shop. Lighted tennis, pro. 18-hole golf, pro, putting green, driving range. Exercise rm; sauna, steam rm. Spa. Refrigerators; microwaves avail. Balconies. Luxury level. Cr cds: A, C, D, DS, ER, JCB, MC, V.

D ⫓ ⯭ ≋ ⯭ ⏃ ⌘ ⋒ SC ⏏

★ ★ ★ **HYATT REGENCY.** *50 Alhambra Plaza (33134).* 305/441-1234; res: 800/233-1234; FAX 305/441-0520. 242 rms, 14 story. Oct-Jan: S $189-$275; D $214-$300; each addl $25; suites $275-$1,800; under 18 free; wkend rates; lower rates rest of yr. Crib free. Valet parking $10, garage $9. TV; cable (premium). Heated pool; whirlpool, poolside serv. Coffee in rms. Restaurant 7 am-11 pm. Bar 11-1 am, Fri, Sat to 2 am; entertainment Wed, Fri, Sat. Ck-out noon. Meeting rms. Business center. Concierge. Gift shop. Exercise equipt; sauna. Some balconies. Cr cds: A, C, D, DS, ER, JCB, MC, V.

D ≋ ⯭ ⏃ ⋒ SC ⏏

★ ★ ★ **OMNI COLONNADE.** *180 Aragon Ave (33134).* 305/441-2600; res: 800/843-6664; FAX 305/445-3929. 157 units, 14 story, 17 suites; guest rms begin on 10th floor. Sept-Apr: S, D $225-$275; each addl $20; suites $325-$700; wkend rates; lower rates rest of yr. Crib free. Garage parking $9, valet $10. TV; cable (premium), VCR avail. Heated pool; whirlpool, poolside serv. Restaurants 6:30-1 am. Rm serv 24 hrs. Bars; entertainment. Ck-out noon. Meeting rms. Business center. In-rm modem link. Concierge. Beauty shop. Exercise equipt; sauna. Health club privileges. Minibars; microwaves avail. Wet bar in suites. Some balconies. European decor; mahogany furnishings. Rotunda off the lobby is part of original Colonnade building (1926). Cr cds: A, C, D, DS, ER, JCB, MC, V.

D ≋ ⯭ ⌘ ⋒ SC ⏏

Restaurants

★ ★ **BANGKOK BANGKOK II.** *157 Giralda Ave (33134), east of downtown.* 305/444-2397. Hrs: 10:30 am-10:30 pm. Closed Thanksgiving. Res accepted. Thai menu. Bar. Semi-a la carte: lunch $6-$12, dinner $15-$25. Complete meal: dinner $45.95. Specialties: roasted duck darling; Earth, Wind and Fire; Name That Tune. Valet parking. Thai decor. Cr cds: A, C, D, MC, V.

D ⋑

★ ★ **BRASSERIE LES HALLES.** *2415 Ponce de Leon Blvd (33134).* 305/461-1099. Hrs: 11:30 am-midnight; Sun brunch 11:30 am-4 pm. Res accepted. French menu. Bar. Wine list. A la carte entrees: lunch $6-$9, dinner $15-$22. Sun brunch $19. Specialties: steak frites, cassoulet toulousain, gigôt d'agneau. Valet parking. Cr cds: A, D, DS, MC, V.

D ⋑

★ ★ **CAFE BARCELONA.** *160 Giralda Ave (33134).* 305/448-0912. Hrs: 11 am-3 pm, 6-11 pm. Res accepted. Spanish menu. Wine, beer. A la carte entrees: lunch $5-$10. Complete meals: lunch, dinner $20-$25. Child's meals. Specializes in seafood, tapas. Pianist. Valet parking. Water colors of Barcelona and oil paintings adorn the dining room. Cr cds: A, C, D, MC, V.

D ⋑

★ ★ **CAFFE ABBRACCI.** *318 Aragon Ave (33134).* 305/441-0700. Hrs: 11:30 am-3 pm, 6 pm-midnight. Res required. Italian menu. Bar. A la carte entrees: lunch $5.50-$14, dinner $7.50-$25. Specialties: costoletta tri-color, trio veneziano. Cr cds: A, D, MC, V.

D ⋑

★ ★ **CAFFE BACI.** *2522 Ponce de Leon Blvd (33134).* 305/442-0600. Hrs: noon-3 pm, 6-11 pm; Fri, Sat from 6 pm. Italian menu. Wine, beer. A la carte entrees: lunch $9-$12, dinner $15-$25. Specialties: red snapper, breaded veal chops. Own pasta. Valet parking. Modern decor; brass vaulted ceiling. Cr cds: A, C, D, MC, V.

D ⌐

★ ★ **CAFFE BUONGIORNO.** *2271 Ponce de Leon Blvd (33134).* 305/442-2033. Hrs: 11:30 am-3 pm, 6:30-10 pm; Sat 6:30-11 pm. Closed Sun. Res required. Northern Italian menu. Wine, beer. A la carte entrees: lunch $4.95-$12, dinner $11.95-$20. Specializes in seafood, pasta. Valet parking. Paintings of Italy. Cr cds: A, MC, V.

D ⌐

★ ★ ★ **COURTYARD CAFE.** *(See Biltmore Westin Hotel)* 305/445-1926. Hrs: 6:30 am-10 pm; Sun brunch 11 am-4 pm. Res accepted. Bar 11-2 am. Wine cellar. Semi-a la carte: bkfst $7.95-$12.95, lunch $8-$18, dinner $18-$22. Sun brunch $39. Specialties: poached chicken, tapas, pasta. Own baking. Entertainment. Valet parking. Outdoor dining. Cr cds: A, C, D, MC, V.

D ⌐ ♥

★ ★ **THE HEIGHTS.** *2530 Ponce de Leon Blvd (33134).* 305/461-1774. Hrs: noon-2:30 pm, 6-11 pm; Fri to midnight, Sat 6 pm-midnight. Closed Sun; most major hols. Res accepted. Eclectic menu. Bar. A la carte entrees: lunch $7-$14, dinner $13-$24. Specialties: sea bass, tuna carpaccio, Colorado rack of lamb. Own baking. Jazz Fri, Sat. Valet parking. Local art on display. Cr cds: A, D, MC, V.

D ⌐

★ ★ **JOHN MARTIN.** *253 Miracle Mile (33134).* 305/445-3777. E-mail JohnMartins@EarthLink.com. Hrs: 11:30 am-midnight; wkends to 1 am. Closed Dec 25. Res accepted. Irish menu. Bar. Complete meals: lunch, dinner $8-$20. Child's meals. Specialties: Gaelic steak, imported Irish oak-smoked salmon. Entertainment. Parking. Authentic Irish pub atmosphere. Cr cds: A, C, D, DS, MC, V.

D ⌐

★ ★ **LA BUSSOLA.** *264 Giralda Ave (33134).* 305/445-8783. Hrs: noon-3 pm, 6-11 pm; Sat, Sun from 6 pm. Closed Thanksgiving, Dec 25. Res accepted. Italian menu. Bar. A la carte entrees: lunch $7-$12, dinner $7-$28. Specialties: pumpkin ravioli with cinnamon butter, roasted peppers with jumbo shrimp. Pianist. Three dining areas; Italian Renaissance decor. Cr cds: A, C, D, MC, V.

D ⌐

★ ★ ★ **LA DORADA.** *177 Giralda Ave (33134).* 305/446-2002. E-mail dorada@worldnet.att.net. Hrs: 11-1 am. Res accepted. Mediterranean seafood menu. Bar. Wine cellar. Complete meal: lunch $18-$35, dinner $45-$80. Specializes in Mediterranean seafood. Piano. Valet parking. Cr cds: A, C, D, DS, ER, JCB, MC, V.

D ⌐

★ ★ ★ **LE FESTIVAL.** *2120 Salzedo St (33134).* 305/442-8545. Hrs: 11:45 am-2:30 pm, 6-10:30 pm; Fri to 11:30 pm; Sat 6-11:30 pm. Closed Sun; major hols. Res accepted; required Fri, Sat. French menu. Serv bar. Wine list. A la carte entrees: lunch $7.50-$14, dinner $15.75-$28.95. Specialties: fresh salmon beurre blanc, grilled veal chop with port wine sauce, chicken a la Normande. Own pastries. Three dining areas decorated with European antiques. Cr cds: A, C, D, DS, MC, V.

D ⌐

✔★ ★ **MELODY INN.** *83 Andalusia Ave (33134).* 305/448-0022. Hrs: 5:30-10 pm; Fri to 11 pm; summer hrs vary. Closed Dec 24, 25. Res accepted. Swiss, continental menu. Beer. Semi-a la carte: dinner $13.50-$24.50. Specializes in veal, seafood, Swiss dishes. Swiss atmosphere. Cr cds: A, C, D, DS, MC, V.

D ⌐

★ ★ **NORMAN'S.** *21 Almeria Ave (33134).* 305/446-6767. Web www.mambotown.com. Hrs: noon-2 pm, 6-10:30 pm; Fri to 11 pm; Sat 6-11 pm. Closed Sun; Jan 1, Dec 25. Res accepted. Bar. Wine list. A la carte entrees: lunch $11-$15. Complete meal: dinner $38-$58. Child's

meals. Specialties: Key West yellow tail, roast pork tenderloin. Asian and European art objects. Cr cds: A, C, D, MC, V.

D ⌐

★ ★ ★ **RESTAURANT ST MICHEL.** *(See Hotel Place St Michel Motor Hotel).* 305/446-6572. Web www.StMichel.com. Hrs: 7-9:30 am, 11 am-10:30 pm; Sat from 1 pm; Sun brunch 11 am-2:30 pm. Res accepted. Continental menu. Wine list. A la carte entrees: bkfst $4.95-$6.50, lunch $6.95-$14.95, dinner $14.95-$29.95. Sun brunch $21.95. Specialties: pan-fried blue crab cakes, roast rack of Australian lamb, sautéed yellowtail snapper. Pianist. Outdoor dining. In historic hotel (1926); 1920s decor. Cr cds: A, C, D, MC, V.

D ⌐

✔★ ★ **THAI ORCHID II.** *317 Miracle Mile (33134).* 305/443-6364. Hrs: 11:30 am-3 pm, 5-10:30 pm; Fri, Sat to 11 pm. Closed Thanksgiving. Res accepted. Thai menu. Wine, beer. A la carte entrees: lunch $4.95-$7.95, dinner $7.25-$16.95. Specializes in fish, macrobiotic dishes. Outdoor dining. Oriental decor. Cr cds: A, MC, V.

D ⌐

Crystal River (D-3)

(See also Homosassa Springs)

Pop 4,044 **Elev** 4 ft **Area code** 352 **Zip** 34428 **E-mail** ncccr@citrus.infi.net
Information Nature Coast Chamber at Crystal River, 28 NW US 19; 352/795-3149.

Favored by Florida residents as a bountiful fishing ground, the area around Crystal River is also a prime diving area. The town stands where the Crystal River meets King's Bay, and both salt- and freshwater fish are abundant. The river is a designated manatee sanctuary, where the endangered species winters from mid-November through March.

What to See and Do

Crystal River State Archaeological Site. Burial mounds, trailside displays and interpretive trails; self-guided tours. Visitor center has Native American artifacts. (Daily) 3400 N Museum Point, 2½ mi W off US 19N, State Park Rd exit. Phone 352/795-3817. Per vehicle ¢

King's Bay. Has 110 springs, including Hunter Spring with a flow of 41 million gallons daily. Fishing, snorkeling and scuba diving.

Motels

★ ★ **BEST WESTERN CRYSTAL RIVER RESORT.** *614 NW US 19, 1 mi N of FL 44.* 352/795-3171; FAX 352/795-3179. E-mail bwcr@citrus.infi.net; web gminet.com/bwest. 96 rms, 2 story. Dec-Easter: S $71-$74; D $75-$78; each addl $5; kit. units $92-$95; under 18 free; lower rates rest of yr. Crib free. Pet accepted; $3/day. TV; cable (premium), VCR avail (movies). Heated pool. Restaurant 6:30 am-8 pm. Bar to 9 pm. Ck-out noon. Coin lndry. Business servs avail. Sundries. Gift shop. Refrigerators avail. Some balconies. Picnic tables, grill. On Crystal River; dock, launching ramp, boats, guides; scuba diving. Cr cds: A, C, D, DS, JCB, MC, V.

D ⟲ 🏊 🏊 🐾 SC

✔★ ★ **COMFORT INN.** *4486 N Suncoast Blvd (US 19/98).* 352/563-1500; FAX 352/563-5426. 66 rms, 2 story. Jan-Apr: S $44.95-$57.95; D $49.95-$67.95; each addl $5; under 18 free; higher rates some hols; lower rates rest of yr. Crib $7. Pet accepted; $5/day. TV; cable (premium). Pool. Complimentary continental bkfst. Ck-out 11 am. Coin lndry. Business servs avail. In-rm modem link. Lighted tennis. Picnic tables. Cr cds: A, D, DS, ER, MC, V.

D ⟲ 🏊 🏊 🐾 SC

Resort

★ ★ ★ **PLANTATION INN & GOLF RESORT.** *9301 W Fort Island Trail (34429), West Fort Island Trail, County 44W, 1/4 mi off US 19/98.* 352/795-4211; FAX 352/795-1368; res: 800/632-6262. Web www.plantation inn.com. 143 rms, 2 story, 12 villas. Feb-mid-Apr: S, D $99-$145; each addl $15; suites $145; villas to 4, $215; golf condos to 6, $310; under 16 free; golf, tennis packages; lower rates rest of yr. Crib free. TV; cable, VCR avail. 2 pools, 1 heated; whirlpool. Complimentary coffee in rms. Dining rm 6 am-2 pm, 5-10 pm. Rm serv. Bar. Ck-out 11 am, ck-in 3 pm. Coin lndry. Convention facilities. Business servs avail. Free airport transportation. Lighted tennis, pro. 27-hole golf, greens fee (incl cart) $40, pro, putting green, driving range. Scuba gear and fishing equipment rentals, fishing guide. Boats avail; dockage. Lawn games. Some refrigerators. Private patios. Picnic tables. On Crystal River. Cr cds: A, C, D, DS, MC, V.

Cypress Gardens

(see Winter Haven)

Dade City (E-4)

(See also Brooksville, Zephyrhills)

Pop 5,633 **Elev** 78 ft **Area code** 352 **Zip** 33525 **Web** www.dadecity.org
Information Greater Dade City Chamber of Commerce, 38035 Meridian Ave; 352/567-3769.

A community filled with moss-hung oaks, camphor trees and azalea bushes, Dade City is also the seat of Pasco County.

What to See and Do

Dade Battlefield State Historic Site. Site is a memorial to Major Francis L. Dade and the more than 100 men who were ambushed and massacred here by Seminoles in 1835. Museum (daily). Nature trails. Picnicking, playground. Tennis, games. Standard hrs, fees. 22 mi N on US 301, off FL 476W in Bushnell. Phone 352/793-4781.

Pioneer Florida Museum. This 25-acre complex contains relics and photographs from pioneer times: clothing, farm implements, wagons; restored 2-story Overstreet House (ca 1864) with period furnishings; one-room school house; 84-yr-old church; old train depot, train engine. Also miniature inaugural ball gowns of Florida's first ladies. (Tues-Sun afternoons; closed major hols) (See ANNUAL EVENTS) 1/2 mi N via US 301N, at 15602 Pioneer Museum Rd. Phone 352/567-0262. ¢

Saint Leo Abbey (1889). Benedictine Abbey named for Pope Leo I, completed in 1948, is an impressive Lombardic-Romanesque building with 21,000-pound cross, carved from Tennessee rose marble, and reproduction of Lourdes Grotto. (Daily) 5 mi SW on FL 52, 4 mi E of I-75, on grounds of Saint Leo College. Phone 352/588-2881. **Donation.**

Annual Events

Kumquat Festival. Arts & crafts, antique cars, cooking contests, petting zoo. Last wkend Jan.

Pasco County Fair. Fairgrounds, 1 mi W on FL 52. 5 days late Feb.

Pioneer Florida Day. Pioneer Florida Museum (see).Commemorates early Florida life with historical exhibits, audiovisual programs; crafts demonstrations, "Cracker" food, traditional music, juried arts & crafts show. Phone 352/567-0262. Labor Day.

Dania (H-6)

(See also Fort Lauderdale, Hollywood, Pompano Beach)

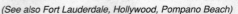

Settled 1896 **Pop** 13,024 **Elev** 11 ft **Area code** 954 **Zip** 33004

Little trace remains of the Danish families that originally settled here and little is left of the crops that at one time made Dania the tomato center of the world. Today, Dania attracts tourists with its antique shopping plaza and proximity to the Atlantic Ocean.

What to See and Do

Jai-Alai Fronton. Parimutuel betting; clubhouse dining. (Tues, Sat evenings; matinees Tues, Sat; closed Sept 1-12) Children over 10 yrs only; must be with parent. 301 E Dania Beach Blvd, at jct US 1 & FL A1A. Phone 954/920-1511. General admission ¢

John U. Lloyd Beach State Recreation Area. A 244-acre park with swimming, skin diving; fishing; boating (marina). Nature trails. Picnicking, concession. Standard hrs, fees. 6503 Dania Beach. 1/2 mi N, off FL A1A (North Ocean Dr). Phone 954/923-2833.

Hotels

★ ★ ★ **HILTON FORT LAUDERDALE AIRPORT.** *1870 Griffin Rd, at Fort Lauderdale Intl Airport.* 954/920-3300; FAX 954/920-3348. E-mail fla1870@aol.com. 388 rms, 8 story. Mid-Dec-early Apr: S, D $120-$225; each addl $10; suites $360-$550; family, wkly, wkend rates; higher rates Super Bowl; lower rates rest of yr. Crib free. TV; cable (premium). Heated pool; whirlpool. Restaurants 6 am-2 pm, 5-11 pm. Bar 11-1 am. Ck-out noon. Convention facilities. Business center. In-rm modem link. Gift shop. Free covered parking; valet parking. Free airport transportation. 2 lighted tennis courts. Exercise equipt. Some refrigerators. Resort-like setting; overlooks waterway. Cr cds: A, C, D, DS, ER, MC, V.

★ ★ **WYNDHAM.** *1825 Griffin Rd, at Fort Lauderdale Intl Airport.* 954/920-3500; FAX 954/920-3571. 250 rms, 12 story. Dec-Apr: S $139-$205; D $149-$215; suites $275-$475; under 12 free; lower rates rest of yr. Crib free. Pet accepted, some restrictions; $50. TV; cable (premium). Pool; whirlpool, poolside serv. Restaurant 6:30 am-10:30 pm. Bar 11 am-midnight. Ck-out noon. Convention facilities. Business servs avail. In-rm modem link. Gift shop. Free airport transportation. Lighted tennis. Golf privileges. Exercise equipt. Some refrigerators. 2-story atrium lobby. Cr cds: A, C, D, DS, ER, MC, V.

Restaurant

★ ★ **LE PETIT CAFE.** *3308 Griffin Rd (33312).* 954/967-9912. Hrs: 11:30 am-2:30 pm; 4:30-10 pm; early-bird dinner 4:30-6:30 pm. Closed Mon; July 4; also Sept. Res accepted. French menu. Wine, beer. Semi-a la carte: lunch $5.50-$7.95, dinner $6.25-$16.95. Specializes in crepes, seafood. French countryside artwork. Totally nonsmoking. Cr cds: MC, V.

Daytona Beach (D-5)

(See also DeLand, New Smyrna Beach, Ormond Beach)

Founded 1870 **Pop** 61,921 **Elev** 10 ft **Area code** 904 **Web** www.daytonabeach-tourism.com
Information Daytona Beach Convention and Visitors Bureau, 126 E Orange Ave, 32114; 904/255-0415 or 800/854-1234.

One of the oldest Floridian resorts, Daytona Beach achieved international fame in the early days of the automobile due to its 23-mile, 500-foot-wide beach, which offered a natural speedway. In 1903, Alexander Winton set the world's record of 68 mph on the Daytona beach. Autos are still allowed on certain sections of the beach (daylight hours only), but the speed limit is 10 mph.

The city, with a triple waterfront—the Atlantic Ocean and two sides of the Halifax River—has developed as a year-round vacation spot, especially popular in spring and summer with vacationing students and families. Deep-sea fishing from charter boats at offshore reefs is enjoyed as well as river fishing on the inland waters and from the six bridges spanning the Halifax River. Supplementing tourism are light industry, Bethune-Cookman College, Embry-Riddle Aeronautical University and a branch campus of the University of Central Florida, Orlando.

What to See and Do

Daytona Beach Kennel Club. Greyhound racing; parimutuel betting. (Mon-Sat evenings; matinees Mon, Wed & Sat) 2201 International Speedway Blvd, W on US 92. Phone 904/252-6484. General admission ¢

Daytona International Speedway. This 2.5 mi, high-speed, banked track, with a grandstand seating 125,000, is a proving ground for car and accessory manufacturers. Track (daily); tours exc during races & special tests. Most racing events Feb, Mar, July, Oct & Dec. (See ANNUAL EVENT) 1801 W International Speedway Blvd, on US 92. Phone 904/253-RACE (tickets) or 904/254-2700. Tour ¢¢ Also here is

   Daytona USA. Features interactive displays on the history and experience of racing such as a NASCAR Online interactive web site exhibit, computer designing of a race car and an IMAX movie depicting race day at the Daytona 500. (Daily; closed Dec 25) 1801 W International Speedway Blvd. Phone 904/947-6800. ¢¢¢¢

Museum of Arts & Sciences. Exhibits include an extensive Cuban collection of fine and folk art; American fine and decorative arts; African art; graphic art; Pleistocene fossils and a 13-ft-tall giant ground sloth skeleton; planetarium with afternoon star shows; Frischer Sculpture Garden. (Daily exc Mon) 1040 Museum Blvd, in Tuscawilla Park. Phone 904/255-0285. ¢¢

Ponce de Leon Inlet & Lighthouse (1887). The lighthouse grounds contain a marine museum with much of the original equipment on display as well as 3 restored keeper's cottages. Visitors may climb to the top of the lighthouse. Beaches; fishing. Picnicking, cafes. (Daily) S of town, 4931 S Peninsula Dr. Phone 904/761-1821. ¢¢

Public beach. Unique in Florida and one of the most unusual in the world, the 23-mi-shoreline of this beach just north and south of the Ponce de Leon Inlet welcomes more than 7.7 million tourists each yr. The water temperature is typically 80°F or warmer during the summer months; ocean lifeguards and beach rangers are on duty yr-round. When dampened by the incoming tide, the sand packs to a consistency firm and smooth enough to drive on, and driving is permitted on 30 mi of strand during daylight hours (Feb-early Nov; fee). Swimming, surfing and surf casting. Phone 904/239-SURF. Beach driving ¢¢

Sugar Mill Gardens. Twelve acres of botanical gardens on grounds of ruined sugar mill (1804); flowering trees include magnolia; other flora. Also dinosaur statues. (Daily) 3½ mi S on US 1 to Port Orange, then 1 mi W on Herbert St. Phone 904/767-1735. **Free.**

Annual Event

Auto races. Daytona International Speedway. Speed weeks with Rolex 24 & Daytona 500, Feb; Daytona 200 (AMA motorcycle races), early Mar; Pepsi 400 stock car race, early July; several other races. Contact Daytona International Speedway, PO Box 2801, 32120-2801; 904/253-RACE.

Motels

★ ★ **ACAPULCO INN.** *2505 S Atlantic Ave (32118). 904/761-2210; FAX 904/761-2216; res: 800/245-3580.* Web www.daytonahotels.com. 133 rms, 8 story, 98 kit. units. Feb-Labor day: S, D $120-$215; each addl $6-$10; under 18 free; lower rates rest of yr. Crib free. TV; cable (premium). Heated pool; wading pool, 2 whirlpools. Free supervised child's activities. Restaurant 7 am-1:30 pm. Bar 4 pm-midnight. Ck-out 11 am. Coin lndry. Bellhops. Valet serv. Gift shop. Golf privileges. Game rm. Lawn games. Refrigerators. Balconies. Picnic tables. Southwestern-style motel; on beach. Cr cds: A, C, D, DS, ER, MC, V.

D ⊁ ≋ ⊠ 🔥 SC

✔ ★ **DREAM INN.** *3217 S Atlantic Ave (32118), 5 mi S on A1A. 904/767-2821; res: 800/767-9738; FAX 904/767-7778.* E-mail dreaminn@travelbase.com; web www.dreaminn.com. 23 rms, 11 with shower only, 2 story, 16 kit. units. Feb-Aug: S, D $35-$69; each addl $5; kit. units $39-$99; higher rates special events; lower rates rest of yr. TV; cable (premium). Complimentary coffee in rms. Restaurant opp open 24 hrs. Ck-out 11 am. Meeting rms. Business servs avail. Coin lndry. 18-hole golf privileges, greens fee $15-$60, pro, putting green. Pool. Lawn games. Refrigerators, microwaves. Some balconies. Picnic tables, grills. On beach. Cr cds: DS, MC, V.

⊁ ≋ ⊠ 🔥 SC

★ **FLAMINGO INN.** *2011 S Atlantic Ave (32118). 904/252-1412; res: 800/682-0919.* E-mail PinkBird@America.com; web www.Daytona-Flamingo.com. 27 rms, 3 story, 20 kits. Feb-Apr, June-Aug: S, D $59; each addl $10; kits. $69; under 12 free; wkly rates; higher rates special events; lower rates rest of yr. Crib $5. TV; cable. Pool. Restaurant opp 7 am-11 pm. Ck-out 10 am. Coin lndry. Balconies. Picnic tables. Swimming beach. Cr cds: DS, MC, V.

≋ 🔥 SC

★ **GRAND PRIX.** *2015 S Atlantic Ave (32118). 904/255-2446; FAX 904/673-6260; res: 800/456-2446.* 41 rms, 2 story, 33 kits. Mar-Apr, June-Aug: S, D $37-$135; each addl $5; kit. units $45-$150; under 16 free; wkly, monthly rates; lower rates rest of yr. Crib free. TV; cable. Heated pool. Complimentary coffee in lobby. Restaurant opp 7 am-11 pm. Ck-out 11 am. Coin lndry. Lawn games. Private patios, balconies. Picnic tables, grills. On beach. Cr cds: A, D, DS, MC, V.

≋ ⊠ 🔥 SC

✔ ★ **GRANDE RESORT AT DAYTONA.** *1299 S Atlantic Ave (32118). 904/255-4545; FAX 904/248-0443.* 96 rms, 5 story, 62 kit. units. Feb-Easter, June-Aug: S, D $55; suites $75-$95; kit. units $65-$80; under 18 free; wkly rates; lower rates rest of yr. Crib free. TV; cable. Heated pool; wading pool. Ck-out 11 am. Coin lndry. On beach. Cr cds: A, DS, MC, V.

≋ ⊠ 🔥 SC

★ ★ **HAMPTON INN-AIRPORT.** *1715 W International Speedway Blvd (US 92) (32114). 904/257-4030; FAX 904/257-5721.* 122 rms, 4 story. S, D $84-$94; under 18 free; higher rates special events. Crib free. TV; cable (premium). Pool; whirlpool. Complimentary continental bkfst. Restaurant adj 11 am-midnight. Ck-out 11 am. Meeting rms. Business servs avail. Valet serv. Free airport transportation. Some refrigerators; microwaves avail. Cr cds: A, C, D, DS, ER, MC, V.

D ≋ ✈ ⊠ 🔥 SC

★ **HOWARD JOHNSON PIRATE'S COVE.** *3501 S Atlantic Ave (32127), opp Port Orange Causeway. 904/767-8740; FAX 904/788-8609.* 135 kit. units, 7 story. Feb-mid-Aug: S, D $79-$99; each addl $10; under 18 free; higher rates special events; lower rates rest of yr. Crib free. TV; cable (premium). Heated pool; wading pool. Restaurant 7-11 pm. Bars noon-2 am; entertainment Mon-Sat. Ck-out 11 am. Coin lndry. Business servs avail. Gift shop. Exercise equipt. Game rm. Private patios, balconies. On beach. Cr cds: A, C, D, DS, MC, V.

[icons]

★ ★ **PERRY'S OCEAN-EDGE RESORT.** *2209 S Atlantic Ave (32118). 904/255-0581; FAX 904/258-7315; res: 800/447-0002.* Web www.perrysoceanedge.com. 205 rms, 2-6 story, 146 kits. Feb-Apr, mid-June-Aug: S, D $65-$126; each addl $10; kit. units $15 addl; varied lower rates rest of yr. Crib $10. TV; cable (premium), VCR avail (movies $2). 3 pools, 1 indoor; whirlpool. Supervised child's activities; ages 5-18. Complimentary continental bkfst. Restaurant 7 am-2 pm. Ck-out 11 am. Coin lndry. Business servs avail. Bellhops. Gift shop. Golf privileges, on-site putting green. Game rm. Lawn games. Microwaves avail. Picnic tables. Oceanfront, beach. Cr cds: A, C, D, DS, MC, V.

[icons]

★ **RED CARPET INN.** *1855 S Ridgewood Ave (32119). 904/767-6681.* 30 rms, 20 kit. units. S $22; D $28; each addl $4; kit. units $33. TV; cable (premium). Pool. Complimentary coffee in lobby. Restaurant nearby. Ck-out 10 am. Cr cds: A, DS, MC, V.

[icons]

✔ **ROYAL HOLIDAY BEACH.** *(3717 S Atlantic Ave, Daytona Beach Shores 32127) 6 mi S on A1A. 904/761-5984; res: 888/761-5987.* 30 rms, 2 story, 26 kits. Feb-Apr & July-Aug: S, D $44-$59; kits. $59-$79; under 16 free; wkly, monthly rates; lower rates rest of yr. Crib free. TV. Pool. Complimentary coffee in rms. Restaurant adj 6:30 am-2 pm. Ck-out 10 am. Exercise equipt. Coin lndry. Refrigerators, microwaves. Balconies. Picnic tables. Swimming beach. Cr cds: A, DS, MC, V.

[icons]

★ ★ ★ **SUN VIKING LODGE.** *2411 S Atlantic Ave (32118). 904/252-6252; FAX 904/252-5463; res: 800/874-4469.* Web www.sunviking.com. 91 rms, 2-8 story, 70 kits. Feb-Sept: S, D $59-$135; each addl $10-$15; suites $88-$179; kit. units $64-$135; under 18 free (limit 2); wkly rates; higher rates special events; lower rates rest of yr. Crib free. TV; cable, VCR avail (movies). 2 heated pools, 1 indoor; wading pool, whirlpool. Playground. Free supervised child's activities. Restaurant 7:30 am-2:30 pm. Ck-out 11 am. Coin lndry. Meeting rm. Business servs avail. Exercise equipt; sauna. Lawn games. Game rms. Refrigerators. Balconies. Picnic tables, grills. 60-ft water slide. Rooftop sun deck; on beach. Cr cds: A, C, D, DS, MC, V.

[icons]

Motor Hotels

★ ★ **BEACHCOMER INN.** *2000 N Atlantic Ave (32118). 904/252-8513; res: 800/245-3575.* Web www.daytonahotels.com. 184 rms, 7 story, 104 kits. Feb-Sept: S, D $83-$113; each addl $6-$10; kit. units $90-$115; under 18 free; lower rates rest of yr. Crib free. TV; cable (premium). Heated pool; wading pool, whirlpool, poolside serv, lifeguard (in season). Free supervised child's activities. Restaurant 7 am-1 pm. Rm serv. Bar. Ck-out 11 am. Coin lndry. Business servs avail. Bellhops. Gift shop. Sundries. Golf privileges. Lawn games. Refrigerators. Balconies. Picnic tables. On ocean. Cr cds: A, C, D, DS, ER, MC, V.

[icons]

★ ★ **BEST WESTERN AKU TIKI INN.** *(2225 S Atlantic Ave, Daytona Beach Shores 32118) 904/252-9631; FAX 904/252-1198.* 132 rms, 5 story. Feb-Apr & June-Aug: S, D $62-$98; each addl $10; kits. $70-$108; under 12 free; higher rates special events; lower rates rest of yr. Crib free. TV; cable (premium). Heated pool; wading pool, poolside serv. Restaurant 7 am-10 pm. Rm serv. Bar. Ck-out 11 am. Business servs avail. Coin lndry. Bellhops. Gift shop. Valet serv. Game rm. Lawn games. Refrigerators. Picnic tables. Swimming beach. Cr cds: A, C, D, DS, MC, V.

[icons]

★ ★ **BEST WESTERN LA PLAYA RESORT.** *2500 N Atlantic Ave (32118). 904/672-0990; FAX 904/677-0982.* Web www.surfsideresorts.com. 239 rms, 9 story, 35 suites, 165 kits. Feb-Apr: S, D $86-$131; each addl $6-$10; suites $134-$180; under 18 free; wkly rates; higher rates special events; lower rates rest of yr. Crib free. TV; cable (premium). Indoor pool; wading pool, whirlpools. Free supervised child's activities (June-Sept); ages 5-12. Restaurant 7 am-1:30 pm. Rooftop bar 5 pm-2 am; entertainment. Ck-out 11 am. Meeting rms. Bellhops. Golf privileges. Exercise equipt; sauna, steam rm. Game rm. Lawn games. Microwaves. Private patios, balconies. Picnic tables. On beach. Cr cds: A, C, D, DS, MC, V.

[icons]

★ **BEST WESTERN MAYAN INN BEACHFRONT.** *103 S Ocean Ave (32118). 904/252-0584; res: 800/443-5323; FAX 904/252-8670.* E-mail bwdaytona@americanhospitality.com; web www.daytona. com. 112 rms, 8 story, 49 kit. units. Feb-Aug: S, D $66-$215; each addl $10; kit. units $70-$225; under 18 free; lower rates rest of yr. Crib free. TV; cable (premium). Pool; wading pool. Supervised child's activities; ages 3 and up. Complimentary continental bkfst. Bar 5 pm-midnight. Ck-out 11 am. Business servs avail. Coin lndry. Balconies. On beach. Cr cds: A, C, D, DS, JCB, MC, V.

[icons]

★ **CASTAWAYS.** *(2043 S Atlantic Ave, Daytona Beach Shores 32118) 2 mi S on FL A1A. 904/254-8480; FAX 904/253-6554; res: 800/407-0342.* Web www.visitdaytona.com. 152 rms, 7 story, 58 kit. units. Feb-Apr, June-Aug: S, D $79-$99; suites $135-$178; kit. units $87-$107; under 18 free; special events (5-day min); lower rates rest of yr. Crib free. Pet accepted, some restrictions. TV; cable (premium), VCR avail. Pool; sauna. Supervised child's activities (mid-June-mid-Aug); ages 5-9. Restaurant 7 am-10 pm. Rm serv. Ck-out 11 am. Coin lndry. Meeting rms. Business servs avail. Game rm. Lawn games. Refrigerators. Balconies. Picnic tables. On beach. Cr cds: A, C, D, DS, MC, V.

[icons]

★ **DAYS INN.** *3357 S Atlantic Ave (32118). 904/767-8737; res: 800/338-4343; FAX 904/756-9612.* E-mail beachball@dockingbay. com. 76 rms, 7 story, 36 kit. units. Feb-Sept: S, D $90-$175; each addl $10; kit. units $100-$185; under 18 free; family rates; package plans; 7-day min (special events); higher rates special events; lower rates rest of yr. Crib free. TV; cable, VCR avail (movies). Complimentary coffee in lobby. Restaurant adj 6-2 am. Ck-out 11 am. Meeting rms. Business servs avail. In-rm modem link. Sundries. Coin lndry. Airport transportation. Pool; whirlpool. Game rm. Lawn games. Refrigerators, microwaves. Balconies. On ocean. Cr cds: A, C, D, DS, ER, JCB, MC, V.

[icons]

★ ★ ★ **HILTON-DAYTONA BEACH.** *2637 S Atlantic Ave (32118). 904/767-7350; FAX 904/760-3651.* 214 units, 11 story. Feb-Labor Day: S, D $99-$189; each addl $15; suites $275-$560; kit. units $170; some wkend rates; higher rates special events; varied lower rates rest of yr. Crib free. TV; cable. Heated pool; wading pool, whirlpool, poolside serv (Mar-Oct). Restaurant 7 am-10 pm; Fri, Sat to 11 pm. Rm serv. Bars 11-1:30 am; entertainment. Ck-out 11 am. Meeting rms. Business servs avail. Bellhops. Valet serv. Gift shop. Beauty shop. Free underground parking. Golf privileges. Exercise equipt. Game rm. Lawn games. Refrigerators; microwaves avail. Private patios, balconies. On beach. Cr cds: A, C, D, DS, ER, JCB, MC, V.

[icons]

★ ★ **HOLIDAY INN SUNSPREE.** *600 N Atlantic Ave (32118). 904/255-4471; FAX 904/253-7543.* Web visitdaytona.com/holidayinn. 322 rms, 14 story. Feb-mid-Apr, mid-June-mid-Sept: S, D $109-$325; under 18 free; golf plans; lower rates rest of yr. Crib free. Pet accepted. TV; cable (premium). Heated pool; poolside serv. Free supervised child's activities (mid-May-Aug); ages 5-12. Complimentary coffee in rms. Restaurant 6 am-10 pm. Rm serv. Bar from noon; entertainment. Ck-out 11 am. Coin lndry. Convention facilities. Business servs avail. Bellhops. Valet serv. Sundries. Golf privileges. Exercise equipt. Game rm. Lawn games. Refrigerators, microwaves. Balconies. On beach. Cr cds: A, C, D, DS, JCB, MC, V.

[icons]

★ ★ ★ **HOLIDAY INN-INDIGO LAKES.** *2620 W International Speedway Blvd (US 92) (32114), at I-95.* 904/258-6333; FAX 904/254-3698. 151 rms, 2 story. Mid-Jan-Apr: S, D $85-$235; each addl $10; kit. units $95-$235; family rates; package plans; lower rates rest of yr. Crib free. TV; cable (premium). Pool; wading pool. Coffee in rms. Restaurants 6-9:30 am, 6-9 pm. Rm serv. Ck-out 11 am, ck-in 3 pm. Coin lndry. Meeting rms. Business servs avail. Valet serv. Free airport transportation. Lawn games. Exercise equipt. Refrigerators. Private patios, balconies. Cr cds: A, C, D, DS, JCB, MC, V.

D ≈ ✗ ⊠ ⛵ SC

★ ★ **HOLIDAY INN-OCEANFRONT.** *2560 N Atlantic Ave (32118).* 904/672-1440; FAX 904/677-8811. 143 kit. units, 4-8 story. Feb-Labor Day: S, D $74-$200; each addl $8; under 18 free; wkly rates; some wkend rates; lower rates rest of yr. Crib free. TV; cable (premium). Heated pool; wading pool, whirlpool. Restaurant adj 6-11 pm. Ck-out 11 am. Coin lndry. Meeting rm. In-rm modem link. Valet serv. Sundries. Health club privileges. Private patios, balconies. On beach. Cr cds: A, C, D, DS, ER, JCB, MC, V.

D ≈ ⊠ ⛵ SC

★ ★ **HOWARD JOHNSON PLAZA.** *701 S Atlantic Ave (32118).* 904/258-8522; res: 800/633-7010; FAX 904/257-9122. Web www.howardjohnson.com. 102 kit. units, 8 story. Mid-Apr-Aug: S, D $79-$129; each addl $10; suite $159; under 16 free; 3-5 day min (hols, special events); higher rates special events; lower rates rest of yr. Crib free. TV; cable (premium). Restaurant open 24 hrs. Bar 11-2 am. Ck-out 11 am. Business servs avail. Coin lndry. Pool; whirlpool. Game rm. Many balconies. On beach. Cr cds: A, D, DS, MC, V.

D ≈ ✗ ⛵ SC

★ ★ **INN ON THE BEACH.** *1615 S Atlantic Ave (32118).* 904/255-0921; FAX 904/255-3849. E-mail res@innonthebeach.com; web www.innonthebeach.com. 195 rms, 7 story, 21 suites, 80 kits. S, D $39.99-$79.99; each addl $6-$10; suites $59.99-$99.99; kit. units $49.99-$89.99; under 18 free; higher rates special events; monthly rates. Crib free. TV; cable, VCR (movies). Heated pool; wading pool. Supervised child's activities (Feb-Aug). Complimentary continental bkfst. Bar 11-2 am. Ck-out 11 am. Coin lndry. Meeting rm. Business servs avail. Bellhops. Valet serv. Exercise equipt. Putting green. Game rm. Lawn games. Balconies. On ocean, beach. Cr cds: A, C, D, DS, ER, JCB, MC, V.

D ≈ ✗ ⊠ ⛵ SC

↙★ ★ ★ **PALM PLAZA OCEANFRONT RESORT.** *3301 S Atlantic Ave (32118), on FL A1A.* 904/767-1711; res: 800/329-8662; FAX 904/756-8394. E-mail palmdbsinc@aol.com; web www.palmplaza.com. 98 kit. units, 11 story. June-Aug: S, D $69-$119; under 18 free; golf plans; higher rates special events; lower rates rest of yr. Crib free. TV; cable (premium). Heated pool; wading pool, whirlpool. Supervised child's activities (May-Sept). Complimentary continental bkfst. Restaurant 7 am-4 pm. Ck-out 11 am. Coin lndry. Business servs avail. Golf privileges. Game rm. Microwaves. Balconies. On ocean, swimming beach. Cr cds: A, C, D, DS, MC, V.

✗ ≈ ⊠ ⛵ SC

★ ★ **QUALITY INN OCEAN PALMS.** *2323 S Atlantic Ave (32118), on FL A1A.* 904/255-0476; res: 800/874-7517; FAX 904/255-3376. Web visitdaytona.com/qualinn. 110 rms, 6 story, 62 kits. S, D $55-$179; suites $179-$220; under 18 free; wkly, monthly rates; higher rates special events. Crib free. Pet accepted. TV; cable. Heated pool; wading pool. Free supervised child's activities (mid-June-mid-Aug); ages 5-12. Complimentary continental bkfst. Ck-out 11 am. Coin lndry. Game rm. Lawn games. Refrigerators, microwaves avail. Private balconies. On beach. Cr cds: A, C, D, DS, MC, V.

D ↙ ≈ ⊠ ⛵ SC

★ **RAMADA INN RESORT-OCEANFRONT.** *2700 N Atlantic Ave (32118).* 904/672-3770; FAX 904/673-7262. 383 rms, 12 story, 74 kits. Feb-mid-Apr, June-Aug: S, D $69-$105; under 18 free; some wkend rates; higher rates special events (3-4-day min), lower rates rest of yr. Crib free. TV; cable. 2 pools, 1 heated; wading pool, poolside serv. Restaurant 6:30 am-2 pm, 5-8 pm. Rm serv. Bar. Ck-out noon. Coin

lndry. Convention facilities. Business servs avail. Sundries. Rec rm. Microwaves. Balconies. On beach. Cr cds: A, C, D, DS, MC, V.

D ≈ ⊠ ⛵ SC

★ **SEAGARDEN INN.** *(3161 S Atlantic Ave, Daytona Beach Shores 32118) on FL A1A.* 904/761-2335; FAX 904/756-6676; res: 800/245-0575. Web www.daytonachamber.com/seagarden.htm. 144 rms, 10 story, 90 kits. Feb-mid-Aug: S, D $97-$109; each addl $6-$10; kit. units $103-$115; under 17 free; higher rates special events; lower rates rest of yr. Crib free. TV; cable (premium). Heated pool; wading pool, whirlpool, poolside serv. Free supervised child's activities; ages 3-16. Coffee in rms. Restaurant 7-11 am. Bar noon-2 am. Ck-out 11 am. Coin lndry. Meeting rms. Business servs avail. Golf privileges. Health club privileges. Private patios, balconies. Picnic tables. On beach. Cr cds: A, C, D, DS, MC, V.

D ✗ ≈ ⊠ ⛵ SC

★ **TREASURE ISLAND INN.** *2025 S Atlantic Ave (32118).* 904/255-8371; FAX 904/255-4984; res: 800/543-5070. Web www.daytonahotels.com. 228 rms, 11 story, 157 kits. Feb-early Apr: S, D $120-$158; each addl $10; suites $165-$200; studio rms $158; kit. units $8 addl; under 18 free; wkly, wkend rates; higher rates special events; lower rates rest of yr. Crib free. TV; cable (premium). 2 pools, 1 heated; wading pool, whirlpools, poolside serv, lifeguard in season. Free supervised child's activities. Restaurant 7 am-2 pm, 5-9:30 pm. Rm serv. Bar 11-2 am; entertainment. Ck-out 11 am. Coin lndry. Meeting rms. Business servs avail. In-rm modem link. Bellhops. Valet serv. Gift shop. Tennis privileges. Golf privileges. Game rm. Lawn games. Refrigerators. Balconies. On ocean, beach. Cr cds: A, C, D, DS, ER, MC, V.

D ✗ ✗ ≈ ⊠ ⛵ SC

★ **TROPICAL WINDS.** *1398 N Atlantic Ave (32118).* 904/258-1016; res: 800/245-6099; FAX 904/255-6462. E-mail beachball@dockingbay.com. 94 kit. units, 8 story. Feb-Sept: S, D, suites $90-$175; each addl $10; under 18 free; 7-day min (hols, special events); higher rates special events; lower rates rest of yr. Crib free. TV; cable, VCR avail (movies). Complimentary coffee in lobby. Restaurant 6 am-2 pm. Rm serv. Ck-out 11 am. Business servs avail. Coin lndry. Airport transportation. Exercise equipt. 2 pools, 1 indoor. Game rm. Lawn games. Balconies. On beach. Cr cds: A, C, D, DS, ER, MC, V.

D ≈ ✗ ⊠ ⛵ SC

Hotels

★ ★ ★ **ADAM'S MARK.** *100 N Atlantic Ave (32118).* 904/254-8200; FAX 904/253-0275. Web www.adamsmark.com. 437 rms, 15 story. S, D $99-$195; each addl $10; suites $159-$1,300; under 18 free; higher rates special events. Crib free. Valet parking $3-$8. TV; cable (premium), VCR avail. Indoor/outdoor pool; whirlpool, poolside serv. Restaurant 7 am-11 pm. Bar 11-2 am; entertainment. Ck-out 11 am. Coin lndry. Convention facilities. Business servs avail. Concierge. Shopping arcade. Airport, RR station, bus depot transportation. Tennis privileges. Golf privileges. Exercise rm; sauna. Health club privileges. Minibars. On beach. Luxury level. Cr cds: A, C, D, DS, JCB, MC, V.

D ✗ ✗ ↙ ≈ ✗ ⊠ ⛵ SC

★ ★ **BAHAMA HOUSE.** *(2001 S Atlantic Ave, Daytona Beach Shores 32118) 1 mi S on A1A.* 904/248-2001; FAX 904/248-0991; res: 800/571-2001. E-mail oceans11@n-jcenter.com; web www.daytonahotels.com. 87 kit. units, 10 story. Mid-Mar-late Apr, mid-June-Aug: S, D $115-$155; suites $160-$205; under 18 free; lower rates rest of yr. Crib free. TV; cable (premium). Heated pool; whirlpool. Supervised child's activities. Complimentary continental bkfst. Restaurant nearby. Ck-out 11 am. Coin lndry. Business servs avail. Microwaves. Balconies. On ocean. Cr cds: A, C, D, DS, ER, MC, V.

D ≈ ⊠ ⛵ SC

★ ★ ★ **RADISSON.** *640 N Atlantic Ave (FL A1A) (32118).* 904/239-9800. 206 rms, 11 story, 52 kit. units. Late May-Labor Day: S, D $69-$139; kit. units $79-$149; under 18 free; family rates; 5-day min (hols); higher rates special events. Crib free. Pet accepted, some restrictions; $25 & $75 deposit. Valet parking $8. TV; cable (premium). Complimentary coffee in rms. Restaurant 6:30 am-10 pm. Bar. Ck-out 11 am. Meeting rms. Business servs avail. Shopping arcade. Gift shop. Coin lndry. Exercise equipt. Pool; wading pool, poolside serv. Game rm. Balconies. On ocean. Cr cds: A, C, D, DS, JCB, MC, V.

⊞ ⬚ ⬚ ⬚ ⬚ SC

★ **RAMADA INN SURFSIDE.** *3125 S Atlantic Ave (32118), on FL A1A.* 904/788-1000; FAX 904/756-9906. Web www.visitdaytona.com/ramada. 119 rms, 7 story, 64 kits. Feb-Mar & mid-June-mid-Aug: S, D $94; suites $151-$161; kits. $104; under 19 free; wkly rates; lower rates rest of yr. Crib free. TV; cable. Heated pool; wading pool, whirlpool, poolside serv. Supervised child's activities (June-Aug); ages 2-12. Restaurant 7 am-9 pm. Bar; entertainment Tues-Sat. Ck-out 11 am. Coin lndry. Meeting rms. Business servs avail. Game rm. Refrigerators. Balconies. On beach. Cr cds: A, C, D, DS, ER, JCB, MC, V.

⊞ ⬚ ⬚ ⬚ SC

Inn

★ ★ **COQUINA INN.** *544 S Palmetto (32114).* 904/254-4969; res: 800/805-7533. Web www.coquinainn.com. 4 rms, 2 story. No rm phones. S, D $80-$110; each addl $20; 2-day min hols. Children over 16 yrs only. TV; cable. Complimentary full bkfst; afternoon refreshments. Ck-out 11 am, ck-in 3-7 pm. Concierge serv. Gift shop. Some fireplaces. Some balconies. Built in 1912; served as a parsonage for many yrs. Grand piano; antiques. Totally nonsmoking. Cr cds: A, MC, V.

⬚ ⬚

Restaurants

★ **ATLANTIC RED SNAPPER.** *2058 S Atlantic Ave (FL A1A) (32118).* 904/254-3130. Hrs: 4-10 pm; early-bird dinner 4-6 pm. Closed Thanksgiving, Dec 25. Res accepted. Seafood menu. Bar. Semi-a la carte: dinner $7.95-$23.95. Child's meals. Specializes in New England style cuisine. Parking. Casual dining. Cr cds: A, DS, MC, V.

⊞ ⬚

★ **AUNT CATFISH'S.** *4009 Halifax Dr (32127), at W end of Port Orange Bridge.* 904/767-4768. Hrs: 11:30 am-10 pm; Sun from 9 am; Sun brunch to 2 pm. Closed Dec 25. Res accepted. Bar. Semi-a la carte: lunch $3.99-$7.89, dinner $7.49-$24.95. Sun brunch $9.99. Child's meals. Specializes in seafood, ribs. Salad bar. Pianist (summer). Southern riverland atmosphere. Antique post office at entrance. Cr cds: A, MC, V.

⊞ SC ⬚

★ ★ **CHART HOUSE.** *1100 Marina Point Dr (32114).* 904/255-9022. Hrs: 5-9:30 pm; Fri, Sat to 10:30 pm; early-bird dinner 5-6 pm. Res accepted. Bar. Semi-a la carte: dinner $14.95-$29.95. Child's meals. Specializes in steaks, seafood, prime rib. Salad bar. Parking. Cr cds: A, C, D, DS, MC, V.

⊞ ⬚

★ ★ **PARK'S SEAFOOD.** *951 N Beach St (32117).* 904/258-7272. E-mail parksseafood.com. Hrs: 5-10 pm; Fri, Sat 4:30-11 pm; Sun from 4 pm; early-bird dinner to 6 pm. Closed Thanksgiving, Dec 25; also 1st 3 wks Dec. Bar. Semi-a la carte: dinner $6.95-$24.95. Child's meals. Specializes in seafood, steak, beef. Rustic setting on waterfront, view of Halifax River; nautical decor. Cr cds: A, D, MC, V.

⊞ ⬚

★ ★ **RICCARDO'S.** *610 Glenview Blvd (32118), near A1A.* 904/253-3035. Hrs: 5-10 pm. Closed Thanksgiving, Dec 24, 25. Res accepted. Northern Italian menu. Wine. Semi-a la carte: dinner $8.95-$19.25. Child's meals. Specializes in veal, shrimp, pasta. Own desserts. Subdued lighting adds to the Mediterranean theme. Family-owned. Cr cds: A, C, D, MC, V.

⊞ ⬚

★ ★ **TOP OF DAYTONA.** *2625 S Atlantic Ave (32118), 3 mi E on A1A.* 904/767-5791. Hrs: noon-11 pm; Sun from 11 am; Sun brunch 11 am-2 pm; early-bird dinner 4-6 pm. Res accepted. Continental menu. Bar. Semi-a la carte: lunch $6.95-$9.95, dinner $12.95-$24.95. Sun brunch $12.95. Child's meals. Specialties: stuffed quail, stuffed chicken breast, shrimp brouchette. Guitar Wed-Sun. Parking. Panoramic view of ocean, beach and Daytona skyline. Cr cds: A, C, D, DS, MC, V.

SC ⬚

Deerfield Beach (G-6)

(See also Boca Raton, Dania, Delray Beach, Fort Lauderdale, Pompano Beach)

Settled 1898 **Pop** 46,325 **Elev** 12 ft **Area code** 954 **Web** www.deerfieldbeach.com
Information Greater Deerfield Beach Chamber of Commerce, 1601 E Hillsboro Blvd, 33441; 954/427-1050.

Twenty settlers established the town of Deerfield Beach in 1898. The Hillsboro River, which formed the northern boundary of Deerfield, was later dredged into a canal that linked the town with Lake Okeechobee, 45 miles to the northwest. Although primarily an agricultural area until the late 1940s, during Prohibition the Hillsboro Canal was an unloading site for rumrunners; federal agents occasionally captured a boatload of liquor. Today, tourists come to Deerfield Beach for the excellent fishing and the beautiful beaches.

What to See and Do

Quiet Waters Park. A 427-acre county park. Swimming, cable water-skiing; fishing; boating (marina, rentals); bicycle rentals. Children's water playground. Miniature golf. Picnicking, concessions; playground. Tent camping (rentals). (Daily) 6601 N Powerline Rd. Phone 954/360-1315. Wkends, hols ¢

Annual Event

Deerfest. Quiet Waters Park. Exhibits, carnival, entertainment, food. 3rd wkend Nov.

Motel

★ **COMFORT SUITES.** *1040 E Newport Center Dr (33442).* 954/570-8887; FAX 954/570-5346. 101 suites, 4 story. Jan-Mar: suites $130-$150; under 18 free; golf plans; lower rates rest of yr. Crib free. Pet accepted, some restrictions. TV; cable (premium), VCR avail (movies). Heated pool; whirlpool. Complimentary continental bkfst. Restaurant adj 6:30 am-10 pm. Bar 5-10 pm. Ck-out noon. Coin lndry. Business servs avail. In-rm modem link. Sundries. Gift shop. 18-hole golf privileges, greens fee $25-$100, pro, putting green. Health club privileges. Refrigerators. Cr cds: A, C, D, DS, ER, JCB, MC, V.

⊞ ⬚ ⬚ ⬚ ⬚ ⬚ ⬚ ⬚ SC

Motor Hotels

★ **QUALITY SUITES.** *1050 E Newport Center Dr (33442).* 954/570-8888; FAX 954/570-5346. 107 suites, 5 story. Jan-Mar: suites $146-$160; under 18 free; golf plans; lower rates rest of yr. Crib free. Pet accepted. TV; cable (premium), VCR (movies). Heated pool; whirlpool. Complimentary bkfst buffet. Restaurant 6:30 am-10 pm. Bar from 5 pm. Ck-out noon. Coin lndry. Meeting rms. Business servs avail. In-rm modem link. Valet serv. Gift shop. 18-hole golf privileges, greens fee $25-$100, pro, putting green, driving range. Exercise equipt. Health club privileges. Refrigerators, microwaves, wet bars. Balconies. Cr cds: A, C, D, DS, ER, JCB, MC, V.

⊞ ⬚ ⬚ ⬚ ⬚ ⬚ ⬚ ⬚ SC

★ ★ **SEABONAY BEACH RESORT.** *(1159 Hillsboro Mile, Hillsboro Beach 33062) S on FL A1A. 954/427-2525; FAX 954/427-3228, ext. 105; res: 800/777-1961.* 78 rms, 6 story, 63 kit. suites. Mid-Dec-Apr: S, D $99; each addl $10; suites $159-$349; under 12 free; wkly, monthly rates; lower rates rest of yr. Crib $10. TV; cable. Heated pool. Complimentary coffee in lobby. Restaurant nearby. Ck-out 11 am. Coin lndry. Business servs avail. In-rm modem link. Free garage parking. Exercise equipt. Microwaves. Balconies. Picnic tables, grills. Private beach; on ocean. Cr cds: A, DS, MC, V.

D ⚓ ≋ ✈ ⊠ 🔥 SC

Hotel

★ ★ **HILTON.** *100 Fairway Dr (33441). 954/427-7700; FAX 954/427-2308.* 221 rms, 8 story. Jan-Mar: S, D $139-$199; each addl $10; family rates; lower rates rest of yr. Crib free. TV; cable (premium). Heated pool; whirlpool, poolside serv. Restaurant 6:30 am-10 pm. Bar from 11 am. Ck-out noon. Meeting rms. Business servs avail. In-rm modem link. Golf privileges. Exercise equipt. Refrigerators. Mirrored lobby; paintings. Balinese sculpture, artifacts. Luxury level. Cr cds: A, C, D, DS, ER, MC, V.

D 🛎 ≋ ✈ ⊠ 🔥 SC

Restaurants

★ ★ ★ **BROOKS.** *500 S Federal Hwy (33441). 954/427-9302.* Hrs: 5:30-10:30 pm. Closed Dec 25. Res accepted. Continental menu. Bar. Wine cellar. A la carte entrees: dinner $19.50-$26.25. Child's meals. Specialties: rack of lamb, roast Indiana duckling, South Carolina trout. Own baking. Valet parking. Totally nonsmoking. Cr cds: A, C, DS, MC, V.

D

★ ★ **CAFE CLAUDE.** *1544 SE 3rd Ct (33441), in Cove Shopping Center. 954/421-7337.* Hrs: 11:30 am-2 pm, 5:15-10 pm. Closed Aug. Res accepted. French menu. Bar. A la carte entrees: lunch $5.95-$13.95, dinner $15.75-$27.95. Specialties: crevettes au safran, canard roti au miel et vinaigre de framboise. Cr cds: A, MC, V.

D

De Funiak Springs (J-2)

Pop 5,120 **Elev** 260 ft **Area code** 850 **Zip** 32435 **Web** www.mwfin.com
Information Walton County Chamber of Commerce, Chautauqua Bldg, Circle Dr, PO Box 29; 850/892-3191.

In 1881, two members of a surveying party seeking a route for the Louisville and Nashville Railroad passed through this area. They were so impressed by the beauty of the location that they envisioned a prosperous settlement and named the site after Mr. DeFuniak, a prominent official of the Louisville & Nashville Railroad. Lake DeFuniak, located in the center of the city, contains several acres of clear water and is said to be one of two naturally round lakes in the world.

What to See and Do

Ponce de Leon Springs State Recreation Area. Within 443-acre park is a natural spring that flows from a horizontal limestone cavity in the center of the pool; the crystal clear water remains at a constant 68°F. Swimming; fishing. Nature trail, ranger-guided walks (on request). Picnicking. Standard hrs, fees. E via US 90, then 1 mi S on FL 181A. Phone 850/836-4281.

Walton-DeFuniak Public Library. Opened in 1887, this library is believed to be the state's oldest public library operating continuously in its original building; some rare books as old as library itself. (Daily exc Sun) 3 Circle Dr. Phone 850/892-3624.

Annual Event

Chautauqua Festival Day. Commemorates the Chautauqua, which brought cultural programs to the area for more than 40 years. Many activities during the preceding three months. Last Sat Apr.

Motel

✔ ★ **BEST WESTERN CROSSROADS INN.** *Box 852 (32433), at jct I-10, US 331. 850/892-5111; FAX 850/892-2439.* 100 rms, 2 story. S, D $42-$52; each addl $5; under 18 free. Crib avail. TV; cable (premium). Pool. Complimentary bkfst. Restaurant 6 am-2 pm, 5-9 pm. Bar 5-11 pm. Ck-out noon. Meeting rm. In-rm modem link. Cr cds: A, C, D, DS, MC, V.

D ≋ ⊠ 🔥 SC

DeLand (D-5)

(See also Altamonte Springs, Daytona Beach, Winter Park)

Founded 1876 **Pop** 16,491 **Elev** 77 ft **Area code** 904
Information DeLand Area Chamber of Commerce, 336 N Woodland Blvd, 32720-3495; 904/734-4331 or 800/749-4350.

Henry A. DeLand, a New York manufacturer with a dream of establishing an "Athens of Florida," chose this site and planted water oaks 50 feet apart along prospective streets. He encouraged the building of a schoolhouse, a venture subsidized by hat manufacturer John B. Stetson. The school, first known as DeLand Academy, continues to thrive as Stetson University. DeLand is largely sustained by the fern, cut foliage and timber industries, manufacturing companies and government and educational services.

What to See and Do

Blue Spring State Park. A 945-acre park with spring on St Johns River. Manatee return each winter. Historic house. Swimming; fishing; canoeing, boating. Nature trails. Picnicking, playground. Camping, cabins. Standard hrs, fees. 5 mi S via US 17/92. Phone 904/775-3663.

DeLand Museum of Art. Exhibits focusing on the fine arts, concerts, classes, workshops, lectures, films and festivals. Tours. (Daily exc Mon; closed major hols) 600 N Woodland Blvd. Phone 904/734-4371. ¢

DeLeon Springs State Recreation Area. Old sugar mill (early 1800s); 50 acres of gardens. Swimming in "fountain of youth," bathhouse, snorkeling; fishing; paddleboats, canoeing (rentals). Hiking, nature trail. Picnicking, concession. Standard hrs, fees. 5 mi N via US 17, on Ponce de Leon Blvd, in DeLeon Springs. Phone 904/985-4212.

Hontoon Island State Park. This 1,650-acre island in St Johns River contains 300-ft-long Timucuan Indian ceremonial mound. Fishing. Nature trails. Picnicking. Tent camping, cabins. Overnight docking. Observation tower. No vehicles; accessible only by ferry boat from parking lot across river (daily; free). Standard hrs, fees. 6 mi SW off FL 44. Phone 904/736-5309.

Houseboat cruises. Two companies rent houseboats. On St Johns River. For information contact Hontoon Landing Resort and Marina, 800/248-2474 (FL) or Holly Bluff Marina, 800/237-5105.

Spring Garden Ranch. At 148 acres, Florida's largest harness training track houses 500 horses; trackside restaurant with observation deck. (Daily) 8 mi N on US 17. Phone 904/985-5654.

Stetson University (1883). (2,100 students) Historic campus includes DeLand Hall, Florida's oldest higher educational building in continuous use; William E. Holler Memorial Fountain, part of the Florida exhibit at the 1939 World's Fair; Gillespie Museum of Minerals (academic yr, daily exc Sun); Duncan Art Gallery (academic yr, daily). Tours. 516 N Woodland Blvd. Phone 904/822-8920.

Annual Events

Manatee Festival. Valentine Park, Orange City. Entertainment, endangered animal displays, children's activities, arts & crafts. Phone 904/775-1112. Late Jan.

DeLand-St Johns River Raft Race. 4 mi W via FL 44. Raft race competition on St Johns River. Mid-Sept.

Volusia County Fair & Youth Show. Fairgrounds, 5 mi E via FL 44. Midway, exhibits, stage shows, livestock show and auction. Phone 904/734-9514. Late Oct-mid-Nov.

Motel

✔★★ **QUALITY INN.** 2801 E New York (32724), off I-4 exit 56. 904/736-3440; FAX 904/736-7484. 112 rms, 2 story. Mid-Dec-Apr: S, D $54.99-$79.99; each addl $5; under 18 free; higher rates: special events, Daytona 500, July 4; lower rates rest of yr. Crib free. Pet accepted, some restrictions; $10. TV; cable (premium), VCR avail (movies $5). Pool; wading pool. Complimentary continental bkfst. Coffee in rms. Restaurant 6:30 am-10 pm. Rm serv. Bar noon-midnight; entertainment. Ck-out 11 am. Coin lndry. Meeting rms. Microwaves avail. Cr cds: A, C, D, DS, ER, JCB, MC, V.

D ✔ ≈ ⊠ 🔥 SC

Hotel

★★★ **HOLIDAY INN.** 350 International Speedway Blvd (32724), on US 92. 904/738-5200; FAX 904/734-7552. 149 rms, 6 story. S, D $69-$99; each addl $10; suites $89-$149; higher rates special events. Crib free. Pet accepted, some restrictions. TV; cable (premium), VCR avail. Pool; whirlpool. Restaurant 6:30 am-midnight. Ck-out noon. Meeting rms. Business servs avail. In-rm modem link. Health club privileges. Some refrigerators. Cr cds: A, C, D, DS, JCB, MC, V.

D ✔ ≈ ⊠ 🔥 SC

Restaurant

★★★ **PONDO'S.** 1915 Old New York Ave (32720). 904/734-1995. Hrs: 5-10 pm; Fri, Sat to 11 pm; Sun 4-9 pm; early-bird dinner to 6:30 pm. Res accepted. Continental menu. Bar. Semi-a la carte: dinner $9.95-$13.95. Child's meals. Specializes in veal, duck. Own pasta. Entertainment Fri, Sat. In historic guest house (1921). Cr cds: A, MC, V.

D 🍴

Delray Beach (G-6)

(See also Boca Raton, Boynton Beach, Palm Beach)

Settled 1895 **Pop** 47,181 **Elev** 20 ft **Area code** 561 **E-mail** chamber@delraybeach.com **Web** www.delraybeach.com

Information Chamber of Commerce, 64 SE 5th Ave, 33483; 561/278-0424.

This placid resort town boasts of beautiful beaches and excellent weather, championship golfing and fishing opportunities along with a historic downtown district. Many noteworthy restaurants and bistros help give Delray Beach a cosmopolitan air.

What to See and Do

Morikami Park. Park includes one-mi, self-guided nature trail. Picnicking. 4000 Morikami Park Rd, off I-95, Linton Blvd exit. Phone 561/495-0233. **Free.** Also here is

The Morikami Museum and Japanese Gardens. Includes gallery, tea ceremony house, theater; bonsai collection and surrounding gardens. (Daily exc Mon). ¢¢

Annual Events

Hatsume Fair. Morikami Park (see). Two-day event featuring Japanese performing arts, food, bonsai exhibits, Asian arts & crafts, exotic plants. Late Feb.

Delray Affair. Arts & crafts and entertainment street festival. Mid-Apr.

Bon Festival. Morikami Park (see). Japanese summer festival features Japanese folk dancing and music, games, food, special displays. Mid-Aug.

Motel

★★ **BREAKERS ON-THE-OCEAN.** 1875 S Ocean Blvd (33483). 561/278-4501; FAX 561/276-6391. 22 kit. suites, 2 story. Feb-Mar: kit. suites $190; each addl $25; lower rates rest of yr. TV; cable. Heated pool. Complimentary continental bkfst. Ck-out 11 am. Free lndry facilities. Business servs avail. Putting green. Rec rm. On ocean; private beach, cabanas. No cr cds accepted.

D ✔ ≈ 🔥

★★ **SEA BREEZE.** 820 N Ocean Blvd (33483). 561/276-7496. 23 kit. units, 1-2 story. Feb-Mar: S, D $74-$194; each addl $15; lower rates rest of yr. Crib $2. TV; cable. Heated pool. Ck-out 11 am. Coin lndry. In-rm modem link. Lawn games. Microwaves. Picnic tables, grills. Ocean opp. Cr cds: MC, V.

≈ 🔥

Motor Hotels

★★ **HOLIDAY INN HIGHLAND BEACH.** (2809 S Ocean Blvd, Highland Beach 33487) 1 mi S on Ocean Blvd. 561/278-6241; FAX 561/278-6241, ext. 431. 114 rms, 3-6 story. Mid-Dec-Apr: S, D $135-$205; each addl $10; under 19 free; varied lower rates rest of yr. Crib free. TV; cable (premium), VCR avail (movies). Heated pool; wading pool. Restaurant 7 am-10 pm. Rm serv. Bar 11-1 am. Ck-out noon. Coin lndry. Meeting rms. Business servs avail. In-rm modem link. Beach shop. Golf privileges. Some refrigerators. Some private patios, balconies. On beach. Cr cds: A, C, D, DS, ER, JCB, MC, V.

D 🍴 ≈ ⊠ 🔥 SC

★★ **SEAGATE HOTEL & BEACH CLUB.** 400 S Ocean Blvd (33483). 561/276-2421; FAX 561/243-4714; res: 800/233-3581. 70 suites, 2-3 story. Feb-Easter: suites $259-$289; studios $169-$179; each addl $15; under 17 free; lower rates rest of yr. Crib free. TV; cable (premium). 2 pools, 1 saltwater. Complimentary continental bkfst. Restaurant 11:30 am-9:30 pm. Supervised child's activities (wkends). Ck-out noon. Guest lndry. Meeting rm. Business servs avail. In-rm modem link. Valet serv. Free valet parking. Opp private beach, water sports rentals; bar. Cr cds: A, C, D, DS, MC, V.

D ≈ ⊠ 🔥 SC

Restaurants

★★★ **DAMIANO'S AT THE TARRIMORE HOUSE.** 52 N Swinton Ave (33444). 561/272-4706. Hrs: 6-10 pm. Closed Mon, Tues; most major hols. Res accepted. Continental menu. Wine, beer. Semi-a la carte: dinner $18-$25. Child's meals. Specialties: Pineapple Grove Florasian lacquered duck, potato and sweet onion-crusted yellow tail snapper, Tarrimore House stone bake piroski turnover. Own desserts. Valet parking. Outdoor dining. Three dining rms with distinct atmospheres: the Russian Room, the Japanese Room and the Julia Room (which pays tribute to old Delray). Cr cds: A, MC, V.

D

★★ **PETER'S STONE CRABS.** 411 E Atlantic Ave (33483). 561/278-0036. Hrs: 4-10 pm; early-bird dinner 4-5:45 pm. Closed Mon. Res accepted. Bar. A la carte entrees: dinner $13-$30. Specializes in seafood. Pianist. Valet parking. Casual dining. Cr cds: A, C, D, DS, MC, V.

D

Destin (J-2)

(See also Fort Walton Beach)

Pop 8,080 **Elev** 33 ft **Area code** 850 **Zip** 32541 **Web**
www.destinchamber.com
Information Chamber of Commerce, 1021 US 98 E, Ste A, PO Box 8,
32540; 850/837-6241.

Perched on a narrow strip of land between Choctawhatchee Bay and the
Gulf of Mexico, Destin has turned from commercial to sport fishing. Trolling
boats ply the waters of the Gulf for king mackerel, cobia, marlin, wahoo and
sailfish. Party boats bring in red snapper and grouper. Destin retains the
atmosphere of the New England birthplace of its founder, Captain Leonard
Destin, who pioneered the snapper fishing industry more than 100 years
ago.

What to See and Do

Eden State Gardens. Overlooking Choctawhatchee Bay, this was once
the site of a large sawmill complex. Eden House, built by William Henry
Wesley in 1897, is restored and furnished with antiques. Mansion tours
(Thurs-Mon). Gardens, picnic area (daily). 24 mi E on US 98, then N on
County 395 to Point Washington, follow signs. Phone 850/231-4214. Tours
¢

Grayton Beach State Recreation Area. Swimming, skin diving; saltwater
fishing. Nature trail. Picnicking. Camping (electric hookups, dump station).
Standard hrs, fees. 20 mi E on US 98, off FL 30A in Santa Rosa Beach.
Phone 850/231-4210.

Annual Events

Seafood Festival. Seafood, entertainment. 1st wkend Oct.

Deep-Sea Fishing Rodeo. $150,000 in prizes. Oct.

Motels

★ ★ **FRANGISTA BEACH INN.** *1860 Old Hwy 98.* 850/654-
5501; FAX 850/654-5876; res: 800/382-2612. 53 rms, 42 suites, 2 cottages. May-Aug: S, D $125-$135; suites $155-$195; cottages $225-$375;
wkly rates; hols (4-day min); lower rates rest of yr. Crib free. TV; cable,
VCR avail. Pool; whirlpool. Complimentary coffee in rms. Rm serv. Restaurant adj 11:30 am-2 pm, 5-10 pm. Ck-out 11 am. Coin lndry. Business
servs avail. In-rm modem link. Refrigerators. Some balconies. Picnic
tables. On beach. Cr cds: A, D, DS, MC, V.

⌨ 🏄 ≈ 🔥

★ **SEA OATS.** *3420 Scenic Hwy 98, 5 mi E on US 98.*
850/837-6655; res: 888/732-6287. 42 rms, 38 kits. Mid-May-early Sept: S, D $80-$120; kit. units
$90-$120; 3-day min in season; wkly rates; lower rates rest of yr. TV;
cable. Heated pool. Ck-out 10 am. Business servs avail. Refrigerators;
microwaves avail. Balconies. Picnic tables. On beach. View of gulf. Cr cds:
DS, MC, V.

≈ 🔥

★ **SLEEP INN.** *10775 Emerald Coast Pkwy, E on US 98.*
850/654-7022; FAX 850/654-7022. 77 rms, 2 story. May-Labor Day: S
$85-$110; D $90-$120; each addl $5; suites $120-$130; family rates; lower
rates rest of yr. TV; cable. Pool. Complimentary continental bkfst. Restaurant nearby. Ck-out 11 am. Coin lndry. Business servs avail. Refrigerator,
wet bar in suites. Cr cds: A, C, D, DS, JCB, MC, V.

⌨ ≈ 🔥 SC

Motor Hotel

★ ★ ★ **HOLIDAY INN.** *1020 US 98E.* 850/837-6181; FAX
850/837-1523. 233 rms, 4 & 9 story. May-Labor Day: S, D $140-$190;

each addl $10; under 18 free; golf plan; lower rates rest of yr. Crib free. TV;
cable (premium). 2 pools, 1 indoor; wading pool, whirlpool. Supervised
child's activities (Memorial Day-Labor Day); ages 5-12. Restaurant 6:30
am-2 pm, 5-10 pm. Rm serv. Bar 11 am-midnight. Ck-out 11 am. Meeting
rms. Business servs avail. In-rm modem link. Bellhops in season. Gift
shop. Tennis privileges. Exercise equipt; sauna. Rec rm. Balconies. On
beach. Cr cds: A, C, D, DS, JCB, MC, V.

⌨ 🏄 ≈ 🏃 🔥 SC

Hotel

★ ★ ★ **HILTON-SANDESTIN BEACH GOLF & TENNIS RE-
SORT.** *4000 Sandestin Blvd S.* 850/267-9500; FAX 850/267-3076; res:
800/367-1271. 598 suites, 15 story. May-Sept: S, D $230-$345; golf, tennis
plans; lower rates rest of yr. Crib free. TV; cable, VCR (movies $6).
Indoor/outdoor pool; wading pool, poolside serv. Supervised child's activities (May-Sept); ages 5-12. Restaurants 7 am-10:30 pm. Bar 11-2 am;
entertainment. Ck-out noon. Convention facilities. Business center. In-rm
modem link. Concierge. Shopping arcade. Valet parking. Tennis, pro.
63-hole golf, greens fee $66, pro, putting green, driving range. Exercise rm.
Health club privileges. Bathrm phones, refrigerators, microwaves, minibars. Private patios, balconies. On beach. Cr cds: A, C, D, DS, MC, V.

🏄 🏃 🏌 ≈ 🏃 🔥 SC 🚣

Inn

★ ★ ★ **HENDERSON PARK INN.** *2700 US 98E, near Henderson
Beach State Park.* 850/654-0400; FAX 850/654-0405; res: 800/336-4853.
35 rms, 3 story. May-early Sept: S, D $180-$279; wkly rates; lower rates
rest of yr. TV; cable. Heated pool. Complimentary bkfst. Complimentary
coffee in rms. Dining rm 7-10 am, 11:30 am-2 pm, 6-9 pm (res required).
Rm serv. Ck-out 11 am, ck-in 3-5 pm. Meeting rm. Business servs avail.
Bellhops. Microwaves. Many balconies. On beach; swimming. Queen
Anne/Victorian-style building. Cr cds: A, DS, MC, V.

⌨ ≈ 🔥

Resorts

★ ★ ★ **SANDESTIN.** *9300 US 98W.* 850/267-8000; res: 800/277-
0800; FAX 850/267-8222. E-mail lifetime@sandestin.com; web www.sand
estin.com. 175 rms in hotel, 525 kit. villas (1-4 bedrm). May-Sept: S, D,
suites $200-$215; tower units $240-$645; villas $220-$440; lower rates
rest of yr. Crib $5. TV; cable. 13 pools; wading pool, whirlpool, poolside
serv. Supervised child's activities (Mar-Sept); ages 4-17. Dining rms 7
am-10 pm (in season). Box lunches. Snack bar. Bar; entertainment. Ck-out
11 am, ck-in 4 pm. Convention facilities. Business center. Grocery. Valet
serv. Sports dir. Tennis, pro. 63-hole golf, greens fee, driving range, putting
green. Sailing, charter boats. Bicycles. Nature trail. Rec rm. Exercise rm;
steam rm, sauna. Refrigerators, microwaves. Private patios, balconies. On
2,400 acres along Gulf, bay shores. Cr cds: A, C, D, DS, MC, V.

⌨ 🏄 🏃 ≈ 🏃 🔥 SC 🚣

★ **SEASCAPE.** *100 Seascape Dr, 7 mi E on Emerald Coast
Pkwy.* 850/837-9181; FAX 850/837-4769; res: 800/874-9106. Web
www.destinweb.com/seascape. 120 kit. cottages. Mar-Oct: cottages $130-
$270 (3-day min hols); wkly rates; lower rates rest of yr. Crib $10. TV;
cable, VCR avail. 5 pools; wading pool. Dining rm 6 am-8 pm. Snack bar.
Bar. Ck-out 11 am, ck-in 4 pm. Grocery, package store 1 mi. Convention
facilities. Business servs avail. Lighted tennis, pro. 18-hole golf, pro,
putting green, driving range. Swimming beach. Bicycle rentals. Exercise
equipt. Microwaves avail. Bathrm phones. Balconies. Grills. On ocean
beach. Cr cds: A, D, MC, V.

🏄 🏌 🏃 ≈ 🏃 🏃

★ ★ **TOPS'L BEACH & RACQUET CLUB.** *9011 US 98W, 10
mi E on US 98.* 850/267-9222; res: 888/867-7535; FAX 850/267-9267.
E-mail rentals@abbott-resorts.com; web www.abbott-resorts.com. 274
rms, 14 story, 125 villas (2-3-bedrm). Memorial Day-Labor Day: S, D, kit.
suites, villas $138-$474; lower rates rest of yr. Crib $5-$8. TV; cable, VCR

(free movies). 4 heated pools, 1 indoor; wading pool, poolside serv, whirlpool. Restaurant 11 am-11 pm. Ck-out 10 am, ck-in 3-5 pm. Grocery 1½ mi. Lndry facilities. Package store. Meeting rms. Business servs avail. Covered parking. Sports dir. 10 lighted clay, 2 hard-surfaced tennis courts, pro. Exercise rm; sauna, steam rm. Private swimming beach. Sailboats. Entertainment. Refrigerators, microwaves; many fireplaces. Private patios, balconies. Gulf view. 55 acres of dunes, beachfront and wooded terrain. Cr cds: A, DS, MC, V.

Restaurants

★ **CAPT. DAVE'S ON THE GULF.** *3796 Old FL 98. 850/837-2627.* Hrs: 4:30-10 pm. Closed Dec 24, 25. Bar. Semi-a la carte: dinner $10-$30. Child's meals. Specializes in broiled, grilled and fried local seafood. Casual decor. Cr cds: A, DS, MC, V.

★ ★ **DESTIN CHOPS.** *320 FL 98 E, on second floor. 850/654-4944.* Web www.marinacafe.com. Hrs: from 5 pm; early-bird dinner 5-6 pm. Closed Jan 1, Dec 25. Res accepted. Steak menu. Bar. Semi-a la carte: dinner $16-$27. Specialties: steaks, chops, seafood. Valet parking. Outdoor dining. Fine dining. Cr cds: A, D, DS, MC, V.

★ ★ **FLAMINGO CAFE.** *414 US 98E. 850/837-0961.* Hrs: 5-10 pm. Closed Dec 25. Res accepted. Continental menu. Bar. Semi-a la carte: dinner $16-$29. Child's meals. Specializes in coastal dishes. Own desserts. Pianist Thurs-Sat. Outdoor dining. On waterfront. Cr cds: A, D, DS, MC, V.

✔★ ★ **LA PAZ.** *950 Gulfshore Dr. 850/837-2247.* Hrs: 11 am-2 pm, 5-10 pm; Sun from 5 pm. Closed Thanksgiving, Dec 25. Mexican menu. Bar. A la carte entrees: lunch, dinner $4.95-$16.95. Specializes in fresh seafood. Patio dining. Southwestern decor; casual atmosphere. Cr cds: A, D, DS, MC, V.

★ ★ **LOUISIANA LAGNIAPPE.** *775 Gulfshore Dr, in Sandpiper Cove. 850/837-0881.* Hrs: 5 pm-closing. Closed Nov-Feb. Cajun menu. Bar. Semi-a la carte: dinner $11.95-$21.95. Child's meals. Specializes in Louisiana seafood, steak, Maine lobster. Own desserts. Valet parking. Outdoor dining overlooking Old Pass Lagoon. Cr cds: A, C, D, DS, MC, V.

★ ★ **MARINA CAFE.** *404 US 98E. 850/837-7960.* Hrs: 5-11 pm. Closed 2 wks Jan. Bar. A la carte entrees: dinner $16-$27. Specializes in seafood, pizza, game. Outdoor dining. Split-level dining room with view of water. Cr cds: A, D, DS, MC, V.

Disney World

(see Walt Disney World)

Dry Tortugas National Park (K-4)

(See also Key West)

(68 mi W of Key West; reached by boat or seaplane)

Covering approximately 64,000 acres of land and water, this national park includes not only the remains of what was once the largest of the 19th-cen-

tury American coastal forts, but also the cluster of seven islands known as the Dry Tortugas.

The coral keys, upon which the fort sits, in 1513 were named "las tortugas" (the turtles) by Ponce de Leon because so many turtles inhabited these bits of land. The "dry" portion of the islands' name warns mariners of a total lack of fresh water. Tropical ocean birds are the chief inhabitants; each year, between February and September, sooty and noddy terns assemble on Bush Key to nest.

Spanish pirates used the Tortugas as a base from which to pillage boats until 1821, when they were driven from the islands. In 1846, the United States, eager to protect its interests in the Gulf of Mexico, began construction of a fort on 10-acre Garden Key. For more than 30 years, laborers worked on the fort, a rampart one-half mile in perimeter with 50-foot-high walls and 3 tiers designed for 450 guns. Called the "Gibraltar of the Gulf," this massive masonry fort was designed for a garrison of 1,500 men. Only partially completed, Fort Jefferson never saw battle. It was occupied by Union troops during the Civil War.

Resting on an unstable foundation of sand and coral boulders, Fort Jefferson's walls began to crack and shift, making it unsuitable for military defense. In 1863, it became a military prison, confining some 2,400 men. Among them was Dr. Samuel Mudd, who was imprisoned on the island after setting the broken leg of John Wilkes Booth, Abraham Lincoln's assassin. Following two yellow fever epidemics and a hurricane, the fort was abandoned in 1874. In the 1880s it was reconditioned for use as a naval base, coaling station and wireless station; the USS *Maine* sailed from the fort for Havana, where she was blown up, triggering the Spanish-American War. The fort became Fort Jefferson National Monument in 1935 and was renamed Dry Tortugas National Park in 1992.

The fort and islands are accessible by boat or seaplane trips from Key West (see). There is camping and a picnic area on Garden Key; campers must bring all supplies, including fresh water. Visitor center (daily). Guided tours. Contact the Park Ranger, PO Box 6208, Key West 33041; 305/242-7700. For transportation information, contact the Greater Key West Chamber of Commerce, 402 Wall St, Old Mallory Sq, Key West 33040; 305/294-2587.

Dunedin (E-3)

(See also Clearwater, St Petersburg, Tampa, Tarpon Springs)

Founded 1870 **Pop** 34,012 **Elev** 11 ft **Area code** 813 **Zip** 34698 **Web** dunedin-fl.com
Information Greater Dunedin Chamber of Commerce, 301 Main St; 813/733-3197.

One of Florida's oldest coastal towns, its name is derived from *Edinburgh*, Scotland. Several buildings in this community are listed on the National Historical Register.

What to See and Do

Caladesi Island State Park. A 607-acre island accessible only by boat. Swimming; boating (dock). Nature trails. Picnicking. No vehicles. Standard hrs, fees. Ferry service from mainland, weather permitting. N via US 19A, W on FL 586 (Dunedin Causeway) to ferry dock on Honeymoon Island. Phone 813/469-5918 or 813/734-5263 (ferry).

Honeymoon Island State Recreation Area. One of the few remaining virgin slash pine stands in south Florida may be observed along the island's northern loop trail. These large trees serve as important nesting sites for the threatened osprey. The island, with more than 208 species of plants and a wide variety of shore birds, including several threatened and endangered species, is a prime area for nature study. Swimming; fishing for flounder, snook, redfish, trout, snapper and tarpon. Nature trails. Picnicking. Ferry service to Caladesi Island State Park. Standard hrs, fees. 2 mi N via US 19A, W on FL 586 (Dunedin Causeway). Phone 813/469-5942 or 813/734-5263 (ferry).

Annual Event

Highland Games & Scottish Festival. Early Apr.

Seasonal Event

Spring training. Dunedin Stadium, 311 Douglas Ave. Toronto Blue Jays baseball spring training; exhibition games. Phone 813/733-9302. Mar.

Motels

★ ★ **BEST WESTERN YACHT HARBOR INN AND SUITES.** *150 Marina Plaza, 3 mi W of US 19 on Main St.* 727/733-4121; FAX 727/736-4365. Web www.advantuscorp.com. 55 rms, 2 story, 36 kits. Feb-Apr: S, D $109; kits. $129; under 12 free; lower rates rest of yr. Crib $10. TV; cable. Heated pool. Complimentary continental bkfst. Restaurant 11:30 am-10 pm. Ck-out 11 am. Business servs avail. In-rm modem link. Some refrigerators, microwaves. Overlooks St Joseph's Sound. Cr cds: A, C, D, DS, MC, V.

✔★ **INN ON THE BAY.** *1420 Bayshore Blvd (US 19A).* 727/734-7689; res: 800/759-5045; FAX 727/734-0972. 42 kit. units, 4 story. Jan-Apr: S, D $74-$85; suites $99; wkly rates; lower rates rest of yr. TV; cable (premium). Heated pool. Restaurant 7 am-2 pm, 5-9 pm; Fri, Sat to 10 pm. Bar. Ck-out 11 am. Coin lndry. Microwaves avail. Balconies. On bay; fishing dock. Cr cds: A, DS, MC, V.

Restaurants

★ ★ ★ **BON APPETIT.** *148 Marina Plaza.* 727/733-2151. Web www.advantuscorp.com. Hrs: 11:30 am-9 pm; Sun brunch 11:30 am-4 pm. Res accepted. Continental menu. Bar. Wine cellar. Semi-a la carte: lunch $4.95-$13.95, dinner $8.99-$26.95. Sun brunch $5.75-$12.95. Child's meals. Specialties: Dover sole, rack of lamb, mixed seafood grill. Valet parking. Outdoor terrace dining. Waterfront dining on Intracoastal Waterway. Cr cds: A, C, D, DS, MC, V.

★ **CAFE ALFRESCO.** *344 Main St, on Pinellas Trail.* 727/736-4299. Web www.advantuscorp.com. Hrs: 11 am-9 pm; Fri to 10 pm; Sat 10 am-10 pm; Sun from 10 am; Sat, Sun brunch to 2 pm. Closed Thanksgiving, Dec 25. Beer, wine. Semi-a la carte: lunch, dinner $2.95-$13.50. Sat, Sun brunch $1.95-$7.50. Specializes in pasta, shrimp, chicken. Outdoor dining. Bistro atmosphere. Cr cds: A, D, DS, ER, JCB, MC, V.

✔★ **SEA SEA RIDERS.** *221 Main St.* 727/734-1445. Hrs: 11:30 am-10 pm; Fri, Sat to 11 pm; Sun brunch to 2 pm. Res accepted. Bar. Semi-a la carte: lunch $4.95-$6.95, dinner $8.95-$14.95. Sun brunch $3.95-$5.95. Child's meals. Specializes in fresh Florida seafood. Outdoor dining on veranda. In (1923) Florida Cracker house, original fireplace. Cr cds: A, MC, V.

Englewood (G-3)

(See also Port Charlotte, Punta Gorda, Venice)

Pop 15,025 **Elev** 13 ft **Area code** 941 **E-mail** eacc@sunline.net **Web** www.charlotte-florida.com/community/echamber.htm
Information Englewood Area Chamber of Commerce, 601 Indiana Ave S, 34223; 941/474-5511 or 800/603-7198.

Motels

✔★ **DAYS INN.** *2540 S McCall Rd (FL 776) (34224).* 941/474-5544; FAX 941/475-2124. 84 rms, 2 story, 48 kits. Feb-mid-Apr: S, D $62-$115; each addl $4; under 13 free; lower rates rest of yr. Crib free. Pet accepted, some restrictions; $4. TV; cable. Heated pool. Playground. Restaurant 6 am-2 pm. Ck-out noon. Business servs avail. Microwaves avail. Private patios; some balconies. Cr cds: A, D, DS, MC, V.

★ **PEARL BEACH.** *7990 Manasota Key Rd (34223).* 941/474-3316; FAX 941/474-3316. 11 kit. units. No rm phones. Late Dec-late Apr: kit. units $90-$110; wkly rates; lower rates rest of yr. TV. Ck-out 10 am. Business servs avail. Microwaves. Some balconies. Picnic tables. On beach. Cr cds: DS, MC, V.

★ **VERANDA INN OF ENGLEWOOD.** *2073 S McCall Rd (FL 776) (34224).* 941/475-6533; res: 800/633-8115. 38 rms, 3 story. Feb-mid-Apr: S, D $85-$90; each addl $6; under 16 free; lower rates rest of yr. Crib free. Pet accepted; $10. TV, cable. Heated pool. Complimentary coffee in lobby. Restaurant adj 11 am-9 pm. Ck-out 11 am. Coin lndry. Business servs avail. Microwaves avail. On creek. Cr cds: A, D, DS, MC, V.

Resort

★ ★ **PALM ISLAND.** *(7092 Placida Rd, Cape Haze 33946) 5 mi S via FL 776 & County Rd 775.* 941/697-4800; FAX 941/697-0696; res: 800/824-5412. 160 kit. villas, 2 story. Mid-Dec-mid-Apr (3-day min): villas $115-$420; wkly rates; package plans; 2-day min off season; lower rates rest of yr. Crib $10. TV; cable, VCR avail (movies). 5 heated pools; whirlpools. 2 playgrounds. Supervised child's activities. Restaurant noon-9:30 pm. Bar to 10 pm. Ck-out 11:30 am, ck-in 2:30 pm. Grocery. Free lndry facilities. Package store. Meeting rm. Business servs avail. Bellhops. Maid serv wkly. Gift shop. Sports dir. Tennis, pro. Golf privileges. Health club privileges. Bicycle rentals. Lawn games. Fishing guides; cleaning. Microwaves. Picnic tables, grills. Swimming beach. On island in Gulf of Mexico. Cr cds: A, MC, V.

Restaurant

✔★ **FLYING BRIDGE II.** *2080 S McCall Rd (FL 776) (34224).* 941/474-2206. Hrs: 11 am-9 pm. Res accepted major hols. Semi-a la carte: lunch $2.65-$6.95, dinner $5.75-$12.95. Child's meals. Specializes in seafood, ribs, steaks. Outdoor dining. On waterfront. Cr cds: DS, MC, V.

Everglades National Park (H-5)

(See also Coral Gables, Miami)

(S of I-75, W of Miami)

This 2,400-square-mile corner of the United States is the largest subtropical wilderness in North America. The park preserves the spectacular half-land, half-water Everglades that once covered most of the southern third of the Florida peninsula.

From Lake Okeechobee to the northern border of the park, much of the glades have been drained and tamed, leaving an incredibly rich blue-black soil responsible for huge sugar, citrus and winter vegetable crops. In addition to the national park, the remaining area, larger than the state of Delaware, has been developed by the South Florida Water Management District into a huge recreation area with hunting, fishing, boating, camping and sightseeing. Easily reached from cities along Florida's east coast are 34 access sites, located along the canals and levees that have been constructed to protect 18 counties from flood and drought. For information write the District at PO Box V, West Palm Beach 33402.

Nowhere else in the world is there an area comparable to this huge, water-sodden wetland with its prairies of saw grass, stands of dwarf cypress, hammocks of cabbage palm, West Indies mahogany, strangler figs and wild orchids. The mood is serene, but the entire expanse teems with water birds, alligators, snakes, marsh rabbits, deer, raccoons, bobcats, turtles, largemouth bass, garfish and panfish. (Wildlife is visible mainly during the winter months.) This is also part of the traditional domain of the Seminole & Miccosukee.

Much of the Everglades is an immense sea of sedges that shoot up 10 feet with barbed blades and needle-sharp edges, appropriately called saw grass. These grassy waters are broken only by clusters of trees and dense vegetation called hammocks. The saw grass glades give way along the coast to huge, shadowy mangrove swamps interlaced by tranquil winding water lanes.

Much of the national park is impenetrable except with an experienced guide; however, the National Park Service has set up trails (all improved or marked), exhibits and facilities that make a safe excursion into the Everglades possible for any visitor. Facilities for the disabled include trails developed to accommodate wheelchairs, ramps to visitor centers, rest rooms and designated campsites.

Accidentally set fires can be a severe danger in the Everglades; ground fires are not permitted. Smoking is also forbidden on nature trails. Pets must be on a leash and are not permitted on the trails or in the backcountry. Hunting is not allowed. Do not feed or disturb the wildlife and stay clear of the alligators— *they are not tame.* Insects, especially mosquitoes, are most plentiful during May-November.

Golden Eagle, Golden Age and Golden Access Passport (see MAKING THE MOST OF YOUR TRIP) and park passport (fee) accepted. Contact the Park Superintendent, 40001 State Rd 9336, Homestead 33034; 305/242-7700. Entrance fee per vehicle (7-day permit) ¢¢¢

What to See and Do

The main road into the park runs southwest from Homestead to Flamingo (50 mi); allow plenty of time. From Homestead it is approx 12 mi on FL 9336 to the Entrance Station. The visitor center has exhibits, orientation programs and information about the Everglades (daily).

Flamingo, with visitor center, museum (daily) and interpretive programs (winter, daily), marina, sightseeing and charter fishing boats, houseboat rentals; it is the starting point for canoe trails. Picnicking, restaurant (Nov-May), lodge, service station. Camping (fee Sept-May; no trailer hookups; dump station; 800/365-2267).

Long Pine Key Area turnoff. Campgrounds (fee; no reservations; dump station); picnicking facilities. Stays at campsites limited to 14 consecutive days, 30 days in a calender year. Campfire talks (mid-Dec-mid-Apr).

Mahogany Hammock. An elevated boardwalk leads into a hardwood hammock with orchids, ferns and strangler figs and a stand of the largest mahogany trees in the US.

Pa-hay-okee. An elevated trail leads to a high platform that offers an excellent view of the Shark River Slough, where many birds and alligators gather; it is an excellent place to take photographs.

Paurotis Pond, with paurotis palms and mangroves. This is the transition zone between fresh and salt water. There is a small lakeside picnic area.

Pineland Trail. Slender slash pines, saw-palmetto and short-leaf fig trees, marked by signs, line this trail.

Royal Palm Station turnoff. Here are the Anhinga Trail, one of the best nature and wildlife trails in the park, and Gumbo Limbo Trail, which leads through a tropical hardwood hammock.

Shark Valley tram tours originate at parking area 30 mi W of Miami on US 41. Two-hr narrated tour along Shark Valley loop road with half-hr stop at observation tower. Abundant wildlife can be seen, especially in winter. No pets. For tram information and reservations phone 305/221-8455. National Park Service entry fee per vehicle (7-day permit) ¢¢

The Western Water Gateway, at Everglades City in the northwest corner of the park, is the starting point for rental-canoe trips along a 99-mi wilderness waterway on the inland route from Everglades City to Flamingo. There is a visitor center. Scenic boat tours leave from the Park Docks, Chokoloskee Causeway on FL 29 (daily). Phone 941/695-2591.

West Lake. An elevated boardwalk leads into a mangrove forest.

Fernandina Beach (B-4)

(See also Amelia Island, Atlantic Beach, Jacksonville)

Settled 1686 **Pop** 8,765 **Elev** 19 ft **Area code** 904 **Zip** 32035 **Web** www.ameliaisland.org
Information Amelia Island-Fernandina Beach-Yulee Chamber of Commerce, 102 Centre St, PO Box 472; 904/277-0717 or 800/226-3542.

The northernmost city on Florida's east coast, Fernandina Beach is the only incorporated city on Amelia Island. It received its name in 1811 from King Ferdinand VII of Spain.

During the course of four centuries, eight flags have flown over this area, starting with the French in 1562, followed by the Spanish and British. In 1812, the Patriots flag flew, followed in short order by General Sir Gregor MacGregor's personal flag, the Green Cross of Florida, and then, for a brief period, the flag of Mexico. The United States formally took possession of the island in 1821. At the outbreak of the Civil War, the Confederate flag was raised over Fernandina and Fort Clinch, but it was lowered in 1862, when the town was the target of a Union fleet.

Today, Fernandina Beach's harbor provides mooring for a large and prosperous shrimping fleet; two local pulp mills produce linerboard for paper containers and chemical cellulose; a 50-block restored Victorian historical district, including redeveloped Centre Street, is located downtown.

What to See and Do

Amelia Island Museum of History. Recited oral history, using artifacts and exhibits, recounts 400 yrs of settlement under 8 flags; materials from 17th-century Spanish mission archeological site; artifacts from 18th-century shipwrecks; 19th-century "Golden Age" decorative arts and photographs. Docent-guided tours. (Daily exc Sun; closed hols) 233 S 3rd St. Phone 904/261-7378. ¢

Beaches. Swimming, surfing; surfcasting. Picnicking. Amusement area. 13 mi of beaches along Atlantic.

Fort Clinch State Park. This 1,100-acre park is the most northeasterly point in Florida. The old fort's brick ramparts offer a view of the Georgia shoreline and the Atlantic Ocean. A living history interpretation is provided by park rangers dressed in Union uniforms of the 1864 garrison. Swimming; fishing from 1,500-ft pier, the shore and jetties. Nature trails. Picnicking. Camping (hookups, dump station). Visitor center. Standard hrs, fees. Entrance on Atlantic Ave off FL A1A. Phone 904/277-7274.

Annual Event

Isle of Eight Flags Shrimp Festival. Blessing of the Shrimp Fleet, art show, folk festival, mock pirates landing. 1st wkend May.

Restaurant

✔★ **DOWN UNDER.** *A1A at Intracoastal Waterway (32034).* 904/261-1001. Hrs: 5-10 pm; Labor Day-Memorial Day to 9 pm. Closed Mon (Labor Day-Memorial Day); Thanksgiving, Dec 25. Res accepted. Bar. Semi-a la carte: dinner $13.95-$17.95. Child's meals. Specializes in seafood. Rustic atmosphere. Cr cds: A, MC, V.

Fisher Island

(see Miami)

Florida Keys (K-4 - J-6)

(Extending SW of Miami along US 1)

E-mail klchamber@aol.com **Web** floridakeys.org
Information Key Largo Chamber of Commerce, Florida Keys Visitor Center, 106000 Overseas Hwy Key Largo 33037; 305/451-1414 or 800/822-1088.

Like a string of coral beads, the Florida Keys sweep in a graceful arc, southwest from a point south of Miami, 100 miles into the Gulf of Mexico. Forty-two beads in this tropical strand are linked by US 1, Florida's Overseas Highway—a road that goes to sea and ends at Key West. The most spectacular over-water drive in the world, this highway divides the blue waters of the Atlantic from the green of the Gulf of Mexico. Forty-two bridges connect the islands. The entire drive can be made in less than half a day, but few can resist the temptation to stop along the way to admire the seascape and landscape.

Until 1912, the Keys remained largely in tranquil isolation—with interludes of high adventure by boisterous buccaneers, devious freebooters and vengeful Indians. That year, one of the great achievements in railroading was completed when Henry Morrison Flagler extended the Florida East Coast Railroad all the way to Key West, where a train ferry continued to Havana. In 1935, a hurricane made a shambles of Flagler's dream; the US Government took over and opened the Overseas Highway in 1938.

Each major Key is different, and each has its special lure for the visitor. The pristine isolation of many of the islands has given way to mainland lifestyle, but travelers can still find peace and quiet along the route.

In November 1990, Congress designated the approximately 2,700 square nautical miles of marine environment surrounding the Florida Keys as Florida Keys National Marine Sanctuary, to address increasing public concern about the escalating threats to each of the natural areas that comprise a healthy marine ecosystem. While some areas will continue to be used in the accustomed way, others will be designated for preservation, restoration or scientific research. For information regarding sanctuary regulations and developments contact Education Dept, Florida Keys National Marine Sanctuary, PO Box 1083, Key Largo 33037.

For additional information on the Keys area, see the following towns included in the *Mobil Travel Guide:* Big Pine Key, Islamorada, Key Largo, Key West, Marathon.

Fort Caroline National Memorial (B-4)

(See also Atlantic Beach, Jacksonville)

(13 mi E of Jacksonville on FL 10, then N on Monument Rd, then E on Fort Caroline Rd)

Fort de la Caroline, a triangular, wood and earthen fortress, once stood near this site. In June 1564, René de Laudonnière established a short-lived foothold for France in the battle for supremacy in the New World. Unfortunately for France, the group of 200 colonists, mostly Huguenots, were more interested in finding mineral wealth than in long-term survival.

Driven by famine and futility, the colonists were about to abandon in August 1565, when reinforcements arrived from France. At the same time, Spanish Captain-General Pedro Menéndez de Avilés was ordered by King Philip II to clear Florida for Spanish colonization. Foiled in his initial efforts to destroy Fort de la Caroline, Menéndez sailed 30 miles south and established a settlement known today as St Augustine. The French tried to attack, but their fleet was destroyed in a storm. Menéndez took 500 men overland to Fort de la Caroline, killed about 140 of the French and took approximately 70 women and children prisoner. An additional 40 to 50 men escaped back to France. About 300 shipwrecked Frenchmen also were captured and slain at Matanzas Inlet (see FORT MATANZAS NATIONAL MONUMENT).

In 1568, a French expedition attacked and burned the former Fort de la Caroline, still in Spanish hands. Florida, however, was to remain in Spain's control almost continuously for the next 200 years. Nearby St Johns Bluff was the scene of later British and Spanish fortifications. Gun batteries were raised on the bluff during both the Civil War and the Spanish-American War.

An outdoor fort exhibit has been constructed along 280 feet of riverfront. Descriptions of the fort by its commander and sketches by Jacques Le Moyne, artist and mapmaker, both of whom escaped the early attacks, served as a blueprint. A visitor center overlooks the St Johns River near the former site of the colony. (Daily; closed Dec 25) For further information contact 13165 Mt Pleasant, Jacksonville 32225; 904/641-7155. **Free.**

Fort Lauderdale (H-6)

(See also Boca Raton, Dania, Hollywood, Pompano Beach)

Pop 149,377 **Elev** 10 ft **Area code** 954 **E-mail** gflcvb@co.broward.fl.us **Web** www.sunny.org
Information Greater Fort Lauderdale Convention & Visitors Bureau, 1850 Eller Dr, Suite 303, 33316; 954/765-4466 or 800/227-8669.

With more than 300 miles of navigable waterways, 23 miles of Atlantic beaches and a myriad of rivers, inlets and man-made canals in the Greater Fort Lauderdale area, the city easily lives up to its nickname "the Venice of America." The abundance of water provides ample port for approximately 40,000 boats, not to mention flotillas of visiting vessels. Water taxis ply waterways to hotels, restaurants and sightseeing attractions. Port Everglades, the deepest and perhaps best-known harbor in the state, is also the world's second largest passenger cruise port. More than one million passengers sail from Fort Lauderdale annually.

Fort Lauderdale was named for Major William Lauderdale, who built a fort in 1838 during the Seminole War. The area remained a sleepy strip of oceanfront until the 1950s and 1960s when college students made it the "spring break capital of the world." More recently, however, Fort Lauderdale has become a recreation area for all ages, as well as a center for commerce and high-tech industry.

What to See and Do

Boating, fishing, diving. Boats of all sizes can be chartered by the hour, day, week or season. Bahia Mar Resort, Pier 66 Resort & Marina, Lauderdale Marina and Marina Bay Club are available for visiting yachtsmen. There are several public fishing piers and boat ramps. Phone 954/765-4466.

Mercedes I Artificial Reef. The *Mercedes I* was sunk in 1985 to provide an artificial reef. This ship lies intact in 97 feet of water and is a popular scuba diving site. 1½ mi offshore of Sunrise Blvd. Phone 954/765-4013.

Lowrance Artificial Reef. 1½ mi offshore of Atlantic Blvd near Pompano Beach. (See POMPANO BEACH)

Butterfly World. Stroll through three acres of lush tropical gardens while thousands of butterflies soar around. Outdoor cafe. Gift shops. (Daily; closed major hols) 3600 W Sample Rd, 10 mi N of Fort Lauderdale in Coconut Creek, off I-95. Phone 954/977-4400. ¢¢¢¢

Bonnet House. 35-acre subtropical, historical estate featuring uniquely decorated rms, tropical birds and live monkeys. (Daily; Sat & Sun afternoons; Closed Mon & Tues) 900 N Birch Rd. Phone 954/563-5393. ¢¢¢

Everglades Holiday Park. Narrated airboat rides, boat rentals, fishing; alligator show; RV campground (fee). (Daily) 21940 Griffin Rd, 20 mi SW of town, off I-95 Griffin Rd W exit. Phone 954/434-8111. ¢¢¢¢

Horseracing. Gulfstream Park, 12 mi S on US 1 at 901 S Federal Hwy in Hallandale (see HOLLYWOOD).

International Swimming Hall of Fame and Aquatic Complex. Leading repository for aquatic displays, photos, sculpture, art and memorabilia; computerized exhibits, film & video presentations, library. Also two Olympic-size public swimming pools (daily; fee). Museum (daily). 1 Hall of Fame Dr, 1 blk S of Las Olas Blvd, W of beach. Phone 954/462-6536 (museum) or 954/468-1580 (pool). Museum ¢¢

Museum of Art. Permanent and changing exhibits. (Tues-Sat, also Sun afternoons; closed hols) 1 E Las Olas Blvd. Phone 954/763-6464 (recording) or 954/525-5500. ¢¢¢

Museum of Discovery and Science and Blockbuster IMAX 3-D Theater. Hands-on science museum with seven permanent exhibit areas, including KidScience, Space Base, Choose Health and Florida Ecoscapes. Features simulated Maneuvering Unit space ride, walk-through simulated Florida habitats and Cut-Away House; traveling exhibitions. Blockbuster IMAX 3-D Theater features large-format films shown on five-story screen (daily; also Thurs-Sat evenings). (Daily; closed Dec 25) 401 SW 2nd St; I-95, Broward Blvd E exit, opp Riverwalk's Esplanade Park. Phone 954/467-6637. ¢¢¢

Recreation areas.

Hugh Taylor Birch State Recreation Area. Approximately 180 acres with access to swimming; fishing; canoeing (fee). Nature trails. Picnicking, pavilion. Standard hrs, fees. E Sunrise Blvd, at FL A1A. Phone 954/564-4521.

Public Beach. Newly renovated 1½-mi stretch from Sunrise Blvd to Seabreeze Blvd has wide pedestrian promenades, bicycle lanes, palm tree landscaping. Swimming; picnicking; cabanas. Atlantic Blvd.

Snyder Park. Swimming; fishing; boating. Nature trails, bicycling. Picnicking. Botanical areas. 3299 SW 4th Ave. Phone 954/468-1585.

Holiday Park. This 86-acre park has a theater (see SEASONAL EVENTS), playing fields, tennis courts. Picnicking, shelters. 1400 E Sunrise Blvd. Phone 954/761-5346.

Markham Park. More than 660 acres. Swimming pool; fishing; boating (ramp), canoeing & paddleboating (rentals). Nature trails, bicycle rentals. Tennis. Picnicking, concession. Camping (dump station). Model airplane field. Pistol/rifle, skeet and trap shooting ranges. (Daily) 13 mi W via I-595 (FL 84), just W of Sawgrass Expy in Sunrise. Phone 954/389-2000. Wkends, hols ¢

Sightseeing trips.

"Lolly Trolley." Trolleys make 90-min narrated route, regularly stopping at points of interest, including Discovery Museum, beaches, hotels and restaurants. (Daily) Phone 954/946-7320. ¢¢¢¢

Jungle Queen **Cruises.** Three-hr cruises (two departures daily); also barbecue-and-shrimp dinner cruise (one departure nightly). Res required. Bahia Mar Yacht Basin, FL A1A. Phone 954/462-5596. Dinner cruise ¢¢¢¢

Annual Events

Air & Sea Show. Aerial acrobatics. Early May.

Winterfest. Month-long festival including a boat parade and downtown New Year's Eve celebration. Phone 954/767-0686. Dec.

Seasonal Events

Spring training. Fort Lauderdale Stadium, 5301 12th Ave NW. Baltimore Orioles baseball spring training; exhibition games. Phone 954/776-1921. Feb-early Apr.

Parker Playhouse. 707 NE 8th St, in Holiday Park. Broadway musicals and plays. Phone 954/764-1441. Nov-Apr.

Motels

★★ **BEST WESTERN OCEANSIDE INN.** *1180 Seabreeze (33316).* 954/525-8115. 101 rms, 5 story. Dec-Apr: S, D $109-$159; each addl $10; suites $150-$190; under 12 free; higher rates special events; lower rates rest of yr. Crib free. TV; cable (premium). Heated pool; poolside serv. Complimentary full bkfst. Restaurant 7 am-3 pm. Bar noon-2 am. Ck-out 11:30 am. Coin lndry. Meeting rms. Business servs avail. Sundries. Valet serv. Free garage parking. Health club privileges. Refrigerators avail. Balconies. Opp beach. Cr cds: A, C, D, DS, ER, JCB, MC, V.

[D] [≈] [⊠] [☎] [SC]

★★ **BEST WESTERN PELICAN BEACH RESORT.** *2000 N Atlantic Blvd (33305).* 954/568-9431; FAX 954/565-2622; res: 800/525-6232. E-mail pelican@aksi.net; web introweb.com/pelican. 110 units in 9 bldgs, 2-6 story. Mid-Dec-Apr: S, D $100-$150; each addl $10; suites $150-$200; kits. $120-$170; under 12 free; wkly rates; higher rates hols; lower rates rest of yr. Crib free. TV; cable. Heated pool. Playground. Complimentary continental bkfst. Restaurant nearby. Ck-out 11 am. Coin lndry. Business servs avail. Concierge. Sundries. On ocean; beach. Cr cds: A, C, D, DS, ER, JCB, MC, V.

[≈] [☎] [SC]

★★ **COURTYARD BY MARRIOTT.** (*7780 SW 6th St, Plantation 33324*) W on FL 595 to Pine Island Rd, N on SW 6th St. 954/475-1100; FAX 954/424-8402. 149 rms, 3 story. Mid-Dec-early Apr: S, D $119-$139; suites $139-$159; under 18 free; lower rates rest of yr. Crib free. TV; cable (premium). Heated pool; whirlpool. Complimentary coffee in rms. Restaurant nearby. Ck-out noon. Coin lndry. Meeting rms. Business servs avail. In-rm modem link. Valet serv. Exercise equipt. Health club privileges. Microwaves avail; refrigerator in suites. Some balconies. Cr cds: A, C, D, DS, MC, V.

[D] [≈] [✕] [⊠] [☎] [SC]

★★ **COURTYARD BY MARRIOTT.** *5001 N Federal Hwy (33308).* 954/771-8100; FAX 954/776-7980. 104 rms, 5 story. Dec-Apr: S, D $129; suites $159; higher rates boat shows; lower rates rest of yr. Crib free. TV; cable (premium). Heated pool; whirlpool. Complimentary coffee in rms. Bar 5-10 pm. Ck-out noon. Coin lndry. Meeting rms. Business servs avail. In-rm modem link. Valet serv. Sundries. Exercise equipt. Refrigerator in suites. Balconies. Cr cds: A, D, DS, MC, V.

[D] [≈] [✕] [⊠] [☎] [SC]

✔ ★ **THE FLAG.** *3011 Granada St (33304).* 954/463-2032; res: 888/298-3405; FAX 954/832-9639. 12 rms, 2 story, 10 kit. units. Mid-Dec-Apr: S, D $59-$89; kit. units $95-$155; under 8 free; wkly rates; 3-day min (hols); higher rates special events; lower rates rest of yr. Crib free. TV; cable, VCR avail (movies). Complimentary continental bkfst. Restaurant nearby. Ck-out 11 am. Coin lndry. Pool. Refrigerators; microwaves avail. Cr cds: A, MC, V.

★ ★ **HAMPTON INN.** *720 E Cypress Creek Rd (33334), I-95, exit 33.* 954/776-7677; FAX 954/776-0805. 122 rms, 4 story. Dec-Apr: S, D $119-$129; under 18 free; lower rates rest of yr. Crib free. TV; cable (premium). Pool; whirlpool. Complimentary continental bkfst. Coffee in rms. Restaurant nearby. Ck-out 11 am. Meeting rm. Business servs avail. In-rm modem link. Valet serv (Mon-Fri). Exercise equipt. Cr cds: A, C, D, DS, MC, V.

⬛ Ⓓ ▨ ✕ ▨ ⓈⒸ

★ ★ **A LITTLE INN BY THE SEA.** *(4546 El Mar Dr, Lauderdale by the Sea 33308)* N on FL A1A. 954/772-2450; FAX 954/938-9354; res: 800/492-0311. E-mail alinn@icanect.net; web travelbase.com/alittleinn. 29 rms, 2-3 story, 7 suites, 12 kits. Late Dec-late Apr: S, D $109; each addl $10; suites $169-$189; kit. units $139-$159; under 12 free; lower rates rest of yr. Crib free. TV; cable. Pool. Complimentary continental bkfst. Restaurant nearby. Ck-out 11 am. Business servs avail. Bicycles. Refrigerators. Some balconies. On beach. Cr cds: A, D, DS, MC, V.

Ⓓ ▨ ▨ ⓈⒸ

★ ★ ★ **RESIDENCE INN BY MARRIOTT.** *(130 N University Dr, Plantation 33324)* approx 3 mi W on FL 842. 954/723-0300; FAX 954/474-7385. 138 suites, 4 story. Mid-Dec-mid-Apr: suites $219-$299; family, wkly rates; lower rates rest of yr. Crib free. Pet accepted; $200. TV; cable (premium). Pool; whirlpool. Complimentary continental bkfst. Complimentary coffee in rms. Restaurant adj 11:30 am-1 pm. Rm serv. Bar. Ck-out noon. Coin lndry. Meeting rms. Business servs avail. In-rm modem link. Valet serv. Sundries. Exercise equipt. Health club privileges. Lawn games. Refrigerators, microwaves. Cr cds: A, D, DS, MC, V.

Ⓓ ▨ ▨ ✕ ▨ ▨ ⓈⒸ

★ **RIVER INN ON THE WATER.** *1180 N Federal Hwy (33304).* 954/564-6411. 58 rms, 2 story, 19 suites. Late Dec-late Apr: S, D $90-$140; each addl $10; suites $140-$350; under 18 free; wkly rates; lower rates rest of yr. Crib free. TV. Complimentary continental bkfst. Restaurant adj 11 am-midnight. Meeting rms. Business servs avail. In-rm modem link. Coin lndry. Golf privileges. Health club privileges. Pool. Refrigerator, microwave in suites. Some balconies. Picnic tables, grills. On river. Cr cds: A, C, D, DS, MC, V.

Ⓓ ▨ ✕ ▨ ▨ ⓈⒸ

★ ★ **VILLAS-BY-THE-SEA.** *(4456 El Mar Drive, Lauderdale-by-the-Sea 33308)* N on FL A1A. 954/772-3550; FAX 954/772-3835; res: 800/247-8963. E-mail vbts@aol.com. 136 rms in 11 buildings, 2-4 story, 67 suites, 39 kit. units. Mid-Dec-mid-Apr: S, D $135-$150; each addl $10; suites $159-$340; under 12 free; lower rates rest of yr. Crib $5. TV; cable, VCR avail. 5 heated pools; whirlpool. Playground. Supervised child's activities; ages 5-12. Complimentary continental bkfst. Bar. Restaurant adj 11 am-11 pm. Ck-out 11 am. Coin lndry. Business servs avail. Concierge. Exercise equipt. Lawn games. Scuba. Refrigerators; balconies. Picnic tables, grills. On ocean; swimming beach. Cr cds: A, C, D, DS, MC, V.

Ⓓ ▨ ✕ ▨ ⓈⒸ

✔★ **WELLESLEY INN.** *(13600 NW 2nd St, Sunrise 33325)* Approx 10 mi W on I-595, 2 mi N on FL 869. 954/845-9929; FAX 954/845-9996. 104 rms, 4 story, 10 suites. Dec-Mar: S, D $115; suites $135; lower rates rest of yr. Crib free. Pet accepted, some restrictions; $10. TV; cable (premium). Heated pool. Complimentary continental bkfst. Complimentary coffee in rms. Ck-out 11 am. Meeting rms. Sundries. Some refrigerators. Cr cds: A, D, DS, MC, V.

Ⓓ ▨ ▨ ▨ ⓈⒸ

✔★ **WELLESLEY INN.** *5070 FL 7N (33319).* 954/484-6909; FAX 954/731-2374. 100 rms, 4 story. Dec-Apr: S, D $49-$99; each addl $5; suites $69-$150.99; under 18 free. TV; cable (premium). Heated pool. Complimentary continental bkfst. Coffee in rms. Restaurant nearby. Ck-out 11 am. Coin lndry. Business servs avail. In-rm modem link. Sundries. Some refrigerators; microwaves avail. Cr cds: A, C, D, DS, MC, V.

Ⓓ ▨ ▨ ▨ ⓈⒸ

★ ★ **WELLESLEY INN-PLANTATION.** *(7901 SW 6th St, Plantation 33324)* W via FL 595 to Pine Island Rd, then N on SW 6th St.

954/473-8257; FAX 954/473-9804; res: 800/444-8888. 106 rms, 4 story, 13 suites. Late Dec-mid-Apr: S, D $89-$119, suites $109-$139; family rates; lower rates rest of yr. Crib free. TV; cable (premium). Heated pool. Complimentary continental bkfst. Complimentary coffee in rms. Restaurant nearby. Ck-out 11 am. Meeting rms. Business servs avail. Valet serv. Health club privileges. Some refrigerators; microwaves avail. Cr cds: A, C, D, DS, ER, MC, V.

Ⓓ ▨ ▨ ▨ ⓈⒸ

Motor Hotels

★ ★ **AMERSUITES.** *1851 SE 10th Ave (33316).* 954/763-7670; res: 800/833-1516; FAX 954/763-6269. 128 suites, 6 story. Jan-Apr: suites $139-$199; each addl $10; under 18 free; higher rates special events; lower rates rest of yr. Crib free. Pet accepted, some restrictions; $10. TV; cable (premium), VCR avail. Complimentary continental bkfst. Complimentary coffee in rms. Restaurant opp 4 pm-midnight. Rm serv. Ck-out 11 am. Meeting rms. Business center. In-rm modem link. Valet serv. Sundries. Coin lndry. Free airport transportation. 36-hole golf privileges, greens fee $35-$60, pro, putting green, driving range. Exercise equipt. Pool. Refrigerators, microwaves, wet bars. Cr cds: A, C, D, DS, JCB, MC, V.

Ⓓ ▨ ✕ ▨ ✈ ▨ ▨ ⓈⒸ ▨

★ ★ **BEST WESTERN MARINA INN.** *2150 SE 17th St Causeway (33316).* 954/525-3484; FAX 954/764-2915. 159 rms, 4 story. Dec-Apr: S, D $89-$149; each addl $10; under 18 free; lower rates rest of yr. Crib free. TV; cable. Pool; whirlpool, poolside serv. Complimentary bkfst. Restaurant 7 am-10 pm. Rm serv. Bars 11-2 am; entertainment. Ck-out 11 am. Coin lndry. Meeting rm. Business servs avail. In-rm modem link. Valet serv. Free airport transportation. Putting green. On Intracoastal Waterway; marina; boating. Cr cds: A, C, D, DS, ER, JCB, MC, V.

Ⓓ ▨ ▨ ▨ ▨ ⓈⒸ

★ **COMFORT SUITES.** *1800 S Federal Hwy (33316), near Ft Lauderdale-Hollywood Intl Airport.* 954/767-8700; FAX 954/767-8629. 111 suites, 7 story. Jan-Apr: S, D $99-$199; each addl $10; under 18 free; lower rates rest of yr. Crib free. TV; cable (premium). Heated pool. Complimentary continental bkfst. Complimentary coffee in rms. Restaurant nearby. Ck-out noon. Meeting rm. Business servs avail. Valet serv. Free airport transportation. Health club privileges. Refrigerators; microwaves avail. Cr cds: A, C, D, DS, ER, MC, V.

▨ ✕ ▨ ▨ ⓈⒸ

★ **DOUBLETREE SUITES.** *555 NW 62nd St (33309).* 954/772-5400. 253 suites, 8 story. Dec-Apr: suites $99-$299; each addl $10; under 18 free; lower rates rest of yr. Crib free. TV; cable (premium), VCR (movies). Heated pool; whirlpool. Complimentary coffee in rms. Restaurant 6:30 am-10 pm. Rm serv. Bar 11 am-11:30 pm. Ck-out noon. Coin lndry. Meeting rms. Business servs avail. In-rm modem link. Bellhops. Sundries. Gift shop. Sauna. Health club privileges. Refrigerators, microwaves. Cr cds: A, D, DS, MC, V.

Ⓓ ▨ ▨ ▨ ⓈⒸ

Hotels

★ **DOUBLETREE GUEST SUITES.** *2670 E Sunrise Blvd (33304).* 954/565-3800; FAX 305/561-0387. Web www.dbltree.com/suites/fll/galeria. 229 kit. suites (1-2 bedrm), 14 story. Mid-Dec-mid-Apr: kit. suites $229-$285; under 18 free; monthly rates; lower rates rest of yr. Crib free. Parking $5; valet $8. Pet accepted; $10. TV; cable (premium). Heated pool; whirlpool, poolside serv. Complimentary coffee in rms. Restaurant 7 am-10 pm. Rm serv 24 hrs. Bar 11 am-midnight. Ck-out noon. Coin lndry. Business servs avail. Concierge. Tennis privileges. Golf privileges. Exercise equipt; sauna. Microwaves, wet bars; balconies. Overlooks Intracoastal Waterway; dockage. Cr cds: A, C, D, DS, JCB, MC, V.

Ⓓ ▨ ✕ ▨ ▨ ✈ ▨ ▨ ⓈⒸ

★ ★ **EMBASSY SUITES.** *1100 SE 17th St (33316), adj to Port Everglades.* 954/527-2700; FAX 954/760-7202. Web www.embassysuites.com. 359 suites, 12 story. Jan-mid-Apr: S, D $209-$229; each addl $10; under 18 free; lower rates rest of yr. Crib free. Valet parking $7. TV; cable (premium). Pool; whirlpool, poolside serv. Complimentary full bkfst. Coffee in rms. Restaurant 11 am-11 pm. Bar to 2 am; entertainment wknds. Ck-out noon. Convention facilities. Business servs avail. In-rm modem link. Concierge. Free airport transportation. Golf privileges. Sauna, steam rm. Health club privileges. Refrigerators, microwaves. Private patios, balconies. Waterfall in atrium. Cr cds: A, C, D, DS, ER, MC, V.

[D] [icons] SC

★ ★ ★ **LAGO MAR RESORT & CLUB.** 1700 S Ocean Lane (33316). 954/523-6511; FAX 954/524-6627; res: 800/255-5246. E-mail lagomar@worldnet.att.net; web travelfile.com/get/lagomar. 170 units, 3-5 story. Dec-Apr: S, D $185-$225; each addl $10; kits. $305-$325; suites $395-$425; lower rates rest of yr. Crib $10. TV; cable. 2 heated pools; poolside serv. Playground. Coffee in rms. Restaurant 7 am-10:30 pm. Bars 11-1 am; entertainment Thurs-Sun. Ck-out noon. Free lndry facilities. Meeting rms. Business center. In-rm modem link. Shopping arcade. Tennis, pro. 18-hole golf privileges. 9-hole miniature golf. Exercise equipt. Game rm. Lawn games. Private patios, balconies. Private dock. Private beach. Located between Lake Mayan & ocean. Cr cds: A, C, D, MC, V.

[D] [icons] SC

★ ★ ★ **MARRIOTT MARINA.** 1881 SE 17th St (33316). 954/463-4000; FAX 954/527-6701. 580 rms, 14 story. Jan-Apr: S, D $195-$225; suites $275-$650; wkend, hol rates; lower rates rest of yr. Crib free. Garage $6.50. TV; cable (premium), VCR avail. Heated pool; whirlpool, poolside serv. Restaurants 6:30 am-11 pm. Bar. Ck-out noon. Coin lndry. Convention facilities. Business servs avail. In-rm modem link. Gift shop. Tennis. Exercise equipt; sauna. Game rm. Minibars. Balconies. Marina. Cr cds: A, C, D, DS, ER, JCB, MC, V.

[D] [icons] SC

★ ★ ★ **MARRIOTT-NORTH.** 6650 N Andrews Ave (33309), in Cypress Park West office complex. 954/771-0440; FAX 954/772-9834. 321 rms, 16 story. Jan-Mar: S, D $169-$259; suites $250-$325; under 18 free; wkend rates; lower rates rest of yr. Crib free. Valet parking $6; garage free. TV; cable (premium), VCR avail. Heated pool; whirlpool, poolside serv. Restaurant 6:30 am-10 pm. Bar. Ck-out noon. Convention facilities. Business servs avail. In-rm modem link. Gift shop. Tennis privileges. Golf privileges. Exercise equipt; sauna. Minibars; some refrigerators; microwaves avail. Balconies. Luxury level. Cr cds: A, C, D, DS, ER, MC, V.

[D] [icons] SC

★ ★ ★ **RADISSON BAHIA MAR BEACH RESORT.** 801 Seabreeze Blvd (33316). 954/764-2233; FAX 954/523-5424. 297 rms, 16 story. Mid-Dec-mid-Apr: S, D $179-$219; each addl $10; suites $500-$700; under 17 free; lower rates rest of yr. Crib free. TV; cable. Heated pool; poolside serv. Coffee in rms. Restaurant 6:30 am-10:30 pm. Bars 11 am-midnight; entertainment wkends. Ck-out noon. Coin lndry. Convention facilities. Business servs avail. In-rm modem link. Barber, beauty shop. Lighted tennis. Golf privileges. Boat rentals. Game rm. Exercise equipt. Minibars; refrigerators, microwaves avail. Many rms with terrace; some balconies. Complete yachting center on 40 acres at Intracoastal Waterway; dock. Ocean opp; overpass to beach. Cr cds: A, C, D, DS, ER, MC, V.

[D] [icons] SC

✔★ ★ ★ **RIVERSIDE.** 620 E Las Olas Blvd (33301). 954/467-0671; FAX 954/462-2148; res: 800/325-3280. E-mail riversidehotel@world net.att.net; web www.riversidehotel.com. 109 rms, 6 story. Late Dec-mid-Apr: S, D $139-$189; each addl $15; suites $239; under 16 free; lower rates rest of yr. Crib free. TV; cable. Pool; poolside serv. Restaurants (see GRILL ROOM ON LAS OLAS and INDIGO). Rm serv 6:30 am-11 pm. Bars. Ck-out 11 am. Meeting rms. Business servs avail. In-rm modem link. Health club privileges. Refrigerators. On New River; dock. Cr cds: A, C, D, MC, V.

[D] [icons] SC

★ ★ **SHERATON INN FT LAUDERDALE-NORTH.** 2440 W Cypress Creek Rd NW (62nd St) (33309), near Executive Airport. 954/772-7770; FAX 954/772-4780. 139 rms, 4 story. Jan-Apr: S, D $125-$135; each addl $5; under 17 free; lower rates rest of yr. Crib free. TV; cable (premium). Heated pool. Coffee in rms. Ck-out noon. Meeting rms. Business servs avail. In-rm modem link. Free airport transportation. Exercise equipt. Health club privileges. Some refrigerators; microwaves avail. Tropical decor. Cr cds: A, C, D, DS, MC, V.

[D] [icons] SC

★ ★ ★ **SHERATON SUITES PLANTATION.** (311 N University Dr, Plantation 33324) 6½ mi W on Broward Blvd, at Fashion Mall. 954/424-3300; FAX 954/452-8887. 263 suites, 9 story. Mid-Dec-mid-Apr: S $209-$254; D $229-$269; each addl $20; under 18 free; wkend rates; lower rates rest of yr. Crib free. TV; cable (premium), VCR. Heated pool; whirlpool, poolside serv. Complimentary coffee in rms. Restaurant 6:30 am-10:30 pm; wkends from 7 am. Rm serv 24 hrs. Bar 11 am-midnight. Ck-out noon. Convention facilities. Business servs avail. In-rm modem link. Free garage, valet parking. Free airport transportation. Exercise equipt; sauna. Refrigerators, microwaves, wet bars. Cr cds: A, C, D, DS, ER, JCB, MC, V.

[D] [icons] SC

★ ★ ★ **SHERATON YANKEE TRADER BEACH RESORT.** 321 N Atlantic Blvd (33304). 954/467-1111; FAX 954/462-2342. 463 rms, 14 & 15 story. Jan-Apr: S, D $149-$239; suites $339-$625; under 17 free; lower rates rest of yr. Crib free. Covered parking $5, valet $8. TV; cable (premium), VCR avail. Heated pools; poolside serv. Supervised child's activities; ages 4-12. Complimentary coffee in rms. Restaurant (see SHULA'S ON THE BEACH). Bar 11-1 am; entertainment. Ck-out 11 am. Coin lndry. Convention facilities. Business servs avail. In-rm modem link. Gift shop. Tennis. 18-hole golf privileges, greens fee $40-$70. Exercise equipt. On ocean; swimming beach. Cr cds: A, C, D, DS, ER, MC, V.

[D] [icons] SC

★ ★ ★ **THE WESTIN, CYPRESS CREEK.** 400 Corporate Dr (33334), I-95 & Cypress Creek Rd. 954/772-1331; FAX 954/772-6867. E-mail laurie.coleman@westin.com. 293 rms, 14 story. Dec-Apr: S, D $155-$275; each addl $15; suites $295-$460; under 18 free; lower rates rest of yr. Crib free. Pet accepted, some restrictions. Valet parking $8. TV; cable (premium). Pool; whirlpool, poolside serv. Coffee in rms. Restaurant 6:30 am-10 pm. Rm serv 24 hrs. Bar 11 am-midnight. Ck-out 1 pm. Convention facilities. Business servs avail. In-rm modem link. Concierge. Tennis privileges. Golf privileges. Exercise equipt; sauna. Minibars; microwaves avail. Some private patios, balconies. Blue-mirrored tile building surrounded by palm trees; 20-ft poolside waterfall, 5-acre lake. Paddleboats. Cr cds: A, C, D, DS, ER, JCB, MC, V.

[D] [icons] SC

Inn

★ ★ **LA CASA DEL MAR.** 3003 Granada (33304-4317). 954/467-2037; FAX 954/467-7439; res: 800/739-0009. E-mail leelarry@ att.net; web www.lacasadelmar.com. 10 rms, 3 with shower only, 2 story, 4 suites. Mid-Dec-mid-Apr (4-day min): S, D $100-$120; suites $135; hol rates; lower rates rest of yr. TV; cable (premium), VCR. Pool. Complimentary full bkfst; evening refreshments. Restaurant nearby. Ck-out 11 am, ck-in 3 pm. Refrigerators. Balconies. Picnic tables, grill. 1 blk to beach. Cr cds: A, MC, V.

[D] [icons] SC

Resorts

★ ★ ★ **HYATT REGENCY PIER 66.** 2301 SE 17th St Causeway (33316), southeast of downtown. 954/525-6666; FAX 954/728-3541; res: 800/327-3796. 388 rms, 17 story. Mid-Dec-Apr: S, D $190-$290; each addl $20; suites $850-$1,200; under 15 free; higher rates special events; lower rates rest of yr. Crib free. Parking $6; valet $8. TV; cable (premium). 2 heated pools; whirlpool, wading pool, poolside serv. Restaurants 6:30 am-midnight. Rm serv 24 hrs. Bars 11-2 am (1 revolving rooftop); entertainment. Ck-out noon, ck-in 4 pm. Coin lndry. Convention facilities. Business center. In-rm modem link. Concierge. Gift shop. Beauty shop. Lighted tennis, pro. 18-hole golf, 9-hole par-3, greens fee $35, pro. Exercise rm;

sauna, steam rm. Spa. Refrigerators; microwaves avail. Many private patios, balconies. 22 acres on Intracoastal Waterway. The rooftop Pier Top Lounge revolves every 66 minutes. Adj to Port Everglades. Cr cds: A, C, D, DS, JCB, MC, V.

★★★ **MARRIOTT'S HARBOR BEACH.** 3030 Holiday Dr (33316). 954/525-4000; FAX 954/766-6152. E-mail mhbrbc@bell south.net. 624 rms, 15 story. Late Dec-Jan: S, D $319-$365; suites $500-$2,200; under 18 free; lower rates rest of yr. Crib free. Garage: self-park $6.36, valet $8.48. TV; cable (premium), VCR avail (movies). Pool; whirlpools, poolside serv. Supervised child's activities; ages 5-12. Dining rms 6:30 am-11 pm (also see SHEFFIELD'S). Rm serv 24 hrs. Bar 11-2 am. Ck-out 11 am, ck-in 4 pm. Convention facilities. Business center. In-rm modem link. Concierge. Shopping arcade. Barber, beauty shop. 5 tennis courts, pro. Golf privileges, pro. Private beach; cabanas. Boats, sailboats. Soc dir. Game rm. Exercise equipt; saunas. Some bathrm phones, refrigerators; microwaves avail. Private patios, balconies. 16 acres of oceanfront property. Antiques, large chandeliers in lobby. Cr cds: A, C, D, DS, ER, MC, V.

★★★ **WYNDHAM RESORT & SPA.** 250 Racquet Club Rd (33326), 1 mi W of I-595, I-75 & Sawgrass Expy. 954/389-3300; FAX 954/384-1416. Web www.wyndham.com. 496 rms in 9 bldgs, 4 story, 108 suites. Jan-mid-Apr: S, D $235-$265; each addl $20; suites $310-$810; under 17 free; some wkend rates; lower rates rest of yr. Crib free. TV; cable (premium). 5 heated pools; whirlpool, poolside serv. Supervised child's activities; ages 5-12. Coffee in rms. Dining rm 7 am-11 pm (also see LA CUCINA TOSCANA). Rm serv. Bar 11-1 am; entertainment. Ck-out noon, ck-in 4 pm. Convention facilities. Business center. In-rm modem link. Valet serv. Concierge. Gift shop. Barber, beauty shop. Airport transportation. Clay tennis courts, many lighted, pro. Two 18-hole golf courses, par 70 & par 72, greens fee $90, pro. Charter excursions avail. Bicycles. Lawn games. Exercise rms; steam rm, sauna. Massage. Minibars. Cr cds: A, C, D, DS, ER, MC, V.

Restaurants

★★ **ARMADILLO CAFE.** (4630 SW 64th Ave, Davie 33314) S on I-95 to Griffin Rd, then 5 mi W. 954/791-4866. Web www.armadillo cafe.com. Hrs: 5-10 pm; wkends to 11 pm. Closed most major hols; Super Bowl Sun. Res required. Southwestern menu. Bar. A la carte entrees: dinner $14-$24. Specialties: smoked barbecued duck, lobster quesadilla, grilled ostrich with dried cherry & port wine sauce. Parking. Outdoor dining. Totally nonsmoking. Cr cds: A, C, D, DS, MC, V.

★ **ARUBA BEACH CAFE.** (1 E Commercial Blvd, Lauder-dale-by-the-Sea 33308) 954/776-0001. Hrs: 11-2 am; Sun brunch 8:30 am-noon. Caribbean menu. Bar. Semi-a la carte: lunch, dinner $2.95-$18.95. Sun brunch $7.95. Specializes in steak, fresh seafood, sushi. Own baking. Entertainment Fri, Sun. Valet parking. Overlooks ocean. Cr cds: A, C, D, DS, MC, V.

★★ **BAR AMICI.** 1301 E Las Olas Blvd (33301). 954/467-3266. Hrs: 11:30-2 am; Sat from 4 pm. Closed Sun. Bar. A la carte entrees: lunch, dinner $3-$13.95. Specializes in bistro fare, gourmet pizza, sandwiches. Valet parking. Outdoor dining. Casual, bistro atmosphere. Cr cds: A.

★★ **BISTRO MEZZA LUNA.** 741 SE 17th St (33316), in shopping center. 954/522-6620. Hrs: 6-11 pm; Fri, Sat to midnight. Res accepted. Bar. A la carte entrees: dinner $8.50-$24. Specializes in prime steaks, fish, homemade pasta. Valet parking. Bistro atmosphere. Cr cds: A, MC, V.

★★ **BLACK ORCHID CAFE.** 2985 N Ocean (33308). 954/561-9398. Hrs: 11:30 am-2:30 pm, 6-10 pm; Fri to 11 pm; Sat 6-11 pm. Res accepted. Contemporary Amer menu. Bar from 6 pm. A la carte entrees: lunch $4.95-$9.95, dinner $13.95-$39.95. Child's meals. Specialties: lobster a la whiskey, tenderloin of buffalo, ostrich. Music Wed-Sun. Parking. Outdoor dining. No cr cds accepted.

★★ **BLUE MOON FISH CO.** (4405 W Tradewinds Ave, Lauderdale-by-the-Sea 33308) 954/267-9888. E-mail skorish@bellsouth.net; web www.introweb/bluemoon. Hrs: 11:30 am-10:30 pm; Fri, Sat to 11 pm; Sun brunch to 3 pm. Res accepted. Bar to 1 am. A la carte entrees: lunch $5-$9, dinner $6-$27. Sun brunch $24.95. Specializes in seafood, lamb. Own desserts, pasta. Jazz Sat, Sun; gospel Sun (brunch). Valet parking. Outdoor dining. On waterfront. Cr cds: A, MC, V.

★★★ **BRASSERIE LA FERME.** 1601 E Sunrise Blvd (33304). 954/764-0987. E-mail henriterrier@mci.2000. Hrs: 5:30-10 pm. Closed Sun. Res accepted. French menu. Serv bar. Wine list. Semi-a la carte: dinner $30-$40. Specializes in Maine lobster, Grand Marnier souffle. Own pastries. Parking. Family-owned. Cr cds: A, D, MC, V.

★★★ **BURT & JACKS.** Berth 23 (33316), I-95 to I-595E, follow signs to Port Everglades. 954/522-5225. Hrs: 5-11 pm; Fri, Sat to midnight. Closed Dec 25. Res accepted. Bar from 4:30 pm. Semi-a la carte: dinner $16.95-$36.95. Specializes in fresh seafood, prime meat. Own baking. Pianist. Valet parking. Spanish mission-style building located at end of pier. Scenic view of port and city skyline. Jacket. Cr cds: A, C, D, DS, MC, V.

★★ **BY WORD OF MOUTH.** 3200 NE 12th Ave (33334). 954/564-3663. Hrs: 11 am-3 pm, 5-10 pm; Sat from 5 pm; Mon, Tues to 2 pm. Closed Sun; major hols; also first 2 wks Aug. Res accepted Wed-Sat. Continental menu. Wine, beer. A la carte entrees: lunch $9.95-$15.95, dinner $18.95-$27.95. Specialties: tomato pesto pate, lobster lasagna, pork loin with raspberry jalapeño. Parking. Totally nonsmoking. Cr cds: A, C, D, DS, MC, V.

★★ **CAFÉ DE GENÈVE.** 1519 S Andrews Ave (33316). 954/522-8928. Hrs: 11:30 am-2:30 pm, 5-10 pm; Sat from 5 pm; early-bird dinner 5-7 pm. Closed Sun. Res accepted. Continental menu. Bar. Semi-a la carte: lunch $6.50-$11.95, dinner $9.95-$23.95. Specializes in veal, fondue, duckling. Parking. Swiss chalet decor. Cr cds: A, C, D, DS, MC, V.

★★ **CAFE SEVILLE.** 2768 E Oakland Park Blvd (33305), at Bayview Dr. 954/565-1148. Hrs: 11:30 am-2 pm, 5-10:30 pm; Sat 5-11 pm; early-bird dinner Mon-Fri 5-7 pm. Closed Sun; some major hols; also 3 wks Aug. Res accepted. Mediterranean menu. Wine, beer. Complete meals: lunch $5.95-$9.95, dinner $11.50-$16.95. Specialties: paella, cazuela de mariscos. Rustic, Spanish atmosphere. Totally nonsmoking. Cr cds: A, C, D, MC, V.

★★★ **CALIFORNIA CAFE BAR & GRILL.** 2301 SE 17th St Causeway (33316). 954/728-3500. Hrs: 11:30 am-3:30 pm, 5:30-10 pm; Sat to 10:30 pm; Sun (brunch) 11 am-3 pm, 5:30-10 pm. Res accepted. Contemporary Amer menu. Bar. Wine cellar. A la carte entrees: lunch $11.95-$17.95, dinner $14.95-$26.95. Sun brunch $8.50-$13.95. Child's meals. Specialties: macadamia nut crusted snapper, pepper grilled tuna, tuna sashimi. Pianist Thurs-Sat. Valet parking. Outdoor dining. Contemporary decor and atmosphere. Cr cds: A, D, DS, MC, V.

★★ **THE CAVES.** 2205 N Federal Hwy (US 1) (33305). 954/561-4622. Hrs: 5-10 pm; Fri, Sat to 11 pm. Res accepted. Bar. A la carte entrees: dinner $12-$30. Child's meals. Specialties: tableside steak Diane, Caveman filet mignon, lobster tail. Salad bar. Dining area resembles actual cave interior; tables set in individual alcoves. Waitstaff dressed as cave dwellers. Family-owned. Cr cds: A, D, MC, V.

[D] [symbol]

★ ★ **CHARLEY'S CRAB.** *3000 NE 32nd Ave (33308). 954/561-4800.* Hrs: 11:30 am-10 pm; wkends to 11 pm; early-bird dinner 4-5:45 pm; Sun brunch 11 am-2:30 pm. Res accepted. Bar. A la carte entrees: lunch $6.75-$16.50, dinner $13.50-$32.50. Complete meals: dinner $11.95-$17.95. Sun brunch $19.95. Child's meals. Specialties: stone crab, live Maine lobster, filet mignon. Valet parking. Outdoor dining. On Intracoastal Waterway, boat dockage. Cr cds: A, C, D, DS, MC, V.

[D] [symbol]

★ ★ ★ **EAST CITY GRILL.** *505 N Atlantic Blvd (33304). 954/565-5569.* Hrs: 9 am-midnight; Sat, Sun brunch to 3 pm; summer hrs vary. Res accepted (dinner). Caribbean, Amer menu. Bar noon-midnight. Wine list. A la carte entrees: bkfst $4-$11, lunch $6.95-$15.95, dinner $16.95-$25.95. Sat, Sun brunch: $4-$18. Specialties: sautéed & honey-glazed snapper, charred tuna, jambalaya. Valet parking. Outdoor dining. View of ocean. Cr cds: A, C, D, DS, MC, V.

[D]

★ ★ ★ **EDUARDO DE SAN ANGEL.** *2822 Commercial Blvd (33308). 954/772-4731.* Hrs: 5:30-10:30 pm. Closed Sun, Mon; major hols; also 2 wks June. Res accepted. Mexican menu. Bar. A la carte entrees: dinner $16.95-$23.95. Specialties: salsa verde, tortilla soup, crab cakes. Intimate dining; antique pieces. Cr cds: A, MC, V.

[D]

✔★ ★ **EVANGELINE.** *211 S Atlantic Blvd (33316). 954/522-7001.* Hrs: 11-2 am; Sun brunch 10:30 am-4 pm. Res accepted. Creole menu. Bar to 2 am. A la carte entrees: lunch $6.50-$14.50, dinner $14.50-$24. Sun brunch $8-$12. Child's meals. Specialities: alligator with flash-fried oysters, smoked rabbit gumbo, stuffed pheasant. Jazz. Valet parking. Outdoor dining overlooking ocean. Cr cds: A, DS, MC, V.

[D]

★ ★ ★ **FRENCH QUARTER.** *215 SE 8th Ave (33301). 954/463-8000.* Hrs: 11:30 am-3 pm, 6-11 pm; Sat from 6 pm. Closed Sun. Res required. French, New Orleans classic menu. Bar. Semi-a la carte: lunch $10-$20, dinner $15.50-$35. Specialty: bouillabaisse Louisianne. Own baking, soups, sauces. Entertainment. Parking. Original residence of city's first mayor (1925). Cr cds: A, C, D, DS, MC, V.

[D]

★ ★ ★ **GIBBY'S STEAKS & SEAFOOD.** *2900 NE 12th Terrace (33334). 954/565-2929.* Hrs: 5-10 pm; Sat, Sun noon-3 pm, 4:30-10 pm. Res accepted. Bar. Semi-a la carte: dinner $14.95-$29.95. Specializes in steak, lamb. Valet parking. Cr cds: A, C, D, MC, V.

[D]

★ ★ ★ **GRILL ROOM ON LAS OLAS.** *(See Riverside Hotel) 954/467-2555.* Hrs: 6-11 pm. Res accepted. Continental menu. Bar. Wine cellar. A la carte entrees: dinner $18.50-$38. Child's meals. Specialties: chateaubriand, veal Oscar. Pianist Wed-Sat. Valet parking. Outdoor dining. Elegant decor. Cr cds: A, C, D, DS, MC, V.

[D] [symbol]

★ ★ **H2O.** *101 S Atlantic Blvd (33316). 954/760-7500.* Hrs: 8 am-11 pm; Fri, Sat to midnight. Mediterranean menu. Bar. A la carte entrees: bkfst, lunch $5.95-$12.95, dinner $8.95-$21.95. Child's meals. Specialties: grilled swordfish, NY strip steak, free-range chicken. Entertainment Thurs-Sat. Outdoor dining on beach. Cr cds: A, C, D, DS, MC, V.

[D] [symbol]

★ ★ ★ **IL TARTUFO.** *2400 Las Olas Blvd (33301). 954/767-9190.* Hrs: 5 pm-midnight; early-bird dinner Mon-Fri 5-6:30 pm. Res accepted. Italian menu. Bar. A la carte entrees: dinner $12-$25. Child's meals. Specialties: lobster ravioli with lobster bisque, tenderloin with truffle cognac

sauce, wood oven-baked snapper. Entertainment evenings. Free valet parking. Outdoor dining. Cr cds: A, D, MC, V.

[D] [symbol]

✔★ ★ **INDIGO.** *(See Riverside Hotel) 954/467-0671.* Hrs: 7 am-11 pm; Fri, Sat to midnight. Eclectic menu. Bar. Semi-a la carte: lunch, dinner $6.95-$18.50. Child's meals. Specialties: baked Indonesian snapper, firecracker noodles, coconut-grilled chicken. Valet parking. Outdoor dining. Decor inspired by hotels of SE Asia. Cr cds: A, D, DS, MC, V.

[D]

★ **KELLY'S LANDING.** *(1305 SE 17th St, Ft Lauderdale 33316) in Southport Shopping Center. 954/760-7009.* Hrs: 11 am-10 pm; Fri, Sat to 11 pm; Sun from noon. Closed Thanksgiving, Dec 25. Beer, wine, specialty drinks. Semi-a la carte: lunch $4.95-$12.95, dinner $6.50-$14.95. Child's meals. Specializes in New England seafood, steak, chicken. New England memorabilia including sports teams. Cr cds: A, C, D, MC, V.

[D] [symbol]

★ ★ ★ **LA BROCHETTE BISTRO.** *(2635 Hiatus Rd, Cooper City 33026) approx 10 mi W on FL 818, in Embassy Mall. 954/435-9090.* Hrs: 5-10 pm. Closed Mon; Jan 1, Dec 25. Res required wkends. Mediterranean menu. Wine list. A la carte entrees: dinner $12-$20. Child's meals. Specialties: rack of lamb, pistachio-crusted Florida snapper, pork chateau with stilton cheese. Bistro decor. Chef-owned. Cr cds: A, DS, MC, V.

[D]

★ ★ ★ **LA COQUILLE.** *1619 E Sunrise Blvd (33304). 954/467-3030.* Hrs: 5:30-10 pm. Res accepted. French menu. A la carte entrees: dinner $14.75-$24.95. Specialties: duck breast with peppercorn sauce, crusty sweetbread with morel. Own baking. Parking. Outdoor cafe dining. Cr cds: A, MC, V.

[D]

★ ★ ★ **LA CUCINA TOSCANA.** *(See Wyndham Resort & Spa) 954/389-3300.* Hrs: 6-10 pm; wkends to 11 pm. Closed Sun. Res accepted. Northern Italian menu. Bar. Wine list. Semi-a la carte: dinner $19.95-$35. Specialties: seafood risotto, veal rib chop, pan-seared yellowtail snapper. Valet parking. Outdoor dining. Cr cds: A, C, D, DS, ER, MC, V.

[D] [symbol]

★ ★ ★ **LA RESERVE.** *3115 NE 32nd Ave (33308). 954/563-6644.* Hrs: 5:45-11 pm. Res accepted. French, Amer menu. Bar. Wine cellar. A la carte entrees: dinner $17.95-$29.95. Specialties: lobster Cabourg, medley of sea scallops, filet de bouef Saint Amour. Outdoor dining. Three-level dining overlooking Intracoastal Waterway. Family-owned. Cr cds: A, D, DS, MC, V.

[D] [symbol]

★ ★ **LA TAVERNETTA.** *926 NE 20th Ave (33304). 954/463-2566.* Web www.showtimeinteractive.com/latavernetta. Hrs: 11:30 am-2:30 pm, 5:30-10:30 pm. Closed Mon, Sun; Easter, Thanksgiving, Dec 25. Res accepted. A la carte entrees: lunch $3.95-$12.95, dinner $17.95-$24.95. Complete meal: dinner $29.95-$31.95. Child's meals. Specialties: shrimp paradiso, veal Federico, chicken ruggiero. Parking. Outdoor dining. Venetian atmosphere. Family-owned since 1978. Cr cds: A, C, D, DS, MC, V.

[D] [symbol]

★ ★ **LE CAFE DE PARIS.** *715 E Las Olas Blvd (33301). 954/467-2900.* Hrs: 11:30 am-2:30 pm, 5:30-10:30 pm; Sun from 5 pm. Res accepted. Continental, French menu. A la carte entrees: lunch $5.95-$19.95, dinner $12-$24. Specialties: beef Wellington, Dover sole, frog legs. Accordianist Mon-Thurs, pianist Fri, Sat. Outdoor dining. Seven distinct dining areas. Family-owned. Cr cds: A, D, DS, MC, V.

[D]

★ ★ ★ **MAI-KAI.** *3599 N Federal Hwy (US 1) (33308). 954/563-3272.* Web www.maikai.com. Hrs: 5 pm-midnight; early-bird dinner 5-6 pm.

Res accepted. Oriental, Amer menu. Bar to 2 am. Wine list. A la carte entrees: dinner $15.50-$29.95. Child's meals. Specialties: fresh Peking duck, sesame charred rare tuna, Maine lobster Tahitienne. Polynesian entertainment (cover in show rm $9.95). Valet parking. Outdoor dining. South Seas setting; exotic gardens. Authentic Polynesian artifacts. Family-owned. Cr cds: A, C, D, DS, MC, V.

D

✔★ ★ **MANGO'S.** *904 E Las Olas Blvd (33301). 954/523-5001.* Web www.lasolasboulevard.com. Hrs: 11 am-midnight; Fri, Sat to 1 am. Bar. A la carte entrees: lunch, dinner $5.95-$17.95. Child's meals. Specialties: Mango seafood salad, Boston lobster pie, snowcrab bisque. Entertainment. Outdoor dining. Split-level. Cr cds: A, MC, V.

D

★ ★ ★ **MARK'S LAS OLAS.** *(1032 E Las Olas Blvd, Ft Lauderdale 33301) 954/463-1000.* Hrs: 11:30 am-2:30 pm, 6-10:30 pm; Fri, Sat to 11:30 pm. Closed Thanksgving, Dec 25. Res accepted. Bar. A la carte entrees: lunch $6-$15, dinner $8-$32. Specialties: crab-crusted grouper, grilled rack of lamb with tapenade sauce, banana leaf wrapped charcoaled dolphin. Valet parking. Modern eclectic decor. Open kitchen. Cr cds: A, D, MC, V.

D

★ ★ **MISTRAL.** *201 S Atlantic Blvd (33316). 954/463-4900.* Hrs: 11-2 am. Serv bar. A la carte entrees: lunch $6-$14, dinner $8-$18. Specialities: pesto-crusted grouper, rack of lamb, paella. Entertainment Fri-Sun. Valet parking. Outdoor dining. Facing ocean. Cr cds: A, DS, MC, V.

D

★ ★ **OASIS CAFE.** *600 Seabreeze Blvd (33316). 954/463-3130.* Web www.oasiscafe.com. Hrs: 11:30 am-11 pm; wkend hrs vary. Bar. Semi-a la carte: lunch, dinner $5.95-$11.95. Specialty: seafood tortellini. Valet parking. All seating is canopied. Outdoor dining. Lit fountain at night. Cr cds: A, C, D, JCB, MC, V.

D ✏

★ ★ **OLD FLORIDA SEAFOOD HOUSE.** *1414 NE 26th St (33305). 954/566-1044.* Hrs: 4:30-9:30 pm. Closed Thanksgiving, Dec 25; also Super Bowl Sun. Bar 4 pm-midnight. Semi-a la carte: dinner $12.95-$27.95. Child's meals. Specializes in local fresh fish, shrimp, fresh swordfish. Raw bar. Parking. Nautical decor; original pencil sketches; artifacts. Cr cds: A, MC, V.

D ⬡

✔★ ★ **PADRINO'S.** *(801 S University Dr, Plantation 33324) W on Broward Blvd to University Dr, in The Fountains Shopping Center. 954/476-5777.* Hrs: 11:30 am-10 pm; Fri to 10:30 pm; Sat noon-10:30 pm; Sun from noon. Closed Mon; some major hols. Semi-a la carte: lunch $4.95-$11.95, dinner $6.95-$11.95. Child's meals. Specializes in Cuban-style pork, steak, vegetarian items. Guitarists Fri, Sat. Cuban scenes on ceramic tile. Totally nonsmoking. Cr cds: A, D, DS, MC, V.

D

★ ★ ★ **PAESANO.** *1301 E Las Olas Blvd (33301). 954/467-3266.* Hrs: 11:30 am-2:30 pm, 6-10:30 pm; Sat from 5:30 pm. Closed Sun. Res accepted. Italian, Amer menu. Bar. Wine cellar. A la carte entrees: lunch $6.95-$10.95, dinner $13.95-$21. Specialities: tuna steak, veal Sinatra, seafood risotto. Pianist. Valet parking. Elegant dining in three dining rms. Family owned. Cr cds: A, MC, V.

⬡

★ ★ ★ **PEBBLES.** *(1280 S Pine Island Rd, Plantation 33324) 954/424-0330.* Hrs: 11:30 am-10 pm; Fri, Sat to 11 pm. Bar. Wine list. A la carte entrees: lunch, dinner $6.50-$19.95. Child's meals. Specializes in pasta, seafood, steaks. Casual atmosphere. Cr cds: A, D, DS, MC, V.

D ⬡

★ ★ ★ **PRIMAVERA.** *830 E Oakland Park Blvd (33334). 954/564-6363.* Hrs: 5:30-10 pm. Closed Mon (summer). Res accepted.

Italian menu. Bar. Semi-a la carte: dinner $16.95-$34.95. Specializes in pasta, beef, chicken. Own baking. European atmosphere. Cr cds: A, D, DS, JCB, MC, V.

D

★ ★ ★ **RUTH'S CHRIS STEAK HOUSE.** *2525 N Federal Hwy (33305). 954/565-2338.* Hrs: 5-10 pm; Fri, Sat to 11 pm. Closed Dec 25; also Super Bowl Sun. Res accepted. Bar. A la carte entrees: dinner $17.50-$29.95. Specializes in steak, lobster, veal chop. Valet parking. Garden view. Cr cds: A, D, JCB, MC, V.

D

✔★ ★ **SAGE.** *2378 N Federal Hwy (33305). 954/565-2299.* Hrs: 11 am-11 pm; Sun brunch to 4 pm. Closed Dec 25. Beer, wine. A la carte entrees: lunch $4.50-$12.95, dinner $4.50-$15.95. Sun brunch $6.50-$12.50. Child's meals. Specialities: braised lamb shank, stuffed roast pork with raspberry sauce. Classical guitarist, pianist. Parking. Outdoor dining. Country French decor. Cr cds: A, DS, MC, V.

D

★ ★ **SEA WATCH.** *6002 N Ocean Blvd (33308). 954/781-2200.* Hrs: 11:30 am-3:30 pm, 5-10 pm; Fri, Sat to 11 pm. Closed Dec 25. Bar. Semi-a la carte: lunch $5-$13.95, dinner $13.50-$31.50. Specializes in fresh local seafood, prime beef. Valet parking. Outdoor dining. Located on the beach. Nautical decor. Cr cds: A, MC, V.

D

★ ★ ★ **SHEFFIELD'S.** *(See Marriott's Harbor Beach Resort) 954/525-4000.* Hrs: 6-10 pm; Fri, Sat to 11 pm. Res accepted. Continental menu. Bar 11-2 am. Wine list. A la carte entrees: dinner $18.95-$52. Specialties: rack of lamb, beef Wellington, Dover sole. Valet parking. Four dining areas decorated in English motif. Cr cds: A, C, D, DS, ER, MC, V.

D SC

★ ★ **SHULA'S ON THE BEACH.** *(See Sheraton Yankee Trader Beach Resort Hotel) 954/355-4000.* Hrs: 7 am-11 pm. Res accepted. Bar 11 am-midnight. Semi-a la carte: bkfst $5.50-$12.95, lunch $7.50-$20, dinner $15.50-$29. Child's meals. Specialties: steak Mary Anne, filet mignon, Chilean salmon. Pianist. Valet parking. Outdoor dining. Overlooks ocean. Cr cds: A, C, D, DS, MC, V.

D ⬡

✔ ★ ★ **SLOOP JOHN B.** *239 S Atlantic Blvd (33316). 954/463-3633.* Web ww.sloopjohnb.com. Hrs: 11 am-midnight; Wed-Sat to 2 am. Seafood menu. Bar. Semi-a la carte: lunch, dinner $5.95-$11.95. Specialties: surf & turf, broiled sampler, seafood fiesta. Folk music Wed-Sat. Outdoor dining. Cr cds: A, C, D, DS, MC, V.

D ⬡

★ ★ **STERLING WORTH CAFE.** *(801 S University Dr, Plantation 33324) in the Fountains Shopping Center. 954/474-7738.* Hrs: 11:30 am-10 pm; Fri, Sat to midnight; Sun to 9 pm; Sun brunch to 3 pm. Closed Mon; Jan 1, Thanksgiving, Dec 25. Bar. A la carte entrees: lunch $6.95-$10.95, dinner $10.95-$22.95. Sun brunch $8.50-$10.95. Child's meals. Specialties: almond chicken salad, baked brie encroute, Caesar salad. Jazz Tues-Sun eves, Sun brunch. Outdoor dining. Continental cuisine with European charm. Cr cds: A, DS, MC, V.

D ⬡

★ ★ **STUDIO ONE CAFE.** *2447 E Sunrise Blvd (33304), across from Galleria Mall. 954/565-2052.* Web www.menusonline.com. Hrs: 5:30-10 pm. Res accepted. French, continental menu. Wine, beer. Complete meals: dinner $15-$20. Child's meals. Specialties: escargot, grilled salmon, black duck with vanilla sauce. Parking. Outdoor dining. Chef-owned. Cr cds: A, DS, MC, V.

D ⬡

★ ★ ★ **TROPICAL ACRES.** *2500 Griffin Rd (33312). 954/761-1744.* Hrs: 4:30-10 pm; Sun 3-9 pm. Closed Dec 24. Res accepted. Bar. A la carte entrees: dinner $7.95-$22.95. Child's meals. Specializes in steak, seafood, chops. Pianist. Family-owned. Cr cds: A, C, D, MC, V.

✔★ ★ **TRY MY THAI CAFE TOO.** *1507 N Federal Hwy (33304), in Del Mar Shopping Plaza.* 954/630-0030. Web www.trymythai.com. Hrs: 11:30 am-2:30 pm, 6-10 pm. Closed Sun; some major hols. Res accepted. Thai menu. Wine, beer. A la carte entrees: lunch $5.95-$7.95, dinner $4.95-$15.95. Specialties: foster care alligator, chiangmai dip, pineapple curry. Thai decor. Totally nonsmoking. Cr cds: A, D, MC, V.

D

★ ★ ★ **YESTERDAY'S.** *3001 E Oakland Park Blvd (33006), on Intracoastal Waterway.* 954/561-4400. Hrs: 5-10:30 pm; Fri, Sat to 11 pm. Res accepted. Continental, Amer menu. Bars. Wine list. Semi-a la carte: dinner $14.95-$29.95. Complete meals: dinner $12.95-$15.95. Specializes in fresh seafood, beef Wellington, rack of lamb. Valet parking. Overlooks Intracoastal Waterway. Cr cds: A, D, DS, MC, V.

D

★ ★ **ZAN(Z)BAR.** *602 E Las Olas Blvd (33301).* 954/767-3377. E-mail mykl@aol.com. Hrs: 11 am-midnight; Fri, Sat to 2 am. Res accepted. South African menu. Wine, beer. A la carte entrees: lunch $3.95-$14.95, dinner $12.95-$29.95. Child's meals. Specializes in seafood, wild boar, alligator. Own desserts. Outdoor dining. South African decor. Cr cds: A, C, D, DS, MC, V.

D

Fort Matanzas National Monument (C-5)

(See also Marineland, St Augustine)

(On Anastasia Island, 14 mi S of St Augustine on FL A1A)

Fort Matanzas National Monument extends over an area of 298 acres that includes the southern tip of Anastasia Island and Rattlesnake Island, where the fort is actually located. By 1569, the first of several successive wooden watchtowers had been erected on the site to detect approaching vessels; the Spanish realized early that access to the Matanzas River through the Matanzas Inlet provided easy access to St Augustine.

The inlet's importance was clearly demonstrated during a British siege in 1740, when Spanish relief ships ran the blockade and reached the starving defenders in time. Between 1740 and 1742 the Spanish built Fort Matanzas to permanently control the inlet. During 1742-1743, British attempts to destroy the fortification failed. Florida did become British by treaty, in 1763, but reverted to the Spanish in 1784. Fort Matanzas served both the British and the Spanish as an outpost.

After the transfer of Florida to the United States in 1821, the unmanned fort fell into ruin. Later, the fort was stabilized in two phases, one in 1916, the other in 1924, when it was designated a national monument. The fort is considered a fine representative of a vanished style of military architecture.

The fort's name, *Matanzas*, means "slaughters" in Spanish and signifies the 1565 surrender of 245 Frenchmen and their subsequent slaughter by the founder of St Augustine, Pedro Menéndez de Avilés.

A visitor center, with exhibits and information on the fort, is located on Anastasia Island, from which the fort is visible; access, however, is possible only by ferry boat (free). (Daily; closed Dec 25) Contact Site Supervisor, 8635 A1AS, St Augustine 32086; 904/471-0116.   **Free.**

Fort Myers (G-4)

(See also Bonita Springs, Cape Coral, Punta Gorda, Sanibel & Captiva Islands)

Founded 1850 **Pop** 45,206 **Elev** 10 ft **Area code** 941

Information Lee County Visitor & Convention Bureau, 2180 W 1st St, Suite 100, 33901; 941/338-3500 or 800/237-6444.

Fifteen miles upstream from the Gulf of Mexico, on the wide Caloosahatchee River, Fort Myers began as a federal post erected after an Indian raid. Later, settlers came to farm within its protective shadow. Tourism, vegetable and flower growing and commercial and sport fishing are major activities of the area today.

What to See and Do

Calusa Nature Center and Planetarium. More than 100 acres of pine flatwoods and bald cypress swamp; Audubon aviary. Planetarium with star shows and laser light and music shows; exhibits; natural history shop; nature trails (2 mi); guided walks. (Daily) On Ortiz Ave, just N of Colonial Blvd near I-75. Phone 941/275-3435.   ¢¢

✪ **Edison/Ford Winter Estates.** Guided tours. (Daily; closed Thanksgiving, Dec 25) 2350 McGregor Blvd; from I-75, exit 22 (Colonial Blvd) to McGregor Blvd and turn right. Phone 941/334-7419. Combination ticket ¢¢¢   includes

Edison Winter House & Botanical Gardens. In 1885, inventor Thomas Edison, ailing at the age of 38, built this 14-acre riverfront estate, where he wintered for the next half-century. The house and guesthouse, designed by Edison, were brought by ship from Maine. Complex includes museum with inventions, mementos and a chemical laboratory; first modern swimming pool in the state; and extraordinary botanical garden with mature specimens from around the world.

Henry Ford Winter House. "Mangoes," the three-and-one-half-acre winter residence of the world's first billionaire, Henry Ford, is next door to the house of Ford's good friend, Thomas Edison. The house reflects the Midwestern, home-grown values of Henry and his wife, Clara, as well as the effect of extraordinary wealth on their lives. The simply-built bungalow is authentically furnished.

Fort Myers Historical Museum. On display are items of local historical significance. (Tues-Sat; closed major hols) 2300 Peck St, in old Atlantic Coastline Railroad Depot. Phone 941/332-5955.   ¢¢

Imaginarium Hands-on Museum and Aquarium. Visitors explore and discover the physical sciences, aquatic sciences and humanities through a series of interactive events. (Daily; closed Mon July-Sept) Cranford Ave at Dr Martin Luther King Jr Blvd. Phone 941/337-3332.   ¢¢¢

JC Cruises. Three-hr narrated ride up Caloosahatchee River; birds, rookeries, wild orchids, alligators. Also cruises on Intracoastal Waterway; some with meals, floor shows, music. (Daily) City Yacht Basin, foot of Lee St. Phone 941/334-7474.   ¢¢¢¢-¢¢¢¢¢

Annual Event

Edison Festival of Light. Tribute to Thomas Edison; includes athletic contests, dances, sailing regattas, entertainment; ends with Parade of Light. Phone 941/334-2999. 2 wks Feb; parade 3rd Sat.

Seasonal Event

Spring training. Lee County Sports Complex, 14100 Six Mile Cypress Pkwy, near Daniels Rd. Minnesota Twins baseball spring training; exhibition games. Phone 941/768-4270. Early Mar-early Apr. City of Palms Park, 2201 Edison Ave. Boston Red Sox spring training; exhibition games. Phone 941/334-4700. Late Feb-Mar.

Motels

✔★ **BAYMONT INN.** *2717 Colonial Blvd (33907). 941/275-3500; FAX 941/275-5426.* 122 rms, 4 story. Jan-Apr: S, D $93; lower rates rest of yr. Crib free. Pet accepted, some restrictions; fee. TV; cable (premium). Pool. Complimentary continental bkfst. Complimentary coffee in rms. Ck-out noon. Meeting rm. Business servs avail. Cr cds: A, C, D, DS, MC, V.

☐ 🖋 ≋ ⩗ 🔥 SC

★ **COMFORT INN.** *11501 S Cleveland Ave (33907). 941/936-3993; FAX 941/936-7234.* Web www.comfortinn.com/hotel/FL425. 80 rms, 2 story. Feb-Apr: S $95-$100; D $100-$105; each addl $10; under 18 free; wknd rates; lower rates rest of yr. Crib free. Pet accepted, some restrictions. TV; cable (premium). Heated pool. Complimentary continental bkfst. Restaurant adj 11 am-11 pm. Ck-out 11 am. Meeting rms. Refrigerators. Cr cds: A, C, D, DS, ER, JCB, MC, V.

☐ 🖋 ≋ ⩗ 🔥 SC

★ ★ **COURTYARD BY MARRIOTT.** *4455 Metro Pkwy (33916). 941/275-8600; FAX 941/275-7087.* 149 rms, 3 story. Mid-Jan-Apr: S, D $120-$135; suites $140-$155; under 12 free. Crib free. TV; cable. Heated pool; whirlpool. Complimentary coffee in rms. Restaurant 6:30-10:30 am; Sat, Sun 7 am-noon. Ck-out noon. Guest lndry. Meeting rms. Business servs avail. In-rm modem link. Exercise equipt. Health club privileges. Refrigerator in suites. Balconies. Cr cds: A, D, DS, MC, V.

☐ ≋ 🏋 ✈ ⩗ 🔥 SC

✔★ **HAMPTON INN.** *13000 N Cleveland Ave (33903). 941/656-4000; FAX 941/656-1612.* 121 rms, 2 story. Dec-Apr: S $99-$119; under 18 free; lower rates rest of yr. Crib free. TV; cable (premium). Pool. Complimentary continental bkfst. Coffee in rms. Restaurant nearby. Ck-out noon. Coin lndry. Business servs avail. On river with view. Cr cds: A, C, D, DS, JCB, MC, V.

☐ ≋ ⩗ 🔥 SC

★ **LA QUINTA.** *4850 Cleveland Ave (33907). 941/275-3300; FAX 941/275-6661.* Web www.travelweb.com/laquinta.html. 130 rms, 2 story. Jan-Apr: S, D $99-$119; each addl $10; under 18 free; lower rates rest of yr. Crib free. Pet accepted, some restrictions. TV; cable (premium). Heated pool. Complimentary continental bkfst. Restaurant nearby. Ck-out 11 am. Meeting rms. Business servs avail. In-rm modem link. Health club privileges. Cr cds: A, C, D, DS, JCB, MC, V.

☐ 🖋 ≋ ⩗ 🔥 SC

★ ★ **RADISSON INN SANIBEL GATEWAY.** *20091 Summerlin Rd (33908). 941/466-1200; FAX 941/466-3797.* E-mail 110424, 3525@compuserve.com; web www.radisson.com. 158 rms, 3 story. Mid-Jan-Apr: S, D $134-$159; under 16 free; lower rates rest of yr. Crib free. Pet accepted, some restrictions; $50. TV; cable (premium). Heated pool; whirlpool. Restaurant 6:30 am-10 pm. Rm serv. Bar 11 am-11pm; Fri, Sat to midnight. Ck-out noon. Coin lndry. Meeting rm. Business servs avail. In-rm modem link. Refrigerators. Cr cds: A, C, D, DS, ER, JCB, MC, V.

☐ 🖋 ≋ ⩗ 🔥 SC

✔★ **TA KI-KI.** *2631 First Street (33916). 941/334-2135; FAX 941/332-1879.* E-mail nshippas@peganet.com; web www.cyberstreet.com/takiki. 23 rms, 5 kits. Mid-Dec-Apr: S, D $65-$67; each addl $5; kit. units $450-$475/wk; lower rates rest of yr. Crib free. Pet accepted, some restrictions. TV; cable. Heated pool. Complimentary coffee. Restaurant nearby. Ck-out 11 am. Business servs avail. Picnic tables, grill. On river; boat dock. Cr cds: A, C, D, DS, MC, V.

🖋 🖋 ≋ ⩗

✔★ ★ **WELLESLEY INN AND SUITES.** *4400 Ford St (33916). 941/278-3949; FAX 941/278-3670; res: 800/444-8888.* 106 rms, 4 story, 15 suites. Mid-Dec-mid-Apr: S, D $105-$115; each addl $10; suites $125-$135; lower rates rest of yr. Pet accepted, some restrictions. TV; cable (premium). Heated pool. Complimentary continental bkfst. Coffee in rms.

Restaurant nearby. Ck-out 11 am. Coin lndry. Meeting rm. Business servs avail. Health club privileges. Some refrigerators. Cr cds: A, C, D, DS, MC, V.

☐ 🖋 ≋ ⩗ 🔥 SC

Motor Hotels

★ ★ **HOLIDAY INN SELECT.** *13051 Bell Tower Dr (33907), in Bell Tower Center. 941/482-2900.* Web www.holiday-inn.com. 227 rms, 5 story. Jan-Apr: S $149-$169; D $159-$179; each addl $10; suites $149-$189; under 18 free; lower rates rest of yr. Crib free. TV; cable (premium), VCR avail. Heated pool. Coffee in rms. Restaurant 6:30 am-midnight. Rm serv. Bar 10-2 am; entertainment. Ck-out noon. Coin lndry. Meeting rms. Business servs avail. In-rm modem link. Concierge. Valet serv. Free airport transportation. Exercise equipt. Health club privileges. Refrigerators; some wet bars. Luxury level. Cr cds: A, C, D, DS, JCB, MC, V.

☐ ≋ 🏋 ✈ ⩗ 🔥 SC

★ ★ **HOLIDAY INN SUNSPREE RESORT.** *2220 W 1st St (33901). 941/334-3434; res: 800/664-7775; FAX 941/334-3844.* E-mail hiftmyers@aol.com. 147 rms, 95 with shower only, 3 story. Jan-Apr: S, D $139-$159; each addl $10; under 12 free; higher rates special events; lower rates rest of yr. Crib free. TV; cable (premium). Pool; wading pool. Playground. Supervised child's activities (Jan-Apr); ages 4-12. Restaurant 7 am-midnight. Bar; entertainment. Ck-out 11 am. Business servs avail. Bellhops. Valet serv. Concierge. Gift shop. Beauty shop. Meeting rms. Business servs avail. Free airport transportation. Exercise equipt. Game rm. Refrigerators; microwaves avail. Cr cds: A, D, DS, JCB, MC, V.

☐ ≋ 🏋 ✈ ⩗ 🔥 SC

★ ★ **RADISSON INN.** *(12635 Cleveland Ave, Ft Meyers 33907) on US 41. 941/936-4300; FAX 941/936-2058.* 192 rms, 5 story. Late Dec-early Apr: S, D $120-$175; suites $165-$195; each addl $10; wknd rates; lower rates rest of yr. Crib avail. TV; cable (premium). Heated pool; poolside serv. Coffee in rms. Restaurant 6:30 am-10 pm. Rm serv. Bar 11-1 am. Ck-out noon. Meeting rms. Business servs avail. In-rm modem link. Bellhops. Gift shop. Valet serv. Coin lndry. Free airport transportation. Golf privileges. Health club privileges. Lawn games. Cr cds: A, C, D, DS, ER, JCB, MC, V.

☐ 🏋 ≋ ⩗ 🔥 SC

Resort

★ ★ ★ **SANIBEL HARBOUR RESORT & SPA.** *17260 Harbour Pointe Dr (33908). 941/466-4000; FAX 941/466-2150; res: 800/767-7777.* E-mail shrs@sanibel-resort.com; web www.sanibel-resort.com. 325 units, 12 story, 83 condo units. Dec-Apr: S, D $275-$315; suites $339; 2-bedrm condo units $339-$599; under 18 free; AP, MAP avail; monthly rates; tennis plans; lower rates rest of yr. Crib free. TV; cable (premium), VCR avail. 4 pools, 1 indoor; whirlpools, poolside serv. Supervised child's activities; ages 5-12. Dining rm 6:30 am-11 pm. Rm serv. Bar 11-2 am. Ck-out noon, ck-in 3 pm. Convention facilities. Business center. In-rm modem link. Bellhops. Valet serv. Concierge. Gift shop. Barber, beauty shop. Valet parking. Sports dir. 13 lighted tennis courts, pro. 36-hole golf privileges, greens fee $40-$100, putting green, driving range. Private beach; marina, fishing pier. Boat cruises avail; paddleboats. Watersports. Bicycles. Entertainment. Exercise rm; steam rm, sauna. Massage. Minibars; microwaves avail. Private patios, balconies. On 80 acres. Cr cds: A, C, D, DS, ER, MC, V.

☐ 🖋 🏋 ✈ ≋ ✈ ⩗ SC 🚶

Restaurants

★ ★ **CHART HOUSE.** *2024 W 1st St (33901). 941/332-1881.* Web www.chart-house.com. Hrs: 11:30 am-3:30 pm, 4:30-10 pm; Fri, Sat to 11 pm; Sun 4:30-9 pm; early-bird dinner 4:30-6 pm. Res accepted. Bar. Semi-a la carte: lunch $6.95-$12.95, dinner $14.95-$31.95. Child's meals.

Specializes in hand-cut steak, fresh seafood, beef. Salad bar. Built over Caloosahatchee River. Cr cds: A, C, D, DS, MC, V.

[D] [⊒]

✔★ ★ **LIGHTHOUSE.** *14301 Port Comfort Rd (33908). 941/489-0770.* Hrs: 11 am-10 pm; Fri, Sat to 11 pm; early-bird dinner 4-6 pm (summer). Closed Dec 25. Res accepted (summer). Steak & seafood menu. Bar to 11 pm. Semi-a la carte: lunch, dinner $5.95-$10.95. Specialties: prime rib, surf & turf, fresh grouper. Piano bar Wed-Sat. Parking. Outdoor dining. On bayou. Cr cds: A, MC, V.

[D] [⊒]

✔★ ★ **MARINER INN.** *3448 Marinatown Lane (33903), off Hancock Bridge Pkwy. 941/997-8300.* Hrs: 11 am-9 pm; Fri, Sat to 10 pm. Res accepted. Bar to midnight. Semi-a la carte: lunch $3.95-$8.95, dinner $6.25-$15.95. Child's meals. Specializes in fresh seafood, beef. Outdoor dining. Occasional entertainment. Parking. Waterfront dining; dockage. New England, nautical decor. Cr cds: A, D, DS, MC, V.

[D] [⊒]

★ ★ **PETER'S LA CUISINE.** *2224 Bay St (33901). 941/332-2228.* Hrs: 11:30 am-2 pm, 5:30-9:30 pm; Sat, Sun from 5:30 pm. Res accepted. Continental menu. Bar 4 pm-2 am. A la carte entrees: lunch $9.95, dinner $24.95-$28.95. Specializes in veal, lamb, fresh seafood. Own pastries. Jazz & blues groups upstairs. Parking. In historic riverfront area; modern decor. Cr cds: A, MC, V.

[D] [⊒]

★ ★ **THE PRAWNBROKER.** *13451 McGregor Blvd (33919). 941/489-2226.* Hrs: 4:30-10 pm; Sun to 9 pm. Closed July 4, Thanksgiving; also Super Bowl Sun. Res accepted. Bar. Semi-a la carte: dinner $10.95-$18.95. Child's meals. Specializes in seafood, steak. Parking. Porch dining overlooks tropical garden and fountain. Cr cds: A, MC, V.

[D] [⊒]

★ ★ **THE VERANDA.** *2nd St & Broadway (33901), opp city hall. 941/332-2065.* Hrs: 11 am-2:30 pm, 5:30-10 pm; Sat from 5:30 pm. Closed Sun exc hols; Dec 25. Res accepted. Continental menu. Bar to 1 am. Wine list. Semi-a la carte: lunch $7.50-$9.50, dinner $13.95-$26.95. Child's meals. Specializes in Southern regional cuisine. Courtyard dining. Own baking. Piano bar. Valet parking (dinner). Turn-of-the-century house; Victorian atmosphere. Cr cds: A, MC, V.

[D] [⊒]

Fort Myers Beach (G-4)

(See also Bonita Springs, Cape Coral, Fort Myers, Naples)

Pop 9,284 **Elev** 5 ft **Area code** 941 **Zip** 33931 **E-mail** fmbeach@usa-chamber.com **Web** www.coconet.com/fmbeach
Information Greater Fort Myers Beach Chamber of Commerce, 17200 San Carlos Blvd; 941/454-7500.

Stretching thinly along the seven-mile sliver of Estero Island, this is a town with the Gulf of Mexico on one side and Estero Bay never more than three blocks away on the other. The 18th-century pirates are gone, but tourists love to poke in the sand for treasure; more likely they find sea shells, starfish and sea horses. The beach stretches the entire length of the island and is considered one of the safest in the state.

What to See and Do

Fishing. From 600-foot public pier in Lynn Hall Park (free); Carl Johnson Park on causeway (fee); surf casting from beach; offshore charter boats avail; moonlight "tarpon hunting" (spring-fall).
Island Rover Excursions. Two to three-hr sailing in the Gulf of Mexico aboard the 72-ft-long schooner *Island Rover.* Day and sunset cruises.

(Three times daily) Adj Snug Harbor Restaurant, San Carlos Blvd, under Mantanzas Bridge. Phone 941/765-7447.   ¢¢¢¢-¢¢¢¢¢

Annual Events

Shrimp Festival. Seven-day event culminating with Blessing of Shrimp Fleet. Mid-Mar.

American Championship Sandsculpting Festival. Early Nov.

Motels

★ ★ ★ **BEST WESTERN PINK SHELL.** *275 Estero Blvd. 941/463-6181; res: 800/237-5786; FAX 941/463-1229.* Web www.best-western.com/best.html. 208 units, 1-7 story, 81 kits, 79 suites, 49 kit. cottages. Late Dec-mid-Apr: S, D, kits $189-$265; each addl $20; apts $319-$359; kit. cottages $289-$429; under 18 free; lower rates rest of yr. Crib free. TV; cable, VCR (movies). 3 pools; wading pool, poolside serv. Playground. Supervised child's activities. Restaurant 7:30 am-9 pm. Ck-out 11 am. Coin lndry. Business servs avail. Sundries. Gift shop. Tennis. Lawn games. Microwaves. Picnic tables, grills. On 12 acres; fishing pier, dockage, water sports. Cr cds: A, C, D, DS, JCB, MC, V.

[D] [➤] [🛉] [≈] [≋] [🛥] [🐾] [SC]

★ **BUCCANEER RESORT INN.** *4864 Estero Blvd. 941/463-5728; FAX 941/463-5756.* Web www.all-florida.com/swbuccaneer.htm. 27 units, 3 story. Late Dec-mid-Apr: S, D $69-$89; each addl $6; suites $89-$169; kits. $92-$149; under 6 free; wkly rates; 1-wk min stay Easter & Christmas; lower rates rest of yr. Crib $6. TV; cable, VCR avail (movies $1). Heated pool. Ck-out 10 am. Business servs avail. Sundries. Coin lndry. Lawn games. Refrigerators; microwaves avail. Some balconies. Picnic tables. On beach. Cr cds: A, DS, MC, V.

[➤] [≋] [🐾] [SC]

★ ★ **NEPTUNE INN.** *2310 Estero Blvd. 941/463-6141; FAX 941/463-7503.* E-mail info@neptuneinn.com; web www.neptuneinn.com. 63 kit. units, 2 story. Mid-Dec-Apr: kit. units $120-$150; each addl $10; under 12 free; monthly rates; lower rates rest of yr. Crib free. TV; cable. 2 pools, 1 heated. Complimentary coffee. Restaurant nearby. Ck-out 11 am. Coin lndry. Business servs avail. Lawn games. Some private patios, balconies. Picnic tables, grills. On Gulf. Cr cds: DS, MC, V.

[D] [≈] [≋] [🐾]

★ ★ **OUTRIGGER BEACH RESORT.** *6200 Estero Blvd. 941/463-3131; FAX 941/463-6577; res: 800/749-3131.* E-mail rooms@outriggerfmb.com; web www.outriggerfmb.com. 144 rms, 1-4 story, 68 kits. No elvtr. Mid-Dec-Apr: S, D $105-$125; each addl $8; kit. units $115-$195; lower rates rest of yr. TV; cable. Heated pool. Restaurant 7 am-8 pm. Bar noon-8 pm. Ck-out 11 am. Coin lndry. Business servs avail. Sundries. Gift shop. Exercise equipt. Putting green. Lawn games. Refrigerators; microwaves avail. On beach. Cr cds: DS, MC, V.

[D] [≈] [🏃] [🐾]

✔★ ★ **SANDPIPER GULF RESORT.** *5550 Estero Blvd. 941/463-5721; res: 800/584-1449; FAX 941/463-5721, ext. 299.* E-mail manager@sandpipergulfresort.com; web www.sandpipergulfresort.com. 63 kit. units, 2-5 story. Mid-Dec-mid-Apr: S, D $108-$133; each addl $7; under 6 free; wkly, monthly rates; higher rates major hols; lower rates rest of yr. Crib free. TV; cable (premium). 2 pools, 1 heated; whirlpool. Complimentary coffee in lobby. Restaurant nearby. Ck-out 11 am. Coin lndry. Business servs avail. Gift shop. Lawn games. Microwaves. Private patios, balconies. Picnic tables. On beach; swimming. Cr cds: DS, MC, V.

[D] [≈] [🐾]

★ ★ **SANTA MARIA.** *7317 Estero Blvd. 941/765-6700; FAX 941/765-6909; res: 800/765-6701.* E-mail sstreamsm@peganet.com; web www.sunstream.com/santamaria. 60 kit. suites (1-, 2- bedrm), 5 story. Late Dec-mid Apr, wkly (7-day min): 1-bedrm $905-$1,610; 2-bedrm $1,015-$2,030; lower rates rest of yr (2-day min). Crib avail. Maid serv (fee). TV; cable, VCR avail. Pool; whirlpool. Sauna. Supervised child's activities. Complimentary coffee in lobby. Restaurant nearby. Ck-out 10 am. Guest

Indry. Business servs avail. Lawn games. Balconies. Picnic tables. Opp beach. Cr cds: A, DS, MC, V.

D ☐ ☐ ☐ SC

Motor Hotels

★ ★ **BEST WESTERN BEACH RESORT.** *684 Estero Blvd. 941/463-6000; FAX 941/463-3013.* E-mail info@bwbeachresort.com; web www.bwbeachresort.com. 75 kit. units, 5 story. Feb-Apr, mid-Dec: S, D $129-$229; under 18 free; lower rates rest of yr. Crib free. Pet accepted, some restrictions. TV; cable (premium). Heated pool. Playground. Complimentary continental bkfst. Restaurant nearby. Ck-out 11 am. Coin Indry. Business servs avail. Game rm. Lawn games. Microwaves. Balconies. Picnic tables, grills. On gulf. Cr cds: A, C, D, DS, MC, V.

D ☐ ☐ ☐ ☐ SC

★ ★ **POINTE ESTERO.** *6640 Estero Blvd. 941/765-1155; FAX 941/765-0657; res: 800/237-5141.* E-mail sstreampe@peganet.com; web www.sunstream.com/pointeestero. 60 1 & 2-bedrm kit. suites, 16 story. Mid-Dec-late-May: 1-bedrm $168-$295, 2-bedrm $198-$410; 7-day min; wkend rates; golf plans; higher rates: special events, hols; lower rates rest of yr (2-day min late Apr-mid-Dec). Crib $5. TV; cable; VCR (movies). Pool; whirlpool. Supervised child's activities; ages 3-18. Complimentary coffee in lobby. Restaurant nearby. Ck-out 10 am. Guest Indry. Business servs avail. Gift shop. Sundries. Lighted tennis. Lawn games. Picnic tables, grills. On ocean; beach. Cr cds: DS, MC, V.

D ☐ ☐ ☐ SC

Restaurants

★ ★ **ANTHONY'S ON THE GULF.** *(3040 Estero Blvd, Ft Myers Beach)* 941/463-2600. Hrs: 11:30 am-10 pm; Fri, Sat to 11 pm. Italian menu. Bar. Semi-a la carte: lunch $5.95-$8.95, dinner $8.95-$18.95. Child's meals. Specializes in veal, pasta, seafood. Parking. Outdoor dining. Built on stilts directly on beach; tropical atmosphere. Cr cds: A, DS, MC, V.

D ☐

★ **BALLENGER'S.** *11390 Summerlin Square Dr, at San Carlos Blvd.* 941/466-2626. Hrs: 4-10 pm; Sun 10 am-9 pm. Bar. Semi-a la carte: dinner $9.75-$15.75. Specializes in fresh local seafood. Salad bar. Parking. Cr cds: A, DS, MC, V.

D ☐

★ ★ **CHARLEY BROWN'S.** *6225 Estero Blvd.* 941/463-6660. Hrs: 5-10 pm. Closed Thanksgiving; also Super Bowl Sun. Semi-a la carte: dinner $10.95-$24.95. Child's meals. Specializes in steak, beef, fresh seafood. Salad bar. Parking. View of Mangrove creek. Cr cds: A, C, D, DS, MC, V.

☐

✔ ★ **THE FISH MONGER.** *19030 San Carlos Blvd.* 941/765-5544. Hrs: 4-10 pm. Closed major hols; Super Bowl Sun. Res accepted. Bar. Semi-a la carte: dinner $8.95-$14.95. Child's meals. Specializes in pasta, seafood. Parking. Cr cds: DS, MC, V.

D ☐

★ ★ **MUCKY DUCK.** *2500 Estero Blvd.* 941/463-5519. Hrs: 5-9:30 pm. Closed Thanksgiving, Dec 25. Bar. Semi-a la carte: dinner $6.95-$16.95. Child's meals. Specializes in fresh seafood, steak, duck. Pianist wkends in season. Parking. Near Gulf. Cr cds: A, D, DS, MC, V.

D ☐

★ ★ **SNUG HARBOR WATERFRONT.** *645 San Carlos Blvd, under Mantanzas Bridge.* 941/463-4343. Web www.snugharbour.com. Hrs: 11:30 am-10 pm. Bar to 2 am. Semi-a la carte: lunch $4.95-$13.95, dinner $10.95-$18.95. Child's meals. Specializes in fresh seafood, pie. Parking. Dock facilities. On waterfront. Cr cds: A, DS, MC, V.

D ☐

Fort Pierce (F-6)

(See also Jensen Beach, Stuart, Vero Beach)

Settled 1837 **Pop** 36,830 **Elev** 24 ft **Area code** 561 **E-mail** slccom@gate.net **Web** www.co.st-lucie.fl.us

Information St Lucie County Chamber of Commerce, 2200 Virginia Ave, 34982; 561/595-9999 or 888/785-8243.

The original Fort Pierce, a US Army garrison established in 1837, during the Seminole War, was located on what is now Indian River Drive. The city formed around the site, with three communities merging into one in 1901. On the west side of the Indian River the city is linked to the ocean and Hutchinson Island beaches by two bridges. It is the marketplace for the cattle ranches, vegetable farms and citrus groves of St Lucie County; tourism and commercial fishing round out the economy.

What to See and Do

Fishing. Surfcasting from 20 mi of beaches. Free fishing balconies on bridge over Indian River, where world's record sea trout was caught. Deep-sea charter boats. Freshwater fishing in St Lucie River, lakes and canal. South jetty fishing pier on south side of Ft Pierce Inlet; also ocean-going inlet.

Fort Pierce Inlet State Recreation Area. More than 300 acres bounded by Atlantic Ocean and Indian River; footbridge to Jack Island. Swimming, skin diving, surfing, dressing rooms, showers; fishing. Nature trails. Picnicking. Standard hrs, fees. 4 mi E, off FL A1A. Phone 561/468-3985.

St Lucie County Historical Museum. Local and state historical exhibits include 1715 Spanish shipwreck artifacts, military material from Old Fort Pierce, Seminole encampment, items from early industries; restored 1907 house, 1919 American-LaFrance fire engine; changing exhibit gallery. (Daily exc Mon; closed most hols) 414 Seaway Dr, in park at E end of South Beach Bridge. Phone 561/462-1795. ¢

Swimming. Of the more than 21 mi of Atlantic coastline along Hutchinson Island, approx 7 mi are accessible to the public.

South Beach, on a barrier island more than 15 mi long, includes South Beach Boardwalk, Waveland Beach, Walton Rocks, Frederick Douglass Park. Paved parking, boardwalks, dressing rooms, showers, concession, restrooms; picnicking. **Free.**

North Beach includes Pepper Beach Park, Jack Island State Preserve and Ft Pierce Inlet State Recreation area. Fishing docks, tennis, picnicking, rest room. **Free.**

County beach accesses include Middle Cove Access, Herman's Bay Access, Normandy Beach Access and Dollman Beach, Avalon Beach, John Brooks Park (all three undeveloped). Swimming; surf fishing; boardwalks. Parking. **Free.**

The Savannas. A 550-acre light marshland. Fishing. Picnicking, playground. Camping (7-day max; fee). Observation tower. Pets on leash only. Park (daily). 1400 E Midway Rd, off US 1. Phone 561/595-5845. Entrance fee per vehicle ¢

Underwater Demolition Team-SEAL Museum. Diving gear, weapons and apparatus of SEAL ("sea, air and land") commandos—successors to US Navy "frogmen" of World War II. Dioramas trace history of the teams; videos of training process. (Daily exc Mon; closed hols) 5 mi NE via US 1 to 3300 N FL A1A, North Hutchinson Island, in Pepper Park. Phone 561/489-3597. ¢

Seasonal Events

Jai-Alai. 1750 S Kings Highway, 1 mi N of FL Tpke. Parimutuel betting. Mon & Wed-Sat evenings; matinees, Mon, Wed & Sat. Restaurant. Phone 561/464-7500 or 800/JAI-ALAI. Jan-Apr.

Spring training. 10 mi S on US 1, at Thomas J White Sports Complex, Peacock Blvd in Port St Lucie. New York Mets baseball spring training; exhibition games. Phone 561/871-2115. Early Mar-early Apr.

Motels

✓★ **COMFORT INN.** 3236 S US 1 (34982). 561/461-2323; FAX 561/464-5151. 61 units, 2 story, 14 kits. Jan-Apr: S, D $73-$78; kit. units $5 addl; under 18 free; lower rates rest of yr. Crib free. TV; cable (premium). Pool; whirlpool. Complimentary continental bkfst. Ck-out 11 am. Coin lndry. Business servs avail. In-rm modem link. Cr cds: A, C, D, DS, ER, MC, V.

★ **DAYS INN.** 6651 Darter Ct (34945), W off I-95 exit 65, just S of Okeechobee Rd. 561/466-4066; res: 800/329-7466; FAX 561/468-3260. Web www.daysinn.com. 125 rms, 2 story. Jan-Apr: S, D $65-$84; each addl $5; under 18 free; lower rates rest of yr. Pet accepted; $10. TV; cable (premium). Heated pool. Coffee in rms. Restaurant 6 am-11 pm; Fri, Sat to 1 am. Ck-out 11 am. Coin lndry. Meeting rms. Business servs avail. Sundries. Some refrigerators. Cr cds: A, C, D, DS, JCB, MC, V.

★★ **DAYS INN.** 1920 Seaway Dr (34949), on South Hutchinson Island. 561/461-8737; FAX 561/460-2218. 31 rms. Mid-Dec-Apr: S, D $89-$95; each addl $6; kits. $107-$135; under 18 free; wkly rates; higher rates: hols (3-day min), special events; lower rates rest of yr. Crib free. TV; cable (premium). Heated pool. Complimentary continental bkfst. Restaurant adj 7 am-10 pm. Ck-out 11 am. Coin lndry. Business servs avail. Lawn games. Microwaves avail. Picnic tables. On water. Cr cds: A, C, D, DS, JCB, MC, V.

★★ **HARBOR LIGHT INN-EDGEWATER MOTEL.** 1160 Seaway Dr (34949), on South Hutchinson Island. 561/468-3555; res: 800/433-0004. 35 units, 2 story, 15 kit. suites. Late Dec-Apr: S, D $49.50-$99.50; each addl $10; suites $77.50-$120; under 16 free (limit 2); wkly rates; lower rates rest of yr. Crib free. TV; cable (premium). Heated pool; whirlpool. Ck-out 11 am. Lawn games. Refrigerators. Balconies. Picnic tables, grills. On inlet; 2 private fishing piers, 2 boat docks. Cr cds: A, C, D, DS, MC, V.

✓★★ **HOLIDAY INN EXPRESS.** 7151 Okeechobee (34945), W off I-95 exit 65. 561/464-5000; FAX 561/461-9573. 100 rms, 2 story. Jan-mid-Apr: S, D $89-$95; under 18 free; lower rates rest of yr. Crib free. Pet accepted, some restrictions. TV; cable (premium). Pool; wading pool. Complimentary continental bkfst. Ck-out noon. Coin lndry. Meeting rms. Sundries. Cr cds: A, C, D, DS, ER, JCB, MC, V.

Inn

★★★ **MELLON PATCH INN.** (3601 N A1A, North Hutchinson Island 34949) 561/461-5231; FAX 561/465-9841; res: 800/656-7824. Web www.swnet.net/mlnptch. 4 rms, 2 story. Rm phones avail. S, D $80-$135; each addl $20; higher rates wkends. Children over 12 yrs only. TV; cable (premium). Complimentary full bkfst. Ck-out 11 am, ck-in 3 pm. Business servs avail. Picnic tables. Swimming beach. Dock. Key West-style house with landscaped grounds overlooking Intracoastal Waterway. Totally non-smoking. Cr cds: A, D, MC, V.

Restaurants

★ **CHUCK'S SEAFOOD.** 822 Seaway Dr, on South Hutchinson Island. 561/461-9484. Hrs: 4-10 pm; early-bird dinner to 6 pm. Closed Mon; some major hols. Bar. Semi-a la carte: dinner $8.95-$24.95. Child's meals. Specialties: shrimp scampi, fried shrimp, baked fresh fish. Entertainment Wed-Sun. Outdoor dining overlooking Fort Pierce Inlet. Family-owned. Cr cds: DS, MC, V.

✓★ **JOHNNY'S CORNER.** (7180 S US 1, Port St Lucie) 1 blk N of Prime Vista Blvd. 561/878-2686. Hrs: 6 am-9 pm; early-bird dinner

Mon-Sat 11 am-5 pm. Closed Dec 25. Italian, Greek, Amer menu. Bar. Semi-a la carte: bkfst $1.95-$4.95, lunch $2.95-$5.25, dinner $4.95-$11.95. Child's meals. Specializes in seafood, steak, chops. Bakery on premises. Cr cds: MC, V.

★★ **MANGROVE MATTIE'S.** 1640 Seaway Dr, on South Hutchinson Island. 561/466-1044. Hrs: 11:30 am-10 pm; early-bird dinner 4:30-6 pm. Res accepted. Bar to 11 pm. Semi-a la carte: lunch $5.99-$9.99, dinner $7.99-$19.99. Specializes in fish, shellfish, aged steak. On Fort Pierce Inlet; view of waterway. Cr cds: A, D, DS, MC, V.

★ **PEKING.** 1012 S US 1 (34950). 561/464-5960. Hrs: 11:30 am-9:30 pm; Fri, Sat to 10 pm. Res accepted. Chinese menu. Wine, beer. Semi-a la carte: lunch $4.25-$6.25, dinner $5.95-$14.95. Specialties: mixed seafood, Hawaiian duck, imperial shrimp. Chinese decor. Cr cds: A, DS, MC, V.

Fort Walton Beach (J-2)

(See also Destin, Pensacola)

Pop 21,471 **Elev** 23 ft **Area code** 850 **Web** interlead.com/fwb-chamber/index.html
Information Greater Fort Walton Beach Chamber of Commerce, 34 Miracle Strip Pkwy SE, PO Box 640, 32549; 850/244-8191.

Fort Walton Beach covers a six-mile stretch of US 98 along Santa Rosa Sound and the Gulf of Mexico in northwest Florida. Archaeological excavations (begun in 1960) of mounds have added historic significance to the city. Temple Mound has yielded artifacts from prehistoric times and between A.D. 1300-1700.

What to See and Do

Air Force Armament Museum. Exhibits include historical aircraft and weapons. Film on history of Eglin AFB is shown continuously (daily, 30-min). (Daily) 13 mi NE via FL 285, on the Eglin Air Force Base. Phone 850/882-4062. **Free.**

Gulfarium. Exhibition of fish and scuba diving shows; trained dolphins; sea lion shows; harbor seals; shark moat; alligator and saltwater fish displays. Exotic bird exhibits; penguin breeding colonies; otters. (Daily; closed Thanksgiving, Dec 25) ½ mi E on US 98, on Okaloosa Island. Phone 850/244-5169. ¢¢¢¢

Indian Temple Mound Museum and Park. Covering an acre of land, this mound served as a major religious and civic center for Native Americans of the area. The ancient temple is recreated in a modern shelter on the original site. On the east flank of the mound a museum houses dioramas and exhibits portraying Native American settlement over a span of 12,000 years. Mound (daily; free). Museum (daily exc Sun; closed Jan 1, Thanksgiving, Dec 25). 139 Miracle Strip Pkwy (US 98), downtown. Phone 850/833-9595. Museum ¢¢

Annual Events

Seafood Festival. Arts & crafts, demonstrations, entertainment, food. Phone 850/244-5319. Mid-Apr.

Billy Bowlegs Pirate Festival. Includes mock pirate assault, parades, treasure hunts, coronation pageant. 7 days early June.

Motels

★★★ **FOUR POINTS BY SHERATON.** 1325 Miracle Strip Pkwy (32548). 850/243-8116; FAX 850/244-3064. 217 rms, 2 story. Mid-May-early Sept: S, D $115-$225; each addl $10; under 18 free; hols (3-day min);

lower rates rest of yr. TV; cable (premium). Pools; poolside serv, whirl-pools. Complimentary full bkfst. Coffee in rms. Restaurant 6 am-11 pm. Rm serv. Bar 4-10 pm. Ck-out noon. Coin lndry. Meeting rms. Business servs avail. In-rm modem link. Bellhops. Valet serv. Exercise equipt. Many refrigerators. Some balconies. Picnic tables. On ocean; beach. Cr cds: A, D, DS, ER, MC, V.

✔★ **HOWARD JOHNSON'S WATERFRONT.** *314 Miracle Strip Pkwy SW (32548).* 850/243-6162; FAX 850/664-2735. 140 rms, 2 story. Late May-Labor Day: S, D $50-$80; each addl $10; under 18 free. TV; cable (premium). Pool. Restaurant open 24 hrs. Ck-out noon. Coin lndry. Meeting rm. Business servs avail. Microwaves avail. Private patios, balconies. Launching ramp; dockage. Cr cds: A, C, D, DS, JCB, MC, V.

✔★ **INN AT FORT WALTON BEACH.** *203 Miracle Strip Pkwy (32548).* 850/244-8663; FAX 850/664-0964. 102 rms, 3 story, 2 kit. units. Mar-Sept: S, kit. units $68; D $63-$73; each addl $5; under 18 free; golf plans; lower rates rest of yr. Crib free. TV; cable (premium). Pool. Complimentary coffee in lobby. Restaurant adj 6 am-midnight. Bar 11-4 am. Ck-out noon. Business servs avail. Cr cds: A, C, D, DS, ER, MC, V.

Motor Hotels

★ ★ **RADISSON.** *1110 Santa Rosa Blvd (32548), on Oklaloosa Island.* 850/243-9181; FAX 850/664-7652. 388 rms, 7 story. Mar-Sept: S $130-$165; D $140-$175; each addl $10; under 18 free; golf plans, min-stay hols; lower rates rest of yr. Crib free. TV; cable (premium). 3 pools; wading pool, poolside serv (in season). Playground. Supervised child's activities (in season); ages 3-12. Complimentary coffee in rms. Restaurant 6 am-10 pm. Rm serv 24 hrs. Bar. Ck-out 11 am. Convention facilities. Business servs avail. In-rm modem link. Bellhops. Gift shop. Valet serv. Tennis. Exercise equipt. Game rm. Balconies. Picnic tables. Cr cds: A, C, D, DS, JCB, MC, V.

★ ★ **RAMADA PLAZA BEACH RESORT.** *1500 Miracle Strip Pkwy SE (32548), 2 mi SE on US 98.* 850/243-9161; FAX 850/243-2391. 335 rms, 2 & 6 story. Apr-Sept: S, D $105-$155; each addl $10; suites $210-$300; under 18 free; lower rates rest of yr. Crib free. TV; cable (premium). 3 pools, 1 indoor; wading pool, whirlpool. Free supervised child's activities (June-Aug); ages 5-12. Coffee in rms. Restaurants 6 am-10 pm. Rm serv. Bars 11 am-midnight; entertainment (seasonal). Ck-out 11 am. Convention facilities. Business servs avail. In-rm modem link. Bellhops. Sundries. Exercise equipt. Microwaves avail. Private patios, balconies. On beach. Cr cds: A, C, D, DS, MC, V.

Restaurants

✔★ **LOS RANCHEROS.** *300 Eglin Pkwy NE (32548).* 850/862-2007. Hrs: 11 am-10 pm; Fri, Sat to 11 pm; Sun to 9 pm. Mexican menu. Bar. Semi-a la carte: lunch $3.25-$5.95, dinner $5.50-$10.50. Child's meals. Specializes in fajitas. Cr cds: A, DS, MC, V.

★ **PANDORA'S STEAK HOUSE.** *1120B Santa Rosa Blvd (32548), on Oklaloosa Island.* 850/244-8669. Hrs: 5-10 pm; wkends to 10:30 pm; early-bird dinner 5-6:30 pm. Closed Mon in winter. Res accepted. Bar. Semi-a la carte: dinner $9.95-$19.95. Specializes in steak, grilled seafood. Bar area inside boat that sits in front of the restaurant. Cr cds: A, C, D, DS, MC, V.

Gainesville (C-4)

(See also Starke)

Settled 1830 **Pop** 84,770 **Elev** 185 ft **Area code** 352 **Web** www.co.alachua.fl.us/~acvacb
Information Alachua County Visitors & Convention Bureau, 30 E University, 32601; 352/374-5231.

The seat of Alachua County, Gainesville is a university city with a variety of industries, including the manufacture of archery equipment.

What to See and Do

Bivens Arm Nature Park. A 57-acre oak hammock sanctuary and marsh with boardwalk and nature trails. (Daily) 3650 S Main St. Phone 352/334-2056. **Free.**

Devil's Millhopper State Geological Site. Giant sinkhole (500 ft wide, 120 ft deep) was formed when the roof of an underground limestone cavern collapsed. The cool environment allows growth of unique lush vegetation. Access to the bottom is by wooden walkway. Interpretive center; nature walks. Nearby is **San Felasco Hammock State Preserve,** with rare flora and fauna; prehistoric Indian sites; nature trails. Standard hrs, fees. 4 mi NW on County 232. Phone 352/955-2008.

Fred Bear Museum. Collection of archery and bow hunting artifacts, Eskimo and African carvings and artwork, wildlife mounts. (Daily; closed major hols) At jct I-75 & Archer Rd. Phone 352/376-2411. ¢¢

Kanapaha Botanical Gardens. A 62-acre botanical garden featuring butterfly garden, large bamboo garden, vinery; hummingbird garden, herb & palm gardens and others. (Daily exc Thurs) 4625 SW 63rd Blvd. Phone 352/372-4981. ¢

Marjorie Kinnan Rawlings State Historic Site. Farmhouse and memorabilia of the author of *The Yearling* and *Cross Creek.* Guided tour (limit 10 per hr). (Oct-July, Thurs-Sun; closed Jan 1, Thanksgiving, Dec 25) 11 mi S on US 441 to Micanopy, then 6 mi E via FL 346, then 4 mi via 325 in Cross Creek. Phone 352/466-3672. ¢

State parks.

O'Leno. The site of an old town, this 5,896-acre park includes a section of the Santa Fe River, which disappears underground through a sink-hole and then emerges nearly three mi to the south. Swimming, fishing. Nature, bridle trails, hiking. Picnicking. Camping (dump station). Standard hrs, fees. 32 mi NW on US 441, 7 mi N of High Springs. Phone 904/454-1853.

Ichetucknee Springs. Crystal-clear springs with limpkins, wood ducks, otters and beavers are found on this 2,241-acre park on the Ichetucknee River. Swimming, scuba and skin diving in Blue Hole (Oct-Mar); canoeing, tubing (daily usage limits on number of people on river). Nature trails; picnicking. Standard hrs, fees. 23 mi NW on US 441 to High Springs, then 14 mi NW off US 27, N of Fort White. Phone 904/497-2511.

Paynes Prairie Preserve. Approx 20,000-acre state preserve is a major wintering ground for sandhill crane. Fishing; boating (ramps; gas motors prohibited), canoeing. Horseback riding, hiking & biking trails. Picnicking. Camping. Visitor center (daily); observation tower. Standard hrs, fees. 10 mi S off US 441 near Micanopy. Phone 352/466-3397.

University of Florida (1853). (40,000 students) A 2,000-acre campus with 16 colleges and 4 schools. University Ave & US 441. Phone 352/392-3261. Located on campus are

Florida Museum of Natural History. Largest museum of natural history in the southeast United States. Features full-scale North Florida Cave exhibit. Object Gallery has fossilized shark's teeth, live reptiles. (Daily; closed Nov 26, Dec 25) (See ANNUAL EVENTS) Hull Rd & SW 34th St. Phone 352/846-2000. **Donation.**

Lake Alice Wildlife Preserve. Alligators, turtles, birds. Picnicking. (Daily) Museum Rd, 1 mi W of SW 13th St.

Samuel P. Harn Museum of Art. Features African and pre-Columbian collections, American paintings as well as contemporary works of art. Film series, lectures and guided gallery tours also avail. (Daily exc Mon; closed major hols) Hull Rd and SW 34 St. Phone 352/392-9826.

Annual Event

Gatornationals. NHRA Drag racing at Gainesville Raceway, just N of 53rd Ave & Waldo Rd. Phone 352/377-0046. Mar.

Motels

★ ★ **CABOT LODGE.** 3726 SW 40th Blvd (32608), I-75 exit 75. 352/375-2400; FAX 352/335-2321; res: 800/843-8735. 208 rms, 3 story. S $56-$66; D $63-$78; each addl $7; under 18 free. Crib free. TV; cable (premium), VCR avail (movies). Pool. Complimentary continental bkfst, coffee. Restaurant nearby. Ck-out 11 am. Meeting rms. Business servs avail. In-rm modem link. Valet serv. Golf privileges. Health club privileges. Cr cds: A, C, D, DS, MC, V.

🄳 🛉🏊🗙🔥 SC

★ ★ **ECONO LODGE UNIVERSITY.** 2649 SW 13th St (32608). 352/373-7816; res: 800/446-6900; FAX 352/372-9099. Web www.hotel choice.com. 53 rms, 2 story. S $36; D $39; each addl $5; under 18 free. Pet accepted, some restrictions. TV; cable (premium). Pool. Complimentary coffee in lobby. Ck-out 11 am. Cr cds: A, C, D, DS, JCB, MC, V.

🄳 🐾🏊🗙🔥 SC

✔ ★ **FAIRFIELD INN BY MARRIOTT.** 6901 NW 4th Blvd (32607), I-75 exit 76. 352/332-8292; FAX 352/332-8292, ext. 709. 135 rms, 3 story. S $46-$60; D $46-$65; each addl $3; under 18 free. Crib free. TV; cable. Heated pool. Complimentary continental bkfst. Restaurant nearby. Ck-out noon. Business servs avail. In-rm modem link. Cr cds: A, D, DS, MC, V.

🄳 🏊🗙🔥 SC

★ ★ **LA QUINTA.** 920 NW 69th Terrace (32605). 352/332-6466; FAX 352/332-7074. 135 rms, 4 story. S $64; D $70; each addl $6; under 18 free. Crib free. Pet accepted. TV; cable, VCR avail (movies). Heated pool. Complimentary continental bkfst. Restaurant adj 11 am-10 pm. Ck-out noon. Meeting rms. In-rm modem link. Valet serv. Health club privileges. Cr cds: A, C, D, DS, MC, V.

🄳 🐾🏊🗙🔥 SC

★ ★ **RESIDENCE INN BY MARRIOTT.** 4001 SW 13th St (32608). 352/371-2101; FAX 352/371-2101, ext. 66. 80 suites, 3 story. 1 & 2 bedrm $99-$160. Crib free. Pet accepted, some restrictions. $50. TV; cable (premium), VCR avail (movies). Pool; whirlpool. Complimentary continental bkfst buffet. Ck-out noon. Coin lndry. Meeting rm. Business servs avail. Valet serv. Exercise equipt. Picnic tables, grill. Cr cds: A, C, D, DS, MC, V.

🄳 🐾🏊🖈🗙🔥 SC

Motor Hotel

★ ★ **HOLIDAY INN-UNIVERSITY CENTER.** 1250 W University Ave (FL 26) (32601). 352/376-1661; FAX 352/336-8717. E-mail hignvuc@ mindspring.com; web www.holiday-inn.com/hotels/gnvue. 167 rms, 6 story. S, D $85-$130; each addl $10; under 18 free; higher rates special events (2-day min). Crib free. TV; cable, VCR avail. Rooftop pool; poolside serv. Restaurant open 24 hrs. Rm serv. Bar. Ck-out noon. Meeting rms. Business servs avail. In-rm modem link. Beauty shop. Free airport, bus depot transportation. University opp. Cr cds: A, C, D, DS, JCB, MC, V.

🄳 🏊🗙🔥 SC

Hotel

★ ★ **UNIVERSITY CENTRE.** 1535 SW Archer Rd (32608). 352/371-3333; FAX 352/371-3712; res: 800/824-5637 (exc FL), 800/251-

4069 (FL). 185 rms, 11 story. S $79; D $89; each addl $8; suites $175-$500; under 19 free. Crib free. TV; cable (premium). Pool; poolside serv. Restaurant 5-10 pm. Bar 11-2 am. Ck-out noon. Meeting rms. Business servs avail. Beauty shop. Free airport, bus depot transportation. Some refrigerators. Balconies. Extensive grounds with decorative pond. Opp medical center. Cr cds: A, C, D, DS, MC, V.

🄳 🏊🗙🔥 SC

Inns

★ ★ **HERLONG MANSION.** (Cholokka Blvd, Micanopy 32667) S on I-75, exit 73, then E to Micanopy. 352/466-3322; FAX 352/466-3322; res: 800/437-5664. 12 rms, 3 with shower only, 3 story, 4 suites, 2 cottages. No rm phones. S, D $55-$115; each addl $20; suites $175-$500; cottage $125-$145. Crib free. TV; VCR avail (free movies). Complimentary full bkfst; afternoon refreshments. Ck-out 11 am, ck-in 3-6 pm. Meeting rm. Lawn games. Antiques, fireplaces. Veranda. Restored vintage mansion (1845). Totally nonsmoking. Cr cds: MC, V.

🄳 🗙🔥

★ ★ **MAGNOLIA PLANTATION.** 309 SE 7th St (32601). 352/375-6653; FAX 352/338-0303; res: 800/201-2379. Web www.magnoliabnb.com. 6 rms, 3 story. Some rm phones. S, D $85-$150; wkly rates. Phone, TV in parlor; cable, VCR. Complimentary full bkfst; afternoon refreshments. Restaurant nearby. Ck-out 11 am, ck-in 2 pm. Restored Second Empire house (1885); antiques. Waterfall, pond with gazebo. Totally nonsmoking. Cr cds: A, MC, V.

🗙🔥 SC

Restaurants

★ ★ **MR. HAN.** 6944 NW 10th Pl (32605). 352/331-6400. Hrs: 11:30 am-10 pm; Fri, Sat to 10:30 pm. Closed Thanksgiving. Res accepted. Chinese, Szechwan menu. Bar. A la carte entrees: lunch $4-$5.25, dinner $7-$26. Specialties: Peking duck, weeping willow chicken. Elegant Chinese decor; photos of celebrities. Overlooks lake. Cr cds: A, D, MC, V.

🄳

★ ★ ★ **SOVEREIGN.** 12 SE 2nd Ave (32601). 352/378-6307. Hrs: 5:30-10 pm; Fri, Sat to 11 pm. Closed Sun; major hols. Res accepted. Continental menu. Bar 5-11 pm. Semi-a la carte: dinner $16-$28. Own baking. Pianist Thurs-Sat. In restored (1878) carriage house. Cr cds: A, C, D, DS, MC, V.

Haines City (E-4)

(See also Lakeland, Lake Wales, Orlando, Winter Haven)

Pop 11,683 **Elev** 161 ft **Area code** 941 **Zip** 33844
Information Chamber of Commerce, 908 US 27N, PO Box 986; 941/422-3751.

Haines City lies at the foot of a range of rolling hills known as "The Ridge" and is in the heart of Florida's citrus country. Originally called "Clay Cut," the town eventually took the name of a South Florida Railroad vice-president and was subsequently made a regular stop on the line. Nearby sand pits, electronics, the hydraulics industry and tourism help diversify the economy.

Annual Event

Heritage Days. Arts & crafts, entertainment. 1st wk Mar.

Motels

★ ★ **COMFORT INN-MAINGATE SOUTH.** (5510 US 27N, Davenport 33837) 9 mi N at jct US 27 & I-4. 941/424-2811; FAX 941/424-1723. 150 rms, 3 story. Mid-Feb-Easter, mid-June-mid-Aug, late Dec: S, D $49.50-$100; lower rates rest of yr. Crib free. TV. Pool. Playground. Ck-out noon. Coin lndry. Meeting rms. Business servs avail. Game rm. Some refrigerators. Cr cds: A, C, D, DS, ER, JCB, MC, V.

D ≈ ⇴ ⚞ SC

★ ★ **HOLIDAY INN EXPRESS HOTEL AND SUITES.** (5225 US 27N, Davenport 33837) 8 mi N on US 27, at I-4 exit 23. 941/424-2120; FAX 941/424-5317. 104 rms, 2 story, 20 suites. Late Dec-late Apr: S $79; D $85; each addl $10; suites $109; under 18 free; lower rates rest of yr. Crib free. TV; cable (premium). Complimentary continental bkfst. Restaurant adj open 24 hrs. Ck-out 11 am. Meeting rms. Business servs avail. Coin lndry. Heated pool. Game rm. Refrigerator, microwave in suites. Some balconies. Cr cds: A, C, D, DS, MC, V.

D ≈ ⇴ ⚞ SC

Resort

★ ★ ★ **GRENELEFE.** 3200 FL 546, 6 mi E of jct US 27, FL 544. 941/422-7511; FAX 941/421-5000; res: 800/237-9549. Web www.grenelefe.com. 800 condo units, 1-2 story. Mid-Jan-Apr: 1-bedrm villa $220; 2-bedrm villa $400; each addl $20; AP, MAP avail; golf, tennis, fishing packages; lower rates rest of yr. Crib free. TV; cable, VCR avail. Heated pool; whirlpool, poolside serv. Playground. Supervised child's activities; ages 4-12. Dining rm (public by res) 7 am-10 pm. Box lunches, snack bar, outdoor buffets, picnics. Bar 11-1 am. Ck-out 11 am, ck-in 3 pm. Lndry facilities in all buildings. Grocery. Package store. Gift shop. Convention facilities. Business center. Airport transportation. 20 tennis courts, 11 lighted, 2 grass, pros. 54-hole golf, pro, putting green, driving ranges. Pier, marina with 26 slips. Boat cruises. Bicycle rentals. 18-hole miniature golf. Lawn games. Activities dir. Entertainment. Movies. Game rms. Exercise equipt; sauna. Massage. Fishing guides. Some refrigerators. Private patios, balconies. 950 acres on Lake Marion. Cr cds: A, C, D, ER, MC, V.

D ➤ ⚞ ⚞ ≈ ⚞ ⇴ ⚞ SC ⚞

Hialeah (H-6)

(See also Coral Gables, Hollywood, Miami, Miami Intl Airport Area)

Founded 1921 **Pop** 188,004 **Elev** 6 ft **Area code** 305
Information Hialeah/Miami Springs/Northwest Dade Area Chamber of Commerce, 59 W 5th St, 33010; 305/887-1515.

Famous for the racetrack that bears its name, Hialeah is the second largest of the municipalities that make up metropolitan Miami. Many appliance manufacturers, food suppliers and department stores have their distribution headquarters in the community. Glenn Curtiss and James H. Bright, aviation pioneers, were the city's founders.

What to See and Do

Hialeah Park. This lush, "old-world" racetrack is home to a famous pink flamingo colony. Visitors may walk through the grounds and view the tropical gardens, flamingo colony, paddocks and related areas. Horse racing (mid-Mar-late May; phone for schedule). Park (Mon-Fri). E 4th Ave between 21st & 32nd Sts. Phone 305/885-8000. Grounds **Free.**

Thompson County Park. Fishing; boating. Biking. Playground. Tent & trailer camping (fee; hookups). Park (daily). Some fees. 16665 NW Krome Ave Ext (FL 997), 2 mi S of US 27. Phone 305/821-5122.

Annual Event

River Cities Festival. Celebrating the Miami River with boat races, demonstrations; Miccosukee Indian activities and exhibits, arts & crafts; all-breed dog & cat show; international foods. 3rd wkend Apr.

Motel

★ ★ **COURTYARD BY MARRIOTT.** 15700 NW 77th Court (33016), W of FL 826 exit 154th St, N on 77th Ct. 305/556-6665; FAX 305/556-0282. 151 rms, 4 story. Jan-mid-Apr: S, D $119; suites $152; lower rates rest of yr. Crib free. TV; cable (premium). Heated pool; whirlpool. Complimentary coffee in rms. Restaurant 6-10 am; wkends 7 am-noon. Ck-out noon. Coin lndry. Meeting rms. Valet serv. Sundries. Exercise equipt. Microwaves avail; refrigerator in suites. Balconies. Cr cds: A, D, DS, MC, V.

D ≈ ✗ ⇴ ⚞ SC

Hotel

★ **PARK PLAZA.** (7707 NW 103rd St, Hialeah Gardens 33016) just W of Palmetto Expy (FL 826). 305/825-1000; res: 800/860-3960; FAX 305/556-6785. 262 rms, 10 story. S, D $69; each addl $10; under 18 free; higher rates special events. Crib free. TV; cable (premium). Pool; whirlpool, poolside serv. Restaurant 7 am-2 pm, 5-11 pm. Bar 4 pm-2 am; entertainment Fri, Sat. Ck-out noon. Meeting rms. Gift shop. Free airport transportation. Tennis. Exercise equipt; sauna. Bathrm phones. Balconies. Cr cds: A, C, D, DS, ER, MC, V.

D ✗ ≈ ✗ ⇴ ⚞ SC

Hollywood (H-6)

(See also Dania, Fort Lauderdale, Miami, Pompano Beach)

Founded 1925 **Pop** 121,697 **Elev** 11 ft **Area code** 954 **Web** www.hollywoodchamber.org
Information Greater Hollywood Chamber of Commerce, 330 N Federal Hwy, 33020; 954/923-4000 or **800/231-5562**.

Born in the real estate boom of the 1920s, Hollywood still rides the crest of tourism. Joseph W. Young, fresh from adventures in California, developed the city and populated it largely by keeping a fleet of 21 buses on the road to bring in prospective buyers. In addition to the lures of beach and busy boulevard, there are several public golf courses in the area, making it a favorite of the golfing set.

What to See and Do

Gulfstream Park. Famous racetrack—home of the Florida Derby—has walking ring decorated with leading stable colors; bronze plaques in Garden of Champions honor great Thoroughbreds. (Mid-Jan-Mar, daily exc Mon; Apr, Tues & Thurs-Sun). US 1 & Hallandale Beach Blvd in Hallandale. Phone 954/454-7000. Grandstand ¢¢

Recreation areas.

Topeekeegee Yugnee Park. Swimming beaches (seasonal), waterslides; marina (rentals). Biking. Picnicking. Tent & trailer camping (fee); store, laundry; dump station. (Daily) 1½ mi NW via I-95, Sheridan St exit, on N Park Rd. Phone 954/985-1980. Wkends & hols ¢

C.B. Smith Park. Swimming beach, waterslides, tube ride; marina (canoe & paddleboat rentals). Racquetball, tennis, miniature golf. Picnicking, concession. Campground (hookups). Outdoor amphitheater. (Daily, weather permitting; some facilities seasonal) 19 mi W via Hollywood Blvd, N on Flamingo Rd in Pembroke Pines. Phone 954/437-2650. Wkends & hols ¢

Annual Events

Canada Fest. International food, performers, arts and crafts display. First wkend Feb.

Caribbean Festival. Shellfish cook-off, Caribbean entertainers. Bimini boat race and kayak race. Early June.

Seasonal Events

Greater Hollywood Philharmonic Orchestra. Young Circle Park bandshell. Pop concerts. Phone 954/921-3404. Dec-Apr.

Dog racing. Hollywood Greyhound Track. US 1 & Pembroke Rd. Phone 954/454-9400. Dec 26-late Apr.

Motel

✔★ ★ **DAYS INN AIRPORT SOUTH.** 2601 N 29th Ave (33020). 954/923-7300; FAX 954/921-6706. 114 rms, 7 story. Mid-Dec-mid-Apr: S, D $99-$150; each addl $10; under 18 free; higher rates: Super Bowl, boat shows; lower rates rest of yr. Crib free. TV; cable. Pool; whirlpool. Complimentary continental bkfst. Restaurant adj open 24 hrs. Bar 4-10 pm. Ck-out noon. Coin lndry. Meeting rms. Business servs avail. In-rm modem link. Exercise equipt. Cr cds: A, C, D, DS, MC, V.

D ⚊ 🏋 ✈ ⚊ 🐾 SC

Motor Hotel

★ ★ **HOWARD JOHNSON PLAZA.** 2501 N Ocean Dr (33019). 954/925-1411; FAX 954/921-5565. 242 rms, 11 story. Late Dec-Apr: S, D $99-$189; each addl $10; under 18 free. Crib free. TV; cable (premium). Heated pool; wading pool; poolside serv. Coffee in rms. Restaurant 6 am-10 pm. Rm serv. Bars 11:30-2 am. Ck-out noon. Coin lndry. Meeting rms. Business servs avail. Bellhops. Valet serv. Sundries. Refrigerators avail. Private patios, balconies. On beach. Cr cds: A, C, D, DS, ER, JCB, MC, V.

D ⚊ ⚊ 🐾 SC

Hotels

★ ★ **CLARION INTRACOASTAL.** 4000 S Ocean Dr (33019). 954/458-1900; FAX 954/458-7222. 309 rms, 10 story. Mid-Dec-early Apr: S $119-$159; D $129-$169; each addl $10; suites $385-$455; family rates; lower rates rest of yr. Crib free. TV; cable (premium). Heated pool; wading pool, whirlpool, poolside serv. Restaurants 7 am-11 pm. Bars 11-2 am. Ck-out noon. Convention facilities. Business center. In-rm modem link. Tennis. Exercise equipt; sauna. Health club privileges. Lawn games. Private patios, balconies. Beach opp. Luxury level. Cr cds: A, C, D, DS, ER, MC, V.

D ⚊ ⚊ ✈ ⚊ 🐾 SC 🏌

★ ★ ★ **HOLIDAY INN.** 2905 Sheridan St (33020). 954/925-9100; FAX 954/925-5512. Web holidayinnfll.com. 150 rms, 6 story, 24 suites. Late Dec-mid-Apr: S, D $124-$174; suites $180-$230; lower rates rest of yr. Crib free. TV; cable (premium). Pool; whirlpool, poolside serv. Complimentary coffee in lobby. Restaurant 6:30 am-11 pm. Bar noon-2 am. Ck-out noon. Coin lndry. Meeting rms. Business center. In-rm modem link. Concierge. Free airport transportation. Exercise equipt. Refrigerator, microwave in suites. Some balconies. Cr cds: A, C, D, DS, ER, JCB, MC, V.

D ⚊ 🏋 ✈ ⚊ 🐾 SC 🏌

Resort

★ ★ **GRAND PALMS GOLF & COUNTRY CLUB.** (110 Grand Palms Dr, Pembroke Pines 33027) I-75 exit 5B. 954/431-8800; res: 800/327-9246; FAX 954/435-5988. Web www.grandpalms.com. 137 rms, 2 story. Late Dec-mid-Apr: S, D $125-$145; each addl $10-$15; suites $185-215; under 16 free; golf plans; lower rates rest of yr. Crib free. TV; cable. Pool. Coffee in rms. Dining rm 6 am-10 pm. Rm serv. Bar. Ck-out

noon, ck-in 3 pm. Grocery 1 mi. Coin lndry. Meeting rms. Business servs avail. In-rm modem link. Bellhops. Valet parking. Sports dir. Lighted tennis, pro. 27-hole golf, greens fee $60-$70, pro, putting green, driving range. Exercise equipt. Massage. Balconies. Grills. Cr cds: A, C, D, DS, MC, V.

D ⚊ 🏋 ⚊ 🏋 ✈ ⚊ 🐾 SC

Restaurants

★ ★ **BAVARIAN VILLAGE.** 1401 N Federal Hwy (US 1) (33020). 954/922-7321. Hrs: 4-11 pm; Sun & hols from noon; early-bird dinner to 5:30 pm. Closed Dec 24. Res accepted. German, Amer menu. Bar. Semi-a la carte: dinner $11.75-$23.75. Child's meals. Specialties: Wienerschnitzel, pork shank, prime rib. Entertainment. Old World, Bavarian decor. Cr cds: A, C, D, DS, MC, V.

D ⚊

★ ★ **DI ANNO'S.** (308 N Federal Hwy, Hallandale 33009) S on US 1. 954/454-5030. Hrs: 4:30-11 pm; early-bird dinner to 7 pm. Res accepted. Italian menu. Bar to 3 am. Semi-a la carte: dinner $7.95-$17.95. Specialties: veal parmigiana, shrimp Fra Diavolo, chicken scarpariello. Entertainment. Valet parking. Casual atmosphere. Cr cds: A, MC, V.

D ⚊

★ ★ **GIORGIO'S GRILL.** 606 N Ocean Dr (33019). 954/929-7030. Hrs: 11:30-4 am; early-bird dinner 4-5:30 pm. Res accepted. Mediterranean menu. Bars. A la carte entrees: lunch $7-$21, dinner $8-$31. Child's meals. Specializes in seafood, steak, pasta. Entertainment. Free valet parking. Outdoor dining. Mediterranean atmosphere. Cr cds: A, C, D, DS, MC, V.

D ⚊

✔★ ★ **LYCHEE GARDEN.** (680 E Hallandale Beach Blvd, Hallandale 33009) S on US 1. 954/457-5900. Hrs: 11:30 am-10 pm; early-bird dinner 3-7 pm. Chinese, Amer menu. Bar. Complete meals: lunch $5-$8.25, dinner $8.25-$15.95. Specialties: twin lobster, Lychee gai pan, cashew chicken. Parking. Cr cds: A, C, D, DS, MC, V.

D ⚊

★ ★ **MARTHA'S SUPPER CLUB ON THE INTRACOASTAL.** 6024 N Ocean Dr (33019). 954/923-5444. E-mail dgrouper@ix.netcom.com. Hrs: 11:30-1 am; sunset dinner 4-5:30 pm; Sun brunch 11 am-3 pm. Res accepted. Continental menu. Bar. Wine cellar. A la carte entrees: lunch $5.50-$12.95, dinner $13.95-$35.95. Sun brunch $18.95. Child's meals. Specialties: porterhouse steak for 2, pecan snapper with tempura shrimp. Entertainment. Valet parking. 2-level dining. Cr cds: A, C, D, DS, MC, V.

D ⚊

★ ★ **MARTHA'S TROPICAL GRILLE.** 6024 N Ocean Dr (33019), on 2nd floor. 954/923-5444. Web dsgrouper@ix.netcom.com. Hrs: 11:30 am-4 pm, 5-11 pm; Fri, Sat to midnight. Res accepted. Caribbean menu. Bar. A la carte entrees: lunch $5.50-$12.95, dinner $9.75-$29.50. Child's meals. Specialties: Florida snapper, roast pork Havana, grilled veal chops. Valet parking. Outdoor dining overlooking Intracoastal Waterway. Cr cds: A, C, D, DS, MC, V.

D ⚊

★ ★ **TAVERNA OPA.** 404 N Ocean Dr (33019). 954/929-4010. Hrs: 4 pm-2 am; Sun from 1 pm. Res accepted. Greek menu. Bar. A la carte entrees: lunch, dinner $4.50-$12. Specialties: grilled lamb, fresh fish, greek pastries. Valet parking. Outdoor dining. Tavern atmosphere. Cr cds: A, C, D, DS, ER, MC, V.

D ⚊

★ ★ **VILLA PERRONE.** (906 E Hallandale Beach Blvd, Hallandale 33009) S on US 1 to Hallandale Beach Blvd, then 1½ mi E. 954/454-8878. Hrs: 4:30 pm-2 am; early-bird dinner 4:30-6:30 pm; also 11:30 am-3 pm Nov-mid-Apr. Italian, Amer menu. Bar. Wine list. Complete meals: dinner $10.95-$26. Specialties: costoletta a la Milanese, orecchiette pasta, surf & turf. Pianist. Valet parking. Roman decor; marble statues & entryway. Family-owned. Cr cds: A, D, MC, V.

D ⊟

Homestead (H-6)

(See also Coral Gables, Key Largo, Miami)

Elev 9 ft **Area code** 305
Information Tropical Everglades Visitor Association, 160 US 1, Florida City 33034; 305/245-9180 or 800/388-9669.

Homestead is the gateway to Everglades National Park, Biscayne National Park and to the Florida Keys.

What to See and Do

Coral Castle. Castle-like structure carved by one man from a native coral reef, using primitive hand tools. Features a perfectly balanced nine-ton swinging rock gate. (Daily) 28655 S Dixie Hwy at SW 286th St. Phone 305/248-6344. ¢¢¢

Everglades National Park (see). 9 mi SW on FL 9336.

Fruit and Spice Park. A 30-acre park contains more than 500 varieties of exotic fruits, herbs, spices and nuts from around the world. Herb garden, banana grove and poisonous plant area. Picnic area. Tours avail by res. (Daily) N on FL 997 at jct 248th St & SW 187th Ave. Phone 305/247-5727. Tours ¢

Annual Event

Marlboro Grand Prix of Miami. Homestead Motor Sports Complex, 1 Speedway Blvd. Phone 305/230-7223 (tickets). Last wk Feb or 1st wk Mar.

Motels

★ ★ **BEST WESTERN.** *(1 Strano Blvd, Florida City 33034) approx 2 mi S on FL 94.* 305/246-5100; res: 888/981-5100; FAX 305/242-0056. E-mail gatewaybw@aol.com. 114 rms, 2 story, 24 suites. Dec-mid-Apr: S, D $84-$99; each addl $10; under 18 free; higher rates special events; lower rates rest of yr. Crib free. TV; cable (premium), VCR avail (movies). Pool; whirlpool. Complimentary continental bkfst. Restaurant adj 6:30 am-2:30 pm. Ck-out noon. Coin lndry. Meeting rms. Business servs avail. Some refrigerators. Cr cds: A, C, D, DS, MC, V.

D ⊠ ⊠ 🐾 SC

★ **DAYS INN.** *51 S Homestead Blvd (33030), SW 320th St & US 1.* 305/245-1260; FAX 305/247-0939. 110 rms, 2 story. Mid-Dec-mid-Apr: S $72; D $86-$99; each addl $10; suite $120; under 16 free; higher rates auto races; lower rates rest of yr. Crib free. Pet accepted, some restrictions. TV; cable (premium). Pool. Complimentary continental bkfst. Restaurant 6:30 am-10:30 pm. Rm serv. Bar 3 pm-2 am; entertainment Thurs-Sat. Ck-out 11 am. Coin lndry. Business servs avail. Cr cds: A, C, D, DS, JCB, MC, V.

D 🐾 ⊠ ⊠ 🐾 SC

★ **HAMPTON INN.** *(124 E Palm Dr, Florida City 33034)* 305/247-8833; FAX 305/247-6456. 122 rms, 2 story. Nov-mid-Apr: S, D $79.95-$95.95; each addl $5; under 18 free; higher rates auto races; lower rates rest of yr. Crib free. Pet accepted, some restrictions. TV; cable (premium). Pool. Complimentary continental bkfst. Restaurant opp 11 am-10 pm. Ck-out noon. Business servs avail. In-rm modem link. Bellhops. Tennis privileges. Golf privileges. Cr cds: A, C, D, DS, MC, V.

D 🐾 🏃 🏄 ⊠ ⊠ 🐾 SC

Restaurants

✔ ★ ★ **CAPRI.** *(935 N Krome Ave, Florida City 33034) approx 2 mi S on FL 94.* 305/247-1544. Hrs: 11 am-10 pm; Fri, Sat to 11 pm; early bird

dinner 4:30-6:30 pm. Closed Sun; Dec 25. Res accepted. Italian, Amer menu. Bar. Semi-a la carte: lunch $5.95-$8.95, dinner $9-$19. Child's meals. Specializes in pizza, seafood. Italian paintings. Family-owned. Cr cds: A, MC, V.

D

★ **MUTINEER.** *(11 SE 1st Ave, Florida City 33034) approx 2 mi S on FL 94.* 305/245-3377. Hrs: 11 am-10 pm; Sun brunch 11 am-2 pm. Res accepted. Bar. Semi-a la carte: lunch $4.95-$7.95, dinner $11.95-$26.95. Buffet (Mon-Sat): lunch $7.50. Sun brunch $7.50. Child's meals. Specializes in seafood, steak. Salad bar. Entertainment Thurs-Sat. Nautical decor; waterfalls. Cr cds: A, D, DS, MC, V.

D

Homosassa Springs (D-3)

(See also Brooksville, Crystal River)

Pop 6,271 **Elev** 6 ft **Area code** 352 **Zip** 34447
Information Homosassa Springs Area Chamber of Commerce, 3495 S Suncoast Blvd, PO Box 709, 34447-0709; 352/628-2666.

What to See and Do

Homosassa Springs State Wildlife Park. This 45-ft-deep spring, with an hourly flow of millions of gallons at 72°F, is the source of the Homosassa River. Scenic boat tours, underwater observatory for view of fish; bird park; manatee, alligator, crocodile and reptile programs; museum & education center. (Daily) 9225 W Fishbowl Dr. Phone 352/628-2311. ¢¢¢

Yulee Sugar Mill Ruins State Historic Site. On six-acre site are remnants of antebellum sugar mill; boiler casing, chimney; engine and connecting gears are scattered. Picnic shelter. On FL 490, W of US 19. Phone 352/795-3817. **Free.**

Motel

★ ★ **HOWARD JOHNSON RIVERSIDE INN RESORT.** *(5297 S Cherokee Way, Homosassa 34487) 3 mi W on FL 490, 3 mi W of US 19/98.* 352/628-2474; FAX 352/628-5208; res: 800/442-2040. 81 rms, 2 story, 8 kits. S, D $80-$115; each addl $10; kit. units $115; under 14 free; wkly rates. Crib $10. Pet accepted; $5. TV; cable. Pool. Restaurant 7 am-9 pm. Bar; entertainment, dancing Fri, Sat. Ck-out 11 am. Coin lndry. Meeting rms. Tennis. Lawn games. Marina; charters, boat tours, guides; free dockage for guests. Cr cds: A, C, D, DS, ER, MC, V.

D 🐾 🐾 🏃 ⊠ 🐾

Hotel

✔ ★ ★ **CROWN.** *(109 N Seminole Ave, Inverness 34450) 15 mi W of I-75 on FL 44.* 352/344-5555; FAX 352/726-4040. E-mail akiss@citris .infi.net; web www.chronicle-online.com/crownhotel.htm. 34 rms, 3 story. Nov-Apr: S $40-$60; D $60-$75; each addl $10; lower rates rest of yr. Crib free. Pet accepted. TV; cable. Pool. Complimentary continental bkfst. Restaurant (see CHURCHILL'S). Bar 11 am-11 pm. Ck-out 11 am. Meeting rms. Business servs avail. Health club privileges. Hotel built in late 19th century; Victorian decor; leaded, cut glass windows in lobby; gold-plated bathrm fixtures. Cr cds: A, C, D, MC, V.

🐾 ⊠ ⊠ 🐾 SC

Restaurant

★ ★ **CHURCHILL'S.** *(See Crown Hotel)* 352/344-5555. E-mail akiss@citrus.infi.net; web www.chronicle-online.com/crownhotel.htm. Hrs: 5:30-9 pm; Sun noon-7 pm. Closed Mon. Res accepted. Continental, traditional English menu. English pub 11:30 am-9 pm; Sun noon-7 pm. Wine list. Semi-a la carte: dinner $8-$20. Child's meals. Specialties:

chicken maison, shellfish caribbean, roast duck. Victorian decor. Cr cds: A, C, D, MC, V.

D ♥

Indian Rocks Beach
(see St Pete Beach)

Islamorada (J-5)

(See also Key Largo)

Pop 1,220 **Elev** 10 ft **Area code** 305 **Zip** 33036 **E-mail** islacc@ix.netcom.com **Web** fla.keys.com
Information Chamber of Commerce, US 1, mile marker 82.5, PO Box 915; 305/664-4503 or 800/322-5397.

Islamorada is made up of 18 miles of coral, limestone and sand on 4 different islands of the Florida Keys. Sport fishing and diving and snorkeling amid coral reefs and shipwrecks are the main tourist attractions. It is the local custom to welcome the spring blossoms of the guaiacum tree, which produces a wood known as lignum vitae that is so dense that it was once used for pulleys and bowling pins. The area got its name, Spanish for purple isles, when early explorers first saw the island as a distant splash of color, which was, perhaps, the purple bloom of the guaiacum tree.

What to See and Do

Hurricane Monument. Memorial to 400 veterans of World War I and others killed in 1935 hurricane while working on Overseas Highway. A few veterans are buried in crypt in center of monument. Ceramic facing on crypt shows map of the Keys. Matecumbe Methodist Church.

Indian Key. State historic site was once seat of Dade County and a salvage area for wrecked ships. With the exception of some stone foundations, all structures on the key were destroyed during a Native American raid in 1840. Boat tour. For schedule phone 305/664-4815 or 305/664-9814 (boat tours). Tour ¢¢¢¢

Lignumvitae Key State Botanical Site. This 332-acre island is covered by a tropical hardwood forest, mostly of West Indian origin, and is named for the lignum vitae, or guaiacum, tree, a gnarled, very hard-wooded species found on this island as well as in the Caribbean and South America. Many unusual plants, some endangered, are protected on this unspoiled key. Boat tour (phone for schedule). Historic house, nature trails. Phone 305/664-4815. Tour ¢¢¢¢

Long Key State Recreation Area. This 965-acre park is noted for excellent fishing. Swimming, diving; boating, self-guided canoe trail. Nature trails, guided walks. Picnicking. Camping. Standard hrs, fees. S on US 1, at mile marker 67.5 near Layton, on Long Key. Phone 305/664-4815.

Scuba diving, snorkeling. Many colorful coral reefs, Gardens #1 and #2, and Herrera, a wreck of a Spanish galleon, may be reached by dive boat.

Theater of the Sea. 90-min show features dolphins and sea lions; land tour with fish native to Keys area; huge shark and ray collection; bottomless boat ride with performing dolphins. Half-hr seminar and swim with dolphins (res suggested). (Daily) On US 1, at mile marker 84.5. Phone 305/664-2431. ¢¢¢¢

Annual Events

Rain Barrel Arts Festival. 3rd wkend Mar.

Indian Key Festival. Mid-Oct.

Motels

★ ★ ★ **CHESAPEAKE RESORT.** 83409 Overseas Hwy (US 1), S of Whale Harbor Bridge, at mile marker 83.5. 305/664-4662; FAX 305/664-8595; res: 800/338-3395. E-mail chesapea@aol.com; web florida-keys.fl.us/chesapea.htm. 65 rms, 2 story, 8 suites, 13 kit. villas (1-2 bedrm). Late Dec-Apr: S, D $150-$220; each addl $20; suites $320-$575; kit. villas $160-$410; lower rates rest of yr. TV; cable (premium). 2 heated pools; whirlpool. Playground. Restaurant adj 6 am-midnight. Ck-out 11 am. Coin lndry. Meeting rm. Tennis. Exercise equipt. Lawn games. Refrigerators. Screened balconies, patios. Picnic tables, grills. Deep-water lagoon with boat ramp. Gardens. On ocean; harbor adj. Cr cds: A, DS, MC, V.

D 🐾 ⚓ ≈ ✈ 🎣 🔥 SC

★ ★ **CORAL BAY.** 75690 Overseas Hwy (US 1), at mile marker 75.5. 305/664-5568; FAX 305/664-3242. E-mail coralbay@terranovanet; web thefloridabay.com/coralbay. 16 rms, 8 kit. units. No rm phones. Dec-Sept: S, D $89-$155; kit. units (2-day min); lower rates rest of yr. TV. Heated pool. Ck-out 11 am. Grills. On Gulf; swimming beach. Cr cds: MC, V.

🐾 ≈ 🔥

✔★ **DROP ANCHOR.** Mile Marker 85, On Overseas Hwy (US 1). 305/664-4863; FAX 305/664-4801. 14 rms, 2 story, 8 kits. Mid-Dec-late Apr: S, D $75-$85; each addl $10; kit. units $85-$105; wkly rates in summer; lower rates rest of yr. TV; cable. Heated pool. Restaurant nearby. Ck-out 11 am. Refrigerators. Some private patios, balconies. Picnic tables, grill. On beach; boat ramp, dock. Cr cds: A, DS, MC, V.

🐾 ≈ 🔥

★ **HARBOR LIGHTS.** 84951 Overseas Hwy. 305/664-3611; FAX 305/664-2703; res: 800/327-7070. Web www.theisle.com. 32 rms, 11 with shower only, 3 story, 22 kit. units, 4 cottages. Late Dec-early Apr: S, D $85-$145; each addl $15; kit. units $120-$145; cottages $100-$120; under 18 free; wkly rates; (3-day min) hols; higher rates special events; lower rates rest of yr. Crib free. TV; cable. Pool. Complimentary coffee in lobby. Ck-out 11 am. Coin lndry. Some refrigerators. Balconies. Picnic tables. On ocean. Cr cds: A, C, D, DS, MC, V.

🐾 ≈ 🔥 SC

★ ★ **HOWARD JOHNSON AT HOLIDAY ISLE.** 84001 Overseas Hwy (US 1) (84001), at mile marker 84.5. 305/664-2711; res: 800/327-7070; FAX 305/664-2703. Web www.theisle.com. 56 rms, 2 story. Mid-Dec-mid-Apr: S, D $140-$175; each addl $15; under 18 free; lower rates rest of yr. Crib free. TV. Heated pool. Playground. Restaurant adj 7 am-11 pm. Ck-out 11 am. Coin lndry. Lawn games. Balconies. On beach. Cr cds: A, C, D, DS, MC, V.

D 🐾 ≈ 🎣 🔥 SC

★ **ISLANDER.** Mile Marker 82.1, On Overseas Hwy (US 1). 305/664-2031; FAX 305/664-5503. 114 units in motel, villas, 92 kits. Mid-Dec-mid-Apr: S, D $74-$98; each addl $7; kit. units $80-$98; under 13 free; lower rates rest of yr. Crib free. TV. 2 heated pools (1 saltwater). Ck-out 11 am. Coin lndry. Meeting rm. Lawn games. Private patios. Grills. Spacious grounds on ocean; pier. Cr cds: A, C, D, MC, V.

🐾 ≈ 🔥

✔★ **KON-TIKI RESORT.** 81200 Overseas Hwy, at mile marker 81. 305/664-4702; FAX 305/664-5305. E-mail kontiki@thefloridakeys.com; web thefloridakeys.com/kontiki. 22 rms, 15 kits. S, D $70-$80; each addl $10; kit. units $100-$195; under 12 free. TV; cable. Heated pool. Restaurant nearby. Ck-out 11 am. Lawn games. Private patios. Picnic tables, grills. On bay; beach, dock. Cr cds: A, DS, MC, V.

🐾 ≈ 🔥

★ **LIME TREE BAY.** (Mile marker 68.5, Long Key 33001) 305/664-4740; FAX 305/664-0750; res: 800/723-4519. E-mail limetree@safari.net. 30 rms, 1-2 story. Late-Dec-Apr: S, D $102; each addl $7; kit. units $110-$235; cottage $160; under 8 free; wkly rates; hols (3-day min); higher rates special events; lower rates rest of yr. Crib free. TV; cable. Pool; whirlpool. Complimentary coffee in lobby. Restaurant 7 am-10 pm.

Bar noon-10 pm. Ck-out 11 am. Lawn games. Some refrigerators. On ocean. Cr cds: A, D, DS, MC, V.

✔ ★ **PLANTATION YACHT HARBOR.** *87000 Overseas Hwy (US 1).* 305/852-2381; res: 800/356-3215; FAX 305/853-5357. E-mail fun@pyh.com; web pyh.com. 56 rms, 1-2 story. S, D $75-$95; each addl $10; houseboats $250-$325; under 12 free. Crib avail. TV; cable. Restaurant (see LATTITUDES). Bar 7 am-11 pm; entertainment Fri-Sun. Ck-out 11 pm. Meeting rms. Lighted tennis. Pool. Playground. Refrigerator, microwave in houseboats. Picnic tables, grills. On bay. Cr cds: A, DS, MC, V.

✔ ★ **SHORELINE.** *81450 Overseas Hwy (US 1), at mile marker 81.* 305/664-4027. 10 units, 4 kits. Mid-Dec-mid-Apr: S, D $62-$90; each addl $7; kits. $70-$80; wkly rates; lower rates rest of yr. TV; cable. Restaurant opp noon-11 pm. Ck-out 11 am. Grills. On Gulf; boat ramp, dock; sunning beach. Cr cds: MC, V.

Motor Hotels

★ ★ **HOLIDAY ISLE.** *84001 Overseas Hwy (US 1), at mile marker 84.* 305/664-2321; FAX 305/664-2703; res: 800/327-7070. Web www.theisle.com. 78 units, 1-5 story, 22 kits. Mid-Dec-mid-Apr: S, D $185; each addl $15; suites $275-$425; kits. $185-$245; under 18 free; wkly rates; lower rates rest of yr. Crib free. TV; cable (premium). Pool. Restaurant (see HORIZON). Bar; entertainment. Ck-out 11 am. Coin lndry. Meeting rm. Business servs avail. Airport transportation. Water sport equipment rentals. Private patios, balconies. On ocean; dock, beach. Cr cds: A, C, D, DS, MC, V.

★ ★ ★ **PELICAN COVE.** *84457 Old Overseas Hwy (US 1), at mile marker 84.5.* 305/664-4435; FAX 305/664-4690. res: 800/445-4690. 63 units, 3 story, 9 suites, 18 kits. Mid-Dec-mid-Apr: S, D $165-$195; each addl $15; suites $285; kit. units $185-$215; under 16 free; wkly rates; lower rates rest of yr. TV; cable. Heated pool; whirlpool, poolside serv. Playground. Complimentary continental bkfst. Coffee in rms. Restaurant 11:30 am-4:30 pm. Bar to 7 pm. Ck-out 11 am. Tennis. Lawn games. Balconies. Picnic tables, grills. On ocean, swimming beach; water sports, fishing, snorkel, diving charters. Cr cds: A, C, D, DS, JCB, MC, V.

Resort

★ ★ ★ **CHEECA LODGE.** *On Overseas Hwy (US 1), at mile marker 82.* 305/664-4651; FAX 305/664-2893; res: 800/327-2888. E-mail cheecalodg@aol.com; web www.cheeca.com. 49 rms in lodge, 4 story, 154 villas, 2 story, 64 kits. Mid-Dec-mid-Apr: S, D $240-$610; each addl $25; kit. units $315-$1,100; under 16 free; AP, MAP avail; golf, tennis, diving plans; lower rates rest of yr. Crib free. TV; cable, VCR (movies avail). 2 heated pools; wading pool, whirlpools, poolside serv. Playground. Supervised child's activities. Dining rms (public by res) 7 am-10:30 pm. Box lunches. Rm serv. Bar noon-midnight. Ck-out 11 am, ck-in 4 pm. Grocery 1 blk. Coin lndry 3 blks. Package store 2 blks. Meeting rms. Business servs avail. In-rm modem link. Bellhops. Valet serv. Concierge. Gift shop. Airport transportation. Lighted tennis. 9-hole golf, greens fee $15, putting green. Beach, boats. Diving shop & gear. On ocean; small boat, sailboat and windsurfing rentals. Soc dir. Fishing guides. Minibars; refrigerator in suites. Balconies. Cr cds: A, C, D, DS, ER, MC, V.

Restaurants

★ ★ **CORAL GRILL.** *MM 83.5 Islamorada, on Overseas Hwy (US 1).* 305/664-4803. Hrs: 4:30-9:30 pm; Sun noon-9 pm. Closed Mon; Dec 25; also Labor Day-mid-Oct. Bar. Semi-a la carte: dinner $15.95-$17.95. Buffet: dinner $15.95-$17.95. Child's meals. Menu service on 1st

floor, buffet on 2nd floor. Specialties: prime rib, steamed shrimp, snow crab clusters. Salad bar. Pianist. Parking. Cr cds: A, D, DS, MC, V.

★ **GREEN TURTLE INN.** *Overseas Hwy (US 1), at mile marker 81.5.* 305/664-9031. Hrs: noon-10 pm. Closed Mon. Semi-a la carte: lunch $5-$20, dinner $10-$30. Specializes in seafood, steak. Cr cds: A, C, D, DS, MC, V.

★ **HORIZON.** *(See Holiday Isle Motor Hotel)* 305/664-2321, ext. 600. Hrs: 7 am-11 pm. Res accepted. Caribbean, Amer menu. Bar to midnight. A la carte entrees: bkfst $4.95-$9.95, lunch $5.95-$10.95, dinner $5.95-$21.95. Child's meals. Specializes in steak, pasta, seafood. Panoramic view of Gulf of Mexico. Cr cds: A, C, D, DS, MC, V.

★ ★ **LATTITUDES.** *(see Plantation Yacht Harbor Motel).* 305/852-2381. Hrs: 7 am-2:30 pm, 5-10 pm. Res accepted. Bar 7-2 am. Semi-a la carte: bkfst $3.25-$7.95, lunch $2.95-$8.25, dinner $9.95-$24.95. Specializes in native seafood. Entertainment wkends. Parking. At marina; overlooks bay. Cr cds: A, D, DS, MC, V.

★ **LORELEI.** *Overseas Hwy (US 1), at mile marker 82.* 305/664-4656. Hrs: 11 am-11 pm. Closed Dec 25. Res accepted. Bar. Semi-a la carte: lunch $4.95-$9.95, dinner $10.95-$29.95. Child's meals. Specializes in steak, seafood. Entertainment. Parking. Outdoor dining. On waterfront. Cr cds: A, C, D, MC, V.

★ ★ **MARKER 88.** *Overseas Hwy (US 1), at mile marker 88.* 305/852-9315. Hrs: 5-10:30 pm. Closed Mon. Res accepted. Continental menu. Bar. Semi-a la carte: dinner $14.95-$30. Child's meals. Specialties: yellowtail Martinique, steak Madagascar, Key lime baked Alaska. Own rolls. Parking. Nautical decor; hatch-covered tables, tropical plants. Overlooks bay. Cr cds: A, C, D, DS, MC, V.

✔ ★ **RIP'S ISLAND.** *Overseas Hwy (US 1), mile marker 84.* 305/664-5300. Hrs: 6 am-11 pm; Fri, Sat to midnight. Bar. Semi-a la carte: lunch, dinner $3.95-$15.95. Specializes in ribs, chicken. Parking. Casual dining. Cr cds: A, C, D, DS, MC, V.

★ **WHALE HARBOR INN.** *Overseas Hwy (US 1), at mile marker 83.5.* 305/664-4959. Hrs: 6 am-noon, 4-9 pm; Fri, Sat to 10 pm; Sun from 11 am; early-bird dinner Mon-Fri 4-5:30 pm. Bar. Bkfst $3.95-$8.95, lunch $3.95-$15.95, dinner $9.95-$21.95. Child's meals. Specializes in seafood. Entertainment. Outdoor raw bar. Parking. Nautical decor. Cr cds: A, C, D, DS, MC, V.

Jacksonville (B-4)

(See also Atlantic Beach, Fernandina Beach, Jacksonville Beach, St Augustine)

Settled 1822 **Pop** 635,230 **Elev** 19 ft **Area code** 904 **E-mail** jaxflcvb@leading.net
Information Jacksonville and the Beaches Convention & Visitors Bureau, 201 E Adams St, 32202; 904/798-9111 or 800/733-2668.

Jacksonville, once primarily an industrial, maritime Southern city, now has a sparkling skyline of skyscrapers; yet the city is still graced with tropical scenery, white sandy beaches and a certain Southern flavor and heritage. The Riverwalk near the St Johns River, Jacksonville's financial focal point, and the Jacksonville Landing, a festive marketplace with events and entertainment, are two manifestations of the city's new image as a modern, prosperous city.

Draped around an S curve of the broad St Johns River, Jacksonville is a major tourist and business center in Florida. The river is the hub for cruise boats and sightseeing excursions. Although 12 miles inland from the mouth of the river, Jacksonville berths freighters, ocean liners and a fleet of shrimp boats.

Under the British flag, Jacksonville was known as Cowford, a name that persisted until the purchase of Florida by the United States, when the town was renamed for Andrew Jackson. In the peace following the Seminole War, the city emerged as a prosperous and boisterous harbor town. Jacksonville was occupied by Union troops four times during the Civil War, but emerged during the Reconstruction period as a popular winter resort.

Transportation

Car Rental Agencies: See IMPORTANT TOLL-FREE NUMBERS.

Public Transportation: Buses (Jacksonville Transportation Authority), phone 904/630-3100.

Airport Information

Jacksonville Intl Airport: Information 904/741-4902; lost and found 904/741-2040; weather 904/741-4311.

What to See and Do

Cummer Museum of Art & Gardens. Contains 14 galleries and the Tudor Room from the original Cummer Mansion. The mansion's formal gardens (2½ acres) were retained as setting for the gallery. Collection ranges from ancient Egypt to the 20th century and features 700 pieces of early Meissen porcelain and important American paintings. Interactive exhibits. (Daily exc Mon; closed major hols, also 1 wk Apr) 826 Riverside Ave. Phone 904/356-6857. ¢¢

Fort Caroline National Memorial (see). 13 mi E on FL 10, then N on Monument Rd.

Industrial Tour. Anheuser-Busch Brewery. Tours of brewery conclude in Hospitality Room for beer tasting. Guided and self-guided tours. (Daily exc Sun; closed hols) 111 Busch Dr, N via I-95 toward airport. Phone 904/751-8118. **Free.**

Jacksonville Museum of Contemporary Art. Exhibits include pre-Columbian artifacts, contemporary paintings, sculpture and graphics. Classes; lectures; film series. Guided tours. (Daily exc Mon; closed most hols) 4160 Boulevard Center Dr. Phone 904/398-8336. ¢¢

Jacksonville University (1934). (2,200 students) This 260-acre riverfront campus houses library of the Jacksonville Historical Society and Charter Marine Science Center. Delius House is restored house of British composer Frederick Delius (1862-1934) (daily, by request). N University Blvd, on E bank of St Johns River. Phone 904/744-3950. Also here is

Alexander Brest Museum. Contains large collection of European and Oriental ivory; changing exhibits of painting, pottery, weaving, sculpture; collections of pre-Columbian artifacts, Steuben glass and American, European and Oriental porcelains. (Daily exc Sun; closed most hols). Phone 904/745-7371. **Free.**

Jacksonville Zoological Gardens. More than 700 mammals, birds and reptiles in natural environments along Trout River. Train ride; animal shows; restaurant. (Daily; closed Thanksgiving, Dec 25) 8605 Zoo Rd via Heckscher Dr, off I-95. Phone 904/757-4463. ¢¢

Kingsley Plantation. Plantation house, kitchen house, barn and tabby slave houses reflect 19th-century life on a Sea Island cotton plantation. Ranger programs. A National Park Service area. Grounds (daily). N on FL A1A, on Fort George Island at 11676 Palmetto Ave; reached by ferry from Mayport or via FL 105 (Heckscher Dr). Phone 904/251-3537.

Little Talbot Island State Park. More than 2,500 acres of wide Atlantic beaches and extensive salt marshes teem with life, including migrating birds and sea turtles. Sand dunes, forests. Swimming, surfing; fishing. Picnicking, playground. Camping (hookups, dump station). Standard hrs, fees. 17 mi NE on FL A1A, near Fort George. Phone 904/251-2320.

Museum of Science and History. Interactive exhibits on science, marine mammals and north Florida history, including health; natural and physical sciences; wildlife; Native Americans; Civil War artifacts from battleship *Maple Leaf.* Free planetarium, science and reptile shows. (Mon-Sat, also Sun afternoons; closed major hols) 1025 Museum Circle. Phone 904/396-7062. ¢¢

Professional sports.

NFL (Jacksonville Jaguars). Alltel Stadium, 1 Stadium Place. Phone 904/633-2000.

The Annabelle Lee. Tours on St Johns River aboard 300-passenger cruise ship. Lunch, dinner and sightseeing cruises. (Fri-Sun; schedule varies rest of wk; closed Dec 25) Phone 904/396-2333 for reservations. ¢¢¢¢-¢¢¢¢¢

Annual Events

Delius Festival. Event features works by the late 19th-century British-born composer, who had lived in Jacksonville; performances by various musical groups; lectures; exhibits. Phone 904/745-7371. 1st wk Mar.

Historic Home Tour. Tour representing work of locally prominent architects and builders between 1870-1930. Phone 904/389-2449. Mid-late Apr.

Riverside Art Festival. Juried art show in variety of media; food, entertainment. Mid- or late Sept.

Jacksonville Jazz Festival. Metropolitan Park, on the river. Early Nov.

Gator Bowl Festival. Alltel Stadium, Haines & Adams Sts. Climaxed by one of the major college football bowl games. Late Dec.

Seasonal Events

Greyhound racing. Nightly exc Tues; matinees Wed, Sat & Sun. Phone 904/646-0001.Year-round seasons rotating among

Jacksonville Kennel Club. 1440 McDuff Ave, N of I-10.

Orange Park Kennel Club. On US 17 at I-295 in Orange Park.

St Johns Greyhound Park. 18 mi S on US 1, at Racetrack Rd in Bayard.

City Neighborhoods

Many of the restaurants, unrated dining establishments and some lodgings listed under Jacksonville include neighborhoods as well as exact street addresses. Geographic descriptions of these areas are given, followed by a table of restaurants arranged by neighborhood.

Baymeadows: Along Baymeadows Rd, east of San Jose Blvd and west of Southside Blvd.

Downtown: South of Beaver St, west of Liberty St, north of the St Johns River and east of Broad St. **South of Downtown:** South of St Johns River. **East of Downtown:** East of Liberty St.

Mandarin: On Mandarin Point south of I-295, east of the St Johns River and Julington Creek.

San Marco/Southbank: Across the St Johns River from Downtown; south of the river, west of US 1A and north of Emerson Rd.

JACKSONVILLE RESTAURANTS BY NEIGHBORHOOD AREAS

(For full description, see alphabetical listings under Restaurants)

BAYMEADOWS
Pagoda. 8617 Baymeadows Rd

SOUTH OF DOWNTOWN
Sterling's Cafe. 3551 St Johns Ave

EAST OF DOWNTOWN
Alhambra Dinner Theatre. 12000 Beach Blvd
Marker 32. 14549 Beach Blvd

MANDARIN
Sebastian's. 10601 San Jose Blvd

SAN MARCO/SOUTHBANK
Café Carmon. 1986 San Marco Blvd
Cafe On The Square. 1974 San Marco Blvd
Crawdaddy's. 1643 Prudential Dr

Note: When a listing is located in a town that does not have its own city heading, it will appear under the city nearest to its location. In these cases, the address and town appear in parenthesis immediately following the name of the establishment.

Motels

✔ ★ **BEST INNS OF AMERICA.** *8220 Dix Ellis Trail (32256), I-95 exit 100, in Baymeadows.* 904/739-3323. 109 rms, 2 story. S $42.88-$48.88; D $49.88-$54.88; each addl $7; under 18 free; wkly rates. Crib free. Pet accepted, some restrictions. TV; cable (premium). Pool. Complimentary continental bkfst. Restaurant nearby. Ck-out 1 pm. Business servs avail. Picnic tables. Cr cds: A, D, DS, JCB, MC, V.

D ✔ ≈ ⅀ 🔥 SC

✔ ★ **BEST WESTERN ORANGE PARK.** *(300 Park Ave, Orange Park 32073)* S on US 17, at I-295 Bypass. 904/264-1211; FAX 904/269-6756. 201 rms, 2 story. S, D $60; each addl $5. Pet accepted; $25. TV; cable (premium). Pool; wading pool. Complimentary coffee in rms. Restaurant 6-11 am, 5-10 pm. Rm serv. Bar. Coin lndry. Meeting rms. Business servs avail. Valet serv. Golf privileges. Some refrigerators, microwaves. Health club privileges. Cr cds: A, C, D, DS, MC, V.

D ✔ ≈ ⅀ 🔥 SC

★ ★ **COURTYARD BY MARRIOTT.** *4600 San Pablo Rd (32224), south of downtown.* 904/223-1700; FAX 904/223-1026. 146 rms, 3 story. S, D $129; suites $159; under 12 free; wkend rates. Crib free. TV; cable (premium). Heated pool; whirlpool. Complimentary coffee in rms. Restaurant 6:30 am-9 pm. Bar from 11 am. Ck-out noon. Coin lndry. Meeting rms. Business servs avail. Valet serv. Exercise equipt. Some refrigerators. Cr cds: A, C, D, DS, MC, V.

D ≈ ✕ ⅀ 🔥 SC

✔ ★ **ECONOMY INNS OF AMERICA.** *4300 Salisbury Rd (32216), in Baymeadows.* 904/281-0198. 123 rms, 3 story. S $42.90; D $49.90. Pet accepted. TV; cable (premium). Heated pool. Complimentary continental bkfst. Ck-out 11 am. Business servs avail. Cr cds: A, MC, V.

D ✔ ≈ ⅀ 🔥 SC

★ **HAMPTON INN.** *4690 Salisbury Rd (32256), in Baymeadows.* 904/281-0443; FAX 904/281-0144. 130 rms, 4 story. S, D $63-$75; under 18 free. TV; cable (premium). Heated pool. Complimentary continental bkfst. Restaurant adj 10 am-10 pm. Ck-out noon. Meeting rms. Business servs avail. In-rm modem link. Microwaves avail. Cr cds: A, C, D, DS, MC, V.

D ≈ ⅀ 🔥 SC

★ ★ **HAMPTON INN.** *6135 Youngerman Circle (32244), I-295 exit 4, south of downtown.* 904/777-5313; FAX 904/778-1545. 122 rms, 2 story. S, D $68-$80; under 18 free. Crib free. TV; cable (premium). Heated pool. Complimentary continental bkfst. Restaurant nearby. Ck-out noon. Meeting rm. Business servs avail. In-rm modem link. Valet serv. Cr cds: A, C, D, DS, MC, V.

D ≈ ⅀ 🔥 SC

★ ★ **HOLIDAY INN-BAYMEADOWS.** *9150 Baymeadows Rd (32256), in Baymeadows.* 904/737-1700; FAX 904/737-0207. 249 rms, 2-4 story. S, D $84-$97; each addl $5; under 19 free; higher rates special events. Crib free. TV; cable, (premium). Pool. Coffee in rms. Restaurant 6:30 am-midnight; Sat, Sun from 7 am. Rm serv. Bar 1 pm-1 am, wkends 11-2 am. Ck-out noon. Coin lndry. Meeting rms. Business servs avail. In-rm modem link. Bellhops. Valet serv. Sundries. Exercise equipt. Microwaves avail. Cr cds: A, C, D, DS, JCB, MC, V.

D ≈ ✕ ⅀ 🔥 SC

★ ★ **HOMEWOOD SUITES.** *8737 Baymeadows Rd (32256), in Baymeadows.* 904/733-9299; FAX 904/448-5889. 116 kit. suites, 2-3 story. Suites $116-$175; wkly, monthly rates; higher rates special events. Crib free. Pet accepted, some restrictions; $75. TV; cable (premium). VCR avail. Pool; whirlpool. Complimentary continental bkfst. Complimentary

coffee in rms. Ck-out noon. Coin lndry. Meeting rms. Business center. In-rm modem link. Valet serv. Exercise equipt. Microwaves. Balconies. Grills. Cr cds: A, C, D, DS, MC, V.

D ✔ ≈ ✕ ⅀ SC 🔥

★ ★ **LA QUINTA.** *8555 Blanding Blvd (32244), south of downtown.* 904/778-9539; FAX 904/779-5214. 122 rms, 2 story. S, D $60-$67; suites $110; under 18 free. Crib free. Pet accepted, some restrictions. TV. Pool. Complimentary continental bkfst. Coffee in rms. Restaurant adj open 24 hrs. Ck-out noon. Meeting rms. Business servs avail. In-rm modem link. Guest lndry. Health club privileges. Microwaves, refrigerators avail. Cr cds: A, D, DS, MC, V.

D ✔ ≈ ⅀ 🔥 SC

★ ★ **LA QUINTA-BAYMEADOWS.** *8255 Dix Ellis Trail (32256), in Baymeadows.* 904/731-9940; FAX 904/731-3854. 106 rms, 2 story. S, D $69-$76; under 18 free. Crib free. Pet accepted. TV; cable (premium). Pool. Complimentary continental bkfst. Restaurant nearby. Ck-out noon. Guest lndry. Business servs avail. In-rm modem link. Valet serv. Health club privileges. Microwaves avail. Cr cds: A, C, D, DS, JCB, MC, V.

D ✔ ≈ ⅀ 🔥 SC

★ ★ **RAMADA INN-MANDARIN CONFERENCE CENTER.** *3130 Hartley Rd (32257), in Mandarin.* 904/268-8080; FAX 904/262-8718. Web www.ramada-inn.com. 150 rms, 2 story. S, D $64-$75; each addl $5; suites $125-$135; family rates. Crib free. Pet accepted, some restrictions; fee. TV; cable. Pool; wading pool. Complimentary full bkfst. Restaurant 6:30 am-2 pm, 5-9 pm; Fri, Sat to 10 pm. Rm serv. Bar 4 pm-midnight; pianist, comedy Tues-Sat. Ck-out noon. Meeting rms. Valet serv. Large stone fireplace in lobby. Cr cds: A, C, D, DS, MC, V.

D ✔ ≈ ⅀ 🔥 SC

✔ ★ **RED ROOF INN.** *6099 Youngerman Circle (32244), south of downtown.* 904/777-1000; FAX 904/777-1005. 108 rms, 2 story. S, D $45.99-$47.99; each addl $6; under 18 free. Crib free. Pet accepted, some restrictions. TV; cable. Complimentary coffee in lobby. Ck-out noon. Business servs avail. In-rm modem link. Cr cds: A, C, D, DS, MC, V.

D ✔ ≈ 🔥

★ ★ **RESIDENCE INN BY MARRIOTT.** *8365 Dix Ellis Trail (32256), in Baymeadows.* 904/733-8088; FAX 904/731-8354. 112 kit. suites, 2 story. Kit. suites $125-$160. Crib free. Pet accepted; $75. TV; cable (premium). Heated pool; whirlpools. Complimentary continental bkfst. Restaurant nearby. Ck-out noon. Coin lndry. Meeting rms. Business servs avail. In-rm modem link. Health club privileges. Microwaves. Grills. Cr cds: A, C, D, DS, JCB, MC, V.

D ✔ ≈ ⅀ 🔥 SC

Motor Hotels

★ ★ **HAMPTON INN-CENTRAL.** *1331 Prudential Dr (32207), I-95 S, exit 108, east of downtown.* 904/396-7770; FAX 904/396-8044. 118 rms, 5 story. S $69-$115; D $69-$125; under 18 free; wkend rates; higher rates special events. Crib free. TV; cable (premium). Complimentary continental bkfst. Complimentary coffee in rms. Restaurant opp 7-1 am. Rm serv 5-10 pm (Mon-Sat). Ck-out noon. Meeting rms. Business servs avail. In-rm modem link. Valet serv. Concierge. Sundries. Pool. Cr cds: A, C, D, DS, MC, V.

≈ ⅀

★ ★ ★ **HOLIDAY INN-AIRPORT NORTH.** *PO Drawer 18409 (32229), 12 mi N on Airport Rd, at I-95, near Intl Airport, north of downtown.* 904/741-4404; FAX 904/741-4907. Web www.travelbase.com/destinations/jacksonville/holiday-airport. 489 rms, 2-6 story. S, D, studio rms $70-$92; under 18 free. Crib free. Pet accepted. TV; cable (premium), VCR avail. 3 pools, 1 indoor/outdoor; poolside serv. Restaurant 6 am-10 pm. Rm serv. Bar 11 am-midnight. Ck-out noon. Coin lndry. Convention facilities. Business center. In-rm modem link. Bellhops. Sundries. Gift shop. Free airport transportation. Lighted tennis. Exercise equipt. Game rm. Luxury level. Cr cds: A, C, D, DS, JCB, MC, V.

Hotels

★ ★ **AMERISUITES.** *8277 Western Way Circle (32256), in Baymeadows.* 904/737-4477; FAX 904/739-1649. 112 suites, 6 story. S, D $79-$109; each addl $10; under 12 free; wkend rates; package plans. Crib free. Pet accepted, some restricitons; $10/day. TV; cable (premium), VCR. Pool. Complimentary continental bkfst. Coffee in rms. Ck-out 11 am. Coin lndry. Meeting rms. Business center. In-rm modem link. Exercise equipment. Refrigerators, microwaves. Cr cds: A, C, D, DS, MC, V.

★ ★ **CLUB HOTEL BY DOUBLETREE.** *4700 Salisbury Rd (32256), in Baymeadows.* 904/281-9700; FAX 904/281-1957. Web www.clubhotels.com. 167 rms, 6 story. S, D $89-$129; each addl $10; suites $129-$169; under 12 free. Crib free. TV; cable (premium). Heated pool; whirlpool. Coffee in rms. Restaurant 6 am-11 pm. Bar 5-11 pm. Ck-out 1 pm. Meeting rms. Business servs avail. In-rm modem link. Exercise equipt. Refrigerator in suites. Cr cds: A, C, D, DS, JCB, MC, V.

★ ★ ★ **EMBASSY SUITES.** *9300 Baymeadows Rd (32256), in Baymeadows.* 904/731-3555; FAX 904/731-4972. 210 kit. suites, 7 story. S, D $89-$169; each addl $10; under 18 free; wkend packages. Crib free. TV; cable (premium). Indoor pool; whirlpool. Complimentary full bkfst. Restaurant 11 am-2 pm, 5:30-10 pm. Rm serv. Bar 2 pm-midnight. Ck-out noon. Meeting rms. Business center. In-rm modem link. Concierge. Gift shop. Exercise equipt; sauna. Microwaves. Balconies. Glass elevators; atrium lobby. Cr cds: A, C, D, DS, JCB, MC, V.

★ ★ ★ **HILTON.** *1201 Riverplace Blvd (32207), in San Marco/Southbank.* 904/398-8800; FAX 904/398-9170. Web hilton.com. 291 rms, 26 with shower only, 10 story. S, D $110-$188; each addl $10; under 18 free. Crib free. Valet parking $9. TV; cable (premium), VCR avail. Comlimentary coffee in lobby. Restaurant 6:30 am-10 pm. Rm serv 24 hrs. Bar 11 am-10 pm; entertainment. Ck-out 11 am. Convention facilities. Business center. In-rm modem link. Concierge. Gift shop. Airport transportation. 18-hole golf privileges, varied greens fee, pro, putting green, driving range. Exercise equipt. Pool; whirlpool, poolside serv. Balconies. On river. Luxury level. Cr cds: A, C, D, DS, MC, V.

★ ★ ★ **MARRIOTT.** *4670 Salisbury Rd (32256), I-95 exit 101, in Baymeadows.* 904/296-2222; FAX 904/296-7561. 256 units, 9 story, 6 suites. S, D $139-$149; suites $195-$295; wkend packages. Crib free. TV; cable (premium), VCR avail. 2 pools, 1 indoor; poolside serv, whirlpool. Restaurant 6:30 am-10 pm; Sat, Sun from 7 am. Bar 11-1 am. Ck-out noon. Convention facilities. Business servs avail. In-rm modem link. Gift shop. Golf privileges, pro, putting green, driving range. Exercise equipt; sauna. Some refrigerators. Cr cds: A, C, D, DS, MC, V.

★ ★ ★ **OMNI.** *245 Water St (32202), downtown.* 904/355-6664; FAX 904/791-4812. 354 rms, 16 story. S $159-$179; D $169-$189; each addl $15; suites from $350; under 18 free; wkend rates. Crib free. Garage $3-$8; valet $8. TV; cable, VCR avail. Heated pool; poolside serv. Restaurant 6:30 am-10:30 pm. Rm serv to 1 am. Bar 11-2. Ck-out noon. Convention facilities. Business servs avail. In-rm modem link. Shopping arcade. Lighted tennis privileges, pro. Golf privileges. Exercise equipt. Health club privileges. Minibars. View of river. Cr cds: A, C, D, DS, JCB, MC, V.

★ ★ ★ **RADISSON RIVERWALK.** *1515 Prudential Dr (32207), east of downtown.* 904/396-5100; FAX 904/396-7154. 322 rms, 5 story. S, D $120-$155; each addl $10; suites $195-$415; under 18 free; wkend rates. Crib free. TV; cable. Pool. Restaurants 6:30 am-2 pm. Rm serv to midnight. Bar 11:30 am-midnight. Ck-out

noon. Convention facilities. Business center. In-rm modem link. Gift shop. Lighted tennis. 18-hole golf privileges, greens fee. Exercise equipt. Some refrigerators, bathrm phones. Balconies. On river. Cr cds: A, C, D, DS, JCB, MC, V.

Inn

★ ★ **CLUB CONTINENTAL.** *(2143 Astor St, Orange Park 32073) I-295 to US 17, 2 mi S to Kingsley, E to Astor St, then S.* 904/264-6070; FAX 904/264-4044; res: 800/877-6070. 22 rms, 2 story, 5 kit. suites. S, D $65-$165; kit. suites $99-$189; monthly rates. Crib $10. TV; cable. Pool; wading pool, poolside serv, lifeguard (in season). Complimentary continental bkfst. Dining rm Tues-Fri 11:30 am-2 pm, 6:30-9 pm; Sun brunch 11 am-2 pm. Ck-out 11 am, ck-in 2 pm. Business servs avail. Lighted tennis, pro. Microwaves. Balconies. Mediterranean-style villa (1923) on 30 acres overlooking St Johns River; pools, reflecting ponds. Cr cds: A, D, DS, MC, V.

Resort

★ **INN AT RAVINES.** *(2932 Ravines Rd, Middleburg 32068) 1 mi E of Blanding Blvd on FL 218.* 904/282-1111; res: 800/728-4631; FAX 904/282-2703. Web www.birdie.com/ravines. 35 rms, 2 story. Feb-May, Oct-Nov: S, D $85-$180; golf plans; lower rates rest of yr. TV; cable. Pool; whirlpool. Dining rm (public by res) 7 am-3 pm. Box lunches, snack bar. Bar 8 am-sundown. Ck-out 11 am, ck-in 3 pm. Meeting rms. Business servs avail. Lighted tennis. 18-hole golf, pro, driving range. In-rm whirlpools, refrigerators; microwaves avail. Private patios, balconies. Cr cds: A, DS, JCB, MC, V.

Restaurants

★ **CAFÉ CARMON.** *1986 San Marco Blvd (32207), in San Marco/Southbank.* 904/399-4488. Hrs: 11 am-11 pm; Fri, Sat to midnight; Sun to 9 pm. Closed major hols. Wine, beer. A la carte entrees: lunch, dinner $5.95-$14.95. Specializes in salads, pasta, chicken. Own baking. Outdoor dining. Cr cds: A, C, D, DS, MC, V.

★ **CAFE ON THE SQUARE.** *1974 San Marco Blvd (32207), in San Marco/Southbank.* 904/399-4848. Hrs: 4 pm-closing. Closed Sun; some major hols. Res accepted. Bar. Semi-a la carte: dinner $12.50-$21.50. Specializes in fresh fish, steak, pasta. Entertainment Tues-Sat. Outdoor dining. Oldest building in San Marco Square (1926). Cr cds: A, C, D, DS, MC, V.

★ **CRAWDADDY'S.** *1643 Prudential Dr (32270), in San Marco/Southbank.* 904/396-3546. Hrs: 11 am-2:30 pm, 5-10 pm; Fri to 11 pm; Sat, Sun from 5 pm; Sun brunch 10 am-2:30 pm. Bars. Semi-a la carte: lunch $4.95-$9.95, dinner $11.95-$19.95. Sun brunch $16.95. Child's meals. Specializes in seafood, beef. Parking. Outdoor dining. Camp shanty decor. On St John's River. Cr cds: A, C, D, DS, MC, V.

✔ ★ ★ **DAVID'S.** *(834 Kingsley Ave, Orange Park 32073) S on US 17 to Kingsley Ave.* 904/264-7431. Hrs: 11 am-2:30 pm, 6-9 pm; Mon, Tues to 2:30 pm; Fri, Sat to 10 pm. Closed Sun; some major hols. Italian, Amer menu. Semi-a la carte: lunch $3.75-$6.25, dinner $8.95-$17.95. Specializes in pasta, seafood. Parking. Cr cds: A, C, D, DS, MC, V.

★ ★ ★ **MARKER 32.** *14549 Beach Blvd (32250), east of downtown.* 904/223-1534. Hrs: 5:30-9:30 pm. Closed some major hols. Res accepted. Bar. Semi-a la carte: dinner $12.95-$24.50. Specializes in seafood, lamb, chicken. Own pasta. Parking. View of water and marshes; pier adj. Artwork displayed. Totally nonsmoking. Cr cds: A, C, D, MC, V.

D

✔★ **PAGODA.** *8617 Baymeadows Rd (32256), in Baymeadows. 904/731-0880.* Hrs: 11 am-10 pm; Fri to 11 pm; Sat noon-11 pm; Sun noon-10 pm. Closed Thanksgiving, Dec 25. Res accepted. Chinese menu. Bar. Semi-a la carte: lunch $4-$5.95, dinner $4.50-$15. Specializes in chicken, seafood combination. Parking. Cr cds: A, C, D, DS, MC, V.

D

✔★ **SEBASTIAN'S.** *10601 San Jose Blvd (32257), in Mandarin Landing Shopping Ctr. 904/268-4458.* Hrs: 5-10 pm; Fri, Sat to 11 pm. Closed Mon; major hols. Res accepted. Italian menu. Wine, beer. Semi-a la carte: dinner $7.95-$15.95. Child's meals. Specializes in pasta, seafood, veal. Cr cds: A, C, D, DS, MC, V.

D **SC**

★★ **STERLING'S CAFE.** *3551 St Johns Ave (32205), south of downtown. 904/387-0700.* Hrs: 11 am-3 pm, 5:30-10 pm; Fri, Sat to 11 pm; Sun to 9 pm. Res accepted Fri, Sat. Continental menu. Bar. Semi-a la carte: lunch $6-$9, dinner $15.95-$24.95. Specializes in fish, pasta, beef. Parking. Outdoor courtyard, patio dining. Totally nonsmoking. Cr cds: A, DS, MC, V.

D

Unrated Dining Spots

ALHAMBRA DINNER THEATRE. *12000 Beach Blvd, east of downtown. 904/641-1212.* Hrs: Tues-Sun cocktails from 6 pm, buffet 6:30 pm, show 8:15 pm; Sat matinee 11 am, buffet 11:30 am, show 1:15 pm; Sun buffet 12:15 pm, show 2 pm. Closed Mon; Jan 1, Dec 25. Res required. Bar. Buffet & show $30.55-$36.75. Menu changes with each show. Professional Equity actors & musicians; Broadway musicals, comedies. Parking. More than 25 yrs of continuous theatrical entertainment. Cr cds: A, DS, MC, V.

SC

THE SISTERS. *(906 Park Ave, Orange Park 32073) 1 mi S of I-295 on US 17. 904/264-7325.* E-mail fabfore@aol.com. Hrs: 11 am-2:30 pm; tea served to 4 pm. Closed Sun & Mon; hols; also 2 wks Sept. Semi-a la carte: lunch $4.50-$6.95. Tea service $6.95. Specializes in salads, sandwiches, quiche. Parking. Outdoor dining. Tea room; Victorian country decor, antique tables. Totally nonsmoking. No cr cds accepted.

D

Jacksonville Beach (B-5)

(See also Atlantic Beach, Jacksonville)

Settled 1884 **Pop** 17,839 **Elev** 9 ft **Area code** 904 **Zip** 32250 **E-mail** jaxflcvb@leading.net **Web** www.jaxcvb.com

Information Jacksonville and the Beaches Convention & Visitors Bureau, 201 E Adams St, Jacksonville 32202; 904/798-9111.

This town, 15 miles east of Jacksonville, has a dual personality—as a suburb for many of Jacksonville's commuters and as an ocean resort. With its neighbors, Atlantic Beach (see), Mayport, Neptune Beach and Ponte Vedra Beach, Jacksonville Beach provides a continuous front of sand and amusement areas sometimes referred to as the beaches of Jacksonville. Fishing tournaments, beach events and a variety of other festivities are held year-round.

What to See and Do

Fishing. Lighted fishing pier 1,200-ft long. Jetties on St Johns River. Charter boats. Between S 5th & 6th Aves.

Pablo Historical Park. Park includes original house built for section foreman of Florida East Coast Railroad, restored with furnishings from the turn of the century; and the old Mayport Depot, with historic railroad exhibits and memorabilia. Adjacent is a steam locomotive. (Daily; closed some hols) 425 Beach Blvd. Phone 904/246-0093. **Donation.**

Annual Events

Beaches Festival Weekend Celebration. Celebration in honor of opening the beaches of Jacksonville; events include sandcastle contests, food and culminating with a spectacular parade. Phone 904/247-6236. Apr.

Players Championship. PGA event. Tournament Player's Club at Ponte Vedra. Phone 904/285-7888.

Motor Hotel

★★★★ **THE LODGE AND CLUB AT PONTE VEDRA BEACH.** *(607 Ponte Vedra Blvd, Ponte Vedra Beach 32082) approx 8 mi S on FL A1A, E on Corona Rd to Ponte Vedra Blvd. 904/273-9500; FAX 904/273-0210; res: 800/243-4304.* E-mail pvlodge@mediaone.net; web www.preferredhotels.com. The look of this plush resort is Mediterranean villa, appealing to an elite clientele whose passions are golf and tennis. All guests rms have ocean views. 66 rms, 2 story, 24 suites. Mid-Feb-mid-Nov: S, D $200-$280; suites $250-$350; under 18 free; package plans; min stay hols, special events; lower rates rest of yr. Crib free. TV; cable. 3 pools; whirlpools, poolside serv, lifeguard. Supervised child's activities (Memorial Day-Labor Day); ages 3-12. Restaurant 7 am-10 pm. Rm serv 24 hrs. Bar 11 am-midnight. Ck-out noon. Meeting rms. Business center. Concierge. Free valet, indoor parking. Tennis privileges. Golf privileges. Exercise rm; saunas. Bathrm phones, refrigerators; microwaves avail; some in-rm whirlpools, minibars, fireplaces. Wet bar in suites. Balconies. Cr cds: A, C, D, DS, MC, V.

D

Resorts

★★★ **MARRIOTT AT SAWGRASS.** *(1000 TPC Blvd, Ponte Vedra Beach 32082) S via FL A1A. 904/285-7777; FAX 904/285-0906; res: 800/457-4653.* 350 rms in hotel, 7 story; 164 villas, 2 story. Feb-June: S, D $195; each addl $20; suites $245-$500; villas $368-$525; under 15 free; tennis & golf plans; higher rates special events; lower rates rest of yr. Crib free. TV; cable (premium), VCR avail. 4 pools, 1 heated; wading pool, whirlpool, poolside serv. Supervised child's activities; ages 3-12. Dining rms 6:30 am-10 pm (also see THE AUGUSTINE ROOM). Box lunches, snack bar. Rm serv to 1 am. Bars 11-1 am. Ck-out noon, ck-in 4 pm. Grocery, coin lndry, package store 1 blk. Convention facilities. Business center. In-rm modem link. Valet serv. Gift shop. Lighted tennis, pro. 99-hole golf, greens fee, pro, shops, putting greens, driving ranges. Miniature golf. Private beach access, boating. 4 stocked ponds. Bicycles. Exercise equipt; steam rm, sauna. Many minibars; some fireplaces. Many private patios, balconies. Cr cds: A, C, D, DS, JCB, MC, V.

D **SC**

★★★ **PONTE VEDRA INN & CLUB.** *(200 Ponte Vedra Blvd, Ponte Vedra Beach 32082) 2 mi S via FL A1A. 904/285-1111; FAX 904/285-2111; res: 800/234-7842.* Established in 1928, this luxurious yet cozy oceanfront resort features third-generation employees serving third-generation guests. 222 units, 2 story, 64 kits. Mar-May: S, D $260-$280; suites $360-$380; golf plans; MAP, AP avail; lower rates rest of yr. Crib $5. TV; cable (premium). 4 pools, 2 heated; wading pool, whirlpool, poolside serv, lifeguard. Playground. Supervised child's activities (June-Sept & hols); ages 4-12. Dining rm 7-10:30 am, 11:30 am-3:30 pm, 6:30-10 pm. Box lunches, snack bar, picnics. Rm serv 24 hrs. Bars 11 am-midnight; entertainment Thurs-Sat. Ck-out noon, ck-in 3 pm. Package store. Convention facilities. Business center. In-rm modem link. Concierge. Gift shops. Valet parking. Airport transportation. Tennis, pro, pro shop. Two 18-hole golf courses, greens fee $90-$110, pro, putting green, driving range, pro shop. Private beach, swimming; boats, rowboats, sailboats, paddleboats. Bicycles. Lawn games. Soc dir; entertainment. Exercise rm; steam rm, sauna. Spa. Refrigerators, minibars, wet bars; some fireplaces;

microwaves avail. Private patios, balconies. Picnic tables. Cr cds: A, C, D, DS, MC, V.

Restaurants

★ ★ ★ **THE AUGUSTINE ROOM.** *(See Marriott At Sawgrass Resort)* *904/285-7777.* Hrs: 6-10 pm. Closed Sun, Mon. Res accepted. French, continental menu. Bar. Wine cellar. Semi-a la carte: dinner $24-$32. Specializes in beef, seafood. Valet parking. Original artwork, fresh floral arrangements. Cr cds: A, C, D, DS, JCB, MC, V.

✔★ ★ **AW SHUCKS.** *(950 Sawgrass Village Dr, Ponte Vedra 32082)* In Sawgrass Village, S on FL A1A. *904/285-3017.* Hrs: 11:30 am-10 pm; Fri, Sat to 11 pm. Closed Thanksgiving, Dec 25. Res accepted. Semi-a la carte: lunch $3.95-$8.95, dinner $9.95-$17.95. Child's meals. Specializes in gourmet seafood, fresh Maine lobster, steak. Parking. Tropical decor with outdoor decks overlooking small lake. Cr cds: A, D, DS, MC, V.

★ **CHIZU.** *1227 S Third St,* on FL A1A. *904/241-8455.* Hrs: 5:30-9:45 pm; Fri, Sat to 10:45 pm. Closed Thanksgiving, Dec 25. Japanese menu. Bar. Semi-a la carte: dinner $9-$23. Child's meals. Specializes in seafood, sushi. Traditional Japanese seating avail. Cr cds: A, D, DS, MC, V.

★ ★ **FIRST STREET GRILLE.** *807 N First St.* 904/246-6555. Hrs: 11:30 am-10 pm; Fri, Sat to 11 pm; Sun from 11 am. Closed Jan 1, Thanksgiving, Dec 25. Bar. Semi-a la carte: lunch $5.95-$9.95, dinner $13.95-$18.95. Child's meals. Specializes in seafood, steak, salads. Outdoor dining overlooking beach. Multi-level dining, original art. Cr cds: A, C, D, DS, MC, V.

★ **KING WU.** *1323 S 3rd St.* 904/246-0567. Hrs: 11 am-9:30 pm; Fri, Sat to 10:30 pm; Sun noon-9 pm. Chinese menu. Bar. A la carte entrees: lunch $2.99-$4.99, dinner $5.50-$16. Specialties: Cantonese pan-fried noodles, chicken with garlic sauce, orange flavored beef. Parking. Chinese decor, red & gold inlay. Cr cds: A, MC, V.

Jensen Beach (F-6)

(See also Fort Pierce, Stuart)

Settled 1871 **Pop** 9,884 **Elev** 50 ft **Area code** 561 **Zip** 34957 **E-mail** Jensen@Metrolink.net **Web** www.metrolinknet/Jensen

Information Chamber of Commerce, 1910 NE Jensen Beach Blvd; 561/334-3444.

Jensen Beach, named for Danish sailor John L. Jensen, who first settled the area, was once a major center of pineapple cultivation. Today, the economy is based on tourism and small retail business.

What to See and Do

Fishing. From charter boats, bridges over Indian and St Lucie Rivers; freshwater fishing in savannas; sport fishing in Gulf Stream; surf fishing along beach; fishing pier at Jensen Beach Causeway.

Hutchinson Island. Connected to the village by a causeway. The island is the waterfront section of Jensen Beach. Swimming (lifeguards); surf casting, shelling. Picnicking. Also Gilbert's Bar House of Refuge (see STUART), a restored historic site (daily exc Mon; fee), and Elliott Museum (see STUART).

Annual Events

Sailfish Powerboat Championships. May.

Pineapple Festival. Contests, street fair, exhibits, amusement rides. 2nd wkend Nov.

Seasonal Event

Turtle Watch. Endangered sea turtles, 200-500 pounds, crawl far up onto the beaches of Hutchinson Island to lay their eggs. Supervised by the Chamber of Commerce. Reservations required. June-July.

Motel

✔★ ★ **BEST WESTERN.** *(7900 S US 1, Port St Lucie 34952)* 2 mi N on US 1. *561/878-7600;* FAX 561/340-0422. 98 suites, 2 story. Mid-Jan-Mar: suites $59-$109; each addl $5; under 12 free; higher rates special events; lower rates rest of yr. Crib free. TV; cable. Heated pool; whirlpool. Complimentary continental bkfst. Restaurant adj 11 am-9 pm. Beer, wine. Ck-out 11 am. Coin lndry. Meeting rm. Business servs avail. In-rm modem link. Health club privileges. Refrigerators; microwaves avail. Cr cds: A, C, D, DS, MC, V.

Motor Hotels

★ ★ ★ **COURTYARD BY MARRIOTT-HUTCHINSON ISLAND.** *10978 S Ocean Dr (FL A1A).* 561/229-1000; FAX 561/229-0253. 110 rms, 8 story. Jan-Apr: S, D $144-$164; each addl $10; under 17 free; lower rates rest of yr. Crib free. TV; cable (premium). Pool; poolside serv. Coffee in rms. Ck-out noon. Coin lndry. Meeting rms. Business servs avail. In-rm modem link. Valet serv. Sundries. Tennis privileges. Golf privileges. Exercise equipt. Refrigerators. Some balconies. Exterior glass elvtr to rooftop cafe. On beach. Cr cds: A, D, DS, MC, V.

★ ★ ★ **HOLIDAY INN OCEANSIDE.** *3793 NE Ocean Blvd,* on FL A1A, on Hutchinson Island. 561/225-3000; res: 800/992-4747; FAX 561/225-1956. E-mail //holiday@siservices.net; web www.holiday-inn.com/hotels/suaos. 177 rms, 4 story. Mid-Jan-mid-Apr: S, D $155-$185; each addl $10; suites $340-$495; under 19 free; varied lower rates rest of yr. Crib free. TV; cable, VCR avail. Heated pool; poolside serv. Restaurant 6 am-10 pm. Rm serv. Bar; entertainment Tues-Sat. Ck-out 11 am. Coin lndry. Meeting rms. Business servs avail. In-rm modem link. Bellhops. Sundries. Gift shop. Lighted tennis. Golf privileges. Exercise equipt. Game rm. Balconies. On ocean. Cr cds: A, C, D, DS, JCB, MC, V.

★ ★ ★ **HOLIDAY INN PORT ST LUCIE.** *(10120 S US 1, Port St Lucie 34952)* 2 mi N on US 1, jct Port St Lucie Blvd. 561/337-2200; FAX 561/335-7872. 142 rms, 5 story, 72 suites. Jan-mid-Apr: S, D $109; each addl $10; suites $119; under 18 free; lower rates rest of yr. Crib free. TV; cable (premium). Heated pool. Coffee in rms. Restaurant 6-11:30 am, 5-10 pm. Rm serv. Bar 4-11 pm. Ck-out noon. Coin lndry. Meeting rms. Sundries. Health club privileges. Wet bars; some refrigerators; microwaves avail. Cr cds: A, C, D, DS, JCB, MC, V.

Inn

★ ★ **HUTCHINSON INN.** *9750 S Ocean Dr (FL A1A),* on Hutchinson Island. 561/229-2000; FAX 561/229-8875. 21 rms, 2 story, 5 suites. Dec-Apr: S, D $90; each addl $20; suites $140-$200; kit. units $140; under 3 free; monthly rates; lower rates rest of yr. Crib free. TV; cable. Heated pool. Complimentary full bkfst. Ck-out 11 am, ck-in 2 pm. Business servs avail. Tennis. Golf privileges, greens fee $23-$40, putting green. Refrigerators; some microwaves. On ocean; miniature waterfall in bkfst area. Cr cds: MC, V.

Restaurants

★ ★ **ADMIRAL'S TABLE.** *4000 NE Indian River Dr.* 561/334-3080. Hrs: 11:30 am-9 pm; Fri, Sat to 10 pm; Sun to 8:30 pm. Closed Dec 25. Bar. Semi-a la carte: lunch $4.10-$8.50, dinner $10.50-$23. Child's meals. Specializes in fresh local seafood, Maine lobster, prime rib. Salad bar. Entertainment Fri, Sat evenings. Nautical decor. View of river. Cr cds: A, C, D, DS, MC, V.

D ⊡ ♥

★ **CONCHY JOE'S SEAFOOD.** *3945 NE Indian River Dr.* 561/334-1130. Hrs: 11:30 am-2:30 pm, 5-10 pm. Closed Thanksgiving, Dec 25; also Super Bowl Sun. Bar. Semi-a la carte: lunch $3.50-$10.95, dinner $8.95-$24.95. Child's meals. Specializes in fresh seafood, steak, Bahamian dishes. Entertainment Wed-Sun. Raw bar. Riverfront dining. Cr cds: A, DS, MC, V.

D ⊡ ♥

★ ★ **LOBSTER SHANTY.** *999 NE Anchorage Dr, off FL 707.* 561/334-6400. Hrs: 11:30 am-9 pm; Fri, Sat to 10 pm; early-bird dinner Mon-Sat 3-6 pm. Closed Thanksgiving. Bar. Semi-a la carte: lunch $3.99-$7.99, dinner $9.99-$16.99. Child's meals. Specializes in Maine lobster, local seafood. Salad bar. Overlooks marina and Indian River. Cr cds: A, D, MC, V.

D ⊡

Jupiter (G-6)

(See also Lake Worth, Palm Beach, West Palm Beach)

Pop 24,986 **Elev** 8 ft **Area code** 561 **Web** jupiterfl.org
Information Jupiter-Tequesta-Juno Beach Chamber of Commerce, 800 N US 1, 33477; 561/746-7111.

Jonathan Dickinson, a Quaker, and his party were swept ashore near the present-day site of Jupiter during a storm in 1696. Captured by Native Americans but set free, the survivors marched 225 miles to St Augustine. Dickinson's tale of his adventures, *God's Protecting Providence,* was widely read in both Europe and America. Jupiter is on the Intracoastal Waterway at the mouth of the scenic Loxahatchee River. A nearly eight-mile stretch of the river, from Riverbend Park in Palm Beach County to the southern boundary of Jonathan Dickinson State Park, forms a component of both the Florida and the National Wild and Scenic Rivers systems.

What to See and Do

Florida History Center & Museum. Exhibits on South Florida culture, Seminole Indians, shipwrecks, railroads; authentic Seminole chickee. (Daily exc Mon; closed hols) On US 1, in Burt Reynolds Park. Phone 561/747-6639. ¢¢ The Historical Society also operates

Jupiter Lighthouse and Museum (1860). This red-brick landmark is one of the oldest lighthouses on the Atlantic coast. Houses local historical artifacts and memorabilia. Tours (Sun-Wed; closed hols). On bluff overlooking Jupiter Inlet. Phone 561/747-8380. ¢¢

Dubois House. Restored pioneer house (ca 1896) built on Jaega Indian mound faces Jupiter Inlet; many original furnishings and personal memorabilia of first occupants. Tours. (Wed & Sun afternoons; closed hols) NE via FL A1A, Jupiter Beach Rd exit to Dubois Rd. Phone 561/747-6639. ¢

Hobe Sound National Wildlife Refuge. This 970-acre refuge contains 3½ mi of undeveloped ocean beach where sea turtles nest. Nature trails. Hobe Sound Nature Center, visitor center; interpretive signs. (Daily) Golden Eagle, Golden Age and Golden Access passports accepted (see MAKING THE MOST OF YOUR TRIP). Approx 5 mi N via US 1, in Hobe Sound. Contact PO Box 645, Hobe Sound 33475; 561/546-6141. Per vehicle ¢¢; Pedestrians **Free.**

Jonathan Dickinson State Park. More than 10,000 acres near where Jonathan Dickinson was shipwrecked between Hobe Sound and the Loxahatchee River; park includes 85-ft-high Hobe Mountain with 25-ft observation tower, pine flatlands and tropical riverfront. Fishing; boating (ramps), canoeing (rentals). Nature trails. Bicycling. Picnicking (shelters), playground, concession. Camping (dump station), cottages. Boat trip (2 hrs). Guided tours at Trapper Nelson Interpretive Site on river, accessible only by boat. Standard hrs, fees. 6 mi N on US 1, in Hobe Sound. Phone 561/546-2771.

Motels

✔★ **BEST WESTERN INTRACOASTAL INN.** *810 US 1 (33477).* 561/575-2936; FAX 561/579-9346. 53 rms, 2 story. Mid-Jan-Apr: S, D $79-$139; each addl $5; under 16 free; lower rates rest of yr. Crib free. TV; cable (premium). Pool. Complimentary continental bkfst. Ck-out 11 am. Lndry facilities. Business servs avail. In-rm modem link. On Intracoastal Waterway; observation deck. Cr cds: A, DS, MC, V.

D ≋ ⇥ ⩗ SC

★ ★ **HAMPTON INN.** *(13801 US 1, Juno Beach 33408)* S on US 1. 561/626-9090; FAX 561/624-9936. Web www.hampton-inn.com. 90 rms, 2 story. Dec-Apr: S, D $105-$165; family rates; lower rates rest of yr. Crib free. TV; cable (premium). Heated pool; whirlpool. Complimentary continental bkfst. Restaurant nearby. Ck-out 11 am. Meeting rms. Business servs avail. In-rm modem link. Sundries. Coin lndry. Exercise equipt. Refrigerators, microwaves. Cr cds: A, C, D, DS, MC, V.

D ≋ ⊀ ⇥ ⩗ SC

★ ★ **HOLIDAY INN EXPRESS.** *(13950 US 1, Juno Beach 33408)* 2½ mi S on US 1. 561/622-4366; res: 800/272-6380; FAX 561/625-5245. 105 rms, 2-3 story, 10 suites. Jan-Mar: S, D $129-$189; suites $189; under 12 free; higher rates special hols; lower rates rest of yr. Crib free. Pet accepted; $25. TV; cable. Complimentary continental bkfst. Restaurant adj 11 am-10 pm. Ck-out 11 am. Business servs avail. In-rm modem link. Coin lndry. Health club privileges. Pool. Many refrigerators, microwaves, wet bars. Cr cds: A, C, D, DS, MC, V.

D ⛵ ≋ ⇥ ⩗ SC

★ ★ **JUPITER CAY RESORT.** *(18903 SE Federal Hwy, Tequesta 33469)* 3 mi N on US 1. 561/747-9085; res: 888/747-9085; FAX 561/575-3374. 36 suites, 2 story. Nov-Apr: suites $99-$149; under 13 free; wkly, monthly rates; lower rates rest of yr. Crib $5. TV; cable. Heated pool. Complimentary continental bkfst. Restaurant nearby. Ck-out 11 am. Coin lndry. Business servs avail. Some in-rm whirlpools. Balconies. On Intracoastal Waterway. Cr cds: A, D, DS, MC, V.

D ⛵ ≋ ⇥ ⩗ SC

Motor Hotel

★ ★ **WELLESLEY INN.** *34 Fisherman's Wharf (33477).* 561/575-7201; FAX 561/575-1169; res: 800/444-8888. 105 rms, 3 story. Mid-Dec-mid-Apr: S $90-$120; D $100-$130; each addl $10; suites $109-$149; under 18 free; wkly rates; diving packages; lower rates rest of yr. TV; cable (premium), VCR avail. Heated pool. Complimentary continental bkfst. Restaurant adj 6 am-11 pm. Ck-out 11 am. Coin lndry. Meeting rm. Business servs avail. In-rm modem link. Golf privileges. Health club privileges. Some refrigerators. Cr cds: A, C, D, DS, JCB, MC, V.

D ⅓ ≋ ⇥ ⩗ SC

Hotel

★ ★ ★ **JUPITER BEACH RESORT.** *5 North A1A (33477),* at Indiantown Rd. 561/746-2511; FAX 561/744-1741; res: 800/228-8810. Web www.jupiterbeachresort.com. 148 rms, 9 story. Jan-Apr: S, D $200-$400; each addl $25; suites $600-$1,000; package plans; lower rates rest of yr. Crib free. TV; cable (premium), VCR avail. Heated pool; poolside serv. Restaurant 6:30 am-10 pm. Bar 11-1 am; entertainment Thurs-Sat. Ck-out noon. Meeting rms. Business servs avail. In-rm modem link. Concierge.

Gift shop. Valet parking. Lighted tennis. Golf privileges. Exercise equipt. Minibars. Balconies. Gazebo overlooks ocean; beach, cabanas. Bicycle rentals. Sailing, snorkeling avail. Cr cds: A, C, D, DS, ER, MC, V.

D 🛏🍴🏊✈🎿🐾 SC

Restaurants

✔★ **BOGART'S HIDEAWAY CAFE.** *725 N FL A1A (33477),* in Alhambra Shopping Center. 561/575-2100. Hrs: 5-10 pm; Fri, Sat to 11 pm. Closed Easter, Thanksgiving, Dec 25. Bar. Semi-a la carte: dinner $6.99-$15.99. Specialties: chicken Francese, veal Marsala. Own desserts. Entertainment Fri, Sat. Autographed pictures of movie stars. Cr cds: DS, MC, V.

D 🍴

★ **BUBBA'S FISH CAMP.** *1511 Old Dixie Hwy (33469),* ¹/₂ blk W of US 1. 561/747-8300. Hrs: 11:30 am-10 pm; Fri, Sat to 11 pm. Closed Thanksgiving. Bar. Semi-a la carte: lunch $4.95-$12.95, dinner $9.95-$34.95. Child's meals. Specializes in seafood, crab & grouper baked in a bag. Parking. Nautical decor; marine artifacts. Cr cds: A, D, DS, MC, V.

D

★ ★ **CHARLEY'S CRAB.** *1000 N US 1 (33477).* 561/744-4710. Hrs: 11:30 am-10 pm; Sunset dinners 3:30-6 pm; Sun 10:30 am-2:30 pm, 3:30-10 pm. Res accepted. Bar to 11 pm. Wine list. Semi-a la carte: lunch $5-$16, dinner $11.50-$26. Sun brunch $21.95. Child's meals. Specializes in fresh seafood, rack of lamb. Own baking, pasta. Valet parking. Outdoor dining. Overlooks Jupiter Inlet. Cr cds: A, C, D, DS, MC, V.

D

★ ★ **COBBLESTONE CAFE.** (*383 Tequesta Dr, Tequesta 33469*) In Gallery Sq North shopping center. 561/747-4419. Hrs: 11:30 am-2:30 pm, 5-9:30 pm. Closed Jan 1, Thanksgiving, Dec 25. Res accepted. French menu. Semi-a la carte: lunch $2.75-$10.95, dinner $12.95-$21.95. Child's meals. Specializes in fresh fish, roast duckling. Own sauces, pastas, soups, desserts. Outdoor dining. Country decor. Totally nonsmoking. Cr cds: A, DS, MC, V.

D

★ ★ **KASHA.** *287 E Indiantown Rd (33477).* 561/744-0605. Hrs: 5:30-10 pm. Closed most major hols; Sun, Mon in summer; also mid-Aug-mid-Sept. Res required. Continental menu. Bar. Wine list. A la carte entrees: dinner $16-$32. Child's meals. Specialties: fresh Dover sole, Florida red snapper, duck a l'Orange. Parking. Elegant dining; floor-to-ceiling windows, original art and crystal chandeliers. Jacket. Cr cds: A, D, DS, MC, V.

D 🍴

✔★ **TOO JAY'S-BLUFF'S SQUARE.** *4050 US 1S (33477),* in Bluff's Sq Plaza. 561/627-5555. Hrs: 8 am-9 pm; Sun brunch to 2 pm. Closed Thanksgiving, Dec 25. Wine, beer. Semi-a la carte: bkfst $1.99-$5.99, lunch $4.99-$7.99, dinner $4.99-$9.99. Sun brunch $4.99-$7.99. Child's meals. Specializes in seafood salad, chicken, deli sandwiches. Parking. Cr cds: A, D, MC, V.

D

Kennedy Space Center (E-5)

(See also Cocoa, Cocoa Beach, Titusville)

(47 mi E of Orlando; 12 mi E of Titusville; 15 mi N of Cape Canaveral. Entrance at visitors center, N or S via US 1 or I-95 exit 78 or 79 to FL 405 NASA Pkwy, then E; N via FL 3; follow signs)

As the launch site for all United States manned space missions since 1968, the Kennedy Space Center on Merritt Island is one of the most historic sites in the world. From here, on July 16, 1969, Apollo 11 astronauts left Earth on man's first voyage to land on the moon. Three Skylab missions, the Apollo/Soyuz Test Project and more than 40 voyages of the space shuttle have all been launched from the Space Center.

The National Aeronautics and Space Administration was established on October 1, 1958. The early focus of NASA's launch operations centered on Cape Canaveral, where manned launches of Project Mercury and Gemini took place. In late 1964, the John F. Kennedy Space Center was relocated to adjacent Merritt Island. The site was selected in 1961 as the launch facility for Apollo, the Moon Mission. Beginning in 1976, these facilities were modified and new ones built to accommodate the launch of the space shuttle. The 140,000-acre John F. Kennedy Space Center is the major launch facility for NASA.

In addition to the historic manned rocket flights, NASA also launches a wide variety of unmanned spacecraft, including weather and communications satellites, orbiting scientific observatories, Earth resources technology satellites and interplanetary probes, such as Galileo and Magellan.

Aside from operational areas, much of Kennedy Space Center is designated a National Wildlife Refuge, portions of which also form part of the Canaveral National Seashore (see TITUSVILLE). Approximately two million visitors annually pass through the Kennedy Space Center Visitor Complex and starting point for the Center's tours, making the Kennedy Space Center one of the major tourist attractions in the state.

What to See and Do

⭐ **Kennedy Space Center Visitor Complex.** The Visitor Complex offers films, exhibits and displays on the past, present and future of space exploration. Available activities include the IMAX Theater, in which the films *The Dream Is Alive, L5: First City in Space, Mission to Mir* are shown on a 70-ft-wide, 5-story-high screen ($7.50); the Gallery of Space Flight, which displays authentic Mercury and Gemini Space capsules; and the outdoor Rocket Garden, where rockets of all types and sizes are displayed. Also at the Visitor Complex are the NASA Art Exhibit, the Space Art Gallery and the 42-ft by 50-ft Astronauts Memorial, with the names of the 16 astronauts who have died in the line of duty etched into the surface. Cafeteria, gift shop. Free cameras; free kennel facilities; free parking. Free wheelchairs avail. (Daily; closed Dec 25) **Free.** From the Visitor Complex visitors may take

Bus tours. There are two regularly scheduled bus tours. **Note:** Tour routes and availability may be altered because of launch operations. Phone 407/452-2121. ¢¢¢¢

Kennedy Space Center Tour includes a stop near space shuttle launch pads A & B, launch complex 39 Observation Gantry, where visitors may take photographs. Also included on this tour is the Apollo/Saturn V Center, which features theatrical presentations, an actual 363-ft Saturn V, an up-close look at NASA technicians working on real space station components, rocket and an intergalactic hands-on gallery.

Cape Canaveral Tour through Cape Canaveral Air Force Station, the site of early space launches, includes the Air Force Space Museum and mission control for the Mercury and Gemini programs.

(For general and launch information contact Kennedy Space Center Visitor Complex, Delaware North Park Services, 32899, phone 407/452-2121.)

Key Biscayne (H-6)

(See also Coral Gables, Hollywood, Miami, Miami Beach)

Pop 8,854 **Elev** 10 ft **Area code** 305 **Zip** 33149 **Web** www.miamiandbeaches.com
Information Chamber of Commerce, 328 Crandon Blvd, Suite 217, 305/361-5207; or the Greater Miami Convention & Visitors Bureau, 701 Brickell Ave, Suite 2700, Miami 33131, phone 305/539-3000 or 800/464-2643.

What to See and Do

Bill Baggs Cape Florida State Recreation Area. Approx 900 acres with historic Cape Florida Lighthouse, southern Florida's oldest structure, and replica of the lightkeeper's dwelling. Tours of lighthouse complex; four departures (Thurs-Mon). Swimming; fishing. Bicycle & nature trails. Picnicking, concession. Standard hrs, fees. 1200 S Crandon Blvd, off US 1, at S end of island. Phone 305/361-5811.

Crandon Park. Beach, cabanas (fee). Golf; marina facilities. Picnic grove, grills, concessions, restaurant. "Pathway to the Sea," specially designed swimming facility for the disabled. (Daily) Parking fee. Phone 305/361-5421.

Annual Event

Lipton Championships. Crandon Park Tennis Center. Major two-week tournament attracting top-ranked players. Phone 305/442-3367. Late Mar.

Hotel

★ ★ ★ **SONESTA BEACH RESORT.** *350 Ocean Dr. 305/361-2021; FAX 305/361-3096; res: 800/766-3782.* E-mail webmaster@sonesta.com; web www.sonesta.com. 292 rms, 8 story. Late Dec-Apr: S, D $255-$395; each addl $35; suites $600-$1,700; under 17 free; lower rates rest of yr. Crib free. Valet parking $12. TV; cable (premium). Heated pool; whirlpool, poolside serv. Playground. Supervised child's activities; ages 5-13. Restaurant (see PURPLE DOLPHIN). Rm serv 7-1 am. Bar noon-1 am; entertainment. Convention facilities. Business center. Concierge. Shopping arcade. Barber, beauty shop. Lighted tennis, pro. 18-hole golf privileges, greens fee $86-$88, pro, putting green, driving range. Exercise rm; sauna. Massage. Game rm. Rec rm. Lawn games. Minibars. Balconies. Picnic tables. On ocean; swimming beach. Cr cds: A, C, D, DS, ER, JCB, MC, V.

Restaurants

★ ★ **PURPLE DOLPHIN.** *(See Sonesta Beach Resort Hotel)* *305/361-2021.* Hrs: 7-11:30 am, noon-3 pm, 6:30-10:30 pm; Sun brunch 11 am-2:30 pm. Res accepted. Continental menu. Bar. A la carte entrees: bkfst $4.50-$9, lunch $4-$14, dinner $12-$21. Sun brunch $27. Serv charge 15%. Child's meals. Specializes in fresh seafood, Florida cuisine. Entertainment. Valet parking. Outdoor dining. Overlooks ocean. Family-owned. Cr cds: A, C, D, DS, ER, JCB, MC, V.

★ ★ **THE RUSTY PELICAN.** *3201 Rickenbacker Causeway.* *305/361-3818.* Hrs: 11 am-11 pm; Fri, Sat to midnight; Sun 5-11 pm; Sun brunch 10:30 am-3 pm. Res accepted. Bar. A la carte entrees: lunch $5.95-$13.95, dinner $15.95-$32.95. Sun brunch $23.95. Child's meals. Specializes in fresh seafood, steak. Pianist, vocalist Tues-Sat. Valet parking. Outdoor dining. View of ocean and Miami skyline. Nautical decor. Family-owned. Cr cds: A, D, DS, MC, V.

Key Largo (J-6)

(See also Islamorada)

Pop 11,336 **Elev** 5-14 ft **Area code** 305 **Zip** 33037 **E-mail** klchamber@aol.com **Web** keylargo.org
Information Key Largo Chamber of Commerce, Florida Keys Visitor Center, 106000 Overseas Hwy; 305/451-1414 or 800/822-1088.

This island at the north end of the Florida Keys (see) is the longest of the chain. Extending some 30 miles, but seldom more than 2 miles wide, it shares its name with the village. The Overseas Highway (US 1) crosses the first bridge at Jewfish Creek to start its southwestward stretch across the keys to Key West. Scattered on the island are marinas catering to the ever-present fishermen and skin divers.

What to See and Do

Dolphins Plus. Research and education center concentrating on the interaction between humans and dolphins; visitors can watch or participate in three to four-hr programs (res required to participate; experienced swimmers only; equipment provided). Min age 10 yrs; under age 18 must be accompanied by an adult. Programs for the disabled. (2 sessions daily) S via Ocean Bay Dr. Phone 305/451-1993. Program participants ¢¢¢¢¢ Non-participant observers ¢¢¢

John Pennekamp Coral Reef State Park. The first underwater park in the US, John Pennekamp lies just off the east coast of Key Largo, parallel to its shore. The 55,011-acre park, covering an area more than 21 mi long and more than 3 mi wide, contains fantastic marine and plant life, 650 varieties of tropical fish, brilliantly colored living coral and the wrecks of many ships—a mecca for skin divers and underwater photographers. Swimming; fishing. Nature trails. Picnicking. Camping. Visitor center. Observation tower. Certified scuba instruction, snorkeling, wading; motorboat and canoe rentals (ramp, marina). Standard hrs, fees. NE off US 1, mile marker 102.5. Phone 305/451-1202. Also in park are

Boat tours over coral reef. Glass-bottom boat cruises (2½ hrs; three departures daily, weather permitting). Scuba and snorkel tours, instruction, rentals; boat rentals. Phone 305/451-1621. Cruises ¢¢¢¢¢

Jules' Undersea Lodge. World's only underwater "hotel," five fathoms deep. Designed to accommodate six divers (introductory diving classes avail), the Lodge has an entertainment center, fully stocked galley, dining area, bathrooms and 42-inch windows. Available for three-hr or overnight stays. Off US 1, mile marker 103.2, adj to John Pennekamp Coral Reef State Park. Contact Jules' Habitat Inc, 51 Shoreland Dr; 305/451-2353. ¢¢¢¢¢

Annual Event

Island Jubilee. Plantation Yacht Harbor, mile marker 87 Bayside. Three-day festival with Caribbean flair; arts & crafts, music, entertainment, concessions. 3rd wkend Nov.

Motels

★ **BAY BREEZE.** *(160 Sterling Rd, Tavernier 33070)* *305/852-5248; res: 800/937-5650; FAX 305/852-5758.* E-mail baybreez@terranova.net; web thefloridakeys.com/baybreeze. 15 rms, 8 with shower only, 1-2 story, 2 suites, 6 cottages. S, D, cottages $89-$139; each addl $10; suites $99-$139; 3-5 day min (hols); higher rates lobster season. TV; cable, VCR avail. Restaurant nearby. Ck-out 11 am. Pool. Refrigerators; microwave in suites. On ocean. Totally nonsmoking. Cr cds: MC, V.

★ ★ **BEST WESTERN THE SUITES AT KEY LARGO.** *201 Ocean Dr, on Overseas Hwy (US 1) at mile marker 100. 305/451-5081; res: 800/462-6079; FAX 305/451-4173.* Web kylsuites.com. 40 kit. suites, 2 story. Mid-Dec-mid-Apr: kit. suites $150-$250; each addl $10; under 12 free; wkly rates; package plans; lower rates rest of yr. Crib free. TV; cable (premium). Pool. Complimentary continental bkfst. Restaurant nearby.

Ck-out 11 am. Covered parking. Balconies. Picnic tables, grills. On canal; marina, dockage. Cr cds: A, C, D, DS, MC, V.

 D ⚓ ≈ ⨯ ⚓ SC

★ ★ **HOLIDAY INN.** *99701 Overseas Hwy (US 1), at mile marker 100.* 305/451-2121; *res:* 800/843-5397; *FAX* 305/451-5592. E-mail hirl@reefnet.com. 132 rms, 2 story. Dec-Apr: S, D $139-$209; each addl $10; under 18 free; lower rates rest of yr. Crib free. TV; cable (premium). 2 heated pools; whirlpool. Restaurant 7 am-10:30 pm. Rm serv. Bar 11 am-10 pm. Ck-out 11 am. Coin lndry. Meeting rms. Sundries. Exercise equipt. On deepwater channel; marina, glass-bottom boat tours. Home port to original African Queen used in Humphrey Bogart movie of same name. Cr cds: A, C, D, DS, ER, JCB, MC, V.

D ⚓ ≈ ⨯ ⨯ ⚓ SC

★ ★ **RAMADA LIMITED RESORT & MARINA.** *99751 Overseas Hwy (US 1), at mile marker 100.* 305/451-3939; *FAX* 305/453-0222. 90 rms, 3 story. Dec-Apr: S, D $129-$169; under 18 free; lower rates rest of yr. Crib avail. TV; cable. Pool. Restaurant adj 7 am-10:30 pm. Ck-out 11 am. Coin lndry. Free covered parking. Balconies. On harbor; glass-bottom boat tours. Cr cds: A, C, D, DS, ER, JCB, MC, V.

D ⚓ ≈ ⨯ ⚓ SC

Motor Hotels

★ ★ **MARINA DEL MAR.** *527 Caribbean Dr, at mile marker 100.* 305/451-4107; *res:* 800/451-3483; *FAX* 305/451-1891. E-mail marina-delmar@msn.com; web www.marinadelmar.com. 76 units, 2-4 story, 28 kit. suites. Dec-Apr: S, D $149-$189; suites $179-$369; wkly rates; lower rates rest of yr. Crib $10. TV; cable. Heated pool; whirlpool, poolside serv. Complimentary continental bkfst. Restaurant 11 am-11 pm. Bar to 1 am; entertainment. Ck-out 11 am. Coin lndry. Meeting rm. Tennis. Exercise equipt. Boat rentals. Refrigerators; many in-rm whirlpools. Some private patios, balconies. Located on a deep-water marina, full-service marina with dive shop, fishing fleet. Cr cds: A, C, D, DS, JCB, MC, V.

D ⚓ ≈ ⨯ ⨯ ⚓ SC

★ ★ **WESTIN BEACH RESORT.** *97000 Overseas Hwy (US 1).* 305/852-5553; *res:* 800/539-5274; *FAX* 305/852-8669. E-mail bwaichul@slcmail.westin.com; web www.1800keylargo.com. 200 rms, 4 story, 10 suites. Mid-Dec-Apr: S, D $250-$300; each addl $15; suites $450; under 17 free; lower rates rest of yr. Crib free. TV; cable (premium). 2 heated pools; whirlpool, poolside serv. Restaurant 6-11 pm. Bar 11 am-2 am. Ck-out noon. Convention facilities. Business servs avail. In-rm modem link. Concierge. Gift shop. Beauty shop. Lighted tennis. Minibars. Private patios, balconies. Caribbean decor. On private beach; pier, dockage. Boat rentals; sailing, windsurfing, scuba diving. 2,000-ft wooded nature trail. Cr cds: A, C, D, DS, ER, MC, V.

D ⚓ ≈ ≈ ⨯ ⚓ SC

Hotel

★ ★ **MARRIOTT'S KEY LARGO BAY BEACH RESORT.** *103800 Overseas Hwy.* 305/453-0000; *FAX* 305/453-0093. 149 rms, 4 story, 21 suites. Early Dec-late Apr: S, D $219-$279; suites $600-$1,000; under 17 free; higher rates auto races; lower rates rest of yr. Crib free. TV; cable (premium), VCR avail. Pool; whirlpool, poolside serv. Complimentary coffee in rms. Restaurant 7 am-11 pm. Bar 11 am-4 am; entertainment. Ck-out noon. Coin lndry. Meeting rms. Business servs avail. In-rm modem link. Concierge. Gift shop. Exercise rm. Game rm. Minibars. Balconies. On beach. Cr cds: A, C, D, DS, ER, JCB, MC, V.

D ⚓ ≈ ⨯ ⨯ ⚓ SC

Restaurant

✔ ★ **MRS. MAC'S KITCHEN.** *Mile Marker 99.4, S on US 1.* 305/451-3722. Hrs: 7 am-9:30 pm. Closed Sun; most major hols. Semi-a la carte: bkfst $2-$7, lunch $2-$8, dinner $5.95-$15.95. Child's meals.

Specialties: meatloaf, lobster, stone crab. Parking. Casual atmosphere. No cr cds accepted.

⊿

Key West (K-4)

(See also Big Pine Key, Marathon)

Founded 1822 **Pop** 24,832 **Elev** 5 ft **Area code** 305 **Zip** 33040

Information Greater Key West Chamber of Commerce, 402 Wall St; 305/294-2587.

This southernmost city of the continental US, on the final inhabited island in the string of Florida Keys, is enjoying its busiest days since 1890, when it was the largest city in Florida. Key West is noted for its nineteenth-century gingerbread houses, first introduced to the island by Bahamian settlers. It is also a city of Cuban foods and dialects that have been assimilated into the culture since the time of the big cigar industry, almost a century ago.

Perhaps Ponce de Leon was the first to spot the island, but Florida Indians often made their way here to trade or battle. The original name was "Cayo Hueso," Spanish for Bone Island. English, Bahamians, Cubans, New Englanders and Southerners came to settle here and prospered from salvaging wrecked ships, cigarmaking, sponge gathering, turtling, shrimping and fishing.

Following its early burst of prosperity, the city went bankrupt in the 1930s; an ambitious rehabilitation program was ended by the hurricane that wiped out the Overseas Railroad. However, completion of the Overseas Highway in 1938, along the existing route of the defunct railroad, signaled the start of Key West's present-day affluence. Today, tourism, followed by shrimping and fishing, sustain the economy.

What to See and Do

Audubon House and Gardens. Gracious antebellum house of sea captain and wrecker John Geiger contains outstanding collection of 18th- and 19th-century furnishings and re-creates the ambiance of the exciting early days of Key West, when Audubon visited the island. Many of the artist's original engravings on display. Admission includes audio cassette tape for self-guided tour. (Daily) 205 Whitehead St, at Greene St. Phone 305/294-2116. ¢¢¢

Curry Mansion (1899). A 26-rm Victorian mansion built for the son of Florida's first millionaire; original Audubon prints, period antiques and Tiffany glass; Ernest Hemingway's elephant gun. Self-guided tours. Guest rooms avail (see INNS). (Daily) 511 Caroline St. Phone 305/294-5349. Tours ¢¢

Dry Tortugas National Park (see). 68 mi W, reached by seasonal boat or seaplane; contact chamber of commerce for information.

East Martello Gallery and Museum. Housed in well-preserved fort constructed in 1861. Changing art exhibits; permanent exhibits depicting history of Florida Keys; antique collections; tropical courtyard garden. Lookout tower. (Daily; closed Dec 25) 3501 S Roosevelt Blvd (FL A1A), at NE end of island. Phone 305/296-3913. ¢¢¢

★ **Ernest Hemingway House Museum** (1851). Spanish-Colonial-style house of native stone purchased in 1931 by Hemingway, an early "discoverer" of Key West who wrote many of his books here, including *For Whom the Bell Tolls* and *The Snows of Kilimanjaro.* Original furnishings, memorabilia; trees and plants from the Caribbean and other parts of the world, most collected and planted by Hemingway. (Daily) 907 Whitehead St. Phone 305/294-1575. ¢¢¢

Fishing. These are some of the best fishing waters in the world. From bridge catwalks, docks, small boats or from many charter boats (fee). Launching ramps at Garrison Bight (fee).

Harry S Truman Little White House. Vacation home of the 33rd president, who spent eleven working vacations in Key West between 1946-

1952. Restored to period with original Truman furnishings. Guided tours; video. (Daily) 111 Front St. Phone 305/294-9911. ¢¢¢

Key West Aquarium. Unique and colorful specimens of sea life from the Gulf of Mexico and the Atlantic Ocean; "touch tank" allows visitors to touch and examine live starfish, horseshoe crabs, sea squirts, sea urchins, conchs and more; watch sharks being hand fed. Guided, narrated tours. (Daily) Whitehead & Front Sts. Phone 305/296-2051. ¢¢¢

Key West Lighthouse Museum. Exhibits depicting the unique maritime history of the Florida Keys. Tower is open to the public. (Daily; closed Dec 25) 938 Whitehead St. Phone 305/294-0012. ¢¢¢

Sightseeing and cruises.

Personalized Tours of Key West and the Keys. Two to three-hr personalized auto or walking tours; also step-on guided bus tours. (Daily) Phone 305/292-8687. ¢¢¢¢

Conch Tour Train. 14-mi narrated tour (1½ hrs) of the island on a trackless train visiting more than 100 sites. (Daily) No pets. Board at Mallory Square Depot, Roosevelt Blvd Depot or Land's End Marina. Phone 305/294-5161. ¢¢¢¢

Old Town Trolley. Narrated, 1½-hour tours of Key West. Departs every 30 min from Mallory Square Depot. (Daily) Phone 305/296-6688. ¢¢¢¢¢

Captain's Corner Charters. Snorkeling (equipment provided), scuba diving, fishing charters; sea planes to Dry Tortugas National Park (see). At foot of Duval St, behind Ocean Key House Hotel. Phone 305/296-8865. ¢¢¢¢

Reef cruises. Two-hr trips in glass-bottom sightseeing boats *Fireball* and *Pride of Key West* from Gulf to ocean over coral reef. Sunset cruises avail. (Daily, weather permitting) From N end of Duval St. For reservations, phone 305/296-6293. ¢¢¢¢¢

Sunset Celebration—Mallory Pier. A roisterous mixture of carnival mid-way and street-theater entertainment by scores of jugglers, magicians, sword-swallowers and others that draws crowds of spectators each night, especially in season. (Nightly, beginning about 2 hrs before sunset until 2 hrs after). 1 blk from end of Duval St.

Swimming. Public areas include Higgs Beach, between White & Reynolds Sts; Smathers Beach, on S Roosevelt Blvd.

Wrecker's Museum (ca 1830). The Oldest House in Key West, built with a unique "conch" construction. Once the house of sea captain and wrecker Francis B. Watlington, the museum now houses displays of Key West's wrecking industry, historic documents, ship models, toys, antiques, furnished 1850s doll house. Also old kitchen house and large garden. (Daily) 322 Duval St. Phone 305/294-9502. ¢¢

Annual Event

Old Island Days. A series of 10 different events that include house and garden tours; orchid & art shows and a conch shell-blowing contest. Contact Old Island Restoration Foundation, PO Box 689, 33041; 305/294-9501. May-Nov.

Motels

★ ★ **BEST WESTERN HIBISCUS.** *1313 Simonton St.* 305/294-3763; FAX 305/293-9243. E-mail hib1313@aol.com. 61 rms, 2 story. Late Dec-Mar; S, D $99-$219; higher rates: hols, Dec 25, Fantasy Fest; lower rates rest of yr. Crib avail. TV; cable. Heated pool. Complimentary continental bkfst. Restaurant opp 7 am-10 pm. Ck-out 11 am. Business servs avail. Refrigerators. Cr cds: A, C, D, DS, ER, MC, V.

D ≈ 🔥 SC

★ ★ **BEST WESTERN KEY AMBASSADOR.** *3755 S Roosevelt Blvd (FL A1A), near Intl Airport.* 305/296-3500; res: 800/432-4315; FAX 305/296-9961. E-mail keyambbw@aol.com; web www.key ambassador.com. 100 rms, 2 story. Dec-Mar; S, D $159-$209; each addl $15; higher rates: hols, special events; lower rates rest of yr. Crib free. TV; cable. Heated pool; poolside serv. Complimentary continental bkfst. Restaurant nearby. Ck-out noon. Coin lndry. Free airport transportation. Lawn

games. Refrigerators. Private screened balconies. Picnic tables, grills. Cr cds: A, C, D, DS, MC, V.

≈ ✈ 🔥 SC

★ ★ **BLUE MARLIN.** *1320 Simonton St.* 305/294-2585; FAX 305/296-1209; res: 800/523-1698 (exc FL), 800/826-5303 (FL). 53 units, 2 story, 10 kits. Late Dec-Apr: S, D $129-$155; kit. units $7-$10 addl (3-night min); under 10 free; higher rates: hols, special events; lower rates rest of yr. Crib $7. TV; cable. Heated pool. Complimentary coffee. Restaurant nearby. Ck-out 11 am. Refrigerators. Cr cds: A, C, D, DS, MC, V.

≈ 🔥 SC

✔ ★ **ECONO LODGE.** *3820 N Roosevelt Blvd (US 1).* 305/294-5511; res: 800/766-7584; FAX 305/296-1939. Web key-west.com//accom/ econo.htm. 145 rms, 6 story, 17 kits. Mid-Dec-late Apr: S, D $119-$325; each addl $10; under 18 free; higher rates: hols, special events; lower rates rest of yr. Crib free. TV; cable. Pool. Restaurant open 24 hrs. Bar. Ck-out 11 am. Coin lndry. Business servs avail. Cr cds: A, C, D, DS, ER, JCB, MC, V.

≈ ⊠ 🔥 SC

★ ★ **HAMPTON INN.** *2801 N Roosevelt Blvd (US 1).* 305/294-2917; FAX 305/296-0221. 159 rms, 2 story. Jan-Apr: S, D $159-$179; under 18 free; higher rates: hols, some special events; lower rates rest of yr. Crib free. TV; cable (premium). Heated pool; whirlpool. Complimentary continental bkfst. Bar noon-11 pm. Ck-out noon. Coin lndry. Gift shop. Some covered parking. Health club privileges. Two-level sun deck overlooking bay. Cr cds: A, C, D, DS, MC, V.

D ≈ ⊠ 🔥 SC

★ ★ ★ **HOLIDAY INN-BEACHSIDE.** *3841 N Roosevelt Blvd (US 1), near Intl Airport.* 305/294-2571; res: 800/292-7706; FAX 305/296-5659. E-mail db_wright@msn.com. 222 rms, 2-3 story. Late Dec-Apr: S, D $169-$265; each addl $10; higher rates: some hols, special events; lower rates rest of yr. Crib free. TV; cable. Pool; whirlpool, poolside bar. Restaurant 7 am-2 pm, 5-10 pm. Rm serv 7 am-10 pm. Bar 11-1 am. Ck-out 11 am. Meeting rms. Lighted tennis. Gift shop. Exercise equipt. Some refrigerators. Private sunning beach; water sport equipt avail. Cr cds: A, C, D, DS, JCB, MC, V.

D ➤ 🐎 ≈ ✈ ⊠ 🔥 SC

★ **HOWARD JOHNSON.** *3031 N Roosevelt Blvd (US 1).* 305/296-6595; FAX 305/296-8351. 64 rms, 2 story. Late Dec-late Apr: S, D $109-$229; each addl $10; under 18 free; higher rates: hols, special events; lower rates rest of yr. Crib free. TV; cable. Pool. Restaurant 6 am-10 pm. Ck-out 11 am. Health club privileges. Private patios, balconies. Courtyard. On Gulf. Cr cds: A, C, D, DS, JCB, MC, V.

≈ 🔥 SC

★ **KEY LODGE.** *1004 Duval St.* 305/296-9915; res: 800/458-1296. 24 rms, 6 kit. units. Mid-Dec-Apr: S, D $140-$163; each addl $15; kit. units $145-$163; higher rates: hols, special events; lower rates rest of yr. Pet accepted; $10/day. TV; cable. Heated pool. Restaurant nearby. Ck-out 11 am. Refrigerators. Cr cds: A, DS, MC, V.

➤ ≈ 🔥

★ ★ **QUALITY INN.** *3850 N Roosevelt Blvd (US 1).* 305/294-6681; res: 800/533-5024; FAX 305/294-5618. E-mail qualityikw@aol.com; web www.travelbase.com/destination/keywest/quality-inn/. 148 rms, 2-4 story. Jan-mid-Apr: S, D $144-$260; each addl $10-$20; kit. units, apts $159-$230; under 18 free; higher rates: hols, special events; lower rates rest of yr. Crib free. TV; cable (premium). Pool. Coffee in rms. Restaurant 6 am-midnight. Rm serv 7 am-10:30 pm. Bar 11:30-2 am. Ck-out 11 am. Coin lndry. Cr cds: A, C, D, DS, ER, JCB, MC, V.

D ≈ ⊠ 🔥

✔ ★ **SANTA MARIA.** *1401 Simonton St, at South St.* 305/296-5678; FAX 305/294-0010; res: 800/821-5397. 51 rms, 2 story, 16 kits. Late Dec-late Apr: S, D $99-$160; each addl $20; kit. units $99-$155; under 12 free; higher rates special events; Dec 25; lower rates rest of yr. Crib $10.

TV; cable. Pool. Restaurant nearby. Bar. Ck-out noon. Balconies. Cr cds: A, C, D, DS, JCB, MC, V.

★ **SOUTH BEACH-OCEANFRONT.** *508 South St. 305/296-5611; FAX 305/294-8272; res: 800/354-4455. Web www.oldtownresorts.com.* 47 rms, 2 story. Mid-Dec-mid-Apr: S $105; D $158-$197; kit. units $170-$197; each addl $10; lower rates rest of yr. Crib free. TV; cable. Pool. Restaurant nearby. Ck-out 11 am. On ocean; pier. Cr cds: A, MC, V.

★ **SOUTHERNMOST.** *1319 Duval St. 305/296-6577; FAX 305/294-8272; res: 800/354-4455. E-mail lamer508@aol.com; web www.oldtownresorts.com.* 127 units, 2-3 story. Late Dec-early Apr: S $105; D $132-$199; each addl $45; lower rates rest of yr. Crib free. TV; cable. 2 heated pools; whirlpool, poolside serv. Bar. Ck-out 11 am. Meeting rm. Concierge. Bicycle rentals. Ocean ½ blk. Cr cds: A, MC, V.

★ **SUGAR LOAF LODGE.** *(Box 148, Sugar Loaf Key 33044) 13 mi NE on Overseas Hwy (US 1), at mile marker 17. 305/745-3211; res: 800/553-6047; FAX 305/745-3389.* 55 rms. 11 kits. Mid-Dec-Apr: S $105; D $110; each addl $10; kit. units $120; under 12 free; lower rates rest of yr. Crib $5. Pet accepted; $10/day. TV; cable. Pool. Restaurant 7:30 am-9 pm. Rm serv. Bar; entertainment Fri-Sat. Ck-out 11 am, ck-in 1 pm. Grocery. Coin lndry. Tennis. Miniature golf. Lawn games. Balconies. Marina; charter boats. Cr cds: A, C, D, DS, MC, V.

Motor Hotels

★ ★ **HOLIDAY INN-LA CONCHA.** *430 Duval St. 305/296-2991; res: 800/745-2191; FAX 305/294-3283. Web laconcha@compuserve.com.* 160 units, 7 story. Mid-Dec-early Apr: S, D $175-$250; each addl $15; suites $175-$300; under 17 free; higher rates special events; lower rates rest of yr. Crib free. TV; cable (premium). Pool; poolside serv. Restaurant 7 am-10 pm. Rm serv. Bar 10-2 am; entertainment. Ck-out 11 am. Meeting rms. Business center. In-rm modem link. Bellhops. Concierge. Gift shop. Free parking. Some balconies. 1920s decor. Cr cds: A, C, D, DS, JCB, MC, V.

★ ★ ★ **OCEAN KEY HOUSE.** *0 Duval St. 305/296-7701; FAX 305/292-7685; res: 800/328-9815. E-mail info@oceankeyhouse; web www.keywest.com/okh.* 100 rms, 5 story. 64 kit. units. Late Dec-mid-Apr: S, D $160; kit. units $340-$700; under 16 free; wkly rates; higher rates hols (2-5 day min), special events; lower rates rest of yr. Crib avail. Garage. TV; cable, VCR (movies). Heated pool; poolside serv. Restaurant 7 am-10 pm. Rm serv. Bar; entertainment. Ck-out noon. Meeting rm. In-rm modem link. Bellhops. Concierge. Sundries. Minibars in kit. units. On ocean. Near airport. Cr cds: A, C, D, DS, MC, V.

★ ★ ★ **PIER HOUSE.** *1 Duval St. 305/296-4600; FAX 305/296-9085; res: 800/327-8340. E-mail phresort@conch.net; web www.pier house.com.* 142 rms, 2 story, 14 suites. Mid-Dec-late Apr: S, D $280-$450; each addl $35; suites $450-$1,500; lower rates rest of yr. Crib free. TV; cable, VCR avail (movies). Heated pool; poolside serv. Restaurant 7:30 am-10 pm. Rm serv. Bars; entertainment. Ck-out noon. Meeting rms. Business servs avail. In-rm modem link. Bellhops. Concierge. Sundries. Gift shop. Beauty shop. Exercise rm; sauna. Massage therapy. Minibars. Private patios, balconies. Private beach; fishing, sailboat charters. Bicycle, moped rentals. Unusual architecture, in Old Town Key West. Cr cds: A, C, D, DS, ER, JCB, MC, V.

Hotels

★ ★ ★ **HILTON RESORT AND MARINA.** *245 Front St. 305/294-4000; res: 888/477-7786; FAX 305/294-4086.* 178 rms, 4 story, 33 suites.

Dec-late Apr: S, D $289-$389; each addl $20; suites $450-$650; under 18 free; wkend rates; higher rates special events; lower rates rest of yr. Crib free. Garage parking $8. TV; cable (premium). Pool; whirlpool, poolside serv. Complimentary coffee in rms. Restaurant 7 am-11 pm. Bar 11-2 am. Ck-out 11 am. Coin lndry. Meeting rms. Business center. In-rm modem link. Concierge. Shopping arcade. Exercise rm. Minibars; some refrigerators. Balconies. On beach. Cr cds: A, C, D, DS, ER, JCB, MC, V.

★ ★ ★ **HYATT.** *601 Front St. 305/296-9900; FAX 305/292-1038. Web www.hyatt.com.* 120 rms, 4 story. Mid-Dec-mid-Apr: S, D $285; each addl $45; suites $445; under 18 free; lower rates rest of yr. Valet parking $6. TV; cable. Heated pool; whirlpool, poolside serv. Restaurant 7 am-10 pm. Bar 11 am-midnight. Ck-out noon. Meeting rms. In-rm modem link. Concierge. Gift shop. Exercise equipt. Refrigerators. Balconies. Bicycle, moped rentals. Sailboat, fishing boat, wave-runner rentals. On gulf; swimming beach. Cr cds: A, C, D, DS, ER, JCB, MC, V.

★ ★ ★ **MARRIOTT REACH.** *1435 Simonton St. 305/296-5000; FAX 305/296-2830; res: 800/874-4118. E-mail reach@key-west.com; web www.key-west.com/reach01.html.* 150 units, 4-5 story, 79 suites. Mid-Dec-mid-Apr: S, D $294-$330; suites $335-$490; under 18 free; lower rates rest of yr. Crib free. TV; cable (premium). Heated pool; whirlpool. Restaurants 7 am-11 pm. Bars; entertainment. Ck-out 11 am. Meeting rms. Business servs avail. In-rm modem link. Concierge. Gift shop. Free covered parking. Exercise rm; sauna, steam rm. Refrigerators; minibar in suites. Private patios, balconies. On ocean beach, with pier; sailboats, windsurfing, snorkeling. Traditional Key West architecture. Cr cds: A, C, D, DS, MC, V.

Inns

★ ★ **ARTIST HOUSE.** *534 Eaton St. 305/296-3977; FAX 305/296-3210; res: 800/582-7882. E-mail artisthse@aol.com; web members.aol.com/artisthse.* 6 rms, 2 story, 4 suites. Mid-Dec-mid-Apr: S, D $145; suites $185-$250; lower rates rest of yr. Children over 12 yrs only. TV; cable, VCR avail (movies). Complimentary continental bkfst. Restaurant nearby. Ck-out 11 am, ck-in 2 pm. Whirlpool. Some balconies. Queen Anne/Victorian mansion, former residence of Key West artist Gene Otto (1890); Oriental rugs. Botanical garden in courtyard. Cr cds: A, D, DS, MC, V.

★ ★ **BLUE PARROT INN.** *916 Elizabeth St. 305/296-0033; res: 800/231-2473; FAX 305/296-5697. Web www.blueparrotinn.com.* 10 rms, 7 with shower only, 2 story. Mid-Dec-Apr: S, D $105-$165; each addl $15; 3-5-day min (wkends, hols); higher rates special events; lower rates rest of yr. Children over 16 yrs only. TV. Complimentary continental bkfst. Restaurant nearby. Ck-out 11 am, ck-in 2 pm. Street parking. Bicycle rentals. Pool. Bathrm phones; many refrigerators. Built in 1884 originally as a private mansion; tropical garden. Cr cds: A, C, D, DS, MC, V.

★ ★ ★ **CENTER COURT.** *916 Center St. 305/296-9292; res: 800/797-8787; FAX 305/294-4104. E-mail centerct@aol.com; web www.center courtkw.com.* 16 rms, 6 with shower only, 1-2 story, 5 suites, 7 kit. units, 1 guest house. Mid-Dec-Apr: S, D $128-$208; each addl $15; suites $178-$208; kit. units $178-$298; guest house $168-$298; 3-7 day min (wkends, hols); higher rates Fantasy Fest; lower rates rest of yr. Crib free. Pet accepted, some restrictions; $10. TV; cable, VCR avail (movies). Complimentary continental bkfst. Restaurant nearby. Ck-out 11 am, ck-in 3 pm. Business servs avail. In-rm modem link. Concierge serv. Street parking. Exercise equipt. Pool; whirlpool. Many refrigerators, microwaves. Built in 1880; local art, tropical foliage. Totally nonsmoking. Cr cds: A, DS, MC, V.

★ ★ ★ **CURRY MANSION.** *511 Caroline St. 305/294-5349; FAX 305/294-4093; res: 800/253-3466. E-mail frontdesk@currymansion.com; web www.currymansion.com.* 28 rms, 2 story. Mid-Dec-mid-Apr: S, D

$160-$275; lower rates rest of yr. TV; cable (premium), VCR avail. Heated pool. Complimentary continental bkfst in courtyard. Restaurant nearby. Pianist. Ck-out 11 am, ck-in 2 pm. Business servs avail. Health club privileges. Refrigerators. Some balconies. Beach access. Victorian-style structure adjoining original mansion (1899); wicker furniture, antiques, sitting rm. Cr cds: A, C, D, DS, JCB, MC, V.

★ ★ **DUVAL HOUSE.** *815 Duval St. 305/294-1666; FAX 305/292-1701; res: 800/223-8825.* Web kwflorida.com/duvalhse.html. 30 rms, 2 story, 3 kit. suites. Dec-Apr: S, D $145-$260; each addl $10; lower rates rest of yr. Children over 12 yrs only. TV in some rms, sitting rm. Pool. Complimentary continental bkfst. Restaurant nearby. Ck-out 11 am, ck-in 3 pm. Private patios, balconies. Historic 1880 Victorian houses; antiques, wicker, individually decorated rms. Cr cds: A, D, DS, JCB, MC, V.

★ ★ **EATON LODGE.** *511 Eaton St, near Intl Airport. 305/292-2170; FAX 305/292-4018; res: 800/294-2170.* Web www.eatonlodge.com. 16 rms, 2-3 story, 3 suites, 3 kit. units. Mid-Dec-mid-Apr: S, D $135-$185; each addl $25; suites $185-$425; kit. units $185-$425; family, wkly rates; higher rates special events; lower rates rest of yr. Adults only. Parking $5. TV; cable. Pool; whirlpool. Complimentary continental bkfst. Restaurant nearby. Ck-out 11 am, ck-in 2 pm. Luggage handling. Concierge serv. Some refrigerators. Balconies. Main House built in 1886 is a fully restored Victorian mansion. Private garden with winding paths and fish pond. Cr cds: A, DS, MC, V.

★ ★ **FRANCES STREET BOTTLE INN.** *535 Frances St. 305/294-8530; FAX 305/294-1628; res: 800/294-8530.* E-mail bottle inn@aol.com; web www.bottleinn.com. 7 rms, 6 with shower only, 2 story. Mid-Dec-Apr (2-5-day min stay): S, D $135-$155; each addl $15; under 12 free; wkend, hol rates; higher rates special events; lower rates rest of yr. Crib free. Pet accepted. TV; cable (premium). Whirlpool. Complimentary continental bkfst. Complimentary coffee in library. Restaurant nearby. Ck-out 11 am, ck-in 2 pm. Balconies. Picnic tables. Victorian conch house built in 1890. Collection of antique bottles and underseas articles. Totally nonsmoking. Cr cds: A, MC, V.

★ ★ ★ **HERON HOUSE.** *512 Simonton St. 305/294-9227; FAX 305/294-5692; res: 800/294-1644.* E-mail heronkyw@aol.com; web fla-keys. com/heronhouse. 23 rms in 4 bldgs, 1-2 story. Dec-Apr: S, D $159-$289; higher rates: hols, Fantasy Fest; lower rates rest of yr. Children over 16 yrs only. Some TV. Pool. Complimentary continental bkfst. Restaurant nearby. Ck-out 11 am, ck-in flexible. Balconies. 3 historical houses (1876); orchid garden. Cr cds: A, C, D, MC, V.

★ ★ **ISLAND CITY HOUSE.** *411 William St. 305/294-5702; FAX 305/294-1289; res: 800/634-8230 (exc FL).* Web www.islandcity house.com. 24 kit. suites, 2-3 story. Late-Dec-late-Apr: kit. suites $165-$285; each addl $20; under 12 free; wkly rates; higher rates: some hols, special events; lower rates rest of yr. TV; VCR avail. Pool; whirlpool. Complimentary continental bkfst. Restaurant nearby. Ck-out 11 am, ck-in 2 pm. Street parking. Balconies. Grills. Houses built in 1880s. Cr cds: A, C, D, DS, MC, V.

✔★ **KEY WEST BED & BREAKFAST.** *415 William St. 305/296-7274; FAX 305/293-0306; res: 800/438-6155.* Web www.key westbandb.com. 8 rms, 4 with bath, 3 story. No rm phones. MAP, mid-Dec-Apr: S $79; D $99-$250; wkly rates in summer; higher rates special events; lower rates rest of yr. Adults only. Complimentary continental bkfst. Restaurants nearby. Ck-out 11 am, ck-in 2-6 pm. Concierge. Street parking. Whirlpool. Sauna. Balconies. Sun decks. Built by shipbuilders (1890). Cr cds: A, C, D, DS, ER, MC, V.

★ ★ **LA MER.** *506 South St. 305/296-5611; FAX 305/294-8272; res: 800/354-4455.* Web lamer508@aol.com. 11 rms, 2 story, 5 kits. Late Dec-Apr: S, D $180-$310, kit. units $240-$310; lower rates rest of yr. Children over 18 yrs only. TV; cable. Pool privileges adj. Complimentary continental bkfst. Restaurant nearby. Ck-out 11 am, ck-in 2 pm. Private balconies, porches. On ocean. Cr cds: A, MC, V.

★ ★ ★ **THE MARQUESA.** *600 Fleming St. 305/292-1919; FAX 305/294-2121; res: 800/869-4631.* Web www.marquesa.com. 27 rms, 2-3 story. No elvtr. Mid-Dec-mid-Apr: S, D $225-$260; suites $325; each addl $20; higher rates some hols; lower rates rest of yr. Children over 12 yrs only. TV; cable. Heated pools. Dining rm (see CAFÉ MARQUESA). Rm serv. Bar. Ck-out noon, ck-in 3 pm. Business servs avail. Bellhops. Valet serv. Concierge. Health club privileges. Minibars. Balconies. Greek-revival architecture. Antiques. Furnishings are a mixture of traditional and tropical. Cr cds: A, D, MC, V.

Resorts

★ ★ ★ ★ **LITTLE PALM ISLAND.** *(28500 Overseas Hwy, Little Torch Key 33042) Accessible only by boat, helicopter or seaplane. A launch to the island departs from the shore station at Little Torch Key, located 28 mi N on Overseas Hwy (US 1) at mile marker 28.5. Pickup service is also avail from the airports in both Key West and Marathon. 305/872-2524; FAX 305/872-4843; res: 800/343-8567.* E-mail getlost@ littlepalmisland.com; web www.littlepalmisland.com. On beautifully land-scaped, palm-fringed Little Munson Island, once a retreat and fishing camp that hosted many a luminary, this small luxury resort consists of an old cypress fishing lodge and thatch-roof villas that stand on stilts 20 feet from the water. Views from the terrace at sunset are spectacular. 28 suites in 14 villas and 1 in greathouse. No rm phones. Mid-Dec-Apr: S, D $595-$650; 2-day min hols; AP, MAP avail; lower rates rest of yr. Children over 16 yrs only. TV; VCR avail (movies). Heated pool; poolside serv. Complimentary coffee in rms. Dining rm 8:30-10 am, 11:30 am-2:30 pm, 7-9:30 pm. Picnics. Rm serv. Bar; entertainment Thurs-Sun. Ck-out 11 am, ck-in 3 pm. Bellhops. Valet serv. Business servs avail. Concierge. Gift shop. Airport transportation. Sports dir. Sailing cruises, boat rentals, scuba trips, swimming beach. Social dir. Exercise equipt; sauna. Massage. Fishing guides; clean & store. Minibars, wet bars. Balconies. Picnic tables. Herb garden. The island is a 15-minute boat ride from Little Torch Key; the launch makes the trip each way once an hour. White sand beach; water sports; nature tours. Dockage avail for 3 deep-draft yachts and 8 shallow-draft boats; complete marine center. Cr cds: A, C, D, DS, MC, V.

★ ★ ★ **MARRIOTT'S CASA MARINA.** *1500 Reynolds St, near Intl Airport. 305/296-3535; FAX 305/296-4633.* E-mail mkwr@ bell south.com; web www.marriott.com. 312 rms. Mid-Dec-mid-Apr: S, D $150-$325; suites $330-$720; under 18 free; lower rates rest of yr. Crib free. Valet parking $9. TV; cable, VCR avail (movies). Heated pools; whirlpool. Free supervised child's activities. Restaurant (see FLAGLER'S). Rm serv 24 hrs (in season). Bar 11-2 am; entertainment. Ck-out 11 am, ck-in 4 pm. Convention facilities. Business servs avail. In-rm modem link. Concierge. Free airport transportation. Lighted tennis, pro. Exercise rm. Sailboats, sailboards. Charter boat, snorkeling & scuba diving trips arranged. Bicycle & moped rentals. Refrigerators. On ocean. Cr cds: A, C, D, DS, JCB, MC, V.

Restaurants

★ ★ ★ **ANTONIA'S.** *615 Duval St. 305/294-6565.* Hrs: 6-10 pm. Closed Thanksgiving. Res accepted. Regional Italian menu. Bar. Wine list. A la carte entrees: dinner $12-$24. Specializes in regional Italian cuisine, local seafood. Own pasta. Family-owned since 1979. Cr cds: A, C, MC, V.

★ ★ **BAGATELLE.** *115 Duval St.* 305/296-6609. Hrs: 11:30 am-3 pm, 5:30-10 pm. Closed Thanksgiving, Dec 25. Res accepted. Caribbean menu. Bars. Semi-a la carte: lunch $6-$12.95, dinner $14.95-$28.95. Specialties: snapper Rangoon, Bahamian conch steak, Jamaican chicken. Outdoor dining. In sea captain's house (1884) in Old Town Key West. Cr cds: A, D, DS, MC, V.

★ ★ **BENIHANA.** *3591 S Roosevelt Blvd (US 1).* 305/294-6400. Hrs: 5:30-10 pm; Fri, Sat to 10:30 pm. Res accepted. Japanese, Amer menu. Bar. Complete meals: dinner $12.95-$27.50. Child's meals. Specializes in steak & seafood prepared tableside. Parking. Japanese decor, artifacts. Garden. Ocean view. Cr cds: A, C, D, DS, MC, V.

★ ★ ★ **CAFE DES ARTISTES.** *1007 Simonton St.* 305/294-7100. Hrs: 6-11 pm. Res accepted. French menu. Bar. A la carte entrees: dinner $23.95-$38.95. Specializes in seafood. Outdoor dining. Cr cds: A, MC, V.

★ ★ ★ **CAFÉ MARQUESA.** *(See The Marquesa Inn)* 305/292-1244. Hrs: 6-11 pm; May-Oct from 7 pm. Res accepted. Bar. Wine list. A la carte entrees: dinner $18-$30. Specializes in fresh local seafood. Parking. Intimate dining area; trompe l'oiel mural on one wall. Totally nonsmoking. Cr cds: A, D, MC, V.

🅳

★ ★ ★ **FLAGLER'S.** *(See Marriott's Casa Marina Resort)* 305/296-3535. Hrs: 7 am-2:30 pm, 6-10:30 pm; Sun brunch 11 am-2 pm. Res accepted. Bar. A la carte entrees: bkfst $5.50-$13.95, lunch $10-$12, dinner $19-$30. Sun brunch $25.95. Child's meals. Specializes in steak, Caribbean seafood. Entertainment. Valet parking. Outdoor dining. Cr cds: A, C, D, DS, MC, V.

🅳 ♥

★ **HALF SHELL RAW BAR.** *231 Margaret St, Lands End Village.* 305/294-7496. Hrs: 11 am-10:30 pm; Sun from noon. Bar. Semi-a la carte: lunch, dinner $5.95-$21.95. Specialties: conch chowder, stone crab claws. Parking. Outdoor dining. Dock. Cr cds: DS, MC, V.

★ ★ ★ **HARBOR VIEW CAFE.** *1 Duval St.* 305/296-4600, ext. 550. Hrs: 7:30 am-10:30 pm. Bar. A la carte entrees: bkfst $6-$12, lunch $7.50-$24, dinner $15-$24. Specializes in fresh local seafood. Guitarist, vocalist (dinner). Outdoor dining overlooking beach, gulf. Cr cds: A, C, D, DS, ER, JCB, MC, V.

🅳

★ ★ **KELLY'S CARIBBEAN.** *301 Whitehead St.* 305/293-8484. Hrs: 11-1 am; Sat, Sun from noon. Caribbean, Amer menu. Bar. Semi-a la carte: lunch $6.50-$10, dinner $9.50-$21.95. Child's meals. Specializes in fresh seafood, beef. Outdoor dining areas include shaded garden & treetop dining. Former Pan American Airways ticket office. Cr cds: A, D, MC, V.

🅳

★ ★ **LOUIE'S BACKYARD.** *700 Waddell Ave.* 305/294-1061. Hrs: 11:30 am-3 pm, 6-10:30 pm; Apr-Oct 11:30 am-3 pm, 6:30-11 pm. Closed Dec 25. Res accepted. Bar. A la carte entrees: lunch $9.50-$16, dinner $27-$35. Specializes in fresh local seafood. Outdoor dining. On oceanfront. Built by early Key West wrecker (1909). Cr cds: A, D, MC, V.

🅳

★ ★ **MARTHA'S.** *3591 S Roosevelt Blvd (FL A1A).* 305/294-3466. Hrs: 5:30-10 pm; Fri, Sat to 10:30 pm. Res accepted. Continental menu. Bar. Semi-a la carte: dinner $13-$27. Child's meals. Specializes in steak, fresh local seafood. Pianist. Parking. Outdoor dining. Overlooks ocean. Cr cds: A, C, D, DS, MC, V.

🅳

✔★ ★ **YO SAKE.** *722 Duval St.* 305/294-2288. Hrs: 6-11 pm. Res accepted. Japanese menu. A la carte entrees: dinner $14-$20. Specialties: tai hei yo, beef yakiniku. Sushi bar. Outdoor dining. Contemporary Japanese decor. Cr cds: A, D, JCB, MC, V.

Kissimmee (E-5)

(See also Haines City, Orlando, Winter Haven)

Pop 30,050 **Elev** 65 ft **Area code** 407

Information Kissimmee-St Cloud Convention and Visitors Bureau, 1925 E Irlo Bronson Memorial Hwy, PO Box 422007, 34742-2007; 407/847-5000 or 800/327-9159.

Although this has been cattle country for more than 75 years (Brahma cattle are raised here), Kissimmee is now known as the gateway to Walt Disney World and several other central Florida attractions.

What to See and Do

Flying Tigers Warbird Restoration Air Museum. Restoration projects, exhibits and hands-on displays of World War II aircraft; bombers, early primary and advanced training aircraft; antique planes. (Daily) 231 N Hoagland Blvd. Phone 407/933-1942. ¢¢¢

Gatorland. More than 5,000 alligators, plus other animals. Snakes of Florida, Gator Jumparoo and Gator Wrestlin' shows; walkway through natural cypress swamp; alligator breeding marsh with three-story observation tower. (Daily) 4 mi N on US 17/92/441. Phone 407/855-5496. ¢¢¢¢

Green Meadows Petting Farm. Two-hr guided tours encourage hands-on experience with more than 200 farm animals, cows for milking, hay rides, pony rides, free pumpkins in Oct. (Daily; closed Thanksgiving, Dec 25) 5 mi S of US 192 on Ponciana Blvd. Phone 407/846-0770. ¢¢¢¢

JungleLand. Assortment of exotic animals and alligators in seven-acre wildlife park. Trail. (Daily) 4 mi W on US 192. Phone 407/396-1012. ¢¢¢

Medieval Life. Living museum of the Middle Ages features thatched-roofed buildings set along cobblestone streets; demonstrations by tradesmen and artisans, medieval artifacts, replicas of torture chamber and devices, dungeon. (Daily) On US 192, E of US 17/92. Phone 407/396-1518 or 407/239-0214 (Orlando). ¢¢¢¢¢

Old Town. Replica turn-of-the-century Florida village with brick-lined streets; specialty shops and restaurants; general store; antique hand-carved wooden carousel, Ferris wheel, Windstorm rollercoaster and Kids Town with 10 rides (fees). (Daily) 7 mi W on US 192. Phone 407/396-4888. **Free.**

Reptile World Serpentarium. Indoor reptile displays; observation of venom laboratories with 1,500 specimens; 3 scheduled venom programs. (Daily exc Mon; closed Thanksgiving, Dec 25, also Sept) E on US 192, 4 mi E of St Cloud. Phone 407/892-6905. ¢¢

Walt Disney World (see). 10 mi NW on US 192.

Water Mania. A 38-acre water theme park featuring raft rides, 72-ft free-fall slide, speed slides, flumes and surfing ride; wave pool; kiddie slide area. Also beach; volleyball courts; miniature golf; picnicking; locker room, showers; first-aid station. (Jan-Nov, daily) On US 192, 1 mi E of I-4. Phone 407/239-8448 or 407/396-2626. ¢¢¢¢¢

Annual Events

Silver Spurs Rodeo. Silver Spurs Arena. Phone 407/67-RODEO. Feb & July.

Bluegrass Festival. Silver Spurs Arena. Mar.

Boating Jamboree. Late Oct.

Seasonal Event

Spring training. Osceola County Stadium, 1000 Bill Beck Blvd. Houston Astros baseball spring training, exhibition games. Phone 407/933-5400. Early Mar-early Apr.

Motels

✔★ **BEST WESTERN.** 2261 E Irlo Bronson Memorial Hwy (34744). 407/846-2221; FAX 407/846-1095. E-mail eagle@phoenixat. com; web www.bestwesternkiss.com. 282 rms, 2-3 story, 9 kit. units. June-Aug: S, D $49.95-$99.95; kit. units $59.95-$109.95; under 19 free; hols (2-3-day min); higher rates Daytona 500; lower rates rest of yr. Crib $4. TV; cable (premium). Heated pool. Playground. Restaurant 7-11 am, 6-10:30 pm. Ck-out 11 am. Coin lndry. Meeting rms. Business servs avail. Gift shop. Free Walt Disney World transportation. Lawn games. Some refrigerators; microwaves avail. Cr cds: A, C, D, DS, MC, V.

🄳 ≋ ⊠ 🔥 SC

✔★ **BEST WESTERN MAINGATE.** 8600 W Irlo Bronson Memorial Hwy (US 192W) (34747). 407/396-0100; FAX 407/396-6718. 299 rms, 2 story. Mid-Feb-late Apr, June-Aug, late Dec: S, D $59-$99; lower rates rest of yr. Crib avail. TV; cable. Pool; wading pool. Restaurant 7-11 am. Ck-out 11 am. Coin lndry. Sundries. Gift shop. Game rm. Cr cds: A, C, D, DS, MC, V.

≋ ⊠ 🔥 SC

✔★★ **COMFORT INN-MAINGATE.** 7571 W Irlo Bronson Memorial Hwy (34747). 407/396-7500; res: 800/223-1628; FAX 407/396-7497. 281 rms, 2 story. S, D $35-$69; higher rates special events. Crib free. TV; cable. Restaurant 7-11 am, 5:30-10 pm. Bar 5 pm-2 am. Ck-out 11 am. Valet serv. Gift shop. Coin lndry. 18-hole golf privileges. Pool. Playground. Game rm. Some refrigerators. Cr cds: A, C, D, DS, ER, JCB, MC, V.

🄳 ≋ 🕴 ≋ ⊠ 🔥 SC

✔★★ **DAYS INN.** 7980 W Irlo Bronson Hwy (US 192) (34747), I-4, exit 25B. 407/396-1000; FAX 407/396-6542. 333 rms, 3 story. Mid-Feb-mid-Aug, late Dec: S, D $79-$159; under 18 free; lower rates rest of yr. Crib free. TV; cable (premium). Pool. Playground. Restaurant 7-11 am, 5:30-9:30 pm. Ck-out 11 am. Coin lndry. Business servs avail. Free Walt Disney World transportation. Exercise equipt. Game rm. Refrigerators; microwaves avail. Picnic tables. Cr cds: A, C, D, DS, ER, MC, V.

≋ 🕴 ≋ ⊠ 🔥 SC

★ **DAYS SUITES.** 5820 Irlo Bronson Memorial Hwy (US 192E) (34746). 407/396-7900; FAX 407/396-1789. Web www. thhotels. com. 603 kit. suites (1-2 bedrm), 2 story. S, D $79-$229. Crib free. TV; cable (premium). 3 pools. Playground. Restaurant 6:30 am-9:30 pm. Ck-out 11 am. Coin lndry. Business servs avail. Gift shop. Airport transportation. Game rm. Refrigerators, microwaves. Private patios, balconies. Picnic tables, grills. Cr cds: A, C, D, DS, ER, JCB, MC, V.

≋ ⊠ 🔥 SC

★ **ECONOMY INNS OF AMERICA.** 5367 W Irlo Bronson Hwy (US 192) (34746). 407/396-4020; FAX 407/396-5450. Web www.ins america.com. 195 rms, 2 story. Apr-Aug: S, D $44.90-$64.90; lower rates rest of yr. TV; cable (premium). Heated pool. Complimentary continental bkfst. Restaurant adj open 24 hrs. Ck-out 11 am. Business servs avail. Picnic tables. Cr cds: A, MC, V.

≋ ⊠ 🔥 SC

★★ **HAMPTON INN.** 3104 Parkway Blvd (34747). 407/396-8484; FAX 407/396-7344. 164 rms, 4 story. Feb-mid-May, mid-June-Aug: S, D $85-$95; under 18 free; higher rates Dec 25-Jan 2; lower rates rest of yr. Crib free. TV; cable (premium). Heated pool. Complimentary continental bkfst. Restaurant nearby. Ck-out 11 am. Health club privileges. Cr cds: A, C, D, DS, MC, V.

🄳 ≋ ⊠ 🔥 SC

✔★★ **HOLIDAY INN EXPRESS.** 2145 E Irlo Bronson Memorial Hwy (34744). 407/846-4646; FAX 407/932-2467. 146 rms, 2 story. S, D $49-$99; each addl $10; under 18 free. Crib free. TV; cable (premium). Pool; wading pool. Complimentary continental bkfst. Restaurant adj open 24 hrs. Ck-out 11 am. Coin lndry. Meeting rms. Business servs avail. Game rm. Cr cds: A, C, D, DS, MC, V.

🄳 ≋ ⊠ 🔥 SC

★★ **HOLIDAY INN HOTEL AND SUITES MAINGATE EAST.** 5678 Irlo Bronson Memorial Hwy (34746). 407/396-4488; res: 800/366-5437 direct national; FAX 407/396-8915. E-mail relax@familyfunhotel.com; web www.familyfunhotel.com. 614 rms, 2 story, 110 suites. Mid-Dec-early Jan, Mar-Apr, June-Aug: S, D $109-$130; suites $175-$225; under 18 free; Easter, Dec 25 (some restrictions); higher rates Daytona 500; lower rates rest of yr. Crib free. Pet accepted. TV; cable, VCR (movies). Restaurant 6:30 am-midnight. Rm serv. Ck-out 11 am. Business servs avail. Bellhops. Valet serv. Free Walt Disney World transportation. Sundries. Gift shop. Coin lndry. Lighted tennis. Pool; wading pool, whirlpool, poolside serv. Playground. Supervised child's activities ages 3-12. Game rm. Refrigerators, microwaves. Cr cds: A, C, D, DS, ER, JCB, MC, V.

🄳 ✈ ♨ 🕴 ≋ ≋ ⊠ 🔥 SC

★★ **HOLIDAY VILLAS.** 2928 Vineland Rd (34746). 407/397-0700; FAX 407/397-0566; res: 800/344-3959. Web www.holidayvillas. com. 190 kit. suites, 2 story. Mid-Feb-early Apr, mid-June-late Aug: kit. suites $189-$239; family rates; higher rates hols; lower rates rest of yr. Crib free. Maid serv $20. TV; cable, VCR (movies $4). Heated pool; whirlpool. Ck-out 11 am. Lighted tennis. Exercise equipt; sauna. Microwaves. Picnic tables. Grills. Cr cds: A, DS, MC, V.

🏃 ≋ 🕴 ≋ ⊠ 🔥 SC

✔★ **HOWARD JOHNSON.** 2323 E Irlo Bronson Memorial Hwy (US 192) (34744). 407/846-4900; FAX 407/846-4900, ext. 333. 200 rms, 2 story. Mid-Feb-mid-Apr, mid-June-mid-Aug, mid-Dec-Jan 1: S, D $49-$84; under 18 free; lower rates rest of yr. Crib free. Pet accepted, some restrictions; $5. Pool. Restaurant 7 am-10 pm. Ck-out noon. Coin lndry. Business servs avail. Game rm. Cr cds: A, C, D, DS, ER, JCB, MC, V.

🄳 ✈ ≋ ⊠ 🔥 SC

✔★★ **HOWARD JOHNSON INN AND SUITES-LAKEFRONT.** 4836 W Irlo Bronson Hwy (34746). 407/396-4762; FAX 407/396-4866. 131 rms, 2 story, 42 kit. suites. S, D $35-$75; each addl $5; kit. suites $50-$120; under 12 free. Crib free. TV; cable. Pool. Playground. Complimentary continental bkfst. Restaurant adj 3 pm-midnight. Ck-out 11 am. Coin lndry. Some in-rm whirlpools. Jet-ski rental avail. On Lake Cecile. Cr cds: A, C, D, DS, MC, V.

🄳 ✈ ≋ ⊠ 🔥 SC

★★ **HOWARD JOHNSON INN-MAINGATE EAST.** 6051 W Irlo Bronson Hwy (US 192) (34747). 407/396-1748; FAX 407/649-8642. Web stay@hajamge.com. 567 rms, 3 story. S, D $75-$115; under 18 free. Crib avail. TV; cable. Heated pool; wading pool, whirlpool. Playground. Restaurant adj 7 am-midnight. Ck-out noon. Coin lndry. Game rm. Some refrigerators. Cr cds: A, C, D, DS, MC, V.

🄳 ≋ ⊠ 🔥 SC

★ **INNS OF AMERICA-MAINGATE.** 2945 Entry Point Blvd (34747). 407/396-7743; FAX 407/396-6307. 117 rms, 3 story. Late May-mid-Aug: S, D $55-$70; suites $69-$90; higher rates wk of Easter & Christmas; lower rates rest of yr. Pet accepted, some restrictions. TV; cable (premium). Heated pool. Complimentary continental bkfst. Restaurant adj 7 am-11 pm. Ck-out 11 am. Coin lndry. Refrigerator in suites. Cr cds: A, MC, V.

🄳 ✈ ≋ ⊠ 🔥 SC

✔★ **LA SUITE.** 2407 W Irlo Bronson Memorial Hwy (34741). 407/933-2400; res: 888/527-8483; FAX 407/933-1474. Web www.lasuite. com. 120 rms, 2 story. Mid-June-early Sept, mid-Dec-Apr: S, D $49-$99; higher rates Dec 25. Crib free. TV; cable (premium). Playground. Complimentary continental bkfst. Restaurant adj open 24 hrs. Ck-out 11 am. Meeting rms. Pool. Game rm. Refrigerators, microwaves. Cr cds: A, C, D, DS, MC, V.

🄳 ≋ ⊠ 🔥 SC

★★ **RESIDENCE INN BY MARRIOTT ON LAKE CECILE.** 4786 W Irlo Bronson Memorial Hwy (US 192W) (34746). 407/396-2056; FAX 407/396-2909. E-mail residence@netpass.com; web www.residence-inn. com. 160 kit. suites, 2 story. Mid-Dec-late Apr, June-Aug: S, D $129-$209;

lower rates rest of yr. Crib free. TV; cable (premium), VCR avail. Pool; whirlpool, poolside serv. Playground. Complimentary continental bkfst. Bar noon-7 pm. Ck-out 11 am. Coin lndry. Business servs avail. In-rm modem link. Valet serv. Game rm. Refrigerators, microwaves; some fireplaces. Balconies. Picnic tables, grills. On Lake Cecile; fishing docks. Cr cds: A, C, D, DS, ER, JCB, MC, V.

D ⚡ ≋ ✈ 🏌 SC

★ **SLEEP INN-MAINGATE.** 8536 W Irlo Bronson Memorial Hwy (US 192) (34747). 407/396-1600; FAX 407/396-1971. 104 rms, all with shower only, 3 story. June-Aug, late Dec-Apr: S, D $69-$150; under 18 free; lower rates rest of yr. Crib free. TV; cable (premium). Pool. Complimentary continental bkfst. Restaurant adj 6 am-midnight. Ck-out 11 am. In-rm modem link. Some refrigerators; microwaves avail. Cr cds: A, C, D, DS, ER, JCB, MC, V.

D ≋ ✈ 🏌 SC

★ **STADIUM INN AND SUITES.** 2039 E Irlo Bronson Memorial Hwy (US 192E) (34744). 407/846-7814; res: 800/785-7567; FAX 407/846-1863. 112 rms, 2 story, 56 kit. studios. S, D, kit. studios $55. Crib free. TV; cable (premium). Pool; whirlpool. Restaurant adj open 24 hrs. Ck-out noon. Meeting rms. Business servs avail. Airport transportation. Game rm. Microwaves avail. Cr cds: A, C, D, DS, ER, JCB, MC, V.

D ≋ ✈ 🏌 SC

★★ **TRAVELODGE SUITES.** 5399 W Irlo Bronson Memorial Hwy (US 192) (34746). 407/396-7666; FAX 407/396-0696. Web www. travelodge.com. 157 suites, 2 story. Feb-Apr & June-Aug: suites $64-$110; higher rates last wk Dec; lower rates rest of yr. Crib free. TV; VCR avail (movies). Heated pool; wading pool, whirlpool. Playground. Complimentary coffee in lobby. Restaurant adj open 24 hrs. Ck-out 11 am. Coin lndry. Meeting rms. Business servs avail. In-rm modem link. Gift shop. Airport transportation; free Walt Disney World transportation. Game rm. Refrigerators, microwaves. Cr cds: A, C, D, DS, ER, MC, V.

D ≋ ✈ 🏌 SC

★★ **WYNFIELD INN MAIN GATE.** 5335 Irlo Bronson Memorial Hwy (US 192) (34746). 407/396-2121; FAX 407/396-1142; res: 800/346-1551. 216 rms, 2-3 story. Late Dec-Apr, June-Aug: S, D $69-$89; each addl $5; under 18 free; lower rates rest of yr. Crib free. TV. Heated pool; wading pool, poolside serv. Complimentary coffee in lobby. Ck-out 11 am. Coin lndry. Business servs avail. Airport transportation; free Walt Disney World transportation. Game rm. Cr cds: A, C, D, DS, MC, V.

D ≋ ✈ 🏌 SC

Motor Hotels

★★ **COURTYARD BY MARRIOTT-MAINGATE.** 7675 W Irlo Bronson (US 192) (34747), I-4 exit 25B. 407/396-4000; FAX 407/396-0714. Web www.orl.com. 198 rms, 5 story. S, D $79-$139; under 18 free. Crib free. TV; cable (premium). Heated pool; wading pool, whirlpool, poolside serv. Playground. Complimentary coffee in rms. Restaurant adj open 24 hrs. Ck-out noon. Meeting rm. Valet serv. Free Walt Disney World transportation. Gift shop. Coin lndry. Exercise equipt. Game rm. Cr cds: A, C, D, DS, JCB, MC, V.

D ≋ 🏃 ✈ 🏌 SC

★★★ **DOUBLETREE GUEST SUITES RESORT-MAINGATE.** 4787 W Irlo Bronson Memorial Hwy (US 192) (34746). 407/397-0555; FAX 407/397-0553. E-mail dtg.som@inspace.net; web www.cyberinn.com/dtgshome.htm. 150 villas, 2 story. Mid-Feb-Apr, late June-late Aug, mid-late Dec: villas $164-$219; lower rates rest of yr. Crib free. TV; cable (premium). Heated pool; whirlpool. Complimentary coffee in rms. Restaurant 7 am-10:30 pm. Bar 6-11 pm. Ck-out noon. Coin lndry. Meeting rms. Concierge. Gift shop. Airport transportation. Lighted tennis. Exercise equipt. Microwaves; balconies. Cr cds: A, D, DS, ER, MC, V.

D 🏃 ≋ 🏃 ✈ 🏌 SC

★★ **FOUR POINTS BY SHERATON.** 4018 W Vine St (Irlo Bronson Memorial Hwy/US 192) (34741). 407/870-2000; FAX 407/870-

2010. 225 rms, 3 & 5 story. Feb-Aug, late Dec: S, D $79-$178; under 18 free; lower rates rest of yr. Crib $6. TV; cable. Heated pool; wading pool, whirlpool, poolside serv. Bar. Ck-out 11 am. Coin lndry. Concierge. Sundries. Airport transportation. Game rm. Refrigerators. Cr cds: A, D, DS, JCB, MC, V.

D ≋ ✈ 🏌 SC

★★ **HOLIDAY INN NIKKI BIRD RESORT.** 7300 Irlo Bronson Memorial Hwy (US 192W) (34747). 407/396-7300; FAX 407/396-7555. 529 rms, 2 story. Feb-Apr, June-Aug, late Dec: S, D $89-$129; under 19 free; lower rates rest of yr. Crib free. TV; cable (premium). 3 heated pools; 2 wading pools, 3 whirlpools. Playground. Rm serv. Bar. Ck-out 11 am. Coin lndry. Bellhops. Valet serv. Sundries. Gift shop. Airport transportation; free Walt Disney World transportation. Lighted tennis. Game rm. Cr cds: A, C, D, DS, ER, JCB, MC, V.

D 🏃 ≋ ✈ 🏌 SC

★★★ **HYATT ORLANDO.** 6375 Irlo Bronson Memorial Hwy (US 192) (34747). 407/396-1234; FAX 407/396-5090. E-mail hyattorl@aol.com; web www.travelweb.com/hyatt.html. 922 rms, 2 story. S, D $109-$179; suites $360-$470; under 18 free. Crib free. TV; cable (premium), VCR avail. 4 heated pools; wading pools, whirlpools, poolside serv. 2 playgrounds. Restaurants 6:30-1 am. Rm serv. Bar; entertainment. Ck-out noon. Coin lndry. Convention facilities. Business center. Bellhops. Valet serv. Sundries. Gift shop. Barber, beauty shop. Valet parking. Airport, Walt Disney World transportation. Lighted tennis. Golf privileges, greens fee. Exercise equipt. Game rm. Balconies. Cr cds: A, C, D, DS, ER, JCB, MC, V.

D 🏃 🎿 ≋ ✈ 🏃 ✈ 🏌 SC 🏌

★★ **QUALITY INN LAKE CECILE.** 4944 W Irlo Bronson Memorial Hwy (US 192) (34746). 407/396-4455; FAX 407/396-2856. 222 rms, 5 story. Mid-Feb-late Apr, June-mid-Aug, late Dec: S, D $69.95-$79.95; under 18 free; lower rates rest of yr. Crib free. TV; cable. Pool. Coffee in rms. Ck-out 11 am. Coin lndry. Game rm. Refrigerators avail. Balconies. On lake; pier, various boats avail. Cr cds: A, C, D, DS, MC, V.

D ⚡ ≋ ✈ 🏌 SC

★★ **QUALITY SUITES MAINGATE EAST.** 5876 W Irlo Bronson Memorial Hwy (US 192W) (34746). 407/396-8040; FAX 407/396-6766. 225 suites (1-2 bedrm), 5 story. Suites $79-$269; under 18 free. Crib $10. TV; cable. Heated pool; wading pool, whirlpool, poolside serv. Playground. Complimentary continental bkfst. Restaurant 6-11 am, 5-10 pm. Ck-out 11 am. Coin lndry. Valet serv. Sundries. Gift shop. Airport transportation. Game rm. Refrigerators, microwaves. Cr cds: A, C, D, DS, ER, JCB, MC, V.

D ≋ ✈ 🏌 SC

★★★ **RADISSON RESORT PARKWAY.** 2900 Parkway Blvd (34747). 407/396-7000; FAX 407/396-6792. 718 rms, 1-8 story. Mid-Feb-Aug & late Dec: S, D $129-$149; each addl $10; under 18 free; Walt Disney World, honeymoon packages; lower rates rest of yr. Crib free. TV. Heated pool; wading pool, 2 whirlpools, poolside serv. Playground. Restaurant 6:30 am-2:30 pm, 5-11 pm. Rm serv. Bar 11-1 am. Ck-out 11 am. Meeting rms. Business center. Bellhops. Valet serv. Gift shop. Lighted tennis. Exercise equipt. Game rm. Minibars; microwaves avail. Located on 20 acres; decorative freshwater ponds. Cr cds: A, C, D, DS, ER, JCB, MC, V.

D 🏃 ≋ ✈ 🏃 ✈ 🏌 SC 🏌

★★ **RAMADA FOUNTAIN PARK HOTEL.** 5150 W Irlo Bronson Memorial Hwy (US 192) (34746). 407/396-1111; FAX 407/396-1607. E-mail dbl@nebula.ispace.com; web www.cyberinn.com/fp/. 401 rms, 4-10 story. Feb-Easter, Jun-Aug, also late Dec: S, D $89; suites $169; lower rates rest of yr. Crib free. TV; cable. Heated pool; wading pool, whirlpool, poolside serv in season. Playground. Restaurant 7-11 am, 5-11 pm. Rm serv. Bar 11 am-midnight. Ck-out 11 am. Coin lndry. Meeting rms. Bellhops. Valet serv. Gift shop. Lighted tennis. Putting green. Game rm. Lawn games. Some refrigerators; microwaves avail. Balconies. Picnic tables. Cr cds: A, C, D, DS, ER, MC, V.

D 🏃 ≋ ✈ 🏌 SC

★ ★ **SHERATON INN-LAKESIDE.** *7769 W Irlo Bronson Memorial Hwy (US 192W) (34747), I-4 exit 25B.* 407/396-2222; FAX 407/239-2650. 651 rms, 2 story. Mid-Feb-Apr, mid-June-late Aug, late Dec: S, D $99-$149; each addl $10; under 18 free; lower rates rest of yr. Crib free. TV; cable (premium). Pools; wading pools, poolside serv. Playgrounds. Seasonal supervised child's activities. Coffee in rms. Restaurant 7-11:30 am, 5-10 pm. Rm serv. Bar 5 pm-1 am. Ck-out 11 am. Coin lndry. Meeting rms. Business servs avail. Bellhops. Valet serv. Sundries. Gift shop. Airport, Walt Disney World transportation. Lighted tennis. Miniature golf. Game rm. Lawn games. Refrigerators. On lake; dock, paddleboats. Cr cds: A, C, D, DS, ER, JCB, MC, V.

D ⓘ ☲ ⚏ ☖ SC

Hotels

★ ★ ★ **DOUBLETREE RESORT-MAINGATE WEST.** *7501 W Irlo Bronson Memorial Hwy (US 192W) (34747), I-4 exit 25B.* 407/396-1400; FAX 407/396-0660. Web www.orlando.com. 580 rms, 7 story. S, D $99-$149; each addl $10; suites $150-$350; under 18 free; package plans. Crib free. TV; cable (premium). Heated pool; whirlpool, poolside serv. Playground. Restaurants 7 am-10 pm. Bar 11-1 am. Ck-out noon. Coin lndry. Convention facilities. Business servs avail. Lighted tennis. Exercise equipt. Game rm. Cr cds: A, C, D, DS, ER, MC, V.

D ⓘ ☲ ✕ ☖ ⚏ SC

★ ★ **RAMADA PLAZA.** *7470 W Irlo Bronson Memorial Hwy (34747).* 407/396-4400; FAX 407/396-4320. 500 rms, 8 story, 13 suites. S, D $80-$145; each addl $15; suites $150-$250; under 18 free; family, wkend rates; Dec 25 (4-day min). Crib free. TV; cable (premium). Complimentary coffee in lobby. Restaurant 6:30-11:30 am, 5-10 pm. Bar. Ck-out 11 am. Convention facilities. Business center. In-rm modem link. Concierge. Gift shop. Coin lndry. Exercise equipt. Pool. Game rm. Lawn games. Refrigerators; some microwaves. Cr cds: A, C, D, DS, ER, MC, V.

D ☲ ✕ ☖ ⚏ SC ☝ ⚞

★ **TRAVELODGE MAIN GATE EAST.** *5711 W Irlo Bronson (US 192) (34746).* 407/396-4222; FAX 407/396-0570. Web www.orlando.com/travelodge. 444 rms, 8 story. Mid-Jan-mid-Apr, June-Aug: S, D $68-$98; higher rates Dec 23-Jan 3; lower rates rest of yr. Crib free. TV; cable (premium). Heated pool; wading pool, whirlpool, sauna. Coffee in rms. Restaurant 7 am-10 pm. Bar 11-2 am; entertainment. Ck-out noon. Coin lndry. Meeting rms. Gift shop. Shopping arcade. Free Walt Disney World transportation. Game rm. Balconies. Cr cds: A, C, D, DS, MC, V.

D ☲ ✕ ⚏ SC

Inn

★ ★ **THE UNICORN.** *8 S Orlando Ave (34741), off US 17/92.* 407/846-1200; FAX 407/846-1773; res: 800/865-7212. E-mail unicorn@gate.net; web touristguide.com/b+b/florida/unicorn. 6 rms, 2 story. S $65-$85; D $75-$95; each addl $10; under 8 free; wkend rates. Crib free. TV; cable. Complimentary full bkfst. Restaurant nearby. Ck-out 11 am, ck-in 4 pm. Business servs avail. Luggage handling. Airport transportation. Colonial-style house built 1901; many English antiques. Cr cds: A, MC.

☖ SC

Restaurants

★ ★ **CHARLEY'S STEAK HOUSE.** *2901 Parkway Blvd (34746), I-4 exit 25A.* 407/396-6055. Hrs: 5-10:30 pm; Fri, Sat to 11 pm. Closed Thanksgiving, Dec 25. Res accepted. Bar. Semi-a la carte: dinner $10.95-$29.95. Child's meals. Specializes in flame-broiled steak, seafood. Parking. Nostalgic atmosphere; old-time portraits, Tiffany lamps. Cr cds: A, MC, V.

D ⚏

★ ★ **KEY W KOOL'S.** *7725 W FL 192 (34746), 3 mi W on I-4, exit 25B.* 407/396-1166. Hrs: 4-11 pm. Res accepted. Bar. Semi-a la carte:

dinner $9.99-$23.95. Child's meals. Specializes in steak, seafood. Open-pit grill; penguin theme. Cr cds: A, D, DS, MC, V.

D ⚏

★ **KOBÉ JAPANESE STEAK HOUSE.** *2901 Parkway Blvd (34746).* 407/396-8088. Hrs: 5-10:30 pm. Res accepted. Japanese menu. Bar. Semi-a la carte: dinner $10.95-$29.95. Child's meals. Specializes in fresh seafood, aged beef, sushi. Parking. Tableside preparation. Garden-like entrance with pool. Cr cds: A, D, DS, MC, V.

D

★ ★ **PACINO'S.** *5795 W FL 192 (34746), I-4 exit FL 192 E.* 407/396-8022. Hrs: 4-11 pm. Italian menu. Bar. Semi-a la carte: dinner $10.95-$24.95. Child's meals. Specializes in steaks. Outdoor dining. Animated puppet show. Cr cds: A, C, D, DS, MC, V.

D ⚏

Unrated Dining Spots

ARABIAN NIGHTS. *6225 W Irlo Bronson Memorial Hwy (US 192W).* 407/239-9223. Dinner show hrs vary each season. Res accepted. Bar. Complete meals: $36.95; children 3-11, $23.95. Specializes in beef, chicken. 25 acts with more than 30 characters; featuring Arabian Dancing Horses, performing Lippizaner horses, "Ben Hur" chariot races. Parking. Arabian-style palace decor. Cr cds: A, DS, ER, MC, V.

D

MEDIEVAL TIMES. *Box 4 (22385), 8 mi W of I-4 on Irlo Bronson Memorial Hwy (US 192).* 407/239-0214; res: 800/327-4024 (exc FL), 800/432-0768 (FL). Dinner show hrs vary each season. Res required. Bar. Complete meals: adult $45; children 3-12, $21; under 3 free. Specialties: roasted chicken flambé, spare ribs. Shows of medieval tournament competitions including ring piercing, javelin throwing, sword fighting and jousting. Parking. Reproduction of 11th-century castle; costumed servers. Cr cds: A, MC, V.

D SC

WILD BILL'S AT FORT LIBERTY. *5260 W Irlo Bronson Memorial Hwy (US 192).* 407/351-5151. Performances: 7 & 9:30 pm. Res accepted. Wine, beer. Complete meals: dinner $36.95; children 3-11, $22.95. Specialty: fried chicken & ribs. Parking. Two hrs of continuous "wild west" entertainment, featuring can-can dancers, cowboys & Indians; seats more than 600. Cr cds: A, D, DS, MC, V.

D SC

Lake Buena Vista

(see Walt Disney World)

Lake City (B-3)

(See also White Springs)

Settled 1824 **Pop** 10,005 **Elev** 196 ft **Area code** 904 **Zip** 32055
Information Columbia County Tourist Development Council, 601 Hall of Fame Dr, PO Box 1847, 32056; 904/758-1312.

A hub for major highways, Lake City was one of the important towns of early Florida. Nearby farms grow tobacco, which is auctioned in summer in Lake City. Forest products are another source of income, and the discovery of large deposits of phosphate has spurred mining operations near the Suwannee River.

What to See and Do

Osceola National Forest. Almost 184,000 acres dotted with ponds and cypress swamps. Swimming; fishing; boating. Hiking. Picnicking. Camping (fee). Fees may be charged at recreation sites. N & E via US 90, US 441 or I-10. Contact USDA Forest Service, 325 John Knox Rd, Suite F-100, Tallahassee, 32333-4061, phone 904/942-9300; or the ranger district office, E on US 90 in Olustee, phone 904/752-2537. In forest is

Olustee Battlefield State Historic Site. Site of important battle during War Between the States, resulting in a major Confederate victory. Museum exhibits depict battle scenes; period displays. Battlefield trail; annual battle reenactment (see ANNUAL EVENTS). (Daily) 15 mi E on US 90. Phone 904/758-0400. **Free.**

Annual Events

Battle of Olustee Reenactment. Mid-Feb.

Alligator Festival. 2nd wkend May.

Motel

★ ★ HOLIDAY INN. *Drawer 1239, On US 90 at jct I-75.* 904/752-3901; FAX 904/752-3901, ext. 7100. 227 rms, 2 story. S $55; D $61; under 18 free. Crib free. TV; cable (premium). 2 pools; wading pool. Playground. Restaurant 6:30 am-2 pm, 5:30-10 pm. Rm serv. Bar 3 pm-1 am, Sun 4-11 pm. Ck-out noon. Coin lndry. Meeting rms. Business servs avail. In-rm modem link. Bellhops. Sundries. Lighted tennis. Golf privileges. Lawn games. 27 acres. Cr cds: A, C, D, DS, JCB, MC, V.

 🖾 🏃 ⛷ 🏊 ⛷ 🔥 SC

Restaurants

★ ROBERT'S DOCK. *On US 90E (32025).* 904/752-7504. Hrs: 11:30 am-9 pm; Sat 5-9 pm; Sun 11 am-2 pm. Closed Mon; some major hols. Wine, beer. Semi-a la carte: lunch, dinner $3.25-$18. Child's meals. Specializes in seafood, chicken. Rustic decor. Situated in pine grove, across hwy from airport. Cr cds: A, MC, V.

★ TEXAS ROAD HOUSE. *On US 90 at jct I-75.* 904/758-0074. Hrs: 11 am-10:30 pm. Closed Dec 25. Res accepted. Bar. A la carte entrees: lunch $3-$8, dinner $4-$15. Child's meals. Specializes in steak. Cr cds: A, DS, MC, V.

🖾 ➘

Lakeland (E-4)

(See also Haines City, Zephyrhills)

Settled 1884 **Pop** 70,576 **Elev** 219 ft **Area code** 941
Information Chamber of Commerce, 35 Lake Morton Dr, PO Box 3607, 33802-3607; 941/688-8551.

Located in central Florida, this city takes its name from the 13 lakes within the city limits. Thousands of acres of citrus groves and several citrus packing and processing plants are in the area. Tourism, agriculture and phosphate mining are integral parts of Lakeland's economy.

What to See and Do

Florida Southern College (1885). (1,600 students) The largest single-site group of structures designed by Frank Lloyd Wright is here, including the Annie Pfeiffer Chapel. Permanent exhibit in Frank Lloyd Wright Visitors Center includes multimedia presentation, photographs and drawings (Tues-Fri, limited hrs Sat & Sun). Guided tours (Thurs, fee). Maps for self-guided tour may be obtained at Visitor Center or Administration Bldg. McDonald St & Johnson Ave. Phone 941/680-4111.

Polk Museum of Art. Collection of Pre-Columbian Art, Oriental and decorative art; contemporary and historical photography, sculpture; changing exhibits. Student Gallery. Lectures, films, performances. (Tues-Sat & Sun afternoons; closed major hols) 800 E Palmetto St. Phone 941/688-7743. **Free.**

Annual Events

Orange Cup Regatta. Lake Hollingsworth. Hydroplane races. Phone 941/499-6035. 1st wkend Apr.

Sun & Fun EAA Fly-In. Lakeland Linder Regional Airport, 4175 Medulla Rd. Week-long convention of aviation enthusiasts; exhibitions, workshops, daily air shows. Phone 941/644-2431. Apr 19-25.

Seasonal Event

Spring training. Marchant Stadium, 2305 Lakeland Hills Blvd. Detroit Tigers baseball spring training; exhibition games. Phone 941/499-8229. Early Mar-early Apr.

Motels

★ ★ BEST WESTERN DIPLOMAT INN. *3311 US 98N (33805).* 941/688-7972; FAX 941/688-8377. 118 rms, 2 story, 2 suites. Feb-Apr: S, D $65-$99; each addl $6; suites $99-$129; under 18 free; lower rates rest of yr. Crib $3. TV; cable (premium). Pool; wading pool. Complimentary continental bkfst. Restaurant 7-11 am. Bar 5 pm-2 am; Sun to midnight; entertainment Fri, Sat. Ck-out 11 am. Meeting rms. Valet serv. Cr cds: A, C, D, DS, ER, JCB, MC, V.

🖾 🏊 ⛷ 🔥 SC

✔ ★ ★ COMFORT INN. *1817 E Memorial Blvd (33801).* 941/688-9221; FAX 914/687-4797. 64 rms, 2 story. Feb-mid-Apr: S, D $58-$69; each addl $5; under 18 free; lower rates rest of yr. Crib free. TV; cable, VCR avail (movies). Pool. Complimentary continental bkfst. Ck-out 11 am. Opp Lake Parker. Cr cds: A, C, D, DS, MC, V.

🖾 🏊 ⛷ 🔥 SC

★ ★ HOLIDAY INN-SOUTH. *3405 S Florida Ave (33803).* 941/646-5731; FAX 941/646-5215. 172 rms, 2 story. S, D $82-$92; each addl $10; under 18 free. Crib free. TV; cable (premium), VCR avail. Pool; whirlpool. Complimentary continental bkfst. Coffee in rms. Restaurant 6:30 am-2 pm, 5-9 pm. Rm serv. Bar; entertainment Tues-Sat. Ck-out noon. Meeting rms. Health club privileges. Refrigerators, microwaves avail. Cr cds: A, C, D, DS, JCB, MC, V.

🖾 🏊 ⛷ 🔥 SC

★ ★ WELLESLEY INN AND SUITES. *3520 N US 98 (33805).* 941/859-3399; FAX 941/859-3483. 106 rms, 6 story, 24 suites. Jan-Apr: S, D $99.99-$109.99; each addl $10; suites $104.99-$159.99; under 18 free; wkend rates. Crib free. Pet accepted; $10. TV; cable (premium). Heated pool. Complimentary continental bkfst. Complimentary coffee in rms. Restaurant nearby. Ck-out 11 am. Coin lndry. Meeting rms. Business servs avail. Health club privileges. Refrigerator in suites; microwaves avail. Cr cds: A, C, D, DS, MC, V.

🖾 🏊 ⛷ 🔥 SC

Restaurant

★ ★ RED FOX GRILL. *1239 E Memorial Blvd (33801).* 941/683-5500. Hrs: 5-9:30 pm; Fri, Sat to 10 pm; Sun 5-9 pm; early-bird dinner 5-7 pm. Closed Dec 25. Res accepted. Bar. Semi-a la carte: dinner $8.95-$24.95. Child's meals. Specializes in steak, seafood. Cr cds: DS, MC, V.

🖾 ➘

Lake Placid (F-5)

(See also Sebring)

Pop 1,158 **Elev** 136 ft **Area code** 941 **Zip** 33862 **E-mail** lpcc@ct.net **Web** www.lake-placid-fl.com

Information Greater Lake Placid Chamber of Commerce, 18 N Oak St, PO Box 187; 941/465-4331 or 800/557-5224.

Located in the central Florida ridge country, halfway between the Atlantic and the Gulf, Lake Placid, with more than 27 freshwater lakes nearby, offers excellent bass fishing and boating.

More than 26 murals have been painted on buildings in the uptown area, portraying Lake Placid's history and heritage.

What to See and Do

Cypress Knee Museum. Museum of sculpture-like natural cypress knees; factory; catwalk in cypress swamp. Tours (daily). 25 mi S on US 27 near Palmdale. Phone 941/675-0128. ¢¢

Historical Society Museum. Four-room museum in historic depot displays exhibits of area history. (Sept-May, Tues-Fri; rest of yr, by appt; closed hols) 19 Park Ave W. Phone 941/465-1771 or -3712. **Free.**

Lake Wales (E-4)

(See also Haines City, Winter Haven)

Pop 9,670 **Elev** 147 ft **Area code** 941 **Zip** 33853 **E-mail** lwacc@digital.net **Web** www.lakewaleschamber.com

Information Lake Wales Area Chamber of Commerce, 340 W Central Ave; 941/676-3445.

Industrial manufacturing, citrus groves and canning make up the commercial life of Lake Wales, but its 23 nearby lakes offer boating, fishing and other recreational sports.

What to See and Do

Babson Park Audubon Center. Nature trails; wildlife museum. (Oct-late Apr, Tues-Sat afternoons & Sat mornings; closed major hols) 7 mi S on US 27A in Babson Park. Phone 941/638-1355. **Free.**

⚡ **Bok Tower Gardens.** The 205-ft Bok Singing Tower, established by Edward W. Bok on top of Iron Mountain, is the highest point on the peninsula. Built of Georgia marble and Florida coquina, it houses a carillon of 57 bells (ranging from 17 lbs to 11 tons) that provides music throughout the day (tower closed to public); an audiovisual presentation of the tower's interior can be seen at the visitors center. Surrounding the tower are 128 acres of landscaped gardens; self-guided nature trail, walking paths; seasonal flowers; bird observatory. Picnic area, restaurant. Pet hostel (fee). (Daily) 3 mi N off US 27A. Phone 941/676-1408. ¢¢

Depot Museum. Built as a passenger station by the Atlantic Coast Line Railroad in 1928, this pink stucco structure now houses memorabilia of early Lake Wales; photographs; turpentine, citrus & ranching exhibits; 1916 train car, 1944 diesel engine, 1926 caboose and old train artifacts. (Daily exc Sun; closed hols) 325 S Scenic Hwy. Phone 941/678-4209. **Free.**

Lake Kissimmee State Park. More than 5,000 acres bordered by lakes Kissimmee, Tiger and Rosalie. The lakes, flood plain prairies, marshes and pine flatwoods form scenic panoramas where wildlife such as white-tailed deer, bald eagles, sand hill cranes and turkey may be seen. Live oak hammocks and swamps offer additional habitat for other wildlife, including bobcats and Florida scrub jays. Fishing; boating (marina, ramp, docks). Hiking. Picnicking, concession. Primitive & improved camping. Observa-

tion platform. Standard hrs, fees. 15 mi E off FL 60, on Camp Mack Rd. Phone 941/696-1112. In the park is

Kissimmee Cow Camp. Re-creation of a Florida frontier cow camp (ca 1875). The history of the region and era is portrayed the way it actually happened by "cow hunters" as they round up scrub cows, share campfire coffee and talk to visitors about their life and work. Tours (Sat, Sun & hols).

Spook Hill. Park car on white line on hill, put into neutral, and watch the car mysteriously roll uphill by itself. **Free.**

Seasonal Event

Black Hills Passion Play. Amphitheater, 2 mi S on US 27A. Same cast as Black Hills, South Dakota, production. Tues, Thurs, Sat & Sun evenings; matinees Wed; extra performance on Good Friday. Phone 941/676-1495 or 800/622-8383. Lenten season, mid-Feb-mid-Apr.

Inn

★ ★ ★ **CHALET SUZANNE.** *3800 Chalet Suzanne Dr, 4 mi N on US 27, E on FL 17A. 941/676-6011; FAX 941/676-1814; res: 800/433-6011.* E-mail info@chaletsuzanne.com; web www.chaletsuzanne.com. 30 rms, 1-2 story, 5 suites. S $139-$195; D $159-$219; each addl $12; suites $195-$219; package plans. Crib $10. TV; cable. Pool; 6 whirlpools, poolside serv. Complimentary full bkfst; afternoon refreshments. Restaurant (see CHALET SUZANNE). Bar. Ck-out 11 am, ck-in 3 pm. Coin lndry. Meeting rms. Business center. Bellhops. Gift shop. Tennis privileges. Golf privileges. Lawn games. Swiss chalet style with steeples, spires, gables, balconies; garden features tiles signed by celebrities. Rms individually decorated, many antiques. On 70 acres overlooking lake; airstrip on grounds. Cr cds: A, C, D, DS, JCB, MC, V.

🄳 🖙 🏌 🏃 🛇 🏊 🚶

Resort

★ ★ **RIVER RANCH.** *24700 FL 60 E (33867), 25 mi E on FL 60. 941/692-1321; res: 800/785-2102; FAX 941/692-9135.* Web www.riverranch.com. 192 units, 1 & 2 story, 80 kits, 58 suites, 30 cottages. S, D $80-$90; suites $115; each addl $5; cottages (1-2 bedrm) $125-$195; under 16 free; wkly, monthly rates. Crib free. TV; cable. 4 pools, poolside serv. Playground. Dining rm 7 am-10 pm. Snack bar. Bar. Entertainment. Ck-out 11 am, ck-in 3 pm. Grocery. Coin lndry. Package store. Meeting rms. Beauty shop. Sports, soc dir. Lighted tennis. 9-hole golf, greens fee $8.50-$12, putting green, driving range. Bicycles (rentals). Game rm. Rec rm. Lawn games. Fishing guides. Ranch cookouts. Hay rides; Sat night rodeos. Microwaves; some fireplaces, private patios. Picnic tables. Grills. Library. 1,500 wooded acres on inland waterway; 5,000-ft lighted airstrip. Cr cds: A, MC, V.

🄳 🖙 ⚡ 🏌 🏃 🛇 🏊 🚶 🛡

Restaurants

★ ★ ★ **CHALET SUZANNE.** *(See Chalet Suzanne Inn) 941/676-6011.* E-mail info@chaletsuzanne.com; web www.chaletsuzanne.com. Hrs: 8-11 am, noon-9:30 pm. Res accepted. Continental, Amer menu. Bar. Wine cellars. Table d'hôte: bkfst $15.95-$17.95, lunch $30-$45, dinner $59-$79. Serv charge 18%. Child's meals. Specialties: chicken Suzanne, lobster Newburg, crab sasse. Own baking, soups. Entertainment Fri, Sat. Chef-owned. Cr cds: A, C, D, DS, JCB, MC, V.

🔳

★ ★ **LEKARICA.** *1650 S Highland Park Dr. 941/676-8281.* E-mail erweaver@highlandparkhills.com; web www.highlandparkhills.com. Hrs: 11 am-2 pm, 6-9 pm; Sun brunch 11 am-2 pm. Closed Mon; Jan 1. Res accepted. Contemporary Amer menu. Bar. Semi-a la carte: lunch $4-$10, dinner $8.50-$25.50. Sun brunch $12.95. Specialties: Applewood grilled filet of ostrich, grouper. Parking. Located in inn. Totally nonsmoking. Cr cds: A, DS, MC, V.

★ ★ ★ **VINTON'S.** *229 E Stuart Ave, at The Marketplace. 941/676-8242.* Hrs: 6-10 pm. Closed Sun; major hols; Aug. Res accepted. French menu. Bar 5-10:30 pm. Wine cellar. Semi-a la carte: dinner $19.95-$23.95. Specialties: filet mignon, shrimp jambalaya. Own baking. New Orleans decor. In historic arcade. Cr cds: A, MC, V.

Lake Worth (G-6)

(See also Boca Raton, Delray Beach, Palm Beach, West Palm Beach)

Settled 1870 **Pop** 28,564 **Elev** 19 ft **Area code** 561
Information Greater Lake Worth Chamber of Commerce, 1702 Lake Worth Rd, 33460; 561/582-4401.

Adjacent to Palm Beach, Lake Worth offers all the advantages of the Gold Coast without straining the budget; a free local transportation system is in use here. On the west shore of saltwater Lake Worth, which is part of the Intracoastal Waterway and separated from the ocean by Palm Beach, the city maintains beach and recreation facilities. Tourism is the principal activity of this town, named for General William J. Worth, a hero of the Seminole and Mexican Wars.

Seasonal Events

Polo. Usually Jan-Apr.

Gulfstream Polo Field. Approx 8 mi W on Lake Worth Rd, 1/4 mi W of Sunshine State Pkwy (FL Tpke). Matches Fri & Sun afternoons. Phone 561/965-2057.

Palm Beach Polo. 12 mi W on Forest Hill Blvd, then left on S Shore Blvd, in Wellington. Matches Sun afternoons. Phone 561/793-1440.

Motel

★ ★ **HOLIDAY INN WEST PALM BEACH TURNPIKE.** *7859 Lake Worth Rd (33467). 561/968-5000;* FAX *561/968-2451.* Web www.holiday-inn.com. 114 rms, 2 story. Jan-Mar: S, D $99-$105; each addl $6; under 19 free; varied lower rates rest of yr. Crib free. TV; cable (premium). Heated pool; poolside serv. Restaurant 7:30 am-2 pm, 4:30-10 pm. Rm serv. Bar 11 am-11 pm, Sun from 2 pm. Ck-out 11 am. Coin lndry. Meeting rms. Business servs avail. In-rm modem link. Tennis. Cr cds: A, C, D, DS, JCB, MC, V.

Restaurant

★ ★ **BOHEMIAN GARDEN.** *(5450 Lake Worth Rd, Green Acres 33463) 561/968-4111.* Hrs: 4:30-10 pm; Sun 4-9 pm; early-bird dinner 5-6 pm. Res accepted. Continental menu. Serv bar. Complete meals: dinner $6.95-$16.95. Child's meals. Specializes in beef, seafood, duck. Outdoor dining. Cr cds: A, C, D, DS, MC, V.

Unrated Dining Spot

JOHN G's. *10 S Ocean Blvd (33460). 561/585-9860.* Web www.johngs.com. Hrs: 7 am-3 pm. Closed Jan 1, Dec 25. Semi-a la carte: bkfst $3.15-$8.50, lunch $4-$14.35. Specialties: cinnamon-nut French toast, eggs Benedict. Outdoor dining. Casual atmosphere; view of ocean. No cr cds accepted.

Leesburg (D-4)

(See also Ocala)

Founded 1856 **Pop** 14,903 **Elev** 79 ft **Area code** 352 **E-mail** chamber@lake-county.org **Web** www.lake-county.org
Information Leesburg Area Chamber of Commerce, 03430 US27/441, Fruitland Park, 34731; 352/787-2131.

The largest city in Lake County with 1,400 named lakes, Leesburg is a base for explorations by skiff, motor launch or houseboat. The economy is based on agriculture and light industry. The largest storage plant in the South for frozen citrus concentrates is located here.

What to See and Do

Lake Griffin State Recreation Area. Approximately 420-acre area noted for its floating islands—marsh plant life floats on dense soil in several feet of water. Fishing; boating, canoeing (rentals). Nature trail. Picnicking. Camping (hookups, dump station). Standard hrs, fees. 3 mi N off US 27/441 in Fruitland Park. Phone 352/360-6760.

Venetian Gardens. An 80-acre park. Miniature islands; swimming pool (fee); boat ramp. Ball fields. Picnicking. Off Dixie Ave. Phone 352/728-9885. **Free.**

Motel

✔★ **BUDGET HOST INN.** *1235 N 14th St (34748), jct US 27, 441. 352/787-3534;* FAX *352/787-0060.* 50 rms, 2 story, 16 kits. Mid-Jan-mid-Apr: S, D $46.50; each addl $4; kits. $51.50; lower rates rest of yr. TV; cable. Pool. Complimentary coffee in lobby. Restaurant nearby. Ck-out 11 am. Coin lndry. Airport transportation. Cr cds: A, DS, MC, V.

Restaurant

★ ★ **VIC'S EMBERS SUPPER CLUB.** *7940 US 441 (34788). 352/728-8989.* Hrs: 4:30-10 pm; Fri, Sat to 11 pm; early-bird dinner to 6 pm; Sun brunch 11:30 am-2:30 pm. Closed most major hols. Bar 3 pm-2 am. Semi-a la carte: dinner $10.95-$17.95. Sun brunch $13.95. Child's meals. Specializes in pasta, seafood, steak. Entertainment Tues-Sat. Valet parking. Cr cds: MC, V.

Live Oak (B-3)

(See also Lake City, White Springs)

Pop 6,332 **Elev** 102 ft **Area code** 904 **Zip** 32060
Information Suwannee County Chamber of Commerce, 106 E Howard St, PO Drawer C; 904/362-3071.

Florida's oldest and largest tobacco market is here, and the town is transformed during July and August by the frenzy of the tobacco auction. Named for a huge live oak that once provided a shaded campground in the area, this is the seat of Suwannee County, which is bordered on three sides by 100 miles of the Suwannee River. This river was picked from an atlas by Stephen Foster and immortalized in his song "Old Folks at Home," which begins "Way down upon the Swanee River..."

What to See and Do

Suwannee River State Park. More than 1,800 acres where the Withlacoochee and Suwannee rivers meet. Suwannee River Canoe Trail, which begins in Georgia, ends at the park (although the river may be canoed south of the park as well). Panoramic view of rivers and wooded uplands. Earthworks of Confederate fort, escarpments overlook river. Fishing; boating (ramp). Nature trails. Picnicking (grills). Camping (electric hookups). Standard hrs, fees. 15 mi W on US 90. Phone 904/362-2746.

Longboat Key (& Lido Beach) (F-3)

(See also Bradenton, Sarasota)

Pop 5,937 **Elev** 9 ft **Area code** 941 **Zip** 34228 **E-mail** director@longboatkeychamber.com **Web** www.longboatkeychamber.com **Information** Chamber of Commerce, 6854 Gulf of Mexico Dr; 941/383-2466.

Situated between Sarasota Bay and the Gulf of Mexico, Longboat Key, nearly 11 miles long, is surrounded by sand beaches. Discovered in 1593 when Hernando De Soto made his historic landing nearby, Longboat Key did not receive recognition until the early 1900s, when circus magnate John Ringling took an interest in surrounding Sarasota. The area's beaches provide good surf fishing and swimming; several charter-boat companies provide full- and half-day trips.

Motels

★ **DIPLOMAT.** *3155 Gulf of Mexico Dr.* 941/383-3791; *res:* 800/344-5418; *FAX* 941/383-0983. 50 kit. units, 1-2 bedrm, 2 story. Feb-Apr: S, D $118-$194; each addl $10; under 12 free; lower rates rest of yr. Crib $5. TV; cable. Heated pool. Restaurant nearby. Ck-out 11 am. Coin lndry. Business servs avail. Microwaves. On beach. Cr cds: DS, MC, V.

★ ★ **HALF MOON BEACH CLUB.** *(2050 Ben Franklin Dr, Sarasota 34236)* 1½ mi W of St Armands Circle in Lido Beach. 941/388-3694; *FAX* 941/388-1938; *res:* 800/358-3245. E-mail info@halfmoon-lido key.com; web www.halfmoon-lidokey.com. 85 rms, 2 story, 12 suites, 30 kits. Late Jan-Apr: S, D $119-$164; each addl $15; suites $229; kit. units $184-$229; under 17 free; lower rates rest of yr. Crib free. TV; cable, VCR avail (movies). Heated pool; poolside serv. Complimentary coffee in rms. Restaurant 7 am-10 pm. Rm serv. Bar 11 am-11 pm; entertainment wkends. Ck-out 11 am. Coin lndry. Meeting rm. Business servs avail. Lawn games. Minibars; some microwaves. Picnic tables. On Gulf; sun deck. Cr cds: A, C, D, DS, ER, MC, V.

★ **HOLIDAY BEACH RESORT.** *4765 Gulf of Mexico Dr.* 941/383-3704; *FAX* 941/383-0546. E-mail hbr4765@aol.com; web www.holidaybeach.com. 24 rms, 22 kits. Late Jan-Apr: S, D $120; each addl $15; suites $130-$170; lower rates rest of yr. Crib $1.50. TV; cable. Heated pool. Restaurant nearby. Ck-out 10 am. Coin lndry. Business servs avail. Tennis. Lawn games. Refrigerators, microwaves. Private patios. On Gulf. Cr cds: MC, V.

★ **SEA CLUB I.** *4141 Gulf of Mexico Dr.* 941/383-2431. 24 kit. units (1-2 bedrm), 1-2 story. Feb-Apr (1-wk min): S, D $97-$182; each addl $10; lower rates rest of yr (3-day min). TV; cable, VCR. Heated pool. Restaurant nearby. Ck-out 10 am. Coin lndry. Business servs avail. Microwaves. Private patios, balconies. On Gulf beach. Cr cds: MC, V.

★ **SEA HORSE BEACH RESORT.** *3453 Gulf of Mexico Dr.* 941/383-2417; *FAX* 941/387-8771. E-mail sresort@aol.com; web www.travelbase.com/destinations/sarasota/seahorse/. 35 kit. units (1-2 bedrm), 2 story. Feb-Apr: 1-bedrm $150; 2-bedrm $190; studio rms $135; lower rates rest of yr. TV; cable. Heated pool. Restaurant opp 11 am-11 pm.

Ck-out 11 am. Coin lndry. Business servs avail. Microwaves. Cr cds: DS, MC, V.

Motor Hotels

★ ★ ★ **HARBOUR VILLA CLUB AT THE BUCCANEER.** *615 Dream Island Rd.* 941/383-9544; *FAX* 941/383-8028; *res:* 800/433-5298. E-mail harbourv@gte.net. 18 suites, 3 story. Mid-Dec-Apr (wkly): suites $1,730-$1,850; each addl $20; monthly rates; lower rates rest of yr. Crib avail. TV; cable. Pool; whirlpool. Ck-out 10 am. Lighted tennis. Private patios, balconies. On Sarasota Bay Intracoastal Waterway; view of yacht harbor marina. Cr cds: A, MC, V.

★ ★ **HARLEY SANDCASTLE.** *(1540 Benjamin Franklin Dr, Sarasota 34236)* 1 mi SW of St Armand Circle Dr in Lido Beach. 941/388-2181; *FAX* 941/388-2655. Web www.harleyhotels.com. 179 rms, 2-4 story. Feb-May: S, D $149-$229; each addl $10; suites $299; under 18 free; lower rates rest of yr. Crib free. TV; cable. 2 pools, 1 heated; poolside serv. Restaurant 7 am-11 pm. Rm serv. Bar 5 pm-1 am; entertainment. Ck-out 11 am. Coin lndry. Meeting rms. Business center. Bellhops. Gift shop. Game rm. Lawn games. Refrigerators. On beach; water sports, boat & bicycle rentals. Cr cds: A, C, D, DS, MC, V.

★ ★ ★ **HILTON BEACH RESORT.** *4711 Gulf of Mexico Dr.* 941/383-2451; *res:* 800/282-3046; *FAX* 941/383-7979. Web www.hilton.com. 102 rms, 5 story. Mid-Dec-Apr: S, D $200-$300; each addl $25; 1-bedrm suites $260-$360; 2-bedrm suites $445-$545; under 18 free; lower rates rest of yr. Crib free. TV; cable (premium). Pool; poolside serv. Coffee in rms. Restaurant 7 am-10 pm. Rm serv. Bar 11 am-midnight; entertainment Thurs-Sat. Ck-out 11 am. Meeting rms. Business servs avail. Bellhops. Valet serv. Sundries. Lawn games. Minibars; refrigerator, microwave in suites. Private patios, balconies. Caribbean decor. On 400-ft beach; cabanas, water sports. Cr cds: A, C, D, DS, MC, V.

★ ★ **HOLIDAY INN-LIDO BEACH.** *(233 Ben Franklin Dr, Sarasota 34236)* 2 blks W of St Armand Circle on Lido Beach. 941/388-5555; *res:* 800/892-9174; *FAX* 941/388-4321. E-mail hilido@gte.net. 140 rms, 7 story. Dec-Apr: S, D $175-$235; suites $215-$245; under 19 free; lower rates rest of yr. Crib avail. TV; cable (premium). Heated pool. Restaurant 6:30 am-10 pm. Rm serv. Bar; entertainment Fri, Sat. Ck-out 11 am. Coin lndry. Meeting rms. Business servs avail. Bellhops. Valet Serv. Concierge. Gift shop. Balconies. Opp Gulf beach. Cr cds: A, C, D, DS, ER, JCB, MC, V.

★ ★ ★ **HOLIDAY INN-LONGBOAT KEY.** *4949 Gulf of Mexico Dr.* 941/383-3771; *res:* 800/465-4436; *FAX* 941/383-7871. E-mail holiday longboat@mindspring.com. 146 rms, 2-3 story. Mid-Dec-Apr: S, D $219-$249; each addl $15; kit. suites $259-$359; under 19 free; lower rates rest of yr. Crib avail. TV; cable (premium). 2 pools, 1 indoor; poolside serv. Restaurant 6:30 am-10 pm. Rm serv. Bars 11-2 am; Fri, Sat entertainment. Ck-out 11 am. Coin lndry. Meeting rms. Business servs avail. Bellhops. Valet serv. Concierge. Sundries. Gift shop. Lighted tennis. Putting green. Exercise equipt; saunas. Lawn games. Bicycles, water sports. Refrigerators; some microwaves. Private patios, balconies. On Gulf beach. Cr cds: A, C, D, DS, ER, JCB, MC, V.

★ ★ ★ **RADISSON LIDO BEACH RESORT.** *(700 Benjamin Franklin Dr, Sarasota 34236)* in Lido Beach. 941/388-2161; *FAX* 941/388-3175. Web www.radisson.com. 116 rms, 4 story, 87 kit. units. Mid-Dec-early Apr: S, D $145; each addl $12.50; kit. units $219-$295; under 16 free; wkly plans; hols (3-day min); higher rates Grand Prix; lower rates rest of yr. Crib free. TV; cable (premium). Pool; poolside serv. Complimentary coffee in rms. Restaurant 6:30 am-9 pm; Fri, Sat to 10 pm. Rm serv. Bar 11:30-2 am. Ck-out noon. Coin lndry. Meeting rms. Business servs avail. In-rm modem link. Bellhops. Airport transportation. Refrigerators; many microwaves. Balconies. On beach. Cr cds: A, D, DS, JCB, MC, V.

Resorts

★ ★ **COLONY BEACH AND TENNIS RESORT.** *1620 Gulf of Mexico Dr, 2 mi N of Longboat Key Bridge. 941/383-6464; res: 800/426-5669; FAX 941/383-7549.* E-mail colonyfl@ix.netcom.com; web www.colonybeachresort.com. 235 kit. apts (1-2 bedrm), 2-6 story. Late Dec-Apr: kit. apts $365-$565; beach houses $850-$975; clubhouses $525; beach units $625-$975; family rates; lower rates rest of yr. Crib $16. TV; cable (premium), VCR avail. Pool; whirlpool, poolside serv. Free supervised child's activities; ages 3-12. Restaurants 7 am-10 pm (also see COLONY). Limited rm serv. Bar 11-2 am; entertainment. Ck-out 11 am, ck-in 4 pm. Grocery. Coin laundry. Meeting rms. Business center. Gift shop. Airport transportation. 21 tennis courts, some lighted, pro, pro shop. Golf privileges. Boat, sailboard, water sport equipt. Bicycle rentals. Exercise rm; steam rm, sauna. Massage. Microwaves. Private patios, balconies. On gulf beach. Cr cds: A, C, D, DS, MC, V.

★ ★ ★ **THE RESORT AT LONGBOAT KEY CLUB.** *301 Gulf of Mexico Dr. 941/383-8821; FAX 941/383-5396; res: 800/237-8821.* Web www.longboatkeyclub.com. This is not simply a refined luxury hotel on 1,000 elaborately landscaped gulfside acres; it's one of the best places to golf in the state, as well as a great place for tennis. 233 units, 4-10 story, 213 kits. Mid-Jan-Apr: S, D $215-$345; suites $315-$445; 1-bedrm suites $350-$515; 2-bedrm suites $480-$735; lower rates rest of yr. TV; cable (premium), VCR avail. Heated pool; whirlpool, poolside serv. Supervised child's activities (mid-Feb-Sept); ages 5-12. Complimentary coffee in rms. Dining rm 7 am-midnight. Box lunches, snack bar. Rm serv from 6:30 am. Bar from 11 am; entertainment. Ck-out 11 am, ck-in 3 pm. Meeting rms. Business servs avail. Valet serv. Concierge. Pro shops. Airport transportation. Activities dir. 38 tennis courts, 6 lighted, pro. 45-hole golf, greens fee $98 (incl cart), pro, putting green, driving range. Private beach, boardwalk; water sports. Boat cruises. Bicycles. Lawn games. Exercise rm; sauna. Massage. Refrigerators, minibars; microwaves avail. Extensive library. Private patios. Bird sanctuary. Cr cds: A, C, D, DS, MC, V.

Restaurants

★ ★ ★ **CHART HOUSE.** *201 Gulf of Mexico Dr. 941/383-5593.* E-mail charthouse@aol.com; web www.charthouse.com. Hrs: 5-10 pm; early-bird dinner to 6 pm; Sun to 9 pm; Sun brunch late Nov-mid May 11 am-2:30 pm. Res accepted. Bar. Semi-a la carte: dinner $16.95-$26.95. Child's meals. Specializes in steak, fresh seafood, beef. Salad bar. Own desserts. Parking. View of gulf. Cr cds: A, C, D, DS, MC, V.

★ ★ **CHEF CALDWELL'S.** *(20 S Adams Dr, St Armands 34236) 941/388-5400.* Hrs: 11:30 am-2 pm, 5-9:30 pm; Sun from 5 pm. Closed 2 wks in Sept. Res accepted. Continental menu. Wine, beer. Semi-a la carte: lunch $5.75-$10.95, dinner $15.95-$23.95. Child's meals. Specializes in fresh seafood, venison, quail. Intimate dining experience; artwork. Cr cds: A, D, DS, MC, V.

★ ★ **COLONY.** *(See Colony Beach And Tennis Resort) 941/383-5558.* E-mail colonyfl@ix.netcom.com; web www.colonybeachresort.com. Hrs: 7-10:30 am, 11:30 am-2:30 pm, 6-9:30 pm; Fri, Sat to 10 pm; Sun brunch 10 am-2 pm. Res accepted. Bar; entertainment. Wine list. A la carte entrees: bkfst $3.95-$10.95, lunch $7.50-$13.95, dinner $19-$31. Sun brunch $24.95. Child's meals. Specialties: pan-roasted snapper, tuna sashimi, pecan-crusted grouper. Valet parking. Outdoor dining. Overlooks gulf beach. Cr cds: A, C, D, DS, MC, V.

★ ★ **EUPHEMIA HAYE.** *5540 Gulf of Mexico Dr. 941/383-3633.* E-mail info@euphemiahaye.com; web www.euphemiahaye.com. Hrs: 5-10:30 pm; summer: 6-10 pm; Fri, Sat 6-10:30 pm; Sun 6-10 pm. Closed Dec 25; also 3 wks after Labor Day. Res accepted. Eclectic menu. Bar. A la carte entrees: dinner $16.75-$26.50. Specialties: peppered steak, duckling in seasonal fruit and nut sauce. Own desserts. Entertainment. Parking. Dessert & gourmet coffee room. Cr cds: C, D, DS, MC, V.

★ ★ **HARRY'S CONTINENTAL KITCHENS.** *525 St Judes Dr. 941/383-0777.* Hrs: 11 am-2:30 pm, 5-9:30 pm; Sun brunch 10 am-3 pm. Closed Dec 25. Res accepted. Continental menu. Wine, beer. Semi-a la carte: lunch $7.95-$15.95, dinner $17.95-$24.95. Specializes in seafood. Parking. Totally nonsmoking. Cr cds: A, MC, V.

★ ★ **MOORE'S STONE CRAB.** *800 Broadway. 941/383-1748.* E-mail mooresrest@earthlink.net; web home.earthlink.net/~mooresrest/. Hrs: 11:30 am-9 pm; Fri, Sat to 9:30 pm; hrs vary May-Oct. Closed Thanksgiving, Dec 25; also Super Bowl Sun. Bar. Semi-a la carte: lunch, dinner $9.95-$21.95. Specializes in fresh seafood, stone crab (in season). Child's meals. Rustic dining on Sarasota Bay; dockage. Family-owned. Cr cds: DS, MC, V.

★ ★ ★ **OSTERIA.** *(29 ½ N Blvd of Presidents, Sarasota (St Armands Key) 34246) St Armands Circle. 941/388-3671.* Hrs: 4-10 pm. Res accepted. Northern Italian menu. Bar. Wine list. Semi-a la carte: dinner $10.95-$21.95. Child's meals. Specializes in fresh seafood, veal, homemade pasta. Own breads. Vocalist, pianist. Upstairs dining area; extensive wine display. Cr cds: A, C, D, DS, MC, V.

★ ★ **POSEIDON.** *3454 Gulf of Mexico. 941/383-2500.* Hrs: 5:30-10 pm. Closed Jan 1. Res accepted. Bar. A la carte entrees: dinner $18.75-$32. Specializes in seafood. Pianist Tues-Sat. Valet parking. Overlooks Intercoastal Waterway. Cr cds: A, C, D, DS, MC, V.

Madeira Beach

(see St Pete Beach)

Marathon (J-5)

(See also Big Pine Key)

Settled 1818 **Pop** 8,857 **Elev** 0-7 ft **Area code** 305 **Zip** 33050 **E-mail** marathincc@aol **Web** florida-keys.fl.us.com

Information Chamber of Commerce, 12222 Overseas Hwy; 305/743-5417 or 800/262-7284.

Transformed from a little fishing village by developers who have spent $15 million in the area, Marathon has become the hub of the Middle Keys. Its name came when an East Coast Railroad engineer groaned "It's getting to be a marathon," after hearing that the construction of the tracks was to continue southward. Today, tourism and commercial and sport fishing are the mainstream of the economy.

What to See and Do

Museum of Natural History of the Florida Keys. Exhibits on coral reefs, shipwrecks, Native Americans, wildlife, pirates; nature trail. Also located here is Florida Keys Children's Museum. (Mon-Sat & Sun afternoons; closed some major hols) 5550 Overseas Hwy (US 1), at mile marker 50. Phone 305/743-9100. ¢¢¢

Motels

★ **CORAL LAGOON.** *12399 Overseas Hwy (US 1). 305/289-0121; FAX 305/289-0195.* E-mail mcdaniel@reefnet.com. 18 kit. units. Late Dec-Mar: S, D $90-$130; each addl $7.50-$10; under 3 free; 7-day min (hols); lower rates rest of yr. Crib avail. TV; cable, VCR (movies). Complimentary coffee in lobby. Ck-out 11 am. Business servs avail. Coin lndry. Tennis. Pool. Microwaves. On ocean. Cr cds: A, DS, MC, V.

★ ★ **HOLIDAY INN.** *13201 Overseas Hwy (US 1) (13201), at mile marker 54. 305/289-0222; res: 800/224-5053; FAX 305/743-5460.* 134 rms, 2 story. Mid-Dec-mid-Apr: S, D $110-$130; each addl $10; under 12 free; higher rates special events; lower rates rest of yr. Crib free. TV; cable. Pool; wading pool. Restaurant 6:30-11:30 am, 5-10 pm. Bar. Ck-out 11 am. Coin lndry. Meeting rm. Business servs avail. In-rm modem link. Gift shop. Refrigerators avail. Dive shop; fishing charters. Cr cds: A, C, D, DS, ER, JCB, MC, V.

★ **RAINBOW BEND RESORT.** *57784 Overseas Hwy (US 1), on Grassy Key, 5 mi NE, at mile marker 58. 305/289-1505; FAX 305/743-0257; res: 800/929-1505.* 24 units, 1-2 story, 20 kits. Mid-Dec-mid-Apr: S, D, kit. units $120-$210; each addl $17.50; lower rates rest of yr. Crib free. Pet accepted. TV; cable (premium), VCR avail (movies). Pool; whirlpool. Complimentary full bkfst. Restaurant 7:30-9:30 am, 5-11 pm. Ck-out noon. Coin lndry. Business servs avail. Picnic tables, grills. On Beach; fishing pier; Boston whaler boats, sailboats, canoes. Cr cds: A, DS, MC, V.

Motor Hotel

★ ★ **SOMBRERO RESORT.** *19 Sombrero Blvd. 305/743-2250; FAX 305/743-2998; res: 800/433-8660.* Web www.fl-web.com/sombrero. 124 units, 1-3 story. Mid-Dec-mid-Apr: S, D $165; each addl $10; 2-bedrm suites $180; under 17 free; lower rates rest of yr. Crib avail. TV; cable. Pool; poolside serv. Restaurant 11 am-2 pm, 6-10 pm. Bar. Ck-out 11 am. Coin lndry. Business servs avail. Lighted tennis. Sauna. Some balconies. Picnic tables. Marina; dockage, full hookups. Cr cds: A, D, DS, MC, V.

Resorts

★ ★ **COCOPLUM BEACH & TENNIS CLUB.** *109 Cocoplum Dr. 305/743-0240; res: 800/228-1587; FAX 305/743-9351.* E-mail cocoplum1@aol.com; web www.cocoplum.com. 20 kit. units, 2 story. Mid-Dec-mid-Apr (3-day min): S, D $200-$350; lower rates rest of yr. Crib avail. Maid serv wkly. TV; cable (premium), VCR avail. Complimentary coffee in rms. Grocery 3½ mi. Guest lndry. Package store 3½ mi. Business servs avail. In-rm modem link. Tennis. Pool. Microwaves. On ocean. Cr cds: A, MC, V.

★ ★ ★ **HAWK'S CAY.** *(Mile Marker 61, Duck Key 33138) 8 mi N on Overseas Hwy (US 1). 305/743-7000; FAX 305/743-5215; res: 800/432-2242.* Web www.hawkscay.com. 176 rms, 2-5 story, 57 villas. Late Dec-late Apr: S, D $220-$375; each addl $20; suites $425-$850; kit. suites $575; villas (3-day min) $375-$475; under 11 free; lower rates rest of yr. Crib free. TV; cable. Heated pool; whirlpools, poolside serv. Supervised child's activities (summer, hols). Coffee in rms. Restaurant 7 am-11 pm. Rm serv. Bar 11-2 am; entertainment. Ck-out 11 am, ck-in 3 pm. Coin lndry. Meeting rms. Business servs avail. In-rm modem link. Concierge. Gift shop. Free airport transportation. Lighted tennis, pro. 18-hole golf privileges. Private beach, swimming. Marina, boats, glass-bottomed boat, charter boat; wave runners, sailing. Scuba diving, snorkeling. Bicycle rentals. Game rm. Refrigerators. Private patios, balconies. On ocean; dolphin training center. Cr cds: A, C, D, DS, MC, V.

Restaurants

★ ★ **KELSEY'S.** *1996 Overseas Hwy (US 1), mile marker 48. 305/743-9018.* Hrs: 6-9:30 pm; Fri, Sat to 10 pm. Closed Mon. Res accepted. Bar. Semi-a la carte: dinner $14.95-$26.95. Child's meals. Specializes in local seafood, beef. Nautical decor. Cr cds: A, DS, MC, V.

D

★ ★ **QUAY.** *12650 Overseas Hwy (US 1), mile marker 54.5. 305/289-1810.* Hrs: 11 am-10 pm; Fri, Sat to 11 pm; early-bird dinner 4-6 pm. Res accepted. Continental menu. Bar. Semi-a la carte: lunch $4.95-$10.50, dinner $8.95-$32.95. Child's meals. Specializes in steak, seafood. Entertainment. Outdoor dining. On Gulf of Mexico. Cr cds: A, C, D, DS, MC, V.

D

Marco Island (H-4)

(See also Naples)

Pop 9,493 **Elev** 10-52 ft **Area code** 941 **Zip** 33937 **Web** www.marco-island-florida.com
Information Marco Island Area Chamber of Commerce, 1102 N Collier Blvd; 941/394-7549.

Marco Island, the largest and northernmost of the Ten Thousand Islands, was once occupied by a cannibalistic tribe that prevented settlement of the island until the late 1800s. Later, the Doxsee Clam Factory established itself on the island, but it wasn't until the 1960s, when dredges were constructed, that Marco became a flourishing community. Today, the island is noted for fishing and shelling and has been developed as a resort area.

What to See and Do

Collier-Seminole State Park. Approx 6,400 acres with historic displays and native plant communities. Fishing; boating (ramp, canoe rentals). Nature trails. Picnicking, concession. Camping (hookups, dump station). Boat tour. Seminole villages nearby. Standard hrs, fees. 12 mi NE on FL 92. Phone 941/394-3397.

Everglades National Park (see). A visitor center is located in Everglades City, S off US 41. Approx 20 mi SE via US 41.

Marco Island Trolley. Narrated, 1¾-hr sightseeing tours; more than 100 points of interest; stops at shopping centers, lodgings, restaurants, attractions; also historic Indian Hills area. (4 trips daily; no trips Dec 25) Phone 941/394-1600 for schedule. All-day pass ¢¢¢

Sightseeing. Island Nature Cruises. A 14-mi, 2-hr cruise aboard the 49-passenger *Island Princess* or 9-passenger *Princess of the Port* through the Ten Thousand Islands. Two departures (daily). Tamiami Trail E to Port of the Islands Hotel. Phone 941/394-3101. ¢¢¢¢

Motels

★ ★ **THE BOATHOUSE.** *1180 Edington Place (34145), in Old Marco Village. 941/642-2400; FAX 941/642-2435; res: 800/528-6345.* E-mail boathousem@aol.com; web www.theboathousemotel.com. 20 rms, 2 story. Nov-May: S, D $82.50-$137.50; each addl $10-$20; wkly rates in season; lower rates rest of yr. Pet accepted, some restrictions; $15. TV; cable. Pool. Restaurant nearby. Ck-out 11 am. Coin lndry. Business servs avail. Some microwaves. Balconies. Picnic tables. Built 1883; French doors, antiques. On entrance to Collier Bay; dockage. Cr cds: MC, V.

★ **FLORIDA PAVILION CLUB CONDOMINIUM.** *1170 Edington Pl (34145), in Old Marco Village. 941/394-3345; FAX 941/394-7472.* E-mail brooms2go@aol.com. 17 kit. condos (1-2 bedrm), 2 story. Dec-Apr (4-day min): S, D $165-$341; family, wkly, monthly rates; lower rates rest of yr. TV; cable, VCR avail. Pool. Ck-out 11 am. Coin lndry. Business servs avail. Private patios, balconies. Dockage (fee). Cr cds: MC, V.

Motor Hotels

★ ★ **EAGLE'S NEST BEACH RESORT.** *410 S Collier Blvd (34145).* 941/394-5167; FAX 941/642-1599; res: 800/448-2736. 96 kit. suites, 10 story. Late Dec-Easter: $199-$335; wkly rates; lower rates rest of yr. TV; cable (premium), VCR (movies). Heated pool; whirlpool. Supervised child's activities; ages 5-10. Restaurant adj. Ck-out 10 am. Business servs avail. Gift shop. Lighted tennis. Exercise rm; sauna. Game rm. Microwaves. Private patios, balconies. Picnic tables, grills. 3 main buildings surround courtyard with fountain, pool, lush landscaping. On beach. Cr cds: A, D, DS, MC, V.

★ **MARCO BAY RESORT.** *1001 N Barfield Dr (34145), at Bald Eagle Dr.* 941/394-8881; FAX 941/394-8909; res: 800/228-0661. Web www.marcobayresort.com. 75 kit. suites (1-2 bedrm), 5 story. Mid-Dec-mid-Apr (wkly): $700-$1,200; under 17 free; lower rates rest of yr. TV; cable (premium). 2 pools; 3 whirlpools. Restaurant 8 am-9 pm. Bars from 11 am. Ck-out 11 am. Coin lndry. Meeting rms. Business servs avail. Tennis. Microwaves. Balconies. On bay. Cr cds: A, MC, V.

Hotels

★ ★ **MARCO ISLAND HILTON BEACH RESORT.** *560 S Collier Blvd (34147).* 941/394-5000; FAX 941/394-5251; res: 800/443-4550. Web www.hilton.com. 294 rms, 11 story. Mid-Dec-Apr: S, D $219-$329; each addl $25; 1-bedrm suite $369; family rates; package plans; lower rates rest of yr. Crib free. TV; cable (premium). Heated pool; whirlpool, poolside serv. Supervised child's activities; ages 3-14. Coffee in rms. Restaurants 7 am-10 pm (also see SANDCASTLES). Bar noon-2 am. Ck-out noon. Convention facilities. Business center. In-rm modem link. Concierge. Gift shop. Drugstore. 3 lighted tennis courts, pro. Golf privileges, greens fee $25-$130, pro, putting green, driving range. Exercise rm; sauna, steam rm. Massage. Bicycles avail. Game rm. Bathrm phones, refrigerators, minibars; microwaves avail. Private patios, balconies. On gulf, fishing by arrangement; beach, water sports. Cr cds: A, C, D, DS, MC, V.

★ ★ **RADISSON SUITE BEACH RESORT.** *600 S Collier Blvd (34145).* 941/394-4100; FAX 941/394-0419. Web www.marcobeachresort.com. 281 units, 12 story. Feb-Apr: S, D $259; 1-bedrm $299-$369; 2-bedrm $489-$509; lower rates rest of yr. Crib $10. TV; cable (premium), VCR avail. Pool; whirlpool, poolside serv. Supervised child's activities; ages 3-12. Restaurants 7 am-10 pm. Bar from 11 am; entertainment. Ck-out noon. Coin lndry. Meeting rms. Business center. In-rm modem link. Concierge. Gift shop. Covered parking. Lighted tennis. Golf privileges, greens fee (incl cart) $60-$120, pro, putting green, driving range. Exercise equipt. Game rm. Balconies. On Gulf; beach. Cr cds: A, C, D, DS, MC, V.

Resort

★ ★ ★ **MARCO ISLAND MARRIOTT RESORT AND GOLF CLUB.** *400 S Collier Blvd (34145).* 941/394-2511; res: 800/438-4373; FAX 941/642-2672. Web www.marriott.com. 735 units, 11 story. Mid-Dec-May: S, D $250-$350; 1-2-bedrm suites $629-$899; 1-, 2-bedrm penthouses $1,000-$1,500; 2-bedrm villas $619-$679; under 18 free; lower rates rest of yr. Crib free. TV; cable (premium), VCR avail. 3 pools, 2 heated; whirlpool, poolside serv. Playgrounds. Supervised child's activities; ages 5-12. Coffee in rms. 5 restaurants 7 am-midnight. Rm serv. Bar 11-2 am; entertainment. Ck-out noon, ck-in 3 pm. Coin lndry. Convention facilities. Business center. In-rm modem link. Valet serv. Concierge. Shopping arcade. Barber, beauty shop. Valet parking. Lighted tennis, pros. 18-hole

golf, greens fee $35-$110, pro. Private gulf beach; water sports (rentals). Bicycle rentals. Lawn games. Soc dir; entertainment. Game rm. Exercise equipt. Massage. Refrigerators, minibars. Private patios, balconies. Ice cream parlor. Cr cds: A, C, D, DS, ER, JCB, MC, V.

Restaurants

★ ★ **BAVARIAN INN.** *960 Winterberry Dr (34145).* 941/394-7233. Hrs: 4:30-10 pm; early-bird dinner 4:30-6 pm. Continental menu. Bar 4:30 pm-2 am. Semi-a la carte: dinner $8.95-$17.50. Child's meals. Specializes in duck, steaks, seafood. German chalet decor. Cr cds: A, C, D, DS, MC, V.

★ ★ **CAFE DE MARCO.** *244 Royal Palm Dr (34145), off Palm St.* 941/394-6262. Hrs: 5-10 pm. Closed Sun off-season; most major hols. Res accepted. Continental menu. Semi-a la carte: dinner $14.95-$20.95. Child's meals. Specializes in fresh Florida seafood. Own desserts. Parking. European atmosphere; stained-glass panels. Cr cds: A, MC, V.

★ ★ ★ **KONRAD'S.** *599 S Collier Blvd (34145).* 941/642-3332. Hrs: 11:30 am-2:30 pm, 5-10 pm; Sun from 5 pm; early-bird dinner 5-6 pm; summer hrs vary. Closed Dec 24, 25; also Super Bowl Sun. Res accepted. Continental menu. Bar. Semi-a la carte: lunch $6.95-$12.95, dinner $13.95-$23.95. Buffet: lunch $8.95. Specializes in seafood, beef, lamb chops. Extensive dessert menu and salad bar. Valet parking. Patio dining with view of landscaped grounds and statuary. Cr cds: A, C, D, DS, MC, V.

★ ★ **MARCO POLO.** *30 Marco Lake Dr (34145).* 941/394-5777. Hrs: 5 pm-2 am. Closed Super Bowl Sun. Res accepted. Continental menu. Bar. Semi-a la carte: dinner $10.95-$21.95. Child's meals. Specializes in veal, steak, fresh seafood. Piano bar. Parking. Cr cds: A, MC, V.

★ ★ ★ **MAREK'S COLLIER HOUSE.** *1121 Bald Eagle Dr (34145).* 941/642-9948. Hrs: 5:30-9:30 pm. Closed Mon, Sun (May-Oct); 1-month Aug or Sept. Res accepted. Modern European menu. Wine list. A la carte entrees: dinner $16.95-$29.95. Specializes in fresh seafood. Parking. Captain Bill Collier's original home (1882). Totally nonsmoking. Cr cds: A, MC, V.

★ ★ ★ **SANDCASTLES.** *(See Marco Island Hilton Beach Resort Hotel)* 941/394-5000. Hrs: 6-10 pm. Res accepted. Continental menu. Bar 5 pm-midnight. Wine list. A la carte entrees: dinner $18-$24. Child's meals. Specializes in fresh seafood, steak, veal. Pianist. Valet parking. View of gulf and pool area. Antiques, paintings. Cr cds: A, C, D, DS, MC, V.

★ **SNOOK INN.** *1215 Bald Eagle Dr (34145).* 941/394-3313. E-mail stuff@snookinn.com; web www.snookinn.com. Hrs: 11 am-10 pm. Closed Thanksgiving, Dec 25. Bar to midnight. Semi-a la carte: lunch $6.25-$8.95, dinner $9.95-$18.95. Child's meals. Specializes in fresh seafood. Salad bar. Entertainment. Outdoor dining. Parking. Nautical decor; aquarium. On Marco River; dockage. Cr cds: A, C, D, DS, MC, V.

✔ ★ **SU'S GARDEN.** *537 Bald Eagle Dr (34145).* 941/394-4666. Hrs: 11:30 am-10 pm. Chinese menu. Wine, beer. Semi-a la carte: lunch $5.25-$5.50, dinner $5.95-$14.95. Sun buffet $7.95. Specializes in Cantonese, Szechwan, Hunan and Mandarin dishes. Oriental decor. Cr cds: A, DS, MC, V.

★ ★ **VITO'S WATERFRONT.** *1079 Bald Eagle Dr (34145).* 941/394-7722. E-mail vistas.com; web www.vitos.com. Hrs: 11:30 am-2 pm, 6-9 pm; Sun from 6 pm. Closed Jan 1, Thanksgiving, Dec 25; also Sun off season. Res accepted. Italian menu. Bar. Wine list. Semi-a la carte: lunch $5.95-$9.95, dinner $13.95-$24.95. Specializes in pasta, seafood, steaks. Parking. Outdoor dining. Many nautical artifacts; view of bay. Cr cds: A, D, DS, MC, V.

Marianna (J-3)

(See also Blountstown)

Founded 1829 **Pop** 6,292 **Elev** 117 ft **Area code** 850 **Zip** 32446 **E-mail** cofc@phonl.com
Information Marianna County Chamber of Commerce, 2928 Jefferson St, PO Box 130, 32447; 850/482-8061.

The Chipola River bisects Marianna, the seat of Jackson County. East is Merritts Mill Pond and its source, an underwater cave at Blue Springs.

What to See and Do

Falling Waters State Recreation Area. More than 150 acres with waterfall that flows into a 100-ft sinkhole, which has moss- and fern-covered walls. Swimming. Nature trails. Picnicking. Camping (dump station). Standard hrs, fees. 15 mi W on I-10 to Chipley, then 3 mi S off FL 77A. Phone 850/638-6130.

Florida Caverns State Park. Approx 1,300-acre park includes a limestone cavern and network of caves with unusual stalactites and stalagmites. Cavern tours (daily). The Chipola River, which helped form the cavern, flows through the park, going underground for a brief distance. Swimming; fishing; boating (ramp). Nature trails. Picnicking. Camping (hookups, dump station). Visitor center. Standard hrs, fees. 3 mi N on FL 166. Phone 850/482-9598 or 482-1228. Cavern tours ¢¢

Three Rivers State Recreation Area. Approx 680 acres on man-made Lake Seminole. Hilly terrain with white-tailed deer, fox squirrel, grey fox and bobwhites. Fishing. Canoeing; boating (ramp). Nature trails. Picnicking. Camping (hookups, dump station). Standard hrs, fees. 25 mi E via US 90 to Sneads, then 2 mi N on FL 271. Phone 850/482-9006.

Motel

★ **COMFORT INN.** 2175 FL 71 (32447), On FL 71N, at jct I-10 exit 21. 850/526-5600; FAX 850/482-7899. 80 rms, 2 story. S $48-$60; D $52-$60; each addl $5; under 18 free. Crib free. Pet accepted. TV; cable (premium). Pool. Complimentary continental bkfst. Restaurant nearby. Ck-out 11 am. Coin lndry. Business servs avail. Cr cds: A, C, D, DS, MC, V.

Restaurant

✔★ **TONY'S.** 4133 W Lafayette. 850/482-2232. Hrs: 6 am-9 pm; Fri to 10 pm; Sat 11 am-10 pm. Closed Sun; major hols. Italian, Amer menu. Beer. Semi-a la carte: bkfst from $2.75, lunch from $4.75, dinner $5.95-$13.95. Child's meals. Specializes in steak, seafood, chicken. Cr cds: A, C, D, DS, MC, V.

Marineland (C-5)

(See also Ormond Beach, St Augustine)

Pop 21 **Elev** 11 ft **Area code** 904

What to See and Do

Fort Matanzas National Monument (see). 4 mi N on FL A1A.
Marineland of Florida. Hundreds of fish of all sizes, including dolphins, sharks, moray eels and barracudas in aquatic communities inhabit two of the world's oldest giant oceanariums; they may be photographed through many surrounding portholes. Trained dolphins exhibit their physical and intellectual prowess, as do performing California sea lions; Marine and freshwater exhibits; tropical penguins; 3-D film in Aquarius Theater; Shell Museum. Oceanfront promenade; lodging; restaurant; campground opp. (Daily) Phone 904/471-1111 or 800/874-0492. ¢¢¢¢¢
Washington Oaks State Gardens. Approx 400 acres; originally a Spanish land grant to Bautista Don Juan Ferreira in 1815. Citrus groves, rose garden, native plants and shrubs. Swimming; fishing. Nature trails. Picnicking. Standard hrs, fees. 2 mi S on FL A1A, just N of Palm Coast. Phone 904/446-6780.

Resort

★★★ **HARBORSIDE INN PALM COAST RESORT.** (300 Clubhouse Dr, Palm Coast 32137) S via I-95 exit 91C. 904/445-3000; res: 800/654-6538; FAX 904/445-9685. Web www.flager.com/pcr.resort.html. 154 units, 3 story. Jan-May, Sept-Nov: S, D $99-$190; each addl $20; under 17 free; golf, tennis plans; higher rates special events (3-5-day min); lower rates rest of yr. TV; cable (premium). 3 pools, 1 heated; wading pool, whirlpool, poolside serv. Playground. Coffee in rms. Restaurant 6:30 am-9:30 pm. Rm serv. Bar 2 pm-1 am; entertainment. Ck-out noon, ck-in 3 pm. Grocery, package store. Meeting rms. Business servs avail. Bellhops. Valet serv. Gift shop. Sports dir. Lighted tennis, 18-court complex with grass, clay and hard surfaces. 4 golf courses, greens fee varies, putting green, driving range, miniature golf. 80-slip marina. Bicycle rentals. Soc dir. Game rm. Exercise equipt; sauna. Minibars. Some private patios, balconies. On Intracoastal Waterway; private beach, club. All rms with view of waterway or marina. Cr cds: A, C, D, DS, MC, V.

Melbourne (E-5)

(See also Cocoa, Cocoa Beach, Vero Beach)

Founded 1878 **Pop** 59,646 **Elev** 21 ft **Area code** 407 **E-mail** mail@melpb-chamber.org **Web** www.melpb-chamber.org
Information Melbourne-Palm Bay Area Chamber of Commerce, 1005 E Strawbridge Ave, 32901; 407/724-5400 or 800/771-9922.

On the Indian River, just west of the Atlantic Ocean and neighbor to both Cape Canaveral and Kennedy Space Center (see), Melbourne has tied its present and future to the space age. Many large electronics firms have been established here in the last decade, making the town a leader in technology. There is fishing from the causeways, the rivers, Lake Washington and the Atlantic Ocean. Boating, sailing, waterskiing, boardsailing and jet skiing are also popular.

What to See and Do

Brevard Zoo. Features more than 200 animals; Paws-On interactive learning area; playground and domesticated animals in Animal Encounters. (Daily; closed major hols) 8225 N Wickham Rd. Phone 407/254-9453. ¢¢

Florida Institute of Technology (1958). (6,000 students) On main campus is the Florida Tech Botanical Garden, which features rare and exotic palms (daily; free). Country Club Rd, 1 mi S of New Haven Ave, US 192. Phone 407/768-8000.

Long Point Park. Approx 120 acres of park including a freshwater lake. Fishing. Picnicking. Playground. Camping facilities (hookups). (Daily) 2 mi N of Sebastian Inlet, 1 mi W on FL A1A. Phone 407/952-4532. Per car ¢

Wickham Park. Approximately 480 acres of parkland with 2 lakes, picnic pavilions, camping facilities. Archery range (free). (Daily) 1 mi W of US 1 on Parkway Dr. Phone 407/255-4307. **Free.**

Annual Event

Melbourne Harbor Festival. A celebration of the Indian River Lagoon's environment. Nov.

Motels

★ ★ **COMFORT INN.** 8298 N Wickham Rd (32940), I-95 exit 74. 407/255-0077; FAX 407/259-9633. E-mail sales@imperialcomfortinn.com. 134 rms, 5 story, 18 suites. Feb-Apr: S $60-$85; D $65-$90; each addl $10; suites $75-$95; under 18 free; wkly rates; golf plans; lower rates rest of yr. TV; cable (premium). Pool. Complimentary continental bkfst. Restaurant 11 am-3 pm, 5-9 pm. Bar 4 pm-midnight. Ck-out 11 am. Coin lndry. Meeting rms. Business servs avail. Bellhops. Airport transportation. Golf privileges, greens fee, pro, putting green, driving range. Health club privileges. Refrigerator in suites; microwaves avail. Cr cds: A, C, D, DS, MC, V.

D 〤 ⊱ ≈ ⊼ ⊼ 🐾 SC

★ ★ **COURTYARD BY MARRIOTT.** 2101 W New Haven Ave (32904), 4 mi E of I-95 exit 71, near Regional Airport. 407/724-6400; FAX 407/984-4006. 146 rms, 3 story. S, D $54-$109; suites $79-$114; wkly rates. Crib free. TV; cable. Pool; whirlpool. Complimentary coffee in rms. Restaurant 6:30-10 am; wkends 7-11 am. Ck-out noon. Meeting rms. Business servs avail. Valet serv. Sundries. Free airport transportation. Exercise equipt. Some refrigerators. Balconies. Picnic tables. Cr cds: A, D, DS, MC, V.

D ≈ ⊼ ⊼ 🐾 SC

✔ ★ ★ **HOLIDAY INN.** 420 S Harbor City Blvd (US 1) (32901). 407/723-5320; FAX 407/724-0581. 100 rms, 1-2 story. Jan-Apr: S, D $59-$79; under 18 free; lower rates rest of yr. Crib free. TV; cable. Pool. Bar. Ck-out 11 am. Microwaves avail. Indian River opp. Cr cds: A, C, D, DS, ER, JCB, MC, V.

D ≈ ⊼ 🐾 SC

Motor Hotels

★ ★ **BEST WESTERN HARBORVIEW.** 964 S Harbor City (32901), near Melbourne Intl Airport. 407/724-4422; FAX 407/951-9974. 122 rms, 5 story. Jan-Mar: S, D $79; eah addl $5; suites $125; under 18 free; lower rates rest of yr. Crib free. TV; cable (premium). Restaurant 7 am-10 pm. Rm. serv. Bar. Ck-out noon. Meeting rms. Business servs avail. In-rm modem link. Valet serv. Free airport transportation. Pool. Cr cds: A, C, D, DS, MC, V.

D ≈ ⊼ ⊼ 🐾 SC

★ ★ **HOLIDAY INN MELBOURNE OCEANFRONT.** (2605 N FL A1A, Indialantic 32903) E on Melbourne Causeway (I-92), then N on FL A1A. 407/777-4100; FAX 407/773-6132. E-mail hi.melbourne.1160@ servicohotels.com. 299 rms, 8 story. S, D $75-$129; suites $109-$189; under 18 free. Crib free. TV; cable. Pool; whirlpool, poolside serv. Complimentary coffee in rms. Restaurant 6:30 am-10 pm. Rm serv. Bar; entertainment Wed-Fri. Ck-out 11 am. Business servs avail. Bellhops. Valet serv. Gift shop. Free airport transportation. Tennis. Exercise equipt. Balconies. On ocean. Cr cds: A, C, D, DS, ER, JCB, MC, V.

D ⊱ ≈ ⊼ ⊼ 🐾 SC

Hotels

★ ★ ★ **HILTON AT RIALTO PLACE.** 200 Rialto Pl (32901), near Regional Airport. 407/768-0200; FAX 407/984-2528. E-mail hotel sunny@aol.com. 240 rms, 8 story. S $109-$139; D $109-$149; each addl $10; suites $250; under 18 free; package plans. Crib free. TV; cable (premium), VCR avail. Pool; whirlpool, poolside serv. Restaurant 6:30 am-midnight. Bar. Ck-out noon. Convention facilities. Business center. In-rm modem link. Gift shop. Free airport transportation. Lighted tennis. Golf privileges. Exercise equipt. Microwaves avail. Some private patios, balconies. Luxury level. Cr cds: A, C, D, DS, ER, JCB, MC, V.

D 〤 ⊱ ≈ ⊼ ⊼ 🐾 SC ⚓

★ ★ ★ **HILTON OCEANFRONT.** (3003 N FL A1A, Indialantic 32903) E via Melbourne Causeway, N on FL A1A. 407/777-5000; FAX 407/777-3713. 118 rms, 11 story. S $90-$130; D $100-$150; each addl $10; suites $130-$170; under 18 free. Crib free. Pet accepted; $25 refundable & $5.50/day. TV; cable (premium). Pool; poolside serv. Restaurant 6:30 am-2 pm, 4-10 pm. Bars 11-2 am; outdoor entertainment Sun. Ck-out noon. Meeting rms. Business servs avail. Golf privileges. Exercise equipt. Balconies. On ocean beach. Cr cds: A, C, D, DS, MC, V.

D ⊱ ⊱ ≈ ⊼ ⊼ 🐾 SC

★ ★ ★ **QUALITY SUITES OCEANFRONT.** (1665 N FL A1A, Indialantic 32903) E via Melbourne Causeway, N on FL A1A. 407/723-4222; FAX 407/768-2438. 208 suites, 9 story. Feb-Apr: suites $89-$189; under 18 free; wkly rates; higher rates hol wkends; lower rates rest of yr. Crib free. Pet accepted. TV; cable (premium), VCR (movies $5.30). Pool; whirlpool, poolside serv. Buffet bkfst. Complimentary coffee in rms. Restaurant 6:30-9:30 am, 11:30 am-2 pm, 5-9 pm. Bar noon-10 pm. Ck-out noon. Coin lndry. Meeting rms. Business servs avail. Gift shop. Health club privileges. Game rm. Minibars; microwaves avail. Balconies. On ocean; swimming beach. Cr cds: A, C, D, DS, ER, JCB, MC, V.

D ⊱ ≈ 🐾 🐾 SC

★ ★ ★ **RADISSON SUITE OCEANFRONT.** 3101 N FL A1A (32903). 407/773-9260; FAX 407/777-3190. 167 suites, 15 story. Jan-Apr: S, D $110-$170; each addl $10; under 18 free; special package plans; lower rates rest of yr. Crib free. TV; cable (premium). Pool; whirlpools, poolside serv. Complimentary coffee in rms. Restaurant 7 am-2 pm, 5-10 pm. Bar noon-10 pm. Ck-out noon. Coin lndry. Meeting rms. Business servs avail. Gift shop. Health club privileges. Microwaves. Balconies. On beach. Cr cds: A, C, D, DS, ER, JCB, MC, V.

D ≈ 🐾 🐾 SC

Restaurants

★ ★ **CHART HOUSE.** 2250 Front St (32901), near US 192 at yacht basin. 407/729-6558. Hrs: 5-9:30 pm; Fri, Sat to 10 pm. Res accepted. Bar. Semi-a la carte: dinner $10.50-$26.95. Child's meals. Specializes in steak, seafood. Salad bar. Parking. On Indian River; view of adj marina. Cr cds: A, C, D, DS, MC, V.

D 🍴

★ **CONCHY JOE'S SEAFOOD.** 1477 Pineapple Ave (32936), Eau Gallie Causeway, at river. 407/253-3131. Hrs: 11:30 am-2:30 pm, 4-10 pm; early-bird dinner to 6 pm. Closed Thanksgiving, Dec 24 (dinner), 25. Bar to 1 am. Semi-a la carte: lunch $3.95-$10.95, dinner $8.95-$24.95. Child's meals. Specializes in fresh seafood, steak, Bahamian dishes. Reggae Thurs-Sun. Parking. Outdoor dining. Casual dining at site of old Oleander Hotel. Cr cds: A, DS, MC, V.

D 🍴

✔ ★ ★ **STRAWBERRY MANSION AND MISTER BEAUJEANS.** 218 E New Haven Ave (32901), downtown. 407/723-1900. E-mail info@strawberrys.com; web www.strawberrys.com. Hrs: 8 am-9 pm; Mon to 5 pm; Sun brunch to 1 pm. Res accepted. Bar. Semi-a la carte: bkfst $4-$8, lunch $4-$7, dinner $9-$15. Sun brunch $4-$8. Child's meals.

Specializes in seafood, steaks, pasta. Outdoor dining in brick courtyard. In historic Victorian mansion. Cr cds: MC, V.

Miami (H-6)

Settled 1870 **Pop** 358,548 **Elev** 5 ft **Area code** 305 **Web** www.miamiandbeaches.com
Information Greater Miami Convention & Visitors Bureau, 701 Brickell Ave, Ste 2700, 33131; 305/539-3000 or 800/464-2643.

Suburbs Coral Gables, Hialeah, Hollywood, Key Biscayne, Miami Beach. (See individual alphabetical listings.)

Metropolitan Miami is part bazaar, part Broadway—a place of bikinis and minks, the habitat of boulevardiers and budgeteers; a New World city made up of both North and South America and its peoples; an international place that provides glamour, excitement and sunburn for about 9.6 million visitors each year. It takes more than 600 hotels and motels, 7,000 restaurants, 650 churches and synagogues, 40 foreign consuls and 35 hospitals to cater to the tourists in this sun-drenched conglomeration of 29 separate municipalities.

Put all its fragments together, and Greater Miami's 2,042-square-mile place in the sun seems like a blazing concoction of suntan oil, sand, glitter and gilt. But beyond this, Miami is a place of gleaming skyscrapers, of more than 3,400 manufacturing firms, 170 banks and a half-billion-dollar agricultural industry. With more than $123 million annually in customs collections, and mighty ties in commerce, it is the prime gateway to Latin America.

To most visitors, Miami is an all-encompassing term, including both the city of Miami and its across-the-bay twin, Miami Beach (see). Actually, each is a separate community and, like most sister cities, each is vigorously different in personality. Miami is the older; still a merry lady, but now more settled and sophisticated. Miami Beach is perpetual youth on a fling.

The city of Miami has a touch of Manhattan to it with its business bustle, its rush-hour traffic and its skyscrapers. This is a city of luxury houses, palm-bordered boulevards, art deco architecture and souvenir shops in the midst of a downtown of new ultramodern office towers, hotels, condominiums and shopping malls.

Biscayne Bay serves as the buffer between the two communities. Along this shore, on the Miami side, runs Biscayne Blvd (US 1), lined with hundreds of stately royal palms—a street where anything from a free glass of orange juice to a $2 million yacht can be casually acquired. The Miami River winds through the heart of the city and seven causeways form lifelines to the sandy shores of Miami Beach. Another causeway links the mainland with Key Biscayne to the south.

Although favored by climate and geography, Miami remained a remote tropical village of frame houses until Henry Morrison Flagler brought his East Coast Railway here in 1896, and turned his hand to community development. Miami's growth was persistent but unspectacular until the 1920s when the great Florida land boom brought 25,000 real estate salesmen to town. In 1925, downtown property was selling at $20,000 a front foot, and $100 million was spent in construction. The bubble burst with a mighty hurricane in 1926, but Miami had the natural assets to come back strong. The city's growth continues at an unflinching pace today, solidly based on year-round tourism, international commerce and trade, industry and agriculture. The Port of Miami is the largest embarkation point for cruise ships in the world.

Transportation

Airport. See MIAMI INTL AIRPORT AREA.

Car Rental Agencies: See IMPORTANT TOLL-FREE NUMBERS.

Public Transportation: Elevated trains and buses (Metro Bus & Rail), phone 305/638-6700.

Rail Passenger Service: Amtrak 800/872-7245.

What to See and Do

American Police Hall of Fame and Museum. Collection of firearms, murder weapons; lie detectors, electric chair; police vehicles; many other exhibits. Memorial to officers killed in the line of duty. (Daily; closed Dec 25) 3801 Biscayne Blvd. Phone 305/573-0070. No charge to police officers and their families. ¢¢¢

Barnacle State Historic Site. Historic house and grounds, former residence of Ralph M. Munroe, Coconut Grove pioneer and yacht designer. Oldest remaining residence in Dade County. Designed for the climate, this is an outstanding example of Caribbean architecture. Tours (Fri-Sun). 5 mi S via I-95, S Miami Ave & S Bayshore Dr to 3485 Main Hwy in Coconut Grove. Phone 305/448-9445. ¢¢

Bayside Marketplace. This 16-acre restaurant, shopping and entertainment complex reflects the South Florida/Caribbean style; more than 150 specialty shops; pushcarts, open-air marketplace, two entertainment pavilions, waterfront promenade, departure point for gondola and boat cruises. (Daily) 401 N Biscayne Blvd, bounded by Biscayne & Port Blvds, on Biscayne Bay. Phone 305/577-3344.

Big Cypress National Preserve. Adjoining the northwest section of Everglades National Park (see), this approx 570,000-acre area is rich in subtropical plant and animal life. The preserve is a favorite spot of bird watchers and photographers. 47 mi W via US 41.

Boating, fishing. More than 600 varieties of saltwater and freshwater fish abound in the waters around metropolitan Miami. Persons may fish from bridges, causeways and piers, or boats may be rented; many tournaments throughout the year. Biscayne Bay offers 370 sq mi of protected water for boating; anything from a skiff to a yacht can be rented; many marinas and launching ramps are scattered about.

Coconut Grove Playhouse. Regional professional theater produces original comedies, dramas and musicals. (Oct-June, Tues-Sat evenings; matinees Wed, Sat, Sun) 3500 Main Hwy. Phone 305/442-4000.

Cruises. Various types of cruises are available, from lunch or dinner cruises to casino cruises to murder/mystery trips; departure point for many Caribbean cruises; rental boats range from intimate sailboats to 140-ft yachts.

Gold Coast Railroad Museum. Collection of railroad cars and memorabilia; *Ferdinand Magellan*, historic armored private car used by Presidents Roosevelt, Truman, Eisenhower and Reagan; various steam locomotives and passenger cars; 20-min train ride (Sat & Sun). 12450 SW 152nd St, just W of FL Tpke. Phone 305/253-0063. ¢¢

Historical Museum of Southern Florida. Participatory exhibits trace man's experiences in southern Florida from prehistoric to modern times. Includes artifacts from prehistoric and Seminole Indian cultures; maritime history; "boom to bust" era of the Roaring '20s and development as an international city. (Mon-Sat, also Sun afternoons; closed Jan 1, Thanksgiving, Dec 25) 101 W Flagler St, in Metro-Dade Cultural Center, downtown. Phone 305/375-1492. ¢¢

Horse racing.

    Calder Race Course. Thoroughbred racing. Parking fee. NW 27th Ave at 210th St, in North Miami, just S of FL Tpke. For schedule, fees phone 305/625-1311.

    Gulfstream Park. Approx 15 mi N via US 1 (Biscayne Blvd), at Hallandale Beach Blvd in Hallandale (see HOLLYWOOD).

Ichimura Japanese Garden. Authentic one-acre Japanese garden and pavilion; many sculptural pieces sent from Japan as gifts—pagoda, statues, waterfall, lagoon. (Daily; hrs vary) On Watson Island, N side of MacArthur Causeway. Phone 305/416-1313. **Free.**

Miami Jai-Alai. Parimutuel betting, courtview restaurant. (Wed-Sat & Mon evenings; matinees Mon, Wed, Fri & Sat) Children under adults only. Parking fee. 3500 NW 37th Ave, at NW 36th St, near airport. Phone 305/633-6400. ¢

Miami Metrozoo. Consists of 290 acres with more than 50 cageless exhibits; features rare white Bengal tigers in a moated area, complete with a replica of an ancient Cambodian temple, and orangutans, elephants, gorillas, chimps, rhinos and bears in areas closely resembling each animal's native habitat. Also free animal shows (three shows daily); elephant

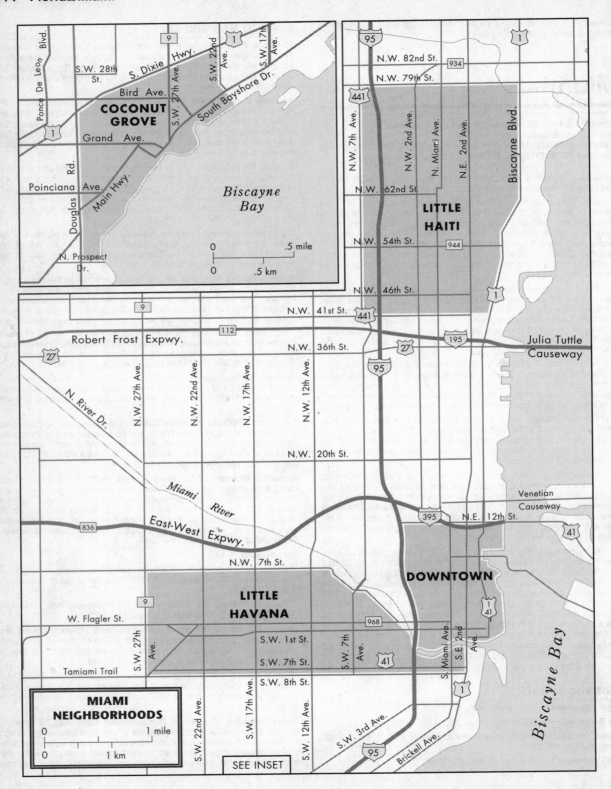

COCONUT GROVE

Ponce De Leon Blvd.

S.W. 28th St.

S. Dixie Hwy.

Bird Ave.

S.W. 27th Ave.

S.W. 22nd Ave.

S.W. 17th Ave.

South Bayshore Dr.

Grand Ave.

Poinciana Ave.

Douglas Rd.

Main Hwy.

N. Prospect Dr.

Biscayne Bay

0   .5 mile

0   .5 km

LITTLE HAITI

N.W. 82nd St.

N.W. 79th St.

N.W. 7th Ave.

N.W. 2nd Ave.

N. Miami Ave.

N.E. 2nd Ave.

Biscayne Blvd.

N.W. 62nd St.

N.W. 54th St.

N.W. 46th St.

N.W. 41st St.

Robert Frost Expwy.

N.W. 36th St.

Julia Tuttle Causeway

N. River Dr.

N.W. 27th Ave.

N.W. 22nd Ave.

N.W. 17th Ave.

N.W. 12th Ave.

N.W. 20th St.

Miami River

East-West Expwy.

N.W. 7th St.

Venetian Causeway

N.E. 12th St.

DOWNTOWN

LITTLE HAVANA

W. Flagler St.

S.W. 27th Ave.

Tamiami Trail

S.W. 1st St.

S.W. 7th St.

S.W. 8th St.

S.W. 7th Ave.

S. Miami Ave.

S.E. 2nd Ave.

Biscayne Bay

S.W. 22nd Ave.

S.W. 17th Ave.

S.W. 12th Ave.

S.W. 3rd Ave.

Brickell Ave.

MIAMI NEIGHBORHOODS

0   1 mile

0   1 km

SEE INSET

rides, elephant show and an ecology theater; children's zoo; monorail system; and observation deck overlooking African Lobe. (Daily) 12400 SW 152nd St (Coral Reef Dr), just W of the FL Tpke exit. Phone 305/251-0400 (recording) or -0401. ¢¢¢

Miami Seaquarium. Tropical marine aquarium on 50 acres of gardens. Home of television's "Flipper"; tanks with viewing windows; tidepool touch tank; killer whale; sea lion & dolphin show. (Daily; shows run continuously) 4400 Rickenbacker Causeway, S on Virginia Key. Phone 305/361-5705. ¢¢¢¢¢

Miami Youth Museum. A hands-on cultural arts museum where children and adults participate in learning experiences that stimulate the imagination and senses. (Daily; closed major hols) 3301 Coral Way, Level U, Miracle Center. Phone 305/446-4386. ¢¢

Miccosukee Indian Village and Airboat Tours. Example of an authentic Indian village depicting the traditional lifestyle of the tribe. Guided tours; demonstrations and exhibits of woodcarving, patchwork, beadwork, basket weaving and doll making; alligator wrestling; museum with artifacts & films; airboat rides (fee). Restaurant featuring authentic Miccosukee dishes as well as standard menu; gift shop. (Daily) (See ANNUAL EVENTS) 25 mi W on US 41 (Tamiami Trail). Phone 305/223-8380 or -8388. Village ¢¢

Monkey Jungle. Unusual setting in which visitors are inside caged walkways and watch nearly 500 monkeys frolic in uncaged freedom; Wild Monkey Swimming Pool, Ape Encounter; three different shows. (Daily) 14805 SW 216th St, W of US 1 & FL Tpke. Phone 305/235-1611. ¢¢¢¢

Museum of Science & Space Transit Planetarium. More than 150 hands-on displays on light, sound, optics, chemistry, biology, physics, energy, the human body, science-technology and invention; live science demonstrations on electricity, anatomy and endangered species; automated slide presentations, animated dioramas and continuous films; Wildlife Center. Planetarium features multimedia astronomy and laser shows (fee); observatory (Sat evenings; free). Museum (daily; closed Thanksgiving, Dec 25) 3280 S Miami Ave, in Coconut Grove area. Phone 305/854-4247 (museum) or -2222 (planetarium). Combined museum/planetarium ¢¢¢

Orange Bowl Stadium. Scene of University of Miami football games (Aug-Jan). 1400 NW 4th St. Phone 305/284-3244 (Univ of Miami).

Parrot Jungle & Gardens. Parrots, macaws, flamingos in natural tropical jungle; walkways through gardens and cactus ravine; trained macaw and cockatoo shows in geodesic dome amphitheater; baby bird training arena; petting zoo, playground. Cafeteria; gift shop. (Daily) 11000 SW 57th Ave, S off US 1. Phone 305/666-7834. ¢¢¢¢

Professional sports.

National League baseball (Florida Marlins). Pro Player Stadium, 2269 NW 199th St. Phone 305/626-7400.

NBA (Miami Heat). Miami Arena, 721 NW First Ave. Phone 305/577-4328.

NFL (Miami Dolphins). Pro Player Stadium, 2269 NW 199th St. Phone 305/452-7000.

NHL (Florida Panthers). Miami Arena, 721 NW First Ave. Phone 954/768-1900.

Recreation areas.

Bayfront Park. Baywalk, laser light tower, amphitheater, fountain. Torch of Friendship symbolizing relationship with Latin American countries; Challenger memorial monument. (Daily) 301 N Biscayne Blvd, at Biscayne Bay. Phone 305/358-7550. **Free.**

Lummus Park. Stone barracks of Fort Dallas, built in 1835 at the mouth of Miami River and once commanded by William Tecumseh Sherman; abandoned in 1838, later moved to this site. Also here is Wagner House, one of the last remaining pioneer structures in Dade County. On Miami River; boat dock. (Daily) 404 NW N River Dr & NW 3rd St. Phone 305/673-7730. **Free.**

New World Center—Bicentennial Park. Fishing; picnicking, playground. Trails. Sculpture fountain. Park (daily). Biscayne Blvd, MacArthur Causeway & NE 9th St, on Biscayne Bay. Phone 305/575-5240. **Free.**

Greynolds Park. Picnicking, grills, concession. New England-style wooden bridge, observation tower; trails. Fishing; boating, paddleboat

rentals; bicycle paths, exercise stations; playground; golf course; bird rookery, bird walks. (Daily) 17530 W Dixie Hwy, in North Miami. Phone 305/945-3425. Parking fee (Sat, Sun & hols) ¢

Sightseeing tours.

Island Queen. Circle cruise (90 min) of Biscayne Bay on the *Island Queen*. Millionaires Row Cruise includes lecture, view of waterfront estates, residential islands, Miami and Miami Beach. (Daily) Departs from Hyatt Regency Hotel, 400 SE 2nd Ave, or Bayside Marketplace. Phone 305/379-5119. ¢¢¢

All Florida Adventure Tours. Customized tours of south Florida; history, nature and ecology emphasis. 8263-B SW 107th Ave. Phone 305/270-0219. ¢¢¢¢¢

Spanish Monastery. Monastery built in 1141 in Segovia, Spain, and purchased by William Randolph Hearst, who had it disassembled, crated and brought to the US. It wasn't reassembled until 1954, after Hearst's death; it is now owned by the Episcopal Church. Formal garden. (Mon-Sat, also Sun afternoons; closed Easter, Thanksgiving, Dec 25) 16711 W Dixie Hwy, in North Miami Beach. Phone 305/945-1462. ¢¢

✪ **Vizcaya Museum and Gardens.** Elaborate 70-rm Italian Renaissance-style villa with extraordinary collection of European furnishings and art objects from the 15th-19th centuries; 10-acre classical Italian garden with fountains, statuary and grottos. House (1914-1916) of James Deering, International Harvester industrialist. (Daily; closed Dec 25) 3251 S Miami Ave, in Coconut Grove area. Phone 305/250-9133. ¢¢¢

Annual Events

Orange Bowl Festival. Pro Player Stadium. Orange Bowl Football Game (Jan 1) and King Orange Jamboree Parade (Dec 31). Two weeks of activities also include tennis tournament, 10K footrace, regatta series and more. Phone 305/371-4600. Dec-early Jan.

Taste of the Grove. Two-day food and music festival in Coconut Grove. Phone 305/444-7270. Mid-Jan.

Coconut Grove Arts Festival. 5 mi S via US 1 in Coconut Grove. 300 artists display their works; entertainment; international foods. Phone 305/447-0401. Mid-Feb.

Doral Ryder Open PGA Golf Tournament. Held on the famed "Blue Monster" course of the Doral Resort & Country Club. Phone 305/477-4653. Mid-Feb-early Mar.

Carnaval Miami/Calle Ocho Festival. Largest Hispanic-culture festival in the US. Includes Carnaval Night in Orange Bowl, Paseo parade and Calle Ocho Festival in Little Havana. Early Mar.

Italian Renaissance Festival. Vizcaya (see). Re-creation of a Renaissance marketplace with arts, crafts, music, plays, food & drink. Phone 305/250-9133. Mar.

Miccosukee Indian Arts Festival. Miccosukee Indian Village (see). More than 20 different tribes gather to perform traditional dances and music; arts & crafts; demonstrations; food. Phone 305/223-8380. Late Dec-early Jan.

Seasonal Events

Greyhound Racing. Flagler Dog Track. On NW 38th Court, at NW 37th Ave & 7th St, near airport. Races nightly; matinees Tues, Thurs, Sat & hols. Phone 305/649-3000. June-Dec.

Opera. Performances at Dade County Auditorium, 2901 W Flagler St. Phone Florida Grand Opera, 305/854-1643. Jan-Apr.

Miami Intl Airport Area

For additional accommodations, see MIAMI INTL AIRPORT AREA, which follows MIAMI.

City Neighborhoods

Many of the restaurants, unrated dining establishments and some lodgings listed under Miami include neighborhoods as well as exact street addresses. Geographic descriptions of these areas are given, followed by a table of restaurants arranged by neighborhood.

Coconut Grove: South of S Dixie Hwy (US 1); west of SW 22nd Ave, north of Biscayne Bay and east of Douglas Rd.

Downtown: South of NE 12th St, west of Biscayne Bay, north of the Miami River and east of I-95. **North of Downtown:** North of I-395. **South of Downtown:** South of US 41. **West of Downtown:** West of I-95.

Little Haiti: South of NW 79th St, west of Biscayne Blvd (US 1), north of NW 41st St and east of NW 7th St.

Little Havana: South of NW 7th St, west of the Miami River, north of SW 8th St and east of SW 27th St.

MIAMI RESTAURANTS BY NEIGHBORHOOD AREAS
(For full description, see alphabetical listings under Restaurants)

COCONUT GROVE
Bocca Di Rosa. 2833 Bird Ave
Cafe Med. 3015 Grand Ave
Cafe Tu Tu Tango. 3015 Grand Ave
Grand Cafe (Grand Bay Hotel). 2669 S Bayshore Dr
Grove Isle. 4 Grove Isle Dr
Mambo Cafe. 3105 Commodore Plaza
Mayfair Grill (Mayfair House Hotel). 3000 Florida Ave
News Cafe. 2901 Forida Ave
Planet Hollywood. 3390 Mary St
Señor Frog's. 3480 Main Hwy
Tuscany. 3484 Main Hwy

DOWNTOWN
Las Tapas. 401 Biscayne Blvd
Le Pavillon (Hotel Inter-Continental). 100 Chopin Plaza
Snappers. 401 Biscayne Blvd

NORTH OF DOWNTOWN
Francis On The Bay. 1279 NE 79th St
Il Tulipano. 11052 Biscayne Blvd (US 1)
Mike Gordon. 1201 NE 79th St
Tony Chan's Water Club (Doubletree Grand Hotel). 1717 N Bayshore Dr

SOUTH OF DOWNTOWN
Fleming. 8511 SW 136th St
Samurai. 8717 SW 136th St
Tropical Chinese. 7991 SW 40th St
Victor's Cafe. 2340 SW 32nd Ave
Wah Shing. 9503 S Dixie Hwy (US 1)

LITTLE HAVANA
Casa Juancho. 2436 SW 8th St

Note: When a listing is located in a town that does not have its own city heading, it will appear under the city nearest to its location. In these cases, the address and town appear in parenthesis immediately following the name of the establishment.

Motels

★ ★ **COURTYARD BY MARRIOTT.** *3929 NW 79th Ave (33166), west of downtown.* 305/477-8118; FAX 305/599-9363. 145 rms, 4 story. Mid-Jan-mid-Apr: S, D $129; suites $149; under 18 free; lower rates rest of yr. Crib free. TV; cable (premium). Heated pool; whirlpool. Complimentary coffee in rms. Bar 5-10 pm. Ck-out noon. Coin lndry. Meeting rm. Business servs avail. In-rm modem link. Valet serv. Sundries. Free airport transportation. Exercise equipt. Refrigerator in suites. Balconies. Cr cds: A, C, D, DS, MC, V.

D ≈ 🏋 🏊 🐾 SC

✔★ ★ **FAIRFIELD INN BY MARRIOTT.** *3959 NW 79th Ave (33166), west of downtown.* 305/599-5200; res: 800/228-2800; FAX 305/436-2935. 135 rms, 3 story. Jan-mid-Apr: S, D $89; under 18 free; lower rates rest of yr. Crib free. TV; cable (premium). Heated pool. Complimentary continental bkfst. Restaurant nearby. Ck-out noon. Business servs avail. In-rm modem link. Free airport transportation. Cr cds: A, C, D, DS, MC, V.

D ≈ 🏊 🐾 SC

✔★ ★ **QUALITY INN-SOUTH.** *14501 S Dixie Hwy (33176), south of downtown.* 305/251-2000; FAX 305/235-2225. 100 rms, 2 story, 14 kits. Dec-Apr: S, D $79-$95; each addl $5; kit. units $95; under 18 free; lower rates rest of yr. Crib free. Pet accepted. TV; cable (premium). Heated pool. Coffee in rms. Restaurant 6:30 am-10 pm; Fri & Sat to 11 pm. Rm serv. Ck-out 11 am. Coin lndry. Cr cds: A, C, D, DS, JCB, MC, V.

🐾 ≈ 🏊 🐾 SC

★ **WELLESLEY INN AT KENDALL.** *11750 Mills Dr (33183), south of downtown.* 305/270-0359; FAX 305/270-1334; res: 800/444-8888. 106 rms, 4 story. S, D $89.99-$99.99; each addl $10; under 12 free. Crib free. TV; cable (premium). Heated pool. Complimentary continental bkfst. Restaurant nearby. Ck-out 11 am. Health club privileges. Cr cds: A, C, D, DS, MC, V.

D ≈ 🏊 🐾 SC

✔★ ★ **WELLESLEY INN AT MIAMI LAKES.** *7925 NW 154th St (33016), north of downtown.* 305/821-8274; res: 800/444-8888; FAX 305/828-2257. 100 rms, 4 story. Jan-Apr: S $89.99-$99.99; D $99.99-$109.99; under 18 free; higher rates special events; lower rates rest of yr. Crib free. Pet accepted. TV; cable (premium). Heated pool. Complimentary continental bkfst. Restaurant adj open 24 hrs. Ck-out 11 am. Coin lndry. Meeting rm. Health club privileges. Valet serv. Refrigerator, microwave in suites. Cr cds: A, C, D, DS, MC, V.

D 🐾 ≈ 🏊 🐾 SC

Motor Hotels

★ ★ **AMERISUITES.** *11520 SW 88th St (33176), south of downtown.* 305/279-8688; FAX 305/279-7907. 67 suites, 5 story. Dec-Apr: suites $129-$149; under 16 free; wkend rates; higher rates Boat Show, Grand Prix; lower rates rest of yr. Crib avail. Pet accepted, some restrictions. TV; cable (premium), VCR. Complimentary continental bkfst. Complimentary coffee in rms. Restaurant nearby. Rm serv 11 am-10 pm. Ck-out 11 am. Meeting rms. Business center. In-rm modem link. Bellhops. Valet serv. Concierge. Coin lndry. Pool. Refrigerators, microwaves, wet bars. Cr cds: A, C, D, DS, MC, V.

D 🐾 ≈ 🏊 SC ⛷

★ ★ **HOLIDAY INN-CALDER/PRO PLAYER STADIUM.** *21485 NW 27th Ave (33056), NW 27th Ave & County Line Rd, north of downtown.* 305/621-5801; FAX 305/624-8202. 214 rms, 9 story. Jan-Mar: S, D $77-$139; each addl $10; under 19 free; lower rates rest of yr. Crib $10. TV; cable (premium). Heated pool. Restaurant 6:30 am-2 pm, 5:30-10 pm. Bar 4 pm-midnight; entertainment. Ck-out noon. Coin lndry. Meeting rms. Business servs avail. In-rm modem link. Bellhops. Valet serv. Exercise equipt. Game rm. Gift shop. Private balconies. Panoramic views of Calder Racetrack and Pro Player Stadium. Cr cds: A, C, D, DS, ER, JCB, MC, V.

D ≈ 🏋 🏊 🐾 SC

Hotels

★ **CLUB HOTEL & SUITES.** *100 SE 4th St (33131), downtown.* 305/374-5100; FAX 305/381-9826; res: 800/222-8733 (exc FL). 134 rms, 16 story, 95 suites. Mid-Dec-Easter: S, D $95-$140; under 12 free; lower rates rest of yr. Crib free. TV; cable (premium). Pool. Restaurant 7 am-11 pm. Bar. Ck-out noon. Meeting rms. Concierge. Exercise equipt. Bathrm phones. On river. Cr cds: A, C, D, DS, MC, V.

D ≈ 🏋 🏊 🐾 SC

★ ★ **DOUBLETREE AT COCONUT GROVE.** *2649 S Bayshore Dr (33133), S on US 1 (S Dixie Hwy) S on SW 27th Ave, then N on S Bayshore Dr, in Coconut Grove.* 305/858-2500; res: 800/222-8733; FAX 305/858-5776. 192 rms, 20 story. S, D $169-$299; each addl $20; under 18 free. Crib free. Valet parking $13. TV; cable (premium), VCR avail. Heated pool; poolside serv. Restaurant 6:30 am-11 pm. Bars from 11 am. Ck-out noon. Meeting rms. Business center. Lighted tennis. Exercise equipt. Microwaves avail. Many balconies with ocean view. Fishing, sailing yachts for charter. Opp Coconut Grove Convention Center. Cr cds: A, C, D, DS, ER, JCB, MC, V.

⊡ ⊞ ≋ ✕ ⊠ ⊠ SC ⛷

★ ★ ★ **DOUBLETREE GRAND HOTEL.** *1717 N Bayshore Dr (33132), north of downtown.* 305/372-0313; FAX 305/372-9455. 227 rms, 42 story, 75 kit. units. Dec-Apr: S, D $129-$149; suites $169-$350; kit. units $175-$375; under 18 free; higher rates Boat Show; lower rates rest of yr. Crib free. TV; cable (premium). Heated pool; whirlpool, poolside serv. Restaurant (see TONY CHAN'S WATER CLUB). Bar. Ck-out noon. Coin lndry. Meeting rms. Business servs avail. Concierge. Gift shop. RR station, bus depot transportation. Exercise rm; sauna. Minibars; refrigerator, wet bar in suites; microwaves avail. Many balconies. On Biscayne Bay. Skywalk connects to Omni International Mall. Cr cds: A, C, D, DS, JCB, MC, V.

⊡ ⊶ ≋ ✕ ⊠ ⊠ SC

★ ★ ★ **GRAND BAY.** *2669 S Bayshore Dr (33133), in Coconut Grove.* 305/858-9600; FAX 305/858-1532; res: 800/327-2788. E-mail grandbay@vcn.net; web www.grandbay.com. This modern high-rise with a stepped facade resembling a Mayan pyramid features traditional furnishings, original art, attentive service and breathtaking views of Biscayne Bay and downtown Miami. 178 rms, 13 story, 47 suites. S, D $205-$300; each addl $20; suites $350-$1,400; under 15 free; package plans. Crib free. TV; cable (premium), VCR (movies avail). Heated pool; whirlpool, poolside serv. Restaurant (see GRAND CAFE). Rm serv 24 hrs. Bar 11:30-2 am; entertainment exc Sun. Ck-out noon. Meeting rms. Business center. In-rm modem link. Concierge. Beauty shop. Exercise equipt; sauna. Massage. Bathrm phones, minibars. Private balconies. Cr cds: A, C, D, MC, V.

⊡ ≋ ✕ ⊠ ⊠ SC

★ ★ ★ **GROVE ISLE CLUB & RESORT.** *4 Grove Isle Dr (33133), in Coconut Grove.* 305/858-8300; FAX 305/858-5908; res: 800/884-7683. 50 rms, 5 story, 4 suites. Dec-mid-Apr: S, D $380; suites $475; under 16 free; lower rates rest of yr. Crib free. TV; cable (premium), VCR. Pool; whirlpool, poolside serv. Complimentary coffee in rms. Restaurant 7:30 am-10 pm. Bar. Ck-out noon. Meeting rms. Business servs avail. Concierge. Gift shop. Barber, beauty shop. Lighted tennis, pro. Exercise equipt. Refrigerators, minibars. Balconies. On Biscayne Bay. Cr cds: A, D, DS, MC, V.

⊡ ⊶ ✕ ≋ ✕ ⊠ ⊠ ⊠

★ ★ ★ **HOTEL INTER-CONTINENTAL.** *100 Chopin Plaza (33131), downtown.* 305/577-1000; FAX 305/577-0384; res: 800/327-3005. 639 rms, 34 story. S $199-$259; D $229-$289; each addl $30; suites $325-$2,900; under 14 free; wkly, wkend rates. Garage; valet parking $12. TV; cable (premium). Heated pool; poolside serv. Restaurant 7 am-11 pm (also see LE PAVILLON). Rm serv 24 hrs. Bar 11:30-am-midnight. Ck-out noon. Convention facilities. Business center. In-rm modem link. Concierge. Exercise rm. Minibars. Cr cds: A, C, D, DS, ER, JCB, MC, V.

⊡ ≋ ✕ ✕ ⊠ ⊠ ⊠

★ ★ **HOWARD JOHNSON.** *1100 Biscayne Blvd (33132), downtown.* 305/358-3080; res: 800/654-2000; FAX 305/358-8631. 115 rms, 7 story. S, D $89-$99; under 18 free; higher rates special events. Crib free. TV; cable (premium). Pool; poolside serv. Restaurant 7 am-10 pm. Bar 4 pm-midnight. Ck-out noon. Coin lndry. Meeting rms. Business servs avail. Balconies. Cr cds: A, C, D, DS, JCB, MC, V.

⊡ ≋ ⊠ ⊠ SC

★ ★ **MARRIOTT BISCAYNE BAY HOTEL & MARINA.** *1633 N Bayshore Dr (33132), downtown.* 305/374-3900; res: 800/228-9290; FAX 305/375-0597. 605 rms, 31 story. Mid-Dec-Apr: S, D $155; suites $400-$1,100; lower rates rest of yr. Covered parking $10; valet parking $12. TV; cable. Heated pool; whirlpool, poolside serv. Restaurant 6:30 am-11 pm. Bar 11-1 am. Ck-out noon. Coin lndry. Convention facilities. Business center. Shopping arcade. Barber, beauty shop. Exercise equipt. Game rm. Minibars; refrigerators avail. Balconies. On Biscayne Bay, marina. Luxury level. Cr cds: A, C, D, DS, ER, JCB, MC, V.

⊡ ⊶ ≋ ✕ ⊠ ⊠ SC ⛷

★ ★ ★ **MARRIOTT-DADELAND.** *9090 S Dadeland Blvd (33156), south of downtown.* 305/670-1035; FAX 305/670-7540. E-mail marrdad@aol.com. 302 rms, 24 story. S, D $164; suites $275-$450; under 18 free. Crib free. Covered parking $8.50; valet $10. TV; cable (premium). Heated pool; whirlpool, poolside serv. Restaurant 6:30 am-11 pm. Bar 2 pm-midnight; entertainment Mon-Fri. Ck-out noon. Meeting rms. Business center. In-rm modem link. Concierge. Free airport, RR station, shopping transportation. Tennis privileges. Golf privileges. Exercise equipt. Game rm. Luxury level. Cr cds: A, C, D, DS, MC, V.

⊡ ≋ ✕ ⊠ ⊠ SC ⛷

★ ★ ★ ★ **MAYFAIR HOUSE.** *3000 Florida Ave (33133), in Coconut Grove.* 305/441-0000; res: 800/433-4555 (exc FL); FAX 305/447-9173. E-mail copyf@bellsouth.net; web www.hotelbook.com. This European-style luxury hotel sits within Mayfair Shops at the Grove, an exclusive open-air shopping mall. Public areas have Tiffany windows, polished mahogany, marble walls and floors, imported crystal and a glassed-in elevator. 179 suites, 5 story. Mid-Dec-Apr: S, D $249-$650; under 12 free; wkend rates; lower rates rest of yr. Crib free. Valet parking $15. TV; cable (premium), VCR (movies avail). Rooftop pool. Restaurant 7 am-11 pm (also see MAYFAIR GRILL). Rm serv 24 hrs. Bars from noon. Ck-out 1 pm. Meeting rms. Business center. Concierge. Shopping arcade. Health club privileges. Massage. Bathrm phones, refrigerators, minibars. Private patios with whirlpool. Cr cds: A, C, D, DS, MC, V.

⊡ ≋ ⊠ ⊠ SC ⛷

★ ★ ★ **SHERATON BISCAYNE BAY.** *495 Brickell Ave (33131), downtown.* 305/373-6000; res: 800/325-3535; FAX 305/374-2279. 598 rms, 18 story. Jan-Mar: S $149-$199; D $159-$209; each addl $20; suites $275 & $375; under 12 free; lower rates rest of yr. Crib free. TV; cable (premium). Heated pool; poolside serv. Restaurant 6:30 am-11:30 pm. Bar 11 am-midnight; entertainment. Ck-out 11 am. Meeting rms. Business servs avail. In-rm modem link. Concierge. Covered parking. Exercise equipt. Microwaves avail. Private patios, balconies. Extensive landscaping; at bayside. Cr cds: A, C, D, DS, ER, MC, V.

⊡ ≋ ✕ ⊠ ⊠ ⊠ SC

★ ★ **WYNDHAM BISCAYNE BAY.** *1601 Biscayne Blvd (33132), north of downtown.* 305/374-0000; FAX 305/374-0020. 528 rms, 28 story. Jan-late Mar: S, D $119-$239; each addl $20; suites $250-$2,700; under 17 free; wkend rates; lower rates rest of yr. Crib free. Valet parking $10.25; self-park $9. TV; cable (premium). Heated rooftop pool; poolside serv. Restaurant 6:30 am-11 pm. Bar. Ck-out noon. Convention facilities. Business center. In-rm modem link. Concierge. Golf privileges. Exercise equipt. Overlooks bay. 3-level shopping, dining, entertainment complex. Luxury level. Cr cds: A, C, D, DS, ER, JCB, MC, V.

⊡ ≋ ✕ ⊠ ⊠ SC ⛷

Inn

★ **MIAMI RIVER INN.** *118 SW South River Dr (33130), downtown.* 305/325-0045; res: 800/468-3589; FAX 305/325-9227. E-mail miami100@ix.netcom.com; web www.travel/base.com. 40 rms in 4 bldgs, 2-3 story. S, D $59-$125; higher rates some special events. TV; cable. Pool; whirlpool. Complimentary continental bkfst. Restaurant nearby. Ck-out noon, ck-in 2 pm. Meeting rm. Business servs avail. Lawn games. Opp river. Restored 1908 houses once owned by Miami's founders. Antiques. Cr cds: A, C, D, DS, MC, V.

⊡ ≋ ⊠ ⊠ SC

Resorts

★ ★ ★ **DON SHULA'S HOTEL & GOLF CLUB.** *(Main St, Miami Lakes 33014) 18 mi NW; N on I-95, W on FL 826 (Palmetto Expy), 1 blk E to Main St.* 305/821-1150; res: 800/247-4852; FAX 305/820-8190. 301 rms, 3 story, 5 kits. Dec-Mar: S, D $229; each addl $10; suites $190-$270; under 12 free; golf package; lower rates rest of yr. Crib $10. TV; cable (premium). 2 pools; whirlpool. Dining rms 6:30 am-11 pm. Snack bars 10 am-7 pm; Fri, Sat from 7 am. Bar 11-2 am. Ck-out noon, ck-in 3 pm. Meeting rms. Business center. Shops. Lighted tennis, pro. Lighted 18-hole golf course, pro, par 3, 2 putting greens, driving range. Exercise rm; sauna, steam rm. Fishing trips. Wet bars; some refrigerators. Private patios, balconies. Luxury level. Cr cds: A, C, D, MC, V.

⊡ 🏌🏃‍♂️≈⛵🏃‍♀️🎿🎣⛷ SC ⛷

★ ★ ★ **DORAL GOLF RESORT AND SPA.** 4400 NW 87th Ave (33178), west of downtown. 305/592-2000; FAX 305/594-4682; res: 800/71-DORAL. Web www.doralgolf.com. 693 rms in 12 bldgs. Dec-Apr: S, D $285-$425; each addl $35; suites $360-$1,500; under 17 free; lower rates rest of yr. Crib free. TV; cable (premium). Heated pool; wading pool, whirlpool, poolside serv. Playground. Supervised child's activities; ages 5-15. Restaurants 6:30 am-midnight. Rm serv 6-1 am. Snack bar, box lunches. 3 bars 11-1:30 am. Ck-out 11 am, ck-in 4 pm. Convention facilities. Business center. Valet serv. 15 tennis courts, 4 lighted, pro. Five 18-hole golf courses, 9-hole par-3 golf, pro, 4 putting greens, lighted driving range, golf school. Bicycle rentals. Lawn games. Soc dir; entertainment, movies. Game rm. Exercise rm; steam rm. Spa. Bathrm phones, refrigerators, minibars. Private patios, balconies. Cr cds: A, C, D, DS, MC, V.

⊡ 🅿 ⛵🏌🏃‍♂️≈🏃‍♀️🎿⛷ 🎣⛷

★ ★ ★ **FISHER ISLAND CLUB.** (1 Fisher Island Dr, Fisher Island 33109) I-95 to MacArthur Causeway, E to ferry terminal. Accesible only by auto ferry, helicopter, boat or seaplane. 305/535-6020; FAX 305/535-6003; res: 800/537-3708. Web www.fisherisland-florida.com. 60 rms, 1-5 story, 4 kit. cottages. Nov-Apr: S $385-$745; D $385-$1,485; suites, cottages $600-$1,485; under 12 free; golf plan; lower rates rest of yr. Crib free. TV; cable (premium), VCR. 4 pools, 1 indoor; whirlpool, poolside serv. Playground. Supervised child's activities; ages 4-10. Complimentary coffee in rms. Dining rm (see VANDERBILT MANSION). Rm serv. Bar 11-2 am; entertainment Wed-Sun. Ck-out noon, ck-in 3 pm. Grocery. Coin lndry. Meeting rms. Business servs avail. In-rm modem link. Bellhops. Valet serv. Concierge. Gift shop. Airport transportation. Sports dir. Lighted tennis, pro. 9-hole golf, greens fee $90, pro, putting green, driving range. Boating. Exercise rm; sauna. Spa. Lawn games. Social dir. Minibars; microwaves avail. Balconies. Bird aviary. Swimming beach. Marina; dockage avail. Cottages (ca 1925) on 200 landscaped acres; former William Vanderbilt estate. Cr cds: A, C, D, MC, V.

⊡ 🅿 ⛵🏌🏃‍♂️≈🏃‍♀️🎿⛷

★ ★ ★ **TURNBERRY ISLE RESORT & CLUB.** (19999 W Country Club Dr, Aventura 33180) Approx 9 mi N via I-95, exit 20 (Ives Dairy Rd), E to US 1 (Biscayne Blvd), to Aventura Blvd. 305/932-6200; FAX 305/933-6560; res: 800/327-7028. E-mail turnbsale@aol.com; web www.turnberryisle.com. This luxurious, gracious and comfortable resort consists of the European-style Marina hotel, the Yacht Club, the Mizner-style Country Club Hotel and the new Mediterranean-style annex, all on 300 secluded acres with subtropical gardens. 340 rms in 3 bldgs, 3-7 story. Late Dec-Apr: Country Club: S, D $395-$495; each addl $50; suites $675-$2,300; Yacht Club: S, D $315; each addl $50; Marina Wing: S, D $355; each addl $50; under 15 free; package plans; lower rates rest of yr. Crib free. TV; cable. 3 pools; whirlpool, poolside serv. Dining rm 7 am-10 pm. Box lunches, snack bar, picnics. Rm serv 24 hrs. Bars 11-1 am. Ck-out noon, ck-in 4 pm. Grocery, package store 1 blk. Coin lndry. Convention facilities. Business center. In-rm modem link. Lighted tennis, pro. 36-hole golf, greens fee $95 ($55 in summer), pro, putting green. Marina, beach, boats, diving, water sports. Entertainment. Exercise rm; sauna, steam rm. Massage. Refrigerators; many in-rm whirlpools. Cr cds: A, C, D, DS, ER, MC, V.

⊡ 🅿 ⛵🏌🏃‍♂️≈🏃‍♀️🎿⛷🎣⛷

Restaurants

★ ★ **BOCCA DI ROSA.** 2833 Bird Ave (33133) in Coconut Grove. 305/444-4222. E-mail juditleon@aol.com. Hrs: 6 pm-midnight. Closed July 4, Dec 25. Res required. Italian menu. Bar. A la carte entrees: dinner $9.95-$29.95. Complete meal: dinner $40-$60. Specialties: risotto, tagliata maremana, tuna Marco Polo. Own baking. Valet parking. Outdoor dining. Stained glass; mirrored walls. Cr cds: A, C, D, DS, MC, V.

⊡ 🍽

✔★ **CAFE MED.** 3015 Grand Ave (33133), in Coconut Grove. 305/443-1770. Hrs: 10 am-midnight; wkends to 1 am. Italian menu. Bar. A la carte entrees: lunch, dinner $3.95-$16.95. Child's meals. Specializes in brick oven pizza, fresh pasta dishes, Mediterranean salads. Own desserts. Outdoor dining. Cr cds: A, D, DS, MC, V.

⊡ 🍽

✔★ ★ **CAFE TU TU TANGO.** 3015 Grand Ave (33133), in Coconut Grove. 305/529-2222. Hrs: 11:30 am-midnight; Fri, Sat to 2 am. International menu. Bar. A la carte entrees: lunch, dinner $2.75-$7.95. Child's meals. Specialties: Barcelona stir-fry, brick oven pizza. Entertainment. Outdoor dining. On 2nd floor of Cocowalk complex. Artist loft motif; painters at work. Cr cds: A, D, MC, V.

⊡ 🍽

★ ★ **CASA JUANCHO.** 2436 SW 8th St (33135), in Little Havana. 305/642-2452. E-mail juancho@casajuancho.com; web www.casajuancho.com. Hrs: noon-midnight; Fri, Sat to 1 am. Res accepted. Spanish menu. Bar. A la carte entrees: lunch $8-$15, dinner $13-$34. Specializes in imported Spanish seafood, tapas. Strolling musicians. Valet parking. Spanish decor. Cr cds: A, C, D, DS, MC, V.

⊡ 🍽

★ ★ ★ **CHEF ALLEN'S.** (19088 NE 29th Ave, Aventura 33137) 1 blk E of Biscayne Blvd off of NE 191st St. 305/935-2900. In this art-deco world of glass block, neon trim, fresh flowers and gallery art, your gaze nevertheless remains riveted on the kitchen. Chef Allen Susser designed it with a picture window 25 feet wide, so you can watch him create new American masterpieces with the help of a wood-burning mesquite grill. Specializes in fresh local seafood, veal chops, dessert soufflés. Own baking. Hrs: 6-10:30 pm. Res accepted. Bar. Wine cellar. A la carte entrees: dinner $24.95-$32.95. Valet parking. Cr cds: A, D, MC, V.

⊡ 🍽

✔★ ★ **FLEMING.** 8511 SW 136th St (33156), in shopping center, south of downtown. 305/232-6444. Hrs: 5:30-10:30 pm. Closed Mon. Res accepted. Danish, continental menu. Bar. Semi-a la carte: dinner $9.95-$19.95. Specialties: Norwegian salmon, duck Danoise. Scandinavian decor. Cr cds: A, MC, V.

⊡ 🍽

★ ★ **FRANCIS ON THE BAY.** 1279 NE 79th St (33138), north of downtown. 305/758-9888. Hrs: 6-10 pm. Closed Sun, Mon. Res accepted. Continental menu. Bar. A la carte entrees: dinner $7.95-$25.95. Specializes in seafood, beef. Band Fri, Sat. Outdoor dining. On bay. Cr cds: A, D, MC, V.

⊡ 🍽

★ ★ ★ **GRAND CAFE.** (See Grand Bay Hotel) 305/858-9600. Hrs: 7 am-11 pm; Fri, Sat to 11:30 pm. Res accepted. Continental menu. Bar 11:30-1 am; Fri, Sat to 2 am. A la carte entrees: bkfst $7.75-$14, lunch $8.75-$19.50, dinner $21-$32. Sun brunch $31-$36. Specializes in beef, chicken, smoked salmon. Own baking. Valet parking. Entertainment. Windows overlook garden area. Cr cds: A, D, MC, V.

⊡ 🍽

★ ★ **GROVE ISLE.** 4 Grove Isle Dr (33133), in Coconut Grove. 305/857-5007. Hrs: 7:30 am-10 pm; Sun brunch 11 am-2:30 pm. Res accepted. Continental menu. Bar. Semi-a la carte: bkfst $3-$12, lunch $6-$15; dinner $6-$25. Sun brunch $6-$17. Child's meals. Valet parking. Outdoor dining. Modern decor. Waterfront dining. Cr cds: A, D, MC, V.

⊡ 🍽

★ ★ ★ **IL TULIPANO.** 11052 Biscayne Blvd (US 1) (33161), north of downtown. 305/893-4811. Hrs: 6-11 pm; Fri, Sat to midnight. Closed Mon; Dec 24; also Sept. Res accepted. Northern Italian menu. Bar. Wine cellar. A la carte entrees: dinner $14-$32. Specialties: pollo scarpariello, osso bucco, snapper. Own baking. Cr cds: A, D, MC, V.

⊡ 🍽

★ ★ ★ **LA PALOMA.** *(10999 Biscayne Blvd, North Miami 33161) N on US 1.* 305/891-0505. E-mail m10999@aol.com. Hrs: 11:30 am-3 pm, 5 pm-midnight. Res accepted. Continental menu. Bar. Wine list. A la carte entrees: lunch $6.95-$15, dinner $12.95-$25. Child's meals. Specialties: lamb chops a la diable, Wienerschnitzel, bouillabaise. Piano bar. Valet parking. Elegant, yet informal dining in three areas. Cr cds: A, D, MC, V.

D ⌐

★ ★ **LAS TAPAS.** *401 Biscayne Blvd (33132), downtown.* 305/372-2737. Hrs: 11:30 am-midnight; Fri, Sat to 1 am. Spanish menu. Bar. Semi-a la carte: lunch $4.95-$9.95, dinner $9.95-$19.95. Specializes in hot & cold tapas, seafood. Strolling minstrels. Outdoor dining. Open kitchen. Spanish contemporary decor. Cr cds: A, C, D, DS, MC, V.

D ⌐

★ ★ **LE PAVILLON.** *(See Hotel Inter-Continental)* 305/372-4494. Hrs: noon-2:30 pm, 7-10 pm; Mon to 2:30 pm; Sat from 7 pm. Closed Sun. Res accepted. Continental menu. Bar. Complete meals: lunch $20. Semi-a la carte: dinner $18-$35. Specializes in fresh seafood, steak, salads. Harpist. Valet parking. Cr cds: A, C, D, DS, ER, JCB, MC, V.

D ⌐

★ ★ **MAMBO CAFE.** *3105 Commodore Plaza (33133), in Coconut Grove.* 305/448-2768. Hrs: 8:30 am-11:30 pm; Fri, Sat 8-1:30 am, Sun brunch 8 am-1 pm. Cuban menu. Semi-a la carte: bkfst $3.50-$7.95, lunch, dinner $4.95-$31.95. Sat, Sun brunch $7.95. Child's meals. Specialties: mariquitas con mojito, zarzuela de mariscos, paella for two. Own baking. Sidewalk dining. Cr cds: A, D, MC, V.

D ⌐

★ ★ **MAYFAIR GRILL.** *(See Mayfair House Hotel)* 305/441-0000. Hrs: 7 am-11 pm. Res accepted. Bar 11-1 am. Wine cellar. A la carte entrees: bkfst $6-$12, lunch $4.95-$13, dinner $16-$26.50. Specializes in seafood, steak. Valet parking. Victorian setting with South Florida accents; stained-glass ceiling. Cr cds: A, C, D, DS, ER, JCB, MC, V.

D ⌐

✔ ★ ★ **MIKE GORDON.** *1201 NE 79th St (33138), north of downtown.* 305/751-4429. Hrs: noon-10 pm; early-bird dinner 3:30-6 pm. Closed Thanksgiving, Dec 25. Bar. Semi-a la carte: lunch $5.95-$16.95, dinner $12.95-$22.95. Child's meals. Specializes in fresh seafood. Valet parking; boat docking. Overlooks bay. Family-owned. Cr cds: A, D, DS, MC, V.

D ⌐

✔ ★ ★ **NEWS CAFE.** *2901 Florida Ave (33133), in Coconut Grove.* 305/774-6397. Open 24 hrs. Eclectic menu. Bar 8-5 am. Semi-a la carte: bkfst $3.95-$8.95, lunch $6.95-$11.25, dinner $6.95-$12.95. Specializes in Middle Eastern cuisine. Mediterranean decor. Cr cds: A, D, MC, V.

D ⌐

★ ★ **SAMURAI.** *8717 SW 136th St (33176), south of downtown.* 305/238-2131. Hrs: noon-2:30 pm, 5:30-10:30 pm; Fri to 11 pm; Sat to 11:30 pm. Res accepted. Japanese menu. Bar. Complete meals: lunch $6.25-$9.95, dinner $12.95-$26. Child's meals. Specializes in steak, chicken, seafood. Parking. Meals prepared in full view of guests. Cr cds: A, C, D, DS, MC, V.

D ⌐

✔ ★ ★ **SEÑOR FROG'S.** *3480 Main Hwy (33133), in Coconut Grove.* 305/448-0990. Hrs: 11:30-1 am; Thurs-Sat to 2 am. Res accepted. Mexican menu. Bar. A la carte entrees: lunch, dinner $7-$15. Specializes in enchiladas, fajitas. Outdoor dining. Mexican cantina decor. Cr cds: A, C, D, MC, V.

D ⌐

★ ★ **SHULA'S STEAK HOUSE.** *(7601 NW 154th St, Miami Lakes 33014) N on I-95, W on FL 826, Miami Lakes exit.* 305/820-8102. Hrs: 7-11 am, 11:30 am-2:30 pm, 6-11 pm; Sat 6-11 pm; Sun 6-10 pm. Closed July 4. Res accepted. Bar. Wine list. A la carte entrees: bkfst $5-$10, lunch $7-$16, dinner $15-$58. Specializes in steak, seafood. Valet parking. Overlooks golf course. Family-owned. Cr cds: A, C, D, MC, V.

D ⌐

★ **SNAPPERS.** *401 Biscayne Blvd (33132), at Pier #5, complex N111, downtown.* 305/379-0605. Hrs: 7:30 am-midnight. Bar. A la carte entrees: lunch $7.95-$13.95, dinner $9.95-$24.95. Child's meals. Specializes in seafood, pasta. Raw bar. Outdoor dining at bayside. On pier. Cr cds: A, D, MC, V.

D ⌐

★ ★ ★ **TONY CHAN'S WATER CLUB.** *(See Doubletree Grand Hotel)* 305/374-8888. Hrs: noon-11 pm; Fri to midnight; Sat 5 pm-midnight; Sun 5-11 pm. Closed Thanksgiving. Chinese menu. Bar. A la carte entrees: lunch $6.95-$30, dinner $9-$40. Specialties: Peking duck, honey walnut shrimp, water club sea bass. Valet parking. Open kitchen. Main dining rm has view marina. Cr cds: A, C, D, DS, MC, V.

D ⌐

★ ★ **TROPICAL CHINESE.** *7991 SW 40th St (33155), south of downtown.* 305/262-7576. Hrs: 11:30 am-10:30 pm; Fri 11 am-11:30 pm; Sat, Sun 10:30 am-10 pm; brunch daily 11 am-3:30 pm. Res accepted. Chinese menu. Bar. Semi-a la carte: lunch $5.25-$8, dinner $6.95-$45. Brunch $2.25-$7.95. Specialties: Peking duck, sizzling black bean, Emperor's prawns. Chinese decor. Cr cds: A, D, MC, V.

D ⌐

★ ★ **TUSCANY CAFE.** *3484 Main Hwy (33133), in Coconut Grove.* 305/445-0022. Hrs: 11:30 am-midnight. Res accepted. Italian menu. Bar. A la carte entrees: lunch $5.95-$12.95, dinner $7.95-$19.95. Complete meals: lunch $10-$15, dinner $20-$30. Child's meals. Specialties: osso buco, snapper Livornese. Parking. Outdoor dining. Cr cds: A, C, D, DS, MC, V.

D ⌐

★ ★ **VANDERBILT MANSION.** *(See Fisher Island Club Resort)* 305/535-6020. Hrs: 7 pm-midnight. Closed Mon, Tues; also June-Sept. Res required. Continental menu. Bar. Wine cellar. A la carte entrees: dinner $18-$45. Specialties: pan-seared snapper with crabmeat, veal chop, rack of lamb. Harpist, bass player Wed-Sat. Valet parking. Outdoor dining. Elegant dining in mansion built for William K. Vanderbilt. Marble floor, chandeliers. Jacket. Cr cds: A, C, D, MC, V.

D ⌐

★ ★ **VICTOR'S CAFE.** *2340 SW 32nd Ave (33145), south of downtown.* 305/445-1313. Hrs: noon-midnight; Fri & Sat to 1 am. Res accepted. Cuban menu. Bar. Wine list. A la carte entrees: lunch $7.95-$16.95, dinner $9.95-$28.95. Child's meals. Specializes in seafood, steak. Entertainment Sat. Valet parking. Original artwork and signed photographs of celebrity guests. Counterpart of NYC restaurant. Cr cds: A, D, MC, V.

D SC ⌐

★ ★ **WAH SHING.** *9503 S Dixie Hwy (US 1) (33156), in Dadeland Plaza, south of downtown.* 305/666-9879. Hrs: 11:30 am-11 pm. Closed Thanksgiving. Chinese menu. Wine, beer. A la carte entrees: lunch $4.95-$6.95, dinner $7.95-$12.95. Specializes in Cantonese, Mandarin & Szechwan dishes. Oriental decor. Cr cds: A, MC, V.

D ⌐

Unrated Dining Spot

PLANET HOLLYWOOD. *3390 Mary St (33133), in Coconut Grove.* 305/445-7277. Hrs: 11:30 am-11:45 pm; Fri, Sat to 12:45 am. Bar. Semi-a la carte: lunch, dinner $4.95-$16.95. Child's meals. Specializes in fajitas, pasta, pizza. TV and movie memorabilia. Cr cds: A, D, DS, JCB, MC, V.

D ⌐

Miami Intl Airport Area (H-6)

(See also Coral Gables, Hialeah, Miami)

Services and Information

Information: 305/876-7000.

Lost and Found: 305/876-7377.

Weather: 305/229-4522.

Airlines: Aces, Aeroflot, Aerolineas Argentinas, AeroMexico, Aeroperu, Air Aruba, Air Atlantic Dominicana, Air Canada, Air Europa, Air France, Air Jamaica, Alitalia, ALM, America West, American, American Eagle, Avensa, Avianca, Aviateca, Bahamasair, BWIA, Canadian Air International, Cayman Airways, City Bird, Comair, Copa, Continental, Delta, Ecuatoriana, El Al, Finnair, Guyana Airways, Gulfstream International, Iberia, Lab, LACSA, Lan Chile, Lauda Air, LTU, Lufthansa, Martinair, Mexicana, Nica, Northwest, Pan Am, Paradise Island Airways, SAETA, Servivensa, South African Airways, Surnam Airways, TACA, Tower Air, Transbrazil, TWA, United, US Airways, Varig, VASP, Virgin Atlantic.

Motels

✔★★ FAIRFIELD INN BY MARRIOTT-SOUTH. *(1201 NW LeJeune Rd, Miami 33126) 305/643-0055; res: 800/228-2800; FAX 305/649-3997.* 282 rms, 3 story. Dec-Apr: S, D $99; suite $125; lower rates rest of yr. Crib free. TV; cable (premium). Pool; poolside serv wkends. Complimentary continental bkfst. Restaurant 6:30-10:30 am. Rm serv. Bar noon-2 am. Ck-out noon. Coin lndry. Convention facilities. Business center. In-rm modem link. Valet serv. Concierge. Sundries. Gift shop. Barber, beauty shop. Free airport transportation. Lighted tennis, pro. Exercise equipt. Cr cds: A, C, D, DS, MC, V.

D ⚹ ≋ ✗ ⚹ ✈ ✗ ⚹ 🖊 SC ⚹

★★ WELLESLEY INN. *(8436 NW 36th St, Miami 33166) N via LeJeune Rd (NW 42nd Ave) to NW 36th St. 305/592-4799; res: 800/444-8888; FAX 305/471-8461.* 106 rms, 4 story, 13 suites. Jan-mid-Apr: S $90; D $99; under 18 free; lower rates rest of yr. Crib free. TV; cable (premium). Pool. Complimentary continental bkfst. Coffee in rms. Ck-out 11 am. Coin lndry. Meeting rm. Business servs avail. In-rm modem link. Valet serv. Free airport transportation. Refrigerator in suites. Cr cds: A, C, D, DS, MC, V.

D ≋ ✗ ⚹ 🖊 SC

Motor Hotels

★★ AMERISUITES. *(3655 NW 82nd Ave, Miami 33166) 305/718-8292; FAX 305/718-8295.* 126 suites, 6 story. Jan-Mar: suites $109-$169; under 18 free; wkly, wkend, hol rates; higher rates Grand Prix Doral Ryder; lower rates rest of yr. Crib free. Pet accepted, some restrictions; $10. TV; cable (premium), VCR. Complimentary continental bkfst. Complimentary coffee in rms. Restaurant adj 9 am-midnight. Ck-out 11 am. Meeting rms. Business center. In-rm modem link. Coin lndry. Free airport transportation. Exercise equipt. Pool. Refrigerators, microwaves. Cr cds: A, C, D, DS, MC, V.

D ⚹ ≋ ⚹ ✈ ✗ ⚹ 🖊 SC ⚹

★★ BEST WESTERN MIAMI AIRPORT INN. *(1550 NW LeJeune Rd, Miami 33126) 305/871-2345; res: 800/327-6087; FAX 305/871-2811.* 208 rms, 6 story. S $84-$104; D $89-$114; each addl $5; under 13 free. Crib free. TV; cable (premium). Pool. Restaurant 6-3 am. Rm serv to midnight. Bar 11-3 am. Ck-out noon. Meeting rms. Business servs avail. In-rm modem link. Bellhops. Sundries. Coin lndry. Airport transportation.

Exercise equipt. Game rm. Bathrm phones; some refrigerators. Cr cds: A, C, D, DS, MC, V.

D ≋ ⚹ ✗ ⚹ 🖊 SC

★ COMFORT INN-EAST. *(5125 NW 36th St, Miami 33166) 305/887-2153; FAX 305/887-3559.* 110 rms, 6 story. Dec-Apr: S $69.95-$109.95; D $75.95-$115.95; each addl $10; under 18 free; wkend, hol rates; golf plans; higher rates Super Bowl; lower rates rest of yr. Crib free. TV; cable (premium). Complimentary continental bkfst. Restaurant nearby. Ck-out noon. Business servs avail. In-rm modem link. Sundries. Coin lndry. Free airport transportation. Golf privileges, greens fee $28-$59, pro, putting green, driving range. Pool privileges. Some refrigerators. Cr cds: A, C, D, DS, ER, JCB, MC, V.

D ⚹⚹ ✗ ⚹ 🖊 SC

★★ COURTYARD BY MARRIOTT-SOUTH. *(1201 NW LeJeune Rd, Miami 33126) 305/642-8200; res: 800/321-2211.* 123 rms, 5 story. Dec-Apr: S, D $119-$139; suite $150; under 18 free; lower rates rest of yr. Crib free. TV; cable (premium). Heated pool; whirlpool, poolside serv wkends. Complimentary coffee in rms. Restaurant 6:30-10:30 am. Rm serv. Bar noon-2 am. Ck-out noon. Coin lndry. Meeting rms. Business center. Valet serv. Concierge. Sundries. Gift shop. Barber, beauty shop. Free airport transportation. Lighted tennis, pro. Exercise equipt. Cr cds: A, C, D, DS, MC, V.

D ⚹✈ ≋ ✗ ⚹ ✗ ⚹ 🖊 SC ⚹

★★ HAMPTON INN AIRPORT-WEST. *(3620 NW 79th Ave, Miami 33166) 305/513-0777; res: 800/426-7806; FAX 305/513-9019.* 129 rms, 6 story. Dec-Apr: S $99-$109; D $109-$119; under 18 free; wkend, hol rates; golf plans; higher rates: Doral Open, Boat Show; lower rates rest of yr. Crib free. Pet accepted, some restrictions. TV; cable (premium), VCR avail. Complimentary continental bkfst. Restaurant adj 7 am-10 pm. Ck-out 11 am. Meeting rms. Business center. In-rm modem link. Valet serv. Free airport transportation. Pool. Some refrigerators; microwaves avail. Cr cds: A, C, D, DS, MC, V.

D ⚹ ≋ ✗ ⚹ 🖊 SC ⚹

Hotels

✔★★ AIRPORT REGENCY. *(1000 NW Le Jeune Rd, Miami 33126) 305/441-1600; FAX 305/443-0766; res: 800/367-1039 (exc FL), 800/432-1192 (FL).* 176 rms, 6 story. S $70-$120; D $85-$125; each addl $10; under 18 free. Crib free. TV; cable (premium). Restaurant 7 am-11 pm; Fri, Sat to midnight. Bar 1 pm-midnight; Fri, Sat 6 pm-4 am; entertainment. Ck-out noon. Meeting rms. Gift shop. Free airport transportation. Pool. Balconies. Cr cds: A, C, D, DS, ER, MC, V.

D ≋ ✗ ⚹ 🖊 SC

★★ CLARION. *(5301 NW 36th St, Miami 33166) 305/871-1000; res: 800/252-7462; FAX 305/871-4971.* Web www.clarcom.com. 103 rms, 7 story. Dec-Apr: S, D $99.95-$185.95; each addl $10; suites $119.95-$175.95; under 18 free; wkend, hol rates; golf plans; lower rates rest of yr. Crib free. TV; cable (premium), VCR avail. Complimentary coffee in rms. Restaurant 11 am-11 pm. Bar from 4 pm. Ck-out noon. Meeting rms. Business center. In-rm modem link. Gift shop. Barber, beauty shop. Coin lndry. Tennis privileges. Golf privileges, greens fee $29-$50, pro, putting green, driving range. Exercise equipt. Pool. Refrigerators, microwaves avail. Cr cds: A, C, D, DS, MC, V.

D ⚹⚹ ≋ ⚹ ✗ ⚹ 🖊 SC ⚹

★★ CLUB HOTEL BY DOUBLETREE. *(1101 NW 57th Ave, Miami 33126) Jct FL 836 & Red Rd exit (57th Ave). 305/266-0000; FAX 305/266-9179.* 266 rms, 10 story. Jan-Mar: S $99-$125; D $109-$135; suites $190-$215; under 18 free; higher rates Boat Show; lower rates rest of yr. Crib free. Pet accepted. TV; cable (premium). Pool; wading pool. Complimentary coffee in rms. Restaurant 6 am-11 pm. Bar 4-11 pm. Ck-out noon. Coin lndry. Meeting rms. Business center. Free airport transportation. Exercise equipt. Refrigerators avail. Cr cds: A, C, D, DS, JCB, MC, V.

D ⚹ ≋ 🏃 🏊 ✈ 🚭 🐾 SC 🚶

★ ★ **COMFORT INN AND SUITES.** *(5301 NW 36th St, Miami 33166) 305/871-6000; res: 800/228-5150; FAX 305/871-4971.* Web www.clarcom.com. 165 rms, 11 story, 12 suites. Dec-Apr: S $89.95-$175.95; D $99.95-$185.95; suites $119.95-$175.95; under 18 free; wkend, hol rates; golf plans; lower rates rest of yr. Crib free. TV; cable (premium), VCR avail. Pool. Complimentary continental bkfst. Restaurant 11 am-11 pm. Bar 4-11 pm. Ck-out noon. Meeting rms. Business center. In-rm modem link. Gift shop. Barber, beauty shop. Coin lndry. Free airport transportation. Tennis. Golf privileges, greens fee $29-$50, pro, putting green, driving range. Exercise equipt. Refrigerators, microwaves avail. Cr cds: A, C, D, DS, MC, V.

D 🏌 🏃 ≋ 🏊 🚭 ✈ 🐾 SC 🚶

★ ★ **EMBASSY SUITES.** *(3974 NW South River Dr, Miami 33142) ½ mi N on LeJeune Rd (NW 42nd Ave), W on NW South River Dr, just E of airport. 305/634-5000; res: 800/362-2779; FAX 305/635-9499.* E-mail orivero@worldnet.att.net; web www.embassysuites.com. 316 suites, 10 story. Oct-mid-Apr: S $139-$249; D $149-$259; each addl $10; under 18 free; lower rates rest of yr. Crib free. TV; cable (premium). Pool; whirlpool. Complimentary full bkfst. Restaurant 11 am-11 pm. Bar to 2 am; entertainment. Ck-out noon. Meeting rms. Business center. In-rm modem link. Airport transportation. Exercise equipt. Cr cds: A, C, D, DS, ER, MC, V.

D ≋ 🏊 ✈ 🐾 SC 🚶

★ ★ **HILTON & TOWERS MIAMI AIRPORT.** *(5101 Blue Lagoon Dr, Miami 33126) S of East-West Expy (Dolphin Expy) via Red Rd (FL 959), E on Blue Lagoon Dr. 305/262-1000; FAX 305/261-6769.* E-mail miah_ds@hilton.com; web www.hilton.com. 500 rms, 14 story, 83 suites. Jan-Apr: S $160-$350; D $180-$370; each addl $20; suites $210-$400; family rates; wkend plans; lower rates rest of yr. Crib free. TV; cable (premium). Pool; whirlpool, poolside serv. Restaurant 6:30 am-11 pm. Rm serv 24 hrs. Bar 9-2 am; Fri, Sat to 5 am; entertainment. Ck-out noon. Convention facilities. Business center. In-rm modem link. Concierge. Gift shop. Valet parking. Free airport transportation. Lighted tennis. Exercise equipt; sauna. Some bathrm phones, refrigerators, minibars; microwaves avail. Private patios, balconies. On lake; marina. Exotic birds in cages, saltwater tanks with exotic fish. Luxury level. Cr cds: A, C, D, DS, ER, JCB, MC, V.

D 🐾 🏃 ≋ 🏊 🏄 ✈ 🐾 SC 🚶

★ ★ **HOLIDAY INN SELECT.** *(950 NW LeJeune Rd, Miami 33126) 305/446-9000; res: 800/428-9582; FAX 305/441-0725.* 304 rms, 6 story. S, D $110; each addl $10; suites $139; under 19 free; wkend rates. Crib free. TV; cable (premium). Pool; whirlpool. Restaurant 6:30 am-2 pm, 5-11 pm. Bar 4 pm-midnight. Ck-out noon. Convention facilities. Business servs avail. Gift shop. Free airport transportation. Exercise equipt; sauna. Luxury level. Cr cds: A, C, D, DS, JCB, MC, V.

D ≋ 🏊 ✈ 🐾 SC

★ ★ **MARRIOTT-AIRPORT.** *(1201 NW LeJeune Rd, Miami 33126) SW of FL 836. 305/649-5000; res: 800/228-9290; FAX 305/642-3369.* 366 rms, 10 story. Dec-Apr: S, D $160-$199; family, wkend rates; lower rates rest of yr. Crib free. TV; cable (premium). Pool; whirlpool. Coffee in rms. Restaurant 6-1 am. Bars 11-2 am. Meeting rms. Business center. In-rm modem link. Gift shop. Barber, beauty shop. Free airport transportation. Lighted tennis, pro. Exercise equipt. Rec rm. Private patios. Luxury level. Cr cds: A, C, D, DS, ER, JCB, MC, V.

D 🐾 ≋ 🏊 🚭 ✈ 🐾 SC 🚶

★ ★ **MIAMI INTERNATIONAL AIRPORT HOTEL.** *(NW 20th St & LeJeune Rd, Miami 33122) in airport terminal, Concourse E. 305/871-4100; FAX 305/871-0800; res: 800/327-1276.* E-mail miahotelresv@miami-airport.com; web www.miahotel.com. 260 rms, 8 story. S $115-$179; D $130-$199; each addl $15; suites $275-$650; under 12 free. Crib free. TV; cable (premium). Pool; whirlpool. Restaurant 7 am-11 pm. Bar 11 am-midnight. Ck-out noon. Coin lndry. Meeting rms. Business center. Drugstore. Barber, beauty

shop. Free airport transportation. Exercise rm; sauna, steam rm. Cr cds: A, C, D, DS, ER, JCB, MC, V.

D ≋ 🚭 🏃 🏊 ✈ 🐾 SC 🚶

★ ★ ★ **RADISSON MART PLAZA.** *(711 NW 72nd Ave, Miami 33126) Just S of East-West Expy (Dolphin Expy/FL 836) on NW 72nd Ave. 305/261-3800; FAX 305/261-7665.* 334 rms, 12 story. S, D $129-$159; each addl $20; suites $159-$399; under 18 free; wkend package. Crib free. TV; cable (premium). Pool; whirlpool, poolside serv. Restaurant 6 am-11 pm. Bars 11-1 am; entertainment. Ck-out noon. Convention facilities. Business center. In-rm modem link. Shopping arcade. Free airport transportation. Lighted tennis. Exercise rm; sauna. Balconies. Luxury level. Cr cds: A, C, D, DS, ER, MC, V.

D 🐾 ≋ 🏃 🏊 ✈ 🐾 SC 🚶

★ ★ ★ **SOFITEL.** *(5800 Blue Lagoon Dr, Miami 33126) S of East-West Expy (Dolphin Expy, FL 836) via Red Rd (FL 959), W on Blue Lagoon Dr. 305/264-4888; FAX 305/262-9049.* 281 rms, 15 story, 27 suites. S, D $179-$225; each addl $30; suites $219-$599; under 17 free; wkend packages. Crib free. Pet accepted, some restrictions. Valet parking $5. TV; cable (premium). Pool. Restaurant 6 am-11 pm. Bar 11-2 am; entertainment. Ck-out noon. Meeting rms. Business center. In-rm modem link. Concierge. Gift shop. Lighted tennis. Exercise equipt. On lagoon. Cr cds: A, C, D, DS, MC, V.

D 🐾 🏃 ≋ 🏊 🚭 🐾 SC 🚶

★ ★ ★ **WYNDHAM-AIRPORT.** *(3900 NW 21st St, Miami 33142) on NW 21st St, just E of LeJeune Rd (NW 42nd Ave), adj to airport. 305/871-3800; res: 800/933-1100; FAX 305/871-0447.* Web www.wyndham.com. 408 rms, 10 story. S, D $95-$225; each addl $15; suites $250-$500; under 18 free. Crib $10. TV; cable (premium). Pool; whirlpool, poolside serv. Restaurant 6 am-11 pm. Rm serv 24 hrs. Bar 11-1 am. Ck-out noon. Convention facilities. Business center. In-rm modem link. Covered parking. Free airport transportation. Lighted tennis. Exercise equipt. Bathrm phone in suites. Golf course adj. On Miami River. Cr cds: A, C, D, DS, ER, JCB, MC, V.

D 🐾 ≋ 🏊 🚭 ✈ 🐾 SC 🚶

Miami Beach (H-6)

(See also Coral Gables, Hollywood, Miami)

Founded 1915 **Pop** 92,639 **Elev** 5 ft **Area code** 305 **E-mail** mbchanber@sobe.com **Web** www.miamibeachchamber.com

Information Chamber of Commerce, 1920 Meridian Ave, 33139, phone 305/672-1270.

Miami Beach is a myriad of hotels, celebrities and sunbathers situated on an island 10 miles long and 1-3 miles wide. The city is an ideal spot from which to sample the sightseeing and recreational opportunities in south Florida and has become an international tourism destination. In the daytime, thousands of people lie in the sun at beaches and pools or enjoy watersports, shopping, museums and sightseeing. In the evening, nightclubs, theater, concerts and world-class dining provide visitors with a variety of entertainment options.

The Miami Beach area was created from what was a wilderness of palmettos: a sandbar infested with snakes and mosquitoes. John S. Collins failed in an attempt to develop avocado groves here and turned to real estate. To join his proposed residential colony with Miami, he built what was then the longest wooden bridge in the US. Collins auctioned off land, then much of it under swamp water, and dredged sand from the bay to transform it into solid ground. This created a yacht basin and several small islands. A pair of elephants, giveaways, super-salesmanship and a talented press agent helped finish the transformation from jungle to resort.

What to See and Do

Bass Museum of Art. Permanent collection ranging from Old Masters to the moderns. Special exhibitions, lectures, performances, films. Tours by appt. (Daily exc Mon; closed hols & day after Thanksgiving) 2121 Park Ave. Phone 305/673-7533 or -7530. ¢¢¢

Jackie Gleason Theater of the Performing Arts. Capacity 2,700. Broadway plays, cultural series, contemporary entertainment. 1700 Washington Ave. For schedule, fees phone 305/673-7300 (box office).

Jungle Queen cruises. Sightseeing cruises to Millionaires Row, Miami Seaquarium, Vizcaya, Bayside Marketplace and Fort Lauderdale. Two cruises (daily). Reservations required; attraction fee included in some cruises. Haulover Park Marina, 10800 Collins Ave. For schedule, fees phone 305/947-6597. ¢¢¢

South Beach. Extends south from the vicinity of Dade Blvd, concentrated mainly along Ocean Dr. This area was spared from demolition through the efforts of citizens and local designers, who began repainting and restoring art deco buildings from the 1920s, '30s and '40s using bright pastel colors. Subsequent redevelopment of the area has transformed the structures into eclectic boutiques, galleries, hotels, nightclubs and restaurants specializing in alfresco dining overlooking the ocean. Within this area is

🔲 **Art Deco District.** A designated national historic district, this is a square-mile concentration of art deco, streamline moderne and Spanish Mediterranean Revival architecture unique in the nation. Former art deco apartment buildings, ballrooms and warehouses have been restored to pastel-and-neon luminosity and sometimes serve as canvases for murals, trompe l'oeil images and elaborate graffiti created by local artists. Special events include classic films, exhibits, music, lectures and fashions. Guided walking tours (Sat mornings). (See ANNUAL EVENTS) From 6th to 23rd Sts, Lenox Court to Ocean Dr. Phone 305/672-2014. Walking tour ¢¢¢

The Wolfsonian. Mediterranean Revival-style building has collection of more than 70,000 European and American objets d'art, including furnishings, architectural elements, murals and poster art. Design from the Industrialist through the Postmodern eras is the focus here. (Daily exc Mon) 1001 Washington Ave at 10th Sts, in South Beach. Phone 305/531-1001. ¢¢

Annual Events

Art Deco Weekend. Art Deco District. A celebration of art deco and popular culture in the 1930s. Vintage cars, music, tours and entertainment throughout the district. 2nd wkend Jan.

Festival of the Arts. Between 80th St & Collins Ave. Art, music and drama. Early Feb.

International Boat Show. Miami Beach Convention Center. Early Feb.

South Florida Auto Show. Miami Beach Convention Center. Nov.

Motels

★★ **BEACHARBOUR RESORT.** 18925 Collins Ave (33160). 305/931-8900; FAX 305/937-1047; res: 800/643-0807 (exc FL). 240 units, 2-4 story, 83 kits. Mid-Dec-late Apr: S, D $85-$115; each addl $10; kit. units $12 addl; under 12 free; lower rates rest of yr. Crib free. TV. 2 pools; wading pool. Restaurant 7:30 am-3 pm, 6-10 pm. Bar 11 am-midnight; entertainment exc Mon. Ck-out noon. Business servs avail. Bellhops. Sundries. Lawn games. Some bathrm phones. Refrigerators. Private patios, balconies. Cr cds: A, C, D, DS, ER, MC, V.

⊠🔥 🔲

★ **MONACO OCEANFRONT.** 17501 Collins Ave (33160), in Sunny Isles. 305/932-2100; FAX 305/931-5519. 113 rms, 2 story, 39 kits. Dec-Apr: S, D $65-$130; each addl $7; kit. units $7 addl; under 12 free; lower rates rest of yr. Crib $7. TV; cable (premium). Heated pool; wading pool. Restaurant 7:30 am-3 pm. Bar 11-1 am. Ck-out noon. Coin lndry. Business servs avail. Bellhops. Sundries. Exercise equipt; sauna.

Rec rm. Lawn games. Refrigerators. On ocean. Cr cds: A, C, D, DS, ER, MC, V.

⊠📡🔥 🔲

★★ **SUEZ.** 18215 Collins Ave (33160), in Sunny Isles. 305/932-0661; FAX 305/937-0058; res: 800/327-5278 (exc FL), 800/432-3661 (FL). 200 rms, 2 story, 68 kits. Mid-Dec-Apr: S, D $67-$98; kit. units $15 addl; lower rates rest of yr. TV; cable (premium). 2 pools, 1 heated; wading pool, poolside serv. Sauna. Playground. Restaurant 7:30 am-10 pm. Bars. Ck-out noon. Coin lndry. Business servs avail. Bellhops. Valet serv. Lighted tennis, pro. Lawn games. Refrigerators. On ocean. Cr cds: A, C, D, ER, MC, V.

🏃⊠📡🔥 🔲

Motor Hotels

★ **HOLIDAY INN-SOUTH BEACH CONVENTION CENTER.** 2201 Collins Ave (33139). 305/534-1511; res: 800/356-6902; FAX 305/532-1403. 355 rms, 3-12 story. Mid-Dec-Apr: S, D $185-$195; each addl $15; suites $390-$400; under 16 free; higher rates special events; lower rates rest of yr. Crib free. TV; cable. Pool; whirlpool, poolside serv. Restaurant 7 am-10 pm. Rm serv. Bar 5 pm-1 am. Ck-out noon. Coin lndry. Business servs avail. In-rm modem link. Bellhops. Valet serv. Sundries. Barber, beauty shop. Gift shop. Lighted tennis. Game rm. On ocean. Cr cds: A, C, D, DS, JCB, MC, V.

D 🏃⊠📡🐾🔥 SC

★★ **INDIAN CREEK.** 2727 Indian Creek Dr (33140). 305/531-2727; FAX 305/531-5651. E-mail indiancreek@travelbase.com; web www.indiancreekhotelmb.com. 61 rms, 3 story, 6 suites. Oct- early May: S, D $130; each addl $10; suites $220; under 12 free; higher rates Super Bowl; lower rates rest of yr. Crib $10. Street parking. TV; cable (premium), VCR avail. Complimentary coffee in lobby. Restaurant (see PAN COAST). Meeting rms. Business servs avail. In-rm modem link. Bellhops. Valet serv. Sundries. Gift shop. Golf privileges. Pool. Refrigerator in suites. Cr cds: A, C, D, DS, JCB, MC, V.

D 🏃⊠🔥 🔲

Hotels

★★★ **THE ALEXANDER.** 5225 Collins Ave (33140). 305/865-6500; res: 800/327-6121; FAX 305/864-8525. Web www.goflorida.com/alexander/. 150 kit. suites, 17 story. Mid-Dec-mid-Apr: 1-bedrm suites $310-$750; 2-bedrm suites $450-$975; 3-4-bedrm suites $950-$1,250; each addl $35; under 17 free; lower rates rest of yr. Crib $10. Garage, valet parking $14. TV; cable (premium). 2 heated pools; whirlpools, poolside serv. Restaurants 7 am-11 pm (also see SHULA'S STEAKHOUSE). Bar 11:30 am-midnight; entertainment. Ck-out noon. Meeting rms. Business center. Concierge. Beauty shop. Golf privileges. Exercise equipt; steam rm, sauna. Refrigerators, microwaves. Private patios, balconies. Elegant decor; many antiques. On ocean; marina, water sport equipt. Cr cds: A, C, D, DS, ER, JCB, MC, V.

D 🏃🎿⊠🏃🐾🔥🏄

★★ **CARDOZO.** 1300 Ocean Dr (33139), in Art Deco District. 305/535-6500; res: 800/782-6500; FAX 305/532-3563. E-mail cardozo @travelbase.com; web www.travelbase.com/destinations/miami-beach/cardozo/. 44 rms, 3 story, 7 suites. S, D $150-$195; suites $300-$620; under 12 free. Valet parking $14. TV; cable (premium), VCR. Restaurant. Bar noon-1 am. Ck-out noon. Business servs avail. In-rm modem link. Health club privileges. Cr cds: A, D, DS, MC, V.

D ⊠🐾 SC

★ **CASA GRANDE.** 834 Ocean Dr (33139). 305/672-7003; res: 800/688-7678; FAX 305/673-3669. E-mail outpost800@aol.com; web www.islandlife.com. 34 kit. suites, 5 story. Oct-May: suites $245-$1,200; under 18 free; lower rates rest of yr. Valet parking $14. TV; cable (premium), VCR. Complimentary coffee in rms. Restaurant 8 am-midnight. Bar. Ck-out noon. Business servs avail. Health club privileges. Refrigerators, microwaves, minibars. Some balconies. In South Beach area. Cr cds: A, C, D, MC, V.

⊡ 🏊 🍴

★ **CASABLANCA ON THE OCEAN.** *6345 Collins Ave (33141). 305/868-0010; res: 808/813-6676; FAX 305/865-7111.* E-mail casablanca@florida.com; web www.florida.com/casablanca/. 288 kit. units, 10 story. Mid-Dec-mid-Apr: kit. units $99-$265; family, wkend, wkly, hol rates; lower rates rest of yr. Crib $15. Valet parking $8. TV; cable (premium). Heated pool. Restaurant 7 am-10:30 pm. Bar 11 am-midnight. Ck-out noon. Meeting rms. Business servs avail. In-rm modem link. Concierge. Gift shop. Coin Indry. Exercise equipt. Refrigerators; some microwaves. On beach. Cr cds: A, C, D, DS, ER, MC, V.

⊡ 🏊 🍴 🏋 🔥 SC

★ ★ ★ **CROWNE PLAZA NEWPORT BEACHSIDE.** *16701 Collins Ave (33160), in Sunny Isles at jct FL A1A, 826. 305/949-1300; FAX 305/956-2733.* 355 rms, 12 story. Mid-Dec-mid-Apr: S, D $145-$180; each addl $10; suites $285-$335; under 18 free; higher rates Feb; lower rates rest of yr. Crib free. Valet parking $5. TV; cable (premium). Pool; wading pool, whirlpool, poolside serv. Supervised child's activities from age 3. Restaurant 7 am-3 pm; dining rm 5:30-11 pm. Bars. Ck-out noon. Coin Indry. Meeting rms. Business servs avail. In-rm modem link. Beauty shop. Exercise rm. Health club privileges. Game rm. Lawn games. Refrigerators; microwaves avail. Many balconies. On ocean; fishing pier; water sport rentals. Cr cds: A, C, D, DS, JCB, MC, V.

⊡ 🏊 🍴 🔥 SC

★ ★ **DELANO.** *1685 Collins Ave (33139). 305/672-2000; FAX 305/532-0099; res: 800/555-5501.* 208 rms, 170 with shower only, 15 story, 30 suites, 8 bungalows. Late Dec-late May: S, D $315-$425; each addl $25; suites $475-$2,250; bungalows $800; under 17 free; wkend, hol rates (min stay hols); higher rates special events; lower rates rest of yr. Crib avail. Valet parking $16. TV; cable (premium), VCR avail (movies). Pool; wading pool, poolside serv. Restaurant (see BLUE DOOR). Rm serv 24 hrs. Bar noon-2 am. Ck-out noon. Meeting rms. Business center. In-rm modem link. Concierge. Gift shop. Exercise rm; sauna. Minibars. Balconies. On beach. Cr cds: A, C, D, DS, JCB, MC, V.

⊡ 🏊 🍴 🔥 🏋

★ ★ ★ **EDEN ROC RESORT.** *4525 Collins Ave (33140). 305/531-0000; FAX 305/531-6955; res: 800/327-8337.* Web florida.com/edenroc. 350 rms, 15 story. Dec-Apr: S, D $200-$375; suites $275-$350; each addl $20; under 17 free; higher rates Dec hols; lower rates rest of yr. Crib free. Valet parking $12. TV; cable (premium). 2 heated pools; poolside serv. Playground. Restaurant 7 am-midnight. Bar. Ck-out 11 am. Convention facilities. Business center. In-rm modem link. Concierge. Beauty salon. Exercise rm. Game rm. Minibars. Balconies. On ocean, swimming beach. Restored landmark hotel. Cr cds: A, D, DS, JCB, MC, V.

⊡ 🏊 🍴 🔥 SC 🏋

★ ★ ★ **FONTAINEBLEAU HILTON RESORT AND TOWERS.** *4441 Collins Ave (33140). 305/538-2000; FAX 305/531-9274.* Web www.hilton.com. 1,206 rms, 17 story. Mid-Nov-May: S $260-$355; D $290-$385; each addl $30; suites $575-$875; family rates; package plans; lower rates rest of yr. Crib free. Pet accepted, some restrictions. Garage $13. TV; cable (premium). Saltwater pool, 1/2-acre heated lagoon pool; whirlpool, poolside serv. Supervised child's activities. Restaurant 6:30-2 am. Bars; entertainment. Ck-out 11 am. Convention facilities. Business center. In-rm modem link. Concierge. Shopping arcade. Barber, beauty shop. 4 lighted tennis courts, pro. Exercise rm; steam rm, sauna. Rec rm. Lawn games. Some refrigerators, minibars; microwaves avail. Balconies. Tropical gardens, rocky waterfall into pool. On ocean; dockage, catamarans, jet skis, paddle boats, para-sailing. Luxury level. Cr cds: A, C, D, DS, ER, JCB, MC, V.

⊡ 🏊 🍴 🏋 🔥 SC

★ ★ **FOUR POINTS BY SHERATON.** *4343 Collins Ave (33140). 305/531-7494; FAX 305/532-0895.* 216 rms, 10 story, 37 suites. Mid-Dec-mid-Apr: S, D $149-$179; suites $199-$360; family, wkend, wkly, hol rates; golf plans; higher rates: Boat Show, Super Bowl; lower rates rest of yr. Crib free. Valet parking $7.50. TV; cable (premium), VCR avail.

Coffee in rms. Restaurant 6:30 am-11 pm. Bar noon-midnight. Ck-out noon. Meeting rms. Business center. Concierge. Gift shop. Tennis privileges. 18-hole par-3 golf privileges, greens fee $37, pro. Pool; whirlpool, poolside serv. Some refrigerators, wet bars. In-rm whirlpool, microwave in suites. Some balconies. On beach. Cr cds: A, D, DS, JCB, MC, V.

⊡ 🏋 🏊 🍴 🔥 SC 🏋

★ ★ ★ **OCEAN FRONT.** *1230 Ocean Dr (33139). 305/672-2579; res: 800/783-1725; FAX 305/672-7665.* E-mail oceanfr@aol.com; web www.travelbase.com/destinations/miami-beach/ocean-front/. 27 rms, 5 story, 19 suites. Nov-May: S, D, suites $155-$515; lower rates rest of yr. Crib avail. Pet accepted, some restrictions. $15. Valet parking $14. TV; cable (premium), VCR. Complimentary continental bkfst. Restaurant 7:30 am-midnight. Bar; jazz Wed-Sun. Ck-out noon. Meeting rms. In-rm modem link. Concierge. Gift shop. Bathrm phones, refrigerators, minibars; some in-rm whirlpools. Some balconies. On beach. Luxury level. Cr cds: A, D, DS, ER, JCB, MC, V.

⊡ 🐾 🔥 🏊

★ ★ **OCEAN SURF.** *7436 Ocean Terrace (33141). 305/886-1648; FAX 305/866-1649.* E-mail info@oceansurf.com; web www.oceansurf.com. 49 rms, 2 with shower only, 3 story. Mid-Dec-mid-Apr: S, D $89-$139; under 12 free; family, wkly rates; higher rates special events; lower rates rest of yr. Crib free. Street parking. TV; cable (premium). Complimentary continental bkfst. Ck-out 11 am. Business servs avail. In-rm modem link. Many refrigerators. Some balconies. Opp ocean. Cr cds: A, D, DS, MC, V.

⊡ 🏊 🔥 SC

★ **RITZ PLAZA.** *1701 Collins Ave (33139). 305/534-3500; res: 800/522-6400; FAX 305/531-6928.* E-mail sales@ritzplaza.com; web www.ritzplaza.com. 132 rms, 12 story. Mid-Dec-mid-Apr: S, D $225-$265; suites $350-$750; under 18 free; family rates; package plans; higher rates Super Bowl; lower rates rest of yr. Pet accepted. Valet/garage parking $10. TV; cable (premium). Complimentary coffee in rms. Restaurant 6 am-11 pm. Bar 4 pm-3 am. Ck-out noon. Meeting rms. Business servs avail. In-rm modem link. Gift shop. Coin Indry. Airport transportation. 18-hole golf privileges. Pool; poolside serv. Refrigerators. Picnic tables. On beach. Cr cds: A, C, D, DS, MC, V.

⊡ 🐾 🏋 🏊 🔥 SC

★ ★ **SEA VIEW.** *(9909 Collins Ave, Bal Harbour 33154) 5 mi N on FL A1A. 305/866-4441; FAX 305/866-1898; res: 800/447-1010.* 200 rms, 14 story, 13 kits. Mid-Dec-mid-Apr: S, D $205-$275; each addl $25; suites $275-$475; under 12 free; lower rates rest of yr. Crib free. TV; cable (premium). Heated pool; poolside serv. Restaurant 7:30 am-3 pm, 6:30-10:30 pm. Bar; entertainment. Ck-out noon. Meeting rms. Business servs avail. Beauty shop. Valet parking $5. Exercise rm. Solarium. Lawn games. Refrigerators. Many balconies. On ocean. Cr cds: A, C, D, MC, V.

🏊 🍴 🏋 🔥

★ **SEACOAST SUITES.** *5101 Collins Ave (33140). 305/865-5152; FAX 305/868-4090; res: 800/523-3671 (exc FL), 800/624-8769 (FL).* E-mail seacoast@sobe.com. 73 kit. suites (1-2 bedrm), 16-17 story. Early Dec-Apr: kit. suites $185-$425; special events, hols (7-day min); lower rates rest of yr. Crib $5. TV; cable (premium). Heated pool. Complimentary coffee in rms. Bar. Ck-out noon. Coin Indry. Valet parking. Lighted tennis. Exercise equipt. Health club privileges. Balconies. On ocean, private beach; marina. Cr cds: A, D, DS, MC, V.

🏋 🏊 🔥

★ ★ ★ **SHERATON-BAL HARBOUR.** *(9701 Collins Ave, Bal Harbour 33154) 5 mi N on FL A1A. 305/865-7511; FAX 305/864-2601.* 644 rms, 15 story. Mid-Dec-mid-Apr: S, D $300-$409; suites $550-$1,500; lower rates rest of yr. Crib free. Pet accepted, some restrictions. Valet parking $12. TV; cable (premium), VCR avail (movies). 2 heated pools; wading pool. Supervised child's activities. Coffee in rms. Restaurants 6:30 am-10 pm (see also AL CARBON). Bars 11-1:30 am. Ck-out noon. Convention facilities. Business center. In-rm modem link. Concierge. Lighted tennis, pro shop. Golf privileges. Exercise equipt. Massage. Game rm. Minibars. Refrigerators avail. Many balconies. Tropical gardens. On 10 acres at oceanfront; boat rental, water sports. Cr cds: A, C, D, DS, ER, JCB, MC, V.

D ⛵ 🏋 🚶 🏊 🎿 🏃 ⛸ 🎣 🚫 SC ⛷

★ ★ ★ **THE TIDES.** *1200 Ocean Dr (33139), 12th St & Ocean Dr.* 305/604-5000. Web www.islandoutpost.com. 45 rms, 10 story, 10 suites. Oct-May: S, D $375-$450; suites $1000-1350; lower rates rest of yr. Crib avail. Pet accepted, some restrictions. Valet parking $10. TV; cable (premium), VCR. Restaurant 6 am-midnight. Rm serv 24 hrs. Bar. Ck-out 1 pm. Meeting rms. Business center. In-rm modem link. Concierge. Shopping arcade. Pool; poolside serv, lifeguard. Bathrm phones, refrigerators, minibars; some microwaves. On beach. Cr cds: A, C, D, DS, MC, V.

D ⛵ 🏊 🎣 🚫 ⛷

★ ★ **WESTIN.** *4833 Collins Ave (33140).* 305/532-3600; FAX 305/535-2766. 424 rms, 18 story, 46 suites. Mid-Dec-mid-Apr: S, D $275-$395; each addl $20-$40; suites $450-$2200; under 18 free; family rates; higher rates special events; lower rates rest of yr. Crib free. Valet parking $13. TV; cable (premium), VCR avail (movies). Complimentary coffee in rms. Restaurants 6:30 am-11 pm. Rm serv 24 hrs. Bar; piano. Ck-out noon. Convention facilities. Business center. In-rm modem link. Shopping arcade. Gift shop. Barber, beauty shop. Coin lndry. Lighted tennis, pro. Exercise rm; sauna. Massage. Heated pool; poolside serv. Supervised child's activities; ages 3-12. Bathrm phones, refrigerators, minibars. Some wet bars. On beach. Cr cds: A, C, D, JCB, MC, V.

D 🏋 🏊 🏃 🎿 ⛸ SC ⛷

Inn

↙ ★ ★ ★ **BAY HARBOR INN.** *(9660 E Bay Harbor Dr, Bay Harbor Islands 33154) N via Collins Ave, near Broad Causeway.* 305/868-4141; FAX 305/867-9094. E-mail bhi@aol.com; web www.jwu.edu/florida. 46 rms, 2 story, 18 suites. Dec-Apr: S, D $149; each addl $25; suites $149-$179; under 10 free; higher rates hols (4-day min); lower rates rest of yr. Crib free. TV; cable. Heated pool. Complimentary continental bkfst. Restaurant (see ISLAND CAFE WATERFRONT TAVERN). Ck-out 11 am, ck-in 3 pm. Business center. In-rm modem link. Refrigerators. Inn (1948) located on scenic Indian Creek. Cr cds: A, C, MC, V.

D ⛵ 🏊 🚫 🐾 ⛷

Restaurants

★ ★ ★ **AL CARBÓN.** *(See Sheraton Bal Harbour Hotel)* 305/865-7511. Hrs: 5:30 pm-1 am; early-bird dinner Sun-Thurs to 7 pm. Res accepted. Continental menu. Bar. Wine list. A la carte entrees: dinner $12-$30. Child's meals. Specializes in veal, steak. Entertainment Thurs-Sun. Valet parking. Outdoor dining. Hand-painted tables. Cr cds: A, C, D, DS, ER, JCB, MC, V.

D 🍽

★ ★ ★ **ASTOR PLACE.** *956 Washington Ave (33139), 10th & Washington.* 305/672-7217. Hrs: 8 am-11 pm; Fri-Sun to midnight; Sun brunch noon-2:30 pm. Res accepted. Bar. Extensive wine list. A la carte entrees: bkfst $8-$12, lunch $15-$25, dinner $15-$30. Sun brunch $20. Specialties: wild mushroom pancakes, corn-crusted snapper, smoked prime rib. Valet parking. Outdoor dining. Atrium. Cr cds: A, C, D, MC, V.

D 🍽

★ ★ **BALANS.** *1022 Lincoln Rd (33139).* 305/534-9191. Hrs: 8 am-midnight; Fri, Sat to 1 am. Res accepted. Continental menu. Bar. A la carte entrees: bkfst $3.50-$6.50, lunch, dinner $5-$15. Specialties: herb-crusted chilean sea bass, hoi-sin pork fillet, Thai salad. Outdoor dining. Cr cds: A, C, D, DS, MC, V.

D 🍽

★ ★ **BELLA LUNA.** *(19575 Biscayne Blvd, Aventura 33180) in Aventura Mall.* 305/792-9330. Hrs: 11:30 am-midnight. Closed Dec 25. Res accepted. Italian menu. Bar. A la carte entrees: lunch $6.95-$12.95,

dinner $6.95-$21.95. Child's meals. Specialties: penne billante, pollo milanese, brick-oven pizza. Valet parking. Cr cds: A, D, MC, V.

D 🍽

★ ★ ★ **BLUE DOOR.** *(See Delano Hotel)* 305/672-2000. Hrs: 7-2 am. Res accepted. Continental menu. Bar from 5 pm. Wine list. Semi-a la carte: bkfst $8-$16.50, lunch $15-$30, dinner $25-$50. Buffet: bkfst $13, lunch $21. Child's meals. Specializes in rack of lamb, grilled swordfish, seared Chilean sea bass. Valet parking. Outdoor dining overlooks garden and pool area. Cr cds: A, MC, V.

🍽

★ ★ **CAFFE DA VINCI.** *(1009 Kane Concourse, Bay Harbor Islands 33154)* 305/861-8166. Hrs: 11:30 am-2:30 pm, 5:30-11 pm; Sat, Sun from 5:30 pm. Res accepted. Italian menu. Bar. A la carte entrees: lunch $5.95-$9.95, dinner $5.95-$22.95. Child's meals. Specializes in chicken, fish, veal. Valet parking. Outdoor dining. Reproductions of da Vinci's artwork. Totally nonsmoking. Cr cds: A, D, MC, V.

D

★ ★ **CAFFÉ MILANO.** *850 Ocean Dr (33139).* 305/532-0707. Hrs: noon-midnight. Res accepted. Italian menu. Bar. Semi-a la carte: lunch $8-$20, dinner $20-$30. Serv charge 15%. Specialties: risotto ai funghi Porcini, cotoletta alla Milanese. Covered patio and sidewalk dining. Art deco furniture on display. Cr cds: A, D, DS, MC, V.

D 🍽

★ ★ ★ **CAFFE SAMBUCA.** *1233 Lincoln Rd (33139).* 305/532-2800. Hrs: 11:30 am-2:30 pm, 6-11:30 pm. Res accepted. Italian menu. A la carte entrees: lunch $5-$15, dinner $10-$26. Specialties: pollo alla Claudia, osso buco in cremolata, dentice crosta di funghi. Own baking. Art-deco decor. Cr cds: A, MC, V.

D 🍽

★ ★ **CARDOZO CAFE.** *(See Cardozo)* 305/538-0553. Hrs: 8 am-midnight; Fri, Sat to 1 am. Res required wkends. Bar. A la carte entrees: lunch $6.95-$12.95, dinner $10.95-$23.95. Specializes in world cuisine. Valet parking. Entertainment Thur-Sun. Outdoor dining. Cr cds: A, C, D, DS, MC, V.

D 🍽

★ ★ **CARPACCIO.** *(9700 Collins Ave, Bal Harbour 33154) in Bal Harbour Shoppes.* 305/867-7777. Hrs: 11:30 am-midnight. Closed Dec 25. Res accepted. Italian menu. Bar. A la carte entrees: lunch $6.95-$12.95, dinner $6.95-$21.95. Child's meals. Specialties: carpaccio di manzo, pennette Harry's bar, fried calamari. Parking. Outdoor dining. Cr cds: A, D, MC, V.

D 🍽

★ ★ **CHRYSANTHEMUM.** *1248 Washington Ave (33139).* 305/531-5656. Hrs: 6-11 pm; Fri, Sat to midnight. Closed Mon; Thanksgiving. Res accepted. Chinese menu. Bar. A la carte entrees: dinner $11-$20. Specializes in beef, chicken, shrimp. Valet parking. Chinese decor. Cr cds: A, C, D, MC, V.

D 🍽

★ ★ ★ **CRYSTAL CAFE.** *726 Arthur Godfrey Rd (33140).* 305/673-8266. Hrs: 5-10 pm; Fri-Sun to 11 pm; early-bird dinner to 6 pm. Closed Mon. Res accepted. Continental menu. Bar. Wine list. Semi-a la carte: dinner $10.95-$24.95. Child's meals. Specialties: osso bucco, rack of lamb, broiled salmon with pistachios. Elegant dining. Chef-owned. Cr cds: A, D, DS, MC, V.

D 🍽

★ ★ **FARFALLA.** *701 Washington Ave (33139).* 305/673-2335. Hrs: 6 pm-midnight; Fri, Sat to 1 am. Closed Dec 25. Res accepted wkends. Italian menu. Bar. Semi-a la carte: dinner $8-$25. Specializes in fresh pasta, fish, wood-burning oven pizza. Casual atmosphere. Cr cds: A, C, D, DS, MC, V.

D 🍽

★ ★ ★ **THE FORGE.** *432 Arthur Godfrey Rd (33140).* 305/538-8533. Hrs: 6 pm-midnight; Fri, Sat to 1 am. Res required. Contemporary Amer menu. Bar from 6 pm. Wine cellar. A la carte entrees: dinner $17.95-$35.95. Child's meals. Specializes in steak, pasta, duck. Own baking. Entertainment. Valet parking. Courtyard dining. Cr cds: A, C, D, MC, V.

D 📷

✔★ ★ **ISLAND CAFE WATERFRONT TAVERN.** *(See Bay Harbor Inn)* 305/867-8883. Hrs: 10:30 am-11 pm; Sun brunch to 2:30 pm. Bar. Semi-a la carte: lunch $5.95-$8.95, dinner $8.95-$18. Sun brunch $15.95. Child's meals. Specialties: grilled vegetable strata, filet mignon. Waterfront dining. Cr cds: A, MC, V.

D 📷

✔★ ★ **LEMON TWIST.** *908 71st St (33141).* 305/868-2075. Hrs: 6 pm-midnight. Res accepted. French menu. Bar. Semi-a la carte: dinner $4-$18.50. Specialties: tian nicois et mozarella, poulet au citron, souris d'agneau confites au thym. Own baking. Bright decor with sculptured ceiling. Cr cds: A, MC, V.

D 📷

★ ★ **MEZZANOTTE.** *1200 Washington Ave (33130).* 305/673-4343. Hrs: 6 pm-midnight; Fri, Sat to 2 am. Closed Thanksgiving. Northern Italian menu. Bar. Semi-a la carte: dinner $12.95-$25.95. Specializes in pasta, veal. Valet parking. Trendy, neon-lit decor; in Art Deco District. Cr cds: A, D, DS, MC, V.

D 📷

★ ★ **NEMO.** *100 Collins Ave (33139).* 305/532-4550. Hrs: noon-3 pm, 7 pm-midnight; Sun 6-11 pm; Sun brunch noon-3 pm. Res required. Bar. A la carte entrees: lunch $6-$12, dinner $16-$21. Sun brunch $19. Specialties: crispy prawns, garlic cured salmon rolls. Valet parking. Outdoor dining. Contemporary decor. Cr cds: A, MC, V.

D 📷

✔★ **NEWS CAFE.** *800 Ocean Dr (33139), in Art Deco District.* 305/538-6397. Open 24 hrs. Bar 8-5 am. A la carte entrees: bkfst $3-$5.50, lunch $4.25-$8.75, dinner $4.25-$10.25. Specializes in Middle Eastern cuisine, salads, sandwiches. Valet parking. Outdoor dining. Cr cds: A, D, MC, V.

D 📷

★ ★ **OSTERIA DEL TEATRO.** *1443 Washington Ave (33139), in Art Deco District.* 305/538-7850. Hrs: 6-11 pm; wkends to midnight. Closed Tues; major hols. Res accepted. Northern Italian menu. A la carte entrees: dinner $12-$28. Child's meals. Specialties: stuffed zucchini blossom with goat cheese, stone crab peppardelle, tuna with a Mediterranean sauce. Valet parking. Cr cds: A, C, D, MC, V.

D 📷

★ ★ ★ **PACIFIC TIME.** *915 Lincoln Rd (33139).* 305/534-5979. This cool, California-style restaurant is packed even on nights something special isn't happening. Twenty-foot cathedral ceilings, abstract paintings, accents of mahogany and brass, plank floors and an open kitchen give this restaurant a special flair. Asian, Amer menu. Specialties: Szechwan grilled grouper, shiitake grilled beef, shrimp Peking pancake. Hrs: 6-11 pm; Fri, Sat to midnight; early-bird dinner to 7 pm. Closed Thanksgiving. Res accepted. Bar. Wine list. A la carte entrees: dinner $11-$25. Child's meals. Street parking. Outdoor dining. Cr cds: A, C, D, MC, V.

D 📷

★ ★ **PALM.** *(9650 E Bay Harbor Dr, Bay Harbor Island 33154)* 305/868-7256. Hrs: 5-10 pm. Closed Thanksgiving. Res accepted; required wkends. Bar. A la carte entrees: dinner $17-$68 Specializes in steak, seafood, pasta. Valet parking. Counterpart to famous New York City restaurant. Caricatures of celebrities. Cr cds: A, C, D, MC, V.

D 📷

★ ★ **PAN COAST.** *(See Indian Creek Motor Hotel).* 305/531-2727. Hrs: 7-11 am, 6-11 pm; May-Sept hrs vary. Closed Tues; some major hols. Res accepted. Caribbean menu. Bkfst buffet $4-$9. A la carte entrees: dinner $14-$22. Serv charge 15%. Child's meals. Specialties: tempura shrimp, mache greens, malanga-crusted Mahi Mahi. Outdoor dining. Intimate atmosphere. Cr cds: A, C, D, DS, MC, V.

D 📷

★ ★ ★ **SHULA'S STEAKHOUSE.** *(See The Alexander Hotel)* 305/861-5252. Web www.goflorida.com/alexander/. Hrs: 7 am-3 pm, 6-11 pm. Res accepted. Bar. Wine list. Semi-a la carte: bkfst $4.75-$14.50, lunch $6.50-$15, dinner $10-$45. Child's meals. Specializes in certified Angus beef, fresh seafood. Valet parking. Oceanfront dining. Cr cds: A, D, MC, V.

D

★ ★ **VAN DYKE CAFE.** *846 Lincoln Rd (33139), in Van Dyke loft hotel.* 305/534-3600. Hrs: 8-1 am; Fri, Sat to 2 am. Continental menu. Bar. A la carte entrees: bkfst $4-$8.75, lunch, dinner $5.75-$11.50. Specialties: fish ceviche with pita chips, smoked salmon. Jazz nightly. Outdoor dining. Cr cds: A, D, MC, V.

D 📷

★ ★ **YUCA.** *501 Lincoln Rd (33139).* 305/532-9822. Hrs: noon-11 pm; Fri, Sat to midnight. Res accepted. Cuban menu. Bar. A la carte entrees: lunch $6-$14, dinner $6-$31. Specialties: Marina's sweet coated plantain, plantain-coated dolphin. Entertainment Fri-Sun. Outdoor dining. Cr cds: A, D, DS, MC, V.

D 📷

★ ★ **ZHIVAGO'S.** *17001 Collins Ave (33160).* 305/949-0711. Hrs: from 5 pm. Closed Mon. Res accepted. Russian & French menu. Bar. A la carte entrees: dinner $15-$30. Specialties: lobster bisque, medallions of rack of lamb, pepper crusted seared sirloin. Valet parking. Dinner theater atmosphere. Cr cds: A, C, D, MC, V.

D SC 📷

Naples (H-4)

(See also Bonita Springs, Marco Island)

Settled 1887 **Pop** 19,505 **Elev** 9 ft **Area code** 941 **E-mail** chamber@naples-online.com **Web** www.naples-online.com
Information Naples Area Chamber of Commerce & Visitors Center, 895 5th Ave S, 34102; 941/262-6141.

Named after the Italian city and complete with a "Bay of Naples," this Gulf of Mexico resort community has grown steadily since 1950. Vacationers enjoy 10 miles of beach and a 1,000-foot fishing pier. Naples is also home to more than 60 golf courses and a stop on the Senior PGA Tour.

What to See and Do

Collier County Museum. Explores 10,000 yrs of Florida history; 4-acre historical park, orchid house, archeological lab, 1910 steam locomotive, 1920s swamp buggy, restored house (1926). (Mon-Fri; closed hols) 3301 Tamiami Trail E (US 41). Phone 941/774-8476. **Free.**

Conservancy Nature Center. Includes natural science museum featuring serpentarium, wildlife, aviary, rehabilitation clinic; trails, free guided boat tours, gift shop. (Hrs vary with season; closed hols) At 14th Ave N, off Goodlette-Frank Rd. Phone 941/262-0304. **Free;** Museum ¢¢

Corkscrew Swamp Sanctuary. This National Audubon Society preserve contains one of the largest stands of mature bald cypress trees; 2-mi boardwalk loops through the swamp; self-guided tour. Picnic area. Visitor center. (Daily) 20 mi NE on County 846. Phone 941/657-3771. ¢¢¢

Jungle Larry's Zoological Park at Caribbean Gardens. A 52-acre botanical garden with animals, birds and plants from around the world; boat tours; wild animal shows; tropical bird circus; lectures. Picnic area, snack bar, petting zoo, gift shop. (Daily; closed Thanksgiving, Dec 25) 1590 Goodlette Rd, E of Coastland Center. Phone 941/262-5409. ¢¢¢¢

Rookery Bay National Estuarine Research Reserve. This 9,400-acre reserve encompasses a variety of habitats, including extensive mangrove forests, sea grasses, salt marshes and upland pine flatwoods; various wildlife and bird species can be observed; slide shows, interpretive displays, nature center with boat & canoe trips (winter) and guided boardwalk tours (fee). Fishing; hiking. (Daily) Approx 5 mi S, on Shell Island Rd. Contact Reserve Manager, 10 Shell Island Rd, 33962; 941/775-8569 (nature center). **Free.**

Annual Events

Collier County Fair. Agriculture and educational displays, entertainment, carnival. Jan.

Swamp Buggy Championship Races. Florida Sports Park. Early Mar, late May & last wkend Oct.

Motels

★ ★ **BEST WESTERN INN.** *2329 Tamiami Trail (US 41) (34103).* 941/261-1148; res: 800/243-1148; FAX 941/262-4684. Web www.bestwesternnaples.com. 80 rms, 2 story. Feb-mid-Apr: S, D $119-$130; suites $169; each addl $10; under 18 free; lower rates rest of yr. Crib $6. TV; cable (premium), VCR (free movies). 2 pools; whirlpools. Complimentary continental bkfst. Coffee in rms. Restaurant adj 5-10 pm. Ck-out 11 am. Business servs avail. In-rm modem link. Health club privileges. Refrigerators, microwaves. Private patios, balconies. Cr cds: A, D, DS, MC, V.

★ ★ **COMFORT INN.** *1221 5th Ave S (34102), on US 41.* 941/649-5800; FAX 941/649-0523. Web www.comfortinnnaples.com. 101 rms, 4 story. S, D $89-$149; each addl $6; under 18 free. Crib free. TV; cable (premium). Pool; whirlpool. Complimentary continental bkfst. Coffee in rms. Restaurant opp 11 am-midnight. Ck-out noon. Coin lndry. Meeting rms. Business servs avail. In-rm modem link. Sundries. Gift shop. Health club privileges. Cr cds: A, C, D, DS, ER, JCB, MC, V.

★ ★ **COMFORT INN SUITES.** *3860 Tollgate Blvd (34114).* 941/353-9500; FAX 941/353-0035. 151 units, 4 story, 8 suites, 53 kits. Mid-Dec-Apr: S, D $99-$110; each addl $8; suites $149-$253; under 18 free; wkly rates; lower rates rest of yr. Crib free. TV; cable. Heated pool; whirlpool, poolside serv. Complimentary continental bkfst. Restaurant adj 6 am-10 pm. Bar 4-10 pm. Ck-out 11 am. Meeting rms. Business servs avail. Gift shop. Tennis privileges. Golf privileges, greens fee from $60 (cart addl), pro, putting green, driving range. Game rm. Wet bars. Balconies. Cr cds: A, C, D, DS, ER, JCB, MC, V.

★ ★ **HAMPTON INN.** *3210 Tamiami Trail (US 41) (34103).* 941/261-8000; FAX 941/261-7802. 107 rms, 4 story. Mid-Dec-Apr: S, D $129-$139; suites $225; under 18 free; lower rates rest of yr. Crib free. TV; cable (premium). Heated pool. Complimentary continental bkfst. Restaurant nearby. Ck-out noon. Meeting rm. Business servs avail. Health club privileges. Some refrigerators; microwaves avail. Cr cds: A, C, D, DS, MC, V.

★ **HOWARD JOHNSON.** *221 9th St S (US 41) (34102).* 941/262-6181; res: 800/206-2883; FAX 941/262-0318. E-mail napleshojo@sprintmail.com. 100 rms, 2 story. Mid-Dec-mid-Apr: S, D $80-$155; under 18 free; lower rates rest of yr. Crib free. Pet accepted, some restrictions; $25. TV; cable (premium). Heated pool; poolside serv. Playground. Restaurant adj. Ck-out noon. Business servs avail. Health club privileges. Lawn games. Bicycle rentals. Some refrigerators; microwaves avail. Private patios, balconies. Cr cds: A, C, D, DS, ER, JCB, MC, V.

✔ ★ **OLDE NAPLES INN.** *801 3rd St S (34102).* 941/262-5194; FAX 941/262-4876; res: 800/637-6036. E-mail oldenap@mediaone.net; web www.bestof.net/naples/hotels/oldnaplesinn. 60 rms, 1-2 story. 45 kits. Dec-Apr: S, D $99; each addl $6; suites $139-$179; kit. units. $109-$129; under 16 free; lower rates rest of yr. Crib $6. TV; cable. 2 heated pools. Complimentary continental bkfst. Restaurant nearby. Ck-out 11 am. Coin lndry. Business servs avail. Lawn games. Bicycle rentals. Refrigerators. Picnic tables, grills. Gulf beach 2 blks. Cr cds: A, C, D, DS, MC, V.

✔ ★ **RED ROOF.** *1925 Davis Blvd (34104).* 941/774-3117; FAX 941/775-5333. E-mail jchizmar@redroofinn.com. 157 rms, 3 story, 29 kits. Dec-Apr: S, D $102-$106; each addl $10; kit. suites $119-$129; under 18 free; lower rates rest of yr. Crib free. Pet accepted, some restrictions. TV; cable (premium). Pool; whirlpool. Restaurant adj 6 am-midnight. Ck-out 11 am. Guest lndry. Business servs avail. Lawn games. Refrigerators. Private patios. Picnic tables. Marina adj. Beach 1 mi. Cr cds: A, C, D, DS, MC, V.

★ ★ **STONEY'S COURTYARD INN.** *2630 N Tamiami Trail (US 41) (34103).* 941/261-3870; FAX 941/261-4932; res: 800/432-3870. Web www.travelbase.com/naples/stoneys/index.ntml. 72 rms, 2 story, 4 suites. Jan-Apr: S, D $90-$105; suites $125; lower rates rest of yr. TV; cable. Heated pool. Complimentary continental bkfst. Restaurant nearby. Ck-out 11 am. Coin lndry. Business servs avail. Refrigerators avail. Cr cds: A, DS, MC, V.

★ ★ **VANDERBILT BEACH RESORT.** *9225 Gulf Shore Dr N (34108), I-75, exit 18.* 941/597-3144; res: 800/243-9076; FAX 941/597-2199. E-mail VBmotel@worldnet.att.com; web www.vanderbiltbeachresort.com. 66 rms in 4 bldgs, 1-4 story, 16 kit. suites. Mid-Dec-Apr: S, D $101-$122; each addl $3-$6; kit. units $104-$230; under 4 free; lower rates rest of yr. Crib $5. TV; cable, VCR avail (movies $6). Pool. Complimentary continental bkfst (motel). Complimentary coffee in motel rms. Restaurant adj 11:30 am-11 pm. Ck-out 11 am. Business servs avail. Coin lndry. Tennis. Refrigerators; some microwaves. Some balconies. Picnic tables. Beachfront property on Gulf. Cr cds: A, MC, V.

★ ★ **VANDERBILT INN ON THE GULF.** *11000 Gulf Shore Dr N (34108), at Vanderbilt Beach.* 941/597-3151; FAX 941/597-3099; res: 800/643-8654. E-mail vandy@naples.net; web www.vanderbiltinn.com. 147 rms, 2 story, 16 kits. Feb-Apr: S, D $180-$195; each addl $10; kit. units $295; under 18 free; lower rates rest of yr. Crib free. TV; cable. Heated pool; wading pool, poolside serv. Restaurant 7 am-10 pm. Rm serv. Bar; entertainment wkends. Ck-out 11 am. Coin lndry. Business servs avail. In-rm modem link. Gift shop. Sundries. Refrigerators. Some balconies. On Gulf. Wiggins Pass State Park adj. Cr cds: A, C, D, DS, MC, V.

★ ★ **WELLESLEY INN.** *1555 5th Ave S (34102).* 941/793-4646; FAX 941/793-5248. 105 rms, 3 story. Late Dec-Apr: S, D $69-$129; under 18 free; lower rates rest of yr. Crib free. Pet accepted, some restrictions; $5. TV; cable (premium). Pool. Complimentary continental bkfst. Coffee in rms. Restaurant adj 11 am-10 pm. Ck-out 11 am. Business servs avail. Health club privileges. Some refrigerators; microwaves avail. Cr cds: A, C, D, DS, JCB, MC, V.

Motor Hotels

★ **COVE INN RESORT & MARINA.** *900 Broad Avenue South (34102), on Naples Bay.* 941/262-7161; res: 800/255-4365; FAX 941/261-6905. Web www.bestof.net/naples/hotels/coveinn. 102 rms, 3 story. Mid-Dec-Apr: S, D $114-$129; kit. units $126-$144; under 18 free; lower rates rest of yr. Crib free. TV; cable (premium). Heated pool; poolside serv. Restaurants 7 am-11 pm. Bar 11 am-9 pm. Ck-out 11 am. Coin lndry. Business servs avail. Bellhops. Sundries. Refrigerators. Picnic tables, grills. Situated on a natural peninsula; most balconies overlook waterway. Cr cds: A, D, DS, MC, V.

[D] [icons] SC

★ ★ ★ **INN AT PELICAN BAY.** *800 Vanderbilt Beach Rd (34108), at US 41.* 941/597-8777; FAX 941/597-8012; res: 800/597-8770. E-mail sales@naplesinn.com; web www.naplesinn.com. 100 rms, 6 story. Mid-Dec-mid-Apr: S, D $125-$250; each addl $20; under 18 free; lower rates rest of yr. Crib $10. TV; cable, VCR avail. Heated pool; wading pool, whirlpool, poolside serv. Complimentary continental bkfst. Restaurant adj 11 am-midnight. Bar 4:30 pm-midnight. Ck-out noon. Meeting rms. In-rm modem link. Bellhops. Concierge. Tennis privileges. 18-hole golf privileges, greens fee $35-$125. Exercise equipt. Microwaves avail. Balconies. Private lake. Cr cds: A, D, DS, MC, V.

[D] [icons] SC

★ ★ ★ **INN OF NAPLES AT PARK SHORE.** *4055 Tamiami Trail N (US 41) (34103).* 941/649-5500; FAX 941/430-0422; res: 800/237-8858. E-mail sstream@peganet.com; web www.sunstream.com. 64 rms, 5 story, 36 suites. Mid-Dec-mid-Apr: S, D $140-$176; under 17 free; lower rates rest of yr. Crib $10. TV; cable (premium), VCR (movies $3.50). Heated pool; poolside serv. Complimentary continental bkfst. Coffee in rms. Restaurant 11:30 am-2:30 pm, 5:30-10 pm; closed Sun. Bar. Ck-out noon. Meeting rms. Business servs avail. Bellhops in season. Exercise equipt. Refrigerators. Private patios, balconies. Spanish-Mediterranean setting. Cr cds: A, C, D, DS, MC, V.

[D] [icons] SC

★ ★ ★ **THE INN ON FIFTH AVE.** *699 5th Ave S (34112).* 941/403-8777; res: 888/403-8778; FAX 941/403-8778. Web www.naplesinn.com. 87 rms, 3 story, 8 suites. Dec-Apr: S, D $150-$250; each addl $20; suites $250-$350; under 18 free; lower rates rest of yr. Crib $5. TV; cable. Restaurant 7 am-midnight. Rm serv. Bar 11-1 am; entertainment. Ck-out noon. Meeting rms. Business servs avail. In-rm modem link. Bellhops. Valet serv. Concierge. Beauty shop. 36-hole golf privileges, greens fee $75, pro, putting green, driving range. Exercise rm; sauna. Massage. Pool. Bathrm phones; some in-rm whirlpools. Balconies. Cr cds: A, C, D, DS, MC, V.

[D] [icons] SC

★ ★ **PARK SHORE RESORT.** *600 Neapolitan Way (34103).* 941/263-2222; res: 800/548-2077; FAX 941/263-0946. E-mail sstreamps@peganet.com; web www.sunstream.com. 156 kit. suites, 2-4 story. Mid-Dec-mid-Apr: 1-bedrm $215; 2-bedrm $235; each addl $10; under 18 free; monthly rates; lower rates rest of yr. Crib free. TV; cable (premium). Heated pool; whirlpool, poolside serv. Supervised child's activities ages 5-16. Restaurant 11:30 am-10 pm. Bar. Ck-out 11 am. Coin lndry. Business servs avail. Tennis. Lawn games. Microwaves. Private patios, balconies. Picnic tables, grills. On 13 landscaped acres; pond, bridge, waterfall. Cr cds: A, D, DS, MC, V.

[D] [icons] SC

★ ★ **QUALITY INN SUITES & GOLF RESORT.** *4100 Golden Gate Pkwy (34116), at FL 951.* 941/455-1010; res: 800/277-0017; FAX 941/455-4038. 181 rms, 2-4 story, 24 suites (1-2 bedrm), 31 kit. units. Mid-Dec-Apr: S, D $95; each addl $8; suites $179-$288; kit. units $139; under 18 free; wkly rates; golf plans; lower rates rest of yr. Crib free. TV; cable. Heated pool; whirlpool, poolside serv. Restaurant 7 am-9 pm. Bar 10:30 am-11 pm; entertainment. Ck-out noon. Meeting rms. Business servs avail. Sundries. Tennis. 18-hole golf, greens fee $60 (incl half-cart), pro, putting green, driving range. Balconies. Cr cds: A, C, D, DS, ER, JCB, MC, V.

[D] [icons] SC

✔ ★ **SEA COURT INN.** *40 Tamiami Trail N (34102).* 941/435-9700; res: 800/325-7595; FAX 941/435-0369. Web www.travelbase.com. 30 rms, 2 with shower only, 3 story, 8 suites. S, D $85-$92; suites $115-$125; under 18 free; family rates; package plans. TV; cable (premium). Complimentary continental bkfst. Restaurant nearby. Meeting rms.

Business servs avail. Tennis. Exercise equipt. Pool. Refrigerators, microwaves, wet bars. Cr cds: A, MC, V.

[D] [icons]

Hotels

★ ★ ★ **EDGEWATER BEACH.** *1901 Gulf Shore Blvd N (34102).* 941/403-2000; res: 800/821-0196; FAX 941/403-2100. Web www.edgewaternaples.com. 126 kit. suites, 4-7 story. Mid-Dec-Apr: 1-bedrm suites $270-$700; 2-bedrm suites $390-$1,500; under 18 free; golf plans; lower rates rest of yr. Crib free. TV; cable (premium), VCR avail. Heated pool; poolside serv. Supervised child's activities (Mid-Dec-Apr). Restaurant 7 am-10 pm. Bar 4 pm-midnight; entertainment. Ck-out noon. Meeting rms. Business servs avail. Gift shop. Valet parking. Tennis privileges. 18-hole golf privileges, greens fee $90-$125 (incl half-cart), putting green, driving range. Exercise equipt. Microwaves. Private patios, balconies. Overlooks Gulf of Mexico. Grand piano in lobby & dining rm; music in afternoons, evenings. Cr cds: A, C, D, DS, MC, V.

[D] [icons] SC

★ ★ ★ **LA PLAYA BEACH RESORT.** *9891 Gulf Shore Dr (34108).* 941/597-3123; res: 800/237-6883; FAX 941/597-6278. Web www.laplayaresort.com. 191 rms, 15 story. Mid-Dec-mid-Apr: S, D $240-$405; each addl $30; under 16 free; lower rates rest of yr. Crib free. Valet parking $10. TV; cable (premium). Restaurant 7 am-10 pm. Bar 11 am-midnight; entertainment Thurs-Sun. Meeting rms. Business servs avail. In-rm modem link. Concierge. Shopping arcade. Coin lndry. Tennis privileges. Golf privileges. Exercise equipt. 2 pools; poolside serv. Supervised child's activities Jun-Aug. Lawn games. Refrigerators, microwaves. Balconies. On beach. Cr cds: A, C, D, ER, JCB, MC, V.

[D] [icons] SC

Inn

★ **INN BY THE SEA.** *287 11th Ave S (34102-7022).* 941/649-4124; res: 800/584-1268. 5 rms, 2 story. Mid-Dec-mid-Apr: S, D $149-$169; suite $189; lower rates rest of yr. Children over 14 yrs only. Complimentary continental bkfst. Restaurant nearby. Ck-out 11 am, ck-in 3 pm. Near beach. Built in 1937 of yellow heart pine. Totally nonsmoking. Cr cds: A, DS, MC, V.

[icons]

Resorts

★ ★ **NAPLES BEACH HOTEL & GOLF CLUB.** *851 Gulf Shore Blvd N (34102).* 941/261-2222; res: 800/237-7600; FAX 941/261-7380. E-mail 104463.1113@compuserve.com; web www.naplesbeachhotel.com. 318 units in 6 bldgs, 2-8 story, 100 kit. units. Mid-Dec-Apr: S, D $205-$325; each addl $15; suites $285-$460; kit. units $235-$355; under 18 free; MAP avail; golf plans; lower rates rest of yr. Crib $10. TV; cable (premium), VCR avail. Heated pool; poolside serv. Free supervised child's activities ages 5-12. Dining rm 7 am-10:30 pm. Box lunches. Snack bar. Picnics. Rm serv 7 am-midnight. Bar noon-1 am; entertainment. Ck-out noon, ck-in 4 pm. Grocery. Coin lndry 1 mi. Package store. Convention facilities. Business servs. In-rm modem link. Bellhops. Valet serv. Concierge. Barber shop. Gift shop. Sports dir. Tennis, pro. 18-hole golf, greens fee $105 (shared cart), pro, putting green, driving range. Health club privileges. Swimming beach. Boats. Bicycle rentals. Lawn games. Soc dir. Rec rm. Game rm. Many refrigerators; microwaves avail. Some balconies. Picnic tables. On Gulf. Cr cds: A, D, DS, MC, V.

[D] [icons]

★ ★ ★ **REGISTRY RESORT NAPLES.** *475 Seagate Dr (34103).* 941/597-3232; FAX 941/597-3147; res: 800/247-9810. E-mail welisten@registryhotels.com; web www.registryhotels.com. 474 rms in main bldg, 18 story, 50 villas. Late Dec-mid-Apr: S, D $355-$495; each addl $25; suites $695-$895; villas $545; under 18 free; package plans; lower rates rest of yr. Crib free. TV; cable (premium), VCR avail (movies). 3 heated pools; whirlpool, poolside serv. Supervised child's activities; ages 5-12. Dining rms 7 am-11 pm (also see LAFITE). Box lunches, snack bar. Rm serv 24 hrs. Bar 11-2 am. Ck-out noon, ck-in 3 pm. Convention facilities. Business center. Valet serv. Concierge. Shopping arcade. Barber, beauty shop. Valet parking. Activities dir. 15 tennis courts, 5 lighted, pro, instruction avail, pro shop. Golf privileges, greens fee $50-$150 (incl cart), putting green. Swimming beach. Boating; water sports avail. Bicycle rentals. Lawn games. Exercise rm; steam rm, sauna. Massage. Entertainment. Minibars, wet bars. Private patios, balconies. Cr cds: A, C, D, DS, ER, JCB, MC, V.

★ ★ ★ ★ ★ **THE RITZ-CARLTON, NAPLES.** *280 Vanderbilt Beach Rd (34108).* 941/598-3300; FAX 941/598-6690; res: 800/241-3333. Web www.ritzcarlton.com. With its classic Mediterranean-style decor, 23 acres of lush seaside gardens and fountains, array of creature comforts and recreational opportunities, this resort exudes elegance while remaining relaxed. The careful, friendly service is directed at making each guest feel comfortable and at ease. 463 units, 14 story. Late Dec-May: S, D $425-$770; each addl $50; suites $850-$4,545; under 17 free; monthly rates, MAP avail; lower rates rest of yr. Crib free. TV; cable (premium), VCR avail. Heated pool; whirlpool, poolside serv. Supervised child's activities; ages 3-16. Dining rms 6:30 am-10 pm (also see THE DINING ROOM and THE GRILL ROOM). Rm serv 24 hrs. Bar 9-1:30 am; entertainment. Ck-out noon, ck-in 3 pm. Convention facilities. Business center. In-rm modem link. Valet serv. Concierge. Gift shop. Barber, beauty shop. Covered parking, valet. Airport transportation. Lighted tennis, pro. 18-hole golf privileges, greens fee $125 (incl cart), pro, putting green, driving range. On white sand beach; water sports. Complimentary bicycles avail. Lawn games. Activities dir. Rec rm. Exercise rm; sauna, steam rm. Massage. Bathrm phones, minibars. Balconies. Luxury level. Cr cds: A, C, D, DS, ER, JCB, MC, V.

★ ★ **WORLD TENNIS CENTER & RESORT.** *4800 Airport-Pulling Rd (34105).* 941/263-1900; FAX 941/649-7855; res: 800/292-6663 (US), 800/621-6665 (CAN). 86 2, 3-bedrm apts, 2 story. Dec-Apr: 1-4 persons $175-$200; wkly, monthly rates; lower rates rest of yr. Pet accepted, some restrictions. Maid serv avail (fee). TV; cable. Heated pool; whirlpool, poolside serv. Ck-out 11 am, ck-in 3 pm. Grocery 1 mi. 16 tennis courts, 10 lighted, pro. Microwaves avail. Private patios, balconies. Mediterranean village atmosphere on 82½ acres. Tennis stadium. Cr cds: A, DS, MC, V.

Restaurants

★ ★ **BAYSIDE.** *4270 Gulf Shore Blvd N (34103), in Village Shopping Center.* 941/649-5552. Web bestofnet.com/naples/dining/bayside/. Hrs: 11:30 am-11 pm; Sun brunch to 2 pm. Res accepted. Continental menu. Bar. A la carte entrees: lunch $6.95-$12.95, dinner $15.95-$26. Sun brunch $6.95-$12.95. Child's meals. Specializes in fresh seafood, lamb, veal. Pianist. Valet parking (dinner). Outdoor dining. View of bay. Cr cds: A, D, DS, MC, V.

★ ★ **BHA! BHA! A PERSIAN BISTRO.** *847 Vanderbilt Beach Rd (34108).* 941/594-5557. Hrs: 11:30 am-3 pm, 5-10 pm; Sun to 9 pm; Sun brunch 11:30 am-3 pm. Closed Mon; Thanksgiving, Dec 25. Res accepted; required (in season). Persian menu. A la carte entrees: lunch $4.95-$10.95, dinner $11.95-$22.95. Sun brunch $15. Specialties: charbroiled lamb, duck fesenjune, Persian cous cous. Parking. Outdoor dining. Oasis atmosphere. Totally nonsmoking. Cr cds: A, MC, V.

★ ★ ★ **CHARDONNAY.** *2331 Tamiami Trail N (US 41) (34103).* 941/261-1744. Hrs: 5:30-10 pm. Closed Sun May-mid-Dec; also Aug. Res accepted. French, continental menu. Bar from 4 pm. Wine cellar. Semi-a la carte: dinner $17.50-$29.75. Specializes in duck, Dover sole, escargot. Own baking. Valet parking. Cr cds: A, D, MC, V.

★ ★ ★ **THE DINING ROOM.** *(See The Ritz-Carlton, Naples Resort)* 941/598-3300. Web ritzcarlton.com. Hrs: 6-10 pm; Sun brunch 10:30 am-2 pm. Res accepted. Bar. Wine cellar. A la carte entrees: dinner $27-$37. Sun brunch $42. Child's meals. Specialties: tandoori salmon, pan-seared ahi tuna. Pianist. Valet parking. Old-World grandeur with chandeliers and oil paintings. Jacket. Cr cds: A, C, D, DS, ER, JCB, MC, V.

✔★ **THE DOCK AT CRAYTON COVE.** *845 12th Ave S (34102), at Naples Bay.* 941/263-9940. Hrs: 11 am-midnight. Closed Dec 25. No A/C. Bar. A la carte entrees: lunch $3.95-$9.95, dinner $6.95-$19.95. Child's meals. Specializes in seafood, hamburgers, steak. Rustic, informal atmosphere. Cr cds: A, DS, MC, V.

★ ★ ★ **THE GRILL ROOM.** *(See The Ritz-Carlton, Naples Resort)* 941/598-3300. Hrs: 6-10 pm. Res accepted. Bar. Wine cellar. A la carte entrees: dinner $19-$36. Child's meals. Specializes in grilled fresh seafood, hand-cut aged beef. Pianist, vocalist. Valet parking. Old English decor; club atmosphere. Jacket. Cr cds: A, C, D, DS, ER, JCB, MC, V.

★ **KELLY'S FISH HOUSE.** *1302 5th Ave S (34102).* 941/774-0494. Hrs: 4:30-10 pm. Closed Thanksgiving, Dec 25; Sept; also Super Bowl Sun. Bar. Semi-a la carte: dinner $10.95-$32.95. Child's meals. Specializes in fresh seafood. Parking. Outdoor dining. Nautical decor; decorated with shells. Overlooks Gordon River. Cr cds: A, MC, V.

★ **L'AUBERGE.** *602 5th Ave S (34102).* 941/261-8148. Hrs: 11 am-2 pm, 5:30-9 pm; July-Sept to 2 pm. Closed Memorial Day; also Sun off season. Res accepted. Southern French menu. Wine list. A la carte entrees: lunch $4.95-$10.95, dinner $17.95-$22.95. Specialties: salmon en papillotte, carré d'agneau (Bearnaise). Ambience of small French village eatery. Cr cds: A, MC, V.

★ ★ ★ **LAFITE.** *(See Registry Resort Naples)* 941/597-3232. Hrs: 6-10:30 pm. Res accepted. Continental menu. Bar. Wine list. A la carte entrees: dinner $26.50-$37.50. Prix fixe: dinner $40. Specializes in fresh seafood, beef, poultry. Harpist. Valet parking. Old World elegance; intimate dining alcoves. Jacket. Cr cds: A, C, D, DS, ER, JCB, MC, V.

★ ★ **LE BISTRO.** *842 Neopolitan Way (34103).* 941/434-7061. Hrs: 5:30-10 pm. Closed Sun; also June 1-Oct 1; most major hols. Res accepted. French menu. Wine, beer. Semi-a la carte: $16.50-$28. Specialties: duck a l'orange, bouillabaisse. Parking. Intimate atmosphere. Cr cds: A, MC, V.

★ ★ **MARGAUX'S.** *3080 Tamiami Trail N (US 41) (34103).* 941/434-2773. Hrs: 11:30 am-2 pm, 5-9 pm; Sat, Sun from 5 pm; early-bird dinner 5-6 pm. Closed July 4, Dec 25. Res accepted. Country French menu. Bar. Semi-a la carte: lunch $5.50-$8.95, dinner $12.95-$18.95. Child's meals. Specialties: bouillabaisse, duck Marseille, veal & lobster. Parking. Intimate atmosphere; French accents. Totally nonsmoking. Cr cds: D, DS, MC, V.

★ ★ **MAXWELL'S ON THE BAY.** *4300 Gulf Shore Blvd N (34103), in Village Shopping Center.* 941/263-1662. Hrs: 11 am-10 pm; Sun brunch 10:30 am-3 pm. Res accepted. Bar. Wine cellar. Semi-a la carte: lunch $8.95-$14.95, dinner $17.95-$27.95. Sun brunch $8.95-$14.95. Child's meals. Specialties: veal & shrimp Maxwell's, lobster, fresh seafood. Valet parking (dinner). Outdoor dining. French country pine furnishings. Overlooks Venetian Bay. Cr cds: A, D, DS, MC, V.

★ ★ **MERRIMAN'S AT TIN CITY.** *1200 5th Ave S (34102).* 941/261-1811. Hrs: 11 am-10 pm. Bar. Semi-a la carte: lunch $6.95-

$17.95, dinner $12.95-$27.95. Specializes in fresh seafood, steak. Parking. On wharf; nautical decor. Cr cds: A, C, D, DS, MC, V.

✔★ **MESON OLÉ.** *2212 Tamiami Trail (US 41) (34103). 941/649-6616.* Hrs: 11 am-3 pm, 5-11 pm; Sat noon-11 pm; Sun noon-10 pm. Closed Thanksgiving, Dec 25. Res accepted. Mexican, Spanish menu. Bar. Semi-a la carte: lunch $5.95-$13.95, dinner $9.95-$17.95. Specialties: "las fajitas olé," en pollo al whiskey, la paella Valenciana. Parking. Mexican/Spanish decor. Cr cds: A, C, D, DS, MC, V.

★ ★ **MICHAEL'S CAFE, BAR & GRILL.** *2950 9th St N (US 41) (34103), at Hibiscus Ctr. 941/434-2550.* Hrs: 5-10 pm; early-bird dinner 5-6 pm. Closed Sun May-Sept; Jan 1, July 4, Dec 25; also Super Bowl Sun. Res accepted. Bar. Semi-a la carte: dinner $14-$26. Specializes in beef, chicken, fresh seafood. Child's meals. Entertainment in season. Parking. Outdoor dining. Contemporary decor. Cr cds: A, D, DS, MC, V.

★ ★ **PACIFIC 41.** *173 9th St S (US 41) (34102). 941/649-5858.* Hrs: 8 am-10 pm. Closed Thanksgiving, Dec 25. Res accepted. Bar. Semi-a la carte: bkfst $2.45-$9.95, lunch $3.95-$8.95, dinner $6.95-$23.95. Child's meals. Specializes in steak, ribs, seafood. Parking. Tropical atmosphere; waterfall in window garden in main dining rm. Cr cds: A, DS, MC, V.

✔★ ★ **THE PALM.** *754 Neapolitan Way (34103). 941/649-6333.* Hrs: 11 am-9 pm; Sun from 8 am. Res accepted. Bar. Semi-a la carte: bkfst $2.75-$6, lunch $4-$8, dinner $8-$16. Child's meals. Specialties: roast turkey, lamb shanks, corned beef. Parking. Cr cds: A, DS, MC, V.

★ **PEWTER MUG.** *12300 N Tamiami Trail (US 41) (34110). 941/597-3017.* Hrs: 5-10 pm. Closed July 4, Thanksgiving, Dec 25; also Super Bowl Sun. Bar. Semi-a la carte: dinner $9.50-$23.95. Child's meals. Specializes in steak, fresh fish. Salad bar. Parking. Cr cds: A, C, D, DS, MC, V.

★ ★ ★ **RISTORANTE CIAO.** *835 4th Ave S (34102), off US 41, exit Tamiami Trail. 941/263-3889.* Hrs: 5:30-10 pm. Closed Easter, Labor Day, Thanksgiving; also July-Aug. Res accepted. Italian menu. Extensive wine list. A la carte entrees: dinner $14-$28. Child's meals. Specialties: calamari al parmigiano, fettucine ciao, osso bucco. Elegant atmosphere. Totally nonsmoking. Cr cds: A, C, D, DS, MC, V.

✔★ **RIVERWALK FISH & ALE HOUSE.** *1200 5th Ave S (34102), at Old Marine Marketplace at Tin City. 941/263-2734.* Hrs: 11 am-11 pm. Closed Dec 24 eve, Dec 25. No A/C. Bar. Semi-a la carte: lunch, dinner $7.25-$19.95. Child's meals. Specializes in seafood. Valet parking in season. Outdoor dining. In complex of restored waterfront warehouses. Cr cds: A, DS, MC, V.

★ ★ ★ **SAVANNAH.** *5200 Tamiami Trail N (34103), in New Gate office bldg. 941/261-2555.* Hrs: 11:30 am-2 pm, 5-10 pm. Closed Mon May-Sept. Res accepted. Southern menu. Serv bar. Wine list. A la carte entrees: dinner $9-$26. Specialties: pan-roasted oyster stew with grits and tasso ham. Four dining rms; fireplace. Cr cds: A, D, DS, MC, V.

★ ★ ★ **ST GEORGE & THE DRAGON.** *936 5th Ave S (34102). 941/262-6546.* Hrs: 11 am-10 pm; Sun 5-9 pm (Jan-Mar). Closed Dec 25. Bar. Wine list. Semi-a la carte: lunch $5.50-$12.95, dinner $10.50-$29.95. Specialties: almond shrimp, conch chowder, prime rib. Own baking. Valet parking. Nautical antiques, decor. Family-owned. Jacket (after 4 pm, main dining rm). Cr cds: A, C, D, MC, V.

★ ★ **TERRA.** *1300 3rd St S (34102), off 13th Ave. 941/262-5500.* E-mail cuisine@sprintmail.com; web bestofnet.com/naples/dining/terra. Hrs: 11:30 am-10 pm. Res accepted. Bar. A la carte entrees: lunch $6.95-$13.95, dinner $9.95-$22.50. Specialty: osso bucco. Own baking. Entertainment Thurs-Sat. Valet parking (dinner). Patio. Cr cds: A, C, D, DS, MC, V.

✔★ **THE'S WATERFRONT CAFE.** *1444 5th Ave S (34102). 941/775-8115.* E-mail wcafe@aol.com; web members.aol.com/wcafe/index/htm. Hrs: 11-1 am; Sat, Sun 8 am-11 pm. No A/C. Bar. A la carte entrees: lunch $4.95-$9.95, dinner $5.95-$21.95. Child's meals. Specializes in fresh seafood. Parking. Outdoor dining. Island atmosphere. Cr cds: A, D, DS, MC, V.

★ ★ ★ **VILLA PESCATORE.** *8920 Tamiami Trail N (US 41) (34108). 941/597-8119.* Web bestofnet.com/naples/dining/villa_pescatore. Hrs: 6-10 pm. Res accepted. Northern Italian, Amer menu. Bar. Wine list. A la carte entrees: dinner $9.95-$25.95. Specializes in Italian cuisine, seafood. Own baking. Entertainment Tues-Sat. Valet parking. Cr cds: A, C, D, DS, MC, V.

New Port Richey (E-3)

(See also Brooksville, Clearwater, Dunedin)

Pop 14,044 **Elev** 11 ft **Area code** 813 **E-mail** chamber@niven.lmsweb.net **Web** westpasco.com
Information West Pasco Chamber of Commerce, 5443 Main St, 34652; 813/842-7651.

Annual Event

Chasco Fiesta. Celebration of the town's Indian heritage. Street parade, boat parade, entertainment, activities, contests, art show, food. Mid-late Mar.

Motels

★ ★ **COMFORT INN GATEWAY.** *6826 US 19N (34652). 727/842-6800; FAX 727/842-5072.* 66 rms, 2 story, 22 kit. units. Feb-Apr: S $62-$72; D $67-$77; each addl $5; kit. units $70-$80; under 19 free; wkly, wkend rates; lower rates rest of yr. Crib free. TV; cable (premium), VCR avail. Heated pool; whirlpool. Sauna. Complimentary continental bkfst. Restaurant adj 11 am-10 pm; Fri, Sat to 11 pm. Ck-out noon. Coin lndry. Meeting rm. Business servs avail. In-rm modem link. Health club privileges. Cr cds: A, C, D, DS, MC, V.

✔★ **DAYS INN AND LODGE.** *(11736 US 19N, Port Richey 34668) on US 19, 1/8 mi S of FL 52. 727/863-1502; res: 800/238-8117.* E-mail aol@daysinn.com; web www.gminet.com/dayspr. 153 rms, 2 story, 32 apts. Feb-Apr: S, D $55-$75; apts $65-$90; under 13 free; monthly rates; lower rates rest of yr. Crib free. Pet accepted; $5/day. TV; cable (premium). Heated pool. Restaurant 6 am-10 pm. Ck-out 11 am. Coin lndry. Business servs avail. In-rm modem link. Health club privileges. Refrigerators, microwaves avail. Cr cds: A, C, D, DS, JCB, MC, V.

✔★ ★ **HOLIDAY INN EXPRESS.** *(10826 US 19N, Port Richey 34668) N on US 19. 727/869-9999; FAX 727/861-0941.* 110 rms, 2 story, 36 kit. units. Jan-Apr: S, D $59-$79; kit. units $79-$129; family, wkly rates; lower rates rest of yr. TV; cable (premium). Heated pool; whirlpool. Complimentary continental bkfst. Restaurant nearby. Ck-out noon. Coin lndry.

Meeting rm. Business servs avail. In-rm modem link. Exercise equipt; sauna. Health club privileges. Game rm. Cr cds: A, C, D, DS, MC, V.

D ≈ ✕ ⊠ SC

New Smyrna Beach (D-5)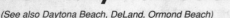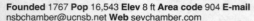

(See also Daytona Beach, DeLand, Ormond Beach)

Founded 1767 **Pop** 16,543 **Elev** 8 ft **Area code** 904 **E-mail** nsbchamber@ucnsb.net **Web** sevchamber.com

Information New Smyrna Beach-Edgewater-Oak Hill Chamber of Commerce, 115 Canal St, 32168; 904/428-2449.

Dr. Andrew Turnbull, a Scottish doctor, brought a group of settlers from Greece, Italy and the Spanish island of Minorca to work on the sugar and indigo plantations he had developed here. He named the community in honor of Smyrna, Greece, his wife's home, but many of the settlers, dissatisfied with the settlement's administration, went to St Augustine in the late 1770s. Today, New Smyrna, with its moss-hung oaks, palms, tropical shrubbery and citrus trees, is a resort center with agricultural resources, commercial fishing and light manufacturing. Canaveral National Seashore (see TITUSVILLE) is located at the end of south beach.

What to See and Do

New Smyrna Speedway. Races every Sat night; also special events during Speed Weeks in Feb. W on FL 44 at jct FL 415. For schedule, fees phone 904/427-4129.

New Smyrna Sugar Mill Ruins State Historic Site. Remains of a large sugar mill destroyed during the Seminole War. Construction of the building began in 1830; it was made of coquina, a native rock made of shells and sand. Today, all that remains is a walking beam from a steam engine and cooking pots. Nature trails. Standard hrs. 2 mi W of US 1, S off FL 44. Phone 904/423-3300.

Annual Event

"Images" Festival of the Arts. Riverside Park & Old Fort Park. Early Mar.

Motels

★ ★ **COASTAL WATERS INN.** 3509 S Atlantic Ave (32169). 904/428-3800; FAX 904/432-5002; res: 800/321-7882. Web www.new-smyrna-beach.com. 40 rms, 3 story, 32 kits. No elvtr. Late Dec-Labor Day: S, D $69; each addl $7.50; 1 & 2-bedrm kit. units $85-$149; under 12 free; wkly rates; higher rates: special events, some hols; lower rates rest of yr. Crib $7.50. TV; cable. Heated pool; wading pool. Complimentary coffee in lobby. Restaurant opp 7 am-11 pm. Business servs avail. Private patios, balconies. Picnic tables. On beach. Cr cds: MC, V.

D ≈ ⊠ SC

✔ ★ **OCEAN AIR.** 1161 N Dixie Frwy (US 1) (32168). 904/428-5748. 14 rms. Mid-Dec-mid-Apr, June-Sept: S, D $34-$50; each addl $5; wkly rates off-season; higher rates special events; lower rates rest of yr. Crib $5. TV; cable. Pool. Complimentary coffee in lobby. Restaurant nearby. Ck-out 11 am. Refrigerators. Picnic tables. Cr cds: A, D, DS, MC, V.

≈ ⊠ ↗ ⊠

Motor Hotels

★ ★ **HOLIDAY INN.** 1401 S Atlantic Ave (32169). 904/426-0020; FAX 904/423-3977. 102 kit. suites, 8 story. Mid-Mar-Aug: suites $89-$110; family rates; higher rates special events; lower rates rest of yr. Crib free. TV; cable. Pool. Complimentary coffee in lobby. Restaurant 7 am-9 pm. Rm serv. Ck-out 11 am. Coin lndry. Meeting rm. Business servs

avail. In-rm modem link. Sundries. Game rm. Refrigerators; microwaves avail. On ocean. Cr cds: A, C, D, DS, JCB, MC, V.

D ≈ ↗ ⊠ SC

★ ★ **ISLANDER BEACH RESORT.** 1601 S Atlantic Ave (32169). 904/427-3452; FAX 904/426-5606; res: 800/831-1719. Web www.islanderbeachresort.com. 114 kit. suites, 7 story. Late Dec-early May, mid-June-Labor Day: suites $60-$120 (3-day min); lower rates rest of yr. Crib free. TV; cable (premium), VCR (movies $3.50). Heated pool; wading pool, whirlpool. Playground. Free supervised child's activities; ages 5 to 12. Restaurant 11 am-9 pm. Bar to midnight. Ck-out 10 am. Coin lndry. Business servs avail. Exercise equipt. Game rm. Lawn games. Microwaves. Many balconies; some private patios. Picnic tables. On beach. Opp shopping center. Cr cds: A, DS, MC, V.

D ≈ ↗ ⊠

Hotels

★ ★ **OCEANIA BEACH CLUB.** 421 S Atlantic Ave (32169). 904/423-8400; FAX 904/423-0254; res: 800/874-1931. Web www.newsmyrnabeach.com. 60 kit. suites (2-bedrm), 8 story. Feb-mid-Apr, late May-early Sept: kit. suites $99-$120; under 12 free; higher rates race wk, hols; wkly rates; lower rates rest of yr. TV; cable (premium), VCR (movies). Heated pool. Restaurant nearby. Ck-out 11 am. Business servs avail. Golf privileges. Exercise equipt. Private patios, balconies. On ocean beach. Cr cds: A, DS, MC, V.

D ↗≈ ↗ ⊠ ⊠ SC

★ ★ ★ **RIVERVIEW.** 103 Flagler Ave (32169). 904/428-5858; FAX 904/423-8927; res: 800/945-7416. E-mail rvhotel@aol.com; web volusia.com/riverview/index.htm. 18 rms, 3 story, 5 suites. S, D $75-$100; suites $110-$150. TV; cable, VCR avail. Pool; poolside serv. Complimentary continental bkfst. Restaurant adj 11:30 am-9:30 pm; Fri, Sat to 10:30 pm. Bar to 11 pm. Ck-out noon. Business servs avail. Airport transportation. On Indian River; private dock. Rms individually decorated. Restored frame building (1885); porches. Elegant turn-of-the-century atmosphere. Cr cds: A, C, D, DS, ER, MC, V.

D ≈ ⊠ SC

Restaurant

★ ★ **NORWOOD'S SEAFOOD.** 400 2nd Ave. 904/428-4621. E-mail wineclub@aol.com. Hrs: 11:30 am-10 pm; early-bird dinner Sun-Fri 4-6 pm. Closed Dec 25. Bar. Semi-a la carte: lunch $3.99-$7.99, dinner $6.59-$22. Child's meals. Specializes in seafood, black Angus beef. Entertainment summer wkends. Tropical, nautical decor. Cr cds: A, C, D, DS, MC, V.

D ↴

Ocala (D-4)

(See also Leesburg, Silver Springs)

Settled 1827 **Pop** 42,045 **Elev** 47 ft **Area code** 352 **E-mail** mmalone@mercury.net **Web** www.ocalacc.com

Information Ocala/Marion County Chamber of Commerce, 110 E Silver Springs Blvd, 34470; 352/629-8051.

In the central highlands of the state, Ocala has become a focal point for excursions in the "ridge" country. There are approximately 500 Thoroughbred breeding and training farms here, in addition to many farms with other horse breeds. The Ocala Breeders Sales Pavilion is host to eight horse sales a year. Along with vegetable and citrus growing, limestone mining and manufacturing of mobile homes are major businesses.

What to See and Do

Appleton Museum of Art. Fifty centuries of fine art and sculpture; galleries dedicated to antiquities, pre-Columbian, African, Oriental and European art; changing exhibits. Guided tours (Tues-Fri). (Tues-Sat, also Sun afternoons; closed some hols) 4333 E Silver Springs Blvd. Phone 352/236-5050. ¢¢

Don Garlits Museum of Drag Racing. Houses racing exhibits, trophies & memorabilia; cars from the beginning of drag racing to the present, starting at the California Dry Lakes in the 1940s and including the finest and most unusual cars in the sport; antique cars. (Daily; closed Dec 25) 13700 SW 16th Ave, 8 mi S via I-75, exit 67. Phone 352/245-8661. ¢¢¢

Horse farm. Ocala Stud Inc. Birthplace of Needles, 1956 Kentucky Derby winner; Carry Back, 1961 Kentucky Derby winner; Roman Brother, 1965 Horse of the Year; and Office Queen, champion 3-yr-old filly of 1970; also training track; horse swimming pool. (Daily exc Sun, limited hrs; closed hols) SW 27th Ave, 2 mi W off FL 200. Phone 352/237-2171. **Free.**

Jai-Alai. Parimutuel betting. (May-Sept, Mon, Wed-Sat evenings; matinees Wed-Mon) Ocala Jai-Alai Fronton, 15 mi N, E of US 441 on FL 318 in Orange Lake. Phone 352/591-2345. General admission ¢

Ocala National Forest. Largest developed area of this approx 430,000-acre forest is Salt Springs, 26 mi E on FL 19. At a constant temperature of 72°F and a flow of 52 million gallons per day, Salt Springs provides swimming, bathhouse; boating (rentals); hiking; picnicking. Camping (some hookups). Juniper Springs and Fern Hammock have a combined daily flow of more than 15 million gallons at a constant 72°F (private canoes allowed, some rentals); swimming, bathhouse; picnicking; camping, trailer facilities; visitor center. Fees may be charged at recreation sites. 10 mi E on FL 40. Contact USDA Forest Service, 227 N Bronough St, Suite 4061, Tallahassee 32301, phone 352/681-7265; or the ranger district office, 17147 E FL 40 in Silver Springs, phone 352/625-2520.

Motels

★ ★ **COURTYARD BY MARRIOT.** *3712 SW 38th Ave (34474), I-75 exit 68.* 352/237-8000; FAX 352/237-0580. 175 rms, 3 story. Mid-Jan-mid-Apr: S, D $65-$95; suites $125-$200; lower rates rest of yr. Crib free. TV; cable (premium). Heated pool; whirlpool. Restaurant 6 am-10 pm. Bar 4-10 pm. Ck-out noon. Coin lndry. Meeting rms. Business servs avail. In-rm modem link. Exercise equipt. Refrigerator in suites. Balconies. Cr cds: A, C, D, DS, JCB, MC, V.

D ≈ ※ ⊠ ※ SC

★ ★ **HAMPTON INN.** *3434 SW College Rd (FL 200) (34474), I-75 exit 68.* 352/854-3200; FAX 352/854-5633. 152 rms, 3 story. Jan-Apr: S, D $60-$70; suites $85-$135; under 18 free; higher rates: Gator International, FL football games; lower rates rest of yr. Crib free. TV; cable (premium), VCR avail. Heated pool. Complimentary continental bkfst. Restaurant opp 11 am-11 pm. Ck-out noon. Coin lndry. Meeting rms. Business center. In-rm modem link. Some refrigerators. Cr cds: A, C, D, DS, MC, V.

D ≈ ⊠ ※ SC 🏃

✔★ ★ **HOLIDAY INN.** *3621 W Silver Springs Blvd (34475).* 352/629-0381; FAX 352/629-0381, ext. 42. 272 rms, 2 story. Jan-Apr: S, D $55-$65; under 18 free; lower rates rest of yr. Crib free. Pet accepted, some restrictions. TV; cable (premium). Heated pool. Restaurant 6 am-10 pm. Rm serv. Bar 1 pm-2 am; entertainment. Ck-out noon. Meeting rms. Business servs avail. In-rm modem link. Bellhops. Free RR station, bus depot transportation. Cr cds: A, C, D, DS, MC, V.

D ✦ ≈ ⊠ ※ SC

✔★ ★ **RAMADA INN AND CONFERENCE CENTER.** *3810 NW Blitchton Rd (34482), I-75 exit 70.* 352/732-3131; FAX 352/732-5692. 124 rms, 2 story. S, D $59-$85; each addl $6; under 18 free; golf plan. TV; cable, VCR avail. Pool; poolside serv. Playground. Restaurant 6:30 am-10 pm. Rm serv. Bar 11:30-2 am; entertainment exc Sun. Ck-out noon. Meeting rms. Business servs avail. Display of baseball and New York Yankees memorabilia. Cr cds: A, C, D, DS, ER, MC, V.

D ≈ ⊠ ※ SC

Hotel

★ ★ ★ **HILTON.** *3600 SW 36th Ave (34474).* 352/854-1400; FAX 352/854-4010. 197 units, 9 story. S, D $89-$129; each addl $10; suites $175-$295; family rates. Crib free. TV; cable (premium). Heated pool; whirlpool, poolside serv. Coffee in rms. Restaurant 6:30 am-10 pm. Bars 11-1 am. Ck-out 11 am. Meeting rms. Business servs avail. In-rm modem link. Gift shop. RR station, bus depot transportation. Lighted tennis, pro. Exercise equipt. Lawn games. Park-like setting. Cr cds: A, C, D, DS, MC, V.

D 🏃 ≈ ※ ⊠ ※ SC

Inn

★ ★ **SEVEN SISTERS.** *820 SE Fort King St (34471).* 352/867-1170; FAX 352/867-5266. E-mail sistersinn@aol.com. 10 rms, some rm phones, 3 story. 3 suites. S, D $115-$185; each addl $25; suites $135-$185; MAP avail. Children over 12 yrs only. TV in club rm; cable, VCR. Complimentary full bkfst; afternoon refreshments. Restaurant nearby. Ck-out 11 am, ck-in 3 pm. Business center. In-rm modem link. Health club privileges. Library, sitting rm. Queen Anne-style, Victorian house (1888); antiques. Porches. Cr cds: A, DS, MC, V.

D ※ ※ 🏃

Restaurants

✔★ ★ **CARMICHAEL'S.** *3105 NE Silver Springs Blvd (34470).* 352/622-3636. Hrs: 6:30-10:30 am, 11:30 am-2:30 pm, 4:30-8:30 pm; early-bird dinner 4:30-6:30 pm. Closed Dec 25. Res accepted. Amer menu. Bar. Semi-a la carte: bkfst $2.39-$4.99, lunch $3.99-$5.99, dinner $4.99-$14.99. Specialities: chicken pot pie, yankee pot roast, meatloaf. Brick fireplace; local historical photographs. Totally nonsmoking. Cr cds: A, DS, MC, V.

D ♥

★ ★ **SHANGHAI.** *815 SW Pine St (34472).* 352/622-2919. Hrs: 11 am-10 pm; Fri & Sat to 11 pm; Sun from 4:30 pm. Closed Thanksgiving. Res accepted. Chinese menu. Bar. A la carte entrees: lunch $3.95-$4.95, dinner $6-$25. Specialties: lobster tail with cream sauce, prawns in love nest, Peking duck. Parking. Chinese decor. Cr cds: A, MC, V.

D ♥

Unrated Dining Spot

HOLIDAY HOUSE. *4011 E Silver Springs Blvd.* 352/236-3014. Hrs: 11 am-8:30 pm. Closed Dec 24 eve. Avg ck: lunch $5.39, dinner $6.69. Specialties: roast beef, turkey, leg of lamb. Salad bar. Parking. Cr cds: A, MC, V.

D

Okeechobee (F-5)

(See also Belle Glade)

Pop 4,943 **Elev** 29 ft **Area code** 941

Information Chamber of Commerce, 55 S Parrott Ave, 34974; 941/763-6464 or 800/871-4403.

Located on the northern shore of Lake Okeechobee, this town's primary industry is agriculture centering on livestock and dairies, some of which offer tours. Okeechobee is a fisherman's paradise and is also popular for boating and duck hunting. Not far from the city is the Brighton Indian Reservation.

What to See and Do

Lake Okeechobee. Covering 730 sq mi, with its deepest point at 22 ft, this is the second largest freshwater lake in the US. Shallow, with many grassy spots and shoals, it is renowned for its bass, crappie, bream & speckled perch. More than 1 million pounds of fish are caught here every year. There are many fishing camps, picnic and parking areas along the shores. S of city.

Annual Events

Speckled Perch Festival. Flagler Park. Fishing contest, parade, art show, rodeo, entertainment. 2nd wkend Mar.

Cattleman's Rodeo. Cattleman's Rodeo Arena, FL 441N. Rodeo, parade, barbecue. Labor Day wkend.

Motels

✔★ BUDGET INN. *201 S Parrott Ave (34974). 941/763-3185.* 24 units. Nov-Apr: S $35-$65; D $45-$75; each addl $5; under 12 free; higher rates special events; lower rates rest of yr. Crib $8. Pet accepted; $5. TV; cable (premium). Pool. Complimentary coffee. Restaurant adj. Ck-out 11 am. Business servs avail. In-rm modem link. Refrigerators; microwaves avail. Cr cds: A, DS, MC, V.

🐾 🏊 ⛷ 🐾 SC

★ ECONOMY INN. *507 N Parrott Ave (34972). 941/763-1148; FAX 941/763-1149.* 24 rms. Feb-Mar: S $49; D $59; Apr-Jan: S $29, D $39; each addl $5; lower rates rest of yr. Pet accepted. TV; cable. Restaurant nearby. Ck-out 11 am. Business servs avail. Cr cds: A, DS, MC, V.

🐾 ⛷ 🐾 SC

Orlando (E-5)

(See also Altamonte Springs, Haines City, Kissimmee, Walt Disney World, Winter Park)

Settled 1837 **Pop** 164,693 **Elev** 106 ft **Area code** 407 **E-mail** info@orlandocvb.com **Web** www.go2orlando.com
Information Orlando/Orange County Convention & Visitors Bureau, 6700 Forum Dr, Suite 100, 32821-8017; 407/363-5800 or -5872.

Orlando was a campground for soldiers during the Seminole Indian War (1835-42), a trading post until 1857, and was then deeded to the county. Since then, it has grown in leaps and bounds, first with the coming of the railroad from Sanford in 1880, then with the establishment of the Kennedy Space Center complex to the southeast.

Orlando is the consistent favorite of a devoted colony of year-round visitors. In fact, major roads have enhanced the city's position as a transportation hub, with easy access to Walt Disney World (see) and other entertainment complexes in the area. The metro area has 300 lakes within its limits and retains an open, park-like atmosphere. While still a shipping center for citrus fruits and winter vegetables, Orlando has developed its own crop of aerospace, defense and electronics industries. Orlando is also the home of the University of Central Florida (1963).

Transportation

Car Rental Agencies: See IMPORTANT TOLL-FREE NUMBERS.
Public Transportation: Buses (Orlando Transit Authority), phone 407/841-8240.
Rail Passenger Service: Amtrak 800/872-7245.

Airport Information

Orlando Intl Airport: Information 407/825-2001; lost and found 407/825-2111; weather 407/851-7510; cash machines, Main Terminal near branch bank office.

What to See and Do

Church Street Market. Two-story marketplace with 17 shops and six restaurants around center courtyard; decor includes streetlamps, benches, fountains, brick walkways. Connected to Church Street Station by second-level footbridge. (Daily) Church St between Orange Ave & Garland. Phone 407/872-3500.

Church Street Station. Complex designed with Victorian atmosphere houses several restaurants and nightclubs, including Rosie O'Grady's Goodtime Emporium, Cheyenne Saloon and Opera House, Apple Annie's Courtyard, Phineas Phogg's Balloon Works, Orchid Garden Ballroom, Crackers Oyster Bar and Wine Cellar, Lili Marlene's Aviators Restaurant & Pub (see RESTAURANTS), Champagne Balloon flights and Commander Ragtime's Midway of Fun, Food and Games; variety of shows and entertainment. Also Church Street Exchange Shopping Emporium. (Daily) 129 W Church St, off I-4 Anderson St/Church St exit. Phone 407/422-2434. Evening cover charge ¢¢¢¢

Gray Line bus tours. Contact PO Box 1671, 32802; 407/422-0744.

Harry P. Leu Gardens. There are 50 acres of stately oaks, flowering shrubs, roses, camellias, orchids and azaleas; desert garden; conservatory. Tours include historic Leu House, restored as a museum to show how people lived in the area from 1910-1930. (Daily; closed Dec 25) 1920 N Forest Ave, at Nebraska. Phone 407/246-2620. ¢¢

Kennedy Space Center (see). 47 mi E via FL 528 to FL 407.

Loch Haven Park. Princeton Blvd & Mills Ave. Here are

Orlando Science Center. Hands-on exhibits, shows, demonstrations in science. Dr Phillips CineDome allows visitors to see remote areas of the earth; Darden Adventure has an interactive theatrical science presentation. Planetarium shows (daily; fee; inquire for schedule). (Daily; closed Dec 25). 777 E Princeton St. Phone 407/514-2000. ¢¢¢

Orange County Historical Museum. Displays of central Florida prehistory, pioneer life, Victorian era; general store; hot-type newspaper composing room; restored 1926 firehouse. (Mon-Sat, also Sun afternoons; closed hols) 812 E Rollins St. Phone 407/897-6350. ¢¢

Orlando Museum of Art. Exhibits of 19th- and 20th-century American art; Pre-Columbian artifacts and African art. (Daily exc Mon; closed some major hols) 2416 N Mills Ave. Phone 407/896-4231. ¢¢

Municipal recreation areas.

Eola Park. Around Lake Eola; illuminated fountain, flowers, band shell, concession. (Daily) Rosalind & Robinson Sts. **Free.**

Turkey Lake Park. Swimming pool; fishing; boating (rentals). Bicycle paths, nature trails. Picnicking, playground, concession. Camping. Petting zoo; ecology center. (Daily) 3401 Hiawassee Rd. Phone 407/299-5594. ¢

Lake Fairview Park. Swimming (fee); boating. Picnicking. Off Lee Rd.

Mystery Fun House. Walk-through participation in 15-rm house featuring crazy-image mirrors, spinning tunnels. Also miniature golf, laser game, arcade; restaurant, gift shops. (Daily) 5767 Major Blvd. Phone 407/351-3355. General admission ¢¢¢;   Combination ticket ¢¢¢¢

Professional sports.

NBA (Orlando Magic). Orlando Arena, 600 W Amelia St. Phone 407/649-3200.

⭐ **Sea World of Florida.** This 150-acre marine park features a killer whale show with the Shamu family; Journey to Atlantis; world's largest collection of dangerous sea creatures in Terrors of the Deep; Penguin Encounter; and Hotel Clyde and Seamore. Wild Artic exhibit explores this region through a simulated flight through the Arctic, encountering polar bears and beluga whales along the way. 3-acre children's play area; water ski show, sky tower; StarLight Laser Spectacular Show; Polynesian Luau dinnershow (nightly). (Daily; all shows several performances/day) 7007 Sea World Dr. Phone 407/351-3600. ¢¢¢¢¢

Skull Kingdom. Walk-through, hands-on, interactive haunted castle with audio and visual special effects. Also face-painting gallery, arcade games. (Daily) 5931 American Way. Phone 407/354-1564. ¢¢¢

✪ **Universal Studios Florida.** A 444-acre lot accommodating more than 40 rides, shows and attractions, 6 working sound stages and realistic street sets from New York City to Hollywood Boulevard. Through technology and special effects, visitors enter the action of such movies as *King Kong, ET, Back to the Future, Terminator 2* and *Jaws,* and experience the FUNtastic World of Hanna-Barbera, Hitchcock 3-D Theatre or The Adventures of Rocky & Bullwinkle. Live shows include Wild, Wild West Stunt Show and Beetlejuice Graveyard Revue; shows for the Nickelodeon cable channel are also produced at the facility. Themed concessions, gift shops and the E-Zone, an entertainment complex with nightclubs. (Daily) 10 mi SW on I-4, exits 29 & 30B, at jct FL Tpke. Phone 407/363-8000. ¢¢¢¢¢

Walt Disney World (see). 22 mi SW on I-4 at FL 535.

Wet 'n Wild. This 25-acre water park features waterfalls, rapids, wind and rain tunnels, wave pools and whirlpools. Beach, lifeguards, lockers, showers; raft and towel rentals; kneeboarding; miniature golf; picnicking. (Daily) 6200 International Dr, off I-4 at FL 435. Phone 407/351-1800. ¢¢¢¢¢

Annual Events

Florida Citrus Bowl. Jan 1.

Zora Neale Hurston Festival of Arts & Humanities. Theatrical performances, educational programs and art exhibits highlight the life and works of America's collectors and interpreters of Southern rural African-American culture. Phone 407/647-3307. Late Jan-early Feb.

Central Florida Fair. Fairgrounds. Horse show, entertainment, midway. Phone 407/295-3247. Late Feb-early Mar.

The Bay Hill Invitational. Bay Hill Golf & Country Club, 900 Bay Hill Blvd. PGA tournament. Phone 407/876-2888. Third wk Mar.

Pioneer Days Folk Festival. On the grounds of Pine Castle Folk Arts Center, 6015 Randolph St. Two-day event features sugar cane grinding and syrup making; traditional crafts demonstrations; bluegrass music and clogging; children's activities & games; food. Phone 407/855-7461. Late Oct.

Additional Visitor Information

Visitors can obtain further information by contacting the Orlando Official Visitor Center, 8723 International Dr, 32819, phone 407/363-5872 or the Orlando/Orange County Convention & Visitors Bureau, 6700 Forum Dr, Suite 100, 32821-8017, phone 407/363-5800. *Orlando Magazine,* available at newsstands, has up-to-date information on cultural events and articles of interest to visitors. For information on the many city parks phone 407/246-2287.

City Neighborhoods

Many of the restaurants, unrated dining establishments and some lodgings listed under Orlando include neighborhoods as well as exact street addresses. Geographic descriptions of Downtown and the International Drive Area are given, followed by a table of restaurants arranged by neighborhood.

Downtown: South of Colonial Dr (FL 50), west of Magnolia Ave (FL 527), north of Holland East-West Expy and east of Parramore Ave. **North of Downtown:** North of FL 50. **South of Downtown:** South of FL 408. **East of Downtown:** East of Magnolia Ave. **West of Downtown:** West of Parramore Ave.

International Drive Area: Area on and around International Drive between the FL Turnpike on the north and I-4 (exit 27A) on the south.

ORLANDO RESTAURANTS BY NEIGHBORHOOD AREAS

(For full description, see alphabetical listings under Restaurants)

DOWNTOWN
Cafe Europa. 55 W Church St
Crackers. 129 W Church St

Le Provence. 50 E Pine St
Lee's Lakeside. 431 E Central Blvd
Lili Marlene's Aviators Restaurant & Pub. 129 W Church St
Manuel's On The 28th. 390 Orange Ave
Vivaldi. 107 Pine St

NORTH OF DOWNTOWN
Del Frisco's. 729 Lee Rd
Straub's Boatyard. 743 Lee Rd

SOUTH OF DOWNTOWN
Charley's Steak House. 6107 S Orange Blossom Trail
Chatham's Place. 7575 Dr Phillips Blvd
Christini's. 7600 Doctor Phillips Blvd
Hard Rock Cafe. 5800 Kirkman Rd
Le Coq Au Vin. 4800 S Orange Ave
Michelangelo's. 4898 Kirkman Rd
Ming Court. 9188 International Dr
Sizzling Wok. 1453 Sand Lake Rd

EAST OF DOWNTOWN
4th Fighter Group Restaurant. 494 Rickenbacker Dr
Bacco. 10065 University Blvd
La Normandie. 2021 E Colonial Dr (FL 50)

INTERNATIONAL DRIVE AREA
Bergamo's. 8445 International Dr
Charlie's Lobster House. 8445 International Dr
Dux (Peabody Orlando). 9801 International Dr
Hanamizuki. 8255 International Dr
King Henry's Feast. 8984 International Dr
La Grille. 8445 International Dr
Passage To India. 5532 International Dr
Siam Orchid. 7575 Republic Dr

Note: When a listing is located in a town that does not have its own city heading, it will appear under the city nearest to its location. In these cases, the address and town appear in parenthesis immediately following the name of the establishment.

Motels

✔★ ★ **BEST WESTERN.** *8421 S Orange Blossom Trail (32809), at Florida Mall, south of downtown.* 407/855-6060; FAX 407/859-5132. 204 rms, 2 story. S, D $49-$119; each addl $7; suites $69-$139; under 18 free. TV; cable. Heated pool; poolside serv. Playground. Bkfst buffet. Ck-out 11 am. Coin lndry. Meeting rms. Business servs avail. Sundries. Gift shop. Free transportation to area attractions. Game rm. Microwaves avail. Florida Mall adj. Cr cds: A, C, D, DS, ER, JCB, MC, V.

🅳 ⊠ 🏊 🔥 **SC**

★ ★ **COMFORT SUITES.** *9350 Turkey Lake Rd (32819), off I-4 exit 29, south of downtown.* 407/351-5050; FAX 407/363-7953. E-mail info@comfortsuites.com; web www.comfortsuitesorlando.com. 215 rms, 3 story. Dec-mid-Apr, mid-June-Aug: S, D $99-$119; lower rates rest of yr. Crib free. TV; cable (premium). Heated pool; wading pool, whirlpool, poolside serv. Playground. Complimentary continental bkfst. Coffee in rms. Bar. Ck-out 11 am. Coin lndry. Business servs avail. Sundries. Airport transportation. Refrigerators. Cr cds: A, C, D, DS, ER, JCB, MC, V.

🅳 ⊠ 🏊 🔥 **SC**

★ ★ **COUNTRY HEARTH INN.** *9861 International Dr (32819), in International Drive Area.* 407/352-0008; FAX 407/352-5449; res: 800/447-1890. 150 rms, 2 story. Late Dec-early Jan, Feb-Apr; S, D $89-$139; each addl $10; under 18 free; lower rates rest of yr. Crib free. TV; cable. Heated pool. Coffee in rms. Restaurant 6:30-10:30 am, 6-10 pm. Rm serv. Bar. Ck-out 11 am. Coin lndry. Meeting rms. Business servs avail. Valet serv. Sundries. Refrigerators. Gazebo. Cr cds: A, C, D, DS, ER, MC, V.

🅳 ⊠ 🏊 🔥 **SC**

★ ★ ★ **COURTYARD BY MARRIOTT.** *7155 Frontage Rd (32812), near Intl Airport, south of downtown.* 407/240-7200; FAX 407/240-8962. 149 rms, 3 story. S, D $89-$129; suites $109-$139; under

18 free; wkend rates. Crib free. TV; cable (premium). Heated pool; whirlpool, poolside serv. Complimentary coffee in rms. Restaurant 6-11 am. Ck-out noon. Coin Indry. Meeting rms. Business servs avail. In-rm modem link. Free airport transportation. Exercise equipt. Some refrigerators. Balconies. Cr cds: A, D, DS, MC, V.

★ **ECONO LODGE-CENTRAL.** 3300 W Colonial Dr (32808), west of downtown. 407/293-7221; FAX 407/293-1166. 102 rms, 1-2 story. Feb-Apr, mid-June-mid-Aug: S $48; D $54; each addl $6; under 18 free; higher rates special events; lower rates rest of yr. Crib free. TV; cable (premium). Pool. Complimentary coffee in lobby. Restaurant adj open 24 hrs. Bar 11-2 am. Ck-out 11 am. Coin Indry. Meeting rm. Business servs avail. Lawn games. Picnic tables. Cr cds: A, C, D, DS, MC, V.

★ **FAIRFIELD INN BY MARRIOTT.** 8342 Jamaican Ct (32819), I-4 exit 29 off International Dr, in International Drive Area. 407/363-1944; FAX 407/363-1944. Web www.fairfieldinn.com. 134 rms, 3 story. Mid-Dec-Aug: S, D $69-$79; under 18 free; lower rates rest of yr. Crib free. TV; cable (premium). Pool. Complimentary continental bkfst. Ck-out noon. Cr cds: A, C, D, DS, MC, V.

★ ★ **GATEWAY INN.** 7050 Kirkman Rd (32819), east of I-4, in International Drive Area. 407/351-2000; FAX 407/363-1835; res: 800/327-3808. 354 rms, 2 story. Feb-mid-Apr, early June-early Sept, mid-Dec-early Jan: S, D $77-97; each addl $6; under 18 free; lower rates rest of yr. Crib $3. Pet accepted, no restrictions. TV; cable (premium). 2 pools, heated; wading pool, poolside serv. Playground. Restaurant 7 am-10 pm. Bar 11:30-2 am; entertainment. Ck-out 11 am. Coin Indry. Meeting rm. Business servs avail. Bellhops. Sundries. Gift shop. Free transportation to area attractions. Miniature golf. Game rm. Lawn games. Picnic tables. Cr cds: A, C, D, ER, MC, V.

★ ★ **HAMPTON INN.** 7110 S Kirkman (32819), in International Drive Area. 407/345-1112; FAX 407/352-6591. 170 rms, 8 story. Feb-late Apr, early June-early Sept, late Dec-early Jan: S $69-$89; D $79-$94; suites $119; under 18 free; lower rates rest of yr. Crib free. TV; cable (premium), VCR avail. Pool; wading pool. Complimentary continental bkfst. Coffee in rms. Restaurant adj open 24 hrs. Ck-out 11 am. Coin Indry. Meeting rms. Business servs avail. In-rm modem link. Gift shop. Free Walt Disney World transportation. Exercise equipt. Game rm. Microwaves avail. Cr cds: A, C, D, DS, MC, V.

★ ★ **HAWTHORN SUITES.** 6435 Westwood Blvd (32821), in International Drive Area. 407/351-6600; FAX 407/351-1977. E-mail hawthorn@aol.com; web www.hawthorn.com. 150 suites, 5 story. 1-2 bedrm: suites $89-$189; under 18 free. Crib free. TV; cable (premium), VCR (movies $5). Heated pool; wading pool, whirlpool. Playground. Complimentary coffee in rms. Restaurant adj 7 am-11 pm. Rm serv 5-11 pm. Ck-out 11 am. Coin Indry. Meeting rms. Business servs avail. Bellhops. Concierge. Sundries. Free Walt Disney World transportation. Exercise equipt. Game rm. Refrigerators, microwaves, wet bars. Cr cds: A, C, D, DS, ER, JCB, MC, V.

★ ★ **HOLIDAY INN-MALL AT CENTRAL PARK.** 7900 S Orange Blossom Trail (32809), south of downtown. 407/859-7900; FAX 407/859-7442. E-mail mcocp@earthlink.com. 266 rms, 2 story. S, D $69-$99; each addl $7; under 18 free. Crib free. TV; cable (premium). Pool; wading pool. Coffee in rms. Restaurant 6:30 am-2 pm, 5:30-10 pm. Rm serv. Bar 5 pm-midnight. Ck-out 11 am. Coin Indry. Meeting rms. Business servs avail. Bellhops. Exercise equipt. Cr cds: A, C, D, DS, JCB, MC, V.

✔★ **INNS OF AMERICA.** 8222 Jamaican Ct (32819), I-4 exit 29 off International Dr, in International Drive Area. 407/345-1172; FAX

407/352-2801. 121 rms, 4 story. Mid-Jan-mid-Apr: S, D $49.90-$85; lower rates rest of yr. TV; cable (premium). Heated pool. Complimentary continental bkfst. Ck-out 11 am. Coin Indry. Business servs avail. Cr cds: A, MC, V.

★ **LA SUITE.** 5858 International Dr (32819), in International Drive Area. 407/351-4410; FAX 407/351-2481. Web www.lasuite.com. 270 rms, 2-4 story. Mid-June-Sept, mid-Dec-Apr: S $39-$109; higher rates some hols; lower rates rest of yr. Crib free. TV; cable (premium). Heated pool; poolside serv. Complimentary continental bkfst. Restaurant adj open 24 hrs. Bar. Ck-out 11 am. Coin Indry. Business servs avail. Airport transportation. Game rm. Some refrigerators, microwaves. Picnic tables. Cr cds: A, C, D, DS, MC, V.

✔★ **RAMADA LIMITED.** 8296 S Orange Blossom Trail (32809), 10 mi S on FL 441, near Florida Mall, south of downtown. 407/240-0570; FAX 407/856-5507. 75 rms, 2 story. Mid-Dec-mid-Apr: S $55-$85; D $59-$89; each addl $6; under 9 free; higher rates special events; lower rates rest of yr. Crib free. TV; cable (premium). Pool. Complimentary continental bkfst. Restaurant nearby. Ck-out noon. Coin Indry. Airport, RR station, bus depot, Walt Disney World transportation. Cr cds: A, C, D, DS, ER, JCB, MC, V.

★ ★ **RAMADA SUITES AT SEAWORLD.** 6800 Villa DeCosta Dr (32821), jct Westwood Blvd & International Dr, in International Drive Area. 407/239-0707; FAX 407/239-8243. Web www.ramadaseaworld.com. 160 kit. suites, 2-3 story. S, D $139-$209; each addl $10; under 18 free; higher rates special events. Crib free. TV; cable (premium). Pool; whirlpool. Playground. Supervised child's activities; ages 3-8. Complimentary continental bkfst. Ck-out noon. Coin Indry. Business center. Sundries. Valet serv. 18-hole golf privileges, greens fee $59-$89. Exercise equipt. Game rm. Microwaves. Balconies. Cr cds: A, C, D, DS, ER, JCB, MC, V.

★ ★ **RESIDENCE INN BY MARRIOTT ORLANDO INTL DRIVE.** 7975 Canada Ave (32819), south of downtown. 407/345-0117; FAX 407/352-2689. E-mail riorlando@bellsouth.net; web marriottresidenceinn.com. 176 kit. suites (studio, 2 bedrm). S, D $104-$199; wkly, monthly rates. Crib free. Pet accepted, some restrictions. Heated pool; whirlpools. Complimentary continental bkfst. Restaurant nearby. Ck-out 11 am. Coin Indry. Meeting rms. Business servs avail. Health club privileges. Valet serv. Many fireplaces; microwaves avail. Balconies. Grills. Lighted sports court. Cr cds: A, C, D, DS, JCB, MC, V.

✔★ ★ **TRAVELODGE CENTROPLEX.** 409 N Magnolia Ave (32801), downtown. 407/423-1671; FAX 407/423-1523. 75 rms, shower only, 2 story. Feb-Apr, June-Aug: S $55; D $65; under 18 free; higher rates special events; lower rates rest of yr. TV; cable (premium). Pool. Complimentary coffee in rms. Restaurant adj. Ck-out 11 am. Business servs avail. In-rm modem link. Coin Indry. Cr cds: A, C, D, DS, ER, JCB, MC, V.

✔★ ★ **WYNFIELD INN.** 6263 Westwood Blvd (32821), in International Drive Area. 407/345-8000; FAX 407/345-1508. Web wwworlando.com/wynfield. 299 rms, 3 story. Feb-late Apr, early June-late Aug: S, D $88-$98; each addl $5; under 18 free; lower rates rest of yr. Crib free. TV. 2 pools, 1 heated; 2 wading pools, poolside serv. Complimentary coffee. Restaurant adj 6:30 am-midnight. Ck-out 11 am. Coin Indry. Business servs avail. Game rm. Cr cds: A, C, D, DS, MC, V.

Motor Hotels

★ ★ **BEST WESTERN PLAZA INTERNATIONAL.** 8738 International Dr (32819), in International Drive Area. 407/345-8195; FAX 407/352-8196. 673 rms, 4 story, 176 kits. Mid-Feb-mid-Apr, mid-June-Aug, mid-Dec-early Jan: S, D $99; suites $119; kit. units $109; under 18 free;

lower rates rest of yr. Crib free. TV; cable. Heated pool; wading pool, whirlpool, poolside serv. Ck-out 11 am. Coin lndry. Bellhops. Gift shop. Free Walt Disney World transportation. Health club privileges. Game rm. Some in-rm whirlpools. Cr cds: A, C, D, DS, MC, V.

[D] [symbols] SC

★ ★ **COLONY PLAZA.** 11100 W Colonial Dr (34761), on FL 50, west of downtown. 407/656-3333; FAX 407/656-2232; res: 800/821-0136. E-mail colony@intelistar.net. 253 kits, 7 story. S, D $65-100; under 18 free; higher rates special events. Crib free. TV; cable (premium). Pool; poolside serv. Playground. Restaurant 7-11 am, 5-10 pm. Bar 4 pm-2 am. Ck-out 11 am. Coin lndry. Meeting rms. Tennis. Exercise equipt. Game rm. Cr cds: A, DS, MC, V.

[D] [symbols] SC

★ ★ **DELTA ORLANDO RESORT.** 5715 Major Blvd (32819), jct FL 435 & I-4 exit 30B at entrance of Universal Studios, south of downtown. 407/351-3340; FAX 407/351-5117; res: 800/634-4763. E-mail delta or@magicnet.net; web www.intpro.com/delta. 800 units, 4 story. Mid-Feb-Apr, mid-June-Aug, late Dec: S, D $118-$198; suites $175-$475; under 18 free; lower rates rest of yr. Crib free. Pet accepted, some restrictions; $25. TV; cable (premium). 3 pools, heated; wading pools, whirlpools, poolside serv. Sauna. Playground. Free supervised child's activities; ages 4-12. Restaurants 6:30 am-midnight. Child's meals. Rm serv. Bar 11:30-2 am; entertainment. Ck-out 11 am. Coin lndry. Convention facilities. Business servs avail. Bellhops. Valet serv. Airport transportation. Concierge. Sundries. Gift shop. Lighted tennis. Golf privileges. Miniature golf. Game rm. Lawn games. Microwaves avail. Private balconies. Cr cds: A, C, D, DS, ER, JCB, MC, V.

[D] [symbols] SC

★ ★ **FLORIDIAN.** 7299 Republic Dr (32819), in International Drive Area. 407/351-5009; FAX 407/363-7807; res: 800/445-7299. 304 rms, 8 story. Feb-Aug, late Dec: S, D $95-$150; lower rates rest of yr. Crib free. TV; cable. Heated pool; poolside serv. Restaurant 7-11 am, 6-11 pm. Rm serv. Bar 6 pm-2 am. Ck-out 11 am. Coin lndry. Meeting rms. Business servs avail. Bellhops. Valet serv. Concierge. Sundries. Gift shop. Airport transportation. Game rm. Cr cds: A, C, D, DS, MC, V.

[D] [symbols] SC

★ ★ **HAMPTON INN.** 5767 T.G. Lee Blvd (32822), near Intl Airport, south of downtown. 407/888-2995; FAX 407/888-2418. 123 rms, 7 story. Jan-May, Oct-Dec: S $99; D $109; higher rates Race Week, Citrus Bowl; lower rates rest of yr. TV; cable (premium). Complimentary continental bkfst. Complimentary coffee in rms. Restaurant nearby. Ck-out 11 am. Meeting rms. Business servs avail. Gift shop. Coin lndry. Free airport transportation. Exercise equipt. Pool. Game rm. Cr cds: A, C, D, DS, MC, V.

[D] [symbols] SC

✔★ ★ **HAMPTON INN.** 6101 Sand Lake Rd (32819), in International Drive Area. 407/363-7886; FAX 407/345-0670. 316 rms, 4 story, 12 suites. Late Apr-Apr, June-mid-Aug: S $59-$89; D $64-$89; each addl $5; suites $109-$149; under 18 free; min stay special events; higher rates: Daytona 500, July 4, Dec 31; lower rates rest of yr. Crib free. TV; cable (premium), VCR avail. Complimentary continental bkfst. Restaurant nearby. Ck-out 11 am. Meeting rms. Business servs avail. Valet serv. Concierge. Sundries. Gift shop. Coin lndry. Exercise equipt. Pool; wading pool. Game rm. Many refrigerators, microwaves. Cr cds: A, C, D, DS, ER, MC, V.

[D] [symbols] SC

✔★ ★ **HAMPTON INN AT UNIVERSAL.** 5621 Windhover Dr (32819), in International Drive Area. 407/351-6716; FAX 407/363-1711. 120 rms, 5 story. Late May-mid-Aug & late Dec-late Mar: S $71; D $79; under 18 free; lower rates rest of yr. Crib free. TV; cable (premium). Heated pool. Complimentary continental bkfst. Restaurant opp 7 am-midnight. Ck-out noon. Meeting rms. Business servs avail. Game rm. Cr cds: A, C, D, DS, MC, V.

[D] [symbols] SC

★ ★ **HARLEY COLONIAL PLAZA.** 2801 E Colonial Dr (32803), 2 mi E of I-4 on FL 50, east of downtown. 407/894-2741; FAX 407/896-9858; res: 800/321-2323. 230 rms, 2 story. S, D $64-$74; suites $75-$149; under 18 free. Crib free. TV; cable (premium); VCR avail. Heated pool; whirlpool. Restaurant 6 am-2:30 pm; wkend hrs vary. Ck-out 11 am. Coin lndry. Meeting rms. Business servs avail. Refrigerators. Cr cds: A, C, D, DS, ER, MC, V.

[D] [symbols]

★ **HOLIDAY INN.** 626 Lee Rd (32810), north of downtown. 407/645-5600; FAX 407/740-7912. 201 rms, 5 story. Jan-mid-Apr: S, D $79-$109; under 18 free; lower rates rest of yr. Crib free. TV; cable (premium), VCR avail. Pool. Restaurant 6 am-2 pm; 5-10 pm. Rm serv. Bar 4 pm-midnight; entertainment Fri-Sat. Ck-out 11 am. Coin lndry. Meeting rms. Business servs avail. Bellhops. Golf privileges, greens fee $18-$30, driving range. Exercise equipt. Game rm. Microwaves avail. Cr cds: A, C, D, DS, JCB, MC, V.

[D] [symbols] SC

★ ★ **HOLIDAY INN-SELECT UNIVERSITY OF CENTRAL FLORIDA.** 12125 High Tech Ave (32817), off University Blvd, east of downtown. 407/275-9000; FAX 407/381-0019. 250 units, 6 story. S, D $140; suites $175; under 18 free. Crib free. TV; cable (premium). Pool; whirlpool. Restaurant 6:30 am-2 pm, 5-11 pm. Rm serv. Bar 11 am-midnight. Ck-out 11 am. Meeting rms. Business center. Bellhops. Airport transportation. Tennis privileges. Golf privileges. Exercise equipt; sauna. Lawn games. Some refrigerators. On lake. Luxury level. Cr cds: A, C, D, DS, JCB, MC, V.

[D] [symbols] SC

★ **HOWARD JOHNSON.** 9956 Hawaiian Court (32819), in International Drive Area. 407/351-5100; FAX 407/352-7188. 222 rms, 2 story, 49 kit. suites. June 20-Aug 20, Late Dec: S, D $89-$129; suites $99-$149; under 18 free; lower rates rest of yr. Crib free. TV; cable. Pool; whirlpool. Playground. Complimentary coffee in lobby. Restaurant nearby. Bar 5:30 pm-1 am. Ck-out noon. Meeting rms. Coin lndry. Valet serv. Exercise equipt. Game rm. Refrigerator in suites. Cr cds: A, C, D, DS, ER, MC, V.

[D] [symbols] SC

★ ★ **MARRIOTT.** 8001 International Dr (32819), off I-4 exit 29, in International Drive Area. 407/351-2420; FAX 407/345-5611. 1,064 units in 16 bldgs, 2 story. Mid-Jan-May 2, Sept 9-Dec: S, D $134; suites $210-$450; under 18 free; lower rates rest of yr. Crib free. TV; cable (premium). 3 pools, heated; 2 wading pools, whirlpool, poolside serv. Playground. Restaurant 6:30 am-2 pm; 4-11 pm. Rm serv. Bar 11-2 am; entertainment. Ck-out 11 am. Coin lndry. Convention facilities. Business center. Bellhops. Sundries. Gift shop. Lighted tennis. Golf privileges. Exercise equipt. Game rm. Balconies. Cr cds: A, C, D, DS, ER, JCB, MC, V.

[D] [symbols] SC

✔★ ★ **QUALITY INN-PLAZA.** 9000 International Dr (32819), in International Drive Area. 407/345-8585; FAX 407/352-6839. 1,020 rms, 4-10 story. S, D $35.95-$89. Crib free. Pet accepted, some restrictions; $5. TV; cable. 3 pools, 2 heated. Restaurant 6:30-10:30 am, 5-9:30 pm. Bar 4 pm-2 am. Ck-out 11 am. Coin lndry. Business servs avail. Gift shop. Health club privileges. Game rm. Cr cds: A, C, D, DS, ER, JCB, MC, V.

[D] [symbols] SC

★ ★ **RADISSON BARCELO.** 8444 International Dr (32819), in International Drive Area. 407/345-0505; FAX 407/352-5894. E-mail radisson-orlando.com. 299 rms, 5 story. S, D $72-$109; each addl $15. Crib free. TV; cable (premium), VCR avail. Pool; poolside serv. Coffee in rms. Restaurant 6:30 am-10 pm. Bar. Ck-out noon. Meeting rms. Business servs avail. In-rm modem link. Gift shop. Lighted tennis. Health club privileges. Refrigerators; microwaves avail. Shopping center opp. Cr cds: A, C, D, DS, ER, JCB, MC, V.

[D] [symbols] SC

✔★ **RODEWAY INN INTERNATIONAL.** 6327 International Drive (32819), in International Drive Area. 407/351-4444; FAX 407/352-

5806. 315 rms, 4-9 story. Mid Dec-Jan 1, June-Sept: S, D $59.95-$75; lower rates rest of yr. Crib free. Pet accepted, some restrictions. TV; cable, VCR (movies). Heated pool. Restaurant 6:30-10:30 am, 5:30-9 pm. Bar 6 pm-midnight. Ck-out 11 am. Coin lndry. Meeting rm. Valet serv. Sundries. Gift shop. Health club privileges. Game rm. Refrigerators avail. Cr cds: A, C, D, DS, ER, JCB, MC, V.

★ ★ ★ **SHERATON WORLD RESORT.** 10100 International Dr (32821), in International Drive Area. 407/352-1100; FAX 407/352-3679. 800 units, 2-3 story. S, D $139-$179; each addl $15; suites $295-$595; under 18 free. Crib free. TV; cable (premium). 3 pools, heated; 2 wading pools, whirlpool, poolside serv. Playground. Restaurants 6:30 am-11 pm. Rm serv. Bar; entertainment. Ck-out 11 am. Coin lndry. Meeting rms. Business center. Bellhops. Sundries. Gift shop. Free Walt Disney World transportation. Lighted tennis. Golf privileges. Miniature golf. Exercise equipt. Game rm. Cr cds: A, C, D, DS, ER, JCB, MC, V.

★ ★ **SUMMERFIELD SUITES.** 8751 Suiteside Dr (32836), west of downtown. 407/238-0777; FAX 407/238-2640. Web www.summerfield-orlando.com. 150 suites, 3 story. No elvtr. Suites $119-$319; higher rates special events. Crib free. TV; cable (premium), VCR (movies). Heated pool; wading pool, whirlpool. Complimentary continental bkfst. Restaurant nearby. Ck-out 11 am. Meeting rms. In-rm modem link. Bellhops. Valet serv. Concierge. Sundries. Gift shop. Coin lndry. Exercise equipt. Game rm. Refrigerators. Cr cds: A, D, DS, JCB, MC, V.

★ ★ **SUMMERFIELD SUITES.** 8480 International Dr (32819), in International Drive Area. 407/352-2400; FAX 407/352-4631; res: 800/830-4964. E-mail sshorlres@mail.att.net; web www.travelbase.com/. 146 kit. suites, 5 story. S, D $119-$319. Crib free. TV; cable (premium), VCR (movies $5). Heated pool; wading pool, whirlpool. Complimentary continental bkfst. Complimentary coffee in rms. Restaurant nearby. Bar 5:30-11 pm. Ck-out 11 am. Meeting rms. Business servs avail. In-rm modem link. Concierge. Gift shop. Grocery. Valet serv. Coin lndry. Exercise equipt. Game rm. Refrigerators; microwaves. Cr cds: A, C, D, DS, JCB, MC, V.

Hotels

★ ★ ★ **ADAM'S MARK.** 1500 Sand Lake Rd (32809), at Florida Mall, south of downtown. 407/859-1500; FAX 407/855-1585. 496 rms, 11 story. S, D $115-$175; each addl $10; under 18 free. Crib free. Valet parking $8. TV; cable (premium). Restaurant 6 am-11 pm. Bar 11 am-midnight. Ck-out noon. Convention facilities. Business center. Concierge. Gift shop. Exercise equipt. Health club privileges. Pool; whirlpool. Bathrm phone, refrigerator in suites. Some balconies. Luxury level. Cr cds: A, C, D, DS, JCB, MC, V.

★ ★ ★ **THE CASTLE DOUBLETREE.** 8629 International Dr (32819), in International Drive Area. 407/345-1511; FAX 407/248-8181. Web www.grandthemehotels. com. 216 rms, 9 story. Feb-Mar, Oct: S, D $149-$179; under 18 free; higher rates special events; lower rates rest of yr. Crib free. TV; cable (premium). Complimentary coffee in rms. Restaurant 10:30 am-11 pm. Bar. Ck-out noon. Meeting rms. Business servs avail. Gift shop. Coin lndry. Free Disney transportation. Airport transportation. Exercise equipt. Pool; whirlpool, poolside serv. Bathrm phones, refrigerators; some microwaves. Cr cds: A, C, D, DS, JCB, MC, V.

★ ★ **CLARION PLAZA.** 9700 International Dr (32819), in International Drive Area. 407/352-9700; FAX 407/351-9111. 810 rms, 14 story. S, D $169-$189; suites $250-$748; under 18 free. Crib free. Valet parking $5.50. TV; cable. Heated pool; whirlpool. Restaurant 6:30 am-10:30 pm. Bar 11-2 am; entertainment. Ck-out noon. Coin lndry. Convention facilities. Business center. Shopping arcade. Airport transportation. Golf privileges,

pro, putting green, driving range. Game rm. Some refrigerators, bathrm phones. Cr cds: A, C, D, DS, ER, JCB, MC, V.

★ ★ ★ **EMBASSY SUITES.** 8978 International Dr (32819), in International Drive Area. 407/352-1400; res: 800/433-7275; FAX 407/363-1120. E-mail essouth@aol.com. 244 kit. suites, 8 story. Suites $129-$209; each addl $15; under 18 free. Crib free. TV; cable (premium). 2 pools, 1 indoor; whirlpool. Complimentary full bkfst. Restaurant 11 am-11 pm. Bar. Ck-out noon. Coin lndry. Meeting rms. Business servs avail. Gift shop. Valet parking. Free Walt Disney World transportation. Exercise equipt; sauna, steam rm. Game rm. Refrigerators, microwaves. Sun deck. Mediterranean-style atrium. Cr cds: A, C, D, DS, MC, V.

★ ★ ★ **EMBASSY SUITES INTERNATIONAL DRIVE.** 8250 Jamaican Ct (32819), I-4 exit 29 off International Dr, in International Drive Area. 407/345-8250; res: 800/327-9797; FAX 407/352-1463. Web www.embassy-suites.com/orlando-jamaican. 246 suites, 8 story. Suites $139-$209; under 18 free; package plans. Crib free. TV; cable (premium). Indoor/outdoor pool; whirlpool, poolside serv. Complimentary full bkfst. Bar 5-11 pm. Ck-out noon. Business servs avail. In-rm modem link. Concierge. Gift shop. Free Walt Disney World transportation. Exercise equipt; sauna. Game rm. Refrigerators; microwaves. Cr cds: A, C, D, DS, JCB, MC, V.

★ ★ **THE ENCLAVE.** 6165 Carrier Dr (32819), south of downtown. 407/351-1155; FAX 407/351-2001; res: 800/457-0077. Web www.prov.com. 321 kit. suites, 10 story. Mid-Dec-mid-Apr, mid-June-mid-Aug: studio & 2-bedrm suites $99-$160; package plans; lower rates rest of yr. Crib $5. TV; cable (premium). 3 pools, 2 heated, 1 indoor; wading pool, whirlpool. Complimentary continental bkfst. Ck-out 11 am. Coin lndry. Meeting rm. Business servs avail. Lighted tennis. Exercise equipt. Game rm. Microwaves avail. Private patios, balconies. On lake. Cr cds: A, C, D, DS, MC, V.

★ ★ **HARLEY.** 151 E Washington St (32801), downtown. 407/841-3220; FAX 407/849-1839. 281 units, 6 story. S, D $99-$109; 2-bedrm suites $140; under 18 free. Crib free. TV; cable (premium). Heated pool; poolside serv. Restaurant 6:30 am-10:30 pm, Fri, Sat to 11 pm. Bar 3 pm-midnight; entertainment. Ck-out 11 am. Meeting rms. Business servs avail. Garage parking. Airport, Walt Disney World transportation. Refrigerators avail. Some balconies. Cr cds: A, C, D, DS, MC, V.

★ ★ **HOLIDAY INN-UNIVERSAL STUDIOS.** 5905 Kirkman Rd (32819), just W of jct FL 435 & I-4 exit 30B, south of downtown. 407/351-3333; res: 800/327-1364; FAX 407/351-3577. 390 units, 10 story. Mid-Feb-mid-Apr, mid-June-mid-Aug, last 2 wks Dec: S, D $119-$169; suites $159-229; under 18 free; lower rates rest of yr. Crib free. TV; cable (premium), VCR (movies). Pool; wading pool. Restaurant 7 am-midnight. Rm serv to 10 pm. Bar. Ck-out noon. Coin lndry. Meeting rms. Business center. Gift shop. Exercise equipt. Health club privileges. Game rm. Private patios, balconies. Near main entrance to Universal Studios Florida. Cr cds: A, C, D, DS, ER, JCB, MC, V.

★ ★ ★ **HYATT REGENCY-ORLANDO INTL AIRPORT.** 9300 Airport Blvd (32827), atop main terminal of Intl Airport, south of downtown. 407/825-1234; FAX 407/856-1672. 446 rms, 10 story. S, D $150-$225; suites $225-$500; under 18 free. Crib avail. Garage parking $10; valet parking $13. TV; cable (premium), VCR avail. Heated pool; whirlpool. Restaurant 6:30 am-11 pm. Rm serv 24 hrs. Bar. Ck-out noon. Convention facilities. Business center. Concierge. Shopping arcade. Golf privileges. Exercise equipt. Bathrm phones; microwaves avail. Balconies. 7-story atrium lobby; airport's main terminal is located 1 level below. Cr cds: A, C, D, DS, ER, JCB, MC, V.

★ ★ ★ **MARRIOTT-DOWNTOWN.** *400 W Livingston St (32801), at Orlando Centroplex Center, downtown.* 407/843-6664; FAX 407/648-5414. 290 rms, 15 story. S $99-$169; D $114-$175; each addl $15; suites $325-$725; under 18 free; package plans. Crib free. Valet parking. TV; cable (premium), VCR avail. Pool; whirlpool, poolside serv. Coffee in rms. Restaurant 6:30 am-10 pm. Bar. Ck-out noon. Convention facilities. Business center. In-rm modem link. Gift shop. Airport transportation. Exercise equipt. Bathrm phones. Refrigerators avail. Landscaped garden terrace. Luxury level. Cr cds: A, C, D, DS, ER, MC, V.

D ⊠ ✈ ⫯ ⌕ SC ⫰

★ ★ ★ **MARRIOTT-ORLANDO AIRPORT.** *7499 Augusta National Dr (32822), near Intl Airport, south of downtown.* 407/851-9000; FAX 407/857-6211. 484 units, 9 story. S, D $79-$209; suites $175-$500; under 18 free; wkend rates. Crib free. TV; cable (premium). Indoor/outdoor pool; wading pool, whirlpool, poolside serv. Restaurant 6 am-11 pm. Bar 11-2 am. Ck-out noon. Convention facilities. Business center. Gift shop. Free airport transportation. Lighted tennis. Exercise equipt; sauna, steam rm. Game rm. Rec rm. Luxury level. Cr cds: A, C, D, DS, ER, JCB, MC, V.

D ⥼ ⊠ ✈ ⫯ ✈ ⌕ SC ⫰

★ ★ ★ **OMNI ROSEN.** *9840 International Dr (32819), in International Drive Area.* 407/204-7234; FAX 407/248-6869. Web www.omnirosen.com. 1,334 rms, 24 story, 80 suites. S, D $205-$285; each addl $15; suites $275-$955; under 18 free. Crib free. Valet/garage parking $7. TV; cable, VCR avail (movies). Pool; wading pool, whirlpool, poolside serv. Restaurant 6:30 am-11 pm. Bar 11 am-2 am. Ck-out 11 am. Coin Indry. Convention facilities. Business center. Concierge. Gift shop. Beauty shop. Lighted tennis. Exercise rm. Refrigerator in suites. Cr cds: A, C, D, DS, JCB, MC, V.

D ⥼ ⊠ ✈ ⌕ ⫰ SC ⫰

★ ★ ★ ★ **PEABODY ORLANDO.** *9801 International Dr (32819), opp Convention & Civic Center, in International Drive Area.* 407/352-4000; FAX 407/351-9177; res: 800/PEABODY. E-mail peab-orl@interramp; web www.peabody-orlando.com. This is an impressive high-rise with sweeping views and extensive grounds. Famous are the resident ducks who parade to the lobby fountain each morning at 11, splash around in it all day and return to their duck palace with fanfare at 5 pm. 891 units, 27 story. S, D $300-$360; each addl $15; suites $495-$1,450; under 18 free; package plans. Crib free. Valet parking $8. TV; cable (premium). Heated pool; wading pool, whirlpool, poolside serv. Restaurant open 24 hrs (also see DUX). Bar 11-2 am; entertainment exc Sun. Ck-out noon. Convention facilities. Business center. In-rm modem link. Shopping arcade. Beauty shop. Lighted tennis, pro shop. 18-hole golf privileges, greens fee. Exercise rm; sauna, steam rm. Massage. Game rm. Refrigerators avail. Luxury level. Cr cds: A, C, D, DS, ER, JCB, MC, V.

D ⫯ ⫰ ⥼ ⊠ ✈ ⌕ ⫰ SC ⫰

★ ★ ★ **RADISSON PLAZA.** *60 S Ivanhoe Blvd (32804), I-4 exit 42, north of downtown.* 407/425-4455; FAX 407/843-0262. 340 rms, 15 story. S, D $158; each addl $15; under 18 free; wkend rates. TV; cable (premium). Heated pool; whirlpool, poolside serv. Coffee in rms. Restaurant 6:30 am-10 pm. Bar. Ck-out noon. Meeting rms. Business servs avail. Concierge. Gift shop. Lighted tennis. Exercise equipt; sauna. Minibars; some refrigerators. Luxury level. Cr cds: A, C, D, DS, ER, MC, V.

D ⥼ ⊠ ✈ ⌕ ⫰ SC

★ ★ ★ **RADISSON TWIN TOWERS.** *5780 Major Blvd (32819), in International Drive Area.* 407/351-1000; res: 800/327-2110; FAX 407/363-0106. 760 rms, 18-19 story. Mid-Jan-Apr: S, D $129-$169; suites $275-$900; under 18 free; lower rates rest of yr. Crib free. TV; cable (premium). Heated pool; wading pool, whirlpool, poolside serv. Playground. Restaurant 7 am-10 pm. Deli 24 hrs. Rm serv 24 hrs. Bar 4:30 pm-2 am; entertainment Tues-Sat. Ck-out noon. Coin Indry. Convention facilities. Business center. In-rm modem link. Shopping arcade. Beauty shop. Airport transportation. Exercise equipt; sauna. Game rm. Refrigerator, wet bar in suites. Located directly in front of Universal Studios entrance. Cr cds: A, C, D, DS, ER, JCB, MC, V.

D ⊠ ✈ ⌕ ⫰ SC ⫰

★ ★ ★ **RENAISSANCE.** *5445 Forbes Place (32812), near Orlando Intl Airport, south of downtown.* 407/240-1000; FAX 407/240-1005. Web www.renaissancehotels.com. 300 rms, 9 story. S, D $129-$189; each addl $15; suites $350-$500; under 18 free. Crib free. TV; cable. Heated pool; whirlpool, poolside serv. Coffee in rms. Restaurant 6 am-11 pm. Bar. Ck-out 1 pm. Convention facilities. Business center. Concierge. Gift shop. Free airport transportation. 36-hole golf privileges. Exercise equipt; sauna. Bathrm phones, minibars. Luxury level. Cr cds: A, C, D, DS, ER, JCB, MC, V.

D ⫯ ⫰ ⊠ ✈ ⌕ ⫰ SC ⫰

★ ★ ★ **RENAISSANCE ORLANDO RESORT.** *6677 Sea Harbor Dr (32821), in International Drive Area.* 407/351-5555; FAX 407/351-9991. 780 rms, 10 story. Late Dec-mid-May: S, D $219-$229; each addl $10; suites $500-$675; under 18 free; lower rates rest of yr. Crib free. TV; cable (premium). Heated pool; wading pool, whirlpool, poolside serv. Supervised child's activities; ages 6 mo-12 yrs. Restaurant open 24 hrs. Bar; entertainment. Ck-out noon. Convention facilities. Business center. In-rm modem link. Shopping arcade. Barber, beauty shop. Airport, Walt Disney World transportation. Lighted tennis. Golf privileges. Exercise rm; sauna. Massage. Game rm. Bathrm phones, minibars. Balconies. Atrium lobby; extensive art collection. Luxury level. Cr cds: A, C, D, DS, ER, JCB, MC, V.

D ⫯ ⫰ ⥼ ⊠ ✈ ⫰ ⌕ ⫰ SC ⫰

✔ ★ **UNIVERSAL TOWER.** *5905 International Dr (32819), at jct FL 435 & I-4, in International Drive Area.* 407/351-2100; res: 800/327-1366; FAX 407/352-2991. 302 units, 21 story. Feb-Aug, late Dec-early Jan: S, D $79-$199; under 18 free; lower rates rest of yr. Crib free. TV; cable (premium). Heated pool; wading pool, poolside serv. Restaurant 6:30-11:30 am. Bar 4:30 pm-2 am; entertainment. Ck-out noon. Coin Indry. Meeting rms. Concierge. Gift shop. Barber, beauty shop. Game rm. Rec rm. Refrigerators avail. Cylindrical building. Cr cds: A, C, D, DS, ER, JCB, MC, V.

D ⊠ ⫰ ⫰ SC

Inns

★ ★ ★ **COURTYARD AT LAKE LUCERNE.** *211 N Lucerne Circle E (32801), near Church St Station, downtown.* 407/648-5188; FAX 407/246-1368; res: 800/444-5289. Web www.orlandohistoricinn.com. 30 units in 3 bldgs, 2 story. S, D $90-$195; suites $165-$225; kit. unit $119. Children over 12 yrs only. TV; cable. Complimentary continental bkfst. Restaurant nearby. Ck-out 11 am, ck-in 3 pm. Meeting rm. Airport, RR station, bus depot transportation. Consists of 4 houses—Victorian, antebellum and art deco—located in historic downtown neighborhood; Victorian Norment-Parry is city's oldest structure (1883). Each guest rm uniquely designed by different artist; large collection of English and American antiques and objets d'art. Gardens. Cr cds: A, D, MC, V.

⫰ ⫰

★ ★ ★ **MEADOW MARSH.** *(940 Tildenville School Rd, Winter Garden 34787) Approx 16 mi W on FL 50.* 407/656-2064; res: 888/656-2064; FAX 407/654-0656. 5 rms, 3 story, 2 suites. No rm phones. S, D $95-$125; each addl $25; suites $190-199; higher rates sports events. Children over 12 yrs only. Complimentary full bkfst. Ck-out 11 am, ck-in 3 pm. Business servs avail. Lawn games. Picnic tables. Built in 1877. Victorian farmhouse; antiques. Totally nonsmoking. Cr cds: DS, MC, V.

D ⫰ ⫰

Resort

★ ★ ★ **WYNDHAM SAFARI RESORT.** *12205 Apopka-Vineland Rd (32836), east of downtown.* 407/239-0444; res: 800/423-3297; FAX 407/239-1778. Web www.wyndhamsafari.com. 489 rms, 15 with shower only, 6 story, 90 suites. S, D $69-$149; suites $99-$179; kit. units $119-$199; under 18 free. Crib free. TV: cable (premium). Complimentary coffee in rms. Restaurant 6:30-11 am, 5-10 pm. Rm serv 6:30 am-11 pm. Bar 3-11 pm. Ck-out 11 am, ck-in 3 pm. Grocery 1 blk. Coin Indry. Package store 1 blk. Convention facilities. Business center. In-rm modem link. Bellhops. Valet serv. Concierge. Exercise equipt. Pool; wading pool, whirlpool, poolside serv. Many refrigerators, microwaves. Many balconies. Cr cds: A, C, D, DS, MC, V.

D ≈ ✕ ≈ ⋈ SC ⚶

Restaurants

★ ★ **4TH FIGHTER GROUP RESTAURANT.** *494 Rickenbacker Dr (37803), east of downtown.* 407/898-4251. Hrs: 11 am-2:30 pm, 4:30-10 pm; Fri, Sat to 11 pm; early-bird dinner to 6:30 pm; Sun brunch 9:30 am-2:30 pm. Res accepted. Bar. Semi-a la carte: lunch $5.95-$10.95, dinner $12.95-$24.95. Sun brunch $16.95. Child's meals. Specializes in steak, fresh seafood. Parking. Modeled after WWII English farmhouse; many air-force, war artifacts. Dedicated to 4th fighter group vets. Overlooks Orlando Executive Airport. Table-side prep. Cr cds: A, C, D, DS, MC, V.

D ⧄

★ ★ ★ **BACCO.** *10065 University Blvd (32817), in Suncrest Village Shopping Center, east of downtown.* 407/678-8833. Hrs: 11:30 am-2 pm, 6-10 pm; Fri, Sat 5-10 pm. Closed Sun, Mon; Easter, Thanksgiving, Dec 25. Res accepted. Italian menu. Bar. A la carte entrees: lunch $15, dinner $10.50-$19.50. Specializes in chicken, beef, fish. Antique furnishings. Cr cds: A, MC, V.

D ⧄

★ ★ ★ **BERGAMO'S.** *8445 International Dr (32819), 8 mi S on I-4, exit 29 at Mercado Shopping Village, in International Drive Area.* 407/352-3805. Hrs: 5-10:30 pm. Closed Dec 25. Res accepted. Italian menu. Bar. Wine cellar. A la carte entrees: dinner $15.95-$27. Child's meals. Specializes in veal, steak, pasta. Own pastries. Outdoor dining. Opera theme with photos and singing servers. Cr cds: A, C, D, DS, MC, V.

D ⧄

✔ ★ ★ **CAFE EUROPA.** *55 W Church St (32801), in Church St Marketplace, downtown.* 407/872-3388. Hrs: 11 am-10 pm; Fri, Sat to 11 pm; Sun from noon. Closed Memorial Day, Dec 25. Res accepted Fri-Sun dinner. Continental menu. Semi-a la carte: lunch $5.25-$8.25, dinner $10-$17. Child's meals. Specialties: goulash, chicken Paprikash. European garden atmosphere. Cr cds: A, C, D, DS, MC, V.

⧄

★ ★ **CHARLEY'S STEAK HOUSE.** *6107 S Orange Blossom Trail (32809), at Oakridge Rd, south of downtown.* 407/851-7130. Hrs: 4:30-10 pm; Fri, Sat to 11 pm. Closed Thanksgiving, Dec 25. Res accepted. Bar. Semi-a la carte: dinner $12.95-$21.95. Child's meals. Specializes in flame-broiled aged steak, fresh seafood. Salad bar. Parking. Antiques. Cr cds: A, MC, V.

D SC ⧄

★ ★ **CHARLIE'S LOBSTER HOUSE.** *8445 International Dr (32819), at Mercado Shopping Village, in International Drive Area.* 407/352-6929. Hrs: 4-10 pm; Fri, Sat to 11 pm. Res accepted. Bar. Semi-a la carte: dinner $12.95-$36.95. Child's meals. Specializes in seafood. Outdoor dining. Nautical decor with wood and brass fixtures. Cr cds: A, C, D, DS, ER, MC, V.

D ⧄

★ ★ ★ **CHATHAM'S PLACE.** *7575 Dr Phillips Blvd (33819), in Phillips Place, south of downtown.* 407/345-2992. Hrs: 11:30 am-2:30 pm, 5:30-10 pm. Closed most major hols. Res accepted. Wine, beer. Semi-a la carte: lunch $7-$12, dinner $20-$40. Specialties: filet mignon, grouper with pecan butter, rack of lamb. Own desserts. Parking. Intricate wrought-iron grillwork on windows. Totally nonsmoking. Cr cds: A, D, DS, MC, V.

D

★ ★ ★ **CHRISTINI'S.** *7600 Doctor Phillips Blvd (32819), 8 mi S on I-4, exit 29 W, south of downtown.* 407/345-8770. Hrs: 6 pm-midnight. Closed most major hols. Res accepted. Italian menu. Bar. Wine cellar. A la carte entrees: dinner $17-$32. Specialties: 26 ounce veal chop, rack of

lamb. Own pasta. Strolling musicians. Valet parking. Italian decor; old world atmosphere. Cr cds: A, C, D, DS, MC, V.

D ⧄

★ ★ **CRACKERS.** *129 W Church St (32801), at Church Street Station, downtown.* 407/422-2434. Web www.churchstreetstation.com. Hrs: 11 am-11:30 pm; Fri, Sat to midnight. Bar. Semi-a la carte: lunch $5.50-$8.95, dinner $7.95-$19.95. Child's meals. Specialties: seafood gumbo, clam chowder, live Maine lobster. Turn-of-the-century carved and paneled bar. Cr cds: A, C, D, DS, JCB, MC, V.

D ⧄

★ ★ ★ **DEL FRISCO'S.** *729 Lee Rd (32810), north of downtown.* 407/645-4443. Hrs: 5-10 pm; wkends to 11 pm. Closed Sun; Jan 1, Memorial Day, Thanksgiving, Dec 25. Bar from 4 pm. A la carte entrees: dinner $15.95-$29.95. Specializes in prime beef, lobster tails. Parking. Steak house atmosphere. Cr cds: A, C, D, DS, MC, V.

D ⧄

★ ★ ★ **DUX.** *(See Peabody Orlando Hotel)* 407/345-4550. Web www.peabody-orlando.com. Expert service and innovative cuisine are the hallmarks of this hotel dining room. The room itself is warm and comfortable, adorned with flowers and crystal chandeliers; around the perimeter is a mural painted with—what else—ducks. Continental menu. Specializes in globally inspired dishes. Hrs: 6-10 pm; Fri, Sat to 11 pm. Closed Sun; also month of Aug. Res accepted. Bar. Wine cellar. Semi-a la carte: dinner $24-$45. Child's meals. Valet parking. Jacket. Totally nonsmoking. Cr cds: A, C, D, DS, ER, JCB, MC, V.

D

★ ★ **HANAMIZUKI.** *8255 International Dr (32819), in International Drive Area.* 407/363-7200. Hrs: 5-10:30 pm. Res accepted. Japanese menu. A la carte entrees: $10-$35. Specializes in Japanese cuisine. Japanese decor. Cr cds: A, D, JCB, MC, V.

D ⧄

★ ★ ★ **LA GRILLE.** *8445 International Dr (32819), 8 mi S on I-4, exit 29, at Mercado Shopping Village, in International Drive Area.* 407/345-0883. Hrs: 6-11 pm. Res accepted. French menu. Bar. Wine cellar. A la carte: dinner $15.95-$23.95. Child's meals. Specialties: rack of lamb, steak frites, tuna Nicoise. Own pastries. Outdoor dining. Medieval European architecture. Cr cds: A, C, D, DS, JCB, MC, V.

D ⧄

★ ★ **LA NORMANDIE.** *2021 E Colonial Dr (FL 50) (32803), east of downtown.* 407/896-9976. Hrs: 11:30 am-2 pm, 5-10 pm; early-bird dinner Mon-Sat to 6:30 pm. Closed Sun; Dec 25. Res accepted. French, continental menu. Bar. Wine list. Semi-a la carte: lunch $7-$11, dinner $11-$25. Specialties: beef Wellington, salmon with lobster sauce, soufflé Grand Marnier. Own baking. Country French decor. Cr cds: A, C, D, DS, ER, MC, V.

D ⧄ ♥

★ ★ **LE COQ AU VIN.** *4800 S Orange Ave (32806), south of downtown.* 407/851-6980. Hrs: 11:30 am-2 pm, 5:30-10 pm; Sat from 5:30 pm; Sun 5-9 pm. Closed Mon; Jan 1, Easter, Dec 25. Res accepted. French, Amer menu. Wine, beer. Semi-a la carte: lunch $6.50-$12.50, dinner $13-$19.50. Child's meals. Parking. French decor. Cr cds: A, C, D, MC, V.

D ⧄

★ ★ ★ **LE PROVENCE.** *50 E Pine St (32801), downtown.* 407/843-1320. E-mail provence@worldramp.net; web www.cenfla.com/res/leprovence. Hrs: 11 am-2 pm, 5:30-9:30 pm; Fri, Sat to 10:30 pm. Closed Sun; some major hols. Res accepted. French menu. Bar. Wine cellar. A la carte entrees: lunch $4.25-$9.95, dinner $14.50-$37. Prix fixe: dinner $27.50 & $58. Child's meals. Specializes in fresh seafood, rack of lamb, veal. Entertainment Fri, Sat. In former bank; large mahogany bar. Cr cds: A, C, D, MC, V.

D ⧄

★ ★ **LEE'S LAKESIDE.** *431 E Central Blvd (32801), downtown.* 407/841-1565. Hrs: 11 am-11 pm; Sat from 5 pm; Sun to 9 pm; early-bird dinner 4-6 pm. Res accepted. Continental menu. Bar. Semi-a la carte: lunch $7.95-$10.95, dinner $16.95-$28.95. Child's meals. Specializes in fresh seafood, beef, veal. Entertainment. Parking. View of skyline across Lake Eola. Cr cds: A, D, DS, MC, V.

D SC ⌂

★ ★ **LILI MARLENE'S AVIATORS RESTAURANT & PUB.** *129 W Church St (32801), at Church Street Station, downtown.* 407/422-2434. Web www.churchstreetstation.com. Hrs: 11 am-4 pm, 5:30-11:30 pm; Fri, Sat to midnight; Sun brunch 10:30 am-3 pm. Bar 11-1 am. Semi-a la carte: lunch $4.95-$9.95. A la carte entrees: dinner $18-$29. Sun brunch $12.95. Child's meals. Specializes in aged beef, fresh grilled Florida seafood. Entertainment. Valet parking. In historic district; antiques, WWI aviation artifacts. Cr cds: A, C, D, DS, JCB, MC, V.

D ⌂

★ ★ ★ **MANUEL'S ON THE 28TH.** *390 Orange Ave (32801), in Barnett Bank Bldg, downtown.* 407/246-6580. Web www.manuels.com. Hrs: 6-10 pm. Closed Sun, Mon; Thanksgiving, Dec 25. Res accepted. Serv bar. Wine list. Semi-a la carte: dinner $26-$32. Specializes in lobster, lamb. Garage parking. View of city. Totally nonsmoking. Cr cds: A, C, D, DS, MC, V.

D

★ ★ ★ **MICHELANGELO'S.** *4898 Kirkman Rd (32811), south of downtown.* 407/297-6666. Web www.abni.netflashmichelangelo. Hrs: 11:30 am-2 pm, 6-11 pm; Sat, Sun 6-11 pm. Closed Jan 1, Dec 25. Res accepted. Italian menu. Bar. Wine cellar. A la carte entrees: lunch $8-$12, dinner $12.95-$28.95. Child's meals. Specializes in traditional northern Italian dishes. Entertainment. Parking. Outdoor dining. Cr cds: A, C, D, DS, JCB, MC, V.

D ⌂

★ ★ ★ **MING COURT.** *9188 International Dr, south of downtown.* 407/351-9988. Hrs: 11 am-2:30 pm, 4:30 pm-midnight. Res accepted. Chinese menu. Bar. Semi-a la carte: lunch $5-$9, dinner $10.95-$19.95. Specialties: Peking duck, dim sum. Chinese performers. Parking. Chinese-style architecture with undulating Great Wall enclosing gardens and waterways. Live seafood tanks. Cr cds: A, C, D, DS, JCB, MC, V.

D ⌂

✔★ ★ **PASSAGE TO INDIA.** *5532 International Dr (32819), in International Drive Area.* 407/351-3456. Web www.destinationusa.com/india1.html. Hrs: 2 pm-midnight; wkends from 1 pm. Res accepted. Indian menu. Wine, beer. A la carte entrees: dinner $12.95-$19.95. Child's meals. Specializes in clay oven preparations, vegetarian dishes. Parking. Richly carved wooden screens, brass. Cr cds: A, C, D, DS, MC, V.

D SC ⌂

★ ★ **SIAM ORCHID.** *7575 Republic Dr (32819), in International Drive Area.* 407/351-0821. Hrs: 5-11 pm. Closed July 4, Dec 25. Res accepted. Thai menu. Bar. Semi-a la carte: dinner $10.25-$24.95. Specialties: Siam Orchid roast duck, fresh seafood. Parking. Thai decor and artifacts. On lake. Cr cds: A, D, DS, MC, V.

D ⌂

✔★ **SIZZLING WOK.** *1453 Sand Lake Rd (32809), south of downtown.* 407/438-8389. Hrs: 11 am-10 pm; Fri, Sat to 10:30 pm. Res accepted hols. Chinese menu. Semi-a la carte: lunch $4.25-$5.50, dinner $4.95-$8.95. Buffet: lunch $4-$7, dinner $9-$11. Child's meals. Specializes in Chinese cuisine. Salad bar. Parking. Cr cds: A, D, DS, MC, V.

D SC ⌂

✔★ ★ **STRAUB'S BOATYARD.** *743 Lee Rd (32810), north of downtown.* 407/628-0067. Hrs: 11 am-10 pm; Fri, Sat to 11 pm; early-bird dinner 4:30-6 pm. Closed Sun; Thanksgiving, Dec 25. Res accepted (dinner). Bar. Semi-a la carte: lunch $4-$9.95, dinner $11.95-$19.95.

Child's meals. Specializes in steak, seafood. Parking. Nautical decor. Cr cds: A, C, D, DS, MC, V.

D ⌂

★ ★ ★ **VIVALDI.** *107 Pine St (32801), downtown.* 407/423-2335. Hrs: 11 am-11 pm; Sat, Sun from 4 pm. Closed Thanksgiving, Dec 25. Res accepted. Italian menu. Bar. A la carte entrees: lunch $6.95-$9.95, dinner $9.90-$22.95. Specialty: Vivaldi's Pride. Parking. Own bread, pasta. Outdoor dining. Intimate gourmet dining. Cr cds: A, D, DS, MC, V.

D SC ⌂

Unrated Dining Spots

HARD ROCK CAFE. *5800 Kirkman Rd (32819), at Universal Studios Florida, south of downtown.* 407/351-7625. Hrs: 11-2 am. Semi-a la carte: lunch, dinner $6.95-$17.99. Child's meals. Specializes in hamburgers, barbecue dishes. Parking. Outdoor dining. Building shaped like an electric guitar; stained-glass windows depict Elvis Presley, Jerry Lee Lewis and Chuck Berry. Rock & roll and entertainment memorabilia throughout. Cr cds: A, D, DS, MC, V.

D ⌂

KING HENRY'S FEAST. *8984 International Dr (32819), in International Drive Area.* 407/351-5151. Dinner show hrs vary each season. Res required. Bar. Complete meals: adult $36.95; children 3-11 $22.95. Specializes in baked chicken, barbecued ribs. Entertainment includes dueling knights, aerial ballerina, jesters. Parking. Medieval palace decor; costumed servers. Cr cds: A, C, D, DS, ER, JCB, MC, V.

Ormond Beach (D-5)

(See also Daytona Beach, DeLand, New Smyrna Beach)

Founded 1875 **Pop** 29,721 **Elev** 22 ft **Area code** 904
Information Chamber of Commerce, 165 W Granada Blvd, 32174; 904/677-3454 or -6362.

John D. Rockefeller, Sr, who died here in 1937 at age 97, spent his twilight years playing golf with intense seriousness and doggedly trying to live to 100. Partly on the Atlantic Ocean, partly on the Halifax River with the Tomoka River at its back, Ormond Beach still boasts of the healthful climate that contributed to Rockefeller's longevity. One of its main assets is its 23-mile, 500-foot-wide public beach. Auto racing was a popular sport in the early 1900s, when world records were set here. A Stanley Steamer went 127.66 miles per hour in January 1906. Today, 18 miles of the beach are open to cars.

What to See and Do

Bulow Plantation Ruins State Historic Site. Bulow Plantation, which flourished in the early 1800s, was destroyed by the Seminole in 1836. Now the ruins of its sugar mill remain on this 109-acre park. Canoe rentals; fishing. Nature trails. Picnicking. Interpretive center. Standard hrs, fees. 8 mi N off FL A1A, on FL 5, S of Flagler Beach. Phone 904/517-2084.

Gamble Rogers Memorial State Recreation Area at Flagler Beach. Approx 145 acres extending across a barrier 3 mi south of town bordered by the Atlantic Ocean and the Intracoastal Waterway. Swimming; fishing; boating (ramp, dock). Nature trails. Picnicking, playground. Camping (hookups, dump station). Standard hrs, fees. 11 mi N on FL A1A, near Flagler Beach. Phone 904/517-2086.

Ormond Memorial Art Museum and Gardens. Changing exhibits include contemporary art, antiques, and special collections; permanent collection of symbolic religious paintings by Malcolm Fraser; four-acre tropical garden. (Daily) 78 E Granada Blvd, 3 blks W of FL A1A. Phone 904/676-3347. ¢

The Casements. Former winter home of John D. Rockefeller, Sr now serves as cultural center for city; historical exhibits include Hungarian

Historic Room, Boy Scout exhibit; changing art displays. (Daily exc Sat afternoons and Sun; closed hols) 25 Riverside Dr. Phone 904/676-3216. **Free.**

Tomoka State Park. Approx 900 acres where the Tomoka and Halifax rivers meet. Site of Indian village of Nocoroco. Museum (daily). Fishing; boating (ramp, dock), canoe rentals. Nature trail. Picnicking, playground. Camping (hookups, dump station). Visitor center. Standard hrs, fees. 3 mi N on FL A1A, off N Beach St. Phone 904/676-4050.

Annual Event

Birthplace of Speed Antique Car Show. Parades, antique car competition, beach sprint races. 3 days Thanksgiving wkend.

Motels

✔★ **BUDGET HOST INN.** 1633 N US 1 (32174), I-95 exit 89. 904/677-7310. 64 rms, 2 story. Jan-Apr: S, D $40-$125; each addl $6; under 18 free. Pet accepted, some restrictions. TV; cable. Pool; wading pool. Playground. Complimentary continental bkfst. Ck-out 11 am. Coin Indry. Private patios; some balconies. Cr cds: A, DS, MC, V.

★ **COMFORT INN INTERSTATE.** 1567 N US 1 (32174), I-95 exit 89. 904/672-8621. 75 rms, 2 story. Feb-Apr: S, D $69.95-$89.95; under 18 free; higher rates: Daytona races, spring break; lower rates rest of yr. Crib free. Pet accepted. TV; cable. Pool. Complimentary continental bkfst. Restaurant adj open 24 hrs. Ck-out noon. Coin Indry. Business servs avail. Lawn games. Cr cds: A, C, D, DS, ER, JCB, MC, V.

★ **COMFORT INN ON THE BEACH.** 507 S Atlantic Ave (FL A1A) (32176). 904/677-8550; FAX 904/673-6260. 49 units, 4 story, 26 kits. Feb-Apr, June-Labor Day: S, D $60-$90; each addl $5; kit. units $65-$95; under 18 free; higher rates: Easter, July 4, special events; lower rates rest of yr. Crib $5. Pet accepted, some restrictions; $5. TV; cable. Heated pool; wading pool. Complimentary continental bkfst. Coffee in rms. Restaurant adj. Ck-out 11 am. Golf privileges. Balconies. On ocean. Cr cds: A, C, D, DS, ER, JCB, MC, V.

✔★ **ECONO LODGE.** 295 S Atlantic Ave (FL A1A) (32176). 904/672-2651; res: 800/847-8811. 58 rms, 4 story, 33 kits. Mid-Feb-Easter, late May-Sept: S, D $62-$70; kit. units $67-$75; each addl $5; wkly rates; higher rates: hols; special events (5-7-day min); lower rates rest of yr. Crib $5. TV; cable. Heated pool; wading pool. Restaurant nearby. Ck-out 11 am. Coin Indry. Private patios. Picnic tables, grills. On ocean, beach. Cr cds: A, D, DS, MC, V.

★ **MAINSAIL.** 281 S Atlantic Ave (FL A1A) (32176). 904/677-2131; res: 800/843-5142. 50 units, 2-4 story, 33 kits. Mar-Apr: S, D $75-$110; each addl $7; kit. units $110-$150; family, wkly rates; higher rates: hols, special events; lower rates rest of yr. TV; cable. Heated pool; wading pool. Restaurant adj. Ck-out 11 am. Coin Indry. Sauna. Private patios, balconies. Picnic tables, grill. On ocean, beach. Cr cds: A, C, D, DS, MC, V.

✔★★ **MAKAI.** 707 S Atlantic Ave (FL A1A) (32176). 904/677-8060; res: 800/799-1112. Web www.webadept.com/makai. 110 rms, 4 story, 61 kits. Feb-Apr, June-Labor Day: S, D $47-$81; each addl $5; suites $90-$162; kit. units $51-$86; under 18 free; higher rates: hols, special events; lower rates rest of yr. Crib $5. TV; cable. Heated pool; wading pool, whirlpool. Restaurant nearby. Ck-out 11 am. Coin Indry. Meeting rm. In-rm modem link. Game rm. Lawn games. Refrigerators. Private patios, balconies. Picnic tables, grills. On beach. Cr cds: A, C, D, DS, ER, MC, V.

★★ **MAVERICK.** 485 S Atlantic Ave (FL A1A) (32176). 904/672-3550. 138 units, 7 story, no ground floor rms, 138 kits. Early Feb-late Apr, mid-June-early Sept: S, D $75-$125; higher rates: Easter, July 4, special events; lower rates rest of yr. Crib free. TV; cable, VCR avail (movies). Heated pool; wading pool, whirlpool. Sauna. Restaurant 7:30 am-2:30 pm. Ck-out 10 am. Coin Indry. Game rm. Lawn games. Refrigerators, microwaves. Private patios, balconies. Picnic tables. On ocean, beach. Cr cds: A, MC, V.

★ **TOPAZ.** (1224 S Ocean Shore Blvd, Flagler Beach 32136) 12 mi N, I-95 exit 91. 904/439-3301; res: 800/555-4735; FAX 904/439-3942. 58 rms, 2 story. S, D $47-$140; each addl $5-$10; kit. units $71-$91; under 12 free; wkly, monthly rates; higher rates: special events, hols. Crib $5. Pet accepted, some restrictions; $10. TV; cable, VCR (free movies). Pool. Restaurant 5:30-9:30 pm; closed Sun, Mon. Ck-out 11 am. Coin Indry. Some balconies. Swimming beach. Cr cds: A, DS, MC, V.

★ **TRADERS INN.** 1355 Ocean Shore Blvd (32176). 904/441-1111; res: 800/881-2494; FAX 904/441-0037. 49 kit. units, 5 story. June-Labor Day: kit. units $60-$80; higher rates special events; lower rates rest of yr. Crib $3. TV; cable, VCR avail (movies $4). Heated pool; wading pool. Restaurant nearby. Ck-out 10 am. Coin Indry. Sundries. Lawn games. Private patios, balconies. Picnic tables, grills. On beach. Cr cds: A, MC, V.

Motor Hotels

★★ **CASA DEL MAR BEACH RESORT.** 621 S Atlantic Ave (FL A1A) (32176). 904/672-4550; FAX 904/672-1418; res: 800/245-1590. 130 kit. units, 7 story. May-Sept: kit. units $83-$155; each addl $8-$10; under 16 free; wkly rates; higher rates: special events, hols; lower rates rest of yr. Crib free. TV; cable (premium). Heated pool; wading pool, whirlpool. Bar. Ck-out 11 am. Coin Indry. Valet serv. Sundries. Game rm. Lawn games. Refrigerators, microwaves. Balconies. On ocean, beach. Cr cds: A, C, D, DS, ER, MC, V.

★ **IVANHOE BEACH RESORT.** 205 S Atlantic Ave (FL A1A) (32176). 904/672-6711; FAX 904/676-9494; res: 800/874-9910. 147 rms, 7 story, 102 kits. Mar-mid-Apr, July-mid-Aug: S, D $60-$75; each addl $5; suites $70-$105; kit. units $65-$90; under 18 free; higher rates: hols, special events (3-7-day min); lower rates rest of yr. Crib $5. TV; cable. Heated pool; wading pool, poolside serv in season. Restaurant 7 am-1 pm. Ck-out 11 am. Coin Indry. Covered parking. Game rm. Lawn games. Refrigerators; microwaves avail. Balconies. On beach. Cr cds: A, MC, V.

Restaurants

✔★★ **JULIAN'S.** 88 S Atlantic Ave (32176). 904/677-6767. Hrs: 4-11 pm. Bar. Semi-a la carte: dinner $8-$16. Child's meals. Specializes in prime beef, seafood. Organist; entertainment exc Mon. Island decor. Family-owned. Cr cds: A, D, DS, MC, V.

★★ **MARIO'S.** 521 S Yonge St (32174). 904/677-2711. Hrs: 11:30 am-2 pm, 4:30-10 pm; Fri, Sat 4:30-11 pm; Sun, Mon from 4:30 pm; early-bird dinner 4:30-6:30 pm. Closed Thanksgiving, Dec 25. Italian, Amer menu. Bar. Semi-a la carte: dinner $8.95-$16.95. Child's meals. Specialties: veal Marsala, veal à la Française. Italian decor; large oil paintings, brass ceiling lights. Family-owned. Cr cds: A, MC, V.

Palatka (C-4)

(See also Gainesville, St Augustine)

Settled 1821 **Pop** 10,201 **Elev** 22 ft **Area code** 904 **Zip** 32177 **Web** www.putnam.special.net/chamber
Information Putnam County Chamber of Commerce, 1100 Reid St, PO Box 550, 32178; 904/328-1503.

The name Palatka is derived from the Native American *pilaklikaha*, meaning "crossing over." The town sits at an elbow of the St Johns River, a mighty mile-wide waterway and one of the few north-flowing rivers in the world. After the Civil War, wintering in Florida became fashionable for rich Easterners, who would travel by train to Jacksonville and then take a 50-mile river-steamer trip to Palatka. The city's role as a resort fell into decline with the opening of the railroad in other sections of Florida. Today, more than 30 fishing camps, resorts and lodges along the St Johns River accommodate fishermen angling for bass.

What to See and Do

Bronson-Mulholland House (1854). Three-story antebellum cypress structure built for one of the first circuit judges of the state. (Tues, Thurs & Sun afternoons; closed hols) 100 Madison St. Phone 904/329-0140. **Free.**

Ravine State Gardens. Thousands of azaleas of many varieties and other ornamental plants bloom on these 182 landscaped acres. Near entrance is Court of States, with 68-ft obelisk at one end and Civic Center at other; 2-mi drive follows edges of 3 ravines penetrated by 6½ mi of paths. Most spectacular in Feb & Mar. Nature trails. Picnicking. (Daily) 1 mi SE, off Moseley Ave on Twigg St. Phone 904/329-3721. ¢ Per car ¢¢

Annual Events

Azalea Festival. Downtown. Parade, festival pageant, crafts show. Mar.

Putnam County Fair. Late Mar.

Blue Crab Festival. Memorial Day wkend.

Motel

★ ★ **HOLIDAY INN RIVERSIDE.** *201 N 1st St. 904/328-3481; FAX 904/328-3481, ext. 315.* 131 rms. S, D $59-$64; under 18 free. Crib free. TV; cable (premium). Pool. Restaurant 6 am-2 pm, 5-10 pm. Rm serv. Bar. Coin lndry. Meeting rms. Business servs avail. In-rm modem link. Bellhops. Valet serv. On river; boat dock. Cr cds: A, C, D, DS, JCB, MC, V.

Palm Beach (G-6)

(See also Jupiter, Lake Worth, West Palm Beach)

Settled 1861 **Pop** 9,814 **Elev** 15 ft **Area code** 561 **Zip** 33480
Information Chamber of Commerce, 45 Cocoanut Row; 561/655-3282.

Although condominiums and office buildings along the main streets have altered the atmosphere of Palm Beach slightly, the image of elegance, beauty and charm remains. Single-family houses and regal estates still dominate the scene, and lush foliage and expert landscaping personify the semi-tropical living. The town prides itself on its world-famous shopping areas: Worth Avenue and the Esplanade, Royal Poinciana Way and South County Road.

Situated on the northern end of a 14-mile-long island, half a mile at its widest point, with Lake Worth to the west and the Atlantic Ocean to the east, Palm Beach probably owes its resort existence to a shipwreck in

1878. The vessel's cargo of coconuts was washed ashore and took root, transforming a barren ribbon of sand into a palm-shadowed haven. Henry Morrison Flagler, the railroad magnate, was the first to recognize the attraction of Palm Beach; he built the famous Royal Poinciana Hotel and directed major civic improvements, including extensive landscaping. The Gulf Stream at Phipps Ocean Park is closer to shore in this area (1-3 miles) than any other point in the US.

What to See and Do

Henry Morrison Flagler Museum (Whitehall). This 55-rm house (1902) was built by Henry Morrison Flagler, developer of the Florida East Coast Railroad. An opulent monument to America's Gilded Age, this marble palace contains porcelains, paintings, silver, glass, dolls, lace, costumes and family memorabilia. Special exhibits illustrate local history and the vast enterprises of the Flagler system. On the grounds is Flagler's private railroad car, refinished and refitted with exact reproductions of the original carpeting, drapery and upholstery materials. (Daily exc Mon; closed Jan 1, Thanksgiving, Dec 25) On Cocoanut Row at Whitehall Way. Phone 561/655-2833. ¢¢¢

Hibel Museum of Art. Located on the shores of Lake Worth, this is the only nonprofit public museum in the world dedicated to the art of a living American woman. Exhibits include paintings, lithographs, drawings, serigraphs, sculpture and porcelain art by Edna Hibel. Also displays of antique Oriental snuff bottles, Italian, English and Oriental furniture, art books and dolls. Gift shop. (Daily exc Mon; closed Dec 25) (See SEASONAL EVENTS) 150 Royal Poinciana Plaza. Phone 561/833-6870. **Free.**

Palm Beach Bicycle Trail. This nearly five-mile, paved trail, beginning south of the Royal Park Bridge at Worth Ave, winds among some of the most beautiful houses in Palm Beach, terminating 2 blks N of the Palm Beach Sailfish Club.

Society of the Four Arts. Complex includes museum, library and gardens; also lectures, films, concerts (Jan-Mar, fee). Galleries (mid-Dec-mid-Apr, daily; fee). Library & gardens (Nov-Apr, daily exc Sun; rest of yr, Mon-Fri; closed most hols). Four Arts Plaza, off Royal Palm Way. Phone 561/655-7226. **Free.**

The Church of Bethesda-by-the-Sea (1925). Church of 15th-century Gothic design with embattlement tower, arched main entrance. Adj is Cluett Memorial Garden with extensive tropical landscaping. (Daily) S County Rd & Barton Ave. Phone 561/655-4554. **Free.**

Seasonal Events

Promenade Concerts. Hibel Museum of Art. Free Classical & light musical concerts by both beginning and established professional musicians. Limited seating; early arrival suggested. Phone 561/833-6870. 2nd Sun each month, Nov-May.

Royal Poinciana Playhouse. 70 Royal Poinciana Plaza. Broadway plays and musicals. Phone 561/659-3310 for tickets. Mid-Dec-Mar.

Motels

★ **BEACHCOMBER.** *3024 S Ocean Blvd (FL A1A). 561/585-4646; FAX 561/547-9438; res: 800/833-7122.* 50 units, 1-2 story, 45 kits. Jan-Apr: S, D $105-$205; each addl $10; lower rates rest of yr. Crib free. TV; cable. Saltwater pool. Restaurant nearby. Ck-out noon. Coin lndry. Business servs avail. Lawn games. Some patios, balconies. On ocean. Cr cds: A, DS, MC, V.

★ **HAWAIIAN OCEAN INN.** *3550 S Ocean Blvd (FL A1A). 561/582-5631; res: 800/457-5631.* E-mail hawaiian@gate.net; web www.worldpubcom/hawaiian. 58 units, 2 story, 8 suites. Jan-Apr: S, D $125; each addl $5; suites $175-$300; studio rms $134; wkly rates; lower rates rest of yr. Crib free. TV; cable (premium). Heated pool; poolside serv. Restaurant 7 am-10 pm. Rm serv. Bar 11 am-midnight. Ck-out 11 am. Business servs avail. Refrigerators. On ocean, swimming beach. Cr cds: A, C, D, DS, ER, MC, V.

Motor Hotel

★ ★ **HOWARD JOHNSON.** *2870 S Ocean Blvd (FL A1A). 561/582-2581; FAX 561/582-7189.* 99 rms, 3 story. Mid-Dec-mid-Apr: S, D $109-$139; under 17 free; package plans; lower rates rest of yr. Crib free. TV; cable (premium). Pool; poolside serv. Restaurant 6:30 am-11 pm. Rm serv. Bar 3 pm-2 am. Ck-out noon. Coin lndry. Business servs avail. Some balconies. Cr cds: A, D, DS, MC, V.

D ≋ ⩫ ⌦ SC

Hotels

★ ★ ★ **BRAZILIAN COURT.** *301 Australian Ave. 561/655-7740; res: 800/552-0335.* 103 rms, 93 with shower only, 2-3 story, 40 suites. Dec-Apr: S, D $275-$335; each addl $30; suites $425-$725; under 16 free; wkend rates; higher rates Super Bowl; lower rates rest of yr. Crib free. Pet accepted, some restrictions; $75. Valet parking $8/day. TV; cable, VCR avail (movies). Restaurant (see CHANCELLOR GRILLE). Rm serv 24 hrs. Bar to midnight; entertainment wkends. Ck-out noon. Meeting rms. Business servs avail. In-rm modem link. Concierge. Beauty shop. Guest lndry. Tennis privileges. 18-hole golf privileges. Exercise rm. Massage. Heated pool. Refrigerators, minibars, wet bars; some microwaves. Some balconies. Cr cds: A, C, D, DS, MC, V.

D ⌦ ⋈ ⅋ ≋ ⩫ ⋇ ⌦ SC

★ ★ ★ ★ **CHESTERFIELD HOTEL.** *363 Cocoanut Row. 561/659-5800; FAX 561/659-6707; res: 800/243-7871.* E-mail chesterpb@aol.com. With a little pretense, a lot of chintz and brass and a superabundance of service, this hotel may be a Mizner copy, but it has an English-country-style elegance all its own. 55 rms, 3 story, 11 suites. Mid-Dec-Apr: S, D $185-$299; suites $529-$1,099; lower rates rest of yr. Crib free. Pet accepted; $150 deposit. TV; cable, VCR avail. Pool; whirlpool, poolside serv. Restaurant 7 am-11 pm (also see THE LEOPARD ROOM). Rm serv 24 hrs. Bar 11-1 am; pianist. Ck-out noon. Meeting rms. Business center. In-rm modem link. Concierge. Free valet parking. Health club privileges. Cigar rm. Library/reading rms. Ocean 3 blks. Cr cds: A, C, D, DS, ER, MC, V.

D ⌦ ≋ ⩫ ⋇ SC ⋌

★ ★ ★ **THE COLONY.** *155 Hammon Ave. 561/655-5430; FAX 561/832-7318; res: 800/521-5525.* 91 rms, 6 story, 14 suites. Mid-Dec-Apr: S, D $255-$305; suites $395-$825; villas $600-$1,600; under 18 free; golf plan; lower rates rest of yr. Parking $10. TV; cable (premium). Heated pool; poolside serv. Restaurant 7 am-10:30 pm; wkends to midnight. Rm serv 24 hrs. Bar 5 pm-1 am; entertainment. Ck-out noon. Meeting rms. Business center. In-rm modem link. Concierge. Barber, beauty shop. Airport, RR station transportation. Lighted tennis privileges. 18-hole golf privileges, greens fee $35-$110, putting green, driving range. Health club privileges. Refrigerators avail. Near ocean. Restored landmark hotel first opened 1947. Cr cds: A, C, D, DS, MC, V.

D ⋈ ⅋ ⋇ ≋ ⩫ ⌦ SC ⋌

★ ★ ★ ★ ★ **THE FOUR SEASONS.** *2800 S Ocean Blvd. 561/582-2800; FAX 561/547-1557.* Web www.fshr.com. This beachside property combines contemporary design with the luxurious detailing of a traditional Floridian resort. There are views of the Atlantic Ocean from many rooms. 210 rms, 4 story. Nov-May: S, D $350-$625; suites $1,200-$2,500; under 17 free; lower rates rest of yr. Crib free. Pet accepted. Valet parking $15. TV; cable (premium), VCR avail (movies). Heated pool; whirlpool, poolside serv. Free supervised child's activities; from age 3. Restaurants 7 am-10 pm (also see THE RESTAURANT AT FOUR SEASONS). Rm serv 24 hrs. Bar 4 pm-midnight; pianist. Ck-out noon. Meeting rms. Business center. In-rm modem link. Concierge. Barber, beauty shop. Airport transportation. Tennis, pro. 18-hole golf privileges, greens fee $80, pro. Exercise rm; sauna, steam rm. Massage. Bathrm phones, minibars. Refrigerators. Balconies. On beach; water sports avail. Cr cds: A, C, D, DS, JCB, MC, V.

D ⌦ ⋈ ⅋ ⋇ ≋ ⩫ ⋇ ⌦ ⋌

★ ★ ★ **HEART OF PALM BEACH.** *160 Royal Palm Way. 561/655-5600; FAX 561/832-1201; res: 800/523-5377.* 88 rms, 2-3 story. Mid-Dec-Apr: S, D $129-$239; each addl $15; suites $275; under 18 free; lower rates rest of yr. Crib free. Pet accepted. TV; cable (premium), VCR (movies). Heated pool; poolside serv. Restaurant 7 am-11 pm. Bar from 11 am. Ck-out noon. Business center. In-rm modem link. Valet serv. Free underground parking. Refrigerators. Bicycle rentals. Private patios, balconies. Cr cds: A, C, D, MC, V.

⋈ ≋ ⩫ ⋇ SC ⋌

★ ★ ★ **HILTON OCEANFRONT RESORT.** *2842 S Ocean Blvd, FL A1A. 561/586-6542; FAX 561/585-0188.* Web www.hilton.com. 134 units, 5 story. Mid-Dec-Apr: S, D $349-$399; suites $499-$1099; family rates; lower rates rest of yr. Crib free. TV; cable (premium), VCR (free movies). Heated pool; whirlpool, poolside serv. Sauna. Coffee in rms. Restaurant 7 am-10 pm. Rm serv. Bar 11 am-11 pm; entertainment wkends in season. Ck-out noon. Meeting rms. Business center. In-rm modem link. Concierge. Valet parking. Tennis. Health club privileges. Refrigerators, minibars; microwaves avail. Private patios, balconies. On ocean beach. Cr cds: A, C, D, DS, MC, V.

D ⌦ ⋈ ≋ ⩫ ⋇ SC ⋌

★ ★ ★ ★ **THE RITZ-CARLTON, PALM BEACH.** *(100 S Ocean Blvd, Manalapan 33462) 8 mi S on US A1A. 561/533-6000; FAX 561/588-4201.* Web www.ritzcarlton.com. Three towers rise above this modern Mediterranean-style beachfront hotel. 270 rms, 6 story, 56 suites. Mid-Dec-Apr: S, D $355-$775; suites $890-$3,500; under 12 free; golf plans; lower rates rest of yr. Crib free. Garage $15/day. TV; cable (premium), VCR avail (movies). Heated pool; whirlpool, poolside serv. Supervised child's activities. Restaurant 6 am-10:30 pm (also see THE RESTAURANT). Rm serv 24 hrs. Bar; entertainment. Ck-out noon. Meeting rms. Business center. In-rm modem link. Concierge. Shopping arcade. Barber, beauty shop. Airport transportation. Lighted tennis. 18-hole golf privileges, greens fee $90-$150, pro, putting green, driving range. Exercise rm; steam rm. Massage. Bathrm phones, minibars. Balconies. Luxury level. Cr cds: A, C, D, DS, ER, JCB, MC, V.

D ⌦ ⋈ ⅋ ⋇ ≋ ⩫ ⋇ ⋈ ⋌

Inns

★ ★ **PALM BEACH HISTORIC INN.** *365 S County Rd (35480). 561/832-4009; FAX 561/832-6255.* 9 rms, 2 story, 4 suites. Mid-Dec-May: S, D $125-$150; suites $175-$225; under 12 free; lower rates rest of yr. TV; cable (premium), VCR avail (movies). Complimentary continental bkfst in rms. Restaurant nearby. Ck-out 11 am, ck-in 2 pm. Concierge serv. Luggage handling. Business servs avail. Refrigerators. Restored 1923 inn. Cr cds: A, C, D, DS, MC, V.

⩫ ⋇ SC

★ ★ **PLAZA.** *215 Brazilian Ave. 561/832-8666; FAX 561/835-8776; res: 800/233-2632.* E-mail plazainn@aol.com; web www.plazainn palmbeach.com. 50 rms, 3 story. Mid-Dec-Apr: S, D $160-$225; each addl $15; suites $275; lower rates rest of yr. Crib free. Pet accepted. TV. Heated pool; whirlpool, poolside serv. Complimentary full bkfst. Dining rm 7:30-10 am. Ck-out noon, ck-in 2 pm. Business servs avail. Bellhops. Health club privileges. Picnic tables. Art deco building (1939); near ocean. Cr cds: A, MC, V.

⌦ ≋ ⩫ ⋇

Resort

★ ★ ★ ★ ★ **THE BREAKERS.** *1 S County Rd. 561/655-6611; FAX 561/659-8403; 800 888/273-2537.* Web www.thebreakers.com. Blending formality with tropical resort ambience, this historic and palatial Italian Renaissance hotel on 140 splendid acres has been frequented by wealthy socialites and celebrities for most of this century. 572 rms, 7 story. Mid-Dec-Apr: S, D $340-$600; each addl $35; suites $550-$2,200; MAP avail; golf, tennis plans; lower rates rest of yr. Crib avail. TV; cable, VCR avail (movies). 3 pools; wading pool, poolside serv, lifeguard. Playground. Supervised child's activities; ages 3 and up. Dining rm 7-10:30 am, 6-10 pm;

beach club lunch from 11:30 am (also see THE FLORENTINE DINING ROOM and SEAFOOD BAR). Box lunches, snack bar, picnics. Rm serv 24 hrs. Bar 11-2 am. Ck-out noon, ck-in 4 pm. Convention facilities. Business center. In-rm modem link. Valet serv. Concierge. Shopping arcade. Barber, beauty shop. Valet parking. Airport transportation. 14 tennis courts, 5 lighted, pro. 36-hole golf, greens fee $90, pro, putting green, driving range. Scuba diving instructor. Bicycle rentals. Lawn games. Soc dir; entertainment, movies. Rec rm. Exercise rm; sauna. Massage. Refrigerators, mini-bars. On ocean, private beach; cabanas, beach club. Cr cds: A, C, D, DS, ER, JCB, MC, V.

Restaurants

★ ★ **AMICI.** *288 S Country Rd. 561/832-0201.* E-mail amici@bellsouth.net; web www.amici-pb.com. Hrs: 11:30 am-3 pm, 5-10:30 pm; Fri, Sat to 11 pm; Sun 5-10:30 pm; early-bird dinner Mon-Thurs 5-7 pm (seasonal). Closed Dec 25. Res accepted; required in season. Northern Italian menu. Bar. A la carte entrees: lunch $7.95-$14.95, dinner $15.95-$31.95. Child's meals. Specialties: risotto with seafood, grilled veal chop, wood-oven roasted portobello mushroom. Valet parking. Cr cds: A, C, D, MC, V.

★ ★ **BICE.** *313½ Worth Ave. 561/835-1600.* Hrs: noon-3 pm, 6-11 pm. Res accepted. Italian menu. Bar from noon. A la carte entrees: lunch $14-$18, dinner $20-$35. Specialties: beef carpaccio, insalata Caprese, tagliolini con gamberetti. Valet parking (dinner). Outdoor courtyard dining. Cr cds: A, D, MC, V.

★ ★ ★ **CAFE CASABLANCA.** *101 N County Rd, corner of Royal Poinciana Way. 561/655-1115.* Hrs: 11:15 am-3 pm, 5:30-10:30 pm; Sat, Sun from 5:30 pm. Res accepted. Mediterranean/continental menu. Bar. Semi-a la carte: lunch $7-$14, dinner $17-$30. Child's meals. Specialties: dill-crusted salmon, oven-braised lamb shank, moussaka. Valet parking. Mural of city of Casablanca; posters from the famous motion picture. Cr cds: A, D, DS, MC, V.

★ ★ ★ **CAFE L'EUROPE.** *331 S County Rd. 561/655-4020.* E-mail lyle@cafeleurope.com; web www.cafeleurope.com. Hrs: noon-2:30 pm, 6-10:30 pm. Res accepted. Continental menu. Bar. Wine cellar. A la carte entrees: lunch $11-$14, dinner $22.50-$33.50. Specialties: pan-seared sesame tuna, braised grouper, rack of lamb. Pianist; jazz Fri, Sat. Valet parking. Old-world atmosphere. Jacket. Cr cds: A, C, D, MC, V.

★ ★ ★ **CHANCELLOR GRILLE.** *(See Brazilian Court Hotel) 561/655-7740.* Hrs: 7 am-11 pm; May-Sept to 10 pm; Sun brunch 11 am-2:30 pm. Res accepted. Bar 11 am-midnight. Wine list. Semi-a la carte: bkfst $8-$13, lunch $8-$16, dinner $18-$35. Sun brunch $12-$22. Child's meals. Specialties: Key West snapper, osso bucco. Own baking. Entertainment Tue, Sat. Valet parking. Outdoor dining. Fish tanks. Jacket. Cr cds: A, C, D, DS, MC, V.

★ ★ ★ **CHARLEY'S CRAB.** *456 S Ocean Blvd (FL A1A). 561/659-1500.* Web www.charleyscrab.com. Hrs: 11:30 am-10 pm; Fri, Sat to 11 pm; Sun 10:30 am-10 pm; Sun brunch 10:30 am-2:30 pm. Res accepted. Bar. Wine list. Semi-a la carte: lunch $7.50-$16.50, dinner $15-$40. Sun brunch $24.95. Child's meals. Specializes in fresh seafood, homemade pasta. Own baking. Valet parking. Oceanfront dining. Cr cds: A, C, D, DS, MC, V.

★ ★ ★ **CHEZ JEAN-PIERRE.** *132 N County Rd. 561/833-1171.* Hrs: 5-10:30 pm. Closed Jan 1, Thanksgiving, Dec 25; also Sun in summer. Res required. French menu. Bar to 2 am. A la carte entrees: dinner $19.50-$32. Child's meals. Specialties: Dover sole, warm shiitake mush-

room salad, foie gras. Valet parking. Split-level bistro dining. Art by Philip Standish Reed. Cr cds: A, D, MC, V.

✔★ ★ **CHUCK & HAROLD'S.** *207 Royal Poinciana Way. 561/659-1440.* Hrs: 7:30 am-midnight; Fri, Sat to 1 am; Sun from 8 am; early-bird dinner 4:30-6 pm. Res accepted. Continental menu. Bar 11:30-1 am. A la carte entrees: bkfst $2-$9.50, lunch $5.50-$12.50, dinner $13.75-$23. Child's meals. Specializes in fresh seafood of the day. Own pasta. Entertainment. Valet parking (dinner). Outdoor dining. Sidewalk cafe. Convertible roof allows for open-air dining. Cr cds: A, C, D, DS, MC, V.

★ ★ **DEMPSEY'S.** *50 Cocoanut Row. 561/835-0400.* Hrs: 11:30 am-11 pm; Sun brunch 10 am-2:30 pm. Bar. Semi-a la carte: lunch $4.50-$11, dinner $8-$22. Sun brunch $4.50-$7.95. Specialties: chicken hash Dempsey, shad roe. Valet parking. Some antiques; original artwork. Cr cds: A, MC, V.

★ ★ **E.R. BRADLEY'S SALOON.** *111 Bradley Place. 561/833-3520.* Hrs: 11-3 am; Sat, Sun from 10 am. Res accepted. Bar. Semi-a la carte: lunch $4.50-$7.50, dinner $7.95-$16.95. Sun brunch $4-$8.95. Child's meals. Specialties: grilled swordfish, sautéed chicken breast, steak. Outdoor dining. Cr cds: A, D, DS, MC, V.

★ ★ ★ **THE FLORENTINE DINING ROOM.** *(See The Breakers Resort) 561/659-8480.* Web www.thebreakers.com. Hrs: 6:30-10:30 pm. Res required. Mediterranean menu. Bar to 2 am. Wine list. Semi-a la carte: dinner $25-$34. Serv charge 18%. Child's meals. Specialties: herbs of Provence crusted rack of lamb, truffled piccata of veal tenderloin, sautéed Mediterranean swordfish steak. Musicians. Valet parking. Hand-carved mahogany bar, Steinway grand piano, 15th-century Flemish tapestry and twelve crystal chandeliers add to elegance of this large dining rm with frescoed ceilings. Jacket. Cr cds: A, C, D, DS, ER, JCB, MC, V.

★ ★ **GALAXY GRILLE.** *350 S County Rd. 561/833-9909.* Hrs: 11:30 am-3:30 pm, 5:30-11 pm; Sun from 5:30 pm; early-bird dinner Sun-Thurs 5:30-7 pm. Closed Dec 25. Res accepted. Bar. Semi-a la carte: lunch $4.95-$9.95, dinner $16.95-$26.95. Specializes in grilled seafood, rotisserie. Valet parking. Cr cds: A, C, D, MC, V.

✔★ **HAMBURGER HEAVEN.** *314 S County Rd. 561/655-5277.* Hrs: 7:30 am-8 pm; May-Oct to 4 pm. Closed Sun; some major hols. Semi-a la carte: bkfst $1.75-$4.75, lunch $3.50-$10, dinner $8.75-$12.95. Specialties: roast turkey, lemon coconut cake. Own soups. No cr cds accepted.

★ ★ ★ **JANEIRO.** *191 Bradley Place. 561/659-5223.* Web www.menusonline.com. Hrs: 6-10 pm; Fri, Sat to midnight. Closed most major hols; summer. Res required Fri, Sat. French menu. Bar. Wine list. A la carte entrees: dinner $28-$40. Specialties: striped bass painted with caviar & lobster sauce; lemon sole fillets woven with tri-color tomato, black squid, and spinach lasagna noodles. Own desserts. Valet parking. Eclectic design and atmosphere; Art deco posters. Jacket required. Totally non-smoking. Cr cds: A, D, MC, V.

★ ★ **THE LEOPARD ROOM.** *(See Chesterfield Hotel) 561/659-5800.* Hrs: 7-10:30 am, 11 am-2:30 pm, 6-11 pm. Res accepted. Continental menu. Bar 11-1 am. A la carte entrees: bkfst $6-$14, lunch $8-$18, dinner $18.95-$40. Specialties: rack of lamb, veal saltimbocca. Pianist. Valet parking. Outdoor dining. Jacket (dinner). Cr cds: A, C, D, DS, ER, MC, V.

★ ★ ★ **RENATO'S.** *87 Via Mizner. 561/655-9752.* Hrs: 11:30 am-3 pm, 6-10:30 pm; Sun from 6 pm. Res accepted. French, Italian menu. Bar. A la carte entrees: lunch $11.50-$18, dinner $19-$28. Child's meals. Specialties: scampi alla griglia, penne alla Caprese, snapper alla Livornese. Pianist exc Mon. Valet parking (dinner). Outdoor dining. Elegant country French atmosphere. Cr cds: A, C, D, DS, MC, V.

D ⊶

★ ★ ★ **THE RESTAURANT.** *(See The Ritz-Carlton, Palm Beach Hotel) 561/533-6000.* Elegant decor features hand-strung crystal chandeliers and museum-quality works of art. The dining room overlooks the Atlantic Ocean. Continental menu. Hrs: 6 am-10 pm; Sun brunch 10:30 am-3:30 pm. Res required. Bar. Extensive wine list. A la carte entrees: bkfst $10-$15, lunch $8.50-$18, dinner $18-$28. Sun brunch $41. Child's meals. Pianist. Valet parking. Cr cds: A, C, D, DS, ER, JCB, MC, V.

D ⊶ ♥

★ ★ ★ **THE RESTAURANT AT FOUR SEASONS.** *(See The Four Seasons Hotel) 561/582-2800.* Web www.fshr.com. Trend-setting cuisine is based on the history and heritage of the Southeast, and a garden on the premises provides fresh fruits and herbs. The dining area overlooks pool and ocean. Southeast regional menu. Specialties: Indian River blue crab, guava-braised short ribs of beef, yellow-tail snapper. Hrs: 6-10:30 pm. Closed Mon, Tues, late May-Nov. Res required. Bar. Extensive wine list. A la carte entrees: dinner $24-$39. Pianist. Valet parking. Jacket. Cr cds: A, C, D, DS, JCB, MC, V.

D ⊶ ♥

★ ★ **SEAFOOD BAR.** *(See Breakers Resort) 561/655-6611.* Web www.thebreakers.com. Hrs: 11-1 am. Closed Tues June-Aug. Res accepted. Seafood menu. Bar. A la carte entrees: lunch, dinner $19-$28. Specializes in fresh seafood. Pianist Thurs-Sat. Valet parking. Oceanfront raw bar designed after plantation homes of "Old Florida." Cr cds: A, C, D, DS, ER, JCB, MC, V.

D ⊶

★ ★ **TA-BOO.** *221 Worth Ave. 561/835-3500.* Hrs: 11:30 am-11 pm; Fri to midnight. Res accepted. Continental menu. Bar. Semi-a la carte: lunch $7.95-$13.95, dinner $14-$24. Specialties: veal Milanaise, roasted rack of lamb Dijonaise, Dover sole Meuniere. Pianist; entertainment Fri, Sat. Valet parking after 6 pm. Five distinct dining areas ranging from informal to formal. Cr cds: A, D, MC, V.

D ⊶ ♥

★ ★ **TESTA'S.** *221 Royal Poinciana Way. 561/832-0992.* Web www.pbol.com. Hrs: 7 am-midnight; early-bird dinner 4-6 pm; Sun brunch 11 am-2:30 pm. Closed Thanksgiving. Res accepted. Italian, Amer menu. Bar from 9 am. Semi-a la carte: bkfst $2.75-$6, lunch $4.50-$10, dinner $10.75-$21.95. Sun brunch $16.95. Child's meals. Specializes in steak, seafood. Valet parking. Outdoor dining. Three individually decorated dining areas. Family-owned since 1921. Cr cds: A, C, D, DS, MC, V.

D ⊶

★ **TOO JAY'S.** *313 Royal Poinciana Plaza, in shopping center. 561/659-7232.* Hrs: 8 am-8 pm. Closed Thanksgiving, Dec 25. Wine, beer. Semi-a la carte: bkfst $1.60-$6.95, lunch $5.50-$8.50, dinner $5.50-$10.50. Child's meals. Specialties: chicken stir-fry, stuffed cabbage. Informal atmosphere. Cr cds: A, C, D, MC, V.

D

Panama City (K-3)

(See also Panama City Beach)

Pop 34,378 **Elev** 29 ft **Area code** 850 **E-mail** info@panamacity.org **Web** www.panamacity.org
Information Bay County Chamber of Commerce, PO Box 1850, 32402; 850/785-5206 or 888/229-7483.

On the cooler northwest panhandle area of the state, this is a popular destination for vacationers and retirees. Panama City is known for its stretches of beautiful nearby beach and is considered one of the best fishing centers in the state. To the west, along the Gulf, are 23 miles of white sand for swimming, fishing and relaxing. With a deepwater harbor, the city also ranks as an important coastal port. Boating is possible in the Gulf, the Intracoastal Waterway and several protected bays, and there are a number of public boat ramps and marinas. Carefully nurtured forests are harvested to supply the city's paper and pulp mill.

What to See and Do

Deer Point Dam. Impounds 5,000-acre stocked lake. Fishing for both salt and freshwater fish from same spot; public boat ramp. 8 mi NE on FL 77A.

Junior Museum of Bay County. Exhibits include reconstructed log cabin with period furnishings, grist and cane mill; changing art & science exhibits. Nature trail through swamp on elevated walkway. (Daily exc Sun; closed hols) 1731 Jenks Ave. Phone 850/769-6128.   **Free.**

Annual Events

Spring Festival of the Arts. McKenzie Park.Entertainment, food, art activities for children, crafts displays. 2 days early May.

Open Spearfishing Tournament. Tyndall Air Force Base. Aug.

Bay County Fair. Fairgrounds. Early Oct.

Motel

★ ★ **COMFORT INN.** *1013 E 23rd St (32405). 850/769-6969; FAX 850/763-4353.* 105 rms, 2 story. May-Sept: S, D $69-$75; each addl $6; under 18 free; higher rates: hols, special events; lower rates rest of yr. Crib free. TV; cable (premium). Pool. Complimentary continental bkfst. Ck-out noon. Coin lndry. Meeting rm. Business servs avail. In-rm modem link. Exercise equipt. Cr cds: A, C, D, DS, ER, JCB, MC, V.

D ≈ 🏃 🚭 🗙 SC

Motor Hotel

★ ★ ★ **HOLIDAY INN SELECT.** *2001 N Cove Blvd (32405). 850/769-0000; FAX 850/763-3828.* E-mail holidayinnsel@panama city.com. 173 rms, 6 story. S, D $85-$95; each addl $7; under 19 free. Crib free. TV; cable (premium). Indoor pool; whirlpool. Complimentary coffee in rms. Restaurant 6 am-2 pm, 5:30-10 pm. Rm serv 6 am-10:30 pm. Bar 3:30 pm-1 am. Ck-out noon. Meeting rms. Business servs avail. In-rm modem link. Bellhops. Free airport transportation. Exercise equipt; sauna. Bathrm phones; microwaves avail. Cr cds: A, C, D, DS, JCB, MC, V.

D ≈ 🏃 🚭 🚭 SC

Restaurants

★ **JP'S FOOD & BREW.** *4701 US 98W (32401). 850/769-3711.* Hrs: 11 am-11 pm. Closed Sun; major hols. Res accepted. Italian, Southwestern menu. Bar. Semi-a la carte: lunch $3.99-$6.99, dinner

$7.99-$15.99. Child's meals. Specializes in sautéed seafood, homemade pastas, hand-cut steak. Cr cds: A, C, D, DS, MC, V.

D ⬛

★ **UNCLE ERNIE'S BAYFRONT GRILL AND BRE-WHOUSE.** *1151 Bayview Ave (32401), at St Andrews Marina.* 850/763-8427. Hrs: 11 am-10:30 pm. Closed Sun; most major hols. Bar. Semi-a la carte: lunch $4.99-$6.95, dinner $4.99-$15.99. Child's meals. Specializes in seafood, steak, pasta. Own beer. Outdoor dining with view of bay. Key West atmosphere. Boat docking avail. Cr cds: A, D, DS, MC, V.

D ⬛

Panama City Beach (K-3)

(See also Panama City)

Pop 4,051 **Area code** 850 **Zip** 32407 **E-mail** pcb@interoz.com **Web** www.panamacitybeachfl.com
Information Convention & Visitors Bureau, PO Box 9473; 850/233-6503 or 800/722-3224.

What to See and Do

Fishing. County Pier, 5 mi W on US 98A. **Panama City Beach City Pier**, 8 mi W on US 98A, a 1600-ft pier (fee). Party and charter boats (inquire locally). Artificial reefs in Gulf. **Dead Lakes State Recreation Area**, 30 mi E on FL 22, then N on FL 71, has excellent fishing for bass, bream and perch; boating; camping. **St Andrews State Recreation Area** (see) has a 450-ft pier. Also fishing from several other piers and bridges.

Gulf World. Sea lion and dolphin shows; dolphin & stingray petting pools; performing parrot show; shark/sea turtle channel; penguins; scuba demonstration. Also tropical gardens. (Feb-Oct, daily) On US 98A, 3 mi E of jct FL 79 at 15412 Front Beach Rd. Phone 850/234-5271. ¢¢¢¢

Miracle Strip Amusement Park. Rides; concessions; arcade. (Memorial Day-Labor Day, daily; mid-Mar-mid-May, Fri-Sat) 5 mi W on US 98A. Phone 850/234-5810 or 800/538-7395. ¢¢¢¢¢   Opp is

Shipwreck Island. Water sports park with a tropical island theme. Unique giant shipwreck. Wave pool, tube ride; Skull Island. (June-Labor Day, daily; Apr, May & early Sept, Sat) On W US 98A. Phone 850/234-0368. ¢¢¢¢¢

Shell Island Trips. Three-hr sightseeing trip; also dinner cruises (June-Labor Day) & fishing and trolling boats. Shell Island trip (Apr-Oct, two trips daily; Feb & Mar, one trip daily; no trips Nov-Jan). Capt Anderson's Marina, Thomas Dr at Grand Lagoon. Phone 850/234-3435. ¢¢¢-¢¢¢¢¢

St Andrews State Recreation Area. A 1,063-acre point of land between Gulf of Mexico and St Andrews Bay with dunes, white sand beaches. Swimming, skin and scuba diving; fishing in surf and from pier & jetties; boating (ramp, dock). Nature trails, guided tours. Picnicking, concession. Camping (dump station). Interpretive center. Standard hrs, fees. 3 mi E, off US 98 at end of FL 3031. Phone 850/233-5140.

Annual Events

Bay Point Billfish Tournament. Mid-late July.

Treasure Island King Mackerel Tournament. Treasure Island Marina. Phone 850/234-6533. Late Sept.

Indian Summer Seafood Festival. 2nd wkend Oct.

Seasonal Event

Greyhound racing. Ebro Greyhound Track. 15 mi N on FL 79 in Ebro. Parimutuels. Trackside dining. Nightly exc Sun & some Tues; matinee Sat & some Wed. Children only with parent. Phone 904/234-3943. Early Mar-early Sept.

Motels

★ **BEST WESTERN DEL CORONADO.** *11815 Front Beach Rd.* 850/234-1600; res: 800/633-0266. 106 rms, 2-3 story. May-Labor Day: S $59-$129; D $79-$139; each addl $10; suites $119-$169; under 12 free; lower rates rest of yr. Crib free. TV; cable. Pool. Restaurant adj 7 am-11 pm. Ck-out 11 am. Business servs avail. Some refrigerators, microwaves. Cr cds: A, C, D, DS, JCB, MC, V.

D ⬛ ⬛ ⬛ SC

★ **BIKINI BEACH RESORT.** *11001 Front Beach Rd.* 850/234-3392; FAX 850/233-2921; res: 800/451-5307. 85 rms, 2-5 story, 67 kit. units. Mar-mid-Apr, mid-May-mid-Sept: S $68.50; D $98.50; suites $125.50; kits. $98.50; higher rates: hols, special events; lower rates rest of yr. Crib free. TV; cable. Pool; poolside serv. Complimentary coffee in lobby. Restaurant adj 10-4 am. Bar 10 am-midnight. Ck-out 11 am. Coin Indry. Meeting rm. Business servs avail. Sundries. Game rm. Lawn games. Balconies. Picnic tables, grills. On beach. Cr cds: A, C, D, DS, MC, V.

D ⬛ ⬛

★ **INN AT ST THOMAS SQUARE.** *8730 Thomas Dr (32408).* 850/234-0349; res: 800/874-8600. E-mail basicmgt@beaches.net. 62 kit. suites, 3 story. Memorial Day-Labor Day: studio $60; efficiency $85; 1-bedrm suites $107; 2-bedrm suites $135; 3-bedrm suites $165; lower rates rest of yr. Crib free. TV; cable. Pool; whirlpool. Sauna. Complimentary coffee in lobby. Restaurant nearby. Ck-out 11 am. Business servs avail. Lighted tennis. Refrigerators; microwaves avail. Many private patios, balconies. On lagoon; dockage. Cr cds: A, C, D, DS, MC, V.

⬛ ⬛ ⬛

★ **PALMETTO.** *17255 Front Beach Rd (32413).* 850/234-2121. 85 units, 2 story, 31 suites, 30 kits. Mid May-Labor Day: S, D $90; each addl $10; suites $114-$160; kits. $92-$118; 3-day min summer months; lower rates rest of yr. Crib free. TV; cable (premium). 2 pools, 1 indoor; wading pool, poolside serv, lifeguard. Complimentary coffee in rms. Restaurant nearby. Ck-out 10:30 am. Coin Indry. Business servs avail. Airport transportation. Game rm. Refrigerators; microwaves avail. Balconies. Picnic tables. Swimming beach. Cr cds: DS, MC, V.

D ⬛ ⬛ ⬛

★ **SHALIMAR PLAZA.** *17545 Front Beach Rd (32413).* 850/234-2133; res: 800/232-2435. 74 units, 3 story, 65 kit units. No elvtr. 1-rm kit. units $49-$89; 2-rm kit. units $69-$180; each addl $5. Crib $5. TV; cable. Heated pool. Restaurant adj 6 am-10 pm. Ck-out 10 am. Business servs avail. Many private patios, balconies. Picnic tables, grills. On Gulf. Cr cds: A, DS, MC, V.

D ⬛ ⬛

Motor Hotels

★ ★ **DAYS INN BEACH.** *12818 Front Beach Rd.* 850/233-3333; FAX 850/233-9568. Web www.daysinn.com. 188 rms, 7 story, 30 kit. units. Mar-Aug: S, D $129-$169; each addl (after 4th person) $10; kits. $129-$169; higher rates: hols, special events; lower rates rest of yr. Crib free. TV; cable (premium). Pool; whirlpool, poolside serv. Bar. Ck-out 11 am. Business servs avail. Sundries. 18-hole golf privileges, putting green, driving range. Health club privileges. Microwaves avail. Balconies. On beach. Cr cds: A, C, D, DS, MC, V.

D ⬛ ⬛ ⬛ ⬛ SC

★ ★ **EDGEWATER BEACH RESORT.** *11212 Front Beach Rd.* 850/235-4044; FAX 850/233-7529; res: 800/874-8686. 478 kit. units, 2-12 story; 163 kit. villas, 1-2 story. Kit. units, villas $108-$368. Crib $5. TV; cable (premium). VCR avail. Pools. Restaurant 7 am-10 pm. Bar. Ck-out 10 am. Lndry facilities. Convention facilities. Business servs avail. Sundries. Lighted tennis, pro. 9- & 18-hole golf, pro, greens fee $65, putting green. Entertainment. Lawn games. Microwaves. Private patios, balconies. Picnic tables. On beach. Cr cds: D, DS, MC, V.

⬛ ⬛ ⬛ ⬛ ⬛

Hotel

★ ★ ★ **HOLIDAY INN SUNSPREE RESORT.** *11127 Front Beach Rd. 850/234-1111; FAX 850/235-1907; res: 800/633-0266.* Web www.paradisefound.com. 340 rms, 15 story. Mar-Sept: S, D $109-$299; each addl $10; suites $750-$1,000; under 19 free; higher rates hols; lower rates rest of yr. Crib free. TV; cable (premium). Pool; whirlpool, poolside serv. Supervised child's activities (Apr-Aug); ages 4-12. Complimentary coffee in rms. Restaurant 7 am-10 pm. Bar from 11 am. Ck-out 11 am. Coin lndry. Meeting rms. Business servs avail. In-rm modem link. Gift shop. 18-hole golf privileges, putting green, driving range. Exercise equipt; sauna. Game rm. Refrigerators; microwaves avail. Wet bar in suites. Balconies. Picnic tables. On beach. Cr cds: A, C, D, DS, JCB, MC, V.

Resort

★ ★ ★ **MARRIOTT'S BAY POINT.** *4200 Marriott Dr (32408). 850/234-3307; FAX 850/233-1308.* 355 rms. Mar-Oct: S, D $119-$139; each addl $20; suites $149-$179; under 18 free; lower rates rest of yr. Crib free. TV; cable (premium). 4 pools, 1 indoor; wading pool, whirlpool, poolside serv. Playground. Supervised child's activities (Mar-Aug); ages 5-12. Coffee in rms. Dining rm 6:30 am-10 pm. Rm serv to 11:30 pm. Box lunches. Snack bar. Picnics. Bars 11 am-midnight; entertainment. Ck-out 11 am, ck-in 4 pm. Grocery. Coin lndry. Convention facilities. In-rm modem link. Valet serv. Airport transportation. Lighted tennis, pro. 36-hole golf, pro, greens fee, putting green, driving range. Marina. Waterskiing. Scuba diving. Sailboats, windsurfers. Deep sea fishing. Bicycle rentals. Lawn games. Game rm. Exercise equipt; sauna, steam rm. Some refrigerators; microwaves avail. Private patios, balconies. Extensive grounds. Cr cds: A, C, D, DS, JCB, MC, V.

Restaurants

★ ★ **BOAR'S HEAD.** *17290 Front Beach Rd (US 98A). 850/234-6628.* Hrs: 4:30-10 pm; off-season to 9 pm. Closed Thanksgiving. Bar. Semi-a la carte: dinner $10.95-$24. Child's meals. Specializes in beef, pork, seafood. Own desserts. Entertainment wkends, 5 days in season. Parking. Old English tavern decor; fireplaces, stuffed boar's head at entrance. Cr cds: A, C, D, DS, MC, V.

✔★ **CAJUN INN.** *477 Beckrich Rd, in the Shoppes at Edgewater. 850/235-9987.* Hrs: 11 am-10 pm. Closed Thanksgiving, Dec 24, 25. Cajun, creole menu. Wine, beer. Semi-a la carte: lunch $4.95-$5.25, dinner $7.95-$14.95. Child's meals. Specialties: blackened fish, red beans & rice, crawfish etoufée. Parking. Outdoor dining. Hand-crafted wooden booths. Cr cds: A, DS, MC, V.

★ ★ **CAPT ANDERSON'S.** *5551 N Lagoon Dr (32408), at Thomas Dr on Grand Lagoon. 850/234-2225.* E-mail captander@aol.com; web www.captanderson.com. Hrs: 4-10 pm. Closed Sun; also Nov-Jan. Bars. Semi-a la carte: dinner $10.95-$34.95. Child's meals. Specialties: charcoal-broiled fish, grilled shrimp, Greek salad. Own baking. Parking. Nautical decor; overlooks waterfront. Family-owned. Cr cds: A, C, D, DS, MC, V.

★ ★ **HAMILTON'S.** *5711 N Lagoon Dr (32408). 850/234-1255.* Hrs: 5-10 pm; summer from 4 pm. Continental menu. Bar. Semi-a la carte: dinner $10.95-$22.95. Child's meals. Specializes in seafood, pasta, mesquite-grilled dishes. Parking. Victorian decor. Overlooks Grand Lagoon. Cr cds: A, DS, MC, V.

✔★ **SWEET BASIL'S.** *11208 Front Beach Rd, in the Shoppes at Edgewater. 850/234-2855.* Hrs: 11 am-10 pm; off-season to 9 pm. Closed wks of Thanksgiving, Dec 25. Italian menu. Bar. Semi-a la carte: lunch $4.95-$6.95, dinner $6.95-$12.95. Child's meals. Specializes in pasta, pizza. Parking. Family dining. Cr cds: A, D, DS, MC, V.

★ **TREASURE SHIP.** *3605 S Thomas Dr (32408), on Grand Lagoon. 850/234-8881.* E-mail tship@interoz.com; web www.interoz. com/treasure.htm. Hrs: 4-10 pm; early-bird dinner 4-5 pm. Bar to 2 am. Semi-a la carte: dinner $9.95-$22.95. Child's meals. Specializes in steak, seafood. Entertainment. Parking. Gift shop. Dining in replica of 16th-century Spanish galleon with views of marina. Cr cds: A, C, D, DS, MC, V.

Unrated Dining Spot

ALL AMERICAN DINER. *10590 W US 98 (10590). 850/235-2443.* Hrs: Open 24 hrs. Semi-a la carte: bkfst $2-$4.95, lunch $3.50, dinner $4.95-$12.95. Child's meals. Specializes in hamburgers, omelets. Salad bar. Parking. 1950s-style diner. No cr cds accepted.

Pensacola (J-1)

(See also Fort Walton Beach; also see Mobile, AL)

Settled 1723 **Pop** 58,165 **Elev** 11 ft **Area code** 850 **Web** www.visitpensacola.com
Information Convention & Visitors Bureau, 1401 E Gregory St, 32501; 850/434-1234 or 800/874-1234.

Pensacola is the Old South blended with a bit of modern Florida and a generous dash of Colonial Spain. With its balconies and jutting balustrades, the city clings to the past—a rich brew of 400 years of history under five flags. Pensacola Bay, the largest, natural, landlocked deep-water harbor in Florida, has been the key to the city's history and development. The Spanish established a settlement here in 1559, which lasted only two years. However, in 1698 they reestablished the site and built a fort. After three battles in 1719, the French took over, but Spain returned in 1723. The British flew their flag in 1763, until Spain returned again in 1781. Andrew Jackson led invasions of this Spanish city in 1814 and 1818, and in 1821 returned to accept Florida as a US territory. During the Civil War, it was captured by Union troops and served as a base for the Union blockade of the Confederate Gulf Coast.

After an extensive study, in 1914 the Navy chose Pensacola as a site for its Naval Air Station—because there were more clear days for flying than at any other available place. Since then, the station has been a major factor in the city's personality and its economy. Today, Pensacola also is host to large chemical and nylon plants, pulp and paper mills, wallboard and plywood factories.

Pensacola is the gateway to "the miracle strip," 100 miles of beach-fringed peninsulas and islands stretching to Panama City, and heavily populated by sun worshipers and sports fishermen. Pensacola Beach, to the east, and Perdido Key, to the west, are primarily resort communities. Beaches on both Santa Rosa Sound (Intracoastal Waterway) and the Gulf of Mexico circle the island.

What to See and Do

Fishing. Pensacola Beach Pier, Pensacola Beach (fee). Pensacola Bay Pier, Wayside Park (fee). Charter boats for big game fishing in Gulf at Pensacola Beach, Bayou Chico and marinas on Gulf Beach Hwy (FL 292).

Greyhound racing. Pensacola Greyhound Track. (Tues, Wed, Fri and Sat evenings) 951 Dog Track Rd, off US 98. Phone 850/455-8595. General admission ¢

Gulf Islands National Seashore. The 1,742 acres include old Ft Pickens (1834), one of largest masonry forts in US, where Geronimo was imprisoned; concrete batteries; tours (daily). Swimming, scuba diving; fishing. Picnicking. Camping (fee). Bookstore, museum with historical & maritime exhibits. No pets on beach or in historic fortifications. Santa Rosa area includes beach with pavilion; swimming, picnicking. Golden Eagle, Golden Age & Golden Access Passport (see MAKING THE MOST OF YOUR TRIP). S on US 98 and FL 399 to Pensacola Beach, then W on Ft Pickens Rd to Ft Pickens Area or E on FL 399 to Santa Rosa Area. Phone 850/934-2600. Per car (Ft Pickens area) **¢¢**

Other areas of the national seashore include Fort Barrancas and other historic fortifications at Naval Air Station; nearly 1,400 acres of forests with picnicking and nature trails, visitors center; at Naval Live Oaks off US 98, E of Gulf Breeze; beach recreation at Perdido Key, SW on FL 292; and picnic and beach areas at Okaloosa area, E of Fort Walton Beach. Contact Superintendent, Gulf Islands National Seashore, 1801 Gulf Breeze Pkwy, Gulf Breeze 32561; 850/934-2600.

Historic Pensacola Village. Historic park contains village buildings (daily exc Sun; closed Jan 1, Thanksgiving, Dec 25). All buildings are included in admission price. Seville Square, E Government & S Alcaniz Sts. Phone 850/444-8905. Admission **¢¢¢** Buildings include

T.T. Wentworth Jr, Florida State Museum. Exhibits on west Florida history, art, architecture and archaeology; Discovery Gallery for children. Guided tours avail. Jefferson & Zaragoza Sts.

Museum of Industry—Museum of Commerce. Converted warehouses contain exhibits depicting Gulf Coast history. 200 E Zaragoza St.

Charles LaValle House (1805). One of the oldest houses in Pensacola; apron roof and plastered interior are typical of French Creole architecture. 205 E Church St.

Dorr House (1871). Post-Civil War classical-revival house; restored with antiques of mid-Victorian era. 311 S Adams St, at Church St.

Quina House. Pre-Civil War house (1825-1860) with period furnishings. 204 S Alcaniz St.

Naval Air Station Pensacola. Home of naval aviation and headquarters for the Naval Education and Training Command. Established first as the Navy Yard in 1826, the easy access to the sea made it a prime site for the construction of wooden ships. Confederate troops retreating from the Navy Yard in 1862 reduced most of the facilities to rubble. Rebuilding began but was destroyed by a great hurricane in 1906; construction was brought to a standstill once again two yrs later by a yellow fever epidemic. Re-opened in 1914 as the first Naval Aeronautic Station, steady growth has produced such additions to the station as the Naval Aviation Depot and many other tenant commands. **Sherman Field** is home of the world-famous precision flying Blue Angels, the Navy's flight demonstration squadron. Phone 850/452-2311. **Free.** Of interest here are

National Museum of Naval Aviation. One of the largest of its kind, this museum features more than 100 historically significant aircraft on display, including the A-1 "Triad," the Navy's first bi-plane, the NC-4 Flying Boat, the first plane to cross the Atlantic, a vintage 1930s Marine Corp fighter, four A-4 Skyhawks (Blue Angels) suspended in a diamond formation and full-size modern-day jets. Museum traces history of naval aviation from dawn of flight to space exploration; naval aviation and space memorabilia; hands-on childrens exhibits; aviation art & photography. Also here is an IMAX theater (fee) and the Naval Aviation Hall of Honor. Gift shop, book store. (Daily; closed Jan 1, Thanksgiving, Dec 25) Phone 800/327-5002. **Free.**

Fort Barrancas (1839-1844). On the site of 18th-century Spanish fortifications, the historic fort and its attached Water Battery, a 19th-century American fort, have been authentically restored and preserved from old drawings, photos, prints and documents from the National Archives. Now part of Gulf Islands National Seashore, the area comprises 65 acres in the middle of the Naval Air Station; approx 40 acres of pine and oak forest; visitor center. Tours avail. Phone 850/455-5167. **Free.**

Old Pensacola Lighthouse (1825). This 176-ft structure is fully automated and remote-controlled from Santa Rosa Island. Owned by the Coast Guard; not open to public.

Pensacola Museum of Art. Housed in the old city jail, the museum has changing art exhibits; library, lectures. (Tues-Sat, Sun afternoons; closed hols) 407 S Jefferson St. Phone 850/432-6247. **¢**

Scenic drive. North via Scenic Hwy (US 90) through Gull Point and east around Escambia Bay; provides bluffs and beach views.

Skin diving and scuba diving. Boats can take divers to the wreck of battleship *Massachusetts*, Russian freighter *San Pablo*, and other spots. Contact the Convention & Visitors Bureau.

St Michael's Cemetery. In use since 1780s; many graves of Spanish settlers. Garden & Alcaniz Sts.

The Zoo. A 50-acre zoo and botanical garden with more than 600 animals including one of the largest lowland gorillas in captivity. Giraffe feeding; petting zoo. Train ride. (Daily; closed Thanksgiving, Dec 25) 15 mi E on US 98, at 5701 Gulf Breeze Pkwy in Gulf Breeze. Phone 850/932-2229. **¢¢¢**

Annual Events

Mardi Gras. Five days of street dances, parades and musical events. 5 days prior to Ash Wed.

SpringFest. May.

Fiesta of the Five Flags. Pageant, parades, waterskiing show, races, sports events. June.

Blue Angels Air Show. US Navy's world-renowned precision flight demonstration team performs; also parachuting and static displays of military and civilian aircraft. July & Nov.

Seafood Festival. Sept.

Pensacola Interstate Fair. Mid-Oct.

Great Gulfcoast Arts Festival. Music, drama; art shows, children's programs. Early Nov.

Motels

★ ★ **BEST WESTERN VILLAGE INN.** *8240 N Davis Hwy (32514), near West Florida Medical Center.* 850/479-1099; FAX 850/479-9320. 142 rms, 3 story, 46 kit. suites. S, D $54-$97. TV; cable (premium). Pool. Complimentary continental bkfst. Restaurant nearby. Ck-out noon. Business servs avail. In-rm modem link. Health club privileges. Refrigerators; microwaves avail. Balconies. Courtyards with walkways. Cr cds: A, C, D, DS, MC, V.

D ⊇ ⋈ 🐾 SC

★ **COMFORT INN & CONFERENCE CENTER.** *(8700 Navarre Pkwy, Navarre 32566)* E on US 98. 850/939-1761; FAX 850/939-2084. 63 rms, 2 story, 6 suites. June-early Sept: S, D $89; each addl $8; suites $103; under 18 free; golf plans; lower rates rest of yr. Crib avail. TV; cable (premium). Pool. Complimentary continental bkfst. Restaurant nearby. Ck-out 11 am. Coin lndry. Business servs avail. Microwaves avail. Refrigerator in suites. Picnic tables. Cr cds: A, C, D, DS, ER, JCB, MC, V.

D ⊇ ⋈ 🐾 SC

★ **COMFORT INN NAS-CORRY.** *3 New Warrington Rd (32506).* 850/455-3233; FAX 850/453-3445. 101 rms, 3 story. S, D $67.50-$75; each addl $6; under 18 free. Crib free. TV; cable. Pool. Coffee in rms. Complimentary continental bkfst. Coffee in rms. Restaurant nearby. Ck-out noon. Coin lndry. Meeting rm. Business servs avail. Many refrigerators, microwaves. Near Pensacola Naval Air Station. Cr cds: A, D, DS, MC, V.

D ⊇ ⋈ 🐾 SC

★ ★ **FAIRFIELD INN BY MARRIOTT.** *7325 N Davis Hwy (32514),* I-10 exit 5. 850/484-8001; FAX 850/484-6008. 63 rms, 3 story. S $59-$67; D $65-$72; suites $67-$72; under 18 free. Crib free. TV; cable (premium). Complimentary continental bkfst. Restaurant adj open 24 hrs. Ck-out noon. In-rm modem link. Valet serv. Indoor pool. Some refrigerators, microwaves. Cr cds: A, C, D, DS, MC, V.

D ⊇ ⋈ 🐾 SC

✔★ ★ **HAMPTON INN.** *7330 Plantation Rd (32504),* at University Mall. 850/477-3333; FAX 850/477-8163. 124 rms, 3 story. S $69; D $79; under 18 free. Crib free. TV; cable (premium). Pool privileges. Complimentary continental bkfst. Coffee in rms. Ck-out noon. Business servs avail.

In-rm modem link. Free airport transportation. Health club privileges. Cr cds: A, C, D, DS, JCB, MC, V.

[D] [icons] [SC]

★ **HOLIDAY INN BAY BEACH.** (51 Gulf Breeze Pkwy, Gulf Breeze 32561) S on US 98, at Pensacola Bay Bridge. 850/932-2214; FAX 850/932-0932. 168 rms, 2 story. May-Sept: S $75-$115; D $85-$125; each addl $15; under 18 free; lower rates rest of yr. Crib free. Pet accepted. TV; cable (premium). Pool; wading pool. Coffee in rms. Restaurant 6 am-3 pm, 5-10 pm. Ck-out noon. Coin lndry. Meeting rms. Business servs avail. In-rm modem link. Health club privileges. Some refrigerators, microwaves. On Pensacola Bay; opp fishing pier. Cr cds: A, C, D, DS, ER, JCB, MC, V.

[D] [icons] [SC]

✔ ★ **HOLIDAY INN EXPRESS.** 6501 Pensacola Blvd (32505). 850/476-7200; FAX 850/476-1277. 214 rms, 2 story. Mar-Sept: S, D $65-$75; under 18 free; golf plans; higher rates major hols; lower rates rest of yr. Crib free. TV; cable (premium). Pool. Complimentary continental bkfst. Coffee in rms. Restaurant nearby. Ck-out noon. Coin lndry. Meeting rms. Business servs avail. In-rm modem link. Exercise equipt. Microwaves avail. Cr cds: A, C, D, DS, ER, JCB, MC, V.

[D] [icons] [SC]

★ ★ **HOLIDAY INN-UNIVERSITY MALL.** 7200 Plantation Rd (32504), at University Mall. 850/474-0100; FAX 850/477-9821. 152 rms, 2 story. S $85; D $95; each addl $6; under 18 free. Crib free. TV; cable (premium). Pool. Restaurant 6 am-10 pm. Bar from 4 pm. Ck-out noon. Coin lndry. Meeting rms. Business servs avail. In-rm modem link. Bellhops. Valet serv. Free airport transportation. Health club privileges. Cr cds: A, C, D, DS, ER, MC, V.

[D] [icons] [SC]

★ **LA QUINTA.** 7750 N Davis Hwy (32514). 850/474-0411; FAX 850/474-1521. 130 rms, 3 story. S $69-$79; D $69-$89; each addl $10; suites $125; under 18 free. Crib free. TV; cable (premium). Pool. Complimentary continental bkfst. Coffee in rms. Restaurant adj open 24 hrs. Ck-out noon. Business servs avail. Microwaves avail. Cr cds: A, C, D, DS, MC, V.

[D] [icons] [SC]

★ ★ **RAMADA INN BAYVIEW.** 7601 Scenic Hwy (32504). 850/477-7155. 150 rms, 2 story. May-Aug: S, D $78; each addl $6; under 18 free; hols (3-day min); lower rates rest of yr. Crib free. Pet accepted, some restrictions. TV; cable. Complimentary coffee in rms. Restaurant 6 am-1 pm, 5-10 pm. Rm serv. Bar 5 pm-1 am; entertainment Tues-Sat. Ck-out noon. Meeting rms. Business servs avail. In-rm modem link. Valet serv. Exercise equipt; sauna. Pool. Some balconies. Cr cds: A, C, D, DS, JCB, MC, V.

[D] [icons] [SC]

✔ ★ **RED ROOF INN.** 7340 Plantation Rd (32504), at University Mall. 850/476-7960; FAX 850/479-4706. Web www.redroofinns.com. 108 rms, 2 story. S, D $49.99-$69.99; each addl $10; under 18 free. Crib free. Pet accepted. TV; cable. Complimentary coffee in lobby. Restaurant nearby. Ck-out noon. Business servs avail. Cr cds: A, C, D, DS, MC, V.

[D] [icons] [SC]

★ ★ **RESIDENCE INN BY MARRIOTT.** 7230 Plantation Rd (32504). 850/479-1000; FAX 850/477-3399. 64 kit. suites, 2 story. S, D $99-$135; wkly, wkend rates. Crib free. TV; cable (premium). Pool; whirlpool. Sauna. Complimentary continental bkfst. Restaurant adj 11-1 am. Ck-out noon. Meeting rms. Business servs avail. In-rm modem link. Sports court. Fireplaces, refrigerators, microwaves. Picnic tables, grills. Cr cds: A, C, D, DS, JCB, MC, V.

[icons] [SC]

✔ ★ **SUPER 8.** 7220 Plantation Rd (32504). 850/476-8038; FAX 850/474-6284. 62 rms, 3 story. Memorial Day-Labor Day: S $37.80-$47; D $39.60-$49; suites $65-$75; under 18 free; family rates; wkly rates; lower rates rest of yr. Crib $5. Pet accepted, some restrictions; $25. TV; cable.

Complimentary coffee in lobby. Restaurant nearby. Ck-out 11 am. Pool. Some refrigerators, microwaves. Cr cds: A, C, D, DS, MC, V.

[D] [icons] [SC]

Motor Hotels

✔ ★ **DAYS INN.** 710 N Palafox St (32501). 850/438-4922; FAX 850/438-7999. 150 rms, 3 story. S $49-$54; D $56-$63; each addl $5; under 12 free; higher rates: hols, special events. Crib free. TV; cable (premium). Pool. Restaurant 6 am-2 pm, 5-10 pm. Ck-out noon. Meeting rms. Business servs avail. Health club privileges. Cr cds: A, C, D, DS, MC, V.

[icons] [SC]

★ ★ **HOLIDAY INN.** 165 Ft Pickens Rd (32561). 850/932-5361; FAX 850/932-7121. 150 rms, 9 story. Easter-Labor Day: S, D $105-$140; each addl $10; under 18 free; wkends, hols (2-3 day min); lower rates rest of yr. Crib free. TV; cable (premium). Complimentary continental bkfst. Complimentary coffee in rms. Restaurant nearby. Bar 3 pm-midnight. Ck-out 11 am. Business servs avail. In-rm modem link. Valet serv. Gift shop. Coin lndry. Lighted tennis. Some refrigerators. Pool. Balconies. On beach. Cr cds: A, C, D, DS, JCB, MC, V.

[D] [icons] [SC]

Hotel

★ ★ ★ **PENSACOLA GRAND HOTEL.** 200 E Gregory St (32501). 850/433-3336; FAX 850/432-7572; res: 800/348-3336. 212 rms, 15 story. S, D $95-$120; each addl $10; suites $175-$408; family rates; package plans. Crib free. Pet accepted, some restrictions; $50. TV; cable (premium). Heated pool. Complimentary coffee in rms. Restaurant 6:30 am-2 pm, 5:30-9:30 pm. Bars 2 pm-2 am. Ck-out 1 pm. Meeting rms. Business servs avail. In-rm modem link. Shopping arcade. Free airport transportation. Exercise equipt. Lobby is restored 1912 Louisville & Nashville Railroad Depot. Cr cds: A, C, D, DS, MC, V.

[D] [icons] [SC]

Inn

★ ★ ★ **NEW WORLD.** 600 S Palafox (32501). 850/432-4111; FAX 850/432-6836. 15 rms, 2 story. S $70-$80; D $80-$85; each addl $10; suites $125; under 18 free. TV; cable (premium). Dining rm 11 am-1:30 pm; closed Sat, Sun. Bar from 5 pm. Ck-out noon, ck-in after 2 pm. Meeting rms. Business servs avail. Bathrm phones. Cr cds: A, MC, V.

[icon]

Restaurants

★ ★ **THE ANGUS.** 1101 Scenic Hwy (US 90E) (32503). 850/432-0539. Hrs: 5-10 pm; Fri, Sat to 11 pm. Closed Sun (exc Sun hols); Dec 25. Res accepted. Greek menu. Bar. Semi-a la carte: dinner $9.95-$34.95. Child's meals. Specializes in seafood, prime rib, steak. Parking. Cr cds: A, DS, MC, V.

[D] [icons]

★ **CHAN'S.** (2½ Via De Luna, Pensacola Beach 32561) S on US 98. 850/932-3525. Hrs: 11 am-11 pm; Fri, Sat to midnight; Sun brunch 10 am-2 pm. Res accepted. Bar. Semi-a la carte: lunch $5-$9, dinner $10-$18. Sun brunch $4.50-$8. Child's meals. Specializes in seafood, salads, pastas. Band Thurs-Sat. Parking. Outdoor dining. View of beach. Family-owned since 1979. Cr cds: A, C, D, DS, MC, V.

[D] [icon]

✔ ★ **CHRIS SEAFOOD GRILLE.** 810 E Gregory St (32501), I-10 exit 110. 850/438-7711. Hrs: 11 am-2 pm, 4-10 pm; Sun (brunch) 11 am-2 pm; early bird dinner 4-6 pm (seasonal). Closed Mon; Jan 1, Thanksgiving, Dec 25. Res accepted. Southwestern menu. Semi-a la carte: lunch, dinner $4.25-$16.95. Sun brunch $9.95. Child's meals. Specialties: Cajun seafood pasta, Greek-style catch, surf & turf combination. Parking. Totally nonsmoking. Cr cds: A, D, DS, MC, V.

✔★ **COFFEE CUP.** *520 E Cervantes St (US 90E) (32501).* *850/432-7060.* Hrs: 5:30 am-noon; Sat to 1 pm. Closed Dec 25. Semi-a la carte: bkfst $2-$4.90. Specializes in bkfst items. Parking. Old-style diner; antique bar stools. Totally nonsmoking. Cr cds: A, C, D, DS, MC, V.

★ **COWBOYS.** *(8673 US 98, Navarre 32566) 5 mi E on US 98.* *850/939-0502.* Hrs: 11 am-2 pm, 4:30-9 pm; Fri, Sat to 9:30 pm; Sun 10:30 am-9 pm. Closed Thanksgiving, Dec 25. Bar. Semi-a la carte: lunch $2.99-$19.99, dinner $5.99-$20.95. Sun brunch $10.95. Child's meals. Specializes in steak, beef, ribs. Parking. Rustic, Western theme. Outdoor dining overlooking water. Cr cds: A, DS, MC, V.

[D] [SC] [🔜]

★ **THE CREAMERY CAFE.** *348 Gulf Breeze Pkwy (US 98) (32561), in shopping center.* *850/932-1525.* Hrs: 8 am-9 pm; Mon, Tues to 2 pm. Closed Thanksgiving, Dec 25. Beer. Semi-a la carte: bkfst $2.75-$6, lunch $3.50-$7, dinner $5-$10.95. Specializes in German dishes, desserts. Own ice cream. Outdoor dining. Family-owned. Cr cds: A, DS, MC, V.

[D] [🔜]

✔★ **CROCKETT'S.** *550 Scenic Hwy (32503).* *850/432-6766.* Hrs: 11 am-2 pm, 5-9 pm; Mon, Sat from 5 pm. Closed most major hols. Bar. Semi-a la carte: lunch $5-$8.99, dinner $8.99-$13.95. Child's meals. Specializes in seafood. View of Escambia Bay. Cr cds: A, DS, MC, V.

[D]

✔★ **DARRYL'S.** *7251 Plantation Rd (32504), at University Mall.* *850/476-1821.* Hrs: 11 am-midnight; Fri, Sat to 1 am. Closed Dec 25. Res accepted. Bar. Semi-a la carte: lunch, dinner $5.50-$15.99. Child's meals. Specializes in steak, seafood, barbecued ribs. Parking. Turn-of-the-century decor. Cr cds: A, C, D, DS, MC, V.

[🔜] [♥]

★ ★ **JAMIE'S.** *424 E Zaragoza St (32501).* *850/434-2911.* Hrs: 11:30 am-2:30 pm, 6-10 pm; Mon from 6 pm. Closed Sun; Thanksgiving, Dec 25. Res accepted. Continental menu. Beer. Wine list. Semi-a la carte: lunch $6.25-$12.50, dinner $17.50-$23.25. Specializes in wild game, fresh seafood. Own pastries. In restored Victorian house (1870). Cr cds: A, DS, MC, V.

[🔜]

★ **JUBILEE BEACHSIDE.** *(400 Quietwater Beach, Pensacola Beach 32561) S on US 98.* *850/934-3108.* Web www.pensacolabeach.com/jubilee. Hrs: 11-2 am; Sun from 10 am. Closed Thanksgiving, Dec 25. Bar. Semi-a la carte: lunch, dinner $5.95-$14.95. Child's meals. Specializes in fresh seafood, ribs, salads. Entertainment Wed-Sun. Parking. Patio dining. Cr cds: A, C, D, DS, MC, V.

[D]

★ ★ **JUBILEE TOPSIDE.** *(400 Quietwater Beach, Pensacola Beach 32561) S on US 98.* *850/934-3108.* Web www.pensacolabeach.com/jubilee. Hrs: 6-10 pm; Fri, Sat to 11 pm; Sun brunch 9 am-2 pm. Closed Thanksgiving, Dec 25. Res accepted Sun-Thurs. Serv bar. Semi-a la carte: dinner $12.95-$24.95. Sun brunch $4.95-$14.95. Child's meals. Specializes in fresh seafood, Angus steak. Parking. 2nd floor dining room overlooking beach. Cr cds: A, C, D, DS, MC, V.

[D] [🔜]

★ ★ **McGUIRE'S IRISH PUB & BREWERY.** *600 E Gregory St (32501).* *850/433-6789.* Hrs: 11-1 am; Fri, Sat to 2 am. Closed Dec 25. Bar. Semi-a la carte: lunch $5.95-$7.95, dinner $6.95-$26.95. Specializes in steak, hamburgers, seafood. Own desserts. Entertainment. Irish pub atmosphere; Tiffany lamps, brass railings. Beer & root beer brewed on premises. Cr cds: A, C, D, DS, MC, V.

[D] [🔜]

✔★ **MESQUITE CHARLIE'S.** *5901 N "W" St (32505).* *850/434-0498.* Hrs: 11 am-10 pm; Fri, Sat to 11 pm. Closed some major hols. Res accepted. Bar. Semi-a la carte: lunch $3.99-$5.99, dinner $6.99-$14.99. Child's meals. Specializes in steak, ribs, shrimp. Parking. Large collection of Remingtons. Cr cds: A, DS, MC, V.

[D] [🔜]

★ ★ **NEW WORLD LANDING.** *600 S Palafox Dr (32501).* *850/434-7736.* Hrs: 11 am-1:30 pm. Closed Sat, Sun; major hols. Res accepted. Bar from 5 pm. Buffet: lunch $5.95. Specializes in beef, chicken, seafood. Elegant dining. Cr cds: A, MC, V.

[D]

✔★ ★ **SKOPELOS ON THE BAY SEAFOOD & STEAK.** *670 Scenic Hwy (US 90E) (32503).* *850/432-6565.* Hrs: 5-10:30 pm; Fri 11:30 am-2:30 pm. Closed Sun, Mon; Dec 25. Res accepted. Bar. Semi-a la carte: dinner $13.95-$19.95. Child's meals. Specializes in seafood, charbroiled steak. Own pastries. Parking. Outdoor dining. Overlooks Escambia Bay. Family-owned. Cr cds: A, DS, MC, V.

[D] [🔜]

Perry (B-2)

Pop 7,151 **Elev** 42 ft **Area code** 904 **Zip** 32347 **E-mail** tacocmbr@perry.gulfnet.com **Web** www.asksam.com/chamber

Information Perry-Taylor County Chamber of Commerce, 428 N Jefferson St, PO Box 892, 32348; 904/584-5366.

What to See and Do

Forest Capital State Cultural Museum. Interprets the story of the forest industry, past, present and future. Exhibits on turpentine production, cutting of virgin forests, cypress swamps and hardwood hammocks; modern forest practices and newly developed techniques are explained; map of the state made of native wood with each of the 67 counties shaped from a different species of Florida tree; visitor center designed in circular shape of a tree; picnic area. (Thurs-Mon) (See ANNUAL EVENT) 204 Forest Park Dr, 1 mi S via US 19, 98. Phone 904/584-3227. ¢ Admission includes

Cracker Homestead. Interpretive site depicts typical early Florida homestead constructed of double-notched, squared logs and furnished in the 1860s period. Outbuildings include smokehouse, barn, corn crib, chicken pen, outhouse. Self-guided tours.

Annual Event

Florida Forest Festival. Forest Capital State Cultural Museum (see). Activities include parade, chainsaw championship competition, antique car show, arts & crafts, races, picnic, fish fry and pageants. Phone 904/584-8733. 4th wkend Oct.

Pompano Beach (G-6)

(See also Boca Raton, Dania, Fort Lauderdale, Hollywood)

Settled 1884 **Pop** 72,411 **Elev** 10 ft **Area code** 954 **Web** www.pompanobeachchamber.com
Information Greater Pompano Beach Chamber of Commerce, 2200 E Atlantic Blvd, 33062; 954/941-2940.

The rapid growth of tourism in this Gold Coast resort has been matched with a comparable increase in year-round residents. Of the town's seven-mile-long ocean beach, more than three remain in the public domain; the rest is fronted with motels. Situated along the Intracoastal Waterway and the Atlantic Ocean, Pompano Beach offers the full range of water sports and fishing activities.

What to See and Do

Butterfly World. Walk among thousands of free-flying butterflies in three, giant, screened aviaries, the largest facility of its kind; botanical vine walk and gardens, breeding laboratory displays, collection of unusual insects. Concessions, gift shop. (Daily; closed Thanksgiving, Dec 25) N on FL Tpke, Sample Rd exit, W to Tradewinds Park at 3600 W Sample Rd, in Coconut Creek. Phone 954/977-4400. ¢¢¢¢

Fishing, boating. Fishing at 887-ft municipal pier, Pompano Beach Blvd, 2 blks N of Atlantic Blvd; Fish City Marina, 2629 N Riverside Dr; Sands Harbor Marina, 125 N Riverside Dr. Deep-sea fishing and charter boat rentals arranged; public launching ramps located at Alsdorf Park, NE 14th St on W side of Intracoastal Waterway.

Goodyear Blimp Visitor Center. Base for the airship *Stars and Stripes*. Visitors are not offered rides, but may view the blimp on the ground. Best time to view blimp in flight is Nov-May. (Daily) 1500 NE 5th Ave. Phone 954/946-8300. **Free.**

Lowrance Artificial Reef. The 435-ft ship *Lowrance* was sunk on Mar 31, 1984, to form one of the largest artificial reefs on the east coast. This reef, in 190 feet of water, is one of the most popular fishing and diving sites in south Florida. Other ships and barges have been sunk off Pompano Beach each year to create additional artificial reefs. 1½ mi offshore of Atlantic Blvd.

State Farmers Market. World's largest wholesale winter vegetable market; visitors may view process, but may not purchase produce. (Daily) Hammondville Rd.

Annual Events

Seafood Festival. Last wkend Apr.

Pompano Beach Fishing Rodeo. Final leg of the south Florida fishing triple crown. Mid-May.

Boat Parade. More than 100 decorated and lighted boats parade up Intracoastal Waterway. 2nd Sun Dec.

Seasonal Event

Horse racing. Pompano Park Racing, off Powerline Rd, W of I-95, Atlantic Blvd exit. Harness racing; 7,500-seat grandstand, dining room. Nightly exc Sun, days vary off-season. Phone 954/972-2000. Oct-Aug.

Motels

★★ **HOLIDAY INN.** 1350 S Ocean Blvd (33068). 954/941-7300. 133 units, 2-3 story, 89 kits. Jan-mid-Apr: S, D $135-$165; each addl $10; kit. units $144-$185; villa units $160-$185; under 19 free; lower rates rest of yr. Crib free. TV; cable (premium). 2 pools, heated; poolside serv. Coffee in rms. Restaurant 7 am-10 pm. Rm serv. Bar 11 am-midnight. Ck-out 11 am. Coin lndry. Meeting rms. Business servs avail. Bellhops. Valet serv. Sundries. 3 tennis courts, pro. Golf privileges, putting green. Lawn games. Private patios, balconies. On ocean beach; marina. Some rms across street. Cr cds: A, C, D, DS, JCB, MC, V.

⊟🛏🏌🏊🏖🎿🏂 SC

✔★ **THREE SISTERS INN.** 2300 NE 10th St (33062). 954/943-3500. 57 rms, 2 story. Jan-mid-Apr: S, D $52-$109; under 12 free; lower rates rest of yr. Crib free. TV. Complimentary continental bkfst. Restaurant nearby. Ck-out 11 am. Business servs avail. Refrigerators avail. Cr cds: A, MC, V.

🔥

Motor Hotels

★ **BEST WESTERN BEACHCOMBER HOTEL & VILLAS.** 1200 S Ocean Blvd (33062). 954/941-7830; FAX 954/942-7680. Web www.bestwestern.com. 147 units, 1-8 story, 68 kit. studio rms, 7 kit. apts,

8 kit. villas (1-2 bedrm). Jan-mid-Apr: S, D $90-$214; studio rms $186-$196; apts, villas for 2-4, $172-$269; each addl $15-$25; lower rates rest of yr. TV; cable (premium), VCR avail (movies). 2 pools, 1 heated; poolside serv. Restaurant 7 am-3 pm, 5-10 pm. Rm serv. Bar; entertainment. Ck-out 11 am. Coin lndry. Meeting rm. In-rm modem link. Bellhops. Gift shop. Putting green. Health club privileges. Lawn games. Many private patios, balconies. 300-ft beach, cabanas. Cr cds: A, C, D, DS, ER, MC, V.

🏊🏖🏂 SC

★ **POMPANO BEACH MOTOR LODGE.** 1112 N Ocean Blvd (33062). 954/943-0630. 58 rms, 6 story, 36 kit. units. Feb-Mar: S, D $99-$109; kit. units $119-$122; under 7 free; hol wkends (4-day min); lower rates rest of yr. Crib $5. TV; cable. Restaurant adj 8 am-1:30 pm, 5-9 pm. Ck-out 11 am. Business servs avail. Coin lndry. 36-hole golf privileges. Game rm. Pool. Lawn games. Many refrigerators; microwave avail. Picnic tables, grills. On beach. Cr cds: A, C, D, DS, MC, V.

D🛏🏊🔥

★ **SANDS HARBOR.** 125 N Riverside Dr (33062). 954/942-9100; FAX 954/785-5657; res: 800/227-3353. Web www.sandsharbor.com. 56 rms, 9 story, 28 kits. Jan-Apr: S, D $89-$139; each addl $10; suites $149-$275; kit. units $99-$139; lower rates rest of yr. Crib free. TV; cable (premium). Pool; poolside serv. Coffee in rms. Restaurant 5-10 pm. Bar 11 am-11 pm. Ck-out 11 am. Business servs avail. Beauty shop. Health club privileges. Boat rentals; scuba diving. Many refrigerators. Balconies. On Intracoastal Waterway; marina. Cr cds: A, C, D, DS, MC, V.

⛵🏊🏂 SC

Restaurants

★★★ **CAFE ARUGULA.** (3150 N Federal Hwy, Lighthouse Point 33064) N on US 1. 954/785-7732. Hrs: 5:30-10 pm; wkends to 10:30 pm. Closed some major hols. Res accepted. A la carte entrees: dinner $9.95-$22.95. Child's meals. Specialties: pecan-crusted yellowtail snapper, jumbo lump crab cakes. Eclectic Mediterranean decor. Chef-owned. Cr cds: A, D, DS, MC, V.

D🔗

★ **CAP'S PLACE.** (2765 NE 28th Ct, Lighthouse Point 33064) N on Federal Hwy (US 1) to NE 24th St, then E and follow signs. 954/941-0418. Hrs: 5:30-10 pm; wkends to 11 pm. Closed Dec 25. Res accepted. Bar. Complete meals: dinner $11.95-$25.50. Specialties: heart of palm salad, filet mignon. Historic restaurant established 1928. Accessible by restaurant's launch or private boat only. Cr cds: A, MC, V.

D🔗

★★ **DARREL & OLIVER'S CAFE MAXX.** 2601 E Atlantic Blvd (33062). 954/782-0606. Contemporary Amer menu. Specialties: caviar pie, grilled veal chop, Norwegian salmon. Own ice cream. Hrs: 5:30-10:30 pm. Closed July 4; Super Bowl Sun. Res accepted. Semi-a la carte: dinner $18.95-$31.95. Valet parking. Open kitchen. Cr cds: A, C, D, DS, MC, V.

D

★★ **JOE'S RIVERSIDE GRILLE.** 125 N Riverside Dr (33062). 954/941-2499. E-mail eaj@msn.com. Hrs: 5-10 pm; Fri, Sat to 11 pm. Res accepted. Continental menu. Bar. Semi-a la carte: dinner $13.95-$28. Specializes in fresh seafood, steak, chicken. Outdoor dining overlooking waterfront. Cr cds: A, D, DS, MC, V.

D🔗

Port Charlotte (G-4)

(See also Arcadia, Punta Gorda)

Pop 41,535 **Elev** 5 ft **Area code** 941 **E-mail** chamber@sunline.net **Web** www.charlotte-florida.com/chamber
Information Charlotte County Chamber of Commerce, 2702 Tamiami Trail, 33952; 627-2222.

Charlotte County has 38 miles of natural shoreline on the Charlotte Harbor, the Peace and Myakka rivers and more than 165 miles of man-made waterways.

Seasonal Event

Spring training. Charlotte County Stadium, 2300 El Jobean Rd. Texas Rangers baseball spring training; exhibition games. Phone 941/625-9500. Early Mar-early Apr.

Motels

✔★★ **DAYS INN.** *1941 Tamiami Trail (33948).* 941/627-8900; FAX 941/743-8503. Web www.daysinn.com/daysinn.html. 126 rms, 3 story. Jan-Mar: S $79-$109; D $89-$114; each addl $5; under 17 free; lower rates rest of yr. Crib free. TV; cable (premium). Heated pool. Complimentary coffee in lobby. Restaurant adj 7-1 am. Rm serv. Ck-out 11 am. Coin lndry. Business servs avail. Exercise equipt. Health club privileges. Refrigerators; microwaves avail. Cr cds: A, C, D, DS, MC, V.

D ⊠ ✗ ⊠ ⊠ SC

★★ **ECONO LODGE.** *4100 Tamiami Trail (33952).* 941/743-2442; FAX 941/743-6376. 60 rms. Late Dec-mid-Apr: S, D $110-$130; each addl $5; under 12 free; lower rates rest of yr. Crib free. TV; cable. Complimentary coffee in lobby. Restaurant nearby. Ck-out 11 am. Meeting rm. Business servs avail. Cr cds: A, C, D, DS, MC, V.

D ⊠ ⊠ SC

★★ **QUALITY INN.** *3400 Tamiami Trail (US 41) (33952).* 941/625-4181; FAX 941/629-1740. 105 rms, 2 story. S, D $75-$110; each addl $6; under 12 free; higher rates special events. Crib free. Pet accepted, some restrictions; $6. TV; cable. Pool. Complimentary continental bkfst. Coffee in rms. Bar. Ck-out noon. Coin lndry. Meeting rms. Business servs avail. Lawn games. Some refrigerators. Cr cds: A, C, D, DS, JCB, MC, V.

D ⊷ ≈ ⊠ ⊠ SC

Motor Hotel

★★ **HAMPTON INN.** *24480 Sandhill Blvd (33983).* 941/627-5600; res: 800/426-7866; FAX 941/627-6883. 73 rms, 3 story. Jan-Mar: S, D $79-$109; under 18 free; lower rates rest of yr. Crib free. TV; cable (premium). Complimentary continental bkfst. Complimentary coffee in rms. Restaurant nearby. Bar 11 am-10 pm. Ck-out 11 am. Business center. Coin lndry. Golf privileges, greens fee $15-$26.50, pro. Health club privileges. Pool. Some refrigerators, microwaves. Some balconies. On pond. Cr cds: A, D, DS, MC, V.

D ✗ ⊠ ⊠ SC ⊁

Restaurant

✔★ **JOHNNY'S DINER & PUB.** *1951 Tamiami Trail (33948).* 941/255-0994. Hrs: 7-1 am. Res accepted. Bar. Semi-a la carte: bkfst $2.79-$5.79, lunch, dinner $6.59-$14.99. Child's meals. Specializes in seafood, steak, ribs. Sports decor. Cr cds: A, D, DS, MC, V.

D ⊠

Punta Gorda (G-4)

(See also Fort Myers, Port Charlotte)

Pop 10,747 **Elev** 61 ft **Area code** 941 **E-mail** chamber@sunline.net **Web** www.charlotte-florida.com/chamber
Information Charlotte County Chamber of Commerce, 2702 Tamiami Trail, Port Charlotte 33952; 941/627-2222.

At the mouth of the Peace River on Charlotte Harbor, this is an increasingly popular resort city. Fishing, boating and all water sports are particularly good here. Cattle raising, commercial fishing, construction and land development are the important industries.

What to See and Do

Babcock Wilderness Adventures. Offers swamp buggy, nature tours (1½ hr) on 90,000-acre ranch; tours go though cypress swamp and woodland areas, view alligators, bison, panther, hawks and other wildlife, commentary by naturalist. Picnic grounds. (Dec-May, daily; rest of yr, daily exc Mon, limited hrs; no tours Easter, Thanksgiving, Dec 25) Advance reservations required. 3 mi NE on US 17, then 18 mi E on FL 74 to FL 31, then 5 mi S. Phone 941/338-6367 (recording) or 941/489-3911. ¢¢¢¢

Fishermen's Village. A 40-store specialty shopping mall built on old city fish docks 1,000 feet into Charlotte Harbor. Pool; 98-slip marina, charter fishing boats & services. Tennis. Several restaurants; lodging. (Daily; closed Dec 25) 1200 W Retta Esplanade. Phone 941/639-8721.

Museum Florida Adventure. Natural history displays, fossils; mounted exhibits including lions, leopards, bears. Lectures. (Daily exc Sun; closed hols) 260 W Retta Esplanade. Phone 941/639-3777. **Free.**

Ponce de Leon Park. Commemorates the landing of Spaniards (1513 & 1521) in the area. Boat ramp. Nature trail. Picnicking. Observation mound; shrine. (Daily) End of W Marion Ave, 3½ mi W on Charlotte Harbor. Phone 941/575-5050. **Free.**

Motel

★★ **DAYS INN.** *26560 N Jones Loop Rd (33950).* 941/637-7200; FAX 941/639-0848. 74 rms, 2 story, 11 kits. Jan-Apr: S $79-$100; D $84-$115; kit. units $99-$175; under 18 free; wkly rates off season; lower rates rest of yr. Crib free. TV; cable (premium). Pool; whirlpool. Playground. Complimentary continental bkfst. Restaurant adj open 24 hrs. Ck-out 11 am. Coin lndry. Business servs avail. In-rm modem link. Cr cds: A, C, D, DS, MC, V.

D ≈ ⊠ ⊠ SC

Motor Hotel

★★ **BEST WESTERN WATERFRONT.** *300 Retta Esplanade (33950).* 941/639-1165; res: 800/525-1022; FAX 941/639-8116. E-mail bestwestern@cyberstreet.com; web www.bestwestern-florida.com. 183 rms, 2-5 story. Jan-Apr: S, D $89-$99; each addl $10; suites $115-$285; under 19 free; lower rates rest of yr. Crib free. Pet accepted, some restrictions; $15. TV; cable (premium). Heated pool. Rm serv. Restaurant 6:30 am-9 pm. Rm serv. Bar; entertainment. Ck-out noon. Coin lndry. Meeting rms. Business servs avail. Valet serv. Sundries. Gift shop. Microwaves avail. Private patios, balconies. On harbor; boat dock. Wilderness tours. Cr cds: A, C, D, DS, JCB, MC, V.

D ⊷ ⊷ ≈ ⊠ ⊠ SC

Resort

★★ **MARINA INN BURNT STORE MARINA.** *3160 Matecumbe Key Rd (33955), 8 mi S of Punta Gorda via Burnt Store Rd (County 765).* 941/575-4488; FAX 941/575-7968; res: 800/859-7529. Web marinainn@juno.com. 401 2-bedrm suites, 3 story. Jan-Apr: 1-bedrm $150-$195; 2-bedrm $275; each addl $10; under 14 free; wkend, wkly, monthly rates;

lower rates rest of yr. Crib avail. TV; cable. Heated pool. Restaurant 11 am-9 pm in season. Bar 11:30-1 am. Ck-out 11 am. Convention facilities. Business servs avail. Grocery. Gift shop. Tennis. 27-hole golf, greens fee $18-$30, pro, putting green, driving range. Exercise equipt. Sailing school; sailing charters. Bicycle rentals. Microwaves. Private patios, balconies. Marina; dockage. Cr cds: A, DS, MC, V.

Restaurant

★ ★ **SALTY'S HARBORSIDE.** *5000 Burnt Store Rd (33955). 941/639-3650.* Hrs: 11:30 am-9 pm; Sun to 8 pm; early-bird dinner 5-6:30 pm. Closed Mon, Tues; June-Oct. Res accepted. Bar. Semi-a la carte: lunch $6.95-$11.95, dinner $10.95-$22.95. Child's meals. Specializes in seafood, veal. Floor to ceiling windows offer view of waterfront and yacht harbor. Cr cds: A, DS, MC, V.

Redington Beach

(see St Pete Beach)

Sanford (D-5)

(See also Altamonte Springs, DeLand, Orlando, Winter Park)

Settled 1837 **Pop** 32,387 **Elev** 29 ft **Area code** 407 **Web** www.sanfordchamber.com
Information Greater Sanford Chamber of Commerce, 400 E 1st St, 32771; 407/322-2212.

Sanford, on the St Johns River and Lake Monroe, was founded near the former site of a federal garrison used for protection against Native Americans. Fishing for shad, bass, bream and perch in the St Johns River is popular. Light industry and the growing tourism industry are important to the town's economy.

What to See and Do

Central Florida Zoological Park. Hundreds of native and exotic animals; children's zoo, reptile exhibit; elevated boardwalk, picnic area. Park (daily; closed Thanksgiving, Dec 25) At I-4 exit 52, 3755 N US 17/92. Phone 407/323-4450. ¢¢¢

Sanford Museum. Exhibits include decorative art objects from New England and Europe (1820-1890); photographs and artifacts relating to town's history; re-created library of town's founder. (Tues-Fri, Sat afternoons; closed hols) 520 E 1st St. Phone 407/302-1000. **Free.**

Riverboat tours.

Rivership *Romance.* Departs from Monroe Harbor Marina. Cruises the St Johns River for regular 3 to 4-hr lunch cruise. Also dinner/dance cruises (Fri & Sat evenings). (Daily) Res required. Phone 407/321-5091. ¢¢¢¢¢

St Johns River Cruises. Narrated nature and wildlife cruises along St Johns River; special cruises. (Daily exc Mon) Res required. Depart from Osteen Bridge at FL 415. Phone 407/330-1612. ¢¢¢¢

Motels

★ ★ **BEST WESTERN DELTONA INN.** *(481 Deltona Blvd, Deltona 32725)* 10 mi N on I-4, exit 53 Deltona. 407/574-6693; FAX 407/860-2687. 131 rms, 2 story. Feb-Apr: S, D $49.95; under 18 free; higher rates special events; lower rates rest of yr. TV; cable (premium). Pool. Restau-

rant 7 am-2 pm, 5:30-10 pm. Bar 11:30-1 am. Ck-out noon. Meeting rms. Golf privileges. Microwaves avail. Lake. Cr cds: A, C, D, DS, MC, V.

★ ★ **COURTYARD BY MARRIOTT.** *(135 International Pkwy, Heathrow 32746)* I-4 exit 50. 407/444-1000; FAX 407/444-5921. 83 rms, 3 story. S, D $91-$98; suites $121-$131; wkend rates; higher rates special events. Crib free. TV; cable (premium), VCR avail. Pool; whirlpool. Complimentary coffee in rms. Restaurant 6:30 am-10:30 pm. Bar 5 pm-midnight. Ck-out noon. Coin lndry. Meeting rms. Exercise equipt. Refrigerator in suites. Balconies. Cr cds: A, C, D, DS, MC, V.

✔★ **DAYS INN.** *4650 W FL 46 (32771),* 1 blk E of I-4. 407/323-6500; FAX 407/323-2962. 119 rms, 2 story. Jan-Mar: S $39-$49; D $42-$60; under 18 free; higher rates special events; lower rates rest of yr. TV; cable (premium). Pool. Restaurant open 24 hrs. Ck-out noon. Sundries. Cr cds: A, C, D, DS, JCB, MC, V.

★ **MARINA.** *530 N Palmetto Ave (32771).* 407/323-1910; FAX 407/322-7076; res: 800/290-1910. 100 rms, 2 story. Feb-Apr: S, D $65-$73; under 18 free; higher rates special events; lower rates rest of yr. Crib free. TV; cable (premium), VCR avail. Pool. Complimentary coffee in rms. Restaurant 6:30 am-2 pm. Rm serv. Bar 11 am-midnight. Ck-out noon. Coin lndry. Meeting rm. Business servs avail. On Lake Monroe; marina, dockage; boat rental; water sports, dinner cruise ship. Cr cds: A, C, D, DS, JCB, MC, V.

Restaurant

★ **CATTLE RANCH FAMILY STEAKHOUSE.** *2700 S Sanford Ave (32773).* 407/321-5761. Hrs: 5-10 pm; wkends to 11 pm. Closed most major hols. Bar. A la carte entrees: dinner $8.50-$19.99. Child's meals. Specializes in steak, chicken, shrimp. Western, cowboy atmosphere; antiques. Cr cds: A, C, D, MC, V.

Sanibel & Captiva Islands (G-4)

(See also Fort Myers)

Pop 5,468 **Elev** 5 ft **Area code** 941 **Zip** Sanibel, 33957; Captiva, 33924
Information Sanibel-Captiva Islands Chamber of Commerce, 1159 Causeway Rd, Sanibel; 941/472-1080.

Sanibel Island, linked to the mainland by a causeway, is considered the third best shelling site in the Western Hemisphere, with deposits on both bay and gulf beaches. North of Sanibel, only a bridge away, is Captiva; legend has it that the pirate Jose Gaspar used the island to harbor his women captives. Together the islands comprise the Sanibel National Wildlife Refuge, haven for more than 200 varieties of birds. The islands are a popular tourist destination, and several marinas line the east pier of Sanibel.

What to See and Do

Bailey-Matthews Shell Museum. Only museum in US devoted entirely to the shells of the world. Major Exhibits like Shells in Tribal Art, Mollusks & Medicine & Man, Kingdom of the Landshells. (Daily; closed Mon) 3075 Sanibel-Captiva Rd, Sanibel Island. Phone 941/395-2233.

Bird Sanctuary and Walk. Tarpon Bay Rd, S side of Sanibel. Tower and trails.

Boat tours. For shelling and bird-watching. Inquire at Chamber of Commerce.

Island Historical Museum. Former "cracker" style homestead restored and furnished to depict lifestyle of early settlers; antique clothing, tin-type photographs, piano. Re-created Cracker village with grocery store, post office, schoolhouse. (Wed-Sat; closed hols) 950 Dunlop Rd, Sanibel Island. Phone 941/472-4648. **Donation.**

J.N. "Ding" Darling National Wildlife Refuge. Five-mile wildlife drive (daily exc Fri); observation tower; walking and canoe trails. Fishing is permitted and crabbing is permitted with use of dipnets only. Feeding of alligators is strictly prohibited. (Daily exc Fri) Golden Eagle, Golden Age and Golden Access passports accepted (see MAKING THE MOST OF YOUR TRIP). Visitor Center 6 mi W of causeway. Phone 941/472-1100. Per vehicle ¢¢

Sanibel-Captiva Conservation Foundation. This 250-acre tract contains 4¹/₂ mi of nature trails along the properties and the Sanibel River. Guided and self-guided tours to explain the ecosystem of the island; native vegetation and wildlife. Special wetlands exhibits; native plant nursery; observation tower and Butterfly House. (Nov-Apr, daily exc Sun; rest of yr, Mon-Fri; closed most major hols) 3333 Sanibel-Captiva Rd, Sanibel Island. Phone 941/472-2329. ¢¢

Annual Event

Sanibel Shell Fair. Serious shell collectors display their wares, including specimen shell and live shell exhibits; contests and prizes. 1st full wkend Mar.

Motels

★ ★ **'TWEEN WATERS INN.** (15951 Captiva Dr, Captiva Island 33924) 941/472-5161; FAX 941/472-0249; res: 800/223-5865. E-mail resv@tween-waters.com; web www.tween-waters.com. 137 rms, 3 story, 97 kit. units. Feb-Apr: S, D $180-$235; each addl $20; suites $270-$485; kit. units $180-$485; under 13 free; lower rates rest of yr. Crib free. Pet accepted, some restrictions; $10/day. TV; cable (premium). Heated pool; wading pool; poolside serv. Complimentary coffee in rms. Restaurant 7:30 am-10 pm. Bar 11-2 am; entertainment. Ck-out noon. Coin lndry. Meeting rms. Business servs avail. Bellhops. Concierge. Gift shop. Lighted tennis; pro. Lawn games. Game rm. Exercise rm. Massage. Balconies. On ocean, swimming beach. Cr cds: A, DS, MC, V.

★ ★ **ISLAND INN.** (3111 Gulf Dr W, Sanibel Island 33957) 941/472-1561; FAX 941/472-0051; res: 800/851-5088. 57 units in motel, lodges, 2 story, 29 kits. MAP, mid-Nov-Apr: S, D $110-$215; each addl $40 (child $20); kit. cottages $190-$280; hol wkends (3-day min); lower rates rest of yr. Crib free. TV; cable. Heated pool. Restaurant 7:30-10:30 am, 6:30-7:45 pm (mid-Nov-Apr only). Ck-out 11 am. Coin lndry. Business servs avail. Tennis. Lawn games. Refrigerators. Screened porches with most units. Library. On beach. Cr cds: A, DS, MC, V.

★ ★ **SANIBEL INN.** (937 E Gulf Dr, Sanibel Island 33957) 941/472-3181; FAX 941/472-5234; res: 800/237-1491. Web www. ssrc.com. 96 units, 3 story, 20 suites. Feb-late Apr: S, D $279-$299; each addl $25; suites $299-$399; under 12 free; higher rates hols (3-day min); lower rates rest of yr. TV; cable (premium). Heated pool. Supervised child's activities; ages 4-12. Complimentary coffee in rms. Restaurant adj 7:30-11 am, 5-10 pm. Bar 11 am-6 pm. Ck-out 11 am. Meeting rms. Business servs avail. Bellhops. Gift shop. Tennis. Golf privileges, greens fee $78. Health club privileges. Refrigerators; microwaves avail. Balconies. Picnic tables. On beach. Cr cds: A, C, D, DS, MC, V.

★ ★ **SANIBEL MOORINGS.** (845 E Gulf Dr, Sanibel Island 33957) 941/472-4119; FAX 941/472-8148; res: 800/237-5144. E-mail sanmoor@sanibelmoorings.com; web www.sanibelmoorings.com. 110 kit. units, 2 story. Late-Dec-Apr (1-wk min): 1-3 bedrm suites $1,190-$2,065/wk; each addl $15; lower rates rest of yr. Crib $8/day. Maid serv

avail. TV; cable, VCR (movies $2). 2 pools, heated; wading pool. Restaurant nearby. Ck-out 11 am. Coin lndry. Business center. Tennis. Screened porches. Grills. On beach; dockage. Cr cds: MC, V.

★ ★ **SANIBEL SIESTA.** (1246 Fulgur St, Sanibel Island 33957) 941/472-4117; FAX 941/472-6826; res: 800/548-2743. E-mail sansiesta@ coconet.com; web www.coconet.com/sanibel-captiva.home.html. 54 condo units (2-bedrm). Mid-Dec-Apr (3-day min): condo units for 4-6, $1,372-$1,764/wk; each addl $70/wk; lower rates rest of yr. Crib avail. TV; cable, VCR. Heated pool. Ck-out 10 am. Coin lndry. Business servs avail. Tennis privileges. Lawn games. Private patios, balconies. Grills. On beach. Cr cds: DS, MC, V.

★ ★ **SEASIDE INN.** (541 E Gulf Dr, Sanibel Island 33957) 941/472-1400; FAX 941/472-6538; res: 800/831-7384. Web www.ssrc.com. 32 rms, 2 story, 10 kits. Feb-Apr: S, D $275; each addl $20; kit. units, apts, cottages $305-$360; wkly rates; lower rates rest of yr. Crib free. TV; cable, VCR (free movies). Heated pool. Complimentary continental bkfst. Coffee in rms. Restaurant nearby. Ck-out 11 am. Coin lndry. Lawn games. Refrigerators. Patios, balconies. Picnic tables, grills. Library. Bicycles. On beach. Cr cds: A, C, D, DS, MC, V.

★ ★ **SONG OF THE SEA.** (863 E Gulf Dr, Sanibel Island 33957) 941/472-2220; FAX 941/472-8569; res: 800/231-1045. Web www. ssrc.com. 30 kit. units, 2 story. Feb-Apr: kit. studios $310-$345; each addl $25; 1-bedrm suites $370; each addl $25; lower rates rest of yr. Crib free. TV; cable, VCR (movies avail). Heated pool; whirlpool. Complimentary continental bkfst. Coffee in rms. Ck-out 11 am. Coin lndry. Business servs avail. Sundries. Tennis privileges. 18-hole golf privileges, greens fee $75. Health club privileges. Library. Screened porches. Bicycles. On beach. Cr cds: A, C, D, DS, MC, V.

Motor Hotel

★ ★ **WEST WIND INN.** (3345 W Gulf Dr, Sanibel Island 33957) 941/472-1541; FAX 941/472-8134; res: 800/824-0476 (exc FL), 800/282-2831 (FL). E-mail wwinn@westwindinn.com; web www.westwind.com. 104 rms, 2 story, 60 kit. units. Late Dec-Apr: S, D $213-$239; kit. units $239-$249; wkly rates; lower rates rest of yr. Crib free. TV; cable (premium). Heated pool; poolside serv. Coffee in rms. Restaurant 8 am-2 pm; Fri, Sat 5-9 pm. Bar. Ck-out 11 am. Coin lndry. Meeting rm. Business servs avail. Tennis. 18-hole golf privileges, greens fee $75-$80 (incl cart). Bicycles, cabanas (fee). Lawn games. Refrigerators. Balconies. Grills. On gulf; beach. Cr cds: A, DS, MC, V.

Resorts

★ ★ ★ **SOUTH SEAS PLANTATION.** (13000 Captiva Rd, Captiva Island 33924) South Seas Plantation Rd, Captiva Island, 19 mi N of Sanibel Causeway at end of Captiva Island. 941/472-5111; FAX 941/472-7541; res: 800/227-8482. Web www.ssrc.com. 106 rms in hotel, 2 story, 450 1-3 bedrm kit. villas, beach & tennis, bayside & marina villas. Early-Feb-late Apr: S, D $175-$305; each addl $25; kit. villas $295-$800; kit. cottages $565-$740; lower rates rest of yr. Crib free. TV; cable (premium), VCR (movies avail). 18 pools, heated; whirlpools, poolside serv at 2 pools. Playground. Supervised child's activities; ages 3-13. Coffee in rms. Dining rm (see CHADWICK'S). Pizza & ice cream parlors; box lunches. Bar 11-1 am. Ck-out 11 am, ck-in 3 pm. Grocery, deli. Coin lndry. Package store. Convention facilities. Business center. Concierge. Shopping arcade. Barber, beauty shop. 19 tennis courts, 4 lighted, pro. Golf, greens fee $120 for 18 holes (incl cart), pro, putting green. Marinas, store; dockage; launching ramp; boats, power motors; waterskiing; wind surfing; para-sailing; jet-skiing, scuba diving; sailing charters; sailing school. Shelling expeditions. Bicycles. Lawn games. Rec dir. Rec rm. Game rm. Entertainment, movies. Exercise rm. Fishing guides, fish clean/shop. Trolley transportation. Refrigerators. Private patios, balconies. Picnic tables, grills. Gracious turn-of-the-century plantation on 330 acres. Elaborate landscaping. 2-mi private beach. Cr cds: A, C, D, DS, MC, V.

★ ★ **SUNDIAL BEACH RESORT.** (1451 Middle Gulf Dr, Sanibel Island 33957) 941/472-4151; FAX 941/472-8892; res: 800/237-4184. 270 condo units, 4 story. Mid-Dec-Apr: 1-bedrm $296-$415; 2-bedrm $399-$560; each addl $20; under 17 free; tennis, golf, package plans; lower rates rest of yr. Crib avail. TV; cable, VCR avail (free movies). 5 pools, heated; whirlpool, poolside serv. Supervised child's activities; ages 3-16. Restaurant 7:30 am-9:30 pm. Bar 11 am-midnight; entertainment. Ck-out 11 am, ck-in 3 pm. Coin lndry. Meeting rms. Business center. Valet serv. Gift shop. Lighted tennis, pro, pro shop. 18-hole golf privileges, greens fee $105 (incl cart), driving range. Boat, watersport equipt rentals. Bicycle rentals. Rec dir. Game rm. Rec rm. Exercise equipt. Fishing, shelling guides. Many private patios, balconies. On Gulf. Cr cds: A, C, D, DS, MC, V.

Restaurants

★ ★ **BELLINI'S.** (11521 Andy Rosse Ln, Captiva Island 33924) 15 mi N on Captiva Rd from Sanibel Causeway. 941/472-6866. Hrs: 5-10 pm. Closed Dec 25. Res accepted. Northern Italian menu. Bar to midnight. A la carte entrees: dinner $10-$25. Child's meals. Specialties: cioppino lombardi mare, lasagne, live maine lobster. Parking. Outdoor dining. Cr cds: A, D, MC, V.

★ **THE BUBBLE ROOM.** (15001 Captiva Rd, Captiva 33924) 941/472-5558. Hrs: 11:30 am-2:30 pm, 5-10 pm. Closed Dec 25. Bar. Semi-a la carte: lunch $5.95-$12.95, dinner $14.95-$27.95. Child's meals. Specializes in fresh fish, aged beef. Memorabilia from the '30s and '40s can be found in this multi-leveled restaurant. Cr cds: A, D, DS, MC, V.

★ ★ **CHADWICK'S.** (See South Seas Plantation Resort) 941/472-7575. Web www.ssrc.com. Hrs: 7:30-10 am, 11 am-2 pm, 5:30-9:30 pm; Sun brunch 9 am-2 pm. Res accepted. Bar. Buffet: bkfst $7.50, lunch $9.50, dinner $21-$23.50. A la carte entrees: lunch $7.25-$10. Complete meals: dinner $23.50. Sun brunch $18.95. Child's meals. Specialties: shrimp scampi, grouper macadamia. Salad bar. Entertainment. Parking. Tropical decor and atmosphere. Family-oriented. Cr cds: A, C, D, DS, MC, V.

★ ★ **JACARANDA.** (1223 Periwinkle Way, Sanibel Island 33957) 941/472-1771. Hrs: 5-10 pm. Closed Dec 25. Res accepted. Continental menu. Bar 4 pm-1 am. Semi-a la carte: dinner $14.95-$24.95. Child's meals. Specializes in seafood, steak, veal. Entertainment. Parking. Outdoor garden dining. Cr cds: A, C, D, DS, MC, V.

★ **JERRY'S OF SANIBEL.** (1700 Periwinkle Way, Sanibel Island 33957) in shopping center. 941/472-9300. Hrs: 6 am-10 pm; early-bird dinner Mon-Sat 4-6 pm. Wine, beer. Semi-a la carte: bkfst $2.99-$6.95, lunch, dinner $3.95-$13.95. Specializes in fresh fish. Salad bar. Family-owned. Cr cds: DS, MC, V.

★ ★ **MAD HATTER.** (6460 Sanibel-Captiva Rd, Sanibel Island 33957) 941/472-0033. Hrs: 5-9:30 pm. Closed Sun in summer; Dec 25; also 2 wks Sept. Res accepted. Beer, wine. A la carte entrees: dinner $17.95-$31.95. Specializes in grilled fish, veal, lamb. Own desserts. Parking. Overlooks gulf. Artists' works on display. Totally nonsmoking. Cr cds: A, D, MC, V.

★ ★ **MATZALUNA.** (1200 Periwinkle Way #4, Sanibel Island 33957) 941/472-1998. Hrs: 4:30-10 pm. Northern and southern Italian

menu. Bar. Semi-a la carte: dinner $9.95-$18.95. Child's meals. Specializes in fresh seafood, pasta, wood-oven pizza. Cr cds: A, MC, V.

★ **TARWINKLES SEAFOOD EMPORIUM.** (2499 Periwinkle Way, Sanibel Island 33957) at Tarpon Bay Rd, 2½ mi W of Causeway. 941/472-1366. Hrs: 4-10 pm. Res accepted. Bar. Semi-a la carte: dinner $12.95-$18.95. Child's meals. Specializes in fresh seafood, pasta, steak. Parking. Tropical decor. Cr cds: A, C, D, DS, MC, V.

★ ★ **TIMBERS.** (703 Tarpon Bay Rd, Sanibel Island 33957) 941/472-3128. Hrs: 4:30-10 pm; off-season from 5 pm. Closed Super Bowl Sun, July 4. Bar 4 pm-1 am. Semi-a la carte: dinner $12.95-$22.95. Child's meals. Specializes in fresh seafood, aged steak. Parking. Retail fish market & seasonal raw bar. Cr cds: A, MC, V.

Sarasota (F-3)

(See also Bradenton, Longboat Key (& Lido Beach), Siesta Key, Venice)

Settled 1856 **Pop** 50,961 **Elev** 27 ft **Area code** 941 **Web** cvb.sarasota.fl.us.com
Information Convention and Visitors Bureau, 655 N Tamiami Trail, 34236; 941/957-1877 or 800/522-9799.

Tourism is the main industry in Sarasota, as it has been since the days before a single house was built and anglers used to pitch tents on the beach. The standard Florida commodities of beach, fishing, golf and sunbathing come in the usual pleasant proportions here, and the city has basis for its claim as "the cradle of golf" since the first Florida course was laid out here in 1886 by Col J. Hamilton Gillespie.

Ever since John Ringling selected the city of Sarasota as winter quarters for his circus (1929-1959), the two have become synonymous in the minds of many. Ringling did much to develop and beautify the area and surrounding islands. Today, culture, the circus and sportfishing make for a rare blend along Sarasota Bay.

What to See and Do

Beaches. There are 13 public beaches in Sarasota county, including Siesta, Lido and Turtle. Longboat Key (see) reached via John Ringling Blvd (FL 780) to St Armands Key, then N on FL 789; 12 mi of beach on Gulf, fishing in surf, from bridges, docks, fishing pier, picnic area. Siesta Key (see), W on Siesta Bridge, S on FL 789. Lido Beach (see), on Lido Key, W on FL 780, then S on Ben Franklin Dr.

Museum of Cars & Music of Yesterday. More than 125 restored antique classic cars and 2,000 mechanical antique music boxes and machines are displayed; turn-of-the-century arcade; tours every ½ hr. (Daily) 5500 N Tamiami Trail (US 41), opp Ringling Museum of Art. Phone 941/355-6228. ¢¢¢

Boating. Cruising, sailing, outboarding in Sarasota Bay and the Gulf of Mexico. Bayfront municipal marina and Island Park, foot of Main St; marinas at frequent intervals along both city and island shores.

Le Barge Cruises. Afternoon cruises (2 hrs) aboard the Le Barge, includes trips around the bird sanctuary, Mangrove Islands and the Keys; also sunset entertainment cruises (ages 2 and older only); galley serves fresh seafood and sandwiches. (Daily; summer, daily exc Mon) Leaves from dock at Marina Jack on US 41. Phone 941/366-6116. ¢¢¢

Marie Selby Botanical Gardens. Features orchids, bromeliads and a wide variety of other exotic plants; 11 acres of outside gardens, including Hibiscus, Banyan Grove, Bamboo Grove, Waterfall Garden; Museum of Botany and the Arts; plant, gift and book shops. (Daily; closed Dec 25) 811 S Palm Ave, just off US 41. Phone 941/366-5730 or -5731. ¢¢¢

Mote Marine Laboratory and Marine Aquarium. Aquariums of marine animals collected throughout the central gulf coast region; 30-ft touch tank; display of sharks' jaws; marine research exhibits; 135,000-gallon shark tank. (Daily; closed Thanksgiving, Dec 25) 1600 Thompson Pkwy. Phone 941/388-2451. ¢¢¢

Myakka River State Park. Approx 28,900 acres encompassing one of country's outstanding wildlife areas and breeding grounds. More than 200 species of birds have been identified in the park's diverse habitats. Turkeys, deer, raccoons and many other animals inhabit the park. Birdwalk along lakeshore; bicycles. Tours of park by boat and tram (res advised). No swimming. Fishing in river and lakes, boat rentals. Picnicking at 4 areas, concession. Vacation cottages, tent & trailer sites (hookups, dump station). Standard hrs, fees. 17 mi E on FL 72. Phone 941/361-6511.

⭐ **Ringling Museum of Art.** The 66-acre estate of John Ringling is a cultural complex, left to the people of Florida at Ringling's death in 1936. On its beautifully landscaped grounds are a sculpture courtyard and a rose garden. (Daily; closed Jan 1, Thanksgiving, Dec 25) 3 mi N on US 41. Phone 941/355-5101. Combination ticket for all facilities ¢¢¢ The museum includes

Ringling Residence (Ca'd'zan) (1924-1926). An elaborate Venetian-Gothic mansion patterned after the Doge's Palace in Venice, Italy. Venetian glass windows; hand-wrought iron work; marble floors and 32 rooms; 4,000-pipe organ; tapestries, period furnishings and art objects from around the world.

Art Gallery. An Italian Renaissance-style villa created by local craftsmen with shiploads of columns, doorways, roof sculptures and marble collected in Italy by John Ringling. One of the most distinguished collections of Baroque art in the Western Hemisphere, assembled by Ringling; also contemporary art; Rubens collection; sculpture garden in courtyard. Admission free on Sat.

Circus Galleries. Extensive collection of circus memorabilia. Multiple galleries include circus wagons, calliopes, costumes, posters and circus-related fine art exhibits.

Sarasota Jungle Gardens. Tropical birds in jungle paradise; more than 5,000 varieties of plants; wild jungle trails; formal gardens; flamingos, swans, peacocks and pelicans roam free; bird and reptile shows; leopards and monkeys; macaws. Kiddie Jungle children's playground. (Daily; closed Dec 25) 3701 Bayshore Rd, 1 mi S of airport on US 41, then 2 blks W on Myrtle St. Phone 941/355-5305. ¢¢¢

Sarasota Visual Art Center. Four galleries display works by Florida artists. (Daily; closed most hols) 707 N Tamiami Trail. Phone 941/365-2032. **Free.**

Annual Events

American Express Invitational. Senior men's Professional Golf Assn, 72-hole championship. Late Feb.

Medieval Fair. Ringling Museum of Art. Re-creates medieval times; theater, equestrian display; entertainment includes singers and dancers, archers, jesters. Early Mar.

Sailor Circus. High school campus. Sarasota school students in full circus program. Late Mar-early Apr.

Sarasota Jazz Festival. Van Wezel Performing Arts Hall. Late Mar-early Apr.

Sarasota Music Festival. Florida West Coast Symphony Center, on bayfront. Internationally renowned guest artists perform with festival chamber and symphony orchestras at the Van Wezel Performing Arts Hall. Contact 709 N Tamiami Trail, 34236; 941/953-4252. June.

Sarasota Sailing Squadron Labor Day Regatta. Largest one-design regatta held on the Florida suncoast. Two days of racing. Phone 941/388-2355. Labor Day wkend.

Seasonal Events

Water-ski shows. Bayfront municipal marina. Phone 941/388-1666. Sun afternoons, Feb-Apr.

Sarasota Opera Association. Sarasota Opera House. Contact 61 N Pineapple Ave, 34236-5716; 941/366-8450. Early Feb-Mar.

Spring training. Ed Smith Sports Complex, 12th St & Tuttle Ave. Cincinnati Reds baseball spring training. Phone 941/366-8451. Early Mar-early Apr.

Asolo Theatre Company. Asolo Center for the Performing Arts, 5555 N Tamiami Trail, adj to Ringling Museum of Art. Professional Equity company presents 7-8 plays. Evening & matinee performances; free tours. For schedule contact 5555 N Tamiami Trail, 34243; 941/351-8000. Sept-June.

Concert Series. Van Wezel Performing Arts Hall, 777 N Tamiami Trail. Varied programs include concerts, films, lectures, plays, ballet. Contact PO Box 699, 34236; 941/953-3366. Oct-June.

Motels

✔ ★ **BEST WESTERN GOLDEN HOST RESORT.** *4675 N Tamiami Trail (34234).* 941/355-5141; res: 800/722-4895; FAX 941/355-9286. 80 rms, 2 story. Feb-mid-Apr: S, D $89-$109; family rates; package plans; hols 3-day min; higher rates July 4; lower rates rest of yr. Crib free. TV; cable (premium). Complimentary continental bkfst. Restaurant adj 7 am-9 pm. Bar 4:30 pm-2 am. Ck-out 11 am. In-rm modem link. Coin lndry. 18-hole golf privileges. Pool. Some refrigerators. Some balconies. Cr cds: A, C, D, DS, MC, V.

D ⛳ ≈ ⊠ 🐾 SC

★ ★ **BEST WESTERN MIDTOWN.** *1425 S Tamiami Trail (34239).* 941/955-9841; FAX 941/954-8948. E-mail bestwestern@earthlink.net; web www.travelweb.com/thisco/bw/10227_b.html. 100 rms, 2-3 story. Jan-Mar: S, D $99-$109; each addl $6; under 18 free; lower rates rest of yr. Crib free. TV; cable (premium). Heated pool. Complimentary continental bkfst. Ck-out 11 am. Business servs avail. Microwaves avail. Cr cds: A, C, D, DS, ER, MC, V.

≈ ⊠ 🐾 SC

✔ ★ **COMFORT INN.** *4800 N Tamiami Trail (34234), near Sarasota-Bradenton Airport.* 941/355-7091; FAX 941/359-1639. 73 rms, 2 story, 16 kit. units. Jan-mid-Apr: S, D $99-$109; kits. $109-$119; under 18 free; lower rates rest of yr. Crib $5. Pet accepted, some restrictions; $5. TV; cable (premium). Heated pool; whirlpool. Complimentary continental bkfst. Restaurant nearby. Ck-out 11 am. Coin lndry. Gift shop. Cr cds: A, C, D, DS, ER, JCB, MC, V.

D 🐾 ≈ ⊠ 🐾 SC

★ ★ **HAMPTON INN-SARASOTA AIRPORT.** *5000 N Tamiami Trail (34234), near Sarasota-Bradenton Airport.* 941/351-7734; FAX 941/351-8820. 97 rms, 3 story. Jan-mid-Apr: S, D $99-$119; under 18 free; dinner theater plans; lower rates rest of yr. Crib free. TV; cable (premium). Heated pool. Complimentary continental bkfst. Restaurant nearby. Ck-out 11 am. Coin lndry. Meeting rm. Business servs avail. Free airport transportation. Exercise equipt. Microwaves avail. Cr cds: A, C, D, DS, ER, MC, V.

D ≈ ⛳ ✈ ⊠ 🐾 SC

★ ★ **HOLIDAY INN SIESTA KEY.** *6600 S Tamiami Trail (34231).* 941/924-4900; FAX 941/923-7774. 132 rms, 4 story. Feb-mid-Apr: S, D $109-$129; lower rates rest of yr. Crib free. TV; cable (premium). Pool; whirlpool. Complimentary coffee in lobby; afternoon refreshments. Restaurant adj open 24 hrs. Bar 5:30-10 pm. Ck-out 11 am. Coin lndry. Meeting rm. Business servs avail. Valet serv. Cr cds: A, D, DS, MC, V.

D ≈ ⊠ 🐾 SC

★ ★ **HOLIDAY INN-AIRPORT/MARINA.** *7150 N Tamiami Trail (34243), near Sarasota-Bradenton Airport.* 941/355-2781; res: 888/818-2781; FAX 941/355-1605. 177 rms, 2 story. Jan-May: S, D $107-$129; suites $175-$375; under 18 free; lower rates rest of yr. Crib free. TV; cable (premium). Pool; poolside serv. Restaurant 6:30 am-10 pm. Rm serv. Bar; entertainment. Ck-out 11 am. Coin lndry. Meeting rms. Bellhops. Valet serv. Free airport transportation. Marina; dockage. Cr cds: A, C, D, DS, JCB, MC, V.

D ≈ ✈ ⊠ 🐾 SC

★ ★ **RAMADA INN-SARASOTA SOUTH.** (1660 S Tamiami Trail, Osprey 34229) S on US 41. 941/966-2121; FAX 941/966-1124. 148 rms, 2 story, 18 kits. Feb-Mid-Apr: S, D $105; kit. units $137-$162; lower rates rest of yr. Crib free. Pet accepted; $25. TV; cable. Heated pool; poolside serv. Restaurant 6:30 am-1 pm, 5-8 pm. Bar 2-10 pm. Ck-out noon. Coin lndry. Meeting rms. Business servs avail. Sundries. Cr cds: A, C, D, DS, MC, V.

🅳 ⛵ 🏊 🏌 🎿 SC

Motor Hotels

★ ★ **HAMPTON INN.** 5995 Cattleridge Rd (34232). 941/371-1900; FAX 941/371-0241. 121 rms, 5 story. Late Dec-mid-Apr: S, D $99-$129; under 18 free; golf plans; higher rates special events; lower rates rest of yr. Crib free. TV; cable (premium). Complimentary continental bkfst. Coffee in rms. Restaurant opp 10-2 am. Bar 5:30-9 pm. Ck-out 11 am. Meeting rms. Business servs avail. In-rm modem link. Valet serv. Coin lndry. Exercise equipt. Pool; whirlpool. Some refrigerators, microwaves. Cr cds: A, C, D, DS, JCB, MC, V.

🏊 🏌 🎿 🅰 SC

★ ★ **WELLESLEY INN.** 1803 N Tamiami Trail (34234), near Sarasota-Bradenton Airport. 941/366-5128; FAX 941/953-4322; res: 800/444-8888. 106 rms, 4 story, 13 suites. Late Dec-early May: S $100; D $110; each addl $10; suites $120-$130; under 18 free; lower rates rest of yr. Crib free. Pet accepted, some restrictions; $10. TV; cable (premium). Heated pool. Complimentary continental bkfst. Coffee in rms. Restaurant nearby. Ck-out 11 am. Business servs avail. Valet serv. Free airport transportation. Health club privileges. Refrigerator, wet bar in suites. Cr cds: A, C, D, DS, MC, V.

🅳 ⛵ 🏊 🏌 🎿 🅰 SC

Hotel

★ ★ ★ **HYATT.** 1000 Blvd of the Arts (34236), on Sarasota Bay. 941/953-1234; res: 800/233-1234; FAX 941/952-1987. Web www.hyatt.com. 297 rms, 11 story. Late Jan-Apr: S $195-$210; D $220-$235; each addl $25; 1-2-bedrm suites $300-$625; under 18 free; wkend rates in season; lower rates rest of yr. Crib free. TV; cable (premium), VCR avail (movies). Heated pool; poolside serv. Restaurant 6:30 am-midnight. Bar. Ck-out noon. Convention facilities. Concierge. Gift shop. Business center. In-rm modem link. Valet parking. Airport transportation. Golf privileges. greens fee varies. Exercise equipt. Some bathrm phones; microwaves avail. Many balconies. Marina; dockage. View of bay. Cr cds: A, C, D, DS, ER, JCB, MC, V.

🅳 ⛵ 🏌 🏊 🏌 🎿 🅰 SC 🚶

Inn

★ ★ ★ **THE CYPRESS.** 621 Gulfstream Ave S (34236). 941/955-4683. Web www.bbonline.com/fl/cypress/. 4 rms, 1 with shower only, 2 story, 1 suite. No rm phones. Mid-Dec-Apr: S, D $190-$205; suites $160-$220; package plans; lower rates rest of yr. Adults only. TV; cable, VCR avail. Complimentary full bkfst. Restaurant nearby. Ck-out 11 am, ck-in 3 pm. Luggage handling. Concierge serv. Bicycles. Built in 1940; antiques. Gardens. Totally nonsmoking. Cr cds: A, DS, MC, V.

🎿 🅰

Cottage Colony

★ ★ **TIMBERWOODS VACATION VILLAS.** 7964 Timberwood Circle (34238), I-75 exit 37, 3 mi W to Beneva Rd, then 2 mi S. 941/923-4966; FAX 941/924-3109; res: 800/824-5444. E-mail timberwd@ix.net com.com; web www.sarasota-online.com/timber.html. 112 villas. Mid-Dec-Apr (1-wk min): $875/wk; lower rates rest of yr. Crib $25/wk. TV; cable. Heated pool; whirlpool. Restaurants nearby. Ck-out 10 am. Lighted tennis.

Clubhouse. Lndry facilities in each villa. Microwaves. Picnic tables, grills. Cr cds: A, C, D, DS, ER, MC, V.

🅳 🚶 🏊 🅰

Restaurants

★ ★ ★ **BIJOU CAFE.** 1287 1st St (34236). 941/366-8111. Hrs: 11:30 am-2 pm, 5-9:30 pm; Fri, Sat to 10:30 pm; Sun 5-9 pm. Closed some major hols; Sun mid-May-early Jan. Res accepted. Continental menu. Bar. Wine list. A la carte entrees: lunch $8.25-$14.75, dinner $15.95-$22.95. Child's meals. Specializes in seafood, roast duck, Black Angus beef. Own pastries. Opp Sarasota Opera House. Cr cds: A, C, D, MC, V.

🅳 ➡ ♥

★ ★ **CAFE BACI.** 4001 S Tamiami Trail (34231), on US 41. 941/921-4848. Hrs: 11:30 am-2:30 pm, 4:30-10 pm; Fri to 11 pm; Sat 4:30-11 pm; Sun from 4:30 pm. Closed Dec 25. Res accepted. Italian menu. Bar. Semi-a la carte: lunch $5.95-$10.95, dinner $10.95-$23.95. Child's meals. Specializes in Northern Italian cooking. Cr cds: A, C, D, DS, MC, V.

🅳 ➡

★ **CAFE CAMPESTRE.** 3164 Bee Ridge Rd (34239). 941/923-5356. Hrs: 11 am-10 pm. Closed Easter, Thanksgiving, Dec 25. Res accepted. Mexican menu. Semi-a la carte: lunch, dinner $2-$16. Specialties: uchepos, chili relleno. Intimate village atmosphere. Cr cds: MC, V.

🅳

★ ★ ★ **CAFE L'EUROPE.** 431 St Armands Circle (34236). 941/388-4415. E-mail leurope@ix.netcom.com; web www.l'europe.net. Hrs: 11 am-4 pm, 5-10 pm; Sun from 10 am. Res accepted. Continental menu. Bar to midnight. Wine list. Semi-a la carte: lunch $8.95-$13.95, dinner $17.95-$25.95. Child's meals. Specialties: New Zealand rack of lamb, bouillabaisse. Own pastries. Pianist & vocalist Tues-Sat. Valet parking. Located in historic bldg; European atmosphere. Cr cds: A, C, D, DS, MC, V.

🅳 ➡

✔★ **CARAGIULO'S.** 69 S Palm Ave (34236), in theater/art district. 941/951-0866. E-mail jcrest@aol.com. Hrs: 11 am-10 pm; Fri to 1 am; Sat 5 pm-1 am; Sun 5-10 pm. Closed some major hols. Italian menu. Bar. Semi-a la carte: lunch, dinner $5.25-$14.95. Specializes in seafood, veal, gourmet pizza. Entertainment Wed-Sun. Outdoor dining. Cr cds: A, C, D, DS, MC, V.

🅳 ➡

★ ★ **CHEZ DANIEL.** 2920 Beneva Rd (34232). 941/924-3224. Hrs: 5-10 pm. Closed some major hols; also Sun (off season). Res accepted. Country French menu. A la carte entrees: dinner $15.95-$23.95. Specialties: bouillabaisse, canard a la orange. Country French atmosphere. Cr cds: DS, ER, MC, V.

🅳 ➡

★ ★ **COASTERS.** 1500 Stickney Point Rd (34231), at Boatyard Shopping Village. 941/925-0300. Hrs: 11:30 am-10 pm. Bar to midnight; Fri, Sat to 1 am. Semi-a la carte: lunch $5.95-$8.50, dinner $12.95-$16.95. Child's meals. Specializes in seafood, grilled selections, pasta. Entertainment. Free valet parking. Outdoor patio dining. Views of Intracoastal Waterway. Cr cds: A, C, D, DS, MC, V.

🅳 ➡

★ ★ **COLUMBIA.** 411 St Armands Circle (34236). 941/388-3987. Hrs: 11 am-11 pm; Sun noon-10 pm; early-bird dinner 4-6 pm. Res accepted. Spanish menu. Bar. Semi-a la carte: lunch $8.95-$14.95, dinner $14.95-$24.95. Child's meals. Specialties: fresh Gulf red snapper Alicante, paella Valenciana. Entertainment Sun. Spanish decor; statuary, paintings, stained-glass windows. Family-owned. Cr cds: A, C, D, DS, MC, V.

🅳 ➡

★ ★ **DAVID MICHAEL'S.** *328 John Ringling Blvd (34236).* 941/388-4429. Hrs: noon-3 pm, 5:30-9 pm. Closed Sun; most major hols; also Mon May-Nov. Res accepted. Serv bar. A la carte entrees: lunch $8.95-$10, dinner $17-$22. Child's meals. Specializes in beef, chicken. Street parking. Outdoor dining. Casual dining. Cr cds: D, DS, MC, V.

★ **EL GRECO CAFE.** *1592 Main St (34236).* 941/365-2234. Hrs: 11 am-10 pm. Closed Sun; major hols. Greek menu. Wine, beer. Semi-a la carte: lunch $4.25-$7.25, dinner $7.95-$16.95. Specialties: lamb shank, Greek salad, moussaka. Informal atmosphere. Cr cds: MC, V.

[D] [⌗]

★ **GASTRONOMIA.** *7119 S Tamiami Trail (34231).* 941/927-8331. Hrs: 11:30 am-10 pm; Sun from 4 pm. Closed Thanksgiving, Dec 25. Italian menu. Wine. A la carte entrees: lunch $4.95-$6.95, dinner $5.95-$11.95. Specializes in pasta. Cr cds: A, C, D, DS, MC, V.

[D] [⌗]

★ ★ **HILLVIEW GRILL.** *1920 Hillview St (34239).* 941/952-0045. Hrs: 11:30 am-2:30 pm, 5-10 pm; Sun 5-9 pm. Closed Sun June-Sept; some major hols. Res accepted. Bar. Semi-a la carte: lunch $4.95-$8.95, dinner $8.95-$18.95. Child's meals. Specializes in fresh fish, pasta, Creole dishes. Outdoor dining. Cr cds: A, DS, MC, V.

[D] [⌗] [♥]

★ **ITALIAN GRILL.** *8620 S Tamiami Trail (US 41) (34238).* 941/966-6565. Hrs: 11 am-10 pm; Fri, Sat to 11 pm; Sun from noon. Closed Easter, Thanksgiving, Dec 25. Res accepted. Italian menu. Wine, beer. Semi-a la carte: lunch $3.95-$5.95, dinner $4.95-$11.95. Child's meals. Specializes in pizza, pasta. Casual, Italian family atmosphere. Cr cds: A, D, DS, MC, V.

[D] [⌗]

★ ★ **JO-TO JAPANESE STEAK HOUSE.** *7971 N Tamiami Trail (34243).* 941/351-4677. Hrs: 5-10 pm; Fri, Sat to 11 pm. Closed July 4, Thanksgiving, Dec. 25; also Super Bowl Sun. Res accepted. Japanese menu. Bar. Semi-a la carte: dinner $10.95-$22.95. Specializes in sushi, authentic Japanese cuisine. Tableside cooking. Japanese decor. Cr cds: A, C, D, MC, V.

[D] [⌗]

★ ★ **MARINA JACK.** *Marina Plaza (34236), on Island Park Pier.* 941/365-4232. Hrs: 11:45 am-10 pm. Closed Dec 25. Res accepted. Continental menu. Bar to 1 am. Wine list. Semi-a la carte: lunch $5.95-$8.95, dinner $10.25-$27.95. Child's meals. Specializes in fresh seafood, veal, beef. Pianist, soloist Tue-Sun. Valet parking. Outdoor dining. On bay. Lunch & dinner cruises avail (see MARINA JACK II DINNER BOAT, Unrated Dining). Cr cds: MC, V.

[D] [⌗]

★ ★ **MICHAEL'S ON EAST.** *1212 East Ave S (34239), in Mid-town Plaza.* 941/366-0007. E-mail michael@bestfood.com; web www.bestfood.com. Hrs: 11:30 am-2 pm, 5-10 pm; Fri to 11 pm; Sat 5-11 pm; Sun to 10 pm. Res accepted. Continental menu. Bar. Wine cellar. A la carte entrees: lunch $7.50-$16.50. Semi-a la carte: dinner $15.50-$28. Specializes in fresh seafood, pasta, steak. Own baking. Piano lounge; jazz (wkends). Valet parking. Contemporary decor. Cr cds: A, D, MC, V.

[D] [⌗] [♥]

★ ★ **MICHAEL'S SEAFOOD GRILLE.** *214 Sarasota Quay (34236).* 941/951-2467. E-mail michael@bestfood.com; web www.bestfood.com. Hrs: 5-10 pm; Fri, Sat to 11 pm. Res accepted. Bar to 2 am. Semi-a la carte: dinner $11.95-$29.95. Prix fixe: $24.95. Child's meals. Specializes in seafood. Entertainment. Valet parking. Outdoor dining. Cr cds: A, C, D, DS, MC, V.

[D] [⌗]

✔ ★ ★ **MOREL.** *3809 S Tuttle Ave (34239).* 941/927-8716. Hrs: 5-10 pm. Closed Sun, Mon; major hols; Sept. Res accepted. Wine, beer. A la carte entrees: dinner $15-$19.75. Specialties: charred smoked Gouda

tuna, hoisin & maple glazed sea bass, lump crab ravioli. Early 20th-century decor. Cr cds: A, D, MC, V.

[D]

★ ★ **NICK'S ON THE WATER.** *230 Sarasota Quay (34236), US 41 & Fruitville Rd.* 941/954-3839. Hrs: 11:30 am-10 pm; Fri, Sat to 11 pm; early-bird dinner 4-5:30 pm. Res accepted. Italian menu. Bar. Semi-a la carte: lunch $5.95-$8.95, dinner $10.95-$22.95. Child's meals. Specialties: cioppino, veal bruschetta. Valet parking. Outdoor dining on wrap-around balcony. Cr cds: A, D, DS, MC, V.

[D] [⌗]

✔ ★ ★ **PRIMO.** *8076 N Tamiami Trail (34243).* 941/359-3690. Hrs: 4-10 pm. Closed Easter, Thanksgiving, Dec 25. Italian menu. Bar. Semi-a la carte: dinner $5.25-$15.95. Child's meals. Specializes in pasta, veal, fresh seafood. Own baking, desserts. Cr cds: A, C, D, DS, MC, V.

[D] [⌗]

✔ ★ **SUGAR AND SPICE.** *4000 Cattlemen Rd (34233).* 941/342-1649. Hrs: 11 am-10 pm. Closed Sun; major hols. Semi-a la carte: lunch, dinner $2.50-$11.95. Child's meals. Specializes in Amish-style dishes. Own desserts. Victorian decor. Totally nonsmoking. Cr cds: DS, MC, V.

[D]

★ **TOMMY BAHAMA'S TROPICAL CAFE.** *300 John Ringling Blvd (34236).* 941/388-2888. Hrs: 11 am-11 pm. Closed Thanksgiving, Dec 25. Res accepted. Caribbean menu. Bar. Semi-a la carte: lunch $7.50-$9.50, dinner $12.95-$20.95. Child's meals. Specialties: mango shrimp salad, pollo island pasta, wha'ja maican pork. Island music. Street parking. Outdoor dining. Caribbean atmosphere and decor. Cr cds: A, MC, V.

[D] [⌗]

Unrated Dining Spot

MARINA JACK II DINNER BOAT. *(See Marina Jack Restaurant)* 941/366-9255. Hrs: noon seating (Jan-May) & 7 pm seating (all-yr). Closed Sept; Dec 25. Res required. Continental menu. Bar. Semi-a la carte: lunch $12 (purchase of 1 lunch entree plus $4 boat fare), dinner $22 (purchase of 1 dinner entree plus $6 boat fare). Specializes in beef, seafood. Guitarist during dinner tours. Dine while cruising aboard 100-ft double-decked sternwheeler, a replica of the steam sternwheel towboat. Excellent view of Sarasota's waterfront & landmarks. Cr cds: MC, V.

[D]

Sebring (F-5)

(See also Lake Placid)

Founded 1912 **Pop** 8,900 **Elev** 131 ft **Area code** 941 **E-mail** sebcc@ct.net **Web** www.sebring.com

Information Chamber of Commerce, 309 S Circle, 33870; 941/385-8448.

With sandy ridge country for citrus, mucklands for vegetables and flowers, and flatlands for cattle, Sebring's (SEE-bring) economy relies upon agriculture, light industry and some tourism. The city has taken over the 2,300 acres that once comprised Hendricks Field Air Force Base and developed them as the Sebring International Raceway, Airport and Industrial Park. The city encircles 3,200-acre Lake Jackson, with 46,000-acre Lake Istokpoga to the southeast.

What to See and Do

Highlands Hammock State Park. Approx 4,600 acres of hardwood hammock and cabbage palms with many orchids and air plants. An outstanding nature park with museum, 5 mi of foot trails, 4 mi of scenic drive, 1-1½-hr conducted wildlife tours by tram. Nature trails; bicycle rentals. Picnic areas (grills, shelters). Camping (hookups, dump station). Standard hrs, fees. 2½ mi W off US 27/98, on FL 634. Phone 941/386-6094.

Annual Event

Sebring 12-Hour Endurance Race. Oldest road race in America. Mid-Mar.

Motels

★ **DAYS INN.** *1406 US 27N (33870).* 941/382-1148. 37 rms, 11 with shower only, 10 kits. Mid-Dec-Apr: S $72-$78; D $85-$95; each addl $7; under 12 free; higher rates special events. Crib $5. TV; cable. Pool. Complimentary coffee in lobby. Restaurant nearby. Ck-out 11 am. Coin lndry. Meeting rm. Business servs avail. Cr cds: A, C, D, DS, JCB, MC, V.

★ **ECONO LODGE.** *(2511 US 27S, Avon Park 33825)* 941/453-2000; FAX 941/453-0820. 58 rms, 2 story, 4 kits. Jan-Apr: S $64.95; D $69.95; each addl $5; under 12 free; wkly rates; higher rates special events; lower rates rest of yr. Crib free. TV. Pool. Complimentary continental bkfst. Ck-out 11 am. Coin lndry. Business servs avail. On Lake Glenada. Cr cds: A, DS, MC, V.

★ ★ **HOLIDAY INN.** *6525 US 27N (33870).* 941/385-4500; FAX 941/382-4793. 148 rms, 2 story. S, D $69-$99; under 18 free; wkend rates; higher rates special events (4-day min). Crib free. TV; cable. VCR avail (movies). Pool; wading pool, poolside serv, sauna. Restaurant 6:30 am-2 pm, 5-9 pm. Rm serv. Bar; entertainment Wed-Sat. Ck-out noon. Coin lndry. Meeting rms. Bellhops. Valet serv. Microwaves avail. Lawn games. Cr cds: A, C, D, DS, JCB, MC, V.

Motor Hotel

★ ★ **INN ON THE LAKES.** *3100 Gulfview Rd (33872), at US 27.* 941/471-9400; FAX 941/471-9400, ext. 195; res: 800/531-5253. 161 rms, 3 story, 14 suites. Jan-mid-Apr: S, D $55-$80; suites $85-$135; wkly, monthly rates; package plans; higher rates special events; lower rates rest of yr. Crib free. Pet accepted, some restrictions. TV; cable (premium), VCR avail. Pool; poolside serv. Restaurant 6:30 am-11 pm. Rm serv. Bar noon-11 pm. Ck-out noon. Coin lndry. Meeting rms. Business servs avail. In-rm modem link. Sundries. 18-hole golf privileges, greens fee $30, putting green, driving range. Exercise equipt. Health club privileges. Refrigerator, microwaves in suites. Overlooks Little Lake Jackson. Cr cds: A, C, D, DS, MC, V.

Siesta Key (F-3)

(See also Bradenton, Sarasota, Venice)

Pop 7,772 **Elev** 10 ft **Area code** 941 **Zip** 34242 **Web** www.sarasota-online.com/siesta
Information Chamber of Commerce, 5100 Ocean Blvd, Suite B; 941/349-3800.

Back in 1907, Harry L. Higel and Captain Louis Roberts launched an advertising campaign to draw vacationers to "the prettiest spot in the world." Although the claim may be disputed, Siesta Key has been hailed as "the island paradise in the Gulf of Mexico," and Crescent Beach has been rated as one of the top three beaches in the world, along with Waikiki and the French Riviera. Shell hunters, snorkelers and anglers usually have great success here. With close proximity to Sarasota and its attractions, Siesta Key is a good base from which to take in the sights.

Motels

★ **BEST WESTERN SIESTA BEACH RESORT.** *5311 Ocean Blvd.* 941/349-3211; FAX 941/349-7915. E-mail odysseys@sprynet.com; web www.sarasota-online.com. 53 units, 1-2 story, 38 kits. Mid-Jan-Apr: S, D $135-$155; kit. units $175-$250; under 12 free; wkly rates; wkend packages off-season; lower rates rest of yr. TV; cable. Pool; whirlpool. Restaurant nearby. Ck-out 11 am. Business servs avail. In-rm modem link. Coin lndry. Picnic tables. Opp Gulf. Cr cds: A, C, D, DS, ER, JCB, MC, V.

★ **CAPTIVA BEACH RESORT.** *6772 Sara Sea Circle.* 941/349-4131; FAX 941/349-8141. E-mail captiva@gte.net. 20 kit. units, 4 suites. 3-day min: S, D $130-$170; each addl $7; suites $210-$290. Crib free. TV; cable. Pool. Ck-out 9:30 am. Business servs avail. Lawn games. Microwaves. Totally nonsmoking. Cr cds: A, MC, V.

★ ★ **CRESCENT VIEW BEACH CLUB.** *6512 Midnight Pass Rd.* 941/349-2000; FAX 941/349-9748; res: 800/344-7171. E-mail cvbclub@earthlink.net. 26 kit. units, 2-4 story. Mid-Dec-early May: kit. units $200-$410; lower rates rest of yr. Crib $6. TV; cable (premium). Heated pool; whirlpool. Complimentary coffee in lobby. Restaurant opp 11 am-11 pm. Ck-out 11 am. Lndry facilities avail. Business servs avail. Balconies. Picnic tables, grills. On beach. Cr cds: A, C, D, DS, ER, MC, V.

★ ★ **TROPICAL SHORES BEACH RESORT.** *6717 Sarasea Circle, S of Stickney Point Bridge.* 941/349-3330; FAX 941/346-0025; res: 800/235-3493. E-mail tropshores@aol.com; web www.tropshores.com. 30 kit. units, 1-2 story. Dec 15-Apr 28: S, D $176-$225; each addl $15; suites $225-$395; wkly rates; lower rates rest of yr. Pet accepted. TV; cable (premium). Heated pool. Restaurant nearby. Ck-out 10 am. Business servs avail. Lawn games. Microwaves. Picnic tables. Cr cds: A, MC, V.

Inn

★ ★ **TURTLE BEACH RESORT.** *9049 Midnight Pass.* 941/349-4554; FAX 941/312-9034. E-mail grubi@ix.netcom.com; web www.sarasota-online.com-/turtle. 6 kit. units, 5 with shower only. Mid-Dec-Apr (7-day min): $1,275-$1,850/wk; 5th addl $15; wkend, nightly rates; lower rates rest of yr. Crib free. Pet accepted. TV; cable, VCR avail. Pool. Complimentary coffee in rms. Restaurant adj 5-10 pm. Ck-out 11 am, ck-in 1 pm. Microwaves, in-rm whirlpools. Patios. Picnic tables. View of bay; gazebo. Totally nonsmoking. Cr cds: A, D, DS, MC, V.

Restaurants

★ ★ **BEACH CAFE AND BAR.** *431 Beach Rd, 2 mi N of Stickney Point Bridge.* 941/349-7117. Hrs: 4-10 pm. Res accepted. Continental, French menu. Bar to 2 am. Semi-a la carte: dinner $5.50-$17.95. Specialties: veal scaloppini, duck with peaches, fresh seafood. Entertainment Tues-Sat. Valet parking. European ambience; garden room, art collection. Cr cds: MC, V.

★ ★ **JAVIER'S.** *6621 Midnight Pass Rd.* 941/349-1792. Hrs: 5-9:30 pm; early-bird dinner to 6 pm. Closed Sun, Mon; some major hols; last wk May; first wk June; first 2 wks in Sept. Res accepted. Wine, beer. Semi-a la carte: dinner $10.95-$18.95. Child's meals. Specializes in fresh seafood, New American dishes with South American flair. Chic, intimate atmosphere. Totally nonsmoking. Cr cds: A, MC, V.

★ **LA TERRAZZA.** *5157 Ocean Blvd.* 941/349-8646. Hrs: 5-10 pm. Closed Dec 25; also 2 weeks in summer. Res accepted. Italian menu. Wine, beer. Semi-a la carte: dinner $10.95-$23.95. Specializes in fresh seafood, veal dishes. Own pasta, baking. Some street parking. Outdoor dining. Italian ambience. Cr cds: A, DS, MC, V.

[D] [⌁]

★ ★ ★ **OPHELIA'S ON THE BAY.** *9105 Midnight Pass Rd, 3 mi S of Stickney Point Bridge.* 941/349-2212. E-mail ophelias@aol.com. Hrs: 5-10 pm. Res accepted. Continental menu. Bar. Wine list. Semi-a la carte: dinner $13.95-$27.95. Child's meals. Specializes in fresh seafood. Valet parking. Outdoor dining. On waterfront; dockage. Cr cds: A, C, D, DS, MC, V.

[D] [⌁]

★ ★ ★ **SUMMERHOUSE.** *6101 Midnight Pass Rd, 1/2 mi N of Stickney Point Bridge.* 941/349-1100. Web www.sarasota-online.com/summer/. Hrs: 5-10 pm; Sun to 9 pm; Sun brunch 11 am-3 pm (in season). Res accepted. Continental menu. Bar to 12:30 am. Wine cellar. Semi-a la carte: dinner $14.50-$23.50. Sun brunch $20. Specializes in fresh seafood, lamb, duck. Own baking. Band. Valet parking. Outdoor dining. Two-story, glass-walled rm overlooks tropical garden. Fine art collection. Cr cds: A, C, D, DS, MC, V.

[D] [⌁] [♥]

★ ★ **SURFRIDER.** *6400 Midnight Pass Rd.* 941/346-1199. Hrs: 5-9:15 pm; early-bird dinner to 6 pm. Closed Sun, Mon; Jan 1, Super Bowl Sun, Dec 25; also last wk May, 1st wk June. Res accepted. Wine, beer. Semi-a la carte: dinner $9.50-$16.95. Child's meals. Specializes in fresh fish, pasta, ribs. Outdoor dining. In 1920s beach house. Totally nonsmoking. Cr cds: A, MC, V.

[D]

★ ★ **TURTLES.** *8875 Midnight Pass Rd.* 941/346-2207. Hrs: 11:30 am-midnight; early-bird dinner 4-6 pm. Res accepted. Bar. Semi-a la carte: lunch $5-$9.45, dinner $7.99-$18.95. Child's meals. Specializes in rack of lamb, local seafood. Entertainment Tues-Sat. Outdoor dining. Waterfront dining with views of bay and mangrove islands. Cr cds: A, DS, MC, V.

[D] [⌁]

Silver Springs (D-4)

(See also Ocala)

Pop 6,421 **Elev** 98 ft **Area code** 352 **E-mail** mmalone@mercury.net **Web** www.ocalacc.com
Information Ocala/Marion County Chamber of Commerce, 110 E Silver Springs Blvd, Ocala 34470; 352/629-8051.

Nearly two million people come to this town each year, principally to see the springs, one of the state's top attractions. This is lake, horse and cattle country, and a Ranger District office of the Ocala National Forest (see OCALA) is located here.

What to See and Do

Silver Springs-Source of the Silver River. This 350-acre multi-theme nature park and national landmark includes the main spring from which flows more than one-half billion gallons of water every 24 hrs. Estimated to be 100,000 yrs old, the spring has one large opening through which water, filtered through limestone, surges to the surface from a 65-ft by 12-ft cavern. Four different 30-min rides let visitors view the area: the famous glass-bottom boats and a jungle cruise pass by 14 springs, various plant and fish species, alligators, waterfowl and exotic wildlife; Lost River Voyage lets visitors experience Florida as it was 1,000 yrs ago; and jeep safari trams take people through a 35-acre rainforest where 30 different species of animals live. In addition, the surrounding park includes the World of Bears exhibit, Kids Ahoy! Playland, entertainment on the Twin Oaks Mansion concert stage and live animal shows. Strollers, wheelchairs avail. (Daily) On FL 40. Phone 352/236-2121 or 800/234-7458. ¢¢¢¢¢

Wild Waters. Water park including 450,000-gallon wave pool, 10 flume rides, children's play area; miniature golf (fee); arcades (fee); 2 volleyball courts; sun decks, picnic area. (Apr-Sept, daily) On FL 40. Phone 352/236-2121 or 800/234-7458. ¢¢¢¢

Motels

✔★ **DAYS INN OCALA EAST.** *5001 E Silver Springs Blvd (FL 40) (34488).* 352/236-2891; FAX 352/236-3546. 56 rms, 2 story. Mid-Jan-mid-Apr, mid-June-early Sept: S $40-$60; D $45-$60; each addl $5; under 18 free; lower rates rest of yr. Crib free. Pet accepted; $5. TV; cable, VCR avail (movies). Pool. Playground. Complimentary coffee in lobby. Restaurant adj 6 am-2 pm. Ck-out 11 am. Coin lndry. Some refrigerators. Ocala National Forest nearby. Cr cds: A, C, D, DS, JCB, MC, V.

[⌁] [≈] [⋈] [🔥] [SC]

★ ★ **HOLIDAY INN.** *5751 E Silver Springs Blvd (FL 40) (34488).* 352/236-2575. E-mail holidaynss@worldnet.att.net. 104 rms, 2 story. Feb-Apr, June-Aug: S, D $52-$79; under 18 free; higher rates hols; lower rates rest of yr. Crib free. Pet accepted. TV; cable, VCR avail (movies). Pool; wading pool, poolside serv. Coffee in rms. Restaurant open 24 hrs. Rm serv. Bar 5-10 pm; closed Sun-Thurs. Ck-out noon. Meeting rms. Business servs avail. In-rm modem link. Bellhops. Valet serv. Fishing guides. Kennels. Cr cds: A, C, D, DS, JCB, MC, V.

[D] [⌁] [≈] [⋈] [🔥] [SC]

★ **KNIGHTS INN.** *PO Box 475 (34488), 5565 E Silver Springs Blvd (FL 40).* 352/236-2616; FAX 352/236-1941. 40 rms, 2 story. Feb-Mar & June-Aug: S $40-$45; D $45-$50; each addl $5; under 18 free; higher rates: races, hols, football wkends, special events; lower rates rest of yr. Crib free. Pet accepted; $10. TV; cable (premium). Pool. Playground. Restaurant adj 7 am-10 pm. Ck-out noon. Lawn games. Some refrigerators. Patios, balconies. Cr cds: A, C, D, DS, JCB, MC, V.

[⌁] [≈] [⋈] [🔥] [SC]

✔★ **SUN PLAZA.** *PO Box 216 (34489), 5461 E Silver Springs Blvd (FL 40).* 352/236-2343; FAX 352/236-1214. 47 rms, 9 kits. Late Dec-Apr, June-Labor Day: S $35-$40; D $38-$50; each addl $5; kit. units $38-$50; lower rates rest of yr. Crib free. Pet accepted; $5. TV. Pool. Playground. Restaurant adj 6 am-11 pm. Ck-out 11 am. Lawn games. Picnic tables, grill. Cr cds: A, C, D, DS, MC, V.

[⌁] [≈] [🔥]

St Augustine (C-5)

(See also Jacksonville, Marineland)

Founded 1565 **Pop** 11,692 **Elev** 6 ft **Area code** 904 **E-mail** tdc@co.st.johns.fl.us; **Web** www.oldcity.com
Information St Johns County Visitors & Convention Bureau, 88 Riberia St, Suite 250, 32084; 904/829-1711 or 800/653-2489.

Spanish towers and steeples, red-capped roofs and low overhanging balconies are reminders of St Augustine's four centuries of history, which began on September 8, 1565, when Don Pedro Menendez de Aviles dropped anchor and rowed ashore. As a symbol of the cultural ties between the United States and Latin nations, and in an effort to establish an Hispanic counterpart to Williamsburg, Virginia, St Augustine (the oldest permanent settlement in the United States) has been restoring important historic areas to their former Spanish charm.

St Augustine was under a Spanish flag longer than it has been under the Stars and Stripes and has possibly retained more of the languid flavor of a Spanish colony than any other city in the US. Mellowed by time and the sun, the city's Spanish-Renaissance architecture continues to overshadow both 19th-century gingerbread and 20th-century neon and plate glass. Old walled gardens, narrow streets, the plaza and horse-drawn surreys all conspire to maintain St Augustine's Old World mood.

Ponce de Leon and his men are believed to have landed in the vicinity of what is now St Augustine in 1513 to fill their casks with water from a local spring. However, the formal history of Spanish settlement began some 50 years later when Menendez arrived, launching St Augustine on a history often marked by bloody violence. Following orders, Menendez wiped out the French Huguenot settlement at Fort Caroline (see), using such violent thoroughness that the River of Dolphins became known as the Matanzas—the Spanish word for "slaughters." (See FORT MATANZAS NATIONAL MONUMENT.) To protect this strategic outpost, the Spanish built Castillo de San Marcos, a massive gray fortress that still dominates the town today. Through the centuries, St Augustine has been attacked, counterattacked, pillaged, burned, betrayed and defended. The Spanish, British, Confederate and US flags all flew over the city.

St Augustine began its more recent history as a fashionable resort when, in the 1880s, Henry Morrison Flagler, the omnipresent personality in Florida history, built two large hotels here and made the city the headquarters of the Florida East Coast Railroad. St Augustine occupies a peninsula with the Matanzas and North rivers on the east and south and the San Sebastian on the west. Still the headquarters for the Florida East Coast Railroad, the city's industries—other than tourism—include food and seafood processing, farming, boat building, printing, bookbinding and aircraft manufacturing.

What to See and Do

Anastasia State Recreation Area. More than 1,000 acres, includes coquina quarries and high white dunes. Swimming; fishing. Nature trails. Picnicking. Camping (hookups, dump station). Standard hrs, fees. 3 mi S on FL A1A. Phone 904/461-2033.

Castillo de San Marcos National Monument. Grim but venerable, Castillo de San Marcos is the symbol of Spain's ubiquitous presence in St Augustine and the rest of Florida. This massive, masonry structure, constructed between 1672-1695, was built to permanently replace a succession of nine wooden fortifications. It was made of coquina, a natural rock of shells and sand. Hispanic artisans and convicts, Native American laborers, black royal slaves and English prisoners erected walls 25 ft high, 14 ft thick at the base, 9 ft at the top, and 4 ft at the parapet. In 1683, before completion, Castillo served as St Augustine's citadel during a pirate raid. Castillo de San Marcos was never conquered. It withstood a 50-day siege when St Augustine was captured by the South Carolinians in 1702, and another siege of 38 days in 1740. During the American Revolution, the British imprisoned "rebels" in the Castillo and felt confident the structure could repulse an American or a Spanish attack. The United States used the fort as a battery in the coastal defense system, as a military prison and as a magazine. Wildcat, the Seminole leader, led an escape from Castillo; Confederate and Union troops occupied it during the Civil War; and American deserters were imprisoned here during the Spanish-American War. As Fort Marion, Castillo de San Marcos was the principal fortification in a regional defense system that reached north to the St Mary's River, south to Matanzas Inlet and west to St Mark's. A unique specimen of a vanished style of military architecture and engineering, it became a national monument in 1924. Area (daily; closed Dec 25). Golden Eagle, Golden Age and Golden Access passports (see MAKING THE MOST OF YOUR TRIP) all available at the Fort. Overlooking Matanzas Bay at jct of Castillo Dr & Avenida Menendez (both are FL A1A). Contact Superintendent, Castillo de San Marcos National Monument, 1 Castillo Dr, 32084; 904/829-6506. ¢¢

Flagler College (1968). (1,400 students) The restored main campus building is the former Ponce de Leon Hotel, built in 1887 by railroad magnate Henry Morrison Flagler. Campus tours (May-mid-Aug, daily; free) begin in the rotunda area of the main building. King St. Phone 904/829-6481.

Fountain of Youth. A 21-acre tropical setting thought to be the first recorded North American landmark. Native American burial grounds; planetarium and discovery globe (both continuous shows); museum, swan pool, Ponce de Leon statue. (Daily; closed Dec 25) 155 Magnolia Ave, at William St. Phone 904/829-3168. ¢¢

Lighthouse Museum of St Augustine. Tours of restored lightkeeper's house; coastal museum with exhibits, video. Visitors can also climb to top of lighthouse tower. Gift shop. (Daily; closed Easter, Thanksgiving, Dec 25)

81 Lighthouse Ave, on Anastasia Island. Phone 904/829-0745. Museum ¢; Museum and tower ¢¢

Lightner Museum. In restored 300-rm former Alcazar Hotel (1888); fountains and gardens on grounds. Natural science exhibits. Victorian village; collections of art, porcelain, 19th-century musical instruments, needlework, ceramics, Tiffany glass, furniture, dolls. (Daily; closed Dec 25) 75 King St. Phone 904/824-2874. ¢¢

Mission of Nombre de Dios. A 208-ft stainless-steel cross marks the site of the founding of St Augustine, September 8, 1565. Here also is the **Shrine of Our Lady of La Leche**, established in 1603 and dedicated to the Motherhood of Mary. (Daily) San Marco Ave, 6 blks N of information center. Phone 904/824-2809. **Free.**

Oldest Wooden Schoolhouse (ca 1760). Served as a private residence and schoolhouse before the Civil War. (Daily; closed Dec 25) 14 St George St. Phone 904/824-0192. ¢

Oldest House (Gonzalez-Alvarez House). Located on a site in use since the early 1600s, the house (built 1700s), furnishings and neighborhood reflect periods of Spanish, British and American ownership; other buildings on site include the Manucy Museum of St Augustine History and the Tovar House, which houses the Museum of Florida's Army. (Daily; closed Dec 25) 14 St Francis St. Phone 904/824-2872. ¢¢

Oldest Store Museum. Turn-of-the-century general store museum; more than 100,000 vintage items on display. (Daily; closed Dec 25) 4 Artillery Lane. Phone 904/829-9729. ¢¢

Pena-Peck House (ca 1700). Home of the Spanish Royal Treasurer; later residence of the Peck family (1837-1930). Original 19th-century; guided tours. (Daily; closed some major hols) 143 St George St. Phone 904/829-5064. ¢¢

Potter's Wax Museum. More than 170 life-size wax figures of famous historical personalities; multi-image presentation; workshop. (Daily; closed Dec 25) 17 King St. Phone 904/829-9056. ¢¢¢

Ripley's Believe It or Not Museum. In historic Castle Warden; three floors of exhibits. (Daily) 19 San Marco Ave, near City Gate. Phone 904/824-1606 or -1607. ¢¢¢

Sightseeing.

Scenic Cruise. Departs from Municipal Marina, Avenida Menendez. One-and-one-quarter-hour tour of waterfront and Matanzas Bay aboard *Victory III*. (Daily; no tours Dec 25) Phone 904/824-1806. ¢¢¢

Sightseeing Trains. Narrated, 7-mi, 1-hr trips; stop-off privileges. Departures every 15 min (daily; no tours Dec 25). 170 San Marco Ave; eight boarding stations. Phone 904/829-6545. ¢¢¢¢

Historical Tours. Narrated, 1-hr tours aboard green & white, open-air trolleys. (Daily; no tours Easter, Dec 24, Dec 25) 167 San Marco Ave. Phone 904/829-3800. ¢¢¢¢

Colee's Horse-drawn Carriage Tours. Departs from Bayfront near entrance to Fort Castillo de San Marco. St Augustine Transfer Co. Lectured tour of historical area lasts approx 1 hr. Night tours avail. (Daily; no tours Easter, Dec 25) Phone 904/829-2818. ¢¢¢

⭐ **Spanish Quarter.** Restoration of 18th-century Spanish colonial village by the Historic St Augustine Preservation Board, a state project. The original settlement was founded in 1565. The following buildings are open (daily; closed Dec 25). Tickets may be purchased at ticket booth on St George St. Phone 904/825-6830. ¢¢¢ Admission includes

Gallegos House. Reconstruction of a two-room tabby house occupied in the 1750s by a Spanish soldier and his family. Daily life-style and household activities of the period are depicted; demonstrations of 18th-century outdoor cooking. 21 St George St.

Gomez House. Reconstruction of 18th-century, one-rm wooden dwelling occupied by a Spanish infantryman in 1763; small neighborhood shop located in a portion of the room where neighbors came to trade or barter. 23 St George St.

Peso de Burgo & Pellicer houses (ca 1780). Two reconstructed frame houses sharing a common center wall. Houses Spanish Quarter Museum Store. 55 St George St.

De Mesa-Sanchez House. One of 33 original surviving colonial houses recently restored; antique furnishings from the early 1800s, when Florida was still a US Territory. 43 St George St.

Gonzales & de Hita houses. The original Gonzalez House, built of native shellstone, is typical of Spanish colonial houses. The interior contains an area with demonstrations of spinning, weaving and textile arts. The de Hita residence is used for special hands-on learning activities. 37 St George St.

Blacksmith Shop. A functioning 18th-century Spanish blacksmith shop, providing hardware for the museum village. This unique Spanish shop is built of tabby, a type of concrete made from oyster shells and lime.

St Augustine Alligator Farm. Farm, established in 1893, offers view of huge alligators and crocodiles; Reptile Show, American Alligator Show, and Snappin' Sam Show; also on the farm are tropical birds, raccoons, monkeys; deer, ducks and goats to feed. (Daily) 2 mi S of the Bridge of Lions on FL A1A, on Anastasia Island. Phone 904/824-3337. ¢¢¢¢

Visitor Information Center. Visitors' guide, maps and descriptive literature available. Continuous film presentation on St Augustine and St Johns County. (Daily; closed Dec 25) 10 Castillo Dr. Phone 904/825-1000. **Free.**

Ximenez-Fatio House (1798). Originally a house and general store built of coquina; used as an inn during 1800s; kitchen in rear is only original remaining in St Augustine. Museum house of the National Society of Colonial Dames of America in the State of Florida. (Feb-Aug, Thurs-Mon) 20 Aviles St. Phone 904/829-3575. **Donation.**

Zorayda Castle (1883). Inspired by the Alhambra in Spain. Cat rug; court of lions; harem quarters. (Daily; closed Dec 25) 83 King St. Phone 904/824-3097. ¢¢

Annual Events

Blessing of the Fleet. Matanzas Bay. Shrimp fleet as well as privately owned boats are blessed. Palm Sunday.

Spanish Night Watch. St George St. Candlelight procession with colorful Spanish costumes commemorates the presence of the Spanish in St Augustine. Mid-June.

Greek Landing Day Festival. St George St. Music, crafts, food. Late June.

British Night Watch. St George St. Grand illumination ceremony. 1st wkend Dec.

Christmas Tour of Homes. Tour of historic and unusual homes, decorated for the holidays. 1st Sun Dec.

Motels

✔★ ★ **BAYFRONT INN.** *138 Avenida Menendez (32084). 904/824-1681; FAX 904/829-8721; res: 800/558-3455.* 39 rms, 2 story. S, D $79-$89; each addl $5; higher rates: hols, special events. Crib $5. TV; cable. Pool; whirlpool. Complimentary coffee in lobby. Restaurant nearby. Ck-out 11 am. Business servs avail. Balconies. Cr cds: A, DS, MC, V.

⊠ ≋ ⊠ 🔥

✔★ ★ **DAYS INN.** *2800 N Ponce de Leon Blvd (32084), in Historical District. 904/829-6581; FAX 904/824-0135.* Web daysinnaug.com. 124 rms, 2 story. S $39-$105; D $44-$105; each addl $5; under 18, $2; under 12 free; higher rates: hols, special events. Crib free. Pet accepted, some restrictions; $10. TV. Pool. Restaurant 6-11:30 am. Ck-out noon. Business servs avail. Sundries. Some refrigerators, microwaves. Picnic tables. Cr cds: A, C, D, DS, JCB, MC, V.

D ▸ ≋ ⊠ 🔥 SC

★ **HOLIDAY INN EXPRESS.** *2310 FL 16 (32095). 904/823-8636; FAX 904/823-8728.* E-mail bp7053@aol.com. 51 rms, 2 story. S, D $49.95-$79.95; each addl $6; under 19 free; higher rates major hols. Crib free. TV; cable (premium). Pool. Complimentary continental bkfst. Restau-

rant nearby. Ck-out 11 am. Business servs avail. In-rm modem link. Microwaves avail. Cr cds: A, C, D, DS, MC, V.

D ≋ ⊠ ⊠ SC

✔★ ★ **MONTEREY INN.** *16 Avenida Menendez (32084), opp Fort Castillo de San Marcos. 904/824-4482; FAX 904/829-8854.* 59 rms, 2 story. Feb-Apr, June-Labor Day: S, D $39-$89; each addl $7; family, wkly rates; higher rates: wkends, hols, special events; lower rates rest of yr. Crib $7. TV; cable. Pool. Restaurant 7 am-9 pm. Ck-out 11 am. Business servs avail. Sundries. Sun deck. Matanzas Bay opp. Cr cds: A, C, D, DS, MC, V.

D ≋ ⊠ 🔥

★ **QUALITY INN ALHAMBRA.** *2700 N Ponce de Leon Blvd (32084). 904/824-2883; res: 800/223-4153.* 77 rms, 2 story. Feb-Apr, June-Labor Day: S $59-$129; D $69-$145; each addl $5; suites $135-$250; under 18 free; higher rates: Daytona races, special events, hols; lower rates rest of yr. Crib free. TV; cable, VCR avail. Pool; whirlpool. Restaurant nearby. Ck-out noon. Business servs avail. Bellhops. Gift shop. Some in-rm whirlpools. Sightseeing train departure area. Cr cds: A, C, D, DS, JCB, MC, V.

D ≋ ⊠ 🔥 SC

Inns

✔★ ★ ★ **CASA DE LA PAZ.** *22 Avenida Menendez (32084). 904/829-2915; res: 800/929-2915.* E-mail delapaz@aug.com; web www.oldcity.com/delapaz. 6 rms, 1 with shower only, 3 story, 2 suites. S, D $89-$189; suites $109-$174. TV; cable. Complimentary full bkfst. Restaurant nearby. Ck-out 11 am, ck-in 3 pm. Concierge. Parking. Mediterranean-style house (1915) overlooking Matanzas Bay; antiques. Totally nonsmoking. Cr cds: A, DS, MC, V.

⊠ 🔥

★ ★ **CEDAR HOUSE.** *79 Cedar St (32084). 904/829-0079; FAX 904/825-0916; res: 800/233-2746.* E-mail russ@aug.com; web www.cedar houseinn.com. 5 rms, 2 story, 1 suite. S, D $69-$129; each addl $15; suite $125-$155. Children over 10 yrs only. TV; VCR avail. Complimentary full bkfst; evening refreshments. Restaurant nearby. Ck-out 11 am, ck-in 3 pm. Concierge serv. Luggage handling. Whirlpool. Bicycles. Some balconies. Restored Victorian house (1893); original floors and woodwork. Cr cds: A, DS, MC, V.

⊠ 🔥

★ ★ **KENWOOD.** *38 Marine St (32084). 904/824-2116; FAX 904/824-1689.* Web www.oldcity.com/kenwood. 14 rms, 3 story. S $65-$95; D $100-$135; each addl $10. Children over 8 yrs only. TV rm; cable. Pool. Complimentary continental bkfst. Restaurant nearby. Ck-out 11 am, ck-in 2 pm. Restored boarding house (1865-1885); many antiques, reproductions; courtyard. In historic district downtown. Totally nonsmoking. Cr cds: DS, MC, V.

≋ ⊠ 🔥

★ ★ **OLD CITY HOUSE.** *115 Cordova St (32084). 904/826-0113; FAX 904/829-3798.* Web www.oldcityhouse.com. 7 rms, 3 with shower only, 2 story. No rm phones. S, D $85-$160; each addl $10; wkly, monthly rates; wkends (2-day min), hols (3-day min). Crib $6. TV; cable. Complimentary full bkfst; afternoon refreshments. Restaurant (see OLD CITY HOUSE). Rm serv. Ck-out 11 am, ck-in 2-9 pm. Business servs avail. Concierge serv. Luggage handling. Balconies. Picnic tables. Colonial revival-style inn built 1873 as stable to a mansion. Totally nonsmoking. Cr cds: A, D, DS, MC, V.

⊠ 🔥

★ ★ **OLD POWDER HOUSE.** *38 Cordova St (32084). 904/824-4149; res: 800/447-4149; FAX 904/825-0143.* E-mail ahowes@aug.com; web www.oldcity.com/powderhouse. 8 rms, 2 story, 2 suites. No rm phones. Mar-Sept, wkends, hols (2-3 day min): S, D $79-$165; each addl $10; suites $125-$165. Children over 8 yrs only. TV avail. Complimentary full bkfst; afternoon refreshments. Restaurant nearby. Ck-out 11 am, ck-in

3 pm. Business servs avail. Built 1899 on site of Spanish colonial powder house that supplied nearby fort. Antiques. Cr cds: DS, MC, V.

★ ★ **ST FRANCIS.** *279 St George St (32084).* 904/824-6068; res: 800/824-6062; FAX 904/810-5525. E-mail innceasd@aug.com; web www.stfrancisinn.com. 16 rms, 3 story, 4 kit. suites. S, D $65-$175; each addl $12; wkly rates. TV; cable. Pool. Complimentary full bkfst. Restaurant nearby. Ck-out noon, ck-in 3 pm. Some in-rm whirlpools. Bicycles. Restored inn (1791) near oldest house in country; library, balconies, courtyard. Antiques & modern furnishings. Totally nonsmoking. Cr cds: A, D, DS, MC, V.

★ ★ ★ **WESTCOTT HOUSE.** *146 Avenida Menendez (32084).* 904/824-4301. Web www.westcotthouse.com. 9 rms, 3 story. D $95-$175. TV; cable. Complimentary continental bkfst. Ck-out 11 am, ck-in 3 pm. Business servs avail. Built in 1885-1890; antiques. Overlooking Matanzas Bay. Cr cds: A, DS, MC, V.

Resort

★ **RADISSON PONCE DE LEON GOLF & CONFERENCE RESORT.** *4000 US 1 N (32095).* 904/824-2821; FAX 904/824-8254. 193 rms, 1-4 story. S, D $79-$199; each addl $10; suites $119-$199; under 17 free; MAP avail; golf plans. Crib free. TV; cable. Pool. Complimentary coffee in rms. Dining rm 6:30 am-2 pm, 5-10 pm. Bar 11-1 am; entertainment wkends. Ck-out noon, ck-in 3 pm. Meeting rms. Business servs avail. In-rm modem link. Bellhops. Valet serv. Sundries. Free local airport transportation. Tennis. Golf, greens fee $60, pro, putting green, 18-hole putting course. Lawn games. Private patios. Cr cds: A, C, D, DS, ER, JCB, MC, V.

Restaurants

✔★ **BARNACLE BILL'S DOWNTOWN.** *14 Castillo Dr (32084).* 904/824-3663. Hrs: 11 am-9 pm; Sun from 4:30 pm. Closed Thanksgiving, Dec 24, 25. Bar. Semi-a la carte: lunch $4.75-$7.95, dinner $8.95-$16.95. Child's meals. Specializes in seafood, chicken, steak. Parking. Nautical decor. Cr cds: A, C, D, DS, MC, V.

★ ★ **BARNACLE BILLS BEACHSIDE.** *451 Beach Blvd (A1A) (32084).* 904/471-2434. Hrs: 4:30-10 pm. Closed Thanksgiving, Dec 24, 25. Bar. Semi-a la carte: dinner $7.95-$15.95. Child's meals. Specializes in seafood. Parking. Picture windows, skylight. Many plants. Cr cds: A, D, DS, MC, V.

✔★ **CAPTAIN JACK'S.** *410 Anastasia Blvd (32084).* 904/829-6846. Hrs: 11:30 am-9 pm; Sat, Sun from noon. Closed Thanksgiving, Dec 25; 1st 2 wks in Dec. Wine, beer. Semi-a la carte: lunch $4.50-$7, dinner $5.99-$21.99. Child's meals. Specializes in seafood, steak, chicken. Parking. Nautical decor. Cr cds: A, C, D, DS, MC, V.

✔★ ★ **COLUMBIA.** *98 St George St (32084).* 904/824-3341. Hrs: 11 am-9 pm; Fri, Sat to 10 pm; Sun brunch to 3 pm. Res accepted. Spanish menu. Bar. Semi-a la carte: lunch $4.95-$7.95, dinner $7.95-$20. Sun brunch $16.95. Child's meals. Specialties: snapper alicante, paella, black bean soup. Parking. In historic area. Spanish decor; balcony around interior courtyard. Bakery. Cr cds: A, C, D, DS, MC, V.

✔★ ★ **CREEKSIDE DINERY.** *160 Nix Boatyard Rd (32084).* 904/829-6113. Hrs: 5-10 pm. Closed Thanksgiving, Dec 25. Bar. Semi-a la carte: dinner $4.99-$15.99. Child's meals. Specializes in seafood, chicken.

Parking. Outdoor dining. Waterfront dining in reproduction turn-of-the-century Florida home. Cr cds: A, C, D, DS, MC, V.

★ ★ **FIDDLERS GREEN.** *2750 Anahma Dr (32095), E of Vilano Bridge.* 904/824-8897. Hrs: 5-10 pm. Closed Thanksgiving, Dec 25. Res accepted Sun-Fri. Bar 5-10 pm. Semi-a la carte: dinner $7.99-$14.95. Specializes in seafood, chicken, steak. Parking. Nautical, Florida decor. View of ocean and St Augustine Inlet. Cr cds: A, D, DS, MC, V.

★ ★ **KING'S FORGE.** *12 Avenida Menendez (32084).* 904/829-1488. Hrs: 11:30 am-10 pm; Fri, Sat 11 am-11 pm. Closed Res accepted. Bar. Semi-a la carte: lunch $4.95-$6.95, dinner $8.95-$14.95. Child's meals. Specializes in chicken, seafood, prime rib. Parking. Also 2nd-floor dining with balcony overlooking Matanzas Bay; view of Castillo de San Marcos. Cr cds: A, DS, MC, V.

★ ★ ★ **LA PARISIENNE.** *60 Hypolita St (32084).* 904/829-0055. Hrs: 11 am-3 pm, 5-10 pm; Mon, Tues to 3 pm. Closed Wed; Dec 25. Res accepted. French menu. Wine. Semi-a la carte: lunch $3.50-$9.95, dinner $9.50-$26. Specializes in croissants, quiches. Own baking. French atmosphere; fireplace. Cr cds: A, DS, MC, V.

★ ★ ★ **LE PAVILLON.** *45 San Marco Ave (32084).* 904/824-6202. Hrs: 11:30 am-2:30 pm, 5-10 pm. Res accepted. Continental menu. Bar. Semi-a la carte: lunch $5.95-$8.50, dinner $7.95-$18.95. Specialties: rack of lamb, bouillabaisse. Own soups, desserts. Parking. Located in former home built 1890. Cr cds: D, DS, MC, V.

★ **O'STEEN'S.** *205 Anastasia Blvd (32084).* 904/829-6974. Hrs: 11 am-8:30 pm. Closed Sun, Mon; Jan 1, Thanksgiving, Dec 25; also 1st wk June. Semi-a la carte: lunch, dinner $5.25-$18.25. Specializes in seafood, fresh vegetables. Fireplace; paintings by local artists. No cr cds accepted.

★ ★ **OLD CITY HOUSE.** *(See Old City House Inn)* 904/826-0781. Web www.oldcityhouse.com. Hrs: 5:30-9 pm; Fri, Sat to 10 pm. Closed most major hols. Res accepted. Continental menu. Bar. Semi-a la carte: dinner $9.95-$24.95. Specializes in pasta, seafood, lamb. Parking. Fireplace. Cr cds: A, D, DS, MC, V.

★ ★ ★ **RAINTREE.** *102 San Marco Ave (32084).* 904/824-7211. Hrs: 5-9:30 pm; Fri, Sat to 10 pm; early-bird dinner 5-6 pm. Closed Dec 25. Res accepted. Bar. Wine list. Semi-a la carte: dinner $9.95-$19.95. Serv charge 15%. Child's meals. Specializes in 10-item menu (changes daily). Own baking. Parking. In historic house (1879) with glassed atrium overlooking courtyard/garden. Cr cds: A, MC, V.

★ ★ **ROSENHOF.** *1824 FL A1A South (32084).* 904/471-4340. Hrs: 5-9 pm; Fri, Sat to 10 pm. Closed Mon; Jan 1, Dec 24, 25. German menu. Beer. Semi-a la carte: dinner $8.95-$16.95. Child's meals. Specializes in veal dishes. Accordian player wkends. Parking. Old World German decor featuring original oils. Cr cds: A, C, D, DS, MC, V.

St Augustine Beach (C-5)

(See also Marineland, St Augustine)

Pop 3,657 **Elev** 10 ft **Area code** 904 **Zip** 32084

Motels

 ★ **BEACHER'S LODGE.** *(6970 S FL A1A, St Augustine 32086)* At jct FL A1A & FL 206. 904/471-8849; FAX 904/471-3002; res: 800/527-8849. E-mail beachers1@aol.com. 118 kit. units, 4 story. Mid-Feb-Sept: kit. units $49-$120; wkly rates; lower rates rest of yr. Crib $5. TV; cable. Pool. Complimentary coffee in lobby. Ck-out 11 am. Coin lndry. Balconies. On beach. Cr cds: DS, MC, V.

★ **BEST WESTERN OCEAN INN.** 3955 FL A1A S. 904/471-8010; FAX 904/460-9124. Web www.bestwestern.com/best.html. 35 rms, 2 story. Feb-early Sept: S, D $59-$89; each addl $6; under 12 free; higher rates major hols; lower rates rest of yr. Crib $10. Pet accepted, some restrictions; $10/day. TV; cable (premium). Pool. Complimentary continental bkfst. Restaurant adj 7:30 am-10 pm. Ck-out 11 am. Business servs avail. Refrigerators, microwaves avail. Cr cds: A, C, D, DS, MC, V.

★ **COMFORT INN.** 901 A1A Beach Blvd. 904/471-1474; FAX 904/461-9659. 70 units, 3 story, 14 kit. units. Feb-Sept: S, D, kit. units $54-$149; each addl $10; under 18 free; higher rates special events; lower rates rest of yr. Crib free. TV; cable (premium). Heated pool; whirlpool. Complimentary continental bkfst. Restaurant nearby. Ck-out 11 am. Coin lndry. Business servs avail. Some refrigerators. Cr cds: A, C, D, DS, JCB, MC, V.

★★ **HOLIDAY INN OCEANFRONT.** 860 A1A Beach Blvd. 904/471-2555; FAX 904/461-8450. 151 rms, 5 story. Feb-mid-Sept: S, D $100-$130; under 18 free; lower rates rest of yr. Crib free. Pet accepted, some restrictions. TV; cable. Pool; poolside serv. Restaurant 7-11:30 am, 5-10 pm. Rm serv. Bar 4 pm-midnight. Ck-out 11 am. Coin lndry. Valet serv. Meeting rms. Business servs avail. Balconies. On beach; ocean views. Cr cds: A, C, D, DS, JCB, MC, V.

★★ **LA FIESTA OCEANSIDE INN.** 810 A1A Beach Blvd. 904/471-2220; FAX 904/471-0186; res: 800/852-6390. 44 rms, 2 story. Feb-Sept: S, D $69-$89; suites $179-$225; 3-day min: Easter, July 4, Daytona "500," Bike Week in Mar; lower rates rest of yr. Crib $5. TV; cable. Pool. Restaurant 7 am-noon. Ck-out 11 am. Coin lndry. Business servs avail. Sundries. Picnic tables. Miniature golf. On ocean beach. Cr cds: C, DS, MC, V.

Restaurants

★★ **ARUANNO'S.** 105 D St. 904/471-9373. Hrs: 5-9:30 pm; wkends to 10 pm. Closed Mon; some major hols. Res accepted. Italian menu. Wine, beer. Semi-a la carte: dinner $7.95-$19.95. Child's meals. Specializes in beef, pasta, seafood. Cr cds: A, DS, MC, V.

✓★ **GREENSTREET'S.** 4320 FL A1A S, Ocean Gate Plaza. 904/471-5573. Hrs: 7:30 am-3:30 pm. Closed Tues; Dec 25; also 1st 2 wks Dec. A la carte entrees: bkfst $1.65-$5.50, lunch $2.50-$6.50. Specializes in deli-style sandwiches, soups, desserts. Garden atmosphere. No cr cds accepted.

★ **GYPSY CAB CO.** 828 Anastasia Blvd. 904/824-8244. Hrs: 4:30-10 pm; Fri to 11 pm; Sat 11 am-11 pm; Sun 10:30 am-10 pm; Sun

brunch to 3 pm. Closed July 4, Dec 25. Bar. Semi-a la carte: dinner $8.99-$16.99. Sun brunch $5.25-$8.25. Child's meals. Specializes in fresh seafood, pasta, unique chicken dishes. Cr cds: A, DS, MC, V.

✓★★ **SALT WATER COWBOY'S.** 299 Dondanville Rd. 904/471-2332. Hrs: 5-10 pm. Closed Thanksgiving; also 2nd wk Dec-Dec 25. Serv bar. Semi-a la carte: dinner $4.95-$15.99. Child's meals. Specializes in fresh seafood. Outdoor dining. Renovated fish camp; on water. Cr cds: A, DS, MC, V.

St Pete Beach (F-3)

(See also Bradenton, St Petersburg, Tampa)

Elev 5 ft **Area code** 813

Information Chamber of Commerce, 6990 Gulf Blvd, St Pete Beach 33706; 813/360-6957.

This strip of islands, connected by bridges and causeways, is separated from the mainland by Boca Ciega Bay. Included here are Indian Rocks Beach, Indian Shores, Madeira Beach, Redington Beach, Redington Shores, St Pete Beach and Treasure Island.

What to See and Do

Suncoast Seabird Sanctuary. Nonprofit organization specializes in care and recuperation of wild birds; largest wild bird hospital in the US. Visitors may observe rehabilitation and behavior of approx 600 birds of more than 76 different species; excellent photographic opportunities. Guided tours (Wed & Sun afternoons). (Daily) N on FL 699 (Gulf Blvd) at 18328 Gulf Blvd in Indian Shores. Phone 813/391-6211.   **Free.**

Motels

★ **ALGIERS.** *(11600 Gulf Blvd, Treasure Island 33706)* N on FL 699 (Gulf Blvd), 9 blks N of Treasure Island Causeway. 727/367-3793. 17 rms, 2 story, 10 kits. Feb-Apr: S, D $77; each addl $5; suites $88-$105; lower rates rest of yr. Crib free. TV; cable. Heated pool. Restaurant nearby. Ck-out 10 am. Coin lndry. Lawn games. Refrigerators, microwaves. On Gulf. Cr cds: MC, V.

★ **ALPAUGH'S GULF BEACH NORTH.** *(1912 Gulf Blvd, Indian Rocks Beach 33785)* N on FL 699 (Gulf Blvd). 727/595-9421. 18 kit. units, 2 story. Dec-Apr: 1-bedrm $88-$97; 2-bedrm $109; each addl $7; under 12, $5; wkly rates; lower rates rest of yr. Crib $4. TV; cable. Restaurant nearby. Ck-out 10 am. Coin lndry. Lawn games. Microwaves. Picnic tables, grills. On beach. Cr cds: DS, MC, V.

★★ **BEACH HAVEN VILLAS.** *(4980 Gulf Blvd, St Pete Beach 33706)* 727/367-8642; FAX 727/360-8202. 18 rms, 14 with shower only, 12 kit. units. Feb-Apr: S, D $75-$125; each addl $10; kit. units $105-$125; under 3 free; wkly rates; 4-day min hols; lower rates rest of yr. Crib $8. TV; cable, VCR (movies). Pool. Restaurant nearby. Ck-out 11 am. Coin lndry. Lawn games. Refrigerators; some microwaves. On beach. Cr cds: MC, V.

★★ **COLONIAL GATEWAY INN.** *(6300 Gulf Blvd, St Pete Beach 33706)* S on FL 699 (Gulf Blvd), 3/4 mi S of St Pete Beach Causeway. 727/367-2711; FAX 727/367-7068; res: 800/237-8918. 200 rms, 1-2 story, 100 kits. Mid-Feb-Apr: S, D $99-$129; each addl $6; kit. units $12 addl; under 12 free; lower rates rest of yr. Crib $6. TV; cable. Pool; wading pool. Restaurant 8-11 am, noon-10 pm. Bar; entertainment.

Ck-out 11 am. Meeting rms. Business servs avail. Sundries. Lawn games. Game rm. On beach. Cr cds: A, C, D, DS, ER, MC, V.

≈ 🐾 SC

★ ★ **DAYS INN ISLAND BEACH RESORT.** (6200 Gulf Blvd, St Pete Beach 33706) S on FL 699 (Gulf Blvd), approx ¾ mi S of St Pete Beach Causeway. 727/367-1902; FAX 727/367-4422. 102 rms, 2 story, 48 kits. Feb-Apr: S, D $98-$148; each addl $20; kit. units $108-$158; under 16 free; lower rates rest of yr. Crib free. TV; cable (premium). 2 heated pools. Coffee in rms. Restaurant noon-1 am. Bars 11-2 am; Sun from noon; entertainment. Ck-out 11 am. Business servs avail. Game rm. Refrigerators. On 5½ acres of tropical gardens; on Gulf. Cr cds: A, C, D, DS, JCB, MC, V.

≈ ≈ 🐾 SC

★ **INN ON THE BEACH.** (1401 Gulf Way, St Pete Beach 33706) At 14th Ave. 727/360-8844. 12 kit. units, 2 story. Jan-Apr: S, D $70-$150 each addl $10; monthly rates; higher rates: Memorial Day, July 4, Dec 25, 31 (3-day min); lower rates rest of yr. TV; cable. Restaurant nearby. Ck-out 11 am. Microwaves avail. Grills. Beach adj. Beach chairs avail. Cr cds: A, D, DS, MC, V.

🐾 SC

★ **ISLAND'S END.** 1 Pass-a-Grille Way (33706), 2 mi S of jct FL 682, FL 699. 727/360-5023; FAX 727/367-7890. 6 cottages, Mid-Dec-May: S, D $90-$175; each addl $15; wkly rates; lower rates rest of yr. Crib $8. TV; cable, VCR (movies $1). Ck-out 11 am. Coin Indry. Business servs avail. Some private patios. Cottages with old-Florida feel. On waterfront 1 blk from Gulf Beach. Cr cds: MC, V.

D ➥ 🐾

✔★ **MALYN.** (282 107th Ave, Treasure Island 33706) N on FL 699 (Gulf Blvd), then ¼ mi E on 107th Ave. 727/367-1974; FAX 727/367-2741. Web www.libertemgt.com. 19 kit. units, 2 story. Jan-May: S, D $64-$85; each addl $6; studio rms $64; wkly rates; lower rates rest of yr. TV; cable. Heated pool. Restaurant nearby. Ck-out 10 am. Coin Indry. Lawn games. Microwaves avail. Picnic tables, grills. Overlooks bay; fishing docks, boat dock $6/day. Bayside cabana. Cr cds: DS, MC, V.

➥ ≈ 🐾

★ **PLAZA BEACH.** (4506 Gulf Blvd, St Pete Beach 33706) on FL 699, ½ mi N of FL682. 727/367-2791; FAX 727/367-3620; res: 800/257-8998. 39 rms, 2 story. Feb-Apr: S, D $81; each addl $5; suites $94; under 4 free; wkly rates; higher rates wkends (3-day min); lower rates rest of yr. Crib free. TV; cable (premium). Heated pool. Complimentary coffee in lobby. Restaurant nearby. Ck-out 11 am. Coin Indry. Lawn games. Refrigerators, microwaves. Picnic tables. On beach. Cr cds: A, DS, MC, V.

D ≈ 🐾 SC

★ ★ **SEA CHEST TREASURE ISLAND.** (11780 Gulf Blvd, Treasure Island 33706) On FL 699 (Gulf Blvd). 727/360-5501; FAX 727/360-8453. 22 rms, 2 story. Jan-Apr: S, D $80-$117; each addl $5; wkly rates; lower rates rest of yr. Crib free. TV; cable (premium). Heated pool. Complimentary coffee in rms. Ck-out 11 am. Coin Indry. Business servs avail. Lawn games. Refrigerators, microwaves. Balconies. Picnic tables, grills. On beach. Cr cds: A, MC, V.

≈ 🐾

★ ★ **SHORELINE ISLAND RESORT.** (14200 Gulf Blvd, Madeira Beach 33708) N on FL 699 (Gulf Blvd), ½ mi S of Madeira Beach Causeway. 727/397-6641; FAX 727/393-9157; res: 800/635-8373. 70 rms in 5 bldgs, 2-5 story, 65 kits. Feb-Apr: S, D $95-$147; each addl $10; studios $116-$175; 1-2 bedrm kit. units $116-$235; wkly rates; monthly rates off-season; lower rates rest of yr. Adults only. TV; cable (premium), VCR. Heated pool. Restaurant nearby. Ck-out 11 am. Coin Indry. Business servs avail. Lawn games. Microwaves avail. Private patios, balconies. Picnic tables. Library. 400 ft of beach. On Gulf. Cr cds: A, DS, MC, V.

≈ 🐾 SC

✔★ **SUNRISE.** (9630 Gulf Blvd, Treasure Island 33706) N on FL 699 (Gulf Blvd). 727/360-9210; res: 800/589-1116. 19 rms, 2 story, 7 kit. units. Feb-mid-Apr: S, D $59; each addl $6; kit. units $68-$75; under 13 free; wkly, monthly rates; lower rates rest of yr. TV; cable. Heated pool. Complimentary coffee in lobby. Restaurant nearby. Ck-out 11 am. Coin Indry. Refrigerators; microwaves avail. Opp bay. Cr cds: A, DS, MC, V.

≈ 🐾

★ **SURFS INN.** (14010 Gulf Blvd, Madeira Beach 33708) N on FL 699 (Gulf Blvd), 1 mi N of Johns Pass Bridge. 727/393-4609; FAX 727/391-8732. E-mail surfsinn@gte.net; web www.beachdirectory.com/surfsinn. 25 rms, 2 story, 18 kits. Feb-Apr: S, D $63; each addl $5; kit. units $68-$106; lower rates rest of yr. TV; cable. Heated pool. Ck-out 10:30 am. Coin Indry. Lawn games. Refrigerators, microwaves avail. Picnic tables, grills. Sun decks. On Gulf; beach. Cr cds: A, DS, MC, V.

≈ ≈ 🐾

★ ★ **THUNDERBIRD BEACH RESORT.** (10700 Gulf Blvd, Treasure Island 33706) On FL 699 (Gulf Blvd). 727/367-1961; FAX 727/367-1961; res: 800/367-2473. E-mail tbird@atlantic.net; web www.go tampabay.com/thunderbird/. 64 rms, 2-3 story, 32 kits. No elvtr. Mid-Feb-Apr: S, D $110-$130; each addl $7; kit. units $120-$140; under 13 free; lower rates rest of yr. Crib free. TV; cable. Heated pool; whirlpool, poolside serv. Restaurant 7 am-3 pm. Bar noon-2 am; entertainment. Ck-out 11 am. Business servs avail. Picnic tables. On beach. Cr cds: A, C, D, DS, MC, V.

≈ 🐾 SC

✔★ ★ **TRAILS END.** (11500 Gulf Blvd, Treasure Island 33706) N on FL 699 (Gulf Blvd), 8 blks N of Treasure Island Causeway. 727/360-5541; FAX 727/360-1508. E-mail flamingles@aol.com. 54 rms, 1-2 story, 32 kits. Feb-Apr: S, D $67-$72; each addl $8; kit. units $75-$92; wkly rates; lower rates rest of yr. Crib free. TV; cable (premium). Heated pool. Restaurant nearby. Ck-out 11 am. Business servs avail. Lawn games. Microwaves avail. Picnic tables, grill. On beach. Cr cds: A, C, D, DS, JCB, MC, V.

≈ 🐾

Motor Hotels

★ ★ ★ **ALDEN BEACH RESORT.** (5900 Gulf Blvd, St Pete Beach 33706) S on FL 699 (Gulf Blvd), ¾ mi S of St Pete Beach Causeway. 727/360-7081; FAX 727/360-5957; res: 800/237-2530 (exc FL), 800/262-3464 (FL). E-mail alden@travelbase.com; web www.travelbase.com/destinations/st-pete/alden. 143 rms, 6 story, 139 kits (1-2 bedrm). Feb-mid-Apr: S, D $103; each addl $10; suites $142-$190; under 12 free; lower rates rest of yr. Crib free. TV; cable (premium), VCR (movies). 2 pools; 2 whirlpools. Complimentary coffee in rms. Restaurant nearby. Bar. Ck-out 11 am. Coin Indry. Meeting room. Business servs avail. Lighted tennis. Game rm. Lawn games. Microwaves. Private patios, balconies. Picnic tables, grills. Sun deck. On Gulf beach. Cr cds: A, C, D, DS, ER, MC, V.

🎾 ≈ ≈ 🐾 SC

★ ★ ★ **BILMAR BEACH RESORT.** (10650 Gulf Blvd, Treasure Island 33706) N on FL 699 (Gulf Blvd) at Treasure Island Causeway. 727/360-5531; FAX 727/360-2915; res: 800/826-9724. E-mail sales@go tampabay.com; web www.gotampabay.com/bilmar/. 176 rms, 3-8 story, 121 kits. Feb-Apr: S, D, studio rms $128, each addl $10; suites $232-$246; kit. units $143-$148; under 18 free; lower rates rest of yr. Crib free. TV; cable (premium). 2 heated pools; whirlpool, poolside serv. Coffee in rms. Restaurant 7 am-10 pm. Rm serv. Bars 11-2 am; entertainment. Ck-out 11 am. Meeting rms. Business servs avail. In-rm modem link. Gift shop. Bellhops. Refrigerators. Some private patios, balconies. On 550-ft beach. Cr cds: A, C, D, MC, V.

D ≈ 🐾

★ ★ **DOLPHIN BEACH RESORT.** (4900 Gulf Blvd, St Pete Beach 33706) on FL 699. 727/360-7011; FAX 727/367-5909; res: 800/237-8916. Web www.dolphinbeach.com. 173 rms, 3 story, 87 kits. Feb-Apr: S, D $100-$120; kit. units $112-$132; family rates; lower rates rest of yr. Crib free. TV; cable. Heated pool; poolside serv. Restaurant 7 am-10 pm. Rm serv. Bar noon-1:30 am; entertainment. Ck-out 11 am. Coin lndry. Meeting rms. Business servs avail. Bellhops. Water sports. Game rm. Lawn games. Some balconies. Picnic tables. Swimming beach. Cr cds: A, C, D, ER, MC, V.

[D] [icons] SC

★ ★ ★ HOLIDAY INN BEACH FRONT RESORT. *(5250 Gulf Blvd, St Pete Beach 33706)* S on FL 699 (Gulf Blvd), approx 1¼ mi S of St Petersburg Beach Causeway. 727/360-1811; FAX 727/360-6919. 156 rms, 11 story. Jan-Apr: S, D $98-$188; suites $178-$328; family rates; lower rates rest of yr. TV; cable (premium). Heated pool; poolside serv. Restaurant 6:30 am-11 pm. Rm serv. Revolving rooftop bar 11-2 am, beachfront bar; entertainment. Ck-out 11 am. Gift shop. Coin lndry. Meeting rms. Business servs avail. In-rm modem link. Bellhops. Sundries. Exercise equipt. Refrigerators; microwaves avail. Balconies. On beach. Cr cds: A, C, D, DS, ER, JCB, MC, V.

[D] [icons] SC

★ ★ ★ HOLIDAY INN-MADEIRA BEACH. *(15208 Gulf Blvd, Madeira Beach 33708)* N on FL 699 (Gulf Blvd), at Madeira Beach Causeway. 727/392-2275; res: 800/360-6658; FAX 727/393-4012. 149 rms, 4 story. Feb-Apr: S, D $110-$163; each addl $10; lower rates rest of yr. Crib free. TV; cable (premium), VCR avail. Heated pool; wading pool, poolside serv, poolside bar, entertainment. Restaurant 6:30 am-10 pm. Rm serv. Bar 11-2 am; Sun from 1 pm. Ck-out 11 am. Coin lndry. Meeting rms. Business servs avail. In-rm modem link. Bellhops. Lighted tennis. Some private patios, balconies. On Gulf; 600-ft beach. Beach activities center. Cr cds: A, C, D, DS, ER, JCB, MC, V.

[D] [icons] SC

★ ★ HOWARD JOHNSON LODGE. *(11125 Gulf Blvd, Treasure Island 33706)* N on FL 699 (Gulf Blvd), 2 blks N of Treasure Island Causeway. 727/360-6971; FAX 727/360-9014. 84 rms, 3 story. Feb-Apr: S, D $94-$102; each addl $10; under 18 free; lower rates rest of yr. Crib free. TV; cable. Heated pool. Restaurant adj 7 am-10 pm. Ck-out noon. Coin lndry. Business servs avail. Valet serv Mon-Fri. Sundries. Game rm. Lawn games. Refrigerators. Private patios, balconies. Fishing dock. City beach opp. Cr cds: A, C, D, DS, MC, V.

[icons] SC

★ ★ RADISSON SANDPIPER BEACH RESORT. *(6000 Gulf Blvd, St Pete Beach 33706)* S on FL 699 (Gulf Blvd), approx ¾ mi S of St Pete Beach Causeway. 727/360-5551; res: 800/237-0707; FAX 727/562-1282. 159 rms, 7 story, 143 kit. suites. Feb-Apr: S, D $155-$207; each addl $15; 1 bedrm kit. suites $235-$299; 2-3 bedrm kit. suites $390-$631; under 17 free; lower rates rest of yr. Crib free. TV; cable, (premium), VCR avail (movies $3). 2 heated pools; poolside serv. Free supervised child's activities; ages 2-12. Coffee in rms. Restaurant 7 am-10 pm. Rm serv. Bar. Ck-out noon. Coin lndry. Meeting rm. Business servs avail. In-rm modem link. Bellhops. Valet serv. Shopping arcade. Free garage parking. Tennis privileges. Exercise equipt. Rec rm. Lawn games. Racquetball court. Some refrigerators. Private patios, balconies. Grill. On beach. Cr cds: A, C, D, DS, ER, JCB, MC, V.

[D] [icons] SC

★ ★ RAMADA INN TREASURE ISLAND. *(12000 Gulf Blvd, Treasure Island 33706)* N on FL 699 (Gulf Blvd), ¾ mi N of Treasure Island Causeway. 727/360-7051; FAX 727/367-6641. 121 rms, 4 story, 23 kits. Mid-Feb-mid-Apr: S, D $130-$140; each addl $10; kit. units $140-$150; under 18 free; lower rates rest of yr. Crib free. TV; cable, VCR (movies $6). Heated pool; whirlpool, poolside serv. Playground. Restaurant 7 am-10 pm. Rm serv. Bar; entertainment Mon-Sat. Ck-out noon. Guest lndry. Business servs avail. Bellhops. Gift shop. Game rm. Lawn games. On Gulf. Cr cds: A, C, D, DS, ER, JCB, MC, V.

[D] [icons] SC

★ ★ ★ TRADE WINDS. *(5500 Gulf Blvd, St Pete Beach 33706)* on FL 699 (Gulf Blvd), 1½ mi N of Pinellas Bayway (FL 682). 727/367-6461; FAX 727/562-1214; res: 800/237-0707. Web www.tradewindsresort.com. 577 rms, 2-7 story, 354 kits. Feb-Apr: S, D $275-$415; 2-bedrm suites $469-$569; under 12 free; lower rates rest of yr. Crib $5. TV; cable

(premium), VCR avail. 4 heated pools; wading pool, poolside serv. Playground. Supervised child's activities; ages 2-18. Restaurants 7 am-10 pm (also see PALM COURT). Rm serv. Bar; entertainment. Ck-out noon. Coin lndry. Valet serv. Convention facilities. Business center. Bellhops. Gift shops. Barber, beauty shop. Tennis, pro. Golf privileges, putting green. Exercise rm; sauna. Beach games. Bathrm phones, refrigerators. Some patios, balconies. Picnic tables, grills. Cr cds: A, C, D, DS, MC, V.

[D] [icons] SC

Hotels

★ ★ ★ DON CESAR BEACH RESORT & SPA. *(3400 Gulf Blvd, St Pete Beach 33706)* Jct FL 682 & FL 699. 727/360-1881; res: 800/637-7200; FAX 727/367-6952. E-mail doheo@attmail.com; web www.doncesar.com. 275 rms, 10 story in 2 bldgs, 70 suites. Feb-Apr: S, D $289-$384; each addl $15; suites $375-$784; penthouse $1,850-$1,950; under 18 free; lower rates rest of yr. Crib free. TV; cable (premium), VCR avail (movies). 3 heated pools; whirlpools. Supervised child's activities; ages 4-12. Restaurant (see MARITANA GRILLE). Rm serv 24 hrs. Bars 11-1 am; Sun from 1 pm; entertainment. Ck-out noon. Convention facilities. Business center. In-rm modem link. Coin lndry. Concierge. Shopping arcade. Valet parking. Tennis privileges. Golf privileges. Exercise rm; sauna. Spa. Game rm. Lawn games. Sailboat rentals. Watersport clinics & rentals. Some refrigerators, minibars. Some balconies. Beach cabanas, boardwalk. Cr cds: A, C, D, DS, ER, JCB, MC, V.

[D] [icons] SC

★ ★ ★ HILTON NORTH REDINGTON BEACH RESORT. *(17120 Gulf Blvd, North Redington Beach 33708)* N on FL 699 (Gulf Blvd), 2 mi S of FL 694 (Park Blvd). 727/391-4000; FAX 727/397-0699. E-mail nrbhr@worldnet.att.net; web www.hilton.com. 125 rms, 6 story. Feb-Apr: S, D $165-$240; family rates; lower rates rest of yr. TV; cable (premium). Heated pool; poolside serv. Complimentary coffee in rms. Restaurant 7 am-2 pm, 5:30-10 pm. Bars 11:30 am-midnight; entertainment. Ck-out 11 am. Meeting rms. Business servs avail. In-rm modem link. Concierge Tues-Sat. Gift shop. Minibars. Balconies. On Gulf; beach. Cr cds: A, C, D, DS, ER, MC, V.

[D] [icons] SC

★ ★ HOLIDAY INN TREASURE ISLAND. *(11908 Gulf Blvd, Treasure Island 33706)* N on FL 699 (Gulf Blvd), ¾ mi N of Treasure Island Causeway. 727/367-2761; FAX 727/367-9446. Web www.holidayinn.com. 110 rms, 9 story. Jan-May: S, D $119-$149; each addl $10; under 19 free; wknd plans; lower rates rest of yr. Crib free. TV; cable (premium). Coffee in rms. Heated pool; whirlpool, poolside serv. Restaurant 7 am-10 pm. Bar 11-midnight; pianist Mon-Sat. Ck-out 11 am. Coin lndry. Business servs avail. In-rm modem link. Concierge. Gift shop. Private patios. On beach. Cr cds: A, C, D, DS, ER, JCB, MC, V.

[D] [icons] SC

Restaurants

★ ★ ★ BRUNELLO. *(3861 Gulf Blvd, St Pete Beach 33706)* 727/367-1851. Hrs: 6-10 pm. Closed Mon; also July 4, Thanksgiving, Dec 25. Res accepted. Italian menu. Bar. Wine list. A la carte entrees: dinner $6-$22. Specializes in tuna, portabella mushrooms, veal. Parking. Elegant decor. Cr cds: A, MC, V.

★ ★ CAPTAIN KOSMAKOS SEAFOOD & STEAK HOUSE. *(9610 Gulf Blvd, Treasure Island 33706)* N on FL 699 (Gulf Blvd) at Blind Pass Bridge. 727/367-3743. Hrs: 3 pm-2 am; Sun 1 pm; early-bird dinner 3-6 pm. Res accepted. Continental menu. Bar. Semi-a la carte: dinner $8.95-$22.95. Child's meals. Specializes in steak, beef, fresh seafood. Entertainment. Parking. View of bay. Cr cds: A, D, MC, V.

[D] [icon]

★ CAPTAIN'S GALLEY. *(660 American Legion Dr, Madeira Beach 33708)* N on FL 699 (Gulf Blvd), E on Madeira Beach Causeway, behind shopping center. 727/398-7220. Hrs: 4-9 pm; Fri, Sat to 10 pm; Sun noon-9 pm; early-bird dinner Mon-Sat 4-5:30 pm. Closed Thanksgiving,

Dec 25. Bar. Semi-a la carte: dinner $5.95-$19.95. Child's meals. Specializes in seafood, steak, ribs. Parking. Nautical decor. Overlooks Intracoastal Waterway. Cr cds: DS, MC, V.

✔★ **DAIQUIRI DECK & OCEANSIDE GRILLE.** (14995 Gulf Blvd, Madeira Beach 33708) N on FL 699 (Gulf Blvd), 1 mi N of Johns Pass Bridge. 727/393-2706. Hrs: 11-2 am; Sun from noon. Bar. Semi-a la carte: lunch, dinner $4.95-$12.95. Specializes in fresh seafood, specialty sandwiches. Entertainment Wed, Sun. Beach-bar atmosphere. Cr cds: A, MC, V.

✔★ **GIGI'S.** (105 107th Ave, Treasure Island 33706) N on FL 699 (Gulf Blvd) to Treasure Island Causeway (107th Ave). 727/360-6905. Hrs: 4-10 pm; Fri, Sat to 11pm; early-bird dinner 4-6 pm. Closed Thanksgiving, Dec 25. Italian menu. Wine, beer. Semi-a la carte: dinner $7.99-$16.99. Child's meals. Specializes in pasta, pizza, seafood. Parking. Copper murals. Family-owned. Cr cds: A, DS, MC, V.

★★ **HURRICANE.** (807 Gulf Way, St Pete Beach 33706) 2 mi S of jct FL 686, FL 699. 727/360-9558. Hrs: 8-2 am. Bars. Semi-a la carte: bkfst $1.75-$6.50, lunch, dinner $2.95-$17.95. Specialties: grouper sandwiches, Maryland crab cakes. Entertainment. Parking. Beachfront dining; sunset cocktail deck. Cr cds: MC, V.

★★ **LEVEROCK'S ON THE BAY.** (565 150th Ave, Madeira Beach 33708) N on FL 699 (Gulf Blvd) to Tom Stuart Causeway (Rt 666). 727/393-0459. Web www.leverocks.com. Hrs: 11:30 am-10 pm; early-bird dinner 3-6 pm. Closed Thanksgiving, Dec 25. Bar. Semi-a la carte: lunch $3.95-$7.95, dinner $6.95-$21.95. Child's meals. Specializes in fresh seafood, steak, ribs. Parking. Overlooks Intracoastal Waterway. Cr cds: A, C, D, DS, MC, V.

★★ **THE LOBSTER POT.** (17814 Gulf Blvd, Redington Shores 33708) N on FL 699 (Gulf Blvd), 1 mi S of FL 694 (Park Blvd). 727/391-8592. Hrs: 4:30-10 pm; Fri, Sat to 11 pm; Sun 4-10 pm; early-bird dinner 4:30-6 pm. Closed most major hols. Res accepted. Serv bar. Wine cellar. Semi-a la carte: dinner $12.75-$28.50. Child's meals. Specializes in fresh seafood, Maine lobster, apple walnut upside-down pie. Own desserts. Valet parking. Cr cds: A, C, D, DS, MC, V.

★★★ **MARITANA GRILLE.** (See Don Cesar Beach Resort & Spa Hotel) 727/360-1882. E-mail doned@attmail.com web www.doncesar.com. Hrs: 5:30-10 pm; Fri, Sat to 11 pm. Sun brunch 10:30 am-2 pm. Res accepted. Bar. Wine cellar. A la carte entrees: dinner $22-$35. Sun brunch $29.95. Child's meals. Specializes in wood-grilled fresh fish, aged meats. Valet parking. Totally nonsmoking. Cr cds: A, C, D, DS, ER, JCB, MC, V.

★★ **PALM COURT.** (See Trade Winds Motor Hotel) 727/367-6461. Web www.tradewindsresort.com. Hrs: 11:30 am-2 pm, 5:30-10 pm; Sun brunch 10 am-2 pm. Res accepted. Mediterranean menu. Bar. Wine list. A la carte entrees: lunch $5-$8, dinner $10-$30. Sun brunch $15.95. Child's meals. Specialties: veal marsala, grilled Atlantic salmon, rack of lamb. Guitarist Fri. Free valet parking. Outdoor dining. Mediterranean decor. Cr cds: A, D, DS, MC, V.

★★ **SCANDIA.** (19829 Gulf Blvd, Indian Shores 33785) N on FL 699 (Gulf Blvd). 727/595-5525. Hrs: 11:30 am-9 pm; Sun noon-8pm. Closed Mon; also Sept. Res accepted. Scandinavian menu. Bar. Semi-a la carte: lunch $5.99-$19.99, dinner $8.99-$19.99. 15% serv chg. Child's meals. Specializes in roast pork, Danish lobster tails, schnitzels. Parking. Gift shop. Cr cds: DS, MC, V.

✔★ **SKIDDER'S.** 5799 Gulf Blvd (33706). 727/360-1029. Hrs: 7 am-11 pm; early-bird dinner 4-6 pm. Res accepted. Continental menu. Bar. Wine list. Semi-a la carte: bkfst $1.95-$5.25, lunch $2.95-$8.95, dinner $6.95-$14.95. Child's meals. Specialties: veal Margarita, steak Diane, zuppa di pescadore. Parking. Outdoor dining. Cr cds: A, D, DS, MC, V.

★★★ **WINE CELLAR.** (17307 Gulf Blvd, North Reddington Beach 33708) on FL 699 (Gulf Blvd) at 173rd Ave. 727/393-3491. Web www.thewinecellar.com. Hrs: 4:30-11 pm; Sun from 4 pm; early-bird dinner to 6 pm. Closed Mon; Jan 1, Dec 24. Res accepted. Continental menu. Bar to 1:30 am. Wine list. A la carte entrees: dinner $14.75-$55. Complete meals: dinner $35. Serv charge 15%. Child's meals. Specialties: beef Wellington, rack of lamb. Valet parking. 7 dining areas, each with decor based on different European country. Cr cds: A, C, D, DS, MC, V.

St Petersburg (F-3)

(See also Bradenton, Clearwater, Dunedin, Tampa)

Founded 1888 **Pop** 238,629 **Elev** 44 ft **Area code** 813
Information St Petersburg Area Chamber of Commerce, 100 2nd Ave N, PO Box 1371, 33731; 813/821-4715.

The fourth largest city in the state and second only to Miami as a winter resort, St Petersburg is host to more than a million visitors each year. Its chief tourist commodity, of course, is sunshine, drawing golf and boating enthusiasts throughout the year; however, it also has the big-city zest of its service and nearby high-tech industries. St Petersburg encompasses a fringe of beaches, parks and yacht basins along Tampa Bay and a string of resort-occupied islands (connected to the mainland by causeways) on the Gulf side, across Boca Ciega Bay. These islands form the St Pete Beach Area (see).

Transportation

St Petersburg/Clearwater Intl Airport: Information 813/535-7600.
Tampa Intl Airport: Information 813/461-5294; lost and found 813/870-8760; cash machines, Landside Building, third level.

Car Rental Agencies: See IMPORTANT TOLL-FREE NUMBERS.

Public Transportation: Buses (Pinellas Suncoast Transit Authority), phone 813/530-9911.

Rail Passenger Service: Amtrak 800/872-7245.

What to See and Do

Boating. Municipal Marina, 300 2nd Ave SE (dock master). Accommodates 610 boats; 500-ft dock for visiting boats. Electric, water & telephone service; phone 813/893-7329. **Municipal ramps:** Crisp Park, 35th Ave NE & Poplar St; Grandview Park, 6th St & 38th Ave S; Lake Maggiore (fresh water), west end of 38th Ave S, off 9th St; Jungle Prada, Elbow Lane N & Park St; Bay Vista, Pinellas Point Dr & 4th St; Coffee Pot Bayou, 4th St & 31st Ave NE; Demens Landing, Bayshore Dr & 1st Ave S; Sunlit Cove, Sunlit Cove Dr & Bay St NE. Phone 813/893-7335.

Florida International Museum. Changing exhibits. Theater. Gift shop. (Daily) 100 2nd St N. For current exhibition information phone 813/821-1448 or 800/777-9882. ¢¢¢¢

Florida's Sunken Gardens. Botanical garden featuring thousands of tropical and subtropical flowers and plants from around the world; exotic and native birds and animals on exhibit throughout the gardens; bird shows, alligator wrestling. Inside the complex is a Biblical wax museum; also fudge kitchen; gift shop; snack bar; stroller rentals. (Daily) 1825 4th St N. Phone 813/896-3186. ¢¢¢

Fort De Soto Park. On five islands reached by Pinellas Bayway (toll), S to Mullet Key. Historical fort grounds offers swimming, modern bathhouses, waterskiing; fishing piers; boating (ramp). Picnicking, grills; concessions, snack bar. Camping (fee; dump station, hookups; 2-wk max Jan-Apr; reservations required in person). No fires on ground; no pets. Phone 813/866-2484 or -2662 (camping). **Free.**

Gray Line bus tours. 6890 142nd Ave N, Largo 33771; 813/535-0208 or 800/282-4051.

Great Explorations. Hands-on museum arranged in six exploration areas; "Touch Tunnel" lets visitors crawl through 100-ft textured maze in total darkness; flexibility and muscle-strength tests, computerized thinking exhibits. Gift shop. (Daily; closed Jan 1, Thanksgiving, Dec 25) 1120 4th St S. Phone 813/821-8885. ¢¢¢

Museum of Fine Arts. Displays include pre-Columbian, European, American, Oriental paintings and sculpture; decorative arts and photography; Georgia O'Keeffe's "Poppy," and a large collection of Steuben glass. Guided tours; films, lectures, concerts. (Daily exc Mon; closed Jan 1, Thanksgiving, Dec 25) 255 Beach Dr NE. Phone 813/896-2667. ¢

Planetarium. One-hr planetarium shows (Sept-Apr, Fri evenings; closed univ hols). Observatory open for telescope viewing after shows (weather permitting). St Petersburg Junior College, off 5th Ave N at 69th St. Phone 813/341-4320. **Free.**

★ **Salvador Dali Museum.** Houses the world's largest and most highly acclaimed collection of works by the famous Spanish artist, Salvador Dali. Oils, drawings, watercolors, graphics and sculptures from 1914-1980; tours. (Daily; closed Thanksgiving, Dec 25) 1000 3rd St S. Phone 813/823-3767. ¢¢¢

Science Center of Pinellas County. Hands-on educational institution stimulating scientific inquiry for children and adults. Facilities include laboratories, museum, live animal exhibits, computer center, nature trail and gardens. (Mon-Fri; closed hols) 7701 22nd Ave N. Phone 813/384-0027. **Free.**

St Petersburg Museum of History. Displays concentrate on the history of St Petersburg; changing exhibits gallery. Tours available. (Daily; closed Jan 1, Thanksgiving, Dec 25) 335 2nd Ave NE. Phone 813/894-1052. ¢¢

Tampa Bay Holocaust Museum. Displays include photographs, testimonies and historical artifacts relating to the Holocaust. Multimedia exhibits; theater. (Daily, Sat-Sun afternoons; closed Rosh Hashana, Yom Kippur, Dec 25) 55 5th St S. Phone 813/820-0100. ¢¢¢

The Pier. A five-story inverted pyramid located at the end of this quarter-mile pier contains observation deck with view of city, restaurants, shops, an aquarium, miniature golf; special events and daily entertainment. Replica of HMS *Bounty* (seasonal docking; fee). Fishing, bait house; boating (rentals), water sports. (Daily) Shuttle trolley. 800 2nd Ave NE. Phone 813/821-6164.

Annual Events

International Folk Fair. Thunderdome. Mar.

Renaissance Festival. Phone 813/586-5423. 6 wkends, early Mar-mid Apr.

Sunshine Festival of States. Late Mar.

Seasonal Event

Concerts. The Florida Orchestra. Bayfront Center, Mahaffey Theatre, 400 1st St S. Classical and pops. Phone 813/892-5798. Sept-May.

Additional Visitor Information

The St Petersburg Area Chamber of Commerce (100 2nd Ave N, PO Box 1371, 33731; 813/821-4715) has free sightseeing literature including maps, brochures, and the comprehensive *Visitors Guide*. Visitor information may be obtained at the Suncoast Welcome Center (2001 Ulmerton Rd; 813/576-1449) and at the Pier (800 2nd Ave NE; 813/821-6164). For a recording of current events phone 813/825-3333.

Motels

✔★ ★ **COMFORT INN.** 1400 34th St N (33713), I-275, exit 12. 727/323-3100; FAX 727/327-5792. 76 rms, 3 story. Jan-Apr: S, D $68-$88; each addl $7; family, wkly rates; lower rates rest of yr. TV; cable (premium). Heated pool; whirlpool. Complimentary continental bkfst. Coffee in rms. Restaurant 6:30-10 am. Ck-out 11 am. Coin lndry. Meeting rms. Business servs avail. In-rm modem link. Health club privileges. Cr cds: A, C, D, DS, MC, V.

D ⌧ ⌧ 🐾 SC

★ ★ **DAYS INN.** 2595 54th Ave N (33714), I-275, exit 14. 727/522-3191; FAX 727/527-6120. Web www.daysinn.com. 155 rms, 2 story. Feb-mid-Apr: S $49-$59; D $49-$65; each addl $5; under 12 free; lower rates rest of yr. Crib free. TV; cable (premium). Pool; wading pool. Restaurant 6 am-10 pm; Sun 6 am-9 pm. Ck-out 11 am. Coin lndry. Meeting rm. Business servs avail. In-rm modem link. Lawn games. Microwaves avail. Picnic tables. Cr cds: A, C, D, DS, JCB, MC, V.

D ⌧ 🐾 SC

★ ★ ★ **HOLIDAY INN SUNSPREE RESORT-MARINA COVE.** 6800 Sunshine Skyway Lane (33711), I-275 exit 3. 727/867-1151; res: 800/227-8045; FAX 727/864-4494. E-mail qzbq76a@prodigy.com; web www.st-pete-sunspree.com. 157 rms, 2 story, 22 kits. Feb-mid-Apr: S, D $99-$179; each addl $10; suites, townhouses $159-$259; under 19 free; lower rates rest of yr. TV; cable (premium). 2 pools; whirlpool, poolside serv. Playground. Supervised child's activities; ages 4-11. Coffee in rms. Restaurant 7-11:30 am, 5-10 pm. Bar; entertainment Thurs-Sat. Ck-out 11 am. Coin lndry. Meeting rms. Business servs avail. Sundries. Gift shop. Lighted tennis. Exercise equipt. Game rm. Lawn games. Refrigerators, bathrm phone in suites; microwaves avail. Private patios, balconies. On bay; water sports, private beach. Marina sailing school, boat charter, deep sea fishing. Attraction tours. Cr cds: A, C, D, DS, ER, JCB, MC, V.

D ⌧ 🐾 ⌧ ⌧ ⌧ 🐾 SC

★ ★ **LA MARK CHARLES.** (6200 34th St N, Pinellas Park 33781) I-275, exit 15. 727/527-7334; FAX 727/526-9294; res: 800/448-6781. 93 rms, 1-2 story, 34 kits. Feb-Apr: S, D $60; each addl $5; suites $65-$70; kit. units $65-$75; under 12 free; lower rates rest of yr. Crib $3. Pet accepted; $35 ($25 refundable). TV; cable (premium). Heated pool; whirlpool. Restaurant 7-10 am. Ck-out 11 am. Meeting rm. Business servs avail. Coin lndry. Sundries. Cr cds: A, DS, MC, V.

🐾 ⌧ 🐾 SC

★ ★ **LA QUINTA INN.** 4999 34th St N (33714), I-275, exit 14. 727/527-8421; FAX 727/527-8851. Web www.laquinta.com. 120 rms, 2 story. Mid-Jan-Apr: S $82; D $92; each addl $10; lower rates rest of yr. Pet accepted, some restrictions. TV; cable (premium). Heated pool. Complimentary continental bkfst. Ck-out 11 am. Coin lndry. Meeting rm. Business servs avail. In-rm modem link. Exercise equipt. Cr cds: A, C, D, DS, MC, V.

🐾 ⌧ ⌧ 🐾 SC

✔★ **VALLEY FORGE.** 6825 Central Ave (33710). 727/345-0135; FAX 727/384-1671. 27 rms, 8 kits. Mid-Jan-mid-Apr: S, D $45-$65; lower rates rest of yr. Crib $5. Pet accepted; $3-$5. TV; cable (premium), VCR avail. Pool. Restaurant nearby. Ck-out 11 am. Business servs avail. Lawn games. Refrigerators; microwaves avail. Private patios. Cr cds: A, DS, MC, V.

Hotel

★ ★ ★ **HILTON.** 333 1st St S (33701). 727/894-5000; FAX 727/894-7655. Web www.hilton.com. 333 units, 15 story, 31 suites. Jan-Apr: S, D $139-$210; each addl $10; suites $210-$449; under 18 free; lower rates rest of yr. Crib free. TV; cable (premium), VCR avail. Heated pool; whirlpool, poolside serv. Restaurant 6:30 am-10:30 pm. Bar. Ck-out noon. Convention facilities. Business servs avail. In-rm modem link. Exercise rm. Refrigerators avail. Overlooks St. Petersburg marina. Cr cds: A, C, D, DS, JCB, MC, V.

Inn

★ ★ **BAY GABLES.** *136 4th Ave NE (33701), downtown, jct 4th Ave NE & Rowland Court NE.* 727/822-8855; res: 800/822-8803; FAX 727/824-7223. 9 rms, 1 with shower only, 3 story, 4 kit. suites. MAP: S, D $85; kit. suites $110-$135; under 18 free; wkly rates. TV. Complimentary continental bkfst. Restaurant adj 7:30 am-3 pm; Sun 9 am-1:30 pm; closed Sat. Ck-out 11 am, ck-in 2 pm. Business servs avail. Refrigerators. 1 blk to Tampa Bay. Restored Victorian house (1910). In historic district. Totally nonsmoking. Cr cds: A, MC, V.

D ✕ ⚓ SC

Resort

★ ★ ★ **RENAISSANCE VINOY RESORT.** *501 Fifth Ave NE (33701), off I-275 onto I-375, then 4th Ave N to Beach Dr, left one block, bayfront.* 727/894-1000; FAX 727/822-2785. Web www.renaissance.com. This 1925 landmark on the National Register of Historic Places has been restored, combining 1920s style with updated amenities and services for '90s lifestyles. Its 14 acres include a 74-slip marina and tropical gardens. 360 units, 7 story. Mid-Jan-Apr: S, D $259-$325; suites $625-$1,750; under 18 free; wkend rates; golf, tennis plans; lower rates rest of yr. Crib free. Garage, overnight; valet parking $12, self-park $8. TV; cable (premium), VCR avail. 2 heated pools; whirlpool, poolside serv. Supervised child's activities (June-Aug); ages 4-12. Complimentary coffee in rms. Restaurants 6 am-11 pm (also see TERRACE ROOM/MARCHAND'S GRILL). Rm serv 24 hrs. Ck-out noon. Lndry facilities. Convention facilities. Business center. In-rm modem link. Concierge. Gift shops. Beauty shop. 12 lighted clay tennis courts, pro. 18-hole golf, greens fee $95 (incl cart), pro, putting green, driving range. Exercise rm; sauna, steam rm. Minibars; wet bar in suites. Cr cds: A, C, D, DS, ER, JCB, MC, V.

D ⚓ ⚐ ✕ ⛵ ≈ ⚓ SC ⚐

Restaurants

★ ★ **BASTA'S.** *1625 4th St S (33701).* 727/894-7880. Hrs: 5-11 pm. Closed some major hols. Res accepted. Northern Italian menu. Bar. A la carte entrees: dinner $13-$24. Specializes in fresh seafood, veal, pasta. Pianist. Italian atmosphere; artwork, mural. Hand-painted ceiling in main dining area. Cr cds: A, D, DS, MC, V.

D ⚐

✔★ ★ **NATIVE SEAFOOD & TRADING COMPANY.** *5901 Sun Blvd (33715), I-275 S exit 4.* 727/866-8772. Hrs: 5-10 pm; Fri to 11 pm. Closed Jan 1, Dec 25. Bar 4 pm-midnight. Semi-a la carte: dinner $9.95-$18.95. Child's meals. Specializes in seafood. Tropical island atmosphere. Cr cds: A, D, DS, MC, V.

⚐

★ ★ **PEPIN.** *4125 4th St N (33703).* 727/821-3773. Hrs: 11 am-11 pm; Sat, Sun from 5 pm. Closed Mon; some major hols. Res accepted. Spanish menu. Bar. Semi-a la carte: lunch $7-$12, dinner $15-$25. Child's meals. Specialties: paella, filet mignon, pork chops. Pianist. Valet parking Fri, Sat. Elegant decor; Spanish tile, tapestry and artwork. Cr cds: A, C, D, DS, MC, V.

D ⚐

★ **SAFFRON'S.** *1700 Park St N (33710), 5 mi W on I-275, exit 12.* 727/345-6400. Hrs: 11 am-10 pm; Sun brunch to 3 pm. Closed Memorial Day, Labor Day. Res accepted. Caribbean menu. Bar. A la carte entrees: lunch $4.95-$9.50, dinner $7.50-$18. Sun brunch $13.95. Child's meals. Specialties: jerk chicken, appleton steak, fish negril. Caribbean band Fri-Tues. Outdoor dining. Casual dining; island art. Cr cds: A, C, D, DS, MC, V.

D ⚐

✔★ **SMOKEY'S TEXAS BAR-B-QUE.** *(8180 49th St N, Pinellas Park 33781) N via 49th St to 82nd Ave.* 727/546-3600. Hrs: 11 am-10

pm. Bar. Semi-a la carte: lunch, dinner $3.50-$13. Specializes in hickory-smoked ribs, chicken, steak. Southwestern decor. Cr cds: MC, V.

D ⚐

★ ★ ★ **TERRACE ROOM/MARCHAND'S GRILL.** *(See Renaissance Vinoy Resort)* 727/894-1000. Hrs: 6 am-3 pm, 5:30-11 pm; early-bird dinner Sun-Thurs 5:30-6:30 pm; Sun brunch 9:30 am-3 pm. Res accepted. Mediterranean menu. Bar 11 am-midnight; Fri, Sat to 1 am; Sun 1-11 pm. Wine list. A la carte entrees: bkfst $5-$11.50, lunch $7.25-$15, dinner $12.50-$23. Sun brunch $29. Child's meals. Specialties: shrimp & scallop ravioli, pan-seared sea bass, macadamia nut-crusted grouper. Contemporary jazz band Thurs-Sat, pianist. Valet parking. In historic building; flower and griffin designs on high ceiling and above column were hand-painted as part of an extensive restoration process. Windows are replicas of original 1920s leaded-glass windows. Cr cds: A, C, D, DS, ER, JCB, MC, V.

D ⚐

Starke (C-4)

(See also Gainesville)

Settled 1857 **Pop** 5,226 **Elev** 160 ft **Area code** 904 **Zip** 32091 **E-mail** bradchamber@daccess.net
Information Starke-Bradford County Chamber of Commerce, 202 S Walnut, PO Box 576; 904/964-5278.

The pine forests that surround Starke have been the source for turpentine stores since the middle of the 18th century. Extensive mining of ilmenite (ore of iron and titanium) and the winter strawberry crop are also mainstays of the economy.

What to See and Do

Camp Blanding Museum. Former training center for nine complete US Army divisions during World War II; museum is refurbished barracks building with photo exhibits and artifacts honoring history of the base and those who trained here. Florida Regimental Memorial is a statue and marble edifice listing Floridians who lost their lives in WWII. Memorial Park is a large area with monuments, displays of weapons and vehicles surrounding a lagoon; fountain and picnic area. (Tues-Fri, also Sat & Sun afternoons; closed Jan 1, Easter, Dec 25) 10 mi E on FL 16. Phone 904/533-3196. **Free.**

Mike Roess Gold Head Branch State Park. This park has several lakes and a wildlife refuge on its approx 1,500 acres; ravine with a nature trail and an old mill site. Swimming, bathhouse; fishing; canoes (rentals). Bicycle rentals. Picnicking. Camping (dump station), family vacation cottages. Standard hrs, fees. 13 mi E on FL 100 to Keystone Heights, then 6 mi NE on FL 21. Phone 352/473-4701.

Annual Event

Bradford County Fair. 5 days Apr.

Motel

★ **BEST WESTERN.** *1290 N Temple Ave (US 301).* 904/964-6744; FAX 904/964-3355. 53 rms, 2 story. S $41-$55; D $53-$65; under 12 free; higher rates special events. Crib free. Pet accepted, some restrictions. TV; cable. Pool. Complimentary continental bkfst. Restaurant nearby. Ck-out 11 am. Business servs avail. In-rm modem link. Some refrigerators. Cr cds: A, C, D, DS, MC, V.

⚐ ≈ ✕ ⚓ SC

Stuart (F-6)

(See also Fort Pierce, Jensen Beach, Jupiter)

Pop 11,936 **Elev** 13 ft **Area code** 561 **Web** goodnature.org
Information Stuart/Martin County Chamber of Commerce, 1650 S Kanner Hwy, 34994; 561/287-1088.

Stuart did not become part of Henry Morrison Flagler's Gold Coast development in the 1890s because the pineapple growers of this area vehemently objected to a railroad going through their lands. Today, the town attracts many fishing enthusiasts and boaters. The St Lucie and Indian rivers meet in Stuart and together they flow through the St Lucie Inlet into the ocean. The bridges and causeways around the town connect Stuart to the attractions and beaches of Hutchinson Island.

What to See and Do

Elliott Museum. Gracious Living Wing; antique autos; shell collection; Seminole artifacts; country store; Americana shops; contemporary art gallery. (Daily; closed major hols) 825 NE Ocean Blvd, Hutchinson Island. Phone 561/225-1961. ¢¢

Gilbert's Bar House of Refuge. Originally a US Life Saving Station, now a historic site restored to the late 1800s; aquarium. (Daily exc Mon; closed hols) 5 mi E on Ocean Blvd to 301 SE MacArthur Blvd on Hutchinson Island, entrance through Indian River Plantation. Phone 561/225-1875. ¢

Annual Event

Martin County Fair. Late Feb-early Mar.

Motels

★ ★ **HOLIDAY INN-DOWNTOWN.** *1209 S Federal Hwy (US 1) (34994).* 561/287-6200; FAX 561/287-6200, ext. 100. 119 rms, 2 story. Feb-Mar: S, D $90-$110; each addl $8; under 19 free; lower rates rest of yr. Crib free. TV; cable (premium). Heated pool. Restaurant 6:30 am-2 pm, 5-10 pm. Rm serv. Bar. Ck-out noon. Coin lndry. Meeting rms. Business servs avail. In-rm modem link. Exercise equipt; sauna. Ocean beach privileges. Cr cds: A, C, D, DS, JCB, MC, V.

D ⊠ ⚡ ⊠ ⚟ SC

★ ★ **HOWARD JOHNSON.** *950 S Federal Hwy (US 1) (34994).* 561/287-3171; FAX 561/220-3594. 80 rms, 2 story. Jan-Mar: S, D $60-$85; under 18 free; lower rates rest of yr. Crib free. TV; cable (premium). Pool. Complimentary continental bkfst. Restaurant 11 am-10 pm. Rm serv. Bar to 11 pm. Ck-out noon. Coin lndry. Meeting rms. Business servs avail. Sundries. Health club privileges. Cr cds: A, C, D, DS, MC, V.

D ⊠ ⊠ ⚟ SC

★ ★ **RAMADA INN.** *1200 S Federal Hwy (34994).* 561/287-6900; res: 800/806-8299. Web www.ramada.com. 120 rms, 2 story. Jan-Apr: S, D $89; each addl $5; suites $119; under 17 free; lower rates rest of yr. Crib free. TV; cable (premium). Complimentary continental bkfst. Restaurant 7 am-10 pm. Rm serv 5-10 pm. Bar 2 pm-midnight; entertainment Wed-Sun. Ck-out noon. Meeting rms. Business servs avail. In-rm modem link. Coin lndry. Health club privileges. Pool. Game rm. Refrigerator, microwave, minibar in suites. Cr cds: A, C, D, DS, MC, V.

D ⊠ ⊠ ⚟ SC

Resort

★ ★ ★ **INDIAN RIVER PLANTATION MARRIOTT RESORT.** *(555 NE Ocean Blvd, Hutchinson Island 34996)* 561/225-3700; FAX 561/225-0003. Web www.marriott.com. 200 hotel units, 4 story, 97 apts (1-2 bedrm). Mid-Jan-mid-Apr: S, D $199-$219; suites $249-$269; 1-2 bedrm kit. units $219-$399; under 18 free; long term rates; lower rates rest of yr. Crib free. TV; cable. 4 pools; whirlpool, poolside serv. Playground.

Supervised child's activities; from age 3. Dining rm 6:30 am-10:30 pm (also see SCALAWAGS). Rm serv to midnight. Box lunches, snack bars, picnics. Bar. Ck-out 11 am, ck-in 3 pm. Grocery. Coin lndry. Convention facilities. Business center. In-rm modem link. Valet serv. Concierge. On-site tram service. Lighted tennis, pro. 18-hole golf, pro, putting green. Private beach. Snorkeling equipt. Deep-sea fishing charters; tour boat; boat rentals. Waterskiing. Bicycles. Activities dir. Exercise equipt. Refrigerators, wet bars. Full-service marina; store. Cr cds: A, C, D, DS, ER, JCB, MC, V.

D ⚡ ⚟ ⚟ ⊠ ⚟ ⚟ ⊠ ⚟ SC ⚟

Restaurants

★ ★ **THE ASHLEY.** *61 SW Osceola St (34994).* 561/221-9476. Hrs: 11:30 am-10 pm; Fri, Sat to 1 am; Sun brunch 8 am-2 pm. Closed Dec 25. Bar. Semi-a la carte: lunch $2.95-$7.95, dinner $6.95-$16.95. Sun brunch $2.95-$5.25. Specialties: osso bucco, duck a l'orange, West Indian stewed chicken. Entertainment Wed-Sun. In historic turn-of-the-century building. Eclectic decor featuring original floor; etched glass windows, doors. Cr cds: A, DS, MC, V.

D ⊠

✔ ★ ★ **CHINA STAR.** *1501 S Federal Hwy (US 1).* 561/283-8378. Hrs: 11 am-10 pm; early-bird dinner 3-6:30 pm; Sun brunch to 2 pm. Res accepted. Chinese menu. Wine, beer. Complete meals: lunch $4.35-4.95, dinner $5.50-$10.95. A la carte entrees: dinner $5.95-$12.95. Sun brunch $5.49. Specialties: Peking duck, lobster Cantonese, orange-flavored beef. Oriental decor; lacquered screens. Cr cds: A, DS, MC, V.

D ⊠ ♥

★ ★ **FLAGLER GRILL.** *47 SW Flagler Ave (34994).* 561/221-9517. Hrs: 5:30-9:30 pm. Closed most major hols. Res accepted. Wine list. A la carte entrees: dinner $15.95-$21. Specialties: pan-seared yellowfin tuna, dry aged rib-eye steak. Open kitchen. Totally nonsmoking. Cr cds: A, MC, V.

D

★ ★ ★ **SCALAWAGS.** *(See Indian River Plantation Marriott Resort)* 561/225-3700. Hrs: 6-10 pm. Res accepted. Continental menu. Bar to midnight. Wine cellar. A la carte entrees: dinner $13.50-$24. Child's meals. Specialties: grilled swordfish, rack of lamb, poached Norwegian salmon. Own baking. Outdoor dining. Display cooking. Large picture windows overlook marina and Indian River. Cr cds: A, C, D, DS, ER, JCB, MC, V.

D ⊠

Sun City Center (F-4)

(See also Bradenton, Tampa, St Petersburg)

Pop 8,326 **Elev** 50 ft **Area code** 813
Information Chamber of Commerce, 1651 Sun City Center Plaza, 33573; 813/634-5111.

Motels

★ ★ **COMFORT INN.** *718 Cypress Village Blvd (33573),* I-75 exit 46B. 813/633-3318; FAX 813/633-2747. 75 rms, 2 story. Jan-Apr: S $89; D $99; each addl $5; kit. units $109; under 17 free; lower rates rest of yr. Crib free. TV; cable (premium). Pool; whirlpool. Complimentary continental bkfst. Restaurant nearby. Ck-out 11 am. Business servs avail. Golf privileges. Microwaves avail. Cr cds: A, C, D, DS, MC, V.

D ⚟ ⊠ ⚟ ⚟ SC

★ ★ **SUN CITY CENTER INN.** *1335 Rickenbacker Drive (33573).* 813/634-3331; FAX 813/634-2053; res: 800/237-8200 (exc FL), 800/282-8040 (FL). 100 rms, 1-2 story. Dec-early May: S $79; D $82; each addl $5; under 17 free; golf plans; lower rates rest of yr. Crib free. Pet accepted, some restrictions; $7.50. TV; cable. Pool. Restaurant 7 am-8 pm. Bar; entertainment. Ck-out 11 am. Meeting rms. Business servs avail. 45-hole golf privileges, putting green. Health club privileges. Some private patios. Some balconies. Cr cds: A, DS, MC, V.

Restaurant

✔★ **DANNY BOYS'.** *(3808 FL 674, Ruskin 33572) W on FL 674, at Cypress Village Shopping Ctr.* 813/633-2697. Hrs: 8 am-8 pm. Closed Thanksgiving, Dec 25. Res accepted. Italian, Amer menu. Wine, beer. Semi-a la carte: bkfst $1.10-$4.95, lunch, dinner $3.25-$12.95. Child's meals. Cr cds: A, DS, MC, V.

Tallahassee (B-1)

Founded 1824 **Pop** 124,773 **Elev** 190 ft **Area code** 850 **Web** www.co.leon.fl.us/visitors/index.html
Information Tallahassee Area Convention and Visitors Bureau, 200 W College Ave, PO Box 1369, 32302; 850/413-9200 or 800/628-2866.

The capital of Florida, Tallahassee retains the grace of plantation days and the echoes of its rustic pioneer past. During the Civil War, this majestic city was the only Confederate capital east of the Mississippi not captured by Union forces. The city, as well as Leon County, are now strongly oriented toward state and local government. Lumber and wood production, food production and printing and publishing maintain its economy.

What to See and Do

Alfred B. Maclay State Gardens. Planted as a private estate garden; outstanding azaleas, camellias, dogwood and others, including some rare plant species, on 308 acres; donated to state in 1953. Museum in house has interpretive display (Jan-Apr). No dogs. The Lake Hall Recreation area has swimming; fishing; boating. Nature trails & gardens. Picnicking. (Daily) 3540 Thomasville Rd, 5½ mi N on US 319. Phone 850/487-4556. ¢¢

Apalachicola National Forest. (See APALACHICOLA) S via US 319.

Edward Ball Wakulla Springs State Park. Located in the heart of this 2,860-acre state park is one of the world's larger and deeper freshwater springs. Glass-bottomed boats allow visitors to see the entrance to the cavern 120 ft below the surface. Wildife observation boat tours encounter alligators, turtles and a variety of birds. Many fossils and artifacts of prehistoric dwellers have been found by skin divers. Facilities include swimming in season; nature trails; picnic area, snack bar, dining rm, lodge and conference center (see MOTELS), gift shop. Glass-bottom boat tour and river boat tour (daily; fees). Standard hrs, fees. 14 mi S on FL 61 to FL 267. Phone 850/922-3633.

First Presbyterian Church (1832). Florida's oldest public building in continuous use; has galleries where slaves worshiped. (Mon-Fri; closed hols) Adams St & Park Ave. Phone 850/222-4504.

Florida Agricultural and Mechanical University (1887). (9,300 students) On campus is the Florida Black Archives, Research Center and Museum (Mon-Fri; closed hols). On M.L. King Blvd & Wahnish Way. Phone 850/599-3000 or -3020 (museum).

Florida State University (1857). (30,000 students) On a 400-acre campus with everything from two supercomputers to its own collegiate circus (see ANNUAL EVENTS). W Tennessee (US 90) & Copeland Sts. Campus tours (Mon-Fri); maps at Visitor Information Center, 1100 University Center, Complex C; 850/644-3246. On campus is

Art Gallery. (Sept-May, daily; rest of yr, daily exc Sun; closed university hols) Fine Arts Bldg, Copeland & W Tennessee Sts. Phone 850/644-6836. **Free.**

Governor's Mansion (1957). Tours during regular session of legislature (Mar-Apr, Mon, Wed & Fri, limited hrs; closed hols). 700 N Adams St. Phone 850/488-4661. **Free.**

Old Capitol Museum. Restored to its 1902 grandeur, the building is now a museum, furnished with authentic period pieces and reproductions of original furniture. Historical exhibits; architectural tours (Sat mornings). (Mon-Sat, also Sun afternoons; closed Thanksgiving, Dec 25) S Monroe St & Apalachee Pkwy. Phone 850/487-1902. **Free.**

LeMoyne Art Foundation. Features works by Florida and Georgia artists. (Daily exc Mon; closed July 4, Dec 25-early Jan; also Aug) 125 N Gadsden St. Phone 850/222-8800. **Free.**

Museum of Florida History. Contains historical artifacts and information about Florida; changing exhibits. (Daily; closed Thanksgiving, Dec 25) 500 S Bronough St, at Pensacola St. Phone 850/488-1484. **Free.**

Natural Bridge State Historic Site. This 8-acre monument on the St Marks River marks the spot where a militia of Confederate forces (mostly young boys and old men) stopped Union troops, barring the way to Tallahassee. The battle (Mar 6, 1865) left Tallahassee as the only Confederate capital east of the Mississippi that never fell into Union hands. Picnicking. (See ANNUAL EVENTS). (Daily) 9 mi S on US 363 to Woodville, then 6 mi E on Natural Bridge Rd. Phone 850/925-6216 or 850/922-6007. **Free.**

San Marcos de Apalache State Historic Site. Site first visited by Panfilo de Narvaez in 1527 and Hernando de Soto in 1539; ruins of fort (1739); museum on site of old federal marine hospital. Picnicking. Nature trails. (Thurs-Mon) 24 mi S via FL 363, on Canal St in St Marks. Phone 904/925-6216 or 850/922-6007. Museum ¢

St Marks National Wildlife Refuge. A 65,000-acre refuge heavily populated with birds, deer, alligators; waterfowl in fall and winter. Freshwater fishing; saltwater boat launching. Nature and primitive walking trails. Picnicking. Visitor center (daily; closed hols). Observation decks. Golden Eagle, Golden Age, Golden Access passports accepted (see MAKING THE MOST OF YOUR TRIP). (Daily) 15 mi S on FL 363 to St Marks, then 3 mi S on County 59. Phone 850/925-6121. Per vehicle ¢¢; Per pedestrian ¢

State Capitol. At top of Tallahassee's second-highest hill, the modern, 22-story capitol building towers above the city; observation level on top floor. Hourly tours (daily). Visitor information center, West Plaza (daily; closed some major hols). Duval St. Phone 850/413-9200. **Free.**

Tallahassee Museum of History & Natural Science. Fifty-two acres with restored 1880s Big Bend farm and 1854 plantation house; gristmill, schoolhouse, church; hands-on Discovery Center; natural habitat zoo with wild animals native to the area, including the endangered Florida panther; gopher nature trail. Visitors center. (See ANNUAL EVENTS) (Daily; closed some major hols) 3945 Museum Dr, on Lake Bradford. Phone 850/575-8684. ¢¢¢

The Columns (1830). Moved from its original site in 1972, this three-story brick mansion once served as a bank, boarding house, doctor's office and restaurant. Restored and furnished with antiques, it now serves as office of the Chamber of Commerce. (Mon-Fri) 100 N Duval St. Phone 850/224-8116.

Annual Events

Natural Bridge Battle Reenactment. Natural Bridge State Historic Site. Reenactment of battle between Confederate and Union forces on this site. 1st Sun Mar.

Springtime Tallahassee. Commemorates founding of city. Parades, concerts, art shows, tours of homes and gardens and numerous other activities in various parts of city. Phone 850/224-5012. 4 wks late Mar-early Apr.

Flying High Circus. Florida State University. Aprox 80 students perform in three-ring circus. Evening & matinee performances. Phone 850/644-4874. 2 wkends Apr.

Spring Farm Days. Tallahassee Museum of History & Natural Science. Focuses on spring activities on 1880s farm; features sheep shearing. Mid-Apr.

Shakespeare Festival. Professional open-air Shakespearean Theatre with guest artists; crafts, sword fights, a living chess match. Early May.

Summer Swamp Stomp. Tallahassee Museum of History & Natural Science. Continuous musical entertainment from bluegrass to folk and "saltwater" music. Mid-July.

North Florida Fair. Fairgrounds. Exhibits, midway. Phone 850/878-3247. Late Oct.

December on the Farm. Tallahassee Museum of History & Natural Science. Focuses on fall activities on 1880s farm; features syrup-making. Early Dec.

Motels

✔★ BEST WESTERN PRIDE INN. *2016 Apalachee Pkwy (32301).* 850/656-6312; FAX 850/942-4312. 78 rms, 2 story. S $41-$53; D $46-$58; each addl $5. TV; cable. Pool. Complimentary continental bkfst. Restaurant adj 6 am-11 pm. Ck-out 11 am. Coin lndry. Meeting rm. Business servs avail. Cr cds: A, D, DS, MC, V.

★ CABOT LODGE. *2735 N Monroe St (32303).* 850/386-8880; FAX 850/386-4254; res: 800/223-1964. 160 rms, 2 story. S $62-$68; D $68-$77; each addl $6; under 10 free. Crib free. TV; cable. Pool. Complimentary continental bkfst. Ck-out noon. Meeting rms. Business servs avail. In-rm modem link. Health club privileges. Microwaves avail. Library, fireplace; veranda overlooking pool. Cr cds: A, C, D, DS, MC, V.

★★ COURTYARD BY MARRIOTT. *1018 Appalachee Pkwy (32301).* 850/222-8822; FAX 850/561-0354. Web www.courtyard.com. 154 rms, 2 story. S, D $94- $118; suites $134-$150; wkend rates. Crib free. TV; cable (premium). Pool; whirlpool. Complimentary coffee in rms. Bar 4-10 pm. Ck-out noon. Coin lndry. Meeting rms. Business servs avail. In-rm modem link. Valet serv. Exercise equipt. Refrigerator in suites. Balconies. Cr cds: A, C, D, DS, MC, V.

★★ LA QUINTA MOTOR INN. *2905 N Monroe (32303).* 850/385-7172; FAX 850/422-2463. 154 units, 3 story. S $61-$71; D $68-$78; each addl $7; under 18 free. Crib avail. Pet accepted, some restrictions. TV; cable (premium). Pool. Complimentary continental bkfst. Restaurant adj 7 am-11 pm. Ck-out noon. Meeting rms. Business servs avail. In-rm modem link. Cr cds: A, D, DS, MC, V.

✔★ RED ROOF INN. *2930 Hospitality St (32303).* 850/385-7884; FAX 850/386-8896. 107 rms, 2 story. S, D $41.99-$48.99; each addl $7; under 18 free. Crib free. Pet accepted, some restrictions. TV. Complimentary coffee in lobby. Ck-out noon. Business servs avail. In-rm modem link. Cr cds: A, C, D, DS, MC, V.

✔★ SHONEY'S INN. *2801 N Monroe (32303).* 850/386-8286; FAX 850/422-1074. Web www.shoneysinn.com. 112 rms, 2 story, 26 suites. S, D $49-$73; each addl $5; suites $80-$150. TV; cable. Pool. Complimentary continental bkfst. Restaurant nearby. Ck-out noon. Coin lndry. Meeting rms. Health club privileges. Sundries. Balconies. Cr cds: A, D, DS, MC, V.

★★ WAKULLA SPRINGS LODGE. *(550 Wakulla Park Dr, Wakulla Springs 32305) at jct FL 61 & FL 267.* 850/224-5950; FAX 850/561-7251. 27 rms, 2 story. S, D $65-$90; suites $250. TV in lobby. Restaurant 7:30-10 am, 11:30 am-2 pm, 6-8:30 pm. Ck-out 11 am. Meeting rms. Business servs avail. Sundries. Picnic tables. Boat tours. Swimming in springs; 2-level diving board. Atmosphere of an old Southern hotel; located in 2,900-acre state park on Wakulla Springs. Cr cds: MC, V.

Lodge

★★ KILLEARN COUNTRY CLUB & INN. *100 Tyron Circle (32308), N off I-10 exit 30, right on Killearny Way, left on Shamrock N to Tyron Circle.* 850/893-2186; FAX 850/893-8267; res: 800/476-4101. 39 rms, 2 story. S, D $80-$150; each addl $10; under 12 free; higher rates football wkends. Crib avail. TV; cable. Pool; wading pool, poolside serv, lifeguard. Restaurant 11 am-9 pm; Sat from 7 am; Sun 7 am-6 pm. Bar. Ck-out noon. Business servs avail. Meeting rms. Lighted tennis, pro. 27-hole golf, pro, greens fee, putting green, driving range. Exercise equipt. Some refrigerators. Microwaves avail. Some balconies. Cr cds: A, DS, MC, V.

Motor Hotels

★★★ HILTON GARDEN INN. *3333 Thomasville Rd (32312).* 850/385-3553; FAX 850/385-4242. 100 rms, 4 story. S $89-$139; D $94-$144; suites $99-$165; under 18 free; higher rates special events. Crib free. TV; cable (premium). Complimentary coffee in rms. Restaurant 6:30-10:30 am. Rm serv 11 am-10 pm. Bar 4-11 pm. Ck-out noon. Meeting rm. Business center. In-rm modem link. Valet serv. Sundries. Coin lndry. Exercise equipt. Pool. Refrigerators, microwaves. Cr cds: A, C, D, DS, JCB, MC, V.

★ RAMADA INN-NORTH. *2900 N Monroe (32303).* 850/386-1027; FAX 850/422-1025. 198 rms, 2-4 story. S, D $87-$92; suites $110-$150; under 18 free. TV. Pool; poolside serv. Restaurant 6:30 am-10 pm. Rm serv. Bar 3-11 pm. Ck-out noon. Meeting rms. Business servs avail. Bellhops. Free airport transportation. Health club privileges. Cr cds: A, C, D, DS, MC, V.

Hotel

★★ RADISSON. *415 N Monroe (32301).* 850/224-6000. 116 units, 7 story. S $101-$140; D $111-$150; each addl $10; suites $140-$195; under 18 free. Crib free. TV; cable. Coffee in rms. Restaurant 6:30 am-10 pm. Bar to 1 am. Ck-out noon. Meeting rms. Business servs avail. In-rm modem link. Concierge. Free airport transportation. Exercise equipt; sauna. Some bathrm phones, refrigerators. Cr cds: A, C, D, DS, ER, MC, V.

Inn

★★★ GOVERNORS INN. *209 S Adams St (32301).* 850/681-6855; FAX 850/222-3105; res: 800/342-7717 (FL). 40 rms, 2-3 story. S $119; D $129-$159; each addl $10; suites $149-$219; wkend rates. Crib free. TV; cable (premium), VCR avail. Complimentary continental bkfst. Ck-out noon, ck-in 3 pm. Meeting rms. Business servs avail. In-rm modem link. Luggage handling. Valet parking. Some fireplaces. Antiques, four-poster beds. Cr cds: A, C, D, DS, MC, V.

Restaurants

★★ ANDREW'S 2ND ACT. *228 S Adams St (32301).* 850/222-3444. Hrs: 11:30 am-1:30 pm, 5:30-10 pm; Fri, Sat to 11 pm; Sun to 9 pm. Closed Thanksgiving, Dec 25, dinner in winter. Res accepted. Continental menu. A la carte entrees: lunch $4.50-$8, dinner $13.50-$27. Child's meals. Specialties: tournedos St Laurent, veal Oscar. Valet parking. Cr cds: A, C, D, MC, V.

✔★ **BARNACLE BILL'S.** *1830 N Monroe St (32303). 850/385-8734.* Hrs: 11 am-11 pm. Closed Dec 25. Bar. Semi-a la carte: lunch $3.95-$6.99, dinner $6.99-$28.95. Child's meals. Specializes in seafood, grilled & smoked fish, chicken. Aquarium. Cr cds: A, D, MC, V.

D SC

✔★ **CAFE DI LORENZO.** *1002 N Monroe St (32303). 850/681-3622.* Hrs: 5-11 pm. Res accepted. Italian menu. Beer, wine. Semi-a la carte: dinner $9-$16. Child's meals. Specializes in seafood, pasta, veal. Outdoor dining. Cr cds: A, MC, V.

✔★ **THE WHARF.** *4141 Appalachee Pkwy (32311). 850/656-2395.* Hrs: 4-9 pm; Fri, Sat to 10 pm; early-bird dinner Mon-Fri 4-6 pm. Closed Thanksgiving, Dec 24-25. Bar. Semi-a la carte: dinner $8.95-$24.95. Child's meals. Specializes in local seafood. Parking. Fish tanks along hallways. Cr cds: A, C, D, DS, MC, V.

D ↩

Unrated Dining Spot

CHEZ PIERRE. *1215 Thomasville Rd (32303). 850/222-0936.* Hrs: 11 am-2:30 pm, 5:30-10 pm. Closed major hols. French menu. Bar. A la carte entrees: lunch $4-$10, dinner $10-$19. Specializes in homemade soup, French pastries. Parking. Country French decor. Cr cds: A, C, D, DS, MC, V.

D

Tampa (E-3)

(See also Clearwater, St Petersburg)

Settled 1824 **Pop** 280,015 **Elev** 57 ft **Area code** 813 **Web** gotampa.com
Information Tampa/Hillsborough Convention & Visitors Association, 400 N Tampa St, Ste 1010, 33602; 813/223-1111, ext 44 or 800/448-2672.

This is the business and vacation hub of Florida's west coast. Tampa, Florida's third largest city and its leading industrial metropolis, has a colorful waterfront and a beautiful bay drive. Within it is Ybor City, a Spanish, Cuban, Italian enclave of narrow streets and cigarmakers, and MacDill Air Force Base, headquarters of the 56th TT Wing, US Special Operations Command and the US Central Command.

Sprawled around the mouth of the Hillsborough River at the head of Tampa Bay, the city traces its origins to Fort Brooke, established to oversee Seminole Indians, who recently had moved here from Georgia and northern Florida. An early center for Florida's cattle industry, Tampa enjoyed brisk trade with Cuba and prospered. However, subjected to hit-and-run raids during the Civil War, the city suffered a decline until 1884, when Henry Plant's narrow-gauge South Florida Railroad reached the city. Determined to outdo his East Coast rival Henry Morrison Flagler, Plant built the opulent Tampa Bay Hotel and opened it with a flamboyance undreamed of in this remote outpost. Teddy Roosevelt trained his Rough Riders in the back yard of the hotel. In 1886, Vincente Martinez Ybor moved his cigar factory and its workers here from Key West. Most of the other cigarmakers moved with him, establishing Ybor City.

Today the port of Tampa handles more than 50 million tons of shipping a year. Its cigar factories turn out three million cigars each working day; two huge breweries are in operation in one of 33 industrial parks; two citrus plants and a variety of other factories are here. Some of the world's largest phosphate mines are nearby, and a new technique to extract uranium from mine wastes has revitalized this industry.

Transportation

Tampa International Airport: Information 813/870-8700; lost and found 813/870-8760; weather 813/645-2506; cash machines, Landside Building, third level.

Car Rental Agencies: See IMPORTANT TOLL-FREE NUMBERS.

Public Transportation: Buses (Hillsborough Area Regional Transit Authority), phone 813/254-4278.

Rail Passenger Service: Amtrak 800/872-7245.

What to See and Do

Adventure Island. This 36-acre water theme park features 4 speed slides, inner-tube slide, slow-winding tube ride, water-sled ride, 16 water flumes; diving platforms; pool that creates 3-5-ft waves for body-and raft surfing; volleyball complex; large children's water play section; lifeguards. Also includes restaurant, picnicking; dressing room, sunbathing; games; gift shop. (Late Mar-mid-Sept, daily; rest of Sept, Sat & Sun) 4545 Bougainvillea Ave, near Busch Gardens. Phone 813/987-5660.   ¢¢¢¢¢

Busch Gardens Tampa. A 335-acre theme park re-creating some of the sites and sounds of Africa. The area is divided into 8 different regions, including the Timbuktu section that has dolphin theater, rides, craftspeople, German restaurant and entertainment center; the Myombe Reserve has gorillas and chimpanzees; the Serengeti Plain is home to Edge of Africa, a 15-acre animal theme park that visitors can take a safari through; and the Morocco section has shops, cafes and the 1,200-seat Moroccan Palace Theater with an ice-skating show. A 7-acre area named Egypt includes a museum, shopping bazaars and an inverted steel roller coaster named "Montu." Throughout the park are an animal nursery, bird garden and rare white tigers; thrill rides including Questor, a flight simulator ride, Tanganyika Tidal Wave flume ride, Kumba, Python, and Scorpion rollercoaster rides, railway, sky trolley and others. (Daily) Parking fee. At Busch Blvd & 40th St, 8 mi N via I-275, then E on Busch Blvd. Phone 813/987-5082. Admission includes all rides, shows, attractions.   ¢¢¢¢¢

Lowry Park. This 105-acre park contains a section with statues of fable and nursery rhyme characters. Also zoo with Asian, primate & Florida sections, aviary and petting zoo; Safety Village/Children's Museum, which teaches school children bicycle safety; and amusement park with rides. Also boat launch, picnicking, playground. Park (daily) Some fees. N Boulevard & W Sligh Ave. Phone 813/935-8441 (museum) or 813/932-0245 (zoo).

MOSI Science Center. Large open-air facility features hundreds of hands-on exhibits and participatory programs on a wide range of scientific subjects. Recent expansion includes MOSIMAX, a 350-seat IMAX Dome theater; exhibits on Florida and its environment; flight and space; a science store and a public library. (Daily, closed Jan 1, Thanksgiving, Dec 25) 4801 E Fowler Ave. Phone 813/987-6300. Museum ¢¢¢   IMAX Theater ¢¢¢

Professional sports.

American League baseball (Tampa Bay Devil Rays). Tropicana Field, 204 16th St S, St Petersburg. Phone 813/825-3250.

NFL (Tampa Bay Buccaneers). Houlihan Stadium, 4201 N Dale Mabry Hwy. Phone 813/870-2700.

NHL (Tampa Bay Lightning). Ice Palace, 401 Channelside Dr. Phone 813/229-2658.

Sightseeing tours.

Gray Line bus tours. Contact 6890 142nd N, Largo 33731; 813/535-0208.

Around the Town. 3450 W Buschwood Park Dr, Suite 115, 33618. For information phone 813/932-7803.

Tampa Tours. 5805 N 50th St, 33610. For information phone 813/621-6667.

Scenic drive. Bayshore Blvd from Platt St Bridge to Gandy Blvd; 6¹/2 miles along Tampa Bay.

Tampa Bay History Center. A history and heritage museum that offers exhibits showing the geographical and multicultural influences that have shaped the region through the centuries. (Daily exc Mon) 225 S Franklin St. Phone 813/228-0097.   **Free.**

Tampa Bay Performing Arts Center. Includes 2,500-seat Festival Hall, 1,000-seat Playhouse Hall, 300-seat Robert and Lorena Jaeb Theater and 100-seat Off Center Theater. The Florida Orchestra performs classical and pop concerts here (Sept-May; phone 813/286-2403); also performances by national artists, touring groups and local artists. 1010 N MacInnes Place. Phone 813/229-7827 or 800/955-1045.

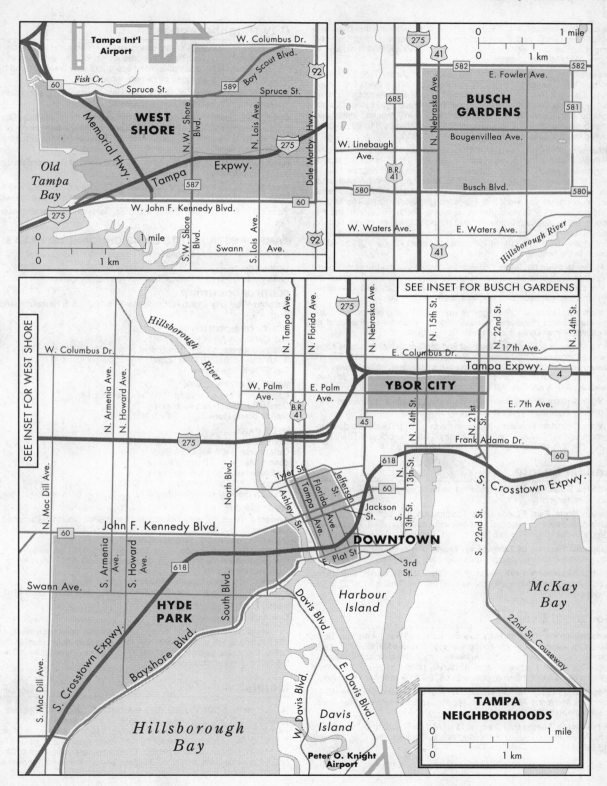

Tampa Int'l Airport

W. Columbus Dr.

Boy Scout Blvd.

92

Fish Cr.

589

Spruce St.

Spruce St.

WEST SHORE

Memorial Hwy.

N.W. Shore Blvd.

N. Lois Ave.

Dale Marby Hwy.

275

60

Tampa Expwy.

587

60

Old Tampa Bay

275

W. John F. Kennedy Blvd.

S.W. Shore Blvd.

S. Lois Ave.

92

Swann Ave.

0   1 mile

0   1 km

275

41

582

E. Fowler Ave.

582

685

N. Nebraska Ave.

BUSCH GARDENS

581

W. Linebaugh Ave.

Bougenvillea Ave.

B.R. 41

580

Busch Blvd.

580

W. Waters Ave.

E. Waters Ave.

41

Hillsborough River

0   1 mile

0   1 km

SEE INSET FOR BUSCH GARDENS

Hillsborough River

275

N. Tampa Ave.

N. Florida Ave.

N. Nebraska Ave.

N. 15th St.

N. 22nd St.

N. 17th Ave.

N. 34th St.

SEE INSET FOR WEST SHORE

W. Columbus Dr.

E. Columbus Dr.

Tampa Expwy.

4

N. Armenia Ave.

N. Howard Ave.

W. Palm Ave.

E. Palm Ave.

YBOR CITY

E. 7th Ave.

B.R. 41

45

N. 14th St.

N. 21st St.

Frank Adamo Dr.

60

275

618

S. Crosstown Expwy.

N. Mac Dill Ave.

North Blvd.

Tyler St.

Ashley St.

Florida Ave.

Tampa Ave.

Jefferson St.

60

N. 13th St.

S. 13th St.

S. 22nd St.

60

John F. Kennedy Blvd.

S. Armenia Ave.

S. Howard Ave.

618

Jackson St.

DOWNTOWN

Swann Ave.

South Blvd.

E. Plat St.

3rd St.

HYDE PARK

Davis Blvd.

Harbour Island

McKay Bay

S. Mac Dill Ave.

S. Crosstown Expwy.

Bayshore Blvd.

W. Davis Blvd.

E. Davis Blvd.

22nd St. Causeway

Hillsborough Bay

Davis Island

Peter O. Knight Airport

TAMPA NEIGHBORHOODS

0   1 mile

0   1 km

Tampa Museum of Art. Traditional and contemporary art; children's exhibitions; Greek and Roman antiquities. Educational programs and films. Tours avail by appt only. (Daily; closed major hols) 600 N Ashley Dr. Phone 813/274-8130. ¢¢

University of South Florida (1956). (34,000 students) This 1,700-acre campus has changing art exhibits in Fine Arts Gallery (Mon-Fri; closed hols), Contemporary Art Museum (Mon-Fri, also Sat afternoons; closed hols), Fine Arts Teaching Gallery (Mon-Fri), Anthropology Museum, Social Science Bldg (Mon-Fri; closed school hols). Film, theater, music and athletic events. Sun Dome entertainment center seats 11,183. 4202 E Fowler Ave (FL 582), 10 mi N. Phone 813/974-2235.

University of Tampa (1931). (1,650 students) Plant Hall, the main building of this 69-acre campus, was the Tampa Bay Hotel, a large, bizarre conglomeration of Victorian, Spanish and Moorish architecture built in 1891 by railroad magnate Henry B. Plant to compete with his east-coast rival Henry Flagler. The structure features several onion-domes, 13 minarets, elaborate filigree work and interlaced gingerbread trim. The 500-rm hotel hosted many famous guests, including Teddy Roosevelt and the Rough Riders, Stephen Crane, Richard Harding Davis and others. Historic walking tour leaves from lobby (Sept-May, Tues & Thurs afternoons). 401 W Kennedy Blvd (US 60), at Hillsborough River. Phone 813/253-6220. **Free.**   In the building is

Henry B. Plant Museum. Showcases original Victorian-era furnishings and decorative art objects amassed by Plant for the hotel; exhibits on Plant's railroad & steamship lines; tours. (Tues-Sat, also Sun afternoons; closed major hols) Phone 813/254-1891. ¢¢

Waterfront. Docks at 139 Twiggs St where stalks of green bananas are unloaded almost daily; shrimp boats unload at docks on the 22nd St Causeway. From Davis Island, Water St or 13th St.

✪ **Ybor City.** A link between the past and present, this area retains some of the atmosphere of the original Cuban settlement. Spanish and Italian are spoken as much as English. Many Spanish restaurants, coffeehouses and cigar factories are here. 2 mi E of downtown; roughly between I-4, 5th Ave, Nebraska Ave & 22nd St. Within the area are

Ybor Square. A complex of shops and restaurants in a restored 19th-century cigar factory. (Daily) Phone 813/247-4497.

Ybor City State Museum. Interprets the beginning (1886) and development of Ybor City and the cigar industry. (Tues-Sat; closed Thanksgiving, Dec 25) 1818 E 9th Ave. Phone 813/247-6323. ¢

Annual Events

Outback Bowl. Tampa Stadium. Post-season college football match-up; other events. Jan 1.

Florida State Fair. Florida State Fairgrounds. US 301 & I-4. County exhibits, livestock shows, orchid show, industrial exposition, amusement rides, entertainment. Phone 813/621-7821. Feb 5-16.

Gasparilla Festival of Tampa Bay. Month-long celebration that begins with a "pirate invasion," parade and street party. Early Feb.

Florida Strawberry Festival. In Plant City. Country music, strawberry delicacies and strawberry shortcake eating contest. Phone 813/752-9194. 10 days early Mar.

Seasonal Events

Baseball spring training. Plant City Stadium, 2 mi S of I-4 on Park Rd in Plant City: Cincinnati Reds spring training, phone 813/752-7337, early Mar-early Apr. Legends Field, Dale Mabry Hwy & Dr Martin Luther King, Jr Blvd: Gulf Coast League, Tampa Yankees, phone 813/875-7753; New York Yankees spring training, phone 813/875-7753, early Mar-early Apr.

Greyhound racing. Tampa Track. 5 mi N at 8300 Nebraska Ave; US 41 Nebraska Ave exit, I-75 Bird St exit . Nightly exc Sun; matinees Mon, Wed, Sat. Phone 813/932-4313. July-Dec.

Horse racing. Tampa Bay Downs. 11 mi NW on FL 580 to Oldsmar, then 1 mi N on Race Track Rd.Thoroughbreds. Parimutuels. Daily. Phone 813/855-4401. Early Dec-early May.

City Neighborhoods

Many of the restaurants, unrated dining establishments and some lodgings listed under Tampa include neighborhoods as well as exact street addresses. Geographic descriptions of these areas are given, followed by a table of restaurants arranged by neighborhood.

Busch Gardens: West of Busch Gardens amusement park; south of Fowler Ave, north of Busch Blvd and east of I-275.

Downtown: South of Tyler St, west of Jefferson St, north of Water St and Harbour Island and east of Ashley St. **North of Downtown:** North of US 275. **South of Downtown:** South of FL 618. **West of Downtown:** West of Hillsborough River.

Hyde Park: South of Kennedy Blvd, west and north of Bayshore Blvd and east of MacDill Ave.

West Shore: On Old Tampa Bay south of Courtney Campbell Pkwy and Tampa Intl Airport, west of Dale Mabry Hwy and north of Kennedy Blvd.

Ybor City: South of I-4, west of 22nd St, north of 7th Ave and east of Nebraska Ave.

TAMPA RESTAURANTS BY NEIGHBORHOOD AREAS

(For full description, see alphabetical listings under Restaurants)

DOWNTOWN
Italianissimo (Hyatt Regency Hotel). 2 Tampa City Center

SOUTH OF DOWNTOWN
Harbour View (Wyndham Harbour Island Hotel). 725 S Harbour Island Blvd

NORTH OF DOWNTOWN
A.J. Catfish. 8751 N Himes Ave
Rumpelmayers. 4812 E Busch Blvd
Sukhothai. 8201-A N Dale Mabry Hwy
Taj. 2734-B Fowler Ave

WEST OF DOWNTOWN
Capdevila's At La Teresita. 3248 W Columbus Dr
Donatello. 232 N Dale Mabry Hwy
Malios Steak House. 301 S Dale Mabry Hwy

HYDE PARK
Bern's Steak House. 1208 S Howard Ave
Colonnade. 3401 Bayshore Blvd
Jimmy Mac's. 113 S Armenia Ave
Le Bordeaux. 1502 S Howard Ave
Miguel's. 3035 W Kennedy
Mise En Place. 442 W Kennedy Blvd

WEST SHORE
Armani's (Hyatt Regency Westshore Hotel). 6200 Courtney Campbell Causeway
CK's (Marriott Airport). Tampa Intl Airport
Landry's Seafood House. 7616 Courtney Campbell Causeway
Oystercatchers (Hyatt Regency Westshore Hotel). 6200 Courtney Campbell Causeway
Ruth's Chris Steak House. 1700 N Westshore Blvd
Shula's Steak House (Wyndham Westshore). 4860 W Kennedy Blvd

YBOR CITY
Columbia. 2117 E 7th Ave

Note: When a listing is located in a town that does not have its own city heading, it will appear under the city nearest to its location. In these cases, the address and town appear in parenthesis immediately following the name of the establishment.

Motels

★ ★ **COURTYARD BY MARRIOTT.** *3805 W Cypress St (33607), I-275, exit 23B, near Intl Airport, in West Shore.* 813/874-0555; FAX 813/870-0685. Web www.marriott.com. 145 rms, 4 story. Jan-Apr: S, D $135-$154; suites $169; under 18 free; lower rates rest of yr. Crib free. TV; cable (premium). Pool; whirlpool. Complimentary coffee in rms. Ck-out noon. Coin lndry. Meeting rms. Business servs avail. In-rm modem link.

Free airport transportation. Exercise equipt. Refrigerator in suites. Some balconies. Cr cds: A, C, D, DS, MC, V.

D ≃ ✕ ✈ ⊠ ⊠ SC

★ **DAYS INN-FAIRGROUNDS.** *9942 Adamo Dr (FL 60) (33619), exit 51 off I-75, west on FL 60, east of downtown.* 813/623-5121; res: 800/831-3297; FAX 813/628-4989. 100 rms, 2 story. Jan-Apr: S $69-$74; D $79-$84; each addl $5; under 18 free; lower rates rest of yr. Crib free. TV; cable (premium). Pool. Complimentary continental bkfst. Coffee in rms. Restaurant adj 6 am-10 pm. Ck-out noon. Coin lndry. Meeting rm. Some refrigerators, microwaves. Cr cds: A, C, D, DS, MC, V.

D ≃ ⊠ 🔥 SC

✔★ **DAYS INN-NORTH.** *701 E Fletcher Ave (33612), I-275 exit 35; near Busch Gardens.* 813/977-1550; FAX 813/977-6556. Web www.flausa.com. 250 rms, 3 story. Jan-Apr: S $39-$59; D $39-$65; each addl $6; wkly rates; lower rates rest of yr. Crib free. Pet accepted, some restrictions. TV; cable (premium). Pool. Complimentary full bkfst. Restaurant 24 hrs. Ck-out noon. Coin lndry. Meeting rms. Business servs avail. Health club privileges. Cr cds: A, D, DS, MC, V.

🐾 ≃ ⊠ 🔥 SC

★★ **DAYS INN-ROCKY POINT ISLAND.** *7627 Courtney Campbell Causeway (33607), in West Shore.* 813/281-0000; res: 800/237-2555; FAX 813/281-1067. Web www.impact.hotel.com. 145 rms, 2 story, 7 suites. Jan-Apr: S, D $89-$109; suites $170; under 17 free; family rates; lower rates rest of yr. Crib free. TV; cable (premium). Restaurant 7 am-10 pm. Rm serv. Bar 11-2 am; Sun from 1 pm; music Sat, Sun. Ck-out noon. Meeting rms. Business servs avail. In-rm modem link. Bellhops. Coin lndry. Free airport transportation. Pool. Refrigerators, microwaves. On beach. Cr cds: A, C, D, DS, MC, V.

D 🐾 ≃ ⊠ 🔥 SC

✔★ **ECONOMY INNS OF AMERICA.** *6606 E Dr Martin Luther King Blvd (33619), I-4 exit 4, east of downtown.* 813/623-6667; FAX 813/623-1495. 128 rms, 2 story. Jan-mid-Apr: S $54.90; D $59.90; lower rates rest of yr. Pet accepted. TV; cable (premium). Heated pool. Complimentary coffee in lobby. Restaurant nearby. Ck-out 11 am. Coin lndry. Cr cds: A, MC, V.

D 🐾 ≃ 🔥 SC

★★ **HAMPTON INN AIRPORT-WESTSHORE.** *4817 W Laurel St (33607), I-275S exit West Shore (21), N to Laurel, in West Shore.* 813/287-0778; FAX 813/287-0882. 134 rms, 6 story. Jan-Apr: S, D $92-$105; under 19 free; higher rates special events; lower rates rest of yr. TV; cable (premium). Pool. Complimentary continental bkfst. Coffee in rms. Ck-out noon. Business servs avail. In-rm modem link. Bellhops. Free airport transportation. Cr cds: A, C, D, DS, MC, V.

D ≃ ✈ ⊠ 🔥 SC

★ **HOLIDAY INN EXPRESS-STADIUM.** *4732 N Dale Mabry Hwy (33614), north of downtown.* 813/877-6061; FAX 813/876-1531. 235 rms, 1-2 story, 40 suites. Late Dec-early Apr: S, D $85-$95; each addl $10; suites $95-$120; under 18 free; lower rates rest of yr. Pet accepted; $20. TV; cable (premium). Pool. Complimentary continental bkfst. Coffee in rms. Restaurant 11 am-11 pm. Ck-out noon. Meeting rms. Business center. In-rm modem link. Bellhops. Valet serv. Free airport transportation. Exercise equipt. Game rm. Microwaves avail. Cr cds: A, C, D, DS, JCB, MC, V.

D 🐾 ≃ ✕ ⊠ 🔥 SC ♿

✔★★ **LA QUINTA INN.** *2904 Melbourne Blvd (33605), I-4 exit 3, east of downtown.* 813/623-3591; FAX 813/620-1375. Web www.travelweb.com/laquinta.html. 128 rms, 3 story. S, D $44-$78; each addl $7; suites $99-$125; under 18 free. Crib free. Pet accepted, some restrictions. TV; cable (premium). Pool. Complimentary continental bkfst. Ck-out noon. Guest lndry. Meeting rms. In-rm modem link. Sundries. Cr cds: A, C, D, DS, MC, V.

D 🐾 ≃ ⊠ ⊠ SC

★ **RED ROOF INN.** *5001 N US 301 (33610), near I-4 exit 6A, east of downtown.* 813/623-5245; FAX 813/623-5240. E-mail i0092@redroofinns.com. 108 rms, 2 story. Jan-Apr: S, D $69.99-$99.99; under 18

free; lower rates rest of yr. Pet accepted, some restrictions. TV; cable (premium). Complimentary coffee. Restaurant adj open 24 hrs. Ck-out noon. Cr cds: A, C, D, DS, MC, V.

D 🐾 ⊠ ⊠

★★ **RESIDENCE INN BY MARRIOTT.** *3075 N Rocky Point Dr (33607), near Intl Airport, west of downtown, off FL 60.* 813/281-5677; FAX 813/289-0266. E-mail notinshow@aol.com; web www.marriott.com. 176 kit. units, 1-2 story. Jan-Apr: S, D $125-$200; family rates; lower rates rest of yr. Crib free. Pet accepted; $150 refundable & $5/day. TV; cable (premium). Pool; whirlpool. Complimentary continental bkfst. Ck-out noon. Coin lndry. Meeting rms. Business servs avail. In-rm modem link. Bellhops. Valet serv Mon-Fri. Free airport transportation. Golf nearby. Health club privileges. Microwaves. Some balconies. Dock; watersports, para-sailing, fishing. On Tampa Bay. Cr cds: A, C, D, DS, MC, V.

D 🐾 ➤ ≃ ✈ ⊠ ⊠ SC

★★ **SAILPORT RESORT.** *2506 Rocky Point Dr (33607), west of downtown.* 813/281-9599; FAX 813/281-9510; res: 800/255-9599. 212 kit. suites (1-2 bedrm), 4 story. S, D $119-$159; under 12 free; wkly, monthly rates. Crib $5; TV; cable (premium). Heated pool. Complimentary continental bkfst. Ck-out 11 am. Coin lndry. Meeting rms. Business servs avail. In-rm modem link. Valet serv. Covered parking. Lighted tennis. Microwaves. Private patios, balconies. Some grills. On bay; dock; all waterfront rms. Cr cds: A, D, MC, V.

➤ ⚡ ≃ 🔥 SC

Motor Hotels

★★ **AMERISUITES-BUSCH GARDENS.** *11408 N 30th St (33612), north of downtown.* 813/979-1922; FAX 813/979-1926. 128 suites, 6 story. Jan-Apr: S $119; D $129; under 18 free; wknd rates; lower rates rest of yr. Crib free. Pet accepted, some restrictions; $50. TV; cable (premium). Complimentary continental bkfst. Complimentary coffee in rms. Restaurant nearby. Ck-out 11 am. Meeting rms. Business center. In-rm modem link. Valet serv. Coin lndry. Exercise equipt. Heated pool. Refrigerators, microwaves, wet bars. Picnic table. Cr cds: A, C, D, DS, JCB, MC, V.

D 🐾 ≃ ✕ ⊠ ⊠ 🔥 SC ♿

★★ **BEST WESTERN RESORT AT BUSCH GARDENS.** *820 E Busch Blvd (33612), jct I-275 & Busch Blvd, north of downtown.* 727/933-4011; FAX 727/932-1784; res: 800/288-4011. 254 rms, 2-4 story. Jan-Apr: S $82.95-$92.95; D $92.95-$102.95; suites $159.95; under 12 free; wkly, wknd rates; higher rates special events; lower rates rest of yr. Crib free. TV; cable (premium). 2 pools, 1 indoor; whirlpool. Coffee in rms. Restaurant 6:30 am-2 pm, 5-10 pm. Rm serv. Bar 5-11 pm. Ck-out 11 am. Coin lndry. Convention facilities. Business center. Bellhops. Valet serv. Sundries. Gift shop. Free Busch Gardens transportation. Lighted tennis. Exercise equipt; sauna. Game rm. Refrigerators, microwaves avail. Cr cds: A, C, D, DS, MC, V.

D ⚡ ≃ ✕ ⊠ 🔥 SC ♿

✔★★ **HOLIDAY INN EXPRESS-SUITES.** *3025 N Rocky Point Dr (33607), west of downtown.* 813/287-8585; res: 888/613-3555; FAX 813/287-8484. 84 rms, 4 story. Jan-Apr: S, D $79-$109; under 18 free; wknd rates; higher rates Superbowl; lower rates rest of yr. Crib free. TV; cable (premium), VCR avail. Complimentary continental bkfst. Complimentary coffee in rms. Restaurant adj 7 am-10 pm. Bar 11-1 am; Sun from 1 pm; music Sat, Sun. Meeting rms. Business center. In-rm modem link. Bellhops. Valet serv. Coin lndry. Free airport transportation. Exercise equipt. Pool. Many refrigerators, microwaves, wet bars. On beach. Cr cds: A, C, D, DS, JCB, MC, V.

D ≃ ✕ ✈ ⊠ 🔥 SC ♿

★★ **QUALITY SUITES.** *3001 University Center Dr (33612), near Busch Gardens, north of downtown.* 813/971-8930; FAX 813/971-8935. 150 suites, 3 story. Suites $99-$159; each addl $7; under 18 free. Crib free. TV; cable (premium), VCR (movies avail). Heated pool; whirlpool. Complimentary full bkfst. Complimentary coffee in rms. Restaurant 6 am-9:30 pm; wkends 6:30 am-10:30 pm. Ck-out noon. Coin lndry. Meeting rms. Business servs avail. In-rm modem link. Bellhops. Valet serv. Sundries. Gift shop. Health club privileges. Refrigerators, microwaves. Balconies. Cr cds: A, C, D, DS, ER, JCB, MC, V.

⊡ ≋ ⊀ 🔥 SC

Hotels

★ ★ **AMERISUITES.** 4811 W Main St (33607), near Intl Airport, west of downtown. 813/282-1037; FAX 813/282-1148. Web www.travelbase.com/destinations/ tampa/amerisuites-airport. 126 suites, 6 story. Jan-Apr: S, D $99-$159; each addl $10; family, wkly, monthly rates; hols (3-day min); lower rates rest of yr. Crib free. Pet accepted, some restrictions. TV; cable (premium). Heated pool. Complimentary continental bkfst. Complimentary coffee in rms. Restaurant adj 5-11 pm. Bar. Ck-out 11 am. Coin lndry. Meeting rms. Business center. In-rm modem link. Free airport transportation. Exercise equipt. Refrigerators, microwaves. Picnic tables. Cr cds: A, C, D, DS, JCB, MC, V.

⊡ 🐾 ≋ ⊀ ✈ 🐾 SC ⚒

★ ★ ★ **CROWNE PLAZA TAMPA-WESTSHORE.** 700 N Westshore Blvd (33609), exit 21 off I-275, near Intl Airport, in West Shore. 813/289-8200; FAX 813/289-9166. 272 rms, 11 story. Jan-Apr: S, D $179-$209; each addl $15; under 18 free; wkend rates; lower rates rest of yr. Crib free. TV; cable (premium). Heated pool; whirlpool. Coffee in rms. Restaurant 6:30 am-11 pm. Bar 11 am-midnight. Ck-out noon. Convention facilities. Business center. In-rm modem link. Valet parking. Free airport transportation. Gift shop. Exercise equipt; sauna. Luxury level. Cr cds: A, C, D, DS, MC, V.

⊡ ≋ ⊀ ✈ 🐾 SC ⚒

★ ★ ★ **DOUBLETREE GUEST SUITES ON TAMPA BAY.** 3050 N Rocky Point Dr W (33607), W on Courtney Campbell Causeway (FL60), near Intl Airport, west of downtown. 813/888-8800; FAX 813/888-8743. Web www.doubletreehotel.com. 203 suites, 7 story. Oct-Apr: S $159; D $179; each addl $20; under 13 free; wkend rates; lower rates rest of yr. Crib free. TV; cable (premium). Heated pool; whirlpool. Restaurant 6:30 am-10 pm. Bar 11 am-midnight. Ck-out noon. Coin lndry. Meeting rms. In-rm modem link. Gift shop. Free airport transportation. Exercise equipt; sauna. Refrigerators; microwaves avail. Sun deck. On bay. Cr cds: A, C, D, DS, MC, V.

⊡ ≋ ⊀ ✈ 🐾 SC

★ ★ ★ **EMBASSY SUITES-TAMPA AIRPORT/WESTSHORE.** 555 N Westshore Blvd (33609), near Intl Airport, in West Shore. 813/875-1555; FAX 813/287-3664. 221 kit. suites, 16 story. Jan-Apr: S, D $159-$179; under 18 free; wkly, monthly, wkend rates; lower rates rest of yr. Crib free. Pet accepted, some restrictions; $15/day. TV; cable (premium). Heated pool; whirlpool; poolside serv. Complimentary full bkfst. Coffee in rms. Restaurant 6:30 am-2 pm, 5-10 pm. Rm serv 6 am-11 pm. Bar noon-midnight. Ck-out noon. Coin lndry. Meeting rms. Business servs avail. In-rm modem link. Gift shop. Free covered parking; valet. Free airport transportation. Exercise equipt; sauna. Health club privileges. Microwaves avail. Balconies. Cr cds: A, C, D, DS, ER, JCB, MC, V.

⊡ 🐾 ≋ ⊀ ✈ 🐾 SC

★ ★ ★ **FOUR POINTS BY SHERATON.** 7401 E Hillsborough Ave (33610), I-4 exit 5, east of downtown. 813/626-0999; FAX 813/622-7893. Web www.sheraton.com. 276 rms, 6 story. Jan-Apr: S, D $159-$169; each addl $10; suites $189-$400; under 18 free; wkend rates; lower rates rest of yr. Crib free. Pet accepted; $45. TV; cable (premium), VCR avail (movies). Pool; whirlpool. Coffee in rms. Restaurant 6:30 am-10:30 pm. Bar 11-2 am. Ck-out noon. Convention facilities. Business center. In-rm modem link. Gift shop. Airport transportation. Exercise equipt. Microwaves avail. Private patios, balconies. Cr cds: A, C, D, DS, JCB, MC, V.

⊡ 🐾 ≋ ⊀ ✈ SC ⚒

★ ★ ★ **HILTON AT METROCENTER.** 2225 N Lois Ave (33607), I-275 exit 22N; near Intl Airport, in West Shore. 813/877-6688; FAX 813/879-3264. Web www.hilton.com. 238 rms, 12 story. Jan-Apr: S $137-$180; D $138-$190; each addl $10; suites $200-$350; family, wkend rates; lower rates rest of yr. Crib free. TV; cable (premium). Pool; whirlpool, poolside serv. Complimentary coffee in rms. Restaurant 6:30 am-11 pm; Sat, Sun from 7 am. Rm serv 24 hrs. Bar noon-midnight. Ck-out noon. Meeting rms. Business servs avail. In-rm modem link. Gift shop. Free airport transportation. Lighted tennis. Exercise equipt. Cr cds: A, C, D, DS, ER, JCB, MC, V.

⊡ 🏃 ≋ ⊀ ✈ 🐾 SC ⚒

★ ★ ★ **HOLIDAY INN SELECT DOWNTOWN.** 111 W Fortune St (33602), adj to Performing Arts Center, downtown. 813/223-1351; FAX 813/221-2000. 312 rms, 14 story. Jan-Apr: S, D $130-$150; each addl $10; suites $219; under 19 free; lower rates rest of yr. Crib free. TV; cable (premium). Pool; whirlpool. Coffee in rms. Restaurant 6 am-11 pm. Bar 4 pm-1 am. Ck-out 11 am. Convention facilities. Business center. In-rm modem link. Gift shop. Free airport transportation. Exercise equipt. Some refrigerators, microwaves. Luxury level. Cr cds: A, C, D, DS, ER, JCB, MC, V.

⊡ ≋ ⊀ ✈ 🐾 SC ⚒

★ ★ ★ **HYATT REGENCY.** 2 Tampa City Center (33602), off I-275 Ashley exit, bear left onto Tampa St to Jackson St, downtown. 813/225-1234; FAX 813/273-0234. Web www.hyatt.com. 520 rms, 17 story. Jan-Apr: S, D $180-$200; each addl $25; 1-bedrm suites $200-$490; 2-bedrm suites $280-$590; under 18 free; wknd rates; lower rates rest of yr. Crib free. TV; cable (premium), VCR avail. Heated pool; whirlpool. Restaurant (see ITALIANISSIMO). Rm serv 24 hrs. Bar. Entertainment Fri-Sat. Ck-out noon. Lndry facilities. Convention facilities. Business center. In-rm modem link. Concierge. Garage, valet parking. Free airport transportation. Exercise equipt. Massage. Some refrigerators. Luxury level. Cr cds: A, C, D, DS, ER, JCB, MC, V.

⊡ ≋ ⊀ ✈ 🔥 SC ⚒

★ ★ ★ **HYATT REGENCY WESTSHORE.** 6200 Courtney Campbell Causeway (33607), near Intl Airport, in West Shore. 813/874-1234; FAX 813/281-9168. Web www.hyatt.com. This large, business-oriented luxury hotel is well placed, nestled next to a 35-acre nature preserve on Tampa Bay. A courtyard with fountains highlights the elaborate landscaping. 400 rms in main bldg, 14 story, 45 casita villas. Jan-May: S $179-$225; D $204-$240; each addl $25; suites $330-$730; casita villas (1-3 bedrm): $179-$730; under 18 free; wknd rates; lower rates rest of yr. Crib free. Covered parking; valet parking $8/night. TV; cable (premium), VCR avail. 2 heated pools; whirlpool, poolside serv. Coffee in rms. Restaurant 6:30 am-11 pm (also see ARMANI'S and OYSTERCATCHERS). Rm serv to midnight. Bar noon-1 am; pianist. Ck-out noon. Convention facilities. Business center. In-rm modem link. Concierge. Gift shop. Free airport transportation. Tennis. Exercise equipt; sauna. Massage. Some refrigerators, minibars. Boat dock. Luxury level. Cr cds: A, C, D, DS, ER, JCB, MC, V.

⊡ 🏃 ≋ ⊀ ✈ 🐾 SC ⚒

★ ★ ★ **MARRIOTT AIRPORT.** At Tampa Intl Airport (33607), 1½ mi N of jct FL 60 & I-275, near Intl Airport, in West Shore. 813/879-5151; FAX 813/873-0945. Web www.marriott.com. 296 rms, 6 story. Jan-Apr: S, D $170-$185; suites $275-$550; under 18 free; wkend rates; lower rates rest of yr. Crib free. TV; cable (premium). Pool; poolside serv. Coffee in rms. Restaurant (see CK'S). Bar 11-1 am. Ck-out 1 pm. Meeting rms. Business center. In-rm modem link. Gift shop. Free airport transportation. Exercise equipt. Refrigerator in some suites. Luxury level. Cr cds: A, C, D, DS, ER, JCB, MC, V.

⊡ ≋ ⊀ ✈ 🔥 SC ⚒

★ ★ ★ **MARRIOTT WESTSHORE.** 1001 N Westshore Blvd (33607), near Intl Airport, off I-275 2 blks, in West Shore. 813/287-2555; FAX 813/289-5464. Web www.marriott.com. 310 rms, 14 story. Jan-May: S, D $165-189; suites $230; under 19 free; wkend, hol rates; lower rates rest of yr. Crib free. TV; cable (premium). 2 pools, 1 indoor. Coffee in rms. Restaurant 6:30 am-midnight. Bar 11:30-2 am. Ck-out 1 pm. Convention facilities. Business servs avail. In-rm modem link. Gift shop. Free airport transportation. Exercise rm. Balconies. Cr cds: A, C, D, DS, ER, JCB, MC, V.

⊡ ≋ ⊀ ✈ 🐾 SC

★ ★ ★ **RADISSON.** 10221 Princess Palm Ave (33610), I-75 exit 52; 1 mi S of I-4, south of downtown. 813/623-6363; res: 800/333-3333; FAX 813/621-7224. Web www.radisson.com. 265 rms, 5 story, 41 suites.

Mid-Jan-mid-Apr: S, D $165-$215; suites $180-$500; under 18 free; wkend rates; lower rates rest of yr. Crib free. TV; cable (premium). Heated pool; wading pool, whirlpool. Restaurant 6:30 am-11 pm. Bar 11-2 am. Ck-out noon. Convention facilities. Business center. In-rm modem link. Concierge. Gift shop. Barber, beauty shop. Free airport transportation. Lighted tennis. Exercise equipt. Refrigerator in suites. Private patios, balconies. Bldg with distinctive curved structure located on 9 acres; 3-story atrium lobby with waterfall. Luxury level. Cr cds: A, C, D, DS, ER, JCB, MC, V.

★ ★ ★ **RADISSON BAY HARBOR.** *7700 Courtney Campbell Causeway (33607), west of downtown.* 813/281-8900; FAX 813/281-0189. 257 rms, 6 story. Jan-Apr: S, D $130-$190; each addl $10; suites $175-$525; under 18 free; lower rates rest of yr. Crib free. TV; cable (premium). Heated pool; poolside serv. Restaurant 6:30 am-midnight. Bar 11 am-midnight, Sun from 1 pm. Ck-out noon. Meeting rms. In-rm modem link. Gift shop. Valet parking. Free airport transportation. Lighted tennis. Exercise equipt. Game rm. Private patios, balconies. On Tampa Bay. Cr cds: A, C, D, DS, MC, V.

★ ★ ★ **WYNDHAM HARBOUR ISLAND.** *725 S Harbour Island Blvd (33602), I-275 exit 25, south of downtown.* 813/229-5000; FAX 813/229-5322. Web www.wyndham.com. 300 rms, 12 story. Jan-May: S, D $199-$245; each addl $20; suites $375-$895; under 18 free; wkend rates; lower rates rest of yr. Crib free. TV; cable. Heated pool; poolside serv. Coffee in rms. Restaurant (see HARBOUR VIEW). Bar. Ck-out noon. Convention facilities. Business servs avail. In-rm modem link. Concierge. Free airport transportation. Tennis privileges. Exercise equipt. Health club privileges. Minibars, wet bars; some bathrm phones; microwaves avail; refrigerator in suites. Cr cds: A, C, D, DS, ER, JCB, MC, V.

★ ★ ★ **WYNDHAM WESTSHORE.** *4860 W Kennedy Blvd (33609), jct Kennedy & West Shore Blvds, near Intl Airport, in West Shore.* 813/286-4400; FAX 813/286-4053. 324 rms, 11 story. Jan-Apr: S, D $159-$195; each addl $15; suites $195-$550; under 18 free; wkend rates; lower rates rest of yr. Crib free. TV; cable (premium). Heated pool; poolside serv. Coffee in rms. Restaurants 6 am-11 pm (also see SHULA'S STEAK HOUSE). Rm serv 24 hrs. Bar 11-2 am; entertainment. Ck-out noon. Convention facilities. Business center. In-rm modem link. Concierge. Shopping arcade. Free airport transportation. Exercise equipt. Health club privileges. Some bathrm phones, refrigerators. Luxury level. Marina. Cr cds: A, C, D, DS, ER, MC, V.

Inn

✔★ ★ **BEHIND THE FENCE.** *(1400 Viola Dr, Brandon 33511) E on I-4, S on I-75, exit 49, S on US 301 to Bloomingdale Ave, left on Countryside to Viola.* 813/685-8201. 5 rms, 3 share bath, 2 story, 2 suites. 3 rm phones. Labor Day-Memorial Day: S, D $59-$72; each addl $10; suites $69-$72; under 10 free; lower rates rest of yr. Pet accepted. TV; cable, VCR avail. Pool. Complimentary continental bkfst; afternoon refreshments. Restaurant nearby. Ck-out 11 am, ck-in 3 pm. Refrigerators, microwaves. House design is New England "Salt Box." Totally nonsmoking. No cr cds accepted.

Resort

★ ★ ★ ★ **SADDLEBROOK RESORT.** *(5700 Saddlebrook Way, Wesley Chapel 33543) 25 mi N of Tampa Airport on I-75, exit 58 then 1 mi E on FL 54.* 813/973-1111; FAX 813/973-4504; res: 800/729-8383. Web www.saddlebrookresort.com. One of Florida's premier tennis and golf resorts, it rests on 480 secluded acres of woodlands, lakes and rolling hills. 552 units, 2 story, 419 with kits., 133 hotel rms, 163 1-bedrm condos, 253 2-bedrm condos. Mid-Jan-Apr: S, D $225-$375; each addl $20; under 13 free; lower rates rest of yr. TV; cable. 4 pools, 3 heated; whirlpool, poolside serv. Playground. Free supervised child's activities; ages 3-12. Dining rm

(public by res) 6:30 am-10:30 pm (see CYPRESS RESTAURANT AND TERRACE ON THE GREEN). Rm serv to 1 am. Bar 11-1 am; entertainment. Ck-out noon, ck-in 3 pm. Convention facilities. Business center. In-rm modem link. Concierge. Grocery 1 mi. Package store. Gift shop. Barber, beauty shop. Valet parking. Airport transportation. Sports dir. Tennis, 45 courts, 5 lighted, pro. Home of Harry Hopman Tennis Academy. 36-hole golf course designed by Arnold Palmer & Dean Refram, pro, putting green, driving range. Home of Arnold Palmer Golf Academy. Nature walks. Bicycle rentals. Game rm. Exercise rm; sauna, steam rm. Massage. Minibars; many refrigerators. Private patios, balconies. Cr cds: A, C, D, DS, MC, V.

Restaurants

★ **A.J. CATFISH.** *8751 N Himes Ave (33614), north of downtown.* 813/932-3474. Hrs: 11:30 am-10 pm; Fri to 11 pm; Sat 5-11 pm; Sun 5-10 pm. Closed Mon; most major hols. Semi-a la carte: lunch $3.95-$7.95, dinner $7.95-$14.95. Child's meals. Specializes in steak, seafood, pasta. Outdoor dining. Cypress wood interior, 2nd floor balcony. Cr cds: A, D, MC, V.

★ ★ ★ **ARMANI'S.** *(See Hyatt Regency Westshore Hotel)* 813/281-9165. Web www.hyatt.com. Hrs: 6-10 pm; Fri, Sat to 11 pm. Closed Sun; some major hols. Res required. Northern Italian menu. Bar 5-11 pm; Fri, Sat to midnight. Semi-a la carte: dinner $25-$45. Child's meals. Specialties: veal Armani, lobster ammiraglia. Antipasta bar. Own baking. Pianist. Valet parking. Outdoor terrace overlooks bay; on rooftop. Jacket. Cr cds: A, C, D, DS, ER, JCB, MC, V.

★ ★ ★ **BERN'S STEAK HOUSE.** *1208 S Howard Ave (33606), 4 blks N of Bayshore Blvd, in Hyde Park.* 813/251-2421. Hrs: 5-11 pm. Closed Dec 25. Res accepted. Bar. Wine cellars. Semi-a la carte: dinner $15-$45 (serv charge). Specializes in organically grown vegetables, aged prime beef, variety of roasted and blended coffees. Own baking, ice cream. Pianist/accordionist. Valet parking. Chef-owned. Antiques, paintings, statuary. Cr cds: A, C, D, DS, MC, V.

✔★ ★ **BOSTON COOKER.** *(3682 Tampa Rd, Oldsmar 34677) FL 584 at Emerald Bay Dr.* 813/855-2311. Hrs: 11:30 am-10 pm; Fri, Sat to 11 pm. Closed Sun; some major hols. Res accepted. New England menu. Bar. Complete meals: lunch $4.95-$7.50, dinner $7.95-$16.95. Child's meals. Specialties: Boston scrod, Ipswich clams, steamed mussels. Nautical decor. Cr cds: A, DS, MC, V.

✔★ **CAPDEVILA'S AT LA TERESITA.** *3248 W Columbus Dr (33607), 1 mi NE on I-275, exit Dale Mabry, E on Columbus Dr, at Lincoln, west of downtown.* 813/875-2007. Hrs: 8 am-10 pm; Fri, Sat to 11 pm. Closed Dec 25. Res accepted. Cuban menu. Bar. Semi-a la carte: bkfst $1-$3.95, lunch $1.25-$6.50, dinner $1.50-$6.50. Child's meals. Specializes in chicken, beef, pork. Valet parking. Spanish/Cuban decor. Family-owned 21 yrs. Cr cds: A, DS, MC, V.

★ ★ ★ **CK'S.** *(See Marriott Airport Hotel)* 813/878-6500. Hrs: 5-10 pm; Fri, Sat to 11 pm; Sun brunch 10:30 am-2:30 pm. Res accepted. Bar from 4 pm. Wine list. A la carte entrees: dinner $13.95-$25.95. Sun brunch $17.95. Child's meals. Specializes in lamb, steaks, fresh fish. Valet parking. Revolving rooftop restaurant on 10th floor. Cr cds: A, C, D, DS, ER, JCB, MC, V.

✔★ ★ **COLONNADE.** *3401 Bayshore Blvd (33629), in Hyde Park.* 813/839-7558. Hrs: 11 am-10 pm; Fri, Sat to 11 pm. Closed Thanksgiving, Dec 25. Bar. Semi-a la carte: lunch $6.99-$7.99, dinner $7.99-$15.99. Child's meals. Specializes in fresh seafood, steak, prime rib. Nautical decor. Overlooks Tampa Bay. Family-owned since 1935. Cr cds: A, C, D, DS, MC, V.

D ⌐

★ ★ ★ **COLUMBIA.** *2117 E 7th Ave (33605), in Ybor City.* 813/248-4961. Hrs: 11 am-10 pm; Fri, Sat to 11 pm; Sun noon-9 pm. Res accepted. Spanish menu. Bar. Wine cellars. Semi-a la carte: lunch $5.95-$7.95, dinner $10.95-$18.95. Cover charge $6 (in dining room with show). Child's meals. Specialties: paella a la Valenciana, snapper alicante, filet mignon Columbia. Flamenco dancers (dinner) exc Sun. Valet parking. Built 1905; building decorated with hand-painted Spanish tiles. Balcony surrounds interior courtyard. Many dining areas; all have antique Spanish-style furnishings. Family-owned. Cr cds: A, C, D, DS, MC, V.

D ⌐

★ ★ ★ **CYPRESS RESTAURANT AND TERRACE ON THE GREEN.** *(See Saddlebrook Resort)* 813/973-1111. Web www.saddlebrookresort.com. Hrs: 6:30 am-3 pm, 6-10 pm; Fri 6-11 pm; Sun, Mon to 3 pm; hrs may vary seasonally. Res accepted. Continental menu. Bar 11-1 am. Semi-a la carte: bkfst $6-$11.50, lunch $8-$14, dinner $20-$30. Serv charge 18%. Child's meals. Specializes in steak, veal, seafood buffet. Pastry shop. Entertainment. Free valet parking. Creative food presentation. Contemporary decor. Lakeside terrace dining overlooking golf course. Cr cds: A, C, D, DS, MC, V.

♥

★ ★ ★ **DONATELLO.** *232 N Dale Mabry Hwy (33609), west of downtown.* 813/875-6660. Web www.tampabaydining.com. Hrs: 11:30 am-2:30 pm, 6-11 pm; Sat, Sun from 6 pm. Closed most major hols; also Super Bowl Sun. Res accepted. Northern Italian menu. Bar. Wine list. A la carte entrees: lunch $5.95-$12.95, dinner $15.95-$31.95. Specializes in hand-rolled pasta, veal chops, fresh seafood. Own baking. Valet parking. Pianist Thurs-Sat. Some tableside cooking. Cr cds: A, C, D, DS, MC, V.

D ⌐

★ ★ **HARBOUR VIEW.** *(See Wyndham Harbour Island Hotel)* 813/229-5001. Hrs: 6:30 am-2 pm, 6-11 pm; Sun brunch 10:30 am-2 pm. Res accepted. Serv bar. A la carte entrees: bkfst $6.25-$10.95, lunch $7-$12.95, dinner $16.50-$24.95. Sun brunch $22.95. Pasta bar (Mon-Fri) $9.95. Child's meals. Specializes in contemporary regional cuisine. Own baking. Valet parking. Private dining rm avail. Waterfront view. Cr cds: A, C, D, DS, ER, JCB, MC, V.

D ⌐ ♥

★ ★ **ITALIANISSIMO.** *(See Hyatt Regency Hotel)* 813/222-4928. Hrs: 5-11 pm. Res accepted. Italian menu. Serv bar. A la carte entrees: dinner $11-$30. Child's meals. Specializes in pasta, beef, lamb. Piano Mon-Fri. Valet parking. Outdoor dining. Elegant dining. Cr cds: A, C, D, DS, ER, JCB, MC, V.

D SC ⌐

★ **JIMMY MAC'S.** *113 S Armenia Ave (33609), in Hyde Park.* 813/879-0591. Hrs: 11:30-2 am; Sat from noon; Sun noon-11 pm. Closed most major hols. Res accepted. Bar 11:30-3 am. Semi-a la carte: lunch $4.95-$7.75, dinner $6.50-$17. Child's meals. Specializes in grilled seasonal seafood, hamburgers, steaks. Entertainment. Parking. Located in 2 restored houses; eclectic decor. Cr cds: A, D, DS, MC, V.

⌐

★ ★ **LANDRY'S SEAFOOD HOUSE.** *7616 Courtney Campbell Causeway (33607), on FL 60, in West Shore.* 813/289-7773. Hrs: 11 am-10 pm; Fri, Sat to 11:15 pm. Closed Dec 25. Bar. Semi-a la carte: lunch $3.99-$10.99, dinner $9.99-$21. Child's meals. Specialties: Pontchartrain red snapper, grouper Mellisa. Entertainment Fri, Sat. Valet parking Fri, Sat. Outdoor dining. 1950s riverwalk atmosphere with New Orleans theme. Cr cds: A, C, D, DS, MC, V.

D ⌐

★ ★ ★ **LE BORDEAUX.** *1502 S Howard Ave (33606), in Hyde Park.* 813/254-4387. Hrs: 5:30-10 pm; Sat to 11 pm; Sun 5-9:30 pm.

Closed most major hols; Aug. Res accepted. French menu. Bar. Wine cellar. A la carte entrees: dinner $13-$26. Specialties: pâté escargot, rack of lamb, veal tenderloin. A la carte entrees: dinner $13-$26. Jazz Fri, Sat. Valet parking. Outdoor dining. Country French atmosphere. Cr cds: A, D, MC, V.

D ⌐

★ ★ **MALIOS STEAK HOUSE.** *301 S Dale Mabry Hwy (33609), west of downtown.* 813/879-3233. Hrs: 11:30 am-2:30 pm, 5-10:30 pm; Fri, Sat 5-11 pm. Closed Sun; most major hols. Res accepted. Bar 11:30-2:30 am. A la carte entrees: lunch $4.95-$7.95, dinner $9.95-$29.95. Specializes in steak, seafood, pasta. Valet parking. Large central lounge with entertainment. Cr cds: A, C, D, DS, MC, V.

D ⌐

★ **MIGUEL'S.** *3035 W Kennedy (33609), in Hyde Park.* 813/876-2587. Hrs: 11 am-10 pm; Fri to 11 pm; Sat noon-11 pm; Sun noon-9 pm. Closed Thanksgiving, Dec 25. Res accepted. Mexican, Amer menu. Wine, beer. Semi-a la carte: lunch $1.70-$7, dinner $5.75-$13.25. Child's meals. Specialties: stuffed jalapeños, quesadillas, tamales. Mexican decor. Cr cds: DS, MC, V.

D ⌐

★ ★ **MISE EN PLACE.** *442 W Kennedy Blvd (33609), in Hyde Park.* 813/254-5373. Hrs: 11 am-3 pm, 5:30-10 pm; Mon to 3 pm; Fri to 11 pm; Sat 5:30-11 pm. Closed Sun; major hols. Bar 5:30 pm-2 am Tues-Sat. Wine list. A la carte entrees: lunch $6.25-$8.55, dinner $13.95-$22.95. Specializes in lamb, grouper, salmon. Contemporary decor. Cr cds: A, C, D, DS, MC, V.

D

★ ★ ★ **OYSTERCATCHERS.** *(See Hyatt Regency Westshore Hotel)* 813/281-9116. Hrs: 11:30 am-2:30 pm, 6-10 pm; Fri, Sat 6-11 pm; Sun from 6 pm; Sun brunch 10:30 am-3 pm. Closed Dec 25. Res accepted. Bar. A la carte entrees: lunch $15-$22, dinner $16-$30. Sun brunch $28. Child's meals. Specializes in fresh seafood, stuffed swordfish. Entertainment Mon-Fri. Valet parking. Overlooks Tampa Bay. Cr cds: A, C, D, DS, ER, JCB, MC, V.

D ⌐

★ ★ **RUMPELMAYERS.** *4812 E Busch Blvd (33617), in Ambassador Square Shopping Center, north of downtown.* 813/989-9563. Hrs: 11 am-11 pm. Res accepted. German menu. Semi-a la carte: lunch $3.95-$8.95, dinner $6.95-$15.95. Child's meals. Specialties: Wienerschnitzel, steak, seafood. Accordionist. Servers in traditional Bavarian outfits. Cr cds: A, C, D, DS, MC, V.

D ⌐

★ ★ ★ **RUTH'S CHRIS STEAK HOUSE.** *1700 N Westshore Blvd (33607), in West Shore.* 813/282-1118. Hrs: 5-10 pm; Fri, Sat to 11 pm. Closed Thanksgiving, Dec 25. Res accepted. Bar. Wine list. A la carte entrees: dinner $15.95-$29.95. Child's meals. Specializes in beef, steak, lamb chops. Valet parking. Elegant decor with antique fixtures. Cr cds: A, D, JCB, MC, V.

D ⌐

★ ★ ★ **SHULA'S STEAK HOUSE.** *(See Wyndham Westshore Hotel)* 813/286-4366. Hrs: 11:30 am-2:30 pm, 5:30-10:30 pm; Sat, Sun 5:30-11 pm. Res accepted. Bar. Wine list. A la carte entrees: lunch $9.50-$21, dinner $25-$64. Child's meals. Specialties: lamb chops, lobster, steak. Valet parking. Cr cds: A, C, D, DS, ER, MC, V.

D

★ ★ **SUKHOTHAI.** *8201-A N Dale Mabry Hwy (33614), north of downtown.* 813/933-7990. Hrs: 11 am-11 pm; Sat, Sun from 5 pm. Closed Labor Day, Thanksgiving, Dec 25. Res accepted. Thai menu. Wine, beer. Semi-a la carte: lunch $4.95-$6.95, dinner $8.95-$19.95. Specializes in seafood. Original Thai tables, pillows. Parking. Cr cds: A, C, D, DS, MC, V.

D ⌐

✔★ ★ **TAJ.** *2734-B Fowler Ave (33612), north of downtown.* *813/971-8483.* Hrs: 11:30 am-2:30 pm, 5-10 pm; Sat, Sun 11:30 am-3 pm, 5-10 pm. Closed Mon; Thanksgiving, Dec 25. Res accepted, required Fri-Sun. Indian menu. Wine, beer. Lunch buffet $6.95-$8.95. A la carte entrees: dinner $7.50-$16.95. Specializes in Tandoori and Bhuna dishes. Own baking. Authentic Indian decor; Tandoori clay oven. Totally nonsmoking. Cr cds: A, MC, V.

D

Tarpon Springs (E-3)

(See also Clearwater, Dunedin, St Petersburg, Tampa)

Founded 1876 **Pop** 17,906 **Elev** 10 ft **Area code** 813 **Web** www.tarponsprings.com
Information Greater Tarpon Springs Chamber of Commerce, 11 E Orange St, 34689, phone 813/937-6109.

Colorfully Hellenic, Tarpon Springs is famous for its sponge industry, which was most prosperous from the early 1900s to the 1940s and continues today. Greek fishermen go far out to sea in their picturesque boats, from which divers plunge to depths of 150 feet to pluck sponges. The city is situated between Lake Tarpon and bayous formed by the Anclote River before it empties into the Gulf of Mexico.

What to See and Do

Dodecanese Blvd. Along the seawall of this waterfront street are anchored shrimp boats and sponge boats decorated with Greek designs. On the other side are restaurants, curio shops, sponge diving exhibitions, boat rides and stacks of sponges.

Inness Paintings. Eleven symbolic paintings by American landscape painter George Inness, Jr (1854-1926); guided tours. (Oct-May, daily exc Mon, limited hrs; closed hols) Universalist Church, 57 Read St, at Grand Blvd. Phone 813/937-4682. ¢

Noell's Ark Chimpanzee Farm. Gorillas, chimpanzees, monkeys, orangutans, baboon, alligator, bear, birds; petting zoo. (Daily) 4612 Pinellas Ave N, approx 2 mi S on US 19A. Phone 813/937-8683. ¢¢

Spongeorama Exhibit Center. Sponge factory, museum on Tarpon Springs, nicknamed "America's sponge-diving birthplace," reproductions of 1900s sponge docks. Specialty shops. Cinematic theater with film of sponge diving industry. (Daily) Sponge docks, 510 Dodecanese Blvd. Phone 813/943-9509. Theater ¢

St Nicholas Greek Orthodox Cathedral (1943). Neo-Byzantine architecture with interior of sculptured Grecian marble. Beautiful iconography and stained-glass windows. (Daily) Proper attire requested. 36 N Pinellas Ave. Phone 813/937-3540.

Annual Event

Festival of the Epiphany. St Nicholas Cathedral. Blessing of the waters at noon, followed by Diving for the Cross Ceremony. Colorfully robed dignitaries, costumed children, acolytes, the Byzantine choir and others proceed through the streets from the church to Spring Bayou. There the Archbishop tosses a golden cross into the waters and the young men of the community plunge in to recover it. A benedictory service at the church is followed by banquets and a ball. Jan 6.

Motels

★ ★ **BEST WESTERN TAHITIAN RESORT.** *(2337 US 19N, Holiday Isle 34691) 1/2 mi N of jct US 19A. 727/937-4121; res: 800/931-0333; FAX 727/937-3806.* 140 rms, 2 story, 18 kits. Feb-mid-Apr: S, D, $69-$99; each addl $5; under 12 free; lower rates rest of yr. Crib $5. Pet accepted; $5. TV; cable. Heated pool. Restaurant 6 am-9 pm. Rm serv. Bar 1 pm-2 am; entertainment Fri, Sat. Ck-out 11 am. Coin lndry. Business servs avail.

Health club privileges. Refrigerators, microwaves. Cr cds: A, C, D, DS, MC, V.

🅳 ⊠ ⊠ 🔥 SC

✔★ **TARPON SHORES INN.** *40346 US 19N (34689). 727/938-2483; FAX 727/938-2486; res: 800/633-3802.* 51 rms, 2 story, 16 kits. Jan-mid-Apr: S, D $38-$60; kits. $39-$58; under 12 free; lower rates rest of yr. Crib $5. TV; cable. Heated pool; whirlpool. Complimentary coffee in lobby. Restaurant nearby. Ck-out 11 am. Coin lndry. Meeting rm. Business servs avail. Sauna. Cr cds: A, DS, MC, V.

🅳 ⊠ ⊠ 🔥 SC

Resort

★ ★ ★ **WESTIN INNISBROOK RESORT.** *(36750 N US 19, Palm Harbor 34684) at Klosterman Rd. 727/942-2000; res: 800/456-2000; FAX 727/942-5576.* 1,000 condo units in 28 lodges, 2-3 story. Jan-Apr: 1-bedrm, 2-bedrm $170-$485; under 19 free; AP, MAP, family, monthly rates; package plans; lower rates rest of yr. Crib free. Pet accepted; some restrictions.TV; cable (premium). 6 pools, heated; poolside serv. Supervised child's activities; ages 4-14. Coffee in rms. 4 dining rms. Rm serv. 2 snack bars. 4 bars; entertainment. Ck-out noon, ck-in 3 pm. Package store. Free lndry facilities. Convention facilities. Business center. Concierge. Gift shop. Airport transportation. 11 tennis courts, 7 lighted, pro, pro shop. 90-hole golf, pro, 5 putting greens, lighted driving range. Miniature golf. Bicycle rentals. Lawn games. Rec dir. Game rm. Exercise rm; sauna. Microwaves avail. Minibars. Private patios, balconies. Wildlife sanctuary with nature walk. Fresh-water stocked lake. Cr cds: A, C, D, DS, ER, JCB, MC, V.

🅳 🖙 🛠 🏌 ⊠ 🚴 🏊 🔥 SC 🚶

Restaurant

★ ★ **LOUIS PAPPAS' RIVERSIDE.** *10 W Dodecanese Blvd (34689), at sponge docks. 727/937-5101.* Hrs: 11:30 am-10 pm; Fri, Sat to 11 pm. Res accepted. Greek, Amer menu. Bar. Semi-a la carte: lunch $5.95-$8.95, dinner $5.95-$21.95. Child's meals. Specializes in lamb, beef, fresh seafood. Entertainment exc Mon. Valet parking. Panoramic view of sponge docks on the Anclote River. Greek decor. Family-owned. Cr cds: A, MC, V.

🅳 🖙

Tavares (D-4)

(See also Clermont, Leesburg)

Founded 1881 **Pop** 7,383 **Elev** 77 ft **Area code** 352 **Zip** 32778 **E-mail** Tchamber@lcia.com
Information Chamber of Commerce, 912 N Sinclair Ave, PO Box 697; 352/343-2531.

Nestled between Lake Dora and Lake Eustis, Tavares is linked to seven nearby lakes by a system of rivers and canals and serves as a base for camping, hunting and fishing expeditions.

What to See and Do

Fishing, boating. Municipal pier, S end of St Clair Abrams Ave; public boat ramps on US 441; Lakes Dora and Eustis, W of town; Tavares Recreation Park on Lake Eustis; Dora Canal Park.

Ocala National Forest (see OCALA). E via FL 44, then N on FL 19. There is a Ranger District office N on FL 19 in Umatilla, phone 352/669-3153.

Motel

✓★ ★ **INN ON THE GREEN.** *700 E Burleigh Blvd, on US 441, W of SR19.* 352/343-6373; FAX 352/343-7216; res: 800/935-2935. 76 rms, 2 story, 14 kit. units. Mid-Dec-mid-Apr: S, D $50-$75; each addl $5; kit. units $15 addl; suites $135; under 12 free; wkly rates; higher rates special events; lower rates rest of yr. Crib $6. TV; cable (premium), VCR avail (movies). Pool. Coffee in lobby. Restaurant nearby. Ck-out 11 am. Coin lndry. Sundries. Putting green. Lawn games. Microwaves avail. Picnic tables. On lake. Cr cds: A, C, D, MC, V.

Motor Hotel

★ ★ **LAKESIDE INN OF MT DORA.** *(100 N Alexander St, Mt Dora 32757) 4 mi S on US 441, then W on Donnelly.* 352/383-4101; FAX 352/735-2642; res: 800/556-5016. E-mail lakeside@magicnet.net; web www.lakeside-inn.com. 86 rms, 2 story. Jan-mid May: S, D $105-$205; each addl $10; MAP avail; golf plans; higher rates special events; lower rates rest of yr. Crib free. TV; cable (premium), VCR avail. Pool. Complimentary continental bkfst. Restaurant 7 am-2:30 pm, 5-9 pm; Fri, Sat to 10 pm. Rm serv. Ck-out 11 am. Business servs avail. Lighted tennis. Golf privileges, pro, putting green. 5 buildings on 5 lakeside acres. Cr cds: A, C, D, DS, MC, V.

Inn

★ ★ ★ **EMERALD HILL INN.** *(27751 Lake Jem Rd, Mount Dora 32757)* 352/383-2777; FAX 352/383-6701. E-mail emerldhill@aol.com; web www.bbonline.com/fl/emeraldhill. 4 rms. No rm phones. S, D $99-$149; wkends, hols, special events (2-day min). TV, VCR in some rms. Complimentary full bkfst. Ck-out 11 am, ck-in 3-6 pm. Some fireplaces. On Lake Victoria. Totally nonsmoking. Cr cds: DS, MC, V.

Resort

★ ★ ★ **MISSION INN GOLF & TENNIS RESORT.** *(10400 CR 48, Howey-in-the-Hills 34737) FL 19, 48, 6½ mi N on FL 19 from FL Tpke exit 285.* 352/324-3101; FAX 352/324-2636; res: 800/874-9053 (exc FL). E-mail reservations@missioninnresort.com; web www.missioninnresort.com. 176 rms, 1-4 story, 15 villas, 15 kits. Feb-Apr: S, D $175-$195; suites $230-$335; villas $320-$380; under 18 free; AP, MAP avail; wkly rates; golf, tennis plans; lower rates rest of yr. Crib free. TV; cable. Heated pool; whirlpool, poolside serv. Playground. Dining rms 6:30 am-10 pm (also see EL CONQUISTADOR). Rm serv. Bar 11 am-midnight; entertainment. Ck-out noon, ck-in 4 pm. Coin lndry. Convention facilities. Business center. Bellhops. Valet serv. Gift shop. Airport transportation. 8 tennis courts, 6 lighted, pro. 36-hole golf course, greens fee, pro, putting green, driving range. Private lakes, motor & sail boats; marina. Yacht cruises 3 times wkly. Bicycle rentals. Lawn games. Exercise equipt. Rec rm. Some refrigerators, fireplaces; wet bar in suites. Private patios, balconies. Picnic tables. Cr cds: A, MC, V.

Restaurant

★ ★ ★ **EL CONQUISTADOR.** *(See Mission Inn Golf & Tennis Resort)* 352/324-3101. E-mail reservations@missioninnresort.com; web www.missioninnresort.com. Hrs: 6-9:30 pm. Res accepted. Continental menu. Bar 4 pm-midnight. Wine list. A la carte entrees: dinner $15-$28. Specializes in fresh seafood, veal. Pianist, vocalists, dancing. Overlooks golf course, small lakes. Elegant decor with Spanish accents. Family-owned. Totally nonsmoking. Cr cds: A, MC, V.

Titusville (D-5)

(See also Cocoa, Cocoa Beach)

Founded 1867 **Pop** 39,394 **Elev** 18 ft **Area code** 407
Information Chamber of Commerce, 2000 S Washington Ave, 32780; 407/267-3036.

Located on the Indian River, Titusville has always been known for its saltwater trout, shrimp and crab. Indian River citrus, grown along its banks, is famous the world over. The sleepy atmosphere of the area was forever changed by Kennedy Space Center and the nearby attractions around Orlando.

What to See and Do

Canaveral National Seashore. Area consists of 24 miles of unspoiled beaches with Apollo Beach at the north (7 mi S of New Smyrna Beach on FL A1A) and Playalinda Beach at the south (12 mi E of Titusville via FL 406 & FL 402); there are no connecting roads between Apollo and Playalinda—the central portion, Klondike Beach, can be reached only by foot, bicycle or on horseback. More than 300 species of birds have been observed within the seashore; Mosquito Lagoon, between the beach and the Intracoastal Waterway, provides a sanctuary for 14 endangered and threatened species. Recreation includes swimming, waterskiing, surfing, beachcombing, crabbing, clamming, shrimping; surf & freshwater fishing; boating (ramps), canoeing. Hiking trails. Picnicking. Primitive camping on beach (Nov-Apr); backcountry camping in some designated areas. Note: Playalinda Beach and other sections may be periodically closed due to NASA launch-related activities; inquire locally. (Daily) 7 mi E of town via FL 402. Contact the Superintendent, 308 Julia St, 32796; 407/267-1110. ¢¢ per vehicle. Adj seashore is

Merritt Island National Wildlife Refuge. Located beneath the Atlantic flyway, the refuge is a sanctuary for wintering waterfowl. Bird watching; waterfowl hunting (in season). Contact Refuge Manager, PO Box 6504, 32782; 407/861-0667.

Kennedy Space Center (see). S on US 1, then 12 mi E on FL 405.

US Astronaut Hall of Fame/US Space Camp. Hall of Fame features historic artifacts, personal mementos of original Mercury astronauts; rare video footage. Multimedia presentation depicts a shuttle mission aboard full-scale orbiter mock-up. **Space Camp** offers children completing grades 4-7 a 5-day program in which participants tour NASA facilities and experience a simulated astronaut training program (advance reservations required). Hall of Fame (daily; closed Dec 25). S on NASA Pkwy. Contact 6225 Vectorspace Blvd, 32780; 407/269-6100. Hall of Fame ¢¢¢

Annual Event

Valiant Air Command Air Show. 6600 Tico Rd, 5 mi S via US 1 or I-95 & US 50 at Space Center Executive Airport. World War II airshow; vintage aircraft in aerial display of formation flying, dog-fights, aerobatics and bombing/strafing runs; pyrotechnics, special effects and current military displays. Phone 407/268-1941. Mar 14-16.

Motels

✓★ ★ **DAYS INN-KENNEDY SPACE CENTER.** *3755 Cheney Hwy (32780), I-95 exit 79.* 407/269-4480; FAX 407/383-0646. 150 rms, 2 story. S $59; D $65; each addl $6; kit. units $64-$69; under 18 free; higher rates special events. Crib free. Pet accepted. TV; cable (premium). Pool. Ck-out 11 am. Coin lndry. Meeting rms. Lawn games. Refrigerators avail. Cr cds: A, C, D, DS, ER, JCB, MC, V.

★ **HOWARD JOHNSON-KENNEDY SPACE CENTER.** *1829 Riverside Dr (US 1) (32780).* 407/267-7900; FAX 407/267-7080. 104 rms, 2 story. Jan-Apr: S $59-$99; D $59-$109; under 18 free; higher rates: Daytona races, shuttle launches, special events; lower rates rest of yr. TV;

cable (premium), VCR avail (movies). Pool. Playground. Restaurant nearby. Bar. Ck-out noon. Coin lndry. Valet serv. Exercise equipt. Refrigerators, microwaves avail. Private patios, balconies. On Indian River; overlooks Kennedy Space Center. Cr cds: A, C, D, DS, ER, JCB, MC, V.

★ ★ **RAMADA INN.** *3500 Cheney Hwy (32780), I-95 exit 79. 407/269-5510; FAX 407/269-3796.* E-mail info@ramadaksc.com; web www.ramadaksc.com. 124 rms, 2 story, 26 kits. S, D $72-$100; each addl $6; suites, kit. units $89-$160; under 18 free; higher rates: Daytona races, space launches. Crib free. TV; cable (premium). Heated pool; whirlpool. Playground. Restaurant open 24 hrs. Rm serv. Bar. Ck-out noon. Coin lndry. Sundries. Meeting rms. In rm modem link. Exercise equipt; sauna. Game rm. Space shuttle exhibit in lobby. Cr cds: A, C, D, DS, MC, V.

★ **RAMADA LIMITED.** *3810 S Washington Ave (US 1) (32780). 407/267-9111; FAX 407/267-0750.* 65 rms, 2 story. S, D $49-$75; under 16 free; higher rates: space launches, race wks, hols. TV; cable (premium). Pool. Complimentary continental bkfst. Ck-out noon. Coin lndry. Business servs avail. Refrigerators, microwaves avail. Picnic tables. Indian River opp. View of launch pads. Cr cds: A, C, D, DS, MC, V.

★ **TRAVELODGE.** *3480 Garden St (32796), I-95 exit 80. 407/269-9310; FAX 407/267-6859; res: 800/267-3297.* 115 rms, 2 story. Feb-Apr: S, D $50-$95; each addl $5; under 12 free; higher rates special events; lower rates rest of yr. Crib free. Pet accepted; $5. TV; cable. Pool. Restaurant 11:30 am-10 pm. Ck-out 11 am. Cr cds: A, C, D, DS, MC, V.

Resort

★ ★ ★ **LA CITA COUNTRY CLUB.** *777 Country Club Dr (32780). 407/383-2582; FAX 407/267-4209.* 39 condo units (1-2-bedrm), 1-2 story. Nov-Apr: S $87-$129; D $109-$149; each addl $20-$30; under 15 free; package plans; varied lower rates rest of yr. TV; cable. Pool; whirlpool. Ck-out noon, ck-in 3 pm. Grocery, package store 1 blk. Meeting rms. Lighted tennis, pro. 18-hole golf, greens fee $25-$60, pro, putting green, driving range. Entertainment. Exercise equipt. Microwaves. Private patios. Shopping center opp. Cr cds: A, D, DS, MC, V.

Restaurants

✔ ★ **DIXIE CROSSROADS.** *1475 Garden St (32796). 407/268-5000.* Hrs: 11 am-10 pm. Closed Thanksgiving, Dec 24, 25. Serv bar. Semi-a la carte: lunch $4.95-$8.95, dinner $7.95-$20.95. Child's meals. Specializes in shrimp, steak, corn fritters. Casual dining. Rustic decor; knotty pine walls, display of mounted fish. Cr cds: A, D, DS, MC, V.

✔ ★ ★ **HARBOR LIGHTS.** *801 Marina Rd (32796), near marina. 407/267-2244.* Hrs: 11 am-10 pm. Res accepted. Bar. Semi-a la carte: lunch $3.99-$8.99, dinner $8.99-$14.99. Child's meals. Specializes in pasta, steamed oysters & clams. Nautical atmosphere. Dining on porch; overlooks marina and Indian River. Cr cds: A, MC, V.

Treasure Island

(see St Pete Beach)

Venice (F-3)

(See also Sarasota)

Pop 16,922 **Elev** 18 ft **Area code** 941 **E-mail** vchamber@netline.net
Information Venice Area Chamber of Commerce, 257 N Tamiami Trail, 34285; 941/488-2236.

Venice retains the spaciousness planned for it in 1924-25 when it was transformed from an obscure fishing village into a retirement city for the Brotherhood of Locomotive Engineers. The retirement project was discontinued after the 1929 stock market crash, but a small-scale economic boom began in 1960 when the Ringling Bros & Barnum and Bailey Circus moved their winter quarters here from Sarasota. Three public beaches and jetties provide swimming and fishing opportunities while beachcombers can find numerous fossilized shark's teeth on shore.

What to See and Do

Oscar Scherer State Recreation Area. Approx 1,400 acres of pine and scrubby flatwoods on the banks of a small tidal creek. Swimming; fishing; canoeing (rentals). Nature trails. Picnicking. Camping (no hookups, dump station). Standard hrs, fees. 6 mi N on US 41 near Osprey. Phone 941/483-5956.

Warm Mineral Springs. Springs produce 9 million gallons of water at 87°F daily. Bathhouse and lockers (fee); Wellness Center. Picnic sites. (Daily; closed Dec 25) 14 mi SE on US 41 to San Servando Ave (I-75 exit 34) in Warm Mineral Springs. Phone 941/426-1692. ¢¢¢

Annual Event

Venetian Sun Fiesta. Parade, entertainment, barbecue, contests, fishing tournament. 2nd wkend in Oct.

Motels

★ ★ ★ **BEST WESTERN SANDBAR BEACH RESORT.** *811 The Esplanade North (34285). 941/488-2251; FAX 941/485-2894.* E-mail bwsandbarest@earthlink.com; web www.travelweb.com/thisco/bw/10186/ 10186_b.html. 44 rms, 1-4 story, 30 kits. Feb-Apr: S $165; D $209; kits. $179-$250; under 18 free; lower rates rest of yr. Crib free. TV; cable (premium). Heated pool. Restaurant 7 am-9 pm. Ck-out 11 am. Coin lndry. Business servs avail. Lawn games. Microwaves. On beach. Cr cds: A, D, DS, MC, V.

✔ ★ ★ **DAYS INN.** *1710 S Tamiami Trail (34293). 941/493-4558; res: 800/329-7466; FAX 941/493-1593.* 73 rms, 5 with shower only, 3 story, 8 kit. units. Late Jan-mid-Apr: S $83-$89; D $89-$99; each addl $10; kit. units $93-$99; under 17 free; higher rates hols; lower rates rest of yr. Crib avail. Pet accepted; $15. TV; cable. Complimentary coffee in lobby. Restaurant 11 am-10 pm; off-season hrs vary. Bar. Ck-out 11 am. Meeting rms. Business servs avail. 18-hole golf privileges. Pool. Some refrigerators, microwaves. Picnic tables. Cr cds: A, C, D, DS, JCB, MC, V.

★ ★ ★ **HOLIDAY INN VENICE.** *455 N US 41 Bypass (34292). 941/485-5411; FAX 941/484-6193.* E-mail odyssey@sprynet.com. 160 rms, 2 story. Jan-Apr: S, D $99-$129; each addl $10; suites $175-$225; under 19 free; wkly rates; lower rates rest of yr. Crib free. TV; cable. Heated pool; whirlpool. Restaurant 6:30-10:30 am, 4-9 pm. Rm serv. Bar; entertainment. Ck-out 11 am. Coin lndry. Meeting rms. Business servs avail. Health club privileges. Lawn games. Dinner theater. Cr cds: A, C, D, DS, JCB, MC, V.

★ ★ **INN AT THE BEACH RESORT.** *725 W Venice Ave (34285). 941/484-8471; FAX 941/484-0593; res: 800/255-8471.* 45 units, 2 story, 15 suites, 13 kits. Jan-Apr: S, D $169; suites $255-$295; each addl

$12.50; kits. $189-$209; under 18 free; lower rates rest of yr. Crib free. Pet accepted, some restrictions; $20. TV; cable (premium). Heated pool. Complimentary coffee in lobby. Ck-out 11 am. Coin lndry. Business servs avail. Lawn games. Picnic tables. Opp beach. Cr cds: A, C, D, DS, MC, V.

Restaurants

✔★ **FLYING BRIDGE.** *(482 Blackburn Point Rd, Osprey 34229) N on US 41. 941/966-7431.* Hrs: 11:30 am-9:30 pm; early-bird dinner 3-5:15 pm. Closed Jan 1, Thanksgiving, Dec 25. Bar. Semi-a la carte: lunch $5-$8, dinner $7.50-$15.95. Child's meals. Specializes in seafood, steak. Multi-tiered dining rm. View of waterway, marina. Cr cds: A, MC, V.

✔★ **LANDMARK.** *133 S Tamiami Trail (Bus US 41) (34285). 941/485-0668.* Hrs: 11 am-midnight; early-bird dinner 4-5:30 pm. Res accepted. Bar. Semi-a la carte: lunch $6.95-$13.95, dinner $12.95-$18.95. Child's meals. Specialties: escargot, prime rib, grilled salmon. Entertainment Tues-Sat (in season). Elegant dining. Cr cds: A, D, DS, ER, MC, V.

✔★ **OYSTER CRACKERS.** *147 E Tampa Ave (34285). 941/486-0909.* Hrs: 11:30 am-9 pm; Sat from 4 pm; early-bird dinner 3:30-5:30 pm (seasonal). Closed Thanksgiving, Dec 25. Res accepted. Seafood menu. Bar. Semi-a la carte: lunch $5.25-$6.95, dinner $8.95-$16.95. Child's meals. Specialties: bouillabaisse, fresh grouper. Entertainment Tues & Sat eves. Parking. Outdoor dining. On Intracoastal Waterway. Cr cds: A, D, DS, MC, V.

★ **SHARKY'S.** *1600 S Harbor Dr (34293), on Venice Pier. 941/488-1456.* Hrs: 11:30 am-9:30 pm; Fri-Sun to 10 pm. Res accepted off season. Bar. Semi-a la carte: lunch $5.95-$8.95, dinner $7.95-$23.95. Child's meals. Specializes in crab cakes, fresh seafood, steak. Entertainment. Outdoor dining. Nautical decor. Shark jaw display, souvenirs. Shell valances. On beach, pier. Cr cds: A, DS, MC, V.

Vero Beach (F-6)

(See also Fort Pierce, Melbourne)

Pop 17,350 **Elev** 20 ft **Area code** 561 **Web** www.vero-beach.fl.us/chamber
Information Indian River County Chamber of Commerce, 1216 21st St, PO Box 2947, 32961; 561/567-3491.

With its broad streets lined with tropical plants and its miles of uncrowded beaches, Vero Beach is a favorite of many perennial Florida visitors. Citrus shipping supplements tourism as a major industry.

What to See and Do

Riverside Park Complex. Boat launch. One-mi jogging trail; tennis & racquetball courts (fee). Picnic pavilions (fireplaces). Site of Riverside Theater and Center for the Arts (fees). Dahlia Lane. Phone 561/567-2144.

Sebastian Inlet State Recreation Area. More than 570 acres, bounded by the Indian River and the Atlantic Ocean. Swimming, surfing, skin diving; saltwater fishing; boat ramp. Picnicking, concession. Tent & trailer camping (hookups, dump station). Standard hrs, fees. 17 mi N on FL A1A, just N of Sebastian. Phone 561/984-4852 or 561/589-9659 (camping). Here is

McLarty Treasure Museum. Exhibits and artifacts of a Spanish treasure fleet downed in this area in 1715; diorama depicts salvage efforts; slide show on history of site; self-guided audio tour. (Daily) Phone 561/589-2147. ¢

Annual Event

Grant Seafood Festival. N via US 1, in Grant. Feb.

Seasonal Event

Spring training. Holman Stadium, Dodgertown, 4000 Walker Ave. Los Angeles Dodgers baseball spring training; exhibition games. Phone 561/569-4900. Early Mar-early Apr.

Motels

★★ **AQUARIUS NORTH.** *3544 Ocean Dr (32963). 561/231-1133.* 28 kit. units, 10 with shower only, 2 story, 10 suites. Feb-Apr: S, D $85-$115; each addl $5; suites $95-$115; under 12 free; wkly rates off season; lower rates rest of yr. Crib $5. TV; cable. Complimentary coffee in lobby. Restaurant opp 6 am-11 pm. Ck-out 11 am. Coin lndry. On beach; swimming. Cr cds: A, C, D, DS, MC, V.

✔★ **AQUARIUS OCEANFRONT RESORT.** *1526 S Ocean Dr (32963). 561/231-5218.* 27 units, 2 story, 25 kits. Feb-Apr: S, D $65; each addl $5; 1 & 2-bedrm $100-$135; under 12 free; wkly rates; some wkend rates; lower rates rest of yr. Crib $5. TV; cable. Heated pool. Restaurant opp 5-10 pm. Ck-out 11 am. Coin lndry. Lawn games. Refrigerators. Picnic tables, grills. On ocean, beach. Cr cds: A, D, DS, MC, V.

★★ **BEST WESTERN.** *8797 20th St (32966), I-95 exit 68 (FL 60). 561/567-8321; FAX 561/569-8558.* 114 rms, 2 story. Feb-mid-Apr: S, D $65-$85; lower rates rest of yr. Crib free. Pet accepted, some restrictions. TV; cable (premium). Heated pool; wading pool. Playground. Restaurant 7 am-9 pm. Rm serv. Bar 3 pm-1 am. Ck-out noon. Coin lndry. Meeting rms. Business servs avail. In-rm modem link. Health club privileges. Lawn games. Cr cds: A, DS, MC, V.

★ **DAYS INN.** *8800 20th St (32966), I-95 exit 68, East FL 60. 561/562-9991; FAX 561/562-0716.* 115 rms, 2 story. Feb-Apr: S $74; D $79; each addl $5; wkly rates; lower rates rest of yr. Pet accepted; $5. TV; cable. Pool. Restaurant 6 am-9 pm; Sun to 2 pm. Ck-out 11 am. Meeting rm. Business servs avail. In-rm modem link. Cr cds: A, C, D, DS, MC, V.

★ **HOJO INN.** *1985 90th Ave (32966), I-95 exit 68. 561/778-1985; FAX 561/778-1998.* 62 rms, 2 story. Feb-Mar: S $69; D $74; each addl $5; under 18 free; wkly rates; lower rates rest of yr. Pet accepted, some restrictions; $5. TV; cable, VCR avail (movies). Complimentary bkfst. Restaurant opp open 24 hrs. Ck-out noon. Coin lndry. Business servs avail. In-rm modem links. Refrigerators. Cr cds: A, C, D, DS, MC, V.

★★ **ISLANDER.** *3101 Ocean Dr (32963). 561/231-4431; res: 800/952-5886.* 16 units, 2 story. Jan-Apr: S, D from $89; each addl $7; lower rates rest of yr. TV; cable (premium). Pool. Complimentary coffee. Restaurant 7 am-7 pm. Ck-out 11 am. Business servs avail. Refrigerators. Microwaves avail. Some balconies. Beach across street. Cr cds: A, MC, V.

★ **SURF AND SAND.** *1516 S Ocean Dr (32963), I-95 exit 68E (FL 60). 561/231-5700; FAX 561/231-9386.* E-mail surf@sunet.net; web www.surfandsand.com. 15 rms, 2 story, 10 kits. Feb-Apr: S, D $65; each addl $10; kit. units $90-$125; wkly rates; lower rates rest of yr. Crib $5. TV; cable. Complimentary coffee. Heated pool. Restaurant opp. Ck-out 11 am. Business servs avail. Lawn games. Refrigerators, microwaves. Grill. On ocean, beach. Cr cds: DS, MC, V.

Motor Hotels

★ ★ **HOLIDAY INN-OCEANSIDE.** *3384 Ocean Dr (32963).* *561/231-2300; res: 888/670-7470; FAX 561/234-8069.* 104 rms, 2 story, 16 kits. Mid-Jan-Apr: S, D $110-$130; suites $210-$295; lower rates rest of yr. TV; cable. Heated pool; wading pool, poolside serv. Restaurant 6:30 am-9 pm. Rm serv. Bar 5 pm-midnight; entertainment. Ck-out 11 am. Coin lndry. Meeting rms. Business servs avail. In-rm modem link. Bellhops. Beauty shop. Health club privileges. Refrigerators; microwave in suites. Private patios, balconies with ocean view. On beach. Cr cds: A, C, D, DS, ER, JCB, MC, V.

D ≈ ⇥ ⌦ SC

★ ★ ★ **PALM COURT RESORT HOTEL.** *3244 Ocean Dr (32963).* *561/231-2800; FAX 561/231-3446.* Web www.palmcourtvero.com. 107 rms, 5 story, 8 kits. Mid-Dec-Apr: S, D $110-$155; kit. units $175; package plans; lower rates rest of yr. TV; cable (premium). Pool. Restaurant 7 am-3 pm. Bar 11 am-8 pm. Ck-out noon. Meeting rms. Business servs avail. In-rm modem link. Exercise equipt. Private patios, balconies. On ocean, beach. Cr cds: A, D, DS, MC, V.

D ≈ ⅄ ⇥ ⌦ SC

Hotel

★ ★ **DOUBLETREE GUEST SUITES.** *3500 Ocean Dr (32963).* *561/231-5666; FAX 561/234-4866.* 55 suites, 4 story. Feb-Apr: 1-, 2-bedrm $205-$295; under 18 free; wkend rates; lower rates rest of yr. Crib free. TV; cable, VCR (movies). Heated pool; wading pool, whirlpool, poolside serv. Restaurant 7 am-10 pm. Ck-out noon. Meeting rms. Business servs avail. In-rm modem link. Garage. Health club privileges. Refrigerators, wet bars; microwaves avail. Private patios, balconies. On ocean, beach. Cr cds: A, C, D, DS, MC, V.

D ≈ ⇥ ⌦ SC

Restaurants

★ **BEACHSIDE.** *3125 Ocean Dr (FL A1A) (32963).* *561/234-4477.* Hrs: 6:30 am-9 pm. Closed Dec 25. Italian, Amer menu. Semi-a la carte: lunch $3.50-$8.95, dinner $5.50-$16.95. Complete meals: bkfst $2.95-$7.95, lunch $3.95-$8.95. Specializes in seafood, lasagne, Key lime pie. Cr cds: A, D, DS, MC, V.

★ ★ **BLACK PEARL.** *2855 Ocean Dr (32963).* *561/234-4426.* Hrs: 11:30 am-2:30 pm, 5:30-10 pm; Sun 5:30-9 pm. Closed most major hols. Res accepted. Beer. Wine list. Semi-a la carte: lunch $6.95-$9.50, dinner $18.50. Specializes in mesquite-grilled local seafood. Own pastries. Parking. Outdoor dining. Eclectic decor. Cr cds: A, C, D, DS, MC, V.

D ⌐

★ ★ ★ **CHEZ YANNICK.** *1605 S Ocean Dr (32963).* *561/234-4115.* Hrs: from 6 pm. Closed Sun. Res accepted. French menu. A la carte entrees: dinner $14.95-$29.95. Specialties: rack of lamb, Dover sole. Pianist Thurs-Sat. Parking. Elegant dining in round dining room; crystal chandelier. Cr cds: A, MC, V.

D ⌐

★ ★ **OCEAN GRILL.** *1050 Sexton Plaza (32963), Hwy 60E.* *561/231-5409.* Hrs: 11:30 am-2:30 pm, 5:45-10 pm; Sat, Sun from 5:45 pm. Bar. Semi-a la carte: lunch $5.95-$13.95, dinner $13.95-$24.95. Child's meals. Specializes in roast duckling, fresh seafood, Japanese trimmed steaks. Parking. Rustic charm; restaurant built by original owner more than 50 yrs ago. Ocean view. Family-owned. Cr cds: A, D, DS, MC, V.

D ⌐

★ ★ **PATIO.** *1103 Miracle Mile (US 1) (32960).* *561/567-7215.* Hrs: 11-1 am; Sun brunch 10:30 am-2:30 pm. Bar. Semi-a la carte: lunch $3.95-$7.50, dinner $7.95-$22.95. Sun champagne brunch $11.95. Child's meals. Specializes in fresh fish, steaks, prime rib. Parking. Outdoor dining.

One of oldest eating establishments in Vero Beach; old Spanish decor. Cr cds: A, DS, MC, V.

D ⌐

★ ★ **TANGOS.** *925 Bougainvillea Lane (32963).* *561/231-1550.* Hrs: 5:30-10 pm; closed Sun-Tues; hrs vary off-season. Closed Sun; most major hols. Res accepted. Contemporary Amer menu. Bar. A la carte entrees: dinner $15-$25. Specializes in seafood, pasta, prime meats. Parking. Covered outdoor dining. Cr cds: A, D, DS, MC, V.

D ⌐

Wakulla Springs
(see Tallahassee)

Walt Disney World (E-4)

(See also Altamonte Springs, Clermont, Haines City, Kissimmee, Orlando, Winter Park)

Area code 407

Information PO Box 10000, Lake Buena Vista, 32830, 407/824-4321; for reservations to many of the lodgings phone W-DISNEY (934-7639).

For the people at Walt Disney World, making dreams come true is a way of life. From its major theme parks to its resort hotels, everything is run with a touch of make-believe in mind. It takes some 35,000 people to keep the Vacation Kingdom going, and every facet of operation is designed to keep visitors happy and content in this gossamer fantasyland.

The Magic Kingdom, the first of the four major parks, offers more than forty-six attractions as well as shows, shops, exhibits, refreshment areas and special theme areas divided into seven "lands": Adventureland, Frontierland, Liberty Square, Fantasyland, Mickey's Starland, Tomorrowland and Main Street, U.S.A. Since its opening in 1971, Walt Disney World has received untold millions of visitors, making it the most popular tourist attraction in the world.

While the Magic Kingdom may be the best known area of the park, it takes up only a fraction of the 28,000-acre resort complex (almost twice the size of Manhattan Island). Combined with Epcot, which opened October 1, 1982, Disney-MGM Studios, which opened May 1, 1989, Animal Kingdom, which opened April 22,1998, and the variety of other new attractions, Walt Disney World is a vacation kingdom unique in all the world. Epcot, the most dramatic Disney project to date, takes visitors through two distinct "worlds." Future World combines rides and attractions, technical innovations, discovery and scientific achievements, bringing to life a world of new ideas, adventures and entertainment. World Showcase brings together eleven celebrated nations re-created in exact detail through architectural landmarks, shops, authentic food and entertainment.

Disney-MGM Studios explores the world of movies and television, both on-stage and off, and includes a working studio. Palm-lined, art deco-style Hollywood Boulevard offers adventure, entertainment, shopping and dining in true Hollywood style. The park offers a mix of cinema nostalgia, sensational stunt work, television magic and backstage wizardry.

Animal Kingdom, Disney's newest theme park, unites fun with a love for animals. After seven years in the making, the park contains forests, streams and waterfalls, tropical jungles and savannahs, where many animals roam. 1,000 birds and mammals representing more than 200 species are present. Animal Kingdom combines close encounters with all kinds of live wild animals with Disney's animated stars plus adventures with prehistoric dinosaurs.

In addition to the Magic Kingdom, Epcot, Disney-MGM Studios and Animal Kingdom, Walt Disney World offers many hotels (see); a campground facility with a water recreation park; a 7,500-acre conservation/wilderness area preserving virgin stands of pine, cypress and bay trees; daily parades and fireworks displays; shopping; and several fine restaurants (see). Activities include relaxing on more than 4 miles of beach, fishing, swimming, sailing, motorboating, waterskiing, tennis, steamboat excursions, ranch and trail rides, picnicking and hiking. There are five 18-hole championship golf courses—collectively referred to as the "Magic Linkdom": the Palm, Magnolia, Lake Buena Vista, Eagle Pines and Osprey Ridge, plus a 9-hole family-play course. All are available for play by the general public.

Walt Disney World's several areas are tied together by a transportation system that includes motorcoaches, 19th-century ferry boats and the famous monorail. Guests at Fort Wilderness Campground and Disney-owned hotels have free use of the transportation system. Special evening shows at Walt Disney World include fireworks, lasers, parades of singers and dancers, moonlight cruises and a variety of after-dark entertainment.

Walt Disney World is open every day of the year with extended hours in summer and during holiday periods. Guided tours are recommended for first-time visitors. Various ticket combinations are available (inquire about details and limits at time of reservation): a One-park/One-day pass to the Magic Kingdom, Epcot, Disney-MGM Studios or Animal Kingdom, $42; a four-day Value Pass with admission to all four of the major theme parks, $157. Admission to each of the smaller parks also by separate fee. Fees for children ages 3-9 are lower; age 2 and under admitted free. Phone 407/824-4321.

Transportation

Orlando Intl Airport: Information 407/825-2001; lost and found 407/825-2111; weather 407/851-7510; cash stations, Main Terminal, near bank office.

Car Rental Agencies: See IMPORTANT TOLL-FREE NUMBERS.

Transportation at Walt Disney World: Monorail, buses, motor launches, basic fare per day $2.50; free to guests at Disney-owned resorts.

Rail Passenger Service: Amtrak 800/872-7245.

What to See and Do

Animal Kingdom. "A New Species of Theme Park" includes

The Tree of Life. Animal Kingdom's centerpiece, 14-stories tall and 50 ft wide at its base. Over 350 animal forms are found within the trunk of the tree. Within The Tree of Life is

It's Tough To Be a Bug. 430-seat theater which offers an adventure into the world of insects through a bug's-eye view.

Safari Village. Island village of themed shops and restaurants.

Dinoland U.S.A. Celebration of America's fascination with dinosaurs. Countdown to Extinction takes guests back 65 million yrs to rescue the last dinosaur from extinction. Children can dig in an open air site in The Boneyard. Shoppers can visit Chester & Hester's Dinosaur Treasures.

Camp Minnie-Mickey. Guests can meet with favorite Disney characters. Stage shows include Festival of the Lion King and Colors of the Wind.

Harambe Village. A contemporary representation of an East Africa coastal town. Coral-walled buildings thatched roofs, hand-lettered signs, narrow-winding streets; African bands. Wildlife Express runs from here to the Conservaton Station. Past the baobab tree is

Kilimanjaro Safaris. Explore more than 110 acres of savannah, forests, rivers, rocky hills and grasslands filled with herds of different animals.

Conservation Station. Guests discover behind-the-scenes operations of the park. Interactive displays, games. Affection Section is the only place where guests will be able to touch live animals under animal specialist supervision.

Blizzard Beach. South of Disney-MGM Studios, this water park has a ski resort in Florida theme. The park's central attraction is Mt Gushmore, a 90-ft "snow-capped" mountain. Summit Plummet is a free-fall speed slide straight down to a splash landing. White-water raft rides, Tike's Peak for young children, an eight-lane water slide called Toboggan Racer and a chair lift can also be found here. Restrooms, showers, lockers, picnicking and restaurants.

Disney Village Marketplace. Located in Lake Buena Vista. A collection of unique shops, restaurants and nightclubs clustered around a lagoon in a resort community. Includes the 50,000-sq-ft World of Disney store with 12 themed areas.

Disney-MGM Studios. Just southwest of Epcot off the main entrance road, this area houses three film and television soundstages of the Walt Disney Company, giving people a chance to watch a film or television show in the making. Various rides and shows let visitors see the backlots, an animation studio, soundstages of famous films and an explanation of stunt work used in major movies. SuperStar Television and the Monster Sound Show allow guests to work with sound effects, trade quips on a sitcom and prepare for stardom in the "Green Room." Children can play on the *Honey, I Shrunk the Kids* Movie Set Adventure, with 30-ft-tall synthetic grass. Twilight Zone's Tower of Terror is a journey into a deserted hotel that ends in a 13-story plunge. Stage shows include Beauty and the Beast, Voyage of the Little Mermaid and Hunchback of Notre Dame.

Epcot. This far-reaching Disney project, the largest of the four theme parks, features these two "worlds."

Future World. Eight themed pavilions present new ideas and technologies in exciting areas such as energy, transportation, communications and imagination; visitors can take a ride through Spaceship Earth, view a 3-D film, take a high-speed simulated flight through the human body, use their imaginations in a state-of-the-art electronic playground, journey through transportation history, take a ride on Test Track that takes guests behind the scenes of automobile testing or participate in various hands-on computer-related exhibits.

World Showcase. These pavilions, surrounding a 40-acre lagoon, showcase some of the world's most fascinating nations—Canada, China, France, Germany, Italy, Japan, Mexico, Morocco, Norway, the United Kingdom and the United States—through treasure-laden shops, enticing restaurants with international specialties, native entertainers, films and attractions.

Fort Wilderness Campground. A 780-acre pine and cypress forest with 785 campsites and 407 "wilderness homes" for rent. The area has swimming pools, beaches; marina, canoeing streams; tennis courts and air-conditioned shower and laundry facilities. All sites have water, power and sewer hookups. Within Fort Wilderness are

River Country. Water slides, flumes, rapids, white-sand beaches and a heated swimming pool round out this Disney version of the "old swimmin' hole."

Discovery Island. An 11-acre island in Bay Lake with exotic birds, animals, flower gardens and nature trails.

Magic Kingdom. Home of Mickey Mouse and Cinderella, includes

Main St, U.S.A. Depicts 1890-1910 America when, electricity and horseless carriages began replacing gas lamps and horse-drawn vehicles. Steam trains depart from Victorian-style station for tour around the Magic Kingdom.

Fantasyland. Dominated by 18-story Cinderella Castle; highlights include Disney characters, It's A Small World and 20,000 Leagues Under the Sea, featuring Captain Nemo's submarine.

Mickey's Starland. Land of Mickey and friends includes tour of Mickey's house, Mickey's dressing room and a live stage show starring the famous mouse and all his animated pals.

Tomorrowland. Featuring Grand Prix Raceway; Astro Orbiter; The Extraterrestrial Alien Encounter and Space Mountain.

Adventureland. Jungle cruises to see "live" lions, hippos and headhunters found on rivers around the world. Swiss Family Tree House affords view of the jungle area. Also features Pirates of the Caribbean.

Frontierland. Re-creation of the Old West when pioneers first arrived; wild west stage show at the Diamond Horseshoe Saloon Revue; a troupe of bears performs a Western hoedown; Big Thunder Mountain Railroad features a runaway train ride through an Old West mining town. Also here is Splash Mountain, a flume ride based on sequences from the Disney film *Song of the South* (1946); guests board eight-passenger hollowed-out logs for a half-mile journey on which they encounter a host of zany characters, including Br'er Rabbit, Br'er Fox and Br'er Bear. The climax of the trip is a thrilling 50-ft, 40-mph drop into the Briar Patch.

Liberty Square. Portrayal of America at the time of its founding; cobblestone streets, colonial shops; Hall of Presidents features 41 life-size, lifelike figures of United States presidents. The Haunted Mansion has an assortment of 999 ghosts, goblins and ghouls waiting to greet visitors.

Nighttime features.

SpectroMagic. Magic Kingdom. Musical parade of performers and floats decorated with millions of twinkling lights, covering such Disney themes as *Fantasia* and *The Little Mermaid.* (Nightly, during extended hrs)

IllumiNations. Epcot. A dramatic 15-min laser, pyrotechnic and water show set to symphonic music, presented around World Showcase Lagoon. (Sat, Sun)

Fantasy in the Sky. Magic Kingdom. Fireworks show above Cinderella Castle expends more than 200 shells in under 5 min. (Nightly, during extended hrs)

Pleasure Island. On the shores of Village Lake, linked to Disney Village Marketplace by footbridge. Six-acre entertainment complex featuring six nightclubs with live music and dancing, shows, comedy, entertainment, shopping and dining. A single cover charge admits guests to all clubs.

Typhoon Lagoon. A 56-acre water park located between Epcot and Disney Village Marketplace. Features world's largest wave pool; 9 waterslides descending from a 95-ft summit; surfing lagoon; saltwater snorkeling in Shark Reef; inner-tube rides. Changing areas, lockers, showers, picnicking and restaurants.

Annual Events

Walt Disney World Village Wine Festival. At Disney Village Marketplace. June.

Fourth of July. Pyrotechnical tour de force over the Seven Seas Lagoon in the Magic Kingdom; also at Disney-MGM Studios and Epcot. July 4.

Walt Disney World Golf Classic. At the "Magic Linkdom." Late Oct.

Halloween. At Disney Village Marketplace. Villains from Disney films, including the Evil Queen from *Snow White and the Seven Dwarfs* and Cruella de Vil from *101 Dalmations,* make appearances after dark. Oct 31.

Festival of the Masters Art Festival. At Disney Village Marketplace. Early Nov.

Motor Hotels

★ ★ **BUENA VISTA SUITES.** *(14450 International Dr, Orlando 32821)* at International Dr & FL 535. 407/239-8588; FAX 407/239-1401; res: 800/537-7737. E-mail reservations@bvsuites.com; web www.buena vistasuites.com. 280 suites, 7 story. Jan-mid-Apr, June-Aug, hols: suites $129-$189; each addl $10; under 18 free; lower rates rest of yr. Crib free. TV; cable (premium), VCR (movies). Pool; whirlpool, poolside serv. Complimentary full bkfst. Rm serv 11 am-11 pm. Restaurant opp 6 am-11 pm. Ck-out 11 am. Coin lndry. Meeting rms. Business servs avail. In-rm modem link. Bellhops. Concierge. Sundries. Gift shop. Free Walt Disney World transportation. Lighted tennis. Golf privileges. Exercise equipt. Game rm. Refrigerators, microwaves. Cr cds: A, C, D, DS, ER, JCB, MC, V.

D ⌘ ⚡ ≈ ✗ ⛵ 🐾 SC

✔★ **COMFORT INN.** *(8442 Palm Pkwy, Lake Buena Vista 32830)* at Vista Ctr. 407/387-7300; res: 800/999-7300; FAX 407/387-7740. Web www.tamarinns.com 640 rms, 5 story. Feb-mid-Apr, June-Aug: S, D up to 4, $59-$85; suites $120; family rates; lower rates rest of yr. Crib free. Pet accepted; $6. TV; cable (premium). 2 pools, 1 heated. Restaurant 6:30-10:30 am, 5:30-9 pm. Bar 5:30 pm-2 am. Ck-out 11 am. Coin lndry. Business servs avail. Valet serv. Sundries. Gift shop. Free Walt Disney World transportation. Game rm. Cr cds: A, C, D, DS, ER, JCB, MC, V.

D ⌦ ≈ 🚫 🐾 SC

★ ★ **DAYS INN.** *(12799 Apopka-Vineland Rd, Orlando 32836)* I-4 exit 27. 407/239-4441; FAX 407/239-0325. E-mail dayslbvhtl@aol.com. 203 rms, 8 story. S, D $164; higher rates special events. Crib free. Pet accepted, some restrictions; $10. TV; cable (premium), VCR (movies

avail). Restaurant 6:30-11 am, 5-10 pm. Ck-out noon. Business servs avail. Free Walt Disney World transportation. Gift shop. Coin lndry. Pool. Playground. Game rm. Balconies. Cr cds: A, C, D, DS, JCB, MC, V.

D ⌦ ≈ 🚫 🐾 SC

★ ★ ★ **HOLIDAY INN LAKE SUN SPREE RESORT.** *(13351 FL 535, Lake Buena Vista 32830)* I-4 exit 27, S on FL 535. 407/239-4500; res: 800/366-6299; FAX 407/239-7713. E-mail max@kidsuites.com; web www.kidsuites.com. 507 rms, 6 story. Mid-Feb-late Apr, mid-June-mid-Aug, late Dec: S, D $106-$168; under 18 free; lower rates rest of yr. Crib free. TV; cable, VCR (movies $6). Heated pool; whirlpools, wading pool, poolside serv. Playground. Supervised child's activities; ages 3-12. Coffee in rms. Restaurant 7 am-10 pm. Rm serv. Bar from 4:30 pm; entertainment. Ck-out 11 am. Coin lndry. Business servs avail. Bellhops. Valet serv. Concierge. Sundries. Free Walt Disney World transportation. Exercise equipt. Game rm. Refrigerators; microwaves. Cr cds: A, C, D, DS, ER, JCB, MC, V.

D ≈ ✗ 🚫 🐾 SC

★ ★ **HOWARD JOHNSON PARK SQUARE INN AND SUITES.** *(8501 Palm Pkwy, Lake Buena Vista 32830)* I-4 exit 27 to FL 535, N to Vista Center. 407/239-6900; res: 800/635-8684; FAX 407/239-1287. Web HoJoLBV.com. 222 rms, 3 story, 86 suites. Jan-Apr, June-Aug, late Dec: S, D $95-155, each addl $10; suites $115-$165; under 12 free; lower rates rest of yr. Crib free. TV. 2 pools, heated; wading pool, whirlpool. Playground. Restaurant 7-11 am. Deli 7 am-10 pm. Rm serv. Bar 5 pm-midnight. Ck-out 11 am. Coin lndry. Meeting rms. Business servs avail. Bellhops. Sundries. Gift shop. Airport, Walt Disney World transportation. Game rm. Lawn games. Refrigerator in suites. Balconies. Landscaped courtyard. Cr cds: A, C, D, DS, ER, JCB, MC, V.

D ≈ 🚫 🐾 SC

Hotels

★ ★ ★ **BUENA VISTA PALACE.** *(1900 Buena Vista Dr, Lake Buena Vista 32830)* in Walt Disney World Village. 407/827-2727; FAX 407/827-6034; res: 800/327-2990. E-mail info@bvp-resort.com; web www.bvp-resort.com. 1,013 rms, 27 story, 128 suites. Feb-Apr, late Dec: S, D $149-$249; suites $249-$850; under 18 free; lower rates rest of yr. Crib free. TV; cable, VCR avail. 3 heated pools; wading pool, whirlpool, poolside serv. Playground. Supervised child's activities; ages 4-12. Coffee in rms. Restaurant open 24 hrs (also see ARTHUR'S 27). Bar 11-2 am; entertainment. Ck-out 11 am. Coin lndry. Convention facilities. Business center. In-rm modem link. Shopping arcade. Barber, beauty shop. Valet parking. Free Walt Disney World transportation. Lighted tennis. 18-hole golf privileges, pro, putting green, driving range, pro shop. Exercise rm; sauna. Game rm. Minibars; some in-rm whirlpools, refrigerators; microwaves avail. Many balconies. Luxury level. Cr cds: A, C, D, DS, MC, V.

D ⌦ 👪 ⚡ ≈ ✗ 🚫 🐾 ⛷

★ ★ ★ **CARIBE ROYALE.** *(14300 International Dr, Orlando 32821)* 2 mi S on I-4 exit 27. 407/238-8000; res: 800/823-8300; FAX 407/238-8050. E-mail cariberoyale.com; web www.cariberoyale.com. 1,218 suites, 10 story. Mid-Dec-mid-Apr: suites $179-$209; under 18 free; lower rates rest of yr. Crib free. TV; cable (premium), VCR avail. Complimentary bkfst buffet. Restaurant 6:30-2 am. Ck-out 11 am. Coin lndry. Convention facilities. Business center. In-rm modem link. Concierge. Free Walt Disney World transportation. Lighted tennis. Golf privileges. Exercise equipt. Heated pool; wading pool, whirlpool, poolside serv, lifeguard. Supervised child's activities. Refrigerators, microwaves, wet bars. Some in-rm whirlpool, minibars. Cr cds: A, C, D, DS, ER, JCB, MC, V.

D 👪 ⚡ ≈ ✗ 🚫 🐾 SC ⛷

✔★ ★ **COURTYARD BY MARRIOTT-WALT DISNEY WORLD VILLAGE.** *(1805 Hotel Plaza Blvd, Lake Buena Vista 32830)* In Walt Disney World Village. 407/828-8888; FAX 407/827-4623. 323 rms, 14 story. S, D $89-$175; suites $250-$395; under 18 free. Crib free. TV; cable (premium). 2 pools; wading pool, whirlpool, poolside serv. Restaurant 6 am-midnight. Rm serv 7 am-10 pm. Bar from 4 pm. Ck-out 11 am. Coin lndry. Convention facilities. Gift shop. Free Walt Disney World transportation. Tennis privileges. Golf privileges. Exercise equipt. Game rm. Many private patios, balconies. Atrium. Cr cds: A, C, D, DS, ER, JCB, MC, V.

D 🛌🍽🏊🎿🍴🏂🏌🎿 SC

★ ★ **DOUBLETREE GUEST SUITES RESORT.** *(2305 Hotel Plaza Blvd, Lake Buena Vista 32830) In Walt Disney World Village. 407/934-1000; FAX 407/934-1015.* E-mail dtorlando@earthlink.net; web www.doubletreehotels.com. 229 suites (1-2 bedrm), 7 story. Late Dec-Apr: S, D $139-$280; each addl $20; lower rates rest of yr. Crib free. TV; cable (premium). Heated pool; wading pool, whirlpool, poolside serv. Playground. Restaurant 7 am-10 pm. Bar 4-11 pm. Ck-out 11 am. Coin lndry. Meeting rms. Business servs avail. Concierge. Gift shop. Free Walt Disney World transportation. Lighted tennis. 18-hole golf privileges, pro, putting green, driving range. Exercise equipt. Game rm. Lawn games. Refrigerators, microwaves. Some private patios. Cr cds: A, C, D, DS, ER, MC, V.

D 🛌🍽🏊🎿🍴🏂🏌🎿 SC

★ ★ **EMBASSY SUITES RESORT.** *(8100 Lake Ave, Orlando 32836) Near jct I-4 & FL 535. 407/239-1144; FAX 407/239-1718.* Web www.embassysuites.com. 280 suites, 6 story. Feb-Apr & mid-Dec-Jan 1: S, D (up to 4 adults) $145-$300; family rates; golf, Disney plans; lower rates rest of yr. Crib free. TV; cable (premium), VCR (movies). Heated pool, indoor/outdoor; wading pool, whirlpool, poolside serv. Playground. Supervised child's activities; ages 3-13. Complimentary full bkfst. Complimentary coffee in rms. Restaurant 11 am-11 pm. Bar 5 pm-midnight. Ck-out 11:30 am. Coin lndry. Meeting rms. Business servs avail. In-rm modem link. Gift shop. Free scheduled shuttle to all Disney theme parks. Lighted tennis. 18-hole golf privileges, pro, putting green, driving range. Exercise equipt; sauna. Game rm. Rec rm. Refrigerators, microwaves. Cr cds: A, C, D, DS, ER, JCB, MC, V.

D 🛌🍽🏊🎿🍴🏂🏌🎿 SC

★ ★ **GROSVENOR RESORT.** *(1850 Hotel Plaza Blvd, Lake Buena Vista 32830) In Walt Disney World Village. 407/828-4444; FAX 407/828-8192; res: 800/624-4109.* E-mail info@grosvenorresort.com; web www.grosvenorresort.com. 626 rms, 19 story. Feb-mid Apr: S, D $160-$215; suites $175-$750; under 18 free; lower rates rest of yr. Crib free. TV; cable, VCR (movies $5). 2 heated pools; wading pool, whirlpool, poolside serv. Playground. Coffee, tea in rms. Restaurant 7 am-10 pm. Deli open 24 hrs. Bar 11-2 am; entertainment in season. Ck-out 11 am. Coin lndry. Convention facilities. Business servs avail. In-rm modem link. Concierge. Shopping arcade. Free Walt Disney World transportation. Lighted tennis. Golf privileges, pro, putting green, driving range. Exercise equipt. Game rm. Lawn games. Activities dir (summer). Sherlock Holmes Museum on grounds. Cr cds: A, C, D, DS, ER, JCB, MC, V.

D 🛌🍽🏊🎿🍴🏂🎿 SC

★ ★ **HILTON AT WALT DISNEY WORLD VILLAGE.** *(1751 Hotel Plaza Blvd, Lake Buena Vista 32830) In Walt Disney World Village. 407/827-4000; FAX 407/827-3890.* Web www.hilton.wdwv.com. 814 rms, 10 story. Mid-Jan-Apr, late Dec: S, D $180-$260; each addl $20; suites $459-$1,500; family rates; lower rates rest of yr. Crib free. TV; cable (premium), 2 heated pools; wading pool, whirlpool, poolside serv. Supervised child's activities; ages 4-11. Restaurant 6:30 am-midnight. Rm serv 24 hrs. Bar 11-2 am. Ck-out 11 am. Coin lndry. Convention facilities. Business center. In-rm modem link. Barber, beauty shop. Valet parking. Free Walt Disney World transportation. Tennis privileges. Golf privileges, pro, putting green, driving range. Exercise equipt. Game rm. Minibars; some bathrm phones, refrigerators; microwaves avail. Some private patios, balconies. Luxury level. Cr cds: A, C, D, DS, ER, JCB, MC, V.

D 🛌🍽🏊🎿🍴🎿 SC

✔★ ★ **RIU ORLANDO.** *(8688 Palm Pkwy, Lake Buena Vista 32836) I-4 exit 27 to FL 535, N to Vista Center. 407/239-8500; res: 888/222-9963; FAX 407/239-8591.* 167 rms, 6 story. S, D $90-$125; each addl $10; under 18 free. Crib free. TV; cable. Heated pool; whirlpool, poolside serv. Restaurant 7-10:30 am, noon-2 pm, 6:30-10:30 pm. Bar to 10:30 pm. Ck-out 11 am. Coin lndry. Meeting rms. Business servs avail. In-rm modem link. Free Walt Disney World transportation. Exercise equipt.

Game rm. Rec rm. Refrigerators avail. Some minibars. Cr cds: A, C, D, DS, ER, JCB, MC, V.

D 🏊🎿🍴🎿🏂 SC

★ ★ ★ **ROYAL PLAZA.** *(1905 Hotel Plaza Blvd, Lake Buena Vista 32830) In Walt Disney World Village. 407/828-2828; FAX 407/827-6338; res: 800/248-7890.* E-mail royresv@aol.com; web www.royalplaza.com. 394 rms, 2-17 story. Feb-Apr: S, D $129-$189; suites $169-$650; lower rates rest of yr. Crib free. TV; cable. Heated pool; whirlpool, poolside serv. Restaurant 6:30 am-midnight. Bar 11-2:00 am; entertainment. Ck-out 11 am. Convention facilities. Business servs avail. Gift shop. Valet parking. Free Walt Disney World transportation. Lighted tennis. 18-hole golf privileges, driving range. Game rm. Lawn games. Some bathrm phones. Refrigerators avail. Balconies. Cr cds: A, C, D, DS, ER, JCB, MC, V.

D 🛌🍽🏊🎿🍴🏂🎿 SC

★ ★ ★ **TRAVELODGE.** *(2000 Hotel Plaza Blvd, Lake Buena Vista 32830) In Walt Disney World Village. 407/828-2424; FAX 407/828-8933.* Web www.travelodgewdw.com. 325 rms, 18 story. S, D $109-$199; suites $299-$399. Crib free. TV; cable (premium). Heated pool; wading pool. Playground. Coffee in rms. Restaurant 7-11 am, 5-11 pm. Bar 4 pm-1:30 am. Ck-out 11 am. Coin lndry. Meeting rms. Concierge. Gift shop. Airport, Walt Disney World transportation. Lighted tennis privileges, pro. 18-hole golf privileges, pro, putting green, driving range. Game rm. Lawn games. Minibars; some refrigerators. Balconies. On lake. Cr cds: A, C, D, DS, ER, JCB, MC, V.

D 🛌🍽🏊🎿🎿 SC

Inn

✔★ ★ ★ **PERRI HOUSE BED & BREAKFAST.** *(10417 FL 535, Orlando 32836) N of I-4 exit 27 on FL 535. 407/876-4830; FAX 407/876-0241; res: 800/780-4830.* E-mail perrihse@iag.net; web www.perri house.com. 8 rms. S, D $89-$119. Crib free. TV; cable. Pool. Complimentary continental bkfst. Ck-out 11 am, ck-in 3 pm. On 4 acres; bird sanctuary. Adj Walt Disney World property. Cr cds: A, D, DS, MC, V.

🏊🎿🎿 SC

Resorts

★ ★ **ALL-STAR MUSIC RESORT.** *(1801 W Buena Vista Blvd, Lake Buena Vista 32830) 407/939-6000; FAX 407/939-7222.* Web www.disney.com. 1,920 rms, 3 story. Mid-Feb-Late Apr, late Dec: S, D $94; each addl $10; under 18 free; golf plan, lower rates rest of yr. Crib free. TV; cable (premium). Heated pool; wading pool, poolside serv, lifeguard. Playground. Restaurant 6 am-midnight. Ck-out 11 am, ck-in 4 pm. Gift shop. Grocery. Coin lndry. Valet serv. Tennis privileges. 99-hole golf privileges, greens fee $85, putting green, driving green. Health club privileges. Game rm. Some refrigerators. Picnic tables. Buildings have musical instrument theme. Cr cds: A, MC, V.

D 🛌🍽🏊🎿🍴🎿

★ ★ **ALL-STAR SPORTS RESORT.** *(1701 W Buena Vista Dr, Lake Buena Vista 32830) 407/939-5000; FAX 407/939-7333.* Web www.disney.com. 1,920 rms, 3 story. Mid-Feb-late Apr, late Dec: S, D $94; each addl $10; golf plans, lower rates rest of yr. Crib free. TV; cable (premium). Heated pool; wading pool, poolside serv, lifeguard. Restaurant 6 am-midnight. Ck-out 11 am, ck-in 4 pm. Gift shop. Grocery. Coin lndry. Valet serv. Tennis privileges. 99-hole golf privileges, greens fee $85. Health club privileges. Some refrigerators. Buildings have various sport themes: baseball, football, tennis, etc. Cr cds: A, MC, V.

D 🛌🍽🏊🎿🍴🎿

★ ★ **DISNEY'S BEACH CLUB RESORT.** *(1800 Epcot Resorts Blvd, Lake Buena Vista 32830) 407/934-8000; FAX 407/934-3850.* Web www.disneyworld.com. 584 rms, 5 story. Mid-Feb-Apr: S, D $314-$485; each addl $25; suites $305-$1,010; under 18 free; Disney packages; higher rates hols; lower rates rest of yr. Crib free. TV; cable (premium), VCR avail. 2 pools; poolside serv. Supervised child's activities; ages 4-12. Dining rm 7 am-10 pm. Rm serv 24 hrs. Bar 11-1 am. Ck-out 11 am, ck-in

3 pm. Coin lndry. Convention facilities. Business center. In-rm modem link. Bellhops. Valet serv. Sundries. Gift shop. Barber, beauty shop. Free valet parking. Free Disney transportation, water transportation to Disney-MGM Studios Theme Park. Lighted tennis. Golf privileges. Mini waterpark; boating, marina. Lawn games. Game rm. Exercise equipt; sauna, steam rm. Bathrm phones, minibars; microwaves avail. Wet bar in suites. Balconies. Located on the shores of a 25-acre man-made lake. Architect Robert A.M. Stern has re-created a New England Village with a turn-of-the-century theme. DISNEY'S BEACH CLUB RESORT meets with DISNEY'S YACHT CLUB RESORT (see) in a central courtyard and shares a Fantasy Lagoon. Cr cds: A, MC, V.

★ ★ ★ **DISNEY'S BOARDWALK INN.** *(2101 N Epcot Resort Blvd, Lake Buena Vista 32830) in Epcot Resort area.* 407/939-5100; FAX 407/939-5155. Web www.disneyworld.com. 378 rms, 5 story. Mid-Feb-Apr, mid-late Dec: S, D $279-$490; each addl $15; suites $650-$1,200; under 18 free; lower rates rest of yr. Crib free. TV; cable (premium), VCR avail (movies). Restaurant (see FLYING FISH CAFE). Rm serv 24 hrs. Bar 11 am-midnight. Ck-out 11 am. Convention facilities. Business center. In-rm modem link. Concierge. Shopping arcade. Coin lndry. Airport transportation. Lighted tennis. 99-hole golf course privileges, pro, putting green, driving range. Exercise rm; sauna. Massage. Pool; wading pool, whirlpool, poolside serv, lifeguard. Supervised child's activities. Game rm. Rec rm. Bathrm phones; some in-rm whirlpools. Balconies. Luxury level. Cr cds: A, MC, V.

★ ★ **DISNEY'S CARIBBEAN BEACH RESORT.** *(900 Cayman Way, Lake Buena Vista 32830) off I-4 exit 26B.* 407/934-3400; FAX 407/934-3288. Web wdw.disney.com\cbr. 2,112 rms in several village groups, 2 story. Mid Feb-late Apr, late Dec: S, D $149-$169; each addl $15; under 18 free, lower rates rest of yr. Crib free. TV; cable. 7 heated pools; wading pool, whirlpool, poolside serv, lifeguard. 4 playgrounds. Coffee in rms. Dining rm 5:30 am-midnight; several dining areas. Bar noon-1:30 am. Ck-out 11 am, ck-in 3 pm. Coin lndry. Business servs avail. Shopping arcade. Tennis privileges. Golf privileges, greens fee. Health club privileges. Marina; boat rentals. Game rm. Minibars. Picnic tables. 1½-acre island-like resort with lake. Each village has a pool and beach area. 1¼-mi promenade around lake; island play area for children in middle of lake. Cr cds: A, MC, V.

★ ★ ★ **DISNEY'S CONTEMPORARY RESORT.** *(Box 10000, Lake Buena Vista 32830) off US 192, I-4 in Walt Disney World.* 407/824-1000; FAX 407/824-3539. Web www.disneyworld.com. 1,041 rms, 14-story tower, 2 3-story bldgs. Mid-Dec-Jan 1, mid-Mar-early Apr: S, D $244-$299; each addl $15; 1-bedrm suites $325-$940; under 18 free; lower rates rest of yr. Crib free. TV; cable (premium). 2 heated pools; wading pool, whirlpool, lifeguard. Playground. Supervised child's activities; ages 3-12. Restaurant (see CALIFORNIA GRILL). Snack bar 24 hrs. Rm serv 24 hrs. Bars noon-1 am. Ck-out 11 am, ck-in 3 pm. Coin lndry. Convention facilities. Business center. In-rm modem link. Shopping arcade. Barber, beauty shop. Valet parking. Lighted tennis, pro. 99-hole golf privileges. Exercise equipt; sauna. Massage. Game rm. Lawn games. Refrigerator in suites. Balconies. Monorail runs through 12-story atrium lobby. On lake. Luxury level. Cr cds: A, MC, V.

★ ★ ★ **DISNEY'S CORONADO SPRINGS.** *(Lake Buena Vista 32830)* 407/939-1000. Web www.disneyworld.com. 1,967 rms, 3 story, 46 suites. Mid-Feb-mid-Apr: S, D $149-$169; each addl $15; suites $298-$625; under 18 free; lower rates rest of yr. Crib free. TV; cable (premium), VCR. Complimentary coffee in rms. Restaurant 7 am-11 pm. Rm serv. Bar; entertainment. Ck-out 11 am, ck-in 3 pm. Grocery. Coin lndry. Convention facilities. Business center. Bellhops. Valet serv. Shopping arcade. Barber, beauty shop. Airport transportation. Boats. Bicycle rentals. Rec rm. Game rm. Exercise rm; sauna. Massage. Spa. Heated pools; whirlpool, poolside serv, lifeguard. Playground. Supervised child's activities; ages 5-12. Many

refrigerators, wet bars; some bathrm phones, in-rm whirlpools. Cr cds: A, MC, V.

★ ★ ★ ★ **DISNEY'S GRAND FLORIDIAN RESORT & SPA.** 4401 Floridian Way (32830), in Walt Disney World. 407/824-3000; FAX 407/824-3186. Web www.disneyworld.com. On the shores of the Seven Seas Lagoon, this looks like a turn-of-the-century summer resort, thanks to a gabled red roof, rambling verandas, cupolas and gingerbread porches and an open-cage elevator. 900 rms: 65 rms in main bldg, 9 suites; 817 rms, 16 suites in 5 lodge bldgs, 4 & 5 story. Mid-Dec-Jan 1, mid-Feb-mid-Apr: S, D $329-$530; each addl $25; suites $990-$1,565; under 18 free; special plans; lower rates rest of yr. Crib free. TV; cable (premium), VCR avail (movies). Heated pool; wading pool, whirlpool, poolside serv, lifeguard. Supervised child's activities (June-Aug); ages 3-12. Dining rms 7 am-11 pm (also see CITRICOS and VICTORIA & ALBERT'S). Rm serv 24 hrs. Bar 11-1 am. Ck-out 11 am, ck-in 3 pm. Coin lndry. Convention facilities. Business center. In-rm modem link. Valet parking. Barber, beauty shop. Monorail to Magic Kingdom, Epcot Center & Disney/MGM Studios. Tennis, clay courts, pro. 99-hole golf privileges, greens fee, pro. Private beach; waterskiing, sailing, marina, boat rentals. Lawn games. Game rm. Exercise rm; steam rm. Massage. Fishing guides. Bathrm phones, minibars; wet bar in suites. Balconies. Kennels avail. On 40 acres. Bldgs #6, #7 and #9 (431 rms) are totally nonsmoking. Luxury level. Cr cds: A, MC, V.

★ ★ ★ **DISNEY'S POLYNESIAN RESORT.** *(Box 10000, Lake Buena Vista 32830) Off US 192, I-4 in Walt Disney World.* 407/824-2000; FAX 407/824-3174. Web www.Disney.com. 853 rms, 2-3 story. S, D $274-$530; each addl $15; suites $395-$1,425; under 18 free; lower rates rest of yr. Crib free. TV; cable, VCR avail. 2 heated pools; wading pool, poolside serv, lifeguard. Playground. Supervised child's activities; ages 3-11. Restaurant open 24 hrs; dining rm 7 am-11 pm (also see 'OHANA). Children's dinner theater. Rm serv 6:30 am-midnight. Bar 1 pm-1:30 am; entertainment. Ck-out 11 am, ck-in 3 pm. In-rm modem link. Coin lndry. Sundries. Shopping arcade. Lighted tennis privileges, pro. 99-hole golf privileges, greens fee, pro. Health club privileges. Fishing (guides avail). Game rm. Balconies. Kennels. On lake; 2 swimming beaches, boat rentals, waterskiing, marina. Monorail access. Luxury level. Cr cds: A, MC, V.

★ ★ **DISNEY'S PORT ORLEANS.** *(1662 Old South Rd, Lake Buena Vista 32830) I-4 exit 26B.* 407/934-7639; FAX 407/934-5353. Web www.disney.com. 1,008 rms in 7 bldgs, 3 story. Mid-Feb-late Apr, late Dec: S, D $149-$169; each addl $15; under 18 free, lower rates rest of yr. Crib free. TV; cable (premium), VCR avail. Pool; wading pool, whirlpool. Sauna. Restaurants 5-10 pm. Bar 11 am-midnight. Ck-out 11 am, ck-in 3 pm. Grocery. Coin lndry. Business servs avail. Bellhops. Gift shop. Lighted tennis privileges, pro. Golf privileges, pro, putting green, driving range. Health club privileges. Boats. Bicycle rentals. Game rm. Located on a canal; ornate row-house buildings with courtyards and intricate railings are reminiscent of the French Quarter in New Orleans; cobblestone streets; trips by flat-bottom boats down river to shops and showplaces. Cr cds: A, MC, V.

★ ★ ★ **DISNEY'S WILDERNESS LODGE.** *(901 Timberline Dr, Lake Buena Vista 32830) in Walt Disney World.* 407/824-3200; FAX 407/824-3232. Web www.disneyworld.com. 728 rms, 7 story. Mid-Feb-late Apr, mid-late Dec: S, D $230-$359; each addl $25; suites $359-$765; golf plan; lower rates rest of yr. Crib free. TV; cable, VCR avail. Heated pool; wading pool, whirlpool, poolside serv, lifeguard. Supervised child's activities; ages 4-12. Restaurant 7:30 am-10 pm. Rm serv 7 am-noon, 4 pm-midnight. Bar 11 am-midnight. Ck-out noon. Bellhops. Valet serv. Shopping arcade. Coin lndry. Lighted tennis privileges. 99-hole golf privileges, greens fee $85, putting green, driving range. Health club privileges. Game rm. Refrigerators, microwaves avail. Some balconies. Picnic tables. Cr cds: A, MC, V.

★ ★ ★ **DISNEY'S YACHT CLUB RESORT.** *(1700 Epcot Resort Blvd, Lake Buena Vista 32830) 5 minute walk to Epcot Center.* 407/934-

7000; FAX 407/934-3450. Web www.disneyworld.com. This refreshingly unstuffy property designed by noted architect Robert A.M. Stern is just right for families. Set on a 25-acre man-made lake, it has a gray clapboard facade, evergreen landscaping and a lighthouse on its pier, recalling the turn-of-the-century New England seacoast. 635 rms, 5 story. Mid-Feb-mid-Apr: S, D $314-$490; each addl $25; suites $495-$1,165; under 18 free; Disney plans; higher rates hols; lower rates rest of yr. Crib free. TV; cable (premium), VCR avail. Pool; whirlpool. Supervised child's activities; ages 4-12. Dining rm 7 am-10 pm (also see YACHTSMAN STEAKHOUSE). Rm serv 24 hrs. Bar 11-1 am. Ck-out 11 am, ck-in 3 pm. Coin lndry. Convention facilities. Business center. In-rm modem link. Bellhops. Valet serv. Concierge. Gift shop. Barber, beauty shop. Free Disney transportation, including water taxi, to Disney-MGM Studios Theme Park & Epcot Center. Lighted tennis. Golf privileges. Mini waterpark; boating, marina. Lawn games. Game rm. Exercise rm; sauna, steam rm. Massage. Bathrm phones, minibars; microwaves avail; wet bar in suites. DISNEY'S YACHT CLUB RESORT meets with DISNEY'S BEACH CLUB RESORT (see) in a central courtyard with a "quiet pool" and shares a Fantasy Lagoon with poolside serv. Luxury level. Cr cds: A, MC, V.

★ ★ ★ **DIXIE LANDINGS.** (1251 Dixie Dr, Lake Buena Vista 32830) I-4 exit 26B. 407/934-6000; FAX 407/934-5024. Web www.disney. com. 2,048 units in 15 bldgs, 2-3 story. Mid Feb-late Apr, late Dec: S, D $149-$169; each addl $15; golf plans, lower rates rest of yr. Crib free. TV; cable (premium), VCR avail. 6 pools; wading pool, whirlpool, poolside serv, lifeguards. Playground. Restaurant 6:30 am-midnight. Bar; entertainment. Ck-out 11 am, ck-in 3 pm. Grocery, package store. Coin lndry. Business servs avail. Bellhops. Gift shop. Lighted tennis, pro. 99-hole golf, greens fee, pro, putting green, driving range. Health club privileges. Boat, bicycle rentals. Game rm. Old South plantation-style project located on the Sassagoula River. Alligator Bayou region is reminiscent of old Cajun country, while Magnolia Bend showcases stately mansions typical of the upriver South. Cr cds: A, MC, V.

★ ★ ★ ★ **HYATT REGENCY GRAND CYPRESS.** (1 Grand Cypress Blvd, Orlando 32836) 2 mi E of I-4 exit 27, Lake Buena Vista exit. 407/239-1234; FAX 407/239-3800. Web www.hyatt.com. Part of what is perhaps the Orlando area's most spectacular resort, this hotel offers virtually every resort amenity and then some. It rests on 1,500 landscaped acres. 750 units, 18 story, 75 suites. Jan-May: S, D $265-$420; suites $650-$3,000; golf plans; lower rates rest of yr. Crib free. Valet parking $10. TV; cable (premium), VCR avail. Heated pool; whirlpool, poolside serv. Supervised child's activities (Memorial Day-Labor Day); ages 3-17. Restaurants (see HEMINGWAY'S and LA COQUINA). Rm serv 24 hrs. Bar; entertainment. Ck-out noon, ck-in 4 pm. Convention facilities. Business center. Valet serv. Concierge. Shopping arcade. Beauty shop. Airport, Walt Disney World transportation. 12 tennis courts, 6 lighted, pro, instruction avail. 45-hole golf, Academy of Golf, pro, putting green, driving range, pitch & putt. Sailing, canoes, paddleboats; rentals avail. Lake with white sand beach. Nature area, Audubon walk; jogging trails. Bicycle rentals. Game rm. Equestrian center; Western and English trails. Exercise rm; sauna, steam rm. Massage. Minibars; microwaves avail. Bathrm phone, refrigerator in some suites. Some private patios. Balconies. Luxury level. Cr cds: A, C, D, DS, ER, JCB, MC, V.

★ ★ ★ **MARRIOTT'S ORLANDO WORLD CENTER.** (8701 World Center Dr, Orlando 32821) I-4 exit 26A, jct FL 536. 407/239-4200; FAX 407/238-8777. Web www.orlando.com/owcm. 1,503 rms, 28 story. S, D $159-$269; suites from $350; under 18 free. Crib free. Valet parking $5, overnight $10. TV; cable (premium), VCR avail. 3 heated pools, 1 indoor; wading pool, poolside serv. Playground. Supervised child's activities; ages 4-12. Dining rms 6 am-11 pm (also see TUSCANY'S). Rm serv 24 hrs. Bar; pianist. Ck-out 11 am, ck-in 4 pm. Coin lndry. Convention facilities. Business center. Concierge. Shopping arcade. Barber, beauty shop. Airport transportation. Lighted tennis, pro. 18-hole golf, greens fee $50-$110, pro, putting green, driving range. 5-acre activity court with pools, lagoon, waterfalls, sun deck. Lawn games. Game rm. Exercise equipt; sauna. Massage. Some refrigerators, minibars. Private patios, balconies.

On 200 landscaped acres; view of many lakes. Cr cds: A, C, D, DS, ER, JCB, MC, V.

★ ★ **RESIDENCE INN BY MARRIOTT.** (8800 Meadow Creek Dr, Orlando 32821) 1 mi S, I-4 exit 27. 407/239-7700; FAX 407/239-7605. 688 kit. villas, 2 story. Mid-Dec-early Jan, mid-Feb-Apr, mid-June-mid-Aug: S, D $179-$219; wkly, monthly rates; lower rates rest of yr. Crib free. Pet accepted, some restrictions. TV; cable (premium), VCR (movies). 3 heated pools; poolside serv. Complimentary coffee in rms. Ck-out 11 am, ck-in 4 pm. Grocery. Coin lndry. Meeting rms. Bellhops. Gift shop. Walt Disney World transportation. Lighted tennis. Golf privileges. Health club privileges. Balconies. Cr cds: A, C, D, DS, JCB, MC, V.

★ ★ ★ ★ **VILLAS OF GRAND CYPRESS.** (1 N Jacaranda, Orlando 32836) N on FL 535. 407/239-4700; FAX 407/239-7219; res: 800/835-7377. E-mail resortinfo@grandcypress.com. web www.grandcypress. com. It's hard to believe that this tranquil, 1,500-acre resort is just minutes from the bustle of Walt Disney World. Spacious villas offer fully equipped kitchens, plush furnishings and private patios overlooking the expansive golf courses. 146 suites, 2 story, 48 kit. units. Late Jan-Apr: S, D, kit. units $370-$1,680; under 18 free; lower rates rest of yr. Crib free. TV; cable (premium), VCR avail (movies). Pool; whirlpool, poolside serv. Complimentary coffee in rms. Restaurant 7 am-10 pm. Rm serv 24 hrs. Box lunches, snacks. Bar from 11 am; entertainment. Ck-out noon, ck-in 4 pm. Bellhops. Valet serv. Concierge. Meeting rms. Business center. Lighted tennis, pro. 45-hole golf course, greens fee $100-140, pro, putting green, driving range. Hiking. Bicycles. Health club privileges. Minibars; some refrigerators; microwaves avail. Balconies. Cr cds: A, C, D, DS, JCB, MC, V.

★ ★ ★ **WALT DISNEY WORLD DOLPHIN.** (1500 Epcot Resorts Blvd, Lake Buena Vista 32830) In Walt Disney World Village, adj Epcot Center. 407/934-4000; FAX 407/934-4099; res: 800/227-1500. E-mail info@swandolphin.com; web www.swandolphin.com. 1,509 rms, 27 story. Mid-Feb-mid-Apr, late Dec: S, D $310-$430; suites from $395-$2,990; under 18 free; Disney packages; lower rates rest of yr. Crib free. TV; cable (premium). 4 pools, 3 heated; wading pool, whirlpool, poolside serv, lifeguard. Playground. Supervised child's activities; ages 4-12. Dining rm 6 pm-midnight. Rm serv 24 hrs. Bars noon-2 am; pianist. Ck-out 11 am, ck-in 3 pm. Coin lndry. Convention facilities. Business center. Concierge. Shopping arcade. Barber, beauty shop. Free Walt Disney World transportation, by both land and water. Lighted tennis. Golf privileges. Exercise rm. Game rm. Rec rm. Minibars; many bathrm phones; wet bar in suites; microwaves avail. Designed by architect Michael Graves as entertainment architecture; the hotel features a waterfall cascading down the front of the building into a pool supported by two dolphin statues. Luxury level. Cr cds: A, C, D, DS, ER, JCB, MC, V.

★ ★ ★ **WALT DISNEY WORLD SWAN.** (1200 Epcot Resorts Blvd, Lake Buena Vista 32830) in Walt Disney World Village, adj Epcot Center. 407/934-3000; FAX 407/934-4499; res: 800/248-SWAN. E-mail info@swandolphin.com; web www.swandolphin.com. 758 rms, 12 story. S, D $310-$430; each addl $25; suites $395-$2,990; Disney packages. Crib free. Valet parking $8. TV; cable (premium), VCR avail. 2 pools, 1 rock-sculptured grotto; wading pool, whirlpool, poolside serv, lifeguard (grotto). Playground. Coffee in rms. Dining rm 6:30 am-11 pm. Rm serv 24 hrs. Bar 4 pm-midnight. Ck-out 11 am, ck-in 3 pm. Convention facilities. Business center. Concierge. Gift shop. Airport transportation. Free transportation, including water taxi, to Epcot Center, Disney-MGM Studios Theme Park and other Kingdom areas. 4 lighted tennis courts. Golf privileges. Exercise rm; sauna. Game rm. Minibars; many bathrm phones; some wet bars. Balconies. Situated on 150-acre resort site. Dramatic style of entertainment architecture; created by Michael Graves; two 28-ton, 47.3-ft swan statues grace the roofline. Luxury level. Cr cds: A, C, D, DS, ER, JCB, MC, V.

Restaurants

★ ★ ★ **ARTHUR'S 27.** *(See Buena Vista Palace Hotel)* 407/827-3450. Web www.bvp-resort.com. Hrs: 6-10 pm. Res accepted. International menu. Bar. Wine cellar. A la carte entrees: dinner $25-$30. Complete meals: dinner $50-$65. Specializes in gourmet dishes, some custom-prepared. Pianist. Valet parking. On 27th floor; view of Walt Disney World. Cr cds: A, C, D, DS, MC, V.

D ⊸

★ ★ ★ **CALIFORNIA GRILL.** *(See Disney's Contemporary Resort)* 407/824-3611. Web www.disneyworld.com. Hrs: 5:30-10 pm. Res accepted. Bar noon-midnight. Wine list. A la carte entrees: dinner $17.75-$28.50. Child's meals. Specializes in chicken, beef, seafood. Valet parking. Rooftop dining; view of the Magic Kingdom. Totally nonsmoking. Cr cds: A, MC, V.

D

★ ★ ★ **CITRICOS.** *(See Disney's Grand Floridian Beach Resort)* 407/824-2989. Web www.disneyworld.com. Hrs: 5:30-10 pm. Res accepted. French Mediterranean menu. Bar. Wine cellar. A la carte entrees: dinner $19-$36. Child's meals. Specialties: six-hr veal shank, lamb & lobster with ratatouille, chocolate ravioli with licorice ice cream. Valet parking. Sophisticated atmosphere. Totally nonsmoking. Cr cds: A, MC, V.

D

★ ★ **CRAB HOUSE.** *(8496 Palm Pkwy, Lake Buena Vista 32831)* I-4 exit 27 to FL 535, N to Vista Center. 407/239-1888. Hrs: 11:30 am-11 pm; Sun from 1 pm. Bar. Semi-a la carte: lunch $4.99-$9.99, dinner $10.99-$19.99. Child's meals. Specializes in beef, fresh seafood, Maryland crab. Salad bar. Valet parking. Patio dining. Rustic, New England-style decor. Cr cds: A, C, D, DS, MC, V.

D ⊸

★ ★ ★ **FLYING FISH CAFE.** *(See Disney's Boardwalk Inn Hotel)* 407/939-2359. Hrs: 5:30-10 pm; Fri, Sat to 10:30 pm. Res accepted. Bar. Extensive wine list. A la carte entrees: dinner $18-$25. Child's meals. Specialties: spice-crusted tuna, red snapper, chocolate lava cake. Own baking. Valet parking. Carnival atmosphere resembling 1930s Coney Island. Totally nonsmoking. Cr cds: A, MC, V.

D

★ ★ **FULTON'S CRAB HOUSE.** *1670 Buena Vista Dr (32830), on Empress Lilly Boat in Walt Disney World Village.* 407/934-2628. Hrs: 8:30 am & 10 am sittings (character bkfst), 11:30 am-4 pm, 5-11 pm. Res accepted (bkfst). Bar 11:30 am-midnight. Complete meal: bkfst $12.95. Semi-a la carte: dinner $15-$33. Child's meals. Specializes in fresh fish, crab, oysters. Valet parking. Nautical decor. Totally nonsmoking. Cr cds: A, MC, V.

D

★ ★ ★ **HEMINGWAY'S.** *(See Hyatt Regency Grand Cypress Resort)* 407/239-1234. Web www.hyatt.com. Hrs: 11:30 am-2:30 pm; Sun, Mon from 6 pm. Res accepted. Bar to 1 am. Extensive wine list. A la carte entrees: lunch $7-$15, dinner $19-$30. Child's meals. Specializes in live Maine lobster, steak. Valet parking. Outdoor dining. Atmosphere of old Key West with ceiling fans, wicker furnishings, tropical palms. Perched atop a rock precipice; multi-level dining overlooks lagoon-like pool. Cr cds: A, C, D, DS, ER, JCB, MC, V.

D ⊸

★ ★ ★ **LA COQUINA.** *(See Hyatt Regency Grand Cypress Resort)* 407/239-1234. Web www.hyatt.com. Hrs: 6:30-10:30 pm; Sun brunch 10:30 am-2:30 pm. Closed Tues, Wed. Res accepted. Bar. Wine list. A la carte entrees: dinner $27-$35. Sun brunch $38. Child's meals. Specialties: steamed petite lobsters with ricotta gnocchi; rack of lamb in herb crust with spinach and red pepper tomato compote. Pianist. Free valet parking. Dining rm with crystal chandeliers and floral centerpieces overlooks lake and grounds. Cr cds: A, C, D, DS, ER, JCB, MC, V.

D

✔★ ★ ★ **'OHANA.** *(See Disney's Polynesian Resort)* 407/824-1334. Hrs: 7:30-11 am, 5-10 pm. Res accepted. South Pacific menu. Bar. Character bkfst buffet: $14.95. Complete meals: dinner $20.95. Child's meals. Own baking. South Pacific decor; stone carvings, open kitchen called the Fire Pit. Overlooks lagoon. Totally nonsmoking. Cr cds: A, MC, V.

D

★ ★ **PEBBLES.** *(12551 SR 535, Lake Buena Vista 32836)* I-4 to FL 535, right to Crossroads Shopping Center. 407/827-1111. Hrs: 11 am-11 pm; Fri, Sat to midnight. Closed Thanksgiving, Dec 25. Bar. Semi-a la carte: lunch, dinner $5.25-$19.95. Child's meals. Specialties: Mediterranean salad, chicken with avocado and sour orange sauce. Parking. Vaulted ceilings. Window alcoves provide semi-private dining with view of lake. Cr cds: A, D, DS, MC, V.

D ⊸

★ ★ **PORTOBELLO YACHT CLUB.** *Pleasure Island (32830), in Walt Disney World Village.* 407/934-8888. Hrs: 11:30 am-midnight. Italian menu. Bar. Semi-a la carte: lunch $4.95-$8.95, dinner $12.95-$22.95. Child's meals. Specializes in seafood. Valet parking. Outdoor dining. Nautical theme. Cr cds: A, MC, V.

D

★ **RAINFOREST CAFE.** *(1800 E Buena Vista Dr, Lake Buena Vista 32830)* I-4 exit 27. 407/827-8500. Web www.rainforestcafe.com. Hrs: 10:30 am-11 pm; Fri, Sat to midnight. Bar. Semi-a la carte: lunch, dinner $7.95-$18.95. Child's meals. Specialties: Rasta Pasta, Rumble in the Jungle, Mojo Bones. Tropical rainforest theme; unique decor. Cr cds: A, D, DS, MC, V.

D

★ ★ **SPOODLES.** *(2101 N Epcot Resort Blvd, Lake Buena Vista 32830)* on Boardwalk. 407/939-2380. Hrs: 7:30-11 am, noon-2 pm, 5-10 pm. Res accepted. Mediterranean menu. Buffet: bkfst $10.95. A la carte entrees: lunch $6.95-$10.95, dinner $7-$21. Child's meals. Specializes in tapas, chicken, beef. Valet parking. Mediterranean decor. Totally nonsmoking. Cr cds: A, MC, V.

★ ★ ★ **TUSCANY'S.** *(See Marriott's Orlando World Center Resort)* 407/239-4200. Hrs: 6-10 pm. Res accepted. Bar. Wine list. Semi-a la carte: dinner $18-$29. Child's meals. Specializes in Northern Italian cuisine. Own baking. Valet parking. Elegant dining; European decor. Cr cds: A, C, D, DS, ER, JCB, MC, V.

D ⊸

★ ★ ★ **VICTORIA & ALBERT'S.** *(See Disney's Grand Floridian Beach Resort)* 407/824-2383. Web www.disneyworld.com. Sittings: 6 & 9 pm. Res required. Contemporary Amer menu. Wine cellar. Complete meals: dinner $80-$100. Child's meals. Own baking. Harpist. Valet parking. Gourmet menu changes daily. Victorian decor. Jacket. Totally nonsmoking. Cr cds: A, MC, V.

D

★ ★ **WOLFGANG PUCK CAFE.** *(1482 E Buena Vista Dr, Lake Buena Vista 32830)* downtown Disney. 407/938-9653. Hrs: 11 am-midnight; Fri, Sat to 1 am. Res accepted. Bar. A la carte entrees: lunch $7.95-$15.95, dinner $9.95-$21.95. Child's meals. Specialties: smoked salmon pizza, cafe pad thai, chinois chicken salad. Valet parking Thurs-Sat eves. Outdoor dining. Totally nonsmoking. Cr cds: A, C, D, MC, V.

D

★ ★ ★ **YACHTSMAN STEAKHOUSE.** *(See Disney's Yacht Club Resort)* 407/934-3356. Web www.disneyworld.com. Hrs: 5:30-10 pm. Res accepted. Bar noon-midnight. Semi-a la carte: dinner $17-$29. Child's meals. Specialties: Kansas City strip steak, porterhouse. Valet parking. Butcher shop in entry for personalized orders. Totally nonsmoking. Cr cds: A, MC, V.

D

Weeki Wachee Spring

(see Brooksville)

West Palm Beach (G-6)

(See also Belle Glade, Boynton Beach, Jupiter, Lake Worth, Palm Beach)

Settled 1880 **Pop** 67,643 **Elev** 21 ft **Area code** 561 **Web** www.palmbeachfl.com
Information Palm Beach County Convention & Visitors Bureau, 1555 Palm Beach Lakes Blvd, Suite 204, 33401; 561/575-4636 or 800/833-5733.

West Palm Beach has developed as a resort city because of its accessibility to nearby beaches and the Intracoastal Waterway, which offers a number of boating opportunities. Golfing also is popular—there are more than 145 courses in Palm Beach County.

What to See and Do

Atlantic Coastal Cruises. Sightseeing cruises on Mississippi paddlewheeler; also lunch and dinner cruises. (Daily; no cruises Dec 25) Res required. I-95 to Blue Heron Blvd, go E to Phil Foster Park. Phone 561/842-0882 or -7827. ¢¢¢¢

Boating. Dockage up to 100 ft. Palm Beach Yacht Club & Marina, 800 N Flagler Dr. Phone 561/655-1944.

Greyhound racing. Palm Beach Kennel Club. Parimutuel wagering and races, simulcast action, poker room; evenings & matinees. (Daily, hours vary) 1111 N Congress Ave at Belvedere Rd. For schedule, fees phone 561/683-2222.

Lion Country Safari. A 500-acre wildlife preserve; 5-mi self-guided auto tour; more than 1,000 African, Asian and American wild animals roam free. Animal nursery, dinosaur exhibit, petting zoo. Animal Theater. *Safari Queen* narrated boat ride; paddleboats. Picnic area, restaurant; curio shop. Camping. (Daily) On Southern Blvd W, 18 mi W of I-95. Phone 561/793-1084. Admission includes all rides and tours. ¢¢¢¢

Norton Museum of Art. Permanent displays include 19th- and 20th-century European paintings; American art from 1900 to present; a distinguished Chinese collection; sculpture patio. (Tues-Sat, also Sun afternoons; closed some major hols) 1451 S Olive Ave. Phone 561/832-5194 or -5196. ¢¢¢

Palm Beach Zoo at Dreher Park. More than 400 animals on 23 acres in natural settings. Petting zoo. (Daily; closed Thanksgiving) 1301 Summit Blvd. Phone 561/533-0887. ¢¢¢

South Florida Science Museum. Dozens of hands-on interactive exhibits; the South Florida Aquarium. Observatory viewing & laser light shows (Fri evenings). Planetarium show (daily, inquire for schedule; fee). Museum (daily; closed Thanksgiving, Dec 25) 4801 Dreher Trail N, off Summit Blvd, between Forest Hill & Southern Blvds. Phone 561/832-1988. ¢¢

Annual Events

South Florida Fair & Exposition. Fairgrounds, 9067 Southern Blvd. Livestock shows, entertainment, midway. Phone 561/793-0333 or 800/527-3247 (FL). Last 2 wks Jan.

SunFest. Flagler Dr. Five-day jazz, art and water festival. Phone 561/659-5980 or -5992. Last wk Apr.

Seasonal Events

Polo. (See LAKE WORTH)

Spring training. Roger Dean Stadium, Donald Ross Rd. Montreal Expos and St Louis Cardinals spring baseball training. Phone 561/775-1818. Exhibition games Late Feb-Mar.

Motels

★ ★ **BEST WESTERN PALM BEACH LAKES.** *1800 Palm Beach Lakes Blvd (33401), I-95 exit 53.* 561/683-8810; FAX 561/478-2580. 135 rms, 2 story. Mid-Jan-mid-Apr: S, D $85-$95; suites $95-$140; under 18 free; lower rates rest of yr. Crib free. TV; cable (premium). Pool. Complimentary continental bkfst. Restaurant adj 11 am-10 pm. Bar. Ck-out noon. Business servs avail. Airport, RR station, bus depot transportation. Health club privileges. Refrigerators. Cr cds: A, C, D, DS, MC, V.

✔★ **CLARION HOTEL & CONFERENCE CENTER.** *(11360 US 1, North Palm Beach 33408)* Jct US 1, PGA Blvd. 561/624-7186; res: 888/696-9692; FAX 561/622-4258. 90 rms, 4 story. Jan-Apr: S, D $129; each addl $10; suites $159; under 18 free; lower rates rest of yr. TV; cable (premium). Complimentary full bkfst. Restaurant opp 6 am-3 pm. Ck-out 11 am. Meeting rms. Business servs avail. In-rm modem link. Valet serv. Exercise equipt. Cr cds: A, C, D, DS, ER, JCB, MC, V.

★ ★ **COURTYARD BY MARRIOTT.** *600 Northpointe Pkwy (33407), I-95 exit 54.* 561/640-9000; FAX 561/471-0122. 149 rms, 3 story. Mid-Jan-mid-Apr: S, D $124; each addl $10; suites $159-$169; under 18 free; long-term rates; lower rates rest of yr. Crib free. TV; cable (premium). Heated pool; whirlpool. Complimentary coffee in rms. Restaurant 6:30-11 am; Sat, Sun 7-11 am. Ck-out noon. Coin lndry. Meeting rms. Business servs avail. In-rm modem link. Sundries. Golf privileges. Exercise equipt. Some refrigerators. Balconies. Cr cds: A, D, DS, MC, V.

✔★ ★ **DAYS INN AIRPORT NORTH.** *2300 45th St (33407), 2 mi N on I-95, exit 54.* 561/689-0450; FAX 561/686-7439. 234 rms, 2 story. Jan-mid-Apr: S, D $79-$109; each addl $10; under 12 free; wkly, monthly rates; lower rates rest of yr. Crib free. Pet accepted; $10; TV; cable (premium). Heated pool; whirlpool. Restaurant 6-10 pm. Ck-out 11 am. Coin lndry. Meeting rms. Business servs avail. Sundries. Cr cds: A, D, DS, MC, V.

★ ★ **DAYS INN OCEANFRONT RESORT.** *(2700 Ocean Dr, Singer Island 33404)* 3 mi N on I-95, exit on Blue Heron Blvd, 4 mi E to Ocean Dr, on Singer Island. 561/848-8661; FAX 561/844-0999. E-mail daysinger@travelbase.com; web www.travelbase.com/daysinger. 165 rms, 2 story. Jan-Apr: S, D, kit. units $129-$179; under 17 free; lower rates rest of yr. Crib free. Pet accepted; $10. TV; cable (premium). Heated pool; whirlpool. Restaurant 6 am-10 pm. Bar 11 am-dusk. Ck-out noon. Business servs avail. Lawn games. Some refrigerators, microwaves. On ocean beach; cabanas. Cr cds: A, C, D, DS, MC, V.

★ **DAYS INN TURNPIKE/AIRPORT.** *6255 Okeechobee Blvd (33417).* 561/686-6000; FAX 561/687-0415. 154 rms, 2 story. Mid-Dec-Apr: S, D $66-$99; each addl $6; under 12 free; wkly, monthly rates; lower rates rest of yr. Crib free. Pet accepted; $10. TV; cable (premium), VCR avail (movies). Heated pool; wading pool; whirlpool. Restaurant 7 am-9 pm. Bar 3-11 pm. Ck-out 11 am. Coin lndry. Meeting rms. Business servs avail. Exercise equipt. Refrigerators avail. Cr cds: A, C, D, DS, JCB, MC, V.

✔★ ★ **FAIRFIELD INN BY MARRIOTT.** *5981 Okeechobee Blvd (33458), FL Tpke exit 99.* 561/697-3388; FAX 561/697-2834. 114 rms, 4 story. Jan-mid-Apr: S, D $75-$119; each addl $10; under 18 free; lower rates rest of yr. Crib free. TV; cable (premium). Heated pool. Complimentary continental bkfst. Ck-out noon. Meeting rm. Business servs avail. In-rm modem link. Free airport transportation. Some refrigerators. Cr cds: A, C, D, DS, MC, V.

★ ★ **HAMPTON INN.** *1505 Belvedere Rd (33406), near Intl Airport.* 561/471-8700; FAX 561/689-7385. 136 rms, 3 story. Dec-Apr: S, D $79-$99; under 18 free; lower rates rest of yr. Crib free. TV; cable (premium). Pool. Complimentary continental bkfst. Ck-out noon. Business servs avail. Airport transportation. Cr cds: A, D, DS, MC, V.

D ≈ ✕ ≍ ⋈ SC

★ ★ **PARKVIEW.** *4710 S Dixie Hwy (US 1) (33405), I-95 exit 50.* 561/833-4644; res: 800/523-8978. 28 rms, 2 story. Mid-Jan-mid-Apr: S $70-$80; D $76-$88; each addl $8; lower rates rest of yr. Crib free. TV; cable. Complimentary continental bkfst. Restaurant adj 7 am-10 pm. Ck-out 11 am. Business servs avail. Refrigerators avail. Opp park. Cr cds: A, DS, MC, V.

≍ ⋈ SC

 ★ **ROYAL INN.** *(675 Royal Palm Beach Blvd, Royal Palm Beach 33411) approx 10 mi W of I-95 on US 98 (Southern Blvd).* 561/793-3000; FAX 561/795-1502; res: 800/428-5389. 85 rms, 1-2 story. Late Dec-Easter: S, D $49.50-$67; kit. units $56-$67; under 12 free; lower rates rest of yr. Crib free. TV; cable (premium). Pool. Restaurant noon-11 pm. Bar 2 pm-1 am. Ck-out noon. Business servs avail. Barber shop. Lawn games. Refrigerators; microwaves avail. Private patios, balconies. Picnic tables. On lake. Cr cds: A, C, D, DS, MC, V.

D ≈ ≍ ⋈

★ ★ **RUTLEDGE INN.** *(3730 N Ocean Dr, Riviera Beach 33404) 3 mi N on US 1 or I-95 to Blue Heron Blvd, 1 mi E to N Ocean Dr, on Singer Island.* 561/848-6621; FAX 561/840-1787; res: 800/348-7946. Web tam...1mbeach/rutledginn.htm. 60 units, 2 story, 36 kits. Mid-Dec-mid-Apr: S, D $84-$120; each addl $10; suites $150-$300; kit. units $90-$120; under 18 free; lower rates rest of yr. Crib free. TV; cable (premium). Heated pool; poolside serv. Restaurant adj 11 am-midnight. Ck-out noon. Coin lndry. Business servs avail. Refrigerators; some microwaves. Private patios, balconies. On beach. Cr cds: A, DS, MC, V.

🏊 ≈ ⋈ SC

★ **TROPICAL ISLE.** *(100 Inlet Way, Palm Beach Shores 33404) 3 mi N on US 1 to Blue Heron Blvd, then E to Ocean Blvd, on Singer Island.* 561/842-2447; FAX 561/842-6026. 25 kit. units. Mid-Dec-Apr: S, D $62-$88; lower rates rest of yr. Crib avail. TV; cable. Restaurant nearby. Ck-out 11:30 am. Guest lndry. Business servs avail. Lawn games. Refrigerators. On ocean. Cr cds: MC, V.

🏊 ⋈

Motor Hotels

★ ★ **COMFORT INN.** *1901 Palm Beach Lakes Blvd (33409), near Intl Airport.* 561/689-6100; FAX 561/686-6177. 157 rms, 6 story. Jan-mid-Apr: S, D $79-$104; each addl $5; under 18 free; lower rates rest of yr. Crib free. Pet accepted, some restrictions. TV; cable (premium). Heated pool. Complimentary continental bkfst. Restaurant 11 am-10 pm. Ck-out noon. Meeting rms. Business servs avail. Valet serv. Refrigerators avail. Health club privileges. Some private patios, balconies. Cr cds: A, D, DS, MC, V.

D 🏊 ≈ ⋈ ⋈ SC

★ ★ **HOLIDAY INN-PALM BEACH AIRPORT.** *1301 Belvedere Rd (33405), off I-95 exit 51, near Intl Airport.* 561/659-3880; FAX 561/655-8886. E-mail hipba@worldnet.att.net; web www.ari.net/holidayinn-west palmbeach. 200 rms, 11 story. Jan-Apr: S, D $79-$139; each addl $10; suites $150; under 18 free; lower rates rest of yr. Crib free. TV; cable (premium). Pool. Coffee in rms. Restaurants 6:30 am-2 pm, 5-10 pm. Rm serv. Bar from 4 pm. Ck-out 11 am. Meeting rms. Business center. In-rm modem link. Bellhops. Free airport transportation. Exercise equipt; sauna. Refrigerators avail. Cr cds: A, C, D, DS, JCB, MC, V.

D ≈ ⋈ ✕ ✕ ⋈ ⋈ SC ⊿

★ ★ **HOLIDAY INN-SUN SPREE RESORT.** *(3700 N Ocean Dr, Singer Island 33404) 3 mi N on I-95, exit 57A E to FL A1A, S 3 mi to N Ocean Dr, on Singer Island.* 561/848-3888; FAX 561/845-9754. E-mail sunspree@siservices.net. 222 rms, 8 story. Mid-Dec-mid-Apr: S, D $149-$199; each addl $10; suites $155-$350; under 19 free; lower rates rest of yr. Crib free. TV; cable (premium). Heated pool; wading pool, poolside serv. Supervised child's activities; ages 5-12. Coffee in rms. Restaurant 7 am-3 pm, 6-9 pm. Rm serv. Bar 11 am-midnight; entertainment. Ck-out noon. Meeting rms. Business servs avail. In-rm modem link. Bellhops. Gift shop. Tennis privileges. Golf privileges. Exercise equipt. Refrigerators. Balconies. On ocean. Cr cds: A, C, D, DS, JCB, MC, V.

D 🏃 ≈ ≈ ✕ ⋈ ⋈ SC

★ ★ **QUALITY RESORT.** *(3800 N Ocean Dr, Riviera Beach 33404) 3 mi N on I-95, exit 55 E to FL A1A S, 3 mi to N Ocean Dr, on Singer Island.* 561/848-5502; FAX 561/863-6560. 125 rms, 4 story. Mid-Dec-Apr: S, D $125-$195; each addl $10; suites $225; under 18 free; lower rates rest of yr. TV; cable (premium). Pool; wading pool, whirlpool, poolside serv. Restaurant 7:30 am-9 pm. Rm serv. Bar. Ck-out noon. Meeting rms. Business servs avail. Sundries. Lighted tennis. Exercise equipt; saunas. Lawn games. Refrigerators. Private patios, balconies. On beach. Cr cds: A, C, D, DS, ER, MC, V.

D 🏃 ≈ ≈ ✕ ⋈ SC

★ ★ **RADISSON SUITE INN-PALM BEACH AIRPORT.** *1808 Australian Ave S (33409), near Intl Airport.* 561/689-6888; FAX 561/683-5783. 175 suites, 6 story. Jan-Apr: suites $109-$139; each addl $5; under 18 free; lower rates rest of yr. Crib free. TV; cable (premium). Heated pool; whirlpool. Complimentary continental bkfst. Coffee in rms. Restaurant 6:30 am-2 pm. Rm serv. Bar 2:30-11:30 pm. Ck-out noon. Meeting rms. Business servs avail. In-rm modem link. Bellhops. Sundries. Gift shop. Free airport transportation. Exercise equipt. Minibars. Cr cds: A, C, D, DS, ER, JCB, MC, V.

D ≈ ≈ 🏃 ✕ ✕ ⋈ SC

Hotels

★ ★ ★ **EMBASSY SUITES.** *(4350 PGA Blvd, Palm Beach Gardens 33410) N on I-95, PGA Blvd exit 57.* 561/622-1000; FAX 561/626-6254. Web www.flhotels.com.palmbeachesembassy.html. 160 suites, 10 story. Jan-Apr: suites $175-$285; under 17 free; monthly, wkly rates; golf plan; lower rates rest of yr. Crib free. TV; cable (premium). Heated pool; wading pool, whirlpool. Complimentary full bkfst. Complimentary coffee in rms. Restaurant 5 am-11 pm. Bars 11-1 am. Ck-out noon. Coin lndry. Meeting rms. Business servs avail. In-rm modem link. Gift shop. Beauty shop. Free garage parking. Tennis. 18-hole golf privileges. Exercise equipt; sauna. Game rm. Refrigerators. Cr cds: A, C, D, DS, ER, MC, V.

D 🏃 🏃 ≈ ≈ 🏃 ⋈ ⋈ SC

★ ★ ★ **HILTON-PALM BEACH AIRPORT.** *150 Australian Ave (33406), near Intl Airport.* 561/684-9400; FAX 561/689-9421. 247 rms, 10 story. Jan-Apr: S, D $129-$199; each addl $10; suites $450-$550; family rates; wkend packages; lower rates rest of yr. TV; cable (premium). Heated pool; poolside serv. Coffee in rms. Restaurant 6:30 am-10 pm. Bar 4 pm-2 am. Ck-out noon. Meeting rms. Business servs avail. In-rm modem link. Gift shop. Valet parking. Free airport transportation. 2 lighted tennis courts. 18-hole golf privileges. Health club privileges. Lawn games. Built around Lake Cloud; dock, waterskiing, recreation area. Cr cds: A, C, D, DS, ER, JCB, MC, V.

D 🏊 🏃 🏃 ≈ ≈ ✕ ⋈ ⋈ SC

★ ★ ★ **MARRIOTT.** *(4000 RCA Blvd, Palm Beach Gardens 33410) N on I-95, PGA exit.* 561/622-8888; FAX 561/622-0052. E-mail pbgm301@aol.com; web www.pbg-marriott.com. 279 rms, 11 story. Jan-Apr: S, D $149-$207; each addl $10; suites $295-$395; under 6 free; golf plan; lower rates rest of yr. Crib free. TV; cable (premium). Coffee in rms. Heated pool; whirlpool, poolside serv. Restaurant 6:30 am-10 pm. Bars 11-3 am; entertainment. Ck-out noon. Convention facilities. Business servs avail. In-rm modem link. Concierge. Gift shop. Tennis privileges. 18-hole golf privileges. Exercise equipt; sauna, steam rm. Health club privileges. Refrigerators avail. Wet bar, bathrm phone in suites. Near beach. Tropical atmosphere. Cr cds: A, C, D, DS, JCB, MC, V.

D 🛉🦺🏊🏋🛫🏊🐾 SC

★ ★ ★ **OMNI.** *1601 Belvedere Rd (33406), near Intl Airport.* 561/689-6400; FAX 561/683-7150. 218 units, 15 story, 108 suites. Dec-Apr: S $149-$189; D $159-$199; each addl $10; suites $189-$229; under 12 free; lower rates rest of yr. Crib free. TV; cable (premium). Heated pool; whirlpool, poolside serv. Coffee in rms. Restaurant 6:30 am-10 pm. Bar. Ck-out noon. Meeting rms. In-rm modem link. Gift shop. Valet, garage parking. Free airport transportation. Lighted tennis. 18-hole golf privileges. Exercise equipt; sauna. Refrigerator, minibar in suites. Balconies. Atrium lobby with 40-ft sculpture. Extensive grounds; elaborate landscaping. Cr cds: A, C, D, DS, ER, MC, V.

D 🛉🦺🏊🏋🛫🏊🐾 SC

★ ★ ★ **SHERATON.** *630 Clearwater Park Rd (33401), near Intl Airport.* 561/833-1234; FAX 561/833-4689. 350 rms, 10 story. Mid-Dec-mid-Apr: S $179; D $189; each addl $15; suites $199-$209; lower rates rest of yr. Crib free. TV; cable (premium). Pool; whirlpool. Restaurant 6:30 am-10:30 pm; Fri, Sat to 11 pm. Bar 11 am-midnight; entertainment Tues-Sat. Ck-out noon. Meeting rms. Business servs avail. In-rm modem link. Gift shop. Free airport transportation. Lighted tennis. Exercise equipt. Some balconies. Cr cds: A, C, D, DS, MC, V.

D 🦺🏊🏋🛫🏊🐾 SC

Inns

★ ★ ★ **HIBISCUS HOUSE.** *501 30th St (33407).* 561/863-5633; res: 800/203-4927. Web www.hibiscushouse.com. 8 units, 2 story. Dec-Apr: S, D $85-$175; wkly rates; lower rates rest of yr. TV; cable. Heated pool. Complimentary full bkfst; evening refreshments. Ck-out noon, ck-in 2 pm. In-rm modem link. Street parking. Microwaves avail. Built 1922 for former mayor; period furnishings and antiques. All rms have balcony or terrace. Cr cds: A, D, MC, V.

🏊🏊🔥

★ ★ **TROPICAL GARDENS.** *419 Thirty-Second St (33407).* 561/848-4064; res: 800/736-4064. E-mail wpbbed@aol.com. 4 rms, 3 with shower only, 1 suite, 1 guest house. No rm phones. Nov-Apr: S, D $65-$125; suite $125; guest house $175; wkly rates; 2-day min (hols); lower rates rest of yr. TV; cable, VCR avail (movies). Complimentary continental bkfst. Ck-out 11 am, ck-in 1 pm. Street parking. Health club privileges. Pool. Some refrigerators, microwaves, minibars. Some balconies. Built in 1937; antiques, tropical plantings. Totally nonsmoking. Cr cds: A, DS, MC, V.

🏊🏊🏋

Resort

★ ★ ★ **PGA NATIONAL RESORT & SPA.** *(400 Ave of the Champions, Palm Beach Gardens 33418) 2 mi W of I-95 on PGA Blvd.* 561/627-2000; FAX 561/622-0261; res: 800/633-9150. Web www.pga-resorts.com. 339 units, 4 story. Early Jan-mid-Apr: S, D $309-$369; each addl $15; kit. cottages $450; each addl $50; under 17 free; lower rates rest of yr. Crib free. TV; cable. Heated pool; wading pool, whirlpool, poolside serv. Supervised child's activities (June-Sept); ages 5-12. Dining rms (see AREZZO and CRAB CATCHER). Bar 11-2 am. Ck-out noon, ck-in 3 pm. Convention facilities. Business center. In-rm modem link. Valet serv. Concierge. Barber, beauty shop. Pro shops. Valet parking. Airport transportation. 19 tennis courts, 12 lighted, pro. 6 golf courses, greens fee $115-$179, pro, 3 putting greens, 3 driving ranges. Boating. Beach volleyball. 5 croquet courts, pro. 3 indoor racquetball/handball courts. Exercise rm; sauna, steam rm. Spa. Refrigerators, minibars; microwaves avail. Balconies. 26-acre lake for sailing; sand beach. Cr cds: A, C, D, DS, ER, JCB, MC, V.

D 🚤🛉🦺🏊🏋🏊🐾 SC 🎿

Restaurants

✔★ **ALEYDA'S.** *1890 Okeechobee Blvd (33409).* 561/688-9033. Hrs: 11 am-10 pm; Fri to 11 pm; Sat 5-11 pm; Sun 5-9 pm. Mexican menu. Serv bar. A la carte entrees: dinner $3.50-$14.95. Child's meals. Specializes in fajitas, burritos, tamales. Authentic Mexican art & decor. Cr cds: A, D, DS, MC, V.

D

★ ★ **AREZZO.** *(See PGA National Resort & Spa)* 561/627-2000. Hrs: 5:30-9:30 pm; early-bird dinner to 7 pm. Res accepted. Italian menu. Bar. A la carte entrees: dinner $10.95-$20.95. Specializes in Italian cuisine. Own baking. Valet parking. Mosaic tiles. Cr cds: A, C, D, DS, ER, JCB, MC, V.

D 🏊♥

★ ★ **BANGKOK O-CHA.** *1687 Forum Pl, E of Palm Beach Mall.* 561/471-3163. Hrs: 11 am-2:30 pm, 5-10 pm; Fri, Sat 5-10:30 pm; Sun 5-9 pm. Closed Thanksgiving. Res accepted. Thai, Chinese menu. Wine, beer. A la carte entrees: lunch $4.95-$6.50, dinner $5.95-$15.95. Child's meals. Specialties: mee krob, tom ka kai, chicken Panang curry. Intimate dining; Thai art and architecture. Cr cds: A, DS, MC, V.

🏊♥

★ ★ **BEEFEEDER'S STEAK PIT & TAVERN.** *3208 Forest Hill Blvd (33406).* 561/964-1900. Hrs: 11:30 am-10 pm; Sun 5-10 pm; Sun, Mon 5-9 pm. Closed Thanksgiving, Dec 25; also Super Bowl Sun. Bar. Semi-a la carte: lunch $4.50-$8.95, dinner $9.95-$29.95. Child's meals. Specializes in beef, steak, lobster. Salad bar. Parking. English pub atmosphere. Cr cds: A, D, DS, MC, V.

D 🏊

★ ★ **THE BUCCANEER.** *(142 Lake Dr, Palm Beach Shores 33404) 3 mi N on US 1 to Blue Heron Blvd, at foot of bridge to Singer Island.* 561/844-3477. Hrs: 11:30 am-10 pm; early-bird dinner Sun-Thurs 5-6:15 pm. Res accepted. Continental menu. Bar. Semi-a la carte: lunch $5.95-$10.95, dinner $12-$24. Child's meals. Specializes in fresh seafood, steak. Valet parking. Nautical decor; view of Intracoastal Waterway. Cr cds: A, C, D, DS, MC, V.

D

★ ★ ★ **CAFE CHARDONNAY.** *(4533 PGA Blvd, Palm Beach Gardens 33410) Jct I-95N, PGA Blvd & Military Trail, in Garden Square Shoppes.* 561/627-2662. Hrs: 11:30 am-2:30 pm, 5:30-10 pm; Sat, Sun from 5:30 pm. Closed Thanksgiving, Dec 25. Res accepted. Wine list. Semi-a la carte: lunch $5.95-$10.95, dinner $16.95-$31.95. Child's meals. Specialties: Macadamia nut-crusted yellow tail snapper, grilled stuffed veal chop. Own baking. Split-level dining areas. Cr cds: A, D, MC, V.

D 🏊

★ ★ **CAFE DU PARC.** *(612 N Federal Hwy (US 1), Lake Park 33403)* 561/845-0529. Hrs: 5:30-10 pm. Closed Sept-mid-Oct; also Sun, Mon Apr-Aug & Sun mid-Oct-Nov. Res accepted. French menu. Wine list. Beer. A la carte entrees: dinner $16.50-$27. Complete meals: dinner $19.95-$28. Specialties: beef Wellington, medallions de veau Normande. Own desserts. French Provincial decor in restored house. Paintings; antique French plate collection. Jacket. Cr cds: A, C, D, MC, V.

D 🏊

★ ★ **CAFE PROTEGE.** *2400 Metrocentre Blvd (33407).* 561/688-2001. Hrs: 11:30 am-2 pm, 5:30-9 pm; Mon to 2 pm; Sat from 5:30 pm. Closed Sun. Res accepted. Bar. Wine list. Semi-a la carte: lunch $8-$13, dinner $16-$27. Buffet: lunch $10.95. Child's meals. Daily and seasonal menu. Parking. At the Florida Culinary Institute; open kitchen to view chefs. Cr cds: A, MC, V.

D

★ ★ ★ **CRAB CATCHER.** *(See PGA National Resort & Spa)* 561/627-2000. Web www.pga-resorts.com. Hrs: 5:30-10 pm. Closed Sun. Res accepted. Bar. Wine list. A la carte entrees: dinner $13.95-$33.95. Specializes in Florida seafood. Own pastries, sauces. Piano bar. Valet parking. Key West decor; handcarved artifacts. Cr cds: A, C, D, DS, ER, JCB, MC, V.

★ **GALLEY.** *90 Lake Dr (33404). 561/848-1492.* Hrs: 7 am-9 pm; Mon, Tues to 2 pm. Closed Thanksgiving, Dec 25. Bar. Semi-a la carte: bkfst $3-$7, lunch $2-$10, dinner $10-$25. Child's meals. Specializes in seafood. Salad bar. Outdoor dining. On marina. Cr cds: A, MC, V.

★ **GREEK VILLAGE.** *6108 S Dixie Hwy (33405). 561/588-5080.* Hrs: 11 am-2:30 pm, 5-9:30 pm; Sat, Sun from 5 pm. Res accepted. Greek menu. Wine, beer. A la carte entrees: lunch $3.95-$9.95, dinner $7.95-$14.95. Specialties: Greek Village salad, moussaka, stuffed grape leaves. Parking. Intimate atmosphere. Cr cds: MC, V.

★★ **MORTON'S STEAKHOUSE.** *777 S Flagler Dr (33401), in Phillips Point Bldg. 561/835-9664.* Hrs: 5:30-11 pm; Sun 5-10 pm. Closed major hols. Res accepted. Bar. Wine list. A la carte entrees: dinner $18-$29. Specialties: porterhouse steak, whole baked Maine lobster, shrimp Alexander. Valet parking. Extensive mahogany and brick dining area; original artwork, Oriental rugs. Cr cds: A, C, JCB, MC, V.

★★ **NO ANCHOVIES.** *(2650 PGA Blvd, Palm Beach Gardens 33410) N on I-95, exit PGA Blvd, then 2 mi E. 561/622-7855.* Hrs: 11:30 am-2:30 pm, 5-11 pm; Sun 5-10 pm. Closed Jan 1, Dec 25. Italian menu. Bar. Semi-a la carte: lunch $4.95-$7.95, dinner $6.95-$16.95. Child's meals. Specialties: scampi Livornese with capellini, veal piccata, rigatoni a la vodka. Parking. Patio dining. Informal dining; eatery only uses fresh ingredients. Cr cds: A, C, D, MC, V.

★★ **PESCATORE.** *200 Clematis St (33401). 561/837-6633.* Hrs: 11:30 am-4 pm, 5-10:30 pm; Fri, Sat to midnight; Sun 5-10:30 pm. Res accepted. Italian menu. Bar. Wine list. A la carte entrees: lunch $6.95-$12.95, dinner $8.95-$20. Specializes in pasta, seafood. Entertainment Fri, Sat. Valet parking wkends. Outdoor dining. Mediterranean atmosphere. Cr cds: A, D, ER, MC, V.

★ **PRONTI'S ITALIAN KITCHEN.** *(1440 Tenth St, Lake Park 33403) N on I-95, exit North Lake. 561/842-3457.* Hrs: 4-10 pm; Fri, Sat to 11 pm. Closed July 4, Thanksgiving, Dec 25. Italian menu. Serv bar. Semi-a la carte: dinner $6.95-$15.95. Child's meals. Specializes in pasta, veal, seafood. Parking. Autographed photos of celebrities adorn the brick walls; NYC artifacts complete the decor. Cr cds: A, DS, MC, V.

★★ **RIVER HOUSE.** *(2373 PGA Blvd, Palm Beach Gardens 33410) I-95N to exit 57, then 2¼ mi E. 561/694-1188.* Hrs: 5-10:30 pm; Sun to 10 pm. Closed Thanksgiving, Dec 25. Bar. Semi-a la carte: dinner $12.95-$28.95. Child's meals. Specialties: fish in parchment, grilled swordfish, lamb chops. Valet parking. On Intracoastal Waterway; boat dock. Cr cds: A, C, D, DS, MC, V.

★★ **RUTH'S CHRIS STEAK HOUSE.** *(661 US 1, North Palm Beach 33408) 561/863-0660.* Web www.ruthschris.com. Hrs: 5-10 pm. Res accepted. Bar. A la carte entrees: dinner $17.95-$29.95. Specializes in steak, prime beef, fresh seafood. Valet parking. Casual steak house atmosphere. Cr cds: A, C, D, ER, JCB, MC, V.

★ **TEXARADO.** *(2450 PGA Blvd, Palm Beach Gardens 33410) 561/775-7772.* Hrs: 5-10 pm; Fri, Sat to 10:30 pm. Closed some hols. Bar. Semi-a la carte: dinner $6.50-$18.95. Child's meals. Specializes in steak, seafood. Southwestern decor. Cr cds: A, MC, V.

★★ **THIS IS IT PUB.** *424 24th St (33407). 561/833-4997.* Hrs: 11:30 am-10 pm; Sat from 5:30 pm. Closed Sun Memorial Day-Labor Day. Res accepted. Bar. Semi-a la carte: lunch $9. Complete meals: dinner $25-$33. Specialties: smoked salmon soup, rack of lamb, seafood chowder. Valet parking. Seascapes, nautical artifacts. Antique bar; English pub atmosphere. Cr cds: A, D, MC, V.

★★★ **VILLA MEDITERRANEA.** *205 Southern Blvd (33405). 561/655-8455.* Hrs: 11 am-2 pm, 4:30-9 pm; Sat from 4:30 pm; early-bird dinner 4:30-6 pm. Closed Mon. Res accepted. Mediterranean menu. Bar. A la carte entrees: lunch $4.95-$9.95, dinner $9-$24. Specializes in steak, fresh seafood, pasta. Entertainment. Valet parking wkends. Mediterranean decor. Original artwork. Cr cds: A, D, DS, MC, V.

★★ **WATERWAY CAFE.** *(2300 PGA Blvd, Palm Beach Gardens 33410) I-95 to PGA Boulevard, then 2 mi E. 561/694-1700.* Web www.waterwaycafe.com. Hrs: 11:30 am-10 pm; wkends to 11 pm. Res accepted. Bar to midnight. A la carte entrees: lunch $6.95-$9.95, dinner $9.95-$17.95. Child's meals. Specialties: grilled shrimp and blackened mahi-mahi, smoked chicken penne pasta, brick oven pizza. Entertainment. Outdoor dining. Open kitchen area with brick oven. On Intracoastal Waterway. Cr cds: A, MC, V.

★★ **ZUCCARELLI'S.** *1937 N Military Trail (33409), in Pine Trail Center. 561/686-7739.* Hrs: 11 am-10 pm; Fri & Sat to 11 pm; Sun from 3:30 pm. Closed most major hols. Res accepted. Italian menu. Semi-a la carte: lunch $3.35-$10.50, dinner $7.50-$25.50. Specializes in fresh seafood, pasta. Own sausage. Murals of Italian scenes. Cr cds: A, MC, V.

White Springs (B-3)

(See also Lake City, Live Oak)

Founded 1826 **Pop** 704 **Elev** 138 ft **Area code** 904 **Zip** 32096

Considered sacred by the Native Americans who came here to recuperate after battle, the springs are esteemed by many for their alleged medicinal qualities. White Springs is on the north bank of the Suwannee River and is headquarters for the Suwannee River Water Management District.

What to See and Do

Stephen Foster State Folk Culture Center. Located on the Suwannee River near the Georgia-Florida state line, this 250-acre center perpetuates the crafts, music and legends of early and contemporary Floridians. A carillon, in a 200-ft tower, gives daily concerts. In the base of tower are two animated dioramas, musical instruments and Foster memorabilia; visitor center has eight animated dioramas. Tours of the visitor center and tower. Special events throughout the yr. (Daily) W edge of city on US 41. Phone 904/397-2733. Per car ¢¢

Annual Event

Florida Folk Festival. Stephen Foster Center (see). Entertaining and educational heritage presentations; traditional singers, tale-tellers, fiddlers, and dancers; craftsmen of native woods and foliage; workshops; puppet shows; ethnic foods. Phone 904/488-1484. Memorial Day wkend.

Winter Haven (E-4)

(See also Haines City, Lakeland, Lake Wales)

Settled 1883 **Pop** 24,725 **Elev** 170 ft **Area code** 941 **Web** www.winterhavenfl.com
Information Chamber of Commerce, 401 Avenue B NW, PO Box 1420, 33882-1420; 941/293-2138.

Attracting more than one million visitors a year—most of whom come to see Cypress Gardens, many of whom stay on to enjoy the freshwater lakes in this area—Winter Haven is a town bolstered by tourism, citrus growing and processing and light manufacturing and distribution.

What to See and Do

⭐ **Cypress Gardens.** Towering cypress trees shelter more than 8,000 varieties of exotic plants and flowers at one of the world's most famous botanical gardens. The 223-acre theme park includes shows, museums, a children's amusement ride and game area; elaborate model railroad; and more than 15 shops in a replica of an antebellum town. Highlights include Wings of Wonder, a butterfly conservatory showcasing up to 1,000 free-flying butterflies daily; Cypress Roots, a museum that imparts the history of Florida's first major attraction; and Kodak's Island in the Sky, a 16-story viewing and photo platform provides a panoramic view of the area. Daily shows include Ski Extreme; Moscow on Ice Live; and Variété Internationalé, featuring entertainment from around the world. Electric boat rides and pontoon boat cruises provide scenic trips through the park. Lovely Southern belles stroll through the lush gardens, which bloom all yr. Strollers; cameras on loan; kennel. Gardens (daily). 4 mi SW on FL 540, off US 27. Phone 941/324-2111. ¢¢¢¢¢

Water Ski Museum/Hall of Fame. Museum depicts the colorful history of water skiing; the Hall of Fame honors the pioneers of the sport. (Mon-Fri; closed hols) 799 Overlook Dr. Phone 941/324-2472. **Free.**

Motels

⭐ **BUDGET HOST DRIFTWOOD MOTOR LODGE.** *970 Cypress Gardens Blvd (FL 540) (33880).* 941/294-4229; FAX 941/293-2089. 22 rms, 2 kits. Dec-Apr: S, D $42-$62; each addl $6; kit. units $8 addl; lower rates rest of yr. Crib $4. Pet accepted. TV; cable. Heated pool. Complimentary continental bkfst. Restaurant adj 11 am-10 pm. Ck-out 11 am. Lawn games. Some refrigerators. Cr cds: A, DS, MC, V.

⭐ **CHAIN OF LAKES BEACH RESORT.** *1823 Cypress Gardens Blvd (33884).* 941/324-6320; FAX 941/324-7894. E-mail colbr@gate.net; web www.chainolakesbeachresort.com/colbr. 25 rms, 2 story, 20 kits. Apr-Mid-Nov: S, D $150-$300; each addl $9; wkly rates; lower rates rest of yr. Crib avail. TV; cable. Heated pool. Restaurant nearby. Ck-out 11 am. Coin lndry. Lawn games. Microwaves; some refrigerators. Private patios. Picnic tables, grill. On Lake Roy; dock. Cr cds: A, DS, MC, V.

⭐ **DAYS INN.** *200 Cypress Gardens Blvd (33880).* 941/299-1151; FAX 941/297-8019. 97 rms, 2 story. Mar-mid-Apr: S $74; D $78; each addl $4; lower rates rest of yr. Crib free. TV; cable. Pool. Complimentary continental bkfst. Ck-out noon. Coin lndry. Meeting rm. Some refrigerators; microwaves avail. Cr cds: A, C, D, DS, JCB, MC, V.

⭐⭐ **GARDEN LODGE.** *2000 Cypress Gardens Blvd (33884).* 941/324-6334; FAX 941/324-9131. 36 rms, 1-2 story, 14 kits. Late Dec-late Apr: S $55-$60; D $60-$65; each addl $8; kit. units $5-$10 addl; wkly rates; lower rates rest of yr. Crib $5. TV; cable. Pool. Complimentary coffee in lobby. Restaurant opp 7 am-10 pm. Ck-out 11 am. Refrigerators. Opp Lake Ina. Cr cds: A, C, D, DS, MC, V.

⭐⭐ **HOLIDAY INN.** *1150 3rd St SW (33880).* 941/294-4451; FAX 941/293-9829. 225 rms, 2 story. Jan-mid-Apr: S, D $69-$129; each addl $10; under 18 free; lower rates rest of yr. Crib free. Pet accepted. TV; cable (premium). Pool; wading pool. Coffee in rms. Restaurant 6:30 am-10 pm. Rm serv. Bar 3 pm-midnight. Ck-out noon. Coin lndry. Meeting rms. Business servs avail. In-rm modem link. Some refrigerators; microwaves avail. Cr cds: A, C, D, DS, JCB, MC, V.

⭐⭐ **HOLIDAY INN CYPRESS GARDENS.** *(339 US 27 N, Dundee 33838) E on FL 542 to US 27.* 941/439-1591; FAX 941/439-5297. E-mail hicypdd@gte.net. 100 rms, 2 story. Jan-Mar: S, D $64-$95; each addl $8; under 18 free; lower rates rest of yr. Crib free. TV; cable (premium). Heated pool; wading pool. Coffee in rms. Restaurant 6:30 am-2 pm, 5-9 pm. Rm serv. Bar; entertainment Tues-Sat. Ck-out 11 am. Meeting rms. Business servs avail. Cr cds: A, C, D, DS, MC, V.

⭐ **HOWARD JOHNSON.** *1300 3rd St SW (US 17S) (33880).* 941/294-7321; FAX 941/299-1673. 98 rms, 2 story. Dec-Apr: S, D $74-$95; each addl $7; under 18 free; lower rates rest of yr. Crib free. Pet accepted. TV; cable (premium). Heated pool; wading pool. Complimentary continental bkfst. Restaurant 11 am-9 pm. Bar 1 pm-2 am. Ck-out noon. Coin lndry. Valet serv. Miniature golf. Game rm. Lawn games. Some refrigerators. Private patios, balconies. Picnic table. Cr cds: A, C, D, DS, ER, JCB, MC, V.

✔⭐ **QUALITY INN TOWN HOUSE.** *975 Cypress Gardens Blvd (33880).* 941/294-4104. 32 rms, 6 kits. Feb-Apr, late Dec: S, D $63.50-$72; each addl $5; lower rates rest of yr. Crib $4. TV; cable. Heated pool. Complimentary continental bkfst. Ck-out 11 am. Coin lndry. Lawn games. Some refrigerators. Cr cds: A, C, D, DS, ER, JCB, MC, V.

⭐ **SCOTTISH INN.** *1901 Cypress Gardens Blvd (33884).* 941/324-3954; FAX 941/324-5998. 23 rms, 8 kit. units, 3 kit. apts. Dec-Apr: S, D $46-$62; each addl $6; kit. units $8 addl; wkly rates; lower rates rest of yr. Crib $4. TV; cable. Complimentary coffee in lobby. Restaurant nearby. Ck-out 11 am. Coin lndry. Refrigerators. Picnic tables, grills. Cr cds: A, DS, MC, V.

Restaurant

⭐⭐ **CHRISTY'S SUNDOWN.** *US 17S (33880), at Ave K & 3rd St SW.* 941/293-0069. Hrs: 11:30 am-10:30 pm; Sat from 5 pm. Closed Sun; major hols. Res accepted. Greek, Amer menu. Bar to 1:30 am. Semi-a la carte: lunch $3.95-$9, dinner $9.95-$26.95. Child's meals. Specializes in fresh seafood, broiled steak, veal. Own baking. Entertainment. Parking. Antiques, artwork. Family-owned. Cr cds: A, DS, MC, V.

Winter Park (D-5)

(See also Altamonte Springs, Orlando)

Founded 1882 **Pop** 22,242 **Elev** 94 ft **Area code** 407 **Web** www.winterparkcc.org
Information Chamber of Commerce, 150 N New York Ave, PO Box 280, 32790; 407/644-8281.

Winter Park is a college town, vacation retreat and artist's haven.

What to See and Do

Rollins College (1885). (2,600 students) Coeducational, private, liberal arts. Knowles Memorial Chapel's Spanish/Mediterranean architecture make it the most distinctive building on campus. Walk of Fame is bordered by more than 500 inscribed stones from birthplaces and houses of famous people. Theater and fine arts museum host plays and exhibitions. Park & Holt Aves, on 67 acres bordering Lake Virginia. Phone 407/646-2000.

Scenic Boat Tour. A narrated 1-hr cruise through canals and three lakes for views of estates, Kraft Azalea Gardens, Rollins College and other sights. Departs hourly. (Daily; no cruises Dec 25) E end of Morse Blvd at Lake Osceola. Phone 407/644-4056. ¢¢¢

The Charles Hosmer Morse Museum of American Art. Turn-of-the-century American arts by Tiffany and other masters include leaded stained-glass windows, blown glass, lamps; pottery; 19th-century American paintings; furniture; also special exhibits. (Tues-Sat, also Sun afternoon; closed hols) 445 Park Ave N. Phone 407/645-5311. ¢¢

Motels

✔★★★ **BEST WESTERN MT VERNON INN.** 110 S Orlando Ave (32789), I-4 exit 45, then 1 mi E to Orlando Ave (US 17/92), turn left 2 blks. 407/647-1166; FAX 407/647-8011. Web www.bestwestern.com/thisco/bw/10020/10020-b.html. 147 rms, 2 story. S $59-$88; D $59-$95; each addl $6; under 18 free; wknd rates. Crib $6. TV; cable (premium). Pool; poolside serv. Restaurant 7 am-2 pm. Rm serv. Bar 11-2 am; entertainment. Ck-out 11 am. Meeting rms. Business servs avail. Valet serv. Sundries. Health club privileges. Many refrigerators. Some balconies. Opp lake. Cr cds: A, C, D, DS, JCB, MC, V.

★★ **DAYS INN.** 901 N Orlando Ave (32789). 407/644-8000; FAX 407/644-0032. 105 rms, 2 story. Feb-mid-Apr: S $69; D $79; each addl $6; under 18 free; higher rates: Daytona 500, art show; lower rates rest of yr. Crib free. TV; cable (premium). Pool. Meeting rm. Business servs avail. Some refrigerators, microwaves. Cr cds: A, C, D, DS, ER, MC, V.

★★ **FAIRFIELD INN BY MARRIOTT.** 951 N Wymore Rd (32789). 407/539-1955. 135 rms, 3 story. S, D $59; under 18 free; higher rates special events. Crib free. TV; cable (premium). Heated pool. Complimentary continental bkfst. Restaurant nearby. Ck-out noon. Business servs avail. Cr cds: A, C, D, DS, MC, V.

Motor Hotel

★★ **LANGFORD.** 300 E New England Ave (32789). 407/644-3400; FAX 407/628-1952. E-mail langford@magicnet.net. 218 rms, 2-7 story, 10 suites, 82 kits. S, D $49.50-$95; each addl $10; suites $200; kits. addl $10; under 18 free; monthly rates; higher rates art show. Crib free. Pet accepted, some restrictions; $25. TV; cable (premium). Heated pool; poolside serv. Sauna, steam rm. Restaurant 7 am-10 pm. Rm serv. Bar 10-1 am; entertainment. Ck-out 11 am. Coin lndry. Meeting rms. Business servs avail. In-rm modem link. Bellhops. Valet serv. Sundries. Beauty shop. Game rm. Balconies. Cr cds: A, D, MC, V.

Hotel

★★★ **PARK PLAZA.** 307 Park Ave S (32789). 407/647-1072; FAX 407/647-4081; res: 800/228-7220. Web www.orl.com/park. 27 rms, 2 story. S, D $80-$200; higher rates special events. Children over 5 yrs only. TV; cable, VCR avail. Complimentary continental bkfst. Restaurant 11:30 am-3 pm, 6-11 pm. Ck-out noon. Business servs avail. In-rm modem link. Concierge. Free valet parking. Balcony. Restored hotel; antiques, oriental rugs, paintings. Flower, chocolate shops in lobby. Rms individually decorated. Overlooks park. Totally nonsmoking. Cr cds: A, D, MC, V.

Inns

★★ **FORTNIGHTLY.** 377 E Fairbanks Ave (32789). 407/645-4440. 5 rms, 2 story, 2 suites. S, D, suites $85-$105; each addl $10; wkly rates. TV in sitting rm. Complimentary full bkfst. Restaurant nearby. Ck-out 11 am, ck-in 2 pm. Restored 1920s house; oak floors, clawfoot bathtubs, pedestal sinks, original fixtures. Totally nonsmoking. Cr cds: MC, V.

★★ **THURSTON HOUSE.** (851 Lake Ave, Maitland 32751) I-4 exit 46 (Lee Rd) E, then N on Wymore, E on Kennedy 3/4 mi. 407/539-1911; FAX 407/539-0365; res: 800/843-2721. E-mail jball54@aol.com; web www.thurstonhouse.com. 4 rms, 2 story. S, D $100-$110. Children over 12 yrs only. TV in sitting rm; cable. Complimentary continental bkfst. Ck-out 11 am, ck-in 3 pm. Business servs avail. In-rm modem link. Restored 1885 Queen Anne Victorian house overlooking lake on secluded wooded property. Antiques; screened porches. Totally nonsmoking. Cr cds: A, MC, V.

Restaurants

✔★★ **CHINA GARDEN.** 118 S Semoran Blvd (32792). 407/671-2120. Hrs: 11:30 am-10 pm; Sat noon-11 pm; Sun from noon. Closed Thanksgiving. Res accepted. Chinese menu. Wine, beer. Semi-a la carte: lunch $4.25-$5.50, dinner $6.25-$15. Specialties: moo shu pork, ginger scallion lobster, braised duck with black mushrooms. Oriental decor. Cr cds: A, DS, MC, V.

★★ **MAISON DES CRÊPES.** 348 N Park Ave (32789). 407/647-4469. Hrs: 11:30 am-3 pm, 5:30-10 pm; Mon to 3 pm; early-bird dinner 5:30-7 pm. Closed Sun; major hols. Res accepted. French menu. Semi-a la carte: lunch $8.25-$13, dinner $12.95-$27. Specialties: filet Royal, crêpes. Country French decor; original artwork. Cr cds: A, C, D, MC, V.

★★ **PARK PLAZA GARDENS.** 319 Park Ave S (32719). 407/645-2475. Web www.orlandoonline.com/parkplaza.htm. Hrs: 11 am-2 pm, 6-10 pm; Fri, Sat to 11 pm, Sun 6-9 pm; Sun brunch 11 am-3 pm. Closed Jan 1, Memorial Day, July 4, Dec 25. Res accepted. Continental menu. Bar 11 am-midnight. Semi-a la carte: lunch $6.95-$12.95. A la carte entrees: dinner $19.95-$28.95. Sun brunch $21.95. Specializes in seafood, veal, beef. Own baking. Pianist Fri-Sun. Glass-enclosed garden dining. Tableside cooking. New Orleans decor. Cr cds: A, C, D, DS, JCB, MC, V.

✔★ **TOUCAN WILLIE'S.** (829 Eyrie St, Oviedo 32765) N on FL 426. 407/366-6225. Hrs: 11 am-midnight; Sun 4-10 pm; Sun brunch 11 am-2 pm; early-bird dinner 4:30-6 pm. Bar to midnight; wkends to 1:30 am. Semi-a la carte: lunch, dinner $5.95-$16.95. Child's meals. Specializes in fresh seafood, barbecued ribs. Entertainment Fri, Sat. Parking. Outdoor dining on porch. Caribbean decor. Cr cds: A, C, D, DS, MC, V.

✔★★ **WINNIE'S ORIENTAL GARDEN.** 1346 Orange Ave (32789). 407/629-2111. Hrs: 11 am-10 pm; Fri to 10:30 pm; Sat 4-10:30 pm. Closed Sun; Memorial Day, Thanksgiving. Res accepted. Chinese menu. Bar. Semi-a la carte: lunch $5.25-$7.95, dinner $7.95-$16.95. Specializes in Pacific Rim cuisine. Contemporary, elegant decor. Totally nonsmoking. Cr cds: A, MC, V.

Zephyrhills (E-4)

(See also Dade City, Lakeland, Tampa)

Pop 8,220 **Elev** 97 ft **Area code** 813 **E-mail** zephcofc@innet.com
Information Chamber of Commerce, 38415 5th Ave, 33540; 813/782-1913.

What to See and Do

Hillsborough River State Park. A 2,994-acre park; one of Florida's oldest. Swinging bridge spans river to nature trail through stands of hammock. The Hillsborough River and rapids are the features of this park. Swimming; fishing; canoeing. Nature trails; biking. Picnic area, concession. Campground (hookups, dump station). Standard hrs, fees. 6 mi SW on US 301. Phone 813/987-6771. Nearby is

Ft Foster Historic Site. Reconstruction of fort (ca 1835) built during Second Seminole War; on original site. Living history presentation. Tours (weather permitting) depart from Hillsborough River State Park. Phone 813/987-6771. ¢¢

Motel

★ ★ **BEST WESTERN.** *5734 Gall Blvd (US 301) (33541), 1/2 mi N of jct FL 54.* 813/782-5527; FAX 813/783-7102. 52 rms, 2 story. Mid-Nov-Apr: S, D $69; each addl $5; under 13 free; lower rates rest of yr. Crib $5. TV; cable (premium). Pool. Complimentary continental bkfst. Restaurant adj 6 am-9 pm. Ck-out 11 am. Meeting rm. Business servs avail. In-rm modem link. Refrigerators. Picnic tables. Cr cds: A, C, D, DS, MC, V.

🏊 ⤨ 🐾 SC

Georgia

Population: 6,478,216
Land area: 58,876 square miles
Elevation: 0-4,784 feet
Highest point: Brasstown Bald Mountain (Between Towns, Union counties)
Entered Union: Fourth of original 13 states (January 1, 1788)
Capital: Atlanta
Motto: Wisdom, Justice and Moderation
State flower: Cherokee rose
State bird: Brown thrasher
State tree: Live oak
State fair: Late October, 1999, in Macon
Time zone: Eastern
Web: www.georgia.org

Georgia, beloved for its antebellum gentility, then devastated by General William Tecumseh Sherman's march to the sea, is now a vibrant, busy state, typifying the economic growth of the New South. Founded with philanthropic and military aims, the only colony where rum and slavery were forbidden, the state nevertheless has the dubious honor of accepting the last shipment of slaves to this country. It boasts Savannah, one of the oldest planned cities in the country, and Atlanta, one of the newest of the South's great cities, rebuilt atop Civil War ashes.

The Georgia Colony was founded by James Oglethorpe on behalf of a private group of English trustees and was named for King George II of England. Georgia's barrier islands not only sheltered the fledgling colony, they provided a bulwark on the Spanish Main for English forts to oppose Spanish Florida and helped end the centuries-old struggle for domination among Spanish, French and English along the South Atlantic Coast.

Today a year-round vacation mecca, the Golden Isles were at times Native American hunting lands, vast sea island plantations, fishing communities isolated after the Civil War and rich men's private preserves. The Colony trustees brought English artisans to found strong colonies at Savannah, Brunswick and Darien, where Scottish Highlanders introduced golf to the New World. The Cherokee made early peace with Oglethorpe and remained within the state to set up the Republic of the Cherokee Nation a century later. Gradually, however, all Native American lands of both Creek and Cherokee were ceded; the Cherokees were banished and their lands, including the capital, distributed by lottery.

From their settlements at Savannah, Brunswick and the coastal islands, Georgia colonists followed the rivers (many of them flowing north) to found inland ports such as Augusta. Colonial boundaries were extended to the Mississippi River by the State of Georgia, but the unfortunate manipulations of land speculators in the legislature deeded all of Mississippi, Alabama, Tennessee, and more, for sale as the Yazoo Tract for one-and-one-half cents an acre. Though repudiated by a subsequent legislature and declared unconstitutional by the Supreme Court, the lands were gone forever, and Georgia no longer extended from the Mississippi to the sea. It is, however, still the largest state east of the Mississippi.

Georgia's lot in the Civil War was a harsh one from the time Sherman opened his campaign in Georgia on May 4, 1864, until he achieved the Union objective of splitting the South from the Mississippi to the sea. Reconstruction ushered in the reign of carpetbaggers and a long, slow recovery.

Georgia boasts many firsts: the *Savannah,* the first steamship to cross the ocean (1819); America's first nuclear-powered merchant ship, the *Savannah* (1959); the first big American gold strike (1828); the cotton gin, invented by Eli Whitney (1793); and the first use of ether as an anesthetic (1842), by Georgia doctor Crawford W. Long.

Georgia produces peanuts, pecans, cotton, peaches, wood pulp and paper products. Near Atlanta, a number of national manufacturing and commercial concerns contribute to a diversified economy. Georgia marble is prized the world over.

Georgia boasts many wonders, from its Blue Ridge vacationlands in the north, where Brasstown Bald Mountain rises 4,784 feet, to the deep "trembling earth" of the ancient and mysterious Okefenokee Swamp bordering Florida. Stone Mountain, a giant hunk of rock that rises from the plain near Atlanta, is the world's largest granite exposure. The coastal Golden Isles, set off by the mysterious Marshes of Glynn, support moss-festooned oaks that grow down to the white sand beaches. Visitors still pan for gold in the country's oldest gold mining town, Dahlonega, and find semiprecious stones in the Blue Ridge.

Historical attractions are everywhere, from the world's largest brick fort near Savannah to the late President Franklin D. Roosevelt's "Little White House" at Warm Springs. There is the infamous Confederate prison at Andersonville and the still lavish splendor of the cottage colony of 60 millionaires of the Jekyll Island Club, now a state-owned resort. The battlefield marking Sherman's campaign before Atlanta and the giant ceremonial mounds of indigenous Native Americans are equally important national shrines.

Tourism is one of Georgia's primary industries. The state's Visitor Information Centers, which are staffed year-round, offer brochures and computerized information to travelers on major highways.

When to Go/Climate

Short winters and mild temperatures are the rule in Georgia. Summers are hot and humid in the southern part of the state; winters can be cold and include snowfall in the northern regions.

AVERAGE HIGH/LOW TEMPERATURES (°F)

ATLANTA

Jan 50/32	**May** 80/59	**Sept** 82/64
Feb 55/35	**June** 86/66	**Oct** 73/52
Mar 64/43	**July** 88/70	**Nov** 63/43
Apr 73/50	**Aug** 87/69	**Dec** 54/35

SAVANNAH

Jan 60/38	**May** 84/63	**Sept** 85/68
Feb 62/41	**June** 89/69	**Oct** 78/57
Mar 70/48	**July** 91/72	**Nov** 70/48
Apr 78/55	**Aug** 90/72	**Dec** 62/41

Parks and Recreation Finder

Directions to and information about the parks and recreation areas below are given under their respective town/city sections. Please refer to those sections for details.

NATIONAL PARK AND RECREATION AREAS

Key to abbreviations: I.H.S. = International Historic Site; I.P.M. = International Peace Memorial; N.B. = National Battlefield; N.B.P. = National Battlefield Park; N.B.C. = National Battlefield & Cemetery; N.C. = National Conservation Area; N.E.M. = National Expansion Memorial; N.F. = National Forest; N.G. = National Grassland; N.H. = National Historical Park; N.H.C. = National Heritage Corridor; N.H.S. = National Historic Site; N.L. = National Lakeshore; N.M. = National Monument; N.M.P. = National Military Park; N.Mem. = National Memorial; N.P. = National Park; N.Pres. = National Preserve; N.R. = National Recreational Area; N.R.R. = National Recreational River; N.Riv. = National River; N.S. = National Seashore; N.S.R. = National Scenic Riverway; N.S.T. = National Scenic Trail; N.Sc. = National Scientific Reserve; N.V.M. = National Volcanic Monument.

Place Name	Listed Under
Andersonville N.H.S.	ANDERSONVILLE
Appalachian N.S.T.	DAHLONEGA
Chattahoochee N.F.	DAHLONEGA
Chickamauga and Chattanooga N.M.P.	same
Cumberland Island N.S.	same
Fort Frederica N.M.	same
Fort Pulaski N.M.	same
Jimmy Carter N.H.S.	AMERICUS
Kennesaw Mountain N.B.P.	same
Martin Luther King, Jr, N.H.S.	ATLANTA
Ocmulgee N.M.	same

STATE PARK AND RECREATION AREAS

Key to abbreviations: I.P. = Interstate Park; S.A.P. = State Archaeological Park; S.B. = State Beach; S.C. = State Conservation Area; S.C.P. = State Conservation Park; S.Cp. = State Campground; S.F. = State Forest; S.G. = State Garden; S.H.A. = State Historic Area; S.H.P. = State Historic Park; S.H.S. = State Historic Site; S.M.P. = State Marine Park; S.N.A. = State Natural Area; S.P. = State Park; S.P.C. = State Public Campground; S.R. = State Reserve; S.R.A. = State Recreation Area; S.Res. = State Reservoir; S.Res.P. = State Resort Park; S.R.P = State Rustic Park.

Place Name	Listed Under
Alexander H. Stephens S.P.	WASHINGTON
Amicalola Falls S.P.	DAHLONEGA
Crooked River S.P.	CUMBERLAND ISLAND N.S.
Florence Marina S.P.	LUMPKIN

CALENDAR HIGHLIGHTS

JANUARY

Georgia Heritage Festival (Savannah). Walking tours, open house at historic sites, crafts show, waterfront festival, parade, concerts, Georgia Day. Phone Historic Savannah Foundation 912/233-7787.

MARCH

Auto racing (Atlanta). Atlanta Motor Speedway. NASCAR Winston Cup, Busch Grand National, IMSA and ARCA events. Phone 770/946-4211.

Cherry Blossom Festival (Macon). Historic tours, concerts, fireworks, hot air ballons, sporting events, parade. Phone 912/751-7429.

Augusta Invitational Rowing Regatta (Augusta). At Augusta Riverfront Marina.

APRIL

Masters Golf Tournament (Augusta). Augusta National Golf Course. Phone 706/667-6000.

Seafood Festival (Savannah). Waterfront. Restaurants offer samples; entertainment, arts and crafts. Contact Savannah Waterfront Association 912/234-0295.

Spring Tour of Homes (Athens). Held by Athens-Clarke Heritage Foundation. Contact Fire Hall #2; phone 706/353-1801 or -1820.

SEPTEMBER

US 10 K Classic and Family Sports Festival (Marietta). Phone 770/432-0100.

OCTOBER

Georgia State Fair (Macon). Central City Park. Grandstand shows, midway, exhibit buildings. Phone 912/746-7184.

DECEMBER

Christmas in Savannah (Savannah). Month-long celebration includes tours of houses, historical presentations, parades, music, caroling and cultural events. Phone 800/444-CHARM.

Fort McAllister S.P.	FORT McALLISTER HISTORIC PARK
Fort Mountain S.P.	CHATSWORTH
Fort Yargo S.P.	WINDER
Franklin D. Roosevelt S.P.	PINE MOUNTAIN
General Coffee S.P.	DOUGLAS
Georgia Veterans Memorial S.P.	CORDELE
Indian Springs S.P.	same
John Tanner S.P.	CARROLLTON
Kolomoki Mounds S.P.	BLAKELY
Laura S. Walker S.P.	WAYCROSS
Red Top Mountain S.P.	CARTERSVILLE
Reed Bingham S.P.	ADEL
Seminole S.P.	BAINBRIDGE
Stephen C. Foster S.P.	OKEFENOKEE SWAMP
Unicoi S.P.	HELEN
Vogel S.P.	DAHLONEGA

Water-related activities, hiking, riding, various other sports, picnicking and visitor centers, as well as camping and rental cottages, are available in many of these areas. Most state parks welcome campers, and there are many comfort stations with hot showers, electric outlets and laundry. All parks listed have trailer dump stations, with the exception of Providence Canyon. Camping is limited to two weeks at any one park. Reservations may be made up to 11 months in advance. Parks are open year round, 7 am-10 pm.

Georgia park vacationers may enjoy cottages at several state parks. These provide complete housekeeping facilities—kitchens with electric ranges and refrigerators, living rooms, one-three bedrooms (linens provided), porches, outdoor grills and picnic tables. They are air-conditioned for summer and heated for winter.

Cottages are available at Amicalola Falls, Black Rock Mountain, Cloudland Canyon, Crooked River, Elijah Clark, Florence Marina, Fort Mountain, Franklin D. Roosevelt, Georgia Veterans Memorial, Hard Labor Creek, Hart, Indian Springs, John Tanner, Little Ocmulgee, Magnolia Springs, Mistletoe, Red Top Mountain, Seminole, Stephen C. Foster, Tugaloo, Unicoi, Vogel and Will-A-Way (in Fort Yargo) parks. Phone 800/864-7275. Cottage reservations can be made up to 11 months in advance; there is a 2-day minimum stay at cottages.

Domestic pets allowed in state parks only if kept on leash not longer than 6 feet and accompanied by owner at all times. No pets allowed in any cottages, site buildings or swimming areas. Fees are subject to change.

Detailed information on state parks may be obtained from the Department of Natural Resources, State Parks & Historic Sites, 205 Butler St SE, Ste 1352, Atlanta 30334; phone 404/656-2770.

FISHING & HUNTING

Georgia's range of fresh and saltwater fishing rivals any other state in variety. There are 26 major reservoirs totaling more than 400,000 acres, and 10 major river systems traverse the state, with thousands of miles of clear, cold-water trout streams and smaller, warm-water streams. Approximately 60,000 small lakes and ponds add to the freshwater total. Some 200 species of freshwater fish are found, 40 of which are considered desirable by game fishermen, including largemouth, shoal and striped bass, as well as crappie and channel catfish. Mountain streams in northern Georgia are a natural source of trout. Fishing in black-water swamp areas in southern Georgia is just as famous for lunker bass and big bream. Coastal waters are good for mackerel, redfish, speckled trout and giant tarpon; no license required.

A state fishing license is required for all freshwater fishing; nonresident: season $24; 7-day permit $7; 1-day permit $3.50; trout stamp (required to fish in trout waters or to keep trout caught): season $13. Fees subject to change. For further information on saltwater fishing contact Dept of Natural Resources, Coastal Resources Division, 1 Conservation Way, Brunswick 31523-8600; 912/264-7218. For further information on freshwater fishing contact Dept of Natural Resources, Wildlife Resources Division, 2123 US 278SE, Social Circle 30279; 770/918-6418.

There is hunting from the Blue Ridge in northern Georgia to the piney woods of the south. Nonresident: season, $59; 7-day, $25; 1-day, $5.50; big game (deer, wild turkey), $118. Preserve license, $12; bow hunting permit, $25. Wildlife Management Area stamp, $73. Waterfowl stamp, $5.50 (federal stamp also required). Fees subject to change. For seasons, bag limits, other details write Dept of Natural Resources, Wildlife Resources Division, 2111 US 278SE, Social Circle 30279; 770/918-6416.

Driving Information

Safety belts are mandatory for all persons in front seat of vehicle and all minors anywhere in vehicle; ages 3 and 4 may use a regulation safety belt; age 2 and under must use an approved safety seat. For further information phone 404/657-9300.

INTERSTATE HIGHWAY SYSTEM

The following alphabetical listing of Georgia towns in *Mobil Travel Guide* shows that these cities are within 10 miles of the indicated Interstate highways. A highway map, however, should be checked for the nearest exit.

Highway Number	Cities/Towns within 10 miles
Interstate 16	Dublin, Macon, Savannah.
Interstate 20	Atlanta, Augusta, Carrollton, Madison.
Interstate 75	Adel, Atlanta, Calhoun, Cartersville, Cordele, Dalton, Forsyth, Macon, Marietta, Perry, Tifton, Valdosta.
Interstate 85	Atlanta, Buford, Commerce, La Grange, Norcross.
Interstate 95	Brunswick, Darien, Jekyll Island, St Simons Island, Savannah.

Additional Visitor Information

For visitor information, including brochures and other materials, contact Dept of Industry, Trade & Tourism, PO Box 1776, Atlanta 30301-1776; phone 404/656-3590 or 800/VISIT-GA. Visitor centers are located in Augusta, Columbus, Kingsland, Lavonia, Plains, Ringgold, Savannah, Sylvania, Tallapoosa, Valdosta and West Point. Information available 8:30 am-5:30 pm.

Adel (G-3)

(See also Tifton, Valdosta)

Pop 5,093 **Elev** 240 ft **Area code** 912 **Zip** 31620 **Web** cookcham@surfsouth.com
Information Adel-Cook County Chamber of Commerce, 100 S Hutchinson Ave, PO Box 461; 912/896-2281.

What to See and Do

Reed Bingham State Park. Park includes 400-acre lake. Waterskiing; fishing; boating (ramp). Nature trails. Picnicking; arboretum. Camping. Standard hrs, fees. 6 mi W off GA 37. Contact Superintendent, Rte 2, Box 394B-1; 912/896-3551.

Motels

★ **DAYS INN.** *I-75 exit 10. 912/896-4574.* 78 rms, 2 story. S, D $34.99-$39.99; each addl $5; under 12 free. Crib $5. Pet accepted; $5. TV; cable (premium), VCR avail (movies). Pool. Restaurant open 24 hrs. Ck-out 11 am. Meeting rm. Business servs avail. Cr cds: A, C, D, DS, MC, V.

D ✶ ≈ ⊠ ⊠ SC

★ **HOWARD JOHNSON.** *I-75 exit 10. 912/896-2244; FAX 912/896-2245.* 70 rms, 2 story. S $32.99-$34.99; D $35.99-$37.99; each addl $5; suite $59.99; under 17 free; wkly rates. Crib $5. Pet accepted; $5. TV; cable. Pool. Complimentary coffee in lobby. Restaurant nearby. Ck-out noon. Cr cds: A, C, D, DS, MC, V.

D ✶ ≈ ⊠ ⊠ SC

✔ ★ **SUPER 8.** *I-75 exit 10. 912/896-4523; FAX 912/896-4524.* 50 rms, 2 story. S $32.99-$34.99; D $35.99-$37.99; each addl $5; under 12 free; wkly rates. Crib $5. Pet accepted; $5. TV; cable. Pool. Complimentary coffee in lobby. Restaurant nearby. Ck-out 11 am. Cr cds: A, C, D, DS, MC, V.

D ✶ ≈ ⊠ ⊠ SC

Albany (F-2)

(See also Americus, Cordele)

Founded 1836 **Pop** 78,122 **Elev** 208 ft **Area code** 912 **E-mail** chamber@albanyga.com
Information Convention & Visitors Bureau, 225 W Broad Ave, 31701; 912/434-8700 or 800/475-8700.

Albany lies in a semi-tropical setting of oaks and pines located in the Plantation Trace region of the state. Colonel Nelson Tift, a Connecticut Yankee, led a party up the Flint River from Apalachicola, Florida, and constructed the first log buildings in Albany. Settlers followed when the

Native Americans were moved to western lands. Paper-shell pecans grown in surrounding Dougherty County have made this the "pecan capital of the world." Surrounded by numerous plantations, the area is also well-known for quail hunting.

What to See and Do

Albany Museum of Art. Permanent and changing exhibits of works by national and regional artists. (Daily exc Mon; closed major hols) 311 Meadowlark Dr. Phone 912/439-8400. **Free.**

Chehaw Park. On 775 acres. Boating. Nature trails. Picnicking. Camping (dump station). 2½ mi NE on GA 91. Per vehicle ¢ Also here is

Chehaw Wild Animal Park. Wildlife preserve (100 acres) where elephant, giraffe, deer, buffalo, llama and other animals roam in natural habitats. Protective trails, elevated walkways. (Daily; closed Dec 25) Phone 912/430-5275. ¢

Lake Chehaw. At the confluence of the Kinchafoonee and Muckalee creeks and the Flint River. Waterskiing; fishing; boating. 2 mi NE off GA 91.

Thronateeska Heritage Center. Sponsors Museum of History and Science. Complex of former railroad buildings houses exhibits on local and natural history and model trains; Discovery Room for children. Also here is Wetherbee Planetarium. (Daily exc Sun; closed major hols) 100 Roosevelt Ave. Phone 912/432-6955. ¢¢

Annual Event

Fall on the Flint Festival. Entertainment, parade, exhibits, athletic contests. Last wkend Sept.

Motels

★ ★ ★ **COMFORT SUITES-MERRY ACRES.** 1400 Dawson Rd (31706). 912/888-3939; res: 888/726-3939; FAX 912/435-4431. Web www.merryacres.com. 62 suites, 2 story. S $89-$104; D $95-$150; each addl $7; under 18 free. Crib $5. TV; cable (premium). Pool privileges. Playground. Complimentary continental bkfst. Complimentary coffee in rms. Restaurant 11 am-2 pm, 5-10 pm. Bar 4 pm-midnight. Ck-out noon. Meeting rms. Business servs avail. In-rm modem link. Valet serv. Airport transportation. Refrigerators. Cr cds: A, C, D, DS, ER, JCB, MC, V.

D ⊠ 🏃 SC

✔ ★ ★ **HAMPTON INN.** 806 North Westover Blvd (31707), at Albany Mall. 912/883-3300; FAX 912/435-4092. 82 rms, 2 story. S $57-$61; D $61-$64; under 18 free; wkend rates. Crib free. TV; cable. Pool. Complimentary continental bkfst. Coffee in rms. Restaurant adj 6 am-midnight. Ck-out noon. Meeting rm. In-rm modem link. Valet serv. Health club privileges. Cr cds: A, D, DS, MC, V.

D ≈ ⊠ 🏃 SC

★ ★ ★ **QUALITY INN MERRY ACRES.** 1500 Dawson Rd (31706). 912/435-7721; res: 888/462-7721; FAX 912/439-9386. Web www.merryacres.com. 108 rms. S $58-$168; D $65-$175; each addl $5; suites $156-$163; under 18 free. Crib $5. TV; cable. Pool; wading pool. Playground. Restaurant 11 am-2 pm, 5-10 pm. Complimentary continental bkfst. Coffee in rms. Bar 4 pm-midnight. Ck-out noon. Meeting rms. Business servs avail. In-rm modem link. Valet serv. Sundries. Exercise equipt. Some refrigerators, wet bars. Cr cds: A, C, D, DS, ER, JCB, MC, V.

D ≈ 🏃 ⊠ 🏃 SC

★ ★ **RAMADA INN.** 2505 N Slappey Blvd (31701-1095). 912/883-3211; FAX 912/439-2806. 158 rms, 2 story. S $54; D $60; each addl $7; suites $75; under 18 free; wkend rates. Crib free. Pet accepted. TV; cable (premium), VCR avail. Pool; wading pool. Coffee in rms. Restaurant 6:30 am-2 pm, 5-10 pm; Sun 7 am-2 pm. Rm serv 7 am-9 pm. Bar 5-10 pm. Ck-out noon. Meeting rms. Business servs avail. In-rm modem link. Bellhops. Valet serv. Free airport transportation. Sundries. Cr cds: A, C, D, DS, ER, JCB, MC, V.

D ✔ ≈ ⊠ 🏃 SC

Motor Hotel

★ ★ **HOLIDAY INN EXPRESS.** 911 E Oglethorpe Blvd (US 19/82 Business) (31705). 912/883-1650; FAX 912/883-1163. 151 rms, 4 story. S, D $56; each addl $5; under 19 free. Crib free. TV; cable (premium). Pool. Complimentary bkfst. Complimentary coffee in rms. Ck-out noon. Meeting rms. Business servs avail. In-rm modem link. Free airport transportation. Refrigerators, microwaves. Tennis privileges. Golf privileges. Cr cds: A, C, D, DS, MC, V.

D 🏃 🏃 ≈ ⊠ 🏃 SC

Americus (F-2)

(See also Albany, Andersonville, Cordele)

Founded 1832 **Pop** 16,512 **Elev** 355 ft **Area code** 912 **Zip** 31709 **E-mail** chamber@americus.americus.net **Web** www.gomm.com/americus
Information Americus-Sumter County Chamber of Commerce, Tourism Division, 400 W Lamar St, Box 724; 912/924-2646or 888/278-6837.

Americus is at the center of an area once known as the "granary of the Creek nations," so called because Native Americans favored this area for the cultivation of maize. The town was named, it is said, either for Americus Vespucius or for the settlers themselves, who were referred to as "merry cusses" for their happy-go-lucky ways. The town flourished in the 1890s. Many Victorian/Gothic-revival buildings remain from that period.

Today, peanuts, corn, cotton, small grain and pecans are grown, and bauxite and kaolin are mined in the area. Americus is also a manufacturing center, producing lumber commodities, metal lighting equipment, heating products and textiles. The town's livestock sales are second in volume in the state. Plains, nine miles west via US 280, is the hometown of the 39th president, Jimmy Carter.

What to See and Do

Americus Historic Driving Tour. Tour features 38 houses of various architectural styles, including Victorian, Greek revival and classical revival. Contact the Chamber of Commerce.

Andersonville National Historic Site. (See ANDERSONVILLE) 11 mi NE on GA 49.

Georgia Southwestern College (1906). (2,600 students) Wheatly & Glessner Sts, 2 mi E of jct US 19, 280. On 187-acre campus with a lake is

Carter Display focusing on former President Jimmy Carter and First Lady Rosalynn Carter; photographs, memorabilia; located in James Earl Carter Library. (Daily exc during school breaks, hols) **Free.**

✪ **Jimmy Carter National Historic Site.** Visitor center is located in Plains High School, where Jimmy and Rosalynn Carter attended grammar and high school. Campaign memorabilia; cassette auto driving tour of Plains available. (Daily; closed Jan 1, Dec 25) 8 mi W on US 280 in Plains. Plains High School is located at 300 N Bond St. Phone 912/824-3413. **Free.**

Motor Hotel

★ ★ ★ **THE WINDSOR.** 125 W Lamar St. 912/924-1555; res: 800/678-8946. 53 units, 3 story. S, D $70; under 15 free. TV; cable (premium). Coffee in rms. Restaurant (see GRAND DINING ROOM). Rm serv. Bar 4 pm-midnight, closed Sun. Ck-out noon. Meeting rms. Business servs avail. In-rm modem link. Bellhops. Valet serv. 3-story atrium lobby. Period-style rms with 12-ft ceilings and ceiling fans. Cr cds: A, D, DS, MC, V.

D ⊠ 🏃 SC

Inn

✔★★★ **PATHWAY INN.** *501 S Lee St.* 912/928-2078; res: 800/889-1466. E-mail pathway@sowega.net; web www.bestinns.com/usa/ga/pathway.html. 5 rms, 2 with shower only, 2 story. S $75-$95; D $87-$125; each addl $20. Pet accepted, some restrictions. TV; cable (premium), VCR avail (movies). Complimentary full bkfst; afternoon refreshments. Complimentary coffee in rms. Ck-out 11 am, ck-in 4 pm. Luggage handling. Concierge serv. Southern mansion built in 1906. Totally nonsmoking. Cr cds: DS, MC, V.

D ✔ ≈ 🖉

Restaurant

★★★ **GRAND DINING ROOM.** *(See The Windsor Motor Hotel)* 912/924-1555. Hrs: 7-10 am, 11:30 am-2 pm, 6:30-9:30 pm; Sun 7-10 am, 11:30 am-2 pm. Res accepted. Continental menu. Bar 4 pm-midnight; closed Sun. Wine list. A la carte entrees: bkfst $3.15-$6.95, dinner $13.95-$26. Buffet: lunch $7.95. Specializes in seafood, desserts. Elegant decor; antique chandeliers, fireplace. Cr cds: A, C, D, DS, MC, V.

D 🖘

Andersonville (E-2)

(See also Americus, Cordele, Perry)

Pop 277 **Elev** 390 ft **Area code** 912 **Zip** 31711

What to See and Do

Andersonville National Historic Site. The Confederate Military Prison, Camp Sumter, was built on a 26-acre tract in early 1864 by soldiers and slaves requisitioned from nearby plantations. The lofty pines that grew in the local sandy soil were cut and used to form a stockade. Built to accommodate 10,000 men, the prison at one time held as many as 33,000. Overcrowding, inadequate food, insufficient medicines and a breakdown of the prisoner exchange system resulted in a high death rate. The site is now a memorial to all prisoners of war throughout history. Included on grounds are escape tunnels and wells dug by prisoners, Confederate earthworks, three reconstructed sections of stockade wall and state monuments. Park (daily). On GA 49. Phone 912/924-0343. **Free.** Also here are

National Prisoner of War Museum. Exhibits, interpretive programs and interactive videos depict the role of military prisoners in the history of the nation (Daily; closed Jan 1, Dec 25). Visitor Center.

Providence Spring. The spring, which bubbled up from the ground after a heavy rain, was said to be in answer to the prisoners' prayers during the summer of 1864.

Andersonville National Cemetery. Graves of more than 17,000 Union soldiers and veterans of US military are in striking contrast to the landscaped grounds. The initial interments were Union soldiers who died in the prison camp. Dedicated as a national cemetery on Aug 17, 1865. ½ mi N of prison site.

Civil War Village of Andersonville. Restored village from the days of the Civil War. Welcome center, pioneer farm, museum (fee), antique shops. (Daily; closed Dec 25) Church St Phone 912/924-2558. **Free.**

Annual Event

Andersonville Historic Fair. Center of town. Civil War reenactments, old time craftsmen, antique dealers; RV campsites. Contact Andersonville Historic Fair, PO Box 6; 912/924-2558. Memorial Day wkend & 1st wkend Oct.

Athens (C-3)

(See also Commerce, Madison, Winder)

Founded 1801 **Pop** 45,734 **Elev** 775 ft **Area code** 706 **E-mail** athensga@negia.net **Web** www.visitathens.com

Information Convention & Visitors Bureau, 300 N Thomas St, 30601, phone 800/653-0603; or Athens Welcome Center, 280 E Dougherty St, 30601, phone 706/353-1820.

Georgia's "Classic City" is the site of the University of Georgia, chartered in 1785. Diversified industry produces nonwoven fabrics, textiles, clocks, electronic components, precision parts, chemicals and animal feed. Lyman Hall, a signer of the Declaration of Independence, proposed the University and Abraham Baldwin, the acknowledged founding father, wrote the charter. Although allotted 10,000 acres by the legislature in 1784, it was another 17 years before Josiah Meigs, Baldwin's successor and first official president, erected a few log buildings, called it Franklin College and held classes under the tolerant eyes of curious Cherokees.

Athens was incorporated in 1806. Its setting on a hill beside the Oconee River is enhanced by towering oaks and elms, white-blossomed magnolias, old-fashioned boxwood gardens and many well-preserved and still-occupied antebellum houses.

What to See and Do

Double-barreled cannon (1863). A unique Civil War weapon cast at Athens' foundry. Believed to be the only double-barreled cannon in the world. City Hall lawn, College & Hancock Aves.

Historic Houses. For tour information contact Athens Welcome Center in Church-Waddel-Brumby House (see) or contact Athens Convention & Visitors Bureau.

Taylor-Grady House (1839). Restored Greek-revival mansion surrounded by 13 columns said to symbolize 13 original states; period furniture. (Mon-Fri; closed major hols) 634 Prince Ave. Phone 706/549-8688. ¢¢

Church-Waddel-Brumby House (ca 1820). Restored Federal-style house thought to be oldest residence in Athens. Houses **Athens Welcome Center,** which has information on self-guided tours of other historic houses and buildings (Mon-Sat, Sun afternoons) 280 E Dougherty St. Phone 706/353-1820.

University President's House (ca 1855). Greek-revival mansion surrounded on three sides by massive Corinthian columns. Extensive gardens and picket fences complement classic design. Private residence. 570 Prince Ave.

Founders Memorial Garden Memorial to founders of Ladies' Garden Club of Athens, the first garden club in the US. 325 S Lumpkin St, on Univ of Georgia campus. Phone 706/542-3631.

Other historic houses in Athens include Ross Crane House (Sigma Alpha Epsilon Fraternity) (1842), 247 Pulaski St; Lucy Cobb Institute (1858), 200 N Milledge Ave; Joseph Henry Lumpkin House (1841), 248 Prince Ave; Old Franklin Hotel (1845), 480 E Broad St; Governor Wilson Lumpkin House (1842), South campus, University of Georgia. University of Georgia, North campus, also has numerous pre-1860 buildings.

Sandy Creek Nature Center. Approximately 200 acres of woods, fields and marshland; includes a live animal exhibit, a 180-yr-old cabin, nature trails. (Mar-late Nov, Mon-Sat; rest of yr, Mon-Fri; closed hols) ½ mi N of Athens bypass, off US 441. Phone 706/613-3615. **Free.**

Sandy Creek Park. Swimming (beach); fishing; boating. Hiking; tennis; basketball. Picnicking, playgrounds. Primitive camping. Walkways. (Daily exc Mon) N on US 441. Phone 706/613-3631. ¢

Tree That Owns Itself. White oak, descendant of original tree, stands on plot deeded to it. Dearing & Finley Sts.

University of Georgia (1785). (30,000 students) Consisting of 13 schools and colleges, the main campus extends more than 2 mi S from the Arch (1858), College Ave & Broad St. Nearby are farms managed by the

College of Agriculture, a forestry preserve and University Research Park. Historic buildings include Demosthenian Hall (1824); chapel (1832), housing an oil painting (17 by 23¹/₂ ft) of the interior of St Peter's Basilica; Old College (1806), oldest building, designed after Connecticut Hall at Yale; Waddel Hall (1821) and Phi Kappa Hall (1834). Phone 706/542-3354. Also on campus are

Butts-Mehre Heritage Museum. Exhibits, video displays and trophy cases display Georgia sports memorabilia. 3rd and 4th floors of Butts-Mehre Heritage Hall, Lumpkin St & Pinecrest Dr. (Mon-Fri & Sat afternoons) Phone 706/542-9094. **Free.**

Georgia Museum of Art. Contains over 8,000 pieces, including Eva Underhill Holbrook Collection; traveling and special exhibits. (Daily exc Mon; closed some major hols, wk of Dec 25) Phone 706/542-4662. **Free.**

State Botanical Garden. Approx 300 acres with natural trails, wildlife and special collections. Gardens (daily); conservatory/visitors center (daily); Callaway Bldg (Mon-Fri). 2450 S Milledge Ave. Phone 706/542-1244. **Free.**

Annual Events

Spring Tour of Homes. Held by Athens-Clarke Heritage Foundation. Contact Fire Hall #2, 489 Prince Ave, 30601; 706/353-1801 or -1820. Last wkend Apr.

Marigold Festival. GA 78 to Cherokee Rd, in Winterville. Arts, crafts, antiques, parades and other events. Phone 706/742-8600. Late June.

Crackerland Tennis Tournament. Dan Magill Tennis Complex, University of Georgia. Juniors, late July-early Aug. Seniors, mid-Aug.

North Georgia Folk Festival. Sandy Creek Park. Phone 706/613-3620. Late Sept or early Oct.

Motel

★ ★ **BEST WESTERN COLONIAL INN.** *170 North Milledge (30601).* 706/546-7311; FAX 706/546-7959. Web www.bestwestern.com/best.html. 69 rms, 2 story. S $54; D $59; each addl $5; under 12 free; higher rates: univ football games, graduation. Crib free. Pet accepted; $10. TV; cable (premium). Pool. Complimentary continental bkfst. Restaurant opp 11 am-11 pm. Ck-out 11 am. In-rm modem link. Refrigerators. Cr cds: A, C, D, DS, MC, V.

Motor Hotels

★ ★ ★ **COURTYARD BY MARRIOTT.** *166 Finley St (30601).* 706/369-7000; FAX 706/548-4224. Web www.courtyard.com. 105 rms, 2-3 story. S, D $74; suites $95-$105; higher rates: univ football games, graduation. Crib free. TV; cable (premium), VCR avail. Pool; whirlpool. Restaurant adj 6:30-10:30 am. Bar. Ck-out noon. Coin lndry. Meeting rms. Business servs avail. In-rm modem link. Free airport transportation. Exercise equipt. Refrigerators; microwaves avail. Cr cds: A, D, DS, ER, MC, V.

★ ★ ★ **HOLIDAY INN.** *197 E Broad St (30603), Broad & Lumpkin Sts.* 706/549-4433; FAX 706/548-3031. 308 rms, 2-6 story. S, D $84-$104; suites $134; under 19 free; wkend rates; higher rates football wkends. Crib free. TV; cable (premium). Indoor pool; whirlpool. Coffee in rms. Restaurant 7 am-2 pm, 5:30-10 pm. Rm serv. Bar 4 pm-1 am; closed Sun. Ck-out noon. Coin lndry. Convention facilities. Business center. In-rm modem link. Free airport transportation. Exercise equipt. Some balconies. Adj to Univ of Georgia. Luxury level. Cr cds: A, C, D, DS, JCB, MC, V.

★ ★ **HOLIDAY INN.** *513 W Broad St (30601), US 29, 78, 129, 441.* 706/546-8122; FAX 706/546-1722, ext. 586. 160 rms, 5 story. S $61-$67, D $67-$73; suites $110; under 18 free; wkend rates; higher rates: graduation, football wkends. Crib free. Pet accepted, some restrictions. TV; cable (premium), VCR avail. Pool. Complimentary coffee in rms.

Restaurant 6:30 am-9:30 pm. Rm serv. Bar 4:30 pm-1 am; entertainment, dancing Tues-Sat. Ck-out noon. Bellhops. Valet serv. Meeting rms. Business servs avail. In-rm modem link. Sundries. Cr cds: A, C, D, DS, ER, JCB, MC, V.

Inns

★ ★ ★ **NICHOLSON HOUSE.** *6295 Jefferson Rd (30607).* 706/353-2200; FAX 706/353-7799. Web bbonline.com/ga/nicholson. 9 rms, 7 with shower only, 2 story; 1 cottage. S, D $75-$85; cottage $95; min stay required special event wkends. Children over 12 yrs only. TV; cable (premium). Complimentary full bkfst. Ck-out 11 am, ck-in 2 pm. Luggage handling. Concierge serv. Free airport transportation. Lawn games. House built 1820 in the Colonial-revival style. Sitting rm; many antiques. Totally nonsmoking. Cr cds: A, DS, JCB, MC, V.

★ ★ ★ **RIVENDELL.** *(3581 S Barnett Shoals Rd, Watkinsville 30677) approx 8 mi S on US 441, then 5 mi W on Barnett Shoals Rd.* 706/769-4522; FAX 706/769-4393. E-mail rivendel@negia.net; web www.negia.net/~rivendel/. 5 rms, 2 share bath, 2 story. Some rm phones. S, D $65-$80; football wkends (2-night min). Children over 10 yrs only. Complimentary full bkfst. Ck-out 11 am, ck-in 5-8 pm. Luggage handling. Concierge serv. English country home set upon 11 woodland acres; on Oconee River. Totally nonsmoking. Cr cds: MC, V.

Restaurants

★ ★ **HARRY BISSETTS.** *279 E Broad St (30601), on GA 78.* 706/353-7065. Hrs: 11:30 am-3 pm, 5:30-10 pm; Mon from 5:30 pm; Fri to 11 pm; Sat, Sun brunch to 3:30 pm, 6-10 pm. Closed Dec 25. Bar. Semi-a la carte: lunch $5.50-$9.50, dinner $12-$24. Sat, Sun brunch $7.95. Specializes in barbecue shrimp, veal, Angus steaks. Storefront building; bar area was once a bank. Cr cds: A, DS, MC, V.

★ **THE LAST RESORT GRILL.** *174 W Clayton St (30601).* 706/549-0810. Hrs: 11 am-3 pm, 5-10 pm; Fri, Sat to 11 pm. Closed some major hols. Bar. Semi-a la carte: lunch $3.95-$6.95, dinner $6.95-$16.95. Child's meals. Specialties: praline chicken, salmon & grits, shiitake roma pasta. Outdoor dining. Eclectic decor. Cr cds: A, MC, V.

Unrated Dining Spot

VARSITY. *1000 W Broad St.* 706/548-6325. Hrs: 10 am-10 pm; Fri, Sat to midnight. Semi-a la carte: bkfst, lunch, dinner: $1-$1.50. Specializes in hot dogs, hamburgers. Outdoor dining. School cafeteria atmosphere; pennant flag display. No cr cds accepted.

Atlanta (C-2)

Founded 1837 **Pop** 394,017 **Elev** 1,050 ft **Area code** 404

Information Convention & Visitors Bureau, 233 Peachtree St NE, Ste 2000, 30303; phone 404/222-6688.

Suburbs Marietta, Norcross. (See individual alphabetical listings.)

When Atlanta was just 27 years old, 90 percent of its houses and buildings were razed by the Union armies after a 117-day siege. Rebuilt by railroads in this century, the city gives an overall impression of 20th-century modernism.

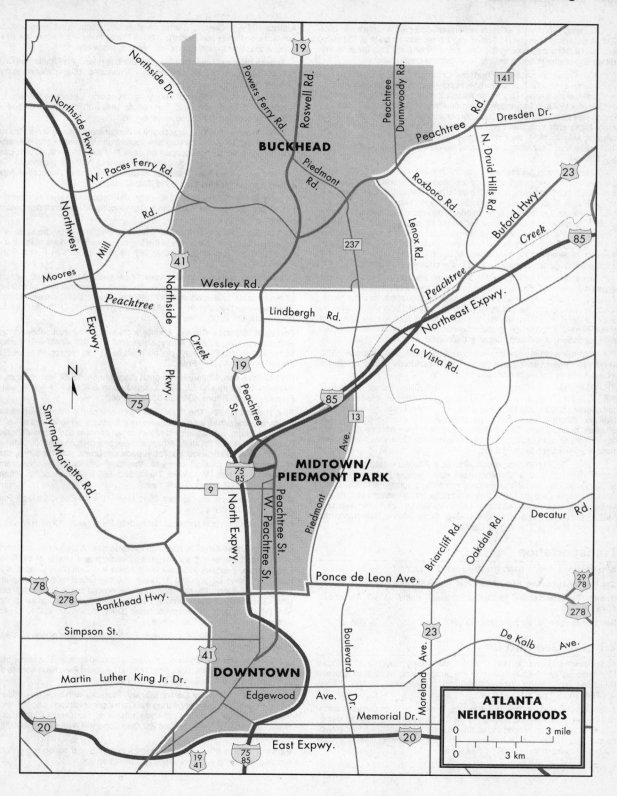

BUCKHEAD

MIDTOWN/
PIEDMONT PARK

DOWNTOWN

**ATLANTA
NEIGHBORHOODS**

0   3 mile

0   3 km

Northside Dr.

Powers Ferry Rd.

Roswell Rd.

Peachtree Dunwoody Rd.

Peachtree Rd.

Dresden Dr.

N. Druid Hills Rd.

Buford Hwy.

Creek

Northside Pkwy.

W. Paces Ferry Rd.

Rd.

Northwest Mill

Piedmont Rd.

Roxboro Rd.

Lenox Rd.

Peachtree

Moores

Peachtree

Expwy.

Wesley Rd.

Lindbergh Rd.

Northeast Expwy.

Creek

La Vista Rd.

Smyrna-Marietta Rd.

Northside Pkwy.

Peachtree St.

North Expwy.

Peachtree St.

W. Peachtree St.

Piedmont Ave.

Briarcliff Rd.

Oakdale Rd.

Decatur Rd.

Ponce de Leon Ave.

Bankhead Hwy.

Simpson St.

Boulevard Dr.

Moreland Ave.

De Kalb Ave.

Martin Luther King Jr. Dr.

Edgewood Ave.

Memorial Dr.

East Expwy.

Standing Peachtree, a Creek settlement, occupied Atlanta's site until 1813. Lieutenant George R. Gilmer led 22 recruits to build a fort here because of difficulties among the Creek and Cherokee. This became the first white settlement and grew into an important trading post.

After Georgia's secession from the Union on January 19, 1861, the city became a manufacturing, storage, supply and transportation center for the Confederate forces. This made Atlanta the target and last real barrier on General William Tecumseh Sherman's march to the sea. Although Atlanta had quartered 60,000 Confederate wounded, it was untouched by actual battle until Sherman began the fierce fighting of the Atlanta Campaign on May 7, 1864, with the engagement at Tunnel Hill, just over the Tennessee line. Despairing of capturing the city by battle, Sherman undertook a siege.

Guns were brought in and Atlanta civilians got a foretaste of 20th-century warfare as the population and defenders alike were subjected to continuous bombardment by the Union's heaviest artillery. People took refuge in cellars, trenches and dugouts. Those who could escaped southward by wagon, foot or train until Union forces seized the railroad 20 miles south at Jonesboro on September 1. General Hood evacuated Atlanta that same night, and the mayor surrendered the city the next day, September 2. Although the terms of surrender promised protection of life and property, Sherman ordered the city evacuated. All but 400 of the 3,600 houses and commercial buildings were destroyed in the subsequent burning.

Many citizens had returned to the city by January of 1865. By June, steps had been taken to reorganize business and repair wrecked railroad facilities. In 1866, Atlanta was made federal headquarters for area reconstruction. During the Reconstruction Convention of 1867-1868, called by General John Pope in Atlanta, the city offered facilities for the state government if it should be chosen the capital. The convention accepted this proposition, and Atlanta became the capital on April 20, 1868.

Atlanta's recovery and expansion as a rail center was begun by 1872, when two more railroads met here. Today, hundreds of manufacturers produce a wide variety of commodities.

Metropolitan Atlanta's population of 2.8 million is as devoted to cultural activities (such as its famed Alliance Theatre) as it is to its many golf courses and its major sports teams. Peachtree Street today considers itself the South's main street and is more Fifth Avenue than Scarlett O'Hara's beloved lane. Skyscrapers, museums, luxury shops and hotels rub shoulders along this concourse where Coca-Cola was first served; there are few peach blossoms left.

There are 29 colleges and universities in Atlanta. Georgia Institute of Technology, home of "a rambling wreck from Georgia Tech and a hell of an engineer," is one of the nation's top technological institutes. Other schools include Georgia State, Emory and Oglethorpe universities. Atlanta University Center is an affiliation of six institutions of higher learning: Atlanta University, Spelman, Morehouse, Clark, Morris Brown and the Interdenominational Theological Center.

Transportation

Airport: See ATLANTA HARTSFIELD AIRPORT AREA.

Car Rental Agencies: See IMPORTANT TOLL-FREE NUMBERS.

Public Transportation: Buses & subway trains (MARTA), phone 404/848-4711.

Rail Passenger Service: Amtrak 800/872-7245.

What to See and Do

A.G. Rhodes Memorial Hall (1903). Outstanding example of Victorian Romanesque architecture. Open to the public during restoration process (Mon-Fri, Sun; closed national hols). 1516 Peachtree St NW. Phone 404/885-7800. ¢¢

Atlanta Botanical Garden. Features 15 acres of outdoor gardens: Japanese, rose, perennial and others. Fuqua Conservatory with tropical, desert and rare plants from around the world; and special exhibit area for carnivorous plants. (Daily exc Mon; closed Jan 1, Thanksgiving, Dec 25) 1345 Piedmont Ave. Phone 404/876-5859. ¢¢¢

Atlanta History Center. Center consists of 5 major structures and 33 acres of woodlands and gardens. 130 W Paces Ferry Rd. Phone 404/814-4000. Admission to entire complex ¢¢¢ On site are

Atlanta History Museum. Historical exhibits relating to Atlanta, the Civil War, Southern folk life and African Americans. (Daily; closed some major hols)

McElreath Hall. Research library, archives and Cherokee Garden Library with gardening and horticulture research collection (Mon-Fri; closed some major hols). Special events.

Swan House (1928), a classically styled mansion is preserved as an example of early 20th-century architecture and decorative arts. Mansion is part of spacious landscaped grounds that include terraces with cascading fountains, formal boxwood garden and Victorian playhouse. On premises is the Philip Trammell Shutze Collection of Decorative Arts. (Daily; closed some major hols) Guided tours.

Tullie Smith Farm. Guided tours of 1840 plantation-style farmhouse, herb gardens, pioneer log cabin and other outbuildings; craft demonstrations.

Atlanta State Farmers' Market. Owned and operated by the state and covering 146 acres, this is one of the largest farmers' markets of its kind in the Southeast. (Daily; closed Dec 25) 10 mi S on I-75 in Forest Park. Phone 404/366-6910. **Free.**

Cable News Network studio tour. View technicians, writers, editors, producers and on-air journalists in the studio headquarters of a 24-hr all-news cable television network (45-min tour). (Daily; closed Easter, Thanksgiving, Dec 25) At 1 CNN Center, Techwood Dr & Marietta St. Phone 404/827-2300. ¢¢¢

Fernbank Science Center. Center includes exhibit hall, observatory, planetarium (fee), science library; also forest area (65 acres) with marked trails. (Hrs for facilities vary; closed most hols) 156 Heaton Park Dr NE. Phone 404/378-4311. **Free.**

Fort McPherson. Military reservation since May 4, 1889. Historical tours (Mon-Fri, by appt). Lee St, US 29, approx 3 mi SW via I-75 & Lakewood Freeway to fort. Phone 404/464-3556. **Free.**

Fox Theatre (1929). The "Fabulous Fox," one of the most lavish movie theaters in the world, was conceived as a Shriners' temple, with a 4,678-seat auditorium, world's largest Moller organ console and three elaborate ballrooms; restored theater's ornate architecture combines exotic Moorish and Egyptian details. Hosts ballet, Broadway shows, summer film series, full spectrum of musical concerts, theatrical events, trade shows and conventions. Tours (Mon, Wed, Thurs, Sat). 660 Peachtree St NE. Phone 404/881-2100 for details. Tours ¢¢

Gray Line bus tours. Contact 2541 Camp Creek Pkwy, College Park 30337; 404/767-0594.

Kennesaw Mountain National Battlefield Park (see). 25 mi NW off US 41.

★ **Martin Luther King, Jr, National Historic Site.** A 2-blk area in memory of the famed leader of the civil rights movement and winner of the Nobel Peace Prize. Features include the Freedom Hall Complex, Chapel of All Faiths, the King Library and Archives and the reflecting pool; films and slides on Dr. King's life and work may be viewed in the screening room (fee). The National Park Service operates an information center; phone 404/331-6922 (daily; closed major hols). (Daily; closed Jan 1, Dec 25) 450 Auburn Ave. 404/331-5190. **Free.**

King Birthplace. 501 Auburn Ave. For tour information phone 404/331-3920. **Free.**

Ebenezer Baptist Church. Dr. King was co-pastor at Ebenezer from 1960-1968. (Daily exc Sun; donation) 407 Auburn Ave. Next door to the church is the gravesite with an eternal flame.

Museum of the Jimmy Carter Library. Museum with exhibits on life in White House, major events during the Carter administration and the life of President Carter. Includes full-scale replica of the Oval Office. (Daily; closed Jan 1, Thanksgiving, Dec 25) One Copenhill Ave. Phone 404/331-0296. ¢¢

Parks in Atlanta offer dogwood blooms in spring and varied recreational facilities, including golf, swimming and picnic areas.

Grant Park. Many miles of walks and roads; visible traces of breastworks built for defense of Atlanta; cyclorama depicting the Battle of Atlanta; Atlanta Zoo with a variety of species. Swimming. Tennis. Picnicking. Park (daily). Zoo (daily; closed Jan 1, Thanksgiving, Dec 25). Cherokee Ave SE. Phone 404/658-7538 or 404/624-5600. Zoo ¢¢¢

Chastain Memorial Park. Swimming. Tennis; golf. Picnicking. Amphitheater. Fees for various activities. Between Powers Ferry Rd & Lake Forrest Dr.

Piedmont Park. Home of the Arts Festival of Atlanta. Swimming (fee). Lake. Tennis (fee). Picnicking. Off of Monroe Dr on Park Dr. Phone 404/875-7275.

Professional sports.

National League baseball (Atlanta Braves). Turner Field, Capitol Ave. Phone 404/522-7630.

NBA (Atlanta Hawks). Georgia Dome, 1 Georgia Dome Dr. Phone 404/827-3800.

NFL (Atlanta Falcons). Georgia Dome, 1 Georgia Dome Dr. Phone 770/945-1111.

Robert W. Woodruff Arts Center. 1280 Peachtree St NE.Largest arts complex in the Southeast; headquarters of Atlanta College of Art and

High Museum of Art. European art from the early Renaissance to the present; Samuel H. Kress, J.J. Haverty, Ralph K. Uhry print collection and Richman collection of African art; photographs; decorative arts; traveling exhibitions. (Daily exc Mon; closed some major hols) Also tours, lectures, films; for schedule phone 404/733-4444. For general information phone 404/733-4400. ¢¢¢

Symphony Hall. Largest auditorium in Arts Center. Permanent home of Atlanta Symphony Orchestra and Chorus; performances (Sept-May & mid-June-mid-Aug). For schedule, ticket information phone 404/733-5000.

Alliance Theatre Company. Six mainstage productions, two studio theater productions and two children's theater productions are presented annually. (Sept-May) For schedule, ticket information phone 404/733-5000.

SciTrek-The Science and Technology Museum of Atlanta. The worlds of science and high technology are examined through self-guided tour of more than 100 "hands-on" exhibits. Traveling exhibits, demonstrations, films, lectures and workshops are frequently offered. (Daily; closed major hols) 395 Piedmont Ave at Pine St. Phone 404/522-5500. ¢¢¢

Six Flags Over Georgia. A family theme park featuring Georgia's history under the flags of England, France, Spain, the Confederacy, Georgia and the US. More than 100 rides, shows and attractions, including the Georgia Cyclone roller coaster, modeled after Coney Island's famous Cyclone; the Ninja roller coaster with five upside down turns; water rides; children's activities; live shows. Restaurants. (Mid-May-early Sept, daily; early Mar-mid-May & early Sept-Oct, wkends only) 12 mi W via I-20, exit 13C Six Flags Pkwy, just beyond Atlanta city limits. Phone 770/948-9290. ¢¢¢¢¢

State Capitol (1884-89). The dome, topped with native gold, is 237 ft high. Inside are historical flags, statues and portraits. Tours (Mon-Fri). Capitol Sq. Phone 404/656-2844. **Free.** On the fourth floor is

Georgia Capitol Museum. Exhibits of wildlife, snakes, fish, rocks, minerals and fossils. Dioramas of Georgia industry. (Call capitol bldg for days open; may change due to extensive restoration) **Free.**

⭐ **Stone Mountain Park.** This 3,200-acre park surrounds the world's largest granite monolith, which rises 825 ft from the plain. A monument to the Confederacy, the deep relief carving on the mountain's face depicts three figures: Gen. Robert E. Lee, Gen. "Stonewall" Jackson and Confederate President Jefferson Davis. It was first undertaken by Gutzon Borglum after the First World War, continued by Augustus Lukeman and completed by Walker Hancock. The top of the mountain is accessible by foot or by cable car (fee). Surrounding the sculpture are: Memorial Hall, a Civil War museum with commentary in seven languages about the mountain and its carving; an antebellum plantation, featuring 19 buildings restored and furnished with 18th- and 19th-century heirlooms, formal and kitchen gardens, cookhouse, slave quarters, country store and other outbuildings; Antique Auto and Music Museum housing cars dating from 1899 and antique mechanical music collection; riverboat *Scarlett O'Hara*, providing

scenic trips around 363-acre lake; scenic railroad with full-size replicas of Civil War trains that make 5-mi trip around base of mountain. Also, a laser show is projected onto the north face of the mountain in 50-min productions (mid-May-Labor Day, nightly; Apr-mid-May & after Labor Day-October, Fri & Sat) and a 732-bell carillon plays concerts (Wed-Sun). In addition, the park has 10 mi of nature trails where wild and domestic animals live on 20 wooded acres; beach with bathhouse, fishing, boat rentals; tennis courts, 36-hole golf course, miniature golf; ice-skating; picnicking, snack bars and 3 restaurants, inn; and campground with tent & trailer sites (hookups, dump station). Most attractions are open daily (addl fees; closed Dec 25). 19 mi E on US 78. For further information contact PO Box 778, Stone Mountain 30086; 770/498-5600. Per vehicle ¢¢¢

⭐ **Underground Atlanta.** A "festival marketplace" featuring shops, pushcart peddlers, restaurants and nightclubs, street entertainers and various attractions. The six-blk area was created in the 1920s, when several viaducts were built over existing streets at second-story level to move traffic above multiple rail crossings. Merchants moved their shops to second floors, relegating first floors to oblivion for nearly half a century. Today's visitor descends onto the cobblestone streets of a Victorian city in perpetual night. On lower Alabama Street the shops are housed in the original, once-forgotten storefronts. Underground Atlanta was first "discovered" in the late 1960s and flourished as a center of nightlife before being closed down in 1981 due to a combination of crime and subway construction. The "rediscovered" Underground combines the original below-ground streets with above-ground plazas, promenades, fountains, more shops and restaurants and a 138-ft light tower. (Daily; closed Dec 25) Bounded by Wall, Central, Peachtree Sts & Martin Luther King, Jr Dr. Phone 404/523-2311.Highlighted here is

The World of Coca-Cola. A square block of interactive displays and exhibits trace history of Coca-Cola from its introduction in 1886 at Jacob's Pharmacy Soda Fountain on Atlanta's Peachtree Street to present; world's largest collection of Coca-Cola memorabilia; movies; old-fashioned soda fountain. (Daily; closed some major hols & 3-4 days during yr for maintenance) 55 Martin Luther King Jr Dr between Central Ave & Washington St, S of the New Georgia Railroad Depot. Phone 404/676-5151. ¢¢

Wren's Nest. Eccentric, Victorian house of Joel Chandler Harris, journalist and transcriber of "Uncle Remus" stories. Original family furnishings, books, photographs. Ongoing restoration. (Daily exc Mon; closed major hols) 1050 Ralph D. Abernathy Blvd SW. Phone 404/753-7735. ¢¢¢

Yellow River Game Ranch. A 24-acre animal preserve on the Yellow River where more than 600 animals roam free in a natural wooded area. Visitors can pet, feed and photograph the animals. Some of the animals at the park include deer, bears, cougars and buffalo. (Daily; closed Jan 1, Thanksgiving, Dec 24,25) 4525 US 78 in Lilburn, approx 17 mi E. Phone 770/972-6643. ¢¢

Annual Events

Auto Racing. Atlanta Motor Speedway. S on I-75, exit 77, then approx 15 mi S on US 19/41. NASCAR Winston Cup, Busch Grand National, IMSA and ARCA events. Phone 770/946-4211. 2 racing wkends, usually Mar & Nov.

Atlanta Steeplechase. At Seven Branches Farm in Cumming. Phone 404/237-7436. 1st Sat Apr.

Atlanta Dogwood Festival. Phone 404/329-0501. Mid-Apr.

BellSouth Golf Classic (see MARIETTA). Early May.

Seasonal Events

Georgia Renaissance Festival. Approx 20 mi S on I-85, exit 12. Hundreds of costumed characters, authentic crafts, games and food in a re-created 16th-century English village. Phone 770/964-8575. 7 wkends, late Apr-early June.

Theater of the Stars. Fox Theatre. Six Broadway musicals with professional casts. For ticket information phone 404/252-8960. Late June-early Nov.

Additional Visitor Information

For information contact the Convention and Visitors Bureau, 233 Peachtree St NE, Suite 2000, 30303; 404/222-6688. Welcome centers are located at Underground Atlanta, at Peachtree Center Mall, at Lenox Square Mall and at the Atlanta Hartsfield Airport.

Atlanta Hartsfield Airport Area

For additional accommodations, see ATLANTA HARTSFIELD AIRPORT AREA, which follows ATLANTA.

City Neighborhoods

Many of the restaurants, unrated dining establishments and some lodgings listed under Atlanta include neighborhoods as well as exact street addresses. Geographic descriptions of these areas are given, followed by a table of restaurants arranged by neighborhood.

Buckhead: South of the northern city limits, west of Lenox and Peachtree Rds, north of Wesley Rd and east of Northside Dr.

Downtown: South of North Ave, west of I-75/I-85, north of I-20 and east of Northside Dr. **North of Downtown:** North of North Ave. **East of Downtown:** East of I-75/I-85.

Midtown/Piedmont Park: South of I-85, west of Piedmont Ave, north of North Ave and east of I-75/85.

ATLANTA RESTAURANTS BY NEIGHBORHOOD AREAS

(For full description, see alphabetical listings under Restaurants)

BUCKHEAD
103 West. 103 W Paces Ferry Rd
Abruzzi Ristorante. 2355 Peachtree Rd NE
Anis. 2974 Grandview Ave
Anthony's. 3109 Piedmont Rd NE
Arugula. 3639 Piedmont Rd NE
Atlanta Fish Market. 265 Pharr Rd
Bacchanalia. 3125 Piedmont Rd
Basil's Mediterranean Cafe. 2985 Grandview Ave
The Bistro. 56 E Andrews Dr NW
Blue Ridge Grill. 1261 W Paces Ferry Rd
Bone's. 3130 Piedmont Rd NE
Brasserie Le Coze. 3393 Peachtree Rd
Buckhead Diner. 3073 Piedmont Rd
The Cabin. 2678 Buford Hwy NE
The Cafe (The Ritz-Carlton, Buckhead Hotel). 3434 Peachtree Rd NE
Cafe Tu Tu Tango. 220 Pharr Rd
Carbo's Cafe. 3717 Roswell Rd
Cassis (Grand Hyatt Hotel). 3300 Peachtree Rd
Chops. 70 W Paces Ferry Rd
The Colonnade. 1879 Cheshire Bridge Rd
Dante's Down The Hatch. 3380 Peachtree Rd NE
The Dining Room (The Ritz-Carlton, Buckhead Hotel). 3434 Peachtree Rd NE
Eclipse Di Luna. 764 Miami Circle
Feeders. 248 Pharr Rd
Fratelli Di Napoli. 2101-B Bennett St
The Frog & Peach Bistro. 3167 Peachtree Blvd
Georgia Grille. 2290 Peachtree Rd
Hedgerose. 490 E Paces Ferry Rd
Imperial Fez. 2285 Peachtree Rd NE
Jim White's Half Shell. 2349 Peachtree Rd NE
Kudzu Cafe. 3215 Peachtree Rd NE
La Grotta. 2637 Peachtree Rd NE
Luna Si. 1931 Peachtree Rd
MacArthur's. 2171 Peachtree Rd
Maggiano's Little Italy. 3368 Peachtree Road NE
McKinnon's Louisiane. 3209 Maple Dr
Nakato. 1776 Cheshire Bridge Rd NE
Nava. 3060 Peachtree Rd
Nino's. 1931 Cheshire Bridge Rd
Ok Cafe. 1284 W Paces Ferry Rd
Palisades. 1829 Peachtree Rd NE

Pano's And Paul's. 1232 W Paces Ferry Rd
Phoenix Brewing Co. 5600 Roswell Road NE
Pricci. 500 Pharr Rd
Prime. 3393 Peachtree Rd NE
Riviera. 519 E Paces Ferry Rd NE
Rock Bottom. 3242 Peachtree Rd
Seeger's. 111 W Paces Ferry Rd
Soto. 3330 Piedmont Rd
South Of France. 2345 Cheshire Bridge Rd
Sundown Cafe. 2165 Cheshire Bridge Rd
Tomtom. 3393 Peachtree Rd
Toulouse. 2293-B Peachtree Rd NE
The Varsity Jr. 1085 Lindbergh Dr NE

DOWNTOWN
City Grill. 50 Hurt Plaza
Dailey's. 17 International Blvd
Haveli. 225 Spring St
Hsu's Gourmet Chinese. 192 Peachtree Center Ave
Lombardi's. 94 Upper Pryor St
Mick's Underground. 75 Upper Alabama St
Mumbo Jumbo Bar And Grill. 89 Park Pl NE
Nikolai's Roof (Hilton & Towers Hotel). 255 Courtland St NE
Pittypat's Porch. 25 International Blvd
The Restaurant (The Ritz-Carlton Hotel). 181 Peachtree St NE
Rio Bravo Grill. 240 Peachtree St

NORTH OF DOWNTOWN
Canoe. 4199 Paces Ferry Rd NW
Circle Sushi. 8725 Roswell Rd
Food Studio. 887 W Marietta St
Horseradish Grill. 4320 Powers Ferry Rd
La Grotta Ravinia (Crowne Plaza Ravinia Hotel). 4355 Ashford Dunwoody Rd
La Paz. 6410 Roswell Rd
McKendrick's. 4505 Ashford Dunwoody Rd
Mi Spia. 4505 Ashford Dunwoody Rd
Ray's On The River. 6700 Powers Ferry Rd
Ruth's Chris Steak House. 5788 Roswell Rd
Soho. 4200 Paces Ferry Rd, Suite 107
Villa Christina. 45 Perimeter Summit Blvd
The Vinings Inn. 3011 Paces Mill Rd
The Waverly Grill (Renaissance Waverly Hotel). 2450 Galleria Pkwy

EAST OF DOWNTOWN
Babette's Cafe. 471 N Highland Ave NE
Dish. 870 N Highland Ave NE
Dusty's Barbecue. 1815 Briarcliff Rd
Harvest. 853 N Highland Ave NE
Petite Auberge. 2935 N Druid Hill Rd
Thai Chili. 2169 Briarcliff Rd NE

MIDTOWN/PIEDMONT PARK
The Abbey. 163 Ponce de Leon Ave NE
Agnes & Muriel's. 1514 Monroe Dr
Camille's. 1186 N Highland Ave
Ciboulette. 1529 Piedmont Ave
Coohill's. 1100 Peachtree St NE
Country Place. 1197 Peachtree St NE
Encore At The Fox. 654 Peachtree St
Fat Matt's. 1811 Piedmont
Gauguin Bistro. 889 W Peachtree
Indigo Coastal Grill. 1397 N Highland Ave
Le Saint Amour. 1620 Piedmont Ave NE
The Mansion. 179 Ponce de Leon Ave
Mary Mac's Tearoom. 224 Ponce de Leon Ave
Meritage (Four Seasons Hotel). 75 Fourteenth St
Nickiemoto's. 990 Piedmont Ave
Pirozki's. 1447 Peachtree Rd NE
Pleasant Peasant. 555 Peachtree St
South City Kitchen. 1144 Crescent Ave
Terra Cotta. 1044 Greenwood Ave
Varsity. 61 North Ave
Veni Vidi Vici. 41 14th St
Zocalo. 187 10th St

Note: When a listing is located in a town that does not have its own city heading, it will appear under the city nearest to its location. In these cases, the address and town appear in parenthesis immediately following the name of the establishment.

Motels

✓★ ★ **COMFORT INN BUCKHEAD.** *2115 Piedmont Rd NE (30324), in Buckhead.* 404/876-4365; FAX 404/873-1007. 186 rms, 3 story. Jan-Sept: S, D $59-$95; each addl $6; suites $99-$149; under 18 free; higher rates special events; lower rates rest of yr. Crib free. TV; cable (premium). Pool. Complimentary continental bkfst. Ck-out noon. Coin lndry. Meeting rms. Business servs avail. Some refrigerators. Cr cds: A, D, DS, MC, V.

D ⤢ ⊠ 🔥 SC

★ ★ **COUNTRY HEARTH INN.** *5793 Roswell Rd NE (30328), in Sandy Springs, north of downtown.* 404/252-6400; FAX 404/851-9306. 82 rms, 5 story. S, D $74-$78; each addl $6; under 18 free; higher rates hols. Crib $7. TV; cable (premium). Pool. Complimentary continental bkfst. Complimentary coffee in rms. Restaurant adj 11:30 am-10:30 pm. Ck-out noon. Meeting rm. Business servs avail. Health club privileges. In-rm modem link. Cr cds: A, C, D, DS, MC, V.

D ⊠ ⊠ 🔥 SC

★ ★ **COURTYARD BY MARRIOTT-NORTHLAKE.** *(4083 La Vista Rd, Tucker 30084) I-285 exit 28, adj to Northlake Festival Mall.* 770/938-1200; FAX 770/934-6497. 128 units, 2 story, 20 suites. S $94; D $104; suites $110-$120; under 18 free; wkly, wkend rates. Crib free. TV; cable (premium). Pool; whirlpool. Complimentary coffee in rms. Restaurant 6:30-10 am, 5-10 pm; Sat, Sun 7 am-noon, 5-10 pm. Bar 4-11 pm. Ck-out noon. Coin lndry. Meeting rms. Business servs avail. In-rm modem link. Valet serv. Exercise equipt. Some refrigerators. Private patios, balconies. Cr cds: A, C, D, DS, MC, V.

D ⊠ 🏃 ⤢ 🔥 SC

✓★ ★ **DAYS INN-SOUTH.** *(6840 Shannon Pkwy S, Union City 30291-2010) 15 mi SW on I-85, exit 13.* 770/964-3777; FAX 770/964-6631. 100 rms, 2 story. S $49-$59; D $57-$63; each addl $5; under 18 free; higher rates Race Wkend. Crib free. TV; cable (premium), VCR avail. Complimentary continental bkfst. Complimentary coffee in rms. Restaurant opp 6 am-10 pm. Ck-out noon. Meeting rms. Coin lndry. Pool. Some refrigerators, microwaves. Cr cds: A, D, DS, MC, V.

D ⤢ ⊠ 🔥

★ ★ ★ **EMORY INN.** *1641 Clifton Rd NE (30329), north of downtown.* 404/712-6700; FAX 404/712-6701; res: 800/933-6679. E-mail sales@ecch.emory.edu. 107 rms, 2 story. S $84-$125; under 18 free. Crib free. TV; cable (premium). Pool; whirlpool. Coffee in rms. Restaurant 7 am-2 pm, 5-10 pm; Sat 7-10 am, 5-10 pm. Rm serv. Ck-out noon. Coin lndry. Convention facilities. Business center. In-rm modem link. Bellhops. Valet serv. Tennis privileges. Health club privileges. Microwaves avail. Antiques. Library/sitting rm. Cr cds: A, C, D, DS, ER, MC, V.

D 🏃 ⤢ ⊠ 🔥 SC 🎿

★ ★ **FAIRFIELD INN BY MARRIOTT.** *1470 Spring St NW (30309), in Midtown/Piedmont Park.* 404/872-5821; FAX 404/874-3602. E-mail fairfieldmidtown@mindspring.com. 182 rms, 4 story. S $64; D $69; each addl $10; under 18 free; higher rates conventions. Crib free. TV; cable (premium). Pool. Complimentary continental bkfst. Ck-out noon. Meeting rms. Business servs avail. Exercise equipt. Some refrigerators. Cr cds: A, C, D, DS, MC, V.

D ⤢ 🏃 ⊠ 🔥 SC

✓★ ★ **HAMPTON INN-BUCKHEAD.** *3398 Piedmont Rd NE (30305), in Buckhead.* 404/233-5656; FAX 404/237-4688. 154 rms, 6 story. S $85-$92; D $90-$102; higher rates: wkends, special events; under 18 free. Crib free. TV; cable (premium). Pool. Complimentary continental bkfst. Coffee in rms. Restaurant adj 11 am-11 pm. Ck-out noon. Meeting

rms. Business servs avail. In-rm modem link. Valet serv. Health club privileges. Cr cds: A, D, DS, MC, V.

D ⤢ ⊠ 🔥 SC

✓★ **RED ROOF INN-DRUID HILLS.** *1960 N Druid Hills Rd (30329), I-85 exit 31, north of downtown.* 404/321-1653; FAX 404/248-9774. 115 rms, 3 story. S, D $48-$65; each addl $6. Crib free. Pet accepted, some restrictions. TV; cable (premium). Complimentary coffee in lobby. Restaurant nearby. Ck-out noon. In-rm modem link. Health club privileges. Cr cds: A, C, D, DS, MC, V.

D 🐾 ⊠ ⊠ 🔥 SC

★ ★ **RESIDENCE INN BY MARRIOTT-DUNWOODY.** *1901 Savoy Dr (30341), I-285 at Chamblee-Dunwoody exit 22, north of downtown.* 770/455-4446; FAX 770/451-5183. 144 kit. suites, 2 story. S, D $99-$119; wkend rates. Crib free. Pet accepted, some restrictions. TV; cable (premium), VCR avail. Heated pool; whirlpools. Complimentary continental bkfst. Ck-out noon. Coin lndry. Meeting rm. Business servs avail. In-rm modem link. Valet serv. Health club privileges. Many fireplaces; microwaves avail. Private patios, balconies. Picnic tables, grills. Cr cds: A, D, DS, MC, V.

D 🐾 ⤢ ⊠ 🔥 SC

★ ★ **STONE MOUNTAIN INN.** *(Robert E Lee Blvd, Stone Mountain 30086) 16 mi E on US 78, Stone Mountain Park exit, in Stone Mountain Park.* 770/469-3311; FAX 770/498-5691; res: 800/722-1000. 92 rms, 2 story. $6 parking fee (required to reach motel). Mid-May-early Sept: S, D $79-$99; each addl $10; under 18 free; lower rates rest of yr. Crib free. TV; cable (premium). Pool. Coffee in rms. Restaurant 7 am-9 pm (hrs vary off-season). Ck-out 11 am. Coin lndry. Meeting rms. Business servs avail. In-rm modem link. Gift shop. Exercise equipt. Lighted tennis. 36-hole golf, pro. Balconies; private patios for poolside rms. Cr cds: A, C, D, DS, JCB, MC, V.

D ➤ 🏒 🎿 ⤢ 🚶 ⊠ 🔥 SC

★ ★ **SUMMERFIELD SUITES.** *505 Pharr Rd NE (30305), in Buckhead.* 404/262-7880; FAX 404/262-3734. 88 suites, 3 story. No elvtr. S, D $199-$239; wkend rates. Crib free. Pet accepted, some restrictions. TV; cable (premium), VCR. Heated pool; whirlpool. Complimentary continental bkfst. Complimentary coffee in rms. Restaurant opp 11 am-midnight. Ck-out 11 am. Coin lndry. Meeting rms. In-rm modem link. Valet serv. Sundries. Exercise equipt. Refrigerators, microwaves. Balconies. Picnic tables, grills. Cr cds: A, C, D, DS, JCB, MC, V.

D 🐾 ⤢ 🏃 ⊠ 🔥 SC

★ ★ **SUMMERFIELD SUITES.** *760 Mt Vernon Hwy NE (30328), north of downtown.* 404/250-0110; FAX 404/250-9335; res: 800/833-4353. 122 kit. suites, 2-3 story. 1-bedrm $159; 2-bedrm $199; wkend rates. Crib free. Pet accepted, some restrictions. TV; cable (premium), VCR (movies $6). Heated pool; whirlpool. Complimentary continental bkfst. Complimentary coffee in rms. Ck-out 11 am. Coin lndry. Meeting rms. Business servs avail. In-rm modem link. Sundries. Exercise equipt. Microwaves avail. Picnic tables, grills. Cr cds: A, C, D, DS, JCB, MC, V.

D 🐾 ⤢ 🏃 ⊠ 🔥 SC

✓★ **SUPER 8-FOREST PARK.** *3701 Jonesboro Rd SE (30354), south of downtown.* 404/361-1111; FAX 404/366-0294. 73 rms, 2 story. S $45-$150; D $50-$150; each addl $5; suites $75-$90; under 18 free. Crib $5. TV; cable (premium). Pool. Complimentary continental bkfst. Restaurant nearby. Ck-out 11 am. Coin lndry. Meeting rms. Business servs avail. In-rm modem link. Sundries. Some refrigerators, microwaves. Cr cds: A, C, D, DS, MC, V.

D ⤢ ⊠ 🔥 SC

★ ★ **TRAVELODGE-DOWNTOWN.** *311 Courtland St NE (30303), downtown.* 404/659-4545; FAX 404/659-5934. E-mail sleepy bear@mindspring.com. 71 rms, 3 story. S $69-$89; D $86-$106; each addl $8; under 18 free; wkend rates. Crib free. TV; cable (premium). Pool. Complimentary continental bkfst. Coffee in rms. Ck-out noon. Valet serv.

Health club privileges. Some balconies. Cr cds: A, C, D, DS, ER, JCB, MC, V.

D ≈ ⋈ ⋒ SC

Motor Hotels

★ ★ ★ **COURTYARD BY MARRIOTT-CUMBERLAND CENTER.** *3000 Cumberland Circle (30339), I-285 Cobb Pkwy exit 13, north of downtown.* 770/952-2555; FAX 770/952-2409. 182 rms, 8 story. S $89; D $109; under 12 free. Crib free. TV; cable (premium). Indoor pool; whirlpool. Complimentary coffee in rms. Restaurant 6:30-10 am, 5-10:30 pm; wkends 7-11 am. Bar 5-11 pm. Ck-out noon. Meeting rms. Business servs avail. In-rm modem link. Valet serv. Sundries. Exercise rm; sauna. Health club privileges. Some refrigerators. Balconies. Cr cds: A, C, D, DS, MC, V.

D ≈ ⊀ ⋈ ⋒ SC

✔★ ★ **FOUR POINTS BY SHERATON.** *3387 Lenox Rd NE (30326), in Buckhead.* 404/261-5500; FAX 404/261-6140; res: 800/241-0200. 180 rms, 2-3 story. S, D $99-$119; each addl $20; suites $99-$260. Crib $10. TV. 2 pools. Complimentary continental bkfst. Ck-out noon. Meeting rms. Business servs avail. Valet serv. Health club privileges. Some refrigerators. Cr cds: A, C, D, DS, MC, V.

D ≈ ⋈ ⋒ SC

✔★ ★ **QUALITY INN-NORTHEAST.** *2960 NE Expy (I-85) (30341), I-85 exit 33, at Shallowford Rd, north of downtown.* 770/451-5231; FAX 770/454-8704. 153 rms, 2 story. S, D $42-$51; family rates. Crib free. TV; cable (premium). Pool. Complimentary continental bkfst. Coffee in rms. Ck-out noon. Coin lndry. Meeting rms. Business servs avail. In-rm modem link. Bellhops. Microwaves avail. Cr cds: A, C, D, DS, MC, V.

D ≈ ⋈ ⋒ SC

✔★ ★ **RAMADA INN-SIX FLAGS.** *4225 Fulton Industrial Blvd (30336), I-20W exit 14, west of downtown.* 404/691-4100; FAX 404/691-2117. 229 rms, 4-5 story. Apr-mid-Sept: S, D $58-$78; each addl $10; lower rates rest of yr. Crib free. TV; cable (premium). Pool. Bar 3 pm-2:30 am; entertainment. Ck-out 11 am. Coin lndry. Meeting rms. Business servs avail. Game rm. Some refrigerators. Grill. Cr cds: A, D, DS, MC, V.

D ≈ ⋈ ⋒ SC

★ ★ ★ **WYNDHAM GARDEN.** *2857 Paces Ferry Rd (30339), I-285 exit 12, north of downtown.* 770/432-5555; FAX 770/436-5558. Web www.travelweb.com. 159 rms, 4 story. S, D $125-$135; suites $149-$150; under 17 free; wkend rates. Crib free. TV; cable (premium). Heated pool; whirlpool; poolside serv. Restaurant 6:30 am-2 pm, 5-10 pm. Rm serv 4-10 pm. Bar 4 pm-midnight. Ck-out noon. Meeting rms. Business servs avail. In-rm modem link. Valet serv. Tennis privileges. Health club privileges. Private patios, balconies. Cr cds: A, C, D, DS, JCB, MC, V.

D ⅍ ≈ ⋈ ⋒ SC

Hotels

★ ★ **BEST WESTERN INN AT THE PEACHTREES.** *330 W Peachtree St NW (30308), downtown.* 404/577-6970; FAX 404/659-3244. 110 rms, 4 story. S $145; D $165; each addl $10; under 18 free. TV; cable (premium). Complimentary full bkfst. Ck-out noon. Meeting rm. Business center. Coin lndry. Covered parking. Airport transportation. Exercise equipt. Health club privileges. Some refrigerators, microwaves. Near Merchandise Mart & Apparel Mart. Cr cds: A, C, D, DS, JCB, MC, V.

D ⊀ ⋈ ⋒ SC ⌂

★ ★ **THE BILTMORE SUITES.** *30 5th St NE (30308), at W Peachtree St, in Midtown/Piedmont Park.* 404/874-0824; FAX 404/872-0067; res: 800/822-0824. 62 kit. suites, 10 story. Kit. suites $109-$299. TV; cable. Complimentary continental bkfst. Restaurant nearby. Ck-out noon. Covered parking. Microwaves. Some balconies. Built 1924; Georgian design with vaulted ceilings, limestone detailing. Cr cds: A, C, D, DS, MC, V.

⋈ ⋒ ⌂

★ ★ **COMFORT INN-DOWNTOWN.** *101 International Blvd (30303), downtown.* 404/524-5555; FAX 404/221-0702. E-mail comfort@ mindspring.com. 260 rms, 11 story. S, D $79-$229; each addl $10; under 18 free; wkend rates. Crib free. Garage in/out $10. TV; cable (premium). Pool; whirlpool. Restaurant 6:30-10:30 am, 11:30 am-1:30 pm, 5:30-10 pm. Bar 4 pm-12:30 am. Ck-out noon. Meeting rms. Business servs avail. In-rm modem link. Gift shop. Exercise equipt. Health club privileges. Adj to Atlanta Market Center and World Congress Center. Cr cds: A, C, D, DS, ER, JCB, MC, V.

D ≈ ⊀ ⋈ ⋒ SC

★ ★ ★ **CROWNE PLAZA RAVINIA.** *4355 Ashford-Dunwoody Rd (30346), 1 blk N I-285 exit 21, adj Perimeter Mall, north of downtown.* 770/395-7700; FAX 770/392-9503. 495 rms, 15 story. S $149-$189; D $159-$199; each addl $10; suites $350-$1,150; under 18 free; wkend rates. Crib free. Valet parking $9. TV; cable (premium), VCR avail. Indoor pool; whirlpool. Restaurants 6 am-11 pm (also see LA GROTTA RAVINIA). Rm serv to 1 am. Bar noon-2 am; entertainment exc Sun. Ck-out noon. Convention facilities. Business center. In-rm modem link. Concierge. Gift shop. Lighted tennis. Exercise equipt; sauna. Microwaves, refrigerator avail. Luxury level. Cr cds: A, C, D, DS, JCB, MC, V.

D ⅍ ≈ ⊀ ⋈ ⋒ SC ⌂

★ ★ **DAYS INN-DOWNTOWN.** *300 Spring St (30308), downtown.* 404/523-1144; FAX 404/577-8495. 263 rms, 10 story. S $89-$199; D $99-$209; each addl $10; under 18 free. Crib free. Garage $8/day. TV; cable (premium). Pool. Coffee in rms. Restaurant 6:30 am-10 pm. Bar 5 pm-midnight. Ck-out 11 am. Meeting rms. Business servs avail. In-rm modem link. Gift shop. Airport, RR station, bus depot transportation. Some refrigerators. Balconies. Cr cds: A, C, D, DS, JCB, MC, V.

D ≈ ⋈ ⋒ SC

★ ★ ★ **DOUBLETREE GUEST SUITE HOTEL-ATLANTA PERIMETER.** *6120 Peachtree-Dunwoody Rd (30328), north of downtown.* 770/668-0808; FAX 770/668-0008. Web www.doubletreehotels.com. 224 suites, 6 story. Suites $69-$159; under 18 free; wkend rates. Crib free. TV; cable (premium), VCR avail. Indoor/outdoor pool; whirlpool. Coffee in rms. Restaurant 6 am-11 pm. Bar 4:30 pm-2 am. Ck-out noon. Coin lndry. Meeting rms. Business center. In-rm modem link. Exercise equipt; sauna. Health club privileges. Refrigerators; microwaves avail. Cr cds: A, C, D, DS, ER, JCB, MC, V.

D ≈ ⊀ ⋈ ⋒ SC ⌂

★ ★ ★ **DOUBLETREE GUEST SUITES-ATLANTA GALLERIA.** *2780 Whitley Rd (30339), I-285 Cobb Pkwy exit 13, north of downtown.* 770/980-1900; FAX 770/980-1528; res: 800/843-5858. 155 suites, 8 story. Suites $169-$189; under 18 free; wkly, wkend rates. Crib free. TV; cable (premium). Pool. Complimentary full bkfst. Complimentary coffee in rms. Restaurant 11 am-2 pm, 5-10 pm. Bar 11-1 am; Sun to 12:30 am; entertainment Tues-Sat. Ck-out noon. Meeting rms. Business servs avail. In-rm modem link. Bathrm phones, in-rm whirlpools, refrigerators. Some private patios, balconies. Cr cds: A, C, D, DS, MC, V.

D ≈ ⋈ ⋒ SC

★ ★ **EMBASSY SUITES.** *3285 Peachtree Rd NE (30305), GA 400, in Buckhead.* 404/261-7733; FAX 404/261-6857. 317 rms, 16 story. Suites $159-$225; under 18 free; wkend rates; higher rates special events. Crib free. TV; cable (premium). 2 pools, 1 indoor; whirlpool. Complimentary full bkfst. Complimentary coffee in rms. Restaurant 11 am-2 pm, 5-10 pm. Bar 11-1 am. Ck-out noon. Coin lndry. Meeting rms. Business servs avail. In-rm modem link. Gift shop. Airport transportation. Exercise equipt; sauna. Health club privileges. Refrigerators, wet bars. Cr cds: A, C, D, DS, JCB, MC, V.

D ≈ ⊀ ⋈ ⋒ SC

★ ★ ★ **EMBASSY SUITES-GALLERIA.** *2815 Akers Mill Rd (30339), I-285 exit 13, north of downtown.* 770/984-9300; FAX 770/955-4183. Web www.embassy-suites.com. 261 suites, 9 story. S $159-$199; D $189-$219; each addl $20; under 18 free; wkend rates. Crib free. TV; cable (premium). Indoor pool; whirlpool. Sauna. Complimentary full bkfst. Restaurant 11 am-10 pm. Bar to midnight. Ck-out noon. Meeting rms. Business servs avail. In-rm modem link. Gift shop. Refrigerators; microwaves avail. Garden atrium, glass elvtrs. Cr cds: A, C, D, DS, MC, V.

⊡ 🏊 ⚊ 🎿 🔥 SC

★ ★ ★ ★ **FOUR SEASONS.** *75 Fourteenth St (30309), Grand Bldg, in Midtown/Piedmont Park.* 404/881-9898; FAX 404/873-4692. Occupying the first 20 floors of the Grand Building, this luxury hotel combines Old World traditions with New South hospitality. A fifth-floor terrace provides skyline views, while the fourth floor boasts a grand ballroom. 244 rms, 19 story. S, D $240-$335; each addl $30; suites $550-$2,000; under 18 free; wkend rates. Crib free. Pet accepted. Garage parking, valet $18. TV; cable (premium), VCR avail. Indoor pool; whirlpool, poolside serv. Restaurant 6:30 am-11 pm (also see MERITAGE). Rm serv 24 hrs. Bar 11:30-1 am; entertainment. Ck-out 1 pm. Meeting rms. Business center. In-rm modem link. Concierge. Gift shop. Barber, beauty shop. Exercise rm; sauna, steam rm. Spa. Refrigerators, minibars. Cr cds: A, C, D, DS, ER, JCB, MC, V.

⊡ 🤾 🏊 🎿 🏋 🔥 SC 🛶

★ ★ ★ **GEORGIAN TERRACE.** *659 Peachtree St (30308), in Midtown/Piedmont Park.* 404/897-1991; res: 800/651-2316; FAX 404/724-9116. Web www.grandheritage.com. 320 kit. suites, 19 story. S $175-$650; D $195-$670; each addl $20; under 18 free; package plans. Crib free. Pet accepted, some restrictions. Valet parking $12; garage $12. TV; cable (premium), VCR avail. Complimentary coffee in rms. Restaurant 11 am-9 pm. Rm serv 24 hrs. Bar 11 am-11 pm. Ck-out noon. Convention facilities. Business center. In-rm modem link. Concierge. Gift shop. Exercise equipt. Heated pool; poolside serv. Bathrm phones, refrigerators, microwaves, minibars. Some balconies. Luxury level. Cr cds: A, C, D, DS, ER, MC, V.

⊡ 🤾 🏊 🎿 🏋 🔥 SC 🛶

★ ★ ★ **GRAND HYATT.** *3300 Peachtree Rd (30305), in Buckhead.* 404/365-8100; FAX 404/233-5686. 439 rms, 25 story. S $189-$285, D $209-$270; each addl $25; suites $485-$2,500; wkend rates. TV; cable (premium), VCR avail. Pet accepted. Pool. Restaurants (see CASSIS). Rm serv 24 hrs. Bars 11-1 am; entertainment, pianist. Ck-out noon. Convention facilities. Business center. In-rm modem link. Concierge. Gift shop. Garage, valet parking. Tennis privileges. Golf privileges. Exercise equipt; sauna. Massage. Bathrm phones, minibars. Luxury level. Cr cds: A, C, D, DS, ER, JCB, MC, V.

⊡ 🤾 🏋 🏌 🏊 🎿 ⚊ 🔥 SC 🛶

★ ★ ★ **HILTON & TOWERS.** *255 Courtland St NE (30303), at Harris St, downtown.* 404/659-2000; FAX 404/222-2868. Web www.hilton.com. 1,224 rms, 30 story. S $139-$295; D $145-$295; each addl $25; suites from $350; family, wkend rates. Crib free. Valet parking $12, garage avail. TV; cable (premium), VCR avail. Pool; whirlpool, poolside serv. Restaurant open 24 hrs; dining rm (see NIKOLAI'S ROOF). Bars 11:30-2 am; Sun 12:30 pm-midnight; entertainment. Ck-out 11 am. Convention facilities. Business center. In-rm modem link. Shopping arcade. Lighted tennis, pro. Exercise rm; sauna. Health club privileges. Some bathrm phones. Balconies. Luxury level. Cr cds: A, C, D, DS, ER, JCB, MC, V.

⊡ 🏌 🏊 🎿 🏋 🎾 🔥 SC 🛶

★ ★ ★ **HOLIDAY INN SELECT.** *4386 Chamblee Dunwoody Rd (30341), I-285, exit 22, north of downtown.* 770/457-6363; FAX 770/936-9592. 250 rms, 5 story. S $129; D $139; each addl $10; suites $225-$400; under 18 free; wkend rates. Crib free. Pet accepted, some restrictions. TV; cable (premium). Heated pool. Complimentary coffee in rms. Restaurant 6 am-2 pm, 5-10 pm; wkends 7 am-2 pm. Bar 4 pm-midnight. Ck-out noon. Coin lndry. Meeting rms. Business servs avail. In-rm modem link. Valet serv. Exercise equipt. Microwaves avail. Cr cds: A, C, D, DS, ER, JCB, MC, V.

⊡ 🤾 🏊 🎿 ⚊ 🔥 SC

★ ★ **HOLIDAY INN-ATLANTA CENTRAL.** *418 Armour Dr NE (30324), in Midtown/Piedmont Park.* 404/873-4661; FAX 404/872-1292. 331 units, 5 story. S, D $79-$119; suites $150-$300; under 19 free; wkend rates. Crib free. TV; cable (premium). Pool; poolside serv. Coffee in rms. Restaurant 6:30 am-2 pm, 5-10 pm. Bar 5-11 pm. Ck-out noon. Coin lndry. Convention facilities. In-rm modem link. Concierge. Gift shop. Barber, beauty shop. Exercise equipt. Refrigerators, microwaves avail. In-rm whirl-

pool, refrigerator, wet bar, fireplace in suites. Balconies. Cr cds: A, C, D, DS, JCB, MC, V.

⊡ 🏊 🎿 🏋 ⚊ 🔥 SC

★ ★ ★ **HOLIDAY INN-BUCKHEAD.** *3377 Peachtree Rd NE (30326), GA 400, in Buckhead.* 404/264-1111; FAX 404/233-7061. E-mail acct.hi.lenox@internetmci.com. 297 rms, 11 story. S, D $119-$149; each addl $10; suites $150-$250; under 18 free; wkend, hol rates; higher rates special events. Crib free. TV; cable (premium), VCR avail. Pool. Complimentary coffee in rms. Restaurant 6 am-2 pm, 5-11 pm. Bar from 5 pm. Ck-out 11 am. Coin lndry. Meeting rms. Business servs avail. In-rm modem link. Concierge. Health club privileges. Many refrigerators. Cr cds: A, C, D, DS, JCB, MC, V.

⊡ 🏊 🎿 ⚊ 🔥 SC

★ ★ ★ **HYATT REGENCY.** *265 Peachtree St NE (30303), in Peachtree Center, downtown.* 404/577-1234; FAX 404/588-4137. Web www.hyatt.com. 1,264 rms, 23 story. S, D $185-$240; each addl $25; suites from $450; under 18 free; wkend rates. Crib free. Garage $17-$20. TV; cable (premium). Pool; poolside serv. Restaurant 6:30-1 am. Bar noon-2 am. Ck-out noon. Convention facilities. Business center. In-rm modem link. Concierge. Gift shop. Exercise equipt. Health club privileges. Minibars; many refrigerators in suites. Many balconies. Luxury level. Cr cds: A, C, D, DS, MC, V.

⊡ 🏊 🏋 🎿 ⚊ 🔥 SC 🛶

★ ★ ★ **J W MARRIOTT.** *3300 Lenox Rd NE (30326), at Peachtree Rd, in Buckhead.* 404/262-3344; FAX 404/262-8689. 371 units, 25 story. S, D $260; suites $300-$1,000; under 18 free. Crib free. Garage $8, valet $14. TV; cable (premium), VCR avail. Indoor pool; whirlpool. Restaurant 6:30 am-10:30 pm. Rm serv 24 hrs. Bar noon-1 am; Fri, Sat to 2 am. Ck-out noon. Convention facilities. Business center. In-rm modem link. Concierge. Valet serv. Shopping arcade. Exercise equipt; sauna. Massage. Bathrm phones, minibars. Luxury level. Cr cds: A, C, D, DS, JCB, MC, V.

⊡ 🏊 🏋 🎿 ⚊ 🔥 SC 🛶

★ ★ ★ **MARRIOTT MARQUIS.** *265 Peachtree Center Ave (30303), downtown.* 404/521-0000; FAX 404/586-6299. 1,671 rms, 47 story. S, D $240-$260; each addl $20; suites $350-$1,500; under 18 free; wkend rates. Crib free. Garage $17. TV; cable (premium), VCR avail. Indoor/outdoor pool; whirlpool, poolside serv. Restaurants 6 am-midnight. Rm serv 24 hrs. Bar 11-2 am, Sun from 12:30 pm. Ck-out noon. Convention facilities. Business center. In-rm modem link. Shopping arcade. Barber, beauty shop. Exercise equipt; sauna. Health club privileges. Refrigerators. Bathrm phone in suites. Luxury level. Cr cds: A, C, D, DS, ER, JCB, MC, V.

⊡ 🏊 🏋 🎿 ⚊ 🔥 SC 🛶

★ ★ ★ **MARRIOTT NORTH CENTRAL.** *2000 Century Blvd NE (30345), I-85 exit 32; in Century Center Park, north of downtown.* 404/325-0000; FAX 404/325-4920. Web www.marriott.com. 287 rms, 15 story. S, D $175; suites from $275; wkend rates. Crib free. TV; cable (premium). Heated pool; poolside serv. Complimentary coffee in lobby. Restaurant 6:30 am-2 pm, 5-11 pm. Bar 2 pm-midnight. Ck-out noon. Convention facilities. Business servs avail. In-rm modem link. Gift shop. Barber. Lighted tennis. Exercise equipt. Some refrigerators. Luxury level. Cr cds: A, C, D, DS, ER, JCB, MC, V.

⊡ 🏌 🏊 🎿 🏋 ⚊ 🔥 SC

★ ★ ★ **OMNI HOTEL AT CNN CENTER.** *100 CNN Center (30335), downtown.* 404/659-0000; FAX 404/525-5050. Web www.omnihotelcnn.com. 458 rms, 15 story. S $250; D $275; each addl from $25; suites $775-$2,200; under 18 free; wkend rates. Crib free. Garage in/out $15-$18. TV; cable (premium), VCR avail. Restaurant 7 am-11 pm. Rm serv 6:30-2 am. Bars 11-1 am. Ck-out noon. Convention facilities. Business center. In-rm modem link. Concierge. Shopping arcade. Barber, beauty shop. Valet parking. Airport transportation. Health club privileges. Bathrm phones, minibars, wet bars. Balconies. Omni Sports Coliseum,

Georgia Dome, Centennial Olympic Park, Georgia World Congress Center adj. Cr cds: A, C, D, DS, ER, JCB, MC, V.

D ⊠ ⊠ SC ⚡

★ ★ ★ **RADISSON HOTEL.** 165 Courtland St (30303), downtown. 404/659-6500; FAX 404/524-1259. E-mail radinfo@radisson.atl.com; web www.radisson.atl.com. 747 rms, 12 story. S $170; D $180; each addl $10; suites $275-$675; under 18 free; wknd rates. Crib free. Covered parking $12. TV; cable (premium). Indoor/outdoor pool; whirlpool, poolside serv. Restaurant 6:30 am-11 pm. Bar 11-2 am; Sun to 12:30 am. Ck-out noon. Convention facilities. Business center. In-rm modem link. Concierge. Barber, beauty shop. Exercise equipt; sauna. Health club privileges. Game rm. Some bathrm phones. Some private patios, balconies. Cr cds: A, C, D, DS, JCB, MC, V.

D ⊠ ⚡ ⊠ ⊠ SC ⚡

↙★ ★ **RADISSON INN-EXECUTIVE PARK.** 2061 N Druid Hills Rd NE (30329), at I-85 exit 31, in Buckhead. 404/321-4174; FAX 404/636-7264. 208 rms, 9 story. S, D $109-$119; under 18 free; wknd rates. Crib free. TV; cable (premium), VCR avail. Pool. Complimentary coffee in rms. Ck-out noon. Meeting rms. Business servs avail. In-rm modem link. Exercise equipt. Near Lenox Square. Luxury level. Cr cds: A, C, D, DS, ER, MC, V.

D ⊠ ⚡ ⊠ ⊠ SC

★ ★ **REGENCY SUITES.** 975 W Peachtree St NE (30309), at 10th St, in Midtown/Piedmont Park. 404/876-5003; FAX 404/817-7511; res: 800/642-3629. E-mail sales@regencysuites.com. 96 kit. suites, 9 story. Suites $159-$179; under 18 free; wknd, monthly rates. Crib free. Garage, covered parking $8. TV; cable (premium). Complimentary continental bkfst. Complimentary coffee in rms. Ck-out 11 am. Coin lndry. Meeting rms. Business servs avail. Exercise equipt. Microwaves. Adj MARTA station. Cr cds: A, C, D, DS, MC, V.

D ⚡ ⊠ ⊠ SC

★ ★ **RENAISSANCE WAVERLY.** 2450 Galleria Pkwy (30339), I-285 exit 13, north of downtown. 770/953-4500; FAX 770/953-0740. Web www.rennaisancehotels.com. 521 rms, 14 story. S $169-$234; D $189-$254; each addl $20; suites $700-$1,400; under 18 free; wknd rates. Crib free. TV; cable (premium), VCR avail. 2 pools, 1 indoor; whirlpool. Complimentary coffee in rms. Restaurant 6 am-10 pm. Rm serv 24 hrs. 3 bars 11:30-1 am. Ck-out noon. Convention facilities. Business center. In-rm modem link. Concierge. Shopping arcade. Exercise equipt; sauna, steam rm. Massage. Racquetball. Bathrm phones; refrigerator in suites. Luxury level. Cr cds: A, C, D, DS, ER, JCB, MC, V.

D ⚡ ⊠ ⚡ ⊠ ⊠ SC ⚡

★ ★ ★ **RENAISSANCE-DOWNTOWN.** 590 W Peachtree St NW (30308), at North Ave, in Midtown/Piedmont Park. 404/881-6000; FAX 404/815-5010. 504 rms, 25 story. S $165-$215; D $180-$240; suites $370-$750; under 18 free; wknd rates. Crib free. Self park $7, valet $12. TV; cable (premium). Pool; poolside serv. Coffee in rms. Restaurant 6:30 am-midnight. Bar from 11 am. Ck-out noon. Meeting rms. Business center. Concierge. Gift shop. Exercise equipt. Health club privileges. Bathrm phones, minibars; some refrigerators, wet bars. Balconies. Luxurious rms; European-style personal service. Luxury level. Cr cds: A, C, D, DS, ER, JCB, MC, V.

D ⚡ ⊠ ⚡ ⚡ SC ⚡

★ ★ ★ ★ **THE RITZ-CARLTON.** 181 Peachtree St NE (30303), downtown. 404/659-0400; FAX 404/688-0400. E-mail zrca@mindspring.com. This quiet retreat in downtown Atlanta has all the important facilities for business travelers and vacationers. The mood at this luxuriously decorated hotel is set by traditional afternoon tea served in an intimate sunken lobby beneath an 18th-century chandelier. 447 rms, 25 story. S, D $186-$265; suites $450-$1,165; under 12 free; wknd, hol rates. Crib free. Valet parking $17, in/out $10. TV; cable (premium), VCR avail. Restaurant (see THE RESTAURANT). Rm serv 24 hrs. Bar 11:30-2 am; entertainment. Ck-out noon. Convention facilities. Business center. In-rm modem link. Concierge. Gift shop. Exercise equipt; steam rm. Massage. Health club

privileges. Refrigerators, minibars. Luxury level. Cr cds: A, C, D, DS, ER, JCB, MC, V.

D ⚡ ⊠ ⊠ ⚡ SC ⚡

★ ★ ★ ★ **THE RITZ-CARLTON, BUCKHEAD.** 3434 Peachtree Rd NE (30326), in Buckhead. 404/237-2700; FAX 404/239-0078. Here is a busy but elegant and eminently comfortable place where you can unwind after a busy day or even spend a busy day. Decorated with the Ritz's signature 18th- and 19th-century antiques, this elegant gem bids a discreet welcome both to visitors and to locals who come to enjoy its many bars and restaurants, including the Dining Room, which serves haute cuisine. 553 rms, 22 story. S, D $175-$215; suites $365-$1,200; under 12 free; wknd rates. Crib free. Valet parking $14; self-park in/out $8. TV; cable (premium), VCR avail. Indoor pool; whirlpool, poolside serv. Restaurants 6:30 am-midnight (also see THE CAFE and THE DINING ROOM). Rm serv 24 hrs. Bar 11-2 am; entertainment. Ck-out noon. Convention facilities. Business center. In-rm modem link. Concierge. Shopping arcade. Airport transportation. Tennis privileges, pro. Golf privileges, greens fee $75-$150. Exercise equipt; sauna, steam rm. Massage. Bathrm phones, minibars. Luxury level. Cr cds: A, C, D, DS, ER, JCB, MC, V.

D ⚡ ⚡ ⊠ ⚡ ⊠ ⊠ SC ⚡

★ ★ ★ **SHERATON COLONY SQUARE.** 188 14th St NE (30361), in Midtown/Piedmont Park. 404/892-6000; FAX 404/872-9192. 467 rms, 27 story. S, D $195-$205; suites $350-$800; under 18 free; wknd rates. Crib free. Valet parking $10. TV; cable (premium), VCR avail. Pool; poolside serv. Restaurant 6:30 am-midnight. Bars 11-1 am; Sun to midnight. Ck-out noon. Convention facilities. Business center. In-rm modem link. Concierge. Shopping arcade. Tennis privileges. Golf privileges. Exercise equipt. Massage. Luxury level. Cr cds: A, C, D, DS, ER, JCB, MC, V.

D ⚡ ⚡ ⊠ ⚡ ⊠ ⊠ SC ⚡

★ ★ ★ **SHERATON MARQUE OF ATLANTA.** 111 Perimeter Center West (30346), I-285 exit 21, north of downtown. 770/396-6800; FAX 770/399-5514; res: 800/683-6100. 274 rms, 12 story, 154 kit. suites. S $99-$165; D $109-$179; each addl $15; kit. suites $99-$165; wknd rates. Crib free. TV; cable (premium). Pool; poolside serv. Complimentary coffee in lobby. Restaurant 6-10 am, noon-2 pm, 6-10 pm. Rm serv 6 am-11 pm. Bar 5:30 pm-midnight. Ck-out noon. Coin lndry. Meeting rms. Business servs avail. Exercise equipt; sauna. Microwaves avail. Balconies. Situated in park-like setting. Cr cds: A, C, D, DS, JCB, MC, V.

D ⊠ ⚡ ⊠ ⚡ SC

★ ★ ★ **SHERATON SUITES-GALLERIA.** 2844 Cobb Pkwy SE (30339), I-285 exit 13, north of downtown. 770/955-3900; FAX 770/916-3165. 278 suites, 17 story. S, D $159; each addl $10; under 18 free; wknd rates. Crib free. TV; cable (premium), VCR avail. 2 pools, 1 indoor; whirlpool, poolside serv. Complimentary coffee in rms. Restaurant 6:30 am-10:30 pm. Bar 11 am-midnight. Ck-out noon. Convention facilities. Business center. In-rm modem link. Gift shop. Free garage parking. Exercise equipt. Refrigerators, microwaves, minibars. Cr cds: A, C, D, DS, ER, MC, V.

D ⊠ ⚡ ⊠ ⚡ ⚡

↙★ ★ **SIERRA SUITES.** 2010 Powers Ferry Rd (30339), NW on I-285 to I-75 exit 110, north of downtown. 770/933-8010; res: 800/474-3772; FAX 770/933-8181. Web www.sierrasuites.com. 89 kit. suites, 3 story. S $49.95-$89.95; D $59.95-$99.95; wkly, wknd rates; higher rates hols. Crib free. TV; cable (premium). Pool. Complimentary coffee in rms. Restaurant nearby. Business servs avail. In-rm modem link. Coin lndry. Exercise equipt. Health club privileges. Pool. Refrigerators, microwaves. Grills. Cr cds: A, C, D, DS, JCB, MC, V.

D ⚡ ⊠ ⚡ SC

★ ★ ★ **SUITE HOTEL-UNDERGROUND.** 54 Peachtree St (30303), at Underground Atlanta, downtown. 404/223-5555; FAX 404/223-0467; res: 800/477-5549. E-mail thesuite@mindspring.com; web www.soramanagement.com/ga/atlanta/index.html. 156 suites, 16 story. S $145-$220; D $155-$230; each addl $10; under 16 free; wknd rates. Crib free. Valet parking $12. TV; cable (premium). Coffee in rms. Restaurant 7-10 am, 5-11 pm. Ck-out noon. Meeting rms. Business servs avail. In-rm modem link. Health club privileges. Bathrm phones. Cr cds: A, C, D, DS, JCB, MC, V.

D ≈ 🏊 🔥

★ ★ ★ **SWISSÔTEL.** *3391 Peachtree Rd NE (30326), in Buckhead.* 404/365-0065; FAX 404/365-8787; res: 800/253-1397. Web www.travelweb.com/thisco/swiss/common/swiss.html. 365 rms, 22 story. S $295-$365; D $315-$385; suites $380-$1,500; under 16 free; wkend rates. Crib free. Garage parking $11, valet $15. TV; cable (premium), VCR avail. Indoor pool; poolside serv. Restaurant 6:30 am-11 pm. Rm serv 24 hrs. Bar 11 am-midnight; Fri, Sat to 1 am. Ck-out noon. Convention facilities. Business center. In-rm modem link. Concierge. Gift shop. Beauty shop. Exercise equipt; steam rm. Bathrm phones, minibars. Art and photo collection. Luxury level. Cr cds: A, C, D, DS, ER, JCB, MC, V.

D 🏊 🏋 🐾 🔥 SC 🎿

★ ★ ★ **TERRACE GARDEN INN.** *3405 Lenox Rd NE (30326), in Buckhead.* 404/261-9250; FAX 404/848-7391; res: 800/241-8260. 361 rms, 10 story. S $135-$195; D $150-$210; suites $275-$495; under 14 free; wkend rates. Crib free. Covered parking $8. Pet accepted, some restrictions. TV; cable (premium). Pool; poolside serv. Restaurant 6:30 am-2 pm, 5-10 pm. Bars noon-2 am. Ck-out noon. Convention facilities. Business center. In-rm modem link. Concierge. Gift shop. Exercise equipt. Some refrigerators, wet bars; bathrm phone in suites. Some balconies. Luxury level. Cr cds: A, C, D, DS, MC, V.

D 🐾 ≈ 🏋 🐾 🔥 SC 🎿

★ ★ ★ **WESTIN ATLANTA NORTH.** *7 Concourse Pkwy (30328), north of downtown.* 770/395-3900; FAX 770/395-3935. 370 rms, 20 story. S $129-$169; D $139-$179; each addl $20; suites $275-$850; under 18 free; wkend rates. Crib free. TV; cable (premium). Heated pool; whirlpool, sauna, poolside serv. Restaurant 6:30 am-11 pm. Rm serv 24 hrs. Bar 4:30 pm-1 am, Sun to 12:30 am; entertainment Mon-Wed. Ck-out noon. Convention facilities. Business servs avail. In-rm modem link. Free parking. Tennis privileges. 18-hole golf privileges, pro. Health club privileges. Some refrigerators. Luxury level. Cr cds: A, C, D, DS, ER, JCB, MC, V.

D 🏋 ⛳ ≈ 🎿 🐾 🐾 SC

★ ★ ★ **WESTIN PEACHTREE PLAZA.** *210 Peachtree St (30303), at International Blvd, downtown.* 404/659-1400; FAX 404/589-7424. Web www.westin.com. 1,068 rms, 73 story. S $185-$205; D $235-$255; each addl $25; suites $385-$1,450; under 18 free; wkend rates. Crib free. Pet accepted, some restrictions. Garage $17; valet, in/out $14. TV; cable (premium), VCR avail. Indoor pool; poolside serv. Restaurants 6 am-11 pm. Rm serv 24 hrs. Bars (1 revolving rooftop) 11-2 am; entertainment. Ck-out 1 pm. Convention facilities. Business center. In-rm modem link. Concierge. Shopping arcade. Exercise equipt; sauna. Massage. Health club privileges. Many bathrm phones; refrigerators avail. 73-story circular tower built around 8-story atrium. Luxury level. Cr cds: A, C, D, DS, ER, JCB, MC, V.

D 🐾 ≈ 🏋 🐾 🔥

★ ★ **THE WYNDHAM GARDEN HOTEL-BUCKHEAD.** *3340 Peachtree Rd NE (30326), in Buckhead.* 404/231-1234; FAX 404/231-5236. 221 rms, 6 story. S, D $124-$134; each addl $10; suites from $159; under 18 free; wkend rates. Crib free. TV; cable (premium). Complimentary coffee in rms. Restaurant 6:30 am-10 pm; Sat, Sun from 7 am. Bar 4 pm-midnight; Sun from noon. Ck-out noon. Meeting rms. Business servs avail. In-rm modem link. Sundries. Health club privileges. Cr cds: A, C, D, DS, JCB, MC, V.

D 🐾 🐾 SC

★ ★ ★ **WYNDHAM MIDTOWN.** *125 10th St (30309), at Peachtree St, in Midtown/Piedmont Park.* 404/873-4800; FAX 404/870-1530. 191 rms, 11 story. S $258; D $278; each addl $10; suites $250-$500; under 18 free; wkly, wkend rates. Crib free. Covered in/out parking $5; valet parking $12. TV; cable (premium), VCR avail. Indoor pool; whirlpool. Complimentary coffee in rms. Restaurant 6:30 am-10 pm; Sat, Sun from 7 am. Bar 4:30 pm-11 pm, Fri, Sat to 1 am. Ck-out noon. Meeting rms. Business

servs avail. In-rm modem link. Exercise equipt; sauna, steam rm. Massage. Many refrigerators. Cr cds: A, C, D, DS, MC, V.

D ≈ 🏋 🐾 🔥

Inns

★ ★ **ANSLEY INN.** *253 15th St NE (30309), north of downtown.* 404/872-9000; FAX 404/892-2318; res: 800/446-5416. E-mail ansleyinn@mindspring.com; web www.ansleyinn.com. 22 rms, 3 story. S, D $100-$150; wkly, monthly rates. TV; cable (premium). Complimentary full bkfst. Restaurant nearby. Ck-out noon, ck-in 3 pm. Business servs avail. In-rm modem link. Luggage handling. Valet serv. Concierge serv. In-rm whirlpools. Turn-of-the-century English Tudor house; art gallery. Cr cds: A, C, D, DS, JCB, MC, V.

D 🐾 🔥

★ ★ **BENTLEY'S BED & BREAKFAST.** *6860 Peachtree Dunwoody Rd (30328), north of downtown.* 770/396-1742. 4 rms. S, D $135. TV in common rm; cable (premium). Complimentary full bkfst. Restaurant nearby. Ck-out varies, ck-in 4 pm. Business servs avail. Luggage handling. Concierge serv. Built in 1930s as a summer home. Totally nonsmoking. No cr cds accepted.

🔥

✔ ★ ★ **BEVERLY HILLS INN.** *65 Sheridan Dr (30305), in Buckhead.* 404/233-8520; FAX 404/233-8659; res: 800/331-8520. Web www.beverlyhillsinn.com. 18 kit. suites, 3 story. S, D $90-$120; each addl $10-$15; wkly, monthly rates. Crib avail. Pet accepted, some restrictions. TV; cable. Pool privileges. Complimentary continental bkfst. Restaurant nearby. Ck-out noon, ck-in 2 pm. Valet serv. Business servs avail. In-rm modem link. Health club privileges. Microwaves avail. Balconies. European-style hotel restored to 1929 ambience. Cr cds: A, C, D, DS, JCB, MC, V.

🐾 🔥

★ ★ ★ **BUCKHEAD INN.** *70 Lenox Pointe NE (30324), 4 mi NE on I-85, exit 28, in Buckhead.* 404/261-8284; res: 888/224-8797; FAX 404/237-9224. E-mail bandb@mindspring.com; web www.georgia-bedandbreakfast.com. 18 rms, 3 story. S, D $85-$105; under 12 free. Crib free. TV; cable (premium), VCR avail. Complimentary continental bkfst. Restaurant nearby. Ck-out 11 am, ck-in 3 pm. Business servs avail. In-rm modem link. Luggage handling. Valet serv. Concierge serv. Lighted tennis privileges, pro. 36-hole golf privileges, pro, putting green, driving range. Health club privileges. Balconies. Cr cds: A, MC, V.

D 🏋 ⛳ 🐾 🐾

★ ★ ★ **GASLIGHT INN.** *1001 St Charles Ave NE (30306), 3 mi NE on I-75 to I-85 exit 96; in Midtown/Piedmont Park.* 404/875-1001; FAX 404/876-1001. E-mail innkeeper@gaslightinn.com; web www.gaslightinn.com. 6 rms, 2 story. 3 suites. S, D $85-$125; each addl $12; suites $149-$195; wkly rates; wkend rates (2-day min). TV; cable (premium), VCR avail. Complimentary continental bkfst. Restaurant nearby. Ck-out noon, ck-in 3 pm. Business servs avail. In-rm modem link. Luggage handling. Street parking. Many refrigerators; some in-rm whirlpools, microwaves, minibars, wet bars, fireplaces. Balconies. Grills. Built in 1903. Totally nonsmoking. Cr cds: A, DS, MC, V.

D 🐾 🐾

★ ★ **KING-KEITH HOUSE.** *889 Edgewood Ave NE (30307), downtown.* 404/688-7330; res: 800/728-3879; FAX 404/584-0730. E-mail kingkeith@mindspring.com; web travelbase.com. 5 rms, 2 share bath, 3 story. S, D $75-$125; each addl $15. TV; cable. Complimentary full bkfst. Restaurant nearby. Ck-out noon, ck-in 2 pm. Luggage handling. Valet serv. Concierge serv. Guest lndry. Street parking. Some refrigerators. Picnic tables, grills. Antiques. Totally nonsmoking. Cr cds: A, MC, V.

🐾 🔥

★ ★ ★ **SERENBE.** *(10950 Hutcheson Ferry Rd, Palmetto 30268) 45 mi SW on I-85, exit 16, follow signs to Spur 14 (S Fulton Pkwy), 13 mi to Rivertown Rd, 2.2 mi then left on Cochran Mill Rd, 4.2 mi to Hutcheson*

Ferry Rd, right 3 mi. 770/463-2610; FAX 770/463-4472. E-mail meet@serenbe.com; web www.serenbe.com. 6 rms, 2 story. S, D $115-$150; each addl $20; 2-day min wkends (Apr-Oct). Premium cable TV in common rm, VCR avail (movies). Complimentary full bkfst; afternoon refreshments. Ck-out 11 am, ck-in 3 pm. Business servs avail. Luggage handling. Concierge serv. Exercise equipt. Pool; whirlpool. Lawn games. Some refrigerators, balconies. Picnic tables, grills. Turn-of-the-century farmhouse built in 1901; 350-acre farm; flower & vegetable gardens; treehouse. Totally nonsmoking. No cr cds accepted.

★★★★ **SHELLMONT.** *821 Piedmont Ave NE (30308), in Midtown/Piedmont Park.* 404/872-9290; FAX 404/872-5379. Web www.innbrook.comgaatl.shellmont. 4 rms, 2 story, carriage house. S, D $110-$120; each addl $25; carriage house $120-$150. Children under 12 in carriage house only. Crib free. TV; cable (premium). Complimentary full bkfst. Restaurant nearby. Ck-out 11 am, ck-in 3 pm. In-rm modem link. Health club privileges. Some patios, balconies. Restored Victorian house (1891); Tiffany windows, antiques, artwork. Totally nonsmoking. Cr cds: A, D, DS, JCB, MC, V.

★★★ **SUGAR MAGNOLIA.** *804 Edgewood Ave NE (30307), east of downtown.* 404/222-0226; FAX 404/681-1067. E-mail DSTAR37866@aol.com. 4 rms, 2 story. S, D 75-$120. Crib free. TV. Complimentary continental bkfst; coffee in library. Ck-out 11 am, ck-in 2 pm. Luggage handling. Concierge serv. Business center. Street parking. Refrigerators; some fireplaces. Balcony. Victorian house (1892) in historic Inman Park district; period furnishings. Totally nonsmoking. No cr cds accepted.

Resort

★★★ **EVERGREEN CONFERENCE RESORT.** *(1 Lakeview Dr, Stone Mountain 30086) E on US 78, in Stone Mountain State Park.* 770/879-9900; FAX 770/464-9013; res: 800/722-1000. E-mail evergreen resort@mindspring.com; web www.evergreenresort.com. 249 rms, 5 story. $6 park entrance fee (required to reach resort). Apr-Oct: S $129; D $149; suites $200-$300; family, wkend, wkly, hol rates; golf plans; lower rates rest of yr. Crib $8. Pet accepted, some restrictions. TV; cable (premium). 2 pools, 1 indoor; wading pool, whirlpool, poolside serv. Coffee in rms. Restaurant 6:30 am-10 pm. Box lunches, snacks, picnics. Rm serv 24 hrs. Bar. Ck-out noon, ck-in 4 pm. Business center. In-rm modem link. Gift shop. Grocery 1 mi. Bellhops. Concierge. Valet serv. Sports dir. Lighted tennis. 36-hole golf, greens fee $45-$55, pro, putting green, driving range. Swimming beach; boats. Hiking. Bicycle rentals. Social dir. Game rm. Exercise equipt. Massage. Health club privileges. Refrigerators. Balconies. Picnic tables. Situated on lake within Stone Mountain State Park. Cr cds: A, C, D, DS, ER, JCB, MC, V.

Restaurants

★★★ **103 WEST.** *103 W Paces Ferry Rd (30305), in Buckhead.* 404/233-5993. Web www.buckheadrestaurants.com. Hrs: 6-11 pm; Fri, Sat from 5:30. Closed Sun; major hols. Res accepted. Contintneal, French menu. Bar. Wine cellar. A la carte entrees: dinner $17-$34.50. Specialties: peppered yellow fin tuna, grilled ostrich loin, baby rack of lamb. Own baking. Pianist. Valet parking. Chef-owned. Cr cds: A, C, D, DS, MC, V.

★★★ **THE ABBEY.** *163 Ponce de Leon Ave NE (30308), at Piedmont Rd & North Ave, in Midtown/Piedmont Park.* 404/876-8831. Hrs: 6-10 pm. Closed major hols. Res accepted. Continental menu. Bar from 5 pm. Wine cellar. A la carte entrees: dinner $18-$28. Specializes in seafood, game, veal. Own baking. Harpist. Valet parking. Former church; 50-ft

arched and vaulted ceiling. Costumed servers. Cr cds: A, C, D, DS, MC, V.

★★★ **ABRUZZI RISTORANTE.** *2355 Peachtree Rd NE (30305), at Peachtree Battle Shopping Center, in Buckhead.* 404/261-8186. Hrs: 11:30 am-2:30 pm, 5:30-10:30 pm; Fri, Sat 5:30-11 pm. Closed Sun; some major hols. Res required. Italian menu. Bar. Semi-a la carte: lunch $20, dinner $45. Specialties: Capellini alla Nico, homemade spinach ravioli, osso buco. Parking. Understated Florentine decor. Jacket. Cr cds: A, D, MC, V.

★★ **AGNES & MURIEL'S.** *1514 Monroe Dr (30324), in Midtown/Piedmont Park.* 404/885-1000. Hrs: 11 am-11 pm; Fri to midnight; Sat 10 am-11 pm; Sun 10 am-11 pm; Sat, Sun brunch 10 am-3 pm. Closed Dec 25. Bar. A la carte entrees: lunch $3.95-$10.95, dinner $3.95-$14.95. Sat, Sun brunch $3.95-$10.95. Specializes in turkey meatloaf, grilled salmon pot pie. 1950s decor. Totally nonsmoking. Cr cds: A, C, D, DS, JCB, MC, V.

★★ **ANIS.** *2974 Grandview Ave (30305), in Buckhead.* 404/233-9889. Hrs: 11:30 am-2:30 pm, 6-10 pm; Fri, Sat to 10:30 pm; Sun brunch to 2:30 pm. Closed some major hols. Southern French menu. Bar. Semi-a la carte: lunch, dinner $7-$15. Sun brunch $6-$12. Specialties: grilled tuna with aioli, bouillabaise. Entertainment Mon, Thurs. Parking. Outdoor dining. European decor. Cr cds: A, D, MC, V.

★★★ **ANTHONY'S.** *3109 Piedmont Rd NE (30305), in Buckhead.* 404/262-7379. E-mail cwik@atlanta.com. Hrs: 6-11 pm. Closed major hols. Res accepted. Continental menu. Bar. Wine cellar. A la carte entrees: dinner $18.95-$29.95. Specializes in wild game, seafood, steak. Own baking. Valet parking. Plantation house (1797); antiques, fireplaces. Cr cds: A, C, D, DS, JCB, MC, V.

★★ **ARUGULA.** *3639 Piedmont Rd NE (30305), in Buckhead.* 404/814-0959. Hrs: 11:30 am-2:30 pm, 5-10 pm; Fri to 11 pm; Sat 5-11 pm. Closed Sun; some major hols. Res accepted. Contemporary Amer menu. Bar. Semi-a la carte: lunch $7-$10.50, dinner $10.50-$19.50. Specialties: Mahi Mahi, tropical mango gazapacho, upside down apple "Gabby." Valet parking. Outdoor dining. Modern decor. Cr cds: A, MC, V.

★★ **ATLANTA FISH MARKET.** *265 Pharr Rd (30305), in Buckhead.* 404/262-3165. Hrs: 11 am-2:30 pm, 5:30-11 pm; Fri to midnight; Sat 11:30 am-midnight; Sun 4-10 pm. Closed Thanksgiving, Dec 25. Bar. Semi-a la carte: lunch $7.50-$25, dinner $12.50-$26.50 Child's meals. Specializes in seafood. Parking. Cr cds: A, C, D, DS, MC, V.

★★ **BABETTE'S CAFE.** *471 N Highland Ave NE (30307), 3½ mi E on Freedom Pkwy, exit 96, S on N Highland Ave, east of downtown.* 404/523-9121. Hrs: 6-10 pm; Fri, Sat to 11 pm; Sun 5-9 pm; Sun brunch 10:30 am-2:30 pm. Closed Mon; some major hols. Bar. Semi-a la carte: dinner $10.25-$18.50. Sun brunch $5.25-$8.50. Child's meals. Specialties: cassoulet, artichoke ravioli, steamed mussels with strawberries and serrano peppers. Romantic dining. Cr cds: A, D, DS, MC, V.

★★★ **BACCHANALIA.** *3125 Piedmont Rd (30305), in Buckhead.* 404/365-0410. Hrs: 6-9:30 pm; Fri, Sat to 10 pm. Closed Sun, Mon; some major hols. Res required. Wine, beer. Prix fixe: dinner $45. Specializes in seafood, game. Own baking. Parking. Original art, antiques; angels highlight the walls & tables. Totally nonsmoking. Cr cds: A, D, MC, V.

✔★ ★ **BASIL'S MEDITERRANEAN CAFE.** *2985 Grandview Ave (30305), in Buckhead.* 404/233-9755. Hrs: 11:30 am-2:30 pm, 6-10 pm; Fri, Sat to 11 pm. Closed some major hols. Res accepted. Mediterranean menu. Bar. A la carte entrees: lunch $4.50-$8.25, dinner $8.25-$13.95. Piano bar. Valet parking. Outdoor dining. Cr cds: A, D, DS, MC, V.

✔★ **THE BEEHIVE.** *(1090 Alpharetta St, Roswell 30075) approx 5 mi NW on Holcomb Bridge Rd (US 140).* 770/594-8765. Hrs: 5-10 pm; Fri, Sat to 11 pm; Sun 5-9 pm. Closed Mon, Tues; most major hols. Bar. Semi-a la carte: dinner $4.95-$15.95. Specializes in trout, sandwiches, fresh pasta. Parking. Converted house. Cr cds: MC, V.

★ ★ **THE BISTRO.** *56 E Andrews Dr NW (30305), in Buckhead.* 404/231-5733. Hrs: 6-11 pm. Closed Sun, Mon; Jan 1, Thanksgiving, Dec 25. Res accepted. French menu. Bar. Semi-a la carte: dinner $18-$28. Specialties: lamb chops, grilled salmon steak, braised filet of Chilean sea bass. Parking. Outdoor dining. Many paintings; antique German mirrors. Cr cds: C, D, DS, JCB, MC, V.

★ ★ **BLUE RIDGE GRILL.** *1261 W Paces Ferry Rd (30327), in Buckhead.* 404/233-5030. Hrs: 11:30 am-2:30 pm, 5:30-11 pm; Sun brunch to 2:30 pm. Closed most major hols. Res accepted. Bar. Semi-a la carte: lunch $9.95-$16.95, dinner $16-$29. Sat, Sun brunch $9-$16. Specializes in fresh seafood, duck, grilled vegetables. Own baking. Adriondack mountain lodge. Cr cds: A, D, DS, MC, V.

★ ★ **BONE'S.** *3130 Piedmont Rd NE (30305), in Buckhead.* 404/237-2663. Hrs: 11:30 am-2:30 pm, 5:30-10:30 pm; Fri, Sat to 11 pm. Closed major hols. Res accepted. Bar. Wine cellar. Semi-a la carte: lunch $8.95-$16.95. A la carte entrees: dinner $21.95-$36. Specializes in aged prime beef, seafood, live Maine lobster. Own desserts. Valet parking. Club atmosphere; wood paneling, fireplace. Cr cds: A, C, D, DS, MC, V.

✔★ ★ **BRASSERIE LE COZE.** *3393 Peachtree Rd (30326), in Lenox Square Mall, in Buckhead.* 404/266-1440. Hrs: 11:30 am-2:30 pm, 5:30-10 pm; Fri 11:30 am-3 pm, 5:30-11 pm; Sat 11:30 am-3:30 pm, 5:30-11 pm. Closed Sun; Thanksgiving, Dec 25. Res accepted. Country French menu. Bar. Wine list. Semi-a la carte: lunch $7.50-$16, dinner $13-$22. Specializes in mussels, coq au vin, desserts. Outdoor dining. Stylish decor. Cr cds: A, D, MC, V.

★ ★ **BUCKHEAD DINER.** *3073 Piedmont Rd (30305), in Buckhead.* 404/262-3336. Web www.buckheadrestaurants.com. Hrs: 11 am-midnight; Sun 10:30 am-10 pm. Closed Thanksgiving, Dec 25. A la carte entrees: lunch $5.95-$14.95, dinner $5.95-$15.95. Specialties: sautéed grouper, veal and wild mushroom meat loaf, white chocolate banana cream pie. Valet parking. Update of classic, stainless steel-wrapped diner. Cr cds: A, C, D, DS, MC, V.

★ ★ **THE CABIN.** *2678 Buford Hwy NE (30324), in Buckhead.* 404/315-7676. Hrs: 11:30 am-2:30 pm, 5:30-10 pm; Fri to 11 pm; Sat 5:30-11 pm. Closed Sun; some major hols. Res accepted. Bar. Semi-a la carte: lunch $4.95-$9.95, dinner $16.95-$28.95. Child's meals. Valet parking (dinner). Specializes in steak, seafood. Log cabin built in 1931. Cr cds: A, C, D, DS, MC, V.

★ ★ ★ **THE CAFE.** *(See The Ritz-Carlton, Buckhead Hotel)* 404/237-2700. Hrs: 6:30 am-11 pm; Sun brunch 11:30 am-2:30 pm. Bar. A la carte entrees: bkfst $7-$15, lunch $10-$22, dinner $20-$30. Sun brunch $38. Child's meals. Specializes in French bistro cuisine. Own pastries. Pianist. Valet parking. Antiques, original art. Totally nonsmoking. Cr cds: A, C, D, DS, ER, JCB, MC, V.

✔★ ★ **CAFE TU TU TANGO.** *220 Pharr Rd (30305), in Buckhead.* 404/841-6222. Web www.cafetututango.com. Hrs: 11:30 am-11 pm; Wed to midnight; Thurs to 1 am; Fri, Sat to 2 am. Eclectic menu. Bar. A la carte entrees: lunch, dinner $3.95-$7.95. Specialties: Cajun chicken egg rolls, Barcelona stir-fry, Hurricane shrimp. Valet parking. Outdoor dining. Artist's studio decor; painters at work. Cr cds: A, D, MC, V.

★ ★ **CAMEAUX LOUISIANA BAR & GRILL.** *(9925 Haynes Bridge Rd, Alpharetta 30022) 25 mi N on GA 400, exit 9.* 770/442-2524. Hrs: 11 am-10 pm; Fri, Sat to 11 pm; Sun 5-10 pm. Closed Jan 1, Dec 25. Res accepted. Cajun menu. Bar. Semi-a la carte: lunch $3.95-$9.95, dinner $8.95-$21.95. Child's meals. Specialties: boiled crawfish, crab cakes, crawfish etouffee. Jazz and blues Tues, Thurs-Sat. Cajun ambience. Cr cds: A, DS, MC, V.

✔★ **CAMILLE'S.** *1186 N Highland Ave (30306), in Midtown/Piedmont Park.* 404/872-7203. Web www.camilles.com. Hrs: 5:30-11 pm. Bar. Semi-a la carte: dinner $10.25-$14.95. Specialties: calamari, linguini with clams, rice balls. Parking. Outdoor dining. Cr cds: A, D, MC, V.

★ ★ ★ **CANOE.** *4199 Paces Ferry Rd NW (30339), north of downtown.* 770/432-2663. E-mail canoe@bellsouth.net. Wonderfully landscaped grounds dotted with walkways and benches add to the outdoor dining experience here. Inside, brick walls, wrought iron and splashes of Southwestern upholstery accent the dining areas. Specialties: slow-roasted Carolina rabbit with swiss chard-country bacon ravioli and balsamic glaze, grilled tuna "steak and potatoes" with roasted pearl onions and sherry vinegar, oak roasted venison with spiced pumpkin puree and apple chestnut compote. Hrs: 10:30 am-2:30 pm, 5:30-10:30 pm; Fri to 11:30 pm; Sat 5:30-11:30 pm; Sun 10 am-2:30 pm (brunch), 5:30-9 pm. Closed Jan 1, Thanksgiving, Dec 25. Res accepted. Bar. Wine list. Semi-a la carte: lunch $7.95-$13.95, dinner $12.95-$19.95. Sun brunch $7.95-$13.50. Valet parking. Outdoor dining. Cr cds: A, C, D, MC, V.

★ ★ ★ **CARBO'S CAFE.** *3717 Roswell Rd (30342), in Buckhead.* 404/231-4433. Web menus.atlanta.com/carboscafe. Hrs: 5:30-10:30 pm; Fri, Sat to 11 pm. Closed major hols. Res accepted. Continental menu. Bar 5 pm-3 am. Wine cellar. Complete meals: dinner $18.95-$29.95. Specializes in seafood, veal, steak. Own baking. Piano bar. Valet parking. European decor; antiques, fireplaces, fountain. Cr cds: A, C, D, MC, V.

★ ★ ★ **CASSIS.** *(See Grand Hyatt Hotel)* 404/365-8100. Hrs: 6:30 am-2:30 pm; Sun brunch 10:30 am-3 pm. Res accepted. Continental menu. Bar. Wine list. A la carte entrees: bkfst $8.25-$16, lunch $8.50-$19. Buffet: bkfst $13. Sun brunch $24.95. Child's meals. Specializes in grilled meats, fish, bistro items. Valet parking. Outdoor dining. View of waterfall and gardens. Cr cds: A, C, D, DS, ER, JCB, MC, V.

★ ★ ★ **CHOPS.** *70 W Paces Ferry Rd (30305), in Buckhead.* 404/262-2675. Web www.buckheadrestaurants.com. Hrs: 11:30 am-2:30 pm, 5:30-11 pm; Fri to midnight; Sat 5:30 pm-midnight; Sun 5-10 pm. Closed some major hols. Res accepted. Bar. A la carte entrees: lunch $7.95-$15.95, dinner $14.75-$34.50. Specializes in steak, lobster, fresh seafood. Own pastries. Valet parking. Art deco motif. Cr cds: A, C, D, DS, MC, V.

★ ★ ★ **CIBOULETTE.** *1529 Piedmont Ave (30324), in Midtown/Piedmont Park.* 404/874-7600. E-mail ciboulette@mindspring.com. Hrs: 6-10 pm; Fri, Sat 5:30-11 pm. Closed Sun; major hols. French menu. Bar. Semi-a la carte: dinner $17-$29. Specialties: nage of fish, duck liver pâté, game. Own desserts. Open kitchen. Elegant atmosphere. Cr cds: A, C, D, DS, MC, V.

★ ★ **CIRCLE SUSHI.** *8725 Roswell Rd (30350), north of downtown.* 770/998-7880. Hrs: noon-2:30 pm, 6-10:30 pm; Fri to 11 pm; Sat 6-11 pm; Sun 5:30-10:30 pm. Closed Memorial Day, Thanksgiving, Dec 25. Res accepted. Japanese menu. Wine, beer. Semi-a la carte: lunch $5.50-$20, dinner $15-$30. Specializes in teriyaki, sushi. Parking. Outdoor dining. Totally nonsmoking. Cr cds: A, C, D, DS, MC, V.

D

★ ★ ★ **CITY GRILL.** *50 Hurt Plaza (30303), in the Hurt Bldg, suite 200, downtown.* 404/524-2489. Hrs: 11:30 am-2:30 pm, 5:30-10 pm; Sat from 5:30 pm. Closed Sun; most major hols. Res accepted. Contemporary Amer menu. Bar. Wine cellar. A la carte entrees: lunch $7-$15, dinner $17-$29. Specialties: blue crab cakes with lemon linguine, mustard-crusted aged New York strip, chocolate pecan soufflé. Own pastries. Valet parking (dinner). Rotunda entrance, bronze chandeliers, marble columns, wall murals. Cr cds: A, C, D, DS, MC, V.

D

✔★ **THE COLONNADE.** *1879 Cheshire Bridge Rd (30324), in Buckhead.* 404/874-5642. Hrs: 11 am-2:30 pm, 5-9 pm; Fri, Sat to 10 pm; Sun 11 am-9 pm. Closed Dec 24-25. Bar. Semi-a la carte: lunch $4.50-$14, dinner $5.95-$16. Specializes in fried chicken, turkey, seafood. Parking. Casual dining. Family-owned. No cr cds accepted.

D

★ ★ **COOHILL'S.** *1100 Peachtree St NE (30309), in Midtown/Piedmont Park.* 404/724-0901. E-mail coohills@coohill.com; web www.coohill.com. Hrs: 11:30 am-2:30 pm, 5:30-9 pm; Fri, Sat to 10 pm. Closed Sun; most major hols. Res accepted. Southern steak house. Bar. Wine list. Semi-a la carte: lunch $8.95-$15.95, dinner $17.95-$28.95. Specializes in chops, prime beef, seafood. Pianist Thurs-Sat. Outdoor dining. Modern decor. Cr cds: A, C, D, DS, MC, V.

D

★ ★ **COUNTRY PLACE.** *1197 Peachtree St NE (30361), Colony Square Complex, in Midtown/Piedmont Park.* 404/881-0144. Hrs: 11:30 am-2:30 pm, 5:30-10 pm; Thurs-Sat 5:30-11 pm; Sun 11 am-3 pm (brunch), 5:30-10 pm. Closed Thanksgiving, Dec 25. Res accepted. Bar. Semi-a la carte: lunch $8.49-$16.49, dinner $14.99-$23.99. Sun brunch $6.95-$13.95. Pianist Thurs-Sat. Parking. Cr cds: A, C, D, DS, MC, V.

D

★ ★ **DAILEY'S.** *17 International Blvd (30303), downtown.* 404/681-3303. Hrs: 11 am-3:30 pm, 5:30-11 pm; Fri, Sat to midnight. Closed major hols. Res accepted. Bar. Semi-a la carte: lunch $4.95-$12.95, dinner $17-$29. Specializes in pepper-crusted swordfish, desserts. Jazz trio, pianist. Converted warehouse; vaulted ceiling. Cr cds: A, C, D, DS, MC, V.

D

★ ★ **DANTE'S DOWN THE HATCH.** *3380 Peachtree Rd NE (30326), across from Lenox Square, in Buckhead.* 404/266-1600. Hrs: 4-11:30 pm; Fri, Sat to 12:30 am; Sun 5-11 pm. Closed Jan 1, Dec 25. Res accepted. Bar. Semi-a la carte: dinner $13-$27. Specializes in mixed fondue dinners. Own desserts. Classical guitarist; jazz trio. Parking. Nautical decor. Antique English, Polish ship figureheads. Ship-board dining within multilevel vessel. Menu translated in 51 languages. Family-owned. Cr cds: A, C, D, DS, MC, V.

D

★ ★ ★ ★ ★ **THE DINING ROOM.** *(See The Ritz-Carlton, Buckhead Hotel)* 404/237-2700. Chef Joel Antunes's daily menu is limited, but it embraces the best that the season offers in elegant surroundings. Traditional European menu with Asian influences. Specializes in light contemporary cuisine. Own baking, pasta, ice cream. Menu changes daily. Hrs: 6-9:30 pm. Closed Sun; major hols. Res accepted. Bar. Wine cellar. Prix fixe: dinner $65-$112. Valet parking. Jacket. Totally nonsmoking. Cr cds: A, C, D, DS, ER, JCB, MC, V.

D

✔★ ★ **DISH.** *870 N Highland Ave NE (30306), east of downtown.* 404/897-3463. Hrs: 5:30-10 pm; Fri, Sat to 11 pm. Closed most major hols. Res accepted. Contemporary Amer menu. Bar. Semi-a la carte: dinner $11-$19. Specialties: grilled prosciutto-wrapped pork filet with carmelized onion relish and potato fluff, creamy wild mushroom risotto. Outdoor dining. Former filling station (1939). Cr cds: A, C, D, MC, V.

D

✔★ **DUSTY'S BARBECUE.** *1815 Briarcliff Rd (30306), east of downtown.* 404/320-6264. Web www.dustys.com. Hrs: 6 am-9 pm; Fri to 10 pm; Sat 7 am-10 pm; Sun from 7 am. Closed Jan 1, Thanksgiving, Dec. 25. Semi-a la carte: lunch, dinner $3.70-$12.25. Child's meals. Specializes in chicken, beef, baby back ribs. Parking. Casual dining. Cr cds: A, D, DS, MC, V.

⎤

✔★ ★ **ECLIPSE DI LUNA.** *764 Miami Circle (30324), 5 mi NW of Piedmont, in Buckhead.* 404/846-0449. Hrs: 11:30 am-3 pm, 5:30-11 pm; Mon to 3 pm; Sun brunch 10 am-4 pm. Closed most major hols. Res accepted. Contemporary Spanish menu. Bar. Semi-a la carte: lunch, dinner $6-$8. Sun brunch $10. Specializes in tapas. Band Fri, Sat. Parking. Outdoor dining. Eclectic decor. Cr cds: A, D, MC, V.

✔★ ★ **EMBERS SEAFOOD GRILLE.** *(234 Hilderbrand Dr, Sandy Springs 30328) N on GA 9.* 404/256-0977. Hrs: 11:30 am-2:30 pm, 6-10:30 pm. Closed Sun. Res accepted. Bar. Semi-a la carte: lunch $5.95-$7.95, dinner $11.95-$19.95. Child's meals. Specializes in seafood, steak. Parking. Modern wall hangings. Cr cds: A, C, D, DS, MC, V.

D ⎤

★ ★ **ENCORE AT THE FOX.** *654 Peachtree St (30308), in Fox building, in Midtown/Piedmont Park.* 404/881-0223. Hrs: 11 am-2 pm, 5-10 pm; Fri to 11 pm. Closed Sat, Sun; Jan 1, Dec 25. Res accepted. Bar. Semi-a la carte: lunch $6-$10, dinner $13-$22. Specialties: grilled filet of beef, crispy sweet & sour calamari, roasted Chilean sea bass. Cr cds: A, D, DS, MC, V.

D ⎤

✔★ **FEEDERS.** *248 Pharr Rd (30305), in Buckhead.* 404/869-8979. Hrs: 11:30 am-midnight; Fri, Sat to 3 am. Closed Mon; most major hols. Res accepted. Barbecue menu. Bar. Semi-a la carte: lunch, dinner $4.95-$14.95. Specializes in smoked chicken, pork, ribs. Thurs comedy; Fri-Sun band. Parking. Outdoor dining. Cr cds: A, MC, V.

D ⎤

★ ★ **FOOD STUDIO.** *887 W Marietta St (30318), north of downtown.* 404/815-6677. Hrs: 5:30-11 pm; Fri, Sat to midnight. Closed most major hols. Res accepted. Bar. Semi-a la carte: dinner $15.95-$25.95. Specialties: ahi tuna tartare, apricot-honey glazed duck, pecan-encrusted halibut. Valet parking. Outdoor dining. Contemporary decor in refurbished 1904 plow factory bldg. Totally nonsmoking. Cr cds: A, D, MC, V.

D

✔★ ★ **FRATELLI DI NAPOLI.** *2101-B Bennett St (30309), in Buckhead.* 404/351-1533. Web www.fratelli.net. Hrs: 5-11 pm; Fri, Sat to midnight; Sun 4-10 pm. Closed Thanksgiving, Dec 25. Italian menu. Bar. Semi-a la carte: dinner $12-$18. Specializes in pasta, veal. Valet parking. Italian decor. Cr cds: A, D, DS, MC, V.

D

★ ★ ★ **THE FROG AND PEACH BISTRO.** *3167 Peachtree Rd NE (30305), in Buckhead.* 404/261-4466. Hrs: 11:30 am-2:30 pm, 5:30-10:30 pm; Sun 11 am-3 pm, 5:30-10:30 pm. Closed Mon; Dec 25. Res accepted. French menu. Bar. Wine list. A la carte entrees: lunch $4.50-$15, dinner $14-$23. Specialties: fruit of the sea baked in parchment paper, grilled salmon filet, braised beef with pureed polenta. Parking. Outdoor dining. Cr cds: A, D, MC, V.

⎤

✔★ ★ **GAUGUIN BISTRO.** *889 W Peachtree (30309), in Midtown/Piedmont Park.* 404/874-5535. Hrs: 11:30 am-2:30 pm, 6-11 pm; Sat 8-11 pm; Sun 10:30 am-2:30 pm. Closed Jan 1, Dec 25. Res accepted. French menu. Bar. Semi-a la carte: lunch $3.15-$8, dinner $11.50-$17.50.

Child's meals. Specialties: osso bucco monkfish stew, goat stew, roasted duck with lychee fruit. Valet parking wkends. Outdoor dining. French island bistro decor. Cr cds: A, D, DS, MC, V.

✔★ GEORGIA GRILLE. 2290 Peachtree Rd (30309), in Buckhead. 404/352-3517. E-mail Richard@menus.atlanta.com; web menus.atlanta.com. Hrs: 6-10 pm; Fri, Sat to 11 pm. Closed Dec 25, Thanksgiving. Southwestern menu. Bar. Semi-a la carte: dinner $5.95-$19.95. Specializes in pork, chicken, seafood. Parking. Outdoor dining. Southwestern decor. Totally nonsmoking. Cr cds: A, MC, V.

✔★ ★ HARVEST. 853 N Highland Ave NE (30306), 5 mi NE on Ponce de Leon to N Highland Ave, east of downtown. 404/876-8244. Hrs: 11:30 am-2:30 pm, 5:30-10 pm; Fri to 11 pm; Sat 5:30-11 pm; Sun brunch 11 am-2:30 pm. Closed Labor Day, Thanksgiving, Dec 25. Contemporary Amer menu. Bar. Semi-a la carte: dinner $10.95-$17.95. Sun brunch $6.95-$10.95. Specialties: seared Chilean sea bass, chicken with honey pecan sauce, chili-rubbed pork tenderloin. Valet parking. Outdoor dining. Paintings, antiques; 3 fireplaces. Totally nonsmoking. Cr cds: A, D, MC, V.

✔★ ★ HAVELI. 225 Spring St (30303), in Gift Mart, downtown. 404/522-4545. Hrs: 11:30 am-2:30 pm, 5:30-10 pm; Sun from 5:30 pm. Closed Dec 25. Indian menu. Bar. Buffet: lunch $6.95. A la carte entrees: dinner $11.95-$15.95. Specialties: chicken tikka, daal maharani, baingan bharta. Parking. Indian decor. Cr cds: A, D, DS, MC, V.

★ ★ ★ HEDGEROSE. 490 E Paces Ferry Rd (30305), in Buckhead. 404/233-7673. Hedgerose's management stands guard vigilantly, scrutinizing the dining room and making sure that the smallest details is attended to promptly. The waiters know that it's important to treat diners graciously resulting in service which is meticulously attentive. Hrs: 6-10 pm; Fri 5:30-10:30 pm; Sun 5:30-9:30 pm. Closed most major hols. Res accepted. French menu. Bar. Wine cellar. A la carte entrees: dinner $16.95-$30.95. Specialties: grilled farm squab with foie gras, John Dory with artichoke & tomato vinegrette, house smoked cod with lettuce sprouts & truffle oil. Valet parking. Outdoor dining. Built in 1930; interior was salvaged from the library of the J. Carroll Payne House. Converted to restaurant in 1976; elegant dining. Totally nonsmoking. Cr cds: A, C, D, DS, MC, V.

★ ★ HORSERADISH GRILL. 4320 Powers Ferry Rd (30342), north of downtown. 770/255-7277. Web www.horseradishgrill.com. Hrs: 11:30 am-10 pm; Fri, Sat 5-11:30 pm; Sun 5-9 pm; Sun brunch 11 am-3 pm. Closed Jan 1, Thanksgiving, Dec 25. Bar. Semi-a la carte: lunch $6.95-$15.95, dinner $15.95-$24.95. Child's meals. Specialties: skillet fried chicken, grilled prime veal chops, lemon chess pie. Parking. Outdoor dining. Modern art, stone fireplace; herb garden area with stone walk. Totally nonsmoking. Cr cds: A, C, D, DS, MC, V.

★ ★ HSU'S GOURMET CHINESE. 192 Peachtree Center Ave (30303), downtown. 404/659-2788. Web www.hsus.com. Hrs: 11:30 am-10:30 pm; Sun 5-10 pm. Closed July 4, Thanksgiving, Dec 25. Res accepted. Chinese menu. Bar. Wine list. A la carte entrees: lunch $5.95-$13.95, dinner $10.95-$18.95. Specialties: Peking Duck, asparagus shrimp in black bean sauce, steamed salmon with ginger sauce. Validated parking (dinner). Chinese decor. Cr cds: A, C, D, DS, MC, V.

★ ★ ★ IMPERIAL FEZ. 2285 Peachtree Rd NE (30309), in Buckhead. 404/351-0870. E-mail rafih@mindspring.com; web www.imperialfez.com. Hrs: 6-11 pm. Res accepted. Moroccan menu. A la carte entrees: dinner $14-$25. Complete meals: dinner $35-$50. Child's meals. Specialties: lamb couscous, shish kebab, fish tagine. Moroccan dancers. Valet parking. Tented ceilings, low tables with silk cushioned seating. Cr cds: A, C, D, DS, JCB, MC, V.

★ INDIGO COASTAL GRILL. 1397 N Highland Ave (30306), in Midtown/Piedmont Park. 404/876-0676. Hrs: 5:30-10 pm; Fri, Sat to 11 pm; Sun brunch 10 am-3 pm. Closed July 4, Thanksgiving, Dec 25. Res accepted. Bar. Semi-a la carte: dinner $12.75-$18.95. Sun brunch $6.95-$10.95. Specializes in seafood, organically grown vegetables, Key lime pie. Outdoor dining. Nautical decor; aquarium. Vintage 1950s jukebox. Cr cds: A, D, MC, V.

★ ★ JIM WHITE'S HALF SHELL. 2349 Peachtree Rd NE (30305), in Peachtree Battle Shopping Center, in Buckhead. 404/237-9924. Hrs: 5-10 pm; Fri, Sat to 11 pm. Closed Sun; most major hols. Bar. Semi-a la carte: dinner $15.95-$29. Child's meals. Specializes in seafood. Parking. Nautical decor. Family-owned. Cr cds: A, D, DS, MC, V.

★ ★ KUDZU CAFE. 3215 Peachtree Rd NE (30305), in Buckhead. 404/262-0661. Hrs: 11 am-10 pm; Fri, Sat to 11 pm; Sat, Sun brunch to 2:30 pm. Closed some major hols. Southern contemporary menu. Bar. Semi-a la carte: lunch $5.50-$16.95, dinner $9.95-$21.95. Sat, Sun brunch $7.95-$16.95. Specializes in grilled chicken, fish, pork chops. Parking. Casual dining. Cr cds: A, D, DS, MC, V.

★ ★ LA GROTTA. 2637 Peachtree Rd NE (30305), in Buckhead. 404/231-1368. Hrs: 6-10:30 pm. Closed Sun; major hols; also last wk June-1st wk July. Res accepted. Northern, regional Italian menu. Bar. Wine list. Semi-a la carte: dinner $15-$25.50. Specializes in veal, seafood, steak. Own pasta, sauces, desserts. Valet parking. Seasonal outdoor dining. Jacket. Totally nonsmoking. Cr cds: A, C, D, DS, MC, V.

★ ★ LA GROTTA RAVINIA. (See Crowne Plaza Ravinia Hotel) 770/395-9925. Web menus.atlanta.com/home/lagrotta.html. Hrs: 11:30 am-2 pm; 5:45-10 pm. Closed Sun; major hols. Res accepted. Northern Italian menu. Serv bar. Wine list. A la carte entrees: lunch $7.95-$13.95, dinner $12.95-$22.95. Specialties: grilled veal chops, portabello mushrooms, fettucine with shrimp & scallops. Valet parking. Outdoor dining. Windows overlook gardens and patio. Cr cds: A, C, D, DS, JCB, MC, V.

★ ★ LA PAZ. 6410 Roswell Rd (30328), in Sandy Springs, north of downtown. 404/256-3555. Web www.lapaz.com. Hrs: 11 am-10 pm; Fri to 11 pm, Sat 5-11 pm, Sun 5-10 pm. Mexican menu. Bar. A la carte entrees: dinner $3.99-$13.99. Child's meals. Parking. Outdoor dining. Cr cds: A, C, D, DS, MC, V.

★ ★ ★ LE SAINT AMOUR. 1620 Piedmont Ave NE (30324), in Midtown/Piedmont Park. 404/881-0300. Hrs: 11 am-2:30 pm, 6-11 pm; Sun brunch to 3 pm. Res accepted; required Fri, Sat night. French menu. Bar. Wine cellar. A la carte entrees: lunch $6-$17, dinner $19-$22. Sun brunch $7-$17. Specialties: duck confit with truffles and sautéed potatoes, boneless rabbit stuffed with baked garlic and figs, trilogie de poisson. Valet parking. Outdoor dining. In antique home; French countryside motif, contemporary French atmosphere. Cr cds: A, MC, V.

★ ★ LOMBARDI'S. 94 Upper Pryor St (30303), downtown. 404/522-6568. Hrs: 11 am-10 pm; Fri to 11 pm; Sat 5-11 pm. Closed some major hols. Res accepted. Italian menu. Bar. A la carte entrees: lunch $8.50-$12.95, dinner $9.95-$16.95. Specializes in pasta, pizza, veal. Parking. Cr cds: A, C, D, MC, V.

✔★ ★ LUNA SI. 1931 Peachtree Rd (30309), in Brookwood Village Shopping Center, in Buckhead. 404/355-5993. Hrs: 5:30-10:30 pm; Fri, Sat to 11 pm. Closed July 4, Thanksgiving, Dec 25. Res required. Eclectic menu. Bar. Semi-a la carte: dinner $12-$21. Specializes in beef, seafood, game. Menu changes monthly. Totally nonsmoking. Cr cds: A, C, D, DS, JCB, MC, V.

★ ★ ★ **MACARTHUR'S.** *2171 Peachtree Rd (30309), in Buckhead. 404/352-3400.* Web www.macarthurs.com. Hrs: 11 am-11 pm; Sun brunch to 3 pm. Closed Thanksgiving, Dec 25. Res accepted. Bar. Wine list. A la carte entrees: lunch $6.50-$10.95, dinner $8.95-$19.95. Sun brunch $4.95-$18.95. Specialties: prime rib MacArthur's style, pecan-crusted grouper, boneless rainbow trout. Valet parking. Outdoor dining. Cr cds: A, D, MC, V.

D ⌐

★ ★ **MAGGIANO'S LITTLE ITALY.** *3368 Peachtree Road NE (30326), 8 mi N on Peachtree Rd, in Buckhead. 404/816-9650.* E-mail maggianoatlanta@mindspring.com; web www.maggianos.net. Hrs: 11:30 am-10 pm; Fri to 11 pm; Sat 11 am-11 pm; Sun from 11 am. Closed Thanksgiving, Dec 25. Res accepted. Italian menu. Bar. A la carte entrees: lunch $3.95-$16.95, dinner $5.95-$29.95. Specialties: calamari fritte, mostaccioli eggplant marinara, New York steak Contadina-style. Valet parking. Outdoor dining. Cr cds: A, C, D, DS, MC, V.

D ⌐

★ ★ ★ **THE MANSION.** *179 Ponce de Leon Ave (30308), in Midtown/Piedmont Park. 404/876-0727.* Hrs: 11 am-2 pm, 6-10 pm; Sat, Sun brunch to 2 pm. Closed Dec 25. Res accepted. Continental menu. Bar 11 am-11 pm. Wine list. Semi-a la carte: lunch $7-$16, dinner $18-$26. Sat, Sun brunch $9-$15. Specializes in fresh seafood, aged beef, lamb. Own baking. Parking. Shingle-style Victorian mansion (1885) with garden, gazebo. Cr cds: A, C, D, DS, MC, V.

D ⌐

✔★ **MARY MAC'S TEAROOM.** *224 Ponce de Leon Ave (30308), in Midtown/Piedmont Park. 404/876-1800.* Hrs: 11 am-9 pm; Sun to 3 pm. Closed major hols. Serv bar. Complete meals: $6-$10. Child's meals. Specializes in baked and fried chicken, fresh vegetables. Own desserts. Pianist. Parking. Informal neighborhood cafe. Family-owned. Totally nonsmoking. Cr cds: A, D, DS, MC, V.

D

★ ★ **McKENDRICK'S.** *4505 Ashford Dunwoody Rd (30346), 10 mi NE on I-285, exit 21, north of downtown. 770/512-8888.* Hrs: 11:30 am-2:30 pm, 5:30-10:30 pm; Fri to 11 pm; Sat 5:30-11 pm; Sun 5:30-10 pm. Closed some major hols. Res accepted. Semi-a la carte: lunch $6.95-$14.95, dinner $15.95-$49. Specialties: cold water lobster tail, porterhouse steak, prime-aged beef. Valet parking. Globe lighting. Cr cds: A, C, D, DS, MC, V.

D ⌐

★ ★ **McKINNON'S LOUISIANE.** *3209 Maple Dr (30305), in Buckhead. 404/237-1313.* Hrs: 6-10 pm; Fri, Sat to 10:30 pm. Closed Sun; major hols. Res accepted. Cajun, Creole menu. Bar. Semi-a la carte: dinner $13.95-$18.95. Specializes in fresh seafood. Parking. Pianist (wkends). Country French decor. Family-owned. Cr cds: A, C, D, DS, MC, V.

D ⌐

★ ★ ★ **MERITAGE.** *(See Four Seasons Hotel) 404/881-9898.* Hrs: 6:30 am-2:30 pm, 6-11 pm; Sun to 10 pm. Res accepted. Bar. Wine cellar. A la carte entrees: bkst $5-$9, lunch $15-$23, dinner $17-$27. Complete meals: 3-course dinner $45. Specialties: rack of lamb, foie gras and smoked duck fricasse, spicy carrots consommé. Pianist. Valet parking. Elegant dining. Cr cds: A, C, D, DS, ER, JCB, MC, V.

D ⌐ ♥

★ ★ ★ **MI SPIA.** *4505 Ashford Dunwoody Rd (30346), in Park Place Shopping Center, north of downtown. 770/393-1333.* Hrs: 11:30 am-2:30 pm, 5-10 pm; Fri to 11 pm; Sat 5-11 pm; Sun 5-10 pm. Closed some major hols. Res accepted. Northern Italian menu. Bar. Semi-a la carte: lunch $7.95-$10.95, dinner $11.95-$21.95. Specialties: honey-glazed salmon, grain mustard marinated pork chops, saffron fettuccine. Outdoor dining. Contemporary decor. Totally nonsmoking. Cr cds: A, C, D, DS, MC, V.

D

✔★ **MICK'S UNDERGROUND.** *75 Upper Alabama St (30303), downtown. 404/525-2825.* Hrs: 11 am-10 pm; Fri, Sat to 12 am; Sun noon-9 pm. Bar. Semi-a la carte: lunch, dinner $3.50-$13.95. Child's meals. Specializes in hamburgers, chicken, pasta. Own desserts. Cr cds: A, D, DS, MC, V.

D ⌐ ♥

★ ★ **MUMBO JUMBO BAR AND GRILL.** *89 Park Pl NE (30303), downtown. 404/523-0330.* E-mail mj89park@aol.com. Hrs: 11:30 am-2:30 pm, 5:30-11:30 pm; Sat, Sun from 5:30 pm. Closed most major hols. Res accepted. Eclectic menu. Bar. Semi-a la carte: lunch $6.95-$14.95, dinner $7.95-$28.50. Specialties: mumbo jumbo gumbo, beef tenderloin. Valet parking (dinner). Spanish decor. Cr cds: A, C, D, DS, MC, V.

D ⌐

★ ★ ★ **NAKATO.** *1776 Cheshire Bridge Rd NE (30324), in Buckhead. 404/873-6582.* Hrs: 5:30-10 pm; Fri, Sat to 11 pm; Sun 5-10 pm. Res accepted. Japanese menu. Bar. Semi-a la carte: dinner $11-$35. Child's meals. Specializes in sushi, teppan. Valet parking. Japanese garden. Cr cds: A, C, D, DS, JCB, MC, V.

D ⌐

★ ★ ★ **NAVA.** *3060 Peachtree Rd (30305), in Buckhead. 404/240-1984.* Hrs: 11 am-2:30 pm, 5:30-11 pm; Fri to midnight; Sat 5 pm-midnight; Sun 5:30-10 pm. Closed most major hols. Res accepted. Southwestern menu. Bar. Wine cellar. Semi-a la carte: lunch $7.25-$15.50, dinner $14.50-$26.95. Specialties: red chile-seared giant scallops, wood-roasted pork tenderloin, sun corn-crusted snapper. Valet parking. Outdoor dining. Genuine New Mexican plaster, sculpture and artwork. Cr cds: A, D, DS, MC, V.

D

✔★ ★ **NICKIEMOTO'S.** *990 Piedmont Ave (30309), in Midtown/Piedmont Park. 404/253-2010.* Hrs: 11:30 am-2:30 pm, 5-11 pm; Sat to 12:30 am; Sun noon-11 pm. Closed Dec 25. Pan-Asian menu. Bar. Wine list. Semi-a la carte: lunch, dinner $4-$16.95 Specializes in sushi, fish, noodle dishes. Parking. Outdoor dining. Cr cds: A, D, DS, JCB, MC, V.

★ ★ ★ **NIKOLAI'S ROOF.** *(See Hilton & Towers Hotel) 404/659-2000.* Web www.hilton.com. Sittings: 6:30 & 9:30 pm. Res accepted. Classic French menu with Russian flair. Wine list. Prix fixe: six-course dinner $62.50. Specialties: turbot à la vapeur sur un lit de chanterelles, la coupe royale de gibier aux airells et poivres, piroshkis. Own baking. Menu recited. Valet parking. Jacket. Elegant decor with views from 30th floor. Cr cds: A, C, D, DS, ER, JCB, MC, V.

D ⌐

✔★ **NINO'S.** *1931 Cheshire Bridge Rd (30324), in Buckhead. 404/874-6505.* Hrs: 5:30-11 pm. Closed Jan 1, July 4, Dec 25. Res accepted. Italian menu. Bar. Semi-a la carte: dinner $8.95-$20.95. Specializes in veal, pasta. Parking. Outdoor dining. Oil paintings, Italian sculpture. Cr cds: A, C, D, DS, MC, V.

⌐

✔★ **OK CAFE.** *1284 W Paces Ferry Rd (30327), in Buckhead. 404/233-2888.* Open 24 hrs. Closed Mon 11 pm-Tues 6 am; some major hols. Wine, beer. Semi-a la carte: bkfst $5-$8, lunch $4-$10, dinner $4.95-$12. Parking. Diner atmosphere. Totally nonsmoking. Cr cds: A, D, DS, MC, V.

D

★ ★ **PALISADES.** *1829 Peachtree Rd NE (30309), in Buckhead. 404/350-6755.* Hrs: 5-10 pm. Closed Dec 25. Res accepted. Continental menu. Bar. Semi-a la carte: dinner $11.95-$22.95. Specializes in fresh fish, steak, crab cakes. Parking. Cr cds: A, C, D, DS, MC, V.

D ⌐

★ ★ ★ **PANO'S AND PAUL'S.** *1232 W Paces Ferry Rd (30327), in Buckhead. 404/261-3662.* Web www.buckheadsrestaurants.com. Hrs: 6-10:30 pm; Fri 6-11 pm; Sat 5:30-11 pm. Closed Sun; major hols. Res accepted. Continental menu. Bar from 5 pm. Wine cellar. Semi-a la carte:

dinner $17.50-$37.50. Specialties: cold water lobster tail, broiled prime veal sirloin steak, flourless chocolate melt cake in chocolate soup. Own baking. Pianist Fri, Sat. Parking. Chef-owned. Cr cds: A, C, D, DS, MC, V.

[D]

★ ★ ★ **PETITE AUBERGE.** *2935 N Druid Hill Rd (30329), Toco Hills Center, east of downtown.* 404/634-6268. Hrs: 11:30 am-2:15 pm, 6-10 pm; Sat from 6 pm. Closed Sun; most major hols. Res accepted. French, continental menu. Bar. Wine list. Semi-a la carte: lunch $5.95-$11.95, dinner $12.50-$19.95. Specializes in beef Wellington, rack of lamb, bouillabaisse maison. European decor. Family-owned. Cr cds: A, C, D, DS, MC, V.

[D] [≣]

✔★ ★ **PHOENIX BREWING CO.** *5600 Roswell Road NE (30342), in Buckhead.* 404/843-2739. Web www.phoenixbrewing.com. Hrs: 11 am-3 pm, 5:30 pm-midnight; Fri to 2 am; Sat noon-2 am; Sun 10:30 am-midnight. Closed Jan 1, Thanksgiving, Dec 25. Res accepted. Bar 11-2 am; Sat, Sun noon-2 am. Semi-a la carte: lunch $5.95-$9.95, dinner $6.95-$22.95. Child's meals. Specializes in buffalo, venison. Own desserts. Outdoor dining. Windows overlook brewing house. Cr cds: A, D, DS, MC, V.

[D] [≣]

★ ★ ★ **PIROZKI'S.** *1447 Peachtree Rd NE (30309), in Midtown/Piedmont Park.* 404/607-0809. Hrs: 11:30 am-3 pm, 5:30-10 pm; Sat 5:30 to 11 pm. Closed Sun; most major hols. Res accepted. Russian menu. Bar. Wine list. Semi-a la carte: lunch $6.95-$9.95, dinner $15.95-$24.95. Specializes in rack of lamb, lobster Alexander, chicken Kiev. Pianist. Outdoor dining. Paintings with Russian theme. Cr cds: A, C, D, MC, V.

[D]

★ ★ **PITTYPAT'S PORCH.** *25 International Blvd (30303), downtown.* 404/525-8228. Hrs: 5-9 pm; Fri, Sat to 10 pm. Closed Labor Day, Dec 25; also July 4 wk, 1 wk in Dec. Res accepted. Southern menu. Bar. Semi-a la carte: dinner $17.95-$23.95. Child's meals. Specialties: fresh coastal fish, Savannah crab cakes, coastal venison pie. Salad bar. Own desserts. Pianist. Parking. Collection of rocking chairs in lounge. Cr cds: A, C, D, DS, MC, V.

★ ★ **PLEASANT PEASANT.** *555 Peachtree St (30308), in Midtown/Piedmont Park.* 404/874-3223. Hrs: 11:30 am-2:30 pm, 5:30-10 pm; Fri to 11 pm; Sat 5:30 pm-11 pm. Closed Thanksgiving, Dec 25. Res accepted. Bar. Semi-a la carte: lunch $6.95-$10.95, dinner $11.95-$20.95. Specialties: lobster sliders, pecan-crusted salmon, seasonal herb chicken. Parking. New York-style bistro. Cr cds: A, C, D, DS, MC, V.

[D] [≣]

★ ★ ★ **PRICCI.** *500 Pharr Rd (30305), in Buckhead.* 404/237-2941. Web www.buckheadrestaurants.com. Hrs: 11 am-11 pm; Fri to midnight; Sat 5 pm-midnight; Sun 5-10 pm. Closed most major hols. Res accepted. Italian menu. Bar. Semi-a la carte: lunch $7.50-$12.95, dinner $14-$23. Own breads. Valet parking. Cr cds: A, C, D, DS, MC, V.

[D] [≣]

★ ★ **PRIME.** *3393 Peachtree Rd NE (30326), in Buckhead.* 404/812-0555. Web www.prime-atlanta.com. Hrs: 11:30 am-2:30 pm, 5-10 pm; Fri to 11 pm; Sat 11:30 am-3 pm, 5-11 pm; Sun noon-9 pm; Sun brunch to 3 pm. Closed some major hols. Res accepted. Japanese, Amer menu. Bar. A la carte entrees: lunch $8.95-$14, dinner $14.95-$32.50. Sun brunch $8.95-$14. Specializes in steak, seafood, sushi. Pianist, saxophonist Fri, Sat. Valet parking. Japanese-American atmosphere. Cr cds: A, C, D, DS, JCB, MC, V.

[D] [≣]

★ ★ **RAY'S ON THE RIVER.** *6700 Powers Ferry Rd (30339), I-285, exit 15; north of downtown.* 770/955-1187. Hrs: 11 am-3 pm, 5:30-10:30 pm; Fri, Sat 5 pm-midnight; Sun 9:30 am-3 pm, 5-10 pm. Closed Dec 25. Bar 11 am-midnight; Fri, Sat to 1 am; Sun 12:30-10 pm. Semi-a la carte: lunch $3.95-$11.95, dinner $14.95-$21.95. Sun brunch $17.95. Child's meals. Specializes in hickory-grilled seafood, steaks. Jazz eves Tues-Sat. Valet parking wkends. Outdoor dining. View of Chattahoochee River. Cr cds: A, C, D, DS, MC, V.

[D] [≣]

★ ★ ★ ★ **THE RESTAURANT.** *(See The Ritz-Carlton Hotel)* 404/659-0400. E-mail zrca@mindspring.com. A private club atmosphere reigns at this hotel restaurant decorated with objets d'art. French, continental menu. Specialties: grilled fresh duck foie gras, seared baby red snapper, grilled Sonoma lamb rack. Own baking, ice cream, pasta. Hrs: 6-10 pm. Closed Sun. Res accepted. Wine cellar. A la carte entrees: dinner $28-$40. Prix fixe: dinner $65 & $90. Valet parking. Jacket. Cr cds: A, C, D, DS, JCB, MC, V.

[D] [≣]

★ ★ **RIO BRAVO GRILL.** *240 Peachtree St (30303), lobby level of Merchandise Mart, downtown.* 404/524-9224. Hrs: 11 am-11 pm; Fri to midnight; Sat noon-11 pm. Closed Thanksgiving, Dec 25. Tex-Mex menu. Bar. Semi-a la carte: lunch $5.95-$7.95, dinner $6.49-$14.99. Child's meals. Specialties: camarones diablo, fajitas. Southwestern decor. Cr cds: A, C, D, DS, MC, V.

[D] [≣]

★ ★ ★ **RIVIERA.** *519 E Paces Ferry Rd NE (30305), in Buckhead.* 404/262-7112. E-mail rivierarestaurant@msn.com; web www.rivierarestaurant.com. Hrs: 6-10 pm; Fri, Sat 5:30-10:30 pm. Closed Sun; most major hols. Res accepted. French, Mediterranean menu. Bar. Wine list. A la carte entrees: dinner $21-$32. Prix fixe: dinner $35. Specialties: sautéed grouper, roast duckling, grilled lamb chops. Valet parking. Outdoor dining. Cozy dining in house with fireplace. Totally nonsmoking. Cr cds: A, MC, V.

[D]

✔★ ★ **ROCK BOTTOM.** *3242 Peachtree Rd (30305), in Buckhead.* 404/264-0253. Hrs: 11:30 am-11 pm; Fri, Sat to midnight. Closed Thanksgiving, Dec 25. Southwestern menu. Bar. Semi-a la carte: lunch, dinner $4.95-$16.95. Child's meals. Specialties: wood-fired pizza, honey chicken sandwich. Valet parking. Outdoor dining. Brewery; pool tables. Cr cds: A, C, D, MC, V.

★ ★ ★ **RUTH'S CHRIS STEAK HOUSE.** *5788 Roswell Rd, in Sandy Springs, north of downtown.* 404/255-0035. E-mail rcshss@aol.com. Hrs: 5-11 pm. Closed July 4, Dec 25. Res accepted. Bar. Wine list. A la carte entrees: dinner $16.95-$29.95. Specializes in prime beef, fresh seafood. Valet parking. Cr cds: A, C, D, DS, MC, V.

[D] [≣]

★ ★ ★ **SEEGER'S.** *111 W Paces Ferry Rd (30305), in Buckhead.* 404/846-9779. With an attractive suburban setting, elegantly modern decor, extremely dedicated service and superb food, Seeger's is well on its way to becoming one of the country's finest places to dine. The overall ambiance is of elegance, light and airiness. Hrs: 6-10 pm. Closed Sun; also most major hols. Res required (wkends). Contemporary Amer menu. Bar. Wine cellar. Complete meals: 3-course dinner $58, 6-course dinner $65-$75. Menu changes daily. Parking. Outdoor dining. In 1938 home; contemporary European decor. Totally nonsmoking. Cr cds: A, D, MC, V.

[D]

★ **SEOUL GARDEN.** *(5938 Buford Hwy, Doraville 30340) 8 mi NE on Buford Hwy.* 770/452-0123. Hrs: 10:30-1 am. Res accepted. Japanese menu. Semi-a la carte: lunch, dinner $5.95-$49.95. Specializes in sushi, Korean & Japanese dishes. Parking. Cr cds: A, MC, V.

[D] [≣]

★ ★ **SOHO.** *4200 Paces Ferry Rd, Suite 107 (30339), in Vinings Jubilee Shopping Center, north of downtown.* 770/801-0069. Hrs: 11:30 am-10:30 pm; Fri to 11 pm; Sat 5-11 pm. Closed most major hols. Contemporary Amer menu. Bar. Wine list. Semi-a la carte: lunch $5-$15, dinner $10-$20. Specialties: salmon wrapped in rice paper, shrimp relleno. Jazz Mon. Parking. Outdoor dining. Contemporary atmosphere. Cr cds: A, C, D, DS, MC, V.

[D] [≣]

★ ★ **SOTO.** *3330 Piedmont Rd (30305), in Buckhead.* 404/233-2005. Hrs: 6-11:30 pm; Fri, Sat to 12:30 am. Closed Sun; most major hols.

Res accepted. Japanese menu. Semi-a la carte: dinner $25-$35. Specializes in sushi. Parking. Cr cds: A, D, DS, JCB, MC, V.

D

★ ★ **SOUTH CITY KITCHEN.** *1144 Crescent Ave (30309), in Midtown/Piedmont Park.* 404/873-7358. Web www.boldamerican.com. Hrs: 11 am-11 pm; Fri, Sat to midnight; Sun brunch to 4 pm. Closed Memorial Day, Thanksgiving, Dec. 25. Res accepted. Bar. Semi-a la carte: lunch $6.75-$13.95, dinner $10.75-$23.95. Sun brunch $7.75-$13.95. Specialties: grilled barbecue swordfish, sauteed shrimp & scallops, old Charleston she-crab soup. Parking. Outdoor dining. Contemporary decor. Cr cds: A, D, MC, V.

★ ★ **SOUTH OF FRANCE.** *2345 Cheshire Bridge Rd (30324), in Buckhead.* 404/325-6963. Hrs: 11:30 am-2 pm, 6-10:30 pm; Fri to 11:30 pm; Sat 6-11:30 pm. Closed Sun; major hols. Res accepted. Country French menu. Bar. A la carte entrees: lunch $7.95-$12.95, dinner $12.95-$24.95. Specialties: bouillabaise a la Marseillaise, rack of lamb, duck with orange sauce. Parking. Entertainment Wed-Sat. Country French decor. Cr cds: A, C, D, DS, MC, V.

✔★ **SUNDOWN CAFE.** *2165 Cheshire Bridge Rd (30324), in Buckhead.* 404/321-1118. Hrs: 11 am-2 pm, 5:30-10 pm; Fri, Sat to 11 pm. Closed Sun; most major hols. Southwestern menu. Bar. Semi-a la carte: lunch $5.95-$9.95, dinner $8.95-$17.95. Specializes in burritos, enchiladas, fajitas. Parking. Outdoor dining. Southwestern decor. Cr cds: A, C, D, MC, V.

✔★ ★ **TERRA COTTA.** *1044 Greenwood Ave (30306), 2 mi NE on Ponce de Leon, in Midtown/Piedmont Park.* 404/853-7888. Hrs: 6-10 pm; Fri, Sat 5:30-10:30 pm; Sun 5:30-9:30 pm. Closed Mon; some major hols. Res accepted. Eclectic menu. Semi-a la carte: dinner $14.50-$20.50. Specialties: Thai crab cake, grilled pork tenderloin, Maine salmon. Contemporary artwork; casual dining. Totally nonsmoking. Cr cds: A, C, D, DS, MC, V.

✔★ ★ **THAI CHILI.** *2169 Briarcliff Rd NE (30329), in Briar Vista Shopping Center, east of downtown.* 404/315-6750. Hrs: 11 am-2:30 pm, 5-10 pm; Fri to 11 pm; Sat, Sun 5-10 pm. Closed Dec 25. Res accepted. Thai menu. Wine, beer. Semi-a la carte: lunch $5.25-$8.95, dinner $6.95-$19.95. Specialties: salmon curry, veggie and tofu delight, spicy pork. Elegant decor. Totally nonsmoking. Cr cds: A, DS, MC, V.

★ ★ **TOMTOM.** *3393 Peachtree Rd (30326), in Lenox Square Mall, in Buckhead.* 404/264-1163. Web menus.atlanta.com/home/tomtom.html. Hrs: 11:30 am-10 pm; wkends to 11 pm. Closed Easter, Thanksgiving, Dec 25. Res accepted. Bar. Semi-a la carte: lunch $7-$11, dinner $8-$16. Specializes in fresh fish, pasta, chicken. Pianist evenings. Valet parking. Outdoor dining. Cr cds: A, C, D, DS, JCB, MC, V.

★ ★ **TOULOUSE.** *2293-B Peachtree Rd NE (30309), in Buckhead.* 404/351-9533. Hrs: 6-10 pm; Fri, Sat to 11 pm; Sun Brunch 11:30 am-2 pm. Closed Jan 1, Dec 25. Res accepted. Bar. Semi-a la carte: dinner $10-$19.95. Specializes in fish, oven-roasted cuisine. Own baking. Outdoor dining. Paintings by local artists. Totally nonsmoking. Cr cds: A, D, MC, V.

★ ★ **VENI VIDI VICI.** *41 14th St (30309), at W Peachtree, in Midtown/Piedmont Park.* 404/875-8424. Web www.buckheadrestaurants.com. Hrs: 11:30 am-11 pm; Fri to midnight; Sat 5 pm-midnight; Sun 5-10 pm. Closed most major hols. Res accepted. Regional Italian menu. Bar 11:30 am-midnight. A la carte entrees: lunch $8.95-$12.95, dinner $12.95-$24.50. Specializes in homemade pasta, antipasta, wood burning rotisserie meats. Jazz Wed, Sun. Valet parking. Outdoor dining. Vaulted ceilings. Open kitchen. Cr cds: A, C, D, DS, MC, V.

★ ★ ★ **VILLA CHRISTINA.** *45 Perimeter Summit Blvd (30319), I-285, exit 21, north of downtown.* 404/303-0133. Hrs: 11:30 am-2 pm, 6-9 pm; Sun 11:30 am-2:30 pm. Closed most major hols. Res accepted. Italian menu. Bar. Wine list. Semi-a la carte: lunch $9-$14, dinner $19-$29. Sun brunch 30. Specializes in steak, fresh seafood, desserts. Valet parking. Outdoor dining. Contemporary decor. Windows overlook 8 acres of gardens, walks and waterfalls. Totally nonsmoking. Cr cds: A, D, DS, MC, V.

✔★ ★ **THE VININGS INN.** *3011 Paces Mill Rd (30339), north of downtown.* 770/438-2282. Hrs: 11:30 am-2:30 pm, 5:30-10 pm. Bar from 5 pm. Semi-a la carte: lunch $6.50-$9.95, dinner $14.95-$27. Specializes in crab cakes, lamb, pasta. Free valet parking. In 1840s house. Original fireplace. Oil paintings. Cr cds: A, DS, MC, V.

★ ★ **VINNY'S ON WINDWARD.** *(5355 Windward Pkwy, Alpharetta 30004)* 770/772-4644. Hrs: 11:30 am-3 pm, 5 pm-midnight; Sun 5-10 pm. Closed July 4, Thanksgiving, Dec 25. Res accepted. Italian menu. Bar. Semi-a la carte: lunch $3.75-$13.25, dinner $9.75-$25.95. Specialties: rack of lamb with raspberry demi-glaze, shrimp and scallops with pumpkin-seed pesto, spinach and ricotta-stuffed veal chop. Valet parking. Outdoor dining. Cr cds: A, DS, MC, V.

★ ★ ★ **THE WAVERLY GRILL.** *(See Renaissance Waverly Hotel)* 770/953-4500. Web www.renaissancehotels.com. Hrs: 6-10 pm. Res accepted. Contemporary Amer menu. Wine list. A la carte entrees: dinner $4-$23. Child's meals. Specialties: crab and shrimp strudel, whole-fried catfish, Mississippi mud pie. Valet parking. Cr cds: A, C, D, DS, ER, JCB, MC, V.

✔★ ★ **YEN JING.** *(5302 Buford Hwy A-6, Doraville 30340) 8 mi NE on Buford Hwy, in Koreatown Plaza.* 770/454-6688. Hrs: 11:30 am-11 pm. Res accepted. Chinese menu. Semi-a la carte: lunch $4.95-$6.95, dinner $2.95-$19.95. Specializes in soup, salad, dumplings. Parking. Cr cds: MC, V.

✔★ **ZOCALO.** *187 10th St (30309), in Midtown/Piedmont Park.* 404/249-7576. Web www.menusonline.com. Hrs: 11:30 am-2:30 pm, 5:30-11 pm; Fri, Sat 11:30 am-midnight; Sun 10:30 am-10 pm. Closed some major hols. Mexican menu. Semi-a la carte: lunch $4.25-$7.75, dinner $7.75-$22.95. Specialties: chiles rellenos, carnos asada, taco bar. Parking. Outdoor dining. Mexican decor. Cr cds: A, C, D, DS, MC, V.

Unrated Dining Spots

FAT MATT'S. *1811 Piedmont (30324), in Midtown/Piedmont Park.* 404/607-1622. E-mail mindspring@fatmatts.com; web www.fatmatts.com. Hrs: 11:30 am-11:30 pm; Fri, Sat to 12:30 am; Sun 2-11:30 pm. Closed Easter, Dec 25. Semi-a la carte: lunch, dinner $3.50-$15. Child's meals. Specializes in fried fish and chicken, barbecue pork. Entertainment nightly. Parking. Outdoor dining. Casual dining; colorful decor. No cr cds accepted.

VARSITY. *61 North Ave, in Midtown/Piedmont Park.* 404/881-1706. Hrs: 9 am-11:30 pm; Fri, Sat to 1:30 am. Specializes in hot dogs, hamburgers, fried peach pie. Avg ck: $4-$4.50. Parking. One of world's largest drive-ins. Graffitiesque decor; tiered seating. Adj Georgia Tech campus. No cr cds accepted.

THE VARSITY JR. *1085 Lindbergh Dr NE (30324), in Buckhead.* 404/261-8843. Hrs: 10 am-11 pm; Fri, Sat to midnight; Sun from 11 am. Closed Thanksgiving, Dec 25. Semi-a la carte: lunch, dinner

$1-$3. Specializes in hot dogs. Parking. Outdoor dining. 1950s drive-in. Family-owned. No cr cds accepted.

D 🔾

Atlanta Hartsfield Airport Area (C-2)

(See also Atlanta)

Services and Information

Information: 404/530-6600.

Lost and Found: 404/530-2100.

Weather: 770/486-8834.

Cash Machines: Concourse A.

Airlines: Aeromexico, Air Canada, Air Jamaica, Air Tran, ALM-Antillean, American, American West, ASA, Austrian, British Airways, Continental, Delta, JAL, Kiwi Intl, KLM Royal Dutch, Korean Air, Lufthansa, Malev Hungarian, Mexicana, Midway, Midwest Express, Northwest, Reno, Sabena, Swissair, TWA, United, USAir, Vanguard, Varig, Western Pacific.

Motels

★ ★ **COURTYARD BY MARRIOTT.** *(2050 Sullivan Rd, College Park 30337) S on I-85 to Riverdale Rd, E to Best Rd, S to Sullivan Rd.* 770/997-2220; FAX 770/994-9743. 144 rms, 3 story. S $99; D $109; suites $125-$135; under 12 free; wkly, wkend rates. Crib free. TV; cable (premium). Indoor pool; whirlpool. Coffee in rms. Restaurant 6:30-10 am; wkends to 11 am. Bar 5-11 pm. Ck-out noon. Coin lndry. Meeting rms. Business servs avail. In-rm modem link. Valet serv. Sundries. Exercise equipt. Some private patios, balconies. Cr cds: A, C, D, DS, MC, V.

D 🔾🏊🏋🛩🔾 SC

✔★ ★ **HAMPTON INN ATLANTA AIRPORT.** *(1888 Sullivan Rd, College Park 30337) S via I-85 exit 18, E on Riverdale Rd, S on Airport Rd.* 770/996-2220; FAX 770/996-2488. 130 units, 4 story. S, D $65-$85; under 18 free. Crib free. TV; cable (premium). Pool. Complimentary continental bkfst. Restaurant adj 11-2 am. Ck-out noon. Meeting rm. Business servs avail. In-rm modem link. Free airport transportation. Exercise equipt. Public park adj. Cr cds: A, C, D, DS, MC, V.

D 🏊🏋🛩🔾🔾 SC

Motor Hotels

★ ★ **DAYS INN.** *(4601 Best Rd, College Park 30337) S on I-85, exit Riverdale Rd W, then N on Best Rd.* 404/761-6500; FAX 404/763-3267. 161 rms, 6 story. S, D $70-$89; each addl (after 4th person) $10; higher rates special events. Crib free. TV; cable (premium). Pool. Playground. Coffee in rms. Restaurant 6 am-10 pm. Rm serv. Bar 5 pm-midnight. Ck-out noon. Meeting rms. Business center. Valet serv. Free airport transportation. Exercise equipt. Many refrigerators. Cr cds: A, C, D, DS, MC, V.

D 🏊🏋🛩🔾🔾 SC 🏋

★ ★ **PARK PLAZA-ATLANTA AIRPORT.** *(1419 Virginia Ave, Atlanta 30337) N on I-85, exit 19 Virginia Ave W.* 404/768-7800; FAX 404/767-5451. 247 rms, 6 story. S, D $69-$89; each addl $10; suites $99-$139; under 12 free. Crib free. TV; cable (premium). Pool. Restaurants 6 am-11 pm. Rm serv. Bar 4 pm-midnight. Ck-out noon. Coin lndry. Meeting rms. Business center. In-rm modem link. Bellhops. Valet serv. Gift shop. Free airport transportation. Exercise equipt. Some in-rm whirlpools. Cr cds: A, C, D, DS, MC, V.

D 🏊🏋🛩🔾🔾 SC 🏋

Hotels

★ ★ ★ **HILTON & TOWERS.** *(1031 Virginia Ave, Atlanta 30354) N on I-85, exit 19 Virginia Ave E.* 404/767-9000; FAX 404/768-0185. 503 rms, 17 story. S $99-$224; D $129-$244; each addl $15; suites $400-$500; family, wkend rates. Crib free. TV; cable (premium), VCR avail. 2 pools, 1 indoor; whirlpool, poolside serv. Coffee in rms. Restaurant 6 am-midnight. Rm serv 24 hrs. Bar 11:30-2 am. Ck-out noon. Convention facilities. Business center. In-rm modem link. Concierge. Gift shop. Barber, beauty shop. Valet parking. Free airport transportation. Lighted tennis. Exercise rm; sauna. Massage. Minibars; some bathrm phones, wet bars; refrigerators avail. Luxury level. Cr cds: A, C, D, DS, ER, JCB, MC, V.

D 🏋🏊🏋🛩🎿🔾 SC 🏋

★ ★ **HOWARD JOHNSON-ATLANTA AIRPORT.** *(1377 Virginia Ave, Atlanta 30344)* 404/762-5111; FAX 404/762-1277. 189 rms, 6 story. S $99; D $109; each addl $10; under 18 free; wkend rates; higher rates special events. Crib free. TV; cable (premium). Pool. Complimentary coffee in lobby. Restaurant 6:30 am-midnight. Bar noon-2 am. Ck-out noon. Coin lndry. Meeting rms. Business servs avail. In-rm modem link. No bellhops. Free airport transportation. Exercise equipt. Cr cds: A, C, D, DS, MC, V.

D 🏊🛩🛩🔾 SC

★ ★ **MARRIOTT-ATLANTA AIRPORT.** *(4711 Best Rd, College Park 30337) S on I-85, exit Riverdale Rd W.* 404/766-7900; FAX 404/209-6808. E-mail bstewart@marriott.com; web www.marriott.com. 638 rms, 15 story. S $139-$165; suites $200-$650; under 18 free; package plans. Crib free. TV; cable (premium), VCR avail. Indoor/outdoor pool; whirlpool, poolside serv. Restaurant 6:30 am-midnight. Bar 5 pm-2 am; Sun 12:30 pm-midnight; entertainment. Ck-out noon. Convention facilities. Business center. In-rm modem link. Concierge. Gift shop. Barber, beauty shop. Valet parking. Free airport transportation. Lighted tennis. Exercise equipt; sauna. Game rm. Refrigerators avail. Some balconies. Luxury level. Cr cds: A, C, D, DS, JCB, MC, V.

D 🏋🏊🏋🛩🛩🔾 SC 🏋

★ ★ ★ **RENAISSANCE ATLANTA HOTEL-CONCOURSE.** *(One Hartsfield Centre Pkwy, Atlanta 30354) I-85 exit 20, at Hartsfield Centre.* 404/209-9999; FAX 404/209-7031. Web www.renaissancehotels.com. 387 rms, 11 story. S $165-$205; D $185-$225; suites $225-$1,450; wkend rates. Crib free. Valet parking $6. TV; cable (premium). 2 pools, 1 indoor; whirlpool, poolside serv. Complimentary coffee in rms. Restaurant 6 am-11 pm. Rm serv 24 hrs. Bar 11-1 am; entertainment exc Sun. Ck-out 1 pm. Convention facilities. Business center. In-rm modem link. Concierge. Gift shop. Exercise equipt; sauna. Massage. Refrigerators, minibars; microwaves avail. Balconies. Luxury level. Cr cds: A, C, D, DS, ER, JCB, MC, V.

D 🏊🛩🛩🔾🔾 SC 🏋

★ ★ **SHERATON GATEWAY.** *(1900 Sullivan Rd, College Park 30337) S on I-85, exit 18.* 770/997-1100; FAX 770/991-5906. Web www.ittsheraton.com-access. 395 rms, 12 story. S $174; D $184; each addl $10; suites $350; under 18 free; wkend rates. Crib $10. Pet accepted, some restrictions. TV; cable (premium). 2 pools, 1 indoor; whirlpool, poolside serv. Complimentary coffee in rms. Restaurant 6 am-10 pm. Rm serv 24 hrs. Bar 11-2 am; entertainment. Ck-out noon. Convention facilities. Business center. In-rm modem link. Concierge. Gift shop. Free airport transportation. 18-hole golf privileges, pro, putting green, driving range. Exercise equipt. Health club privileges. Microwaves avail; refrigerator in suites. Cr cds: A, C, D, DS, ER, JCB, MC, V.

D 🏋🏌🏊🏋🛩🛩🔾 SC 🏋

★ ★ ★ **WESTIN.** *(4736 Best Rd, Atlanta 30337) S on I-85, exit Riverdale Rd W.* 404/762-7676; FAX 404/763-4199. 495 units, 10 story. S, D $170-$199; suites $175-$600; wkend plans. Crib free. Pet accepted, some restrictions. TV; cable (premium), VCR avail. Indoor/outdoor pool; whirlpool, poolside serv. Complimentary coffee in rms. Restaurant 6:30 am-11 pm; Sun from 12:30 pm. Rm serv 24 hrs. Bar 11-2 am. Ck-out noon. Convention facilities. Business center. In-rm modem link. Gift shop. Free airport transportation. Exercise equipt; sauna. Minibars; some bathrm phones; microwave in suites. Luxury level. Cr cds: A, C, D, DS, ER, JCB, MC, V.

D 🛏 ≋ ✈ ✈ ⋈ 🖐 SC 🏃

Augusta (C-5)

Founded 1736 **Pop** 44,639 **Elev** 414 ft **Area code** 706 **E-mail** amcvb@augustaga.org **Web** www.augustaga.org
Information Metropolitan Convention & Visitors Bureau, 32 Eighth St, Ste 200, PO Box 1331,-1331; 706/823-6600 or 800/726-0243.

Augusta was the second town marked off for settlement by General James E. Oglethorpe. Today, it is as famed for golf as for its red Georgia clay bricks. The city has been a military outpost and upriver trading town, the leading 18th-century tobacco center, a river shipping point for cotton, the powder works for the Confederacy, an industrial center for the new south and a winter resort.

During the Revolution, the town changed hands several times, but Fort Augusta, renamed Fort Cornwallis by its British captors, was finally surrendered to "Lighthorse Harry" Lee's Continentals on June 5, 1781.

The Civil War played havoc with many of the wealthy families who had contributed to the Confederate cause. To help revive their depleted bank accounts, some Summerville residents opened their houses to paying guests. Attracted by Augusta's mild winter climate, northern visitors began an annual migration in increasing numbers, and by the turn of the century, Augusta had become a popular winter resort. Many wealthy northerners built winter residences here in the 1920s. Golf courses and country clubs added to the lure. The Masters Tournament attracts the interest of golfers worldwide.

Augusta's many firsts include the state's first medical academy (chartered 1828); the first and oldest newspaper in the South to be published continuously, the *Augusta Chronicle* (1785); the first steamboat to be launched in southern waters (1790), invented and built by William Longstreet; and the experimental site for one of Eli Whitney's early cotton gins.

Augusta lies at the head of navigation on the Savannah River. Its importance as a cotton market, a producer of cotton textiles, kaolin tiles and brick has been enhanced by diversified manufacturing, processing of cottonseed, farm products and fertilizers. Fort Gordon, an army base southwest of the city, also contributes to the area's economy. With the Medical College of Georgia, Augusta is a leading medical center in the Southeast.

What to See and Do

Augusta-Richmond County Museum(1802). Historic and natural science collections. (Daily exc Mon; closed hols) 560 Reynolds St. Phone 706/722-8454. ¢¢

Augusta State University (1925). (5,600 students) Site of Augusta Arsenal (1826-1955), of which portions are preserved. 2500 Walton Way, between Katharine St & Arsenal Ave. Phone 706/737-1444

Confederate Powder Works Chimney. A memorial honoring war dead, this brick chimney is all that remains of what was once the second-largest powder factory in the world. 1717 Goodrich St.

Gertrude Herbert Institute of Art. Old Ware's Folly Mansion (1818) houses changing exhibits; works by local artists. (Tues-Sat; closed major hols) 506 Telfair St. Phone 706/722-5495. **Donation.**

Harris House (ca 1795). House of Ezekiel Harris, tobacco merchant. Period furnishings. Tours (Tues-Fri; also Sat afternoons) 1822 Broad St. Phone 706/724-0436. ¢

Meadow Garden. House (1791-1804) of George Walton, signer of the Declaration of Independence. Period furnishings. Guided tours (Mon-Fri; also Sat by appt). 1320 Independence Dr. Phone 706/724-4174. ¢¢

National Science Center's Fort Discovery. An innovative hands-on science, communications and technology center with 250 interactive exhibits; high-tech theater; Computer World; KidScape for children ages 3-7.

Also here is a Teacher Resource Center, traveling exhibits and a science store. (Daily; closed Thanksgiving, Dec 25) One Seventh St. Phone 706/821-0200. ¢¢¢

St Paul's Episcopal Church (1750). Granite Celtic cross in churchyard marks site of fort, and the spot where Augusta began, established by Oglethorpe in 1736 in honor of Princess Augusta. Oglethorpe Park, a recreational area on the Savannah river, is located behind the church; picnicking. 605 Reynolds St. Phone 706/724-2485.

Annual Events

Augusta Invitational Rowing Regatta. At Augusta Riverfront Marina. Late Mar or early Apr.

Masters Golf Tournament. Augusta National Golf Course. 1st full wk Apr. Phone 706/667-6000.

Seasonal Events

Augusta Symphony Orchestra. Phone 706/826-4705. Fall-spring.

Augusta Opera Association. Phone 706/826-4710. Fall-spring.

Motels

★ ★ **COURTYARD BY MARRIOTT.** 1045 Stevens Creek (30907), I-20 at Washington Rd. 706/737-3737; FAX 706/738-7851. 130 rms, 2 story. S, D $69; each addl $10; suites $84-$94; wkend rates. TV; cable (premium). Pool; whirlpool. Restaurant 6-9:30 am; Sat 7 am-noon; Sun 7 am-1 pm. Bar; closed Sat, Sun. Ck-out noon. Coin lndry. Meeting rms. Business servs avail. Valet serv. Exercise equipt. Health club privileges. Refrigerators avail. Private patios, balconies. Cr cds: A, C, D, DS, MC, V.

D ≋ ✈ ⋈ 🖐 SC

★ **DAYS INN.** 3026 Washington Rd (30907), I-20, exit 65. 706/738-0131; FAX 706/738-0131, ext. 303. 124 rms, 2 story. S, D $45-$65; each addl $5; crib free. TV; cable (premium). Pool. Complimentary full bkfst. Complimentary coffee in rms. Restaurant 6 am-10 pm. Ck-out 11 am. Refrigerators, microwaves; some in-rm whirlpools. Cr cds: A, C, D, DS, MC, V.

D ≋ ⋈ 🖐 SC

✔★ ★ **HOLIDAY INN EXPRESS.** 1103 15th Street (30901). 706/724-5560; FAX 706/774-6821. 42 rms, 2 story, 4 suites. S, D $54; each addl $5; suites $58; under 19 free. Crib $5. TV; cable (premium). Complimentary continental bkfst. Restaurant nearby. Ck-out noon. Business servs avail. In-rm modem link. Refrigerators, microwaves. Cr cds: A, C, D, DS, JCB, MC, V.

D ⋈ 🖐 SC

✔★ **KNIGHT'S INN.** 210 Boy Scout Rd (30909), I-20, exit 65. 706/737-3166; FAX 706/731-9204. 109 rms, 10 kits. S $21.95, D $26.95; kits. $32.95-$50.95; wkly rates. Pet accepted. TV; cable. Pool. Complimentary coffee. Restaurant nearby. Ck-out 11 am. Coin lndry. Cr cds: A, C, DS, JCB, MC, V.

D 🛏 ≋ ⋈ 🖐 SC

★ **VALU-LODGE.** 1365 Gordon Hwy (30901). 706/722-4344; FAX 706/724-4437. 146 rms, 2 story. S $36.95-$42.95; D $39.95-$45.95; each addl $3; under 17 free; wkend, wkly rates. Crib free. Pet accepted. TV; cable (premium). Pool. Restaurant 6 am-10 pm. Rm serv. Bar 4 pm-1 am. Ck-out 11 am. Some refrigerators; microwaves avail. Cr cds: A, C, D, DS, MC, V.

D 🛏 ≋ ⋈ 🖐 SC

Motor Hotels

★ ★ **AMERISUITES.** 1062 Claussen Rd (30907), I-20, exit 66 off Clausen Road. 706/733-4656; FAX 706/736-1133. 111 suites, 6 story. S $59; D $64; each addl $5; under 12 free; wkend rates. Pet accepted. TV;

cable (premium), VCR avail. Pool; whirlpool. Complimentary bkfst. Complimentary coffee in rms. Restaurant nearby. Ck-out noon. Coin lndry. Meeting rms. Business center. Health club privileges. Exercise equipt. Refrigerators, microwaves. Picnic table. Business suites avail. Cr cds: A, C, D, DS, JCB, MC, V.

★ ★ ★ **RADISSON SUITES INN.** 3038 Washington Rd (30907), at I-20. 706/868-1800; FAX 706/868-9300. 176 units, 4 story, 152 suites. S $59-$99; D $69-$109; each addl $10; under 18 free. Crib free. Pet accepted; $25. TV; cable (premium). Pool. Complimentary bkfst. Coffee in rms. Restaurant 6:30-9:30 am, 5 pm-9 pm; Sat & Sun from 7 am. Rm serv. Bar 5-7 pm. Ck-out noon. Coin lndry. Meeting rms. Business center. In-rm modem link. Health club privileges. Some wet bars. Bathrm phone, refrigerator, microwave in suites. Cr cds: A, C, D, DS, MC, V.

Hotels

★ ★ ★ **RADISSON RIVERFRONT.** 2 Tenth St (30901). 706/722-8900; FAX 706/823-6513. E-mail imp1155@aol.com; web www.radisson.com/augustariverfront. 237 rms, 11 story. S, D $119; suites $135-$475. Crib free. Pet accepted, some restrictions. TV; cable (premium). Pool. Complimentary coffee in rms. Restaurant 6:30 am-2 pm, 5:30-11 pm. Bar 11-1 am; Sun 12:30 pm-midnight. Ck-out noon. Meeting rms. Business servs avail. In-rm modem link. Golf privileges, greens fee $40-$60, putting green, driving range. Exercise equipt; saunas. Health club privileges. Some refrigerators. On Savannah River. Cr cds: A, C, D, DS, ER, JCB, MC, V.

★ ★ ★ **SHERATON.** 2651 Perimeter Pkwy (30909), I-520 Wheeler Rd exit. 706/855-8100; FAX 706/860-1720. 179 rms, 30 suites. S, D $104; each addl $10; suites $159; under 17 free. Crib free. Pet accepted, some restrictions. TV; cable (premium), VCR in suites. 2 pools, 1 indoor. Complimentary coffee in rms. Restaurant 6:30 am-10:30 pm. Bars. Ck-out noon. Coin lndry. Convention facilities. Business center. In-rm modem link. Concierge. Gift shop. Free airport transportation. Exercise equipt; sauna. Refrigerator, microwave in suites. Cr cds: A, C, D, DS, JCB, MC, V.

Inns

✔★ ★ **1810 WEST INN.** (254 N Seymour Dr, Thomson 30824) 30 mi W on I-20 exit 59. 706/595-3156. Web www.bbonline.com/ga/1810west/index.html. 11 rms, 2 story, 2 suites. S $55-$65, D $65-$75; each addl $10; suites $69-$75; guest house $325; wkly rates; higher rates special events. Children over 12 yrs only. TV; cable (premium), VCR (avail) in common rm. Complimentary continental bkfst. Restaurant nearby. Ck-out noon, ck-in 3 pm. In-rm modem link. Concierge serv. Golf privileges, pro, putting green, driving range. Some fireplaces, balconies. Picnic tables, grills. Restored farmhouse (1810); antiques. Totally nonsmoking. Cr cds: A, DS, JCB, MC, V.

★ ★ **AZALEA INN.** 312-316 Greene St (30901). 706/724-3454. E-mail azalea@theazaleainn.com; web www.theazaleainn.com. 21 rms, 3 story, 2 kit. units. S, D $79-$125; each addl $10; kit. units $79-$125; honeymoon plans. TV; cable (premium). Complimentary continental bkfst in rms. Ck-out 11 am. Meeting rm. Business servs avail. Bellhops. Concierge serv. Whirlpool. Some refrigerators, fireplaces. Grills. Turn-of-the-century building (1895) in Olde Town area, near River Walk. Cr cds: A, MC, V.

★ ★ ★ **ROSEMARY & LOOKAWAY HALL.** (804 Carolina Ave, North Augusta SC 29841) 2 mi N on GA 25. 803/278-6222; FAX 803/278-4877; res: 800/531-5578. 23 rms in 2 bldgs, 2 story. S, D $75-$195. Children over 12 yrs only. TV; cable. Complimentary full bkfst; refreshments. Restaurant nearby. Ck-out 11 am, ck-in 3 pm. Concierge serv.

Luggage handling. Business servs avail. Golf privileges, pro, putting green, driving range. Health club privileges. Two inns (1898 & 1902) restored and furnished with period pieces. Landscaped grounds. Totally nonsmoking. Cr cds: A, C, D, DS, MC, V.

Restaurants

★ ★ ★ **CALVERTS.** 475 Highland Ave (30909), in Surrey Center. 706/738-4514. Hrs: 5-10 pm. Closed Sun; major hols. Res accepted. Continental menu. Bar. Wine list. Semi-a la carte: dinner $11.95-$25.95. Specializes in roast rack of lamb, seafood, prime rib. Family-owned. Cr cds: A, D, MC, V.

★ ★ ★ **LA MAISON.** 404 Telfair St (30901). 706/722-4805. Hrs: 6-10 pm. Closed Sun; some major hols. Res accepted. Continental menu. Bar. Wine cellar. Semi-a la carte: dinner $14.50-$35. Specializes in rack of lamb, fresh game, smoked salmon in potato crust with herb sauce. In restored Victorian home (ca 1800). Cr cds: A, D, DS, MC, V.

Bainbridge (G-2)

(See also Thomasville; also see Tallahassee, FL)

Founded 1829 **Pop** 10,712 **Elev** 135 ft **Area code** 912 **Zip** 31717 **E-mail** bchamber@surfsouth.com **Web** www.bainbridgega.com/chamber

Information Bainbridge-Decatur County Chamber of Commerce, PO Box 736, 31718; 912/246-4774 or 800/243-4774.

On the banks of 37,500-acre Lake Seminole, Bainbridge is Georgia's first inland port. It is a town of giant water oaks and live oaks on the Flint River. Andrew Jackson's troops built an earthworks defense (Ft Hughes) near the present town during the Indian Wars (1817-1821). The town was later named in honor of William Bainbridge, commander of the frigate *Constitution*. The forests were so rich in this area that Bainbridge was known as the wealthiest town in the state when fortunes were made in lumbering in the early 20th century.

What to See and Do

Earl May Boat Basin & Park. This 600-acre park on Lake Seminole has exhibit of turn-of-the-century steam engines and locomotives. Beach swimming; boating (ramps). Volleyball court; playing fields. Camping (hookups). Visitor center (Mon-Sat; closed hols). W Shotwell St at bypass.

Seminole State Park. Lake Seminole, shallow by Georgia standards, holds a greater number of fish species than any other lake in the state. Swimming beach, waterskiing; fishing; boating. Miniature golf. Picnicking, concession. Camping, cottages. Standard hrs, fees. 23 mi W on GA 253. Contact Superintendent, Rte 2, Donalsonville 31745; 912/861-3137.

Annual Events

Riverside Arts Festival. Arts festival featuring a different state each year. 1st wk May.

Decatur County Fall Festival & Fair. Carnival, rides, exhibits, livestock show. Mid-Oct.

Motels

✔★ **BEST WESTERN.** 751 W Shotwell St. 912/246-0015. 53 rms, 2 story. S $39-$45; D $44-$45; each addl $5; suites $66; under 19 free; wkly rates; higher rates Bass Fishing Tournament. Crib free. TV; cable. Pool; whirlpool. Complimentary continental bkfst. Restaurant nearby. Ck-out 11 am. Meeting rms. Business servs avail. Refrigerator, wet bar in suites. Cr cds: A, C, D, DS, JCB, MC, V.

★ ★ **CHARTER HOUSE INN.** *1401 Tallahassee Hwy, at jct US 27S, 84 Bypass.* 912/246-8550; FAX 912/246-0260; res: 800/768-8550. E-mail chi@brainbridgega.com; web www.brainbridgega.com/chi. 124 rms, 2 story. S $45-$50; each addl $5; suites $95-$135; under 18 free. Crib free. TV; cable (premium). Pool. Restaurant 6 am-2 pm, 5-10 pm. Bar 4 pm-midnight; closed Sun. Ck-out noon. Valet serv. Meeting rms. Business servs avail. Cr cds: A, C, D, DS, MC, V.

Blakely (G-1)

(See also Dothan, AL)

Founded 1826 **Pop** 5,595 **Elev** 275 ft **Area code** 912 **Zip** 31723 **E-mail** earlycoc@sawega.net **Web** www.blakelyearlychamber.com

Information Chamber of Commerce, 52 Court Square, PO Box 189; 912/723-3741.

Named for US Navy Captain Johnston Blakeley, a hero of the War of 1812, this is an important peanut producing area.

What to See and Do

Coheelee Creek Covered Bridge. Southernmost standing covered bridge in US, built in 1891. Old River Rd, 9 mi SW via GA 62.

Courthouse Square. On the grounds stands what may be the world's only monument honoring the peanut and a

Confederate Flag Pole. The South's last remaining wooden confederate flag pole, erected in 1861.

Kolomoki Mounds State Park. Native American mounds, temple mound and some excavation indicate a settlement here between A.D. 800-1200. Swimming pool; fishing; boating (ramps, dock) on Kolomoki Lake. Trails. Picnicking. Camping. Standard hrs, fees. 6 mi N off US 27. Contact Superintendent, Rte 1, Box 114; 912/723-5296. In park is

Indian Museum. Exhibits explain artifacts and civilization of Kolomoki, Weeden Island and Swift Creek cultures. Entry into excavated burial mound. (Daily exc Mon; closed Jan 1, Thanksgiving, Dec 25) ¢

Inn

★ ★ **TARRER INN.** *(155 S Cuthbert St, Colquitt 31737) 15 mi S on GA 27.* 912/758-2888; res: 888/282-7737; FAX 912/758-2825. Web www.TFN.net/tarrer. 12 rms, 2 story. 1 kit. unit. S $89; D $105; kit. unit $125; golf plans; higher rates special events. Crib $10. TV; cable (premium), VCR avail. Complimentary full bkfst. Complimentary coffee in rms. Restaurant Wed, Thurs 11:30 am-2 pm; Fri 11:30 am-2 pm, 6:30-9 pm; Sat 6:30-9 pm; Sun brunch 11:30 am-2 pm. Rm serv 7 am-11 pm. Ck-out 11 am, ck-in 3 pm. Business servs avail. In-rm modem link. Luggage handling. Valet serv. Concierge serv. Coin lndry. Tennis privileges. 18-hole golf privileges, pro, putting green, driving range. Lawn games. Fireplaces. Built in 1861; burned in 1902, rebuilt in 1905. Totally nonsmoking. Cr cds: A, C, D, DS, MC, V.

Restaurant

✔ ★ **OUR PLACE.** *310 S Main St, in Sawyer Shopping Center.* 912/723-8880. Hrs: 5 am-9:30 pm; Sun to 2 pm. Closed most major hols. Semi-a la carte: bkfst $2-$5, lunch, dinner $2.50-$10.75. Buffet: lunch

$5.80. Child's meals. Specializes in fried chicken, hamburgers, steak. Cr cds: MC, V.

Brunswick (G-6)

(See also Golden Isles, St Simons Island)

Settled 1771 **Pop** 16,433 **Elev** 10 ft **Area code** 912 **E-mail** bgislesvisitorsb@technonet.com **Web** www.bgislesvisitorsb.com

Information Brunswick-Golden Isles Visitors Bureau, 4 Glynn Ave, 31520, phone 912/265-0620 or 800/933-2627.

Brunswick, on the southern third of Georgia's seacoast, separated from the "Golden Isles" by the Marshes of Glynn and the Intracoastal Waterway, was laid out in 1771 by the Colonial Council of the Royal Province of Georgia. Named to honor George II of the House of Brunswick (Hanover), it later became the seat of Glynn County, named in honor of John Glynn, member of the British Parliament and sympathizer with the colonists' struggle for independence.

Gateway to St Simons Island, Jekyll Island and Sea Island (see all), Brunswick is also a manufacturing and seafood processing town. Among its principal products are pulp, paper, lumber machinery, lumber products and processed seafood. Its harbor is a full oceangoing seaport, as well as a home port to coastal fishing and shrimping fleets. Brunswick is known as one of the shrimp capitals of the world. Natural beauty is enhanced by plantings of palms and flowering shrubs along main avenues, contrasting with moss-covered ancient oaks in spacious parks.

What to See and Do

Cumberland Island National Seashore (see). S, off the coast.

Fort Frederica National Monument (see). 12 mi NE via St Simons/Sea Island Causeway (toll).

James Oglethorpe Monument. Honors founder of Georgia. Queens Square, E side of Newcastle St.

Lover's Oak. Giant oak said to be more than 900 yrs old; the trunk, at a point 3 ft above ground, measures 13 ft in diameter. Albany & Prince Sts.

Marshes of Glynn separate Brunswick from St Simons Island, Sea Island, Little St Simons Island and Jekyll Island. Traversed by causeways connecting with US 17, the vast saltwater marshes are bisected by several rivers and the Intracoastal Waterway. Of them Sidney Lanier wrote "Oh, like to the greatness of God is the greatness within the range of the marshes, the liberal marshes of Glynn." Marshes of Glynn Overlook Park has picnic facilities, view of marshes.

Mary Miller Doll Museum. Collection of 4,000 dolls, dollhouses, miniatures, boats and toys; exhibit subjects include antique dolls, foreign dolls and modern doll artists. (Daily exc Sun; closed Jan 1, Thanksgiving, Dec 25) 1523 Glynn Ave. Phone 912/267-7569. ¢

Motels

✔ ★ ★ **BEST WESTERN INN.** *5323 New Jesup Hwy (31523).* 912/264-0144; FAX 912/262-0992. 143 rms, 2 story. S $45-$55; D $49-$59; each addl $4; under 12 free. Crib free. Pet accepted. TV; cable. Pool; wading pool. Complimentary continental bkfst. Restaurant nearby. Ck-out 11 am. Coin lndry. Picnic tables. Cr cds: A, D, DS, MC, V.

★ ★ **COMFORT INN.** *5308 New Jesup Hwy (US 341) (31525), at I-95 Jesup exit 7B.* 912/264-6540; FAX 912/264-9296. 118 rms, 5 story. S $49-$79; D $59-$99; each addl $6; under 18 free. Crib $6. Pet accepted. TV; cable (premium). Pool. Complimentary continental bkfst. Restaurant adj open 24 hrs. Ck-out noon. Meeting rms. Business servs avail. In-rm modem link. Cr cds: A, C, D, DS, JCB, MC, V.

★ ★ **HAMPTON INN.** 112 Tourist Dr (31520), I-95, exit 7A. 912/261-0002; FAX 912/265-5599. 128 rms, 3 story. S $60; D $68; under 18 free. Crib avail. TV; cable (premium). Pool. Coffee in rms. Complimentary continental bkfst. Restaurant adj 6 am-10 pm. Ck-out noon. Meeting rms. Business servs avail. Some refrigerators. Cr cds: A, C, D, DS, MC, V.

[D] [≈] [≈] [🐾] [SC]

★ ★ **THE JAMESON INN.** 661 Scranton Rd (31520), 2 mi E of I-95, exit 8. 912/267-0800; res: 800/526-3766; FAX 912/265-1922. 60 rms, 2 story. S $58; D $63; each addl $5; suites $115-145; under 16 free. Crib free. TV; cable (premium), VCR avail (movies). Pool. Complimentary continental bkfst. Restaurant nearby. Ck-out 11 am. Business servs avail. In-rm modem link. Exercise equipt. Some refrigerators; microwaves avail. Cr cds: A, C, D, DS, MC, V.

[D] [≈] [✕] [≈] [🐾] [SC]

✔ ★ ★ **QUALITY INN.** 125 Venture Dr (31525), I-95 exit 8. 912/265-4600; res: 888/394-8495; FAX 912/265-8268. E-mail relax@ qualityinn.com. 83 rms, 2 story. S $55-$75; D $59-$89; each addl $6; under 17 free. TV; cable (premium). Pool. Complimentary continental bkfst. Complimentary coffee in rms. Ck-out 11 am. Meeting rm. In-rm modem link. Some refrigerators; microwaves avail. Cr cds: A, D, DS, MC, V.

[D] [≈] [≈] [🐾] [SC]

★ **SLEEP INN.** 5272 New Jesup Hwy (31523), I-95, exit 7B. 912/261-0670; FAX 912/264-0441. 93 rms, 90 with shower only, 2 story. S $49-$79; D $59-$89; under 18 free. Crib $2. Pet accepted. TV; cable. Pool. Complimentary continental bkfst. Restaurant adj open 24 hrs. Ck-out noon. Business center. In-rm modem link. Valet serv. Cr cds: A, C, D, DS, ER, JCB, MC, V.

[D] [🐾] [≈] [≈] [🐾] [SC] [🚶]

Hotel

★ ★ **EMBASSY SUITES.** 500 Mall Blvd (31525), I-95 exit 8, near Glynco Jet Port Airport. 912/264-6100; FAX 912/267-1615. E-mail embassy@darientel.net; web www.embassy-suites.com. 130 suites, 5 story. S, D $149; each addl $10; under 16 free. Crib free. Pet accepted. TV; cable (premium). Pool. Complimentary full bkfst. Complimentary coffee in rms. Ck-out noon. Meeting rms. Business servs avail. In-rm modem link. Free airport transportation. Exercise equipt. Health club privileges. Refrigerators, microwaves, wet bars; some in-rm whirlpools. Skylit atrium lobby. Cr cds: A, C, D, DS, MC, V.

[D] [🐾] [≈] [✕] [≈] [🐾] [SC]

Inn

★ ★ **BRUNSWICK MANOR.** 825 Egmont St (31520). 912/265-6889. 4 rms, 2 story. No rm phones. S, D $75-$100; 2-night package. Children over 12 yrs only. Some TVs. Whirlpool. Complimentary full bkfst; afternoon refreshments. Ck-out noon, ck-in 3 pm. Some street parking. Antique furnishings, reproductions. Restored Victorian residence (1886) in Old Town section, opp Halifax Square. Totally nonsmoking. Cr cds: MC, V.

[≈] [🐾]

Restaurants

★ **CAPTAIN JOE'S.** 5296 New Jesup Hwy (US 341) (31523). 912/264-8771. Hrs: 11 am-10 pm. Closed Dec 25. Res accepted. Semi-a la carte: lunch $4-$12.75, dinner $7-$14.75. Child's meals. Specializes in seafood, steak. Salad bar. Parking. Nautical decor. Cr cds: C, D, DS, MC, V.

[D] [≈]

✔ ★ **MATTEO'S ITALIAN RESTAURANT.** 5448 New Jesup Hwy (31523), I-95 & US 341, exit 7B. 912/267-0248. Hrs: 11 am-10 pm. Closed Sun; most major hols. Italian menu. Wine, beer. Semi-a la carte: lunch, dinner $3.25-$10.50. Specializes in pizza, spaghetti, cannoli. Park-

ing. Italian cafe atmosphere; wrought-iron booths. Totally nonsmoking. Cr cds: A, MC, V.

★ ★ **NEW CHINA.** 3202 Glynn Ave (US 17) (31520). 912/265-6722. Hrs: 11 am-10:30 pm; Fri, Sat to 11 pm. Chinese menu. Wine, beer. Semi-a la carte: lunch $3.50-$5.75, dinner $5.50-$9.50. Child's meals. Specialties: Oriental bird nest, kung bo ding. Parking. Chinese decor. Family owned. Cr cds: A, C, D, MC, V.

[≈]

★ **OYSTER BOX.** 2129 Glynn Ave (US 17) (31520). 912/264-3698. Hrs: 11:30 am-10 pm. Closed Sun; Thanksgiving, Dec 25. Wine, beer. Semi-a la carte: lunch $4.50-$6, dinner $8.25-$15.95. Child's meals. Specializes in seafood, chicken wings. Parking. Nautical decor. Cr cds: DS, MC, V.

[≈]

✔ ★ ★ **WILSONS SEAFOOD RESTAURANT.** 3848 Darien Hwy (31521). 912/267-0801. Hrs: 5-10 pm. Closed Mon. Bar from 3 pm. Semi-a la carte: dinner $8.95-$21. Child's meals. Specializes in seafood, steak. Parking. Cr cds: MC, V.

[D] [≈]

Buford (B-3)

(See also Atlanta, Gainesville)

Pop 8,771 **Elev** 1,187 ft **Area code** 770 **Zip** 30518 **E-mail** info@gcvb.org **Web** www.gcvb.org

Information Gwinnett Convention & Visitors Bureau, 1505 Lakes Pkwy, Ste 110, Lawrenceville 30043; 770/277-6212 or 888/494-6638.

What to See and Do

Lake Lanier Islands. A 1,200-acre, yr-round resort. Swimming, waterskiing; beach and water park with wave pool, 10 waterslides and other attractions; fishing; boating (ramps, rentals). Horseback riding; two 18-hole golf courses, tennis. Picnicking; hotel; resort (see); cottages. Tent & trailer camping (hookups). Special events are held May-Oct. Fees for some activities. N of town, on Lake Lanier. For further information contact 6950 Holiday Rd, Lake Lanier Islands, 30518; 770/932-7200.

Winery tours. Chateau Elan Winery and Resort. Tours, tastings; restaurants; 18-hole golf course (fee); special events (fee). (See RESORTS) (Daily; closed Thanksgiving, Dec 25) 1½ mi NW on I-85, exit 48, Braselton. Phone 800/233-WINE. **Free.**

Motels

★ **AMERICAN INN.** 4267 GA 20. 770/932-0111. 40 rms, 2 story. S $43.55; D $49.95. Crib free. TV; cable (premium). Restaurant adj 7 am-10 pm. Ck-out 11 am. In-rm modem link. Cr cds: A, DS, MC, V.

[D] [≈] [🐾] [SC]

★ ★ **HOLIDAY INN.** (2955 GA 317, Suwanee 30174) I-85 exit 44. 770/945-4921; FAX 770/945-0440. 120 rms, 2 story. S $71-$75; D $81-$85; each addl $6; under 18 free. Crib $6. TV; cable (premium). Pool; wading pool. Restaurant 6:30 am-2 pm, 5-10 pm. Rm serv. Bar 3:30 pm-1 am; Fri, Sat to 1 am. Ck-out 11 am. Coin lndry. Meeting rms. Business servs avail. Valet serv. Sundries. Putting green. Microwaves avail. Cr cds: A, C, D, DS, ER, JCB, MC, V.

[D] [≈] [≈] [🐾] [SC]

Inn

★ ★ ★ **WHITWORTH.** (6593 McEver Rd, Flowery Branch 30542) NE on I-985 exit 2, N on 347, then N on McEver Rd. 770/967-2386; FAX 770/967-2649. E-mail visit@whitworthinn.com; web www.whitworthinn.

com. 10 rms, 3 story. No rm phones. S, D $55-$75; each addl $10; under 12 free; monthly rates. Crib free. TV; VCR avail. Complimentary full bkfst. Ck-out 11 am, ck-in 3 pm. Business servs avail. Luggage handling. Balconies. Picnic tables, grills. Contemporary country inn. Library. Totally non-smoking. Cr cds: A, MC, V.

[D] [symbols]

Resorts

★ ★ ★ ★ **INN AT CHATEAU ELAN.** (100 Rue Charlemagne, Braselton 30517) N on I-85, exit 48. 770/932-0900; FAX 770/271-6000; res: 800/233-9463. Web www.chateauelan.com. This 16th-century chateau-style building on a 3,100-acre property includes its own vineyards and winery. The interior is designed as an open-air French street market. 310 rms, 5 story. Mid-May-mid Sept: S, D $170-$195; suites $225-$250; wkend, hol rates; golf plan; lower rates rest of yr. Crib free. TV; cable (premium), VCR avail. 4 pools, 2 indoor; whirlpools, poolside serv. Playground. Supervised child's activities (May-Aug). Complimentary coffee in rms. Restaurant (see CHATEAU ELAN'S LE CLOS). Rm serv 24 hrs. Bar 11 am-11:45 pm; entertainment in season. Ck-out noon, ck-in 3 pm. Gift shop. Convention facilities. Business center. In-rm modem link. Bellhops. Valet serv. Concierge. Airport transportation. Lighted tennis, pro. 63-hole golf, 9-hole par-3 golf, greens fee $65-$125, pro, putting green, driving range. Exercise rm; sauna. Massage. Bicycle rentals. Hiking trails. Lawn games. Rec rm. Game rm. Minibars. Picnic tables. Art gallery; 2 ballrms. Cr cds: A, C, D, DS, JCB, MC, V.

[D] [symbols] [SC] [symbol]

★ ★ ★ **LAKE LANIER ISLANDS HILTON RESORT.** (7000 Holiday Rd, Lake Lanier Islands) I-85 N to I-985 N, exit 1. 770/945-8787; FAX 770/932-5471. 224 rms, 4 story. Apr-Oct: S, D $139-$159. Crib free. TV; cable (premium). Heated pool; wading pool, whirlpool, poolside serv. Playground. Supervised child's activities (Memorial Day-Labor Day). Coffee in rms. Dining rm 6:30 am-10 pm. Box lunch, snack bar, picnics. Rm serv. Bar 11-1 am. Ck-out noon, ck-in 3 pm. Grocery 1 mi. Package store 5 mi. Convention facilities. Business center. In-rm modem link. Bellhops. Valet serv. Concierge. Gift shop. Lighted tennis. 18-hole golf, greens fee $55 (incl cart), pro, putting green, driving range. Beach, boats, water skiing, swimming. Hiking. Bicycles (rentals). Lawn games. Exercise equipt; sauna. Some refrigerators. Balconies. Picnic tables, grills. Water park nearby. On lake. Cr cds: A, C, D, DS, ER, MC, V.

[D] [symbols] [SC] [symbol]

★ ★ ★ **RENAISSANCE PINEISLE RESORT.** (9000 Holiday Rd, Lake Lanier Islands) 3 mi N on GA 13, then 3 mi W on GA 347. 770/945-8921; FAX 770/945-0351. Web www.renaissancehotels.com. 250 rms, 5 story. S $79-$119; D $89-$149; each addl $20; 1-, 2-bedrm suites $175-$548; under 18 free; MAP, golf, tennis, other plans avail. Crib free. TV; cable (premium), VCR avail. Indoor/outdoor pool; whirlpool, poolside serv. Supervised child's activities (late Mar-late Nov); ages 4-18. Complimentary coffee. Dining rm 6:30-10 pm (also see BREEZES). Box lunches; snack bar. Rm serv 24 hrs. Bar 11-2 am; Sat to midnight; Sun 12:30 pm-midnight. Afternoon tea. Ck-out noon, ck-in 3 pm. Concierge. Lndry avail. Valet parking. Convention facilities. Business center. In-rm modem link. Gift shop. Tennis, pro. 18-hole golf, greens fee $49-$59 (incl cart), pro, driving range, putting green. Swimming, private beach, waterskiing; water park adj. Boats, motors, sailboats, canoes, pontoon boats, houseboats, docks; instruction avail. Complimentary sunset cruises. Bicycles. Horseback riding lessons. Lawn games. Soc dir; entertainment. Game rm. Exercise equipt; sauna. Massage. Picnic tables. Private patios, balconies. Many decks. Cr cds: A, C, D, DS, ER, JCB, MC, V.

[D] [symbols] [SC] [symbol]

Restaurants

★ ★ ★ **BREEZES.** (See Renaissance Pineisle Resort) 770/945-8921. Web www.pineisle.com. Hrs: 6:30 am-10 pm; Sun brunch 11 am-2:30 pm (Apr-Oct). Res accepted. Bar 11-2 am; Sat to midnight; Sun 12:30 pm-midnight. A la carte entrees: bkfst $6.95-$10.95, lunch $7.95-$14, dinner $15-$26.95. Sun brunch $24.95. Serv charge 15%. Specializes in

grilled steak, seafood. Own baking. Two-piece band Tues-Sat (Mar-Oct). Braille menu. Valet parking. View of Lake Lanier. Cr cds: A, C, D, DS, ER, JCB, MC, V.

[D] [symbol]

★ ★ ★ **CHATEAU ELAN'S LE CLOS.** (See Inn At Chateau Elan Resort) 770/932-0900. E-mail chateau@chateauelan.com; web www.chateau elan.com. Hrs: 6-10 pm. Closed Sun-Tues. Res required. Classical French menu. Wine list. Complete meals: 8-course dinner $88. Specializes in genuine classical French cuisine. Festive atmosphere of an authentic French chateau. Located in a winery complex with gift shop, museum and wine tasting. Cr cds: A, C, D, DS, JCB, MC, V.

[D] [symbol]

Calhoun (B-1)

(See also Dalton, Rome)

Pop 7,135 **Elev** 715 ft **Area code** 706 **Zip** 30701 **Web** www.gordonchamber.org
Information Gordon County Chamber of Commerce, 300 S Wall St; 706/625-3200or 800/887-3811.

Once called Oothcaloga, "place of the beaver dams," the name was changed in 1850 to honor John Caldwell Calhoun, Secretary of State to President John Tyler. Although the town was directly in the path of General Sherman's 1864 march to the sea, Calhoun was not destroyed. Now Calhoun is the seat of Gordon County and center of a dairy, beef cattle and poultry raising area. The town has a major carpet industry and several major manufacturing companies that provide a wide range of products.

What to See and Do

New Echota State Historic Site (restoration of final Eastern Cherokee capital) (1825-38). Includes the Worcester house (1828), the Council House, the print shop, courthouse, the Vann Tavern (1805), an 1830s log store and a museum-orientation center. Citizens of Calhoun bought the 200-acre site in the early 1950s and donated it to the state. After establishing a government in 1817, the legislature of the Cherokee Indian Nation in 1825 established a capital surrounding the site of their Council House. The written form of the Cherokee language, created by the brilliant Sequoyah, had been developed by 1821, and the print shop was built in 1827. The first issue of the Cherokee newspaper, the *Cherokee Phoenix*, was printed in this shop in 1828 in both Cherokee and English; the paper continued publication until 1834. Samuel A. Worcester, a most able missionary, arrived from Boston in 1827 and built a house, which is the only original building still standing. The Vann Tavern, built by Cherokees at another location, was moved to the park as part of their restoration. The Cherokee Nation had a legislative hall, a supreme court house, a mission and several other buildings at New Echota. At the height of Cherokee prosperity, gold was found in Cherokee territory, then including parts of Georgia, North Carolina, Alabama and Tennessee. In 1835, after a long legal battle, the Cherokees were forced to agree to sell their territory and move to Oklahoma. In the winter of 1838-39 the Cherokees were driven to their new location over the "Trail of Tears," one-fourth of them dying en route. Many hid out in the Great Smoky Mountains; their descendants now form the Eastern Cherokees. The buildings of the restored New Echota are furnished authentically and are a dramatic reconstruction of a remarkable episode in Native American history. (Tues-Sat, also Sun afternoons; closed Jan 1, Thanksgiving, Dec 25) Tours. 1/2 mi E of I-75, exit 131 on GA 225. Contact Site Superintendent, 1211 Chatsworth Hwy NE; 706/624-1321. ¢¢

Resaca Confederate Cemetery. Site of the Civil War battle that opened the way to Atlanta for General Sherman. Civil War markers and cemetery on the Civil War Discovery Trail. (Daily) 5 mi N on I-75, Resaca exit (133). **Free.**

Motels

✔★ **DAYS INN.** *742 GA 53 SE, at I-75 exit 129. 706/629-8271.* 120 rms, 2 story. S $30-$42; D $35-$49; each addl $5; suites $65; under 12 free; lower rates May & Sept. Crib free. Pet accepted; $4. TV; cable. Pool. Playground. Ck-out noon. Coin lndry. Business servs avail. Some refrigerators. Cr cds: A, C, D, DS, ER, MC, V.

★ **HOWARD JOHNSON.** *Redbud Rd, on Redbud Rd, I-75 exit 130. 706/629-9191; FAX 706/629-0873.* 99 rms, 2 story. S $49; D $54; each addl $5; under 18 free. Crib free. Pet accepted. TV; cable (premium). Pool. Restaurant 6:30 am-2 pm, 5-9 pm. Rm serv. Ck-out noon. Meeting rms. Business servs avail. In-rm modem link. Bellhops. Valet serv. Cr cds: A, C, D, DS, JCB, MC, V.

✔★★ **JAMESON INN.** *189 Jameson St SE, I-75, exit 129. 706/629-8133; FAX 706/629-7985.* Web www.jamesonsinns.com. 59 rms, 2 story. S $52; D $56; each addl $4; suite $70; under 12 free. Crib free. TV; cable (premium), VCR avail. Pool. Complimentary continental bkfst. Restaurant adj open 24 hrs. Ck-out 11 am. Business servs avail. In-rm modem link. Exercise equipt. Some refrigerators, microwaves. Cr cds: A, C, D, DS, MC, V.

✔★★ **QUALITY INN.** *915 GA 53 E, E off I-75 exit 129. 706/629-9501; res: 800/225-4686; FAX 706/629-9501.* 100 rms, 2 story. S $40-$50; D $50-$60; each addl $5; under 18 free. Crib free. Pet accepted, some restrictions; $5. TV; cable (premium). Pool. Complimentary continental bkfst. Restaurant 11 am-midnight. Rm serv. Bar 4 pm-midnight. Ck-out 11 am. Coin lndry. Meeting rms. Business servs avail. In-rm modem link. Exercise equipt. Cr cds: A, C, D, DS, JCB, MC, V.

Restaurant

✔★ **PENG'S PAVILLION.** *1120 South Wall St, I-75 exit 129. 706/629-1453.* Hrs: 11 am-9 pm; wkends to 9:30 pm. Closed Sun; some major hols. Res accepted. Chinese menu. Semi-a la carte: lunch $4.25-$4.75, dinner $6.50-$9.25. Specialty: Mongolian beef. Parking. Chinese decor; murals, lanterns. Cr cds: A, C, D, DS, JCB, MC, V.

Carrollton (C-1)

Pop 16,029 **Elev** 1,116 ft **Area code** 770 **Zip** 30117 **Web** www.carroll-ga.org
Information Carroll County Chamber of Commerce, 200 Northside Dr; 770/832-2446.

Carrollton was named in honor of Charles Carroll, one of the signers of the Declaration of Independence. The town serves as a regional retail, service, manufacturing and health care center for several counties in western Georgia and eastern Alabama. Carrollton is home to Southwire, one of the nation's largest privately owned rod and cable manufacturing companies. The world's largest tape and record manufacturing plant, owned by Sony, is located here as well.

What to See and Do

John Tanner State Park. Two lakes offer the longest beach in the state park system. Swimming; fishing; boating (rentals). Picnicking. Camping, motel. Standard hrs, fees. 6 mi W off GA 16. Contact Superintendent, 354 Tanner's Beach Rd; 770/830-2222.

State University of West Georgia (1933). (7,500 students) A unit of the state university system. On campus are John F. Kennedy Memorial Chapel and

Thomas Bonner House (ca 1840). Restored plantation house, campus information center. (Mon-Fri; closed hols, school breaks) Maple St. Phone 770/836-6464.

Motel

✔★★ **COMFORT INN.** *(128 GA 61, Villa Rica 30180) N on GA 61, at jct I-20. 770/459-8000; FAX 770/459-8413.* 64 rms, 2 story. Memorial Day-mid-Sept: S $49-$69; D $59-$79; each addl $6; under 18 free; higher rates auto races; lower rates rest of yr. Crib $6. TV; cable (premium), VCR avail. Pool. Complimentary continental bkfst. Restaurant opp 6 am-11 pm. Ck-out 11 am. Business servs avail. In-rm modem link. Some in-rm whirlpools, refrigerators. Cr cds: A, C, D, DS, ER, JCB, MC, V.

Restaurant

★★ **MAPLE STREET MANSION.** *401 Maple St. 770/834-2657.* Hrs: 11 am-midnight; Sat from 4 pm. Closed Sun; Jan 1, Dec 24, 25. Res accepted. Bar. Semi-a la carte: lunch $3.95-$6.95, dinner $5.95-$21.95. Specializes in prime rib, Maple Hill pie. Parking. In restored house (1894) built by Georgian industrialist Leroy Mandeville. Cr cds: A, C, D, DS, MC, V.

Cartersville (B-2)

(See also Atlanta, Marietta, Rome)

Founded 1832 **Pop** 12,035 **Elev** 787 ft **Area code** 770 **Zip** 30120 **E-mail** cvb@notatlanta.org **Web** www.notatlanta.org
Information Cartersville/Bartow County Convention & Visitors Bureau, PO Box 200397; 770/387-1357 or 800/733-2280.

Cartersville is in the center of an area rich in minerals. Its economy is based upon textile manufacturing, plastics, the quarrying of limestone and the mining of ocher, barite and manganese. An Anheuser-Busch brewery also contributes to the economy.

What to See and Do

Allatoona Lake (US Army Corps of Engineers). Swimming, waterskiing; fishing; boating (ramps). Hiking trails, overlook. Picnicking. Camping (fee). Headquarters is 3 mi N on I-75, exit 125, then E on GA 20, then 4 mi S on Spur 20. Contact Park Ranger, PO Box 487; 770/382-4700.

Etowah Indian Mounds Historic Site & Archaeological Area. The most impressive of more than 100 settlements in the Etowah Valley, this village was occupied from A.D. 1000-1500. It was the home of several thousand people of a relatively advanced culture. Six earthen pyramids grouped around two public squares, the largest of which occupies several acres, served as funeral mounds, bases for temples and the residences of the chiefs. Museum displays artifacts from the excavations; crafts, foods, way of life of the Etowah; painted white marble mortuary. (Daily exc Mon; closed Jan 1, Thanksgiving, Dec 25) 3 mi S, off GA 113, 61. Phone 770/387-3747. ¢

Kennesaw Mountain National Battlefield Park (see). Approx 20 mi SE off US 41.

Red Top Mountain State Lodge Park. Swimming, waterskiing; boating (ramps, dock, marina). Trails; miniature golf. Picnicking, concession. Restaurant. Lodge. Camping, cottages. Standard hrs, fees. 2 mi E of I-75, exit 123. Phone 770/975-0055.

William Weinman Mineral Museum. Displays of cut gemstones, minerals and rocks from Georgia and around the world; simulated limestone cave with waterfall. (Daily exc Mon; closed hols) I-75 exit 126, 51 Mineral Museum Dr. Phone 770/386-0576. ¢¢

Motels

✔★ **BUDGET HOST INN.** *851 Cass/White Rd, I-75N exit 127.* 770/386-0350. 92 rms, 3 story. S $21.95-$49.95; D $26.95-$89.95; each addl $5. Crib $2. Pet accepted; $2. TV; cable. Pool. Restaurant 6 am-2 pm, 5-9 pm. Ck-out 11 am. Coin lndry. Cr cds: A, DS, MC, V.

✪ ≋ ⊠ ⋈ SC

✔★★ **COMFORT INN.** *28 GA 20 Spur SE (30184).* 770/387-1800. 60 rms, 2 story. S $32-$48; D $39-$60; each addl $5; under 18 free; higher rates special events. TV; cable. Pool. Complimentary continental bkfst. Restaurant nearby. Ck-out 11 am. Some refrigerators, microwaves. Cr cds: A, C, D, DS, MC, V.

D ≋ ⊠ ⋈ SC

✔★★ **DAYS INN.** *5618 GA 20 SE, at jct I-75 exit 125.* 770/382-1824; FAX 770/606-9132. 52 rms, 2 story. Mar-Aug, Dec: S $55; D $60; each addl $5; under 12 free; higher rates: baseball, football games; lower rates rest of yr. Crib free. TV; cable (premium). Pool. Complimentary continental bkfst. Restaurant adj 6 am-11 pm; wkends to 2 am. Ck-out noon. Some refrigerators. Cr cds: A, D, DS, MC, V.

D ≋ ⊠ ⋈ SC

★★ **HOLIDAY INN.** *2336 US 411 NE, jct I-75 exit 126.* 770/386-0830; FAX 770/386-0867. 144 rms, 2 story. S, D $67; each addl $6; under 19 free. Crib free. Pet accepted. TV; cable (premium). Pool. Coffee in lobby. Restaurant 6 am-10 pm. Rm serv. Bar 5 pm-midnight. Ck-out noon. Meeting rms. Business servs avail. In-rm modem link. Valet serv. Sundries. Exercise equipt. Health club privileges. Lawn games. Whirlpool in suites. Cr cds: A, C, D, DS, JCB, MC, V.

D ✪ ≋ ✗ ⊠ ⋈ SC

★★ **RAMADA LIMITED.** *45 GA 20 Spur SE (30121), at jct I-75 exit 125.* 770/382-1515; FAX 770/382-1515, ext. 406. 50 rms, 2 story. S $42-$75, D $45-$105; each addl $8; under 12 free. Crib free. TV; cable (premium). Pool. Complimentary continental breakfast. Restaurant nearby. Ck-out 11 am. Meeting rm. Business servs avail. In-rm modem link. Cr cds: A, C, D, DS, ER, JCB, MC, V.

D ≋ ⊠ ⋈ SC

Restaurant

✔★ **MORRELL'S.** *22 GA 294, I-75 & GA 20, exit 125.* 770/382-1222. Hrs: 6 am-10 pm. Closed Thanksgiving, Dec 25. Semi-a la carte: bkfst $1.50-$4.50, lunch $4.25-$5.95, dinner $5.95-$15.95. Child's meals. Specializes in prime rib, barbecued pork & chicken. Parking. Cr cds: A, D, DS, MC, V.

Chatsworth (A-2)

(See also Calhoun, Dalton; also see Chattanooga, TN)

Pop 2,865 **Elev** 750 ft **Area code** 706 **Zip** 30705 **E-mail** mchamber@northga.net
Information Chatsworth-Murray County Chamber of Commerce, 126 N Third Ave; 706/695-6060.

Murray County has a strong carpet industry. Almost a third of the land is forest and mountains. Opportunities for fishing, hunting, camping, backpacking and mountain biking abound in the surrounding Cohutta Wilderness and woodlands. A Ranger District office of the Chattahoochee National Forest is located in Chatsworth. Talcum, a mineral that most people know only as a comfort to the skin, was once mined here in large quantities.

What to See and Do

Carters Lake. Swimming; fishing; boating (ramps). Hiking trails, overlooks. Camping (mid-Apr-late Oct; fee). For more information visit Resource Manager's office at dam site. 15 mi S, off US 411. Phone 706/334-2248.

Chattahoochee National Forest. (See DAHLONEGA)

Fort Mountain State Park. A mountain park with ruins of a prehistoric stone wall; observation tower. Swimming; fishing; paddleboats (rentals). Self-guided nature trail. Picnicking. Cabins, camping. Standard hrs, fees. 7 mi E via GA 52. Contact Superintendent, 181 Fort Mountain Park Rd; 706/695-2621.

Vann House State Historic Site (1804). This brick house was the showplace of the Cherokee Nation. James Vann was half Scottish, half Cherokee. His chief contribution to the tribe was his help in establishing the nearby Moravian Mission for the education of the young Cherokees. The three-story house, with foot-thick brick walls, is modified Georgian in style; partly furnished. (Daily exc Mon; closed Jan 1, Thanksgiving, Dec 25) 3 mi W on GA 52-A at jct GA 225 in Spring Place.Contact Manager, 82 GA 225 N; 706/695-2598. ¢

Annual Event

Appalachian Wagon Train. 1 mi E via US 76. Horse and mule shows, trail rides, square dancing, parade. Phone 706/695-7122. Late June-early July.

Lodge

★★ **COHUTTA LODGE.** *500 Cochise Trail, 10 mi E on GA 52.* 706/695-9601; FAX 706/695-0913. 61 rms, 2-3 story. May-Dec: S, D $69-$99; each addl $8; suites $99; kit. units $105-$125; cottage $165; under 12 free; Oct wkends (2-day min); lower rates rest of yr. Crib free. TV. Indoor pool. Complimentary coffee in rms. Restaurant (see COHUTTA DINING ROOM). Ck-out 11 am. Coin lndry. Meeting rms. Business servs avail. Gift shop. Lighted tennis. Game rm. Lawn games. Many refrigerators. Balconies. Picnic tables. Cr cds: A, D, DS, MC, V.

D ✦ ✪ ≋ ⊠ ⋈ SC

Restaurant

✔★★ **COHUTTA DINING ROOM.** *(See Cohutta Lodge)* 706/695-9601. Hrs: 11:30 am-3 pm, 5-9 pm; Fri to 9:30 pm; Sat 8-10:30 am, 11:30 am-3 pm, 5-9:30 pm; Sun 8-10:30 am, 11:30 am-3 pm, 5-9 pm. Closed Dec 24, 25. Semi-a la carte: bkfst 4.95-$6.95, lunch $1.50-$6.25, dinner $5.75-$15.75. Buffet: bkfst $5.95. Specializes in prime rib, seafood. Salad bar. Pianist Fri, Sat. Parking. Cr cds: A, D, DS, MC, V.

 D

Chickamauga and Chattanooga National Military Park (A-1)

(See also Dalton; also see Chattanooga, TN)

E-mail chch_administration@nps.gov **Web** www.nps.gov/chch/

(9 mi S of Chattanooga, TN on US 27)

Established in 1890, this is the oldest and largest national military park in the United States. The two-day battle fought at Chickamauga was one of the Civil War's fiercest, with 36,000 casualties, and was the greatest success of Confederate armies in the West. However, the inability of General Braxton Bragg to follow up the success of September 19 and 20, 1863, and his defeat two months later on Missionary Ridge at Chattanooga, Tennessee, meant the loss of a strategic railway center and opened the gateway to a Union advance into the deep South.

General Bragg had evacuated Chattanooga on September 9 to maintain rail communications southward after Union Commander Rosecrans had abruptly crossed the Tennessee River southwest of the city. However, with the arrival of reinforcements from Lee's army in the East giving him a numerical advantage, Bragg turned back north to surprise Rosecrans' scattered forces. On September 18, the two armies stumbled into each other on the west bank of the Chickamauga Creek.

By the morning of September 19, Union troops attacked and were driven back in heavy fighting. Confederate troops broke the Union line the morning of the 20th, sweeping the entire right wing and part of the center from the field. Union troops on the left, with the aid of the reserve corps, all under the command of General George H. Thomas, took up new positions on Snodgrass Hill, holding under terrific assaults by Confederates until the Union army was able to retreat in good order to Chattanooga. Thomas earned the nickname "Rock of Chickamauga."

US Highway 27 extends more than three miles through the 5,400-acre Chickamauga Battlefield, where the battle has been commemorated by markers, monuments, tablets and artillery pieces. Woods and fields are kept as close as possible to the way they were in wartime, and some old buildings lend added atmosphere.

Chickamauga Battlefield is but one of 17 areas forming the National Military Park. Other major areas (all in Tennessee) are Point Park on Lookout Mountain, the Reservations on Missionary Ridge, Signal Point on Signal Mountain and Orchard Knob in Chattanooga—totaling nearly 3,000 acres.

The Chickamauga visitor center, on US 27 at the north entrance to the battlefield, is the logical starting point for auto tours. The center has the Fuller Collection of American Military Shoulder Arms, consisting of 355 weapons, as well as a 26-minute multimedia program (fee) describing the Battle of Chickamauga. Visitor center (daily; closed Dec 25). Park (daily). The National Park Service also offers guided tours, walks, evening programs and musket/cannon firing demonstrations (June-Aug). For further information contact PO Box 2128, Fort Oglethorpe 30742; 706/866-9241. **Free.**

Clayton (A-3)

(See also Hiawassee, Toccoa)

Pop 1,613 **Elev** 1,925 ft **Area code** 706 **Zip** 30525 **Web** www.gamountains.com/rabun
Information Rabun County Chamber of Commerce, Box 750, phone 706/782-4812; a Rabun County Welcome Center is located on US 441 N, phone 706/782-5113 or -4812.

Located in the mountainous and forested northeast corner of Georgia, Clayton offers visitors a wide variety of activities, including hiking, mountain climbing, camping, boating, fishing, hunting, skiing and whitewater rafting. A Ranger District office of the Chattahoochee National Forest (see DAHLONEGA) is located in Clayton.

What to See and Do

Chattooga Wild and Scenic River. Originating in the mountains of North Carolina, the Chattooga tumbles southward 57 mi to its terminus, Lake Tugaloo, between Georgia and South Carolina. Designated a Wild and Scenic River by Congress in 1974, the Chattooga is one of the few remaining free-flowing streams in the Southeast. Scenery along the river is spectacular, with gorges, waterfalls and unusual rock formations. 8 mi SE via US 76.

Foxfire Museum and Center. Located in replica of log cabin, the museum contains artifacts and crafts of early Appalachian life, including the inner workings of an old grist mill. (Daily exc Sun; closed some hols) 2 mi N on US 441, in Mountain City. Phone 706/746-5828. Museum **Free.** Center ¢¢

Raft trips. Southeastern Expeditions. Whitewater raft trips on the Chattooga River in northeast Georgia ranging in length from half-day to three-days. (Mar-Oct) Contact 50 Executive Park South, Suite 5016, Atlanta 30329; 404/329-0433 or 800/868-7238.   ¢¢¢¢¢

Annual Event

Homemakers' Harvest Festival. 6 mi N on US 23, 441 in Dillard. Mountain arts & crafts. 3 wkends Oct.

Columbus (E-1)

(See also Pine Mountain (Harris Co))

Founded 1827 **Pop** 178,681 **Elev** 250 ft **Area code** 706 **E-mail** ccvb@msn.com **Web** columbusga.com/ccvb
Information Tourist Division, Convention and Visitors Bureau, 1000 Bay Ave, PO Box 2768 31902, phone 706/322-1613 or 800/999-1613; or the Georgia Welcome Center, 1751 Williams Rd; 24-hour visitors information hotline, phone 706/322-3181.

Power from the falls of the Chattahoochee River feeds the industries of this dynamic city. With a nine-foot-deep navigable channel to the Gulf of Mexico, it is at the head of navigation on the Chattahoochee. Originally a settlement of the Creek Indians, the site was chosen as a border stronghold by Governor Forsyth in 1828. The city reached a peak of frenzied manufacturing and commerce between 1861 and 1864, when it supplied the Confederate Army with shoes, caps, swords and pistols.

The Columbus Iron Works (1853) supplied Columbus and the surrounding area with cast iron products, farming equipment, steam engines and industrial and building supplies. It was a major supplier of cannons for the Confederate States during the Civil War. Reconstruction created havoc for a time, but by 1874 Columbus' industries were more numerous and varied than before the war: from 1880 until 1920, a commercial ice-making machine was produced in the town; and by the beginning of World War II,

Columbus was a great iron-working center and the second largest producer of cotton in the South.

Much of the original city plan of 1827 is still evident, with streets 99 to 164 feet wide flanked by magnificent trees. Dogwood and wisteria add color in the spring. The atmosphere is exemplified by the brick-lined streets and gaslights in the 28-block historic district and by the Victorian gardens, gazebos and open air amphitheaters on the Chattahoochee Promenade along the banks of the river.

What to See and Do

Columbus Convention and Trade Center. Converted from the historic Columbus Iron Works. Exhibit space, banquet facilities, outdoor amphitheater. 801 Front Ave. Phone 706/327-4522.

The Columbus Museum. Features Chattahoochee Legacy, a regional history gallery with re-created period settings; fine and decorative arts galleries; and Transformations, a youth-oriented participatory gallery. (Daily exc Mon; closed major hols) 1251 Wynnton Rd. Phone 706/649-0713. **Free.**

Fort Benning. Largest infantry post in the US, established during World War I, the fort was named for Confederate General Henry L. Benning of Columbus. Infantry School; demonstrations of Airborne 5000 at Jump Tower (Mon mornings). 5 mi S on US 27. For information phone 706/545-2958. **Free.** Here is

National Infantry Museum. Exhibits of US infantry weapons, uniforms, equipment from the Revolutionary War to the War in the Gulf; experimental and developmental weapons; collection of foreign weapons and equipment. (Daily; closed most major hols) Phone 706/545-2958. **Free.**

Springer Opera House (1871). Restored Victorian theater in which many famous performers have appeared, including Shakespearean actor Edwin Booth; museum. Guided tours. 103 10th St at 1st Ave. For performance schedule, fee information phone 706/327-3688 (box office).

Woodruff Museum of Civil War Naval History. Salvaged remains of Confederate gunboats *Jackson* and *Chattahoochee;* relics, ship models, uniforms, paintings and other exhibits on Confederate naval operations. (Daily exc Mon; closed Thanksgiving, Dec 25) 202 4th St. Phone 706/327-9798. **Donation.**

Annual Event

Riverfest Weekend. At riverfront. Last wkend Apr.

Motels

✔★ **BAYMONT INN.** *2919 Warm Springs Rd (31909). 706/323-4344; FAX 706/596-9622.* 102 rms, 3 story. S $43.95-$48.95; D $51.95-$56.95; suites $58.95-$63.95; under 18 free. Crib free. Pet accepted, some restrictions. TV; cable. Pool. Complimentary continental bkfst. Complimentary coffee in rms. Restaurant opp 11 am-10 pm. Ck-out noon. Meeting rm. Business servs avail. In-rm modem link. Valet serv. Refrigerator, microwave in suites. Cr cds: A, C, D, DS, MC, V.

[D] [✦] [≈] [≧] [⚲] [SC]

★ **COMFORT INN.** *3443 B Macon Rd (31907), I-185 exit 4. 706/568-3300; FAX 706/563-2388.* 66 rms, 3 story. S $55.95; D $59.95; each addl $4; suites $99.95; under 18 free. Crib free. TV; cable. Pool. Complimentary continental bkfst. Complimentary coffee in rms. Restaurant opp open 24 hrs. Ck-out noon. Business servs avail. Valet serv. Exercise equipt. Refrigerators. Near airport. Cr cds: A, C, D, DS, ER, JCB, MC, V.

[D] [≈] [✈] [≧] [⚲] [SC]

★ **COURTYARD BY MARRIOTT.** *3501 Courtyard Way (31904), adj to Peachtree Mall. 706/323-2323; FAX 706/327-6030.* 139 rms, 2 story. S $72-$82; D, suites $99.95; under 18 free; wkend rates. Crib free. TV; cable, VCR. Pool. Restaurant 6:30-10 am, 5-10 pm; Sat, Sun 7 am-noon. Bar 5-10 pm. Ck-out noon. Coin lndry. Meeting rms. In-rm

modem link. Valet serv. Exercise equipt. Some refrigerators. Private patios, balconies. Cr cds: A, D, DS, MC, V.

[D] [≈] [✈] [≧] [⚲] [SC]

★★ **HAMPTON INN-COLUMBUS AIRPORT.** *5585 Whitesville Rd (31904), I-185 exit 6, near Metropolitan Airport. 706/576-5303; FAX 706/596-8076.* 119 rms, 2 story. S $64; D $69; under 18 free. Crib $5. TV; cable (premium), VCR. Pool. Complimentary continental bkfst. Restaurant nearby. Ck-out noon. Meeting rm. Business servs avail. In-rm modem link. Sundries. Free airport transportation. Health club privileges. Cr cds: A, C, D, DS, MC, V.

[D] [≈] [✈] [≧] [⚲] [SC]

✔★ **LA QUINTA.** *3201 Macon Rd (31906), I-185 exit 4. 706/568-1740; FAX 706/569-7434.* 122 rms, 2 story. S, D $59; suites $85; under 18 free. Crib free. Pet accepted. TV; cable (premium). Pool. Complimentary continental bkfst. Restaurant adj open 24 hrs. Ck-out noon. Coin lndry. Business servs avail. In-rm modem link. Valet serv. Some refrigerators. Grills. Cr cds: A, C, D, DS, MC, V.

[D] [✦] [≈] [≧] [⚲] [SC]

Hotels

★★★ **HILTON.** *800 Front Ave (31901). 706/324-1800; FAX 706/576-4413.* 177 rms, 6 story. S $84-$126; D $94-$136; each addl $10; suites $125-$375; family, wkend rates. Crib free. TV; cable (premium). Pool. Restaurant 6:30 am-2 pm, 5-10:30 pm. Bar noon-midnight. Ck-out noon. Meeting rms. Business servs avail. In-rm modem link. Free airport, bus depot transportation. Incorporates 100-yr-old grist mill into design. Convention Ctr (former Columbus Iron Works facility) opp. Cr cds: A, C, D, DS, MC, V.

[D] [≈] [≧] [⚲] [SC]

★★★ **SHERATON AIRPORT.** *5351 Simons Blvd (31904), I-185 exit 6, near Metropolitan Airport. 706/327-6868; FAX 706/327-0041.* 178 rms, 5 story. S, D $80-$84; each addl $5; under 18 free. Crib free. TV; cable. Heated pool; whirlpool. Restaurant 6:30 am-2 pm, 5-9:30 pm; Sat, Sun from 7 am. Bar 4 pm-1 am. Ck-out noon. Meeting rms. Business servs avail. In-rm modem link. Free airport, bus depot transportation. Health club privileges. Game rm. Some refrigerators. Cr cds: A, C, D, DS, ER, JCB, MC, V.

[D] [≈] [✈] [≧] [⚲] [SC]

Restaurants

★★★ **BLUDAU'S GOETCHIUS HOUSE.** *405 Broadway (31901). 706/324-4863.* Hrs: 5-9:45 pm; Fri, Sat to 10:45 pm. Closed Sun. Res accepted. Continental menu. Bar. Semi-a la carte: dinner $13.95-$39.95. Specializes in fresh seafood, veal. Parking. Outdoor dining. In restored antebellum mansion (1839). Cr cds: A, D, DS, MC, V.

[⛶]

✔★★ **MALONE'S.** *2955 Warm Springs Rd (31909). 706/324-3250.* Hrs: 11-1 am; Fri, Sat to 2 am; Sun to midnight. Closed Thanksgiving, Dec 25. Bar. Semi-a la carte: lunch $5.95-$8.95, dinner $8.95-$15.95. Child's meals. Specializes in fajitas, fresh seafood, steak. Parking. Outdoor dining. Cr cds: A, D, DS, MC, V.

[D] [⛶]

Unrated Dining Spot

COUNTRY BBQ. *Jct Hamilton & Weems Rds, at Main Street Village. 706/660-1415.* Hrs: 11 am-10 pm; Fri, Sat to 11 pm. Closed some major hols. Res accepted. Semi-a la carte: lunch, dinner $6-$8. Child's meals. Specializes in barbecued chicken, ribs & beef. Outdoor dining. Western decor. Cr cds: MC, V.

[D]

Commerce (B-3)

(See also Athens, Gainesville)

Pop 4,108 **Elev** 931 ft **Area code** 706 **Zip** 30529

What to See and Do

Crawford W. Long Medical Museum. Museum contains diorama of Dr. Long's first use of ether as an anesthetic in surgery, a enormous breakthrough in medicine. Also here are documents, artifacts and history of anesthesia exhibit. Entrance is in Jackson County Historical Society building, which has other exhibits on local history. A third building has an 1840s doctor's office, an apothecary shop, a 19th-century general store exhibit and a herb garden. (Tues-Sat; closed legal hols) 10 mi SW via GA 15, on College St in Jefferson or 5 mi S on I-85, exit 50. Phone 706/367-5307. **Donation.**

Motels

★ ★ **HOLIDAY INN EXPRESS.** *30747 US 441S, S at I-85, exit 53. 706/335-5183; FAX 706/335-6588.* 96 rms, 2 story. S, D $52-$85; under 18 free; higher rates special events. Crib free. Pet accepted, some restrictions. TV; cable (premium). Pool. Complimentary continental bkfst. Ck-out noon. Coin lndry. Meeting rm. Business servs avail. In-rm modem link. Exercise equipt. Microwaves avail. Cr cds: A, D, DS, MC, V.

D ✔ ≈ ⊀ ⊠ ⋒ SC

✔★ **HOWARD JOHNSON.** *30591 US 441, 3 mi N at I-85. 706/335-5581; FAX 706/335-7889.* 120 rms, 2 story. S $40-$55; D $45-$74; each addl $5; under 18 free. Crib free. Pet accepted. TV; cable (premium). Pool; wading pool. Complimentary continental bkfst. Restaurant 6 am-10 pm. Ck-out noon. Microwaves avail. Cr cds: A, C, D, DS, MC, V.

D ✔ ≈ ⊠ ⋒ SC

Cordele (F-3)

(See also Albany, Perry)

Founded 1888 **Pop** 10,321 **Elev** 319 ft **Area code** 912 **Zip** 31015 **E-mail** cccofc@sowega.net
Information Cordele-Crisp Tourism Commission, 302 E 16th Ave, PO Box 158; 912/273-3526.

Watermelons, sweet potatoes, soybeans, pecans, cotton, peanuts, corn and cantaloupes are produced in Crisp County, of which Cordele is the seat. The local state farmers market sells more watermelons than any other market in the state; Cordele residents thus refer to their city as the "Watermelon Capital of the World." Garment making and the manufacture of enormous baling presses for scrap metals, agricultural implements, air conditioners, foundry products, mobile homes, livestock feed, fiberglass items, steel fittings and several other industries are locally important.

What to See and Do

Georgia Veterans Memorial State Park. Swimming pool, waterskiing; fishing; boating; golf. Picnicking, concession. Camping, cabins. Museum; model airplane field with historic aircraft. Standard hrs, fees. 9 mi W via US 280. Contact Park Manager, 2459-A Hwy 280 West; 912/276-2371.

Annual Event

Watermelon Festival. Parade; watermelon-eating, seed-spitting and largest watermelon contests; fishing rodeo; Miss Heart of Georgia contest; arts & crafts; entertainment. Early-mid-July.

Motels

★ ★ **COMFORT INN.** *1601 16th Ave E, I-75 exit 33. 912/273-2371; FAX 912/273-8351.* 59 rms, 2 story. Mid-June-Aug: S, D $60; each addl $5; suites $80-$95; under 18 free. Crib $5. TV; cable (premium), VCR avail (movies). Pool. Complimentary continental bkfst. Restaurant opp 6 am-11 pm. Ck-out 11 am. Meeting rm. Business servs avail. In-rm modem link. Some refrigerators; microwaves avail. Cr cds: A, C, D, DS, ER, JCB, MC, V.

D ≈ ⊠ ⋒ SC

★ ★ **HOLIDAY INN.** *1711 16th Ave E, at jct US 280, I-75 exit 33. 912/273-4117; FAX 912/273-1344.* 187 rms, 2 story. S, D $50; golf plans. Crib free. Pet accepted. TV; cable (premium). Pool. Restaurant 6 am-10 pm. Rm serv. Ck-out noon. Meeting rms. Business servs avail. In-rm modem link. Valet serv. Sundries. Cr cds: A, D, DS, JCB, MC, V.

D ✔ ≈ ⊠ ⋒ SC

✔★ **SUPER 8.** *566 Farmers Market Rd, I-75 exit 35. 912/276-1008; FAX 912/276-0222.* 120 rms, 2 story. S $32.95; D $36.95-$39.95; under 10 free. TV; cable (premium). Pool. Complimentary continental bkfst. Ck-out 11 am. Cr cds: A, C, D, DS, MC, V.

≈ ⊠ ⋒ SC

Restaurants

★ ★ **DAPHNE LODGE.** *US 280W. 912/273-2596.* Hrs: 5:30-10 pm. Closed Sun, Mon; some major hols. Res accepted. Semi-a la carte: dinner $7.95-$18.95. Specializes in sautéed scallops, bacon-baked oysters. Plantation manor house surrounded by pines. Cr cds: A, D, DS, MC, V.

★ **OLDE INN.** *2536 US 280W. 912/273-1229.* Hrs: 6-10 pm; Fri, Sat from 5:30 pm. Closed Sun, Mon; July 4, Thanksgiving, Dec 25. Res accepted. Setups. Wine, beer. Semi-a la carte: dinner $9-$21.75. Child's meals. Specializes in seafood, steak. Late 1800s building with original fireplace. Cr cds: A, MC, V.

Cumberland Island National Seashore (G-6)

(See also Brunswick, Jekyll Island, St Simons Island)

(Off the coast, NE of St Marys)

Cumberland Island National Seashore, off the coast of Georgia, is an island 16 miles long and 1.5 to 3 miles wide. It is accessible by passenger tour boat, which operates year round. Mainland departures are from St Marys (fee); reservations by phone are necessary.

A visit to the island is a walking experience, and there are no restaurants or shops. The island's western side is fringed with salt marsh, and white sand beaches face the Atlantic Ocean. The interior is forested, primarily by live oak; interspersed are freshwater marshes and sloughs. Activities include viewing the scenery and wildlife, swimming and exploring historical areas led by a ranger. Native Americans, Spanish and English have all lived on the island; most structures date from the pre-Civil War plantation era, although there are turn-of-the-century buildings built by the Thomas Carnegie family. Camping (daily); reservations by phone necessary. Ferry (Mid-Mar-Sept, daily; winter, Thurs-Mon; closed Dec 25) For further information contact the Superintendent, PO Box 806, St Marys 31558; 912/882-4335.

Crooked River State Park. Swimming pool, water sports; fishing in coastal tidewaters; boating. Hiking. Picnicking. Camping, cottages. 3 mi W of St Marys on GA 40, then 8 mi N on GA 40 Spur. Contact Superintendent, 3092 Spur 40, St Marys 31558; 912/882-4335.

Dahlonega (B-3)

(See also Gainesville)

Settled 1833 **Pop** 3,086 **Elev** 1,454 ft **Area code** 706 **Zip** 30533 **Web** www.dahlonega.org
Information Dahlonega-Lumpkin County Chamber of Commerce, 13 Park St S; 706/864-3711.

Gold fever struck this area in 1828, 20 years before California's Sutter's Mill discovery. Dahlonega, derived from the Cherokee for the color yellow, yielded so much ore that the federal government established a local mint, which produced $6,115,569 in gold coins from 1838 to 1861. Dahlonega is the seat of Lumpkin County, where tourism, manufacturing, higher education and agri-business are the major sources of employment. A US Forest Service Visitor Center is located in Dahlonega.

What to See and Do

Amicalola Falls State Park. Highest waterfall in the eastern US (729 ft). Trout fishing. Hiking trails. Picnicking, concession, restaurant. Camping, cabins, lodge. 20 mi W off GA 52. For fee information, contact Superintendent, Star Rte, Box 215, Dawsonville 30534; 706/265-8888.

Chattahoochee National Forest. This vast forest (748,608 acres) includes Georgia's Blue Ridge Mountains toward the north, which have elevations ranging from 1,000 to nearly 5,000 ft. Because the forest ranges from the Piedmont to mountainous areas, the Chattahoochee has a diversity of trees and wildlife. There are 25 developed camping areas, 24 picnicking areas, 10 wilderness areas and 6 swimming beaches. For the Chattahoochee-Oconee National Forest Recreation Area directory, contact the US Forest Service, 508 Oak St NW, Gainesville 30501; 770/536-0541. Camping and swimming fees at developed recreation sites. In the forest are

Anna Ruby Falls. Approx 1,570 acres surrounding a double waterfall, with drops of 50 and 153 ft. This scenic area is enhanced by laurel, wild azaleas, dogwood and rhododendron. Visitor center. Off GA 356, 6 mi N of Helen. Parking fee ¢

Track Rock Gap. Well-preserved rock carvings of ancient Indian origin; figures resemble animal and bird tracks, crosses, circles and human footprints. Off US 76, 8 mi SW of Young Harris.

Appalachian National Scenic Trail. Eleven lean-tos are maintained along the 79 mi marking southern portion of the trail. Following the crest of the Blue Ridge divide, the trail begins outside Dahlonega and continues for 2,000 mi to Mount Katahdin, Maine.

Dahlonega Courthouse Gold Museum State Historic Site. Exhibits on first major gold rush; display of gold coins minted in Dahlonega. Film shown every half-hour. (Daily; closed Jan 1, Thanksgiving, Dec 25) On the Square, in old Lumpkin County Courthouse (1836). Contact Manager, Public Square, Box 1; 706/864-2257. ¢¢

Gold panning.

Consolidated Gold Mines. Underground mine tour (40-45 min) through tunnel network; displays of original equipment used. Instructors avail for gold panning. (Daily; closed Dec 25) 125 Consolidated Gold Mine Rd, at jcn GA 52, US 19 & GA 9. Phone 706/864-8473. ¢¢

Crisson's Gold Mine. Gold and gem panning; indoor panning (winter). Demonstration of working stamp mill, over 100 yrs old. Gift shop. (Daily; closed Dec 25) 2 1/2 mi N via US 19 to end of Wimpy Mill Rd, then 1 mi E. Phone 706/864-6363 or -7998. ¢¢

Gold Miners' Camp. Gold panning near the Chestatee River in an authentic mining setting. (May-Oct, daily) 2 1/2 mi S via GA 60. Phone 706/864-6373. ¢

Lake Winfield Scott. A US Forest Service Recreation Area with an 18-acre lake in the Blue Ridge Mountains. Swimming, bathhouse; fishing.

Picnicking. Campsites (fee). (May-Oct) 15 mi N on US 19, 129, then 4 mi SW on GA 180. Contact the Ranger District Office, Box 9, Blairsville 30512; 706/745-6928. Parking ¢

North Georgia College and State University (1873). (3,500 students) Part of the state university system, North Georgia College's administration building, Price Memorial, was built on the foundation of the old US Branch Mint; unique gold steeple. Liberal arts and military college. College Ave. Phone 706/864-1800.

Vogel State Park. Rugged area in the heart of north Georgia's mountains. At the foot of Blood and Slaughter mountains, 22-acre Lake Trahlyta has swimming, bathhouse; fishing, boating. Picnicking, grills; playground. Camping, 36 furnished cabins. Standard hrs, fees. 25 mi N off US 19/129, S of Blairsville. Contact Superintendent, 7485 Vogel State Park Rd, Blairsville 30512; 706/745-2628. Parking ¢

Annual Events

Gold Panning Competition. Consolidated Gold Mine. 3rd wkend Apr.

Gold Rush Days. 3rd wkend Oct.

Motel

★ **HOJO INN.** 20 Mountain Drive Hwy (GA 60 S). 706/864-4343. 60 rms, 2 story. S $37-$125; D $45-$125; each addl $5; under 18 free. TV; cable (premium). Pool. Complimentary coffee in lobby. Restaurant adj 6 am-midnight. Ck-out noon. Some refrigerators. Cr cds: A, C, D, DS, MC, V.

D ⟲ 🏊 🐾 SC

Inn

★ ★ **SMITH HOUSE.** 84 S Chestatee St. 706/867-7000; res: 800/852-9577; FAX 706/864-7564. 16 rms, 2 story. Apr-Nov: S $65; D $75; under 16 free; higher rates Gold Rush; lower rates rest of yr. TV; cable (premium). Complimentary continental bkfst. Coffee in rms. Restaurant (see SMITH HOUSE). Ck-out 11 am, ck-in until 10 pm. Gift shop. Pool. Some in-rm whirlpools. Built on a gold mine. Totally nonsmoking. Cr cds: A, DS, MC, V.

D ⟲ 🏊 🐾 🔥

Resort

★ ★ **FORREST HILLS MOUNTAIN HIDEWAY.** 135 Forrest Hills Rd, 12 mi W on GA 52, then right on Wesley Chapel Rd. 706/864-6456; FAX 706/864-5405; res: 800/654-6313. E-mail lindagad@stc.net; web www.foresths.com. 27 kit. cottages (1-4 bedrm). June, Aug, Oct, Nov MAP: S, D $89-$185; wkly rates; higher rates special events; lower rates rest of yr. TV; VCR (movies $3.50). Pool. Complimentary coffee in rms. Dining rm 8:30-10:30 am, 6-8 pm. Ck-out 11 am, ck-in 3 pm. Grocery 4 mi. Meeting rms. Business center. Maid serv bi-wkly. Gift shop. Tennis. Hiking. Microwaves; many in-rm whirlpools, fireplaces. Porches. Picnic tables. Grills. Surrounded by north Georgia mountain forest. Cr cds: A, DS, MC, V.

D 🏌 ⛷ 🏊 🐾 SC 🛶

Restaurant

✓★ **SMITH HOUSE.** (See Smith House Inn) 706/867-7000. Hrs: 11 am-3 pm, 4-7:30 pm; Fri, Sat 11 am-3 pm, 4:30-8 pm; Sun 11 am-7:30 pm; winter hrs vary. Closed Mon. Southern menu. Complete meals: lunch $10.25-$13.95, dinner $11.50-$14.50. Specializes in country cooking. Family-style dining in Blue Ridge Mt tradition. Family-owned. Totally nonsmoking. Cr cds: A, DS, MC, V.

D

Dalton (A-1)

(See also Calhoun; also see Chattanooga, TN)

Founded 1837 **Pop** 21,761 **Elev** 759 ft **Area code** 706 **E-mail** daltoncvb@nwga.com **Web** www.nwgeorgia.com/daltoncvb/

Information Convention and Visitors Bureau, 2211 Dug Gap Battle Rd, PO Box 2046, 30722-2046; 706/272-7676 or 800/331-3258.

Once a part of the Cherokee Nation, Dalton was involved in fierce battles and skirmishes in the Civil War as Union forces advanced on Atlanta. Today, Dalton has more than 100 carpet outlets and manufactures a large portion of the world's carpets. Dalton also produces other tufted textiles, chemicals, latex, thread and yarn.

What to See and Do

Chickamauga and Chattanooga National Military Park (see). 23 mi N via I-75, GA 2, then 2 mi S via US 27.

Crown Garden and Archives. Headquarters of the Whitfield-Murray Historical Society. Genealogical library; changing exhibits include Civil War items; permanent exhibit on the history of bedspread tufting in the area. (Tues-Fri; closed Jan 1, wk of July 4, Thanksgiving, wk of Dec 25) 715 Chattanooga Ave, 2 mi N via I-75 and US 41, Walnut Ave exit. Phone 706/278-0217. **Donation.**

Annual Event

Prater's Mill Country Fair. 10 mi NE on GA 2. Arts & crafts show, food, late 1800s entertainment; canoeing on Coahulla Creek, pony rides, exhibits; 3-story gristmill in operation. Phone 706/275-6455. Mother's Day wkend & Columbus Day wkend.

Motels

✔★ ★ **BEST WESTERN.** *2106 Chattanooga Rd (30720), at I-75 Rocky Face exit 137.* 706/226-5022. 99 rms, 2 story. S $40; D $45; each addl $5; under 12 free. Crib $6. Pet accepted. TV; cable. Heated pool. Playground. Restaurant 6-10 am, 5-9:30 pm. Rm serv. Bar 4 pm-midnight; entertainment Fri, Sat. Ck-out noon. Beauty shop. Coin lndry. Meeting rms. Business servs avail. In-rm modem link. Sundries. Cr cds: A, C, D, DS, MC, V.

D ✔ ≋ ⊠ 🔥 SC

★ ★ **HOLIDAY INN.** *515 Holiday Dr (30720), I-75 exit 136.* 706/278-0500; FAX 706/226-0279. 199 rms, 2 story. S $59-$69; D $64-$72; under 19 free; wkend rates. Crib free. Pet accepted. TV; cable (premium). Pool; wading pool. Coffee in rms. Restaurant 6:30 am-1:30 pm, 5:30-10 pm. Rm serv. Bar 5-10 pm, closed Sun. Ck-out noon. Coin lndry. Meeting rms. Business servs avail. In-rm modem link. Valet serv. Exercise equipt. Cr cds: A, C, D, DS, JCB, MC, V.

D ✔ ≋ 🕴 ⊠ 🔥 SC

★ ★ **HOWARD JOHNSON.** *2107 Chattanooga Rd (30720), at I-75 exit 137.* 706/278-1448; res: 800/446-4656; FAX 706/226-9716. 106 rms, 2 story. S $33.95-$39.95; D $45.95-$49.95; under 18 free. Crib free. Pet accepted, some restrictions. TV; cable. Pool; wading pool. Restaurant 6 am-2 pm, 5:30-9:30 pm. Rm serv. Bar 5 pm-midnight. Ck-out 11 am. Health club privileges. Picnic tables. Cr cds: A, C, DS, MC, V.

D ✔ ≋ ⊠ 🔥 SC

Restaurant

✔★ ★ **HISTORIC DALTON DEPOT TRACKSIDE CAFE.** *110 Depot St (30720).* 706/226-3160. Hrs: 11 am-midnight. Closed Sun; most major hols. Res accepted. Bar. Semi-a la carte: lunch $6-$12, dinner $8-$15. Child's meals. Specialties: baby back ribs, prime rib, fresh fish.

Band Fri, Sat. Parking. Train depot atmosphere and decor. Cr cds: A, D, DS, MC, V.

D ⊡

Darien (G-6)

(See also Brunswick, Jekyll Island, St Simons Island, Sea Island)

Founded 1736 **Pop** 1,783 **Elev** 20 ft **Area code** 912 **Zip** 31305 **E-mail** McIntosh@McIntoshcounty.com **Web** www.mcintoshcounty.com

Information McIntosh Chamber of Commerce, PO Box 1497; 912/437-4192.

James Oglethorpe recruited Scots Highlanders to protect Georgia's frontier on the Altamaha River in 1736. Calling their town Darien, the Scots guarded Savannah from Spanish and native attack and carved out large plantations from the south Georgia wilderness. After 1800, Darien thrived as a great timber port until the early 20th century. Today, shrimp boats dock in the river over which Darien Scots once kept watch.

What to See and Do

Fort King George State Historic Site (1721). South Carolina scouts built this fort near an abandoned Native American village and Spanish mission to block Spanish and French expansion into Georgia, thereby establishing the foundation for the later English Colony of Georgia. The fort and its blockhouse have been entirely reconstructed to original form. Museum interprets the periods of Native American, Spanish and British occupations, the settlement of Darien and Georgia's timber industry. (Daily exc Mon; closed Jan 1, Thanksgiving, Dec 25) 1½ mi E of US 17 on Fort King George Dr. Contact Superintendent, PO Box 711; 912/437-4770. ¢

Golden Isles (see). SE off US 17.

Hofwyl-Broadfield Plantation State Historic Site (1807). The evolution of this working rice plantation (1807-1973) is depicted through tours of the 1851 plantation house, museum and trails. Tours (daily exc Mon; closed Jan 1, Thanksgiving, Dec 25). 6 mi S on US 17. Contact Manager, 5556 US 17N, Brunswick 31525; 912/264-7333. ¢

Annual Event

Blessing of the Shrimp Fleet. At Darien Bridge. Apr or May.

Douglas (F-4)

Founded 1858 **Pop** 10,464 **Elev** 259 ft **Area code** 912 **Zip** 31533 **E-mail** chamber@almatel.net **Web** www.douglasga.org

Information Chamber of Commerce, 46 John Coffee Rd, PO Box 2470, 31534; 912/384-1873.

The town's central location between I-75 and I-95 has helped Douglas develop into a leading trade and distribution center for the southeast. A number of Fortune 500 companies operate within Coffee County.

What to See and Do

General Coffee State Park. A 1,510 acre park on the Seventeen-Mile River in Coffee County. Swimming pool; fishing. Nature trails. Picnicking, playgrounds. Camping. Lodging. Standard hrs, fees. 6 mi E on GA 32. Contact Manager, Rte 2, Box 83, Nicholls 31554; 912/384-7082.

Motels

★ **DAYS INN.** *907 N Peterson Ave.* 912/384-5190. 70 rms, 2 story. S, D $36-$45; each addl $5; under 12 free. Crib free. Pet accepted.

TV; cable (premium), VCR (movies). Pool. Complimentary continental bkfst. Restaurant adj 6 am-midnight. Ck-out noon. Health club privileges. Microwaves avail. Cr cds: A, C, D, DS, MC, V.

★ ★ **HOLIDAY INN.** US 441S. 912/384-9100. 100 rms, 2 story. S $54; D $59; each addl $5; under 18 free. Crib free. Pet accepted, some restrictions. TV; cable (premium). Pool. Restaurant 6-10 am, 11 am-2 pm, 5-10 pm. Rm serv. Bar 4 pm-midnight. Ck-out noon. Meeting rms. Business servs avail. In-rm modem link. Free airport transportation. Some refrigerators; microwaves avail. Picnic tables. Cr cds: A, C, D, DS, MC, V.

✔★ ★ **INN AT DOUGLAS.** 1009 N Peterson Ave. 912/384-2621. 100 rms, 2 story. June-Aug: S $42-$49; D $47-$54; each addl $5; lower rates rest of yr. Crib free. Pet accepted. TV; cable (premium). Pool. Restaurant 6 am-midnight. Bar 4 pm-2 am; entertainment. Ck-out noon. Meeting rms. Grills, picnic tables. Cr cds: A, C, D, DS, MC, V.

Dublin (E-4)

Pop 16,312 **Elev** 228 ft **Area code** 912 **E-mail** chamber@dublin-georgia.com
Information Dublin-Laurens County Chamber of Commerce, PO Box 818, 31040; 912/272-5546.

The seat of Laurens County, Dublin sits on land once occupied by Creek Indians. Area industries manufacture a wide range of goods, including textiles, carpeting, missile control systems and computer components. The first aluminum extrusion plant in the US is located here. Agricultural products include soybeans, wheat, grain, peanuts, corn, cotton and tobacco.

What to See and Do

Dublin-Laurens Museum. Local history museum featuring Native American artifacts, art, textiles and relics from early settlers. (Tues-Fri; closed Jan 1, Thanksgiving, Dec 25) Bellevue & Academy at Church. Phone 912/272-9242. **Free.**

Fish Trap Cut. Believed to have been built between 1000 B.C. and A.D. 1500, this large rectangular mound, smaller round mound and canal may have been used as an aboriginal fish trap. Oconee River, GA 19.

Historic buildings. Greek-revival and Victorian houses can be found along Bellevue Avenue.

Annual Event

St Patrick's Festival. Includes parade, ball, contests, golf tournaments, arts & crafts show, square dancing and entertainment. Mar.

Motel

✔★ ★ **HOLIDAY INN.** (31021). 3 mi S on US 319/441 at jct I-16. 912/272-7862; FAX 912/272-1077. 124 rms, 2 story. S $54; D $59; each addl $5; suites $79; under 18 free; wkly rates. Crib free. Pet accepted. TV; cable (premium). Pool. Complimentary bkfst. Restaurant 6:30-9:30 am, 11:30 am-2 pm, 6-9 pm. Rm serv. Bar 5 pm-1 am; entertainment. Ck-out noon. Meeting rms. Business servs avail. In-rm modem link. Valet serv. Airport transportation. Exercise equipt. Health club privileges. Cr cds: A, C, D, DS, JCB, MC, V.

Eatonton (D-3)

(See also Madison, Milledgeville)

Pop 4,737 **Elev** 575 ft **Area code** 706 **Zip** 31024 **E-mail** epchamber@oconee.com **Web** www.oconee.com/epchamber
Information Eatonton-Putnam Chamber of Commerce, 105 Sumter St, PO Box 4088; 706/485-7701 or -4875.

In the early 19th century large tracts of land in this area were acquired and put under cultivation; by the mid-1800s the town of Eatonton had become a center of planter culture, that archetypal romantic concept of cotton fields, mansions, wealth and southern grace. Joel Chandler Harris was born in Eatonton in 1848. In creating the character "Uncle Remus" to retell the "Br'er Rabbit" and "Br'er Fox" folk tales heard on the plantation, he successfully immortalized the traditional ways of the Old South.

Eatonton is also the hometown of Alice Walker, author of *The Color Purple*, an acclaimed depiction of the South of a different time. Eatonton, the seat of Putnam County, is known as the largest dairy producer in the state.

What to See and Do

Alice Walker: A Driving Tour. Driving tour past the author's birthplace, church and house where she grew up. Contact the Chamber of Commerce for brochure and information; 706/485-7701.

Indian Springs State Park (see). 35 mi W via GA 16 to Jackson, then 5 mi SE on GA 42.

Lake Oconee. Lawrence Shoals Recreation Area. E on GA 16 & N on GA 44 (see MADISON). **Lake Sinclair.** S on US 441 (see MILLEDGEVILLE). Both Georgia Power Co projects created by the impoundment of the Oconee River.

Rock Eagle Effigy. This 8-ft-high mound of milky white quartz is shaped like a great prone bird, wings spread, head turned eastward, 102 ft from head to tail and 120 ft wingtip to wingtip. Archaeologists estimate the monument is more than 5,000 yrs old and was probably used by Native Americans for religious ceremonies. It may be viewed from an observation tower. 7 mi N on US 441, located in Rock Eagle 4-H Center. Phone 706/485-2831. **Free.**

Uncle Remus Museum. Log cabin made from two original slave cabins. Reconstruction of cabin fireplace; shadow boxes with illustrations of 12 tales; mementos of era, first editions; diorama of old plantation; other relics. (June-Aug, daily; rest of yr, daily exc Tues) 3 blks S of courthouse on US 441 in Turner Park. Phone 706/485-6856. ¢

Annual Event

Putnam County Dairy Festival. Parade, dairy and farming-related contests, arts & crafts fair, entertainment. 1st Sat June.

Forsyth (D-3)

(See also Macon)

Pop 4,268 **Elev** 705 ft **Area code** 912 **Zip** 31029 **Web** www.hom.net/monroe
Information Forsyth-Monroe County Chamber of Commerce, 267 Tift College Dr, PO Box 811; 912/994-9239.

What to See and Do

Indian Springs State Park (see). 17 mi N on GA 42.

Jarrell Plantation State Historic Site. Authentic plantation with 20 historic buildings dating from 1847-1940. Plain-style plantation house, sawmill, grist mill, blacksmith shop, farm animals. Seasonal demonstrations.

(Daily exc Mon; closed Jan 1, Thanksgiving, Dec 25) 18 mi E of I-75 exit 60 on GA 18E, then N on Jarrell Plantation Rd. Phone 912/986-5172. ¢

The Whistle Stop Cafe. Town of Juliette, GA was where the movie *Fried Green Tomatoes* was filmed. Cafe and other stores along McCrackin St. Cafe (Mon-Sat & Sun afternoons). I-75, exit 61, then 8 mi E to Juliette. Phone 912/994-3670.

Motels

★ ★ **BEST WESTERN HILLTOP INN.** *951 Hwy 42N, At jct I-75, exit 63, & GA 42.* 912/994-9260. 120 rms, 2 story. S, D $40-$75; each addl $6; under 12 free. Crib $6. TV; cable. Pool; wading pool. Ck-out noon. Business servs avail. In-rm modem link. Cr cds: A, C, D, DS, MC, V.

☒ ☒ ☒ SC

↙★ ★ **HAMPTON INN.** *520 Holiday Circle, at I-75 exit 61.* 912/994-9697; FAX 912/994-3594. 124 rms, 4 story. S $49; D $52-$56; under 18 free. Crib free. Pet accepted. TV; cable (premium). Pool privileges. Complimentary continental bkfst. Ck-out noon. Meeting rm. In-rm modem link. Health club privileges. Cr cds: A, C, D, DS, MC, V.

D ☒ ☒ ☒ SC

★ ★ **HOLIDAY INN.** *480 Holiday Circle, at I-75 exit 61, Tift College Dr & Juliette Rd.* 912/994-5691; FAX 912/994-3254. 120 rms, 2 story. S, D $59-$69; each addl $5. Crib free. Pet accepted, some restrictions. TV; cable (premium). Pool; wading pool. Coffee in rms. Restaurant 6 am-10 pm. Rm serv. Bar 4 pm-midnight; closed Sun. Ck-out noon. Coin lndry. Meeting rms. Business center. In-rm modem link. Exercise equipt. Golf privileges. Game rm. Chapel on premises. Cr cds: A, C, D, DS, JCB, MC, V.

D ☒ ☒ ☒ ☒ ☒ SC ☒

Unrated Dining Spot

WHISTLE STOP CAFE. *(McCracklin St, Juliette 31046)* 3 mi E. 912/994-3670. Hrs: 8 am-2 pm; Sun noon-7 pm. Closed some major hols. Semi-a la carte: bkfst $2-$3.75, lunch $1.95-$6.95. Specializes in barbecue ribs, country cooking. Film site of Fried Green Tomatoes. No cr cds accepted.

D ☒

Fort Frederica National Monument (G-6)

(See also Brunswick, Jekyll Island, St Simons Island, Sea Island)

(12 mi NE of Brunswick via St Simons/Sea Island Causeway-toll)

Fort Frederica marked the southern boundary of British Colonial North America. It was carefully planned by the Trustees in London in 1736 and included the town of Frederica, named after Frederick the Prince of Wales.

Having picked the site of the fort on a bluff commanding the Frederica River, General James Oglethorpe returned to England and helped select families to build and settle it. Forty-four men and 72 women and children landed at St Simons Island on March 16, 1736. In 1738 a regiment of 650 British soldiers arrived. The fort was then strengthened with "tabby" (a kind of cement made of lime, oyster shells, sand and water) and the whole town was enclosed with earth and timber works from 10 to 13 feet high that included towers and a moat.

Oglethorpe used Fort Frederica as a command post for his invasion of Florida. He built other forts on St Simons and other islands and attacked Spanish outposts to the south. In July 1742, Spaniards launched an attack on Fort Frederica, but Oglethorpe repulsed this with an ambush at Bloody Marsh, ending Spanish attempts to gain control of Georgia.

Frederica flourished as a military town until after the peace of 1748. With the withdrawal of the regiment the following year, the shopkeepers and tradesman at Frederica had to move elsewhere. The town did not long survive these losses. Archaeological excavations have exposed some of it and stabilization work has been done by the National Park Service. Outdoor exhibits make it easy to visualize the town as it was, and the visitor center has exhibits, touch computers and a film dealing with its life and history. Self-guided audio tour (fee). (Daily; closed Dec 25) Contact the Superintendent, Rte 9, Box 286-C, St Simons Island 31522; 912/638-3639. Golden Age Passport (see MAKING THE MOST OF YOUR TRIP). Entrance per vehicle ¢¢

Fort McAllister Historic Park (F-6)

(See also Savannah)

(25 mi S of Savannah, via GA 144 from I-95 or US 17; 10 mi E of Richmond Hill off US 17)

This Confederate fort, built for the defense of Savannah, stands on the left bank of the Great Ogeechee River, commanding the river's mouth. Fort McAllister's fall on December 13, 1864, marked the end of Sherman's march to the sea, opening communications between the Union Army and the fleet and rendering further defense of Savannah hopeless.

Prior to this, McAllister had proved that its type of massive earthwork fortifications could stand up against the heaviest naval ordnance. It protected the blockade-running ship *Nashville* from pursuit by Union gunboats in July and November 1862. It successfully resisted the attacks of *Monitor*-type ironclads of the Union Navy in 1863. The USS *Montauk* shelled the fort with the heaviest shells ever fired by a naval vessel against a shore work up to that time. The fort sustained only one casualty. There were huge holes in its parapets, but the damage was minor. Its gun emplacements were separated by large "traverses," several used to house powder magazines. The fort that seemed to be "carved out of solid earth" was termed "a truly formidable work" by a Union naval officer in 1864. General Sherman called the capture of the fort and overpowering its garrison ". . .the handsomest thing I have seen in this war." Union losses were 24 killed, 110 wounded (mostly by mines outside the fort); the Confederate garrison of 230 men had 70 casualties—16 killed and 54 wounded—in the 15-minute battle.

The earthworks have been restored to approximate conditions of 1863-1864. A museum containing mementos of the *Nashville* and the fort was completed in 1963 and opened on the centennial of the great bombardment. (Tues-Sat, also Sun afternoon; closed Thanksgiving, Dec 25; fee) Fort McAllister has a campground and day-use facilities (fee); boating (ramps, dock). For further information contact the Superintendent, 3894 Fort McAllister Rd, Richmond Hill 31324; 912/727-2339. ¢

Fort Pulaski National Monument (F-6)

(See also Savannah)

(15 mi E of Savannah off US 80)

A unit of the Department of the Interior's National Park Service, Fort Pulaski National Monument was established by President Coolidge in 1924. The site, named in honor of Revolutionary war hero Casimir Pulaski, commemorates an international turning point in the history of fortification and artillery. It was here, on April 11, 1862, that newly developed rifled cannons easily overtook a masonry fortification. After centuries of use throughout the world, both masonry forts and smoothbore cannons were obsolete.

Most visitors begin the tour at the visitor center, which contains a small museum, an information desk and a bookstore featuring more than 300 items on the Civil War and other site-related and regional subjects.

Restored to its mid-19th-century appearance, the fort contains several rooms, or casemates, depicting garrison life during its Confederate (1861-1862) and Union (1862-1875) occupations. This exhibit includes an officer's quarters and mess, medical dispensary, chapel, quartermaster's office, supply room and enlisted men's quarters. Other displays include several examples of smooth-bore and rifled artillery and carriages. While self-guided tours are available year-round, ranger conducted programs and demonstrations are presented daily in the summer.

There are three major trails in the monument. The nature trail is a quarter-mile paved loop through several historic sites. The picnic trail is a half-mile paved trail from the visitor center to the picnic and recreation area, which borders the vast salt marshes and forested hammocks of the Savannah River estuary. The third trail follows the historic dike originally surveyed by Robert E. Lee. A walk on any segment of the trail provides excellent opportunities to see a wide variety of plants and wildlife, as well as scenic views of the fort.

Fishing, boating and other water-related activities are offered at the park. The north channel shoreline and the bridge approaches at the south channel are the best fishing locations. A boat ramp and fishing dock just off US 80 at Lazaretto Creek provide more opportunities for fishing.

All facilities are open daily except Dec 25. Contact Superintendent, PO Box 30757, Savannah 31410; 912/786-5787. Entrance fee per person ¢

Gainesville (B-3)

(See also Buford, Dahlonega)

Pop 17,885 **Elev** 1,249 ft **Area code** 770 **E-mail** lhh@applied.com
Information Gainesville/Hall County Convention & Visitors Bureau, 424 Green St, 30501; 770/536-5209.

On the shore of 38,000-acre Lake Sidney Lanier, Gainesville is a poultry producing and marketing center with a variety of industries. It is also the headquarters for the Chattahoochee National Forest (see DAHLONEGA). Contact the Forest Supervisor, US Forest Service, 508 Oak St, 30501; 770/536-0541.

What to See and Do

Brenau University (1878). (2,000 students) Liberal arts residential college for women with coed evening and weekend programs; off-campus, graduate and undergraduate divisions. On campus is Brenau Academy, a four-year preparatory high school for girls. Pearce Auditorium (1897) has fine acoustics, stained glass windows and ceiling frescoes. Trustee Library has displays of American art. 1 Centennial Circle. Phone 770/534-6299.

Green Street Historical District. A broad street with Victorian and classical-revival houses dating from the late 19th and early 20th centuries. Here is

Green Street Station. Home of Georgia Mountains Historical and Cultural Trust. Houses historical and arts and crafts exhibits of northeast Georgia as well as the Mark Trail Memorial Exhibit. (Tues-Sat; closed major hols) Phone 770/536-0889. ¢

Lake Lanier Islands. W edge of town (see BUFORD).

Seasonal Event

Road Atlanta. 8 mi S via GA 53. Sports car and motorcycle racing. Also street-driving and road racing training programs. Phone 770/967-6143. Mar-Nov.

Motel

✔★★ **HOLIDAY INN.** *726 Jesse Jewell Pkwy (30501).* 770/536-4451; FAX 770/538-2880. 132 rms, 2-3 story. S $63-$100; D $68-$105; each addl $5; under 19 free. Crib free. Pet accepted. TV; cable (premium), VCR avail. Pool. Restaurant 6:30 am-9 pm. Rm serv. Bar. Ck-out noon. Coin lndry. Meeting rms. In-rm modem link. Bellhops. Valet serv. Free RR station, bus depot transportation. Cr cds: A, C, D, DS, JCB, MC, V.

D ✔ ≈ ⊠ 🐾 SC

Motor Hotel

★★★ **BEST WESTERN-LANIER CENTRE HOTEL.** *400 E E Butler Pkwy (30501).* 770/531-0907; FAX 770/531-0788. Web www.best-western.com/best.html. 122 rms, 4 story. S $69-$115; D $70-$125; under 18 free; golf plans. Crib free. TV; cable (premium), VCR avail. Pool; poolside serv. Complimentary coffee in rms. Restaurant 6:30 am-10 pm. Rm serv. Bar from 4:30 pm; Fri, Sat to 11 pm. Ck-out noon. Meeting rms. Business servs avail. Valet serv. Sundries. Free RR station, bus depot transportation. Lighted tennis privileges. 18-hole golf privileges, greens fee, pro, putting green, driving range. Exercise equipt. Some in-rm whirlpools. Cr cds: A, C, D, DS, MC, V.

D 🏋 ✔ ≈ ✕ ⊠ 🐾 SC

Inn

★★★ **DUNLAP HOUSE.** *635 Green St (30501).* 770/536-0200; res: 800/276-2935; FAX 770/503-7857. E-mail dunlaphouse@mindspring. com; web www.bestinns.net/. 10 rms, 2 story. S $95-$150; D $105-$155. TV; cable. Complimentary full bkfst. Complimentary coffee in rms. Restaurant opp 5:30-10 pm. Ck-out 11 am, ck-in 3 pm. Business servs avail. In-rm modem link. Built 1910. Totally nonsmoking. Cr cds: A, DS, MC, V.

D ⊠ 🐾 SC

Restaurants

★★ **POOR RICHARD'S.** *1702 Park Hill Dr (30501).* 770/532-0499. Hrs: 5-10 pm; Fri, Sat to 11 pm. Closed Sun; most major hols. Res accepted Mon-Thurs. Bar 4:30 pm-midnight. Semi-a la carte: dinner $5.95-$36.95. Complete meals: dinner $9.95-$16.95. Child's meals. Specializes in prime rib, steaks, seafood. Cr cds: A, DS, MC, V.

D

★★★ **RUDOLPH'S.** *700 Green St (30501).* 770/534-2226. Hrs: 5:30-10 pm; Fri, Sat to 11 pm; Sun brunch 11 am-2 pm. Closed most major hols. Res accepted. Bar. Wine list. Semi-a la carte: dinner $12.95-$17.95. Child's meals. Specialty: steak Rudolph. Own baking. In restored historic residence (1915). Cr cds: A, DS, MC, V.

D ➘

Golden Isles (F-6)

(See also Brunswick, Jekyll Island, St Simons Island, Sea Island)

Four barrier subtropical islands off Georgia's coast at Brunswick. Best known of the group are Sea Island (see), St Simons Island (see) and Jekyll Island (see), all of which may be reached by road. Others are Cumberland, Little St Simons Island, Ossabaw, St Catherine's and Sapelo, reached only by water.

Native Americans hunted on these islands for giant turtles, waterfowl, deer and other animals. Spaniards established a chain of missions, which existed for about a century, the largest on St Simons. The French made half-hearted efforts to settle on the islands. James Oglethorpe built Fort Frederica (see) on St Simons in 1736 and later defeated Spanish forces attempting to recapture the island.

Now the Golden Isles are resort areas, offering beautiful scenery, swimming, a wide variety of sports facilities and accomodations.

Helen (B-3)

(See also Toccoa)

Pop 300 **Elev** 1,446 ft **Area code** 706 **Zip** 30545 **Web** www.WhiteCounty.com/Helen
Information Helen/White County Convention & Visitors Bureau, 726 Brucken St, PO Box 730; 706/878-2181 or 800/858-8027.

The natural setting of the mountains and the Chattahoochee River helped create the atmosphere for this logging town, transformed into a charming alpine village. Helen was reborn in 1969 when the citizens, with the help of a local artist, decided to improve the town's appearance.

The result is the relaxed atmosphere of a small Bavarian town. Quaint cobblestone streets, gift shops with an international flavor, craftsmen, restaurants and festivals—a bit of the Old World in the heart of the mountains of northeast Georgia.

What To See and Do

Anna Ruby Falls. In Chattahoochee National Forest (see DAHLONEGA).

Babyland General Hospital. Authentic turn-of-the-century hospital, home of the original "Cabbage Patch Kids"—soft-sculptured "babies" created by artist Xavier Roberts. (Daily; closed Dec 24 & most hols) 73 W Underwood St, 9 mi SW via GA 75N, on US 129 in Cleveland. Phone 706/865-2171. **Free.**

Museum of the Hills & Fantasy Kingdom. Authentic reconstruction of rural and village lifestyle in North Georgia at the turn of the century. (Daily; closed Dec 25) Main St, in The Castle complex. Phone 706/878-3140. ¢¢

Nacoochee Indian Mound. Located in former center of the Cherokee Nation. 1 mi SE on GA 17.

Richard B. Russell Scenic Highway. Highway winds around mountainsides, offering spectacular scenic views. 5 mi N of Helen.

Stovall Covered Bridge over Chickamauga Creek. The smallest covered bridge in Georgia. 7 mi E on GA 255.

Unicoi State Park. A 1,081-acre park adjacent to Anna Ruby Falls. Swimming beach; fishing; paddleboat (rentals), canoeing (rentals). Nature and hiking trails. Picnicking. Camping, cottages, lodge/conference center (see MOTELS), restaurant, craft shop. Programs on natural resources, folk culture. 2 mi NE on GA 356. Standard hrs, fees. Contact Director of Sales, PO Box 849; 878-2201.

Annual Events

Volksmarch. Bavarian walk in the forest. 3rd wkend Apr.

Hot Air Balloon Race & Festival. 1st wkend June.

Seasonal Events

Fasching Karnival. German Mardi Gras. Jan-Feb.

Oktoberfest. German music & beer festival; one of the longest running Oktoberfests in the country. Sept-Oct.

Motels

★ ★ **CASTLE INN.** 8590 Main St. 706/878-3140; FAX 706/878-3130. 12 rms, 2 story. Sept-Oct (2-day min wkends): S, D $108; each addl $10; under 16 free; golf, package plans; lower rates rest of yr. Crib $3. TV; cable (premium). Coffee in rms. Restaurant 11:30 am-midnight. Ck-out 11 am. Cr cds: A, MC, V.

★ ★ **COMFORT INN.** Edelweiss Drive. 706/878-8000; FAX 706/878-1231. E-mail helenga@stc.net; web www.stc.net/~helenga/ci/. 60 rms, 2 story. Mid-Sept-Oct: S, D, $89-$119; each addl $5; under 18 free; lower rates rest of yr. Crib $5. TV; cable (premium). Pool. Complimentary continental bkfst. Restaurant nearby. Ck-out 11 am. Meeting rm. Some refrigerators. Cr cds: A, C, D, DS, MC, V.

🅳 ⤬ ⤬ ⤬ SC

✔ ★ **HEIDI.** 8820 Main St, 4 blks W of town center. 706/878-2689; FAX 706/878-1238. E-mail windmill@stc.net. 14 rms, 2 story. Sept-Oct (2-day min wkends): S, D $45-$259; each addl $5; under 10 free; higher rates hols; lower rates rest of yr. TV; cable (premium), VCR avail. Heated pool. Restaurant nearby. Ck-out 11 am. Cr cds: A, DS, MC, V.

🅳 ⤬ ⤬ ⤬ SC

★ ★ **UNICOI STATE PARK LODGE.** Unicoi State Park, 1 mi N on Ga 75, 2 mi E on GA 356. 706/878-2201; FAX 706/878-1897; res: 800/864-7275. 100 rms, 2-3 story; 30 kit. units. Apr-Nov: S, D $69-$110; each addl $6; under 12 free; kit. units $65-$85 (2-day min; 1-wk min June-Aug); lower rates rest of yr. Parking $2. TV; cable, VCR avail (movies). Coffee in rms. Restaurant 7 am-8 pm. Ck-out 11 am. Meeting rms. Sundries. Lighted tennis. Access to all facilities of state park. Game rm. Cr cds: A, D, DS, MC, V.

🅳 ⤬ ⤬ ⤬ ⤬

Inn

✔ ★ ★ **THE BURNS-SUTTON INN.** (855 Washington St, Clarkesville 30523) 15 mi E on TN 17 to TN 75. 706/754-5565; FAX 706/754-9698. Web georgiamagazine.com/burns-sutton. 7 rms, 2 share bath, 3 story, 3 suites. May-Oct: S, D $65-$95; each addl $20; suites $75-$150; under 8 free; wkly plans; lower rates rest of yr. Cable TV in common rm; VCR avail (movies). Complimentary full bkfst. Restaurant 11 am-2:30 pm, 5:30-10 pm. Business servs avail. Luggage handling. Some fireplaces. Picnic tables, grills. Built in 1901; Victorian style and decor. Totally nonsmoking. Cr cds: MC, V.

⤬ ⤬ SC

Restaurant

★ ★ **HOFBRAUHAUS.** 1 Main St. 706/878-2248. E-mail charlene@stc.net. Hrs: 5-10 pm; Fri, Sat to 10:30 pm; Sun 3-9 pm. Closed Dec 25. Res accepted. Continental menu. Bar 3 pm-1 am. Semi-a la carte: dinner $10.75-$19.95. Child's meals. Specializes in prime rib, veal, seafood. German decor. Cr cds: A, C, D, DS, MC, V.

🅳 ⤴

Hiawassee (A-3)

(See also Clayton)

Pop 547 **Elev** 1,980 ft **Area code** 706 **Zip** 30546

A picturesque mountain town in the heart of Georgia's "Little Switzerland," Hiawassee is on Lake Chatuge, surrounded by Chattahoochee National Forest (see DAHLONEGA). Its backdrop is a range of the Blue Ridge Mountains, topped by Brasstown Bald Mt, Georgia's highest peak. Rock hunting, including hunting for the highly prized amethyst crystal, is a favorite activity in surrounding Towns County. Mountaineers of North Georgia gather from 26 surrounding counties to participate in a fair, the rule of which is "everybody can bring something."

What to See and Do

Brasstown Bald Mountain-Visitor Information Center. At 4,784 ft, this is Georgia's highest peak. Observation deck affords a view of four states.

Visitor Center has interpretive programs presented in mountain-top theater and exhibit hall. Parking/shuttle fee. (June-Oct, daily; late Apr-May, wkends only, weather permitting) S on GA 17, 75, then W on GA 180, then N on GA 180 spur. Phone 706/896-2556. **Free.**

Lake Chatuge. This approx 7,000-acre TVA lake provides fishing, boating. Camping. W edge of town.

Annual Events

Georgia Mountain Fair. Individual accomplishment and "friendlier living" is theme of gathering of mountain farm people; arts & crafts, farm produce, flowers, minerals, Native American relics; board splitting, soap and hominy making, quilting; general store, still, farm museum, midway, music hall; entertainment, parade. Camping, beach and tennis courts at Georgia Mountain Fairgrounds and Towns County Recreation Park. Phone 706/896-4191. 12 days early Aug.

Fall Celebration. At the fairgrounds. Phone 706/896-4191. Ten days mid-Oct.

Motel

★ ★ ★ **FIELDSTONE INN.** *3499 US 76, 3 mi W on US 76. 706/896-2262; FAX 706/896-4128.* 66 rms, 2 story. Apr-Nov: S, D $89-$115; each addl $7; under 14 free; lower rates rest of yr. Crib free. TV; cable (premium), VCR avail. Pool. Playground. Complimentary coffee in lobby. Restaurant adj 7 am-3 pm, 5-9 pm; Fri, Sat to 10 pm. Ck-out 11 am. Meeting rm. Business servs avail. Street parking. Lighted tennis. Exercise equipt. Lawn games. Microwaves avail. Patios, balconies. Picnic tables. On Lake Chatuge. Cr cds: A, C, D, DS, MC, V.

⊡ 🐾 🏃 ≋ 🏋 🐾 🅂🅲

Lodge

✔★ **SALALE.** *1340 Palmer Place US 76E, 1½ mi S on US 76E. 706/896-3943; FAX 706/896-4773.* 4 rms, 2 story. July-Oct: S $29-$69; D $34-$74; each addl $5; under 12 free; higher rates: country music season, fall foliage; lower rates rest of yr. Pet accepted, some restrictions. TV; cable (premium). Restaurant nearby. Ck-out 11 am. Refrigerators, microwaves. On lake; swimming. Cr cds: A, DS, MC, V.

🐾 🐾 🐾

Resort

★ ★ ★ **BRASSTOWN VALLEY.** *(6321 US 76, Young Harris 30582)* Approx 5 mi W on US 76. *706/379-9900; FAX 706/379-9999; res: 800/201-3205.* Web www.brasstownvalley.com. 102 rms in main bldg, 5 story, 8 kit. cottages. Apr-mid-Nov: S, D $129-$149; each addl $10; suites $200-$250; kit. cottages $139-$159; under 18 free; golf plans; lower rates rest of yr. Crib free. TV; cable (premium). Indoor/outdoor pool; whirlpool, poolside serv. Playground. Supervised child's activities (June-Sept); ages 4-12. Complimentary coffee in rms. Restaurants 6 am-11 pm. Box lunches, snacks, picnics. Bar from 11 am. Ck-out noon, ck-in 4 pm. Grocery. Coin lndry. Bellhops. Valet serv. Concierge. Gift shop. Convention facilities. Business center. In-rm modem link. Sports dir. Lighted tennis, pro. 18-hole golf, greens fee $55-$65, putting green, driving range. Hiking. Lawn games. Social dir. Rec rm. Game rm. Exercise rm; sauna. Some refrigerators; microwaves avail. Balconies. Picnic tables. Located in Blue Ridge Mountains. Cr cds: A, C, D, DS, ER, JCB, MC, V.

⊡ 🐾 🎿 🏃 ≋ 🏋 🐾 🐾 🅂🅲 🏃

Indian Springs State Park (D-3)

(5 mi SE of Jackson on GA 42)

Called "the oldest state park in the United States," this was originally a gathering place for Creek Native Americans, who valued sulphur springs for curative powers. General William McIntosh, a Creek, headed the encampment in this area in 1800. In 1821, McIntosh signed a treaty ceding most of the Creek lands between the Flint and Ocmulgee rivers and north to the Chattahoochee. In 1825, he relinquished the rest of the Creek land in Georgia.

The state disposed of all Native American lands except 10 acres called Indian Springs Reserve. Butts County citizens bought an adjoining 513 acres, donating it to the state for a park with a mineral spring, a 105-acre lake and a museum (summer only). Swimming beach; fishing, boating (rentals). Nature trails. Picnicking. Camping, cottages. Standard hrs, fees. Contact Superintendent, 678 Lake Clark Rd, Flovilla 30216; 770/504-2277.

Jekyll Island (G-6)

(See also Brunswick, Golden Isles, St Simons Island, Sea Island)

Pop 1500 (est) **Elev** 5 ft **Area code** 912 **E-mail** jekyll@darientel.net **Web** www.jekyllisland.com
Information Jekyll Island Convention & Visitors Bureau, PO Box 13186, 31527; 912/635-3636 or 800/841-6586.

Connected to the mainland by a causeway, Jekyll Island, the smallest of Georgia's coastal islands (see GOLDEN ISLES) with 5,600 acres of highlands and 10,000 acres of marshland, was favored by Native Americans for hunting and fishing. Spanish missionaries arrived in the late 16th and early 17th centuries and established a mission. In 1734, during an expedition southward, General James Oglethorpe passed by the island and named it for his friend and financial supporter, Sir Joseph Jekyll. Later, William Horton, one of Oglethorpe's officers, established a plantation on the island.

Horton's land grant passed to several owners before the island was sold to Christophe du Bignon, a Frenchman who was escaping the French Revolution. It remained in the du Bignon family as a plantation for almost a century. In 1858, the slave ship *Wanderer* arrived at the island and unloaded the last major cargo of slaves ever to land in the United States. In 1886, John Eugene du Bignon sold the island to a group of wealthy businessmen from the northeast, who formed the Jekyll Island Club.

Club members who wintered at Jekyll in exclusive privacy from early January to early April included J.P. Morgan, William Rockefeller, Edwin Gould, Joseph Pulitzer and R.T. Crane, Jr. Some built fabulous "cottages," many of which are still standing. But by World War II, the club had been abandoned for economic and social reasons, and in 1947 the island was sold to the state. The Jekyll Island Authority was created to conserve beaches and manage the island while maintaining it as a year-round resort.

What to See and Do

Cumberland Island National Seashore (see). S, off the coast.

Horton House. Ruins of former house (1742) of William Horton, sent from St Simons as captain by General James Oglethorpe. On Jekyll he established an outpost and plantation. Horton became major of all British forces at Fort Frederica after Oglethorpe's return to England. This house was later occupied by the du Bignon family as part of their plantation. NW side of Island.

Jekyll Island Club Historic District. Once one of the nation's most exclusive resorts, this restored district is a memorable example of turn-of-the-century wealth. Exhibition buildings and shops are open daily (closed Jan 1, Dec 25). Tours are available (daily, fee; tickets, information at the Visitors Center, the former Jekyll Island Club stables) for Mistletoe Cottage (1900), Indian Mound (or Rockefeller) Cottage (1892), du Bignon Cottage (1884) and the Faith Chapel (1904). Period rooms and changing exhibits can be viewed in several houses.

Public facilities. Beachfront bathhouses, cable water skiing; pier fishing; charter boats for offshore and inlet fishing and also sightseeing cruises. Bicycle trails, rentals; golf, driving range; miniature golf; 13 clay tennis courts, pro shop. Picnicking on east shore; shopping center. Camping at north end. Some fees.

Summer Waves. Eleven-acre water park featuring wave pool, enclosed speed slide, serpentine slides, tubing river, children's pool; picnicking, concessions. (Late May-early Sept, daily) 210 S Riverview Dr. Phone 912/635-2074. ¢¢¢¢

Annual Events

Country by the Sea Music Festival. Top country music stars perform on Jekyll's Beach. Early June.

Beach Music Festival. Famous beach music groups perform all afternoon. Late Aug.

Motel

★ ★ **COMFORT INN ISLAND SUITES.** 711 Beachview Dr (31527). 912/635-2211; FAX 912/635-2381. Web www.motelproperties.com. 180 suites, 2 story, 78 kits. Mid-May-mid-Aug: S, D $99-$179; each addl $10; kits. $149-$189; under 18 free; wkly rates; lower rates rest of yr. Crib $4. Pet accepted; $10. TV; cable. Pool; wading pool, whirlpools. Playground. Complimentary continental bkfst. Restaurant 6 am-11 pm. Ck-out 11 am. Coin lndry. Meeting rms. Sundries. Airport transportation. Tennis privileges. Golf privileges, pro, putting green, driving range. Refrigerators, microwaves; some in-rm whirlpools. Private patios, balconies. On ocean. Cr cds: A, C, D, DS, MC, V.

D ⟋ ⬤ 🏃 ⚡ ≋ ➶ ⊠ ⊼ SC

Motor Hotels

★ ★ ★ **CLARION RESORT BUCCANEER.** 85 S Beachview Dr (31527), I-95 exit 6. 912/635-2261; FAX 912/635-3230. Web www.motelproperties.com. 206 rms, 2-4 story, 120 kits. Early May-mid-Aug: S, D $119-$179; each addl $10; under 19 free; wkly rates; lower rates rest of yr. Crib $4. TV; cable. Pool; wading pool, poolside serv (in season). Playground. Supervised child's activities (June-Aug); ages 4-12. Restaurant 7 am-10 pm. Ck-out 11 am. Coin lndry. Meeting rms. Business servs avail. In-rm modem link. Bellhops. Sundries. Airport transportation. Tennis. 18-hole golf privileges, pro, putting green. Game rm. Lawn games. Microwaves avail. Private patios, balconies. Beachfront. Cr cds: A, C, D, DS, MC, V.

D ⟋ 🏃 ⚡ ≋ ⊠ ⊼ SC

✔★ ★ ★ **HOLIDAY INN BEACH RESORT.** 200 S Beachview Dr (31527). 912/635-3311; FAX 912/635-2901. E-mail hi.jekyll.island.1207@servicehotels.com; web www.traveler.net/htio/custom/service/1207.html. 205 units, 2-4 story. May-mid-Sept: S, D $119-129; each addl $10; lower rates rest of yr; under 18 free. Crib free. Pet accepted; $7.50. TV; cable (premium). Pool; wading pool, poolside serv (in season). Playground. Restaurant 7 am-2 pm, 5:30-10 pm. Rm serv. Bar 5 pm-2 am; entertainment. Ck-out 11 am. Lndry facilities. Meeting rms. Business servs avail. In-rm modem link. Bellhops. Sundries. Gift shop. Tennis. Bicycles. Private patios, balconies. On beach. Cr cds: A, C, D, DS, MC, V.

D ⟋ ⬤ 🏃 ≋ ⊠ ⊼ SC

Resorts

★ ★ ★ **JEKYLL ISLAND CLUB HOTEL.** 371 Riverview Dr (31527). 912/635-2600; FAX 912/635-2818; res: 800/535-9547. Web www.jekyllclub.com. 134 units, 4 story, 20 suites. Mar-Aug: S, D $129-$189; each addl $20; suites $189-$259; under 17 free; MAP, AP, golf plans; lower rates rest of yr. Crib free. TV; cable, VCR (movies avail). Heated pool; poolside serv. Supervised child's activities (June-Aug); ages 5-12. Dining rm 7 am-2 pm, 6-10 pm (also see GRAND DINING ROOM). Bar 3 pm-midnight; closed Sun. Ck-out noon, ck-in 4 pm. Meeting rms. Business servs avail. In-rm modem link. Concierge. Shopping arcade. Valet parking. Airport transportation. 9 tennis courts, 1 indoor & 5 lighted. Three 18-hole golf courses & one 9-hole course, greens fee $29, cart $26, pro, putting green, driving range. Marina; deep sea and sport fishing. Swimming beach. Bicycle rentals; croquet. Originally founded as an exclusive retreat for members of high society; historic club house (1887) has been restored. Cr cds: A, C, D, DS, JCB, MC, V.

D ⟋ 🏃 ⚡ ≋ ➶ ⊼ SC

★ ★ ★ **VILLAS BY THE SEA.** 1175 N Beachview Dr (31527). 912/635-2521; FAX 912/635-2569; res: 800/841-6262. Web www.jekyllisland.com. 166 kit. villas, 1-2 story. Late Mar-early Sept: 1-bedrm $99-$154, 2-bedrm $174-$189, 3-bedrm $224-$239; wkly: 1-bedrm $594-$924, 2-bedrm $1,044-$1,134; 3-bedrm $1,344-$1,434; package plans; lower rates rest of yr. Crib $7. Pet accepted; fee. TV; cable, VCR avail. Pool; wading pool, whirlpool. Playground. Dining rm 7 am-2 pm, 5-10 pm. Bar. Ck-out 11 am, ck-in 4 pm. Grocery 3 mi. Coin lndry. Package store 3 mi. Convention facilities. Business servs avail. Gift shop. Lighted tennis privileges, pro. Golf privileges, pro. Bicycle rentals. Private beach. Microwaves. Private patios, balconies. Picnic tables, grills. On 17 acres. Cr cds: A, C, D, DS, MC, V.

D ⟋ ⬤ 🏃 ⚡ ≋ ⊠ ⊼ SC

Restaurants

★ ★ **BLACKBEARD'S.** 200 N Beachview Dr (31527). 912/635-3522. Hrs: 11 am-10 pm. Bar. Semi-a la carte: lunch $3.50-$7.50, dinner $4.95-$18.50. Child's meals. Specializes in coastal seafood, steak. Parking. Nautical decor. View of ocean, dunes and beach. Cr cds: A, DS, MC, V.

D ⊼

★ ★ **GRAND DINING ROOM.** (See Jekyll Island Club Resort) 912/635-2600. Web www.jekyllclub.com. Hrs: 7 am-2 pm, 6-10 pm; Sun brunch 10:45 am-2 pm. Res accepted. Bar. Wine list. Semi-a la carte: bkfst $7.95-$9.95, lunch $5.95-$12.95, dinner $18.75-$29.95. Sun brunch $15.95. Child's meals. Specializes in fresh seafood, beef, pork. Own baking. Pianist. Valet parking. White columned dining rm; fireplaces, crystal wall lamps. Jacket (dinner). Totally nonsmoking. Cr cds: A, C, D, DS, MC, V.

D

✔★ **LATITUDE 31.** 1 Pier Rd (31527), in historic district. 912/635-3800. Hrs: 5-10 pm. Closed some major hols. Res accepted. Continental menu. Bar. Semi-a la carte: dinner $8.95-$17.95. Child's meals. Specialties: stuffed flounder, romano-crusted chicken, desert fire fettucine. On pier overlooking Jekyll River. Cr cds: DS, MC, V.

D ⊼

✔ **ZACHRY'S.** 44 Beachview Dr (31527). 912/635-3128. Hrs: 11 am-9 pm; Fri, Sat to 10 pm; winter to 8 pm. Closed Mother's Day, Thanksgiving, Dec 25. Wine, beer. Semi-a la carte: lunch, dinner $2.50-$14.95. Child's meals. Specializes in fresh seafood, chicken, steak. Salad bar. Cr cds: DS, MC, V.

 ⊼

Kennesaw Mountain National Battlefield Park (C-2)

(Approx 3 mi NW of Marietta off US 41 or I-75 exit 116)

At Kennesaw Mountain in June of 1864, General William Tecumseh Sherman executed the last of a series of flanking maneuvers that were started 100 miles to the north on May 7. The Battle of Kennesaw Mountain stalled but did not halt General Sherman's invasion of Georgia. Kennesaw Mountain National Battlefield Park commemorates the 1864 Atlanta campaign.

In a series of flanking maneuvers and minor battles in May and June, Sherman's 100,000-man Union Army forced the 65,000-man Confederate army, under the command of General Joseph E. Johnston, back from Dalton to the vicinity of Kennesaw Mountain, 20 miles north of Atlanta. On June 19, Johnston took position and dug in, anchoring his right flank on the steep mountain slopes and extending his left flank several miles to the south. He trusted that strong fortifications and rugged terrain would make up for the disparity in numbers.

The Confederates abandoned their positions after a heavy day's fighting and occupied strong points between Kennesaw and Lost mountains. Sherman first tried to march around to an area just south of the Confederate position, but Johnston shifted 11,000 troops to counter the maneuver. In fierce fighting at Kolb's Farm on June 22, Confederate attacks were repulsed, but Sherman was temporarily stymied.

Although the Confederate entrenchments seemed strong, Sherman suspected that they were weakly held. A sharp frontal attack, he decided, might break through and destroy Johnston's entire army. On the morning of June 27, after a heavy artillery bombardment, Sherman struck the Confederate line at two places simultaneously. At Pigeon Hill, 5,500 attackers were quickly driven under cover by sheets of Southern bullets. Two miles to the south, 8,000 Union infantrymen stormed up Cheatham Hill and for a few minutes engaged the Confederates in hand-to-hand combat on top of their earthworks. Casualties were so severe that the location was nicknamed "Dead Angle." By noon both attacks had failed. Sherman had lost 3,000 men, Johnston only 500.

Sherman reverted to his flanking strategy, and on July 2 the Confederates withdrew, eventually to Atlanta. The siege and fall of Atlanta soon followed. Sherman then began his devastating "March to the Sea."

The Visitor Center, on Old US 41 and Stilesboro Rd, north of Kennesaw Mountain, has exhibits, an audiovisual program and information (daily; closed Dec 25). A road leads to the top of Kennesaw Mountain (daily; Mon-Fri, drive or walk; Sat & Sun, bus leaves every 1/2 hr between the months of Feb and Nov, or walk—no driving). (The Cheatham Hill area, in the south-central section of the park, has the same hours as the Kennesaw Mountain road; closed Dec 25).

Park (daily; closed Dec 25). Self-guided tours. For additional information contact Park Ranger, 900 Kennesaw Mountain Dr, Kennesaw 30152-4854; 770/427-4686. **Free.**

La Grange (D-1)

(See also Pine Mountain (Harris Co))

Settled 1828 **Pop** 25,597 **Elev** 772 ft **Area code** 706 **Zip** 30240 **E-mail** mellody@mindspring.com **Web** www.lagrange-ga.org

Information La Grange-Troup County Chamber of Commerce, 111 Bull St, Box 636, 30241-0636; 706/884-8671.

La Grange is said to be the only town in the Confederacy that organized its own female military company. Legend has it that La Grange was so loyal to the Confederacy that every man marched off to battle. A women's home guard was named for Nancy Hart, Revolutionary heroine. When the defenseless city was about to be invaded by Wilson's Raiders, the Nancy Harts marched out to the fray. The Union colonel, named La Grange, was so affected by this female defense that he marched on without burning the city.

What to See and Do

Bellevue (1852-1853). Greek-revival house of US Senator Benjamin Harvey Hill; period furnishings. (Tues-Sat; closed hols) 204 Ben Hill St. Phone 706/884-1832. ¢¢

Chattahoochee Valley Art Museum. Art museum housed in remodeled 1800s jail. Changing exhibits by local, national and international artists. (Tues-Sat; closed major hols) 112 Hines St. Phone 706/882-3267. **Free.**

West Point Lake. Approx 26,000 acres with 525 mi of shoreline. Swimming; fishing, hunting; boating. Camping (fee). W on GA 109. Phone 706/645-2937.

Motels

✓★ BEST WESTERN LA GRANGE INN. *1601 Lafayette Pkwy (30241), I-85 exit 4.* 706/882-9540; FAX 706/882-3929. 101 rms, 2 story. S $40-$45; D $45-$50; each addl $5; under 12 free. Crib free. TV; cable. Pool. Complimentary continental bkfst. Restaurant nearby. Ck-out 11 am. Meeting rms. Business serves avail. Health club privileges. Cr cds: A, C, D, DS, ER, MC, V.

D ⛵ 🏋 🔥 SC

✓★ ★ RAMADA INN. *1513 Lafayette Pkwy, GA 109 at I-85.* 706/884-6175; FAX 706/884-1106. 146 rms, 2 story. S, D $55-$65; each addl $8; suites $140. Crib free. TV; cable. Pool. Complimentary coffee in rms. Restaurant 6:30 am-2 pm, 5:30-10 pm. Rm serv. Bar 4:30 pm-2 am. Ck-out noon. Meeting rms. Business servs avail. In-rm modem link. Valet serv. Exercise equipt. Some refrigerators. Cr cds: A, C, D, DS, JCB, MC, V.

D ⛵ 🏃 🏋 🔥 SC

Lumpkin (F-2)

(See also Americus, Columbus; also see Eufaula, AL)

Pop 1,250 **Elev** 593 ft **Area code** 912 **Zip** 31815

What to See and Do

Lake Walter F. George. This 45,000-acre lake, stretching south along the border of Georgia and Alabama, was created by damming the Chattahoochee River. Fishing is good for bass, bream, crappie and catfish, and the lake's 640-mi shoreline provides countless hidden coves and inlets. Approx 18 mi W via GA 39C or approx 30 mi SW via GA 27. Phone 912/768-2516. Various state parks are situated on the lake's border including

Florence Marina State Park. More than 140 acres at the northern end of Lake Walter F. George. Swimming pool; fishing; boating, johnboat rentals (fee). 18-hole miniature golf (fee); tennis. Camping, cottages. Contact Manager, Rte 1, Box 36, Omaha 31821; 912/838-4244.

Providence Canyon State Conservation Park. Georgia's "Little Grand Canyon" has spectacular erosion gullies up to 150 ft deep. Hiking. Picnicking. Interpretive center (daily). Standard hrs, fees. 7 mi W via GA 39C. Contact Superintendent, Rte 1, Box 158; 912/838-6202.

Westville. Living history village featuring buildings circa 1850; decorative arts and work skills of early Georgia. Demonstrations by craftsworkers include quilting, weaving, candlemaking, potterymaking, blacksmithing, and basket weaving; syrup making in season. (Daily exc Mon; closed some major hols; also early Jan) Phone 912/838-6310. ¢¢¢

Annual Events

Westville events. Westville has many varied events throughout the year. Phone 912/838-6310. Of special interest are the Spring Festival (early Apr), the May Day celebration (early May), Independence Day (July 4), "Fair of 1850" (late Oct-early Nov) and a variety of Christmas activities (Dec).

Macon (D-3)

Founded 1823 **Pop** 106,612 **Elev** 325 ft **Area code** 912

Information Macon-Bibb County Convention & Visitors Bureau, Terminal Station, 200 Cherry St, PO Box 6354, 31208; 912/743-3401 or 800/768-3401.

Macon began as a trading post. It served as a fort and rallying point for troops in the War of 1812; later it became a river landing for shipping to the seacoast by oar-propelled flat-bottom boats; then Macon became a major regional cotton market. Having launched *The Pioneer*, a forerunner of all Southern river steamers, Macon was not content to remain just a port. In 1838 a railroad linked Macon with Forsyth; five years later it was connected by rail to Savannah. In 1848, a third line, the Southwestern, connected Macon with the fertile southwest section of the state. The town had become a major railroad center.

Macon's role in the Civil War was to manufacture and distribute quartermaster supplies and ordnance. Harnesses, small weapons, cannon and shot were produced, and the city harbored $1.5 million in Confederate gold. In 1864 refugees poured in from devastated north Georgia. In July and November, Union forces were twice repulsed. The city finally surrendered to Wilson's Raiders in April 1865.

Sidney Lanier was born and lived here, practicing law before turning to poetry. Macon is also the hometown of rock 'n' roll singer Little Richard and soul singer Otis Redding.

What to See and Do

City Hall (1836). Main entrance of classical-revival building is flanked by panels depicting history of Macon area. Building was state capitol Nov 18, 1864-Mar 11, 1865, during the last session of the Georgia General Assembly under the Confederate States of America. Tours. (Mon-Fri; closed hols) 700 Poplar St. Phone 912/751-7170. **Free.**

Georgia Music Hall of Fame. Georgia's musical heritage is explored through different exhibits such as the Soda Fountain playing songs of the 50s, the Jazz Club, Gospel Chapel and Rythm & Blues Revue. Videos can be selected for viewing in the Georgia Theater. (Daily; closed Jan 1, Thanksgiving, Dec 25, 26) 200 Martin Luther King, Jr Blvd. Phone 912/738-0017. ¢¢¢

Grand Opera House. Originally the Academy of Music (1884), theater was restored in 1970. 651 Mulberry St. Phone 912/752-5470.

Hay House (1855-59). An Italian Renaissance-revival villa with 24 rms; elaborate ornamental plaster, woodwork, stained glass; ornate period furnishings and objets d'art. (Daily; closed major hols) 934 Georgia Ave. Phone 912/742-8155. ¢¢¢

Lake Tobesofkee. A 1,750-acre lake and a 650-acre park. Swimming, waterskiing; fishing; boating (launch). Nature trails; tennis. Picnicking. Camping (hookups). (Daily) 3 mi W via I-475, exit GA 74. Phone 912/474-8770. Fee for some activities. General admission ¢¢

Macon Historic District. District comprises nearly all of old Macon; 48 buildings and houses have been cited for architectural excellence and listed on National Register of Historic Places; an additional 575 structures have been noted for architectural significance. Walking and driving tours noted on Heritage Tour Markers. For tour maps contact the Convention & Visitors Bureau. Downtown.

Macon Museum of Arts and Sciences & Mark Smith Planetarium. Three galleries with permanent and changing art and science exhibits; displays of live amphibians, birds, reptiles and small mammals; nature trails; observatory. Planetarium shows. (Daily; closed Jan 1, Dec 25) 4182 Forsyth Rd. Phone 912/477-3232. ¢¢

Mercer University (1833). (6,100 students) Founded as Mercer Institute in Penfield, moved to Macon in 1871. Liberal arts, business, law, engineering and medicine are offered at Macon campus; also campus in Atlanta. 1400 Coleman Ave. Phone 912/752-2715.

Ocmulgee National Monument (see). 2 mi E on US 80, Alt 129.

Old Cannonball House & Macon-Confederate Museum (1853). Greek-revival house struck by Union cannonball in 1864. Museum contains Civil War relics and Macon historical items. (Daily exc Sun; closed Jan 1, Thanksgiving, Dec 25) 856 Mulberry St. Phone 912/745-5982. ¢¢

Sidney Lanier Cottage (1840). Gothic-revival house was birthplace of the nationally known poet; period furnishings. Headquarters of Middle Georgia Historical Society. (Daily exc Sun; closed hols) 935 High St. Phone 912/743-3851. ¢¢

Sightseeing tours.

Heart of Georgia Tours. Operated by the Middle Georgia Historical Society, 935 High St. Guides avail (fee) for private tours of city or for bus tours. Phone 912/743-3851.

Sidney's Tours of Historic Macon. Operated by the Macon-Bibb County Convention & Visitors Bureau. Examples of Greek-revival architecture, Victorian cottages, Italianate mansions, antebellum houses; statues, monuments, other landmarks left standing by General Sherman on his march to the sea. (Daily exc Sun; no tours some major hols) 200 Cherry St. Phone 912/743-3401 or 800/768-3401. ¢¢¢

Tubman African American Museum. Features African American art, African artifacts and traveling exhibits on the history and culture of African American people. Resource center, workshops and tours (by appt). (Daily; closed Jan 1, Thanksgiving, Dec 25) 340 Walnut St. Phone 912/743-8544. ¢¢

Wesleyan College (1836). (500 women) This 4-yr liberal arts college was chartered to grant degrees to women. Campus tours by appt. 4760 Forsyth Rd, on US 41. Phone 912/477-1110.

Annual Events

Cherry Blossom Festival. Historic tours, concerts, fireworks, hot air balloons, sporting events, parade. Phone 912/751-7429. Mar 20-29.

Georgia State Fair. Central City Park. Grandstand shows, midway, exhibit buildings. Phone 912/746-7184. Oct 19-25.

Motels

★ ★ ★ **BEST WESTERN RIVERSIDE INN.** *2400 Riverside Dr (31204), I-75 exit 54.* 912/743-6311; FAX 912/743-9420. 122 rms, 2 story. S, D $54; under 18 free. Crib free. TV; cable (premium). Pool. Complimentary coffee in rms. Restaurant 6:30 am-9 pm. Rm serv. Bar 5 pm-midnight. Ck-out noon. Coin lndry. Meeting rms. Business servs avail. In-rm modem link. Valet serv. Health club privileges. Refrigerators; microwaves avail. Cr cds: A, C, D, DS, MC, V.

D ≈ ⊠ 🕊 SC

★ ★ **COMFORT INN-NORTH.** *2690 Riverside Dr (31204), I-75 exit 54.* 912/746-8855; FAX 912/746-8881; res: 800/847-6443. 120 rms, 3 story. June-Dec: S $59; D $64; under 18 free; higher rates Cherry Blossom Festival; lower rates rest of yr. Crib free. TV; cable (premium). Pool. Complimentary continental bkfst. Complimentary coffee in rms. Bar 4-10 pm; closed Sun. Ck-out noon. Meeting rms. Business servs avail. In-rm modem link. Some refrigerators; microwaves avail. Cr cds: A, C, D, DS, JCB, MC, V.

D ≈ ⊠ 🕊 SC

★ ★ **COURTYARD BY MARRIOTT.** *3990 Sheraton Dr (31210), I-75 exit 55A.* 912/477-8899; FAX 912/477-4684. 108 rms, 3 story. S $84; D $94; suites $119; wkend rates. Crib free. TV; cable (premium). Pool; whirlpool. Complimentary coffee in rms. Bar 5-10 pm. Ck-out noon. Guest

Indry. Meeting rm. Business servs avail. In-rm modem link. Valet serv. Exercise equipt. Health club privileges. Some refrigerators; microwaves avail. Balconies. Cr cds: A, C, D, DS, MC, V.

D ≈ ✗ ⇕ ⚡ SC

✔★ ★ **HAMPTON INN.** 3680 Riverside Dr (31210), I-75 exit 55A. 912/471-0660; FAX 912/471-2528. 151 rms, 2 story. S $59-$69; D $65-$69; under 18 free. Crib free. Pet accepted; $10. TV; cable. Pool. Complimentary continental bkfst. Coffee in rms. Ck-out noon. Business servs avail. In-rm modem link. Valet serv. Health club privileges. Cr cds: A, D, DS, MC, V.

D ✦ ≈ ⇕ ⚡ SC

✔★ ★ **RODEWAY INN.** 4999 Eisenhower Pkwy (31206), I-475 exit 1. 912/781-4343; FAX 912/784-8140. 55 rms, 2 story. S $38-$42; D $48-$54; each addl $4; under 18 free; higher rates Cherry Blossom Festival. Crib $4. Pet accepted. TV; cable (premium), VCR avail (movies). Pool. Complimentary continental bkfst. Restaurant nearby. Ck-out 11 am. Coin Indry. Business servs avail. Refrigerators, microwaves. Cr cds: A, C, D, DS, MC, V.

D ✦ ≈ ⇕ ⚡ SC

Motor Hotel

✔★ ★ **HOLIDAY INN EXPRESS.** 2720 Riverside Dr (31298), I-75 exit 54. 912/743-1482; FAX 912/745-3967. 93 rms, 6 story. S, D $51-$69; each addl $6; suites $69; under 18 free. Crib free. Pet accepted. TV; cable (premium). Pool. Complimentary continental bkfst. Ck-out noon. Meeting rm. Business servs avail. In-rm modem link. Valet serv. Health club privileges. Cr cds: A, C, D, DS, MC, V.

D ✦ ≈ ⇕ ⚡ SC

Hotel

★ ★ ★ **CROWNE PLAZA.** 108 First St (31201). 912/746-1461; FAX 912/738-2460. Web www.impachotels.com. 298 units, 16 story. S, D $79-$109; each addl $10; suites $175-$279; under 18 free. Crib free. Valet parking $6; self-park $5. TV; cable (premium). Pool. Restaurants 7 am-10 pm. Bar 4 pm-2 am; entertainment. Ck-out noon. Convention facilities. In-rm modem link. Gift shop. Airport transportation. Exercise equipt; sauna. Luxury level. Cr cds: A, C, D, DS, JCB, MC, V.

D ≈ ✗ ⇕ ⚡ SC

Inn

★ ★ ★ ★ **1842 INN.** 353 College St (31201). 912/741-1842; FAX 912/741-1842, ext. 41; res: 800/336-1842. The 1842 Inn offers the amenities of a grand hotel with the charm of a country inn and gracious Southern hospitality. The Greek-Revival antebellum house is filled with fine English antiques, Oriental carpets, tapestries and paintings. Rooms are individually decorated and strikingly beautiful. 21 rms, 2 story. S $115-$175; D $125-$185; each addl $10. Children over 12 yrs only. TV; cable (premium), VCR avail. Complimentary continental bkfst. Restaurant nearby. Ck-out 11 am, ck-in 3 pm. Business servs avail. Valet serv. Health club privileges. Some in-rm whirlpools. Cr cds: A, MC, V.

D ⇕ ⚡ SC

Restaurants

✔★ ★ **GREEN JACKET.** 325 5th St (31201). 912/746-4680. Hrs: 11 am-10 pm; Fri to 11 pm; Sat 5-11 pm; Sun buffet to 3 pm. Closed Dec 25. Res accepted. Bar. Semi-a la carte: lunch, dinner $4.99-$34.95. Buffet: Sun $9.95. Specializes in prime rib, seafood, chicken. Salad bar. Golf motif. Cr cds: A, D, DS, MC, V.

D ⌐

★ ★ ★ **NATALIA'S.** 2720 Riverside Dr (31210). 912/741-1380. Hrs: 6-10:30 pm. Closed Sun; some major hols, July 4th wk. Res accepted.

Northern Italian menu. Bar. Semi-a la carte: dinner $12.50-$25. Specializes in lamb chops, fish in parchment. Antiques. Paintings, photographs on display. Cr cds: A, MC, V.

D ⌐

★ ★ **STEAK AND ALE.** 3086 Riverside Dr (31201), I-75 exit 54. 912/477-1728. Hrs: 11 am-2 pm, 4-10 pm; Fri to 11 pm; Sat 4-11 pm; Sun noon-10 pm; early bird dinner Mon-Sat 4-6 pm. Res accepted. Bar. Semi-a la carte: lunch $5.50-$13, dinner $7.95-$19.99. Child's meals. Specializes in prime rib, grilled steak, fish. Salad bar. Old English decor. Cr cds: A, C, D, DS, MC, V.

D ⌐

Madison (C-3)

(See also Athens, Eatonton)

Pop 3,483 **Elev** 667 ft **Area code** 706 **Zip** 30650
Information Welcome Center, 115 E Jefferson, PO Box 826; 706/342-4454 or 800/709-7406.

General Sherman spared Madison on his Civil War march to the sea. The result is a contemporary city with a wealth of well-preserved Antebellum and Victorian residences. Several movies have been filmed in the town to take advantage of the 19th-century atmosphere.

What to See and Do

Lake Oconee. Approx 19,000-acre lake with 374 mi of shoreline was created by the impoundment of the Oconee River. Beach swimming; fishing; boating, marinas. Picnicking. Camping. E on I-20. For further information phone 706/485-8704. Some fees at recreation areas. Parking ¢

Madison-Morgan Cultural Center. Romanesque-revival school building (1895) with art galleries, restored schoolroom, museum of local history, original auditorium and ongoing schedule of performances. (Daily exc Mon; closed major hols) 434 S Main St. Phone 706/342-4743. ¢¢

Annual Event

Spring Tour of Homes. Historic houses, scenic gardens, period furnishings and antiques. 3rd wkend Apr.

Holiday Tour of Homes. Historic private homes. 1st wkend Dec.

Motels

✔★ ★ **DAYS INN.** 2001 Eatonton Hwy, 2 mi S at jct US 129/441, I-20 exit 51. 706/342-1839; FAX 706/342-1839, ext. 100. 77 rms, 2 story. S, D $49.95; each addl $5; under 18 free; higher rates special events. Crib free. Pet accepted; $10. TV; cable (premium). Pool; wading pool. Restaurant 6:30-9:30 am, 11 am-3 pm, 5-8:30 pm. Ck-out noon. Cr cds: A, C, D, DS, MC, V.

D ✦ ≈ ⇕ ⚡ SC

★ ★ **HOLIDAY INN EXPRESS.** (10111 Alcovy Rd, Covington 30209) 27 mi on I-20 exit 45A. 770/787-4900; FAX 770/385-9805. E-mail hie@mindspring.com. 50 rms, 2 story, 25 suites. S, D $62; each addl $5; suites $67; under 18 free. Crib $5. Pet accepted, some restrictions; $25. TV; cable (premium). Complimentary continental bkfst, coffee in rms. Restaurant adj 11 am-10 pm. Ck-out noon. Meeting rms. Business servs avail. In-rm modem link. Valet serv. Coin Indry. Exercise equipt. Pool. Refrigerators, microwaves. Cr cds: A, C, D, DS, JCB, MC, V.

D ✦ ≈ ✗ ⇕ ⚡ SC

Inns

★ ★ **BRADY.** *250 N Second St. 706/342-4400; res: 706/342-9287.* 7 rms. No rm phones. S $65; D $75; suite $150. TV in sitting rm; cable, VCR avail (movies). Complimentary full bkfst. Restaurant nearby. Ck-out noon, ck-in 6 pm. Health club privileges. Restored Victorian cottage in historic downtown. Cr cds: A, DS, JCB, MC, V.

★ ★ **BURNETT PLACE.** *317 Old Post Rd. 706/342-4034.* 3 rms, 2 story. S $75; D $85; each addl $10. TV; cable (premium), VCR avail (movies). Complimentary full bkfst; afternoon refreshments. Restaurant nearby. Ck-out 11 am, ck-in 3 pm. Picnic tables, grills. Federal-style house (ca 1830) typical of the Piedmont region. Cr cds: MC, V.

Marietta (C-2)

(See also Atlanta, Norcross)

Founded 1834 **Pop** 44,129 **Elev** 1,128 ft **Area code** 770 **Web** www.cobbcvb.org
Information Cobb County Convention & Visitors Bureau, 1100 Circle 75 Pkwy, Ste 125, PO Box 672827, 30006-0048; 770/933-7228 or 800/451-3480. A welcome center is located at 4 Depot St, phone 770/429-1115.

What to See and Do

Kennesaw Civil War Museum. The L & N steam locomotive *General*, permanently housed here, was taken from this spot in 1862 by Union raiders in an attempt to cut Confederate supply lines. The raiders were chased and captured by the train crew. Includes exhibits and video about the raid. (Daily; closed major hols) 6 mi N via US 41 or I-75 to exit 118, at 2829 Cherokee St in Kennesaw. Phone 770/427-2117 or 800/742-6897. ¢¢

Kennesaw Mountain National Battlefield Park (see). Approx 3 mi NW off US 41 or I-75, follow signs.

White Water. Water theme park with 40 rides; body flumes, rapids ride, wave pool, float. (Memorial Day-Labor Day, daily; May, wkends) Marietta Pkwy, I-75 exit 113. Phone 770/424-WAVE. ¢¢¢¢ Adj is

American Adventures. Children's amusement park with over a dozen rides. (Daily; closed some major hols) Fee for various activities. Phone 770/424-6683. Parking ¢

Annual Event

US 10K Classic and Family Sports Festival. Phone 770/432-0100. Labor Day wkend.

Motels

✔ ★ **BEST INNS OF AMERICA.** *1255 Franklin Rd (30067), I-75 exit 111. 770/955-0004; FAX 770/955-0004, ext. 345; res: 800/237-8466.* 116 rms, 3 story. S $43.88-$59.88; D $50.88-$69.88; under 18 free. Crib free. TV; cable (premium). Pool. Complimentary coffee in lobby. Restaurant nearby. Ck-out 1 pm. In-rm modem link. Microwaves avail. Cr cds: A, D, DS, MC, V.

★ ★ **BEST WESTERN BRADBURY SUITES.** *(4500 Circle 75 Pkwy, Atlanta 30339) I-75 exit 110, north of downtown. 770/956-9919; FAX 770/955-3270.* 247 rms in 2 bldgs, 3-5 story. S, D $55-$89; each addl $5; suites $75; under 6 free. Crib free. TV; cable (premium). Pool; whirlpool. Complimentary full bkfst buffet. Coffee in rms. Restaurant nearby. Ck-out noon. Coin Indry. Meeting rms. Business servs avail. In-rm modem link.

Health club privileges. Some refrigerators; microwaves avail. Cr cds: A, D, DS, MC, V.

★ **ECONO LODGE.** *1940 Leland Dr (30067), I-75 exit 110. 770/952-0052; FAX 770/952-0501.* 108 rms, 3 story. S $50; D $55; each addl $5; under 16 free; wkly rates; higher rates special events. TV; cable (premium). Restaurant adj 6 am-4 pm. Ck-out 11 am. Coin Indry. Meeting rms. Sundries. Cr cds: A, D, DS, MC, V.

★ ★ **HAMPTON INN.** *455 Franklin Rd (30067), I-75 exit 112. 770/425-9977; FAX 770/427-2545.* 140 rms, 4 story. S, D $69-$79; under 18 free. Crib free. TV; cable (premium). Pool; wading pool. Complimentary continental bkfst. Restaurant nearby. Ck-out noon. Meeting rm. Business servs avail. In-rm modem link. Valet serv. Health club privileges. Microwaves avail. Cr cds: A, C, D, DS, ER, MC, V.

★ ★ **HAWTHORN SUITES-ATLANTA NORTHWEST.** *(1500 Parkwood Circle, Atlanta 30339) I-75 exit 110, north of downtown. 770/952-9595; FAX 770/984-2335.* E-mail atlanta-041@rfsmgmt.com; web www.hawthorne.com. 280 rms, 2-3 story. S, D $99; suites $135-$195; wkend, monthly rates. Crib free. Pet accepted; $100. TV; cable (premium). Heated pool; whirlpool. Complimentary full bkfst. Restaurant nearby. Ck-out noon. Coin Indry. Meeting rms. In-rm modem link. Valet serv. Lighted tennis. Exercise equipt. Health club privileges. Refrigerators, microwaves. Private patios, balconies. Picnic tables, grills. Elaborate landscaping, flowers. Cr cds: A, C, D, DS, JCB, MC, V.

★ ★ **LA QUINTA.** *2170 Delk Rd (30067), I-75 N Delk Rd exit 111. 770/951-0026; FAX 770/952-5372.* 130 rms, 3 story. S $60-$70; D $65-$75; each addl $6; under 18 free. Crib free. Pet accepted, some restrictions. TV; cable (premium). Pool. Complimentary continental bkfst. Restaurant adj 6 am-10 pm; wkends to 11 pm. Ck-out noon. Meeting rm. In-rm modem link. Valet serv. Some refrigerators, microwaves. Cr cds: A, C, D, DS, MC, V.

★ ★ **WINDSOR INN.** *(2655 Cobb Pkwy, Kennesaw 30152) approx 5 mi N on US 41. 770/424-6330; FAX 770/419-8837; res: 800/494-3767.* 31 rms. Mar-Sept: S $40-$45; D $40-$55; each addl $5; suite $70; under 5 free; higher rates special events; lower rates rest of yr. TV; cable (premium). Pool; wading pool. Continental bkfst. Complimentary coffee in rms. Rm serv. Ck-out 11 am. Refrigerators; microwaves avail. Picnic tables. Cr cds: A, DS, MC, V.

Motor Hotel

★ ★ ★ **WYNDHAM GARDEN-ATLANTA NORTHWEST.** *1775 Parkway Place (30067), I-75 exit 112. 770/428-4400; FAX 770/428-9782.* 218 rms, 10 story. S, D $99-$109; under 12 free; wkend rates. Crib free. TV; cable (premium). Pool. Coffee in rms. Restaurant 6:30 am-10 pm. Bar 4 pm-midnight; Sun 4 pm-midnight. Ck-out noon. Meeting rms. Business servs avail. In-rm modem link. Bellhops. Valet serv. Exercise equipt. Some refrigerators. Some balconies. Cr cds: A, C, D, DS, JCB, MC, V.

Hotels

★ ★ **HOLIDAY INN.** *2265 Kingston Ct (30067), I-75 exit 111. 770/952-7581; FAX 770/952-1301.* Web www.atl.ixl.com/holiday-inn/atldl. 196 rms, 5-7 story, 55 suites. S, D $109; each addl $10; suites $99-$199; under 18 free; higher rates special events. Crib free. TV; cable (premium). Pool. Complimentary coffee in rms. Restaurant 6:30 am-2 pm, 5-10 pm; wkends from 7 am. Bar 5 pm-midnight. Ck-out noon. Meeting rms. Business servs avail. In-rm modem link. Exercise equipt. Cr cds: A, D, DS, MC, V.

★ ★ ★ **HYATT REGENCY SUITES-PERIMETER NORTHWEST.** *2999 Windy Hill Rd (30067), I-75N to Windy Hill exit 110, north of downtown.* 770/956-1234; FAX 770/956-9479. E-mail dhewitt@hycntpo.hyatt. com; web www.hyatt.com. 200 suites, 7 story. S $89-$165; D $89-$190; under 18 free; wkend rates. Crib free. TV; cable (premium). Heated pool; whirlpool. Complimentary coffee in rms. Restaurant 6:30 am-11 pm. Bar 11:30 am-midnight. Ck-out noon. Meeting rms. Business center. In-rm modem link. Tennis privileges. Golf privileges. Exercise equipt; sauna. Health club privileges. Refrigerators; some microwaves. Cr cds: A, C, D, DS, JCB, MC, V.

★ ★ ★ **MARIETTA CONFERENCE CENTER AND RESORT.** *500 Powder Springs St (30064).* 770/427-2500; FAX 770/429-9577. E-mail mccr@atlanta.com; web www.mariettaresort.com. 199 rms, 6 story. S $159-$204; D $169-$219; each addl $15; suites $250-$1,250; under 18 free; wkend, hol rates; golf plans. Crib free. Valet parking $3-$10. TV; cable (premium), VCR avail. Complimentary coffee in rms. Restaurant 6:30 am-10 pm. Rm serv 24 hrs. Bar noon-1 am; entertainment. Ck-out 11 am. Meeting rms. Business center. In-rm modem link. Concierge. Gift shop. Lighted tennis. 18-hole golf, greens fee $37.50-$55, pro, putting green, driving range. Exercise equipt; sauna. Massage. Pool; whirlpool, poolside serv. Lawn games. Refrigerators, minibars. Cr cds: A, C, D, DS, MC, V.

Inn

★ ★ ★ **WHITLOCK INN.** *57 Whitlock Ave (30064), 1 blk W of town square; in National Register Historic District.* 770/428-1495; FAX 770/919-9620. Web www.mindspring.com/~whitlockinn/. 5 rms, 2 story. S, D $100-$125. Children over 12 yrs only. TV; cable (premium). Complimentary continental bkfst. Restaurant nearby. Ck-out 11 am, ck-in 3 pm. Business servs avail. In-rm modem link. Luggage handling. Concierge serv. Gift shop. Lawn games. Victorian mansion built in 1900. Totally nonsmoking. Cr cds: A, DS, MC, V.

Restaurants

★ ★ ★ **1848 HOUSE.** *780 S Cobb Dr (30060), entrance on Pearl St at Cobb Pkwy.* 770/428-1848. Web www.1848house.com. Hrs: 6-9:30 pm; Sun (brunch) 10:30 am-2:30 pm, 5:30-8 pm. Closed Mon; Jan 1, Dec 25. Res accepted. Bar from 5:30 pm. Wine cellar. A la carte entrees: dinner $13.95-$25.95. Sun brunch $19.95. Child's meals. Specialties: Charleston she-crab soup, house-smoked center-cut pork chop, Savannah rock shrimp cake. Own baking. Valet parking. Ten dining rooms in Greek-revival plantation house completed in 1848; 13 landscaped acres. Cr cds: A, C, D, DS, JCB, MC, V.

✔★ ★ **FOOD MERCHANT.** *2143-C Roswell Rd (30062).* 770/579-5515. Hrs: 11:30 am-2:30 pm, 5-9:30 pm; Fri to 10 pm; Sat 5-10 pm. Closed Sun; Thanksgiving, Dec 25. Continental menu. Wine, beer. Semi-a la carte: lunch, dinner $3.50-$13.95. Child's meals. Specialties: seafood stew, bayou Angus sirloin, vegetarian farfalle pasta. Outdoor dining. Contemporary murals. Totally nonsmoking. Cr cds: A, DS, MC, V.

✔★ ★ **GRAZIE.** *1000 Whitlock Ave (30064).* 770/499-8585. Hrs: 11 am-2 pm, 4 pm-midnight; Fri, Sat to 1 am; Sun 11 am-2 pm (brunch), 3-10 pm. Closed most major hols. Res accepted. Italian menu. Bar. Semi-a la carte: lunch $3-$7, dinner $8-$18. Sun brunch $5-$7. Specializes in fresh fish, steak, pasta. Pianist; vocalists Fri, Sat. Cr cds: A, C, D, DS, MC, V.

★ ★ **LA STRADA.** *2930 Johnson Ferry Rd NE (30067).* 770/640-7008. Hrs: 5-10 pm; Fri, Sat to 11 pm. Closed most major hols. Italian menu. Bar. Semi-a la carte: dinner $7.95-$14.95. Child's meals. Specializes in stuffed shrimp Fra Diavolo, soft shell crab, tiramisu. Cr cds: A, C, D, DS, MC, V.

✔★ **OLD SOUTH BAR-B-Q.** *(601 Burbank Circle, Smyrna 30080) approx 5 mi S off Cobb Pkwy (US 41) on Windy Hill Rd.* 770/435-4215. Hrs: 11 am-9:30 pm. Closed Mon; some major hols. Semi-a la carte: lunch, dinner $2.50-$7.50. Child's meals. Specializes in beef, chicken, pork. Parking. Casual dining. Family-owned. Cr cds: MC, V.

✔★ ★ **SHILLING'S ON THE SQUARE.** *19 North Park Square (30060).* 770/428-9520. Hrs: 11 am-midnight; Fri, Sat to 1 am; Sun brunch 10:30 am-2 pm. Closed Jan 1, Dec 25. Res accepted. Bar to 1 am. Semi-a la carte: lunch $5.95-$7.95, dinner $8.95-$19.95. Sun brunch $4.50-$6.95. Specializes in steak, fresh seafood. Tavern decor; century-old wood bar, stained glass panels, tin ceiling. Cr cds: A, C, D, DS, MC, V.

Milledgeville (D-3)

(See also Eatonton, Macon)

Founded 1803 **Pop** 17,727 **Elev** 335 ft **Area code** 912 **Zip** 31061 **Web** www.milledgevillega.com/cvb.htm
Information Convention & Visitors Bureau, 200 W Hancock St, Box 219, phone 912/452-4687 or 800/653-1804.

Milledgeville was laid out to be the state capital and served in that capacity from 1804 through 1868. When the state records were transferred to Milledgeville from Louisville in 1807, wagons were escorted by troops of cavalry from Washington, DC.

Milledgeville's houses typify the development of Southern architecture; the earliest structures had small stoops; houses of the next period had two porches, one above the other; with the third period, the two-story columns become Greek porticos, the second story, a balcony. Later, porches became broad, multi-columned verandas, extending across the front and even around to the sides and back of the house.

What to See and Do

Georgia College (1889). (5,500 students) Occupies one of four twenty-acre plots "reserved for public use" when the city was laid out. The Museum and Archives of Georgia Education is located on campus. 231 W Hancock St. Phone 912/453-5350. Also located on campus is

Old Governor's Mansion. Greek-revival residence of Georgia governors from 1839 to 1868. Guided tours. (Tues-Sat, also Sun afternoons; closed hols, Thanksgiving wkend, wk of Dec 25) 120 S Clark St. Phone 912/453-4545. ¢¢

Historic Guided Trolley Tour. Includes stops at St Stephens Episcopal Church and Stetson-Sanford House. Tour departs from the Convention & Visitors Bureau office, 200 W Hancock. The office also has information on walking tours. Trolley tour (Tues-Fri mornings, Sat afternoons). ¢¢¢

Lake Sinclair. This 15,330-acre lake with 417 mi of shoreline was created by the impoundment of the Oconee River. Fishing; boating, marinas. Camping. N on US 441, GA 24. Phone 912/452-1605.

Annual Event

Browns Crossing Craftsmen Fair. 9 mi W via GA 22. Features original works, including paintings, weavings, pottery, woodcarvings, graphics. 3rd wkend Oct.

Motels

★ ★ **HOLIDAY INN.** 2627 N Columbia, approx 4 mi N. 912/452-3502; FAX 912/453-3591. 170 rms, 2 story. S $64, D $69; each addl $5; suites $125; under 18 free. Crib free. TV; cable (premium). Pool; wading pool. Restaurant 6 am-2 pm, 5:30-9 pm. Rm serv. Bar. Ck-out noon. Meeting rms. Business servs avail. In-rm modem link. Valet serv. Wet bar, whirlpool in some suites. Cr cds: A, C, D, DS, JCB, MC, V.

D ≈ ⊠ ⋒ SC

★ ★ **JAMESON INN.** 2551 N Columbia St. 912/453-8471; FAX 912/453-8482; res: 800/541-3268. 100 rms, 2 story, 2 kit. units. S $51; D $56; each addl $4; suites $95-$147; under 14 free; wkly rates avail. Crib $5. TV; cable (premium). Pool; wading pool, whirlpool. Complimentary continental bkfst. Ck-out 11 am. Meeting rms. Business servs avail. Lighted tennis. Exercise equipt; sauna. Cr cds: A, D, DS, MC, V.

D ≈ ⊠ ⊀ ⊠ ⋒ SC

Norcross (C-2)

(See also Atlanta, Buford, Winder)

Pop 5,947 **Elev** 1,057 ft **Area code** 770 **Web** www.norcrossgeorgia-gvt.com
Information City of Norcross, 65 Lawrenceville St, 30071; 770/448-2122.

Norcross, a suburb of Atlanta, is located approximately 20 miles northeast of the city. Citizens have preserved many old residences; there is a 112-acre Historic District here with a restored downtown square.

Motels

★ ★ **BEST WESTERN BRADBURY INN.** 5985 Oakbrook Pkwy (30093), I-85 exit 37. 770/662-8175; FAX 770/840-1183. 121 rms, 1-3 story. S, D $59-$89; suites $89-$119; under 18 free; wkend rates. Crib free. TV; cable (premium). Pool. Complimentary full bkfst. Complimentary coffee in rms. Ck-out noon. Coin lndry. Meeting rms. Business servs avail. In-rm modem link. Valet serv. Exercise equipt. Health club privileges. Some refrigerators; microwaves avail. Cr cds: A, C, D, DS, MC, V.

D ≈ ⊀ ⊠ ⋒ SC

★ ★ **CLUBHOUSE INN.** 5945 Oakbrook Pkwy (30093), I-85 exit 37. 770/368-9400; FAX 770/416-7370. 147 rms, 2-3 story, 25 kit. suites. S, D $79-$89; each addl $10; kit. suites $94; under 18 free. Crib free. TV; cable (premium). Pool; whirlpool. Complimentary full bkfst. Restaurant adj 11 am-11 pm. Ck-out noon. Coin lndry. Meeting rms. Business servs avail. Valet serv. Microwave, wet bar in suites. Balconies. Picnic tables, grills. Cr cds: A, C, D, DS, JCB, MC, V.

D ≈ ⊠ ⋒ SC

★ ★ **COURTYARD BY MARRIOTT-JIMMY CARTER BLVD.** 6235 McDonough Dr (30093), I-85 exit 37. 770/242-7172; FAX 770/840-8768. 122 rms, 2 story. S, D $82; suites $102; under 18 free; wkend rates. Crib free. TV; cable (premium), VCR avail. Pool; whirlpool. Restaurant 6:30-10 am; Sat, Sun 7-11 am. Bar Mon-Fri 5-11 pm. Ck-out noon. Coin lndry. Meeting rms. Business servs avail. In-rm modem link. Valet serv. Sundries. Exercise equipt. Health club privileges. Bathrm phone in suites. Private patios, balconies. Cr cds: A, C, D, DS, MC, V.

D ≈ ⊀ ⊠ ⋒ SC

✔★ ★ **FAIRFIELD INN BY MARRIOTT.** 6650 Bay Circle Dr (30071), I-285 exit 23 B. 770/441-1999. 135 rms, 3 story. S, D $42-$49; under 18 free. Crib free. TV; cable (premium). Pool. Complimentary continental bkfst. Restaurant nearby. Ck-out noon. Business servs avail. In-rm modem link. Valet serv. Sundries. Cr cds: A, C, D, DS, MC, V.

D ≈ ⊠ ⋒ SC

★ ★ **HOMEWOOD SUITES-PEACHTREE CORNERS.** 450 Technology Pkwy (30092). 770/448-4663; FAX 770/242-6979. Web www.homewood-suites.com. 92 suites, 2-3 story. Suites $110-$195; wkend rates. Crib free. Pet accepted, some restrictions; $50. TV; cable. Pool; whirlpool. Complimentary continental bkfst. Complimentary coffee in rms. Restaurant nearby. Ck-out noon. Coin lndry. Meeting rms. Business center. In-rm modem link. Valet serv. Sundries. Exercise equipt. Health club privileges. Refrigerators, microwaves. Picnic tables, grills. Cr cds: A, C, D, DS, MC, V.

D ✔ ≈ ⊀ ⊠ ⋒ SC ⊀

★ ★ **LA QUINTA.** 5375 Peachtree Industrial Blvd (30092). 770/449-5144; FAX 770/840-8576. Web www.laquinta.com. 130 rms, 3 story. S, D $59-$66; each addl $7; suites $100; under 18 free. Crib free. TV; cable (premium). Pool. Complimentary continental bkfst. Restaurant nearby. Ck-out noon. Meeting rms. Business servs avail. In-rm modem link. Sundries. Some refrigerators. Cr cds: A, C, D, DS, MC, V.

D ≈ ⊠ ⋒ SC

✔★ ★ **QUALITY INN.** 6045 Oakbrook Pkwy (30093), I-85 exit 37. 770/449-7322; FAX 770/368-1868. 108 rms, 2 story. S, D $49-$89; each addl $10; wkly rates; higher rates special events. Crib free. TV; cable. Pool. Complimentary continental bkfst. Complimentary coffee in rms. Restaurant adj open 24 hrs. Ck-out 11 am. Guest lndry. Business servs avail. In-rm modem link. Sundries. Refrigerators, microwaves avail. Cr cds: A, C, D, DS, ER, JCB, MC, V.

D ≈ ⊠ ⋒ SC

✔★ **RED ROOF INN.** 5171 Brook Hollow Pkwy (30071), I-85 exit 38. 770/448-8944; FAX 770/448-8955. 115 rms, 3 story. S $40.99; D $55.99-$59.99; each addl $7; under 18 free. Crib free. Pet accepted, some restrictions. TV; cable (premium). Complimentary coffee in lobby. Restaurant nearby. Ck-out noon. Sundries. Cr cds: A, C, D, DS, MC, V.

D ✔ ⊠ ⋒

Motor Hotels

★ ★ ★ **AMBERLEY SUITE HOTEL.** 5885 Oakbrook Pkwy (30093), I-85 exit 37. 770/263-0515; FAX 770/263-0185; res: 800/365-0659. 177 suites, 3 story. S, D $59-$139; under 18 free; wkend, wkly rates. Crib free. TV; cable (premium). Pool; whirlpool. Complimentary full bkfst. Restaurant 6:30 am-1:30 pm, 5-9 pm, Sat, Sun 7:30-10:30 am. Bar 5-11 pm, closed Fri, Sat. Ck-out noon. Coin lndry. Meeting rms. Business center. In-rm modem link. Valet serv. Sundries. Exercise equipt; sauna. Health club privileges. Refrigerators. Cr cds: A, C, D, DS, ER, MC, V.

D ≈ ⊀ ⊠ ⋒ SC ⊀

★ ★ **AMERISUITES.** (3390 Venture Parkway, Duluth 30096) 2 mi N on I-85, exit 40. 770/623-6800; FAX 770/623-0911; res: 800/833-1516. 114 suites, 6 story. S $99-$129; D $109-$139; higher rates special events. Crib avail. TV; cable (premium), VCR (movies $6). Pool. Complimentary continental bkfst. Complimentary coffee in rms. Restaurant opp 11 am-10 pm. Ck-out noon. Meeting rms. Business center. In-rm modem link. Exercise equipt. Health club privileges. Refrigerators, microwaves. Cr cds: A, C, D, DS, JCB, MC, V.

D ✔ ≈ ⊀ ⊠ ⋒ SC ⊀

★ ★ **BEST WESTERN BRADBURY SUITES.** (2060 Crescent Centre Blvd, Tucker 30084) 5 mi S to I-285 exit 28. 770/496-1070; FAX 770/939-9947. 113 suites, 6 story. Apr-Nov: S $76.95-$124.95; D $81.95-$135.95; under 15 free; higher rates special events; lower rates rest of yr. Crib free. TV; cable (premium). Pool; whirlpool. Complimentary full bkfst. Complimentary coffee in rms. Restaurant nearby. Ck-out noon. Coin lndry. Meeting rms. Business servs avail. In-rm modem link. Valet serv. Sundries. Refrigerators. Cr cds: A, C, D, DS, ER, JCB, MC, V.

D ≈ ⊠ ⋒ SC

Hotels

★ ★ ★ **ATLANTA MARRIOTT GWINNETT PLACE.** *(1775 Pleasant Hill Rd, Duluth 30096) Approx 6 mi NE via I-85 exit 40, then NW on Pleasant Hill Rd, adj to Gwinnett Mall.* 770/923-1775; FAX 770/923-0017. 426 rms, 8-17 story. S, D $149-$189; suites $225-$325; wkend rates. Crib free. TV; cable (premium). Indoor/outdoor pool; whirlpool, poolside serv. Restaurant 6:30 am-10 pm. Bar 5 pm-2 am; Sun to midnight; entertainment. Ck-out noon. Convention facilities. Business center. In-rm modem link. Lndry facilities. Gift shop. Covered parking. Exercise equipt; sauna. Some balconies. On 11 landscaped acres. Luxury level. Cr cds: A, D, DS, ER, JCB, MC, V.

D ≈ ⅄ ⅄ ⅄ SC ⅄

★ ★ ★ **HILTON NORTHEAST ATLANTA.** *5993 Peachtree Industrial Blvd (30092).* 770/447-4747; FAX 770/448-8853. 272 rms, 10 story. S, D $94-$144; each addl $10; suites $185-$295; family, wkend rates. TV; cable (premium). Indoor/outdoor pool; whirlpool, poolside serv. Restaurant 6:30 am-10 pm. Bar 11-12:30 am. Ck-out noon. Convention facilities. Business center. In-rm modem link. Gift shop. Golf privileges. Exercise equipt; sauna. Cr cds: A, C, D, DS, MC, V.

D ⅄ ≈ ⅄ ⅄ ⅄ SC ⅄

★ ★ ★ **HOLIDAY INN.** *(1075 Holcomb Bridge Rd, Roswell 30076) NW on Holcomb Bridge Rd.* 770/992-9600; FAX 770/993-6539. 173 rms, 7 story. S, D $119-$139; each addl $10; suites $139-$250; under 18 free; wkend rates. Crib free. TV; cable (premium). Pool. Complimentary coffee in lobby. Restaurant 6:30 am-10:30 pm. Bar noon-midnight. Ck-out noon. Meeting rms. Business servs avail. In-rm modem link. Exercise equipt. Health club privileges. Refrigerators avail. Cr cds: A, C, D, DS, JCB, MC, V.

D ≈ ⅄ ⅄ ⅄ SC

★ ★ ★ **HOLIDAY INN SELECT-PEACHTREE CORNERS.** *6050 Peachtree Industrial Blvd NW (30071).* 770/448-4400; FAX 770/840-7292. Web www.hiselect.com/atlantapeachtreecorners. 246 rms, 8 story. S $99-$139; D $109-$149; suites $250-$259; under 18 free; wkly, wkend rates. Crib free. TV; cable (premium), VCR avail. Indoor/outdoor pool; whirlpool. Restaurant 6:30 am-2 pm, 5:30-11 pm. Rm serv 6 am-midnight. Bar from 2 pm. Ck-out noon. Meeting rms. Business servs avail. In-rm modem link. Concierge. Exercise equipt. Some microwaves. Luxury level. Cr cds: A, C, D, DS, JCB, MC, V.

D ≈ ⅄ ⅄ ⅄ SC

★ ★ ★ **HOMEWOOD SUITES.** *(10775 Davis Dr, Alpharetta 30004) 8 mi NW on 400 exit 8.* 770/998-1622; FAX 770/998-7834. 112 kit. suites, 6 story. S $79-$109; D $89-$119; each addl $10; suites $79-$119; under 18 free; family rates; package plans. Crib free. Pet accepted. $50. TV; cable (premium), VCR avail. Complimentary continental bkfst. Complimentary coffee in rms. Restaurant nearby. Ck-out noon. Meeting rms. Business center. In-rm modem link. Gift shop. Coin lndry. Exercise equipt. Pool. Refrigerators, microwaves. Some balconies. Grills. Cr cds: A, D, DS, MC, V.

D ✈ ≈ ⅄ ⅄ ⅄ SC ⅄

★ ★ ★ **MARRIOTT.** *475 Technology Pkwy (30092), in Technology Park.* 770/263-8558; FAX 770/263-0766. 222 rms, 6 story. S $124; suites $200-$250; under 12 free. Crib free. TV; cable (premium). Indoor pool. Restaurant 6:30-9 am, 11 am-2 pm, 5-10 pm. Bar 4 pm-midnight. Ck-out noon. Meeting rms. Business servs avail. In-rm modem link. Concierge. Gift shop. Exercise equipt; sauna. Refrigerators avail. Cr cds: A, C, D, DS, JCB, MC, V.

D ≈ ⅄ ⅄ ⅄ SC

Restaurants

★ ★ **BROOKWOOD GRILL.** *7050 Jimmy Carter Blvd (30092).* 770/449-0102. Hrs: 11 am-10:30 pm; Fri, Sat to 11 pm; Sun to 10 pm. Closed Thanksgiving, Dec 25. Bar. Semi-a la carte: lunch, dinner $7.95-$18.95. Child's meals. Specializes in hickory-grilled steaks & chicken,

baby back ribs, fresh seafood. Own desserts. Outdoor dining. Cr cds: A, C, D, DS, MC, V.

D ⅄

★ ★ **DICK & HARRY'S.** *(1570 Holcomb Bridge Rd, Roswell 30076) in Holcomb Woods Village shopping center.* 770/641-8757. Hrs: 11:30 am-2 pm, 5:30-10 pm; Fri to 11:30 pm; Sat 5:30-11:30 pm. Closed Sun; major hols. Res accepted. Contemporary Amer menu. Bar. Semi-a la carte: lunch $6-$12, dinner $12-$20. Child's meals. Specialties: crab cakes, barbecued salmon, emu. Valet parking Fri, Sat. Outdoor dining. Casual dining. Cr cds: A, C, D, DS, MC, V.

D

★ ★ **DOMINICK'S.** *95 S Peachtree St (30071).* 770/449-1611. Hrs: 11:30 am-3 pm, 5-10 pm; Sat from 5 pm; Sun 5-9 pm. Closed Dec 25. Res accepted. Italian menu. Bar. Semi-a la carte: lunch $5.50-$21.50, dinner $11-$21.50. Child's meals. Specialties: Dominick's chicken, spedini bread, Dominick's ravioli. Parking. Originally a hardware store; original brick, original tin tiled ceiling; 175 yrs old. Cr cds: A, D, DS, MC, V.

D ⅄

★ ★ **THE GECKO.** *(11950 Jones Bridge Rd, Suite 112, Alpharetta 30202) in Seven Winds Shopping Center.* 770/772-6050. Hrs: 11:30 am-2 pm, 5-10 pm; Sat 5-11 pm; Sun 5-9 pm. Closed Mon; Jan 1, Thanksgiving, Dec 25. Res accepted. Continental menu. Bar. Semi-a la carte: lunch $6.95-$12.95, dinner $15-$24. Child's meals. Specialties: lobster bisque, black angus New York strip steak, sautéed grouper with jumbo lump crab. Jazz Fri, Sat eves. Parking. Outdoor dining. Contemporary decor. Cr cds: A, D, DS, MC, V.

D ⅄

★ ★ ★ **HI LIFE.** *3380 Holcomb Bridge Rd (30092), in Corners Court Shopping Center.* 770/409-0101. E-mail hilife@mindspring.com. Hrs: 11 am-10 pm; Wed-Fri to 11 pm; Sat 4 pm-midnight. Closed Jan 1, Thanksgiving, Dec 25. Res accepted. Bar. Wine list. Semi-a la carte: lunch $4-$15, dinner $4-$22. Child's meals. Specialties: Maine lobster, lemon grass & shellfish stew, tuna poke. Parking. Outdoor dining. Contemporary American decor. Cr cds: A, D, MC, V.

D

★ ★ **KILLER CREEK CHOP HOUSE.** *(1700 Mansell Rd, Alpharetta 30004) 8 mi NW on GA 400 exit 8.* 770/649-0064. Hrs: 5-11 pm; Fri to midnight; Sat 4 pm-midnight; Sun 4-11 pm. Closed major hols. Bar. Semi-a la carte: dinner $12.95-$24.95. Child's meals. Specializes in steak, chops, seafood. Valet parking. Outdoor dining. Features an open kitchen. Cr cds: A, D, DS, MC, V.

D ⅄

★ ★ ★ **LICKSKILLET FARM.** *(1380 Old Roswell Rd, Roswell 30077) Approx 5 mi NW on Holcomb Bridge Rd (US 140).* 770/475-6484. Hrs: 11:30 am-2 pm, 6-9 pm; Mon 6-10 pm; Sat 5:30-10 pm; Sun 5:30-9 pm; Sun brunch 10:30 am-2 pm. Closed July 4, Dec 25. Res accepted. Continental menu. Bar. Semi-a la carte: lunch $7.95-$9.95, dinner $14.95-$22.95. Sun brunch $19.95. Specialties: Australian rack of lamb, penne salmon, steak. Pianist Sun brunch. Parking. Outdoor dining overlooking landscaped grounds that feature herb and flower gardens. 1846 farm house furnished with many antiques; original fireplaces. Family-owned. Totally nonsmoking. Cr cds: A, D, DS, MC, V.

★ ★ ★ **SERENADES.** *(10595 Old Alabama Rd Connector, Alpharetta 30202) GA 400, exit 8.* 770/552-6030. Web www.serenades.net. Hrs: 6:30-11 pm; Sun 11:30 am-2:30 pm, 6:30-11 pm. Closed Mon; most major hols. Res accepted. Eclectic menu. Bar. Semi-a la carte: dinner $17.95-$32. Specializes in seafood, game, pasta. Parking. Elegant atmosphere. Cr cds: A, C, D, DS, MC, V.

D ⅄

✔ ★ **SOUTHSTREET.** *(2750 Buford Hwy, Duluth 30096) 5 mi NE on Buford Hwy.* 770/495-0997. Hrs: 11 am-10 pm; Sun from 10 am; Sun brunch 10 am-3 pm. Closed Thanksgiving, Dec 25. Contemporary southern menu. Bar. Semi-a la carte: lunch $4.95-$8.95, dinner $5.95-$15.95. Sun brunch $5.95-$8.95. Child's meals. Specialties: grilled chicken with blackberry barbecue sauce, reuben sandwich, grilled pepper-cured pork loin. Parking. Outdoor dining. Totally nonsmoking. Cr cds: A, D, DS, MC, V.

D

★ ★ ★ **VAN GOGH'S.** *(70 W Crossville Rd, Roswell 30075)* Approx 5 mi NW on Holcomb Bridge Rd (US 140). 770/993-1156. Hrs: 11:30 am-midnight; Sun 5-10 pm. Closed some major hols. Res accepted. Bar. Wine list. Semi-a la carte: lunch $4.95-$13.95, dinner $13.95-$25.95. Child's meals. Specializes in seafood, grilled portobello mushrooms, crab cakes. Own desserts. Valet parking. European ambiance. Cr cds: A, DS, MC, V.

D

Ocmulgee National Monument (D-3)

(2 mi E of Macon on US 80, Alt 129)

Ocmulgee, the most scientifically excavated of the South's major Native American sites, shows evidence of 12,000 years of settlement, including 6 successive occupations from at least 10,000 B.C. to 1825. The major remains consist of 9 ceremonial mounds, a funeral mound and a restored ceremonial earthlodge of the early Mississippian Period (A.D. 900 to 1100).

Exhibits and dioramas in the museum depict this sequence: Paleo-Indian Period, from more than 12,000 years ago, when Ice Age hunters trailing mammoth and other now-extinct game arrived using stone-tipped spears. During the Archaic Period, after the Ice Age ended, hunter-gathering people hunted small game and supplemented their diet with mussels, fish, seeds, berries and nuts. They made polished stone tools and camped along the streams. By 2000 B.C., crude pottery was fashioned. During the Woodland Period (beginning 1000 B.C.), some plants were cultivated, villages were larger and mounds were being built. Pottery was stamped with elaborate designs carved into wooden paddles. The Early Mississippian Period began about A.D. 900, when invaders brought cultivated corn, beans, squash and tobacco to the Macon Plateau. They built a large town with burial and temple mounds and circular, earth-covered council chambers. This ceremonial center declined around A.D. 1100. Late Mississippian Period villagers of the Lamar Culture combined elements of the Mississippian and older Woodland ways of life. They may have been direct ancestors of the historic Creek who lived here when Europeans first settled Georgia. The Creek soon became involved in the struggle between France, Spain and England for possession of the New World.

Exhibits and dioramas in the museum show the Native American from earliest origins to his removal to Oklahoma in the early 1800s. Great Temple Mound, more than 40 feet high, is the largest in the park. An audio program is conducted in the restored earthlodge, which was the Mississippian council chamber. (Daily; closed Jan 1, Dec 25) For information, contact the Superintendent, 1207 Emery Hwy, Macon 31217; 912/752-8257.

Okefenokee Swamp (G-4)

(See also Waycross)

(In SE corner of state, S of Waycross, E of Valdosta)

Web www.fws.gov

Information Refuge Manager, Rte 2, Box 3330, Folkston 31537; 912/496-7836.

One of the largest preserved freshwater wetlands in the United States, the Okefenokee Swamp encompasses more than 700 square miles, stretching an average of 25 miles in width and 35 miles in length. The swamp's southern border is beyond the Florida line. Called "land of trembling earth" by Native Americans, its lakes of dark brown water, lush with moss-draped cypress, are headwaters for the Suwannee and St Marys rivers. The swamp embraces vast marshes, termed "prairies," which comprise 60,000 acres.

What to See and Do

Okefenokee National Wildlife Refuge occupies more than 90 percent of the swamp region and harbors bears, deer, bobcats, alligators and aquatic birds. Naturalists have discovered many rare plants on the swamp floor, which has been described as "the most beautiful and fantastic landscape in the world." The cypress stand mile after mile, their dense formations broken by watery "prairies" or covered by deposits of peat on the swamp's floor ranging to 15 ft in thickness. It is possible to cause small trees and shrubs to shake by stamping on the "trembling earth"; these trees take root in the crust of peat beds and never reach the solid bottom. Such forests are interspersed with varied swamp vegetation. The bay, one of the swamp's most distinctive trees, blooms from May to October, producing a white flower in contrast to its rich evergreen foliage. Aquatic flowers, such as yellow spatterdock and white water lily, blend with pickerel-weed and golden-club and swamp iris in the spring. The swamp is also the home of the sandhill crane and round-tailed muskrat. (Hrs vary with season; phone for details) Phone 912/496-7836. Per vehicle ¢¢

Okefenokee Swamp Park. This park, located on Cowhouse Island, has a serpentarium and reptile shows. Guided boat tours (fee); canoe rentals. Cypress boardwalk into swamp to 90-ft-high observation tower. Picnicking. Interpretive centers, video. (Daily) No overnight facilities. Camping available at nearby Laura S. Walker State Park (see WAYCROSS). Phone 912/283-0583. Admission fee ¢¢¢

Stephen C. Foster State Park. Park offers access to Billy's Lake, Minnie's Lake and Big Water (daily during daylight hours without a guide). Fishing; boating (rentals, basin, dock, ramp), canoeing (rentals), sightseeing boat tours. Nature trails. Picnicking, concession. Camping, cabins. Museum. Standard rms, fees. Contact 912/637-5274.

Suwannee Canal Recreation Area. Recreation Area provides entry to the Chesser, Grand, Mizell and Chase prairies, where small lakes and "gator holes" offer some of the nation's finest bird watching. Area also has restored swamp homestead and guided swamp tours. Boating (ramp, boat and motor rentals), canoeing, guided boat tours. Nature trails, boardwalk (3/4 mi) with observation tower. Picnicking. Visitor center. (Daily; closed Dec 25) Fees for some activities. Phone 912/496-7836. Per vehicle ¢¢

Wilderness canoeing. There are 7 overnight stops and trips avail from 2 to 5 days (3-day limit Mar & Apr); wooden platforms for campsites. March to May and October through early November are most popular times. By advance reservation (two months) and special permit from Refuge Manager. Phone 912/496-3331. Fee per person per night ¢¢¢

Perry (E-3)

(See also Andersonville, Cordele, Macon)

Pop 9,452 **Elev** 337 ft **Area code** 912 **Zip** 31069 **Web** www.perryga.com

Information Perry Area Convention & Visitors Bureau, 101 General Courtney Hodges Blvd, PO Box 1619; 912/988-8000.

The early-blooming wildflowers and trees of March and April have made Perry a favorite stopover place for spring motorists. The town is full of stately houses and historical churches. Perry is known as the "Crossroads of Georgia" because of its location near the geographic center of the state.

What to See and Do

Massee Lane Gardens. Ten-acre camellia garden reaches height of bloom between November and March; large greenhouse, Japanese garden, rose garden. Colonial-style headquarters contains more than 300 sculptures of Boehm and other porcelains, other items. Headquarters include the Annabelle Lundy Fetterman Educational Museum; exhibition hall (rare books; porcelain); auditorium with presentation on history of gardens; gift shop. Buildings (Nov-Mar, daily; rest of yr, Mon-Fri); grounds (daily). 14 mi W on GA 127 to Marshallville, then 3 mi N on GA 49. Phone 912/967-2722 or -2358. ¢¢

⭐ **The Andersonville Trail.** Along drive are American Camellia Society gardens, two state parks, antebellum houses and Andersonville National Historic Site. For information contact the Chamber of Commerce. A 75-mi loop drive from Perry to Cordele (see).

Annual Events

Mossy Creek Barnyard Festival. Deep Piney Woods, N on I-75, exit 43A, 3 mi E. Semiannual event with craftsmen, artists, entertainment and demonstrations. Phone 912/922-8265. 2 days late Apr & 2 days late Oct.

Old Fashioned Christmas at the Crossroads. Community Christmas tree, parade, candlelight service. Dec.

Motels

★ ★ **COMFORT INN.** 1602 Sam Nunn Blvd. 912/987-7710; FAX 912/987-2624. 102 rms, 2 story, 12 suites. S, D $45-$80; each addl $5; suites $69-$90; under 18 free. Crib free. TV; cable (premium). Indoor pool; whirlpool. Complimentary continental bkfst. Restaurant nearby. Ck-out 11 am. Coin lndry. Meeting rm. Business servs avail. In-rm modem link. Valet serv. Sundries. Exercise equipt; sauna. Refrigerators; some wet bars. Cr cds: A, C, D, DS, JCB, MC, V.

🅳 ≈ 🏃 ≈ 🐾 SC

✔★ ★ **DAYS INN.** 102 Valley Dr, US 341 at I-75 exit 43. 912/987-2142; FAX 912/987-0468. 80 rms, 2 story. S, D $41-$52; each addl $5; under 18 free. Crib free. TV; cable. Pool; wading pool. Complimentary coffee. Complimentary continental bkfst. Restaurant nearby. Ck-out noon. Business servs avail. Private patios, balconies. Cr cds: A, C, D, DS, JCB, MC, V.

≈ ≈ 🐾 SC

✔★ ★ **HOLIDAY INN.** 200 Valley Dr, US 341 I-75 exit 43. 912/987-3313; FAX 912/988-8269. 203 rms, 2 story. S, D $54; under 18 free. Crib free. TV; cable (premium). Pool. Complimentary coffee in lobby. Restaurant 6-10 am, 11 am-2 pm, 5-10 pm. Rm serv. Bar 4:30 pm-12:30 am. Coin lndry. Meeting rms. Business servs avail. Valet serv. Sundries. Exercise equipt. Some refrigerators. Cr cds: A, C, D, DS, JCB, MC, V.

🅳 ≈ 🏃 ≈ 🐾 SC

✔★ ★ **NEW PERRY.** 800 Main St. 912/987-1000. 39 hotel rms, 3 story, 17 motel rms. S $28-$45; D $39-$49; each addl $2. Crib $2. Pet accepted; $5/day. TV; cable. Pool. Restaurant (see NEW PERRY). Ck-out noon. Meeting rms. Built in 1925; landscaped grounds. Cr cds: A, MC, V.

🐾 ≈ 🐾

★ ★ ★ **QUALITY INN.** 1504 Sam Nunn Blvd, US 341 at I-75, exit 43. 912/987-1345; FAX 912/987-5875. 70 rms, 1-2 story. No elvtr. S $35-$55; D $45-$55; each addl $5; suites $55-$75; under 18 free. Crib free. TV; cable. Pool; wading pool. Complimentary continental bkfst. Restaurant 11:30 am-1 pm, 5-10 pm. Ck-out 11 am. Business servs avail. Some refrigerators. Landscaped gardens. On 15 acres. Cr cds: A, C, D, DS, MC, V.

🅳 ≈ ≈ 🐾 SC

✔★ ★ **RAMADA LIMITED.** 100 Marketplace Dr, I-75 exit 43. 912/987-8400; FAX 912/987-3133. 60 rms, 2 story. S $44; D $48; each addl $4; under 18 free; higher rates special events. Crib avail. Pet accepted, some restrictions; $5. TV; cable (premium). Complimentary continental bkfst. Restaurant adj 6 am-10 pm. Ck-out 11 am. Meeting rm. In-rm modem link. Valet serv. Golf privileges. Indoor pool; whirlpool. Bathrm phones; many refrigerators, microwaves. Cr cds: A, D, DS, MC, V.

🅳 🐾 🏃 ≈ ≈ 🐾 SC

✔★ ★ **TRAVELODGE.** 100 Westview Lane, I-75 exit 42. 912/987-7355; FAX 912/987-7250. 62 rms, 2 story. May-Oct: S $39; D $47; each addl $5; suites $52; under 17 free; higher rates fair wk. Crib free. TV; cable.

Pool. Complimentary continental bkfst. Complimentary coffee in rms. Restaurant adj 24 hrs. Ck-out 11 am. Coin lndry. Business servs avail. In-rm modem link. Refrigerator. Cr cds: A, C, D, DS, MC, V.

🅳 ≈ ≈ 🐾 SC

Inn

✔★ ★ **THE EVANS-CANTRELL HOUSE.** (300 College St, Fort Valley 31030) 12 mi NW on US 341. 912/822-0611; res: 888/923-0611; FAX 912/822-9925. 4 rms, 2 story, 1 suite. S, D $65-$75; suite $95. Children over 10 yrs only. TV; cable (premium). Complimentary full bkfst. Ck-out 11 am, ck-in 3 pm. Luggage handling. Coincierge serv. Coin lndry. Built in 1916; Mr. Evans was known as the "Peach King" in early 1920s. Cr cds: A, DS, MC, V.

≈ 🐾

Restaurant

✔★ ★ **NEW PERRY.** (See New Perry Motel) 912/987-1000; res: 800/877-3779. Hrs: 7-10 am, 11:30 am-2:30 pm, 5:30-9 pm; Sun, hols from 11 am. Res accepted. Semi-a la carte: bkfst $3.75-$5.50, lunch $6.60-$7.25, dinner $9.85-$12.85. Specializes in fried chicken, country ham. Overlooks pool, gardens. Cr cds: A, MC, V.

🅳

Pine Mountain (Harris Co) (D-1)

(See also Columbus, La Grange)

Pop 875 **Elev** 860 ft **Area code** 706 **Zip** 31822

What to See and Do

⭐ **Callaway Gardens.** This distinctive public garden and resort, consisting of 14,000 acres of gardens, woodlands, lakes, recreation areas and wildlife, was conceived by prominent textile industrialist Cason J. Callaway to be "the finest garden on earth since Adam was a boy." Originally, in the 1930s, the family's weekend vacation spot, Callaway and his wife Virginia expanded the area and opened it to the public in 1952. Today, Callaway Gardens is home to more than 50 varieties of butterflies, 230 varieties of birds and more than 100 species of plantlife, including the rare plunifolia azalea, indigenous to the area. The complex offers swimming, boating and other water recreation around 13 lakes, including 175-acre Mountain Creek Lake and the white sand beach of Robin Lake; 23 mi of roads and paths for hiking or jogging; 63 holes of golf (a 9-hole and three 18-hole courses); 17 lighted tennis courts and 2 indoor racquetball courts; skeet and trapshooting ranges, hunting for deer or quail on 1,000-acre preserve; picnicking, country store; cottages, villas and resort (see), dining pavilion; and 5,000-ft paved and lighted runway and terminal. On US 27. Also on garden grounds are

Cecil B. Day Butterfly Center. An 8,000-sq-ft, glass-enclosed conservatory housing up to 1,000 free-flying butterflies, as well as ground pheasants; exotic plants and waterfalls.

Ida Cason Callaway Memorial Chapel, a woodland chapel patterned after rural wayside chapels of the 16th and 17th centuries; organ concerts year round. **Pioneer Log Cabin** is an authentic 18th-century structure in which life of early Georgia settlers is demonstrated.

Gardens (daily); Robin Lake Beach (June-Labor Day, daily; wkends; seperate fee includes entrance to gardens). Special events include Florida State University Circus at Robin Lake Beach (June-Labor Day); rates may be higher during special events wkends. Bus tours of gardens available. Phone 706/663-2281 or 800/225-5292. ¢¢¢¢

John S. Sibley Horticultural Center. Five acres displaying unique collections of exotic and native plants, seasonal flowerbeds and lush green lawns; also sculpture garden and 22-ft waterfall.

Mr. Cason's Vegetable Garden. Vegetable garden (7½ acres) that produces hundreds of varieties of fruits, vegetables and herbs; setting for "Victory Garden South" television show.

Franklin D. Roosevelt State Park. One of the largest parks in the state system has many historic buildings and King's Gap Indian trail. Swimming pool; fishing. Hiking, bridle & nature trails. Picnicking. Camping, cottages. Standard hrs, fees. 5 mi SE off jct US 27, GA 190. Contact Superintendent, 2970 Hwy 190E; 706/663-4858.

✪ **Little White House Historic Site.** Cottage in which President Franklin D. Roosevelt died on Apr 12, 1945, is preserved as it was on the day he died. On display is original furniture, memorabilia and the portrait on which Elizabeth Shoumatoff was working when the president was stricken with a massive cerebral hemorrhage. A film about Roosevelt's life at Warm Springs and in Georgia is shown at the F.D. Roosevelt Museum and Theater. Picnic area, snack bar. (Daily; closed Jan 1, Thanksgiving, Dec 25) Approx 15 mi E on GA 18 & GA 194, then ½ mi S on GA 85W in Warm Springs. Phone 706/655-5870. ¢¢

Motels

★ ★ **DAVIS INN.** 5585 State Park Rd, jct US 27S & State Park Rd. 706/663-2522; res: 888/346-2668; FAX 706/663-4726. 23 rms, 1-2 story, 10 kit. units, 15 condos (1-2 bedrm). S, D $70-$80; each addl $10; kit. units, condos $90-$185; under 12 free; wkends (2-day min). TV; cable (premium). Swimming privileges. Complimentary coffee in lobby. Restaurant nearby. Ck-out noon. Meeting rms. Lighted tennis privileges. Golf privileges, pro, putting green, driving range. Health club privileges. Picnic tables, grills. Adj Callaway Gardens. No cr cds accepted.

🛉 🏃 🖼 🏊

★ **VALLEY INN.** (14420 US 27, Hamilton 31811) 6 mi S on US 27. 706/628-4454; res: 800/944-9393. E-mail valley-inn-resort@juno.com. 20 rms, 4 kits. Mar-Dec; S, D $55-$72; each addl $12; kit. cottages $105-$120; under 6 free; wkly rates; lower rates rest of yr. Crib $4. TV; cable. Pool. Playground. Coffee in rms. Ck-out noon. Sundries. Tennis privileges. 63-hole golf privileges. Health club privileges. Picnic tables, grills. On 22-acre lake with flat-bottom boats. Cr cds: MC, V.

🗅 🏖 🛉 🏃 🏊 🔥

Resort

★ ★ **CALLAWAY GARDENS.** US 27, S on US 27, 1 mi S of GA 18. 706/663-2281; FAX 706/663-8114; res: 800/225-5292. E-mail reservations@callawaygardens.com; web www.callawaygardens.com. 349 rms, 1-3 story, 155 cottages (2-bedrm), 49 villas. Mid-Mar-mid-Apr & mid-Nov-late Dec: S, D $111-$121; each addl $15; suites $154-$200; luxury villas (1-4 bedrm) $136-$350; cottages $111-$184; under 18 free; MAP rates, golf, tennis plans; lower rates rest of yr. Crib free. TV; cable. 3 pools; wading pool, lifeguard in summer. Playground. Supervised child's activities (June-mid-Aug); ages 6 months-18 yrs. 8 dining rms 6:30 am-10 pm (also see GEORGIA ROOM). Box lunches, snack bar. Bar 5 pm-1 am, closed Sun. Ck-out noon, ck-in 4 pm. Grocery 1 mi. Coin lndry. Package store nearby. Convention facilities. Business center. Bellhops. Valet serv. Concierge. Local airport transportation. Lighted tennis, pro. Three 18-hole, one 9-hole golf, greens fee $75-$110 (incl cart), pros. Swimming, private beach, waterskiing. Paddle boats, sailboats. Bicycles avail; 7-mi bicycle trail. Horseback riding nearby. Skeet & trap shooting. Soc dir; entertainment, movies. Rec rm. Exercise equipt. Refrigerators avail. Private patios, balconies. Picnic tables, grills. On 14,000 acres; butterfly conservatory on site. Cr cds: A, D, DS, MC, V.

🗅 🏖 🛉 🏃 🏊 🕴 🏂 🎿 🚵 SC 🎣

Restaurants

★ ★ **THE BULLOCH HOUSE.** (US 27, Warm Springs 31830) 15 mi E on GA 18, then S on GA 85. 706/655-9068. Hrs: 11 am-2:30 pm; Fri, Sat also 5-8:30 pm. Closed most major hols. Res accepted. Semi-a la carte: lunch $4.50, dinner $6.95-$8.95. Buffet: lunch $5.95, dinner $7.95. Child's meals. Specializes in Southern cooking. Salad bar. Parking. Outdoor dining. House built 1892; original floors and fireplaces. Totally nonsmoking. Cr cds: A, DS, MC, V.

🗅

★ ★ ★ **GEORGIA ROOM.** (See Callaway Gardens Resort) 706/663-2281. Web www.callawaygardens.com. Hrs: 6-10 pm. Closed Sun. Res accepted. New Southern menu. Serv bar. Wine list. A la carte entrees: dinner $18-$28. Specializes in sautéed veal chop, breast of duck confit. Own baking. Cr cds: A, D, DS, MC, V.

🗅

★ ★ ★ **OAK TREE VICTORIAN RESTAURANT.** (US 27, Hamilton 31811) 5 mi S of Callaway Gardens. 706/628-4218. Hrs: 6-9:30 pm. Closed Sun; major hols. Res accepted. Continental menu. Serv bar. Wine cellar. Semi-a la carte: dinner $7.95-$23.95. Specializes in veal pirozhki, onion soup, prime rib. Victorian house (1871). Totally nonsmoking. Cr cds: A, C, D, DS, MC, V.

🗅

✔★ **VICTORIAN TEA ROOM.** (Broad St, Warm Springs 31830) 15 mi E on GA 18, then S on GA 85. 706/655-2319. Hrs: 11:30 am-3:30 pm; Fri, Sat to 8 pm. Closed Mon; Jan 1, Thanksgiving, Dec 25. Semi-a la carte: lunch $2.95-$5.95. Buffet: lunch $5.95-$6.95; dinner (Fri, Sat) $6.96-$7.96. Child's meals. Specializes in grilled chicken sandwiches, salads, desserts. Salad bar. In 1906 building; many antiques. Totally nonsmoking. Cr cds: MC, V.

🗅

Plains
(see Americus)

Rome (B-1)

(See also Calhoun, Cartersville)

Founded 1834 **Pop** 30,326 **Elev** 605 ft **Area code** 706 **Zip** 30161 **E-mail** goromega@romegeorgia.com **Web** www.romegeorgia.com

Information Greater Rome Convention & Visitors Bureau, 402 Civic Center Hill, PO Box 5823, 30162-5823; 706/295-5576 or 800/444-1834.

According to legend, five men, seven hills, three rivers, a spring and a hat were the equation that led to the founding of Rome, Georgia. The seven hills suggested that "Rome" be one of the names drawn from the hat by the five founders, two of whom had discovered the site at the junction of three rivers.

Nobles' Foundry Lathe, one of the few that produced Confederate cannons, is on display on Civic Center Hill and is a reminder of Sherman's occupation. Rome fell despite the frantic ride of Georgia's Paul Revere, a mail carrier named John E. Wisdom, who rode 67 miles by horse from Gadsden, Alabama, in 11 hours to warn "the Yankees are coming."

What to See and Do

Berry College (1902). (1,800 students). Campus, forest preserves and 100 buildings comprise more than 26,000 acres, one of the largest campuses in the world. Old overshot waterwheel is one of the largest in the world. On US 27. Phone 706/291-1883. Close to campus is

Oak Hill and the Martha Berry Museum. Oak Hill is the antebellum plantation house of Martha Berry, the founder of Berry College. Manicured lawns, formal gardens and nature trails. The museum is located on the grounds of Oak Hill and serves as the reception center for visitors. (Mon-Sat & Sun afternoons) Veterans Memorial Hwy & US 27. Phone 706/291-1883. ¢¢

Capitoline Wolf Statue. Replica of the famous statue of Romulus and Remus in Rome, Italy. Presented by that city as a gift to Rome, Georgia in 1929. In front of City Hall.

Chieftains Museum. Eighteenth-century house of prominent Cherokee leader Major Ridge; artifacts with emphasis on Cherokee history. (Tues-Sat; closed major hols) 501 Riverside Pkwy, N off US 27. Phone 706/291-9494. ¢¢

The Old Town Clock (1871) and Clocktower Museum. Surmounting 104-ft high water tower of brick and superstructure of cypress wood, clock face is 9 ft in diameter. Bronze striking bell is 32 inches high, 40 inches in diameter at rim. Tower was built to hold the city's water supply and is located atop one of Rome's seven hills. Now the water tank houses a museum with artifacts from Rome's history. (Apr-Nov, wkends; also by appt) Phone 706/236-4416.

Annual Event

Heritage Holidays. River rides, parade, tours, wagon train, arts & crafts fair, music. Mid-Oct.

Motor Hotels

✔★ ★ **DAYS INN.** *840 Turner McCall Blvd, at Broad St (US 27/GA 20).* 706/295-0400; FAX 706/295-0400, ext. 255. 107 rms, 5 story. S $46; D $51; each addl $5; suites $90-$120; under 12 free. Crib free. TV; cable (premium). Pool. Complimentary continental bkfst. Ck-out 11 am. Coin lndry. Meeting rms. Business servs avail. Valet serv (Mon-Fri). Cr cds: A, C, D, DS, MC, V.

🄳 ⊵ 🛉 🐾 SC

★ ★ **HOLIDAY INN-SKYTOP.** *US 411E, 2 mi E of town center.* 706/295-1100; FAX 706/291-1100. 200 rms, 2 story. S $59.95; D $65.95; each addl $6; under 18 free. Crib free. Pet accepted, some restrictions. TV; cable (premium). Indoor/outdoor pool; whirlpool, poolside serv. Restaurant 6:30 am-1:30 pm, 5:30-10 pm. Rm serv. Bar noon-1:30 am, Sat to midnight; entertainment Tues-Sat. Ck-out noon. Coin lndry. Meeting rms. Business center. Bellhops. Valet serv. Sundries. 18-hole golf privileges, pro. Exercise equipt; sauna. Cr cds: A, C, D, DS, JCB, MC, V.

🄳 ⊵ 🛉 ✈ ⊵ 🏌 ⊵ 🐾 SC 🏃

✔★ **RAMADA INN.** *707 Turner McCall Blvd (US 27/GA 20) (30165).* 706/232-0444; res: 800/272-6232; FAX 706/232-3872. 155 rms, 2 story. S $60; D $65; each addl $5; under 18 free. Crib free. TV; cable (premium). Pool. Restaurant open 24 hrs. Ck-out noon. Free lndry facilities. Meeting rms. Business servs avail. Valet serv. Exercise equipt. Cr cds: A, C, D, DS, ER, JCB, MC, V.

⊵ 🏃 ✈ ⊵ 🐾 SC

St Simons Island (G-6)

(See also Brunswick, Golden Isles, Jekyll Island, Sea Island)

Pop 12,026 **Elev** 0-30 ft **Area code** 912 **Zip** 31522 **E-mail** bgislesvisitorsb@technonet.com **Web** bgislesvisitorsb.com

Information St Simons Visitors Center, 530 B Beachview Dr, Neptune Park; 800/933-2627.

One of Georgia's Golden Isles (see), St Simons Island has been under five flags: Spanish, French, British, United States and Confederate States of America. Fragments of each culture remain.

John and Charles Wesley preached under St Simons' oaks before a church was built at Frederica, and later Aaron Burr spent a month at Hampton's Point after killing Alexander Hamilton in a duel. St Simons' plantations flourished and were noted for the luxurious and sporting life of planters from about 1800 to the Civil War. Cotton and slavery collapsed after Sherman's forces razed the estates. Former slave quarters remained; inhabitants turned to fishing and garden crops for subsistence as St Simons was nearly forgotten until the 20th century.

What to See and Do

Coastal Alliance for the Arts. Exhibitions of works by regional artists, traveling exhibits, lectures. (Daily exc Sun; closed most major hols) 319 Mallory St. Phone 912/638-8770. **Free.**

Cumberland Island National Seashore (see). S, off the coast.

Fort Frederica National Monument (see). N end of island.

Gascoigne Bluff. This is a low-wooded, shell-covered bank named for Captain James Gascoigne, commander of HMS *Hawk*, which convoyed the two ships bringing settlers (1736). Great live oaks cut here were used to build first US Navy vessels, including the *Constitution* ("Old Ironsides") (1794). St Simons Marina is open to the public. Where the bridge crosses the Frederica River, SW side of island.

Museum of Coastal History. Housed in restored 1872 lightkeeper's house; exhibits on history of St Simons lighthouse and Golden Isles. (Daily; closed most hols) 101 12th St. Phone 912/638-4666. ¢¢ Includes

    St Simons Lighthouse. The original lighthouse (1810), which was 75 ft high, was destroyed by Confederate troops in 1861 to prevent it from guiding Union invaders onto the island. The present lighthouse, 104 ft high, has been in continuous operation, except during wartime, since 1872. Visitors may climb to the top. S end of island.

Annual Events

Homes & Gardens Tour. Tour of houses and gardens on St Simons Island and Sea Island. Varies each yr. Phone 912/638-3166. Mid-Mar.

Sunshine Festival. Neptune Park. Juried arts & crafts exhibits; food; fireworks on July 4. Wkend closest to July 4.

Georgia Sea Island Festival. Neptune Park. Traditional crafts and music. Phone 912-638-9014. 3rd wkend Aug.

Golden Isles Art Festival. Neptune Park. Juried arts and crafts exhibits, demonstrations, entertainment, food. Mid-Oct.

Motels

★ ★ **DAYS INN.** *1701 Frederica Rd.* 912/634-0660; FAX 912/638-7115. 101 rms, 2 story. Mar-Sept: S, D $89; each addl $10; under 12 free; lower rates rest of yr. Crib free. TV; cable (premium). Pool. Complimentary continental bkfst. Complimentary coffee in rms. Restaurant adj open 24 hrs. Ck-out noon. Meeting rms. Business servs avail. Bicycle rentals. Refrigerators, microwaves. Cr cds: A, D, DS, MC, V.

🄳 ⊵ 🐾 SC

★ ★ **ISLAND INN.** *301 Main St, in Plantation Village.* 912/638-7805; res: 800/673-6323. Web www.stsimonsdestinations.com. 74 units, 2 story, 12 kits. May-Sept: S, D $76-$96; each addl $10; under $86-$96; under 18 free; golf packages; lower rates rest of yr. Crib free. TV; cable. Pool; whirlpool. Playground. Complimentary continental bkfst. Ck-out 11 am. Business servs avail. Health club privileges. Cr cds: A, DS, MC, V.

🄳 ⊵ 🐾 SC

✔★ **QUEEN'S COURT.** *437 Kings Way.* 912/638-8459; FAX 912/638-0054. 23 rms, 2 story. S $50; D $56; each addl $3-$4; suites $64; kit. units $72. TV; cable. Pool. Restaurant nearby. Ck-out 11 am. Some refrigerators. Cr cds: MC, V.

⊵ 🔥

★ **SEA GATE INN.** *1014 Ocean Blvd.* 912/638-8661; FAX 912/638-4932. Web www.travelbase.com/destinations/st-simons/seagate. 48 units, 2-4 story, 16 kits. Early Mar-Sept: S, D $60-$130; each addl $7; suites $80-$320; kit. units $70-$320; under 10 free; lower rates rest of yr. Crib free. TV; cable. Pool; wading pool. Complimentary continental bkfst. Ck-out noon. Lawn games. Some refrigerators; microwaves avail. Balconies. On beach. Cr cds: A, MC, V.

⊵ 🔥

Hotel

★ ★ ★ **KING & PRINCE BEACH AND GOLF RESORT.** *201 Arnold Rd.* 912/638-3631; FAX 912/634-1720; res: 800/342-0212. Web www.kingandprince.com. 184 units, 4 story. Mar-early Nov: S, D $120-$160; kit. villas $275-$380; higher rates wkends; lower rates rest of yr. Crib free. TV; cable (premium), VCR avail. 5 pools, 1 indoor; whirlpool, poolside dining (May-Sept). Coffee in rms. Restaurant 7-10:30 am, 11:30 am-10 pm. Bar 11 am-midnight; Sun 1-9 pm. Ck-out 11 am. Meeting rms. Business servs avail. Airport transportation. 4 tennis courts. 18-hole golf, greens fee $55, pro. Exercise equipt. Some refrigerators. Some private patios, balconies. Resort-type hotel (1935); on ocean. Cr cds: A, D, DS, JCB, MC, V.

Inn

★ ★ **SAINT SIMONS INN.** *609 Beachview Dr, near lighthouse.* 912/638-1101; FAX 912/638-0943. 34 rms, 3 story. Mid-Mar-Oct: S, D $79-$105; each addl $7.50; under 12 free; 2-day min summer; lower rates rest of yr. Crib $5. TV. Pool. Complimentary continental bkfst. Restaurant nearby. Ck-out 11 am, ck-in 3 pm. Business servs avail. Refrigerators, microwaves. Within walking distance from attractions, beach. Cr cds: A, C, D, DS, MC, V.

Resort

★ ★ ★ **SEA PALMS GOLF & TENNIS RESORT.** *5445 Frederica Rd.* 912/638-3351; FAX 912/634-8029; res: 800/841-6268. Web www.gacoast.seapalms. 155 units, 1-3 story, 77 kit. villas. Mar-Oct: S $129; D $139; 1-bedrm $169; 2-bedrm $268; under 14 free; golf, tennis plans; lower rates rest of yr. Crib $10. TV; cable, VCR avail (movies). 3 pools; poolside serv. Playground. Dining rm 7 am-10:30 pm. Box lunches, snack bar, outdoor buffets. Bar 11 am-midnight. Ck-out 4 pm, ck-in 4 pm. Convention facilities. Business servs avail. In-rm modem link. 12 clay tennis courts, 3 lighted, pro, clinics. 27-hole golf, greens fee $40, golf cart $17, pro, putting greens, driving range. Private beach. Skeet shooting nearby. Exercise equipt; sauna. Private patios, balconies. Cr cds: A, C, D, MC, V.

Restaurants

★ ★ **ALFONZA'S OLDE PLANTATION SUPPER CLUB.** *171 Harrington Lane.* 912/638-9883. Hrs: 6-10:30 pm. Closed Sun; Thanksgiving, Dec 25. Res accepted. Bar. Semi-a la carte: dinner $12.50-$20. Specializes in pork chops, catfish, steak. Singers Thurs, Sat. Valet parking. 1930s roadhouse nightclub ambience. Cr cds: D, DS, MC, V.

★ ★ ★ **ALLEGRO.** *2465 Demere Rd.* 912/638-7097. Hrs: 5:30 pm-close. Closed Mon; some major hols; also first wk Jan. Res accepted. Continental menu. Bar. Wine list. A la carte entrees: dinner $12.95-$22.95. Specialties: Angus beef, seafood, pasta. Parking. Modern art on display. Cr cds: A, MC, V.

★ **BENNIE'S RED BARN.** *5514 Frederica Rd.* 912/638-2844. Hrs: 5:30-10:30 pm. Closed most major hols. Res accepted. Bar; entertainment Wed-Sat. Semi-a la carte: dinner $9.95-$19.75. Child's meals. Specializes in steak, lamb & pork chops, seafood, chicken. Parking. Family-owned. Rustic country ambience. Cr cds: DS, MC, V.

★ ★ **BLANCHE'S COURTYARD.** *440 Ocean Blvd.* 912/638-3030. Hrs: 5:30-9:30 pm; winter to 9 pm. Closed Thanksgiving, Dec 24-25. Res accepted. Bar. Semi-a la carte: dinner $11.50-$20. Specializes in broiled and grilled fresh seafood, steak. Own desserts. Entertainment Sat. Parking. Victorian nautical decor; antiques; outdoor courtyard. Totally nonsmoking. Cr cds: A, D, MC, V.

✔ ★ **BROGEN'S FOOD & SPIRITS.** *200 Pier Alley, in Pier Village.* 912/638-1660. Hrs: 11:30-2 am. Closed Sun Oct-Apr; Jan 1, Easter, Dec 25. Bar. A la carte entrees: lunch, dinner $2.95-$6.95. Specialties: hamburgers, chicken Swiss sandwiches. Outdoor dining. View of pier. Cr cds: A, DS, MC, V.

★ ★ **CHELSEA.** *1226 Ocean Blvd.* 912/638-2047. Hrs: 5:30-closing; early bird dinner 5:30-6:30 pm. Res accepted. Continental menu. Bar. Semi-a la carte: dinner $8.95-$21.95. Child's meals. Specializes in seafood, pasta, prime rib. Parking. Cr cds: DS, MC, V.

★ ★ **J. MAC'S.** *407 Mallery St.* 912/634-0403. E-mail jmac@technet.com. Hrs: 5:30-10 pm. Closed Sun; most major hols. Res accepted. Bar. A la carte entrees: dinner $12.95-$27.95. Specializes in seafood, crab cakes, rack of lamb. Bistro atmosphere. Cr cds: A, MC, V.

★ **KYOTO JAPANESE SEAFOOD & STEAK HOUSE.** *202 Retreat Village Center, Frederica Rd.* 912/638-0885. Hrs: 5-10 pm; Fri to 11 pm; Sat 4:30-10:30 pm; Sun 4:30-9:30 pm; early-bird dinner 5-6 pm. Closed Thanksgiving, Dec 25; also Super Bowl Sun. Res accepted. Japanese menu. Bar. Semi-a la carte: dinner $9.95-$25.50. Child's meals. Specializes in seafood, steak, chicken. Parking. Sushi bar. Tableside preparation. Traditional Japanese decor. Cr cds: A, C, D, DS, MC, V.

Savannah (F-6)

Founded 1733 **Pop** 137,560 **Elev** 42 ft **Area code** 912 **E-mail** cvb@savga.com **Web** www.savcvb.com

Information Savannah Area Convention & Visitors Bureau, 222 W Oglethorpe Ave, PO Box 1628, 31402-1628; 912/944-0456 or 800/444-2427.

Savannah has a wealth of history and architecture that few American cities can match. Even fewer have managed to preserve the same air of colonial grace and charm. The city's many rich, green parks are blooming legacies of the brilliance of its founder, General James E. Oglethorpe, who landed at Yamacraw Bluff with 120 settlers on February 12, 1733. His plan for the colony was to make the "inner city" spacious, beautiful and all that a city should be. Bull Street, named for Colonel William Bull, one of Oglethorpe's aides, stretches south from the high bluffs overlooking the Savannah River and is punctuated by five handsome squares and Forsyth Park.

Savannah then changed its outer garb of wood palisades to a gray "Savannah brick" fort surmounting the bluff. By Revolutionary times, wharves served ocean trade, and sailors caroused in seamen's inns. The town had its liberty pole and a patriots' battallion when news of Lexington came. The Declaration of Independence led to Savannah's designation as capital of the new state. By December, however, the British had retaken the city with 2,000 troops, and the Royal Governor, who had fled earlier, returned. An attempt to recapture Savannah by American troops failed, and more than 1,000 Americans and 700 Frenchmen were killed. General "Mad Anthony" Wayne's forces finally drove the British from Savannah in 1782.

In 1795, tobacco culture and Eli Whitney's cotton gin brought prosperity back to Savannah. Meanwhile, the city's growth followed the orderly pattern laid out by Colonel Bull. By the first decade of the new century, classical-revival or Regency-style architecture had superseded Georgian colonial. Savannah, with new forts protecting the estuary and strengthening Fort Wayne on the bluff, fared better during the War of 1812. Afterwards, architect William Jay and master builder Isaiah Davenport added splendid mansions that fronted palm-lined squares. The steamboat *Enterprise* plied upriver from here to Augusta in 1816; and three years later, on May 22, 1819, the SS *Savannah* set sail from Savannah for Liverpool to be the first steamer to cross the Atlantic. Savannah had become the leading market and shipping point for cotton, naval stores and tobacco, and prosperity increased until the Civil War.

Throughout the war, Savannah tried to hold its own. Fort Pulaski (see), which the Confederates took control of even before Secession, was retaken by a Union artillery assault on April 11, 1862, and became a Union military prison. Despite repeated Union naval battering, the Confederates held Fort McAllister (see) until Sherman marched to the sea and captured it on December 13, 1864. Although Confederate troops resisted for three days after Sherman demanded Savannah's surrender, Union forces eventually occupied the city, and the Confederates were forced to escape to Hutchison Island.

Reconstruction was painful, but 20 years later cotton was king again. Surrounding pine forests produced lumber and resins; the Cotton and Naval Stores Exchange was launched in 1882 while financiers and brokers strode the streets with confidence. By the 20th century, Savannah turned to manufacturing. With more than 200 industries by World War II, the city's prosperity has been measured by the activity of its port, which included shipbuilding booms during both world wars. Extensive developments by the Georgia Port Authority in the past decade have contributed to the city's commercial, industrial and shipping growth.

Today, more than 1,400 historically and architecturally significant buildings have been restored in Savannah's historic district, making it one of the largest urban historic landmark districts in the country. Another area, the Victorian district, south of the historic district, offers some of the best examples of post-Civil War Victorian architecture in the country. The city that launched the Girl Scouts of America also plays host to modern Girl Scouts, who visit the shrine of founder Juliette Gordon Low.

What to See and Do

Andrew Low House (ca 1848). Built for Andrew Low, this was later the residence of Juliette Gordon Low, founder of Girl Scouts of America. Period furnishings. (Daily exc Thurs; closed most hols; also mid-late Dec) 329 Abercorn St. Phone 912/233-6854. ¢¢

Christ Episcopal Church (1838). The mother church of Georgia, the congregation dates from 1733. Among early rectors were John Wesley and George Whitfield. The present church is the third building erected on this site. (Tues & Fri, limited hrs) Johnson Square between E St Julian & E Congress Sts. Phone 912/232-4131.

City Hall (1905). A gold dome tops the four-story neoclassic facade of this building, which replaced the original 1799 structure. A tablet outside commemorates sailing of the SS *Savannah;* a model is displayed in the Council Chamber. Another tablet is dedicated to the *John Randolph,* the first iron-sided vessel launched in American waters (1834). (Mon-Fri) Bull & Bay Sts. **Free.**

Colonial Park Cemetery (1753). This was the colony's first and only burial ground for many years; Button Gwinnett, a signer of the Declaration of Independence, is buried in cemetery, as are other distinguished Georgians. Closed since 1853, it has been a city park since 1896. E Oglethorpe & Abercorn Sts.

Congregation Mickve Israel. Only Gothic-style synagogue in US contains Torah scroll brought to America by congregation founders, Portuguese and German Jews who came to Savannah in 1733. Synagogue museum has portraits, religious objects, documents, letters from Presidents Washington, Jefferson, Madison. Guided tours (Mon-Fri). 20 E Gordon St, E side of Monterey Sq. Phone 912/233-1547. **Free.**

Davenport House (1815-1820). Built by master builder Isaiah Davenport, this is one of the finest examples of federal architecture in Savannah. Saved from demolition in 1955 by the Historic Savannah Foundation, it is now restored and furnished with period antiques. Gardens. (Daily; closed major hols) 324 E State St. Phone 912/236-8097. ¢¢

Factors Walk. Named by cotton factors of the 19th century, this row of business houses "on the Bay" is accessible by a network of iron bridgeways over cobblestone ramps. Between Bull & E Broad Sts.

Fort McAllister Historic Park (see). 25 mi S via GA 144.

Fort Pulaski National Monument (see). 15 mi E off US 80.

Georgia Historical Society. Research library and archives for Savannah and Georgia history and genealogy. (Tues-Sat) 501 Whitaker St. Phone 912/651-2128. **Free.**

Green-Meldrim House. Antebellum house used by General Sherman during occupation of Savannah (1864-1865) is now Parish House of St John's Church. Tours. (Tues & Thurs-Sat; closed hols, occasionally for parish activities, also last 2 wks before Easter) 14 W Macon St. Phone 912/233-3845. Tours ¢¢

Historic Savannah Waterfront Area. Restoration of the riverfront bluff to preserve and stabilize the historic waterfront includes a 9-blk brick concourse of parks, studios, museums, shops, restaurants and pubs. John P. Rousakis Riverfront Plaza.

Juliette Gordon Low Birthplace (1818-1821). Restored Regency town house was birthplace, in 1860, of the founder of Girl Scouts of the USA. Many original Gordon family pieces. Garden restored to Victorian period. (Thurs-Tues; closed some major hols) 142 Bull St. Phone 912/233-4501. ¢¢

Laurel Grove Cemetery (South). Possibly the oldest black cemetery currently in use; both antebellum slave and free black graves. Buried here is Andrew Bryan (1716-1812), pioneer Baptist preacher. 37th & Ogeechee Rds.

Owens-Thomas House (1816-1819). Authentically furnished Regency-style house designed by William Jay. Lafayette was an overnight guest in 1825. Walled garden is designed and planted in 1820s style. (Daily exc Mon; closed major hols, also Jan) 124 Abercorn St. Phone 912/233-9743. ¢¢

Savannah History Museum. This 19th-century railroad shed was renovated to house historical orientation center. Mural in lobby chronicles major events in Savannah's 250-yr history. (Daily; closed Jan 1, Thanksgiving, Dec 25). 303 Martin Luther King Jr Blvd, in Battlefield Park, adj Savannah Visitors Center. Phone 912/238-1779. ¢¢ Here are

   Auxiliary Theater. Special audio-visual presentations.

   Exhibit Hall. Artifacts, antiques and memorabilia from Savannah's past; pre-colonial Native American artifacts, Revolutionary and Civil war uniforms and weapons; 1890 Baldwin locomotive; replica of the SS *Savannah*, first steamboat to cross the Atlantic.

   Main Theater. Orientation film provides an overview of the history of Savannah from 1733 to the present as seen through the eyes of General James E. Oglethorpe.

Savannah National Wildlife Refuge. N via US 17 or US 17A, across the Savannah River in South Carolina.

Savannah Science Museum. Exhibits of live reptiles and amphibians; exhibits on the natural, physical, medical and technological sciences. Planetarium shows (Sat & Sun afternoons). (Tues-Sat, also Sun afternoons; closed hols) 4405 Paulsen St. Phone 912/355-6705. ¢¢

Ships of the Sea Museum. Ship models, figureheads; scrimshaw, sea artifacts; ship's carpenter shop. (Daily exc Mon; closed some major hols) 41 Martin Luther King Blvd. Phone 912/232-1511. ¢¢

Sightseeing tours.

   Touring Savannah. Various guided bus tours of Historic Landmark district and other areas. Tours depart from Visitors Center (see ADDITIONAL VISITOR INFORMATION) and downtown hotels and inns. (Daily; closed St Patrick's Day, Thanksgiving, Dec 25) 514 Berrien St. For details, reservations phone 912/234-8128. ¢¢¢-¢¢¢¢

   Gray Line bus tours. Contact 215 W Boundary St, 31401; 912/234-8687.

Telfair Museum of Art. Site of Royal Governor's residence from 1760 to end of Revolutionary War. Regency Mansion (1818) is one of three surviving buildings in Savannah by William Jay, English architect. Period rooms with family furnishings, silverware, porcelains; Octagon Room. Telfair is the oldest public art museum in the southeast, with a permanent collection of 18th-, 19th- and 20th-century American and European paintings and sculpture; prints, silver, decorative arts. Concerts, lectures; tours. (Daily exc Mon; closed major hols) 121 Barnard St. Phone 912/232-1177. ¢¢

Trustees' Garden Site. Original site of 10-acre experimental garden modeled in 1733 after the Chelsea Gardens in London by colonists who hoped to produce silk, wine and drugs. Peach trees planted in garden were responsible for Georgia's peach industry. Fort Wayne occupied the site in 1762. Not of military importance until the Revolution, the fort was named for General "Mad Anthony" Wayne. Strengthened by the British (1779), the Americans rebuilt it during the War of 1812. The massive buttressed brick walls later served as the foundation for a municipal gas company building. The **Pirates' House** (1734), former inn for visiting seamen, has been restored and is a restaurant; Robert Louis Stevenson referred to the inn in *Treasure Island.* E Broad St.

US Customs House (1850). Erected on site of colony's first public building. The granite columns' carved capitals were modeled from tobacco leaves. Tablet on Bull Street marks site where John Wesley preached his first Savannah sermon; tablet on Bay Street marks site of Oglethorpe's headquarters. Bull & E Bay Sts.

Wormsloe State Historic Site. Remains of early fortified 18th-century tabby house. (Tabby is a kind of cement made from lime, oyster shells, sand and water.) Visitor center exhibits outline history of site and of Noble Jones family, owners for more than 200 yrs. (Daily exc Mon) 8 mi SE on Skidaway Rd. Contact Manager, 7601 Skidaway Rd, 31406; 912/353-3023. ¢

Annual Events

Georgia Heritage Festival. Walking tours, open house at historic sites, crafts show, waterfront festival, parade, concerts, Georgia Day. Late Jan-mid-Feb.

St Patrick's Day Parade. Rivals New York City's in size. Mar.

Savannah Tour of Homes & Gardens. Sponsored by Christ Episcopal Church with Historic Savannah Foundation. Day and candlelight tours of more than 30 private houses and gardens. Contact 18 Abercorn St, 31401; 912/234-8054. Early Apr.

Seafood Festival. Waterfront. Restaurants offer samples; entertainment, arts & crafts. Contact Savannah Waterfront Association, 912/234-0295. Early Apr.

Walking Tour of Old Savannah Gardens. Includes eight private walled gardens in historic Savannah, tea at antebellum Green-Meldrim House. Phone 912/238-0248. Early Apr.

Night In Old Savannah. At the Savannah Visitors Center. Foods of more than 25 countries; entertainment includes jazz, country and rhythm and blues. Mid-Apr.

Savannah Scottish Games & Highland Gathering. Old Fort Jackson, 2 mi E via President St extension. The clans gather for a weekend of Highland games, piping, drumming, dancing and the traditional "Kirkin' o' th' Tartans." 2nd Sat May.

Christmas in Savannah. Month-long celebration includes tours of houses, historical presentations, parades, music, caroling and cultural events. Dec.

Additional Visitor Information

The Savannah Visitors Center, 301 Martin Luther King, Jr Blvd, is open daily, providing information on area attractions (including a free visitors guide with translations in French, German, Spanish and Japanese). All guided bus tours depart from the center on a regular basis.

Visitor information is also available from the Savannah Area Convention & Visitors Bureau, PO Box 1628, 31402-1628; 912/944-0456 or 800/444-2427.

Motels

✔★ ★ **BAYMONT INN.** 8484 Abercorn St (31406). 912/927-7660; FAX 912/927-6392. 103 rms, 3 story. S $45.95; D $51.95; under 18 free. Crib free. Pet accepted, some restrictions. TV; cable (premium). Pool. Complimentary continental bkfst. Complimentary coffee in rms. Restau-

rant nearby. Ck-out noon. Coin lndry. Meeting rm. In-rm modem link. Valet serv. Some refrigerators. Cr cds: A, C, D, DS, MC, V.

★ ★ **CLUBHOUSE INN.** 6800 Abercorn St (31405). 912/356-1234; FAX 912/352-2828. 122 rms, 2 story, 16 suites. S, D $74-$84; each addl $10; suites $89-$99; under 16 free; wkend rates special events. Crib free. TV; cable (premium). Pool; whirlpool. Complimentary full bkfst. Restaurant opp 11 am-10 pm. Ck-out noon. Coin lndry. Meeting rms. Business servs avail. In-rm modem link. Health club privileges. Refrigerator, wet bar in suites. Balconies. Grills. Cr cds: A, C, D, DS, MC, V.

★ ★ **COURTYARD BY MARRIOTT.** 6703 Abercorn St (31405). 912/354-7878; FAX 912/354-1432. 144 rms, 3 story, 12 suites. Feb-Nov: S $88; D $98; suites $102-$112; wkend rates; lower rates rest of yr. Crib free. TV; cable. Pool; whirlpool. Restaurant 6:30-10 am, 5-10 pm; Sat 7-11 am, 5-10 pm; Sun 7 am-noon. Bar 5-10 pm; closed Sun. Ck-out noon. Coin lndry. Meeting rms. Business servs avail. In-rm modem link. Valet serv. Guest lndry. Sundries. Exercise equipt. Private patios, balconies. Cr cds: A, C, D, DS, MC, V.

✔★ **DAYS INN SOUTHSIDE.** 11750 Abercorn (31419), at Mercy Blvd. 912/927-7720; FAX 912/925-8424. 114 rms, 2 story. S $55; D $60; each addl $5; under 12 free. Crib free. TV; cable (premium). Complimentary continental bkfst. Restaurant nearby. Ck-out 11 am. Whirlpool. St Joseph's hospital adj. Cr cds: A, D, DS, MC, V.

✔★ **FAIRFIELD INN BY MARRIOTT.** 2 Lee Blvd (31405), at Abercorn Rd. 912/353-7100. 135 rms, 3 story. Mar-Aug: S, D $59-$70; each addl $5; under 18 free; higher rates: wkends, special events; lower rates rest of yr. Crib free. TV; cable (premium). Pool. Complimentary continental bkfst. Ck-out noon. Business servs avail. In-rm modem link. Health club privileges. Cr cds: A, D, DS, MC, V.

★ ★ **HAMPTON INN.** 201 Stephenson Ave (31405). 912/355-4100; FAX 912/356-5385. 129 rms, 2 story. S $59; D $69; under 18 free; higher rates special events. Crib free. TV; cable (premium). Pool. Complimentary continental bkfst. Restaurant adj 11 am-10 pm. Ck-out noon. Meeting rms. Business servs avail. In-rm modem link. Health club privileges. Cr cds: A, C, D, DS, MC, V.

★ ★ **HAMPTON INN.** 17007 Abercorn St (31419), I-95 exit 16. 912/925-1212; FAX 912/925-1227. 62 rms, 2 story. S $58-$74; D $61-$84. Crib free. TV; cable (premium). Pool. Complimentary continental bkfst. Complimentary coffee in lobby. Restaurant adj 7 am-10 pm. Ck-out 11 am. Business servs avail. Cr cds: A, C, D, DS, MC, V.

★ ★ **HOMEWOOD SUITES.** 5820 White Bluff Rd (31405). 912/353-8500; FAX 912/354-3821. 106 kit. suites, 2-3 story. S, D $109-$159; under 18 free; wkend rates. Crib free. TV; cable, VCR. Pool; whirlpool. Complimentary continental bkfst. Complimentary coffee in rms. Restaurant adj 11 am-11 pm. Ck-out 11 am. Coin lndry. Meeting rms. Business center. In-rm modem link. Valet serv. Sundries. Exercise equipt. Sports court. Microwaves. Cr cds: A, C, D, DS, JCB, MC, V.

★ **QUAIL RUN LODGE.** 1130 Bob Harmon Rd (31408), E via I-16, exit Dean Forest Rd, 3 mi N, adj Savannah Intl Airport. 912/964-1421; res: 800/627-7035; FAX 912/966-5646. 171 rms, 2 story. S $60; D $65; each addl $8; suites $80-$90; under 16 free. Crib free. TV; cable (premium). Pool. Restaurant 6-10 am, 11 am-2 pm, 5:30-8:30 pm. Bar 2 pm-midnight. Ck-out noon. Meeting rms. Business servs avail. Bellhops. Valet serv. Free airport transportation. Microwaves avail. Private patios, balconies. Cr cds: A, C, D, DS, MC, V.

★ **SUPER 8.** *15 Fort Argyle Rd (31419), I-95 at GA 204 (exit 16).* 912/927-8550; FAX 912/921-0135. 61 rms, 2 story. S $43; D $53; each addl $5; under 12 free; higher rates wkends. Crib $4. TV; cable (premium). Pool. Complimentary continental bkfst. Restaurant adj open 24 hrs. Ck-out 11 am. Cr cds: A, C, D, DS, MC, V.

D ⊠ ⊠ ⊠ SC

✔★ **TRAVELODGE.** *390 Canebrake Rd (31419), I-95 exit 16.* 912/927-2999; FAX 912/927-9830. 56 rms, 2 story. S $45-$50; D $55-$60; each addl $5; under 17 free. Crib free. Pet accepted, some restrictions; $5. TV; cable (premium). Pool. Complimentary continental bkfst. Complimentary coffee in rms. Restaurant opp 6 am-midnight. Ck-out 11 am. Cr cds: A, D, DS, MC, V.

D ⊠ ⊠ ⊠ ⊠ SC

Motor Hotel

★★ **DAYS INN.** *201 W Bay St (31401).* 912/236-4440; FAX 912/232-2725. 253 rms, 7 story, 57 kit. suites. S, D $57-$150; each addl $10; kit. suites $99-$150; higher rates special events. Crib free. TV; cable (premium). Pool. Restaurant. Rm serv 7 am-noon. Ck-out noon. Meeting rms. Free garage parking. Health club privileges. Cr cds: A, C, D, DS, JCB, MC, V.

D ⊠ ⊠ ⊠ SC

Hotels

★★★ **HOLIDAY INN-MULBERRY.** *601 E Bay St (31401).* 912/238-1200; FAX 912/236-2184. Web www.savannahhotel.com. 122 rms, 3 story, 26 suites. Mid-Feb-Oct: S $135-$179; D $145-$189; suites $165-$225; under 18 free; package plans; higher rates special events; lower rates rest of yr. Crib free. TV; cable (premium). Pool. Complimentary coffee. Restaurant 7 am-2 pm, 6-9:30 pm. Bar. Ck-out noon. Meeting rms. Business servs avail. In-rm modem link. Health club privileges. Refrigerator in suites. Early 1800s Victorian structure, in the Historic District. Elegant Old Savannah decor; many objets d'art, antiques, paintings. Cr cds: A, D, DS, JCB, MC, V.

D ⊠ ⊠ ⊠ SC

★★★ **HYATT REGENCY.** *2 W Bay St (31401), on riverfront.* 912/238-1234; FAX 912/944-3678. 347 rms, 7 story. Mar-June, Sept-Nov: S $155-$200; D $180-$225; each addl $25; suites $234-$900; under 18 free; wkend rates; lower rates rest of yr. TV; cable (premium). Indoor pool. Restaurant 6:30 am-10 pm; Fri, Sat to midnight; Sun 9 am-3 pm. Bar noon-1 am, Sun noon-midnight; entertainment Tues-Sat. Ck-out noon. Convention facilities. Business center. In-rm modem link. Concierge. Shopping arcade. Garage parking; valet $12. Lighted tennis privileges, pro. 18-hole golf privileges, pro, putting green. Exercise equipt. Some refrigerators. Heliports. Cr cds: A, C, D, DS, JCB, MC, V.

D 🏋 ⊠ 🎿 ⊠ ⊠ SC 🛶

★★★ **MARRIOTT RIVERFRONT.** *100 General McIntosh Blvd (31401).* 912/233-7722; FAX 912/233-3765. 383 rms, 8 story, 46 suites. S, D $145-$190; each addl $20; suites $219-$519; under 18 free. Crib free. Garage (fee). TV; cable (premium). 2 pools, 1 indoor; whirlpool, poolside serv. Restaurant 6:30 am-midnight. Bar 3-10 pm. Ck-out 11 am. Convention facilities. Business servs avail. In-rm modem link. Concierge. Shopping arcade. Exercise equipt. Wet bar in suites. Balconies. On river. Cr cds: A, C, D, DS, MC, V.

D ⊠ 🎿 ⊠ ⊠ SC

Inns

★★ **17 HUNDRED 90.** *307 E President St (31401).* 912/236-7122; FAX 912/236-7123; res: 800/487-1790. 14 units, 3 story. S, D $119-$189. Crib free. TV; cable (premium). Complimentary continental bkfst. Dining rm 11:30 am-2 pm, 6-10 pm; Sat, Sun from 6 pm. Bar noon-1

am. Ck-out 11 am, ck-in 3 pm. Refrigerators; some fireplaces. Antiques. Cr cds: A, MC, V.

🔥 SC

★★★ **BALLASTONE.** *14 E Oglethorpe Ave (31401).* 912/236-1484; FAX 912/236-4626; res: 800/822-4553. Web www.ballastone.com. 17 rms, 4 story. S, D $195-$255; each addl $20; suites $315. Children over 16 yrs only. TV; cable, VCR (free movies). Complimentary full bkfst. Restaurant nearby. Bar. Ck-out 11 am, ck-in 3 pm. Concierge. Health club privileges. Some in-rm whirlpools, fireplaces. Victorian mansion (1838) with period antiques. Courtyard garden with fountain. Cr cds: A, MC, V.

🔥

✔★★ **BED AND BREAKFAST INN.** *117 W Gordon St (31401).* 912/238-0518; FAX 912/233-2537. 14 rms, 4 story. No elvtr. S $80-$105; D $85-$110; each addl $12. Crib $8. TV; cable. Complimentary full bkfst. Restaurant nearby. Ck-out 11 am, ck-in 2 pm. Some refrigerators. Restored 1853 Federal town house in the Historic District. Totally nonsmoking. Cr cds: A, DS, MC, V.

🔥

★★★ **EAST BAY INN.** *225 E Bay St (31401).* 912/238-1225; FAX 912/232-2709; res: 800/500-1225. 28 rms, 3 story. S, D $109-$129; each addl $10; under 12 free. Pet accepted, some restrictions; $25. TV; cable. Complimentary continental bkfst. Dining rm 11 am-3 pm; dinner hrs vary; closed Sun. Ck-out 11 am, ck-in 3 pm. Business servs avail. In-rm modem link. Luggage handling. Built in 1853; formerly a cotton warehouse. Antiques. Opp historic waterfront of Savannah River. Cr cds: A, C, D, DS, JCB, MC, V.

🐾 ⊠ ⊠ SC

✔★★★ **ELIZA THOMPSON HOUSE.** *5 W Jones St (31401).* 912/236-3620; FAX 912/238-1920; res: 800/348-9378. Web www.bbonline.com. 25 units, 3 story. S, D $89-$199; each addl $20; under 12 free. TV; cable (premium). Complimentary full bkfst; afternoon refreshments. Ck-out 11 am, ck-in 3 pm. Restored 1847 home; period furniture, many antiques. Courtyard with fountain. Cr cds: MC, V.

🔥

★★★ **FOLEY HOUSE.** *14 W Hull St (31401).* 912/232-6622; FAX 912/231-1218; res: 800/647-3708. Web www.bbonline.com/ga/savannah/foley/index.html. 19 rms, 3-4 story. No elvtr. S, D $135-$250; each addl $15; under 12 free. TV; VCR avail (free movies). Complimentary continental bkfst. Ck-out noon, ck-in 3 pm. In-rm modem link. Luggage handling. Fireplaces, some in-rm whirlpools. Some private patios, balconies. Restored 1896 home and carriage house in heart of Historic District. Individually decorated rms; antiques, artwork. Totally nonsmoking. Cr cds: A, D, MC, V.

🔥

★★★ **GASTONIAN.** *220 E Gaston St (31401).* 912/232-2869; res: 800/322-6603; FAX 912/232-0710. Web www.gastonian.com. 17 units, 4 story. Children over 12 yrs only. TV; cable. Complimentary full bkfst; afternoon refreshments. Ck-out noon, ck-in 3 pm. Business servs avail. Concierge serv. Gift shop. Whirlpool. Health club privileges. Fireplaces; many in-rm whirlpools. Balconies. Each rm individually decorated. Totally nonsmoking. Cr cds: A, DS, MC, V.

D ⊠ 🔥

★★★★ **THE KEHOE HOUSE.** *123 Habersham St (31401).* 912/232-1020; FAX 912/231-0208; res: 800/820-1020. Built in 1892 for an iron-mill owner, this Victorian mansion is furnished with many antiques and reproductions. 15 rms, 2 & 5 story, 2 suites. S, D $195-$250; each addl $35. Crib free. TV; cable. Complimentary full bkfst; afternoon refreshments. Restaurant opp noon-10 pm. Ck-out 11 am, ck-in 3 pm. Luggage handling. Concierge serv. Meeting rm. Business servs avail. Health club privileges. Totally nonsmoking. Cr cds: A, C, D, DS, JCB, MC, V.

D ⊠ 🔥 SC

★★★ **MAGNOLIA PLACE.** *503 Whitaker St (31401).* 912/236-7674; FAX 912/236-1145; res: 800/238-7674 (exc GA). E-mail b.b.magno lia@mci2000.com; web www.magnoliaplaceinn.com. 13 rms, 3 story. S, D $135-$250; each addl $25. Children over 11 yrs only. TV; cable, VCR (movies). Complimentary continental bkfst. Ck-out 11 am, ck-in 2:30 pm. Concierge serv. Fireplaces; some in-rm whirlpools. Private patios, balconies. Built in 1878; many antiques. Cr cds: A, DS, MC, V.

★ ★ ★ **MANOR HOUSE.** *201 W Liberty St (31401), 9 blks S on W Liberty St.* 912/233-9597; res: 800/462-3595; FAX 912/236-9419. 5 suites, 3 story. Suites $185-$225. Children over 12 yrs only. TV; cable, VCR (movies). Pet accepted. Complimentary continental bkfst. Restaurant nearby. Ck-out 11 am, ck-in 2 pm. In-rm modem link. Luggage handling. Valet serv. Concierge serv. Refrigerators, fireplaces; some in-rm whirlpools, minibars, wet bars. Balconies. Built for the Lester Byrd family, housed federal officers during Sherman's "march to the sea." Cr cds: A, MC, V.

★ ★ **OLDE HARBOUR.** *508 E Factors Walk (31401).* 912/234-4100; FAX 912/233-5979; res: 800/553-6533. Web www.oldeharbourinn.com. 24 kit. suites, 3 story. S, D $175-$215; each addl $10; under 12 free; wkly, monthly rates; package plans. Crib free. Pet accepted, some restrictions; $35. TV; cable (premium). Complimentary continental bkfst; refreshments. Business servs avail. Balconies. Antiques. Built in 1892, originally housed offices and warehouse of an oil company. Cr cds: A, D, DS, MC, V.

★ ★ **PRESIDENT'S QUARTERS.** *225 E President St (31401).* 912/233-1600; FAX 912/238-0849; res: 800/233-1776. E-mail pqinn@aol.com; web www.presidentsquarters.com. 9 rms, 4 story, 7 suites. S, D $147-$157; each addl $20; suites $177-$195; under 10 free. Crib free. TV; cable (premium), VCR (free movies). Complimentary continental bkfst. Ck-out 11 am, ck-in 2 pm. Business servs avail. In-rm modem link. Health club privileges. Refrigerators; some in-rm whirlpools. Private patios, balconies. Built 1855. Cr cds: A, D, DS, MC, V.

★ ★ **RIVER STREET INN.** *124 E River St (31401).* 912/234-6400; FAX 912/234-1478; res: 800/253-4229. 44 rms, 5 story. S, D $129-$189; each addl $10; under 12 free; higher rates wkend closest to Mar 17. Crib free. TV; cable (premium). Complimentary full bkfst; afternoon refreshments. Dining rms 7 am-10 pm; Sat, Sun 8 am-11 pm. Ck-out noon, ck-in 4 pm. Business servs avail. Luggage handling. Valet serv. Concierge serv. Health club privileges. Microwaves avail. Balconies. On river. Converted cotton warehouse (1817); variety of decors & furnishings; canopy beds, Oriental rugs. Cr cds: A, C, D, MC, V.

Restaurants

★ ★ ★ **45 SOUTH.** *20 E Broad St (31401), on grounds of Pirates' House Restaurant.* 912/233-1881. Hrs: 6-9 pm; Fri, Sat to 9:30 pm. Closed Sun; major hols. Res accepted. Bar. Wine list. A la carte entrees: dinner $18.50-$29.50. Specialties: grilled Ahi tuna with foie gras, seared breast of duck with ginger beets, sliced breast of pheasant with wild mushrooms. Own baking. Valet parking. In 1852 building. Jacket. Cr cds: A, C, D, DS, MC, V.

★ ★ **BISTRO SAVANNAH.** *309 W Congress St (31401).* 912/233-6266. Hrs: 6-10:30 pm; Fri, Sat 5:30-11 pm. Res accepted. Bar. A la carte entrees: dinner $12.95-$21.95. Bistro atmosphere. Local art on display. Cr cds: A, MC, V.

★ ★ **CHART HOUSE.** *202 W Bay Street (31401).* 912/234-6686. Hrs: 5-10 pm; Fri, Sat to 11 pm. Res accepted. Bar. A la carte entrees: dinner $14.95-$19.95. Child's meals. Specializes in steak, seafood, prime rib. Nautical decor; beamed ceilings, artwork. 3 floors. On historic waterfront. Covered balcony over Savannah River. Cr cds: A, C, D, DS, MC, V.

★ **DAMON'S.** *401 Mall Blvd (31406), Suite 101.* 912/354-3331. Web www.damons.com. Hrs: 11 am-10 pm; Fri, Sat to 11 pm. Closed Thanksgiving, Dec 25. Bar. Semi-a la carte: lunch, dinner $4.99-$19.99. Child's meals. Specializes in barbecued ribs, onion loaf, sandwiches. Parking. Outdoor dining. Cr cds: A, DS, MC, V.

★ ★ ★ **ELIZABETH ON 37TH.** *105 E 37th St (31401).* 912/236-5547. Web www.elizabethon37th.com. This elegant dining room, accented with Oriental rugs, marble fireplaces and classical music, is booked weeks in advance. Chef Elizabeth Terry's ingredients are always fresh and baking is done on the premises. Specializes in local seafood, poultry, lamb. Own baking. Hrs: 6-10 pm. Closed major hols. Res accepted. Semi-a la carte: dinner $22.50-$29.50. Parking. Totally nonsmoking. Cr cds: A, D, DS, MC, V.

★ ★ **GARIBALDI'S CAFE.** *315 W Congress (31401).* 912/232-7118. Hrs: 5:30-10:30 pm; Fri, Sat to midnight. Res accepted. Italian menu. Bar. A la carte entrees: dinner $8.95-$24.95. Specializes in fresh fish, veal, pasta. Own desserts. Former 1871 Germania firehouse in historic district. Italian cafe decor. 1842 antique mirror, paintings. Cr cds: A, MC, V.

★ ★ **JOHNNY HARRIS.** *1651 E Victory Dr (31404).* 912/354-7810. Hrs: 11:30 am-10:30 pm; Fri, Sat to midnight. Closed Sun; Jan 1, Dec 25. Res accepted. Bar. Semi-a la carte: lunch $4.95-$7.95, dinner $7.95-$18.95. Child's meals. Specializes in barbecue, prime rib, seafood. Entertainment Fri, Sat. Jacket (Sat night in main dining rm). 1930s night club atmosphere. Savannah's oldest continuously operating restaurant. Cr cds: A, D, DS, MC, V.

★ ★ ★ **OLDE PINK HOUSE.** *23 Abercorn St (31412).* 912/232-4286. Hrs: 6-10:30 pm. Res accepted. Southern menu. Bar from 5 pm. A la carte entrees: dinner $14.95-$22.95. Specializes in seafood, beef, veal. Jazz pianist Tues-Sun. Restored 18th-century mansion. Totally nonsmoking. Cr cds: A, MC, V.

★ **PEARL'S ELEGANT PELICAN.** *7000 La Roche (31406).* 912/352-8221. Hrs: 5-10 pm. Closed Jan 1, Thanksgiving, Dec 25. Bar. Semi-a la carte: dinner $9.95-$17.95. Child's meals. Specializes in seafood. Parking. Multi-level dining rm provides view of the Herb River and marshlands. Family-owned. Cr cds: A, C, D, DS, MC, V.

★ ★ **RIVER HOUSE.** *125 W River St (31401).* 912/234-1900. Hrs: 11 am-10 pm; Fri, Sat to 11 pm; Sun from noon. Closed Thanksgiving, Dec 25. Res accepted. Bar. Semi-a la carte: lunch $6-$13, dinner $13.95-$23.95. Child's meals. Specializes in seafood, poultry, steak. In an old cotton warehouse. Cr cds: A, C, D, MC, V.

★ ★ **RIVER'S END.** *3122 River Dr (31404).* 912/354-2973. Web www.riversend.com. Hrs: 5-10 pm; Fri, Sat to 11 pm. Closed Sun; Thanksgiving, Dec 24, 25. Res accepted. Bar 4-11 pm; Fri, Sat to midnight. Wine list. A la carte entrees: dinner $10.95-$19.95. Child's meals. Specializes in seafood, steak, pasta. Own baking. Pianist. Parking. Overlooks Intracoastal Waterway; dockage. Cr cds: A, C, D, DS, MC, V.

★ ★ **SEASONS OF SAVANNAH.** *315 W Saint Julian St (31401), city market.* 912/233-2626. Web www.savannahcitymarket.org. Hrs: 11:30 am-2:30 pm, 6-10 pm; Fri, Sat to 10 pm. Sun 11:30 am-3 pm; 5:30-9 pm. Res accepted. Bar. Semi-a la carte: lunch $5.95-$9.95, dinner

$14.95-$22.95. Specializes in steak, seafood, pasta. Outdoor dining. Local artwork. Cr cds: A, DS, MC, V.

★ ★ **SHRIMP FACTORY.** *313 E River St (31401). 912/236-4229.* Hrs: 11 am-10 pm; Fri, Sat to 11 pm; Sun noon-10 pm. Closed Thanksgiving, Dec 25. Bar. Semi-a la carte: lunch $5.50-$13.90, dinner $14.90-$23.90. Child's meals. Specialties: pine bark stew, fresh fish and shrimp with special sauces, lobster. Located on river. Cr cds: A, C, D, DS, MC, V.

✔★ **WILLIAMS SEAFOOD.** *8010 Tybee Rd (31410). 912/897-2219.* Hrs: 11:30 am-9:30 pm; Sun 11 am-9 pm. Closed Thanksgiving, Dec 25. Bar. Semi-a la carte: lunch, dinner $5.25-$17.95. Child's meals. Specializes in seafood, chicken, beef. Casual atmosphere. Nautical prints. Family-owned. Cr cds: A, D, DS, MC, V.

[D] [SC] ⌐

Unrated Dining Spot

MRS WILKES' DINING ROOM. *107 W Jones St. 912/232-5997.* Hrs: 8-9 am, 11 am-3 pm. Closed Sat, Sun; major hols. Southern cooking. Complete meals: bkfst $5, lunch $8. Boarding house-style seating and service. Large variety of noted Southern dishes: barbecued pork chops, fried chicken, turnip greens, biscuits, cornbread, banana pudding. Own desserts. 1870 brick house; original wallpaper. Clippings of articles about the boarding house, famous guests. No cr cds accepted.

Sea Island (G-6)

(See also Brunswick, Golden Isles, Jekyll Island, St Simons Island)

Pop 750 (est) **Elev** 11 ft **Area code** 912 **Zip** 31561

Resort

★ ★ ★ ★ **THE CLOISTER.** *9 mi E of US 17. 912/638-3611; FAX 912/638-5159; res: 800/SEA-ISLA.* Web www.seaisland.com. Separated from St. Simons Island by a narrow waterway, this famed upper-crust resort comprises a Spanish Mediterranean hotel, hundreds of privately owned cottages and villas available for rent, and abundant recreational facilities. The grand old resort makes a point of Southern hospitality. 286 rms, 1-3 story, 200 kit. cottages. AP, mid-Mar-late May: S $274-$640; D $324-$700; each addl $72; 6-12 yrs, $26; 3-5 yrs, $18; under 2 free; spa, golf, tennis plans; lower rates rest of yr. Serv charge 15% per day. Garage avail; free parking. TV; cable, VCR avail (movies $5). 2 pools, 1 heated; wading pool, whirlpool, poolside serv, lifeguard. Free supervised child's activities (late May-early Sept); ages 3-11. Dining rm 7:30-9:30 am, noon-2 pm, 7-9:30 pm (also see CLOISTER MAIN DINING ROOM). Box lunches, snack bar, outdoor buffets. Rm serv 6:30 am-midnight. Bar 2:30 pm-12:30 am; closed Sun. Ck-out noon, ck-in 4 pm. Convention facilities. Business center. In-rm modem link. Valet serv. Package store. Grocery 1 mi. Airport, RR station, bus depot transportation. Sports dir. Tennis, pro, pro shop. 54-hole golf, greens fee $90 (incl cart), shop, putting greens, driving range, pro shop. Private beach. Sailboats, charter boats; dock. Nature walks. Bicycles. Lawn games. Trap & skeet shooting; instruction. Soc dir; entertainment, dancing (instruction), movies on Sun. Rec rm. Exercise rm; sauna, steam rm. Spa. Beach club; lockers avail; steam bath. Private patios, balconies. No cr cds accepted.

[D] [→] ⊀ ⟰ ⟷ ⟿ ✕ ⟐ ⟐ ⟰

Restaurant

★ ★ **CLOISTER MAIN DINING ROOM.** *(See The Cloister Resort) 912/638-3611.* Web www.seaisland.com. Hrs: 7:30-9:30 am, noon-1:30 pm, 7-9 pm; hrs vary by season. Res required. Continental menu. Bar.

Wine cellar. Complete meals: bkfst $16, lunch $21, dinner $52. Child's meals. Specializes in seafood, prime rib, steak. Own baking. Orchestra exc Sun. Valet parking. American colonial decor. Menu changes daily. Family-owned. Jacket. Cr cds: MC, V.

[D] ⌐ ♥

Statesboro (E-5)

Settled 1796 **Pop** 15,854 **Elev** 258 ft **Area code** 912 **Zip** 30458
Information Convention and Visitors Bureau, 322 S Main St, PO Box 1516; 912/489-1869.

What to See and Do

Georgia Southern University (1906). (14,000 students) On campus are art department gallery (Mon-Fri; closed hols); museum (daily exc Sat; closed hols); planetarium (by appt); Herty Nature Trail (daily); Center for Wildlife Education and Raptor Center (daily exc Sat; closed hols; phone 912/681-0831); and a botanical garden (daily; closed hols). 1/2 mi S on US 301. Phone 912/681-5611.

Annual Event

Regional Ogeechee Fair. Fairgrounds, GA 67.2nd wk Oct.

Motels

★ ★ **COMFORT INN.** *316 S Main St. 912/489-2626; FAX 912/489-2626, ext. 300.* 65 rms, 2 story, 8 kits. S, D $45-$60; each addl $5; kits. $60; under 18 free; higher rates special events. Crib free. TV; cable (premium), VCR (movies avail). Pool. Complimentary bkfst buffet. Complimentary coffee in rms. Ck-out 11 am. Business servs avail. In-rm modem link. Coin lndry. Health club privileges. Refrigerators, microwaves. Cr cds: A, C, D, DS, MC, V.

[D] ⟷ ⟿ ⟐ [SC]

✔★ **DAYS INN.** *461 S Main St. 912/764-5666; FAX 912/489-8193.* 44 rms, 1-2 story. S $36-$52; D $38-$64; each addl $5; under 17 free. Crib free. Pet accepted. TV; cable (premium), VCR avail (movies). Pool. Complimentary continental bkfst. Restaurant adj 11 am-10 pm. Ck-out 11 am. Cr cds: A, C, D, DS, JCB, MC, V.

⟵ ⟷ ⟿ ⟐ [SC]

★ ★ **JAMESON INN.** *1 Jameson Ave. 912/681-7900; FAX 912/681-7905; res: 800/526-3766.* 39 rms, 2 story. S $51; D $56; each addl $5; suites $97-$137; under 12 free. Crib free. TV; cable (premium). Pool. Complimentary continental bkfst. Restaurant nearby. Ck-out 11 am. Business servs avail. In-rm modem link. Exercise equipt. Opp Georgia Southern College. Cr cds: A, D, DS, MC, V.

[D] ⟷ ⊀ ⟿ ⟐ [SC]

✔★ ★ **RAMADA INN.** *230 S Main St (US 25/301). 912/764-6121; FAX 912/764-6121, ext. 509.* 129 rms, 2 story. S, D $50; each addl $3; under 18 free. Crib free. Pet accepted, some restrictions. TV; cable (premium). Pool; wading pool. Complimentary bkfst buffet. Restaurant 6:30 am-2 pm, 5-10 pm. Rm serv. Bar 5 pm-midnight. Ck-out noon. Coin lndry. Meeting rms. Business servs avail. In-rm modem link. Valet serv. Cr cds: A, C, D, DS, MC, V.

[D] ⟵ ⟷ ⟿ ⟐ [SC]

Inn

★ ★ **STATESBORO INN.** *106 S Main St. 912/489-8628; FAX 912/489-4785; res: 800/846-9466.* Web www.statesboroinn.com. 18 rms, 2 story. S, D $75-$120; each addl $10. Crib free. TV; cable (premium),

VCR avail. Complimentary full bkfst. Dining rm (public by res). Rm serv. Ck-out 11 am, ck-in 2 pm. Business servs avail. In-rm modem link. Health club privileges. Some in-rm whirlpools, fireplaces. Private patios. Built 1904. Many antiques. Cr cds: A, DS, MC, V.

⬛ SC

Thomasville (H-3)

(See also Bainbridge; also see Tallahassee, FL)

Pop 17,457 **Elev** 285 ft **Area code** 912 **Zip** 31792

Information Welcome Center, 135 N Broad St, PO Box 1540, 31799; 912/225-3919.

What to See and Do

Big Oak. Giant live oak is 68 ft tall, has a limb spread of 162 ft and a trunk circumference of 24 ft. The approximately 310-yr-old tree was enrolled as a member of the National Life Oak Society in 1936. Corner of N Crawford and E Monroe Sts, one blk behind Post Office and Federal Courthouse.

Lapham-Patterson House State Historic Site (1885). Restored three-story Victorian house features decorative shingle-work, elaborate chinoiserie porches, fanciful gables and cantilevered balconies; built by Chicago merchant as resort cottage. Tours on the hour. (Daily exc Mon; closed Jan 1, Thanksgiving, Dec 25) 626 N Dawson St. Phone 912/225-4004. ¢¢

Pebble Hill Plantation. Historic plantation dates from 1820s; elaborate Greek-revival house furnished with art, antiques, porcelains, crystal, silver and Native American relics belonging to Hanna family of Ohio, who rebuilt house, guest houses, stables and garages after a fire in the 1930s. Gardens; livestock. Wagon rides; tours (daily exc Mon; closed Thanksgiving, Dec 24-25, also Sept; must be over 6 yrs of age). 5 mi SW via US 319. Phone 912/226-2344. Grounds ¢¢ House ¢¢¢

Thomas County Museum of History. Five buildings on property include a log house with period furnishings; an 1877 frame house furnished in middle-class fashion of period; an 1893 Victorian bowling alley; a garage housing historic vehicles; and a 1920s mansion, which houses the main museum. Photographs, period costumes, artifacts. (Closed Jan 1, Easter, Thanksgiving, Dec 24-25, also last wk Sept) 725 N Dawson St. Phone 912/226-7664. ¢¢

Thomasville Cultural Center. A center for visual and performing arts. Facilities include art galleries with permanent and changing exhibits; children's room; and 550-seat auditorium. Concerts, musicals, children's programs, art classes and other programs are offered. Galleries, building tours (daily exc hols; fee). 600 E Washington St. Phone 912/226-0588. **Free.**

Annual Event

Rose Festival. Parade, rose show, arts & crafts. Late Apr.

Motels

✔★ **DAYS INN.** *(35 US 84E, Cairo 31728) 13 mi W on US 84. 912/377-4400.* 34 rms, 2 story. S $40; D $45; each addl $5; suites $55-$65; under 12 free; higher rates: Rose Parade, Rattlesnake Roundup, Mule Day. Crib free. TV; cable. Pool. Complimentary coffee in lobby. Restaurant opp 6 am-11 pm. Ck-out 11 am. Business servs avail. Cr cds: A, D, DS, JCB, MC, V.

D ⬛⬛⬛ SC

★★ **HOLIDAY INN.** *15138 US 19S. 912/226-7111; FAX 912/226-7257.* 147 rms, 2 story. S $64; D $69; each addl $5; suite $130; under 19 free; wkend rates; higher rates: Rose Festival, Sun Belt Expo (Oct). Crib free. TV; cable. Pool; whirlpool. Restaurant 6:30 am-2 pm, 5:30-10 pm. Rm serv. Bar 4:30 pm-midnight; closed Sun; entertainment.

Ck-out noon. Coin lndry. Meeting rms. Business servs avail. In-rm modem link. Valet serv. Cr cds: A, C, D, DS, JCB, MC, V.

D ⬛⬛⬛ SC

Inns

★★★ **1884 PAXTON HOUSE.** *445 Remington Ave. 912/226-5197.* Web www.1884paxtonhouseinn.com. 8 rms, 2 story, 1 suite, 1 kit. unit. S $85-$95; D $90-$110; suite $125-$185; kit. unit $185; wkend (2-day min). Children over 12 yrs only. TV; cable (premium), VCR avail. Complimentary full bkfst. Restaurant nearby. Ck-out 11 am, ck-in 3-6 pm. Gift shop. Indoor pool. Built in 1884. Extensive porcelain collection. Totally nonsmoking. Cr cds: A, MC, V.

⬛⬛⬛

★★ **GRAND VICTORIA.** *817 S Hansell St. 912/226-7460.* 4 rms, 1 with shower only, 2 story. No rm phones. S $65-$85; D $70-$90; each addl $10; under 3 free; special event wkends (2-day min). Cable TV in library, VCR avail (movies). Complimentary full bkfst. Restaurant nearby. Ck-out 11 am, ck-in 3 pm. Lighted tennis privileges. 18-hole golf privileges, pro, putting green, driving range. Victorian house built in 1893 with wrap-around porch. Totally nonsmoking. No cr cds accepted.

⬛⬛⬛⬛

★★ **SERENDIPITY COTTAGE.** *339 E Jefferson St, NE of Broad, in Dawson St historic area. 912/226-8111; res: 800/383-7377; FAX 912/226-2656.* Web www.bbhost.com/serendipity. 3 rms, 1 with shower only, 2 story. S $75; D $80. Children over 13 yrs only. TV; cable (premium); VCR avail (movies). Complimentary full bkfst. Restaurant nearby. Ck-out 11 am, ck-in 4-6 pm. Luggage handling. Lighted tennis privileges. 18-hole golf privileges; greens fee $36-$46, pro, putting green, driving range. Bicycles. Fireplaces. Foursquare house built in 1906; antiques. Totally nonsmoking. Cr cds: A, DS, MC, V.

⬛⬛⬛⬛⬛

★★ **SUSINA PLANTATION.** *1420 Meridian Rd, 12 mi SW via US 319, then 1 mi N via GA 93, then W on GA 156, follow signs. 912/377-9644.* 8 rms, 2 story. No rm phones. MAP: S $125; D $150. Pool. Ck-out noon, ck-in 2 pm. Lighted tennis. Picnic tables, grills. 1841 plantation house set amid 115 acres of lawns, oaks and magnolias. No cr cds accepted.

⬛⬛⬛⬛

Resort

★★★ **MELHANA PLANTATION.** *301 Showboat Ln. 912/226-4585; res: 888/920-3030; FAX 912/226-4585.* E-mail infomelhanna.com; web www.melhanna.com. 30 rms, 1-2 story, 10 suites. S, D $250-$350; suites $400-$450; under 5 free; Crib avail. TV; cable (premium), VCR avail. Complimentary full bkfst. Complimentary coffee in rms. Restaurant 6-10 pm. Box lunches. Snack bar. Picnics. Rm serv 24 hrs. Wine, beer. Ck-out noon, ck-in 3 pm. Meeting rms. Business center. In-rm modem link. Bellhops. Valet serv. Concierge. Shopping arcade. Airport transportation. Tennis, pro. Hiking. Horse stables. Bicycle rentals. Lawn games. Soc dir. Exercise equipt. Massage. Carriage rides. Fishing/hunting guides nearby. Indoor pool; poolside serv. Supervised child's activities (June-Sept). Many in-rm whirlpools, refrigerators, minibars; some fireplaces. Picnic tables, grills. Totally nonsmoking. Cr cds: A, C, D, DS, JCB, MC, V.

D ⬛⬛⬛⬛⬛⬛

Restaurants

★★ **HARRISON'S.** *119 N Broad. 912/226-0074.* Hrs: 11:30 am-2 pm, 5:30-9 pm. Closed Sun; Jan 1, Thanksgiving, Dec 25. Res accepted. Bar. Northern Italian menu. A la carte entrees: lunch, dinner $9.50-$16.95. Specialties: fettucini Mileo, pollo e salsiccia con melanzane, vitello al popi. Own baking. Entertainment Thurs, Fri. Dining in mid-1800s hotel bldg. Cr cds: A, MC, V.

D ⊐

✔★ ★ **PLAZA.** *217 S Broad St. 912/226-5153.* Hrs: 6 am-10 pm; Sun 7 am-2:30 pm. Closed some major hols. Greek, Amer menu. Bar. Semi-a la carte: bkfst $2.50-$7, lunch $4-$6, dinner $6.50-$16.95. Buffet: lunch $4.50. Child's meals. Specializes in fresh seafood, Greek salad, Western steak. Salad bar. Own soups, sauces. Entertainment Fri. Parking. Family-owned. Cr cds: A, DS, MC, V.

D ⊐

Tifton (G-3)

(See also Adel)

Pop 14,215 **Elev** 357 ft **Area code** 912 **Zip** 31794 **Web** www.surfsouth.com/business/tiftchamber
Information Tifton-Tift County Chamber of Commerce, 100 Central Ave, PO Box 165, 31793; 912/382-6200.

What to See and Do

Georgia Agrirama, 19th-Century Living History Museum. Operating exhibits include farms & farmhouses, one-room school, gristmill, newspaper office, blacksmith shop, church, cotton gin, sawmill, turpentine still, country store, drugstore, variety works and more from 1870-1910. Logging train runs spring through fall. Costumed interpreters. (Tues-Sat, also Sun afternoons; closed Jan 1, Thanksgiving, Dec 22-25). 8th St at I-75, exit 20. Phone 912/386-3344. ¢¢¢

Motels

★ ★ **COMFORT INN.** *1104 King Rd, I-75 exit 19. 912/382-4410; FAX 912/382-4410, ext. 102.* 91 rms, 2 story. S $49; D $57; each addl $5; suites $89-$98; under 18 free; wkend rates; higher rates Agricultural Expo. Pet accepted; $10. TV; cable. Indoor/outdoor pool; whirlpool. Complimentary continental bkfst. Ck-out 11 am. Meeting rm. Business servs avail. Refrigerator, wet bar in suites. Cr cds: A, D, DS, MC, V.

D ✔ ≈ ⋈ 🕭 SC

✔★ **DAYS INN.** *1008 W 8th St, I-75 exit 20. 912/382-7210; FAX 912/386-8146.* 72 rms, 2 story. S $40; D $45; each addl $5; under 12 free; higher rates special events. TV; cable. Pool. Complimentary continental bkfst. Ck-out noon. Cr cds: A, D, DS, MC, V.

≈ ⋈ 🕭 SC

✔★ ★ **RAMADA LIMITED.** *1211 Hwy 82W, 2 mi W on US 82 at jct I-75 exit 18. 912/382-8500; FAX 912/386-5913.* 100 units, 2 story. S, D $50-$65; each addl $5; under 12 free. Crib free. TV; cable (premium). Pool. Complimentary bkfst. Bar 4 pm-2 am; closed Sun; entertainment. Ck-out noon. Meeting rms. Business center. Cr cds: A, C, D, DS, MC, V.

≈ ⋈ 🕭 SC 🕴

Restaurants

✔★ **CHARLES SEAFOOD.** *701 W 7th St. 912/382-9696.* Hrs: 11 am-2 pm, 5-10 pm. Closed Sun; July 4, Dec 25. Semi-a la carte: lunch, dinner $2.29-$9.95. Specializes in seafood, BBQ sandwiches. Cr cds: MC, V.

D ⊐

★ **CHINA GARDEN.** *1020 W 2nd St, I-75 exit 19. 912/382-1010.* Hrs: 11 am-2 pm, 5-10 pm. Closed July 4, Thanksgiving, Dec 25; also Chinese New Year. Chinese menu. A la carte entrees: lunch, dinner

$4.50-$12.99. Buffet: lunch $4.99, dinner $10.95. Specializes in beef, chicken. Cr cds: A, D, DS, MC, V.

D ⊐

Toccoa (B-3)

(See also Clayton, Commerce, Gainesville)

Pop 8,266 **Elev** 1,017 ft **Area code** 706 **Zip** 30577
Information Toccoa-Stephens County Chamber of Commerce, 901 E Currahee St, PO Box 577; 706/886-2132.

What to See and Do

Hartwell Lake. This 56,000-acre reservoir with 962-mi of shoreline was created by a dam on the Savannah River. Swimming, waterskiing; fishing; boating (ramps, marinas). Picnicking. Numerous campsites (Mar-Nov; fee) surround lake. Reservoir (daily). 6 mi E on US 123 to lake; continue approx 21 mi E on same road to access Twin Lakes campground, follow signs. Phone 706/376-4788.

Toccoa Falls College (1907). (911 students) On November 6, 1977, a 40-year-old earthen dam above the college collapsed, spewing tons of water over the 186-foot Toccoa Falls and inundating the campus—one of the worst such disasters in Georgia history. There is no longer a lake or dam above the falls.

Toccoa Falls is open to the public (daily; closed Dec 25). NW edge of town off GA 17A. Phone 706/886-6831. Toccoa Falls ¢

Traveler's Rest State Historic Site. Plantation house (ca 1840) built on land granted in 1785 to Jesse Walton, a Revolutionary soldier and political leader. Two-story structure covers 6,000 sq ft. Later owned and enlarged by Devereaux Jarrett, it served as a stagecoach inn and post office. Museum (daily exc Mon-Wed; closed Jan 1, Thanksgiving, Dec 25). 6 mi NE off US 123. Phone 706/886-2256. ¢

Motels

★ **DAYS INN.** *GA 17. 706/886-9461; FAX 706/282-0907.* 78 rms, 2 story. Early Apr-Nov: S $36; D $45; each addl $5; under 15 free; lower rates rest of yr. Crib $5. TV; cable (premium). Pool. Complimentary continental bkfst. Ck-out 11 am. Meeting rms. Cr cds: A, D, MC, V.

D ≈ ⋈ 🕭 SC

★ ★ **SHONEY'S INN.** *(14227 Jones St, Lavonia 30553) 20 mi SE on GA 17 exit 58. 706/356-8848; FAX 706/356-2951.* 60 rms, 2 story. S $40-$53; D $45-$64; each addl $5; under 18 free; higher rates special events. Crib free. Pet accepted; $10. TV; cable (premium). Pool. Coffee in lobby. Restaurant adj 6 am-midnight. Ck-out noon. Meeting rms. Business servs avail. In-rm modem link. Some refrigerators; microwave in suites. Cr cds: A, D, DS, MC, V.

D ✔ ≈ ⋈ 🕭 SC

Tybee Island (F-6)

(See also Savannah)

Pop 2,842 **Elev** 17 ft **Area code** 912 **Zip** 31328 **E-mail** cvb@savga.com **Web** www.savcvb.com

Information Savannah Area Convention & Visitors Bureau, 222 W Oglethorpe Ave, PO Box 1628, Savannah 31402-1628; 912/944-0456 or 800/444-2427.

A popular year-round Georgia resort has evolved on this V-shaped sandbar fronting the Atlantic for nearly four miles and the Savannah River for over two miles. The beach runs the entire length of the island; its north end is marked by old coastal defenses, a museum and a lighthouse at the tip. Reached by a causeway from Savannah and US 80, the beach has a boardwalk, fishing pier, amusements, hotels, motels and vacation cottages.

What to See and Do

Fort Pulaski National Monument (see). 3 mi W on US 80.

Tybee Museum and Lighthouse. Museum is housed in a coastal artillery battery built 1898. Battery Garland is one of six gun emplacements that made up Fort Screven. Museum traces history of Tybee from colonial times to 1945; exhibits on Martello Tower, Civil War, Fort Screven; doll and gun collections. The lighthouse is one of the oldest active lighthouses in the US; visitors may climb to the top for a scenic view of Tybee and historic Fort Screven. Exhibits and gift shop in 1880s lighthouse keeper's cottage. (Daily exc Tues; closed Jan 1, Thanksgiving, Dec 25). N end of island. Phone 912/786-5801. ¢¢

Motel

★ ★ **BEST WESTERN DUNES INN.** 1409 Butler Ave. 912/786-4591; FAX 912/786-4593. 32 rms, 2 story, 14 kit. units. Apr-Sept: S, D $79-$125; kit. units $89-$135; under 12 free; wkly rates; higher rates: special events, hols (3-day min); lower rates rest of yr. Crib $5. TV; cable, VCR avail (movies). Pool. Complimentary coffee in lobby. Restaurant adj 5 am-10 pm. Business servs avail. In-rm modem link. Refrigerators avail. Balconies. Opp beach. Cr cds: A, C, D, DS, MC, V.

Inn

★ **HUNTER HOUSE.** 1701 Butler Ave. 912/786-7515. 4 rms (1 with kit.), 2 story. No rm phones. Memorial Day-Labor Day: S, D $75-$95; kit. unit $115; lower rates rest of yr. TV; cable (premium). Complimentary continental bkfst. Restaurant (see HUNTER HOUSE). Ck-out noon, ck-in 2 pm. Seaside inn built in 1910. Cr cds: A, MC, V.

Restaurant

✔★ **BREAKFAST CLUB.** 1500 Butler Ave. 912/786-5984. Hrs: 6 am-1 pm. Closed Dec 25. Semi-a la carte: bkfst $2.35-$8.95. Child's meals. Specialties: eggs Florentine, the Grill Cleaner's Special. Old-time diner atmosphere. Family-owned. Cr cds: DS, MC, V.

★ ★ **HUNTER HOUSE.** (See Hunter House Inn) 912/786-7515. Hrs: 6-10 pm; wkend hrs vary. Closed most major hols. Res required. Bar. Semi-a la carte: dinner $10-$18. Specializes in seafood, steak. Jazz ensemble some wkends. Outdoor dining. Cr cds: A, MC, V.

★ **MACELWEE'S SEAFOOD HOUSE.** 101 Lovell Ave (US 80). 912/786-4259. Hrs: 3-11 pm; Sat, Sun 11:30 am-10:30 pm. Closed Easter, Thanksgiving, Dec 25. Bar. Semi-a la carte: dinner $6.99-$19.95. Child's meals. Specializes in grilled, fried and steamed seafood & steak. View of ocean. Cr cds: A, D, DS, MC, V.

Valdosta (H-3)

(See also Adel)

Settled 1860 **Pop** 39,806 **Elev** 229 ft **Area code** 912 **E-mail** hhampton@mail.datasys.net **Web** www.datasys.net/valdtourism

Information Valdosta-Lowndes County Convention & Visitors Bureau, 1703 Norman Dr, Suite F, PO Box 1964, 31603-1964; 912/245-0513 or 800/569-8687.

When local citizens discovered that surveyors had left the town off the railroad right-of-way, they lost no time in moving the town four miles east of the original community (then called Troupville). Named for Val de Aosta (Vale of Beauty), the governor's estate, Valdosta later became a rail center with seven branch lines of three systems. One of the state's most prosperous small cities, Valdosta's products include timber, tobacco and cattle. Agriculture, tourism, Valdosta State University and Moody Air Force Base, 12 miles to the north, also contribute to the economy. Valdosta is in the center of a large wooded area with many lakes nearby.

What to See and Do

Barber House (1915). Restored neo-classical house serves as offices for Valdosta-Lowndes County Chamber of Commerce; elaborate woodwork, original light fixtures and furniture. Self-guided tours. (Mon-Fri) 416 N Ashley St. Phone 912/247-8100. **Free.**

Converse Dalton Ferrell House (1902). Neo-classical house with wide two-story porch that wraps around front and two sides. Interior has 20-ft ceilings, 14-foot high pocket doors, golden-oak woodwork, some original light fixtures. (By appt only) Contact the Convention & Visitors Center. 305 N Patterson St.

Lowndes County Historical Society Museum. Originally a Carnegie library, now contains collection of artifacts from Civil War to present; genealogical library. (Mon-Fri; closed major hols) 305 W Central Ave. Phone 912/247-4780. ¢

The Crescent (Valdosta Garden Center) (1898). Neo-classical house named for the dramatic, two-story, crescent-shaped porch supported by 13 columns. House includes grand staircase, second-floor bathroom with gold-leafed tiles and fireplace, and ballroom on third floor. In garden are chapel and octagonal school house. (Mon-Fri; also by appt) 904 N Patterson St. Phone 912/244-6747. ¢

Motels

✔★ ★ **BEST WESTERN KING OF THE ROAD.** 1403 N St Augustine Rd (31601), 1 blk W of jct GA 133, I-75 exit 5. 912/244-7600; FAX 912/245-1734. Web www.bestwestern.com. 137 units, 3 story. S $34-$44; D $39-$49; each addl $3; under 12 free. Crib $2. Pet accepted. TV; cable. Complimentary continental bkfst. Pool. Playground. Restaurant 5-9 pm. Rm serv. Bar 4 pm-midnight; closed Sun; entertainment. Ck-out 11 am. Meeting rms. Business servs avail. Sundries. Airport transportation. Some refrigerators. Cr cds: A, C, D, DS, MC, V.

✔★ ★ **BEST WESTERN LAKE PARK INN.** (6972 Bellville Rd, Lake Park 31636) S on I-75 exit 1. 912/559-4939; FAX 912/559-4944. 60 rms, 2 story. S, D $39-$42; under 18 free; family rates. Crib free. TV; cable (premium), VCR avail (movies). Complimentary continental bkfst. Complimentary coffee in rms. Restaurant adj open 24 hrs. Ck-out 11 am. In-rm modem link. Pool. Cr cds: A, D, DS, MC, V.

★ ★ **CLUBHOUSE INN.** 1800 ClubHouse Dr (31601), I-75 at GA 94, exit 5. 912/247-7755; FAX 912/245-1359; res: 800/258-2466. 121 rms, 2 story, 17 suites. S, D $58-$68; suites $76-$86; each addl $5; under 16 free; wkly rates; golf plans. Crib free. TV; cable (premium). Pool; whirlpool. Complimentary bkfst buffet; evening refreshments. Ck-out noon.

Meeting rms. Business center. In-rm modem link. Refrigerator in suites. Some private patios, balconies. Cr cds: A, C, D, DS, MC, V.

[D] [icons] SC [icon]

★ ★ **COMFORT INN.** *2101 W Hill Ave (31603), at jct US 84, I-75 exit 4.* 912/242-1212; FAX 912/242-2639. 138 rms, 2 story. S $46-$50; D $50-$57; each addl $5; suites $90; under 18 free. TV; cable (premium). Pool. Coffee in rms. Complimentary continental bkfst. Bar 11 am-11 pm. Ck-out noon. Business center. Valet serv. Guest lndry. Airport transportation. Lawn games. Cr cds: A, C, D, DS, MC, V.

[D] [icons] SC [icon]

★ ★ **HAMPTON INN.** *1705 Gornto Rd (31601), I-75, exit 5, adj Valdosta Mall.* 912/244-8800; FAX 912/244-6602. 102 rms, 3 story. S $56; D $61; under 18 free. Crib free. TV; cable (premium). Pool. Complimentary continental bkfst. Coffee in rms. Restaurant adj 6 am-11 pm. Ck-out noon. Business servs avail. In-rm modem link. Valet serv. Health club privileges. Cr cds: A, C, D, DS, MC, V.

[D] [icons] SC

✔★ ★ ★ **QUALITY INN-SOUTH.** *1902 W Hill (31601), I-75 at US 84, exit 4.* 912/244-4520; FAX 912/247-2404. 48 rms, 2 story. S $34.95-$49.95; D $37.95-$54.95; each addl $4; under 17 free. Crib $4. Pet accepted. TV; cable. Pool. Playground. Complimentary continental bkfst. Restaurant 11 am-2 pm, 5-10 pm. Bar 2-11 pm; Sat to midnight; closed Sun. Ck-out noon. Business servs avail. Cr cds: A, C, D, DS, MC, V.

[D] [icons] SC

★ ★ **RAMADA INN.** *2008 W Hill Ave (31601), jct US 84, I-75 exit 4.* 912/242-1225; FAX 912/247-2755. 102 rms, 2 story. S $44; D $49; under 18 free; golf plans. Crib free. Pet accepted; $5. TV; cable. Complimentary continental bkfst. Pool. Rm serv. Ck-out noon. Business servs avail. Health club privileges. Valet serv. Cr cds: A, C, D, DS, MC, V.

[icons] SC

✔★ **SHONEY'S INN.** *1828 W Hill Ave (31601), I-75 exit 4.* 912/244-7711; FAX 912/244-0361; res: 800/222-2222. 96 rms, 2 story. S $38-$46; D $42-$50; each addl $5; suite $65-$75; under 18 free. Crib free. TV; cable. Pool. Restaurant adj 6 am-midnight. Ck-out noon. Meeting rm. Business servs avail. Cr cds: A, D, DS, MC, V.

[D] [icons]

★ **TRAVELODGE.** *1330 N St Augustine Rd (31601), I-75 exit 5.* 912/242-3464. 88 rms, 2 story. S $34-$41; D $38-$51; each addl $4; under 18 free. Crib free. Pet accepted. TV; cable (premium). Pool. Complimentary full bkfst. Coffee in rms. Restaurant. Bar. Ck-out noon. Business servs avail. Valet serv. Some refrigerators. Balconies. Cr cds: A, C, D, DS, JCB, MC, V.

[D] [icons] SC

Restaurants

★ ★ **CHARLIE TRIPPER'S.** *4479 N Valdosta Rd (31602).* 912/247-0366. Hrs: 6-10 pm. Closed Sun; some major hols. Res accepted. Bar from 5 pm. Semi-a la carte: dinner $12.95-$16.95. Specializes in Angus beef, seafood, steak. Parking. Cr cds: A, C, D, DS, MC, V.

[D] [icon]

★ ★ **JP MULLDOONS.** *1405 Gornto Rd (31602).* 912/247-6677. E-mail mullis@www.valuu.net. Hrs: 4-11 pm. Closed Sun; major hols. Res accepted. Bar. Semi-a la carte: dinner $7.95-$16.95. Specializes in chicken, steak, fresh seafood. Pianist. Parking. Cr cds: A, MC, V.

[D] [icon]

★ ★ **MOM & DAD'S.** *4143 N Valdosta Rd (31602).* 912/333-0848. Hrs: 5-10 pm. Closed Sun, Mon; most major hols. Italian menu. Bar. Semi-a la carte: dinner $6.95-$14. Child's meals. Specializes in fish, veal, beef. Parking. Cr cds: A, D, DS, MC, V.

[D] [icon]

Warm Springs

(see Pine Mountain (Harris Co))

Washington (C-4)

(See also Athens)

Settled 1769 **Pop** 4,279 **Elev** 618 ft **Area code** 706 **Zip** 30673 **Web** www.washingtonga.org
Information Washington-Wilkes Chamber of Commerce, 104 Liberty St, Box 661; 706/678-2013.

The first city incorporated in the name of George Washington, it was the site of the Confederacy's last cabinet meeting (May 5, 1865) and the home of the South's first woman newspaper editor (Sarah Hillhouse of *The Monitor*, who printed editorials about the weather). Natives refer to this town as "Washington-Wilkes" (it is in Wilkes County) to distinguish it from the nation's capital.

Settlers first built a stockade called Heard's Fort. Elijah Clark led them in resistance to British troops, enabling patriots to hold Wilkes County when the rest of Georgia fell in 1779 (Kettle Creek Battleground). The last Confederate cabinet meeting convened in the Heard Building with President Davis and 14 officials on May 5, 1865. On June 4, Union soldiers seized $100,000 of the $500,000 in gold remaining in the Confederate Treasury. Legend persists that the rest of the gold (not recovered when Davis was captured at Irwinville) is buried in or near Washington.

What to See and Do

Callaway Plantation. Complete working plantation complex includes red brick Greek-revival mansion (1869); gray frame "Federal plainstyle" house (ca 1790) with period furnishings; hewn log kitchen (ca 1785) with utensils, agricultural equipment. RV parking (hookups). (Daily exc Mon; closed major hols) For further information contact the Chamber of Commerce. 5 mi W on US 78. ¢¢

Courthouse Square. On square are historic markers noting last cabinet meeting of Confederacy; inscription of first land-grant record; capstone from cotton factory (1811); World War II Memorial; Hill House (ca 1784), first property owned by a woman in northeast Georgia; and a Vietnam Memorial.

J. Strom Thurmond Dam and Lake. Swimming; fishing; boating (ramps). Hiking. Picnicking. Camping (yr-round; fee). For information contact Resource Manager's Office (E end of dam), Thurmond Lake, Rte 1, Box 12, Clarks Hill, SC 29821. 16 mi NE on US 378 to Lincolnton, then S on GA 47, E on GA 150. Phone 800/533-3478.

Kettle Creek Battleground. Marker indicates site of a decisive battle of Revolutionary War. 8 mi SW on Kettle Creek, off GA 44.

Robert Toombs House State Historic Site (1797). Restored residence of unreconstructed Confederate statesman and soldier. Frame Federal-era house with Greek-revival portico; period furniture, exhibits, video. (Tues-Sat, also Sun afternoons; closed major hols) 216 E Robert Toombs Ave. Contact Superintendent, PO Box 605; 706/678-2226. ¢

State parks.

Elijah Clark. Park includes log-cabin museum with colonial life demonstrations. Swimming beach, waterskiing; fishing; boating (ramp). Nature trails. Picnicking. Camping; cottages. Standard hrs, fees. 23 mi NE on US 378, on western shore of Clark Hill Lake. Contact Manager, Rte 4, Box 293, Lincolnton 30817; 706/359-3458.

Alexander H. Stephens. In 1,190-acre park is Liberty Hall (ca 1830), restored house of A.H. Stephens, Vice-President of the Confederacy; Confederate Museum (Tues-Sat, also Sun afternoons; closed Thanksgiving, Dec 25; fee). Fishing; boating, rentals. Nature trails. Picnicking. Camping. Standard hrs, fees. 19 mi SW on GA 47 to Crawfordville, then ½ mi N.Contact Superintendent, PO Box 283, Crawfordville 30631; 706/456-2602.

Washington-Wilkes Historical Museum. Located in white frame, antebellum house (ca 1836), the museum includes period furnishings, Civil War mementos, Native American items, earthenware. (Tues-Sat, also Sun afternoons; closed Jan 1, Thanksgiving, Dec 25) 308 E Robert Toombs Ave. Phone 706/678-2105. ¢

Motel

★ ★ **JAMESON INN.** *115 Ann Denard Dr. 706/678-7925; res: 800/541-3268.* 41 rms, 2 story. S $52; D $56; each addl $4; suites $111-$147; under 12 free; higher rates Masters Tournament. Crib $4. TV; cable. Complimentary continental bkfst. Restaurant adj open 24 hrs. Ck-out 11 am. Some refrigerators. Cr cds: A, D, DS, MC, V.

D ⊠ ⋒ SC

Waycross (G-5)

Settled 1818 **Pop** 16,410 **Elev** 135 ft **Area code** 912 **Zip** 31501 **Web** www.okefenokeeswamp.com
Information Tourism & Conference Bureau, 200 Lee Ave, PO Box 137, 31502; 912/283-3742.

The name Waycross reflects the town's strategic location at the intersection of nine railroads and five highways. Situated at the edge of the Okefenokee Swamp, the town's early settlers put up blockhouses to protect themselves from local Native Americans. The production of naval stores and the marketing of furs were of prime importance before Okefenokee became a national wildlife refuge. Today, the economy of Waycross is based on a diversity of industries, including timber, railroad, mobile homes and tourism.

What to See and Do

Laura S. Walker State Park. Within the park is a 106-acre lake. Swimming pool, waterskiing; fishing; boating. Golfing. Picnicking, playground. Camping. Standard hrs, fees. 9 mi SE via US 82 & GA 177. Contact Manager, 5653 Laura Walker Rd; 912/287-4900.

Okefenokee Heritage Center. Exhibits on Okefenokee area history; art gallery with changing exhibits; social science room with exhibit on Native Americans of South Georgia; 1912 train depot and railroad cars; turn-of-the-century print shop; nature trails; Power House building; 1840s pioneer house. (Daily; closed major hols) 2 mi W on US 82 to N Augusta Ave. Phone 912/285-4260. ¢

Okefenokee Swamp (see). S via US 1/23.

Southern Forest World. Exhibits, with audiovisual displays, detail development and history of forestry in the South; logging locomotive, fire tower, 38-ft model of a loblolly pine, giant cypress tree. Nature trails. (Daily; closed major hols) 2 mi W between US 1 & US 82 on N Augusta Ave. Phone 912/285-4056. ¢

Annual Events

Okefenokee Spring Fling. Okefenokee Swamp Park (see OKEFENOKEE SWAMP). Fish fry, theater, crafts. Every Sat in Mar, Apr, May.

Pogofest. Parade, exhibits, barbecue. Oct.

Motels

★ ★ **HOLIDAY INN.** *1725 Memorial Dr, at jct US 84. 912/283-4490; FAX 912/283-4490, ext. 197.* Web www.okeswamp.com. 148 rms, 2 story. S $45-$50; D $51-$55; each addl $5; under 19 free. Crib free. Pet accepted. TV; cable (premium). Pool. Complimentary full bkfst. Coffee in rms. Restaurant 6 am-2 pm, 5-9:30 pm. Rm serv. Bar 3 pm-midnight, Sat from 5 pm; closed Sun. Ck-out noon. Coin lndry. Meeting rms. In-rm modem link. Bellhops. Valet serv. Sundries. Airport, bus depot transportation. Exercise equipt. Health club privileges. Putting green. Game rm. Microwaves avail. Some private patios, balconies. Cr cds: A, C, D, DS, JCB, MC, V.

D ✏ ≈ 🏋 ⊠ ⋒ SC

★ **PINE CREST.** *1761 Memorial Dr (US 1/23). 912/283-3580.* 30 rms. S $28; D $33; each addl $3; under 18 free. Crib $3. TV; cable (premium). Pool. Restaurant adj 6 am-10 pm. Ck-out noon. Health club privileges. Cr cds: A, D, MC, V.

≈ ⋒ SC

Winder (C-3)

(See also Athens, Atlanta)

Pop 7,373 **Elev** 984 ft **Area code** 770 **Zip** 30680 **E-mail** mcartmill@mindspring.com
Information Barrow County Chamber of Commerce, 6 Porter St, PO Box 456, phone 770/867-9444.

What to See and Do

Fort Yargo State Park. The park is named for a fort of hand-hewn pine logs built during Native American uprisings in the 1790s. Swimming, beach; fishing; boating and canoeing (rentals). Nature trails. Picnicking. Camping. 1 mi S via GA 81. Contact Manager; 770/867-3489. At the N end is

Will-A-Way Recreation Area. Designed to benefit disabled persons. Swimming pool; fishing; boating. Nature trails. Picnicking. Camping area for disabled and special chairs for water access. For hrs, fees phone 770/867-5313.

Motel

★ **DAYS INN.** *(802 N Broad St, Monroe 30655) US 11 N at US 78. 770/267-3666; FAX 770/267-7189.* 45 rms, 2 story. S, D $45-$55; each addl $5; under 17 free; wkly rates. Crib free. Pet accepted, some restrictions; $5. TV; cable (premium). Complimentary continental bkfst. Restaurant nearby. Meeting rms. Business servs avail. In-rm modem link. Pool. Some refrigerators, microwaves. Cr cds: A, DS, MC, V.

D ✏ ≈ ⊠ ⋒ SC

Kentucky

Population: 3,685,296
Land area: 40,409 square miles
Elevation: 257-4,145 feet
Highest point: Black Mountain (Harlan County)
Entered Union: June 1, 1792 (15th state)
Capital: Frankfort
Motto: United We Stand, Divided We Fall
Nickname: Bluegrass State
State flower: Goldenrod
State bird: Kentucky cardinal
State fair: 10 days late August, 1999, in Louisville
Time zone: Eastern and Central
Web: www.kentuckytourism.com

The spirits of native sons Abraham Lincoln, Daniel Boone and Henry Clay are still present in many aspects of modern-day Kentucky. Known for such traditions as mountain music, mint juleps and the Derby, Kentucky's rich heritage has not faded over time. Although the bluegrass is blue only for a short time in the spring, and although few self-respecting Kentuckians will dilute a good bourbon with sugar and mint leaves, Kentucky has not sought to distance itself from its history. To many, this is still the land where Lincoln was born, where Zachary Taylor spent his youth and where Harriet Beecher Stowe witnessed the auctioning of slaves and found the inspiration to write *Uncle Tom's Cabin.* Such pioneers and visionaries continue to be revered today perhaps more so in Kentucky than anywhere else. The state itself has been assured immortality through the words of Stephen Foster's song, "My Old Kentucky Home."

Kentucky stretches from Virginia to Missouri, a geographic and historic bridge in the westward flow of American settlement. The state can be divided into four sections: the Bluegrass, the south central cave country, the eastern mountains and western lakes. Each differs drastically in geography, culture and economics. A circular area in the north central portion of the state, the Lexington plain, is bluegrass country, home of great horses and gentlemen-farmers. A predominantly rural nature has remained even though a patina of industry has been imposed, thanks to generous tax laws that have added industrial muscle to almost every major community. The great dams of the Tennessee Valley Authority have harnessed floods, generated cheap power, lured chemical plants and created new vacation resources.

More than 450 million pounds of burley and dark tobacco are typically grown in Kentucky each year. The principal crop is followed by corn, soybeans and wheat. Cattle, hogs, sheep and poultry round out the farm family. Not all of Kentucky's corn is served on the cob; much of it winds up as bourbon whiskey, respected and treasured in much of the world. Kentucky is a major mining state as well, with rich deposits of bituminous coal, petroleum, natural gas, fluorspar, natural cement and clay. Tobacco and food products, electronic equipment, transportation equipment, chemicals and machinery are the principal factory products.

The Cumberland Gap, a natural passageway through the mountains that sealed the Kentucky wilderness off from Virginia, was the gateway of the pioneers. Dr. Thomas Walker, the first recorded explorer to make a thorough land expedition into the state, arrived in 1750. Daniel Boone and a company of axmen hacked the Wilderness Road through the Cumberland Gap and far into the wilds. The first permanent settlement was at Harrodsburg in 1774, followed quickly by Boonesborough in 1775. Richard Henderson, founder of the Transylvania company, asked Congress to recognize Transylvania as the fourteenth state; instead Virginia claimed Kentucky as one of its counties, and Transylvania passed into history. Finally, in 1792 Congress admitted Kentucky as a state. The Civil War found Kentucky for the Union but against abolition. It remained officially with the North, but fought on both sides.

When to Go/Climate

Kentucky enjoys a temperate climate with four distinct seasons. Winter snowfall ranges from 5 to 10 inches in the southwestern part of the state to as much as 40 inches in the highest elevations. Thunderstorms are common in the Ohio River Valley in spring and summer.

AVERAGE HIGH/LOW TEMPERATURES (°F)
LOUISVILLE

Jan 40/23	**May** 76/55	**Sept** 80/59
Feb 45/27	**June** 84/63	**Oct** 69/46
Mar 56/36	**July** 87/67	**Nov** 57/37
Apr 67/45	**Aug** 86/66	**Dec** 45/29

Parks and Recreation Finder

Directions to and information about the parks and recreation areas below are given under their respective town/city sections. Please refer to those sections for details.

CALENDAR HIGHLIGHTS

MARCH

Jim Beam Stakes Race (Covington). Turfway Park Race Track in Florence. One of the largest pursed Thoroughbred races for three-year-olds. Race culminates week-long festival. Phone 606/371-0200.

APRIL

Rolex-Kentucky Event and Trade Fair (Lexington). Three-day endurance test for horse and rider in dressage, cross-country and stadium jumping. Fair features boutiques. Phone 606/233-2362.

Kentucky Derby Festival (Louisville). Two-week celebration with Pegasus Parade, Great Steamboat Race, Great Balloon Race, mini-marathon, concerts and sports tournaments. Contact Kentucky Derby Festival; phone 502/584-6383 or 800/928-FEST.

MAY

Governor's Derby Breakfast (Frankfort). Breakfast, entertainment and Kentucky crafts. Phone 502/564-2611.

JUNE

Capital Expo Festival (Frankfort). Capital Plaza Complex. Traditional music, country music, fiddling; workshops, demonstrations, arts and crafts; balloon race, dancing, games, contests, puppets, museum exhibitions, ethnic and regional foods, entertainment. Phone 502/875-868?

Festival of the Bluegrass (Lexington). Kentucky Horse Park. Top names in Bluegrass music, with more than 20 bands appearing. Includes special shows for children; crafts; workshops with the musicians. The 600-acre park has more than 750 electric hookups for campers. Phone 606/846-4995.

AUGUST

Kentucky Heartland Festival (Elizabethtown). Freeman Lake Park. Antique auto show, arts and crafts, races, hot air balloon, bluegrass music, games and food. Phone 502/765-4334 or 502/769-2396.

Kentucky State Fair (Louisville). Livestock shows; championship horse show; home and fine arts exhibits; midway, entertainment. Contact VP of Expositions; phone 502/367-5180.

SEPTEMBER

Riverfest (Covington). One of the largest fireworks displays in the country; shot from barges moored on the Ohio River. Phone 513/621-9326.

OCTOBER

Big River Arts & Crafts Festival (Henderson). Audubon State Park. More than 250 exhibitors. Phone 502/026-4433.

Daniel Boone Festival (Barbourville). Celebrates Boones search for a route through Kentucky. Square dancing, musket shooting, reenactment of Native American treaty signing, horse show, parade, old time fiddling, long rifle shoot between neighboring states, exhibits, antique displays, arts and crafts, parade, entertainment, homemade candies and cakes. The Cherokee make annual pilgrimage to city. Phone 606/546-4300.

NATIONAL PARK AND RECREATION AREAS

Key to abbreviations: I.H.S. = International Historic Site; I.P.M. = International Peace Memorial; N.B. = National Battlefield; N.B.P. = National Battlefield Park; N.B.C. = National Battlefield & Cemetery; N.C. = National Conservation Area; N.E.M. = National Expansion Memorial; N.F. = National Forest; N.G. = National Grassland; N.H. = National Historical Park; N.H.C. = National Heritage Corridor; N.H.S. = National Historic Site; N.L. = National Lakeshore; N.M. = National Monument; N.M.P. = National Military Park; N.Mem. = National Memorial; N.P. = National Park; N.Pres. = National Preserve; N.R. = National Recreational Area; N.R.R. = National Recreational River; N.Riv. = National River; N.S. = National Seashore;

N.S.R. = National Scenic Riverway; N.S.T. = National Scenic Trail; N.Sc. = National Scientific Reserve; N.V.M. = National Volcanic Monument.

Place Name	Listed Under
Abraham Lincoln Birthplace N.H.S.	same
Big South Fork N.R.	DANIEL BOONE NATIONAL FOREST
Cumberland Gap N.H.	same
Daniel Boone N.F.	same
Land Between the Lakes	same
Mammoth Cave N.P.	same

STATE PARK AND RECREATION AREAS

Key to abbreviations: I.P. = Interstate Park; S.A.P. = State Archaeological Park; S.B. = State Beach; S.C. = State Conservation Area; S.C.P. = State Conservation Park; S.Cp. = State Campground; S.F. = State Forest; S.G. = State Garden; S.H.A. = State Historic Area; S.H.P. = State Historic Park; S.H.S. = State Historic Site; S.M.P. = State Marine Park; S.N.A. = State Natural Area; S.P. = State Park; S.P.C. = State Public Campground; S.R. = State Reserve; S.R.A. = State Recreation Area; S.Res. = State Reservoir; S.Res.P. = State Resort Park; S.R.P = State Rustic Park.

Place Name	Listed Under
Barren River Lake S.Res.P.	GLASGOW
Ben Hawes S.P.	OWENSBORO
Big Bone Lick S.P.	WALTON
Blue Licks Battlefield S.P.	MAYSVILLE
Breaks I.P.	same
Buckhorn Lake S.Res.P.	HAZARD
Carter Caves S.R.P.	OLIVE HILL
Cumberland Falls S.Res.P.	same
Dale Hollow Lake S.Res.P.	MONTICELLO
E.P. "Tom" Sawyer S.P.	LOUISVILLE
Fort Boonesborough S.P.	WINCHESTER
General Burnside S.P.	SOMERSET
General Butler S.Res.P.	CARROLLTON
Grayson Lake S.P.	OLIVE HILL
Green River Lake S.P.	CAMPBELLSVILLE
Greenbo Lake S.Res.P.	ASHLAND
Jenny Wiley S.Res.P.	PRESTONSBURG
John James Audubon S.P.	HENDERSON
Kenlake S.Res.P.	same
Kentucky Dam Village S.Res.P.	GILBERTSVILLE
Kincaid Lake S.P.	WILLIAMSTOWN
Lake Barkley S.Res.P.	CADIZ
Lake Cumberland S.Res.P.	JAMESTOWN
Lake Malone S.P.	GREENVILLE
Levi Jackson Wilderness Road S.P.	LONDON
Lincoln Homestead S.P.	BARDSTOWN
My Old Kentucky Home S.P.	BARDSTOWN
Natural Bridge S.Res.P.	same
Old Fort Harrod S.P..	HARRODSBURG
Pennyrile Forest S.Res.P.	MADISONVILLE
Pine Mountain S.Res.P.	PINEVILLE
Rough River Dam S.Res.P.	same

Water-related activities, hiking, riding and various other sports, picnicking and camping are available in many of these areas. Eighteen areas have lodges and/or cottages (rates vary; phone 800/255-PARK for information); 30 have tent and trailer sites (Apr-Oct: $12 for two persons; $1 each addl person over 16 years; sr citizens rate; electricity and water included; primitive camping $8.50; rates subject to change). Thirteen state parks have campgrounds open year-round. Campsites are rented on a first-come, first-served basis; pets on leash only. No entrance fee is charged at state parks. For further information on state parks or camping, contact the Kentucky Department of Parks, 500 Mero St, Frankfort 40601; 502/564-2172 or 800/255-PARKincluding the Canadian provinces of Ontario and Quebec.

FISHING & HUNTING

Mountain streams, giant lakes and major rivers all invite the angler and are productive throughout the year. Both largemouth bass and crappie can be found throughout the state. Lake Cumberland (see SOMERSET) has walleye; Laurel River Lake (see CORBIN), Lake Cumberland tailwaters and Paintsville Lake have trout; Buckhorn, Cave Run (see MOREHEAD) and Green River lakes have muskie; Lake Barkley, Kentucky Lake (see GILBERTSVILLE) and tailwaters have sauger and Lake Cumberland has striped bass. Statewide nonresident fishing license: $30; trout stamp $5; nonresident 3-day fishing license $12.50; 15-day license $20; no fishing license required for children under age 16. Annual nonresident hunting license: $95; deer permit with two tags, gun or archery $21; turkey permit $17.50; 5-day small game license $27.50. For open season dates and other details contact the Department of Fish and Wildlife Resources, #1 Game Farm Rd, Frankfort 40601; phone 502/564-4336 or 800/858-1549.

Tennessee Valley Authority Recreation Sites

Many of Kentucky's major recreation areas have developed around projects of the Tennessee Valley Authority. The flood-control and power projects in the west have created Kentucky Lake (see GILBERTSVILLE, KENLAKE STATE RESORT PARK), with a scenic shoreline of 2,380 miles, big Lake Barkley (see CADIZ) and Land Between the Lakes (see). The TVA (Land Between the Lakes, 100 Van Morgan Dr, Golden Pond, KY 42211; phone 502/924-2000) will furnish material on the authority and its lakes, including recreation maps. Navigation charts are available at nominal cost from Map Sales, TVA, 101 Haney Bldg, Chattanooga, TN 37402-2801.

Driving Information

Children under 40 inches in height must be in an approved safety seat anywhere in vehicle. In addition, all persons anywhere in vehicle are required to use safety belts. For further information phone 502/695-6356.

INTERSTATE HIGHWAY SYSTEM

The following alphabetical listing of Kentucky towns in *Mobil Travel Guide* shows that these cities are within 10 miles of the indicated Interstate highways. A highway map should, however, be checked for the nearest exit.

Highway Number	Cities/Towns within 10 miles
Interstate 24	Cadiz, Gilbertsville, Hopkinsville, Paducah.
Interstate 64	Ashland, Frankfort, Georgetown, Lexington, Louisville, Morehead, Olive Hill, Winchester.
Interstate 65:	Bowling Green, Cave City, Elizabethtown, Glasgow, Hodgenville, Horse Cave, Louisville, Mammoth Cave Natl Park, Park City, Shepherdsville.
Interstate 71	Carrollton, Covington, Louisville, Walton.
Interstate 75	Berea, Corbin, Covington, Georgetown, Lexington, London, Mount Vernon, Richmond, Walton, Williamsburg, Williamstown.

Additional Visitor Information

The Department of Travel, Dept MR, PO Box 2011, Frankfort 40602, phone 800/225-8747, distributes literature and information, including a list of the state's many interesting festivals and fairs. The *Kentucky Official Vacation Guide* is informative, comprehensive and is revised annually.

There are eight welcome centers in Kentucky; visitors who stop by will find information and brochures most helpful in planning stops at points of interest. Their locations are as follows: Florence Welcome Center, I-75 southbound exit 180, Walton; Franklin Welcome Center, I-65 northbound exit 2, Franklin; Hopkinsville Welcome Center, I-24 westbound exit 89, Hopkinsville; Grayson Welcome Center, I-64 westbound exit 181, Grayson; Shelby County Welcome Center, I-64 eastbound exit 28, Shelbyville; Bullitt Co. Welcome Center, I-65 southbound exit 116, Shepherdsville; Whitehaven Welcome Center, I-24 eastbound and US 45, Paducah; and Williamsburg Welcome Center, I-75 northbound exit 11, Williamsburg.

Abraham Lincoln Birthplace National Historic Site (D-6)

(See also Elizabethtown, Hodgenville)

Web www.nps.gov/abli lincomj.htm

(3 mi S of Hodgenville on US 31E/KY 61)

On February 12, 1809, the Sinking Spring Farm, named after a small limestone spring, became the birthplace of Abraham Lincoln, the 16th President of the United States. Less than three years later, in 1811, Thomas Lincoln, the President's father, moved the family to Knob Creek Farm, located about ten miles northeast. Later moves eventually took the Lincoln family to Indiana and Illinois.

The Lincoln Farm Association purchased the farm in 1905. In 1916 the Lincoln Farm Association deeded the farm to the War Department and was later transferred to the National Park Service in 1933. Today 110 acres of the original Lincoln Farm are contained within the 116-acre park.

Visitor Center Audiovisual program (18 min) and exhibits explore Lincoln's background and environment. Thomas Lincoln's Bible is on display.

More than 100,000 citizens contributed funds to construct the granite and marble Memorial Building in 1911. Inside is the log cabin originally believed to be the Lincoln birthplace; research has revealed that this is most likely not the case. The cabin was disassembled, moved, exhibited and stored many times before being reconstructed permanently inside the Memorial Building.

(Daily; closed Thanksgiving, Dec 25) For specific hours and possible holiday closures contact the Superintendent, 2995 Lincoln Farm Rd, Hodgenville 42748; 502/358-3137.   **Free.**

Annual Events

Martin Luther King's Birthday. Sun, mid-Jan.

Lincoln's Birthday. Wreath-laying ceremony. Afternoon of Feb 12.

Founders Day. Festivities commemorating the park's founding (July 17,1916). Wkend nearest July 17.

Ashland (C-9)

(See also Olive Hill)

Settled 1815 **Pop** 23,622 **Elev** 548 ft **Area code** 606 **E-mail** aacvb@ramlink.net
Information Ashland Area Convention & Visitors Bureau, 728 Greenup Ave, PO Box 987, 41105; 606/329-1007 or 800/377-6249.

Set in the highlands of northeastern Kentucky, on the Ohio River, Ashland is an industrial city that produces oil, steel and chemicals.

What to See and Do

Central Park. A 47-acre park with prehistoric Native American mounds. Sport facilities; playgrounds, picnicking. Phone 606/327-2046.

Covered bridges.

Bennett's Mill Bridge. Built in 1855 to service mill customers, bridge spans Tygarts Creek. At 195 ft, this is one of Kentucky's longest single-span covered bridges; original footings and frame intact. Closed to traffic. 8 mi W on KY 125 off KY 7.

Oldtown Bridge. Built 1880 to Burr's design; 194-ft, dual-span bridge crosses Little Sandy River. Closed to traffic. 14 mi W via US 23, then 9 mi S on KY 1.

Greenbo Lake State Resort Park. A 3,330-acre park, with 225-acre lake, has early buffalo (pig-iron) furnace. Swimming pool (Memorial Day-Labor Day); fishing; boating (marina). Hiking, bicycle rentals; tennis. Picnicking, playground, lodge. Tent & trailer sites (Apr-Oct). Recreation program for children. 18 mi W via US 23 to KY 1. Phone 606/473-7324.

Kentucky Highlands Museum. Displays trace history and cultural heritage of the region. Period clothing; Native American artifacts; WW II memorabilia; industrial exhibits. Gift shop. (Tues-Sat; closed major hols) 1624 Winchester. Phone 606/329-8888. **Free.**

Paramount Arts Center. Historical 1930s art-deco theatre. Hosts childrens events, concerts. Tours. (Daily) 1300 Winchester Ave. Phone 606/324-3175.

Annual Event

Poage Landing Days Festival. Central Park. Fiddle festival, national and local entertainers, arts & crafts, children's activities. 3rd wkend Sept.

Motels

★ ★ **DAYS INN.** *12700 KY 180 (41102).* 606/928-3600; FAX 606/928-6515. E-mail ash@musselmanhotels.com; web www.musselmanhotels.com. 63 rms, 2 story. S $46-$59; D $52-$64; each addl $5; under 18 free. Crib free. Pet accepted; $5. TV; cable (premium), VCR avail (movies). Pool. Complimentary continental bkfst. Complimentary coffee in rms. Restaurant nearby. Ck-out noon. Coin lndry. Meeting rms. Business center. In-rm modem link. Exercise equipt. Some refrigerators, microwaves. Picnic tables. Cr cds: A, C, D, DS, MC, V.

D ⊯ ≋ ⋈ ⋈ SC ⏃

★ ★ **FAIRFIELD INN BY MARRIOTT.** *10945 US 60 (41102), I-64 exit 185 to US 60.* 606/928-1222. 63 rms, 3 story, 8 suites. S $55-$60; D $60-$65; each addl $6; suites $65-$75; under 18 free. Crib avail. TV; cable (premium). Complimentary continental bkfst. Restaurant adj 6 am-11 pm. Ck-out noon. Meeting rms. Business servs avail. Sundries. Indoor pool; whirlpool. Game rm. Refrigerators, microwaves in suites. Cr cds: A, C, D, DS, ER, JCB, MC, V.

D ≋ ⋈ ⋈ SC

✔ ★ ★ **KNIGHTS INN.** *7216 US 60 (41102).* 606/928-9501; FAX 606/928-4436. 124 rms. S $38; D $43; kit. units $42-$47; each addl $5; under 18 free. Crib free. Pet accepted; $5. TV; cable (premium). Pool. Complimentary continental bkfst. Restaurant nearby. Ck-out noon. Meet-

ing rms. Business servs avail. Refrigerators. Cr cds: A, C, D, DS, ER, MC, V.

D ⊯ ≋ ⋈ ⋈ ⋈ SC

Hotel

★ ★ **ASHLAND PLAZA.** *1 Ashland Plaza (41101), I-64 exit 185.* 606/329-0055; res: 800/346-6133; FAX 606/325-4513. 157 rms, 10 story. S $78-$80; D $84-$88; each addl $6; under 18 free; wkend, hol plans; higher rate special events. Crib $6. TV; cable (premium), VCR avail. Complimentary coffee in lobby. Restaurant 6 am-2 pm, 5-10 pm; Sun to 9 pm. Bar 4 pm-1:30 am; closed Sun. Ck-out noon. Meeting rms. Business servs avail. Free airport, RR station transportation. Health club privileges. Cr cds: A, C, D, DS, MC, V.

D ⋈ ⋈ SC

Resort

★ ★ **GREENBO LAKE STATE RESORT PARK.** *(HC 60, Box 562, Greenup 41144)* 606/473-7324; res: 800/325-0083; FAX 606/473-7741. 36 rms, 3 story. Mid-May-Aug: S $53-$58; D $63-$68; each addl $5; under 16 free; golf plan; lower rates rest of yr. TV; cable. Complimentary coffee in lobby. Restaurant 7 am-9 pm. Box lunches. Grocery 2 mi. Coin lndry 2 mi. Meeting rms. Business servs avail. Shopping arcade. Tennis privileges. 18-hole golf privileges, greens fee $13, pro. Boats. Hiking. Bicycle rentals. Lawn games. Social dir. Rec rm. Game rm. Pool; wading pool, lifeguard. Playground. Supervised child's activities. Many balconies. On lake. Cr cds: A, C, D, DS, MC, V.

D ⊯ ⏃⏃ ⋈ ≋ ⋈ ⋈ SC

Restaurant

✔ ★ ★ **DRAGON PALACE.** *807 Carter Ave (41101).* 606/329-8081. Hrs: 11 am-10 pm; Fri, Sat noon-11 pm; Sun noon-9 pm. Chinese, Amer menu. Bar. Semi-a la carte: lunch $2.55-$5.25. A la carte entrees: dinner $6.50-$14.95. Specialties: orange chicken, seafood Imperial, sizzling combo. Cr cds: A, DS, MC, V.

D

Barbourville (E-8)

(See also Corbin, Pineville)

Founded 1800 **Pop** 3,658 **Elev** 986 ft **Area code** 606 **Zip** 40906
Information Knox County Chamber of Commerce, 196 Daniel Boone Dr, Suite 205; 606/546-4300.

In the valley of the scenic Cumberland River, Barbourville is protected by a $2.5-million flood wall built around the city. Tobacco, coal mining and timber are the area's major industries. The city has also produced two Kentucky governors, a lieutenant governor, three US congressmen, and many other statesmen who served outside Kentucky.

What to See and Do

Daniel Boone National Forest (see). 24 mi NW on US 25.

Dr. Thomas Walker State Historic Site. Replica of original log cabin built in 1750 by Dr. Thomas Walker; surrounded by 12 acres of parkland. Miniature golf (fee). Picnic area, shelter, playground. Grounds (daily). 5 mi SW on KY 459. Phone 606/546-4400. **Free.**

Annual Event

Daniel Boone Festival. Celebrates Boone's search for a route through Kentucky. Square dancing, musket shooting, reenactment of Native

American treaty signing, horse show, parade, old time fiddling, long rifle shoot between neighboring states, exhibits, antique displays, arts & crafts, parade, entertainment, homemade candies & cakes. The Cherokee make annual pilgrimage to city. 7 days early Oct.

Bardstown (D-6)

(See also Elizabethtown)

Settled 1775 **Pop** 6,801 **Elev** 647 ft **Area code** 502 **Zip** 40004 **E-mail** tourism@bardstown.com **Web** www.win.net/bardstown

Information Bardstown-Nelson County Tourist & Convention Commission, PO Box 867; 502/348-4877 or 800/638-4877.

One of Kentucky's oldest settlements, Bardstown includes many historic sites. It is the seat of Nelson County, home of four bourbon distilleries. Today, the chief agricultural product is tobacco.

What to See and Do

Bernheim Forest. 14 mi NW on KY 245 in Shepherdsville (see).

Jim Beam American Outpost. Visitors can tour the historic Beam family home and stroll the grounds. Craft shop. (Daily; closed some hols) 15 mi NW on KY 245 in Clermont. Phone 502/543-9877. **Free.**

Lincoln Homestead State Park. In a compound framed by split rail fences is a replica of the cabin built on this land, which was originally settled in 1782 by Abraham Lincoln, Sr, grandfather of the President. This was the home of Thomas Lincoln until he was 25. Furnished in pioneer style, including several pieces made by Thomas Lincoln. Also, the Berry House, home of Nancy Hanks during her courtship by Thomas Lincoln; pioneer relics, photostatic copies of the Thomas and Nancy Lincoln marriage bonds. A replica of the blacksmith and carpenter shop where Thomas Lincoln worked is also in the compound. Houses (May-Sept, daily; Oct, wkends). The 150-acre park offers 18-hole golf (daily, fee). Picnic facilities, playground. 20 mi SE on US 150 to KY 528. Phone 606/336-7461. Museum ¢

My Old Kentucky Dinner Train. Scenic dining excursions aboard elegant, restored dining cars from the 1940s. Round trip through countryside includes four-course meal; five-course meal Fri & Sat evenings. (Feb-Dec, daily exc Mon) Departs from 602 N 3rd St. Phone 502/348-7300. ¢¢¢¢¢

My Old Kentucky Home State Park. The composer Stephen Foster occasionally visited his cousin, Judge John Rowan, at the stately house, Federal Hill (1795). These visits may have inspired him to write "My Old Kentucky Home," a melody that is a lasting favorite. The house and its 290 acres of grounds are now a state park. Attendants wear period costumes; period furnishings. Golf course. Picnic area, playground. Tent & trailer sites (standard fees). Guided tour (fee). Gardens; amphitheater (see SEASONAL EVENT). (Daily; closed Jan 1, Thanksgiving, wk of Dec 25) 1 mi E on US 150. For information contact Superintendent, PO Box 323; 502/348-3502. Grounds **Free.**

Spalding Hall (ca 1825). Once part of St Joseph College; used as hospital in Civil War. Former dormitory; now houses art and pottery shop. (May-Oct, daily; rest of yr, daily exc Mon) Just off N 5th St. Phone 502/348-2999. **Free.** Also here are

    Oscar Getz Museum of Whiskey History. Copper stills, manuscripts, documents, bottles and advertising art chronicle the history of whiskey from pre-colonial days to Prohibition era. (May-Oct, daily; rest of yr, daily exc Mon) 114 N 5th St. Phone 502/348-2999. **Free.**

    Bardstown Historical Museum. Features items covering 200 years of local history. Exhibits include Native American artifacts, Lincoln papers concerning Lincoln-Reed suit, John Fitch papers and replica of first steamboat, Stephen Foster memorabilia, tools and utensils of Trappist Monks, Civil War artifacts, gifts of King Louis Phillipe and King Charles X of France, pioneer items, period costumes (1850s-1890s), natural science display. (May-Oct, daily; rest of yr, daily exc Mon) Phone 502/348-2999. **Free.**

St Joseph Proto-Cathedral (1816). First Catholic cathedral west of the Allegheny Mountains. Paintings donated by Pope Leo XII. (Daily) 310 W Stephen Foster, at jct US 31E, 62. Phone 502/348-3126.

The Mansion. House of Ben Johnson, a powerful political figure of Kentucky's past, was site of raising of first Confederate flag in 1861. Tours. Overnight stays avail. (Daily; closed Dec 25) 1003 N Third St. Phone 502/348-2586. ¢¢

Wickland (1813-1817). Stately Georgian mansion, residence of two Kentucky governors, Charles A. Wickliffe and J.W. Beckham, and former Louisiana governor, R.C. Wickliffe (all of one family). Handsomely furnished with many original antiques. (Appt only; closed major hols) E on US 62. Phone 502/348-5428. ¢¢

Seasonal Event

Stephen Foster, The Musical. J. Dan Talbott Amphitheater, in My Old Kentucky Home State Park. Musical with 50 Foster melodies, tracing composer's triumphs and romance. Nightly exc Mon; Sat also matinee. In the event of rain, indoor theater is used. Phone 502/348-5971 or 800/626-1563 for prices, reservations. Early June-early Sept.

Motels

★ ★ **BEST WESTERN GENERAL NELSON.** *411 W Stephen Foster Ave (US 62).* 502/348-3977; res: 800/225-3977. 52 rms, 2 story, 4 kits. May-Oct: S, D $59-$79; lower rates rest of yr. Crib free. TV; cable (premium), VCR avail. Pool. Business servs avail. In-rm modem link. Coffee in lobby. Restaurant adj 6:30 am-9 pm. Ck-out 11 am. Coin lndry. Business servs avail. In-rm modem link. Sundries. Refrigerators avail. Cr cds: A, C, D, DS, MC, V.

D ≈ ⊠ ⚒ SC

★ ★ **HOLIDAY INN.** *1875 New Haven Rd, 2 mi S on US 31E exit 21 at Bluegrass Pkwy.* 502/348-9253; FAX 502/348-5478. E-mail hibard@cube3.net. 102 rms, 2 story. May-Sept: S, D $59-$89; each addl $5; under 19 free; lower rates rest of yr. Crib free. Pet accepted, some restrictions. TV; cable (premium), VCR avail (movies). Pool. Playground. Restaurant 6 am-2 pm, 5-9 pm; Fri, Sat to 10 pm. Bar. Ck-out 11 am. Meeting rms. Business servs avail. In-rm modem link. 9-hole par 3 golf, driving range. Exercise equipt. Some refrigerators, microwaves Cr cds: A, C, D, DS, JCB, MC, V.

D ⚑ ⚓ ≈ ⚒ SC

✔ ★ **OLD BARDSTOWN INN.** *510 E Stephen Foster Ave (US 150E), off US 150E.* 502/349-0776; res: 800/894-1601. 34 rms, 2 story. S $38-$50; D $38-$54; each addl $5; under 16 free. Crib $5. TV; cable. Pool. Complimentary coffee in lobby. Restaurant nearby. Ck-out 11 am. Cr cds: A, MC, V.

D ≈ ⊠ ⚒

★ ★ **PARKVIEW.** *418 E Stephen Foster Ave (US 62), at jct US 150.* 502/348-5983; FAX 502/349-6973; res: 800/732-2384. 38 rms, 1-2 story, 10 kit. units. June-Labor Day: S $50; D $55; each addl $5; suites, kit. units $65-$85; lower rates rest of yr. Crib free. Pet accepted. TV; cable. Pool. Complimentary continental bkfst. Restaurant 11 am-9 pm. Bar. Ck-out 11 am. Coin lndry. Refrigerators, wet bars. My Old Kentucky Home State Park opp. Cr cds: A, DS, MC, V.

⚑ ≈ ⊠ ⚒ SC

Motor Hotel

★ ★ **HAMPTON INN.** *985 Chambers Blvd, I-65 exit 112.* 502/349-0100; FAX 502/349-1191. 106 rms, 2 story. June-Oct: S $62; D $68; higher rates special events; lower rates rest of yr. Crib free. Pet accepted. TV; cable (premium), VCR avail. Indoor pool. Complimentary continental bkfst. Complimentary coffee in rms. Ck-out noon. Meeting rms. Business servs avail. In-rm modem link. Valet serv Mon-Fri. Exercise equipt. Refrigerators, microwaves avail. Cr cds: A, C, D, DS, JCB, MC, V.

D ⚑ ≈ ⚓ ⊠ ⚒ SC

Inns

★ ★ **JAILER'S INN.** *111 W Stephen Foster Ave (US 62).* 502/348-5551; res: 800/948-5551; FAX 502/348-1852. E-mail cpaul@ jailersinn.com; web www.jailersinn.com. 6 rms. No rm phones. S, D $65–$105; each addl $5–$10. Closed Jan. Crib free. TV; cable, VCR avail. Complimentary full bkfst; afternoon refreshments. Restaurant adj 11 am–9 pm. Ck-out 11 am, ck-in 2 pm. Some in-rm whirlpools. Built 1819 as jail, then converted to jailer's residence. Antiques, oriental rugs. Cr cds: A, DS, MC, V.

⊠ 🔥

★ **McLEAN HOUSE.** *107 W Stephen Foster Ave (US 62).* 502/348-3494; res: 800/482-8376. 7 rms, 2 story. S, D $80–$125. TV; cable. Complimentary continental bkfst. Ck-out 11 am, ck-in 2 pm. Colonial furnishings; antiques. In original post office building built 1812. Cr cds: MC, V.

🔥

Restaurant

✔ ★ ★ **KURTZ.** *418 E Stephen Foster.* 502/348-8964. Hrs: 11 am–9 pm. Closed Dec 25. Res accepted. Bar. Semi-a la carte: lunch $5.95–$8.95, dinner $9.95–$15.95. Specializes in country ham, fried chicken, biscuit pudding with bourbon sauce. Parking. State park adj. Cr cds: A, DS, MC, V.

D ⊐

Berea (D-7)

(See also Mount Vernon, Richmond)

Settled 1855 **Pop** 9,126 **Elev** 1,034 ft **Area code** 606 **Zip** 40403 **Web** www.4berea.com
Information Tourist and Convention Commission, 201 N Broadway; 606/986-2540 or 800/598-5263.

Berea College and diverse industry provide the income for this community in the foothills of the Cumberland Mountains and the Daniel Boone National Forest. Designated the "Folk Arts and Crafts Capital of Kentucky" by the state legislature, Berea boasts more than 155 antique shops, 40 craft shops and working studios. Indian Fort Mountain nearby is the site of prehistoric fortifications. A Ranger District office of the Daniel Boone National Forest (see) is located here.

What to See and Do

Churchill Weavers. Established 1922, Churchill is one of the nation's oldest producers of handwoven goods. Self-guided tours through loom-house (Mon-Fri; closed Dec 25). Gift shop and outlet shop (daily; closed Dec 25). Lorraine Ct, exit I-75 to US 25N. Phone 606/986-3127. **Free.**

The Studio Craftspeople of Berea. An organization of craftspeople working in various media invite visitors to visit their studios. The Tourist and Convention Commission has a list of studios open to the public.

Annual Events

Kentucky Guild of Artists & Craftsmen's Fair. Indian Fort Theater. Crafts, art, folk dances, singing. Phone 606/986-3192. 3rd wkend May and 2nd wkend Oct.

Berea Craft Festival. Indian Fort Theater, at Berea College. Entertainment, regional food, crafts demonstrations. Phone 606/986-2258. Three days mid-July.

Celebration of Traditional Music Festival. Features traditional music, dancers, concerts. Last wkend Oct.

Motel

★ ★ **DAYS INN.** *I-75 exit 77, at jct KY 595.* 606/986-7373; FAX 606/986-3144. 60 rms, 2 story. S $43–$45; D $49–$51; each addl $5; family rates. Crib free. Pet accepted; $5. TV. Pool. Complimentary coffee in lobby. Restaurant adj. Ck-out 11 am. Meeting rm. Business servs avail. Miniature golf. Cr cds: A, C, D, DS, MC, V.

D ✔ ⊠ ⊠ 🔥 SC

✔ ★ **HOLIDAY.** *1/2 mi E of I-75 exit 76 on KY 21.* 606/986-9311. E-mail holmotel@aol.com. 62 rms. S, D $45; each addl $5; suites $56. Crib $5. TV; cable. Pool. Restaurant adj 7 am–10 pm. Ck-out 11 am. Cr cds: A, MC, V.

D ⊠ ⊠ 🔥

Hotel

★ ★ ★ **BOONE TAVERN.** *Main & Prospect Sts (40404), 1 mi E of I-75 exit 76, on KY 21.* 606/986-9358; FAX 606/986-7711; res: 800/366-9358. Web www.4berea.com/tavern. 58 rms. S $55–$80; D $65–$90; each addl $10; under 12 free. Crib $10. TV. Restaurant 7-9:30 am, 11:30 am-2 pm, 6-8 pm. Ck-out 11 am. Meeting rms. Gift shop. Health club privileges. Established 1909. Operated by Berea College; most furniture handmade by students. Cr cds: A, C, D, DS, MC, V.

D ⊠ 🔥 SC

Restaurants

✔ ★ **DINNER BELL.** *I-75 exit 76.* 606/986-2777. E-mail rstew59348@aol.com. Hrs: 7 am-10 pm; winter hrs vary. Semi-a la carte: bkfst $1.65–$5.95, lunch $1.99–$4.95, dinner $4.50–$11.95. Child's meals. Specializes in country cooking. Parking. Country and antique shop. Cr cds: MC, V.

D ⊐

★ **PAPALENO'S.** *108 Center St, adj Berea College.* 606/986-4497. Hrs: 11 am-11 pm; Fri, Sat to midnight; Sun noon-11 pm. Closed Thanksgiving, Dec 25. Italian menu. Semi-a la carte: lunch, dinner $1.65–$12.50. Child's meals. Specializes in soups, salads, pizza. Cr cds: A, DS, MC, V.

SC

Bowling Green (E-5)

Founded 1780 **Pop** 40,641 **Elev** 496 ft **Area code** 502 **E-mail** bowlinggreen.chamber.ky.net **Web** www.bowlinggreen.chamber.ky.net
Information Bowling Green Area Chamber of Commerce, 812 State St, PO Box 51, 42102; 502/781-3200.

In the early days of the community, county court was held in the house of Robert Moore, a founder of the town, and visiting lawyers would idle away their time bowling on the lawn—hence the name. A cultural center for southern Kentucky with a variety of industries, Bowling Green is also sustained by Warren County's dairy cattle, livestock and tobacco farms. For a short time, it was the Confederate capital of Kentucky.

What to See and Do

Beech Bend Park. Water park includes swimming pool, waterslide, paddleboats, eight rides. Miniature golf. Picnic area. Camping. Separate fee for each activity. (Late May-early Sept, daily) Beech Bend Rd. Phone 502/781-7634. ¢

Capitol Arts Center. Restored art-deco building; national and local live presentations, gallery exhibits. (Mon-Fri; closed hols) Admission varies with event. 416 E Main. Phone 502/782-2787.

Historic Riverview at Hobson Grove (1857). House in Italianate style, furnished with collection of Victorian furniture from 1860-1890. (Feb-mid-Dec, daily exc Mon; closed hols) 1100 W Main Ave, in Hobson Grove Park. Phone 502/843-5565. ¢¢

⊠ **National Corvette Museum.** Hands-on educational exhibits and displays on history of this classic American car. More than 50 vintage cars. (Daily; closed Jan 1, Thanksgiving, Dec 25) I-65 exit 28. Phone 502/781-7973. ¢¢¢

Western Kentucky University (1906). (15,800 students) High on a hill, Western Kentucky University was built around the site of a Civil War fort. College St & 15th St. Phone 502/745-0111. On campus are

Kentucky Museum. Collections include costumes, implements, art works and textiles relating to the cultural history of Kentucky and the region. Exhibits, tours, special programs. Gift shop. (Daily exc Mon; closed univ hols) Kentucky Bldg, Kentucky St. Phone 502/745-2592. ¢ In same building is

Kentucky Library. Contains 30,000 books, manuscripts, maps, broadsides, photographs, sheet music, scrapbooks, materials relating to Kentucky and to genealogical research of Kentucky families. (Daily exc Sun; closed univ hols) Phone 502/745-2592. **Free.**

Hardin Planetarium. State St. Varying programs year-round; phone 502/745-4044 for schedule & fees.

Motels

✓★ ★ **BEST WESTERN CONTINENTAL INN.** 700 Interstate Dr (42102), I-65N exit 28, at US 31W. 502/781-5200; FAX 502/782-0314. 100 rms, 2 story. S $40-$50; D $50-$70; each addl $3; higher rates special events. Complimentary continental bkfst. Crib $3. TV; cable. Heated pool; wading pool. Restaurant open 24 hrs. Rm serv. Ck-out noon. Business servs avail. Cr cds: A, D, DS, MC, V.

D ⊠ ⊠ 🔥 SC

★ ★ **BEST WESTERN MOTOR INN.** 166 Cumberland Trace Rd (42102), 1 blk E of I-65 exit 22. 502/782-3800; FAX 502/782-2384; res: 800/343-2937. 179 rms, 2-3 story. S, D $62-$69; suites $99-$110. Crib free. TV; cable. 2 pools, 1 indoor; wading pool, whirlpool. Playground. Restaurant open 24 hrs. Rm serv. Ck-out noon. Coin lndry. Meeting rms. Sundries. Gift shop. Tennis. Exercise equipt; sauna. Game rm. Lawn games. Some refrigerators. Enclosed courtyard. Cr cds: A, C, D, DS, MC, V.

D 🏌 ⊠ 🏃 🎿 SC

★ ★ **FAIRFIELD INN BY MARRIOTT.** 1940 Mel Browning St (42104), I-65 exit 22. 502/782-6933; FAX 502/782-6967. 105 rms, 3 story. S $52; D $59; under 18 free. Crib free. TV; cable (premium). Heated pool. Complimentary continental bkfst. Restaurant adj 6 am-10 pm. Ck-out noon. Meeting rms. Business servs avail. In-rm modem link. Refrigerator avail. Cr cds: A, D, DS, MC, V.

D ⊠ ⊠ 🔥 SC

★ ★ **HAMPTON INN.** 233 Three Springs Rd (42104), I-65 exit 22, W on KY 231. 502/842-4100; FAX 502/782-3377. 131 rms, 4 story. S $64; D $74; under 18 free; higher rates special events. Crib avail. TV. Pool. Complimentary continental bkfst. Coffee in rms. Restaurant nearby. Meeting rms. Ck-out noon. Business servs avail. In-rm modem link. Health club privileges. Cr cds: A, C, D, DS, MC, V.

D ⊠ ⊠ 🔥 SC

★ ★ **HOLIDAY INN I-65.** 3240 Scottsville Rd (42104), 2¾ mi SE on US 231, 1 blk W of I-65 exit 22. 502/781-1500; FAX 502/842-0030. E-mail bghotel@aol.com. 107 rms, 2 story. S $49-$80; D $90; each addl $10; under 19 free. Crib free. Pet accepted. TV; cable (premium). Pool; wading pool. Restaurant 6:30-10 am, 5-9 pm. Rm serv. Bar 5-10 pm. Ck-out noon. Business servs avail. In-rm modem link. Sundries. Exercise equipt. Cr cds: A, C, D, DS, JCB, MC, V.

D 🐾 ⊠ 🏃 🎿 SC

✓★ ★ **NEW'S INN.** 3160 Scottsville Rd (42104), 2½ mi E on US 231; 1 blk W of I-65 exit 22. 502/781-3460; FAX 502/781-3463; res:

800/443-3701. 52 rms. S $41; D $45-$59; each addl $3; under 16 free; higher rates special events. Crib free. Pet accepted, some restrictions. TV; cable (premium). Pool. Playground. Complimentary continental bkfst. Restaurant adj 6 am-11 pm. Ck-out 11 am. Business servs avail. Free airport transportation. Refrigerators. Picnic tables, grills. Cr cds: A, DS, MC, V.

D 🐾 ⊠ ⊠ 🏃 SC

Motor Hotel

★ **GREENWOOD EXECUTIVE INN.** 1000 Executive Way (42102), 2¾ mi SE, just off US 231; 1 blk W of I-65 exit 22. 502/781-6610; FAX 502/781-7985; res: 800/354-4394. 150 rms, 4 story. S $45-$55; D $55-$65; each addl $5; suites $95-$130; higher rates special events. Crib $5. TV; cable (premium), VCR avail (movies). Pool. Restaurant 6 am-2 pm, 5-10 pm. Rm serv. Bar noon-1 am; Fri, Sat to 2 am; entertainment. Ck-out noon. Meeting rms. Business servs avail. Airport, bus depot transportation. Cr cds: A, C, D, DS, MC, V.

D ⊠ 🏃 🔥 SC

Restaurants

★ ★ **ANDREW'S.** 2019 Scottsville Rd (42104). 502/781-7680. Hrs: 4:30-9:30 pm; Fri, Sat to 10 pm. Closed Sun. Bar 3:30 pm-midnight. Semi-a la carte: dinner $4.95-$19.95. Child's meals. Specializes in seafood, beef, flambé cooking. Red oak paneling with stained & beveled glass. Cr cds: A, D, DS, MC, V.

D 🍴

✓★ ★ **MARIAH'S.** 801 State St (42102). 502/842-6878. Hrs: 11 am-10 pm; Fri, Sat to 11 pm; Sun to 9 pm. Closed Memorial Day, Labor Day, Dec 25. Bar 11-1 am. Semi-a la carte: lunch $6.95-$10, dinner $9.95-$15.95. Child's meals. Specializes in steak, seafood, salad. Parking. Historic home from 1800s; large mural of downtown in early 1940s. Cr cds: A, D, DS, MC, V.

D 🍴

Breaks Interstate Park (D-10)

(See also Pikeville)

(7 mi SE of Elkhorn City, KY and 8 mi N of Haysi, VA on KY-VA 80)

Where the Russell Fork of the Big Sandy River plunges through the mountains is called the "Grand Canyon of the South," the major focus of this 4,600-acre park on the Kentucky-Virginia border. From the entrance, a paved road winds through an evergreen forest and then skirts the canyon rim. Overlooks provide a spectacular view of the "Towers," a huge pyramid of rocks. Within the park are extraordinary rock formations, caves, springs, a profusion of rhododendron and, of course, the 5-miles-long, 1,600-ft-deep gorge.

The visitor center houses historical and natural exhibits, including a coal exhibit (Apr-Oct, daily). Laurel Lake is stocked with bass and bluegill. Swimming pool; pedal boats. Hiking, bridle trails, mountain bike trails. Picnicking, playground. Camping (Apr-Oct, fee); motor lodge, cottages (year-round), restaurant, gift shop. Park (daily); facilities (Apr-late Dec, daily). For further information contact Breaks Interstate Park, PO Box 100, Breaks, VA 24607; 540/865-4413 or 800/982-5122. Memorial Day-Labor Day, per car ¢

Cadiz (E-3)

(See also Gilbertsville, Land Between The Lakes)

Pop 2,148 **Elev** 423 ft **Area code** 502

Information Cadiz-Trigg County Tourist Commission, PO Box 735, phone 502/522-3892; or visit Tourist Information Center, US 68E at I-24 interchange.

With the development of "Land Between The Lakes," a 170,000-acre wooded peninsula between the Tennessee Valley Authority's Kentucky Lake and the Army Corps of Engineers' Lake Barkley on the Cumberland River, Cadiz became a staging area for the major recreation project. The area covers much of Trigg County, of which Cadiz is the seat.

What to See and Do

Barkley Dam, Lock and Lake. 35 mi NW in Gilbertsville (see). On lakeshore is

Lake Barkley State Resort Park. A 3,700-acre park on a 57,920-acre lake. Swimming beach, pool, bathhouse (seasonal); fishing; boating, canoeing (ramps, rentals, marina). Hiking, backpacking, horseback riding (seasonal); 18-hole golf course (yr-round); tennis, trapshooting, shuffleboard, basketball. Picnicking, restaurant, cottages, lodge (see RESORT). Camping (fee). Children's programs. Lighted airstrip. Standard fees. 7 mi W on KY 80 to KY 1489. Phone 502/924-1131 or 800/325-1708.

Kenlake State Resort Park (see). 16 mi SW on US 68, KY 80.

Original Log Cabin. Four-rm log cabin, furnished with 18th- and 19th-century artifacts, was occupied by a single family for more than a century. (Mon-Fri; closed major hols) 22 Main St. Phone 502/522-3892. **Free.**

Recreation areas.

Cadiz Public Use Area. Fishing; launching ramp. Playground, picnic area. On US 68 on W side of town. **Free.**

Hurricane Creek Public Use Area. Swimming; launching ramp. Playground. Improved campsites (fee). (Apr-mid-Oct, daily) Golden Age Passport accepted (see MAKING THE MOST OF YOUR TRIP). 12 mi NW via KY 274. Phone 502/522-8821.

Motel

★ ★ **COUNTRY INN BY CARLSON.** *154 Hospitality Lane (42211), I-24 exit 65. 502/522-7007; FAX 502/522-3893; res: 800/707-0129.* 48 rms, 2 story. S $52; D $57; each addl $5; under 18 free. Crib free. Pet accepted. TV; cable (premium). Pool. Complimentary continental bkfst. Coffee in rms. Restaurant adj. Ck-out noon. Business servs avail. Cr cds: A, C, D, DS, MC, V.

[D] [⊙] [≈] [⊼] [🔥] [SC]

Resort

★ ★ ★ **LAKE BARKLEY LODGE.** *3500 State Park Rd (42211), 10 mi NW on KY 1489, 3 1/2 mi N of US 68 in Lake Barkley State Resort Park. 502/924-1131; FAX 502/924-0013; res: 800/325-1708.* Web www.state.ky.us. 124 rms, 2 story, 13 kit. cottages. Apr-Oct: S $59-$74; D $69-$84; each addl $5; suites $160; kit. cottages $150; under 16 free; some lower rates rest of yr. Crib free. TV. Pool; wading pool, whirlpool, lifeguard in summer. Child's program; playground. Dining rm 7-10:30 am, 11:30 am-2:30 pm, 5-9 pm. Ck-out noon (cottages 11 am), ck-in 4 pm. Coin lndry. Meeting rms. Business servs avail. Maid serv in lodge. Free transportation to lodge from park airport. Lighted tennis. 18-hole golf, greens fee $20. Beach; waterskiing; boats. Lawn games. Trap shooting. Soc dir; entertainment. Rec rm. Exercise rm; sauna, steam rm. Some private patios, balconies. Picnic tables. State-owned; facilities of park available. Cr cds: A, C, D, DS, MC, V.

[D] [⊙] [➳] [🏃] [⛷] [✕] [⊼] [🔥] [SC]

Restaurant

✔★ **SHERLOCK'S BUFFET AND GRILL.** *136 Hospitality Lane (42211). 502/522-8420.* Hrs: 10:30 am-9 pm; Sat, Sun from 6 am. Closed Jan 1, Dec 25. Res accepted. Semi-a la carte: bkfst $1.95-$5.95, lunch $3.50-$4.95, dinner $5.25-$12.95. Child's meals. Specializes in ham, fish. Salad bar. Modern country atmosphere. Cr cds: A, DS, MC, V.

[D] [⊸]

Campbellsville (D-6)

(See also Jamestown)

Pop 9,577 **Elev** 813 ft **Area code** 502 **Zip** 42718 **Web** www.campbellsvilleky.com
Information Taylor County Tourist Commision, Court St & Broadway, PO Box 4021, 42719; 502/465-3786 or 800/738-4719.

Located geographically in the heart of Kentucky, Campbellsville is near the junction of the Pennyrile, Bluegrass and Knobs regions of the state. Nearby, at Tebbs Bend, the Battle of Green River was fought on July 4, 1863. Also in the vicinity is the town of Greensburg, with its interesting historic district dating to the 18th century.

What to See and Do

Green River Lake State Park. Beach; fishing; marina (rentals). Picnicking. Camping. (Daily) Standard fees. 6 mi S on KY 55. Phone 502/465-8255.

Motels

★ ★ **BEST WESTERN.** *1400 E Broadway (US 68). 502/465-7001.* 60 rms. S $52; each addl $5; suites $55-$89; under 18 free. Crib free. TV; cable (premium). Pool; whirlpool. Playground. Complimentary continental bkfst. Restaurant nearby. Ck-out 11 am. Meeting rms. Business servs avail. In-rm modem link. Some refrigerators, microwaves. Cr cds: A, C, D, DS, MC, V.

[D] [≈] [⊼] [🔥] [SC]

✔★ **LAKEVIEW.** *1291 Old Lebanon Rd, 1 mi N on KY 289, across from lake. 502/465-8139; res: 800/242-2874.* 16 rms. S $36; D $40; each addl $2; under 12 free. Crib free. TV; cable (premium). Complimentary continental bkfst. Coffee in rms. Restaurant nearby. Ck-out 11 am. Some refrigerators. Cr cds: A, DS, MC, V.

[⊼] [🔥] [SC]

Restaurant

✔★ **CANDLESTICK.** *350 W Broadway (US 68). 502/465-7777.* Hrs: 11 am-9 pm; Fri, Sat to 10 pm. Res accepted. Semi-a la carte: lunch $1.95-$7.95, dinner $2.50-$15.95. Buffet: Sat $11.95, Sun (lunch) $7.95. Child's meals. Specializes in beef, seafood, regional dishes. Salad bar. Cr cds: DS, MC, V.

[SC] [⊸]

Carrollton (C-6)

Founded 1794 **Pop** 3,715 **Elev** 469 ft **Area code** 502 **Zip** 41008 **E-mail** carrollkytour@kih.net
Information Carroll County Tourism Commission, PO Box 293; 502/732-7036 or 800/325-4290.

At the confluence of the Ohio and Kentucky rivers, this tree-shaded residential town is named in honor of Charles Carroll. Originally from Carrollton, Maryland, Carroll was one of the signers of the Declaration of Independence.

What to See and Do

General Butler State Resort Park. A 791-acre memorial to William O. Butler, native of Carrollton and hero of Battle of New Orleans. Within the park is a 30-acre lake. Swimming; fishing; boating (rentals). Nature trails; 9-hole golf (fee), tennis. Ski area (fee). Picnic sites, playground, grocery adj; cottages, lodge & dining room (see RESORT). Tent & trailer camping (daily, standard fees). Recreation program. 2 mi S on KY 227. For fees or information phone 502/732-4384.

Historic District. Self-guided auto tour of historic sites and houses. Tour begins at Old Stone Jail, corner of Highland & Court Sts. Tourist center on 2nd floor houses small museum on local history.   **Free.**

Annual Events

Kentucky Scottish Weekend. Celebration of Scottish heritage includes pipe bands, bagpipers; Scottish athletic competition, Celtic music; British auto show. Phone 502/239-2665. 2nd wkend May.

Blues to the Point—Two Rivers Blues Festival. Point Park. Two-day event with regional and national blues music performances. Early Sept.

Motels

★ **DAYS INN.** 61 Inn Rd, I-71 exit 44. 502/732-9301; FAX 502/732-5596. 84 rms. S, D $55; each addl $6; under 19 free; higher rates special events. Crib free. TV; cable (premium). Pool. Complimentary bkfst buffet. Ck-out noon. Meeting rms. Business servs avail. In-rm modem link. Downhill ski 2 mi. Microwaves avail. Cr cds: A, C, D, DS, MC, V.

[D] [≠] [≈] [⋈] [⋈] [SC]

★ ★ **HOLIDAY INN EXPRESS.** 141 Inn Rd, at I-71 exit 44. 502/732-6661; FAX 502/732-6661. 62 rms, 2 story. S, D $59; each addl $6; under 19 free; some wkend rates; higher rates special events. Crib free. Pet accepted, some restrictions. TV; cable (premium). Complimentary continental bkfst. Restaurant nearby. Ck-out noon. Meeting rm. Business servs avail. In-rm modem link. Downhill ski 2 mi. Microwaves avail. Cr cds: A, C, D, DS, JCB, MC, V.

[D] [≠] [≈] [⋈] [⋈] [SC]

Inn

✔★ **CARROLLTON INN.** 3rd & Main Sts. 502/732-6905. 11 rms. S $39.95; D $49.95; each addl $5; under 16 free; higher rates special events. Crib free. TV; cable. Restaurant (see CARROLLTON INN). Bar. Ck-out 11 am, ck-in noon. Business servs avail. Cr cds: A, MC, V.

[🔥]

Resort

★ ★ **GENERAL BUTLER LODGE.** 2 mi N of I-71 exit 44, in General Butler State Resort Park. 502/732-4384; FAX 502/732-4270; res: 800/325-0078. 56 rms in 2-3 story lodge, 23 kit. cottages. No elvtr in lodge. S $55; D $65; each addl $5; kit. cottages $73-$140; under 17 free. Crib free. TV; cable (premium), VCR avail. Pool; wading pool, lifeguard in summer. Playground. Free supervised child's activities (late May-early Sept). Dining rm 7 am-9 pm. Ck-out noon; cottages 11 am. Meeting rm. Business center. Gift shop. Lighted tennis. 9-hole golf, greens fee $10, miniature golf. Swimming in lake; boats, paddleboats. Downhill ski on site. Private patios, balconies. Picnic tables, grills. State-owned; all facilities of state park. Cr cds: A, C, D, DS, MC, V.

[D] [≠] [∠] [⋏] [⋈] [≈] [⋈] [⋈] [SC] [⋈]

Restaurant

✔★ ★ **CARROLLTON INN.** (See Carrollton Inn) 502/732-6905. Hrs: 11 am-10 pm; Fri & Sat to 11 pm; Sun 10 am-9 pm. Closed Dec 25. Res accepted. Bar. Semi-a la carte: lunch $3-$6, dinner $5.95-$14.95. Child's meals. Specializes in beef, seafood, bbq ribs. Cr cds: A, MC, V.

Cave City (E-5)

(See also Glasgow, Horse Cave, Park City)

Pop 1,953 **Elev** 636 ft **Area code** 502 **Zip** 42127 **E-mail** cavecity@mail.ivprog.com **Web** cavecity.com
Information Cave City Convention Center, PO Box 518; 502/773-3131 or 800/346-8908.

Located in the heart of Cave Country, this village primarily serves tourists passing through the region en route to Mammoth Cave and other commercially-operated caves nearby.

What to See and Do

Crystal Onyx Cave. Helectites, stalagmites, stalactites, onyx columns, rare crystal onyx rimstone formations; Native American burial site dating from 680 B.C. Temperature in cave 54°F. Guided tours every 45 min. Improved & primitive camping adj (fee). (Feb-Dec, daily; closed Thanksgiving, Dec 25) 2 mi SE on KY 90, off I-65. Phone 502/773-2359. Guided tours ¢¢

Kentucky Action Park. Chairlift to top of mountain, slide downhill in individual alpine sleds with braking system. Go-carts, bumper boats, bumper cars (fees); horseback riding (fee). (Memorial Day-Labor Day, daily; Easter-Memorial Day, Labor Day-Oct, wkends) 1½ mi W on KY 70. Phone 502/773-2636.   ¢¢

Mammoth Cave Chair Lift and Guntown Mountain. Lift ascends 1,350 feet to Guntown Mountain. On grounds is authentic reproduction of 1880s frontier town; museums, saloon, entertainment. Train ride (fee). Water slide. Onyx Cave tours (Apr-Nov, daily). (Memorial Day-Labor Day, daily; May-Memorial Day & Labor Day-mid-Oct, Sat, Sun only) At jct KY 70, I-65. Phone 502/773-3530. Admission includes chair lift.   ¢¢¢

Mammoth Cave National Park (see). 10 mi W via I-65, KY 70.

Motels

★ **BEST WESTERN KENTUCKY INN.** 1009 Doyle Ave, I-65 exit 53. 502/773-3161. 50 rms. Mid-May-early Sept: S $59-$69; D $64-$69; each addl $5; under 12 free; higher rates special events; lower rates rest of yr. Crib $5. TV; cable. Pool; wading pool. Complimentary coffee in lobby. Restaurant opp 5 am-11 pm. Ck-out 11 am. Coin lndry. Cr cds: A, C, D, DS, MC, V.

[≈] [⋈] [⋈] [SC]

★ **DAYS INN.** 822 Mammoth Cave St, ¾ mi W on KY 70; 2 blks NE of I-65 exit 53. 502/773-2151. 110 rms, 2 story. Late May-early Sept: S $56; D $66; each addl $5; under 12 free; lower rates rest of yr. Crib free. Pet accepted. TV; cable (premium); VCR avail (movies). Heated pool; wading pool. Restaurant 6 am-10 pm (seasonal). Ck-out noon. Coin lndry.

Meeting rms. Business servs avail. Game rm. Some in rm whirlpools. Private patios, balconies. Cr cds: A, C, D, DS, JCB, MC, V.

▣ ▨ ◪ ◪ SC

★ **HOLIDAY INN EXPRESS.** 102 Happy Valley Rd, I-65 exit 53. 502/773-3101; FAX 502/773-6082. E-mail cav@musselmanhotels.com; web musselmanhotels.com. 105 rms, 2 story. Memorial Day-Labor Day: S, D $62-$67; each addl $5; under 18 free; higher rates Highland Games; lower rates rest of yr. Crib free. Pet accepted; $7. TV; cable (premium). Complimentary continental bkfst. Complimentary coffee in rms. Restaurant nearby. Ck-out 11 am. Meeting rms. Business servs avail. In-rm modem link. Coin lndry. Heated pool. Game rm. Some refrigerators, microwaves. Picnic tables, grills. Cr cds: A, C, D, DS, JCB, MC, V.

D ▣ ▨ ◪ ◪ SC

✔★ **QUALITY INN.** 1006A Doyle Ave, W on KY 70, 90. 502/773-2181; FAX 502/773-3200; res: 800/321-4245. 100 rms, 2 story. Memorial Day-Labor Day: S $42-$62; D $48-$68; each addl $6; under 12 free; higher rates special events; lower rates rest of yr. Crib $6. Pet accepted. TV; cable (premium). Pool. Playground. Restaurant to 11 pm. Ck-out 11 am. Business servs avail. Game rm. Picnic tables. Cr cds: A, C, D, DS, MC, V.

D ▣ ▨ ◪ ◪ SC

★ **SUPER 8.** (88 Stockpen Rd, Munfordville 42765) I-65 exit 65. 502/524-4888; FAX 502/524-5888. 50 rms, 2 story. May-mid-Sept: S $47; D $51; each addl $4; under 12 free; higher rates special events; lower rates rest of yr. Crib free. Pet accepted; $6. TV; cable (premium). Complimentary continental bkfst. Restaurant nearby. Ck-out 11 am. Business servs avail. Some in-rm whirlpools. Cr cds: A, C, D, DS, MC, V.

D ▣ ▨ ◪ SC

Restaurant

★ **SAHARA STEAK HOUSE.** 413 E Happy Valley St. 502/773-3450. Hrs: 11 am-9 pm; Sat from 3 pm; Sun from 11:30 am. Closed Thanksgiving, Dec 25. Semi-a la carte: lunch $2.95-$6.95, dinner $4.95-$23.95. Child's meals. Specializes in steak, seafood. Salad bar. Cr cds: A, DS, MC, V.

▨

Corbin (E-8)

(See also Barbourville, London, Williamsburg)

Settled 1883 **Pop** 7,419 **Elev** 1,080 ft **Area code** 606 **Zip** 40701 **E-mail** corbinoed@2geton.net
Information Tourist & Convention Commission, 101 N Depot St; 606/528-6390 or 800/528-7123.

What to See and Do

Colonel Harland Sanders' Original Restaurant (1940). Authentic restoration of the first Kentucky Fried Chicken restaurant. Displays include original kitchen, artifacts, motel room. Original dining area is still in use. (Daily; closed Dec 25) 2 mi N on US 25. **Free.**

Cumberland Falls State Resort Park (see). 19 mi SW via US 18W, KY 90.

Laurel River Lake. A 5,600-acre lake with fishing; boating (launch, rentals). Hiking, recreation areas. Picnicking. Camping (fee). (See ANNUAL EVENT) Approx 10 mi W, in Daniel Boone National Forest (see); access from I-75, US 25W, KY 312 & KY 192. Contact the US Army Corps of Engineers, Resource Manager, 1433 Laurel Lake Rd, London 40741; 606/864-6412. For camping information, contact London District Ranger, US Forest Service, PO Box 907, London 40741; 606/864-4163. **Free.**

Annual Event

Nibroc Festival. Costumes, mountain arts & crafts, parade, horse shows, square dancing, beauty pageant, midway, entertainment, food booths. Boat races on Laurel River Lake. Early Aug.

Motels

✔★ ★ **BEST WESTERN CORBIN INN.** 2630 Cumberland Falls Rd, I-75 exit 25. 606/528-2100; res: 888/528-2100; FAX 606/523-1704. E-mail bestwest@2geton.net; web www.2geton.net/bestwest. 63 rms, 2 story. S, D $49.99; under 12 free. Crib free. TV; cable (premium). Pool. Complimentary continental bkfst. Complimentary coffee in rms. Ck-out 11 am. Business servs avail. Some refrigerators; microwaves avail. Cr cds: A, C, D, DS, MC, V.

D ▨ ◪ ◪ SC

★ **KNIGHTS INN.** 37 Hwy 770, I-75 exit 29. 606/523-1500; FAX 606/523-5818. 109 rms, 10 kits. S $37.75; D $44.95; each addl $6; kit. units $49; under 18 free; wkly rates. Crib $2. TV; cable (premium). Pool. Restaurant nearby. Ck-out noon. Cr cds: A, C, D, DS, MC, V.

D ▨ ◪ ◪ SC

Covington (Cincinnati Airport Area) (B-7)

(See also Walton)

Founded 1815 **Pop** 43,264 **Elev** 531 ft **Area code** 606 **E-mail** info@nkycvb.com **Web** www.nkycvb.com/
Information Northern Kentucky Convention and Visitors Bureau, 50 E RiverCenter Blvd, Suite 40, 41011; 606/261-4677 or 800/782-9659.

This town is linked to Cincinnati, Ohio, by five broad bridges spanning the Ohio River. Named for a hero of the War of 1812, Covington in its early days had many German settlers who left their mark on the city. East of the city, the Licking River meets the Ohio. The suspension bridge (1867) that crosses from Third and Greenup streets to Cincinnati is the prototype of the Brooklyn Bridge in New York City. The adjacent riverfront area includes Covington Landing, a floating restaurant-entertainment complex.

What to See and Do

Cathedral Basilica of the Assumption (1901). Patterned after the Abbey of St Denis and the Cathedral of Notre Dame, France, the basilica has massive doors, classic stained-glass windows (including one of the largest in the world), murals and mosaics by local and foreign artists. (Daily exc hols) Guided tours (Sun, after 10 am mass; also by appt). Madison Ave & 12th St. Phone 606/431-2060. Tour ¢

Devou Park. A 550-acre park with lake overlooking the Ohio River. Golf (fee), tennis. Picnic grounds. Lookout point, outdoor concerts (mid-June-mid-Aug). (Daily) Western Ave. Phone 606/292-2151. **Free.** In park is

> **Behringer-Crawford Museum.** Exhibits on local archaeology, paleontology, history, fine art and wildlife. (Daily exc Mon) 1600 Montague Rd. Phone 606/491-4003. ¢

MainStrasse Village. Approx 5 sq blks in Covington's old German area. Historic district of residences, shops and restaurants in more than 20 restored buildings dating from mid-late 1800s. (See ANNUAL EVENTS) Phone 606/491-0458. Also featured is the

> **Carroll Chimes Bell Tower.** Completed in 1979, this 100-ft tower has a 43-bell carillon and mechanical figures that portray the legend of the Pied Piper of Hamelin. Philadelphia St, W end of Village.

Oldenberg Brewery/Museum. Functioning micro brewery with guided tours; large brewing memorabilia collection; replica 1930s beer truck; beer garden (seasonal); pub; gift shop. (Daily) 4 mi S on I-75, Buttermilk Pike exit in Ft Mitchell. Phone 606/341-2802. Museum tour ¢¢

Riverboat cruises. Sightseeing cruises on the Ohio River; also lunch, dinner and moonlight cruises. Full-day and half-day cruises by appt. Contact BB Riverboats, 1 Madison Ave, 41011, phone 606/261-8500; or Queen City Riverboats, 303 O'Fallon St, PO Box 131, Dayton 41074, phone 606/292-8687. ¢¢¢

Annual Events

Jim Beam Stakes Race. Turfway Park Race Track in Florence. One of the largest pursed Thoroughbred races for three-yr-olds. Race culminates week-long festival. Phone 606/371-0200. Last Sat in Mar.

Maifest. MainStrasse Village. Traditional German spring festival with entertainment, arts & crafts, food, games and rides. Phone 606/491-0458. 3rd wkend May.

Riverfest. Banks of Ohio River. One of the largest fireworks displays in the country; shot from barges moored on river. Labor Day wkend.

Oktoberfest. MainStrasse Village. Entertainment, arts & crafts, food. Early Sept.

Seasonal Event

Horse racing. Turfway Park Race Course. 3 mi SW at 7500 Turfway in Florence. Thoroughbred racing Wed-Sun. Phone 606/371-0200 or 800/733-0200. Early Sept-early Oct & late Nov-early Apr.

Motels

★ **BEST WESTERN.** (7821 Commerce Dr, Florence 41042) I-75/71 exit 181, 1 blk E to Commerce Dr. 606/525-0090; FAX 606/525-6743. 51 rms, 3 story. June-Sept: S, D $59-$69; each addl $5; under 12 free; higher rates special events; lower rates rest of yr. Crib free. TV; cable (premium). Complimentary continental bkfst. Restaurant nearby. Ck-out 11 am. Business servs avail. Pool. Some bathrm phones, in-rm whirlpools, refrigerators, wet bars. Cr cds: A, C, D, DS, MC, V.

D ⊠ ⚓ 🐾 SC

✔★ ★ **CROSS COUNTRY INN.** (7810 Commerce Dr, Florence 41042) I-75 exit 181. 606/283-2030; FAX 606/283-0171. 112 rms, 2 story. S $36.99-$43.99; D $48.99-$50.99; each addl $7; under 18 free. Crib free. TV; cable (premium). Heated pool. Complimentary coffee in lobby. Restaurant nearby. Ck-out noon. Business servs avail. In-rm modem link. Cr cds: A, C, D, DS, MC, V.

D ⊠ ⚓ 🐾 SC

★ ★ **COURTYARD BY MARRIOTT.** 46 Cavalier Blvd (41042), I-71/75 exit 182. 606/371-6464; res: 800/321-2211; FAX 606/371-3443. 78 rms, 3 story. S, D $99-$149; suites $165-$200; under 18 free; higher rates Jazzfest (3-day min). Crib free. TV; cable (premium). Complimentary coffee in rms. Restaurant adj 7 am-11 pm. Ck-out noon. Meeting rms. Business servs avail. In-rm modem link. Valet serv. Guest lndry. Exercise equipt. Indoor pool; whirlpool. Bathrm phones; some in-rm whirlpools, refrigerators, microwaves. Cr cds: A, C, D, MC, V.

D ⊠ 🍴 🐾 SC

★ ★ **FAIRFIELD INN BY MARRIOTT-FLORENCE.** (50 Cavalier Blvd, Florence 41042) I-75 exit 182. 606/371-4800. 135 rms, 3 story. S, D $52-$68; under 18 free; higher rates special events. Crib free. TV; cable (premium). Heated pool. Complimentary continental bkfst. Restaurant adj 11 am-10 pm. Ck-out noon. Meeting rm. Business servs avail. In-rm modem link. Valet serv. Health club privileges. Cr cds: A, C, D, DS, MC, V.

D ⊠ ⚓ 🐾 SC

★ ★ **HAMPTON INN.** 200 Crescent Ave (41011), On I-75/71 exit 192. 606/581-7800; FAX 606/581-8282. 151 rms, 6 story. S $79-$84; D $84-$91; under 18 free; wkend rates (summer); higher rates special events. Crib free. TV; cable (premium). Complimentary continental bkfst. Coffee in rms. Restaurant nearby. Ck-out noon. Meeting rms. Business servs avail. In-rm modem link. Valet serv (Mon-Fri). Exercise equipt. Indoor pool. Cr cds: A, C, D, DS, JCB, MC, V.

D ⊠ 🍴 🐾 🐾 SC

★ ★ **HAMPTON INN-CINCINNATI SOUTH.** (7393 Turfway Rd, Florence 41042) I-75 exit 182. 606/283-1600. Web www.hampton-inn. com. 117 rms, 4 story. S, D $76-$79; under 18 free; higher rates: special events, Dec 31. Crib free. TV; cable (premium). Pool. Complimentary continental bkfst. Coffee in rms. Restaurant adj 7-2 am. Ck-out noon. Meeting rms. Business servs avail. Sundries. Free airport transportation. Health club privileges. Cr cds: A, C, D, DS, MC, V.

D ⊠ ⚓ 🐾 SC

★ ★ ★ **HOLIDAY INN-SOUTH.** (2100 Dixie Hwy, Ft Mitchell 41011) 8 mi SW on I-75/71, exit 188B. 606/331-1500; FAX 606/331-2259. 214 rms, 2 story. S, D $109-$129; under 18 free; family, wkend rates; higher rates: special events, Jazz Festival. Crib free. TV; cable. Indoor pool; whirlpool. Playground. Complimentary coffee in rms. Restaurant 6 am-2 pm, 5-11 pm. Rm serv. Ck-out 11 am. Meeting rms. Business servs avail. In-rm modem link. Bellhops. Valet serv. Sundries. Free airport transportation. Exercise equipt. Health club privileges. Game rm. Cr cds: A, C, D, DS, JCB, MC, V.

D ⊠ 🍴 🐾 🐾 SC

✔★ **KNIGHTS INN.** (8049 Dream St, Florence 41042) Jct I-75/71 and US 42/127; exit 180. 606/371-9711; FAX 606/371-4325. 116 rms, 10 kits. S, D $37-$62; each addl $6; kit. units $48-$58; under 18 free. Crib free. Pet accepted, some restrictions. TV; cable (premium). Pool. Restaurant nearby. Ck-out noon. Meeting rm. Business servs avail. Some microwaves. Cr cds: A, C, D, DS, MC, V.

D 🐾 ⚓ 🐾 🐾 SC

★ ★ ★ **RESIDENCE INN BY MARRIOTT.** (2811 Circleport Dr, Erlanger 41018) W on I-275 exit 2. 606/282-7400; res: 800/331-3131; FAX 606/282-1790. 96 suites, 3 story. No elvtr. Suites $79-$179; higher rates special events. Crib free. Pet accepted; $100. TV; cable (premium), VCR avail. Heated pool; whirlpool. Complimentary continental bkfst. Complimentary coffee in rms. Ck-out noon. Meeting rms. Business servs avail. In-rm modem link. Valet serv. Sundries. Coin lndry. Free airport transportation. Exercise equipt. Refrigerators, microwaves; some fireplaces. Picnic tables, grills. Cr cds: A, C, D, DS, MC, V.

D 🐾 ⚓ 🍴 🐾 🐾 SC

★ ★ **SIGNATURE INN.** (30 Cavalier Ct, Florence 41042) I-75/71, exit 182 (Turfway Rd). 606/371-0081. 125 rms, 2 story. S, D $65-$75; each addl $7; under 18 free; wkend rates; higher rates special events. Crib free. TV; cable (premium); VCR avail. Pool. Complimentary continental bkfst. Restaurant adj 5:30 am-10:30 pm. Ck-out noon. Meeting rms. Business center. In-rm modem link. Valet serv. Free airport transportation. Health club privileges. Cr cds: A, C, D, DS, MC, V.

D ⊠ 🐾 SC 🚶

Motor Hotel

★ ★ **DRAWBRIDGE ESTATE.** (2477 Royal Dr, Ft Mitchell 41017) at I-75/71 exit 186. 606/341-2800; FAX 606/341-5644; res: 800/354-9793 (exc KY), 800/352-9866 (KY). Web www.thedrawbridge. com. 505 rms, 2-4 story. S, D $93-$132; each addl $10; suites $210-$275; under 18 free; wkend rates; Jazz Fest (2-day min). Crib free. TV; cable (premium). 3 pools, 1 indoor; whirlpool, poolside serv, lifeguard. Restaurant open 24 hrs. Rm serv 6:30 am-11 pm. Bars 11:30-2 am; Sun 1 pm-midnight; entertainment. Ck-out noon. Convention facilities. Business servs avail. Bellhops. Valet serv. Shopping arcade. Free airport transportation. Lighted tennis. Exercise equipt; sauna. Lawn games. Tudor decor. Oldenberg brewery adj. Luxury level. Cr cds: A, C, D, DS, JCB, MC, V.

D 🐾 ⚓ 🍴 🐾 🐾 SC

Hotels

★ ★ **COMMONWEALTH HILTON.** *(7373 Turfway Rd, Florence 41042) I-75 exit 182, at Turfway Rd.* 606/371-4400; FAX 606/371-3361. Web www.hilton.com. 206 units, 5 story. S $99-$129; D $109-139; each addl $10; suites $159-$399; family, wkend rates. Crib free. TV; cable (premium). Pool; poolside serv. Coffee in rms. Restaurant 6:30 am-11 pm. Bar; entertainment. Ck-out noon. Meeting rms. Business servs avail. In-rm modem link. Bellhops. Concierge. Gift shop. Free airport transportation. Tennis. Exercise equipt; sauna. Some refrigerators; microwaves avail. Elaborate landscaping. Original artwork. Luxury level. Cr cds: A, C, D, DS, JCB, MC, V.

⊡ 🏌 ⊠ ✕ ⊠ ⊠ SC

★ ★ **EMBASSY SUITES AT RIVERCENTER.** *10 E RiverCenter Blvd (41011).* 606/261-8400; FAX 606/261-8486. Web www.embassy suites.com. 226 suites, 8 story. Suites $149-$169; under 18 free; wkend rates; higher rates special events. Crib free. TV; cable (premium). Indoor pool; whirlpool. Complimentary full bkfst. Complimentary coffee in rms. Restaurant 7-1 am; Sun to midnight. Bar; entertainment. Ck-out noon. Coin lndry. Meeting rms. Business servs avail. In-rm modem link. Gift shop. Free garage. Exercise equipt; sauna. Refrigerators, wet bars, microwaves. Cr cds: A, C, D, DS, JCB, MC, V.

⊡ ⊠ ✕ ⊠ ⊠ SC

★ ★ **HOLIDAY INN-CINCINNATI AIRPORT.** *(1717 Airport Exchange Blvd, Erlanger 41018) I-275 exit Mineola Pike.* 606/371-2233; FAX 606/371-5002. E-mail cvgap@fuse.net; web www.holiday-inn.com. 306 rms, 6 story. S, D $95-$119; suites $149-$175; under 18 free; higher rates special events. Crib free. TV; cable (premium). Indoor pool; whirlpool. Complimentary coffee in rms. Restaurant 6 am-11 pm. Bar. Ck-out noon. Coin lndry. Convention facilities. Business center. In-rm modem link. Gift shop. Free airport transportation. Exercise equipt; sauna. Microwaves avail. Minibar in suites. Cr cds: A, C, D, DS, JCB, MC, V.

⊡ ⊠ ✕ ⊠ ⊠ SC ✈

★ ★ **QUALITY HOTEL-RIVERVIEW.** *666 5th St (41011), at I-71/75 exit 192.* 606/491-1200; FAX 606/491-0326. 236 rms, 18 story. S, D $74-$104; suites $199; under 18 free. Crib free. TV; cable (premium). Indoor/outdoor pool; whirlpool, poolside serv. Coffee in rms. Restaurants 7-1 am (also see RIVERVIEW ROOM). Rm serv to 11 pm. Bars from 11 am. Ck-out 11 am. Meeting rms. Business servs avail. In-rm modem link. Gift shop. Barber. Free airport transportation. Exercise equipt. Rec rm. Cr cds: A, C, D, DS, JCB, MC, V.

⊡ ⊠ ✕ ⊠ ⊠ SC

Restaurants

★ ★ **DEE FELICE CAFE.** *529 Main St (41011).* 606/261-2365. Hrs: 11 am-2:30 pm, 5 pm-closing; Sat, Sun 5 pm-midnight. Closed major hols. Res accepted. Continental menu. Bar. Semi-a la carte: lunch $5.95-$9.95, dinner $12.95-$18.95. Specializes in Creole and Cajun dishes. Own pasta. Jazz nightly. Street parking. Bistro cafe atmosphere. Cr cds: A, D, MC, V.

⊡ ⊡

★ ★ **MIKE FINK.** *Foot of Greenup St (41011), near Covington Landing.* 606/261-4212. Hrs: 11 am-10 pm; Fri, Sat to 11 pm; Sun 10 am-9 pm. Res accepted. Bar. Semi-a la carte: lunch $5-$9, dinner $11-$29. Specializes in fresh seafood. Raw bar. Parking. Old paddlewheel steamer, permanently moored. Scenic view of Cincinnati. Cr cds: A, C, D, DS, JCB, MC, V.

⊡

✔★ **ORIENTAL WOK.** *(317 Buttermilk Pike, Fort Mitchell 41017) SW via I-75 exit 186, 3 blks E on Buttermilk Pike.* 606/331-3000. Hrs: 11 am-10 pm; Fri to 11 pm; Sat 4-11 pm; Sun 11:30 am-10 pm. Closed Thanksgiving, Dec 25. Res accepted. Chinese, Amer menu. Bar. Semi-a la carte: lunch $4.95-$7.50, dinner $7.50-$16.95. Child's meals. Special-

izes in Cantonese & Szechwan dishes. Entertainment Fri, Sat. Parking. Outdoor dining. Fountain with goldfish. Cr cds: A, C, D, DS, MC, V.

⊡

★ ★ **RIVERVIEW ROOM.** *(See Quality Hotel-Riverview)* 606/491-5300. Hrs: 11:30 am-2 pm, 5-10 pm; Fri, Sat to 11 pm; Sun 5-9 pm; Sun brunch 9:30 am-2:30 pm. Closed Dec 25. Res accepted. Bar. Wine list. Semi-a la carte: lunch $4.95-$9.95, dinner $16.95-$24.95. Sun brunch $13.95. Child's meals. Specializes in steak, seafood. Own desserts. Harpist. Parking. Revolving restaurant overlooking river, Cincinnati skyline. Cr cds: A, C, D, DS, MC, V.

⊡

★ ★ **SOUTH BEACH GRILL AT THE WATERFRONT.** *14 Pete Rose Pier (41011), on river.* 606/581-1414. Hrs: 5:30-10 pm; Fri to 11 pm; Sat 5-11 pm; Sun 5-9 pm. Res accepted. Bar. Semi-a la carte: dinner $16.95-$31.50. Specializes in seafood, steak, chops. Raw, sushi bar. Valet parking. Pianist Tues-Sat. Outdoor dining. Elegant, 2-story floating restaurant with panoramic view of Cincinnati skyline; Art Deco with tropical accents. Cr cds: A, C, D, DS, MC, V.

⊡ ⊡ ♥

★ ★ **SPAZZI.** *14 Pete Rose Pier (41011).* 606/291-9025. Hrs: 5:30-10 pm; Fri to 11 pm; Sat 5-11 pm; Sun 5-9 pm. Closed some major hols. Res accepted. Regional Italian menu. Bar. Wine list. A la carte entrees: dinner $11.95-$22. Specializes in pasta, beef, seafood. Valet parking. Italian tapestries. Open kitchen. Cr cds: A, C, D, DS, MC, V.

⊡

Unrated Dining Spot

BB RIVERBOATS. *1 Madison Ave, Covington Landing, on riverfront.* 606/261-8500; res: 800/261-8586. E-mail bbriver@one.net; web www.bbriverboats.com. Hrs: May-Oct: lunch cruise noon-2 pm; dinner cruise (nightly) 7-9:30 pm. Limited cruises Nov-Apr. Res required. Bar. Complete meals: lunch $19.50-$20.50, dinner $27.95-$34.95. Child's meals. Specializes in beef, chicken. Entertainment. Parking. Dinner cruises on Ohio River, at the Port of Cincinnati. Cr cds: A, C, D, DS, MC, V.

⊡ SC

Cumberland Falls State Resort Park (E-7)

(See also Corbin, Williamsburg)

(19 mi SW of Corbin via US 25W, KY 90)

In this 1,657-acre park on the Cumberland River is a magnificent waterfall, 65 feet high and 125 feet wide, amid beautiful scenery. Surrounded by Daniel Boone National Forest (see), this awesome waterfall is the second largest east of the Rockies. By night, when the moon is full and the sky clear, a mysterious moonbow appears in the mist. This is the only place in the Western Hemisphere where this phenomenon can be seen. Swimming pool (seasonal); fishing. Nature trails; nature center; riding (seasonal); tennis. Picnicking, playground, lodge (see RESORT), cottages. Tent & trailer campsites (standard fees). For information phone 800/325-0063.

What to See and Do

Big South Fork National River/Recreation Area. Approx 12 mi W on KY 90, then approx 25 mi S on US 27 to Oneida, TN, then 20 mi W on TN 297. (See JAMESTOWN, TN)

Blue Heron Mining Community. Re-created mid-20th Century mining town where 300 miners were once employed. Depot has exhibits on history of town with scale models, photographs. Town features giant coal tipple built in 1937 and metal-frame representations of miners' houses, church, school, company store. Snack bar & gift shop (Apr-Oct). A scenic railway line connects Blue Heron with the town of Stearns (see SOMERSET). In Big South Fork National River/Recreation Area (KY side); S via US 27 and KY 92 to Stearns, then 9 mi W on KY 742 (Mine 18 Rd). Phone 606/376-3787 (KY) or 931/879-3625 (TN). **Free.**

Sheltowee Trace Outfitters. River rafting, canoeing and "funyak" trips in the scenic Cumberland River Gorge below the falls; Big South Fork Gorge, Rockcastle River. Five- to seven-hr trips, appointments necessary. (Memorial Day-Sept; daily; Apr-mid-May & Sept-Oct, Sat & Sun). For information contact Sheltowee Trace Outfitters, PO Box 1060, Whitley City 42653; 606/376-5567 or 800/541-7238. ¢¢¢¢

Resort

✔★ ★ **DUPONT LODGE.** (7351 KY 90, Corbin 40701) In Cumberland Falls State Resort Park. 606/528-4121; FAX 606/528-0704; res: 800/325-0063. 52 rms in 3-story lodge, 26 kit. cottages. Apr-Oct: S $55; D $65; each addl $5; kit. cottages for 1-4, $67-$81; cottages for 6-8, $130; under 17 free; lower lodge rates Nov-Mar. Closed 5 days late Dec. Crib free. TV. Pool; wading pool, lifeguard. Dining rm 7-10:30 am, 11:30 am-4 pm, 5-8 pm. Ck-out noon, cottages 11 am; ck-in 4 pm. Meeting rms. Business servs avail. Gift shop. Tennis. Lawn games. Rec dir. Rec rm. Hiking trails. Fireplace in most cottages. On river. State-operated. Cr cds: A, C, D, DS, MC, V.

D 🏃 🏊 ☁ 🎿 🏖 SC

Cumberland Gap National Historical Park (E-8)

(See also Pineville; also see Harrogate, TN)

(1/4 mi S of Middlesboro on US 25E)

Web www.nps.gov/cuga/index.htm

Information Park Superintendent, US 25E, Box 1848, Middlesboro 40965; 606/248-2817.

Cumberland Gap, a natural passage through the mountain barrier that effectively sealed off the infant American coastal colonies, was the open door to western development. Through this pass first came Dr. Thomas Walker in 1750, followed by Daniel Boone in 1769. In 1775, Boone and 30 axmen cut a 208-mile swath through the forest from Kingsport, Tennessee, to the Kentucky River, passing through the Cumberland Gap. Settlers poured through the pass and along Boone's "Wilderness Road," and in 1777 Kentucky became Virginia's westernmost county. Although pioneers were harassed by Native Americans during the Revolution, travel over the Wilderness Road continued to increase and became heavier than ever. After the Revolution, the main stream of western settlement poured through Cumberland Gap and slowed only when more direct northerly routes were opened. During the Civil War, the gap was a strategic point, changing hands several times.

Nearly 22,300 acres of this historic and dramatically beautiful countryside in Kentucky, Tennessee and Virginia have been set aside as a national historical park. More than 50 miles of hiking trails provide a variety of walks, long and short. Park (daily; closed Jan 1, Dec 25).

What to See and Do

Camping. Tables, fireplaces, water and bathhouse. 14-day limit. Off US 58. ¢¢¢¢

Civil War fortifications. Throughout the Gap area.

Hensley Settlement. An isolated mountain community, now a restored historic site, that is accessible by hiking 3.5 mi up the Chadwell Gap trail or by driving up a jeep road.

Pinnacle Overlook. Broad vistas of mountains and forests viewed from a high peak jutting above the Cumberland valley. Vehicles over 20 ft in length and all trailers are prohibited.

Tri-State Peak. View of meeting point of Kentucky, Virginia and Tennessee.

Visitor Center. Historical exhibits, audiovisual program. (Closed some major hols) At W end of park (near Middlesboro).

Daniel Boone National Forest (C-8)

(See also Hazard, London, Morehead, Williamsburg)

(Stretches roughly north-south from Morehead on US 60 to Whitley City on US 27)

Within these 692,164 acres is some of the most spectacular scenery in Kentucky, from the Cave Run and Laurel River lakes to the Natural Arch Scenic Area. The forest includes the Red River Gorge Geological Area, known for its natural arches. The gorge has colorful rock formations and cliffs that average 100 to 300 feet high. A scenic loop drive of the gorge begins north of Natural Bridge State Resort Park (see) on KY 77. The nearest camping facilities (fee) are located at Koomer Ridge, on KY 15 between the Slade (33) and Beattyville (40) exits of Mt Parkway.

The Sheltowee Trace National Recreation Trail runs generally north to south, beginning near Morehead (see) and continuing to Pickett State Rustic Park, TN (see JAMESTOWN, TN), a total distance of more than 260 miles. Forest Development Road 918, the main road into the Zilpo Recreation Area, has been designated a National Scenic Byway. The 11.2-mile road features a pleasant, winding trip through Kentucky hardwood forest, with interpretive signs and pull-overs with views of Cave Run Lake.

Cave Run Lake (see MOREHEAD) has swimming beaches, boat ramps, and camping at Twin Knobs and Zilpo recreation areas. Laurel River Lake (see CORBIN) has boat ramps and camping areas at Holly Bay and Grove (vehicle access). Clay Lick (Cave Run Lake), Grove, White Oak (Laurel River Lake) have boat-in camping. Hunting and fishing permitted in most parts of the forest under Kentucky regulations; backpacking is permitted on forest trails. For further information contact the Forest Supervisor, 1700 Bypass Rd, Winchester 40391; 606/745-3100 or 800/255-7275.

Danville (D-7)

(See also Harrodsburg)

Founded 1775 **Pop** 12,420 **Elev** 989 ft **Area code** 606 **Zip** 40422 **E-mail** tourism@searnet.com **Web** www.danville-ky.com

Information Danville-Boyle County Convention & Visitors Bureau, 304 S 4th St; 606/236-7794 or 800/755-0076.

Birthplace of Kentucky government, Danville is near the geographical center of the state. Ten years after the city was founded, it became the first capital of the Kentucky district of Virginia. Later, nine conventions were held leading to admission of the state to the Union. From 1775 to 1792, Danville was the most important center in Kentucky, the major settlement on the Wilderness Road. "Firsts" seem to come naturally to Danville, which claims the state's first college, first log courthouse, first post office, first brick courthouse, first school for the deaf and first law school.

One of the largest tobacco markets in the state, Danville has also attracted several industrial plants.

What to See and Do

Constitution Square State Shrine. Authentic reproduction of Kentucky's first courthouse square stands at exact site where first state constitution was framed and adopted in 1792. Original post office; replicas of jail, courthouse, meetinghouse; restored row house, Dr Goldsmith House and Grayson Tavern. Governor's Circle has a bronze plaque of each Kentucky governor. Museum store, art gallery. (Daily) On US 127 in center of town, 134 S Second. Phone 606/239-7089. **Free.**

Herrington Lake. Formed by Dix Dam, one of the world's largest rock-filled dams, Herrington has 333 mi of shoreline. Balanced fish population maintained through conservation program. Fishing (fee); boat launch (fee; rentals). Camping (hookups), cabins. 3 mi N off KY 33. Phone 606/236-4286. **Free.**

Kids Farm Education Center. A working farm open to the public to experience wildlife management techniques, exotic animals, and wild game in a natural setting. (Daily) 636 Quirks Run Rd. Phone 606/236-1414. **¢¢**

McDowell House and Apothecary Shop. Residence and shop of Dr. Ephraim McDowell, noted surgeon of the early 19th century. Restored and refurbished with period pieces. Large apothecary ware collection. Gardens include trees, wildflowers and herbs of the period. (Mar-Oct, daily; rest of yr, daily exc Mon; closed Jan 1, Easter, Thanksgiving, Dec 25) 125 S 2nd St. Phone 606/236-2804. **¢¢**

Perryville Battlefield State Historic Site. A 100-acre park, once a field, appears much as it did Oct 8, 1862, when Confederate forces under General Braxton Bragg and Union troops under General Don Carlos Buell clashed. A total of 4,241 Union soldiers and 1,822 Confederate troops were killed, wounded or missing. Still standing are the Crawford House, used by Bragg as headquarters, and Bottom House, center of some of the heaviest fighting. Mock battle is staged each year (wkend nearest October 8). A 30-acre area at the north end of what was the battle line includes a memorial erected in 1902 to the Confederate dead and one raised in 1931 to the Union dead. Museum with artifacts from battle, 9-by-9-ft, detailed battle map, battle dioramas (fee). Hiking. Picnicking, playground. Self-guided tours. (Apr-Oct, daily; rest of yr by appt) 10 mi W on US 150, 4 mi N on US 68. Phone 606/332-8631. **Free.**

Pioneer Playhouse Village-of-the-Arts. Reproduction of an 18th-century Kentucky village on a 200-acre site; drama school, museum. Camping (fee). (See SEASONAL EVENT) (May-mid-Oct, daily) 1 mi S on Stanford Ave, US 150. Phone 606/236-2747. **Free.**

Seasonal Event

Pioneer Playhouse. Pioneer Playhouse Village-of-the-Arts. Summer stock; Broadway comedies, musicals. Tues-Sat evenings. Phone 606/236-2747. Mid-June-late Aug.

Motels

★ **DAYS INN.** *4th St, at jct US 127S, 127 Bypass, 150 Bypass. 606/236-8601; FAX 606/236-0314.* 81 rms, 2 story. S, D $55-$65; each addl $6; under 19 free. Crib free. Pet accepted. TV; cable (premium). Pool. Coffee in rms. Restaurant open 24 hrs. Ck-out noon. Meeting rms. Business servs avail. In-rm modem link. Refrigerators, microwaves avail. Cr cds: A, D, DS, JCB, MC, V.

D ⟋ ≋ ⊠ 🐾 SC

★ **HOLIDAY INN EXPRESS.** *96 Daniel Dr. 606/236-8600; FAX 606/236-4299.* 63 rms. S, D $55-$69; under 19 free. Crib free. TV; cable (premium). Pool; whirlpool. Sauna. Complimentary continental bkfst. Ck-out noon. Meeting rms. Business servs avail. Coin lndry. Microwaves avail. Cr cds: A, D, DS, JCB, MC, V.

D ≋ ⊠ 🐾 SC

✓★ **SUPER 8.** *3663 US 150, at US 127 Bypass. 606/236-8881.* 49 units, 2 story. S $41.88; D $51.88-$56.88; each addl $5; under 12 free. Crib free. Pet accepted, some restrictions. TV; cable (premium). Complimentary coffee. Restaurant nearby. Ck-out 11 am. Meeting rms. Business

servs avail. Valet serv. Guest lndry. Some refrigerators; microwaves avail. Cr cds: A, C, D, DS, MC, V.

D ⟋ ≋ 🐾 SC

Elizabethtown (D-6)

(See also Bardstown, Fort Knox, Hodgenville)

Founded 1797 **Pop** 18,167 **Elev** 731 ft **Area code** 502 **Zip** 42701
Information Elizabethtown Tourism & Convention Bureau, 1030 N Mulberry St; 502/765-2175 or 800/437-0092.

The Lincoln story has deep roots in this town. Thomas Lincoln, the President's father, owned property and worked in Elizabethtown; it is the town to which Thomas Lincoln brought his bride, Nancy Hanks, immediately after their marriage. Abe's older sister Sarah was born in Elizabethtown. After his first wife's death, Thomas Lincoln returned to marry Sarah Bush Johnston.

What to See and Do

Abraham Lincoln Birthplace National Historic Site (see). 13 mi SE via US 31 or KY 61.

Brown-Pusey Community House (1825). This former stagecoach inn is an excellent example of Georgian-colonial architecture; General George Custer lived here from 1871-1873. Restored as a historical genealogy library (fee) and community house; garden. (Daily exc Sun; closed hols) 128 N Main St, at Poplar St. Phone 502/765-2515. **Free.**

Lincoln Heritage House. Double log cabin (1789, 1805) was home of Hardin Thomas. Unusual trim work done by Thomas Lincoln. Pioneer implements, early surveying equipment, period furniture. Park facilities include pavilions, paddle and row boats, canoes. (June-Sept, daily exc Mon) 1 mi N on US 31W in Freeman Lake Park. For information contact the Tourism & Convention Bureau. **Free.**

Schmidt's Coca-Cola Museum. Very large private collection of Coca Cola memorabilia includes several thousand items. Complete 1890s marble ice cream parlor; complete tray collection; stained glass chandelier; three-foot, Tiffany-style bottle. Lobby contains magnificent collection of *koi* (carp) in Japanese garden. (Mon-Fri; closed most major hols) 2½ mi W on US 31. Phone 502/737-4000. **¢**

Annual Events

Hardin County Fair. Hardin County Fairgrounds. Mid-July.

Kentucky Heartland Festival. Freeman Lake Park. Antique auto show, arts & crafts, canoe race, running event, hot air balloon, bluegrass music, games, food. Phone 502/765-4334 or 502/769-2391. Last full wkend Aug.

Motels

✓★ **BEST WESTERN CARDINAL INN.** *642 E Dixie. 502/765-6139; FAX 502/737-9944.* 54 rms, 2 story. S, D $44-$49; each addl $4; under 18 free; higher rates Kentucky Derby. Crib free. Pet accepted, some restrictions; $25 deposit. TV; cable (premium). Complimentary continental bkfst. Coffee in rms. Pool. Playground. Ck-out 11:30 am. Coin lndry. Cr cds: A, C, D, DS, MC, V.

⟋ ≋ ⊠ 🐾 SC

★★ **COMFORT INN.** *1043 Executive Dr, I-65 exit 94. 502/769-3030; res: 800/682-5285; FAX 502/769-2516.* 133 rms, 2 story. S, D $63.95-$79.95; each addl $6; under 18 free; higher rates Kentucky Derby. Crib free. Pet accepted. TV; cable (premium). Indoor pool. Complimentary continental bkfst. Restaurant adj 6 am-11 pm. Ck-out 11:30 am. Coin lndry. Meeting rms. Business servs avail. Indoor putting green. Game rm. Many refrigerators; some wet bars. Cr cds: A, C, D, DS, ER, JCB, MC, V.

D ⟋ ≋ ⊠ 🐾 SC

★ **DAYS INN.** *2010 N Mulberry, at jct I-65, KY 62 (exit 94).* 502/769-5522; FAX 502/769-3211. 121 rms, 2 story. S $38-$43; D $43-$50; each addl $5; higher rates Derby wknd. Crib free. Pet accepted; $5. TV; cable (premium). Pool. Playground. Restaurant open 24 hrs. Ck-out 11 am. Coin lndry. Sundries. Gift shop. Game rm. Cr cds: A, C, D, DS, JCB, MC, V.

D ⮌ ≈ ⋈ 🖊 SC

Motor Hotel

★ ★ **HAMPTON INN.** *1035 Executive Dr.* 502/765-6663; FAX 502/769-3151. 60 rms. S, D $59-$69; under 18 free; higher rates Kentucky Derby. Crib free. TV; cable (premium). Indoor pool; whirlpool. Complimentary continental bkfst. Complimentary coffee in rms. Restaurant nearby. Ck-out 11 am. Meeting rms. Business center. Some refrigerators, microwaves. Cr cds: A, C, D, DS, MC, V.

D ≈ ⋈ 🖊 🚶

Restaurants

★ ★ **GREEN BAMBOO.** *902 N Dixie, in Governor's Shopping Center.* 502/769-3457. Hrs: 11 am-2:30 pm, 4:30-9:30 pm. Closed Thanksgiving, Dec 25. Chinese menu. Semi-a la carte: lunch $4.25-$4.50, dinner $7.25-$18. Child's meals. Specialties: Mongolian beef, mandarin chicken, lobster. Oriental decor. Cr cds: A, DS, MC, V.

SC ⥢

✔★ **JERRY'S.** *654 E Dixie Hwy (US 31E).* 502/769-2336. Hrs: Open 24 hrs. Closed Dec 25. Semi-a la carte: bkfst $2.50-$5.65, lunch $3.65-$5.65, dinner $4.65-$8.50. Child's meals. Specialties: J-Boy, Husky, strawberry pie. Parking. Cr cds: A, D, DS, MC, V.

SC ⥢

★ ★ **STONE HEARTH.** *1001 N Mulberry.* 502/765-4898. Hrs: 11 am-2 pm, 5-9 pm; Sun 11 am-3 pm. Closed Jan 1, Dec 25. Semi-a la carte: lunch $5.75-$6.75, dinner $11.95-$18.95. Specializes in beef, seafood. Salad bar. Old English decor. Cr cds: A, C, D, DS, MC, V.

D ⥢

Florence

(see Covington (Cincinnati Airport Area))

Fort Knox (D-5)

(See also Elizabethtown, Louisville, Shepherdsville)

Elev 740 ft **Area code** 502 **Zip** 40121 **Web** www.knox.army.mil

Information Public Affairs Office, US Army Armor Center & Fort Knox, PO Box 995; 502/624-4788 or -3051.

This military post, established in 1918, is home for the US Army Armor Center and School and the Army's home of Mounted Warfare. Named for Major General Henry Knox, first Secretary of War, the post has been a major installation since 1932, when mechanization of the Army began.

What to See and Do

Patton Museum of Cavalry and Armor. The Armor Branch Museum was named in honor of General George S. Patton, Jr. Collection includes US and foreign armored equipment, weapons, art and uniforms; mementos of General Patton's military career, including the sedan in which he was riding when he was fatally injured in 1945. Also on display are a 10-by-12-ft section of the Berlin Wall and foreign armored equipment from Operation

Desert Storm. (Daily; closed Jan 1, Dec 24-25, 31) Building 4554, Fayette Ave. Phone 502/624-3812. **Free.**

United States Bullion Depository. Two-story granite, steel and concrete building. Opened in 1937, the building houses part of the nation's gold reserves. The depository and the surrounding grounds are not open to the public. Gold Vault Rd.

Annual Event

Armored Vehicle Presentation. Patton Museum.Operational armored vehicle demonstration features restored World War II tanks and authentically uniformed troops. July 4.

Motor Hotel

★ ★ **QUALITY INN.** *(438 S Dixie Blvd, Radcliff 40160) 2¹/₂ mi S on US 31E.* 502/351-8211; FAX 502/351-3227. 83 rms, 3 story. No elvtr. May-Aug: S, D $52-$80; each addl $3; suites $57-$80; under 18 free; higher rates Kentucky Derby. Crib free. TV; cable (premium). Pool. Complimentary continental bkfst. Coffee in rms. Restaurant nearby. Ck-out noon. Meeting rms. Business servs avail. Valet serv. Sundries. Game rm. Cr cds: A, C, D, DS, JCB, MC, V.

D ≈ ⋈ 🖊 SC

Frankfort (C-7)

(See also Lexington)

Founded 1786 **Pop** 25,968 **Elev** 510 ft **Area code** 502 **Zip** 40601

Information Frankfort/Franklin County Tourist and Convention Commisssion, 100 Capital Ave; 502/875-8687.

Frankfort is split by the Kentucky River, which meanders through the city. Although rich farmlands funnel burley tobacco and corn through Frankfort, the chief crop is politics, especially when the legislature is in session. Frankfort was chosen as the state capital in 1792 as a compromise to settle the rival claims of Lexington and Louisville. Frankfort was briefly held by the Confederates during the Civil War. Later, the "corn liquor" industry blossomed in this area, utilizing water from flowing limestone springs. Bourbon distilleries carry on this tradition.

What to See and Do

Daniel Boone's Grave. Monument to Boone and his wife. Boone died in Missouri but his remains were brought here in 1845. In Frankfort Cemetery, 215 E Main St.

Kentucky Military History Museum. Exhibits trace Kentucky's involvement in military conflicts through two centuries. Weapons, flags, uniforms. (Daily; closed major hols) Old State Arsenal, E Main St. Phone 502/564-3265. **Free.**

Kentucky State University (1886). (2,550 students) Liberal studies institution. Jackson Hall (1887) has art and photo gallery exhibits (Sept-mid-May); King Farouk butterfly collection in Carver Hall. Jackson Hall and Hume Hall (1909) on historic register. E Main St. Phone 502/227-6000.

Kentucky Vietnam Veterans Memorial. Unique memorial is a 14-ft sundial that casts a shadow across veterans' names on the anniversary of their death. Memorial contains more than 1,000 names. Adj to State Library & Archives, 300 Coffee Tree Rd.

Liberty Hall (ca 1796). Fine example of Georgian architecture, built by the first US senator from Kentucky, John Brown, is completely restored to its original state and furnished with family heirlooms. Period gardens. (Mar-Dec, daily exc Mon; closed some major hols) 218 Wilkinson St, at W Main St. Phone 502/227-2560. ¢¢ On the same block is

Orlando Brown House (1835). Early Greek-revival house built for Orlando Brown, son of Senator John Brown; original furnishings and artifacts. (Mar-Dec, daily exc Mon; closed some major hols) 202 Wilkinson St. Phone 502/227-2560. ¢¢ Combination ticket avail for both houses.

Old Governor's Mansion (1798). Georgian-style residence of 33 governors until 1914, when the new mansion was built. Restored to the style of the 1800s. Tours (Tues & Thurs afternoons; closed hols). 420 High St. Phone 502/564-3449. **Free.**

Old State Capitol Building. Kentucky's third capitol building, erected in 1827-1829, was used as the capitol from 1829-1909 and was the first Greek-revival statehouse west of the Alleghenies. Completely restored and furnished in period style, the building features an unusual self-balanced double stairway. (Mon-Sat, also Sun afternoons) Broadway & Lewis Sts. **Free.** In the Old Capitol Annex are

Kentucky History Museum. Exhibits pertaining to the history and development of the state and the culture of its people. (Mon-Sat, also Sun afternoons; closed major hols) Phone 502/564-3016. **Free.**

Library. Manuscripts, maps, photographs and special collections cover Kentucky's history; genealogy section. (Daily exc Sun; closed major hols) Phone 502/564-3016. **Free.**

State Capitol (1910). Building noted for Ionic columns and the high central dome on an Ionic peristyle, topped with a lantern cupola. In the rotunda are statues of Abraham Lincoln, Jefferson Davis, Henry Clay, Dr. Ephraim McDowell and Alben Barkley, vice-president under Harry S Truman. Guided tours. (Mon-Sat & Sun afternoons; closed major hols) Capitol Ave, on an elevation overlooking the Kentucky River. Phone 502/564-3449. **Free.** On grounds are

Floral Clock. Functioning outdoor timepiece is adorned with thousands of plants and elevated above reflecting pool. Mechanism moves a 530-pound minute hand and a 420-pound hour hand. Visitors toss thousands of dollars in coins into the pool, all of which is turned over to state child-care agencies.

Governor's Mansion (1914). Official residence of the Governor is styled after the Petit Trianon, Marie Antoinette's villa at Versailles. Guided tours (Tues & Thurs mornings). Phone 502/564-3449. **Free.**

Annual Events

Governor's Derby Breakfast. State Capitol. Breakfast, entertainment and Kentucky crafts. Phone 502/564-2611. 1st Sat May.

Capital Expo Festival. Capital Plaza Complex. Traditional music, country music, fiddling; workshops, demonstrations, arts & crafts; balloon race, dancing, games, contests, puppets, museum exhibitions, ethnic & regional foods, entertainment. 1st full wkend June.

Motels

★ ★ **BEST WESTERN PARKSIDE INN.** *80 Chenault Rd, I-64 exit 58.* 502/695-6111; res: 800/528-1234. 98 rms, 2 story. S, D $48-$65; each addl $5; suites $75-$85; under 12 free; higher rates Kentucky Derby. Crib free. TV; cable (premium). Indoor/outdoor pool; whirlpool. Complimentary continental bkfst. Ck-out noon. Lndry facilities. Meeting rms. Business servs avail. Airport transportation. Exercise equipt. Game rm. Refrigerator avail. Cr cds: A, C, D, DS, ER, JCB, MC, V.

D ⊠ ✕ ⊠ ⊠ SC

★ **BLUEGRASS INN.** *635 Versailles Rd.* 502/695-1800; FAX 502/695-3628; res: 800/322-1802. 62 rms, 2 story. S $36-$42; D $42-$48; each addl $6; under 14 free; higher rates Kentucky Derby. Pet accepted. TV; cable. Pool. Complimentary coffee in lobby. Restaurant adj 9 am-10 pm. Ck-out noon. Business servs avail. Some refrigerators. Cr cds: A, C, D, DS, ER, MC, V.

🐾 ⊠ ⊠ ⊠ SC

✔★ **DAYS INN.** *1051 US 127S, I-64 exit 53B.* 502/875-2200. 122 rms, 2 story. S $38; D $44; each addl $6; age 13-17, $1; under 12 free.

Crib free. TV; cable. Pool. Continental bkfst. Ck-out 11 am. Sundries. Cr cds: A, C, D, DS, MC, V.

⊠ ⊠ ⊠ SC

Hotel

★ ★ ★ **HOLIDAY INN-CAPITAL PLAZA.** *405 Wilkinson Blvd.* 502/227-5100; FAX 502/875-7147. 189 rms, 8 story. S, D $85; each addl $10; suites $100-$175; higher rates Kentucky Derby. Crib free. TV; cable (premium). Heated pool; whirlpool. Coffee in rms. Restaurants 6 am-1:30 pm, 5-9:30 pm. Bar 5-11:30 pm, Sun to 11 pm. Ck-out noon. Meeting rms. Business servs avail. In-rm modem link. Shopping arcade. Covered parking. Exercise equipt, sauna. Game rm. Some refrigerators. Cr cds: A, C, D, DS, JCB, MC, V.

D ⊠ ✕ ⊠ ⊠ SC

Restaurant

✔★ **JIM'S SEAFOOD.** *950 Wilkinson Blvd.* 502/223-7448. Hrs: 11 am-2 pm, 4-10 pm; Sat from 4 pm. Closed Sun; major hols. Res accepted. Wine, beer. Semi-a la carte: lunch $3.95-$6.95, dinner $7.95-$13.95. Child's meals. Specializes in surf & turf. Outdoor dining. View of river. Family-owned. Cr cds: A, DS, MC, V.

D

Georgetown (C-7)

(See also Frankfort, Lexington, Paris)

Settled 1776 **Pop** 11,414 **Elev** 871 ft **Area code** 502 **Zip** 40324 **E-mail** geoscott@uky.campus.mci.net
Information Georgetown/Scott County Tourism Commission, 401 Outlet Center Dr, Suite 240; 502/863-2547 or 888/863-8600.

Royal Spring's crystal-clear water flows in the center of this city. This spring attracted pioneer settlers who established an outpost at Georgetown and rebuffed frequent Native American attacks. The town was named for George Washington and was incorporated in 1790 by the Virginia legislature. Today it remains a quiet college town, with a large portion of the business area designated as a historic district.

What to See and Do

Cardome Centre. Former house of Civil War Governor J.F. Robinson and later home of the Academy of the Sisters of the Visitation. Now houses **Georgetown and Scott County Museum** (daily; closed major hols) and serves as community center. (Mon-Fri, also by appt; closed major hols) 800 Cincinnati Pike, I-75 exit 125/126, on US 25N. Phone 502/863-1575. **Free.**

Royal Spring Park. Location of Royal Spring, largest in Kentucky and source of city water since 1775. Former site of McClelland's Fort (1776), first paper mill in the West, pioneer classical music school and state's first ropewalk. Reputed site of first bourbon distillation in 1789. Cabin of former slave relocated and restored here for use as an information center (mid-May-mid-Oct, daily exc Mon). Picnicking. (Daily) Water St. Phone 502/863-2547.

Scott County Courthouse (1877). Designed in Second Empire style by Thomas Boyd of Pittsburgh. Part of the historic business district. (Mon-Fri; closed hols) 101 E Main St, at Broadway. Phone 502/863-7850. **Free.**

Toyota Motor Manufacturing, Kentucky, Inc. About 400,000 cars and 350,000 engines are made here annually. The Visitor Center has interactive exhibits. One-hr tours of the plant (ages 8 and up) include video presentation and tram ride through different levels of production. Visitor Center (Mon-Fri). Tours (res are required; Tues & Thurs). 1001 Cherry Blossom Way. Phone 502/868-3027 or 800/TMM-4485. **Free.**

Motor Hotel

★ **SHONEY'S INN.** *200 Shoney Dr, At jct I-75 & US 62.* 502/868-9800; FAX 502/868-9800, ext. 141; res: 800/222-2222. 104 rms, 3 story, 15 suites. S $55.95; D $60.95; under 18 free. TV; cable. Pool. Complimentary coffee in lobby. Restaurant adj 6 am-11 pm. Ck-out noon. Meeting rms. Business servs avail. In-rm modem link. Cr cds: A, C, D, DS, ER, MC, V.

⊡ 🏊 ⚒ 🐾 SC

Gilbertsville (E-3)

(See also Cadiz, Land Between The Lakes, Paducah)

Pop 500 (est) **Elev** 343 ft **Area code** 502 **Zip** 42044 **E-mail** marshall@ldd.net **Web** www.kentuckylake.com/mccc/index.htm
Information Marshall County Chamber of Commerce, Inc, 17 US 68 W, Benton 42025; 502/527-7665.

Fishing parties heading for Kentucky Lake stop in Gilbertsville for last-minute provisions. The area also caters to tourists bound for the resorts and state parks. Chemical plants have been built nearby, utilizing Kentucky Dam's hydroelectric power.

What to See and Do

Barkley Lock and Dam. A 1,004-mi shoreline created by damming of the Cumberland River; navigation lock, canal, hydroelectric generating plant, flood control and recreation areas; information & visitor center. 5 mi E. Contact the Resource Manager, PO Box 218, Grand Rivers 42045; 502/362-4236. **Free.**

Kenlake State Resort Park. (see). SE on Purchase Pkwy, US 68.

Kentucky Dam. Longest dam in the TVA system, 22 mi upstream from Paducah; 206 ft high, 8,422 ft long, built at cost of $118 million, created lake 184 mi long with 2,380 mi of shoreline. Regulates flow of water from Tennessee River into the Ohio River. Carries US 62/641 across northern end of Kentucky Lake. Viewing balcony (daily); tours of powerhouse (by appt). Phone 502/362-4221. **Free.**

Kentucky Dam Village State Resort Park. A 1,352-acre park on a 160,300-acre lake. Fishing. Swimming beach, pool, bathhouse (seasonal), waterskiing; boating (rentals, launching ramps, docks). Hiking; 18-hole and miniature golf (seasonal fee), tennis. Picnicking, playground, shops, grocery. Camping, lodge (see RESORT), cottages. Supervised recreation. Lighted 4,000-ft airstrip. Just S of town off US 62/641 on Kentucky Lake. For fees and information phone 502/362-4271.

Resort

★ ★ **KENTUCKY DAM VILLAGE.** *Box 69, ¾ mi W of Kentucky Dam on US 62/641; 2 mi E of I-24 exit 27.* 502/362-4271; FAX 502/362-8747; res: 800/325-0146. 86 lodge rms, 2 story; 70 kit. cottages. Apr-Oct: S $58; D $68; each addl $5; kit. cottages for 2-8, $77-$154; under 16 free; lower rates rest of yr. Crib free. TV. Pool; wading pool, lifeguard in season. Dining rm 7 am-9 pm. Ck-out noon (cottages 11 am), ck-in 4 pm. Convention facilities. Airport transportation. Lighted tennis. 18-hole golf, greens fee $15. Miniature golf. Lawn games. Game rm. Many microwaves. Private patios, balconies. Picnic tables. On lake; beach, marina. State-owned; all state park facilities avail. Cr cds: A, C, D, DS, MC, V.

🏄 ⛷ 🚶 ⛳ 🏊 🐾 SC

Restaurant

★ **PATTI'S.** *(JH O'Bryan Ave, Grand River 42045)* I-24 exit 31, on US 453. 502/362-8844. Hrs: 10:30 am-9 pm. Closed wk of Dec 25.

Res accepted. Semi-a la carte: lunch $5.50-$10.99, dinner $10.99-$18.99. Gift shops. Stained glass, antiques. Family-owned. No cr cds accepted.

Ⓓ

Glasgow (E-5)

(See also Cave City, Horse Cave, Mammoth Cave National Park, Park City)

Settled 1799 **Pop** 12,351 **Elev** 790 ft **Area code** 502 **Zip** 42141
Information Glasgow-Barren County Chamber of Commerce, 118 E Public Square; 502/651-3161.

Glasgow was one of the first towns to be settled in the "barrens," then an almost treeless plateau west of the bluegrass section of Kentucky. Today, lumber products are important in Glasgow although tobacco is the leading money crop, followed by dairy products.

What to See and Do

Barren River Dam and Lake. Impounds waters of Barren River and its tributaries. There is good bass fishing; boating (ramps); water sports. Picnic areas. Camping, lodge, cabins (most have fee). 12 mi SW on US 31E. Contact 11088 Finney Rd; 502/646-2055. Other recreation areas and campsites include Baileys Point, Beaver Creek, Browns Ford (no campsites), the Narrows, Peninsula (no campsites), the Tailwater, Walnut Creek and

Barren River Lake State Resort Park. Approx 2,100 acres with a 10,000-acre lake. Swimming beach, pool; fishing; boating (rentals). Hiking, horseback riding, bicycle trails; 18-hole golf course, tennis. Picnicking, playground. Tent & trailer sites (Apr-Oct, standard fees), cottages, lodge (see RESORT). Some fees. Phone 502/646-2151.

Annual Event

Highland Games and Gathering of Scottish Clans. 14 mi S via US 31E in Barren River Lake State Resort Park (see). Six-day festival. Wkend following Memorial Day.

Motels

★ **DAYS INN.** *105 Days Inn Blvd.* 502/651-1757; FAX 502/651-1755. E-mail gla@musslemanhotels.com; web www.mussleman hotels.com. 59 rms, 2 story. S, D $49-$61; each addl $6; suites $55-$65; under 18 free; higher rates Highland Games. Crib free. TV; cable (premium). Complimentary coffee in rms. Restaurant adj 6 am-10 pm. Ck-out noon. Meeting rms. Business servs avail. In-rm modem link. Valet serv. Indoor pool; whirlpool. Some in-rm whirlpools, refrigerators, microwaves. Cr cds: A, C, D, DS, MC, V.

⊡ 🏊 ⚒ 🐾 SC

✔★ **FAMILY BUDGET INN.** *1003 W Main, ½ mi W on US 68; ½ blk W of US 31E Bypass.* 502/651-5191; FAX 502/651-9233; res: 800/452-7469. 80 rms, 2 story. S $34-$50; D $40-$55; each addl $5; under 13 free. Pet accepted; $5. TV; cable. Heated pool. Restaurant. Ck-out 11 am. Coin lndry. Meeting rms. Business servs avail. In-rm modem link. Cr cds: A, DS, MC, V.

🐾 🏊 ⚒ 🐾 SC

Inn

★ ★ ★ **FOUR SEASONS COUNTRY INN.** *4107 Scottsville Rd (US 31E).* 502/678-1000; FAX 502/678-1017. 21 rms, 3 story, 5 suites. S, D $70-$78; each addl $5; suites $125; wkly rates. Crib $5. TV; cable (premium). Heated pool. Complimentary continental bkfst. Restaurant nearby. Ck-out noon, ck-in 2 pm. Business servs avail. Refrigerators; some in-rm whirlpools. Antique reproductions. Cr cds: A, C, D, DS, MC, V.

D ≈ ⊠ 🐾 SC

Resort

★ ★ ★ **BARREN RIVER LAKE LODGE.** (1149 State Park Rd, Lucas 42156) 12 mi SW on US 31E, in state park. 502/646-2151; FAX 502/646-3645; res: 800/325-0057. 51 rms, 1-3 story, 22 kit. cottages. S $62; D $72; each addl $5; 2-bedrm kit. cottages (up to 6) $140-$170; under 17 free. Closed 5 days wk of Dec 25. Crib free. TV. Pool; wading pool, lifeguard. Free supervised child's activities. Dining rm 7 am-9 pm. Ck-out noon (cottages 11 am), ck-in 4 pm. Meeting rms. Business servs avail. Lighted tennis. 18-hole golf, greens fee $19. Gift shop. Rec rm. Private patios, balconies. Picnic tables. On lake. State-owned; all facilities of state park avail. Cr cds: A, C, D, DS, MC, V.

D 🏌 🏃 🏊 ≈ ⊠ 🐾 SC

Restaurant

✓★ ★ **BOLTON'S LANDING.** 2433 Scottsville Rd, 1½ mi S on US 31E. 502/651-8008. Hrs: 11 am-2 pm, 5-8:30 pm; Sat from 5 pm. Closed Sun; most major hols. Semi-a la carte: lunch $5.75-$7.29, dinner $6.50-$14.95. Child's meals. Specializes in chicken, catfish, pasta. Original art work. Cr cds: A, D, DS, MC, V.

D ⤴

Greenville (E-4)

(See also Hopkinsville, Madisonville)

Settled 1799 **Pop** 4,689 **Elev** 538 ft **Area code** 502 **Zip** 42345
Information Chamber of Commerce, PO Box 313; 502/338-5422.

Located in the heart of the western Kentucky coal, oil and natural gas fields, Greenville is the seat of Muhlenberg County. There is good hunting and fishing in the area.

What to See and Do

Lake Malone State Park. A 325-acre park on 788-acre Lake Malone; located in a hardwood tree forest, with tall pines on scenic cliffs. A natural rock bridge, steep sandstone bluffs and a wooded shoreline can be seen from a ride on the lake. Swimming beach; fishing for bass, bluegill, crappie; boating (ramp, rentals, motors). Hiking trail. Picnicking, playground. Tent & trailer camping (Apr-mid-Nov). (Daily) Standard fees. 8 mi S on KY 973, between US 431 and KY 181. For information contact the Park Superintendent, Dunmor 42339; 502/657-2111.

Harrodsburg (D-7)

(See also Danville)

Founded 1774 **Pop** 7,335 **Elev** 886 ft **Area code** 606 **Zip** 40330 **Web** www.harrodsburgky.com
Information Harrodsburg/Mercer County Tourist Commission, 103 S Main St, PO Box 283; 606/734-2364 or 800/355-9192.

When James Harrod and a troop of surveyors came here early in 1774 and established a township, they were creating Kentucky's first permanent white settlement. Here, the first corn in Kentucky was grown, the first English school was established and the first gristmill in the area was operated. Today the state's oldest city, its sulphur springs and historical

sites make it a busy tourist town. Tobacco, cattle, and horse-breeding are important to the economy.

What to See and Do

Harrodsburg Pottery and Craft Shop. Demonstrations of candle-dipping; herbal and wreath arrangements; other crafts. Herbal garden; greenhouse. (Mar-Dec, daily; rest of yr, wkends; closed Easter, Thanksgiving, Dec 25) 1026 Lexington Rd. Phone 606/734-9991. **Free.**

Morgan Row (1807-1845). Probably the oldest standing row house west of the Alleghenies; once a stagecoach stop and tavern. Houses Harrodsburg Historical Society Museum (Tues-Sat). 220-222 S Chiles St, behind courthouse. Phone 606/734-5985. **Free.**

Old Fort Harrod State Park. This 28-acre park includes a reproduction of Old Fort Harrod in an area known as Old Fort Hill, site of the original fort (1774). The stockade shelters Ann McGinty Block House, George Rogers Clark Block House, James Harrod Block House and the first school, complete with hand-hewn benches. Authentic cooking utensils, tools and furniture are displayed in the cabins. Mansion Museum includes Lincoln Room, Confederate Room, gun collection, Native American artifacts. Lincoln Marriage Temple shelters the log cabin in which Abraham Lincoln's parents were married on June 12, 1806 (moved from its original site in Beech Fork). Pioneer Cemetery. Picnic facilities, playground, gift shop. Living history crafts program in fort (mid-Apr-late Oct). Museum (mid-Mar-Nov, daily; fort (daily; closed Thanksgiving, wk of Dec 25; also Mon in Jan). On US 68/127 in town. Phone 606/734-3314. ¢¢

Old Mud Meeting House (1800). First Dutch Reformed Church west of the Alleghenies. The original mud-thatch walls have been restored. (By appt only) 4 mi S off US 68. Phone 606/734-5985. **Free.**

Shaker Village of Pleasant Hill (1805-1910). Thirty-three buildings (1805-1859) including frame, brick and stone houses. Center Family House has exhibits; Trustees' House (see RESTAURANT) has twin spiral staircases. Craft shops with reproductions of Shaker furniture, Kentucky craft items; craft demonstrations; lodging in 15 restored buildings. Year-round calendar of special events including music, dance and Sept wkend big events. (Daily; closed Dec 24, 25) Sternwheeler offers one-hour excursions on Kentucky River (Late Apr-Oct; fee). 7 mi NE on US 68. Phone 606/734-5411. ¢¢¢

Annual Event

Pioneer Days Festival. 3rd wkend Aug.

Seasonal Event

The Legend of Daniel Boone. James Harrod Amphitheater, in Old Fort Harrod State Park (see). Outdoor drama traces the story of Boone. Daily exc Mon. For information contact PO Box 365; 606/734-3346 or 800/852-6663. Mid-June-Aug.

Motel

✓★ ★ **BEST WESTERN.** 1680 Danville Rd, 3 mi S on US 127. 606/734-9431; FAX 606/734-5559. Web www.bestwestern.com/best.html. 69 rms, 3 story. S $53-$57; D $58-$62; each addl $5; under 12 free. Crib free. TV; cable (premium). Pool. Complimentary continental bkfst. Restaurant adj 6:30 am-10 pm. Ck-out 11 am. Business servs avail. Valet serv. Many refrigerators; microwaves avail. Balconies. Miniature golf course adj. Cr cds: A, C, D, DS, MC, V.

D ≈ ⊠ 🐾 SC

Motor Hotel

★ ★ **INN AT SHAKER VILLAGE.** 3501 Lexington Rd, Shaker Village of Pleasant Hill. 606/734-5411; res: 800/734-5611. Web www.shakervillageky.org. 81 rms in 15 bldgs, 1-4 story. S $56-$80; D $60-$80; each addl $10; suites $110-$200; under 18 free. Closed Dec 24, 25. Crib free. TV. Restaurant (see TRUSTEES' OFFICE AT PLEASANT HILL). Ck-out 11 am. Meeting rms. Riverboat cruises. 30 restored buildings (ca 1800) furnished with Shaker reproductions, hand-woven rugs and curtains; some trundle beds. Cr cds: MC, V.

Inn

★ ★ ★ **BEAUMONT.** *638 Beaumont Inn Dr, off US 127.* 606/734-3381; *FAX* 606/734-6897; *res: 800/352-3992.* 33 rms. S $65-$85; D $85-$110; each addl $25; under 12, $15. Closed late Dec-Feb. TV; cable. Pool; wading pool, lifeguard. Dining rm (public by res). Ck-out noon. Meeting rms. Business servs avail. Gift shop. Golf privileges. Lawn games. Rms are in 4 buildings; main building furnished with antiques. Cr cds: A, D, DS, MC, V.

Restaurant

★ ★ **TRUSTEES' HOUSE AT PLEASANT HILL.** *(See Inn At Shaker Village Motor Hotel)* 606/734-5411. Web www.tourky.com.shaker village/. Hrs: 7:30-9:30 am, 11:30 am-2:30 pm, 5:30-8:30 pm. Closed Dec 24, 25. Res accepted. Semi-a la carte: lunch $6.50-$8.75. Complete meals: dinner $11.50-$18. Child's meals. Specializes in traditional Kentucky and Shaker dishes. Restored Shaker village; Shaker decor. Totally nonsmoking. Cr cds: MC, V.

D

Hazard (D-9)

Pop 5,416 **Elev** 867 ft **Area code** 606 **Zip** 41701

Information Hazard-Perry County Chamber of Commerce & Tourism Commission, 601 Main St, Suite 3; 606/439-2659.

In rugged mountain country, Hazard is a coal mining town, a trading center and the seat of Perry County. Both town and county were named for Commodore Oliver Hazard Perry, naval hero of the War of 1812.

What to See and Do

Bobby Davis Memorial Park. Picnic area, reflecting pool, WW II Memorial, 400 varieties of shrubs and plants. (Daily) Walnut St. In the park is

Bobby Davis Park Museum. Community museum housing local historical artifacts and photographs relating to life on Kentucky River waterways. (Mon-Fri; closed most hols) Phone 606/439-4325. **Free.**

Buckhorn Lake State Resort Park. This 856-acre park encompasses a 1,200-acre lake. Swimming beach, pool, bathhouse (seasonal); fishing; boating (ramp, motors, rentals). Hiking; bicycle rentals, miniature golf, tennis. Picnicking, playground. Lodge (see RESORT), cottages. 25 mi NW via KY 15/28. For fees and information phone 606/398-7510.

Carr Fork Lake. A 710-acre lake. Beach; fishing; boating (ramps, marina). Picnic shelters. Camping (hookups, dump station; fee). Observation points. Some facilities seasonal. 15 mi SE. Phone 606/642-3308.

Daniel Boone National Forest (see). 15 mi W on KY 80.

Annual Event

Black Gold Festival. On Main St. Celebrates local coal resources. Food and craft booths, games, entertainment, carnival, parade. Phone 606/436-0161. 3rd full wkend Sept.

Motels

★ ★ **HOLIDAY INN.** *200 Dawahare Dr, off Daniel Boone Pkwy.* 606/436-4428. 81 rms, 2 story. S, D $54-$70; each addl $6; suites $125-$186; under 16 free. Crib avail. TV; cable. 2 pools, 1 indoor; whirlpool.

Restaurant 5:30 am-11 pm. Rm serv. Bar 3 pm-midnight. Ck-out 11 am. Meeting rms. Business servs avail. In-rm modem link. Sundries. Cr cds: A, C, D, DS, JCB, MC, V.

✔ ★ **SUPER 8.** *125 Village Lane, off Daniel Boone Pkwy.* 606/436-8888; *FAX* 606/439-0768. 86 rms, 2 story, 11 suites. S $43.88-$48.88; D $46.88-54.88; each addl $3; suites $49.88-$78.88; under 12 free. Crib free. TV; cable (premium). Coffee in rms. Complimentary continental bkfst. Restaurant nearby. Ck-out 11 am. Business servs avail. Cr cds: A, C, D, DS, MC, V.

Resort

★ ★ **BUCKHORN LODGE.** *(4441 KY Hwy 1833, Buckhorn 41721)* 25 mi W on KY 28, in Buckhorn Lake State Resort Park. 606/398-7510; *FAX* 606/398-7077; *res: 800/325-0058.* 36 rms, 2 story. Memorial Day-Labor Day: S $53; D $63; each addl $5; cottages $104-$146; under 16 free; lower rates rest of yr. Crib free. TV; cable (premium). Pool; wading pool, lifeguard. Supervised child's activities (Memorial Day-Labor Day). Dining rm 7 am-9 pm. Ck-out noon. Meeting rms. Business servs avail. Gift shop. Tennis. Miniature golf. Game rm. Rec rm. Lawn games. Balconies. Picnic tables, grills. On lake; beach facilities, boat rental. State-owned; all facilities of state park avail. Cr cds: A, C, D, DS, MC, V.

Henderson (D-4)

(See also Owensboro)

Founded 1797 **Pop** 25,945 **Elev** 409 ft **Area code** 502 **Zip** 42420 **E-mail** gotour@henderson.net **Web** www.go-henderson.com

Information Tourist Commission, 2961 US 41N; 502/826-3128 or 800/648-3128.

Henderson was developed by the Transylvania Company and named for its chief executive, Colonel Richard Henderson. This town along the banks of the Ohio River has long attracted residents, most notably naturalist John James Audubon, W.C. Handy, well-known "father of the Blues" and A.B. "Happy" Chandler, former governor and commissioner of baseball.

What to See and Do

John James Audubon State Park. Here stand 692 acres of massive hardwood trees, woodland plants, nature preserve, densely forested tracts and two lakes favored by migratory birds and described in Audubon's writings. Swimming beach, bathhouse (seasonal); fishing; paddleboat rentals (seasonal). Nine-hole golf (yr-round; fee). Picnicking, playground. Tent & trailer camping (standard fees), cottages (yr-round). Supervised recreation; guided nature walks. (Daily) Some fees. 2 mi N on US 41. Phone 502/826-2247. **Free.**

Annual Events

W.C. Handy Blues & Barbecue Festival. Mid-June.

Bluegrass in the Park. Audubon Mill Park. 1st wkend Aug.

Big River Arts & Crafts Festival. Audubon State Park (see). More than 250 exhibitors. Early Oct.

Seasonal Event

Horse Racing. Ellis Park. 5 mi N on US 41. Thoroughbred racing. Daily exc Mon. Phone 812/425-1456. Early July-Labor Day.

Motels

★ ★ **DAYS INN.** *2044 US 41N. 502/826-6600; FAX 502/826-3055.* 117 rms, 2 story. S, D $50-$80; each addl $6; suites $70-$100; under 12 free. Crib free. Pet accepted; $5. TV; cable (premium). Pool. Coffee in rms. Restaurant 6 am-2 pm, 5-9 pm; Sun to 3 pm. Rm serv. Bar 11-2 am; entertainment. Ck-out 11 am. Coin lndry. Meeting rms. Business center. Valet serv. Some refrigerators. Cr cds: A, C, D, DS, MC, V.

D ⚏ ≈ ⊠ 🔥 SC

✔ ★ **SCOTTISH INN.** *2820 US 41N. 502/827-1806; FAX 502/827-8192.* 60 rms, 1-2 story. S $35; D $40-$45; each addl $3; under 10 free. Crib $5. Pet accepted; $5. TV; cable (premium), VCR avail (movies). Pool; wading pool. Complimentary coffee in lobby. Restaurant nearby. Ck-out 11 am. Business servs avail. Cr cds: A, C, D, DS, MC, V.

⚏ ≈ ⊠ 🔥 SC

Hodgenville (D-6)

(See also Elizabethtown)

Founded 1789 **Pop** 2,721 **Elev** 730 ft **Area code** 502 **Zip** 42748
Information LaRue County Chamber of Commerce, 72 Lincoln Square, PO Box 176; 502/358-3411.

Robert Hodgen built a mill and tavern here and entertained many prominent people. Young Abraham Lincoln often came to the mill with corn to be ground from his father's farm seven miles away. Soon after Hodgen's death in 1810, the settlement surrounding his tavern adopted his name and was known thereafter as Hodgenville. In 1909 a bronze statue of Lincoln was erected on the town square.

What to See and Do

Abraham Lincoln Birthplace National Historic Site (see). 3 mi S on US 31E (KY 61).

Lincoln Jamboree. Family entertainment featuring traditional and modern country music. (Sat evenings; res recommended in summer) 2 mi S on US 31E. Phone 502/358-3545. ¢¢¢

Lincoln Museum. Dioramas depicting events in Lincoln's life; memorabilia; special exhibits. (Daily; closed Jan 1, Thanksgiving, Dec 25) 66 Lincoln Square. Phone 502/358-3163. ¢¢

⭐ **Lincoln's Boyhood Home.** Replica of the log cabin where Lincoln lived for five years (1811-1816) during his childhood; contains historic items and antiques. (Apr-Oct, daily) 7 mi NE on US 31E, on Knob Creek Farm. Phone 502/549-3741. ¢

Annual Events

Founder's Day. Lincoln Birthplace N.H.S. Arts, crafts, music. Wkend nearest July 17.

Lincoln Days Celebration. Railsplitting competition; pioneer games; classic car show; arts and crafts exhibits; parade. 2nd wkend Oct.

Hopkinsville (E-4)

(See also Cadiz; also see Clarksville, TN)

Founded 1797 **Pop** 29,809 **Elev** 548 ft **Area code** 502 **Zip** 42240 **E-mail** commercecenter.org **Web** http://.ci.hopkinsville.ky.us
Information Hopkinsville-Christian County Chamber of Commerce, 1209 S Virginia St, PO Box 1382; 502/885-9096 or 800/842-9959.

The tobacco auctioneers' chant has long been the theme song of Hopkinsville. Industry has moved in, and Hopkinsville now manufactures precision springs, magnetic wire, lighting fixtures, bowling balls, hardwood, plastic and cement products, non-woven textiles, wearing apparel and hydraulic motors. Tobacco redrying, flour and cornmeal milling are also done here. Fort Campbell military post has played an important role in the city's growth.

Hopkinsville was the site of the Night Rider War, brought on by farmers' discontent at the low prices they received for their dark tobacco. They raided the town in December 1907, burning several warehouses. In 1911, the culprits were tried and their group disbanded. Hopkinsville was a stop on the "Trail of Tears." The site of the Cherokee encampment is now a park with a museum and memorial dedicated to those who lost thier lives. Famous sons of the town include Adlai Stevenson, Vice President of the United States 1892-1897; Edgar Cayce, famous clairvoyant, who is buried here; Colonel Wil Starling, Chief of the White House Secret Service 1914-1944; and Ned Breathitt, Governor of Kentucky 1963-1967.

What to See and Do

Fort Campbell. One of the nation's largest military installations (105,000 acres); home of 101st Airborne Div (Air Assault). Wickham Hall houses Don F. Pratt Museum, which displays historic military items (daily; closed Jan 1, Dec 25). 16 mi S on US 41A, in both KY and TN. Phone 502/798-2151. **Free.**

Jefferson Davis Monument State Shrine (see). 11 mi E on US 68 in Fairview.

Pennyrile Forest State Resort Park. Approx 17 mi NW on KY 109 (see MADISONVILLE).

Pennyroyal Area Museum. Exhibits feature area's agriculture and industries, Native American artifacts, miniature circus, old railroad items. Civil War items; 1898 law office furniture; Edgar Cayce exhibit, books. (Daily exc Sun; closed most hols) 217 E 9th St. Phone 502/887-4270. ¢

Annual Events

Dogwood Festival. Features bike tours along the Dogwood Trail, band concerts and historical walking tours. Phone 502/885-9096. Last 2 wks Apr.

Little River Days. Downtown. Festival consists of road races, canoe races; arts and crafts; entertainment; square dance; children's events. Early May.

Western Kentucky State Fair. Midway, rides, concerts, local exhibits and events. 1st wk Aug.

Motels

★ ★ **BEST WESTERN.** *4101 Ft Campbell Blvd (US 41A). 502/886-9000.* 111 rms, 3 story. S, D $50; each addl $5; under 12 free. Crib free. Pet accepted, some restrictions. TV; cable (premium). Pool. Continental bkfst. Restaurant nearby. Bar 5-10 pm. Ck-out noon. Meeting rms. Business servs avail. Health club privileges. Cr cds: A, C, D, DS, MC, V.

D ⚏ ≈ ⊠ 🔥 SC

✔ ★ **HOLIDAY INN.** *2910 Ft Campbell Blvd (US 41A). 502/886-4413.* 101 rms, 5 story. S, D $49-$79; each addl $6; under 19 free. Crib free. Pet accepted. TV; cable (premium). Indoor pool. Restaurant 6 am-

1:30 pm, 5-9:30 pm. Rm serv. Bar 4 pm-midnight. Ck-out noon. Meeting rms. Business servs avail. In-rm modem link. Valet serv. Sundries. Exercise equipt; sauna. Cr cds: A, C, D, DS, JCB, MC, V.

⊡ ⛷ ≋ 🏃 ⛷ ⊠ SC

Restaurant

✔★ **WOODSHED.** *1821 W Seventh St.* 502/885-8144. Hrs: 5 am-8 pm. Closed Sun; major hols. Semi-a la carte: bkfst $3-$4.50, lunch, dinner $3.50-$9.95. Specializes in barbecue, ham, corn bread. No cr cds accepted.

⊡ ⊴

Horse Cave (E-5)

(See also Cave City, Glasgow)

Pop 2,284 **Elev** 132 ft **Area code** 502 **Zip** 42749

Tobacco, livestock and caves are important sources of local income. The town took its name from a nearby cave, which provided water for the area's first settlers ("horse" meant large).

What to See and Do

Horse Cave Theatre. Southern Kentucky's resident professional festival theatre. Six of the season's plays run in rotating repertory in summer. Art gallery; concessions. (June-Nov, nightly exc Mon; matinees Sat, Sun; phone ahead for current schedule) I-65 exit 58, downtown. Phone 800/342-2177 for schedule, reservations. ¢¢¢¢

★ **Kentucky Down Under/Mammoth Onyx Cave.** Exotic bird garden; wallabies, emus, sheep and other animals in Australian outback setting. Petting zoo; bison and elk overlook. (Apr-Oct, daily) Guided cave tour (45 min) includes Mammoth Onyx Column (45 ft high); colorful stalactites, stalagmites, flowstone and hanging bridges; cave temperature approximately 60°F. Tours (daily; closed Jan 1, Dec 25) 2 mi NW on KY 218, just E of I-65, exit 58. Phone 502/786-2634 or 800/762-2869. ¢¢¢¢

Jamestown (E-6)

(See also Somerset)

Pop 1,641 **Elev** 1,024 ft **Area code** 502 **Zip** 42629 **Web** www.lakecumberlandvacation.com
Information Russell County Tourist Commission, 650 S KY 127, PO Box 64, Russell Springs 42642; 502/866-4333.

What to See and Do

Wolf Creek Dam. US Army Corps of Engineers dam; 258 ft high, 5,736 ft long, draining a 5,789-sq-mi area and creating 101-mi-long Lake Cumberland (see SOMERSET). Camping (mid-Mar-Nov; fee). Visitor center. 12 mi S via US 127. Phone 606/679-6337. On N shore of lake is

Lake Cumberland State Resort Park. More than 3,000 acres on a 50,250-acre lake. Swimming pools; fishing; boating (ramps, rentals, dock). Hiking, riding (seasonal), 9-hole par-3 and miniature golf (seasonal), tennis, shuffleboard. bicycling (rentals). Picnicking, playground, lodge (see RESORTS), rental houseboats, cottages. Tent & trailer camping (Apr-Nov; standard fees). Nature center, supervised recreation. 14 mi S on US 127. For rates and information phone 502/343-3111 or 800/325-1709.

Motel

★ **CUMBERLAND LODGE.** *(US 127 & Cumberland Pkwy, Russell Springs 42642)* N on US 127. 502/866-4208; FAX 502/866-4206. 53 rms, 2 story. S $40; D $50; each addl $5; under 12 free; higher rates wkends, special events. Crib free. TV; cable (premium), VCR avail (movies). Pool. Complimentary continental bkfst. Complimentary coffee in rms. Restaurant adj 5 am-11 pm. Ck-out 11 am. Meeting rm. Exercise equipt. Some refrigerators. Cr cds: A, DS, MC, V.

⊡ ≋ 🏃 ⊠ 🏄

Resorts

★★ **JAMESTOWN RESORT & MARINA.** *3677 S KY 92, 4 mi S on KY 92E.* 502/343-5253; FAX 502/343-5252. E-mail jrmarina@duocounty.com; web www.jamestown-marina.com. 40 rms in main bldg, 2 story, 4 kit. units, 18 kit. cottages (1-3 bedrm). Memorial Day-Labor Day, EP: S, D $129.95-$139.95; each addl $10; kit. units $149.95-$169.95; kit. cottages $69.95-$109.95; under 16 free; lower rates rest of yr. Crib free. TV; cable, VCR. Pool. Playground. Complimentary coffee in rms. Restaurant adj (seasonal) 7 am-10 pm. Ck-out 10 am, ck-in 2 pm. Grocery. Coin lndry. Meeting rms. Gift shop. Tennis. Boats. Waterskiing. Lake swimming. Hiking. Lawn games. 19-hole miniature golf. Fishing guides. Refrigerators; some minibars. Balconies. Grills. A 300-acre lakeside development; more than 800 boat slips. Cr cds: A, DS, MC, V.

⊡ ⛷ 🏃 ≋ ⊠ 🏄

★★★ **LAKE CUMBERLAND STATE RESORT PARK.** *5465 State Park Rd (42629-7801), 10 mi S, in Lake Cumberland State Park.* 502/343-3111; FAX 502/343-5510; res: 800/325-1709. Web www.ky stateparks.com. 63 rms in lodge, 13 in annex, 30 kit. cottages (1-2 bedrm). Apr-Oct: S $54-$72; D $64-$82; each addl $5; cottages for 2-4, $81-$130; under 16 free; lower lodge rates rest of yr. Crib free. TV; cable. 2 pools, 1 indoor; 2 wading pools. Supervised child's activities (Memorial Day-Labor Day). Dining rm 7-10:30 am, 11:30 am-2:30 pm, 5-9 pm. Ck-out noon, cottages 11 am, ck-in 4 pm. Coin lndry. Convention facilities. Business servs avail. Gift shop. Tennis. 9-hole golf, greens fee $8, putting green. Exercise equipt. Miniature golf $2.50. Waterskiing. Marina; boat, houseboat rental. Lawn games. Soc dir. Entertainment. Rec rm. Children's program. Balconies overlook lake. State-owned; all facilities of state park avail. Cr cds: A, C, D, DS, MC, V.

⊡ ⛷ ⫟ ≋ 🏃 ⊠ 🏄 SC

Jefferson Davis Monument State Shrine (E-4)

(See also Hopkinsville)

(10 mi E of Hopkinsville on US 68 in Fairview)

The monument, a cast-concrete obelisk 351 feet tall, ranks as the fourth tallest obelisk in the country and the tallest of such material. It marks the birthplace of Jefferson Davis, the only President of the Confederate States of America. Overlooking a 19-acre park, the monument was built at a cost of $200,000 raised by public subscription and was dedicated in 1924. Visitors may take an elevator to the top (fee).

The son of a Revolutionary War officer, Jefferson Davis was born here in 1808, less than 100 miles from Abraham Lincoln's birthplace. Davis graduated from West Point, became a successful cotton planter in Mississippi, was elected to the US Senate and was Secretary of War in President Franklin Pierce's Cabinet. Elected President of the Confederacy, he served for the duration of the war, was captured in Georgia and imprisoned for two years. Picnic area; playground. (May-Oct, daily) Phone 502/886-1765.

Kenlake State Resort Park (E-3)

(See also Cadiz, Land Between The Lakes)

(16 mi NE of Murray on KY 94)

Located 16 miles northeast of Murray (see), Kenlake State Resort Park lies on 1,800 acres with a four-mile shoreline on 160,300-acre Kentucky Lake. Pool, bathhouse (seasonal), waterskiing; fishing; boating (ramps, rentals, marina). Hiking trail; 9-hole golf (rentals), shuffleboard, tennis (indoor, outdoor, shop). Picnicking, playgrounds, cottages, dining room, lodge (see RESORT). Tent & trailer sites (Apr-Oct, standard fees). For rates and information phone 502/474-2211 or 800/325-0143.

Motel

✔★ **EARLY AMERICAN.** *(16749 US Hwy 68, Aurora 42048) At jct US 68, KY 80 & jct KY 94.* 502/474-2241. 18 rms, 7 kits. Late May-early Sept: S $37.95; D $41.95-$63.95; each addl $5; kit. units $48.95-$68.95; under 12 free; wkly rates; lower rates rest of yr. Crib free. Pet accepted. TV; cable. Pool. Playground. Complimentary coffee in rms. Restaurant adj 6 am-9 pm. Ck-out 10 am. Rec rm. Lawn games. Picnic tables, grills. Cr cds: A, DS, MC, V.

⟆ ≋ 🔥 SC

Resort

★★ **KENLAKE.** *542 Kenlake Rd (42048), On KY 94 at jct US 68.* 502/474-2211; FAX 502/474-2018; res: 800/325-0143. 48 rms in lodge, 1 story, 34 cottages. S $57; D $67; each addl $5.45; 1-3 bedrm cottages $81-$119; lower rates rest of yr. Closed Christmas wk. Crib free. TV. Pool; wading pool. Playground. Dining rm 7 am-9 pm. Ck-out noon (lodge rms), 11 am (cottages); ck-in 4 pm (lodge rms & cottages). Meeting rms. Lighted tennis, some indoor. 9-hole golf, greens fee $10, putting green. Lawn games. Rec rm. Picnic tables, grills. State-owned; all state park facilities avail. Cr cds: A, C, D, DS, MC, V.

D 🏃 ⛷ ≋ ⛷ 🔥 SC

Restaurant

★★ **BRASS LANTERN.** *(16593 US 68E, Aurora 42048) on US 68 at jct KY 80.* 502/474-2773. E-mail lantern1@ldd.net. Hrs: 5-9 pm. Closed Mon, Tues exc mid-June-mid-Aug; also closed late Dec-late Mar. Res accepted. Semi-a la carte: dinner $9.50-$24.95. Child's meals. Specialties: prime rib, filet mignon. Salad bar. Cr cds: A, C, D, DS, MC, V.

D ⏍

Land Between The Lakes (E-3)

(See also Cadiz, Gilbertsville; also see Paris, TN)

Information Land Between The Lakes, 100 Van Morgan Dr, Golden Pond 42211; 800/LBL-7077.

A 170,000-acre wooded peninsula, running 40 miles from north to south, located between Kentucky Lake and Lake Barkley in western Kentucky and Tennessee, Land Between The Lakes is one of the largest outdoor recreation areas in the country.

There are four major family campgrounds: Hillman Ferry, Piney, Energy Lake (yr-round; electric hookups; fee) and Wranglers campground that is equipped for horseback riders. Eleven other lake access areas offer more primitive camping (fee). All areas offer swimming; fishing; boating, ramps. Picnic facilities. Family campgrounds have planned recreation programs (summer).

There is a 5,000-acre wooded Environmental Education Area that includes The Nature Station, which presents interpretive displays of native plant and animal life. Within this area are several nature trails. Elk and Bison Prairie is a drive-through wildlife viewing area featuring native plants and wildlife (daily; fee). Nature center (Mar-Nov, daily; fee).

What to See and Do

Golden Pond Visitor Center. Main orientation center for Land Between The Lakes visitors. Planetarium presentation (Mar-Dec, fee). Seasonal programs. Visitor center (daily).

The Homeplace-1850. Living history farm. (Apr-Nov, daily) 17 mi SE of Aurora via US 68, Land Between The Lakes exit. ¢¢

The Nature Station. Interpretive displays of native animals and plants. (Mar-Nov, daily) 14 mi NE of Aurora via US 68, Land Between the Lakes exit. ¢¢

Lexington (C-7)

(See also Frankfort, Paris, Richmond, Winchester)

Founded 1779 **Pop** 225,366 **Elev** 983 ft **Area code** 606
Information Lexington Convention & Visitors Bureau, 301 E Vine St, 40507; 606/233-1221 or 800/845-3959.

A midland metropolis rooted in the production of tobacco and Thoroughbreds, Lexington is a gracious city, decorated with rich bluegrass and dotted with aristocratic old houses. The legendary steel-blue tint of the bluegrass is perceptible only in May's early-morning sunshine, but throughout spring, summer and fall it is unrivaled for turf and pasture.

An exploring party, camping here in 1775, got news of the Battle of Lexington and so named the spot. The city was established four years later, rapidly becoming a center for barter and a major producer of hemp (used by New England's clipper ships). Lexington cashed in on its tobacco crop when smoking became popular during the Civil War. Pioneers who settled here brought their best horses with them from Maryland and Virginia; as they grew wealthy, they imported blooded lines from abroad to improve the breed. The first races were held in Lexington in 1780, and the first jockey club was organized in 1797.

Lexington is the world's largest burley tobacco market, with well over 100 million pounds sold each year. Precious bluegrass seed, beef cattle and sheep are also merchandised in Lexington. More than 50 major industries, manufacturing everything from peanut butter and bourbon to air brakes and ink jet printers, are located here.

What to See and Do

⊠ **Ashland** (1806). Estate on 20 acres of woodland was the home of Henry Clay, statesman, orator and would-be president. Ashland, occupied by the Clay family for five generations, is furnished with family possessions and furniture. The estate was named for the ash trees that surround it. A number of outbuildings still stand. (Daily; closed hols, also Jan) Richmond Rd (E Main St), at Sycamore Rd. Phone 606/266-8581. ¢¢¢

Headley-Whitney Museum. Unusual buildings house display of bibelots (small decorative objects) executed in precious metals and jewels; Oriental porcelains, paintings, decorative arts, shell grotto, special exhibits; library. (Daily exc Mon; closed most hols). 4435 Old Frankfort Pike, 4½ mi NW of New Circle Rd. Phone 606/255-6653. ¢¢

Horse farms. More than 400 in area, most concentrated in Lexington-Fayette County. Although the majority are Thoroughbred farms, other varieties such as standardbreds, American saddle horses, Arabians, Morgans and quarter horses are bred and raised here as well. Farms may be seen by taking one of the many tours offered by tour companies in Lexington.

Hunt-Morgan House (ca 1812-1814). In Gratz Park area, a historic district with antebellum residences. Federal-period mansion with a cantilevered elliptical staircase and fanlight doorway. Built for John Wesley Hunt, Kentucky's first millionaire. Later occupied by his grandson, General John Hunt Morgan, known as the "Thunderbolt of the Confederacy." Nobel Prize-winning geneticist Thomas Hunt Morgan was also born in this house. Family furniture, portraits and porcelain. Walled courtyard garden. Gift shop. (Daily exc hols; closed hols, late Dec-Feb) 201 N Mill St, at W 2nd St. Phone 606/233-3290. ¢¢

✖ **Kentucky Horse Park.** More than 1,000 acres of beautiful bluegrass fill the park; features Man O' War grave and memorial, visitors' information center with wide-screen film presentation *Thou Shalt Fly Without Wings.* Also located within park are the International Museum of the Horse, Parade of Breeds (seasonal), Calumet Trophy Collection, Sears Collection of hand-carved miniatures; Hall of Champions stable that houses famous Thoroughbreds and standardbreds; walking farm tour, antique carriage display. Swimming. Tennis, ball courts. Picnic area, playgrounds. Campground (fee). Special events (see ANNUAL EVENTS); horsedrawn rides (fee). (Mid-Mar-Oct, daily; rest of yr, Wed-Sun; closed Jan 1, Thanksgiving, late Dec) Parking fee (seasonal). 6 mi N via I-75, Kentucky Horse Park exit 120, on Iron Works Pike. Contact Director, 4089 Iron Works Rd, 40511; 606/233-4303 or 800/568-8813. General admission ¢¢¢ Also on grounds is

American Saddle Horse Museum. Museum dedicated to the American Saddlebred horse, Kentucky's only native breed. Contemporary exhibits on the development and current uses of the American Saddlebred. Multimedia presentation. Gift shop. (May-Sept, daily; rest of yr, Wed-Sun; closed Jan 1, Thanksgiving, Dec 24-25) 4093 Iron Works Pike. Phone 606/259-2746. ¢¢

Lexington Cemetery. Buried on these 170 acres are Henry Clay, John C. Breckinridge, General John Hunt Morgan, the Todds (Mrs. Abraham Lincoln's family), coach Adolph Rupp and many other notable persons. Also interred are 500 Confederate and 1,110 Union veterans. Sunken gardens, lily pools, four-acre flower garden, extensive plantings of spring-flowering trees and shrubs. (Daily) 833 W Main St, on US 421. Phone 606/255-5522.

Mary Todd Lincoln House. Childhood residence of Mary Todd Lincoln is authentically restored; period furnishings, personal items. (Mid-Mar-Nov, Tues-Sat; closed major hols) 578 W Main St. Phone 606/233-9999. ¢¢

Opera House (1886). Restored and reconstructed opera house is a regional performing arts center; performances include Broadway shows and special events. (Sept-June) 401 W Short St. Contact Lexington Center Corp, Performing Arts, 430 W Vine St, 40507; 606/233-4567.

Sightseeing tours. There are many tour companies that offer tours of working horse farms in the Lexington area. Many of these companies also offer historic sightseeing tours. For more information contact the Convention & Visitors Bureau.

Transylvania University (1780). (926 students) The oldest institution of higher learning west of the Allegheny Mountains, it has educated two US vice-presidents, 36 state and territorial governors, 34 ambassadors, 50 senators, 112 members of the US House of Representatives and Confederate President Jefferson Davis. Thomas Jefferson was one of Transylvania's early supporters. Henry Clay taught law courses and was a member of the university's governing board. Administration Building, "Old Morrison" (1833), Greek-revival architecture, was used as hospital during Civil War. Tours of campus (by appt). N Broadway & 3rd St. Phone 606/233-8120.

University of Kentucky (1865). (24,000 students) Area of S Limestone St & Euclid Ave. For information on bus and walking tours phone 606/257-3595. Free. On campus are

William S. Webb Museum of Anthropology. Exhibits include cultural history of Kentucky and evolution of man. (Mon-Fri; closed hols) Lafferty Hall. Phone 606/257-7112. **Free.**

Art Museum. Permanent collections; special exhibitions. (Daily exc Mon; closed hols & Dec 26-Jan 2) Singletary Center for the Arts, Euclid Ave & Rose St. Phone 606/257-5716. **Free.**

Victorian Square. Shopping area located in downtown restoration project. Specialty stores; restaurants; Children's Museum (phone 606/258-3253); parking in 400-car garage with covered walkway into mall. Vine St, across

from Triangle Park, the Convention Center and Rupp Arena. Phone 606/252-7575.

Waveland State Historic Site. Greek-revival mansion (1847) with three original outbuildings. Exhibits depict plantation life of 1840s. Playground. (Mar-Dec, Mon-Sat & Sun afternoons) 225 Waveland Museum Lane. Phone 606/272-3611. ¢¢

Annual Events

Blue Grass Stakes. Keeneland Race Course (see SEASONAL EVENTS). Three-yr-olds; one of last major prep races before Kentucky Derby. Mid-Apr.

Rolex-Kentucky Event & Trade Fair. Kentucky Horse Park. Three-day endurance test for horse and rider in dressage, cross-country and stadium jumping. Fair features boutiques. Phone 606/233-2362. Late Apr.

High Hope Steeplechase. Kentucky Horse Park. Mid-May.

Egyptian Event. Kentucky Horse Park. Activities highlighting rare Egyptian Arabian horses. Show classes, Walk of Stallions, Breeder's Sale, native costumes, seminars, art auction and Egyptian Bazaar. Early June.

Festival of the Bluegrass. Kentucky Horse Park. Campground. Top names in Bluegrass music, with more than 20 bands appearing. Includes special shows for children; crafts; workshops with the musicians. The 600-acre park has more than 750 electric hookups for campers. For information, tickets, contact PO Box 644, Georgetown 40324; 606/846-4995. 2nd full wkend June.

Junior League Horse Show. The Red Mile Harness Track. Outdoor Saddlebred horse show. Contact PO Box 1092, 40589; 606/252-1893. Six days early-mid-July.

Grand Circuit Meet. The Red Mile Track (see SEASONAL EVENTS). Features Kentucky Futurity race, the final leg of trotting's Triple Crown. Daily exc Sun. Phone 606/255-0752. 2 wks, late Sept-early Oct.

Seasonal Events

Thoroughbred racing. Keeneland Race Course, 6 mi W on US 60. Phone 606/254-3412. 3 wks Apr & 3 wks Oct.

Harness racing. The Red Mile Harness Track, 1200 Red Mile Rd, 1½ mi S on US 68. Also site of Grand Circuit racing (see ANNUAL EVENTS). Phone 606/255-0752. Night racing (May & late Sept-early Oct, Wed-Sat).

Motels

✔★ ★ **BEST WESTERN REGENCY.** *2241 Elkhorn (40505), I-75 exit 110.* 606/293-2202; FAX 606/293-1821. 112 rms, 2 story. S $54-$74; D $59-$79; suite $139; under 18 free. Crib free. Pet accepted; $10. TV; cable (premium). Pool; whirlpool. Sauna. Complimentary continental bkfst. Restaurant nearby. Ck-out 11 am. Coin lndry. Meeting rms. Business servs avail. Cr cds: A, C, D, DS, MC, V.

D ⚐ ≈ ⊠ ⚞ SC

★ ★ ★ **CAMBERLEY CLUB HOTEL.** *120 W 2nd St (40507).* 606/231-1777; FAX 606/233-7593; res: 800/555-8000. 44 rms, 3 story, 6 suites. S, D $130; each addl $10; suites $250-$325; under 12 free. Crib free. TV; cable (premium). Complimentary continental bkfst. Restaurant 7-9:30 am, 5-10 pm; Fri to 11 pm; Sat 7-11 am, 5-11 pm; Sun 7-11 am. Ck-out noon. Meeting rms. Business servs avail. In-rm modem link. Free airport transportation. Health club privileges. Elegantly restored building (1916). Cr cds: A, C, D, DS, JCB, MC, V.

D ⊠ ⚞ SC

★ ★ **COMFORT INN.** *2381 Buena Vista (40505), I-75 exit 110.* 606/299-0302; res: 800/394-8403; FAX 606/299-2306. 124 rms, 3 story. S $59-$69; D $69-$89; each addl $7; under 18 free. Crib free. TV; cable (premium). Indoor pool; whirlpool. Complimentary continental bkfst. Restaurant nearby. Ck-out noon. Meeting rms. Business servs avail. Exercise equipt. Refrigerators, microwaves avail. Cr cds: A, C, D, DS, MC, V.

D ≈ ⚞ ⊠ ⚞ SC

★ ★ **COURTYARD BY MARRIOTT.** *775 Newtown Ct (40511). 606/253-4646; FAX 606/253-9118.* 146 rms, 3 story. S $59-$99; D $69-$109; suites $94-$125; under 18 free. Crib free. TV; cable (premium). Indoor pool; whirlpool. Complimentary coffee in rms. Bar 4-11 pm. Ck-out noon. Coin lndry. Meeting rms. Business servs avail. In-rm modem link. Valet serv. Sundries. Exercise equipt. Some refrigerators. Balconies. Cr cds: A, C, D, DS, JCB, MC, V.

[D] [symbols] SC

✔ ★ **DAYS INN-SOUTH.** *5575 Athens Boonesboro Rd (40509), I-75 exit 104. 606/263-3100; FAX 606/263-3120.* Web www.daysinn.com. 56 rms, 2 story. S $40-$60; D $45-$65; each addl $5; family rates; higher rates special events. Crib free. Pet accepted. TV. Complimentary continental bkfst. Restaurant nearby. Ck-out 11 am. Business servs avail. In-rm modem link. Some microwaves. Cr cds: A, C, D, DS, MC, V.

[D] [symbols] SC

★ **HAMPTON INN.** *2251 Elkhorn Rd (40505), I-75 exit 110. 606/299-2613; FAX 606/299-9664.* Web www.hampton-inn.com. 125 rms, 5 story. S $69-$79; D $79-$89; under 18 free. Crib free. TV; cable (premium), VCR avail. Indoor pool. Complimentary continental bkfst. Restaurant adj open 24 hrs. Ck-out noon. Meeting rm. In-rm modem link. Exercise equipt. Microwaves avail. Cr cds: A, C, D, DS, MC, V.

[D] [symbols] SC

★ **HOLIDAY INN-NORTH.** *1950 Newtown Pike (40511), ½ blk S of I-75 exit 115. 606/233-0512; FAX 606/231-9285.* 303 rms, 2 story. S $109.95; D $114.95; suites $250; under 18 free. Crib free. Pet accepted, some restrictions. TV; cable (premium). Indoor pool; whirlpool. Supervised child's activities (Memorial Day-Labor Day). Coffee in rms. Restaurant 6 am-2 pm, 5-10 pm. Rm serv. Bar 2 pm-1 am. Ck-out noon. Coin lndry. Convention facilities. Business center. In-rm modem link. Bellhops. Sundries. Gift shop. Putting green. Exercise equipt; sauna. Game rm. Some refrigerators, microwaves. Cr cds: A, C, D, DS, JCB, MC, V.

[D] [symbols] SC

★ ★ **HOLIDAY INN-SOUTH.** *5532 Athens Boonesboro Rd (40509), I-75 exit 104. 606/263-5241; FAX 606/263-4333.* 149 rms, 2 story. S, D $60-$79; each addl $6; under 18 free; higher rates: horse racing, special events. Crib free. Pet accepted, some restrictions. TV; cable (premium). Pool; whirlpool. Restaurant 6 am-2 pm, 5-10 pm; Sat, Sun 7 am-2 pm. Rm serv. Bar; entertainment Tues-Sat. Coin lndry. Meeting rms. Business servs avail. In-rm modem link. Valet serv. Exercise equipt; sauna. Sundries. Cr cds: A, C, D, DS, JCB, MC, V.

[D] [symbols] SC

★ ★ **LA QUINTA INN.** *1919 Stanton Way (40511), I-64/75 exit 115. 606/231-7551; FAX 606/281-6002.* Web www.laquinta.com. 129 rms, 2 story. S $64; D $68; each addl $8; under 18 free; higher rates some wkends. Crib free. Pet accepted, some restrictions. TV; cable. Pool. Complimentary continental bkfst. Coffee in rms. Restaurant adj 6 am-10 pm; wkends to 11 pm. Ck-out noon. Business servs avail. In-rm modem link. Valet serv. Guest lndry. Cr cds: A, D, DS, MC, V.

[D] [symbols] SC

✔ ★ **MICROTEL.** *2240 Buena Vista Rd (40505), I-75 exit 110. 606/299-9600; FAX 606/299-8719; res: 800/844-8608.* Web www.microtel inn.com. 99 rms, 2 story. Apr-Oct: S $37.95; D $42.95; under 16 free; lower rates rest of yr. Crib free. TV; cable. Coffee in lobby. Restaurant adj open 24 hrs. Ck-out noon. In-rm modem link. Cr cds: A, C, D, DS, MC, V.

[D] [symbols]

★ ★ **QUALITY INN-NORTHWEST.** *1050 Newtown Pike (KY 922) (40511), I-75/I-64 exit 115. 606/233-0561; FAX 606/231-6125.* 109 rms, 2 story. S, D $40.50-$75.95; each addl $5; under 19 free. Crib $1. Pet accepted. TV; cable. Heated pool; lifeguard in season. Playground. Coffee in rms. Complimentary continental bkfst. Ck-out noon. Meeting rms. Business servs avail. Valet serv. Sundries. Gift shop. Some refrigerators, microwaves. Cr cds: A, C, D, DS, JCB, MC, V.

[D] [symbols] SC

✔★ **RED ROOF INN.** *483 Haggard Ln (40505), US 27, 68 at jct I-64, I-75 exit 113. 606/293-2626; FAX 606/299-8353.* Web www.redroof inns.com. 108 rms, 2 story. S $35.99-$45.99; D $41.99-$61.99; each addl $7; under 18 free. Crib free. Pet accepted, some restrictions. TV; cable (premium). Complimentary coffee in lobby. Restaurant nearby. Ck-out noon. Business servs avail. Cr cds: A, C, D, DS, MC, V.

[D] [symbols]

★ **SHONEY'S INN.** *2753 Richmond Rd (40509), jct US 25 & KY 4. 606/269-4999; FAX 606/268-2346.* 102 rms, 2 story. S $57-$67; D $62-$72; each addl $5; under 18 free. Crib free. TV; cable. Pool. Complimentary coffee in lobby. Restaurant adj 6 am-midnight; wkends to 2 am. Ck-out noon. Meeting rms. Business servs avail. Valet serv. Sundries. Cr cds: A, C, D, DS, MC, V.

[D] [symbols] SC

★ ★ **SPRINGS INN.** *2020 Harrodsburg Rd (US 68) (40503). 606/277-5751; FAX 606/277-3142; res: 800/354-9503.* 196 rms, 2 story. S $58; D $68; suites $88-$160. Crib free. TV; cable. Pool; wading pool. Restaurant 6:30 am-10 pm; Sun 7 am-8:30 pm. Rm serv. Bar 11 am-midnight; entertainment Wed-Sat. Ck-out noon. Meeting rms. Business servs avail. Valet serv. Gift shop. Free airport transportation. Cr cds: A, D, DS, MC, V.

[D] [symbols] SC

★ **SUPER 8.** *2351 Buena Vista Rd (40505), I-75 exit 110. 606/299-6241.* Web www.super8.com. 62 rms, 2 story. Apr-Oct: S $41.99; D $50.99-$60.99; each addl $5; under 12 free; wkly rates; higher rates horse racing; lower rates rest of yr. Crib free. Pet accepted. TV; cable (premium). Complimentary coffee in lobby. Restaurant adj open 24 hrs. Ck-out 11 am. Cr cds: A, C, D, DS, MC, V.

[D] [symbols] SC

Motor Hotels

★ ★ **CAMPBELL HOUSE INN, SUITES & GOLF CLUB.** *1375 Harrodsburg Rd (US 68) (40504). 606/255-4281; FAX 606/254-4368; res: 800/354-9235 (exc KY), 800/432-9254 (KY).* 370 rms, 3 story. S $59-$89; D $69-$99; each addl $10; suites $89-$189; under 12 free. Crib free. TV; cable. Heated pool; poolside serv. Restaurants 6 am-10 pm. Rm serv. Bar 9-1 am; entertainment. Ck-out noon. Coin lndry. Convention facilities. Business servs avail. In-rm modem link. Bellhops. Valet serv. Sundries. Gift shop. Barber, beauty shop. Free airport transportation. Tennis. 18-hole golf, pro. Exercise equipt. Game rm. Bathrm phones, refrigerators. Cr cds: A, C, D, DS, ER, JCB, MC, V.

[D] [symbols]

★ ★ **HARLEY.** *2143 N Broadway (US 27/68) (40505), I-75 exit 113. 606/299-1261; FAX 606/293-0048.* 146 rms, 2-3 story. S, D $100-$110; each addl $10; under 18 free; wkend rates. Crib free. TV; cable (premium). Indoor/outdoor pools; whirlpool. Restaurant 6:30 am-2 pm, 5-10 pm; Fri, Sat to 11 pm. Rm serv. Bar 4:30 pm-midnight; entertainment Fri, Sat. Ck-out 11 am. Meeting rms. In-rm modem link. Bellhops. Valet serv. Free airport transportation. Lighted tennis. Putting green. Exercise equipt; sauna. Rec rm. Balconies. Cr cds: A, C, D, DS, JCB, MC, V.

[D] [symbols] SC

Hotels

★ ★ ★ **HILTON SUITES OF LEXINGTON GREEN.** *3195 Nicholasville Rd (US 27) (40503). 606/271-4000; FAX 606/273-2975.* E-mail hiltonsuites@juno.com; web www.hilton.com. 174 suites, 6 story. S $115-$165; D $125-$180; each addl $10; family rates; wkend package plans; higher rates: Kentucky Derby, race season. Crib free. TV; cable (premium). Pool; poolside serv. Coffee in rms. Restaurant 6:30 am-2 pm, 5-10 pm. Bar 2 pm-1 am. Ck-out noon. Meeting rms. Business center. In-rm modem link. Free airport, bus depot transportation. Exercise equipt; sauna. Refrigerators. Cr cds: A, C, D, DS, ER, JCB, MC, V.

[D] [symbols] SC

★ ★ ★ **HYATT REGENCY.** *401 W High St (40507). 606/253-1234; FAX 606/233-7974.* 365 rms, 16 story. S $140; D $183; suites $275-$650; under 18 free; wkend plans. Crib free. TV; cable (premium), VCR avail. Indoor pool. Restaurants 6 am-10:30 pm. Bar 11-1 am. Ck-out noon. Convention facilities. Business center. In-rm modem link. Concierge. Shopping arcade. Free airport transportation. Exercise equipt. Sun deck. Luxury level. Cr cds: A, C, D, DS, ER, JCB, MC, V.

⊡ ⩬ ⅺ ⅻ ⅹ SC ⋊

★ ★ ★ **RADISSON PLAZA.** *369 W Vine St (40507). 606/231-9000; FAX 606/281-3737.* Web www.radisson.com. 367 rms, 22 story. S $155; D $165; each addl $10; suites $190-$390; under 18 free; wkend rates. Crib free. Pet accepted. Valet parking $8. TV; cable (premium), VCR avail (movies). Indoor pool; whirlpool, poolside serv. Coffee in rms. Restaurant 6 am-11 pm. Rm serv to 1 am; wkends to 2 am. Bar 11:30-1 am; entertainment. Ck-out noon. Convention facilities. Business center. Concierge. Gift shop. Free airport transportation. Lighted tennis privileges. Exercise equipt; sauna. Health club privileges. Rec rm. Some refrigerators. Wet bar in suites. Atrium with fountains. Luxury level. Cr cds: A, C, D, DS, ER, JCB, MC, V.

⊡ ⚐ ⚒ ⩬ ⅹ ⅺ ⅻ SC ⋊

★ ★ ★ **SHERATON SUITES.** *2601 Richmond Rd (40509), near jct New Circle Rd (KY 4) & Richmond Rd. 606/268-0060; res: 800/262-3774; FAX 606/268-6209.* 155 suites, 5 story. S, D $115-$170; each addl $10; under 18 free. Crib free. TV; cable. Heated pool; whirlpools. Complimentary coffee in rms. Restaurant. Bar; pianist, Sat. Ck-out noon. Meeting rms. Business servs avail. In-rm modem link. Free airport transportation. Exercise equipt. Health club privileges. Bathrm phones, refrigerators, some wet bars; microwaves avail. Balconies. Cr cds: A, C, D, DS, JCB, MC, V.

⊡ ⩬ ⅺ ⅻ ⅹ SC

Inns

★ ★ **ROSE HILL INN.** *(233 Rose Hill, Versailles 40383) 15 mi W on US 60, turn left on Main St, turn right on Rose Hill. 606/873-5957; res: 800/307-0460; FAX 606/873-3063.* E-mail innkeepers@rosehillinn.com; web www.rosehillinn.com. 5 rms, 1 with shower only, 2 story, 1 suite, 1 kit. unit, 1 guest house. S $75-$125; D, kit. unit, guest house $100-$120; each addl $10; suite $125-$150; 2-day min (racing season). Crib free. Pet accepted, some restrictions. TV; cable (premium), VCR avail (movies). Complimentary full bkfst. Restaurant nearby. Ck-out noon, ck-in 3 pm. Business servs avail. Lawn games. Some in-rm whirlpools; microwaves avail. Picnic tables, grills. Built in 1823; 3 acres. Totally nonsmoking. Cr cds: A, MC, V.

⚐ ⅹ ⋊

★ ★ **SILLS INN.** *(270 Montgomery Ave, Versailles 40383) approx 15 mi W on US 60 to Versailles; 2 blks S of courthouse on Main St, left on Montgomery Ave. 606/873-4478; FAX 606/873-7099; res: 800/526-9801.* E-mail sillsinn@aol.com; web www.sillsinn.com. 12 rms, 3 story. S, D $79-$159; each addl $25; wkly rates; higher rates Kentucky Derby. TV; cable, VCR. Complimentary full bkfst. Complimentary coffee in rms. Ck-out 11 am. Meeting rms. Business center. In-rm modem link. Luggage handling. Valet service. Concierge serv. Free airport transportation. Health club privileges. Some refrigerators, minibars, microwaves avail. Balconies. Restored Victorian-style house. Totally nonsmoking. Cr cds: A, C, D, DS, JCB, MC, V.

ⅹ ⅺ SC ⋊

Resort

★ ★ ★ ★ **MARRIOTT'S GRIFFIN GATE RESORT.** *1800 Newtown Pike (KY 922) (40511), I-64 & I-75 exit 115. 606/231-5100; FAX 606/255-9944.* Web www.marriott.com/lex. This gleaming, contemporary resort caters to those who like a mix of activities and comfort. The lobby has an atrium with waterfalls, mahogany tables and leather chairs. 409 rms, 7 story. S $110-$154; D $129-$169; suite $295-$850; under 18 free; golf plans. Crib free. Pet accepted, some restrictions; $40. TV; cable (premium). 2 pools, 1 indoor; whirlpool, poolside serv. Playground. Supervised

child's activities (summer). Dining rm 6 am-11 pm (also see MANSION AT GRIFFIN GATE). Rm serv. Bar 11-1 am. Ck-out noon. Coin lndry. Convention facilities. Business center. In-rm modem link. Valet serv. Gift shop. Barber, beauty shop. Package store 1 mi. Airport transportation. Sports dir. Lighted tennis, pro. 18-hole golf, greens fee $28-$62, pro, putting green. Seasonal activities incl walking tours, pool activities. Game rm. Exercise rm; sauna. Refrigerator in suites. Private patios, balconies. Picnic tables. Luxury level. Cr cds: A, C, D, DS, JCB, MC, V.

⊡ ⚐ ⚒ ⅻ ⩬ ⅹ ⅺ ⅹ SC ⋊

Restaurants

★ ★ **A-LA LUCIE.** *159 N Limestone St (40507), at Church St. 606/252-5277.* Hrs: 6-10 pm. Closed Sun; major hols. Res accepted. Continental menu. Bar. Semi-a la carte: dinner $13.95-$22. Specializes in fresh seafood, ethnic foods. Intimate cafe. Cr cds: A, C, D, DS, MC, V.

⊐

★ ★ **BRAVO'S OF LEXINGTON.** *401 W Main St (40507), Victorian Square. 606/255-2222.* Hrs: 5:30-10 pm; Fri, Sat to 11 pm. Closed Sun; some major hols. Res accepted. Northern Italian menu. Bar. Semi-a la carte: dinner $10.95-$19.95. Specializes in osso buco, veal, seafood. Terrace dining on balcony overlooking atrium. Cr cds: A, C, D, DS, MC, V.

⊡ SC ⊐

★ ★ ★ **COACH HOUSE.** *855 S Broadway (US 68) (40504). 606/252-7777.* Hrs: 11 am-2:30 pm, 5-10 pm; Sat from 5 pm. Closed Thanksgiving, Dec 25. Res accepted. Continental menu. Bar 11 am-midnight; Fri, Sat to 1 am. Wine cellar. Semi-a la carte: lunch $5.50-$8.95, dinner $13.50-$25. Specializes in tuna, rack of lamb. Jazz band Fri, Sat. Family-owned. Cr cds: A, C, D, DS, MC, V.

⊡ ⊐

✔★ ★ **DARRYL'S 1891 RESTAURANT & TAVERN.** *3292 Nicholasville Rd (US 27) (40503), 1 blk S of New Circle Rd. 606/272-1891.* Hrs: 11-1 am; Sun to 10 pm. Closed Dec 25. Res accepted. Bar. Semi-a la carte: lunch $3.99-$9.99, dinner $6.79-$15.99. Child's meals. Specialties: prime rib, pork ribs. Parking. Old English building. Braille menu. Cr cds: A, C, D, DS, MC, V.

⊡ ⊐ ♥

★ ★ **DE SHA'S.** *101 N Broadway (40507). 606/259-3771.* E-mail DeShas2@hlc.com; web www.deshas.com. Hrs: 11 am-11 pm; Fri, Sat to midnight; Sun to 10 pm. Closed Thanksgiving, Dec 25. Bar. Semi-a la carte: lunch $3.95-$8.95, dinner $13.95-$19.95. Child's meals. Specializes in regional dishes. Validated parking. In Victorian Square. Antique bar; oak staircase to upper level. View of park. Cr cds: A, D, DS, MC, V.

⊡ ⊐

★ ★ **DUDLEY'S.** *380 S Mill St (40508), in Dudley Square. 606/252-1010.* Hrs: 11:30 am-2:30 pm, 5:30-10 pm; Fri, Sat to 11 pm. Closed major hols. Res accepted. Continental menu. Bar. Semi-a la carte: lunch $5.50-$9.50, dinner $13-$23. Specializes in seafood, beef, pasta. Parking. Outdoor dining on tree-shaded patio. Restored school (1851); paintings. Cr cds: A, D, MC, V.

⊡ ⊐

★ ★ **MALONE'S.** *3347 Tates Creek Rd (40502), in shopping center. 606/335-6500.* Hrs: 5-10 pm; Fri to 11 pm; Sat 4-11 pm; Sun 11 am-9 pm; Sun brunch 11 am-2 pm. Closed some major hols. Serv bar. Res accepted. Semi-a la carte: dinner $6.95-$25.95. Sun brunch $5.95. Child's meals. Specializes in steak, pasta, seafood. Parking. Cr cds: A, MC, V.

⊡ ⊐

★ ★ ★ **MANSION AT GRIFFIN GATE.** *(See Marriott's Griffin Gate Resort) 606/288-6142.* Hrs: 6-10 pm; Fri, Sat to 10:30 pm. Res accepted. Continental menu. Bar. Wine list. Semi-a la carte: dinner $23.95-$38.95. Specializes in beef, game, fresh seafood. Valet parking. Greek-revival mansion built 1873; antiques; crystal chandeliers. Cr cds: A, C, D, DS, JCB, MC, V.

D **SC** **⊸**

★ ★ **RAFFERTY'S.** *2420 Nicholasville Rd (US 27) (40503). 606/278-9427.* Hrs: 11 am-10:30 pm; Fri, Sat to 11:30 pm. Closed Thanksgiving, Dec 25. Bar to midnight; Fri, Sat to 1 am; Sun to 11 pm. Semi-a la carte: lunch, dinner $4.95-$14.99. Child's meals. Specialties: Danish baby back pork ribs, prime rib. Outdoor dining. Cr cds: A, D, DS, MC, V.

D **⊸**

✔ ★ ★ **REGATTA SEAFOOD GRILLE.** *3199 Nicholasville Rd (US 27) (40503), in Lexington Green Mall. 606/273-7875.* Hrs: 11:30 am-10 pm; Fri, Sat to 11 pm. Closed Dec 25. Res accepted. Bar; Sun from 1 pm. Semi-a la carte: lunch $5.95-$8.95, dinner $8.95-$16.95. Child's meals. Specializes in fresh seafood, pasta. Outdoor dining overlooking lake. Cr cds: A, D, DS, MC, V.

D **⊸**

✔ ★ ★ **TONY ROMA'S.** *3199 Nicholasville Rd (40503). 606/272-7526.* E-mail trlexington@msn.com. Hrs: 11 am-10 pm; Fri, Sat to 11 pm. Closed Thanksgiving, Dec 25. Bar. Semi-a la carte: lunch $4.99-$8.99, dinner $6.99-$15.99. Child's meals. Specializes in ribs, chicken. Cr cds: A, D, DS, MC, V.

D **⊸**

London (E-8)

(See also Corbin)

Founded 1825 **Pop** 5,757 **Elev** 1,255 ft **Area code** 606 **Zip** 40741 **Web** www.tourky.com/london
Information London-Laurel County Tourist Commission, 140 W Daniel Boone Parkway; 606/878-6900 or 800/348-0095.

London, is a County seat of Daniel Boone National Forest (see). A Ranger District office of the forest is located in London.

What to See and Do

Canoe trips. Canoe trips on the Rockcastle River, ranging from three hours to three days; rentals. Contact Rockcastle Adventures, PO Box 662; 606/864-9407. ¢¢¢¢- ¢¢¢¢¢

Daniel Boone National Forest (see). 10 mi E on Daniel Boone Pkwy.

Levi Jackson Wilderness Road State Park. A 896-acre park. Descendants of pioneer farmer Levi Jackson deeded some of this land to the state as a historical shrine to those who carved homes out of the wilderness. Boone's Trace and Wilderness Road pioneer trails converge within the park. Recreational facilities include swimming pool (fee); bathhouse. Hiking; archery range; miniature golf (Apr-Oct, fee). Picnicking, playgrounds. Camping (tent & trailer sites). Supervised recreation (Memorial Day-Labor Day). Standard fees. 3 mi S on US 25, exit 38 off I-75. Phone 606/878-8000. Here are

Mountain Life Museum. Split-rail fences enclose rustic cabins with household furnishings, pioneer relics, farm tools, Native American artifacts; smokehouse, blacksmith shop, barn with prairie schooner. (Apr-Oct, daily) Phone 606/878-8000. ¢

McHargue's Mill. One of the largest collections of millstones in the world. Mill built in 1812, reconstructed on present site in 1939. Tours and demonstrations. (Memorial Day-Labor Day, daily) **Free.**

Motels

✔ ★ **BEST WESTERN HARVEST INN.** *207 W KY 80, ¼ mi E of I-75 exit 41. 606/864-2222; FAX 606/878-2825.* 100 rms, 2 story. June-Oct: S $51; D $60; each addl $5; lower rates rest of yr. Crib $3. TV; cable (premium). Indoor pool; whirlpool. Complimentary continental bkfst.

Restaurant 7 am-9 pm. Ck-out noon. Meeting rms. Cr cds: A, C, D, DS, MC, V.

D **≋** **⊠** **⬟** **SC**

✔ ★ **BUDGET HOST-WESTGATE INN.** *254 W Daniel Boone Pkwy, exit 41 on KY 80. 606/878-7330; res: 800/283-4678.* E-mail mail@budgethost.com; web www.budgethost.com. 46 rms, 2 story. Memorial Day-Oct: S $39.30; D $46.95; each addl $4; under 12 free; wkly rates; lower rates rest of yr. Crib free. Pet accepted, some restrictions. TV; cable (premium). Complimentary continental bkfst. Restaurant adj 6 am-11 pm. Ck-out noon. Pool. Cr cds: A, C, D, DS, MC, V.

D **⬤** **≋** **⊠** **⬟** **SC**

★ ★ **COMFORT SUITES.** *1918 US 192, I-75 exit 38. 606/877-7848; FAX 606/877-7907.* 62 rms, 3 story. S, D $61-$99; under 18 free; higher rates hols, special events. Crib free. TV; cable (premium). Indoor pool. Complimentary continental bkfst. Complimentary coffee in rms. Restaurant nearby. Ck-out noon. Valet serv. Coin lndry. Meeting rms. Business servs avail. In-rm modem link. Refrigerators. Cr cds: A, C, D, DS, MC, V.

D **≋** **⊠** **⬟** **SC**

★ ★ **HAMPTON INN.** *2075 US 192, I-75 exit 38. 606/877-1000; FAX 606/864-8560.* 82 rms, 2 story. S $51.95-$59.95; D $61.95-$71.95; under 18 free. Crib free. TV; cable (premium). Heated pool. Complimentary continental bkfst. Coffee in rms. Restaurant opp 6 am-10 pm. Ck-out noon. Meeting rms. Business servs avail. In-rm modem link. Health club privileges. Some refrigerators, whirlpools. Cr cds: A, C, D, DS, MC, V.

D **≋** **⊠** **⬟** **SC**

★ ★ **HOLIDAY INN EXPRESS.** *400 GOP Dr, jct I-75 & KY 80. 606/878-7678; FAX 606/878-7654.* 60 rms, 2 story. S, D $58-$68. Crib avail. Pet accepted. TV; cable (premium). Indoor/outdoor pool. Complimentary continental bkfst. Restaurant opp 6 am-11 pm. Ck-out 11 am. Business servs avail. Game rm. Cr cds: A, C, D, DS, JCB, MC, V.

D **⬤** **≋** **⊠** **⬟** **SC**

Louisville (C-6)

(See also Fort Knox, Shepherdsville)

Founded 1778 **Pop** 269,063 **Elev** 462 ft **Area code** 502 **E-mail** info@louisville-visitors.com **Web** www.louisville-visitors.com
Information Convention and Visitors Bureau, 400 S First St, 40202; 502/582-3732 or 800/792-5595.

Louisville is a unique city. It has southern graces and a determined dedication to music and the arts, but to the world, Louisville is "Derby City" for at least two weeks of every year. Since the first running on May 17, 1875, the Kentucky Derby has generated tremendous excitement. Modeled after England's Epsom Derby, it is the oldest race in continuous existence in the US. The first Saturday in May each year, world attention focuses on Churchill Downs as the classic "run for the roses" is played out against its backdrop of Edwardian towers and antique grandstands.

The social highlight of a very social city, Derby festivities are a glamorous mélange of carnival, fashion show, spectacle and celebration of the horse. From the opening strains of "My Old Kentucky Home," played before the big race, until the final toast of bourbon is made, Louisville takes on a uniquely festive character. Afterward, the center of Thoroughbred racing quickly returns to normalcy—a city southern in manner, midwestern in pace.

Situated at the falls of the Ohio River, Louisville is a city long nurtured by river traffic. The Spanish, French, English, Scottish, Irish and Germans all had roles in its exploration, settlement and development. George Rogers Clark established the first real settlement, a base for military operations against the British, on a spit of land above the falls, now entirely erased by the river. Named after Louis XVI of France, the settlement became an important portage point around the falls; later a canal bypassed them. Today, the McAlpine Locks and Dam provide modern navigation around the falls of the Ohio.

Louisville is a top producer of bourbon and a leader in synthetic rubber, paint and varnish, cigarettes, home appliances and aluminum for home use.

This is a community that takes its culture seriously, with a public subscription Fund for the Arts subsidizing the Tony Award-winning Actors Theater. The city also boasts the Kentucky Center for the Arts, home of ballet, opera, art and music groups and other cultural organizations.

Transportation

Car Rental Agencies: See IMPORTANT TOLL-FREE NUMBERS.

Public Transportation: Buses (Transit Authority of River City), phone 502/585-1234.

Airport Information

Louisville International Airport: Information 502/367-4636; lost and found 502/368-6524; weather 502/968-6025.

What to See and Do

American Printing House for the Blind. The largest and oldest (1858) publishing house for the blind. In addition to books and music in Braille, it issues talking books, magazines, large type textbooks and educational aids. Tours (Mon-Fri; closed hols). 1839 Frankfort Ave, 3 mi E. Phone 502/895-2405. **Free.**

Bellarmine College (1950). (2,300 students) A 115-acre campus. Liberal arts and sciences. The campus houses the Thomas Merton Studies Center, with his manuscripts, drawings, tapes and published works (Tues-Fri, by appt; closed hols); phone 502/452-8187. Guided campus tours (by appt). Newburg Rd, 5 mi SE. Phone 502/452-8000.

Cave Hill Cemetery. Burial ground of George Rogers Clark. Colonel Harland Sanders, of fried-chicken fame, is also buried here. Rare trees, shrubs and plants; swans, geese, ducks. (Daily) 701 Baxter Ave, at E end of Broadway. Phone 502/451-5630.

⭐ **Churchill Downs.** Founded in 1875, this historic and world-famous Thoroughbred race track is the home of the Kentucky Derby, "the most exciting two minutes in sports." (See ANNUAL EVENTS) Spring race meet, late Apr-June; fall race meet, late Oct-late Nov; Kentucky Derby, 1st Sat May. 700 Central Ave. Phone 502/636-4400. ¢-¢¢ Adj is

⭐ **Kentucky Derby Museum.** Features exhibits on Thoroughbred racing and the Kentucky Derby. Multi-image show, hands-on exhibits, artifacts, educational programs, tours and special events. Outdoor paddock area with Thoroughbred. Tours of Churchill downs (weather permitting). Gift shop; cafe serving lunch (wkdays). (Daily; closed Thanksgiving, Oaks & Derby Days, Dec 25) Phone 502/637-1111 or 502/637-7097. ¢¢

Colonel Harland Sanders Museum. Artifacts and memorabilia relating to Colonel Harland Sanders and Kentucky Fried Chicken. Audiovisual displays, 28-min film "Portrait of a Legend." (Mon-Thurs, limited hrs Fri; closed hols and 1st Fri in May) 1441 Gardiner Lane. Phone 502/456-8353. **Free.**

E.P. "Tom" Sawyer State Park. Approx 370 acres with swimming pool. Tennis; archery range; BMX track; ballfields; gymnasium, games area. Picnicking. Some fees. 3000 Freys Hill Rd. Phone 502/426-8950.

Farmington (1810). Federal-style house built from plans drawn by Thomas Jefferson. Abraham Lincoln visited here in 1841. Furnished with pre-1820 antiques; hidden stairway, octagonal rooms; museum room; blacksmith shop, stone barn, 19th-century garden. Guided tour (daily; closed some hols) Grounds and gardens (daily; free). 3033 Bardstown Rd N, at jct Watterson Expwy (I-264), 6 mi SE on US 31E. Phone 502/452-9920. ¢¢

Historic districts. Features renovated Victorian housing; West Main Street Historic District is a concentration of cast iron buildings being renovated on Main Street between 1st and 8th streets; Butchertown is a renovated 19th-century German community between Market St & Story Avenue; Cherokee Triangle is a well-preserved Victorian neighborhood with diverse architectural details; and Portland is an early settlement and commercial port with Irish and French heritage. Old Louisville, between Breckinridge and 9th Sts, near Central Park.

Jefferson County Courthouse (1835-1860). Designed by Gideon Shryock in Greek-revival style. Cast iron floor in rotunda supports statue of Henry Clay. Magnificent cast-iron monumental stair and balustrade in 68-foot rotunda. Statues of Thomas Jefferson and Louis XVI, as well as war memorial on grounds. Guided tours (by appt). (Mon-Fri; closed major hols) Jefferson St between 5th & 6th Sts. Phone 502/574-5761. **Free.**

Kentucky Center for the Arts. Three stages present national and international performers showcasing a wide range of music, dance and drama. Distinctive glass-arched lobby features a collection of 20th-century sculpture and provides a panoramic view of Ohio River and Falls Fountain. Restaurant, gift shop, parking garage. 5 Riverfront Plaza. For schedule and ticket information phone 502/584-7777 or 800/775-7777.

Kentucky Fair and Exposition Center. More than one million sq-ft complex includes coliseum, exposition halls, stadium, amusement park. More than 1,500 events take place throughout the year, including Univ of Louisville football, basketball, Louisville Riverfrogs and Milwaukee Brewers minor league affiliate, the Louisville Redbirds. I-65S at I-264W. Phone 502/367-5000.

Kentucky Kingdom—The Thrill Park. Amusement and water park with more than 110 rides and attractions, including 5 roller coasters. (Memorial Day-Labor Day, daily; early Apr-Memorial Day, Fri eves, Sat & Sun; Labor Day-late Sept, Sat & Sun) Adj to Kentucky Fair and Exposition Center, 937 Phillips Ln. Phone 502/366-7508. ¢¢¢¢¢

Locust Grove (ca 1790). Home of General George Rogers Clark from 1809-1818. Handsome Georgian mansion on 55 acres; original paneling, staircase; authentic furnishings; garden; 8 restored outbuildings. Visitors center features audiovisual program. (Daily; closed hols, Derby Day) 6 mi NE on River Rd, then 1 mi SW at 561 Blankenbaker. Phone 502/897-9845. ¢¢

Louisville Falls Fountain. World's largest floating fountain sprays water 375 ft high. Light shows, with more than 100 colored lights, offered nightly. (May-Nov) On the Ohio River, between Clark Memorial Bridge and Conrail Bridge.

Louisville Presbyterian Theological Seminary (1853). (250 students) On 52-acre campus is Gardencourt, a renovated turn-of-the-century mansion, and the Archaeological Museum, with collection of Palestinian pottery (daily; closed hols). 1044 Alta Vista Rd, 1/2 mi off US 60 Business, adj to Cherokee Park. Phone 502/895-3411. **Free.**

Louisville Science Center. Hands-on scientific exhibits; aerospace hall; IMAX four-story screen film theater (fee); Egyptian mummy's tomb; World We Create interactive exhibit. (Daily; closed Thanksgiving, Dec 24 & 25) 727 W Main St. Phone 502/561-6111. ¢¢

Louisville Slugger Museum & Bat Factory. Manufacturers of Louisville Slugger baseball bats and Power-bilt golf clubs. No cameras. Children over 8 yrs only; must be accompanied by adult. Tours (Mon-Sat; closed major hols). 800 W Main St. Phone 502/588-7228. ¢¢

Louisville Zoo. Modern zoo exhibits more than 1,600 animals in naturalistic settings. In HerpAquarium are simulated water, desert and rain forest ecosystems. Islands exhibit highlights endangered species and habitats. Camel and elephant rides (summer). (Daily; closed Jan 1, Thanksgiving, Dec 25). 1100 Trevilian Way, 7 mi SE via I-65, I-264 to Poplar Level Road North. Phone 502/459-2181. ¢¢¢

Otter Creek Park. A 3,000-acre park located on the site of Rock Haven, a town destroyed by 1937 flood. Much of the park that fronts on the Ohio River consists of steep cliffs or very wooded banks. Otter Creek is a small, deeply entrenched stream with steep banks. Artifacts found here indicate that many Native American tribes used the Otter Creek area as hunting and fishing grounds. Swimming pools; fishing; boating (ramp). Miniature golf, tennis, basketball. Picnic facilities. Tent & trailer sites, cabins, lodge and restaurant. Nature center (Mar-Nov; daily exc Mon), wildlife area. Park (daily). 30 mi SW via US 31W and KY 1638, near Fort Knox. For fees, information contact Park Manager, 850 Otter Creek Park Rd, Vine Grove 40175; 502/583-3577. **Free.**

Sightseeing.

Riverboat excursion. Two-hr afternoon trips on sternwheeler, *Belle of Louisville.* (Memorial Day-Labor Day, daily exc Mon); sunset cruise (Tues & Thurs); dance cruise (Sat). Riverfront Plaza, wharf, 4th St and River Rd. For rates and schedules phone 502/625-2355 or 502/574-BELL.

Gray Line bus tours. For information and reservations phone 502/589-7433.

Spalding University (1814). (1,400 students) Liberal arts college. On campus is Whitestone Mansion (1871), a Renaissance-revival house with period furniture (Mon-Fri; closed hols), art gallery. 851 S 4th St. Phone 502/585-9911. **Free.**

The Filson Club. Historical library (fee); manuscript collection, photographs and prints collection. (Daily exc Sun; closed major hols) 1310 S Third St. Phone 502/635-5083. Mansion tour **Free.**

Thomas Edison House. Restored 1850 cottage where Edison lived while working for Western Union after the Civil War. Bedroom furnished in the period; four display rooms with Edison memorabilia and inventions: phonographs, records and cylinders, early bulb collection. (Limited hrs; call for appt) 731 E Washington. Phone 502/585-5247. ¢

University of Louisville (1798). (23,000 students) On Belknap Campus is the Ekstrom Library, with the John Patterson rare book collection, original town charter signed by Thomas Jefferson and the Photo Archives, one of the largest collections of photographs in the country. Also here is an enlarged cast of Rodin's sculpture *The Thinker;* a Foucault pendulum more than 73 feet high, demonstrating the Earth's rotation; and the largest concert organ in the Midwest. Two art galleries feature works by students and locals as well as national and international artists (daily exc Sat). The grave of Supreme Court Justice Louis D. Brandeis is located under the School of Law portico. 3 mi S at 3rd St & Eastern Pkwy. Contact information centers at 3rd St entrance or at corner 1st & Brandeis Sts; 502/852-6565. Also on campus are

J.B. Speed Art Museum. Oldest & largest in state. Traditional and modern art, English Renaissance Room, sculpture collection, Kentucky artists; special exhibits. Cafe, shop and bookstore; tours on request. (Daily exc Mon; closed hols) 2035 S 3rd St. Phone 502/636-2893. **Free.**

Rauch Memorial Planetarium. Planetarium shows (Sat afternoons). Phone 502/852-6665. ¢¢

Water Tower. Restored tower and pumping station built in the classic style in 1860. Tower houses Louisville Visual Art Association, Center for Contemporary Art. Exhibits vary. (Daily; closed major hols) Zorn Ave & River Road. Phone 502/896-2146. **Free.**

Zachary Taylor National Cemetery. The 12th President of the US is buried here, near the site where he lived from infancy to adulthood. The Taylor family plot is surrounded by this national cemetery, established 1928. (Daily) 4701 Brownsboro Rd, 7 mi E on US 42. Phone 502/893-3852.

Annual Events

Kentucky Derby Festival. Two-week celebration with Pegasus Parade, Great Steamboat Race (between *Belle of Louisville* and *Delta Queen*), Great Balloon Race, mini-marathon, concerts, sports tournaments. For information on tickets for festival events contact Kentucky Derby Festival, 1001 S 3rd St, 40203; phone 502/584-6383 or 800/928-FEST. Early May.

Kentucky Derby. Churchill Downs. The first jewel in the Triple Crown. Contact Churchill Downs, 700 Central Ave, 40208; 502/636-4400. 1st Sat May.

Kentucky State Fair. Kentucky Fair & Exposition Center. Livestock shows; championship horse show; home & fine arts exhibits; midway, entertainment. Contact VP of Expositions, PO Box 37130, 40233; 502/367-5180. 10 days late Aug.

Corn Island Storytelling Festival. Recaptures bygone days of yarnspinning. Events held at various sites in city. Programs include ghost stories at night in Long Run Park. For information contact Festival Director, 12019 Donohue Ave, 40243; 502/245-0643. Sept 20-21.

Seasonal Events

Performing arts. Louisville Orchestra (502/587-8681), Kentucky Opera (502/584-4500), Broadway Series (502/584-7469), Louisville Ballet (502/456-4520); all at Kentucky Center for the Arts; 502/584-7777. Actors Theatre, 316 W Main St, phone 502/584-1265. Kentucky Shakespeare Festival, free plays in Central Park, daily exc Sun, mid-June-early Aug; phone 502/634-8237.

Horse racing. Churchill Downs (see).

Additional Visitor Information

The Louisville Convention & Visitors Bureau, 400 S First St, 40202, phone 502/582-3732 or 800/792-5595, provides literature and information. Also available is information about several unique areas of special interest, such as Old Louisville, Butchertown, Phoenix Hill, Cherokee Triangle and the Main Street Preservation District.

The Convention & Visitors Bureau also operates three visitor information centers that can be found on westbound I-64, in the central lobby of Louisville International Airport and downtown at 1st & Liberty Sts.

For information on parks and course in the area, phone the Metropolitan Park and Recreation Board, 502/459-0440.

City Neighborhoods

Many of the restaurants, unrated dining establishments and some lodgings listed under Louisville include neighborhoods as well as exact street addresses. Geographic descriptions of these areas are given, followed by a table of restaurants arranged by neighborhood.

Downtown: South of the Ohio River, west of Shelby St, north of Oak St and east of 9th St. **South of Downtown:** South of Oak St. **East of Downtown:** East of Shelby St.

Old Louisville: South of Breckenridge St, west of I-65, north of Eastern Pkwy and east of 9th St.

LOUISVILLE RESTAURANTS BY NEIGHBORHOOD AREAS

(For full description, see alphabetical listings under Restaurants)

DOWNTOWN
The English Grill (The Camberley Brown). 335 W Broadway
Kunz's Fourth & Market. 115 S 4th St
Lynn's Paradise Cafe. 984 Barret Ave
Old Spaghetti Factory. 235 W Market St
Timothy's. 826 E Broadway
Vincenzo's. 150 S 5th St

SOUTH OF DOWNTOWN
Fifth Quarter Steakhouse. 1241 Durrett Lane
Jessie's. 9609 Dixie Hwy
Koreana Ii. 5009 Preston Hwy
Masterson's. 1830 S 3rd St
Uptown Cafe. 1624 Bardstown Rd

EAST OF DOWNTOWN
Asiatique. 106 Sears Ave
Cafe Metro. 1700 Bardstown Rd
Cafe Mimosa. 1216 Bardstown Rd
Darryl's 1815 Restaurant. 3110 Bardstown Rd
Equestrian Grille. 1582 Bardstown
Ferd Grisanti. 10212 Taylorsville Rd
Le Relais. 2817 Taylorsville Rd
Lilly's. 1147 Bardstown Rd
Mamma Grisanti. 3938 DuPont Circle
Sichuan Garden. 9850 Linn Station Rd
Thai Siam. 3002½ Bardstown Rd
Winston's. 3101 Bardstown Rd

Note: When a listing is located in a town that does not have its own city heading, it will appear under the city nearest to its location. In these cases, the address and town appear in parenthesis immediately following the name of the establishment.

Motels

★ ★ **BEST WESTERN BROWNSBORO INN.** *4805 Brownsboro Rd (40207), north of downtown. 502/893-2551; res: 800/528-*

1234; FAX 502/895-2417. 144 rms, 2 story, 16 suites. S, D $75-$95; suites $95-$110; under 18 free; family rates; higher rates Kentucky Derby; lower rates winter. Crib avail. TV; cable (premium). Complimentary coffee in lobby. Restaurant 7 am-9 pm. Rm serv. Bar 4 pm-2 am; entertainment. Ck-out 11 am. Meeting rms. Business servs avail. Valet serv. Coin lndry. Free airport transportation. Exercise equipt. Pool; whirlpool, lifeguard. Microwaves avail; in-rm whirlpool, refrigerator, microwave in suites. Cr cds: A, D, DS, MC, V.

★ ★ **BEST WESTERN SIGNATURE INN-EAST.** 1301 Kentucky Mills Dr (40299), I-64 exit 17, east of downtown. 502/267-8100. Web www.bestwestern.com/best.html. 119 rms, 3 story. S $66-$72; D $73-$80; under 18 free. Crib free. TV; cable (premium). Coffee in rms. Indoor pool; whirlpool. Complimentary continental bkfst. Restaurant adj 6:30 am-10 pm. Ck-out noon. Coin lndry. Meeting rms. Business center. In-rm modem link. Valet serv. Exercise equipt; sauna. Golf privileges. Some refrigerators; microwaves avail. Cr cds: A, C, D, DS, JCB, MC, V.

★ ★ **COURTYARD BY MARRIOTT.** 9608 Blairwood Rd (40222), I-64 Hurstbourne Ln exit 15, east of downtown. 502/429-5926. 151 rms, 4 story. S, D $109; suites $125; under 18 free; wkend rates. Crib free. TV; cable (premium). Pool; whirlpool. Complimentary coffee in rms. Bar 5:30-10 pm. Ck-out noon. Coin lndry. Meeting rms. Business servs avail. In-rm modem link. Valet serv. Exercise equipt. Health club privileges. Refrigerators; microwaves avail. Cr cds: A, D, DS, MC, V.

★ ★ **FAIRFIELD INN BY MARRIOTT.** 9400 Blairwood Rd (40222), I-64 exit 15, east of downtown. 502/339-1900; FAX 502/3391900. 105 rms, 3 story. S, D $60-$85; each addl $10; under 18 free. Crib free. TV; cable (premium). Pool. Continental bkfst. Restaurant adj 6 am-11 pm. Ck-out noon. Meeting rms. In-rm modem link. Lndry facilities. Cr cds: A, D, DS, MC, V.

★ ★ **HAMPTON INN.** 1902 Embassy Square Blvd (40299), I-64 Hurstbourne Lane exit 15, east of downtown. 502/491-2577; FAX 502/491-1325. 119 rms, 2 story. S $65; D $77; under 18 free. Crib free. TV; cable (premium). Pool. Continental bkfst. Coffee in rms. Restaurant nearby. Ck-out noon. Meeting rm. Business servs avail. In-rm modem link. Microwaves avail. Cr cds: A, C, D, DS, MC, V.

✔ ★ **RED ROOF INN.** 9330 Blairwood Rd (40222), 1 blk N of I-64 exit 15, east of downtown. 502/426-7621; FAX 502/426-7933. 108 rms, 2 story. S $35.99-$69.99; D $43.99-$79.99; each addl $7-$9; under 18 free. Crib free. Pet accepted. TV; cable. Complimentary coffee. Restaurant nearby. Ck-out noon. Business servs avail. In-rm modem link. Cr cds: A, C, D, DS, MC, V.

★ ★ **RESIDENCE INN BY MARRIOTT.** 120 N Hurstbourne Pkwy (40222), east of downtown. 502/425-1821; FAX 502/425-1672. 96 kit. suites, 2 story. 1-bedrm $106-$120; 2-bedrm $119-$149; family rates; wkend rates. Crib free. Pet accepted. TV; cable (premium). Heated pool; whirlpool, lifeguard. Complimentary continental bkfst. Ck-out noon. Coin lndry. Business servs avail. In-rm modem link. Valet serv. Sport court. Health club privileges. Refrigerators, microwaves, fireplaces. Grills. Cr cds: A, C, D, DS, JCB, MC, V.

★ ★ **SIGNATURE INN-SOUTH.** 6515 Signature Dr (40213), I-65 exit 128, south of downtown. 502/968-4100. 123 rms, 2 story. S $67-$70; D $74-$77; under 18 free; wkend rates Dec-Feb. Crib free. TV; cable (premium). Pool. Complimentary continental bkfst. Restaurant adj 6 am-11 pm. Ck-out noon. Meeting rms. Business center. In-rm modem link. Valet serv. Sundries. Free airport transportation. Health club privileges. Refrigerators, microwaves. Cr cds: A, D, DS, JCB, MC, V.

✔ ★ **SUPER 8.** 4800 Preston Hwy (40213), off I-65 exit 130, south of downtown. 502/968-0088; FAX 502/968-0088, ext. 347. 100 rms, 3 story. S $43.88; D $53.88; each addl $5; under 12 free. Crib free. Pet accepted, some restrictions. TV; cable (premium). Complimentary coffee in lobby. Restaurant opp open 24 hrs. Ck-out 11 am. Business servs avail. In-rm modem link. Free airport transportation. Cr cds: A, C, D, DS, MC, V.

✔ ★ **TRAVELODGE.** 9340 Blairwood Rd (40222), east of downtown. 502/425-8010; FAX 502/425-2689. 108 rms, 3 story. S, D $47-$75; each addl $6; under 18 free; higher rates Kentucky Derby. Crib free. Pet accepted; $25 deposit. TV; cable (premium). Complimentary continental bkfst. Complimentary coffee in rms. Restaurant nearby. Ck-out noon. Meeting rms. Business servs avail. Valet serv. Heated pool; whirlpool. Some refrigerators. Cr cds: A, C, D, DS, ER, JCB, MC, V.

Motor Hotels

★ ★ **AMERISUITES.** 701 S Hurstbourne Pkwy (40222), east of downtown. 502/426-0119; FAX 502/426-3013; res: 800/833-1516. 123 kit. units, 5 story. June-Aug: S, D $84-$128; each addl $10; higher rates special events; lower rates rest of yr. Crib free. TV; cable (premium), VCR (movies). Heated pool. Complimentary continental bkfst. Complimentary coffee in suites. Restaurant nearby. Ck-out noon. Meeting rms. Business center. Coin lndry. Free airport transportation. Exercise equipt. Refrigerators, microwaves. Cr cds: A, C, D, DS, MC, V.

★ ★ **BRECKINRIDGE INN.** 2800 Breckinridge Lane (40220), I-264 exit 18A, south of downtown. 502/456-5050; FAX 502/451-1577. 123 rms, 2 story. S, D $65-$95; each addl $7; under 12 free. Crib $7. Pet accepted; $50. TV; cable. 2 pools, 1 indoor; lifeguard. Restaurant 7 am-1:30 pm, 5-9 pm. Rm serv. Bar. Ck-out noon. Meeting rms. Business servs avail. Valet serv. Coin lndry. Sundries. Gift shop. Barber shop. Free airport transportation. Lighted tennis. Exercise equipt, sauna. Cr cds: A, C, D, DS, MC, V.

★ ★ **COMFORT SUITES.** 1850 Resource Way (40299), east of downtown. 502/266-6509; FAX 502/266-9014. E-mail blk@musselman hotels.com; web www.musselmanhotel.com. 70 suites. S, D $79-$159. Crib free. TV; cable (premium). Indoor pool; whirlpool. Complimentary continental bkfst. Complimentary coffee in rms. Restaurant nearby. Ck-out 11 am. Business center. Free airport transportation. Refrigerators, microwaves. Cr cds: A, C, D, DS, JCB, MC, V.

★ ★ ★ **EXECUTIVE INN.** 978 Phillips Lane (40209), I-65 & I-264 exit Fair/Expo Center, south of downtown. 502/367-6161; FAX 502/363-1880; res: 800/626-2706. E-mail toetken@execinn.win.net; web www.win.net/~execinn/. 465 rms, 2-6 story. S $85; D $95; each addl $10; suites $109-$282; under 18 free. Crib free. Pet accepted. TV; cable, VCR avail. 2 pools, 1 indoor; wading pool, poolside serv, lifeguard. Restaurants 6:30 am-midnight. Rm serv. Bar 11 am-midnight, closed Sun. Ck-out 1 pm. Convention facilities. Business servs avail. Bellhops. Sundries. Gift shop. Barber, beauty shop. Free airport transportation. Exercise rm; sauna. Lawn games. Some private patios, balconies. Tudor-inspired architecture. Cr cds: A, C, D, DS, MC, V.

★ ★ ★ **EXECUTIVE WEST.** 830 Phillips Lane (40209), south of downtown. 502/367-2251; res: 800/633-8723; FAX 502/363-2087; res: 800/626-2708 (exc KY). E-mail exwest@iglou.com; web wl.iglou.com/ex-west. 611 rms, 8 story. S, D $84-$124; suites $105-$240; under 17 free. Crib free. Pet accepted; $100. TV; cable. Indoor/outdoor pool; poolside serv, lifeguard. Restaurant 6:30 am-11 pm. Rm serv. Bar; entertainment. Ck-out noon. Convention facilities. Business servs avail. In-rm modem link. Bellhops. Gift shop. Barber, beauty shop. Free airport transportation.

Health club privileges. Refrigerator in suites. Kentucky Kingdom Amusement Park opp. Cr cds: A, C, D, DS, MC, V.

[D] [icons]

★★ **HAMPTON INN.** 800 Phillips Lane (40209), near Louisville Intl Airport, south of downtown. 502/366-8100; FAX 502/366-0700. 130 rms, 4 story. S $79-$89; D $84-$94; under 18 free; wkend rates; higher rates: summer, special events. Crib free. TV; cable (premium). Coffee in rms. Pool; lifeguard. Complimentary continental bkfst. Restaurant nearby. Ck-out noon. Meeting rm. Business servs avail. Free airport transportation. Exercise equipt. Cr cds: A, C, D, DS, MC, V.

[D] [icons]

★★ **HOLIDAY INN.** 1325 S Hurstbourne Pkwy (40222), at I-64 exit 15, east of downtown. 502/426-2600; FAX 502/423-1605. 267 rms, 7 story. S, D $99-$125; suites $125-$275; under 18 free. Crib free. Pet accepted, some restrictions. TV; cable (premium). Indoor pool; lifeguard. Coffee in rms. Restaurant 6:30 am-10 pm. Rm serv. Bar noon-midnight. Ck-out noon. Meeting rms. Business servs avail. In-rm modem link. Bellhops. Valet serv. Free airport transportation. Exercise equipt, sauna. Refrigerator in suites. Cr cds: A, C, D, DS, JCB, MC, V.

[D] [icons]

★★ **HOLIDAY INN AIRPORT-EAST.** 1465 Gardiner Lane (40213), east of downtown. 502/452-6361; FAX 502/451-1541. 200 rms, 3 story. S, D $98; each addl $7; under 18 free; wkend rates. Crib free. Pet accepted. TV; cable (premium). Pool; poolside serv, lifeguard. Complimentary coffee in rms. Restaurant 11 am-11 pm. Rm serv. Bar to midnight. Ck-out noon. Coin lndry. Meeting rms. Business servs avail. In-rm modem link. Bellhops. Valet serv. Free airport transportation. Tennis. Exercise equipt. Game rm. Cr cds: A, C, D, DS, JCB, MC, V.

[D] [icons]

✔★ **WILSON INN.** 9802 Bunsen Pkwy (40299), I-64 exit 15, east of downtown. 502/499-0000; FAX 502/493-2905; res: 800/945-7667. 108 rms, 5 story, 30 suites, 38 kit. units. S, D $44.95; each addl $5; suites $54.95; kit. units $44.95; under 19 free. Crib free. Pet accepted, some restrictions. TV; cable (premium). Complimentary continental bkfst 6-10 am. Restaurant nearby. Ck-out noon. Meeting rms. Business servs avail. In-rm modem link. Free airport transportation. Refrigerators; microwaves avail. Cr cds: A, D, DS, JCB, MC, V.

[D] [icons]

Hotels

★★★★ **THE CAMBERLEY BROWN.** 335 W Broadway (40202), downtown. 502/583-1234; FAX 502/587-7006; res: 800/866-7666. Web www.camberleyhotels.com. This elegantly restored 1923 hotel has Old English-style furnishings, artwork, atmosphere and service. 292 rms, 16 story. S, D $189-$199; suites from $425; wkend, family rates. Crib free. Covered parking $10/day; valet $15. TV; cable. Restaurants 6:30 am-11 pm (also see THE ENGLISH GRILL). Rm serv 24 hrs. Bar 11-1 am. Ck-out 11 am. Convention facilities. Business center. In-rm modem link. Shopping arcade. Barber, beauty shop. Airport transportation. Exercise equipt. Health club privileges. Refrigerator in suites. Luxury level. Cr cds: A, C, D, DS, ER, JCB, MC, V.

[D] [icons]

★★ **GALT HOUSE.** 140 4th St (40202), at River Rd, downtown. 502/589-5200; FAX 502/589-3444; res: 800/626-1814. 656 rms, 25 story. S $110; D $120; each addl $10; suites $275; under 16 free. Crib free. TV; cable. Pool; lifeguard. Restaurants 6:30 am-midnight; dining rm 5:30-10:30 pm. Bar 11:30-1 am. Ck-out noon. Convention facilities. Shopping arcade. Garage parking. Refrigerator in suites. Overlooks Ohio River. Cr cds: A, C, D, DS, ER, JCB, MC, V.

[D] [icons]

★★ **GALT HOUSE EAST.** 141 N 4th St (40202), downtown. 502/589-5200; FAX 502/585-4266; res: 800/843-4258. E-mail info@ galthouse.com. 600 suites, 18 story. S $145; D $160; each addl $10; 2-bedrm suites $475; under 16 free. Crib free. TV; cable. Pool privileges

adj. Restaurant adj 6:30 am-midnight. Bar from 11 am. Ck-out noon. Garage parking. Refrigerators, wet bars. Some private patios, balconies. Overlooks Ohio River. 18-story atrium. Cr cds: A, C, D, DS, ER, JCB, MC, V.

[D] [icons]

★★ **HOLIDAY INN-DOWNTOWN.** 120 W Broadway (40202), downtown. 502/582-2241; res: 800/626-1558; FAX 502/584-8591. 287 rms, 12 story. S $95-$115; D $103-$125; each addl $10; suites $350; under 18 free. Crib free. Pet accepted. TV; cable, VCR avail. Indoor pool; lifeguard. Coffee in rms. Restaurant 6 am-11 pm. Bar 11-2 am. Ck-out noon. Convention facilities. Business servs avail. In-rm modem link. Gift shop. Barber. Free airport transportation. Exercise equipt. Health club privileges. Some refrigerators. Some balconies. Luxury level. Cr cds: A, C, D, DS, JCB, MC, V.

[D] [icons]

★★★ **HYATT REGENCY.** 320 W Jefferson St (40202), downtown. 502/587-3434; FAX 502/581-0133. Web www.hyatt.com. 388 rms, 18 story. S $89-$180; each addl $25; suites $250-$650; under 18 free. Crib free. TV; cable (premium), VCR avail. Indoor pool; whirlpool. Restaurants 6:30 am-midnight. Bars 11-2 am; Sun to midnight. Ck-out noon. Convention facilities. Business center. In-rm modem link. Concierge. Gift shop. Tennis. Exercise equipt. Garage. Access to shopping center via enclosed walkway. Modern design. Luxury level. Cr cds: A, C, D, DS, JCB, MC, V.

[D] [icons]

★★ **MARRIOTT-EAST.** 1903 Embassy Square Blvd (40299), E of I-264 at jct I-64, Hurstbourne Lane (exit 15), east of downtown. 502/499-6220; FAX 502/499-2480. 254 rms, 10 story. S, D $109-$139; under 18 free. Crib free. TV; cable (premium). Indoor pool; poolside serv, lifeguard. Restaurant 6:30 am-2 pm, 5-10 pm. Bar 2 pm-2 am. Ck-out 11 am. Convention facilities. Business servs avail. In-rm modem link. Concierge. Exercise equipt. Balconies. Cr cds: A, C, D, DS, MC, V.

[D] [icons]

★★★ **SEELBACH HILTON.** 500 Fourth Ave (40202), downtown. 502/585-3200; FAX 502/585-9239; res: 800/333-3399. Web www.hilton. com. The lobby in this restored hotel, originally opened in 1905, has eight murals by Arthur Thomas depicting Kentucky pioneers and Native Americans. Rooms have four-poster beds, armoires and marble baths. 321 rms, 11 story. S $170-$230; D $180-$230; each addl $10; suites $210-$510; under 18 free; package plans. Crib free. Pet accepted; $50 deposit. Parking $10; valet $14. TV; cable (premium), VCR avail. Pool privileges. Restaurants 6:30 am-midnight. Bar 4 pm-2 am; entertainment. Ck-out 1 pm. Convention facilities. Business center. In-rm modem link. Concierge. Shopping arcade. Free airport transportation. Health club privileges. Luxury level. Cr cds: A, C, D, DS, JCB, MC, V.

[D] [icons]

Inns

★★ **THE COLUMBINE.** 1707 S Third St (40208), in Old Louisville. 502/635-5000; res: 800/635-5010. E-mail colum bine@ntr.net; web www.bbonline.com/ky/columbine. 5 rms, 1 with shower only, 3 story, 1 suite. S $65-$80; D $70-$95; suite $70-$115; wkly, wkend rates. Children over 12 yrs only. TV; cable, VCR (movies). Complimentary full bkfst. Ck-out 11 am, ck-in 3 pm. Business servs avail. In-rm modem link. House built in 1900 with full-length porch. English garden. Cr cds: A, D, DS, MC, V.

[icons]

★★ **OLD LOUISVILLE.** 1359 S 3rd St (40208), in Old Louisville. 502/635-1574; FAX 502/637-5892. E-mail oldlouinn@aol.com; web www.digifax.com/oli.html. 10 rms, 3 story. No rm phones. D $75-$95; suites $110-$195; under 12 free. Crib free. TV in sitting rm; VCR avail (movies). Complimentary full bkfst. Restaurant nearby. Ck-out noon, ck-in 3 pm. Business servs avail. Exercise equipt. Some in-rm whirlpools.

Individually decorated rms in Victorian house (1901); antique furnishings. Ceiling murals. Cr cds: A, DS, MC, V.

🏃🏊♨️

★ ★ **WOODHAVEN.** *401 S Hubbards Lane (40207), east of downtown.* 502/895-1011; res: 888/895-1011. Web www.bbonline.com/ ky/woodhaven. 7 rms, 2 story. S, D $70-150. Crib free. Pet accepted. TV; cable (premium). Complimentary full bkfst. Complimentary coffee in rms. Ck-out 11:30 am, ck-in 3 pm. Gothic-revival house built in 1853. Totally nonsmoking. Cr cds: A, MC, V.

🔄🏊♨️

Restaurants

★ ★ **ASIATIQUE.** *106 Sears Ave (40207), east of downtown.* 502/899-3578. E-mail pslooi@iglow.com. Hrs: 5-10:30 pm; Mon to 10 pm; Fri, Sat to 11:30 pm, Sun to 10 pm. Closed most major hols. Res accepted. Pacific Rim menu. Bar. Semi-a la carte: dinner $15-$18. Child's meals. Specialties: wok seared Pacific salmon, roasted Mandarin Quail, ginger-dusted soft-shell crab. Parking. Elegant atmosphere; modern art decor. Cr cds: A, C, D, MC, V.

D ⬛

★ ★ ★ **CAFE METRO.** *1700 Bardstown Rd (40205), in Highland area, east of downtown.* 502/458-4830. Hrs: 6-10 pm; Fri, Sat to 11 pm. Closed Sun; hols. Res accepted. Continental menu. Bar. A la carte entrees: dinner $18.95. Specialties: grilled swordfish, salmon with cucumber caper dill sauce, jaegerschnitzel. Parking. Collection of pre-WWI German posters. Cr cds: A, D, DS, MC, V.

D ⬛

✔★ **CAFE MIMOSA.** *1216 Bardstown Rd (40204), east of downtown.* 502/458-2233. Hrs: 11 am-10 pm; Fri to 11 pm; Sat noon-11 pm; Sun noon-10 pm, brunch to 2 pm. Vietnamese, Chinese menu. Sushi bar. Semi-a la carte: lunch, dinner $4.50-$10.95. Sun brunch $6.95. Child's meals. Specializes in chicken, pork, shrimp. Parking. Vietnamese artwork. Cr cds: A, D, DS, MC, V.

D ⬛

✔★ **DARRYL'S 1815 RESTAURANT.** *3110 Bardstown Rd (40205), I-264 exit 16, east of downtown.* 502/458-1815. Hrs: 11 am-11 pm; Fri, Sat to 12:30 am. Bar. Semi-a la carte: lunch $4.99-$9.99, dinner $4.99-$18.99. Child's meals. Specializes in steak, chicken, ribs. Cr cds: A, D, DS, MC, V.

D ⬛

★ ★ **THE ENGLISH GRILL.** *(See The Camberley Brown Hotel)* 502/583-1234. Web www.camberleyhotels.com. Hrs: 5-11 pm; Sun to 10 pm. Res accepted. Bar. Semi-a la carte: dinner $17.25-$24.95. Specializes in fresh seafood, rack of lamb, steak. Seasonal menus feature regional foods. English motif; leaded and stained-glass windows, artwork featuring English scenes and Thoroughbred horses. Totally nonsmoking. Cr cds: A, C, D, DS, ER, JCB, MC, V.

D

★ ★ **EQUESTRIAN GRILLE.** *1582 Bardstown (40205), at Bonniecastle Rd, east of downtown.* 502/454-7455. Hrs: 5-11 pm; Fri, Sat to midnight. Closed Sun; major hols. Res accepted. Bar. Wine list. A la carte entrees: dinner $11-$26. Complete meals: dinner $25-$50. Specialties: free range chicken, double-cut pork chop, New York strip steak. Own baking. Offers 151 martinis. Upscale atmosphere features original equestrian artwork. Cr cds: A, C, D, MC, V.

D ⬛

★ ★ ★ **FERD GRISANTI.** *10212 Taylorsville Rd (40299), east of downtown.* 502/267-0050. E-mail grisanti@iglou.com; web www.ferd grisanti.com. Hrs: 5-10 pm; Fri, Sat to 11 pm. Closed Sun. Northern Italian menu. Res accepted. Bar. Wine list. Semi-a la carte: dinner $8.50-$18.95. Child's meals. Specializes in veal, pasta. Own baking. Parking. Contempo-

rary Italian decor; artwork. In historic Jeffersontown. Cr cds: A, C, D, DS, MC, V.

D ⬛

★ ★ **FIFTH QUARTER STEAKHOUSE.** *1241 Durrett Lane (40213), south of downtown.* 502/361-2363. Hrs: 11 am-10 pm; Fri to 11 pm; Sat 4-11 pm. Closed Dec 25. Bar. Semi-a la carte: lunch $4.59-$7.99, dinner $8.99-$19.99. Specialty: prime rib. Salad bar. Guitarist exc Sun. Parking. Rustic decor. Cr cds: A, C, D, DS, MC, V.

D SC ⬛

✔★ **JESSIE'S.** *9609 Dixie Hwy (40272), south of downtown.* 502/937-6332. Hrs: 5:30 am-9 pm; Sun 7 am-3 pm. Closed Thanksgiving, Dec 24-26; also July 4 wk. A la carte entrees: bkfst $1.95-$4.95, lunch, dinner $1.75-$5.95. Family-owned. Cr cds: MC, V.

D SC ⬛

✔★ **KOREANA II.** *5009 Preston Hwy (40213), south of downtown.* 502/968-9686. Hrs: 11 am-10 pm; Sat from noon; Sun from 5 pm. Closed Easter, Thanksgiving, Dec 25. Res accepted. Korean menu. Beer. Semi-a la carte: lunch $4.99-$8.99, dinner $7.25-$13.95. Child's meals. Specializes in beef, pork, chicken. Parking. Cr cds: A, DS, MC, V.

D ⬛

★ ★ ★ **KUNZ'S FOURTH & MARKET.** *115 S 4th St (40202), at Market St, downtown.* 502/585-5555. Hrs: 11 am-10:30 pm; Fri, Sat 4-11:30 pm; Sun 4-10 pm. Closed Dec 25. Res accepted. Continental menu. Bar. Semi-a la carte: lunch $5.95-$8.95, dinner $10.95-$24.95. Child's meals. Specializes in seafood, steak. Raw bar. Salad bar (lunch). Own breads. Family-owned since 1892. Cr cds: A, C, D, DS, MC, V.

D ⬛

★ ★ ★ **LE RELAIS.** *2817 Taylorsville Rd (40205), at Bowman Field, I-264 exit 17, Taylorsville Rd, east of downtown.* 502/451-9020. Hrs: 11:30 am-2:30 pm, 5:30-10 pm; Fri, Sat 5:30-10:30 pm; Sun 5:30-9 pm. Closed Mon; major hols. Res accepted. French menu. Bar. A la carte entrees: lunch $4.25-$10.25, dinner $14-$22.50. Specializes in fish, crab cakes, lamb chops. Parking. Outdoor dining. Formerly room in airport administration building. View of landing strip. Cr cds: A, D, MC, V.

D ⬛

★ ★ ★ ★ **LILLY'S.** *1147 Bardstown Rd (40204), east of downtown.* 502/451-0447. E-mail lillyslp@aol.com. The menu here changes biweekly and is filled with inventive dishes made with fresh, homegrown ingredients. The vaguely art deco-style dining room is decked in shades of green, black and purple. Specialties: pork tenderloin marinated and grilled in seasonal sauces, rack of lamb with demi-glaze. Hrs: 11 am-3 pm, 5:30-10 pm; Fri, Sat to 11 pm. Closed Sun, Mon; most major hols; also 2 wks in Aug. Res accepted. Semi-a la carte: lunch $10-$15, dinner $25-$36. Cr cds: A, DS, MC, V.

⬛

✔★ **LYNN'S PARADISE CAFE.** *984 Barret Ave (40204), downtown.* 502/583-3447. Hrs: 8 am-2:30 pm, 5:30-10 pm; Tues, Wed, Sun to 2:30 pm. Closed Mon; also Thanksgiving, Dec 25. Res accepted. Eclectic menu. Bar. Semi-a la carte: bkfst, lunch $4.50-$9, dinner $8-$15. Child's meals. Specialties: breakfast burrito, portobella wrap, walnut-crusted chicken. Parking. Outdoor dining. Colorful decor; casual atmosphere. Cr cds: MC, V.

D ⬛

✔★ ★ **MAMMA GRISANTI.** *3938 DuPont Circle (40207), east of downtown.* 502/893-0141. Hrs: 11:30 am-2 pm, 5-10 pm; Sat 3-11 pm; Sun 11:30 am-9 pm. Res accepted. Italian menu. Bar. Semi-a la carte: lunch $4.95-$8.50, dinner $6-$16. Buffet: lunch $6.25. Child's meals. Specialties: lasagne, fettucini Alfredo, veal parmesan. Own pasta. Family-owned. Cr cds: A, C, D, DS, MC, V.

⬛ ♥

★ ★ **MASTERSON'S.** *1830 S 3rd St (40208), south of downtown.* 502/636-2511. E-mail sales@mastersons.com; web www.mastersons.com.

Hrs: 11 am-9 pm; Mon to 4 pm; Sun 11:30 am-4 pm. Closed some major hols. Res accepted. Greek, Amer menu. Bar. Semi-a la carte: lunch $3.25-$9.75, dinner $9.25-$19.75. Buffet: lunch $7. Sun brunch $9. Child's meals. Specializes in regional cooking, Greek dishes. Parking. Outdoor dining. Near Univ of Louisville. Family-owned and operated for 60 yrs. Cr cds: A, C, D, DS, MC, V.

D SC

✔★ **OLD SPAGHETTI FACTORY.** 235 W Market St (40202), downtown. 502/581-1070. Hrs: 11:30 am-2 pm, 5-10 pm; Fri to 11 pm; Sat noon-11 pm; Sun 12:30-10 pm. Closed Thanksgiving, Dec 24, 25. Italian menu. Bar. Semi-a la carte: lunch $3.25-$5.45. Complete meals: dinner $4.75-$9.25. Child's meals. Specializes in spaghetti. Cr cds: A, D, DS, MC, V.

D

✔★ **SICHUAN GARDEN.** 9850 Linn Station Rd (40223), in Plainview Shopping Center, east of downtown. 502/426-6767. Hrs: 11:30 am-9:30 pm; Fri, Sat to 10:30 pm; Sun brunch noon-2 pm. Closed Thanksgiving. Res accepted. Chinese, Thai menu. Bar. Semi-a la carte: lunch $4.75-$5.95, dinner $5.95-$12.95. Sun brunch $6.95. Specialties: Sichuan orange beef, Mandarin seafood-in-a-net, beef tenders. Pianist Fri, Sat. Frosted-glass rm dividers. Cr cds: A, D, DS, MC, V.

D

✔★ **THAI SIAM.** 3002½ Bardstown Rd (40205), in shopping center, east of downtown. 502/458-6871. Hrs: 11 am-2 pm, 5-9 pm; Fri, Sat to 10 pm; Sun 5-9 pm. Closed Mon; most major hols. Res accepted. Thai menu. Wine, beer. Semi-a la carte: lunch $6.50-$7, dinner $8.50-$16. Specializes in traditional Thai dishes. Parking. Casual dining. Cr cds: DS, MC, V.

D

★★ **TIMOTHY'S.** 826 E Broadway (40204), downtown. 502/561-0880. Hrs: 11:30 am-11 pm; Fri to midnight; Sat 5:30 pm-midnight. Closed Sun; Easter, Thanksgiving, Dec 25. Res accepted. Italian, Amer menu. Bar. Semi-a la carte: lunch $5.95-$10.95, dinner $7.95-$24.95. Specializes in pasta, fresh seafood, white chili. Parking. Outdoor dining. Contemporary decor; vintage bar. Cr cds: A, D, MC, V.

D

★★ **UPTOWN CAFE.** 1624 Bardstown Rd (40205), south of downtown. 502/458-4212. Hrs: 11:30 am-11 pm; Fri, Sat to midnight. Closed Sun; most major hols. Continental menu. Bar. Semi-a la carte: lunch $6.25-$9.75, dinner $6.25-$17.95. Specialties: duck ravioli, salmon croquettes, veal pockets. Parking. Converted store front. Cr cds: A, D, DS, MC, V.

D

★★★ **VINCENZO'S.** 150 S 5th St (40202), downtown. 502/580-1350. E-mail vgabriele@aol.com; web onguide.com/net/vincenzo.htm. Highly skilled kitchen and dining room staff and an elegant, relaxed atmosphere are the benchmarks of this Louisville favorite. Diners can choose a simple meal or a multi-course culinary tour of traditional Italian dishes. Eurospa cuisine is available for those who prefer lighter fare. Continental menu. Specialties: crêpes Agostino, veal Gabriele. Own baking. Hrs: 11:30 am-2:30 pm, 5:30-11 pm; Fri, Sat 5:30 pm-midnight. Closed Sun; major hols. Res accepted. Wine list. A la carte entrees: lunch $6.95-$11.95, dinner $16.95-$24.95. Pianist Fri, Sat. Valet parking (dinner). Cr cds: A, C, D, DS, MC, V.

D ♥

★★ **WINSTON'S.** 3101 Bardstown Rd (40205), in Sullivan College, east of downtown. 502/456-0980. Hrs: 11 am-2:30 pm, 5:30-10 pm; Sun brunch 9:30 am-2:30 pm. Closed Mon-Thurs; most major hols. Res accepted. Bar. Semi-a la carte: lunch $8-$14, dinner $10-$30. Sun brunch $10. Child's meals. Specializes in local and regional dishes. Parking. Operated by senior culinary students. Totally nonsmoking. Cr cds: A, C, D, DS, MC, V.

D

Madisonville (D-4)

Founded 1807 **Pop** 16,200 **Elev** 470 ft **Area code** 502 **Zip** 42431 **E-mail** chamber@wka.com **Web** www.madisonvillenet.com
Information Madisonville-Hopkins County Chamber of Commerce, 15 E Center St; 502/821-3435.

In a region of hills, rivers and creek bottoms, and in the center of a coal-mining area, Madisonville is a growing industrial center and a marketplace for loose-leaf tobacco. Between the Tradewater and the Pond rivers, the town is named for President James Madison.

What to See and Do

Historical Library. More than 4,000 items are on display, including Civil War material, old maps and photos and a 150-gallon whiskey still confiscated in Hopkins County. Special events. (Mon-Fri afternoons) 107 Union St. Phone 502/821-3986. ¢

Pennyrile Forest State Resort Park. An 863-acre park surrounding a 55-acre lake. Swimming beach, pool, bathhouse (seasonal); fishing; boating (no motors), rentals. Hiking, riding; 9-hole & miniature golf (seasonal, rentals), tennis. Picnicking, playground, grocery, cottages & lodge (see RESORT). Tent & trailer sites (Apr-Oct, standard fees), cottages. Supervised recreation. 10 mi S on US 41, then 14 mi W on Western Kentucky Pkwy, then 7 mi S on KY 109. For fees and information phone 502/797-3421 or 800/325-1711.

Annual Event

Hopkins County Fair. Last wk July-first wk Aug.

Motels

✔★★ **BEST WESTERN PENNYRILE INN.** (Pennyrile Pkwy, Mortons Gap 42440) 6 mi S on Pennyrile Pkwy, exit 37. 502/258-5201; FAX 502/258-9072. 60 rms, 2 story. S $35; D $40-$49; each addl $3; under 12 free. Crib free. Pet accepted. TV; cable (premium), VCR avail (movies). Pool. Complimentary bkfst buffet. Coffee in rms. Restaurant open 24 hrs. Ck-out noon. Meeting rm. Business servs avail. Refrigerators avail. Cr cds: A, D, DS, MC, V.

D ✔ ≈ ⋈ SC

★★ **DAYS INN.** 1900 Lantaff Blvd, US 41 Bypass exit 44. 502/821-8620; FAX 502/825-9282. 143 rms, 2 story. S $52-$57; D $57-$62; each addl $5; suites $90-$120. Crib free. Pet accepted. TV; cable (premium). Indoor pool. Sauna. Complimentary continental bkfst. Restaurant 6-10 am, 11 am-2 pm, 5-10 pm; Sat 6-10 am, 5-10 pm; Sun to 2 pm. Rm serv. Ck-out noon. Meeting rms. Business servs avail. Sundries. Health club privileges. Cr cds: A, C, D, DS, MC, V.

D ✔ ≈ ⋈ SC

Resort

★★ **PENNYRILE LODGE.** (20781 Pennyrile Lodge Rd, Dawson Springs 42408) 9 mi S of Dawson Springs on County Rd 398 in Pennyrile State Forest, 2 mi S of KY 109. 502/797-3421; FAX 502/797-3413; res: 800/325-1711. 24 lodge rms, 2 story, 13 kit. cottages. Memorial Day-Labor Day: S $56; D $66; each addl $5; kit. cottages $87-$100; under 16 free; higher rates hol wkends; lower rates rest of yr. Crib free. TV. Pool; lifeguard. Dining rm 7-10:30 am, 11:30 am-2:30 pm, 5-9 pm. Ck-out noon, cottages 11 am, ck-in 4 pm. Meeting rms. Tennis. 9-hole golf, greens fee $6. Mountain biking. Miniature golf. Lawn games. Private patios, balconies. Picnic tables, grills. State-owned property; all state park facilities avail. Cr cds: A, DS, MC, V.

 SC

Restaurant

✔★ ★ **BARTHOLOMEW'S.** *51 S Main. 502/821-1061.* Hrs: 11 am-2:30 pm, 5-9:30 pm; Fri to 11 pm; Sat noon-11 pm. Closed Sun; most major hols. Bar. Semi-a la carte: lunch $6-$9, dinner $11-$20. Child's meals. Specializes in prime rib, pork chops, seafood. Parking. English pub atmosphere. Cr cds: A, DS, MC, V.

D ⌐

Mammoth Cave National Park (D-5)

(See also Cave City, Horse Cave, Park City)

Web www.nps.gov/maca

(On KY 70, 10 mi W of Cave City or 8 mi NW of Park City on KY 255)

This enormous underground complex of intertwining passages, totaling more than 350 miles in length, was carved by mildly acidic water trickling for thousands of years through limestone. Species of colorless, eyeless fish, crayfish and other creatures make their home within. Visible are the remains of a crude system used to mine 400,000 pounds of nitrate to make gunpowder for use in the War of 1812. The cave was the scene of an experiment aimed at the cure of tuberculosis. Mushroom growing was also attempted within the cave.

Above ground the park consists of 52,830 acres with sinkholes, rivers, 70 miles of hiking trails. Picnicking; lodging (see MOTEL). Camping (Mar-Dec, daily; some fees). An orientation movie is offered at the visitor center (daily exc Dec 25), phone 502/758-2328. Evening programs are conducted by park interpreters (summer; spring & fall, wkends).

Ranger-led trips of Mammoth Cave vary greatly in distance and length. Trails are solid, fairly smooth and require stooping or bending in places. Most tours involve steps and extensive walking; many are considered strenuous; proper footwear is recommended (no sandals); a sweater or wrap is also advised, even though it may be a hot August day above ground. Tours are conducted by experienced National Park Service interpreters. Contact Superintendent, Mammoth Cave 42259.

What to See and Do

Miss Green River **Boat Trip.** Round-trip cruise (60 min) through scenic and wildlife areas of the park. (Apr-Oct, daily) Advance tickets may be purchased at visitor center. Phone 502/758-2243. ¢¢

🔲 **Cave tours** depart from the visitor center (schedules vary with season; no tours Dec 25), phone 502/758-2328. Advance reservations are highly recommended. Tickets may be purchased in advance through Destinet Outlets; phone 800/967-2283. (The following is a partial list of available cave tours.)

Frozen Niagara. This moderately strenuous tour (2 hrs) explores huges pits and domes and decorative dripstone formations. ¢¢¢

Historic. A 2-mi guided tour highlighting the cave's rich human history; artifacts of Native Americans, early explorers; ruins of mining operations. ¢¢¢

Travertine. Quarter-mile Travertine (1 hr) is considered an easy tour through Drapery Room, Frozen Niagara and Crystal Lake. Designed for those unable to take many steps. ¢¢¢

Violet City. A 3-mi lantern-light tour (3 hrs) of historic features, including tuberclosis hospital huts and some of the cave's largest rooms and passageways. Inquire for schedule. ¢¢¢

Motel

★ **MAMMOTH CAVE HOTEL.** *10 mi W of US 31W (42259), I-65 exit 53 on KY 70 to park entrance, or exit 48 on KY 255 to entrance,* then 3 mi inside park. 502/758-2225; FAX 502/758-2301. 42 rms, 2 story. 20-rm motor lodge. S, D $62-$72; each addl $7; cottages: S, D $46-$52; family rates. Crib $5. TV. Restaurants 7 am-7:30 pm. Ck-out noon. Coin lndry (summer). Meeting rms (winter). Business servs avail. Gift shop. Tennis. Lawn games. Private patios, balconies. Cr cds: A, C, D, DS, MC, V.

D 🏃 ⊠ 🔥

Mayfield (E-2)

(See also Murray)

Settled 1823 **Pop** 9,935 **Elev** 492 ft **Area code** 502 **Zip** 42066 **E-mail** graves@ldd.net **Web** www.ldd.net/commerce/mayfield

Information Mayfield-Graves County Chamber of Commerce, 201 E College; 502/247-6101.

Rich clay fields in the area provide clay for all parts of the country. Tobacco is an important crop in this area.

What to See and Do

Wooldridge Monuments. Eccentric horse trader and breeder Henry C. Wooldridge is buried here. Near the stone vault, in which he is interred, are life-size statues of his parents, his brothers, five girls, his favorite dogs, a deer, a fox and a statue of himself mounted on a favorite horse—all facing east. (Daily) In Maplewood Cemetery, N end of town on US 45.

Motel

★ **DAYS INN.** *1101 Houseman St, 2 mi W on US 45 Bypass, at jct KY 121. 502/247-3700; FAX 502/247-3135.* 80 rms, 2 story. May-Oct: S $48; D $55; each addl $7; under 18 free; lower rates rest of yr. Crib free. TV; cable. Pool. Restaurant 6 am-2 pm, 5-10 pm. Rm serv. Ck-out noon. Meeting rms. In-rm modem link. Valet serv. Lawn games. Cr cds: A, C, D, DS, ER, JCB, MC, V.

D ⊠ ⊠ 🔥 SC

Maysville (C-8)

(See also Covington, Lexington)

Founded 1787 **Pop** 7,169 **Elev** 514 ft **Area code** 606 **Zip** 41056
Information Tourism Commission, 216 Bridge St; 606/564-9411.

This Ohio River town, first known as Limestone, was established by the Virginia Legislature. By 1792 it had become a leading port of entry for Kentucky settlers. Daniel Boone and his wife maintained a tavern in the town for several years. Maysville is now an important burley tobacco market. Many buildings and sites in the 8-block historic district are included on the National Historic Register.

What to See and Do

Blue Licks Battlefield State Park. Approx 150 acres on the site of one of the bloodiest battles of the frontier and last Kentucky battle of the Revolutionary War (Aug 19, 1782, one year after Cornwallis' surrender). A monument in the park honors pioneers killed in an ambush. Also here is a museum with exhibits and displays depicting history of the area from the Ice Age through the Revolution. Recreational facilities include swimming pool; fishing. Miniature golf. Picnic shelters, playground. Camping (standard fees). (Apr-Oct, daily) 26 mi SW on US 68. Phone 606/289-5507. Museum ¢

Historic Washington. The original seat of Mason County, Washington was founded in 1786 and soon was the second largest town in Kentucky, with 119 cabins. Restored buildings include Paxton Inn (1810), Albert Sidney Johnston House (1797), Old Church Museum (1848), Mefford Fort, Simon Kenton Trading store and the Cane Brake, thought to be one of the original cabins of 1790. Guided tours (mid-Mar-Dec, daily). (See ANNUAL EVENTS) 4 mi S on US 68.Contact Old Washington, Inc, PO Box 227, Washington 41096; 606/759-7411. ¢¢

Mason County Museum. Restored building (1876) houses art gallery, local historical exhibits, genealogical library. (Apr-Dec, daily exc Sun; rest of yr, daily exc Mon; closed hols) 215 Sutton St. Phone 606/564-5865. ¢

The Piedmont Art Gallery. Located in one of the oldest settlements on the Ohio River, the gallery houses contemporary works by national and regional artists and craftspeople; antiques, paintings, sculpture, ceramics, American folk art. (Thurs-Sun, afternoons) 16 mi NE via KY 8E in Augusta at 115 W Riverside Dr. Phone 606/756-2216. **Free.**

Annual Events

Sternwheeler Annual Regatta. 16 mi NE in Augusta. Mid-June.

Simon Kenton Festival. Historic Washington. 3rd wkend Sept.

Monticello (E-7)

Pop 5,357 **Elev** 923 ft **Area code** 606 **Zip** 42633

Information Monticello-Wayne County Chamber of Commerce, PO Box 566; 606/348-3064 or 888/326-8689.

What to See and Do

Dale Hollow Lake State Resort Park. A 3,398-acre park on a 27,700-acre lake. Swimming pool; boat rentals, marina (fee). Playground. Camping (hookups, dump station). Standard fees. SE via KY 90, 449. Phone 502/433-7431.

Motel

✔★ ★ **GRIDER HILL DOCK & INDIAN CREEK LODGE.** *(Albany 42602) 20 mi W on KY 90, then 5 mi N on KY 734, 1266, on Lake Cumberland. 606/387-5501; FAX 606/387-7023.* 22 rms, 2 story, 12 kit. cottages, 20 houseboats. S $34-$48; D $42-$62; each addl $6; kit. cottages for 2-10, $50-$136; houseboats for 6-12, $475-$2,000 (3-day wkends; deposit required). Closed Nov-Mar. TV; cable. Restaurant 6 am-9 pm. Ck-out noon. On lake; swimming, boats, motors, dockage. Cr cds: A, DS, MC, V.

Morehead (C-8)

(See also Olive Hill)

Pop 8,357 **Elev** 748 ft **Area code** 606 **Zip** 40351

Information Tourism Commission, 150 E 1st St; 606/784-6221.

Seat of Rowan County, Morehead is a university town and a provisioning point for lumbermen and tourists visiting the northern portions of Daniel Boone National Forest (see). A Ranger District office for the forest is located in Morehead.

What to See and Do

Cave Run Lake. An 8,270-acre lake created by the impoundment of the Licking River. Beach, bathhouse and seasonal interpretive programs at Twin Knobs and Zilpo campgrounds; fishing for bass and muskie; 12 boat ramps, 2 marinas with boat rentals. Hiking. Picnicking. Camping at Twin Knobs and Zilpo campgrounds, boat-in camping at Clay Lick campground.

Morehead Visitor Center, on KY 801, has exhibits, information. Scenic roads and views, including Forest Development Road 918, designated a National Scenic Byway. (Mid-Apr-Oct, daily) Some fees. In Daniel Boone National Forest (see), 10 mi SW via US 60 then S on KY 801; or S on KY 211. For information contact the Morehead Ranger District, US Forest Service, 2375 KY 801S; phone 606/784-5624. Per car ¢¢

Minor Clark State Fish Hatchery. Largemouth bass, smallmouth bass, walleye, muskellunge and rockfish are reared here; on display in exhibition pool. (May-Sept, Mon-Fri; closed most hols) 10 mi SW on US 60, then 2 mi S on KY 801. Phone 606/784-6872. **Free.**

Morehead State University (1922). (7,800 students) One-rm schoolhouse (by appt); Folk Art Museum, 1st floor of Claypool-Young Art Bldg (Mon-Fri). Just off I-64, in center of town. Phone 606/783-2221. Also on campus is

MSU Appalachian Collection. Fifth floor of Camden Carroll Library Tower. Collection includes books, periodicals, geneaological materials, government documents. Special holdings devoted to authors James Still and Jesse Stuart, displays of regional art. (Daily) **Free.**

Annual Events

Appalachian Celebration. Week devoted to history & heritage of Appalachia in Kentucky; dances, concerts, arts & crafts, exhibitions. Late June.

Kentucky Hardwood Festival. Appalachian arts & crafts, pageant, parade, contests, antiques, logging contests. 2nd wkend Sept.

Motels

✔★ **DAYS INN.** *170 Toms Dr, I-64 exit 137. 606/783-1484.* 50 rms, 2 story. S $44; D $55; under 12 free; higher rates univ graduation. Crib free. TV; cable (premium). Complimentary continental bkfst. Restaurant adj 6 am-11 pm. Ck-out 11 am. Coin lndry. Some refrigerators. Cr cds: A, C, D, DS, MC, V.

D ⊠ ⦰ SC

★ **HOLIDAY INN.** *1698 Flemingsburg Rd, jct I-64, KY 32. 606/784-7591; FAX 606/783-1859.* 141 rms, 2 story. S, D $55-$65; each addl $6; under 19 free; higher rates special events. Crib free. TV; cable (premium). Pool. Restaurant 6:30 am-2 pm, 5-9 pm. Rm serv. Ck-out noon. Meeting rms. Business servs avail. In-rm modem link. Cr cds: A, C, D, DS, JCB, MC, V.

D ≋ ⊠ ⦰ SC

★ **SUPER 8.** *602 Fraley Dr, I-64 exit 137. 606/784-8882; FAX 606/784-9882.* 56 rms, 3 story. S $37.88-$43.88; D $46.88-$54.88; under 12 free; higher rates special events. Crib free. TV; cable (premium). Complimentary coffee in lobby. Restaurant opp 7 am-10 pm. Ck-out noon. Coin lndry. Cr cds: A, C, D, DS, MC, V.

D ⊠ ⦰ SC

Mount Vernon (D-7)

(See also Berea)

Pop 2,654 **Elev** 1,156 ft **Area code** 606 **Zip** 40456

What to See and Do

William Whitley House Historic Site (1785-1792). First brick house west of the Alleghenies, building was used as a protective fort from Native Americans and as a haven for travelers on the Wilderness Road. Was called Sportsman's Hill because of the circular racetrack built nearby (first in US), which ran counter-clockwise, unlike those in England. Panels symbolizing each of the 13 original states are over the mantel in parlor. Restored and furnished with period pieces. (Memorial Day-Labor Day, daily; rest of yr, daily exc Mon) Picnicking, playground. 15 mi NW on US 150. Phone 606/355-2881. ¢¢

Motels

★ **ECONO LODGE.** *1630 Richmond St, US 25 & I-75 exit 62. 606/256-4621.* 35 rms, 2-3 story. S 29.50-$32, D $36-$40.50; family rates; higher rates: hol wkends, special events. Crib $5. Pet accepted, some restrictions. TV; cable. Pool. Complimentary coffee in lobby. Restaurant nearby. Ck-out 11 am. Cr cds: A, C, D, DS, ER, JCB, MC, V.

D ✔ ≈ ⨯ 🎿 SC

✔★ ★ **KASTLE INN.** *E of I-75 exit 59. 606/256-5156.* 50 rms, 2 story. S $36-$44; D $44-$54; each addl $8; under 12 free. Pet accepted, some restrictions. TV; cable (premium), VCR avail (movies). Pool. Restaurant 6 am-10 pm. Ck-out 11 am. Sundries. Cr cds: A, C, D, DS, ER, JCB, MC, V.

✔ ≈ ⨯ 🎿 SC

Murray (E-3)

(See also Mayfield)

Pop 14,439 **Elev** 515 ft **Area code** 502 **Zip** 42071 **E-mail** murtour@ldd.net
Information Murray Tourism Commission, PO Box 190; 502/759-2199 or 800/651-1603.

In Murray, in 1892, Nathan B. Stubblefield made the first radio broadcast in history. Rainey T. Wells, attorney for the Woodmen of the World, was about one mile away when he heard Stubblefield's voice saying "Hello Rainey! Hello Rainey!" Wells was astounded, and urged Stubblefield to patent his invention. Because of delays and ill-advised deals while perfecting his invention, Stubblefield was not the first to obtain the patent. He finally received one in 1908, but died in poverty in 1928. This is the home of Murray State University (1922), of which Rainey Wells was the second president.

What to See and Do

Kenlake State Resort Park (see). 16 mi NE on KY 94.

Land Between The Lakes (see). 20 mi NE off KY 94.

National Museum, Boy Scouts of America. Houses the 54 original Norman Rockwell paintings of the scouting movement; several thousand items of scouting memorabilia and artifacts. (Mar-Nov, daily exc Mon; closed Easter, Thanksgiving) N 16th Street on Murray State University campus. Phone 502/762-3383. ¢¢

Annual Events

Calloway County Fair. June.

Freedom Fest. July 4th.

Motels

★ **DAYS INN.** *517 S 12th St, US 641S. 502/753-6706; res: 800/329-7466.* S $47.50-$60; D $52.50-$65; each addl $5; under 13 free; higher rates special events. Crib free. Pet accepted; $5. TV; cable (premium). Complimentary continental bkfst. Coffee in rms. Restaurant nearby. Ck-out 11 am. Business servs avail. Pool. Health club privileges. Some in-rm whirlpool, refrigerators, microwaves. Cr cds: A, C, D, DS, JCB, MC, V.

D ✔ ≈ ⨯ 🎿 SC

✔★ **PLAZA COURT.** *502 S 12 St, US 641S. 502/753-2682.* 40 rms, 2 story. S $33; D $36.30; each addl $5; wkly plans; higher rates special events. Crib $6. Pet accepted, some restrictions. TV; cable (pre-

mium). Complimentary coffee in lobby. Restaurant opp 6-2 am. Ck-out noon. Cr cds: A, DS, MC, V.

✔ 🎿

✔★ **SHONEY'S INN.** *1503 N 12th St. 502/753-5353.* 67 rms, 2 story. S $44-$48; D $49-$53; each addl $5; higher rates special events; crib free. Pet accepted; $5; TV; cable (premium). Complimentary coffee in lobby. Restaurant adj 6 am-10 pm. Ck-out noon. Meeting rms. Business servs avail. In-rm modem link. Pool. Cr cds: A, C, D, DS, MC, V.

D ✔ ≈ ⨯ 🔥 SC

Restaurant

✔★ **SEVEN SEAS.** *1901 N 12th St, 2 mi NW on US 641. 502/753-4141.* E-mail pauld@mursuky.campus.mci.net. Hrs: 4-9 pm; Sun 11 am-2 pm. Closed Mon, Tues; also some major hols. Semi-a la carte: dinner $6.29-$16.95. Child's meals. Specializes in grand buffet, Angus beef, seafood. Cr cds: A, DS, MC, V.

SC ⊣

Natural Bridge State Resort Park (D-8)

(See also Winchester)

(On KY 11 near Slade)

Surrounded by 1,899 acres and a 54-acre lake in Daniel Boone National Forest (see), the natural bridge is 78 feet long and 65 feet high. The park has balanced rock and native hemlocks. Swimming pool (seasonal); fishing; boating. Nature trails and center (no pets are allowed on the trails). Picnicking, playground; dining room; cottages, lodge (see RESORT). Tent & trailer sites (Apr-Oct; standard fees), central service buildings. Skylift (mid-Apr-Oct, daily; fee); square dance pavilion; festivals. For prices, information phone 606/663-2214 or 800/325-1710.

Resort

★ ★ **HEMLOCK LODGE.** *(2135 Natural Bridge Rd, Slade 40376) 2 mi S of Mountain Pkwy on KY 11, in Natural Bridge State Resort Park. 606/663-2214; FAX 606/663-5037; res: 800/325-1710.* Web www.state.ky.us/agencies/park/parkhome.htm. 35 rms, 2 story, 10 kit. cottages. Memorial Day-Labor Day: S $57; D $67; each addl $5; kit. cottages $75-$105; under 16 free; lower rates rest of yr. Closed Christmas hols. Crib free. TV; cable. Pool; wading pool, lifeguard. Playground. Supervised child's activities (Memorial Day- Labor Day). Dining rm 7-10:30 am, 11:30 am-4 pm, 5-9 pm. Ck-out noon, cottages 11 am, ck-in 4 pm. Meeting rms. Business servs avail. Miniature golf. Balconies. Picnic tables, grills. State-owned property; all park facilities avail. Cr cds: A, C, D, DS, MC, V.

D ≈ ⨯ 🎿 SC

Olive Hill (C-9)

(See also Morehead)

Pop 1,809 **Elev** 160 ft **Area code** 606 **Zip** 41164

What to See and Do

Carter Caves State Resort Park. This 1,350-acre park lies in a region of cliffs, streams and many caves. Pool (seasonal); boating (rentals); fishing, canoe trips. Nine-hole and miniature golf, tennis, shuffleboard. Picnicking, playground, cottages, lodge (see RESORT). Tent & trailer sites (standard fees); central service building. Planned recreation, films, dances, festivals. Several guided cave tours. (Daily; closed late Dec) Some fees. 7 mi NE via US 60, KY 182. Phone 606/286-4411.

Grayson Lake State Park. A 1,500-acre park and 1,512-acre lake. Fishing; boating (boat launch). Hiking. Picnicking, playground. Camping (hookups, dump station). 15 mi E via US 60, then 10 mi S on KY 7. Phone 606/474-9727.

Resort

★ ★ **CAVELAND LODGE.** *344 Caveland Dr, 3 mi N on KY 182, 5 mi NE of I-64 exit 161, in Carter Caves State Resort Park. 606/286-4411; FAX 606/286-8165; res: 800/325-0059.* Web www.kystateparks.com. 28 rms in lodge, 2 story, 15 kit. cottages. Memorial Day-Labor Day & special events: S $57; D $67; each addl $5; kit. cottages $75-$95; under 16 free; lower rates rest of yr. Crib free. TV. 2 pools; wading pool, lifeguard. Playground. Ck-out noon, cottages 11 am, ck-in 4 pm. Meeting rms. Business servs avail. Gift shop. Tennis. 9-hole golf, greens fee $11, putting green, miniature golf. Refrigerator in cottages. Private patios, balconies. Picnic tables, grills. State-owned property; all facilities of park avail. Cr cds: A, C, D, DS, MC, V.

Owensboro (D-4)

Settled 1800 **Pop** 53,549 **Elev** 401 ft **Area code** 502 **Zip** 42303
Information Owensboro-Daviess County Tourist Commission, 215 E 2nd St; 502/926-1100 or 800/489-1131.

Third largest city in Kentucky, Owensboro serves as the major industrial, commercial and agricultural hub of western Kentucky. A progressive arts program has provided Owensboro with a symphony orchestra, fine art museum, dance theatre, science museum and theater workshop. In spring the many historic houses along tree-arched Griffith Avenue are brightened by dogwood and azalea blossoms.

Once known as Yellow Banks from the color of the clay on the Ohio River's high banks, the town saw clashes between Union and Confederate troops during the Civil War. An earlier clash between the values of the North and South occured when Harriet Beecher Stowe found inspiration for her novel *Uncle Tom's Cabin* after a visit to a local plantation.

What to See and Do

Ben Hawes State Park. Approx 300 acres with hiking; 9-hole, 18-hole golf (fee, rentals). Picnicking, playground. 4 mi W off US 60. Phone 502/684-9808 or 502/685-2011 (golf).

Owensboro Area Museum of Science & History. Live reptiles, insects; archaeological, geological and ornithological displays; historic items. Gift shop. (Daily exc Mon; closed major hols) 220 Daviess St. Phone 502/687-2732. **Donation.**

Owensboro Museum of Fine Art. Permanent collection includes 16th-20th-century American, French and English paintings, drawings, sculpture, graphic and decorative arts. Special collection of 19th- and 20th-century regional art; Appalachian folk art. (Daily exc Mon; closed major hols) 901 Frederica St. Phone 502/685-3181. ¢

Windy Hollow Recreation Area. Area of 214 acres offers swimming, 240-ft water slide (Memorial Day-Labor Day, fee); fishing. Miniature golf (fee). Grocery. Tent & trailer camping (fee). Park (Apr-Oct, daily). 10 mi SW off KY 81. Phone 502/785-4150.

Annual Events

International Bar-B-Q Festival. Cooks compete with recipes for mutton, chicken, burgoo. Also, tobacco spitting, pie-eating, fiddling contests. Arts & crafts, music, dancing. Early May.

Daviess County Fair. 4 days late July-early Aug.

Bluegrass Blast. On riverfront in English Park. Bluegrass musicians perform. Phone 502/926-1100. Late Sept.

Seasonal Event

Owensboro Symphony Orchestra. RiverPark Center. Includes guest appearances by renowned artists, ballet companies. Phone 502/684-0661. Oct-Apr.

Motels

✔★ **DAYS INN.** *3720 New Hartford Rd, jct US 60 Bypass & US 231. 502/684-9621; FAX 502/684-9626.* 122 rms, 2 story. S $44; D $48; each addl $4; under 18 free. Crib free. TV; cable (premium). Pool. Complimentary coffee in rms. Restaurant 6 am-9 pm. Rm serv 5-9 pm. Ck-out noon. Business servs avail. In-rm modem link. Cr cds: A, D, DS, MC, V.

★ ★ **HOLIDAY INN.** *3136 W 2nd St (42301). 502/685-3941; FAX 502/926-2917.* 145 rms, 2 story. S, D $59-$69; suites $95; under 19 free. Crib free. Pet accepted. TV; cable (premium). Indoor pool; whirlpool. Playground. Coffee in rms. Restaurant 6 am-2 pm, 5-9 pm; Sun 6 am-2 pm. Rm serv. Bar 3 pm-2 am; closed Sun. Ck-out noon. Meeting rms. Business center. In-rm modem link. Exercise equipt; sauna. Cr cds: A, C, D, DS, JCB, MC, V.

Motor Hotel

★ ★ ★ **THE EXECUTIVE INN.** *1 Executive Blvd (42301). 502/926-8000; FAX 502/926-6442; res: 800/626-1936.* 550 rms, 2-7 story S, D $39-$65; suites $85-$135; under 18 free. Crib free. TV; cable (premium). 2 pools, 1 indoor. Restaurants 6 am-10 pm. Rm serv. Bar 4 pm-2 am; closed Sun; entertainment. Ck-out 11 am. Convention facilities. Business center. Bellhops. Shopping arcade. Free airport transportation. Indoor tennis. Exercise equipt; sauna, steam rm. Game rm. Refrigerators. Patios, balconies. On river. Cr cds: A, D, DS, MC, V.

Restaurants

★ ★ **BRIARPATCH.** *2760 Veach Rd. 502/685-3329.* E-mail buntin@mindspring.com. Hrs: 11 am-2 pm, 5-9:30 pm; Fri to 10:30 pm; Sat 4:30-10:30 pm. Closed Thanksgiving, Dec 25. Bar. Semi-a la carte: lunch $3.50-$6.95, dinner $7.95-$18.95. Child's meals. Specializes in steak, seafood. Salad bar. Parking. Cr cds: A, D, DS, MC, V.

★ ★ **COLBY'S.** *202 W Third St. 502/685-4239.* Hrs: 11 am-10 pm; Fri, Sat to 11 pm. Closed most major hols. Bar. Semi-a la carte: lunch $6-$10, dinner $9-$18. Child's meals. Specializes in fresh seafood, Angus beef. Historic house (1895); restored. Antiques. Cr cds: A, DS, MC, V.

✔★ **MOONLITE BAR B-Q.** *2840 W Parish Ave (42301). 502/684-8143.* Web www.moonlite.com. Hrs: 9 am-9 pm; Fri, Sat to 9:30 pm; Sun 9 am-3 pm; Sun brunch 10 am-2:30 pm. Closed most major hols. Wine, beer. Semi-a la carte: lunch, dinner $3.10-$10.95. Sun brunch $8.95. Child's meals. Specializes in mutton, ribs, chicken. Parking. Family-owned. Cr cds: A, D, DS, MC, V.

★ **RUBY TUESDAY.** *5000 Frederica St (US 431) (42301), in Towne Square Mall. 502/926-8325.* Hrs: 11 am-10 pm; Fri, Sat to 11 pm; Sun to 8:30 pm. Res accepted. Semi-a la carte: lunch $4-$8, dinner $10-$18. Child's meals. Specializes in steak, fajitas, chicken. Salad bar. Cr cds: A, C, D, DS, MC, V.

✔★★ **TROTTER'S.** *1100 Walnut St (42301), in Cigar Factory Complex. 502/685-2771.* Hrs: 11 am-10 pm; Fri, Sat to 11 pm; early-bird dinner Mon-Thurs 4-7 pm. Closed Sun; most major hols. Bar 11 am-11 pm; Fri, Sat to midnight. Semi-a la carte: lunch $4.95-$9.95, dinner $9.95-$16.95. Child's meals. Specializes in pasta, seafood, beef. Parking. Race track theme. Cr cds: A, D, MC, V.

Paducah (E-2)

(See also Gilbertsville)

Founded 1827 **Pop** 27,256 **Elev** 339 ft **Area code** 502 **E-mail** fun@Paducah-tourism.org **Web** www.Paducah-tourism.org
Information Paducah-McCracken County Convention and Visitors Bureau, 128 Broadway, PO Box 90, 42002; 502/443-8783 or 800/723-8224.

Paducah, historic gateway to western Kentucky, has been shaped and influenced by its location at the convergence of the Ohio and Tennessee rivers. The waters have brought both prosperity and ruin in the form of disastrous floods; the worst occurred in 1937.

Explorer William Clark laid out the town site and named it after his Chickasaw friend, Chief Paduke. Paducah quickly developed as a shipping center and was a strategic point hotly contested during the Civil War. TVA dams have tamed the rivers and created the recreation areas of the Land Between The Lakes (see). Timber, tobacco, soybeans, coal and livestock flow through Paducah as they have for more than a century.

Paducah is perhaps most famous as the birthplace of author and actor Irvin S. Cobb, known for his witty humor and beloved "Old Judge Priest" stories.

What to See and Do

Market House (1905). S 2nd St & Broadway. Now a cultural center housing

Market House Museum. Early Americana, including complete interior of drugstore more than 100 yrs old. River lore, Alben Barkley and Irvin S. Cobb memorabilia, Native American artifacts, old tools. (Mar-Dec, daily exc Mon; closed major hols) Phone 502/443-7759. ¢

Yeiser Arts Center. Monthly changing exhibits; collection ranges from European masters to regional artists. Gift shop. Tours. (Daily exc Mon; closed major hols). Phone 502/442-2453. ¢

Market House Theatre. A 250-seat professionally-directed community playhouse. (All yr) Phone 502/444-6828. ¢¢¢

Memorials.

Irvin S. Cobb Memorial. Oak Grove Cemetery.

Alben W. Barkley Monument. The senator and vice-president was one of Paducah's most famous citizens. 28th & Jefferson Sts.

Chief Paduke Statue. Memorial to the Chickasaw chief by Lorado Taft. 19th & Jefferson Sts.

Museum of the American Quilter's Society. More than 200 quilts exhibited. Special exhibits scheduled regularly. Gift shop. (Apr-Oct, daily exc Mon; rest of yr, Tues-Sat; closed Jan 1, Thanksgiving, Dec 25) 215 Jefferson St. Phone 502/442-8856. ¢¢

Red Line Scenic Tour. Self-guided driving tour (with map) of city points of interest, including Market House and City Hall, designed by Edward Durell Stone. Obtain tour folders at the Visitors Bureau,128 Broadway, 42001; 502/443-8783.

Whitehaven. Antebellum mansion remodeled in classical-revival style in 1903; elaborate plasterwork, stained glass, 1860s furnishings. State uses a portion of the house as a tourist welcome center and rest area. Tours (afternoons). (Daily; closed Jan 1, Thanksgiving, Dec 24, 25) I-24, exit 7. Phone 502/554-2077. **Free.**

Annual Events

Dogwood Trail Celebration. Blossoming of dogwood and azalea is celebrated with a 12-mi trail, spotlighted at night. Driving tours begin at Paducah City Hall. Mid-Apr.

Kiwanis West Kentucky-McCracken County Fair. Carson Park, 301 Joe Clifton Dr. Society & Western horse shows; harness racing; motorcycle racing; gospel singing. Last full wk June.

Summer Festival. Hot air balloons, symphony & fireworks, free entertainment nightly. Events along river front and throughout city. Last wk July.

Seasonal Event

Players Bluegrass Downs. 2 mi W at 32nd & Park Ave. Parimutuel horse racing. Thurs-Sun. Phone 502/444-7117. Oct.

Motels

★★ **COURTYARD BY MARRIOTT.** *3835 Technology Dr (42001), 1 mi E at I-24, exit 4. 502/442-3600; FAX 502/442-3619.* 100 rms, 3 story. S $69; D $79; under 18 free; higher rates special events. Crib free. TV; cable (premium). Complimentary coffee in rms. Restaurant nearby. Bar 5-10 pm; entertainment Mon-Sat. Ck-out noon. Valet serv. Guest lndry. Exercise equipt. Indoor pool; whirlpool. Some in-rm whirlpools, refrigerators, microwaves. Cr cds: A, C, D, DS, MC, V.

✔★ **DAYS INN.** *3901 Hinkleville Rd (42001), 3½ mi E on US 60, at I-24. 502/442-7501; FAX 502/442-7500.* 122 rms, 2 story. S $45-$50; D $50-$55; each addl $5; under 18 free. Crib free. TV; cable (premium). Pool. Complimentary continental bkfst. Restaurant adj 11 am-10 pm. Ck-out noon. Business servs avail. Refrigerators avail. Cr cds: A, D, DS, MC, V.

✔★ **DENTON.** *2550 Lone Oak Rd (42003), 1 mi S of I-24 exit 7. 502/554-1626; res: 800/788-1626.* E-mail dentonmo@uci.net. 34 rms, 2 story. S $47-$52; D $52-$59; each addl $7; under 13 free; package plans; higher rates special events. Crib avail. TV; cable (premium). Complimentary coffee in lobby. Restaurant nearby. Business servs avail. Health club privileges. Refrigerators avail. Cr cds: A, C, D, DS, MC, V.

★ **DRURY INN.** *3975 Hinkleville Rd (42001). 502/443-3313.* Web www.drury-inn.com. 118 rms, 5 story. S $59-$70; D $65-$80 each addl $8; suites $70-$80; under 18 free. Crib free. Pet accepted. TV; cable. Indoor pool; whirlpool. Complimentary full bkfst. Ck-out noon. Health club privileges. Cr cds: A, C, D, DS, MC, V.

★★ **HOLIDAY INN EXPRESS.** *3994 Hinkleville Rd (42001), I-24 and US 60, exit 4. 502/442-8874; FAX 502/443-3367.* E-mail pahex@ apex.net; web www.midamcorp.com/holidayinnexpress. 76 rms, 3 story. S $80.50; D $90.50; each addl $10; under 18 free; higher rates special events. Crib avail. Pet accepted, some restrictions. TV; cable (premium), VCR avail. Complimentary continental bkfst. Ck-out 11 am. Meeting rm. Business servs avail. Coin lndry. Health club privileges. Indoor pool; whirlpool. Game rm. Bathrm phones, refrigerators, microwaves, minibars; some in-rm whirlpools. Cr cds: A, C, D, DS, JCB, MC, V.

✔★ **QUALITY INN.** *1380 Irvin Cobb Dr (42003), W on I-24, exit 7. 502/443-8751; FAX 502/442-0133.* 101 rms, 2 story. Mar-Nov: S $39.99-$48.99; D $48.99-$58.99; each addl $7; family, wkly rates; higher rates special events; lower rates rest of yr. Crib avail. Pet accepted, some restrictions. TV; cable (premium). Complimentary continental bkfst. Restaurant nearby. Ck-out 11 am. Meeting rms. Business servs avail. Coin lndry. Pool. Cr cds: A, C, D, DS, MC, V.

★ **SUPER 8.** *5125 Old Cairo Rd (42001), E on I-24, exit 3.* 502/575-9605. 42 rms, 2 story. S $45-$50; D $50-$60; each addl $5; under 12 free; higher rates special events. Crib $7. TV; cable (premium). Complimentary continental bkfst. Restaurant opp 6 am-10 pm. Ck-out 11 am. Business servs avail. Refrigerators, microwaves. Cr cds: A, D, DS, MC, V.

🆗 🐾 SC

Motor Hotel

★ ★ **J.R.'S EXECUTIVE INN.** *1 Executive Blvd (42001), 10 mi W of I-24 exit 16.* 502/443-8000; res: 800/866-3636; FAX 502/444-5317. E-mail bige@apex.net; web www.jrsexecutiveinn.com. 399 rms, 4 story, 34 suites. S $59-$64; D $69-$74; each addl $5; suites $125; under 12 free; wkend plans; higher rates special events. Crib avail. TV; cable (premium). Restaurant 6 am-10 pm. Bar 11 am-10 pm; Fri, Sat to 2 am; closed Sun; entertainment Sat. Ck-out noon. Convention facilities. Business servs avail. Bellhops. Sundries. Shopping arcade. Gift shop. Grocery store. Barber, beauty shop. Coin lndry. Free airport transportation. Exercise equipt. Indoor pool. Game rm. Refrigerators; minibars, wet bars in suites. Balconies. On River. Cr cds: A, C, D, MC, V.

D 🆗 🐾 SC

Restaurants

✔★ **C.C. COHEN.** *103 Market House Sq (42001).* 502/442-6391. E-mail alan_raidt@prodigy.com. Hrs: 11 am-9 pm; Fri, Sat to 10 pm. Closed Sun; closed some major hols. Res accepted. Bar. Semi-a la carte: lunch $3.50-$6.50, dinner $9.50-$20. Child's meals. Specializes in beef, seafood, steaks. Entertainment Fri, Sat. In Cohen Bldg (ca 1870); early decorative metalwork. Many antiques. Cr cds: A, DS, MC, V.

D 🖻 ♥

★ **JEREMIAH'S.** *225 Broadway.* 502/443-3991. Hrs: 4-9:30 pm; Fri, Sat to 10:30 pm. Closed Sun; Dec 25. Res accepted. Bar to 2 am. Semi-a la carte: dinner $11.99-$20.99. Specializes in charcoal-grilled steak, frog legs. Own brewery. Former bank (1800s); rustic decor. Cr cds: A, D, DS, MC, V.

🖻

✔★ **NINTH STREET HOUSE.** *323 N 9th St.* 502/442-9019. Hrs: 11 am-2 pm; Fri, Sat also 5-10 pm. Closed Sun, Mon; most major hols. Res accepted. Bar. Semi-a la carte: lunch $3.50-$7.95, dinner $8.95-$18. Specializes in Southern cuisine, 3-5 course dinners. Own baking. Historic house (1886); restored. Antiques. Cr cds: D, MC, V.

★ ★ **THE PINES.** *900 N 32nd St.* 502/442-9304. Hrs: 11:30 am-2 pm, 5-10 pm; Sat from 5 pm. Closed Sun; major hols. Continental menu. Bar. Semi-a la carte: lunch $4.50-$12, dinner $11-$25. Child's meals. Specializes in steak, seafood. Salad bar. Own ice cream. Parking. Cr cds: A, C, D, DS, MC, V.

D 🖻

★ ★ **WHALER'S CATCH.** *123 N 2nd St (42001).* 502/444-7701. Hrs: 11 am-2 pm, 5-9 pm; Fri to 10 pm; Sat 5-10 pm. Closed Sun; major hols. Res accepted. Bar. Semi-a la carte: lunch $4.99-$6.99, dinner $11.95-$32.95. Child's meals. Specializes in Southern-style seafood. Outdoor dining. New Orleans atmosphere. Cr cds: A, MC, V.

Paris (C-7)

(See also Georgetown, Lexington)

Founded 1789 **Pop** 8,730 **Elev** 845 ft **Area code** 606 **Zip** 40361
Information Paris-Bourbon County Chamber of Commerce, 525 High St, #114; 606/987-3205.

Both Paris and Bourbon County were named in appreciation of France's aid to the colonies during the Revolution. While the French dynasty is long gone, the whiskey made in this county is a lasting tribute to the royal name. In early days, the limited herds of livestock could not consume all the corn produced, and the surplus grain was used to make corn liquor. Corn liquor made in Paris in 1790 had such respected qualities that soon all Kentucky corn whiskey came to be called bourbon. Fine tobacco and Thoroughbred horse farms are also important to the economy of this town in the Bluegrass region.

What to See and Do

Duncan Tavern Historic Shrine. Includes Duncan Tavern (1788) and adjoining Anne Duncan House (1800). Daniel Boone and many leading figures of the day were entertained in this tavern. The Anne Duncan House was built flush to the wall of the tavern by the innkeeper's widow, who ran the tavern for many years after his death. Both the tavern, which is made of local limestone, and the old clapboard house of log construction have been restored and furnished with period pieces. (Tues-Sat; closed hols) 323 High St. Phone 1593. Both houses ¢

Old Cane Ridge Meeting House (1791). Birthplace of the Christian Church (Disciples of Christ). Original log meetinghouse has been restored within an outer building of stone. In the early 1800s, revival meetings outside Old Cane Ridge attracted 20,000 to 30,000 persons at a time. Tours (by appt). 8 mi E on KY 537. Phone 606/987-5350. **Free.**

Annual Events

Central Kentucky Steam and Gas Engine Show. Bourbon County Park. Old operating farm machinery; steam traction engines; old gasoline tractors; threshing grain; flea market; country music. July.

Bourbon County Fair. Carnival; farm and craft exhibits. Late July.

Motel

★ **HOWARD JOHNSON.** *2011 Alverson Dr.* 606/987-0779; FAX 606/987-0779. Web www.hojo.com. 49 rms, 2 story. S $47-$55; D $52-$60; each addl $5; under 18 free. Crib avail. TV; cable. Pool. Complimentary continental bkfst. Coffee in rms. Restaurant opp 6 am-10 pm. Ck-out noon. Meeting rm. Business servs avail. Cr cds: A, C, D, DS, JCB, MC, V.

D 🏊 🆗 🐾 SC

Inns

★ ★ **AMELIA'S FIELD.** *617 Cynthiana Rd.* 606/987-5778; FAX 606/987-9075. 4 rms, 2 story. S, D $75-$100. Closed Jan-mid-Feb. TV in common rm. Complimentary full bkfst. Restaurant Thurs-Sun noon-2 pm, 6-9:30 pm. Ck-out 12:30 pm, ck-in 3 pm. Luggage handling. Lawn games. Built in 1936, colonial revival. Cr cds: A, D, MC, V.

D 🐾

★ ★ **ROSEDALE.** *1917 Cypress St.* 606/987-1845; res: 800/644-1862. Web www.cre8iv.com/rosedale.html. 4 rms, 2 share baths, 2 story. S $65; D $65-$90; each addl $15; family, wkly rates. Children over 12 yrs only. TV in common rm; TV, VCR avail (movies). Complimentary full bkfst. Restaurant nearby. Ck-out noon, ck-in 3 pm. Luggage handling. Gift shop. Guest lndry. Lawn games. Built in 1862, previously home of Civil War general. Cr cds: MC, V.

Park City (E-5)

(See also Bowling Green)

Pop 549 **Elev** 650 ft **Area code** 502 **Zip** 42160

What to See and Do

Kentucky Diamond Caverns. Guided tours of projecting peaks, rock palaces and some of the world's largest stalactites and stalagmites. Constant 54°F, smooth walks, handrails. 1 mi NW on KY 255. For schedule phone 502/749-2891. ¢¢¢

Mammoth Cave National Park (see). 2 mi N on KY 70.

Resort

★ ★ **PARK MAMMOTH.** *I 65 and US 31W, 1½ mi S just off US 31W; 1½ mi SE of I-65 Park City exit 48.* 502/749-4101; FAX 502/749-2524. 92 rms, 2 story. June-Oct: S $45; D $58; each addl $5; under 18 free; golf plan; lower rates rest of yr. Crib free. TV; cable, VCR avail (movies). Indoor pool; wading pool. Sauna. Playground. Dining rm 7-10 am, 11:30 am-1 pm, 5-8:30 pm. Ck-out noon. Meeting rms. Business servs avail. Gift shop. Lighted tennis. 36-hole golf, greens fee $10. Miniature golf. Lawn games. Rec rm. Miniature train ride. On 2,000 acres. Cr cds: A, C, D, DS, MC, V.

🏊 🎿 🏌 ⛷ 🏊 🛶 🎾 SC

Pikeville (D-9)

(See also Prestonsburg)

Founded 1824 **Pop** 6,324 **Elev** 685 ft **Area code** 606 **Zip** 41501 **E-mail** pikechamb@kymtnnet.org **Web** www.kymtnnet.org/PikeB.html

Information Pike County Chamber of Commerce, 225 College St, Suite 2; 606/432-5504.

Location of the notorious Hatfield-McCoy feud, Pikeville sits astride the Levisa Fork of the Big Sandy River and is the seat of Pike County, a leading producer of deep-mined coal. The town was named for Zebulon M. Pike, the explorer.

What to See and Do

Breaks Interstate Park (see). S on US 460.

Fishtrap Lake. Created by US Army Corps of Engineers dam on Levisa Fork of Big Sandy River, the lake offers fishing; boating (marina). Picnicking, playground, ballfields. Camping. (Daily) 15 mi SE via US 460 on KY 1789. Phone 606/437-7496. **Free.**

Grapevine Recreation Area. Boating. Picnicking, playground. Camping (May-Sept; fee). In Phyllis, S via KY 194. Phone 606/437-7496.

Annual Event

Hillbilly Days Spring Festival. Antique car show, music, arts & crafts. 3rd wkend Apr.

Motor Hotel

★ ★ **LANDMARK INN.** *146 S Mayo Trail.* 606/432-2545; res: 800/831-1469. 103 rms, 4 story. S $55; D $65; each addl $10; under 12 free. Crib free. Pet accepted, some restrictions. TV; cable (premium), VCR avail (movies). Pool. Rooftop restaurant 6 am-10 pm; Sun to 3 pm. Rm serv. Bar; entertainment. Ck-out noon. Coin lndry. Sundries. Meeting rms. Valet serv. Some balconies. Cr cds: A, C, D, DS, MC, V.

D 🏌 🏊 🛶 🎾 SC

Pineville (E-8)

(See also Barbourville)

Settled 1799 **Pop** 2,198 **Elev** 1,015 ft **Area code** 606 **Zip** 40977

In 1797 the Kentucky legislature authorized funds for the construction of a tollhouse on the Wilderness Road at a gap called the Narrows. Pineville grew around the tollhouse, which was abandoned in 1830.

What to See and Do

Bell Theatre (1939). Restored Art-Deco movie house. 114 W Kentucky Ave. For schedule phone 606/337-1319. ¢

Pine Mountain State Resort Park. Approx 1,500-acre park, surrounded by 12,000-acre Kentucky Ridge State Forest, has nature center, supervised recreation and the Laurel Cove Amphitheater. Swimming pool (seasonal). Nine-hole and miniature golf, shuffleboard. Picnicking, playgrounds, cottages, lodge (see RESORT). Camping (Apr-Oct, standard fees), central service building. (See ANNUAL EVENT) 1 mi S on US 25E. Phone 606/337-3066 or 800/325-1712.

Annual Event

Mountain Laurel Festival. Pine Mountain State Resort Park. College women from entire state compete for Festival Queen title. Parade, art exhibits, contests, sporting events, concerts. Memorial Day wkend.

Resort

★ ★ **EVANS LODGE.** *1050 Pine Mt State Park Rd, 1 mi S on US 25E.* 606/337-3066; FAX 606/337-7250; res: 800/325-1712. 30 rms, 2 story, 19 1-2 bedrm kit. cottages. Memorial Day-Labor Day: S $59; D $69; each addl $5.46; kit. cottages $85-$99; under 16 free; lower lodge rates rest of yr. Crib free. TV; cable. Pool; lifeguard. Supervised child's activities (June-Aug). Meeting rm. Business servs avail. Dining rm 7 am-9 pm; Sun 7-10:30 am, noon-3 pm, 5-9 pm. Ck-out noon, cottages 11 am, ck-in 4 pm. 9-hole golf, greens fee $11, carts $10, miniature golf. Lawn games. Rec rm. Balconies, patios. Picnic tables. State-owned; all park facilities avail. Cr cds: A, C, D, DS, MC, V.

D 🏌 🏊 🛶 🎾 SC

Prestonsburg (D-9)

(See also Pikeville)

Settled 1791 **Pop** 3,558 **Elev** 642 ft **Area code** 606 **Zip** 41653

Information Floyd County Chamber of Commerce, 245 North Lake Dr; 606/886-0364.

Prestonsburg, located between the Big Sandy River and forested hills, is surrounded by coal, oil and natural gas fields. In 1862, Colonel James A. Garfield achieved a decisive Union victory nearby; the first major triumph for the Union cause in the Civil War. This victory elevated Garfield to the rank of general and started him on the road to the presidency.

What to See and Do

Jenny Wiley State Resort Park. Mountainous terrain spanning more than 1,600 acres. Swimming pool (seasonal); fishing in 1,150-acre Dewey Lake; boating (rentals, ramp, dock). Nine-hole golf (seasonal, fee), shuffleboard. Picnicking, playground, cottages, lodge (see RESORT). Tent & trailer sites (Apr-Oct, standard fees). Skylift (Memorial Day-Labor Day, daily; rest of yr, wkends only, weather permitting; fee); amphitheater (see SEASONAL EVENT); recreational programs. 2 mi S on US 23, then 3 mi N on KY 3. Phone 606/886-2711 or 800/325-0142 (reservations).

Mountain Arts Center. Performance theater seats 1,060. Home of the Kentucky Opry; variety of entertainment scheduled yr-round. One Hal Rogers Dr. For schedule and tickets phone 606/886-2623. ¢¢¢-¢¢¢¢¢

Annual Event

Kentucky Apple Festival. In Paintsville, 11 mi N via US 23/460. Parade, amusement rides, antique car show, arts & crafts, flea market, 5K run, postage cancellation, square dancing, music and entertainment. Phone 606/789-4355. 1st Sat Oct.

Seasonal Event

Jenny Wiley Theatre. Jenny Wiley State Resort Park (see). Broadway musicals. For schedule contact General Mgr, PO Box 22; 606/886-9274. Mid-June-late Aug.

Motel

✔★ **DAYS INN.** *(512 South Mayo Trail, Paintsville 41240) 12 mi N on US 23/460.* 606/789-3551; FAX 606/789-9299. 72 rms, 2 story. S $45-$70; D $55-$70; each addl $5; under 12 free; higher rates Apple Festival. Crib free. Pet accepted. TV; cable (premium). Pool. Complimentary continental bkfst. Restaurant opp 6 am-9:30 pm. Ck-out 11 am. Business servs avail. Exercise equipt. Cr cds: A, C, D, DS, MC, V.

D ✉ ≈ ✗ ⋈ 🔥 SC

Motor Hotels

★★ **CARRIAGE HOUSE.** *(624 2nd St, Paintsville 41240) Off US 23.* 606/789-4242; FAX 606/789-6788; res: 800/951-4242. E-mail chhotel@itiseasy.com; web www.carriagehousehotel.com. 129 rms, 3 story. S $52; D $60; each addl $3; suites $120-$130; under 12 free. Crib free. TV; cable. Indoor/outdoor pool; whirlpool, poolside serv. Restaurant 6 am-9 pm; Sun to 3 pm. Rm serv. Ck-out 11 am. Coin lndry. Meeting rms. Business servs avail. Gift shop. Exercise equipt. Balconies. Cr cds: A, C, D, DS, MC, V.

D ≈ ✗ ⋈ 🏊

★★ **HOLIDAY INN.** *575 US 23S.* 606/886-0001; FAX 606/886-9850. 117 rms, 3 story. S, D $66; each addl $6; under 19 free. Crib free. Pet accepted, some restrictions. TV; cable. Heated pool; whirlpool, poolside serv. Restaurant 6 am-10 pm. Rm serv from 7 am. Bar; entertainment Thurs, Fri. Ck-out noon. Coin lndry. Meeting rms. Business servs avail. In-rm modem link. Exercise equipt. Refrigerators avail. Cr cds: A, C, D, DS, JCB, MC, V.

D ✉ ≈ ✗ ⋈ 🔥 SC

Resort

★★ **MAY LODGE.** *39 Jenny Wiley Rd, 2 mi S on US 23, then 1½ mi N on KY 3, in Jenny Wiley State Resort Park.* 606/886-2711; res: 800/325-0142. 49 rms, 2 story, 18 kit. cottages (1-2 bedrm). Memorial Day-Labor Day: S $65; D $67; each addl $5; kit. cottages $85-$95; under 16 free; rates vary rest of yr. Crib free. TV; cable (premium). 2 pools; wading pool. Playground. Supervised child's activities (Memorial Day-Labor Day). Dining rm 7 am-9 pm. Ck-out noon, cottages 11 am, ck-in 4 pm. Meeting rms. Business servs avail. Gift shop. Social dir. 9-hole golf, greens fee $10. Lawn games. Private patios, balconies. Picnic tables, grills, hiking trails. On lake. State-owned; all park facilities avail. Cr cds: A, C, D, DS, MC, V.

D ✉ ✗ ≈ ⋈ 🔥 SC

Richmond (D-7)

(See also Berea, Lexington, Winchester)

Founded 1798 **Pop** 21,155 **Elev** 975 ft **Area code** 606 **Zip** 40475 **Web** www.richmond-ky.com
Information Tourism & Visitor Center, 345 Lancaster Ave; 606/626-8474 or 800/866-3705.

Scene of a major Civil War battle—the first Confederate victory in Kentucky—Richmond is an industrial and agricultural center and the home of Eastern Kentucky University (1906).

What to See and Do

Courthouse (1849). Greek-revival courthouse in downtown historic district was used as a hospital by Union and Confederate forces during Civil War. Courthouse Square, Main St between N 1st & N 2nd Sts. In lobby is

Squire Boone Rock. One of the Wilderness Road markers.

Hummel Planetarium and Space Theater. One of the largest and most sophisticated planetariums in the US; state of the art projection and audio systems; large-format film system. Public programs (Thurs-Sun). Kit Carson Dr, on Eastern Kentucky Univ campus. Phone 606/622-1547. ¢¢

White Hall State Historic House. Restored 44-room house of Cassius M. Clay (1810-1903), emancipationist, diplomat and publisher of *The True American,* an antislavery newspaper. The 1799 Georgian house incorporates an Italianate addition from 1860s. Period furnishings, some original; personal mementos. Picnicking. (Apr-Labor Day, daily; after Labor Day-Oct, Wed-Sun) 9 mi N; I-75 exit 95. Phone 606/623-9178. ¢¢

Annual Event

Madison County Fair & Horse Show. Last wk July.

Motels

★ **BEST WESTERN ROAD STAR INN.** *1751 Lexington Rd, near I-75 exit 90/90A.* 606/623-9121; res: 800/575-5339; FAX 606/623-3160. 95 rms, 2 story. S, D $59; under 17 free. Crib free. Pet accepted. TV; cable (premium). Heated pool. Continental bkfst. Coffee in rms. Restaurant nearby. Ck-out noon. Meeting rm. Business servs avail. In-rm modem link. Some refrigerators. Cr cds: A, C, D, DS, MC, V.

D ✉ ≈ ⋈ 🔥 SC

✔★ **DAYS INN.** *2109 Belmont Dr, I-75 exit 90B.* 606/624-5769; FAX 606/624-1406. 70 rms, 2 story. S $42; D $47; each addl $5; under 18 free. Pet accepted, some restrictions; $5. TV; cable (premium). Pool. Restaurant adj open 24 hrs. Ck-out 11 am. Meeting rm. Business servs avail. Cr cds: A, C, D, DS, JCB, MC, V.

D ✉ ≈ ⋈ 🔥 SC

★★ **HOLIDAY INN.** *100 Eastern Bypass (KY 876), I-75 exit 87.* 606/623-9220; FAX 606/624-1458. 141 rms, 2 story. S, D $59; each addl $5; under 19 free. Crib free. TV; cable. Pool. Coffee in rms. Restaurant 6:30-10:30 am, 5-9 pm. Ck-out 11 am. Meeting rms. Business servs avail. In-rm modem link. Bellhops. Some refrigerators. Picnic tables. Near Eastern Kentucky Univ. Cr cds: A, C, D, DS, JCB, MC, V.

D ≈ ⋈ 🔥 SC

★ **SUPER 8.** *107 N Keeneland, I-75, exit 90B.* 606/624-1550; FAX 606/624-1553. 63 rms, 2 story. S $39.88; D $49.88; each addl $5; under 18 free; weekly rates; higher rates college events, races. Crib free. Pet accepted; $5. TV; cable (premium). Complimentary continental bkfst. Restaurant adj open 24 hrs. Ck-out 11 am. Cr cds: A, C, D, DS, MC, V.

D ✉ ⋈ 🔥 SC

Rough River Dam State Resort Park (D-5)

(On KY 79 at NE end of Rough River Lake)

This 637-acre park is at the northeast end of 4,860-acre Rough River Lake, on KY 79. Beach with bathhouse, pool (seasonal); fishing; boat dock (ramps, rentals). Hiking; fitness trail; 9-hole golf, pro shop, driving range, miniature golf; tennis, shuffleboard. Picnicking, playgrounds, lodge (see RESORT), dining room, cottages. Tent & trailer camping (Apr-Oct, standard fees); central service building. Planned recreation. For fees and information phone 502/257-2311.

Resort

★ ★ **ROUGH RIVER LODGE.** *(450 Lodge Road, Falls of Rough 40119)* off KY 79 in park. 502/257-2311; FAX 502/257-8682; res: 800/325-1713. Web www.kystateparks.com. 40 rms, 2 story, 17 kit. cottages. Memorial Day-Labor Day: S $59; D $69; each addl $5; kit. cottages $97-$110; under 16 free; lower rates rest of yr. Closed Christmas wk. Crib free. TV; cable. Pool; lifeguard. Playground. Dining rm 7-10:30 am, 11:30 am-4 pm, 5-9 pm; Sun noon-9 pm; winter to 8 pm. Ck-out noon, cottages 11 am, ck-in 4 pm. Coin lndry. Meeting rms. Business servs avail. Lighted tennis. 9-hole golf, greens fee $9, driving range. Miniature golf. Airstrip. Private patios, balconies. Picnic tables, grills (cottages). State-owned property; all facilities of park avail. On lake; marina & boat rental. Cr cds: A, C, D, DS, MC, V.

D ➤ 👫 👫 ≈ ✈ ✈ 🔥 SC

Shepherdsville (C-6)

(See also Elizabethtown, Fort Knox, Louisville)

Pop 4,805 **Elev** 449 ft **Area code** 502 **Zip** 40165

Shepherdsville is the seat of Bulitt County, which was named for Thomas Bullitt, who established Bullitt's Lick in 1773. Salt was produced from this site of prehistoric animal licks. A state information center is located here.

What to See and Do

Bernheim Arboretum and Research Forest. This 2,000-acre arboretum offers a nature center with trails, a nature museum (daily), waterfowl lakes and a 12,000-acre research forest. The 200-acre landscape arboretum features 1,800 species of plants. (Daily; closed Jan 1, Dec 25) 6 mi S on I-65, exit 112, then 1 mi E on KY 245. Phone 502/543-2451. Mon-Fri (free); Sat, Sun & hols per vehicle ¢¢

Motel

★ ★ **BEST WESTERN-SOUTH.** *211 S Lakeview Dr, I-65 exit 117.* 502/543-7097; FAX 502/543-2407. 85 rms, 2 story. S $53; D $58; each addl $4; suites $66-$70; under 12 free; higher rates Kentucky Derby. Crib free. TV; cable (premium). Pool; wading pool. Restaurant 6:30 am-2 pm, 5-10 pm; Sun 6:30 am-2 pm, 5-9 pm. Rm serv. Bar 4 pm-midnight; entertainment Thurs-Sat. Ck-out noon. Meeting rm. Business servs avail. Cr cds: A, C, D, DS, MC, V.

D ≈ 🔀 🐾 SC

Somerset (E-7)

(See also Jamestown, London)

Founded 1801 **Pop** 10,733 **Elev** 975 ft **Area code** 606 **Zip** 42501
Information Somerset/Pulaski Convention & Visitors Bureau, 522 Ogden St; 606/679-6394 or 800/642-6287.

Centrally located, Somerset is only four miles from Lake Cumberland. Many of the state's most popular attractions are within an hour's drive. A Ranger District office of the Daniel Boone National Forest (see) is located in Somerset.

What to See and Do

Beaver Creek Wilderness. On 4,791 acres below the cliff lines of the Beaver Creek Drainage within the Daniel Boone National Forest (see). Vertical sandstone cliffs, rockhouses; streams, waterfalls; flowering trees, shrubs and plants; variety of game and wildlife. Trail, compass hiking; backpacking; scenic overlooks. (Daily) 15 mi S on US 27. Phone 606/679-2010. **Free.**

General Burnside State Park. On General Burnside Island in Lake Cumberland. Swimming pool; fishing; boating (ramps). 18-hole golf. Picnicking, playground. Tent & trailer sites (Apr-Oct, standard fees). Recreation program (June-Labor Day). 10 mi S on US 27. Phone 606/561-4104 or -4192.

Lake Cumberland. Man-made lake with 1,255 miles of shoreline has five recreation areas with campsites (mid-Apr-Oct). Swimming; fishing; commercial docks; houseboats, boats, motors for rent. Picnicking. 10 mi S. Phone 606/679-6337.

Motels

★ ★ **DAYS INN SOMERSET.** *125 N US 27.* 606/678-2052; FAX 606/678-8477. 53 rms, 2-3 story. No elvtr. S, D $64; under 12 free. Crib free. TV; cable (premium). Indoor pool; whirlpool. Complimentary continental bkfst. Restaurant nearby. Ck-out 11 am. Business servs avail. In-rm modem link. Coin lndry. Cr cds: A, C, D, DS, MC, V.

D ≈ 🔀 🐾 SC

★ ★ **LANDMARK INN.** *1201 S US 27, 1 mi S of KY 80.* 606/678-8115. 157 rms, 2 story. S $48, D $54; each addl $6; suites $75; under 12 free. Crib free. TV; cable (premium). Pool. Playground. Restaurant 11 am-10 pm. Ck-out 11 am. Coin lndry. Business servs avail. In-rm modem link. Free local airport transportation. Cr cds: A, C, D, DS, JCB, MC, V.

D ≈ 🔀 🐾 SC

✔★ **SOMERSET LODGE.** *725 S US 27.* 606/678-4195; FAX 606/679-3299. 100 rms, 1-2 story. S $42; D $50; each addl $5; under 12 free. Pet accepted; $85. TV; cable (premium). Pool; wading pool. Playground. Restaurant 6 am-9 pm. Rm serv. Ck-out noon. Meeting rms. Business servs avail. Lawn games. Cr cds: A, C, D, DS, MC, V.

D ➤ ≈ ✈ 🔥 SC

South Union (E-5)

(See also Bowling Green)

Founded 1807 **Elev** 608 ft **Area code** 502 **Zip** 42283
Information Logan County Chamber of Commerce, 116 S Main St, Russellville 42276; 502/726-2206.

The Shakers, officially the United Society of Believers in Christ's Second Appearing, settled this town as a religious community. Craftsmen and farmers of great skill and ingenuity, the Shakers were widely known both for the quality of their products and for their religious observances. When "moved by the spirit" they performed a dance that gave them the name Shakers. Celibacy was part of the religious observance. By 1922 the community had dwindled to only nine members. The property was sold at auction, and the remaining members dispersed. Nearby are many historic buildings, including the Red River Meeting House in Adairville; the Bibb House and the Old Southern Bank in Russellville, robbed by the James Gang in 1868.

What to See and Do

Shaker Museum. Located in original 1824 building, museum houses Shaker crafts, furniture, textiles and tools. (Mar-mid-Dec, daily; rest of yr, by appt; closed Thanksgiving) On US 68. Phone 502/542-4167. ¢¢

Annual Events

Shaker Festival. Tour of historic buildings; Shaker foods, music; craft demonstrations. June.

Tobacco Festival. 12 mi SW on US 68 in Russellville. Parade; reenactment of the Jesse James bank robbery; house tours in historic district; tobacco displays; antiques; arts & crafts exhibits; bicycle rides; run (5 mi); fun run (1 mi); entertainment. One wk mid-Oct.

Inn

★ **SHAKER TAVERN.** KY 73. 502/542-6801. 6 rms, 5 share bath, 2 story. No rm phones. S, D $65-$75; wkly rates. TV in common rm. Complimentary full bkfst. Ck-out 9 am, ck-in 5 pm. Built 1869. Totally nonsmoking. Cr cds: MC, V.

Walton (B-7)

(See also Covington (Cincinnati Airport Area))

Pop 2,034 **Elev** 930 ft **Area code** 606 **Zip** 41094

What to See and Do

Big Bone Lick State Park. On 525 acres. Museum and diorama explain prehistoric mammal life preserved in the soft sulphur spring earth around the salt lick (daily; closed Jan); displays of Ice Age formations. Swimming pool (seasonal, campers only). Tennis (free). Picnicking. Camping (standard fees). Supervised recreation (summer). 7 mi W on KY 338. Phone 606/384-3522. Museum ¢

Motels

✔★ **DAYS INN RICHWOOD.** 11177 Frontage Rd, Jct I-75, KY 338 exit 175. 606/485-4151. 137 rms, 2 story. S, D $39-$55; each addl $7. Crib free. Pet accepted. TV; cable. Pool. Playground. Restaurant adj open 24 hrs. Ck-out 11 am. Sundries. Cr cds: A, C, D, DS, MC, V.

★ **ECONO LODGE.** 11165 Frontage Rd, jct I-75, KY 338 exit 175. 606/485-4123; FAX 606/485-9322. 60 rms, 2 story. S $38-$65; D $44-$95; each addl $5; under 18 free; higher rates special events. Crib free. TV; cable (premium). Pool. Playground. Complimentary continental bkfst. Restaurant open 24 hrs. Ck-out 11 am. Business servs avail. Cr cds: A, C, D, DS, MC, V.

Wickliffe (E-2)

(See also Paducah)

Pop 851 **Elev** 330 ft **Area code** 502 **Zip** 42087

On high ground, Wickliffe is near the confluence of the Ohio and the Mississippi rivers. The Lewis and Clark Expedition's Fort Jefferson (1789) was at a nearby site, now marked, one mile south on US 51.

What to See and Do

Wickliffe Mounds. Remnants of a Mississippian culture of 1,000 yrs ago. Museum exhibits, pottery, ongoing excavations. (Mar-Nov, daily; closed Thanksgiving) On US 51/60/62 in NW area of city. Phone 502/335-3681. ¢¢

Williamsburg (E-8)

(See also Corbin)

Founded 1817 **Pop** 5,493 **Elev** 951 ft **Area code** 606 **Zip** 40769
Information Tourist & Convention Commission, PO Box 2; 606/549-0530.

Shadowed by ridges that rise nearly 2,000 feet, Williamsburg is the seat of Whitley County. Both town and county are named in honor of William Whitley, pioneer.

What to See and Do

Cumberland River, which runs through Williamsburg and then 18 mi N to Cumberland Falls State Resort Park (see), offers one of the most remote and rustic float trips in the US.

Daniel Boone National Forest (see). N via US 75, E via Daniel Boone Pkwy.

Motels

✔★ ★ **BEST WESTERN CONVENIENT MOTOR LODGE.** 1½ blks W of I-75 exit 11. 606/549-1500; FAX 606/549-8312. 86 rms, 2 story. S $36; D $45; each addl $4; under 12 free. Crib free. TV; cable (premium). Pool. Continental bkfst. Restaurant opp open 24 hrs. Ck-out 11 am. Business servs avail. Cr cds: A, C, D, DS, MC, V.

★ ★ **HOLIDAY INN EXPRESS.** 30 KY 92W, I-75 exit 11. 606/549-3450; FAX 606/549-8161. 100 rms, 2-3 story. No elvtr. S, D $65; under 18 free. Crib free. Pet accepted. TV; cable (premium). Pool. Complimentary continental bkfst. Rm serv. Ck-out noon. Meeting rms. Business servs avail. In-rm modem link. Cr cds: A, C, D, DS, JCB, MC, V.

Williamstown (C-7)

(See also Covington (Cincinnati Airport Area))

Settled 1820 **Pop** 3,023 **Elev** 974 ft **Area code** 606 **Zip** 41097
Information Grant County Chamber of Commerce, 149 N Main St, PO Box 365; 606/824-3322.

What to See and Do

Kincaid Lake State Park. An 850-acre park with 183-acre lake stocked with bass, bluegill, crappie, channel catfish. Swimming pool (seasonal;

fee); fishing; boating (dock, rentals, max 16-ft and 10-HP motor). Hiking; miniature golf. Camping (Apr-Oct). Amphitheater; planned recreation. 17 mi NE via KY 22, then 3 mi N off US 27. Phone 606/654-3531.

Lloyd Wildlife Management Area. A 1,200-acre area with archery and shooting ranges (shooting allowed only during sponsored events). Five-acre lake with fishing for catfish, bass and bluegill. Hunting. Forty acres of virgin timberland includes monument to founder Curtis Lloyd; hiking trails. (Daily) 10 mi N via US 25, E at Gardnersville Rd (KY 491) exit. Phone 606/428-3193. **Free.**

Motel

 DAYS INN. *211 W KY 36, 1-75 exit 154. 606/824-5025; FAX 606/824-5028.* 50 rms, 1-2 story. S $36-$40; D $45-$51; each addl $5; under 12 free. Crib free. Pet accepted, some restrictions. TV; cable. Pool. Coffee in lobby. Restaurant adj. Ck-out 11 am. Cr cds: A, C, D, DS, MC, V.

Restaurant

★ **COUNTRY GRILL.** *(21 Taft Hwy, Dry Ridge 41035) 2 mi N on 1-75, exit 159. 606/824-6000.* Hrs: 9 am-10 pm; Fri-Sun from 8 am. Closed some major hols. Res accepted. Semi-a la carte: bkfst $2.85-$7.75, lunch $4.50-$6.95, dinner $6.50-$13.95. Child's meals. Specializes in chicken, pasta, homemade soup. Cr cds: A, DS, MC, V.

Winchester (C-7)

(See also Lexington)

Pop 15,799 **Elev** 972 ft **Area code** 606 **Zip** 40391
Information Winchester-Clark County Tourism Commission, 2 S Maple; 606/744-0556.

Winchester is the location of several industrial plants. Nearby coal and gas fields and fertile farmland also contribute to the economy. Henry Clay made his first and last Kentucky speeches in the town. The Forest Supervisor's office of the Daniel Boone National Forest (see) is located in Winchester.

What to See and Do

Fort Boonesborough State Park. Site of settlement where Daniel Boone defended his fort against Native American sieges. The fort houses craft shops where costumed "pioneers" produce wares; a museum with Boone memorabilia and other historical items; and an audiovisual program (Apr-Labor Day, daily; after Labor Day-Oct, Wed-Sun). Exhibits in cabins and blockhouses recreate life at the fort. Sand beach, swimming pool, bathhouse; fishing; boating (ramp, dock). Miniature golf. Picnicking, playground; snack bar. Tent & trailer sites (standard fees). Rec dir; special events all yr. 9 mi SW via KY 627, located on the Kentucky River. Phone 606/527-3131. Museum ¢¢

Historic Main Street. Street has a number of restored buildings, most of the Victorian era, and unique shops (daily exc Sun). Walking tour avail.

Natural Bridge State Resort Park (see). 35 mi E via KY 15, 77 in Slade.

Old Stone Church. Built in the late 1700s, this famous landmark in the Boonesboro section of Clark County is the oldest active church west of the Allegheny Mountains. Daniel Boone and his family worshiped here. 6 mi S off KY 627.

Annual Event

Daniel Boone Pioneer Festival. College & Lykins Parks. Juried arts & crafts, antiques, street dance, 5K run, 2-mi walk, bicycle race, concerts, music, food, fireworks. Phone 606/744-0556. Labor Day wknd.

Motels

★★ **HAMPTON INN.** *1025 Early Dr. 606/745-2000; FAX 606/745-2001.* 60 rms, 2 story. S $56-$66; D $59-$69; under 18 free; higher rates special events. Crib avail. TV; cable (premium). Pool. Complimentary continental bkfst. Coffee in rms. Restaurant adj 6 am-10 pm. Ck-out 11 am. Coin lndry. Meeting rooms. Business servs avail. Valet serv. Sundries. Exercise equipt. Cr cds: A, C, D, DS, MC, V.

★★ **HOLIDAY INN.** *1100 Interstate Dr, I-64 E, exit 96. 606/744-9111; FAX 606/745-1369.* 64 rms, 2 story. S, D $59; under 19 free; higher rates special events. Crib free. Pet accepted. TV; cable (premium). Pool. Complimentary coffee in rms. Restaurant 6:30 am-1 pm, 6-8:30 pm; Sat 7-10:30 am; Sun 7 am-2 pm. Rm serv. Ck-out 11 am. Coin lndry. Meeting rms. Business servs avail. Some refrigerators. Cr cds: A, C, D, DS, MC, V.

Restaurant

★ **HALL'S ON THE RIVER.** *(1225 Athens-Boonesborough Rd, Boonesborough) 8 mi S on KY 627, adj to Boonesborough State Park. 606/527-6620.* Hrs: 11:30 am-10 pm; Fri, Sat to 11 pm; Sun noon-8 pm. Closed Thanksgiving, Dec 25. Bar. Semi-a la carte: lunch $2.95-$6.50, dinner $9.95-$14.95. Child's meals. Specializes in seafood, steak. Outdoor dining. Overlooks Howard's Creek. Family-owned. Cr cds: A, MC, V.

Mississippi

Population: 2,573,216
Land area: 47,234 square miles
Elevation: 0-806 feet
Highest point: Woodall Mt (Tishomingo County)
Entered Union: December 10, 1817 (20th state)
Capital: Jackson
Motto: By valor and arms
Nickname: Magnolia State
State flower: Magnolia
State bird: Mockingbird
State tree: Magnolia
State fair: Early October 1999, in Jackson
Time zone: Central
Web: www.mississippi.org

Bearded Spaniards in rusted armor followed De Soto across Mississippi in search of gold 80 years before the *Mayflower* landed in Massachusetts. De Soto died in the fruitless search. Pierre Le Moyne, Sieur d'Iberville, established Mississippi's first permanent settlement near Biloxi in 1699. There was no gold to be found, but the mighty Mississippi River had created something of infinitely greater value; an immense valley of rich, productive land—land on which cotton could be grown. It was cotton that established the great plantations, but while cotton still ranks first in agricultural production, the state also produces forestry, poultry, soybeans and catfish. However, manufacturing is the number one industry in the state.

Andrew Jackson became a hero in Mississippi after he defeated the Creek Indian nation and was again honored during a triumphal return through the state after winning the Battle of New Orleans in 1815. Mississippians enthusiastically named their capital after "Old Hickory" and they entertained him royally when he returned as an elder statesman in 1840.

For two years northern Mississippi was the scene of some of the fiercest fighting in the Civil War. Following the Union defeat of Confederate forces at the Battle of Shiloh (Tennessee) in April 1862, General Ulysses S. Grant moved southwest into Mississippi. The following year, Grant besieged Vicksburg for 47 days. When the city finally fell, the fate of the Confederacy, according to some historians, was sealed. Yet battles still seesawed across and up and down the beleaguered state as railroads and telegraph lines were sliced by Northern raiders. Mississippi was left in shambles. It was after General William Tecumseh Sherman burned Jackson that he said, "War is Hell!" For Mississippi the war was indeed hell, and the Reconstruction period was nearly as chaotic.

Today Mississippi's subtropical Gulf Coast provides vast quantities of shrimp and oysters; it is also a tremendously popular resort and vacation area. Fishing is good in many streams, and hunting for waterfowl along the Mississippi River and for deer in other areas is also excellent. The state has beautiful forests, the antebellum traditions and pageantry of Natchez, the beautiful Natchez Trace Parkway and many other attractions.

When to Go/Climate

Mild winters and hot summers are the norm in Mississippi. Rain is common, but snow is unusual. Hurricane season runs from June through October along the Gulf Coast.

AVERAGE HIGH/LOW TEMPERATURES (°F)

JACKSON

Jan 56/33	**May** 84/60	**Sept** 88/64
Feb 60/36	**June** 91/67	**Oct** 79/50
Mar 69/44	**July** 92/71	**Nov** 69/42
Apr 77/52	**Aug** 92/70	**Dec** 60/36

TUPELO

Jan 49/31	**May** 81/60	**Sept** 85/63
Feb 55/34	**June** 88/67	**Oct** 75/50
Mar 64/43	**July** 91/71	**Nov** 64/42
Apr 74/51	**Aug** 90/69	**Dec** 53/34

Parks and Recreation Finder

Directions to and information about the parks and recreation areas below are given under their respective town/city sections. Please refer to those sections for details.

NATIONAL PARK AND RECREATION AREAS

Key to abbreviations: I.H.S. = International Historic Site; I.P.M. = International Peace Memorial; N.B. = National Battlefield; N.B.P. = National Battlefield Park; N.B.C. = National Battlefield & Cemetery; N.C. = National Conservation Area; N.E.M. = National Expansion Memorial; N.F. = National Forest; N.G. = National Grassland; N.H. = National Historical Park; N.H.C. = National Heritage Corridor; N.H.S. = National Historic Site; N.L.

CALENDAR HIGHLIGHTS

MARCH

Spring Pilgrimage (Vicksburg). Twelve antebellum houses are open to the public at this time. Three tours daily. Contact Convention and Visitors Bureau; phone 601/636-9421 or 800/221-3536.

National Cutting Horse Association Show (Jackson). Entries from across the US participate in amateur to professional rider competitions. Phone 817/244-6933.

MAY

Blessing of the Fleet (Biloxi). Hundreds of vessels manned by descendants of settlers participate in this ritual of European origin.

Siege Re-enactment (Vicksburg). 500 persons reenact the siege of Vicksburg. Contact Convention and Visitors Bureau; phone 601/636-9421 or 800/221-3536.

JUNE

Delta Jubilee (Clarksdale). Statewide arts & crafts festival; Mississippi championship pork barbecue cooking contest; 5K run; antique car show. Contact Convention and Visitors Bureau; phone 601/627-7337 or 800/626-3764.

JULY

Mississippi Deep-Sea Fishing Rodeo (Gulfport). Fisherman from US, Canada and Latin America compete in various types of sportfishing. Phone 228/388-2271 or 228/863-2713.

SEPTEMBER

Delta Blues and Heritage Festival (Greenville). Showcase of Blues greats. Phone 601/335-3523.

OCTOBER

Mississippi State Fair (Jackson). Agricultural and industrial exhibits and contests; entertainment. Phone 601/961-4000.

Great Mississippi River Balloon Race Weekend (Natchez). Food, music, entertainment. Contact Convention and Visitors Bureau; phone 601/446-6345 or 800/647-6724.

Mississippi-Alabama State Fair (Meridian). Mississippi-Alabama Fairgrounds. Agricultural exhibits, carnival. Phone 601/693-5465.

= National Lakeshore; N.M. = National Monument; N.M.P. = National Military Park; N.Mem. = National Memorial; N.P. = National Park; N.Pres. = National Preserve; N.R. = National Recreational Area; N.R.R. = National Recreational River; N.Riv. = National River; N.S. = National Seashore; N.S.R. = National Scenic Riverway; N.S.T. = National Scenic Trail; N.Sc. = National Scientific Reserve; N.V.M. = National Volcanic Monument.

Place Name	Listed Under
Bienville N.F.	MENDENHALL
Brices Cross Roads N.B.C.	TUPELO
Delta N.F.	YAZOO CITY
De Soto N.F.	HATTIESBURG
Gulf Islands N.S.	same
Holly Springs N.F.	HOLLY SPRINGS
Homochitto N.F.	NATCHEZ
Natchez Trace Parkway	same
Tombigbee N.F.	LOUISVILLE
Tupelo N.B.	TUPELO
Vicksburg N.M.P. & Cemetery	VICKSBURG

STATE PARK AND RECREATION AREAS

Key to abbreviations: I.P. = Interstate Park; S.A.P. = State Archaeological Park; S.B. = State Beach; S.C. = State Conservation Area; S.C.P. = State Conservation Park; S.Cp. = State Campground; S.F. = State Forest; S.G. = State Garden; S.H.A. = State Historic Area; S.H.P. = State Historic Park; S.H.S. = State Historic Site; S.M.P. = State Marine Park; S.N.A. = State Natural Area; S.P. = State Park; S.P.C. = State Public Campground; S.R. = State Reserve; S.R.A. = State Recreation Area; S.Res. = State Reservoir; S.Res.P. = State Resort Park; S.R.P = State Rustic Park.

Place Name	Listed Under
Buccaneer S.P.	PASS CHRISTIAN
Clarkco S.P.	MERIDIAN
George Payne Cossar and John W. Kyle S.P.	SARDIS
Golden Memorial S.P.	PHILADELPHIA
Great River Road S.P.	CLEVELAND
Holmes County S.P.	KOSCIUSKO
Hugh White S.P.	GRENADA
Lake Lowndes S.P.	COLUMBUS
Legion S.P.	LOUISVILLE
Leroy Percy S.P.	GREENVILLE
Natchez S.P.	NATCHEZ
Paul B. Johnson S.P.	HATTIESBURG
Percy Quin S.P.	MCCOMB
Tombigbee and Trace S.P.	TUPELO
Wall Doxey S.P.	HOLLY SPRINGS

Water-related activities, hiking, various other sports, picnicking and visitor centers, as well as camping, are available in many of these areas. State parks provide fishing (free); boating, rentals ($6/day); launching ($5); swimming ($2; children $1); picnicking; tent & trailer facilities ($11-$14/night; 14-day max); primitive tent camping ($6-$8) and cabins ($30-$70/night; 14-day max). Pets on leash only; not allowed in cabin or on property. Scattered throughout the state are 89 roadside parks with picnic facilities. For further information contact Information Services and Marketing, Dept of Wildlife, Fisheries and Parks, PO Box 451, Jackson 39205-0451; 800/467-2757.

FISHING & HUNTING

Anglers find limitless possibilities in Mississippi. There are no closed seasons, and size limits are imposed on game fish in only some areas (except sea-run striped bass and black bass on a few state waters). The Chickasawhay, Pearl, Homochitto and Pascagoula rivers are endless sources for largemouth bass, crappie, bluegill, bream and catfish, as are six large reservoirs and more than 170,000 acres of lakes. There are fishing camps at many lakes and reservoirs and on the Gulf Coast, where boats, bait and tackle are available. Complete charter services for deep-sea fishing and fishing piers are featured along US 90 as well as at Gulf Coast resorts. Nonresident fishing license, 16 yrs & over: annual, $25; 3-day, $6.

Hunting on some one million acres of the more than 30 state-managed public hunting areas is seasonal: quail, late Nov-late Feb; wild turkey (gobblers only), late Feb-late Apr; squirrel, mid-Oct-mid-Jan; deer, usually Oct-Jan; duck, reservoir areas and major river lowlands, usually Dec-Jan; dove, Sept-Oct and winter. Public waterfowl management areas are located on some reservoirs and river lowlands. Licenses for nonresidents: all game (annual $225, 5-day $105); small game (annual $75, 5-day $30); archery and primitive firearms (must also purchase annual all-game permit) $30; waterfowl, state waterfowl stamp required $5. For detailed information contact the Dept of Wildlife Fisheries and Parks, PO Box 451, Jackson 39205-0451; 601/362-9212.

Driving Information

Safety belts are mandatory for front seat passengers. Children under 4 years must be in an approved safety seat anywhere in vehicle. In addition, safety belts are mandatory for all persons anywhere in vehicle when traveling on the Natchez Trace Parkway. For further information phone 601/987-1336.

INTERSTATE HIGHWAY SYSTEM

The following alphabetical listing of Mississippi towns in *Mobil Travel Guide* shows that these cities are within 10 miles of the indicated Interstate highways. A highway map should, however, be checked for the nearest exit.

Highway Number	Cities/Towns within 10 miles
Interstate 10:	Biloxi, Gulfport, Ocean Springs, Pascagoula, Pass Christian.
Interstate 20:	Jackson, Meridian, Vicksburg.
Interstate 55:	Grenada, Jackson, McComb, Sardis.
Interstate 59:	Hattiesburg, Laurel, Meridian.

Additional Visitor Information

Information booklets are available from the Division of Tourism, PO Box 1705, Ocean Springs 39566; 800/WARMEST.

There are 11 welcome centers in Mississippi; visitors who stop by will receive information, brochures and personal assistance in planning stops at points of interest. Their locations are as follows: at the northern end of the state, on I-55 south of Hernando; along the southern border, on I-55 south of Chatawa, on I-59 north of Nicholson, on I-10 at Waveland and on I-10 at Pascagoula; by the eastern border, on I-20 east of Toomsuba; in the western section, on US 82 & Reed Rd in Greenville, on I-20 near Vicksburg, on US 61 Bypass & Seargent S. Prentiss Dr north of Natchez and on I-78 west of border. Centers are open 8 am-5 pm, daily. For information on road conditions phone the Mississippi Highway Patrol, 601/987-1212.

Biloxi (J-5)

(See also Gulfport, Ocean Springs, Pascagoula, Pass Christian)

Settled 1699 **Pop** 46,319 **Elev** 25 ft **Area code** 228 **E-mail** visitor@biloxi.ms.us **Web** biloxi.ms.us
Information Visitors Center, 710 Beach Blvd, 39530; 228/374-3105 or 800/BILOXI-3.

The oldest town in the Mississippi Valley, Biloxi has been a popular resort since the 1840s. It has, since the 1870s, been a leading oyster and shrimp fishing headquarters; shrimp were first canned here in 1883.

The Sieur d'Iberville's first French fort was established at Ocean Springs, just east of Biloxi. In 1721 the third shipment of "Cassette girls" (so called after the boxes or "cassettes" in which they carried their possessions) landed at Ship Island, 12 miles south in the Gulf of Mexico. These 89 girls, carefully selected by a French bishop, were sent to become wives to the settlers. The area continues to reflect a strong ethnic heritage representing the eight flags that have flown over Biloxi during the past 300 years.

Magnolia trees, camellias, azaleas, roses and crepe myrtle bloom along Biloxi's streets among the oaks draped with Spanish moss. There is freshwater, saltwater and deep-sea fishing all year; crabbing, floundering and mullet net casting. Biloxi is the home of Keesler AFB, the electronics and computer training center of the US Air Force. In recent years, casinos have become a popular attraction in Biloxi and many have been built along the Gulf of Mexico beach.

What to See and Do

★ **"Beauvoir"—Jefferson Davis Home and Presidential Library.** Estate where the Confederate president spent the last 12 yrs of his life. From 1903-1957, "Beauvoir" also served as the Mississippi soldiers' home for Confederate veterans and their widows. Adjoining museums have Davis and Confederate artifacts. The Library Pavilion, where Davis wrote *The Rise and Fall of the Confederate Government* and *A Short History of the Confederate States of America*, contains his desk and books. Landscaped grounds covering 57 acres contain house, museums, 2 pavilions, Confederate cemetery with Tomb of the Unknown Soldier of the Confederate States of America and Presidential Library. (Daily; closed Dec 25) 2244 Beach Blvd (US 90). Phone 228/388-1313. ¢¢¢

Gulf Coast Research Lab/J.L. Scott Marine Education Center & Aquarium. Facility features more than 40 aquariums showcasing native fish and other creatures. Also here is a 42,000-gallon Gulf of Mexico tank, featuring sharks, sea turtles and eels; seashell collection and hands-on exhibits for children. (Daily exc Sun; closed hols) 1535 Beach Blvd. Phone 228/374-5550. ¢¢

Gulf Islands National Seashore (see).

Harrison County Sand Beach. This 300-ft-wide white sand beach stretches the entire 26-mi length of the county; a seawall separates the beach from the highway.

Old Biloxi Cemetery. Burial ground of French pioneer families of Biloxi and the Gulf Coast. John Cuevas, hero of Cat Island (War of 1812), is buried here. Carter Ave between Father Ryan Ave & Cemetery St.

Small Craft Harbor. View fishing boats unloading day's catch of Gulf game fish. Deep-sea fishing charter boats. Jct Main St, US 90.

Tullis-Toledano Manor (1856). Historic antebellum mansion; oak-shaded grounds; period furniture. (Mon-Fri; closed hols). 360 Beach Blvd. Phone 228/435-6293. ¢

Annual Events

Mardi Gras. Carnival and parade. Shrove Tuesday. Feb.

Garden Club Pilgrimage. Guided tour of historic houses, sites and gardens. Mar or Apr.

Blessing of the Fleet. Gulf of Mexico. Hundreds of vessels manned by descendants of settlers participate in this ritual of European origin. 1st wkend May.

Seafood Festival. Point Cadet Plaza, E on US 90. Arts & crafts show, entertainment, seafood booths, contests. Last wkend Sept.

Motels

★ **BREAKERS INN.** *2506 Beach Blvd (US 90) (39531).* 228/388-6320; res: 800/624-5031. Web www.gcww.com/breakers. 28 kit. suites, 1-2 story. May-Sept: S, D $121-$171; higher rates: Memorial Day wkend, July 4, Labor Day; lower rates rest of yr. Pet accepted. TV; cable. Pool; wading pool. Playground. Restaurant nearby. Ck-out 11 am. Lndry facilities in rms. Business servs avail. In-rm modem link. Tennis. Lawn games. Opp gulf. Cr cds: A, C, D, DS, MC, V.

⬚ ⬚ ⬚ ⬚ ⬚ SC

★★ **COMFORT INN.** *1648 Beach Blvd (39531), on US 90.* 228/432-1993; FAX 228/432-2297. Web comfortinnbiloxi@digiscape.com. 68 rms, 2 story. June-Aug: S, D $65-$145; each addl $8-$12; kits. $70-$150; under 18 free; higher rates hols (3-day min); lower rates rest of yr. Crib free. TV; cable (premium). Pool; whirlpool. Complimentary continental bkfst. Restaurant nearby. Ck-out 11 am. Balconies. Beach opp. Cr cds: A, D, DS, MC, V.

D ⬚ ⬚ ⬚ SC

⬚★★ **DAYS INN.** *2046 Beach Blvd (US 90) (39531).* 228/385-1155; FAX 228/385-2532. 166 rms, 3 story, 83 kit. Suites. S, D $64-$139; each addl $5; kit. suites $89-$159; under 18 free; golf plans. Crib free. TV; cable (premium). Pool. Complimentary continental bkfst. Ck-out noon. Coin lndry. Business servs avail. Tennis. Balconies. Opp beach and gulf. Cr cds: A, D, DS, MC, V.

D ⬚ ⬚ ⬚ ⬚ SC

★★ **EDGEWATER INN.** *1936 Beach Blvd (US 90) (39531).* 228/388-1100; FAX 228/385-2406; res: 800/323-9676. E-mail edge inn@aol.com; web www.gcww.com/edgewaterinn/. 65 rms, 3 story. Mar-Sept: S, D $69-$159; each addl $6; suites $129-$199; under 13 free; wkly rates; package plans; higher rates hols; lower rates rest of yr. Crib $6. TV; cable. Indoor/outdoor pool. Restaurant open 24 hrs. Ck-out noon. Exercise equipt; sauna. Refrigerators. On Gulf; opp beach. Cr cds: A, C, D, DS, MC, V.

D ⬚ ⬚ ⬚ ⬚ SC

✓★ ★ **QUALITY INN-EMERALD BEACH.** *1865 Beach Blvd (US 90) (39531).* 228/388-3212; FAX 228/388-6541. 62 rms, 2 story. Apr-early Sept: S, D $60-$80; each addl $10; lower rates rest of yr. Crib $10. TV; cable (premium). Heated pool; poolside serv. Restaurant 7 am-2 pm, 5-9 pm. Rm serv. Bar from 5 pm. Ck-out noon. Meeting rms. Business servs avail. In-rm modem link. Bellhops. Sundries. On Gulf; private sand beach. Cr cds: A, C, D, DS, ER, MC, V.

D ✓ ≈ ⋈ 🏂 SC

Motor Hotel

★ ★ **HOLIDAY INN.** *2400 Beach Blvd (39531).* 228/388-3551; FAX 228/385-2032. 268 rms, 4 story. S $59-$64; D $93-$98; each addl $10; golf plan; higher rates hols (3-day min). Crib avail. TV; cable. Pool; poolside serv. Playground. Restaurant. Rm serv. Bar 4:30 pm-midnight; entertainment. Coin lndry. Meeting rms. Business servs avail. In-rm modem link. Bellhops. Valet serv. Free airport transportation. Game rm. Refrigerators avail. Balconies. Opp ocean. Cr cds: A, C, D, DS, ER, JCB, MC, V.

D ≈ 🏂 SC

Hotels

★ ★ **GRAND CASINO.** *265 Beach Blvd (39530).* 228/432-2500; FAX 228/435-8901; res: 800/946-2946. 491 rms, 12 story. S $59-$129; D $69-$139; each addl $10; suites $160-$220; under 16 free; wkday rates. Crib free. TV; cable. Pool; whirlpool, lifeguard. Supervised child's activities; ages 6 wks-12 yrs. Complimentary coffee in lobby. Restaurant 7 am-10 pm. Bar. Ck-out 11 am. Convention facilities. Business servs avail. Concierge. Shopping arcade. Beauty shop. Free airport transportation. Exercise equipt; sauna. Game rm. Rec rm. Refrigerator in suites. Balconies. On ocean. Cr cds: A, C, D, DS, ER, JCB, MC, V.

D ≈ ✈ ⋈ 🏂 ≋

Restaurants

★ **CUCO'S.** *1851 Beach Rd (39531).* 228/388-1982. Hrs: 11 am-11 pm; Fri, Sat to midnight; Sun to 10 pm. Closed Thanksgiving, Dec 25. Res accepted. Mexican menu. Bar. Semi-a la carte: lunch $4.50-$6, dinner $5.95-$9.95. Specializes in chimichangas, fajitas, fried ice cream. Mexican artwork on walls. Cr cds: A, C, D, DS, MC, V.

D ⊸

★ ★ **THE FRENCH CONNECTION.** *1891 Pass Christian Rd (39531).* 228/388-6367. Hrs: 5:30-9:30 pm; Fri, Sat to 10 pm. Closed Sun, Mon; most major hols. French, continental menu. Bar. Semi-a la carte: dinner $13.95-$28.95. Child's meals. Specialties: Tar Babies, smoked oysters, shrimp Robert. Own baking. Parking. Outdoor dining. Open-hearth cooking. Antiques. On grounds that were once part of Beauvoir, estate of Jefferson Davis. Cr cds: A, C, D, DS, MC, V.

⊸

★ **HOOK, LINE & SINKER.** *2030 Beach Blvd (US 90).* 228/388-3757. Hrs: 11 am-10 pm; Fri, Sat to 11 pm. Closed Mon; also 1 wk in Dec. Bar. Semi-a la carte: lunch $5-$20, dinner $10-$22. Child's meals. Specializes in seafood. Oyster bar. Parking. Nautical decor; view of gulf. Family-owned. Cr cds: A, C, D, DS, MC, V.

D ⊸

★ ★ **MARY MAHONEY'S OLD FRENCH HOUSE.** *Rue Magnolia & US 90.* 228/374-0163. Hrs: 11 am-10 pm. Closed Sun; Dec 24, 25. Continental menu. Bar. Wine cellar. Semi-a la carte: lunch $7.95-$10.95, dinner $14.95-$28.95. Complete meals: lunch $7.95-$10.95. Child's meals. Specialties: half lobster Georgo, stuffed red snapper, seafood gumbo. Own bread pudding. Parking. Outdoor dining. Colonial house & slave quarters built 1737; antiques, fireplaces. Family-owned. Cr cds: A, C, D, DS, MC, V.

D ⊸

✓★ ★ **O'CHARLEY'S.** *2590 Beach Blvd (US 90), at Edgewater Mall.* 228/388-7883. Hrs: 11 am-midnight; Fri to 1 am, Sat 9-1 am; Sun 9 am-10 pm; Sat brunch to 1 pm; Sun brunch to 3 pm. Bar. Semi-a la carte: lunch $3.99-$9.99, dinner $7.99-$16.95. Sat, Sun brunch $3.99-$12.99. Child's meals. Specializes in beef, seafood. Outdoor dining with view of gulf. Cr cds: A, C, D, DS, MC, V.

D SC

Brices Cross Roads National Battlefield Site
(see Tupelo)

Clarksdale (B-3)

(See also Cleveland)

Founded 1869 **Pop** 19,717 **Elev** 175 ft **Area code** 601 **Zip** 38614 **Web** www.clarksdale.com/tourism
Information Coahoma County Tourism Commission, 1540 Desoto, PO Box 160; 601/627-7337 or 800/626-3764.

Named for John Clark, an Englishman who laid out the town in 1869, Clarksdale shared dual status with Friars Point as Coahoma County seat from 1892 until 1930. Sunflower Landing near Clarksdale is said to be the site where De Soto discovered the Mississippi River.

Clarksdale is located in the heart of the rich delta farmland, one of the state's top-ranking areas in cotton, soybean and grain production. Three lakes in the area make this a water sports center.

What to See and Do

Carnegie Public Library. (Daily exc Sun; closed major hols) 114 Delta Ave. Phone 601/624-4461. Located within the library are

Delta Blues Museum. Videotapes, recordings and memorabilia about blues music. Permanent and changing exhibits; performances. **Free.**

Archaeology Museum. Native American pottery and other artifacts on exhibit. Collection of books and reports on Lower Mississippi Valley archaeology. **Free.**

North Delta Museum. Archaeological and historical exhibits of early Delta life, including Native American artifacts, three original log buildings and Civil War artifacts. (Tues-Fri, Sat afternoons) Friars Point-Clarksdale Rd, 12 mi NW in Friars Point. Phone 601/383-2233. ¢

Annual Event

Delta Jubilee. Statewide arts & crafts festival; Mississippi championship pork barbecue cooking contest; 5K run; antique car show. First wkend June.

Motels

✓★ ★ **HAMPTON INN.** *710 S State St, ½ mi S on US 61.* 601/627-9292; FAX 601/627-9292, ext. 650. 93 rms, 2 story. S $56-$62; D $62-$68; each addl $6; under 18 free. Crib free. TV; cable. Indoor/outdoor pool; whirlpool. Complimentary continental bkfst. Restaurant 6 am-11 pm. Rm serv. Ck-out noon. Coin lndry. Meeting rms. Business servs avail. In-rm modem link. Exercise equipt; weights, bicycles. Some refrigerators. Some balconies. Cr cds: A, C, D, DS, JCB, MC, V.

D ≈ ✈ ⋈ 🏂 SC

✔★ ★ **LADY LUCK.** *(777 Lady Luck Pkwy, Lula 38644) approx 20 mi N on US 61, W on US 49.* 601/363-4600; FAX 601/363-2768; res: 800/789-5825. 172 rms, 2 story. S, D $39-$69; each addl $10; suites $49-$79; under 18 free; higher rates blues fest. Crib free. TV; cable (premium). Pool. Complimentary coffee in lobby. Restaurant 11 am-11 pm. Bar open 24 hrs; entertainment. Ck-out noon. Coin lndry. Meeting rms. Business center. Bellhops. Valet serv. Concierge. Sundries. Gift shop. Golf privileges. Exercise equipt. Game rm. Refrigerators. On river. Cr cds: A, DS, MC, V.

Cleveland (C-2)

(See also Clarksdale)

Pop 15,384 **Elev** 142 ft **Area code** 601 **Zip** 38732
Information Chamber of Commerce, Third St, PO Box 490; 601/843-2712 or 800/295-7473.

What to See and Do

Delta State University (1924). (4,200 students) MS 8. Phone 601/846-3000. On campus is

Wright Art Gallery. Exhibits works by southern artists.

Bologna Performing Arts Center. Performances in music, theatre and dance. MS 8W. For schedule phone 601/846-4626. ¢¢¢¢

Great River Road State Park. The 800-acre park is situated on the bluffs of the Mississippi River and has the state's largest campground inside the levee. Fishing in Perry Martin Lake; boating (ramp, rentals). Nature, bicycle trails. Picnicking (shelters), playground, playing field, snack bar, lodge, coin lndry. Improved & primitive camping. Four-level observation tower. Standard fees. 18 mi W on MS 8 in Rosedale. Phone 601/759-6762.

Motel

✔★ **CLEVELAND INN.** *US 61S, 1 mi S on US 61.* 601/846-1411; FAX 601/843-1713. 119 rms, 2 story. S $41-$50; D $46-$55; each addl $5; under 18 free. Crib free. TV; cable. Pool. Restaurant 6 am-2 pm, 6-9 pm; closed wkends. Rm serv. Bar 5-11 pm; closed wkends. Ck-out noon. Business servs avail. In-rm modem link. Cr cds: A, C, D, DS, MC, V.

Columbus (C-5)

(See also Starkville)

Settled 1817 **Pop** 23,799 **Elev** 200 ft **Area code** 601 **E-mail** ccvb@tilc.com **Web** www.friendship.columbus.ms.us
Information Columbus Convention & Visitors Bureau, PO Box 789, 39703; 601/329-1191 or 800/327-2686(exc MS).

On the Tennessee-Tombigbee Waterway (also on the Buttahatchie and Luxapalila), Columbus progressed from a trading post to an educational center and repository for traditions and architecture of the Old South.

Mentioned in the state's oldest records, Columbus' site early became a stopover on the Military Road ordered built by Andrew Jackson between New Orleans and Nashville (1817-1820). It was first called "Possum Town" because Native Americans thought that the tavernkeeper who served them looked like a wizened old possum. Columbus welcomed its first steamboat, the *Cotton Plant*, in 1822, a year after Mississippi's first public school, Franklin Academy, was established in the town.

Commerce and education went forward together. The Columbus Female Institute, founded in 1847, later became the first state-supported school in the US to offer education exclusively to women—Mississippi University for Women (1884). Columbus was a favored place for planters to build imposing houses, and in antebellum days it became the cultural center of the rich Black Prairie. During the Civil War a large Confederate arsenal was located in the town, and the state capital was moved here after Jackson fell. Columbus Air Force Base, an ATC training facility, is nine miles north.

What to See and Do

Blewett-Harrison-Lee Museum. Contains articles of local history as well as Civil War exhibits. (Fri; closed hols) 316 7th St N. Phone 601/327-8888. ¢¢

Friendship Cemetery. Where first Memorial Day, Apr 25, 1866, was said to have been observed, as women of Columbus gathered to decorate graves of Union and Confederate soldiers alike. 4th St S & 13th Ave.

Historic houses. Columbus boasts more than 100 antebellum houses. Some are open for tours (daily; fee). For information, free 30-min auto tour map and narrative of houses contact the Convention & Visitors Bureau. Tour fee per home ¢¢

Lake Lowndes State Park. One of the finest recreation complexes among all the state parks. Approx 600 acres with a 150-acre lake. Swimming beach, waterskiing; fishing; boating (ramps, rentals). Nature trail, tennis, game fields. Picnicking, playground, concession, indoor recreation complex, coin laundry. Improved & primitive camping, cabins. Standard fees. 6 mi SE off MS 69. Phone 601/328-2110 or 601/328-9182.

Waverley Plantation (1852). Mansion with twin, circular, self-supporting stairways leading to a 65-ft-high, octagonal observation cupola; original gold-leaf mirrors and Italian marble mantels. (Daily) 10 mi NW via US 45, MS 50 near West Point. Phone 601/494-1399. ¢¢¢

Annual Event

Pilgrimage. Costumed guides conduct tours through 15 historic houses. Special events. 1st 2 wks of Apr.

Motels

✔★ **COMFORT INN.** *1210 US 45N (39701).* 601/329-2422; FAX 601/327-0311. 64 rms, 2 story. S ,D $53-57; each addl $4; under 12 free. Crib free. TV; cable. Complimentary continental bkfst. Restaurant opp 11 am-9 pm. Ck-out 11 am. Meeting rms. Business servs avail. In-rm modem links. Cr cds: A, C, D, DS, MC, V.

★ ★ **HOLIDAY INN.** *506 US 45N (39701), 1/4 mi S off US 82 Bypass.* 601/328-5202; FAX 601/241-4979. 153 rms, 2 story. S, D $62-68; each addl $5. Crib free. TV; cable (premium). Pool. Restaurant 6 am-2 pm, 5:30-10 pm. Rm serv. Bar 4 pm-midnight. Ck-out noon. Meeting rms. Business servs avail. Valet serv. Cr cds: A, D, DS, MC, V.

Restaurant

✔★ **HARVEY'S.** *200 Main St.* 601/327-1639. Hrs: 11 am-9:30 pm; Fri, Sat to 10 pm. Closed Sun; some major hols. Res accepted. Bar 4:30-11 pm; Fri, Sat to midnight. Semi-a la carte: lunch $4.95-$9.95, dinner $6.95-$14.95. Child's meals. Specializes in beef, seafood, salads. Restored tannery; antiques. Cr cds: A, DS, MC, V.

Corinth (A-5)

Founded 1854 **Pop** 11,820 **Elev** 455 ft **Area code** 601 **Zip** 38834 **E-mail** tourism@tsixroads.com **Web** www.corinth.net

Information Corinth Area Tourism Promotion Council, 810 Tate St, PO Box 1089, 38835-1089; 601/287-5269.

The Memphis and Charleston and the Mobile and Ohio railroads selected this spot as a junction point, calling the town Cross City. Later the name was changed to honor the Greek city.

After being defeated at the Battle of Shiloh (April 6-7, 1862), Confederate General P.G.T. Beauregard retreated to Corinth. On October 3-4, 1862, Union forces, aiming at Vicksburg, took the town and held it until January 25, 1864. The only effort made to regain Corinth by the Confederates ended in defeat.

What to See and Do

Battery Robinett. Union fort constructed on inner defense lines during Battle of Corinth (1862). Monuments mark spots where Confederate heroes died; headstones commemorate color-bearers who fell while trying to plant flag during battle. W on Linden St. **Free.**

Curlee House (1857). Restored antebellum house; served as headquarters for Generals Bragg, Halleck and Hood during Civil War. (Daily; closed Dec 25) 705 Jackson St. Phone 601/287-9501. **¢¢**

Jacinto Courthouse (1854). Fine example of early federal architecture was first courthouse for old Tishomingo County; later used as both school and church. (Daily exc Mon) 15 mi SE in Jacinto. **Free.**

Motel

✔★★ **EXECUTIVE INN.** US 72, jct US 45 Bypass. 601/286-6071; res: 800/354-3932; FAX 601/286-9608. 70 rms, 2-3 story, 6 kits. S $42; D $47; each addl $5; kits $60; under 12 free. Crib free. TV; cable (premium). Pool. Restaurant 11 am-2 pm, 5-9 pm. Rm serv. Ck-out 11 am. Meeting rms. Cr cds: A, C, D, DS, MC, V.

⊠ ≋ ⊠ 🔥

Greenville (D-2)

Settled 1828 **Pop** 45,226 **Elev** 125 ft **Area code** 601

Information Greenville Area Chamber of Commerce, PO Box 933, 38702-0933, phone 601/378-3141 or the Washington County Convention & Visitors Bureau, 410 Washington Ave, 38702, phone 601/334-2711.

Greenville, which is not even on the Mississippi, is the state's largest river port. The Mississippi River was, in 1935, finally broken of its habit of stealing whole areas of the town, block by block. Levees forced the channel six miles westward and left a lake for a harbor. Before this, in 1927, the whole town was under water for 70 days. The first Greenville settlement was on the Blantonia Plantation (1828), which was purchased for the site of the third county seat. The first was flooded out; the second burned during shelling by Union gunboats in 1863.

What to See and Do

Birthplace of the Frog Exhibit. Muppet memorabilia from collectors and the family of the late Jim Henson, creator of the Muppets. (Memorial Day-Labor Day, daily; rest of yr, Mon-Fri) 8 mi E via US 82, in Leland. Phone 601/686-2687. **Donation.**

Leroy Percy State Park. The oldest of Mississippi's state parks is composed of approx 2,400 acres. One of the four hot artesian wells provides water for an alligator pond (view from boardwalk). Nature trails lead through Delta lowlands. Nearby is live alligator exhibit. Swimming pool (Memorial Day-Labor Day, daily); fishing, hunting; boating (rentals). Picnicking (shelters), playground, game field, snack bar, restaurant, lodge, coin lndry. Improved & primitive camping, cabins. Standard fees. 18 mi S on MS 1, then 6 mi E on MS 12. Phone 601/827-5436.

River Road Queen. Replica of 19th-century paddlewheel steamboat. Built for 1984 World's Fair; now serves as town's welcome center. (Daily) 7 mi E of bridge via us 82. Phone 601/332-2378.

Winterville Mounds State Park. One of the largest groups of Native American mounds in the Mississippi Valley, the area was a religious site and economic and military center for thousands of Native Americans of the Mississippian era, who disappeared sometime after De Soto's exploration. Great Temple mound, 55 ft high, is surrounded by 10 smaller mounds used for a variety of purposes. Picnicking (shelters), concession, playground. Museum houses artifacts from mound site and adjoining territory (Wed-Sat & Sun afternoons; closed Dec 25) 5 mi N off MS 1. Phone 601/334-4684. Museum **¢**

Annual Event

Delta Blues and Heritage Festival. Showcase of Blues greats. Phone 601/335-3523. 3rd wkend Sept.

Motels

★★ **HAMPTON INN.** 2701 US 82E (38701). 601/334-1818; FAX 601/332-1761. 120 units, 2 story. S, D $52-$58; each addl $7; studio rms $59-$66; under 12 free. Crib free. TV; cable. Pool. Complimentary continental bkfst. Ck-out noon. Meeting rm. Business center. In-rm modem link. Cr cds: A, D, DS, MC, V.

D ≋ ⊠ 🔥 SC 🏃

★★ **HOLIDAY INN EXPRESS.** 2428 US 82E (38701). 601/334-6900; FAX 601/332-5863. 119 rms, 2 story, 13 suites. S, D $47-$59; each addl $6; suites $67-$74; under 17 free. Crib $5. TV; cable. Heated indoor/outdoor pool; wading pool, whirlpool. Complimentary continental bkfst. Complimentary coffee in rms. Ck-out noon. Coin lndry. Meeting rms. Business servs avail. In-rm modem link. Exercise equipt. Health club privileges. Refrigerators. Cr cds: A, C, D, DS, JCB, MC, V.

D ≋ 🏃 ⊠ 🔥

★★ **RAMADA INN.** 2700 US 82E (38701). 601/332-4411; FAX 601/332-4411, ext. 171. 121 rms, 2 story. S $47-$50; D $52-$55; each addl $5. Crib free. TV; cable. Pool. Playground. Complimentary full bkfst (wkdays). Restaurant 6 am-10 pm. Rm serv. Bar 4 pm-2 am; closed Sun. Ck-out noon. Meeting rms. Business servs avail. In-rm modem link. Sundries. Airport transportation. Some refrigerators. Cr cds: A, C, D, DS, JCB, MC, V.

D ≋ ⊠ 🔥 SC

Restaurant

✔★ **SHERMAN'S.** 1400 S Main St (38701). 601/332-6924. Hrs: 11 am-2 pm, 5-10 pm. Closed Sun; major hols. Italian, Amer menu. Bar. Semi-a la carte: lunch $5-$8, dinner $11-$18. Child's meals. Specializes in steak, seafood. Informal atmosphere. Wildlife prints. Family-owned. Cr cds: A, D, DS, MC, V.

D

Greenwood (C-3)

(See also Grenada)

Settled 1834 **Pop** 18,906 **Elev** 140 ft **Area code** 601 **Zip** 38930 **E-mail** gcvb@netdoor.com **Web** www.netdoor.com/com/gcvb
Information Convention & Visitors Bureau, PO Drawer 739; 601/453-9198 or 800/748-9064.

Lying on both banks of the Yazoo River and surrounded by rich, black delta lands, Greenwood was a river port shipping cotton before the Civil War and a rail center after Reconstruction.

The town grew from a river landing established on 162 acres of land bought for $1.25 an acre by John Williams. Planters who used his landing to ship their cotton included Choctaw Chief Greenwood Leflore. After a quarrel about Williams' storage methods, the chief built his own landing with a warehouse three miles up the river, calling it Point Leflore. However, the original landing flourished and absorbed the trade of its rival. Today Greenwood is one of the nation's largest cotton markets.

What to See and Do

Cottonlandia Museum. Exhibits highlight the history of the Mississippi Delta, its people and its land from 10,000 B.C. to the present. Also Mississippi art exhibit; garden; gift shop. (Daily) 2 mi W on US 49E, US 82 Bypass W. Phone 601/453-0925. ¢¢

Florewood River Plantation. Re-creation of 1850s plantation and outbuildings; crops worked and harvested; cotton museum; steam engine displays; crafts demonstrations. Tours (Mar-Nov, daily exc Mon; limited tours rest of yr). 2 mi W on US 82. Phone 601/455-3821. ¢¢

Motels

✔★ **COMFORT INN.** *401 US 82W. 601/453-5974; FAX 601/455-6401.* 60 rms, 2 story. S $47-$49; D $49-$53; each addl $5; under 18 free; wkly rates. Crib $3. TV; cable. Pool. Complimentary continental bkfst. Restaurant opp 6 am-10 pm. Ck-out noon. Business servs avail. In-rm modem link. Park, picnic grounds opp. Cr cds: A, C, D, DS, JCB, MC, V.

D 🌊 🚫 🔥 SC

★★ **HAMPTON INN.** *635 US 82W. 601/455-5777; FAX 601/455-4239.* 100 rms, 2 story. S $50-$52; D $56-$58; under 18 free. Crib free. TV; cable. Indoor/outdoor pool; wading pool. Complimentary continental bkfst. Restaurant 6 am-11 pm. Rm serv. Ck-out noon. Coin lndry. Meeting rms. Business servs avail. In-rm modem link. Valet serv. Tennis. Exercise equipt. Refrigerators. Some balconies. Cr cds: A, C, D, DS, MC, V.

D 🏃 🌊 🍴 🚫 🔥 SC

Restaurant

★★ **CRYSTAL GRILL, INC.** *423 Carrollton Ave. 601/453-6530.* Hrs: 10:30 am-10 pm. Closed Mon; most major hols & Dec 24. Res accepted. Bar from 11 am. Semi-a la carte: lunch $4.55-$7.45, dinner $4.75-$18.50. Child's meals. Specializes in seafood, steak. Family-owned. Cr cds: A, DS, MC, V.

 D ♥

Grenada (C-4)

(See also Greenwood)

Pop 10,864 **Elev** 195 ft **Area code** 601 **Zip** 38901 **E-mail** gtourism@aol.com
Information Grenada Tourism Commission, 1321 Sunset Plaza, Ste JJ, PO Box 1824; 601/226-2571 or 800/373-2571.

The economy of Grenada had from early days been based on cotton. Today, it is diversified; industry and tourism, as well as agriculture, support this town located on the eastern edge of the Mississippi Delta. Founded as two towns by political rivals, the two communities united in 1836. The union was literally symbolized by a wedding in which the bride came from one town and the groom from the other. Confederate General John C. Pemberton headquartered in Grenada while opposing Grant's second Vicksburg campaign.

What to See and Do

Grenada Lake. Covers approx 35,000 acres, with 200 mi of shoreline. Swimming, water sports; fishing, hunting; boat launch. Fitness trails; archery, tennis, ball fields. Picnicking. Primitive & improved camping (fee at some sites). Visitor center at Grenada Dam on Scenic Loop 333. (Daily) 5 mi NE off MS 8. Phone 601/226-5911. **Free.** On lake is

Hugh White State Park. A 1,581-acre park with swimming beach, pool, waterskiing; fishing; boating (ramp, rentals). Nature, bicycle trails; tennis nearby. Picnicking (shelter), playground, lodge. Primitive & improved camping, cabins, camp store. Standard fees. 5 mi E on MS 8. Phone 601/226-4934.

Historic Old Grenada. Motor and walking tour of houses and churches. For brochure contact Chamber of Commerce.

Annual Event

Thunder on Water Festival. Grenada Lake. Parade, children's fishing rodeo, antique car show, boat light parade and several speed boat races. 2nd wkend June.

Motels

★★ **BEST WESTERN MOTOR INN.** *1750 Sunset Dr, I-55 exit 206. 601/226-7816; FAX 601/226-5623.* 61 rms, 2 story. S $42-$49; D $54-$66. Crib $5. Pet accepted, some restrictions. TV; cable. Pool. Complimentary full bkfst. Restaurant 6 am-10 pm. Rm serv. Ck-out noon. Meeting rms. Business servs avail. In-rm modem link. Lawn games. Cr cds: A, C, D, DS, MC, V.

🐾 🌊 🚫 🔥 SC

✔★ **COMFORT INN.** *1552 Sunset Dr. 601/226-1683; FAX 601/226-9484.* 66 rms, 2 story. S $52-$90; D $55-$90; each addl $5; under 18 free; lower rates rest of yr. Crib $5. TV; cable. Pool; whirlpool. Complimentary continental bkfst. Restaurant nearby. Ck-out noon. Business servs avail. Refrigerators. Cr cds: A, C, D, DS, ER, JCB, MC, V.

D 🌊 🚫 🔥 SC

✔★ **DAYS INN.** *1632 Sunset Dr. 601/226-8888; FAX 601/227-9592.* 53 rms, 2 story. S $45-$69; D $55-$79; each addl $7; under 18 free. Crib free. TV; cable. Pool; whirlpool. Restaurants nearby. Ck-out noon. Refrigerators, microwaves avail. Cr cds: A, C, D, DS, ER, JCB, MC, V.

D 🌊 🚫 🔥 SC

★★ **HOLIDAY INN.** *1796 Sunset Dr, MS 7/8, 1/8 mi E of I-55 exit 206. 601/226-2851; FAX 601/226-5058.* 130 rms, 2 story. S, D $50-$75; each addl $7; suites $165; under 18 free. Crib free. TV; cable (premium), VCR avail. Indoor pool; wading pool. Restaurant 6 am-2 pm, 5-10 pm. Rm serv. Bar. Ck-out noon. Coin lndry. Meeting rms. Business servs avail. In-rm modem link. Airport transportation. Cr cds: A, C, D, DS, JCB, MC, V.

D 🌊 🚫 🔥 SC

Gulf Islands National Seashore (J-5)

(See also Biloxi, Gulfport, Ocean Springs)

Information Park Office, 3500 Park Rd, Ocean Springs 39564; 601/875-0821.

Headquarters and campground for the Mississippi district of this beautiful area are in Ocean Springs. Sparkling beaches, coastal marshes and wildlife sanctuaries may be found on the four offshore islands (Petit Bois, Horn, East and West Ship) and the mainland area (Davis Bayou). The mainland areas are open year round and are accessible from US 90.

In 1969, Hurricane Camille split Ship Island in two, leaving East Ship and West Ship Islands. Ship Island was once a base for French exploration and settlement (1699-1753) of the Gulf Coast from Mobile, Alabama, to the mouth of the Mississippi River. What is now East Ship Island once served as the staging area for a 50-ship British armada and an unsuccessful attempt to capture New Orleans in 1815 at the end of the War of 1812.

On West Ship Island is Fort Massachusetts. Construction of this brick coastal defense began in 1859, prior to the outbreak of the Civil War. Two years later the Mississippi militia took control of the fort from the US Army Corps of Engineers after the state seceded from the Union. The Confederates later fortified it, naming it Fort Twiggs in honor of the New Orleans Confederate general. Repeated threats from Northern forces caused the Confederates to withdraw in September 1861. The fort was then reoccupied by Union soldiers, who called it Fort Massachusetts. For a time, the area east of the fort served as a prisoner-of-war camp, confining some 4,300 Confederate prisoners at one point. Completed in 1866, the fort was never fully armed. Free tours of the fort are offered daily (Mar-Nov). Concession boats run to Fort Massachusetts and West Ship Island from Gulfport (Mar-Oct), depending on weather conditions.

All four offshore islands are accessible year round by boat only and are open to wilderness camping (except on West Ship Island), surf fishing, surf swimming (Memorial Day-Labor Day), boating, picnicking and hiking. No motor vehicles or glass are allowed on the islands. Horn and Petit Bois are designated as wilderness areas, and special restrictions apply.

The mainland campground has water and electric hookups (fee) at 51 sites, a public boat dock and picnic areas. The visitor center offers audiovisual programs, exhibits, boardwalks and nature trails. Pets are allowed on leash only. **Free.**

Gulfport (J-5)

(See also Biloxi, Ocean Springs, Pass Christian)

Founded 1880 **Pop** 40,775 **Elev** 20 ft **Area code** 601
Information Chamber of Commerce, 1401 20th Ave, PO Drawer FF, 39502; 228/863-2933.

Although chosen as an ideal site for a port and a railroad terminus in 1887, it was 1902 before the Gulf & Ship Island Railroad's New York owner fulfilled the plan. As a planned city, Gulfport has broad streets laid out in a regular rectangular pattern paralleling the seawall. This was in marked contrast to the narrow-streeted antebellum towns along the rest of the coast. When completed, the railroad, which ran through sparsely settled sections rich in timber, transformed southern Mississippi.

Gulfport turned to the resort business in the 1920s and had a real estate boom in 1925 when the Illinois Central Railroad bought the Gulf & Ship Island line. The boom collapsed a year later after having produced Gulfport's tower apartments and many hotels. After World War II, luxury motels took over. With the Mississippi Sound and a great number of lakes, rivers, bays and bayous within a few minutes drive from downtown, and with excellent facilities for deep-sea fishing, Gulfport is a fisherman's paradise.

Mississippi City, which has been incorporated into Gulfport, was the scene of the bare-knuckles fight for the heavyweight championship of the world on February 7, 1882, when John L. Sullivan beat Paddy Ryan under the live oaks now at the corner of US 90 and Texas Street.

What to See and Do

Boat trips. Passenger ferry leaves from Gulfport Yacht Harbor for trips to Ship Island. (Mar-Oct) Schedule varies; for information contact Ship Island Excursions, PO Box 1467, 39502; 228/864-1014 (recording), or 228/864-3797 (office). Round trip ¢¢¢¢

Gulf Islands National Seashore (see).

⭐ **John C. Stennis Space Center.** Second-largest NASA field installation. Testing site of Saturn V, first and second stages for the Apollo manned lunar program, including those for Apollo 11, which landed first men on moon in 1969. Original test stands were later modified to develop and test space shuttle main engines. The Stennis Space Center hosts NASA and 18 federal and state agencies involved in oceanographic, environmental and national defense programs. Visitor Center with 90-ft Space Tower; films, demonstrations; indoor, outdoor exhibits; guided tours (daily; closed Easter, Thanksgiving, Dec 25). 38 mi W via I-10. Phone 228/688-2370. **Free.**

Port of Gulfport. Extends seaward from jct US 49, 90, located equidistant between New Orleans and Mobile, AL. One of the largest banana import facilities in the US; the projected depth of the channel is 32 ft; the depth of the harbor is 30 ft at mean low water with a tidal variation of approx two ft. The 1,320-ft wide harbor separates the port's two parallel piers; 11 berths are available.

Small Craft Harbor. Launching ramps, charter boats and pleasure craft docking. Jct US 49, 90. Adj is

Marine Life Oceanarium. Dolphin and sea lion feedings, giant reef tank, underwater divers, touch pool. Also Aqua Stadium with exotic birds and Captain Crooked's SS *Gravity*. (Daily; closed Dec 25) US 90 at US 49, in Jones Memorial Park. Phone 228/863-0651. ¢¢¢

Annual Events

Spring Pilgrimage. Tours of antebellum houses, gardens. Contact Biloxi Community Center for details; 228/432-5836. Late Mar-early Apr.

Mississippi Deep-Sea Fishing Rodeo. Small Craft Harbor. Fishermen from US, Canada and Latin America compete in various types of sportfishing. Phone 228/388-2271 or 228/863-2713. Early July.

Motor Hotels

✔⭐ ⭐ **BEST WESTERN BEACH VIEW INN.** *2922 W Beach Blvd (US 90) (39501).* 228/864-4650; FAX 228/863-6867. E-mail bchview@ aol.com. 150 rms, 5 story. Mid-Feb-Mar, mid-May-Labor Day: S, D $75-$95; each addl $6; suites $130-$150; under 16 free; higher rates wknds; lower rates rest of yr. Crib free. TV; cable. Pool. Bar 10-6 am. Ck-out noon. Meeting rms. Overlooks harbor. Cr cds: A, C, D, DS, MC, V.

≈ ⊠ ⊠ 🐾 SC

⭐ ⭐ **HOLIDAY INN-BEACHFRONT.** *1600 E Beach Blvd (39501).* 228/864-4310; FAX 228/865-0525. 229 rms, 2-5 story. May-Labor Day: S, D $73-$120; each addl $5; under 19 free; lower rates rest of yr. Crib free. TV; cable. Pool; wading pool, poolside serv. Restaurant 6 am-10 pm. Rm serv. Bar 4 pm-1 am. Ck-out noon. Coin lndry. Meeting rms. In-modem link. Bellhops. Game rm. Opp beach. Cr cds: A, C, D, DS, JCB, MC, V.

D ≈ ⊠ ⊠ 🐾 SC

Hotel

⭐ ⭐ **GRAND CASINO.** *3215 W Beach Blvd (39501).* 228/870-7200; FAX 228/870-7220; res: 800/354-2450. Web grandcasinos.com. 407 rms, 18 story. S, D $69-$139; each addl $20; suites $179-$279; under 18 free; wkend rates; higher rates major hols. Crib free. TV; cable (premium), VCR avail (movies). Indoor pool; wading pool, whirlpool, poolside serv. Supervised child's activities; ages 6 months-12. Complimentary coffee in lobby. Restaurant 6:30 am-11 pm. Bar. Ck-out 11 am. Convention facilities. Business servs avail. In-rm modem link. Concierge. Shopping arcade. Beauty shop. Free airport transportation. Exercise equipt; sauna. Game rm. Refrigerator in suites. On ocean. Cr cds: A, D, DS, MC, V.

Inn

✓★ **RED CREEK.** *(7416 Red Creek Rd, Long Beach 39560)* Approx 5 mi W on US 90, N on Menge Ave to Red Creek Rd. 228/452-3080; FAX 228/452-4450; res: 800/729-9670. E-mail karlmertz@aol.com; web members.aol.com./karlmertz. 5 rms, 3 story. No rm phones. S, D $49-$99. Complimentary continental bkfst. Complimentary coffee in rms. Ck-out, ck-in by arrangement. Business servs avail. Lawn games. French colonial house (1899) with 6 fireplaces, antique furnishings; 64-ft front porch. Situated on 11 acres of magnolia trees and ancient live oaks. Totally nonsmoking. No cr cds accepted.

Restaurants

★ ★ ★ **VRAZEL'S.** 3206 W Beach Blvd (US 90) (39501). 228/863-2229. E-mail wvrazel@aol.com; web www.gcww.com/vrazels/. Hrs: 11 am-2 pm, 5-10 pm; Sat from 5 pm. Closed Sun; some major hols. Res accepted. Continental menu. Wine list. A la carte entrees: lunch $5.95-$13.95, dinner $12.95-$18.95. Specializes in steak, fresh seafood, veal. Elegant dining rm with views of gardens, beach. Cr cds: A, C, D, DS, MC, V.

✓★ **WHITE CAP.** Gulfport Yacht Harbor (39501). 228/863-4652. Hrs: 11:30 am-9 pm; Fri, Sat to 10 pm; Sun from noon. Closed Tues; Jan 1, Thanksgiving; also last 2 wks Dec. Bar. Semi-a la carte: lunch $4.95-$5.95, dinner $10-$15. Child's meals. Specializes in seafood. Oyster bar. On pier. Nautical decor. Family-owned. Cr cds: DS, MC, V.

Hattiesburg (G-4)

Founded 1882 **Pop** 41,882 **Elev** 161 ft **Area code** 601 **E-mail** adp@hattiesburg-adp.org **Web** www.hattiesburg-adp.org

Information Area Development Partnership-Chamber Division, 1 Convention Center, PO Box 751, 39403; 800/238-4288.

Once known as Twin Forks and Gordonville, the settlement was renamed by an early settler in honor of his wife, Hattie. When railroads were routed through Hattiesburg during the late 19th century, the town began to thrive. Unlike other towns that came and went with the lumber boom of the 1920s, Hattiesburg was able to diversify its economic base with a number of industries. The University of Southern Mississippi makes the town the educational center of the southern sector of the state.

What to See and Do

De Soto National Forest. Approx 500,000 acres. Black Creek Float Trip offers 50 mi of scenic streams. Black Creek Trail has 41 mi of trails, 10 of which go through 5,000 acres of Black Creek Wilderness. Fees may be charged at designated recreation sites. Swimming; fishing. Hiking, bridle trails. Picnicking. Primitive camping. Ranger District offices are located in Laurel, Wiggins and McHenry. 10 mi SE on US 49. Contact Forest Supervisor, 100 W Capitol St, Suite 1141, Jackson 39269; 601/965-4391 or -5514.

Paul B. Johnson State Park. More than 805 acres of pine forest. A spring-fed lake provides excellent facilities for water sports. Swimming beach, waterskiing; fishing; boating (ramp, rentals). Nature trail. Picnicking

(shelters), playground, playing fields, snack bar, lodge with game rm, coin lndry. Improved & primitive camping, cabins. Visitor center. Standard fees. 15 mi S off US 49. Phone 601/582-7721.

University of Southern Mississippi (1910). (12,000 students) Library houses large collection of original illustrations and manuscripts for children's books by authors and artists from here and abroad. American Rose Society garden on campus, blooms spring-mid-Dec. Also Science & Technology Bldg, Performing Arts Center, Danforth Chapel, Polymer Research Center, art gallery, natatorium and golf course. 2700 Hardy St. For tours phone 601/266-4491.

Motels

✓★ **COMFORT INN.** 6595 US 49 (39401). 601/268-2170. 119 rms, 2 story. S, D $50-$64; each addl $6; suites $90-$100; under 18 free. Crib free. Pet accepted, some restrictions. TV; cable (premium). Pool. Complimentary full bkfst. Restaurant 6 am-9:30 pm. Rm serv. Bar 5 pm-midnight; entertainment Fri, Sat. Ck-out noon. Coin lndry. Meeting rms. Business servs avail. Valet serv. Golf privileges. Cr cds: A, C, D, DS, MC, V.

✓★ **HAMPTON INN.** 4301 Hardy St (39402). 601/264-8080; FAX 601/268-9916. 155 units, 2 story. S $55-$75; D $63-$75; under 18 free. Crib free. TV; cable. Pool. Complimentary continental bkfst. Ck-out noon. Meeting rm. Business servs avail. In-rm modem link. Health club privileges. Cr cds: A, C, D, DS, MC, V.

★ ★ **HOLIDAY INN.** 6563 US 49 (39401), off I-59 exit 67A. 601/268-2850; FAX 601/268-2823. E-mail hiuniv@netdoor.com. 128 rms, 2 story. S, D $62.99; each addl $6; under 18 free. Crib free. TV; cable. Pool; whirlpool. Restaurant 6:30 am-2 pm, 5-10 pm. Rm serv. Bar 4:30 pm-midnight; entertainment. Ck-out noon. Meeting rms. Business servs avail. Lighted tennis. Some refrigerators. Cr cds: A, C, D, DS, JCB, MC, V.

Restaurants

✓★ ★ **CHESTERFIELD'S.** 2507 Hardy St. 601/582-2778. Hrs: 11 am-11 pm; Sun to 10 pm. Closed Thanksgiving, Dec 25. Bar to midnight. Semi-a la carte: lunch, dinner $4.25-$14.95. Child's meals. Specializes in beef, steak, seafood. Cr cds: A, C, D, DS, MC, V.

★ ★ **CRESCENT CITY GRILL.** 3810 Hardy St (39402). 601/264-0656. Hrs: 11 am-10 pm; Fri, Sat to 11 pm. Closed Thanksgiving, Dec 25. French, creole menu. Bar to 2 am. Semi-a la carte: lunch $12-$20, dinner $12-$20. Child's meals. Specializes in steak, pasta, seafood. Local original art. Casual, elegant dining. Cr cds: A, DS, MC, V.

✓★ ★ **ROCKET CITY DINER.** 4700 Hardy St, at the Arbor in Turtle Creek Shopping Ctr. 601/264-7893. Hrs: 6 am-10 pm; Fri, Sat to 11 pm. Closed Dec 25. Beer. Semi-a la carte: bkfst, lunch, dinner $3.50-$10.95. Child's meals. Specializes in hamburgers, country-fried steak. 1950s atmosphere. Cr cds: A, DS, MC, V.

Holly Springs (A-4)

(See also Memphis, TN)

Founded 1835 **Pop** 7,261 **Elev** 609 ft **Area code** 601 **Zip** 38635
Information Chamber of Commerce, 154 S Memphis; 601/252-2943.

Holly Springs crowns the ridge along which a Native American trail once led from the Mississippi to the tribal home of the Chickasaw Nation. William Randolph, descendant of Virginia's famed John Randolph, is credited with founding the town.

Wealth from cotton went into buying more and more land, driving up real estate prices. Soon lawyers, who were needed to cope with squabbles over land and deeds, outnumbered all other professionals. The town skipped the frontier stage as Georgian and Greek-revival mansions rose instead of log cabins.

Holly Springs suffered 61 raids during the Civil War; the most devastating was by a Southern force led by Confederate General Van Dorn in 1862; the Confederates destroyed General Grant's supply base, delaying the fall of Vicksburg by a year.

What to See and Do

Holly Springs National Forest. Intensive erosion-control measures are carried out within this 152,200-acre area. Fishing, large and small game hunting; boating at Puskus, Chewalla and Tillatoba lakes. Picnicking. Primitive camping. Fees are charged at designated recreation sites. Contact Forest Supervisor, 100 W Capitol St, Suite 1141, Jackson 39269; 601/965-4391.

Kate Freeman Clark Art Gallery. Endowed by the artist to permanently house her works, the gallery contains more than 1,000 paintings done while Clark studied under William Merritt Chase in New York in the early 1900s. Clark returned to her native Holly Springs in 1923 and simply stored her work until her death 40 yrs later. Also here are three canvasses by Chase and one by Rockwell Kent. College Ave. For schedule inquire at Bank of Holly Springs, phone 601/252-2511 or First State Bank, phone 601/252-4211. ¢

Marshall County Historical Museum. Local historical artifacts; Civil War Room; quilts; dolls; toys; antique clothing; wildlife exhibits. Library. (Daily exc Sun; closed wk before Christmas) 220 E College Ave at Randolph St. Phone 601/252-3669. ¢

Rust College (1866). (1,075 students) Site of campground for General Grant's troops. On campus is Leontyne Price Library, which houses the Roy Wilkins Collection on civil rights. Tours. Memphis & Rust Aves. Phone 601/252-8000, ext 4074.

Wall Doxey State Park. Park covering 850 acres located on a spring-fed lake. Swimming beach (3-level diving pier); fishing; boating (ramp, rentals). Nature trail. Picnicking (shelters), playground, playing field, snack bar, lodge. Improved & primitive camping, cabins. Standard fees. 7 mi S off MS 7. Phone 601/252-4231. Per car ¢

Annual Events

Pilgrimage. Historic houses and gardens open to visitors. For schedule and fee information phone 601/252-2943. Mid-Apr.

Kudzu Festival. Arts and crafts, carnival, live music, barbeque. Late July.

Jackson (E-3)

(See also Mendenhall)

Founded 1821 **Pop** 196,637 **Elev** 294 ft **Area code** 601 **Web** www.visitjackson.com
Information Chamber of Commerce, 201 S President St, 39205, phone 601/948-7575; or the Convention & Visitors Bureau, PO Box 1450, 39215, phone 601/960-1891 or 800/354-7695.

The beautiful site of Jackson, along the bluffs above the Pearl River, was selected as a perfect location for commerce by a young French Canadian trader. Although Louis LeFleur succeeded in his aim and set up a trading post after his exploratory voyage up the Pearl from the Gulf of Mexico, the city has throughout its existence been a center of government, rather than business.

It is impossible to separate the town's history from its role as state capital; it was designated such as soon as the state's boundaries had expanded sufficiently, by the ceding of Native American lands, to make Jackson the state's geographical center. The first session of the legislature held in the town convened in January of 1822. By then the city had already been named for Andrew Jackson, idol of Mississippi, and laid out in a checkerboard pattern in accordance with Thomas Jefferson's recommendation to Governor Claiborne 17 years earlier. Evidence still remains of the original plan, which reserved every other square as a park or green.

There were attempts in 1829 to move the capital to Clinton and in the following year to Port Gibson, but these were averted by a legislative act of 1832 that named Jackson as the capital until 1850—by which time it had a permanent stature. Andrew Jackson addressed the legislature in what is now the Old Capitol in 1840, the year after its completion, and a Mississippi Convention assembled to consider Henry Clay's last compromise in 1850. The building was the scene of the Secession Convention in January 1861.

Jackson was the junction of two great railroads by the time of the Civil War; it played an important role as Confederate capital of Mississippi until it was besieged in 1863, when the capital was removed and the city destroyed. All that was recorded in Jackson of the state's turbulent politics and government went up in smoke when General Sherman's army reduced the city to ashes, bringing it the ironic nickname, "Chimneyville."

The so-called "Black and Tan" convention that met at Jackson in January 1868, was the first political organization in Mississippi with black representation. It framed a constitution under which Mississippi lived for 22 years, giving blacks the franchise and enabling a few to attain high political office. In the same year, the governor was ejected from his office, and the carpetbaggers reigned until 1876. Jefferson Davis made his last public appearance in Jackson in 1884.

With the coming of the 20th century and half a dozen railroads connecting Jackson with the whole South, the population doubled within five years. Further growth came with the discovery of natural gas fields in 1930. The Ross Barnett Reservoir, covering 31,000 acres in central Mississippi, created tourist and recreational attractions as well as residential and industrial sites in the greater Jackson area.

What to See and Do

Battlefield Park. Site of Civil War battle; original cannon and trenches. Porter St between Langley Ave & Terry Rd.

Davis Planetarium. Programs change quarterly; 230-seat auditorium. (Daily; closed major hols) 201 E Pascagoula St. Phone 601/960-1550. ¢¢

Governor's Mansion (1842). Restored to original plan and Greek-revival style; antiques and period furnishings. Grounds occupy entire block and feature gardens, gazebos; tours. (Tues-Fri, mornings only; closed during official state functions) 300 E Capitol St, between N Congress & N West Sts. Phone 601/359-3175. **Free.**

Jackson Zoological Park. More than 400 mammals, birds and reptiles in naturalized habitats. (Daily; closed Jan 1, Dec 25) 2918 W Capitol St. Phone 601/352-2580. ¢¢

Manship House. Restored Gothic-revival cottage (ca 1855), was residence of Charles Henry Manship, mayor of Jackson during the Civil War. Period furnishings; fine examples of wood graining and marbling. (Tues-Sat; closed major hols) 420 E Fortification St. Phone 601/961-4724. **Free.**

Mississippi Agriculture & Forestry Museum and National Agricultural Aviation Museum. Complex, covering 39 acres, includes museum exhibit center, forest trail, 1920s living history town and farm. Picnicking. (Daily; closed Jan 1, Dec 25) 1 mi NE on I-55, exit 98 at Lakeland Dr. Phone 601/354-6113 or 800/844-8687. ¢¢

Mississippi Museum of Art. Exhibitions of 19th- and 20th-century works by local, regional, national and international artists. Special exhibitions; sculpture garden; hands-on children's gallery; restaurant, gallery programs, films; instruction, sales gallery. (Daily exc Mon; closed most major hols) 201 E Pascagoula. Phone 601/960-1515. ¢¢

Mississippi Petrified Forest. Surface erosion exposed giant (up to 6 ft in diameter) petrified logs that were deposited in Mississippi area as driftwood by a prehistoric river. Self-guided nature trail. Museum at visitor center has dioramas; wood, gem, mineral, fossil displays; ultraviolet (black light) room. Picnicking. Camping. Gift shop. (Daily; closed Dec 25) 11 mi N on US 49, 1½ mi W via access road. Phone 601/879-8189. ¢¢

Mississippi Sports Hall of Fame and Museum. A variety of interactive exhibits can be found here such as touch-screen television kiosks that access archival sports footage. Through interactive technology, visitors can play championship golf courses, soccer or pitch horseshoes. (Daily exc Mon) 11152 Lakeland Dr. Phone 601/982-8264 or 800/280-FAME. ¢¢

Municipal Art Gallery. Changing exhibits in a variety of media displayed in antebellum house. (Tues-Sat, also Sun afternoons; closed major hols, Fri of Thanksgiving wk; also Aug) 839 N State St. Phone 601/960-1582. **Free.**

Museum of Natural Science. Collections, designed for research and education, cover Mississippi's vertebrates, invertebrates, plants and fossils. Exhibits and aquariums depict ecological story of region; educational programs and workshops offered for all ages. Professional library. Division of Mississippi Department of Wildlife Conservation. (Daily exc Sun; closed Jan 1, July 4, Thanksgiving, Dec 25) 111 N Jefferson St. Phone 601/354-7303. **Free.**

Mynelle Gardens. A five-acre display garden with thousands of azaleas, camellias, daylilies, flowering trees and perennials; reflecting pools and statuary; Oriental garden, miniature flower gardens and an all-white garden. Turn-of-the-century Westbrook House is open for viewing. Changing art & photography exhibits. Gift shop. Picnicking. (Daily; closed some major hols) 4736 Clinton Blvd, 2 blks off MS 220. Phone 601/960-1894. ¢

Old Capitol. Houses State Historical Museum. Exhibits tracing state history housed in restored Greek-revival building that was state capitol from 1839 to 1903; collection of Jefferson Davis memorabilia. Monthly exhibits. (Daily; closed major hols) E end of Capitol St at State St. Phone 601/359-6920. **Free.** Adj are

Confederate Monument (1891). Built with money raised by women of Mississippi and by legislative appropriations.

Archives and History Building. Houses state archives and history collections, research library. Phone 601/359-6850.

Ross R. Barnett Reservoir. Reservoir (43 mi in length) created by damming Pearl River. Swimming, waterskiing; fishing; boating. Picnicking. Camping. Standard fees. (Daily) 7 mi N on I-55, 3 mi E on Natchez Trace Pkwy. Phone 601/354-3448 or 601/856-6574.

Smith Robertson Museum. History and culture of African-American Mississippians from Africa to present; large collection of photos, books, documents, art & crafts. (Mon-Fri, Sat mornings, Sun afternoons; closed major hols) 528 Bloom St. Phone 601/960-1457. ¢

State Capitol (1903). Impeccably restored in 1979, the lavish, beaux-arts capitol building was patterned after the national capitol in Washington. Houses legislature and governor's office. Tours (Mon-Fri). 400 High St. Phone 601/359-3114. **Free.**

The Oaks House Museum (1846). Greek-revival cottage, built of hand-hewn timber by James H. Boyd, former mayor of Jackson, was occupied by General Sherman during the siege of 1863. Period furniture; garden. (Tues-Sat; closed Jan 1, Thanksgiving, Dec 25) 823 N Jefferson St. Phone 601/353-9339. ¢

Annual Events

Dixie National Livestock Show. Mississippi Coliseum. Late Jan-mid Feb. Rodeo 2nd wk Feb.

National Cutting Horse Association Show. Mississippi Coliseum. Entries from across the US participate in amateur to professional rider competitions. Late Mar.

Mississippi State Fair. State Fairgrounds, Jefferson St. Agricultural and industrial exhibits and contests; midway, entertainment. Phone 601/961-4000. Early Oct.

Motels

✔★ **BEST WESTERN-NORTHEAST.** *Box 16275 (39236), 5035 I-55N.* 601/982-1011; FAX 601/982-1011, ext. 199. 133 rms, 2 story. S $46-$50; D $48-$54; each addl $5; suites $70-$100; under 17 free. Crib free. Pet accepted. TV; cable (premium). Pool. Restaurant 6 am-9 pm; closed Sat, Sun. Rm serv. Bar 5 pm-midnight. Ck-out noon. Coin lndry. Meeting rms. Business servs avail. In-rm modem link. Valet serv. Cr cds: A, C, D, DS, MC, V.

D ✔ ⩬ ⩬ ⊠ SC

✔★ **ECONO LODGE.** *2450 US 80W (39204).* 601/353-0340. 40 rms. S $39-$59; D $45-$70; each addl $5; under 12 free. Crib $5. TV; cable. Complimentary continental bkfst. Restaurant nearby. Ck-out 11 am. Business servs avail. Cr cds: A, D, DS, JCB, MC, V.

D ⊠ 🛁 SC

✔★ **HOLIDAY INN EXPRESS.** *310 Greymont Ave (39202), I-55N, exit 96C west.* 601/948-4466; FAX 601/948-4466; res: 800/333-9457. 110 rms, 5 story. S $43.95-$55.95; D $50.95-$55.95; each addl $7; under 18 free. Crib free. TV; cable (premium). Complimentary continental bkfst. Restaurant opp 11 am-9 pm. Ck-out noon. Meeting rms. Business servs avail. Some wet bars. Cr cds: A, C, D, DS, MC, V.

D ⊠ 🛁 SC

★★ **LA QUINTA MOTOR INN.** *150 Angle St (39204), I-20W, exit 43S.* 601/373-6110; FAX 601/373-6115. 101 rms, 2-3 story. S $51; D $57; each addl $6; under 18 free. Crib free. Pet accepted. TV; cable. Pool. Ck-out noon. Business servs avail. In-rm modem link. Valet serv. Airport transportation. Cr cds: A, C, D, DS, MC, V.

D ✔ ⩬ ⩬ 🛁 SC

★★ **LA QUINTA-NORTH.** *616 Briarwood Dr (39236), just E off I-55N.* 601/957-1741; FAX 601/956-5746. 145 rms, 2 story. S, D $56-64; each addl $8; under 17 free. Crib free. Pet accepted. TV; cable (premium). Pool. Restaurant adj. Ck-out noon. Business servs avail. In-rm modem link. Cr cds: A, C, D, DS, MC, V.

D ✔ ⩬ ⩬ ⊠ SC

★★ **RESIDENCE INN BY MARRIOTT.** *881 E River Place (39202), I-55N, exit 96B east.* 601/355-3599; FAX 601/355-5127. 120 kit. suites, 2 story. S, D $85-$149; wkly, monthly rates. Crib free. TV; cable (premium). Pool. Playground. Complimentary continental bkfst. Ck-out noon. Coin lndry. Meeting rms. Business servs avail. In-rm modem link. Health club privileges. Fireplaces. Some private patios, balconies. Cr cds: A, C, D, DS, JCB, MC, V.

D ⩬ 🐕 ⊠ 🛁 SC

Motor Hotel

★★ **CABOT LODGE MILLSAPS.** *2375 N State St (39202).* 601/948-8650; FAX 601/948-8650, ext. 198; res: 800/874-4737. 205 rms, 6 story. S $53-71; D $61-$77; each addl $8; under 12 free; wkend rates. TV. Pool; wading pool. Complimentary continental bkfst. Ck-out noon.

Coin lndry. Meeting rms. Business servs avail. In-rm modem links. Bell-hops. Opp University Medical Center. Cr cds: A, C, D, DS, MC, V.

D ⊠ ⊠ ⊠ SC

Hotels

★ ★ ★ **EDISON WALTHALL.** *225 E Capitol St (39201). 601/948-6161; FAX 601/948-0088; res: 800/932-6161.* 208 rms, 8 story. S $69-$75; D $79-$85; each addl $8; suites $90-$185; under 18 free. Crib free. Pet accepted. TV; cable. Pool; whirlpool. Restaurant 6:30 am-10 pm; Sat, Sun from 7 am. Bar from 4 pm; pianist Mon-Fri. Ck-out noon. Meeting rms. Business servs avail. In-rm modem link. Gift shop. Barber. Free covered parking. Free airport transportation. Exercise equipt. Cr cds: A, C, D, DS, MC, V.

D ⊡ ⊠ ⊀ ⊀ ⊠ ⊠ SC

★ ★ **HILTON.** *1001 County Line Rd (39211). 601/957-2800; FAX 601/957-3191.* 300 rms, 14 story. S $85-$115; D $95-$125; each addl $10; suites $255-$350; under 18 free; wkend rates. Crib free. TV; cable. Pool; whirlpool. Restaurants 6 am-10 pm. Bar 11-1 am; entertainment. Ck-out 1 pm. Convention facilities. Business center. Concierge. Barber, beauty shop. Free airport, RR station, bus depot transportation. Tennis privileges. 18-hole golf privileges, driving range. Health club privileges. Bathrm phones, refrigerators. Luxury level. Cr cds: A, C, D, DS, MC, V.

D ⊀ ⊀ ⊀ ⊠ ⊠ ⊀

Inn

★ ★ ★ **MILLSAPS BUIE HOUSE.** *628 N State St (39202). 601/352-0221; FAX 601/352-0221; res: 800/784-0221.* 11 units, 3 story. S $85-$155; D $100-$170. Children over 12 yrs only. TV; cable (premium). Complimentary full bkfst; afternoon refreshments. Ck-out 11 am, ck-in 2 pm. Meeting rms. Business servs avail. In-rm modem link. Some refrigerators. Private patios, balconies. Picnic tables. Victorian architecture. Restored house built 1888; antique furnishings. Cr cds: A, D, DS, MC, V.

D ⊠ ⊠

Restaurants

★ ★ **DENNERY'S.** *330 Greymont Ave. 601/354-2527.* Hrs: 11 am-10 pm; Sat from 5 pm. Closed Sun; major hols. Res accepted. Serv bar. Semi-a la carte: lunch $7-$10, dinner $11.50-$21.50. Child's meals. Specializes in seafood, beef. Own baking. Parking. Grecian theme. Family-owned. Cr cds: A, C, D, MC, V.

D ♥

★ ★ **IRON HORSE GRILL.** *320 W Pearl St (39203). 601/355-8419.* Hrs: 11 am-10 pm; Fri, Sat to 11 pm. Closed Sun; major hols. Southwestern menu. Bar. Semi-a la carte: lunch $4.95-$19.95, dinner $5.95-$19.95. Child's meals. Specialties: grilled catfish with red bell pepper sauce, fajitas. Pianist Fri, Sat. Parking. Cr cds: A, C, D, MC, V.

D ⊡

★ ★ ★ **NICK'S.** *1501 Lakeland Dr. 601/981-8017.* E-mail nixrest@bellsouth.net. Hrs: 11 am-2 pm, 6-10 pm; Fri, Sat 6-10:30 pm. Closed Sun; major hols. Bar. Wine list. Semi-a la carte: lunch $7-$13, dinner $14-$25. Child's meals. Specializes in seafood, beef, veal. Own desserts. Parking. Cr cds: A, D, MC, V.

D

✔★ ★ **POETS.** *1855 Lakeland Dr (55645). 601/982-9711.* Hrs: 11:30-1 am. Closed Sun, Mon; major hols. Bar. A la carte entrees: lunch, dinner $3.25-$14.95. Specialties: scampi, shrimp, crabmeat. Entertainment. Parking. Outdoor dining. Antique bar, fixtures; stained glass, Tiffany lamps, tin ceiling. Cr cds: A, C, D, DS, MC, V.

D

✔★ ★ **PRIMOS RESTAURANT AT NORTHGATE.** *4330 N State St. 601/982-2064.* Hrs: 11 am-10 pm; Fri, Sat to 10:30 pm; Closed July 4,

Dec 25. Res accepted. Bar. Semi-a la carte: lunch, dinner $6.50-$15.50. Complete meals: lunch $4.95-$15.50. Child's meals. Specializes in salads, seafood, steak. Parking. Country French decor. Cr cds: A, MC, V.

D

★ ★ **TICO'S.** *1536 E County Line Rd. 601/956-1030.* Hrs: 4:30-10:30 pm; Fri, Sat to 11 pm. Closed Sun; major hols. Res accepted Fri, Sat. Bar. Semi-a la carte: dinner $8.95-$19.50. Specializes in steak, fresh seafood. Own desserts. Parking. Lodge style; fireplace, beamed ceilings. Cr cds: A, D, DS, MC, V.

D

Unrated Dining Spot

COCK OF THE WALK. *PO Box 12705 (39236), 15 mi N via I-55, Natchez Trace exit to Ross Barnett Reservoir. 601/856-5500.* Web www.thevirtualmenu.com/cockofthewalk. Hrs: 5-9 pm; Fri, Sat to 10 pm. Closed Thanksgiving, Dec 24, 25. A la carte entrees: dinner from $8.95. Child's meals. Specializes in catfish, pickles, mustard greens. Parking. Rustic decor. Cr cds: A, DS, MC, V.

D ⊡

Kosciusko (D-4)

(See also Louisville)

Pop 6,986 **Elev** 488 ft **Area code** 601 **Zip** 39090 **E-mail** chamber@kopower.com **Web** www.kopower.com/coc/coc.htm
Information Kosciusko-Attala Chamber of Commerce, 301 E Jefferson, PO Box 696; 601/289-2981.

What to See and Do

Holmes County State Park. Approx 450-acre park has 2 lakes. Swimming beach; fishing; boating (rentals). Nature trails; archery range. Picnicking (shelters), playground, skating rink (call for schedule), coin lndry. Camping (water, electric hookups), cabins. Standard fees. 25 mi W on MS 12, then S on US 51, between US 51 & I-55. Phone 601/653-3351.

Kosciusko Museum-Information Center. Museum features information on the area, Natchez Trace Pkwy and Polish general Tadeusz Kosciuszko; revolving displays. (Daily; closed Dec 25) 1½ mi S via S Huntington St, Natchez Trace Pkwy exit. Contact Chamber of Commerce. **Free.**

Annual Event

Central Mississippi Fair. Central Mississippi Fairgrounds. Phone 601/289-2981. July.

Laurel (F-5)

(See also Hattiesburg)

Settled 1882 **Pop** 18,827 **Elev** 246 ft **Area code** 601 **E-mail** edajones@teclink.com **Web** www.joneseda.com
Information Jones County Chamber of Commerce, PO Box 527, 39441; 601/428-0574.

Laurel was built by two sawmill men in the piney woods of southeastern Mississippi after Reconstruction. Pushing through northeast Mississippi's pinelands, they picked a spot on the Southern Railroad that they thought was the forest's center. They called it Laurel for the abundant flowering shrubs, but it remained a rough lumber camp for a decade. Laurel bloomed after a midwestern company took over the lumber mill, laying out streets and encouraging workers to buy houses. The ladies of Laurel organized the state's first garden club in the 1890s.

Laurel has been fortunate in the development of a reforestation program and diversified industry.

What to See and Do

Lauren Rogers Museum of Art. Collections of 19th- and 20th-century American and European paintings, 18th-century Japanese woodblock prints, English Georgian silver, Native American baskets. (Daily exc Mon; closed major hols) 5th Ave & 7th St. Phone 601/649-6374. **Free.**

Landrum's Homestead. Recreation of a late 1800s settlement. Blacksmith shop, watermill gristmill, gem mining, general store. (Daily; closed major hols) 1356 MS 15 S. Phone 601/649-2546. **¢¢**

Motor Hotel

✔★ ★ **RAMADA INN SAWMILL.** *1105 Sawmill Rd (39440). 601/649-9100; FAX 601/649-6045.* 207 rms, 1-4 story. S $44; D $49; each addl $5; studio rms $50-$100; under 18 free. Crib free. TV; cable. Pool; poolside serv. Restaurant 6 am-10 pm; Sun to 9 pm. Rm serv. Bar 11-1 am; entertainment, Tues-Sat. Ck-out 1 pm. Meeting rms. Business servs avail. Valet serv. Some refrigerators. Cr cds: A, C, D, DS, MC, V.

D ≈ 🏊 🐾

Restaurant

★ ★ **PARKER HOUSE.** *3115 Audubon Dr (33940). 601/649-0261.* Hrs: 6-9 pm; Fri, Sat to 9:30 pm. Closed Sun, Mon; major hols. Res accepted. Continental menu. Bar 5 pm-midnight. A la carte entrees: dinner $6.95-$19.95. Child's meals. Specializes in seafood, steak, stuffed mushrooms. Parking. Cr cds: A, C, D, DS, MC, V.

Louisville (D-5)

Pop 7,169 **Elev** 525 ft **Area code** 601 **Zip** 39339 **Web** www.coclwc.com

Information Louisville-Winston County Chamber of Commerce, 311 W Park, PO Box 551; 601/773-3921.

What to See and Do

Legion State Park. One of the first parks developed by the Civilian Conservation Corps; original stone lodge still in use. Swimming beach; two fishing lakes; boating (ramp, rentals). Nature trail. Picnicking (shelters). Tent camping, cabins. (Daily) Standard fees. On Old MS 25. Phone 601/773-8323.

Nanih Waiya State Park. Legendary birthplace of the Choctaw and site of their Sacred Mound; area occupied from approx the time of Christ until arrival of Europeans. Swinging bridge leads to cave under mound. Picnicking (shelters). Near Pearl River. (Daily; closed Dec 25) 18 mi SE via MS 397. Contact Site Manager, Rte 3, Box 251-A; 601/773-7988. **Free.**

Tombigbee National Forest. This southern section of the forest contains Choctaw Lake. Swimming (fee); fishing; boating. Picnicking. Camping (Mar-mid-Nov; hookups, fee; dump station). Fees are charged at recreation sites. There is a Ranger District station near Ackerman and another section of the forest S of Tupelo (see). N on MS 15, which borders W side of forest. Contact Forest Supervisor, 100 W Capitol St, Suite 1141, Jackson 39269, phone 601/965-4391; or contact the District Ranger, US Forest Service, Rte 1, Box 98A, Ackerman 39735, phone 601/285-3264. Day use **¢¢**

Resort

✔★ ★ **LAKE TIAK O'KHATA.** *213 Smyth Lake Rd, ¼ mi off MS 15 Bypass S. 601/773-7853; res: 888/845-6151; FAX 601/773-4555.* 80

rms, 2 story; duplex cottages. S $44-$75; D $49-$75; each addl $4; kit. cottages $45; wkly rates. Crib $5. TV in hotel rms, lobby; cable (premium). Dining rm 6 am-10 pm. Snack bar. Ck-out 11 am. Grocery 1 mi. Meeting rms. Business servs avail. Tennis. Private beach; swimming classes (summer), waterslide, lifeguard; boating (ramps, rentals), pedal boats. Nature trails. Picnic tables. 400 acre pine forest; 5 lakes. Cr cds: A, D, DS, MC, V.

D 🐾 🏊 🛷 🐾 SC

McComb (G-3)

Founded 1872 **Pop** 11,591 **Elev** 460 ft **Area code** 601 **Zip** 39649 **E-mail** pcedd@telapex.com **Web** www.telapex.com/~pcedd

Information Chamber of Commerce, 617 Delaware Ave, PO Box 83; 601/684-2291 or 800/399-4404.

What to See and Do

Bogue Chitto Water Park. Swimming; tubing, canoeing. Nature trail. Picnicking, playground, pavilion. Primitive/improved camping, cabins (fee). Visitor center. (Daily) 12 mi E on US 98. Phone 601/684-9568. Per car **¢**

Percy Quin State Park. Park covering 1,700 acres on 700-acre Tangipahoa Lake in oak and pine forests. Lodge area includes arboretum and Liberty White Railroad Museum, housed in a caboose. Pool, bathhouse, waterskiing; fishing; boating (ramp, rentals). Nature; miniature golf, 27-hole golf course. Picnicking (shelters), snack bar, playing field, lodge. Improved & primitive camping, cabins. Standard fees. 6 mi S on I-55, exit 13. Phone 601/684-3931.

Annual Event

Lighted Azalea Trail. In keeping with the Japanese tradition of lighting cherry blossoms, McComb citizens illuminate their azaleas; arts festival, music programs. Two wks mid-Mar.

Motel

✔★ **HOLIDAY INN.** *1900 Delaware (39648), I-55 exit 17. 601/684-6211; FAX 601/684-0408.* 143 rms, 2 story. S, D $48; suites $75. Crib free. TV; cable. Pool. Restaurant 6 am-2 pm, 5-10 pm. Rm serv. Bar 5 pm-midnight. Ck-out noon. Coin lndry. Business servs avail. In-rm modem link. Exercise equipt. Cr cds: A, C, D, DS, JCB, MC, V.

D ≈ 🏋 🛷 🐾 SC

Unrated Dining Spot

DINNER BELL. *229 5th Ave (39648). 601/684-4883.* Hrs: 11 am-2 pm; 5:30-8 pm; Apr-Sept hrs vary. Closed Mon; July 4, Dec 23-mid-Jan. Buffet: lunch, dinner $8-$11. Child's meals. Specializes in Southern home-style cooking. Totally nonsmoking. No cr cds accepted.

Mendenhall (F-4)

(See also Jackson)

Pop 2,463 **Elev** 323 ft **Area code** 601 **Zip** 39114

What to See and Do

Bienville National Forest. This central Mississippi tract of 178,374 acres has numerous forest management demonstration areas of second-growth pine and hardwood. Swimming; boating. Hiking, bridle trails. Picnicking. Camping. Ranger District office is located in Forest. NW on US 49 to MS 13, then N. For information contact District Ranger, Bienville Ranger

District, 3473 Hwy 35S, Forest 39074; 601/469-3811. Two major recreation areas are

Shongelo. A five-acre lake. Swimming (fee), bathhouse; fishing. Picnicking. Camping (fee). 22 mi E & N via MS 540, 35.

Marathon. A 58-acre lake. Swimming (fee); fishing; boating. Picnicking. Camping (fee). 47 mi NE via MS 540, 18, 501, forest service roads.

D'Lo Water Park. Park includes 85 acres. Swimming, bathhouse; fishing; canoeing (rentals). Nature trails, lighted playing fields. Picnicking. Camping (hookups; fee). (Daily; closed Jan 1, Thanksgiving, Dec 25) 3 mi NW via US 49. Phone 601/847-4310. **Free.**

Meridian (E-5)

Settled 1831 **Pop** 41,036 **Elev** 333 ft **Area code** 601 **E-mail** embdcl@cybertron.com **Web** www.cybertron.com/city.mdn

Information East Mississippi Development Corporation, 1915 Front St, Union Station, 39302; 601/693-1306 or 800/748-9970.

Founded at the junction of two railroads, Meridian is now an industrial, agricultural and retailing center in the heart of the South's finest timber-growing country.

What to See and Do

Bienville National Forest. 45 mi W off I-20 (see MENDENHALL).

Clarkco State Park. Park covering 815 acres situated on 65-acre lake. Swimming beach, waterskiing; fishing; boating (ramp, rentals). Nature trail; lighted tennis. Picnicking (shelters), playground, playing field, lodge, coin lndry. Primitive & improved camping, cabins (each with lake pier). Standard fees. 18 mi S off US 45. Phone 601/776-6651.

Jimmie Rodgers Museum. Fashioned after an old train depot, the museum houses souvenirs and memorabilia of the "Father of Country Music," including a rare Martin 00045 guitar. (Daily; closed Jan 1, Thanksgiving, Dec 25) 19th St & 41st Ave, in Highland Park. Phone 601/485-1808. **¢**

Meridian Museum of Art. Permanent and changing exhibits of paintings, graphics, photographs, sculpture and crafts by regional artists. (Tues-Sun, afternoons; closed hols) 25th Ave at 7th St. Phone 601/693-1501. **Free.**

Merrehope. Stately 20-rm mansion, begun in 1859, features unusual woodwork, handsome columns, mantels and stairway. (Daily exc Sun; closed most major hols) Special Christmas tours. 905 Martin Luther King, Jr Memorial Dr. Phone 601/483-8439. **¢¢** Nearby is

Frank W. Williams House. Victorian home (ca 1886) features stained glass, oak paneling, parquet floors and detailed gingerbread. (Days same as Merrehope) Admission to both houses **¢¢**

Okatibbee Dam and Reservoir. A 3,800-acre lake with swimming (seasonal), waterskiing, water slides; fishing; boating (ramps, marina). Picnicking, lodging. Camping at Twiltley Branch Park (fee; phone 601/626-8068) and at Okatibbee Water Park (seasonal, fee; phone 601/737-2370). 7 mi NW off MS 19. Phone 601/626-8431.

Annual Events

Arts in the Park. Concerts, plays, art shows, children's programs. 1st wkend Apr.

Jimmie Rodgers Memorial Festival. Country and western music. Last wkend May.

Mississippi-Alabama State Fair. Agricultural exhibits, carnival. Oct.

Motels

✔★ **BAYMONT INN.** 1400 Roebuck Dr (39301). 601/693-2300; FAX 601/485-2534. 102 rms, 3 story. S $32.95-$37.95; D $35.95-$40.95; under 18 free. Crib free. TV; cable. Pool. Restaurant adj open 24 hrs.

Ck-out noon. Meeting rms. Business servs avail. In-rm modem link. Cr cds: A, C, D, DS, MC, V.

D ≈ ⊠ ⊠ SC

✔★ ★ **BEST WESTERN.** 2219 S Frontage Rd (39301), at jct I-20, I-59. 601/693-3210. 120 rms, 2 story. S $42-$53; D $47-$57; each addl $5; under 12 free. Crib free. TV; cable. Pool. Restaurant 6 am-10 pm; Sun to 3 pm. Bar 4 pm-1 am; closed Sun; entertainment. Ck-out noon. Meeting rms. Sundries. Cr cds: A, C, D, DS, MC, V.

≈ ⊠ ⊠ SC

★ ★ **HOLIDAY INN EXPRESS.** 1401 Roebuck Dr (39302), US 45 at jct I-20, I-59. 601/693-4521; FAX 601/693-4521, ext. 7625. 172 rms, 1-2 story. S, D $49-$54; under 12 free. Crib free. TV; cable (premium). Pool. Playground. Coffee in rms. Ck-out noon. Coin lndry. Meeting rms. Business servs avail. In-rm modem link. Valet serv. Cr cds: A, C, D, DS, JCB, MC, V.

D ✦ ≈ ⊠ ⊠ SC

★ **HOWARD JOHNSON.** Box 588 (39305), 2 mi E, exit 154 at I-59, I-20. 601/483-8281. 142 rms, 2 story. S $45-$54; D $47-$58; each addl $4; suites $95-$250; under 18 free. Crib free. TV. Indoor pool; whirlpool. Restaurant 6 am-10 pm. Bar 11-1 am; entertainment exc Sun. Ck-out noon. Coin lndry. Meeting rms. Business servs avail. Sundries. Private patios, balconies. Cr cds: A, C, D, DS, JCB, MC, V.

≈ ⊠ ⊠ SC

✔★ **RAMADA LIMITED.** 2915 St Paul St (39301). 601/485-2722; FAX 601/485-3960. 50 units, 2 story. S $48.98; D $52.98; each addl $5; under 12 free. Crib free. TV; cable. Pool; whirlpool. Ck-out noon. Business servs avail. Exercise equipt; sauna. Cr cds: A, D, DS, MC, V.

D ≈ 🏃 ⊠ ⊠ SC

Restaurant

★ ★ **WEIDMANN'S.** 210 22nd Ave (39301). 601/693-1751. Hrs: 7 am-9:30 pm. Closed most major hols. Bar. Semi-a la carte: bkfst $2.85-$5, lunch $5-$10, dinner $8-$16. Child's meals. Specialties: crab Belvedere, trout almandine. Cr cds: A, C, D, DS, MC, V.

D

Natchez (G-1)

Settled 1716 **Pop** 19,460 **Elev** 215 ft **Area code** 601 **Zip** 39120 **E-mail** ncvb@bkbank.com **Web** www.natchez.ms.us

Information Convention and Visitors Bureau; 640 S Canal, Box C, PO Box 1485; 601/446-6345 or 800/647-6724.

Natchez lives in the enchantment of the Old South, a plantation atmosphere where everything seems beautiful and romantic. Greek-revival mansions, manicured gardens and lawns, tree-shaded streets and southern hospitality abound in this museum of the antebellum South.

Natchez, named for a Native American tribe, is also a manufacturing town with a history of trapping, trading, hunting and farming. French, Spanish, English, Confederate and US flags have flown over this town, one of the oldest in the Mississippi Valley. Vestiges of the Spanish influence can still be seen along South Wall Street, near Washington Street, a charming neighborhood once restricted to the Spanish dons. The city's modern stores and buildings serve to emphasize how lovingly the citizens of Natchez have preserved their past.

What to See and Do

🔲 **Canal Street Depot.** Houses official Natchez Pilgrimage Tour and Tourist Headquarters. (Daily) Information on historic Natchez and the surrounding area. Offers tours (fee) of 15 antebellum mansions and tickets for spring, fall and Christmas pilgrimages (see ANNUAL EVENTS). Corner of Canal & State St.

Dunleith (ca 1856). National Historic Landmark. Restored antebellum, Greek-revival mansion completely surrounded by colonnaded galleries. Estate includes 40 acres of green pastures and wooded bayous within Natchez. French and English antiques. (Daily; closed Thanksgiving, Dec 25) Guest rms (see INNS). 84 Homochitto St. Phone 601/446-8500 or 800/433-2445 (exc MS). Tours ¢¢

Emerald Mound. This eight-acre Mississippian mound, the second largest in the US, dates roughly from 1250-1600. Unlike earlier peoples, who constructed mounds to cover tombs and burials, the Mississippians (ancestors of the Natchez, Creek and Choctaw) built mounds to support temples and ceremonial buildings. When DeSoto passed through this area in the 1540s the flat-topped temple mounds were still in use. (Daily) 12 mi NE on Natchez Trace Pkwy (see). Phone 601/680-4025.   **Free.**

Grand Village of the Natchez. Museum, archaeological site, nature trails, picnic area, gift shop. (Daily; closed Jan 1, Thanksgiving, Dec 25) 400 Jefferson Davis Blvd. Phone 601/446-6502.   **Free.**

Historic Jefferson College. The Jefferson College campus was the site, in 1817, of the first state Constitutional Convention. Jefferson Davis was among the famous Mississippians who attended the college. No longer in use as a school, the buildings are being restored as a historic site. A museum interprets the early history of the territory, state and campus; nature trails; picnicking. (Daily; closed Jan 1, Thanksgiving, Dec 25) 6 mi E on US 61 in Washington. Phone 601/442-2901.   **Free.**

Historic Springfield Plantation (1786-1790). Believed to be first mansion erected in Mississippi; remains nearly intact with little remodeling over the years; original hand-carved woodwork. Built for Thomas Marston Green, Jr, wealthy planter from Virginia; site of Andrew Jackson's wedding. Displays include Civil War equipment, railroad memorabilia, narrow-gauge locomotive. (Daily; closed Dec 25) 20 mi NE via US 61, Natchez Trace Pkwy, then 12 mi N on MS 553. Phone 601/786-3802.   ¢¢¢

Homochitto National Forest. This 189,000-acre forest is located near the picturesquely eroded loess country. Visitors view the regular timber management activities. Swimming (Clear Springs Recreation Area); fishing and hunting. Picnicking, camping (Clear Springs Recreation Area). Fees may be charged at recreation sites. Ranger District offices are located in Meadville and Gloster. NE & SE via US 84, 98, MS 33. Contact Forest Supervisor, 100 W Capitol St, Suite 1141, Jackson 39269; 601/965-4391.

Lady Luck **Riverboat Casino.** On riverfront, 21 Silver St. Phone 601/445-0605 or 800/722-5825.

Longwood. Enormous, Italianate detailed "octagon house" crowned with an onion dome. Under construction at start of Civil War, interiors were never completed above first floor; ca 1840 furnishings. Owned and operated by the Pilgrimage Garden Club. (Daily; days vary during Pilgrimages) (See ANNUAL EVENTS) Lower Woodville Rd.   ¢¢

Magnolia Hall (1858). Last great mansion to be erected in city before outbreak of Civil War, house is an outstanding example of Greek-revival architecture; period antiques; costume museum. (Daily) S Pearl at Washington. Phone 601/442-6672.   ¢¢

Monmouth (ca 1818). Registered as a National Historic Landmark, the monumental, Greek-revival house and auxiliary buildings, once owned by Mexican War hero Gen. John Anthony Quitman, have been completely restored; antique furnishings; extensive gardens. Guest rms (see INNS). Tours (daily; closed Dec 25). 36 Melrose Ave. Phone 601/442-5852 or 800/828-4531.   ¢¢

Mount Locust. Earliest inn on the Trace; restored to 1810s appearance. Interpretive program. (Feb-Nov, daily; grounds only, Dec-Jan) 15 mi NE on Natchez Trace Pkwy (see). Phone 601/680-4025.   **Free.**

Natchez State Park. Park has horse trails believed to be abandoned plantation roads that lead to Brandon Hall, house of the first native Mississippi governor, Gerard Brandon (1826-1831). Fishing lake; boating (ramp, rentals). Nature trail. Picnicking. Primitive & improved camping, cabins. Standard fees. 10 mi N off US 61. Phone 601/442-2658.

Ravennaside (ca 1880). Designed by original owner for entertainment on lavish scale; restored; most of original furniture retained. (Sept-June, daily) Guest rms (see INNS). 601 S Union St. Phone 601/442-8015. Tours   ¢¢

Rosalie (1820-1823). Red brick, Georgian mansion with Greek-revival portico served as headquarters for Union Army during occupation of Natchez. Original furnishings date from 1857; gardens on bluff above Mississippi. (Daily; closed Thanksgiving, Dec 24, 25) Fees vary during scheduled times at the Pilgrimages (see ANNUAL EVENTS). 100 Orleans St. Phone 601/445-4555.   ¢¢

Stanton Hall (1851-1857). Highly elaborate antebellum mansion surrounded by giant oaks; original chandeliers, marble mantels, Sheffield hardware, French mirrors. Owned and operated by the Pilgrimage Garden Club. (Daily; days & fees vary during pilgrimages) (See ANNUAL EVENTS) 401 High St. Phone 601/446-6631 or 800/647-6742.   ¢¢

The House on Ellicott Hill. Site where, in 1797, Andrew Ellicott raised the first American flag in the lower Mississippi Valley. Built in 1798, the house overlooks both the Mississippi and the terminus of the Natchez Trace. Restored and authentically furnished. (Daily) Jefferson & Canal Sts. Phone 601/442-2011.   ¢¢

Annual Events

Pilgrimages. Headquarters, Canal Street Depot. Tours of antebellum houses sponsored by the Natchez Pilgrimage Assn (daily). Also Confederate Pageant at City Auditorium (Mon, Wed, Fri, Sat). Contact PO Box 347 or phone 800/647-6742 for details. Mar-early Apr; Fall Pilgrimage mid-Oct; Christmas Dec.

Great Mississippi River Balloon Race Weekend. Oct.

Seasonal Event

Natchez Opera Festival. Entire month of May.

Motels

✔★ **HOWARD JOHNSON.** *45 Seargent Prentiss Drive, US 61, at jct US 65, 84, 98.* 601/442-1691; res: 800/541-1720; FAX 601/445-5895. 131 units, 1-2 story. S $41-$53; D $41-$61; each addl $5; suites $60-$75; under 12 free. TV; cable, VCR avail. Pool. Ck-out noon. Meeting rms. Business center. In-rm modem link. Cr cds: A, C, D, DS, MC, V.

D ≋ ⇌ 🐾 SC 🚶

★★ **RAMADA INN HILLTOP.** *Box 1263, 130 John R. Junkin Dr, at Mississippi River bridge.* 601/446-6311; FAX 601/446-6321. 162 rms, 1-3 story. No elvtr. S $48-$60; D $48-$70; each addl $5; suites $140; under 18 free. Crib free. Pet accepted, some restrictions. TV; cable (premium), VCR avail. Pool; wading pool, poolside serv. Restaurant 6 am-10 pm. Rm serv. Bar; entertainment Fri, Sat. Ck-out 1 pm. Coin lndry. Meeting rms. Business servs avail. In-rm modem link. Sundries. Airport, bus depot transportation. Some refrigerators. On hilltop overlooking Mississippi River. Cr cds: A, C, D, DS, JCB, MC, V.

D ⟲ ≋ ⇌ 🐾 SC

★★ **SUPER 8.** *271 D'Evereaux Dr (US 61N).* 601/442-3686; FAX 601/446-9998. 139 rms, 2 story. S $47-$70; D $53-$76; each addl $6; under 18 free. Crib free. TV; cable. Pool. Restaurant 6 am-8:30 pm. Rm serv. Ck-out noon. Meeting rm. Business servs avail. In-rm modem link. Cr cds: A, C, D, DS, JCB, MC, V.

D ≋ ⇌ 🐾 SC

Hotels

✔★★ **LADY LUCK.** *645 S Canal St.* 601/445-0605; FAX 601/442-9823. 147 units, 6 story. S $55-$65; D $69; each addl $5; suites $155; under 18 free. Crib free. TV; cable. Pool; whirlpool, poolside serv. Restaurant 6:30 am-2 pm. Ck-out 1 pm. Meeting rms. Business servs avail. Casino. Cr cds: A, C, D, DS, MC, V.

D ≋ ⇌ 🐾 SC

★★ **NATCHEZ EOLA.** *110 N Pearl St.* 601/445-6000; FAX 601/446-5310; res: 800/888-9140. 125 rms, 7 story. S, D $75-$195; suites $120-$225. Crib free. Pet accepted. TV; cable. Restaurant 7 am-2 pm, 5-9 pm. Bar 5:30 pm-midnight. Ck-out 11 am. Meeting rms. Balconies; many with view of river. Classic architecture; antique furniture. Cr cds: A, C, D, MC, V.

D ⮐ ⛶ ⛲ SC

Inns

★ ★ ★ **THE BRIARS.** *31 Irving Ln. 601/446-9654; FAX 601/442-1290; res: 800/634-1818.* 14 rms, 1-2 story, 2 suites. S, D $135-$220; each addl $45; suites $200-$220. Children over 12 yrs only. TV; cable (premium). Pool. Complimentary full bkfst. Complimentary coffee in rms. Restaurant nearby. Ck-out 11 am, ck-in 2 pm. Luggage handling. Balconies. Picnic tables. Early Southern plantation-style mansion built between 1814 and 1818. Residence where Jefferson Davis married in 1845. Totally nonsmoking. Cr cds: A, MC, V.

D ⛲ ⛶ ⛲

★ ★ **THE BURN.** *712 N Union. 601/442-1344; FAX 601/445-0606; res: 800/654-8859.* 7 rms, 2 story. No rm phones. S $85; D $95-$130; each addl $20. Closed Dec 25. Children over 12 yrs only. TV. Pool. Complimentary bkfst. Ck-out 11 am, ck-in 2-6 pm. Business servs avail. Early Greek-revival house (1834) with semi-spiral staircase in central hall; used as headquarters and hospital by Union troops during Civil War; antique furnishings. Gardens with many rare camellias. Free tour of house. Cr cds: A, DS, MC, V.

⛲ ⛲

★ ★ ★ **DUNLEITH.** *84 Homochitto St. 601/446-8500; res: 800/433-2445.* 11 rms, 2 story. S, D $95-$140; each addl $15. Closed Easter, Thanksgiving, Dec 24-25. Children over 18 yrs only. TV; cable (premium). Complimentary full bkfst. Ck-out 11 am, ck-in 1-6 pm. Balconies. Antebellum mansion (ca 1856) on 40 acres; formal gardens, courtyard. Greek-revival architecture; rms individually decorated; antique furnishings; fireplaces. Cr cds: DS, MC, V.

⛲

★ **LINDEN.** *1 Linden Place. 601/445-5472; res: 800/254-6336.* 7 rms, 2 story. No rm phones. S, D $90-$120; each addl $30. Children over 10 yrs only. Complimentary full bkfst. Ck-out 11 am, ck-in 1 pm. Business servs avail. Antebellum house (ca 1800); antique furnishings; set among mossy oaks, cedars and magnolias. Free tour of house. No cr cds accepted.

D ⛲ ⛲

★ ★ ★ **MONMOUTH.** *36 Melrose Ave. 601/442-5852; FAX 601/446-7762; res: 800/828-4531.* E-mail luxury@monmouthplantation. com; web www.monmouthplantation.com. 27 rms, 2 story. S, D $125-$255; each addl $35. Children over 14 yrs only. TV. Complimentary bkfst. Serv bar. Ck-out 11 am, ck-in 3 pm. Business servs avail. Greek-revival mansion (1818) with column-supported galleries on front & back; antique furnishings, Civil War memorabilia; extensive gardens. Free tour of mansion. Cr cds: A, C, D, DS, MC, V.

D ⮕ ⛲ ⛲

★ ★ **PLEASANT HILL.** *310 S Pearl. 601/442-7674; FAX 601/442-2266; res: 800/621-7952.* 4 rms. S, D $90-$110; each addl $25; wkly rates. Complimentary Southern bkfst. Ck-out 11 am, ck-in 3-5 pm. Business servs avail. Greek-revival house (1835); antiques; rms individually decorated. Tour of house. Cr cds: MC, V.

⛲ ⛲

★ ★ **RAVENNASIDE.** *601 S Union St. 601/442-8015.* 8 rms, 3 story. S, D $85-$115; each addl $20. Crib free. TV. Whirlpool. Complimentary full bkfst. Ck-out 11 am, ck-in 3 pm. Colonial revival mansion built circa 1895; many original furnishings. Cr cds: MC, V.

⛲ ⛲

Restaurants

✔★ ★ **CARRIAGE HOUSE.** *401 High St. 601/445-5151.* Hrs: 11 am-2:30 pm. Closed Jan 1, July 4. Res accepted. Bar. Semi-a la carte: lunch $3.50-$10.95. Specializes in southern fried chicken, ham. On grounds of Stanton Hall, owned by the Pilgrimage Garden Club. Cr cds: A, MC, V.

D

✔★ **COCK OF THE WALK.** *200 N Broadway, on the Mississippi River. 601/446-8920.* Hrs: 5-9 pm; Sun to 8 pm. Closed most major hols. Limited menu. Serv bar. Complete meals: dinner $9-$15.95. Child's meals. Specializes in catfish. Entertainment. Parking. Rustic decor; old train station on river. Cr cds: A, C, D, DS, JCB, MC, V.

D

★ **NATCHEZ LANDING.** *61 Silver St. 601/442-6639.* Hrs: 5-10 pm; Fri-Sun 11:30 am-2 pm, 5-10 pm; spring & fall pilgrimages 11:30 am-2 pm, 5-10 pm. Closed Thanksgiving, Dec 25. Serv bar. Semi-a la carte: lunch, dinner $4.95-$20. Child's meals. Specializes in barbecued ribs, catfish. Parking. Rustic decor. Cr cds: A, MC, V.

D

Natchez Trace Parkway (G-2 - A-6)

One of the earliest "interstates," the Natchez Trace stretched from Natchez, Mississippi to Nashville, Tennessee and was the most heavily traveled road in the Old Southwest from approximately 1785 to 1820. Boatmen floated their products downriver to Natchez or New Orleans, sold them and walked or rode home over the Natchez Trace. A "trace" is a trail or road. This one was shown on French maps as far back as 1733. It was still in use, to some extent, as late as the 1830s, although its importance diminished after the invention of the steam engine.

When completed, the Natchez Trace Parkway, operated by the National Park Service, will be a magnificent 445-mile-long road. At this writing about 430 miles are paved and open, most of them in Mississippi; a continuous stretch of 341 miles is open between Jackson, MS and TN 100 south of Nashville, Tennessee. A 79-mile stretch is open west of Jackson, MS to near Natchez, MS.

The parkway crosses and recrosses the original trace, passing many points of historic interest, including Emerald Mound (see NATCHEZ).

The parkway headquarters and visitor center are five miles north of Tupelo, at jct US 45 Business (sign reads US 145) and the parkway. Interpretive facilities include a visitor center with exhibits depicting the history of the trace and an audiovisual program that tells the story of the trace (daily; closed Dec 25; free). Park Service personnel can furnish information on self-guided trails, wayside exhibits, interpretive programs, camping and picnicking facilities along the parkway. For further information contact Superintendent, 2680 Natchez Trace Pkwy, Tupelo 38801; 601/680-4025 or 800/305-7417.

Ocean Springs (J-5)

(See also Biloxi, Gulfport, Pascagoula)

Pop 14,658 **Elev** 20 ft **Area code** 228 **Zip** 39566 **Web** www.lillypr.com/oschamber

Information Chamber of Commerce, 1000 Washington Ave, PO Box 187; 228/875-4424.

This is the site of Old Biloxi, settled by d'Iberville in 1699. The site of the original Fort Maurepas was verified by the discovery here of cannons dredged from the bay and cannonballs unearthed from the land.

Although some soldiers and settlers remained after the French colonial capital was moved to Mobile in 1702, the area languished until the first large influx of summer visitors arrived in the 1850s. It has since become a popular resort.

Headquarters and campground for the Mississippi District of the Gulf Islands National Seashore (see) are in Ocean Springs.

What to See and Do

Shearwater Pottery. Established in 1928. Displays include thrown glazed ware by founder Peter Anderson and his son Jim; original paintings and block prints by Peter's brothers, James McConnell Anderson and Walter Anderson. (Mon-Sat & Sun afternoons; closed major hols) 102 Shearwater Dr. Phone 228/875-7320. **Free.**

Annual Events

Garden and Home Pilgrimage. Late Mar or early Apr.

Anniversary of the Landing of d'Iberville. Pageant, street fair and other activities commemorating the 1699 event. Last wkend Apr.

Restaurants

★ ★ **GERMAINE'S.** *1203 Bienville Blvd (US 90) (39564).* *228/875-4426.* E-mail germaines@worldnet.att.net. Hrs: 11:30 am-2 pm, 6-10 pm; Sun to 2 pm. Res accepted. Closed Mon; major hols. Creole, Amer menu. Bar. Semi-a la carte: lunch, dinner $10-$21.95. Child's meals. Specializes in crabmeat, stuffed mushrooms. Display of antique clocks; changing exhibits of Gulf Coast art. Cr cds: A, DS, MC, V.

★ ★ **JOCELYN'S.** *US 90E (39564).* *228/875-1925.* Hrs: 5-10 pm. Closed Sun-Mon. French creole menu. Bar. Semi-a la carte: dinner $10-$18. Child's meals. Specializes in seafood. Renovated cottage (1890s). Casual dining. No cr cds accepted.

Oxford (B-4)

Settled 1836 **Pop** 9,984 **Elev** 416 ft **Area code** 601 **Zip** 38655 **E-mail** tourism@oxfordcenter.com **Web** www.ci.oxford.ms.us/

Information Oxford Tourism Council, PO Box 965; 601/234-4680 or 800/758-9177.

Oxford was named for the English university city in an effort to lure the University of Mississippi to the site; in 1848 the university was opened. Today, "Ole Miss," with its forested, hilly 1,194-acre campus, dominates the area, and the town that boasted an opera house before the Civil War still reveres its role as a university town.

William Faulkner, Nobel Prize winning author, lived near the university at "Rowan Oak." Many landmarks of his fictional Yoknapatawpha County can be found in surrounding Lafayette County.

What to See and Do

⭐ **Rowan Oak.** Residence of William Faulkner from 1930-1962; furnishings and memorabilia are as they were at the time of Faulkner's death. Maintained by the University of Mississippi. (Daily exc Mon; closed university hols) Old Taylor Rd, 1½ mi SE. Phone 601/234-3284. **Free.**

University of Mississippi (1848). (10,000 students) Greek-revival style buildings grouped around the Lyceum Building. Newer buildings follow the classical-revival style. 1 mi W on University Ave. Phone 601/232-7236. On campus are

Blues Archive. Extensive collection of blues recordings and related material. Three major collections form the nucleus of the archive: The B.B. King Collections, The Kenneth S. Goldstein Folklore Collection and The Living Blues Archival Collection. (Mon-Fri; closed university hols) Farley Hall, Grove Loop. Phone 601/232-7753. **Free.**

University Museums. Housed in two adjoining buildings, the collections include Greek and Roman antiquities, antique scientific instruments, other historic objects; also African-American, Caribbean and Southern folk art. (Daily exc Mon; closed university hols) Phone 601/232-7073. **Free.**

University Archives. Historical and literary works of and by Mississippians; works by William Faulkner in 35 languages, exhibit of his awards, including Nobel Prize, manuscripts and first editions. (Mon-Fri; closed university hols) University Library. Phone 601/232-7408. **Free.**

Annual Event

Faulkner Conference. Center for Study of Southern Culture, University of Mississippi. Various programs celebrate the author's accomplishments. Phone 601/232-7282. Last wk July.

Motels

✔ ★ ★ **BEST WESTERN OXFORD INN.** *1101 Frontage Rd.* *601/234-9500; FAX 601/236-2772.* 100 rms, 2 story. S $45-$52, D $49-$60; each addl $5; under 12 free; higher rates college football games. Crib free. TV; cable. Pool. Complimentary coffee in rms. Restaurant 6 am-9 pm. Rm serv. Bar 2 pm-midnight; Thurs, Fri to 1 am. Ck-out noon. Meeting rms. Business servs avail. Cr cds: A, C, D, DS, ER, JCB, MC, V.

🏊 ⊠ 🎿 **SC**

★ ★ **DOWNTOWN INN.** *400 N Lamar.* *601/234-3031; FAX 601/234-2834; res: 800/606-1497.* 123 rms, 2 story. S, D $63-$85; under 19 free. Crib free. TV; cable (premium), VCR avail. Pool. Restaurant 6 am-2 pm, 5-9 pm. Rm serv. Bar 4 pm-midnight. Ck-out 1 pm. Coin lndry. Meeting rms. Business servs avail. In-rm modem link. Valet serv. Free airport transportation. Cr cds: A, C, D, DS, JCB, MC, V.

D 🏊 ⊠ 🎿 **SC**

★ **RAMADA INN.** *2201 Jackson Ave W.* *601/234-7013; FAX 601/236-4378.* 116 rms, 2 story. S $49-$51; D $55-$57; each addl $6; suites $115; under 12 free; higher rates football wkends. Crib free. TV; cable. Pool. Ck-out noon. Business servs avail. Cr cds: A, C, D, DS, JCB, MC, V.

D 🏊 ⊠ 🎿 **SC**

Inn

✔ ★ ★ **OLIVER-BRITT HOUSE.** *512 Van Buren Ave.* *601/234-8043; FAX 601/281-8065.* 5 rms, 2 story. No rm phones. S, D $45-$65; higher rates wkends. Pet accepted, some restrictions. TV; cable. Complimentary full bkfst. Restaurant nearby. Ck-out 11 am, ck-in 2 pm. Business servs avail. Restored manor house built 1905; some period furnishings. Cr cds: A, DS, MC, V.

🐾 ⊠ 🎿 **SC**

Restaurant

★ ★ **DOWNTOWN GRILL.** *110 Courthouse Square. 601/234-2659.* Hrs: 9 am-10 pm. Closed Sun; some major hols. Res accepted. Bar to midnight; Thurs, Fri to 1 am. Semi-a la carte: lunch $5.95-$9.95, dinner $11.95-$25.95. Specialties: catfish Lafitte, filet Paulette. Entertainment Thurs-Sat. Elegant dining. On Oxford Square. Cr cds: A, DS, MC, V.

D

Pascagoula (J-5)

(See also Biloxi, Ocean Springs; also see Mobile, AL)

Pop 25,899 **Elev** 15 ft **Area code** 228 **Zip** 39567
Information Jackson County Chamber of Commerce, 825 Denny Ave, PO Box 480, 39568-0480; 228/762-3391.

This resort, shipbuilding center and port offers fresh and salt water fishing, swimming and many other recreational opportunities. The city has a long and fascinating history. Pine ridges and mysterious bayous surround it, and its "singing river" is famous.

The Pascagoula River gives forth a peculiar singing music, which resembles a swarm of bees in flight. According to legend, the Pascagoula Indians (for whom the city is named) had a young chieftain who wooed and won a princess of the neighboring Biloxi tribe, even though she was betrothed. The Biloxi chief, enraged, attacked the Pascagoula tribe with an overwhelming force. The Pascagoula, realizing they could not win, joined hands and walked, singing, into the river to their death.

What to See and Do

Mississippi Sandhill Crane National Wildlife Refuge. Established to protect endangered cranes, the refuge's three units total 18,000 acres. Visitor center has slide programs (by request), wildlife exhibit, paintings and maps (Mon-Fri; closed legal hols). Tours (Jan-Feb, by appt). Also here is wildlife trail (3/4 mi) with interpretive panels; outdoor exhibit; birdwatching. Off Gautier-Vancleave Rd, 1/2 mi N of I-10 exit 61, follow signs. Contact Manager, 7200 Crane Lane, Gautier 39564; 228/497-6322. **Free.**

Old Spanish Fort and Museum (1718). Built by the French, later captured by the Spanish, the fort's walls of massive cypress timbers cemented with oyster shells, mud and moss are 18 inches thick. Said to be the oldest structure in the Mississippi Valley. Museum has Native American relics, historic items. (Daily ; closed major hols) 4602 Fort St, 5 blks N of US 90. Phone 228/769-1505. ¢

Scranton Museum. Nautical, marine and wetlands exhibits housed in restored shrimp boat. (Tues-Sat, Sun afternoons; closed hols) River Park at Pascagoula River. Phone 228/762-6017 or 228/938-6612. **Free.**

🔲 **Singing River.** Singing sound is best heard on late summer and autumn nights. The music seems to increase in volume, coming nearer until it seems to be underfoot. Scientists have said it could be made by fish, sand scraping the hard slate bottom, natural gas escaping from sand bed or current sucked past a hidden cave. None of the explanations offered have been proven. Pascagoula River, 2 blks W of courthouse.

Annual Events

Mardi Gras. Month leading to Ash Wednesday.

Garden Club Pilgrimage. Tours of Historic houses and gardens in town. Late Mar-early Apr.

River Jamboree. In Moss Point, N on MS 63. Arts & crafts, games. First Sat in May.

Jackson County Fair. Fairgrounds. Mid-Oct.

Motels

★ **DAYS INN.** *(6700 MS 63, Moss Point 39563) at I-10 exit 69.* 601/475-0077; FAX 601/475-3783. 54 rms, 2 story. S, D $55.95-$70; each addl $5; under 12 free. Crib free. TV; cable. Pool. Complimentary continental bkfst. Restaurant adj 7 am-10 pm. Ck-out 11 am. Some refrigerators. Cr cds: A, D, DS, MC, V.

D ⟰ ≋ ⚞ SC

✓★ ★ ★ **LA FONT INN.** *2703 Denny Ave, 2703 Denny Ave.* 228/762-7111; FAX 228/934-4324; res: 800/647-6077 (exc MS), 800/821-3668 (MS). 192 rms, 2 story, 13 kits. S $61-$78; D $66-$78; each addl $5; suites $121-$148; under 14 free. Crib free. Pet accepted. TV; cable (premium). Pool; wading pool, whirlpool, poolside serv. Playground. Complimentary coffee in rms. Restaurant 6 am-10 pm. Rm serv. Bar 11 am-midnight. Ck-out 1 pm. Coin lndry. Meeting rms. Business servs avail. In-rm modem link. Bellhops. Valet serv. Sundries. Lighted tennis. 18-hole golf privileges. Exercise equipt; steam rm, sauna. Lawn games. Refrigerators. Cr cds: A, C, D, DS, MC, V.

D ⚟ ⚞ ⚐ ≋ ⚞ ⚟ ⚞ SC

Restaurants

✓★ **FILLETS.** *1911 Denny Ave.* 228/769-0280. Hrs: 11 am-9 pm; Fri, Sat to 10 pm. Closed Jan 1, July 4, Thanksgiving, Dec 25. Res accepted. Semi-a la carte: lunch, dinner $2-$13. Specializes in seafood platter, po boys. Casual dining. Cr cds: A, D, DS, MC, V.

D SC ⚞

★ ★ **TIKI RESTAURANT, LOUNGE & MARINA.** *(3212 Mary Walker Dr, Gautier 39553) 4 mi W off US 90.* 228/497-1591. Hrs: 11 am-10 pm; Fri, Sat to midnight. Closed Jan 1, Dec 24, 25. Res accepted. Bar to 1 am. Semi-a la carte: lunch $4.50-$6.95, dinner $5.95-$20.95. Child's meals. Specializes in fresh seafood, steak. Entertainment Tues-Sun. On bayou. Family-owned. Cr cds: A, C, D, DS, MC, V.

D SC ⚞

Pass Christian (J-4)

(See also Gulfport)

Settled 1704 **Pop** 5,557 **Elev** 10 ft **Area code** 228 **Zip** 39571
Information Chamber of Commerce, PO Box 307; 228/452-2252.

The town was a resort before the Civil War and the site of the South's first yacht club, which was founded in 1849. It is Mrs. Jane Murphy Manders who is generally credited with the "bed sheet surrender" of Pass Christian on April 4, 1862; attempting to save the city from further shelling by the Union fleet after the Confederate forces evacuated, Mrs. Murphy waved a sheet from her doorway. Pass Christian has hosted six vacationing US presidents—Jackson, Taylor, Grant, Theodore Roosevelt, Wilson and Truman. The world's largest oyster reef is offshore.

What to See and Do

Buccaneer State Park. Located on the Gulf of Mexico, the park features two waterslides. Swimming beach, pool, wading pool; gulf fishing for speckled trout, flounder, redfish, crab, shrimp. Nature, bicycle trails; lighted tennis. Picnicking (shelters), playground, basketball courts, snack bar, lodge with game room, coin lndry. Primitive & improved camping. Standard fees. 20 mi W on US 90 in Waveland. Phone 228/467-3822.

The Friendship Oak. The oak's 16-ft trunk and 5-ft-plus-diameter limbs dwarf Hardy Hall. A plaque dates the tree back to 1487, five years before Columbus' arrival to the new world. Legend proclaims that those who enter the tree's shadow shall remain lifetime friends. Wooden platform provides a peaceful haven. American poet Vachel Lindsay regularly held classes in the shade of the majestic oak. 6 mi E on US 90, located on the Univ of Southern Mississippi's Gulf Park campus, beside Hardy Hall in Long Beach.

Annual Events

Mardi Gras. Carnival Ball and Parade. Sat, Sun before Shrove Tuesday.

Garden Club Pilgrimage. Information at Chamber of Commerce Bldg, Small Craft Harbor. Visits to several historic houses and gardens in town. Late Mar.

Blessing of the Fleet. Festival; boat decorations competition; band; entertainment. Last Sun May.

Seafood Festival. Entertainment. Mid-July.

Motel

★ ★ **CASINO MAGIC INN.** (711 Casino Magic Dr, Bay St Louis 39520) 9 mi W on US 90. 228/466-0891; FAX 228/466-0870; res: 800/5-MAGIC-5. E-mail webmaster@casinomagic.com; web www.casinomagic.com. 201 rms, 4 story. S, D $65-$119; each addl $5; suites $175-$195; under 18 free; wkend rates; higher rates hols. Crib free. TV; cable. Heated pool; whirlpool. Complimentary coffee in rms. Restaurant adj 24 hrs. Ck-out 11 am. Meeting rms. Bellhops. Gift shop. Coin lndry. Some refrigerators. Cr cds: A, C, D, DS, MC, V.

D ⚄ ⚊ ⚊ ⚊ SC

Restaurant

★ **ANNIE'S.** 120 W Bayview. 228/452-2062. Hrs: 11:30 am-10 pm; Sun to 9 pm. Closed Mon; also Dec. Res accepted. Continental menu. Bar. Semi-a la carte: lunch, dinner $4.50-$16.50. Child's meals. Specializes in seafood, steak, veal. Mission bells from old Southern plantations displayed on patio. Family-owned. Cr cds: A, DS, MC, V.

Philadelphia (E-5)

(See also Louisville, Meridian)

Pop 6,758 **Elev** 424 ft **Area code** 601 **Zip** 39350
Information Philadelphia-Neshoba County Chamber of Commerce, 410 Poplar Ave, Suite 101, PO Box 51; 601/656-1742.

This town was settled on Choctaw land. Several thousand Choctaws continue to live in the area. The Choctaw tribe, which once numbered more than 25,000, ceded its lands to the United States by the Treaty of Dancing Rabbit Creek in 1830. The Choctaw Indian Agency, which was founded shortly after the treaty was signed, is located in Philadelphia.

What to See and Do

Golden Memorial State Park. Park covering 120 acres on Golden Lake. Developed as a memorial to one-room schoolhouse that operated on this site after the Civil War. Swimming beach; fishing; boating (rentals). Nature, bicycle trails. Picnicking (shelters), playground. Standard fees. (Wed-Sun) Approx 20 mi SW via MS 21, 5 mi E of Walnut Grove off MS 35. Phone 601/253-2237.

Annual Events

Choctaw Indian Fair. Choctaw Indian Reservation, 8 mi W via MS 16. Entertainment; arts & crafts; cultural programs; princess pageant; music. Mid-July.

Neshoba County Fair. 8 1/2 mi SW via MS 21S. Early Aug.

Port Gibson (F-2)

(See also Vicksburg)

Settled 1788 **Pop** 1,810 **Elev** 120 ft **Area code** 601 **Zip** 39150
Information Port Gibson-Claiborne County Chamber of Commerce, PO Box 491; 601/437-4351.

Many antebellum houses and buildings remain in Port Gibson, lending support to the story that General Grant spared the town on his march to Vicksburg with the words: "It's too beautiful to burn."

The Samuel Gibson House (ca 1805), oldest existing structure in town, has been restored and now houses the Port Gibson-Claiborne County Chamber of Commerce and Visitor Information Center.

What to See and Do

✪ **Antebellum houses.** Open year round by appointment; special schedule during Spring Pilgrimage. Phone 601/437-4351.   ¢¢

Energy Central. On grounds of Grand Gulf Nuclear Station. Exhibits and hands-on displays about nuclear energy and electricity. (Mon-Fri) 2 mi N on US 61 to Grand Gulf Rd. Phone 601/437-6393 or -6317.   **Free.**

First Presbyterian Church (1859). Gold-leaf hand with a finger pointing skyward tops the steeple; interior features old slave gallery and chandeliers taken from the steamboat *Robert E. Lee.* Church & Walnut Sts. **Free.**

Grand Gulf Military Park. This site marks the former town of Grand Gulf, which lost 55 of 75 city blocks to Mississippi floods between 1855 and 1860. The Confederacy chose to fortify the banks when the population was only 160 and the town was dying. In the spring of 1862, Admiral David G. Farragut sent his powerful naval squadron upriver; Baton Rouge and Natchez fell, but Vicksburg refused to surrender. Confederate artillery and supporting troops were sent to Grand Gulf, where intermittent fighting between Union warships and Confederate shore batteries continued until a Union column landed at Bayou Pierre, marched on Grand Gulf and burned what remained of the town. War returned to Grand Gulf when Admiral D.D. Porter's ironclads opened fire on forts Cobun and Wade on the morning of Apr 29, 1863. After more than five hrs, two ironclads were disabled and the guns of Fort Wade silenced. The park today includes fortifications, an observation tower, a cemetery, sawmill, dog-trot house, memorial chapel, water wheel and grist mill, a carriage house with vehicles used by the Confederates, a four-rm cottage reconstructed from early days of Grand Gulf and several other pre-Civil War buildings. A museum in the visitor center displays Civil War, Native American and prehistoric artifacts (daily; closed Jan 1, Thanksgiving, Dec 25; fee). Park (daily). Picnic facilities, 42 camper pads (hookups). 8 mi NW off US 61. Phone 601/437-5911. Park ¢; camping ¢¢¢.

Oak Square (ca 1850). Restored 30-rm mansion with 6 fluted, Corinthian columns, each standing 22 ft tall. Antique furnishings from the 18th and 19th centuries. Extensive grounds, courtyard, gazebo. Guest rms avail (see INNS). Tours by appt. 1207 Church St, 1 mi off Natchez Trace Pkwy. Phone 601/437-4350 or 800/729-0240.   ¢¢

Rosswood Plantation (1857). Classic Greek-revival mansion designed by David Shroder, architect of Windsor, features columned galleries, 10 fireplaces, 15-ft ceilings, a winding stairway and slave quarters in the basement. The first owner's diary has survived and offers details of antebellum life on a cotton plantation. The 14 rms are furnished with antiques. Guest rms avail (see INNS). (Tours Mar-Dec; closed some hols) 9 mi S on US 61 to Lorman, then 2 1/2 mi E on MS 552. Phone 800/533-5889. Tours ¢¢¢

The Ruins of Windsor. 23 stately columns are all that is left of a four-story mansion built in 1860 at a cost of $175,000 and destroyed by fire in 1890. Its proximity and size made it a natural marker for Mississippi River pilots, including Samuel Clemens. Old Rodney Rd.

Annual Event

Spring Pilgrimage. Tours of historic houses. Phone 601/437-4351 for dates. Early spring.

Inns

★ ★ ★ **CANEMOUNT PLANTATION.** *(Rte 2, MS 552W, Lorman 39096) 10 mi S on US 61, 8 mi W on MS 552. 601/877-3784; FAX 601/877-2010; res: 800/423-0684 (exc MS).* E-mail cmount@vicksburg.com; web www.canemount.com. 3 cottages; 2 suites. No rm phones. MAP: S, D $165-$195; each addl $75. Children over 12 yrs only. TV; VCR avail. Heated pool. Complimentary coffee in rm. Ck-out noon, ck-in 2 pm. Business servs avail. Valet serv. On 10,000-acre working plantation. Built 1855; fireplaces. Totally nonsmoking. Cr cds: MC, V.

✔★ ★ **OAK SQUARE COUNTRY INN.** *1207 Church St. 601/437-4350; FAX 601/437-5768; res: 800/729-0240.* 12 rms, 2 story. S, D $85-$120. TV; cable. Complimentary bkfst. Ck-out 11 am. Restored antebellum mansion (ca 1850) and guest house; antique furnishings. Courtyard, fountain, gazebo, massive oak trees. Free tour of mansion, grounds. Cr cds: A, DS, MC, V.

★ ★ **ROSSWOOD PLANTATION.** *(MS 552E, Lorman 39096) 2 1/2 mi E on MS 552. 601/437-4215; FAX 601/437-6888; res: 800/533-5889.* E-mail whylander@aol.com; web www.rosswood.net. 4 rms, 2 story. S, D $115-$135. TV; VCR (movies). Heated pool; whirlpool. Complimentary full bkfst. Complimentary coffee in rms. Ck-out 11 am, ck-in 2-5 pm. Landmark Greek-revival mansion (1857) on working Christmas tree plantation. Many antiques. Cr cds: A, DS, MC, V.

Restaurant

★ **OLD DEPOT.** *1202 Market St. 601/437-4711.* Hrs: 11 am-9 pm; Fri, Sat to 10 pm. Closed Sun; major hols. Res accepted Fri, Sat. Bar. Semi-a la carte: lunch, dinner $3.95-$15.75. Child's meals. Specializes in steak, seafood, red beans & rice. Parking. Cr cds: A, DS, MC, V.

Sardis (B-3)

Pop 2,128 **Elev** 379 ft **Area code** 601 **Zip** 38666
Information Chamber of Commerce, 114 W Lee St, PO Box 377; 601/487-3451.

What to See and Do

Enid Lake and Dam. Shoreline with swimming; boating. Picnicking. Camping (hookups; fee). Amphitheater. Golden Age and Golden Access passports accepted (see MAKING THE MOST OF YOUR TRIP). Dam is part of the Yazoo Basin Flood Control Plan. 21 mi S on I-55, then 1 mi E. Phone 601/563-4571. On S shore of lake is

George Payne Cossar State Park. Park covering 900 acres situated on a peninsula jutting into Enid Lake. Swimming pool, waterskiing; fishing; boating (ramp). Nature, bicycle trails (rentals); miniature golf. Picnicking (shelters), playground, concession, restaurant (yr round, Wed-Sun), lodge, coin lndry. Improved camping, cabins. Standard fees. 25 mi S on I-55, then 4 mi E on MS 32. Phone 601/623-7356.

Heflin House Museum (1858). One of the few remaining antebellum structures in Sardis and Panola County; houses exhibits on history of Panola County from Native American times through 1900. (Mon-Fri by appt; closed hols) Contact Chamber of Commerce. 304 S Main. Phone 601/487-3451. **Donation.**

Sardis Lake and Dam. This lake, with a 260-mi shoreline formed by damming the Little Tallahatchie River, is part of the Yazoo Basin flood control project. Noted for its natural white sand beaches. Swimming, waterskiing; fishing; boating (launching ramps). Picnicking. Camping (some fees). Interpretive programs. 9 mi E off I-55. Phone 601/563-4531. **Free.** Overlooking the lake is

John W. Kyle State Park. Pool (summer, daily exc Mon), waterskiing; fishing; boating (ramps). Nature trails; lighted tennis. Picnicking (shelters), playground, playing field, snack bar, lodge, coin lndry. Improved camping, cabins. Standard fees. On 740 acres overlooking Sardis Lake. Phone 601/487-1345.

Motel

✔★ ★ **BEST WESTERN SARDIS INN.** *Box 279, 1/8 mi W on MS 315 at I-55, exit 252. 601/487-2424; FAX 601/487-2424.* 79 rms, 2 story. S $35-$38; D $38-$50; each addl $6; under 12 free. Crib free. TV; cable (premium), VCR (movies). Pool; wading pool. Restaurant 6 am-10 pm. Rm serv. Bar 4 pm-midnight. Ck-out 11 am. Business servs avail. Some refrigerators. Cr cds: A, C, D, DS, MC, V.

Starkville (C-5)

(See also Columbus)

Founded 1831 **Pop** 18,458 **Elev** 374 ft **Area code** 601 **Zip** 39759 **Web** www.starkville.org
Information Visitors & Convention Council, 322 University Dr; 601/323-3322 or 800/649-8687.

Starkville is the seat of Oktibbeha County and the home of Mississippi State University.

What to See and Do

Mississippi State University (1878). (14,000 students) Originally Mississippi Agricultural and Mechanical College, it became a state university in 1958. On a 4,200-acre tract, approximately 750 acres make up the campus; the Mississippi Agricultural and Forestry Experiment Station utilizes much of the remaining land for cultivation, pasture and buildings. On campus are the Dunn-Seiler Geology Museum, Cobb Institute of Archaeology, University Art Gallery and the Chapel of Memories. 1 mi E, on University Dr. Phone 601/325-2323.

National Wildlife Refuge. This 48,000-acre refuge, which includes 1,200-acre Bluff Lake, offers space for more than 200 species of birds, including waterfowl, wild turkey, the endangered bald eagle and red-cockaded woodpecker, as well as alligators and deer. Fishing (Mar-Oct), hunting (fall; some fees). Hiking. Refuge (daily). SE off MS 25; follow signs from stadium at Mississippi State Univ. Phone 601/323-5548. **Free.**

Oktibbeha County Heritage Museum. Artifacts from the county's past housed in the former GM&O railroad station. (Tues-Thurs; or by appt; closed hols) Fellowship & Russell Sts. Phone 601/323-0211. **Free.**

Motel

✔★ ★ **HOLIDAY INN.** *Box 751, MS 12 & Montgomery St, opp MSU. 601/323-6161; FAX 601/323-8073.* 173 rms, 2 story. S, D $55; each addl $6; under 18 free; higher rates football wknds. Crib free. Pet accepted. TV; cable (premium). Pool. Restaurant 6 am-2 pm, 5-10 pm. Rm serv. Bar 5 pm-midnight; closed Sun. Ck-out noon. Meeting rms. Business servs avail. Cr cds: A, C, D, DS, JCB, MC, V.

Inn

★ ★ **STATE HOUSE HOTEL.** *Box 2002, Main & Jackson Sts. 601/323-2000; FAX 601/323-4948; res: 800/722-1903.* 43 units, 3 story, 9 suites. S $45-$70; D $55-$72; each addl $3-$10; suites $74-110; under 13 free; higher rates football wkends. Crib $8. TV, cable. Dining rm 6:30 am-2 pm, 6-9:30 pm. Ck-out noon, ck-in 2 pm. Refrigerators. Balconies. Antique furnishings; courtyard. Cr cds: A, C, D, DS, MC, V.

D ⛅ 🔥 SC

Restaurant

✔★ ★ **HARVEY'S.** *406 MS 12. 601/323-1639.* Hrs: 11 am-9:30 pm; Fri, Sat to 10 pm. Closed Sun; most major hols. Res accepted. Bar 5 pm-midnight. Semi-a la carte: lunch $4.95-$9.95, dinner $5.95-$15.95. Child's meals. Specializes in steak, seafood, pasta. Cr cds: A, DS, MC, V.

D

Tupelo (B-5)

Settled 1833 **Pop** 30,685 **Elev** 290 ft **Area code** 601 **Zip** 38801 **Web** www.Tupelo.net
Information Convention & Visitors Bureau, 399 E Main St, PO Drawer 47, 38802; 601/841-6521 or 800/533-0611.

Tupelo is built on what was formerly Chickasaw land. On May 26, 1736, two forces of French colonists and their Choctaw allies unsuccessfully attacked the Chickasaw in an attempt to rescue prisoners and avenge an attack by the Natchez on the French settlement of Natchez. Failure to conquer the Chickasaw prevented the extension of French authority into northern Alabama, Mississippi and western Tennessee.

When the town was ceded by the Treaty of Pontotoc in 1832, settlers moved in and began farming. After the Battle of Shiloh, April 6-7, 1862, Confederate General P.G.T. Beauregard and his defeated troops retreated to Tupelo.

This was the first city to sign for TVA power—on October 11, 1933. Less than four months later service was begun at a tremendous savings. Tupelo is also the birthplace of Elvis Presley.

What to See and Do

Brices Cross Roads National Battlefield Site. One-acre site overlooks terrain where Confederate soldiers defeated an attacking Union force. Marker with texts and maps identifies landmarks. Adj cemetery is burial site of over 100 identified Confederate soldiers. (Daily) 17 mi N on US 45 to Baldwyn, then 6 mi W on MS 370. **Free.**

Elvis Presley Park and Museum. In park is small white frame house where Presley lived for the first three years of his life. Museum houses collection of Elvis memorabilia. Chapel (free). (Daily; buildings closed Thanksgiving & Dec 25) 306 Elvis Presley Dr. Phone 601/841-1245. House ¢; Museum ¢¢

Natchez Trace Parkway Visitor Center. 5 mi N at jct Pkwy, US 45 Business (see NATCHEZ TRACE PARKWAY).

Oren Dunn Museum of Tupelo. Displays include NASA space equipment used in Apollo missions; Elvis Presley room; reproductions of Western Union office, general store, train station, log cabin; Civil War and Chickasaw items. (Daily; closed some hols) 2 mi W via MS 6 at Ballard Park. Phone 601/841-6438. ¢

Pvt John Allen National Fish Hatchery. This federal hatchery, one of the oldest (1902), operates 15 ponds totaling 17 acres. A warmwater hatchery, it produces striped and largemouth bass, bluegill and redear; it distributes one million fish annually for use in management of reservoirs and coastal waters. (Daily) 111 Elizabeth St. Phone 601/842-1341. **Free.**

Tombigbee National Forest. This section of the forest, along with a tract to the south on MS 15 near Louisville (see), totals 66,341 acres. Davis Lake provides swimming (fee); fishing. Picnicking. Camping (electric hookups; fee; dump station). Recreation area (Mar-mid-Nov). Standard fees are charged at recreation sites. A Ranger District office is located in Ackerman. 20 mi S, off Natchez Trace Pkwy. Contact Forest Supervisor, 100 W Capitol St, Suite 1141, Jackson 39269; 601/965-4391. Day use ¢¢

Tombigbee State Park. A 702-acre park with a 102-acre spring-fed lake. Swimming beach (summer, daily). Fishing; boating (ramp, rentals). Nature trail; tennis; archery range. Picnicking (shelters), playground, snack bar, lodge. Primitive & improved camping, cabins. Standard fees. 6 mi SE off MS 6. Phone 601/842-7669.

Trace State Park. On 2,500 acres with a 600-acre lake. Swimming beach, waterskiing; fishing for bass, catfish, redear, bluegill and crappie; boating (ramp, rentals). Hiking, horseriding trail; golf. Picnicking. Tent & trailer camping (electric and water hookups, dump station), cabins. Standard fees. 10 mi W via MS 6. Phone 601/489-2958.

Tupelo National Battlefield. One-acre tract near area where Confederate line was formed to attack Union position. Marker with texts and maps explains battle. (Daily) 1 mi W on MS 6. **Free.**

Motels

★ ★ **COMFORT INN.** *1190 N Gloster. 601/842-5100; FAX 601/844-0554.* 83 rms, 2 story. S $50-$59; D $53-$65; each addl $4; under 18 free. Crib free. TV; cable (premium). Complimentary continental bkfst. Ck-out 11 am. Meeting rms. Business servs avail. In-rm modem link. Cr cds: A, C, D, DS, MC, V.

D ⛅ 🔥 SC

✔★ **HOLIDAY INN EXPRESS.** *923 N Gloster St, jct US 45, 78. 601/842-8811; FAX 601/844-6884.* E-mail tupms@aol.com. 124 rms, 2 story. Feb-Aug: S $50; D $54; each addl $7; under 12 free; lower rates rest of yr. Pet accepted; $7/day. TV; cable (premium). Pool. Complimentary continental bkfst. Coin lndry. Meeting rms. Business servs avail. Cr cds: A, D, DS, MC, V.

D 🐾 ⛅ 🔥 SC

★ ★ **RAMADA INN.** *854 Gloster St N, jct US 45, 78. 601/844-4111; FAX 601/844-4111, ext. 2496.* 230 rms, 3 story. No elvtr. S $47; D $57; each addl $5; suites $115-$175; studio rms $55-$80; under 18 free. Crib free. TV; cable (premium), VCR avail. Pool; wading pool, poolside serv. Restaurant 6 am-10 pm. Rm serv. Bar 4 pm-midnight; entertainment. Ck-out 1 pm. Coin lndry. Convention facilities. Business center. In-rm modem link. Valet serv. Sundries. Free airport transportation. Exercise equipt. Cr cds: A, C, D, DS, JCB, MC, V.

D ⛅ 🏃 🔥 SC 🚶

✔★ **RED ROOF INN.** *1500 McCullough Blvd. 601/844-1904; FAX 601/844-0139.* 100 units, 2 story. S $38-$52; D $43-$56; each addl $5; under 16 free; wkly rates; higher rates special events. Crib free. TV; cable. Pool. Ck-out noon. Coin lndry. Business servs avail. In-rm modem link. Cr cds: A, D, DS, MC, V.

D ⛅ 🔥 🐾

Motor Hotel

✔★ ★ **EXECUTIVE INN.** *1011 N Gloster. 601/841-2222; FAX 601/844-7836; res: 800/533-3220.* 115 rms, 5 story. S, D $60-$79; suites $170-$225; under 18 free. Crib free. TV; cable (premium). Indoor pool; whirlpool. Sauna. Restaurant 6 am-10 pm; Sat, Sun 7 am-2 pm. Rm serv 7 am-2 pm, 5-10 pm. Bar 4 pm-midnight; closed Sun. Ck-out noon. Meeting rms. Business servs avail. In-rm modem link. Bellhops. Cr cds: A, C, D, DS, JCB, MC, V.

D ⛅ 🔥 SC

Inn

★ ★ **MOCKINGBIRD INN.** *305 N Gloster. 601/841-0286; FAX 601/840-4158.* 7 rms, 2 story. S, D $65-$125; each addl $10; wkend rates. Children over 10 yrs only. Pet accepted, some restrictions; $10. TV; cable. Complimentary full bkfst; afternoon refreshments. Restaurant opp 11 am-10 pm. Ck-out noon, ck-in 3-9 pm. Business servs avail. Built in 1925; porch, gazebo. Cr cds: A, DS, MC, V.

D ☞ ⋈ ⋉ SC

Restaurants

★ **JEFFERSON PLACE.** *823 Jefferson St. 601/844-8696.* Hrs: 11 am-midnight. Closed Sun; Thanksgiving, Dec 25. Bar. Semi-a la carte: lunch $3.95-$9.95, dinner $5.25-$14.95. Specializes in steak, chicken, shrimp. Cr cds: A, D, MC, V.

✔ ★ **PAPA VANELLI'S.** *1302 N Gloster. 601/844-4410.* Hrs: 11 am-10 pm. Closed Dec 25. Italian, Greek menu. Bar. A la carte entrees: lunch, dinner $4.95-$15.95. Child's meals. Specializes in pizza, pasta buffet. Family-owned. Cr cds: A, D, DS, MC, V.

D ♥

Unrated Dining Spot

MALONE'S FISH & STEAK HOUSE. *1349 MS 41. 601/842-2747.* Hrs: 5-10 pm. Closed Sun, Mon; Thanksgiving; also 2 wks late Dec. Semi-a la carte: dinner $3.95-$12.95. Child's meals. Specializes in steak, catfish. Salad bar. Cr cds: MC, V.

D

Vicksburg (E-2)

(See also Port Gibson)

Settled 1790 **Pop** 20,908 **Elev** 200 ft **Area code** 601 **Zip** 39180 **E-mail** cvb@vicksburg.org **Web** www.vicksburg.org/cvb

Information Convention & Visitors Bureau, PO Box 110, 39181; 601/636-9421 or 800/221-3536.

In June 1862, the Union controlled the Mississippi River with the exception of Vicksburg, which was in Confederate hands. The location of the town, partly on high bluffs above the river, made it impossible to move traffic up or down the river without subjecting the boats to withering fire from strong Confederate batteries. This position made it possible to maintain communication lines with Louisiana, which were vital to the Confederacy.

Grant's purpose was to gain complete control of the Mississippi as a waterway and, in doing so, to split the South. In June, Admiral David Farragut sent his fleet of Union gunboats upriver from New Orleans and shelled the town; he was, however, forced to withdraw before taking the city or silencing its guns. General William Tecumseh Sherman, also attempting to take Vicksburg, moved along the west banks of the river, south from Memphis with 30,000 troops. He was repulsed. Meanwhile, Grant's supply lines were being broken and harassed by Confederate cavalry.

Grant was now desperate. He had to take Vicksburg. He ordered Admiral David Porter to move his gunboats south from Memphis and to pass Vicksburg at night. The boats were sighted; two transports were lost. The others got through, and Grant, with an army west of the river, now had transportation across the river. Once in Mississippi, the Union army, living off the land, moved around Vicksburg in a series of brilliant diversionary maneuvers that kept the Confederate cavalry busy accomplishing nothing. Grant now took Jackson and moved toward Vicksburg from the east. He attacked the city with three corps, setting the time of attack and synchronizing watches to make sure all attacked together. But his forces were driven back.

Grant was a more modern and committed general than most of the other Union commanders in the war. He would settle for nothing less than total victory, unconditional surrender of the city of Vicksburg. He realized that to take Vicksburg, the town must be starved; so he surrounded it and laid siege. For 47 days and nights Grant pounded Vicksburg with mortar and cannon fire; and the populace, hiding in caves, nearly starved.

The caves dug by the residents of Vicksburg and the Union army's trenches and tunneling were made easier because the city was built on loess, a wind-blown silt that forms a compacted but soft soil. Grant dug tunnels and planted mines under Confederate positions, but only one charge was set off. On July 4, the Confederates agreed to surrender the city. On that day the South's cause was dealt a mighty blow from which it never recovered.

Modern Vicksburg is nearly surrounded by the Vicksburg National Military Park, which is as much a part of the town as the streets and antebellum houses. Originally an important river port, Vicksburg has a fascinating riverfront along the Mississippi River and the Yazoo Canal. Plan to spend several days; the town offers much to see and do.

What to See and Do

✪ **Antebellum houses.**

Martha Vick House (1830). Built by the daughter of the founder of Vicksburg, Newit Vick. Greek-revival facade; restored original interior furnished with 18th- and 19th-century antiques; outstanding art collection. (Daily; closed some hols) 1300 Grove St. Phone 601/638-7036. ¢¢

McRaven Home Civil War Tour Home. Heaviest-shelled house during Siege of Vicksburg; provides an architectural record of Vicksburg history, from frontier cottage (1797) to Empire (1836) and finally to elegant Greek-revival townhouse (1849); many original furnishings. Original brick walks surround the house; garden of live oaks, boxwood, magnolia and many plants. Guided tours. (Mar-Nov, daily) 1445 Harrison St. Phone 601/636-1663. ¢¢

Cedar Grove (1840). Elegant mansion shelled by Union gunboats in siege; restored, but a cannonball is still lodged in parlor wall; roof garden with view of Mississippi and Yazoo rivers; tea room; many original furnishings. Over four acres of formal gardens; courtyards, fountains, gazebos. (Daily) Guest rms avail (see INNS). 2200 Oak St. Phone 601/636-1000 or 800/862-1300. Guided tours ¢¢

Anchuca (1830). Restored Greek-revival mansion furnished with period antiques and gas-burning chandeliers. Landscaped gardens, brick courtyard. (Daily; closed Dec 25) Guest rms (see INNS). 1010 First East St. Phone 601/661-0111. Guided tours ¢¢

Duff Green (1856). Mansion of Paladian architecture shelled by Union forces during siege, then used as hospital for remainder of the war. Restored; antique furnishings. Guided tours. High tea & tour (by reservation). Guest rms avail (see INNS). (Daily) 1114 First East St. Phone 601/636-6968 or 800/992-0037. ¢¢

Biedenharn Museum of Coca-Cola Memorabilia. Building in which Coca-Cola was first bottled in 1894. Restored candy store; old-fashioned soda fountain; collection of Coca-Cola advertising and memorabilia. (Daily; closed Jan 1, Easter, Thanksgiving, Dec 25) 1107 Washington St. Phone 601/638-6514. ¢

Old Court House Museum (1858). Built with slave labor, this building offers a view of the Yazoo Canal from its hilltop position. Here Grant raised the US flag on July 4, 1863, signifying the end of fighting after 47 days. Courthouse now houses an extensive display of Americana: Confederate Room contains weapons, documents on the siege of Vicksburg; also Pioneer Room; Furniture Room; Native American displays and objets d'art. (Daily; closed Jan 1, Thanksgiving, Dec 24-25) Court Square, 1008 Cherry St. Phone 601/636-0741. ¢

Tourist Information Center. Furnishes free information, maps and brochures on points of interest and historic houses. Guide service (fee). House (daily; closed Jan 1, Thanksgiving, Dec 25). Clay St at I-20. For information contact PO Box 110; 601/636-9421 or 800/221-3536.

"The Vanishing Glory." 30-min dramatization of Civil War siege of Vicksburg; story based upon diaries and writings of people who lived through the campaign; wide-screen production, quadraphonic sound. (Shown every hour, daily) 717 Clay St. Phone 601/634-1863. ¢¢

⭐ **Vicksburg National Military Park & Cemetery.** This historic park, the site of Union siege lines and a brave Confederate defense, borders the eastern and northern sections of the city. A visitor center is at the park entrance, on Clay St at I-20. Museum; exhibits and audiovisual aids. Self-guided, 16-mi tour. (Daily; closed Dec 25) Phone 601/636-0583. Per vehicle ¢¢ Within park is

Cairo Museum. The Union ironclad USS *Cairo,* which sank in 1862, was raised in 1964 and subsequently was restored. An audiovisual program and more than 1,000 artifacts from the sunken gunboat can be viewed inside the museum. (Daily; closed Dec 25) Phone 601/636-2199. **Free.**

Waterways Experiment Station. Principal research and testing laboratory of the US Army Corps of Engineers. Research ranges from hydraulics and soils to wetlands, and from concrete and military vehicles to environmental relationships. River, harbor and flood control projects are studied on scale models, some with wave and tide-making machines, others with model towboats. Guided tours (Mon-Fri, mid-morning-early afternoon; closed hols); also self-guided tours. Visitor center (daily). 2 mi S of I-20 on Halls Ferry Rd. Phone 601/634-2502. **Free.**

Annual Events

Spring Pilgrimage. Twelve antebellum houses are open to the public at this time. Three tours daily. Late Mar-early Apr.

Siege Re-enactment. 500 persons re-enact the siege of Vicksburg. Memorial Day wkend.

Motels

✔★ **DAYS INN.** *2 Pemberton Place. 601/634-1622; FAX 601/638-4337.* 86 units, 2 story, 20 suites. June-Aug: S $45-$50; D $50-$55; each addl $5; suites $55-$60; under 12 free; lower rates rest of yr. Crib free. TV; cable. Pool. Restaurant adj 6 am-midnight. Ck-out 11 am. Business servs avail. Cr cds: A, D, DS, MC, V.

D ≋ 🚭 SC

★ ★ **PARK INN INTERNATIONAL.** *4137 I-20 Frontage Rd, exit 4B. 601/638-5811; FAX 601/638-9249.* 117 rms, 2 story. S $35-$57; D $45-$67; each addl $5; under 16 free. Crib free. Pet accepted. TV; cable (premium). Pool. Complimentary bkfst buffet. Restaurant 6:30-9:30 am, 5-9 pm. Rm serv 5-9 pm. Bar 5-11 pm; entertainment. Ck-out 12:30 pm. Meeting rms. Business servs. In-rm modem link. Bellhops. Airport transportation. Some refrigerators. Cr cds: A, C, D, DS, MC, V.

🐾 ≋ 🚭 🔥 SC

✔★ ★ **QUALITY INN.** *2390 S Frontage Rd, at I-20. 601/634-8607; FAX 601/634-6053.* 70 rms, 2 story. S $40-$50; D $45-$55; each addl $10; under 18 free. Crib $10. TV; cable. Pool; whirlpool. Sauna. Continental bkfst. Ck-out 11 am. Business servs avail. Refrigerators. Cr cds: A, D, DS, MC, V.

D ≋ 🚭 🔥 SC

★ **SUPER 8.** *4127 I-20 Frontage Rd. 601/638-5077; FAX 601/638-5077.* 62 rms, 2 story. S $45.88; D $52.88-$58.88; each addl $4; under 12 free; wkly rates. Crib free. TV; cable. Pool. Restaurant nearby. Ck-out 11 am. Business servs avail. Cr cds: A, C, D, DS, MC, V.

D ≋ 🚭 🔥 SC

Motor Hotel

★ ★ **HOLIDAY INN.** *3330 Clay St. 601/636-4551; FAX 601/636-4552.* 173 rms, 2 story. S, D $65-$72; each addl $7; under 18 free. Crib free. Pet accepted. TV; cable (premium). Indoor pool. Sauna. Restaurant 6 am-10 pm. Rm serv. Bar 3 pm-midnight. Ck-out noon. Coin lndry. Meeting rms. Business servs avail. In-rm modem link. Bellhops. Game rm. Cr cds: A, C, D, DS, JCB, MC, V.

D 🐾 ≋ 🚭 🔥 SC

Inns

★ ★ ★ **ANCHUCA.** *1010 First East St. 601/661-0111; res: 888/686-0111; FAX 601/630-4121.* 6 rms, 2 story. S, D $85-$300; each addl $20. Crib free. TV; cable (premium). Pool; whirlpool. Complimentary bkfst. Ck-out noon, ck-in 2 pm. Business servs avail. Greek-revival house (1830). Gas-lit chandeliers, period antiques and artifacts. Tour of house. Cr cds: MC, V.

≋ 🔥

★ ★ ★ **ANNABELLE BED & BREAKFAST.** *501 Speed St, in Historic River View Garden District. 601/638-2000; FAX 601/636-5054; res: 800/791-2000.* E-mail annabelle@vicksburg.com; web www.missbab.com/annabelle. 7 rms, 2 story, 1 suite. Mar-Nov: S $85-$120; D $93-$125; each addl $20; suite $125; lower rates rest of yr. Complimentary full bkfst; afternoon refreshments. Restaurant nearby. Ck-out 11 am, ck-in 2 pm. Luggage handling. Picnic tables. Victorian-Italianate house built in 1868. Period antiques. Totally nonsmoking. Cr cds: A, C, D, DS, MC, V.

≋ 🚭 🔥 🚭

★ ★ ★ **CEDAR GROVE MANSION.** *2200 Oak St. 601/636-1000; FAX 601/634-6126; res: 800/862-1300 (exc MS), 800/448-2820 (MS).* Web cedargroveinn.com. 30 rms, 4 story. S $80-$155; D $90-$165; each addl $20. TV; cable (premium). Pool. Complimentary bkfst. Restaurant 6-9 pm. Ck-out noon, ck-in 2 pm. Business servs avail. Tennis. Exercise equipt. Antebellum mansion built 1840. Many original antiques; gas-burning chandeliers. Formal gardens, gazebos, fountains, statues. River view. Cr cds: A, DS, MC, V.

🏃 ≋ 🎾 🚭 🔥

★ ★ **THE CORNERS.** *601 Klein St. 601/636-7421; FAX 601/636-7232; res: 800/444-7421.* 15 rms, 2 story. S $95; D $105; each addl $20; suites $120. TV; cable. Complimentary full bkfst. Restaurant nearby. Ck-out 11 am, ck-in 2 pm. Business servs avail. Luggage handling. 1 blk from river. Built 1872 as a wedding gift. Antiques; extensive gardens. Totally nonsmoking. Cr cds: A, C, D, DS, MC, V.

D 🚭 🔥

★ ★ ★ **DUFF GREEN MANSION.** *1114 First East St. 601/638-6662; FAX 601/634-1061; res: 800/992-0037.* 7 units, 3 story. Mar-Nov: S, D $65-$160; each addl $10; suites $120-$160; under 5 free; wkly plan; lower rates rest of yr. Pet accepted. TV; cable, VCR avail. Pool; whirlpool. Complimentary full bkfst. Restaurant nearby. Ck-out 11 am, ck-in 3 pm. Business center. Paladian mansion (1856), used as both Confederate and Union hospital during Civil war, was shelled during siege; completely restored, many antiques. Cr cds: A, MC, V.

D 🐾 ≋ 🚭 🔥 🏃

Restaurants

★ ★ **CEDAR GROVE.** *2200 Oak St. 601/636-1000.* Web cedar groveinn.com. Hrs: 6-9 pm. Res required. Bar. Semi-a la carte: dinner $16.95-$24.95. Specializes in prime rib, filet mignon, New Orleans-style cooking. Parking. Split-level dining rm in antebellum mansion (1840). Cr cds: A, D, DS, MC, V.

D

★ ★ **EDDIE MONSOUR'S.** *1903 G Mission 66. 601/638-1571.* Hrs: 11 am-2 pm, 5:30-10 pm; Sat from 5:30 pm. Closed Sun; major hols. Res accepted. Lebanese, Amer menu. Bar. Semi-a la carte: lunch $5-$6, dinner $8.50-$25. Child's meals. Specializes in steak, seafood. Salad bar. Parking. Country-French decor. Cr cds: A, MC, V.

D

★ ★ **MAXWELL'S.** *4207 E Clay St. 601/636-1344.* Hrs: 11 am-10 pm; Sat from 5 pm. Closed Sun; major hols. Bar 4:30-11 pm. Semi-a la carte: lunch $5.50-$8.75, dinner $10.95-$24.95. Lunch buffet $6.50. Child's meals. Specializes in seafood, pasta, prime rib. Salad bar. Parking. Cr cds: A, C, D, DS, MC, V.

✔★ **WALNUT HILLS ROUND TABLES.** *1214 Adams St. 601/638-4910.* Hrs: 11 am-9 pm; Sun to 2 pm. Closed Sat; most major hols. Bar. A la carte: lunch, dinner $5.95-$15.95. Child's meals. Specializes in Southern cooking, fried chicken. Parking. Built 1880. Cr cds: A, C, D, DS, MC, V.

D

Woodville (G-2)

(See also Natchez)

Founded 1811 **Pop** 1,393 **Elev** 410 ft **Area code** 601 **Zip** 39669 **E-mail** Wilkmuseum@aol.com
Information Woodville Civic Club, PO Box 1055; 601/888-3998.

First settled in the 18th century, Woodville grew steadily and became the seat of Wilkinson County. It is the home of *The Woodville Republican,* the oldest newspaper and the oldest business institution in Mississippi. The town still has many beautiful 19th-century houses, and some of the state's first churches. These include the Woodville Baptist (1809), the Woodville Methodist (1824) and St Paul's Episcopal (1823), which has an Erben organ, installed in 1837.

What to See and Do

★ **Rosemont Plantation** (ca 1810). The home of Jefferson Davis and his family. His parents, Samuel and Jane Davis, moved to Woodville and built the house when the boy was 2 yrs old. The Confederate president grew up here and returned to visit his family throughout his life. Many family furnishings remain, including a spinning wheel that belonged to Jane Davis. Original working atmosphere of the 300-acre plantation. Five generations of the Davis family are buried here. (Mar-mid-Dec, Mon-Fri) 1 mi E on MS 24 (Main St). ¢¢¢

Wilkinson County Museum. Housed in Greek revival-style building; changing exhibits, period room settings. (Mon-Fri, also Sat mornings) Court House Square. Phone 601/888-3998.   **Free.**

Yazoo City (D-3)

(See also Jackson)

Founded 1823 **Pop** 12,427 **Elev** 120 ft **Area code** 601 **Zip** 39194
Information Yazoo County Chamber of Commerce, 212 E Broadway St, PO Box 172; 601/746-1273.

What to See and Do

Casey Jones Railroad Museum. Site of famous 1900 Casey Jones train wreck. Now state-owned museum covering story of wreck; local railroad history, folklore and artifacts; 1923 steam locomotive on display. (Daily exc Sun; closed most major hols) 10901 Vaughan Rd #1, in Vaughan, approx 15 mi E on MS 16. Phone 601/673-9864.   ¢

Delta National Forest. Numerous small lakes, streams and greentree reservoirs contained on 59,500 acres. Fishing, hunting for squirrel, raccoon, turkey, waterfowl, rabbit, woodcock, deer. Blue Lake picnic area and walking trail; Sweetgum, Overcup Oak and Green Ash natural areas. Primitive camping (fee). W via US 49, 61, MS 16. A Ranger District office is located in Rolling Fork, phone 601/873-6256. Contact Forest Supervisor, 100 W Capitol St, Suite 1141, Jackson 39269; 601/965-4391.   **Free.**

Yazoo Historical Museum. Exhibits cover history of Yazoo County from prehistoric time to present; Civil War artifacts; fossils. Tours. (Mon-Fri; closed Jan 1, Thanksgiving, Dec 24-26) Triangle Cultural Center, 332 N Main St. Phone 601/746-2273.   **Free.**

Tennessee

Population: 4,877,185
Land area: 42,244 square miles
Elevation: 182-6,643 feet
Highest point: Clingmans Dome (Sevier County)
Entered Union: June 1, 1796 (16th state)
Capital: Nashville
Nickname: Volunteer State
State flower: Iris
State bird: Mockingbird
State tree: Tulip poplar
State fair: Mid-September 1999, in Nashville
Time zone: Eastern and Central

Handsomely rugged and rough-hewn, Tennessee reveals itself most characteristically in a 480-mile stretch from Mountain City at its northeastern boundary, southwest to Memphis and the Mississippi River, with its twisting western shore. In a place of individualistic, strong-minded people, history and legend blend into folklore based on the feats of Davy Crockett, Daniel Boone, Andrew Jackson and Sam Houston. It is a state of mountain ballads and big-city ballet, of waterpowered mills and atomic energy plants.

The state's economy and its basic patterns of life and leisure were electrified in the 1930s by the Tennessee Valley Authority, that depression-born, often denounced and often praised grand-scale public power, flood control and navigation project. TVA harnessed rampaging rivers, saved cities from the annual plague of floods, created a broad system for navigation and produced inexpensive power and a treasury of recreational facilities. TVA altered the mainstream of the state's economy, achieving a dramatic switch from agriculture to industry. Cheap power, of course, sparked that revolution. Today, Tennessee has manufacturing payrolls in excess of farm income. Chemicals, textiles, foods, apparel, tourism, healthcare, printing and publishing, metalworking and lumber products are its chief industries.

Farms and forests still produce more than 50 different crops, but the emphasis is changing from cotton and tobacco to livestock. With more than 200 species of trees, Tennessee is the nation's hardwood producing center. Mining is also a leading industry in Tennessee, with limestone the major product. The state also ranks high in the production of zinc, pyrite, ball clay, phosphate rock and marble.

In 1541, it is believed, the explorer DeSoto planted the flag of Spain on the banks of the Mississippi, near what is now Memphis. Although French traders explored the Tennessee Valley, it was their English counterparts who came over the mountain ranges, settling among the Cherokee and establishing a claim to the area. By the end of the 17th century, the Tennessee region was a territory of North Carolina. With the construction of Fort Loudoun (1756), the first Anglo-American fort garrisoned west of the Alleghenies, settlement began. The first permanent colonies were established near the Watauga River in 1769 and 1771 and are known as the Watauga settlements.

The free-spirited settlers in the outlying regions found themselves far from the seat of their formal government in eastern North Carolina. Dissatisfied and insecure, they formed the independent state of Franklin in 1784. But formal recognition of the independent state was never to come. After four chaotic years, the federal government took over and in 1790 established "The Territory of the United States South of the River Ohio." Tennessee was admitted to the Union six years later. Among the first representatives it sent to Washington was a raw backwoodsman named Andrew Jackson.

During the War of 1812, Tennessee riflemen volunteered in such great numbers that Tennesee was henceforth called the "Volunteer State," and Andrew Jackson emerged from the war a national hero.

Although there was strong abolitionist sentiment in parts of the state, Tennessee finally seceded in 1861 and became a battleground; some of the bloodiest battles of the war, including Shiloh, Stones River, Missionary Ridge, Fort Donelson and the Battle of Franklin, were fought within the state's boundaries. In 1866, shortly after former Tennessee governor Andrew Johnson became president, the state was accepted back into the Union.

When to Go/Climate

Tennessee usually experiences cool winters and warm summers. There is little variation in temperatures from north to south, however temperatures do drop from west to east due to the rise in elevation. There is occasionally significant snowfall in the eastern mountains. The following temperature chart offers a representative sampling of high/low temperatures in the state.

AVERAGE HIGH/LOW TEMPERATURES (°F)
KNOXVILLE

Jan 46/26	May 78/53	Sept 81/59
Feb 51/29	June 85/62	Oct 71/46
Mar 61/37	July 87/66	Nov 60/38
Apr 70/45	Aug 87/65	Dec 50/30

MEMPHIS

Jan 49/31	May 81/61	Sept 84/65
Feb 54/35	June 89/69	Oct 74/52
Mar 63/43	July 92/73	Nov 62/43
Apr 73/52	Aug 91/71	Dec 53/35

Parks and Recreation Finder

Directions to and information about the parks and recreation areas below are given under their respective town/city sections. Please refer to those sections for details.

NATIONAL PARK AND RECREATION AREAS

Key to abbreviations: I.H.S. = International Historic Site; I.P.M. = International Peace Memorial; N.B. = National Battlefield; N.B.P. = National Battlefield Park; N.B.C. = National Battlefield & Cemetery; N.C. = National Conservation Area; N.E.M. = National Expansion Memorial; N.F. = National Forest; N.G. = National Grassland; N.H. = National Historical Park; N.H.C. = National Heritage Corridor; N.H.S. = National Historic Site; N.L. = National Lakeshore; N.M. = National Monument; N.M.P. = National Military Park; N.Mem. = National Memorial; N.P. = National Park; N.Pres. = National Preserve; N.R. = National Recreational Area; N.R.R. = National Recreational River; N.Riv. = National River; N.S. = National Seashore; N.S.R. = National Scenic Riverway; N.S.T. = National Scenic Trail; N.Sc. = National Scientific Reserve; N.V.M. = National Volcanic Monument.

Place Name	Listed Under
Andrew Johnson N.H.S.	same
Big South Fork N.R.	JAMESTOWN
Cherokee N.F.	same
Fort Donelson N.B.C.	same
Great Smoky Mountains N.P.	same
Shiloh N.M.P.	same
Stones River N.B.	MURFREESBORO

STATE PARK AND RECREATION AREAS

Key to abbreviations: I.P. = Interstate Park; S.A.P. = State Archaeological Park; S.B. = State Beach; S.C. = State Conservation Area; S.C.P. = State Conservation Park; S.Cp. = State Campground; S.F. = State Forest; S.G. = State Garden; S.H.A. = State Historic Area; S.H.P. = State Historic Park; S.H.S. = State Historic Site; S.M.P. = State Marine Park; S.N.A. = State Natural Area; S.P. = State Park; S.P.C. = State Public Campground; S.R. = State Reserve; S.R.A. = State Recreation Area; S.Res. = State Reservoir; S.Res.P. = State Resort Park; S.R.P. = State Rustic Park.

Place Name	Listed Under
Bledsoe Creek S.P.	GALLATIN
Booker T. Washington S.P.	CHATTANOOGA
Burgess Falls S.N.A.	COOKEVILLE
Cedars of Lebanon S.P.	LEBANON
Chickasaw S.R.P.	JACKSON
Cove Lake S.P.	CARYVILLE
Cumberland Mountain S.P.	CROSSVILLE
David Crockett S.P.	LAWRENCEBURG
Davy Crockett Birthplace S.P.	GREENVILLE
Fall Creek Falls S.Res.P.	McMINNVILLE
Fort Pillow S.H.A.	COVINGTON
Frozen Head S.P.	OAK RIDGE
Harrison Bay S.P.	CHATTANOOGA
Henry Horton S.Res.P.	LEWISBURG
Indian Mountain S.P.	JELLICO
Meeman-Shelby Forest S.P.	MEMPHIS
Montgomery Bell S.Res.P.	DICKSON
Natchez Trace S.Res.P.	same
Nathan Bedford Forrest S.P.	PARIS
Old Stone Fort S.A.P.	MANCHESTER
Panther Creek S.P.	MORRISTOWN
Paris Landing S.P.	PARIS
Pickett S.R.P.	JAMESTOWN
Pickwick Landing S.Res.P.	SAVANNAH
Reelfoot Lake S.P.	TIPTONVILLE
Roan Mountain S.P.	ELIZABETHTON
Rock Island S.R.P.	McMINNVILLE
South Cumberland S.P.	MONTEAGLE
Standing Stone S.P.	CELINA
T.O. Fuller S.P.	MEMPHIS
Warriors' Path S.P.	KINGSPORT

CALENDAR HIGHLIGHTS

APRIL

Dogwood Arts Festival (Knoxville). Arts and crafts exhibits and shows; over 80 public and private gardens on display; music; parades; sporting events; more than 60 miles of marked dogwood trails or auto or free bus tours; special children's and senior citizen activities. Phone 423/637-4561.

MAY

Memphis in May International Festival (Memphis). Month-long celebration of the cultural and artistic heritage of Memphis. Major events occur weekends, but activities are held daily. Includes The Beale St Music Festival, World Championship Barbecue Cooking Contest and Sunset Symphony. Phone 901/525-4611.

JUNE

Int'l Country Music Fan Fair (Nashville). Country music fans have opportunity to mix and mingle with their favorite stars. Autograph sessions, special concerts. Phone 615/889-7503.

Riverbend Festival (Chattanooga). Music & sporting events, children's activities, fireworks display. Phone 423/265-4112.

AUGUST

Tennessee Walking Horse National Celebration (Shelbyville). More than 2,100 horses participate. Events conclude with crowning ceremonies for world grand champion walking horse. Phone 931/684-5915.

SEPTEMBER

Labor Day Fest (Memphis). Beale St. Memphis musicians perform rhythm and blues, jazz, country and rock at clubs and restaurants throughout the historic district. Phone 901/526-0110.

Tennessee State Fair (Nashville). Phone 615/862-8980.

Tennessee Valley Fair (Knoxville). Chilhowee Park. Entertainment; livestock and agricultural shows; contests, exhibits, fireworks and carnival rides. Phone 423/637-5840.

Mid-South Fair and Exposition (Memphis). Mid-South Fairgrounds. Agricultural, commercial, industrial exhibits; rides and concerts. Largest rodeo east of the Mississippi. Phone 901/274-8800.

OCTOBER

National Storytelling Festival (Johnson City). Three-day gathering from across the nation features some of the country's best storytellers. Phone 423/753-2171.

Fall Color Cruise & Folk Festival (Chattanooga). Riverboat trips, arts and crafts, entertainment. Phone 423/892-0223.

NOVEMBER

A Country Christmas (Nashville). At Opryland Hotel. Offers events ranging from a musical stage show to an art, antique & craft show. Phone 615/871-7637.

Water-related activities, hiking, riding, various other sports, picnicking and visitor centers, as well as camping, are available in many of these areas. Most state parks have supervised swimming (June-Labor Day; $1.50-$2.25), golf in resort parks (18 holes, $19; 9 holes, $10), boating ($2.25-$3/hr), fishing and tent camping (1-2 persons, one must be over 17 yrs; $6-$14/day, each addl over 7 yrs, 50¢; 2-wk max). Cabins, rustic to very modern, are available in several parks (daily; $50-$135; reservations should be made at park of choice; 1-night deposit required; $5 surcharge added for 1-night-only rental). Reservations for camping at some parks. There is also camping in Cherokee National Forest and Great Smoky Mountains National Park (see both). For further information contact the Tennessee Dept of Environment & Conservation, Bureau of State Parks, 401 Church St, 7th floor, Nashville 37243-0446; 615/532-0001, 800/421-6683 or 888/TN-PARKS.

SKI AREA

Place Name	Listed Under
Ober Gatlinburg Ski Resort	GATLINBURG

FISHING & HUNTING

There are more than 30 different kinds of fish in the state's mountain streams and lakes, including striped, largemouth, smallmouth and white bass, rainbow trout, walleye, muskie, crappie and catfish. Nonresident licenses: 3-day all species, $20.50; 10-day all species, $30.50; 3-day, no trout $10.50; 10-day, no trout $15.50; annual, no trout $26; annual, all species $51.

Within the constraints of season and limits, everything from squirrel and deer to wild boar can be hunted. Nonresident licenses: 7-day small game and water fowl, $30.50; annual small game and water fowl, $56; 7-day all game, $105.50; annual all game, $156. For detailed information contact the Tennessee Wildlife Resources Agency, Ellington Agricultural Center, PO Box 40747, Nashville 37204; 615/781-6500.

Driving Information

Safety belts are mandatory for all persons in front seat of vehicle. Children under 4 years must be in a child/passenger restraint system meeting Federal Motor Vehicle Safety Standards. For further information phone 615/741-3073.

INTERSTATE HIGHWAY SYSTEM

The following alphabetical listing of Tennessee towns and parks in *Mobil Travel Guide* shows that these cities are within 10 miles of the indicated Interstate highways. A highway map should be checked, however, for the nearest exit.

Highway Number	Cities/Towns within 10 miles
Interstate 24	Chattanooga, Clarksville, Manchester, Monteagle, Murfreesboro, Nashville.
Interstate 40	Cherokee Natl Forest, Cookeville, Crossville, Dickson, Hurricane Mills, Jackson, Knoxville, Lebanon, Lenoir City, Memphis, Nashville, Natchez Trace State Resort Park, Oak Ridge, Sevierville.
Interstate 65	Columbia, Franklin, Lewisburg, Nashville.
Interstate 75	Caryville, Chattanooga, Cleveland, Jellico, Knoxville, Lenoir City, Sweetwater.
Interstate 81	Kingsport, Morristown.

Additional Visitor Information

The Department of Tourist Development, 320 6th Ave N, 5th floor, Rachel Jackson Bldg, Nashville 37243, publishes a state map and a Tennessee vacation guide magazine highlighting attractions, historic sites and major events and will provide information on vacationing in Tennessee; phone 615/741-2158.

The TVA and the US Army Corps of Engineers have transformed muddy rivers into lovely lakes, making Tennessee home to the "Great Lakes of the South" with more than 29 big lakes in the public province. Also, TVA has developed Land Between The Lakes (see under KENTUCKY), a giant national recreation area spanning the Kentucky-Tennessee border.

There are 13 welcome centers in Tennessee; visitors may find the information and brochures helpful in their state travels. These centers operate year round; they are located on interstate highway entrances to the state.

Andrew Johnson National Historic Site (D-9)

(See also Greeneville)

(Monument Ave, College & Depot Sts in Greeneville)

The tailor shop, two houses and the burial place of the 17th president of the United States are preserved. Apprenticed to a tailor during his youth, Andrew Johnson came to Greeneville from his native Raleigh, NC, in 1826. After years of service in local, state and federal governments, Senator Johnson chose to remain loyal to the Union when Tennessee seceded. After serving as military governor of Tennessee, Johnson was elected vice-president in 1864. On April 15, 1865, he became president following the assassination of Abraham Lincoln. Continued opposition to the radical program of Reconstruction led to his impeachment in 1868. Acquitted by the Senate, he continued to serve as president until 1869. In 1875, Andrew Johnson became the only former president to be elected to the US Senate.

What to See and Do

Grave and monument. An eagle-capped marker sits over the President's grave. Members of his immediate family are also buried in what is now a national cemetery. (Daily) Monument Ave.

Park area. Camping (mid-Mar-Oct) nearby at Kinser Park, phone 423/639-5912, or call US Forest Service, 423/638-4109. For further information about the Historic Site contact Superintendent, PO Box 1088, Greeneville 37744; 423/638-3551.

Visitor Center. The visitor center houses the Johnson tailor shop, preserved with some original furnishings and tools of the craft, as well as a museum with exhibits and memorabilia relating to Johnson's career. (Daily; closed Jan 1, Thanksgiving, Dec 25) Opp is the Johnson house (1830s-1851), occupied during his career as a tailor and as a congressman. Depot & College Sts.   **Free.**

Johnson Homestead. Occupied by Johnson family from 1851 to 1875, except during Civil War and presidential years, the house is restored and furnished with family heirlooms. (Daily; closed Jan 1, Thanksgiving, Dec 25) Tickets at Visitor Center. Main St.   ¢

Caryville (D-7)

Pop 1,751 **Elev** 1,095 ft **Area code** 423 **Zip** 37714

What to See and Do

Cove Lake State Park. Approx 1,500 acres include 300-acre Cove Lake, where hundreds of Canada geese winter. Pool, wading pool, lifeguard; fishing; boat rentals. Nature trails, programs. Picnicking, concession, restaurant, playground, game courts. Camping, tent & trailer sites. Standard fees. N, off US 25W. Phone 423/566-9701.

Motels

★ **BUDGET HOST INN.** *115 Woods Ave, I-75 exit 134.* 423/562-9595; res: 800/283-4678; FAX 423/566-0515. 22 rms, 2 story. Mar-Dec: S $26-$32; D $28-$34; each addl $4; higher rates special events; lower rates rest of yr. Crib $4. Pet accepted. TV; cable (premium). Restaurant nearby. Ck-out 10:30 am. Business servs avail. Cr cds: A, DS, MC, V.

★ ★ **DAYS INN.** *(221 Colonial Ln, Lake City 37769) Approx 10 mi S on I-75 exit 129.* 423/426-2816; res: 800/329-7466; FAX 423/426-4626. 60 rms, 2 story. Mar-Oct: S $45-$65; D $55-$69; each addl $5; under 12 free; higher rates special events; lower rates rest of yr. Crib free. TV; cable (premium). Pool. Complimentary continental bkfst. Restaurant nearby. Ck-out 11 am. Sundries. Cr cds: A, C, D, DS, MC, V.

★ ★ **HAMPTON INN.** *4459 Veterans Memorial Hwy.* 423/562-9888; FAX 423/562-7474. 64 rms, 2 story. May-Sept: S, D $64-$74; each addl $10; suites $89-$99; under 16 free; family, wkly rates; package plans; higher rates special events; lower rates rest of yr. Crib free. TV; cable (premium), VCR avail. Complimentary coffee in rms. Complimentary full bkfst. Restaurant nearby. Ck-out 11 am. Meeting rms. Business servs avail. In-rm modem link. Sundries. Coin lndry. Golf privileges. Exercise equipt. Heated pool; whirlpool. Some bathrm phones, refrigerators, microwaves, fireplaces. Picnic tables, grills. Cr cds: A, C, D, DS, MC, V.

✔ ★ **LAKEVIEW INN.** *276 John McGee Blvd, at US 25W, I-75 exit 134.* 423/562-9456; res: 800/431-6887. 92 rms, 2 story. No elvtr. S, D $29-$49; each addl $5; under 16 free. Crib $3. TV; cable. Pool. Ck-out 11:30 am. Coin lndry. Business servs avail. Some refrigerators, microwaves. Cr cds: A, C, D, DS, MC, V.

★ ★ **SUPER 8.** *200 John McGee Blvd, TN 63, I-75 exit 134.* 423/562-8476; FAX 423/562-8870. 98 rms, 2 story. S, D $35-$50; each addl $5. Crib free. Pet accepted; $5. TV; cable (premium). Pool; wading pool. Playground. Complimentary continental bkfst. Ck-out noon. Meeting rms. Business servs avail. Cr cds: A, C, D, DS, JCB, MC, V.

Celina (C-6)

Pop 1,493 **Elev** 562 ft **Area code** 931 **Zip** 38551

Located in the scenic Upper Cumberland section of Tennessee, Celina is the location of the first law office of Cordell Hull, the revered statesman. Involved in both agriculture (especially cattle raising and truck farming) and industry (notably work clothes and denim sportswear), Celina is also noted for its nearby recreational facilities.

What to See and Do

Dale Hollow Lake. Controlling and harnessing the Obey River is a concrete dam 200 ft high and 1,717 ft long; it creates a 61-mi-long lake with 620 mi of shoreline. Swimming, bathhouse; fishing, hunting; boating (14 commercial docks). Primitive and improved camping (May-Oct; fee; dump station). (Daily) Headquarters are 3 mi E on TN 53. For fees and information phone 931/243-3136.

Dale Hollow National Fish Hatchery. More than 300,000 pounds of rainbow, browns and lake trout are raised annually for stocking streams and reservoirs; aquarium, visitor center. (Daily) 2 mi N off TN 53. Phone 931/243-2443. **Free.**

Old Mulkey Meeting House State Historic Site (KY) (1798). Oldest log meetinghouse in Kentucky, built by Baptist settlers from the Carolinas. Construction is 12-cornered with half-hewn logs. Hannah Boone, sister of

Daniel Boone, and 15 soldiers of the Revolutionary War are buried in adjacent graveyard. Picnicking, playground. (Daily) 7 mi NW on TN 52, then 10 mi N on TN 51, KY 163 in Tompkinsville, KY. Phone 502/487-8481. **Free.**

Standing Stone State Park. Approx 11,000 acres of virgin forest. Swimming pool, bathhouse; fishing; boating (rentals). Hiking; tennis. Picnicking, playground, concessions. Tent & trailer sites, cabins. Standard fees. 10 mi S on TN 52. Phone 931/823-6347.

Resort

★ **CEDAR HILL.** *2371 Cedar Hill Rd, 3½ mi N on TN 53.* 931/243-3201; res: 800/872-8393. E-mail rrroberts@twlakes.net; web www.cedarhill-resort.com. 37 1-4 rm kit. cottages; 10 motel rms, 4 kits. Memorial Day wknd-Labor Day: cottages (no towels; maid serv avail) for 2-6, $50-$170; motel S, D $50-$60; each addl $6; kit. units $55-$65; wkly rates; lower rates rest of yr. Pet accepted. TV. Pool (open to public); lifeguard. Dining rm 6 am-8:30 pm. Box lunches, snack bar. Ck-out 10 am, ck-in 1 pm. Grocery ¼ mi. Sports dir. Boats, motors, guides; waterskiing. Lawn games. Houseboats (drive your own) for 6-12 (3-day min) $125-$500; $450-$3,695 wkly. On Dale Hollow Lake. Cr cds: MC, V.

Chattanooga (E-6)

Settled 1835 **Pop** 152,466 **Elev** 685 ft **Area code** 423 **E-mail** cvb@chattanooga.net **Web** www.chattanooga.net/cvb

Information Chattanooga Area Convention & Visitors Bureau, 2 Broad St, 37402; 423/756-8687 or 800/322-3344.

Walled in on three sides by the Appalachian Mountains and the Cumberland Plateau, Chattanooga is a diversified city. It is the birthplace of miniature golf, the site of the first Coca-Cola bottling plant and has the steepest passenger incline railway in the country.

It's a city celebrated in song and heralded in history. The Cherokees called it *Tsatanugi* (rock coming to a point), describing Lookout Mountain, which stands like a sentinel over the city. They called the creek here "Chickamauga" ("river of blood").

Cherokee Chief John Ross founded the city. One of the starting points of the tragic "Trail of Tears" was from Chattanooga; Native Americans from three states were herded by Federal troops and forced to march in bitter winter to distant Oklahoma. The Battle of Chickamauga in the fall of 1863 was one of the turning points of the Civil War. It ended when the Union forces overpowered the entrenched Confederate forces on Missionary Ridge; there were more than 34,500 casualties. Sherman's march to the sea began immediately thereafter.

Chattanooga emerged as an important industrial city at the end of the Civil War, when soldiers from both sides returned to stake their futures in this commercially strategic city. Only 1,500 persons lived in Chattanooga at the war's end, but by 1880 the city had 77 industries.

In 1878, Adolph S. Ochs moved to Chattanooga from Knoxville, purchased the *Chattanooga Times* and made it one of the state's most influential newspapers. Although he later went on to publish the *New York Times,* Ochs retained control of the Chattanooga journal until his death in 1935.

Sparked by the Tennessee Valley Authority, the city's greatest period of growth began in the 1930s. In the past few years, millions of dollars have been spent along Chattanooga's riverfront, making it a popular visitor destination.

What to See and Do

Chattanooga African-American History Museum. Educational institution that portrays African-American contributions to the growth of Chattanooga and the nation. (Daily) 200 M. L. King Blvd. Phone 423/266-8658. ¢¢

Booker T. Washington State Park. More than 350 acres on Chickamauga Lake. Swimming pools; fishing; boating (rentals, launch). Nature trail. Picnicking, playground, lodge. Some facilities seasonal. Standard fees. 13 mi NE on TN 58. Phone 423/894-4955.

Chattanooga Choo-Choo. Converted 1909 train station with hotel (see MOTOR HOTELS) and restaurants. Formal gardens, fountains, pools, turn-of-the-century shops, gaslights, trolley ride (fee), model railroad (fee). Terminal Station, 1400 Market St. Phone 423/266-5000 or 800/872-2529.

Chester Frost Park. Swimming, sand beach, bathhouse; fishing; boating (ramps). Hiking. Picnicking, concessions. Camping (fee; electricity, water). Islands in park are accessible by causeways. 2318 Gold Point Circle; 17 mi NE off I-75 exit 4, then TN 153 to Hixson Pike, N to Gold Point Circle, on W shore of Chickamauga Lake. Phone 423/842-0177. **Free.**

Chickamauga and Chattanooga National Military Park (see under GEORGIA).

Creative Discovery Museum. Encourages children to learn about their world hands-on through creativity and individual achievement. Exhibit areas include Artist's Studio, Inventor's Workshop, Musician's Studio and Scientist's Field Laboratory. (May-Aug, daily; rest of yr, daily exc Mon) 321 Chestnut St. Phone 423/756-2738. **¢¢¢**

Harrison Bay State Park. More than 1,200 acres on Chickamauga Lake. Swimming pool; fishing; boating (ramp, rentals, marina). Picnicking, playground, snack bar, restaurant, camp store (all seasonal). Camping. Recreation building (seasonal). Standard fees. 11 mi NE off TN 58. Phone 423/344-6214 or -2272.

Houston Museum of Decorative Arts. Glass, porcelain, pottery, music boxes, dolls, collection of pitchers; country-style furniture. (Daily; closed major hols) 201 High St, in Bluff View Art District. Phone 423/267-7176. **¢¢**

Hunter Museum of Art. Paintings, sculpture, glass, drawings; permanent collection of major American artists; changing exhibits. Gift shop. (Daily exc Mon; closed most hols) 10 Bluff View, in Bluff View Art District. Phone 423/267-0968. **¢¢**

International Towing and Recovery Hall of Fame and Museum. Antique vehicles on display; history of wreckers and tow trucks. (Daily) 401 Broad St. Phone 423/267-3132. **¢¢**

★ **Lookout Mountain.** Mountain towers more than 2,120 ft above the city, offering clear-day views of Tennessee, Georgia, North Carolina, South Carolina and Alabama. During the Civil War, the "Battle above the Clouds" was fought on the slope. S of town via Ochs Hwy & Scenic Hwy.

Lookout Mountain Incline Railway. World's steepest passenger incline railway climbs Lookout Mountain to 2,100-ft altitude; near top, grade is at 72.7° angle; passengers ride glass-roofed cars; Smoky Mountains (200 mi away) can be seen from Upper Station observation deck. Round trip approx 30 min. (Daily; closed Dec 25) Lower station at 3917 St Elmo Ave. Phone 423/821-4224. **¢¢¢**

Point Park. View of Chattanooga and Moccasin Bend from observatory. Monuments, plaques, museum tell story of battle. Visitor Center. Part of Chickamauga and Chattanooga National Military Park (see under GEORGIA). (Daily; closed Dec 25) Lookout Mt. Phone 423/821-7786. **¢**

Cravens House (1866). Oldest surviving structure on mountain, restored with period furnishings. Original house (1856), center of the "Battle Above the Clouds," was largely destroyed; the present structure was erected on the original foundations in 1866. (Apr-Oct, daily) Golden Eagle Passport (see MAKING THE MOST OF YOUR TRIP). On Lookout Mt. Phone 423/821-7786. **¢**

Ruby Falls-Lookout Mountain Caverns. Under the battlefield are twin caves with onyx formations, giant stalactites and stalagmites of various hues; at 1,120 ft below surface Ruby Falls is a 145-ft waterfall inside Lookout Mountain Caverns. View of city from tower above entrance building. Guided tours. (Daily; closed Dec 25) Scenic Hwy TN 148, on Lookout Mt. Phone 423/821-2544. **¢¢¢**

Rock City Gardens. Fourteen acres of mountaintop trails and vistas. Fairyland Caverns and Mother Goose Village, rock formations, swinging bridge, observation point. Restaurant; shops. (Daily; closed Dec 25) 2½ mi S on TN 58, on Lookout Mt. Phone 706/820-2531. **¢¢¢**

Chattanooga Nature Center at Reflection Riding. Park meant for leisurely driving offers winding three-mile drive with vistas: historic sites, trees, wildflowers, shrubs, reflecting pools. Also wetland walkway; nature center; animal diorama, solar energy display; hiking trails; programs. (Daily) Garden Rd, 6 mi SW, near jct US 11/64, US 41 & US 72, on Lookout Mt. Phone 423/821-1160. **¢¢**

Battles for Chattanooga Museum. Automated, three-dimensional display re-creates Civil War Battles of Chattanooga using 5,000 miniature soldiers, flashing lights, smoking cannons and crackling rifles. Also here are dioramas of area history prior to Civil War. (Daily; closed Dec 25) 1110 E Brow Rd, adj to Point Park. Phone 423/820-2531. **¢¢**

National Knife Museum. Permanent display of knives of every age and description; also changing exhibits. (Daily exc Sun; closed hols) 7201 Shallowford Rd. Phone 423/892-5007. **¢**

Nickajack Dam and Lake. TVA dam impounds lake with 192 mi of shoreline and 10,370 acres of water surface. Fishing; boat launch. Visitor lobby at navigation lock (daily). 25 mi W on US 41, 64, 72 or I-24. Phone 423/942-1633. **Free.**

Raccoon Mountain.

Raccoon Mountain Pumped-Storage Plant. Raccoon Mountain is the largest of the TVA's rock-filled dams, measuring 230 ft high and 8,500 ft long. Water pumped from the Tennessee River flows from the reservoir atop the mountain to the powerhouse below. Cut 1,350 ft inside the mountain, the powerhouse chamber has four of the largest reversible pump-turbines in the world. Visitor center and picnic area atop mountain (daylight hrs); fishing at base of mountain; overlooks with spectacular views of Tennessee River gorge and Chattanooga. 6 mi W. Phone 423/825-3100. **Free.**

Raccoon Mountain Caverns and Campground. Guided tours offer views of beautiful formations, stalagmites and stalactites; also "wild" cave tours through undeveloped sections. Full-facility campground (fee). (Daily) Approx 5 mi W; exit 174 off I-24, 1 mi N on TN 41. Phone 423/821-9403 or 423/821-CAVE. Cave tour **¢¢¢**

Raccoon Mountain Alpine Slide. Chairlift to top of mountain and personal-control sled ride (½ mi) to bottom. (Mid-May-Labor Day, daily; Mar-mid-May & early Sept-Nov, wkends only) Phone 423/825-5666. **¢¢**

Grand Prix of Chattanooga. Three-quarter scale Formula cars race against clock on challenging half-mile track; also go-carts. Must have valid driver's license. (Same days as Alpine Slide) Phone 423/825-5666. Per lap **¢¢**

Signal Point. Mountain was used for signaling by Cherokees and later by Confederates. View of "Grand Canyon of the Tennessee" can be seen by looking almost straight down to the Tennessee River from Signal Point Military Park, off St James Blvd. 9 mi N on Ridgeway Ave (US 127).

***Southern Bell* riverboat.** Sightseeing, breakfast, lunch and dinner cruises on 500-passenger riverboat. (Apr-Dec, daily) 2 Riverfront Pkwy, Pier 2. For schedule phone 423/266-4488 or 800/766-2784. **¢¢¢-¢¢¢¢¢**

★ **Tennessee Aquarium.** First major freshwater life center in the country, focusing primarily on the natural habitats and wildlife of the Tennessee River and related ecosystems. Within this 130,000-sq-ft complex are more than 9,000 animals in their natural habitats. The Aquarium re-creates riverine habitats in 7 major freshwater tanks and 2 terrestial environments and is organized into 5 major galleries: **Appalachian Cove Forest** re-creates the mountain source of the Tennessee River; **Tennessee River Gallery** examines the river at midstream and compares the "original" river with the river as it now exists; **Discovery Falls** is a series of interactive displays and small tanks; **Mississipi Delta** explores the river as it slows to meet the sea; and **Rivers of the World** explores 6 of the world's great river systems. Highlight of the Aquarium is the 60-ft-high central canyon, designed to give visitors a sense of immersion into the river. (Daily; closed Thanksgiving, Dec 25). 1 Broad St, on the banks of the Tennessee River. Phone 423/265-0695 or 800/262-0695. **¢¢¢¢** Adj is

IMAX 3D Theater. Six-story movie screen. Discounted combination tickets with the Tennessee Aquarium are available. (Daily) 201 Chestnut St. Phone 800/262-0695. **¢¢¢**

Tennessee Valley Railroad. The South's largest operating historic railroad, with steam locomotives, diesels, passenger coaches of various types. Trains take passengers on a six-mile ride, including tunnel. Audiovisual show, displays; gift shop. (June-Labor Day, daily; Apr-May & Sept-mid-Nov, Mon-Fri) 4119 Cromwell Rd. Phone 423/894-8028. ¢¢¢

University of Tennessee at Chattanooga (1886). (7,800 students) Fine Arts Center has Arena stage for entertainment and special events. Tours of campus by appt. 615 McCallie Ave. Phone 423/755-4662.

Annual Events

Kaleidoscope. Downtown at Ross's Landing. Creative festival for children including interactive and educational activities. Phone 423/756-2212. Early May.

Riverbend Festival. Music & sporting events, children's activities, fireworks display. Phone 423/265-4112. Late June.

Fall Color Cruise & Folk Festival. Riverboat trips, arts & crafts, entertainment. Phone 423/892-0223. Last 2 wkends Oct.

Seasonal Events

Theatrical, musical productions. Tivoli Theater, 709 Broad St. Variety of events, including plays, concerts, opera; box office, phone 423/757-5042. Chattanooga Theatre Centre, 400 River St, box office, phone 423/267-8534. Memorial Auditorium, 399 McCallie Ave; box office, phone 423/756-5050. Chattanooga Symphony and Opera Assn, 25 concerts and 2 opera productions yearly, phone 423/267-8583. Backstage Playhouse, 3264 Brainerd Rd, dinner theater, phone 423/629-1565.

Motels

✔★ **BUDGET HOST INN.** (395 Main St, Kimball 37347) 20 mi W on I-24, exit 152. 423/837-7185; res: 800/759-5804. 64 rms, 2 story. Mid-Apr-mid-Sept: S, D $40-$55; each addl $5; under 12 free; lower rates rest of yr. Crib free. TV; cable (premium). Complimentary continental bkfst. Restaurant nearby. Ck-out 11 am. Business servs avail. In-rm modem link. Coin lndry. Pool. Some refrigerators, microwaves. Cr cds: A, C, D, DS, ER, MC, V.

D ⊠ ⌇ 🔥 SC

✔★ **CHANTICLEER INN.** (1300 Mockingbird Lane, Lookout Mountain 30750) 8 mi S on GA 157, 3 mi from foot of mountain. 706/820-2015; FAX 706/820-1060. 16 rms. S $35-$48; D $40-$86; each addl $6. TV; cable. Pool. Complimentary continental bkfst. Restaurant nearby. Ck-out 11 am. Picnic tables, grill. Cr cds: A, MC, V.

⌇ 🔥 SC

★★ **COMFORT INN.** 7717 Lee Hwy (37421). 423/894-5454; FAX 423/499-9597. 64 rms, 2 story. S, D $40-$58; each addl $5; under 18 free; higher rates: hol wkends, special events. Crib free. Pet accepted; $5. TV; cable (premium). Pool. Complimentary continental bkfst. Restaurant adj open 24 hrs. Ck-out 11 am. Microwaves avail. Cr cds: A, C, D, DS, ER, JCB, MC, V.

D ✔ ⌇ ⌇ 🔥 SC

★★ **COMFORT SUITES.** 7324 Shallowford Rd (37421), I-75 exit 5. 423/892-1500; FAX 423/892-0111. 62 rms, 2 story. June-Aug: S $59-$83; D $68-$88; each addl $12; under 12 free; higher rates special events; lower rates rest of yr. Crib free. TV; cable (premium), VCR avail. Indoor pool. Complimentary continental bkfst. Coffee in rms. Restaurant adj 6 am-9:30 pm. Ck-out 11 am. Coin lndry. Meeting rms. Business servs avail. Exercise equipt. Refrigerators, microwaves. Cr cds: A, C, D, DS, ER, JCB, MC, V.

D ⌇ ⌇ ⌇ 🔥 SC

✔★★ **DAYS INN AIRPORT.** 7725 Lee Hwy (37421). 423/899-2288. Web www.daysinn.com. 80 rms, 2 story. June-Aug: S $48-$58; D $58-$78; each addl $5; under 12 free; lower rates rest of yr. Crib avail. Pet accepted, some restrictions; $5. TV; cable (premium). Indoor pool; whirlpool. Complimentary continental bkfst. Restaurant nearby. Ck-out 11 am. Microwaves avail. Cr cds: A, C, D, DS, ER, MC, V.

D ✔ ⌇ ⌇ 🔥 SC

★★ **DAYS INN RIVERGATE-AQUARIUM.** 901 Carter St (37402), at M.L. King Blvd. 423/266-7331; FAX 423/266-9357. 135 rms, 3 story. S $50-$75; D $65-$95; each addl $6; suites $75-$115; under 13 free; higher rates special events. Crib free. TV; cable (premium). Pool. Complimentary continental bkfst. Coffee in rms. Ck-out 11 am. Meeting rms. Business servs avail. Microwaves, refrigerators avail. Cr cds: A, D, DS, MC, V.

D ⌇ ⌇ 🔥 SC

✔★ **ECONO LODGE.** 1417 St Thomas (37412), I-75 exit 1. 423/894-1417. 89 rms, 2 story. S $29.95-$59.95; D $34.95-$59.95; each addl $5; under 12 free. Pet accepted, some restrictions. TV; cable (premium). Pool. Complimentary continental bkfst. Restaurant nearby. Ck-out 11 am. Cr cds: A, C, D, DS, MC, V.

D ✔ ⌇ ⌇ 🔥 SC

★★ **HAMPTON INN.** 7013 Shallowford Rd (37421), near Lovell Field Airport. 423/855-0095; FAX 423/874-7600. 167 rms, 2 story. S $69-$73; D $79-$83; under 18 free; higher rates special events. Crib free. TV; cable (premium). Pool. Complimentary continental bkfst. Coffee in rms. Restaurant adj open 24 hrs. Ck-out 11 am. Meeting rms. Exercise equipt. Airport transportation. Cr cds: A, C, D, DS, MC, V.

D ⌇ ⌇ ⌇ 🔥 SC

★★★ **HOLIDAY INN-LOOKOUT MOUNTAIN.** 3800 Cummings Hwy (37419), I-24 exit 174. 423/821-3531; FAX 423/821-8403. 162 rms, 2 story. S $64-$72; D $71-$79; each addl $7; suites from $81; under 19 free. Crib free. TV; cable (premium). Pool. Rm serv. Bar 5 pm-midnight; entertainment. Ck-out 11 am. Meeting rms. Exercise equipt. Game rm. Volleyball, basketball. Picnic tables. Cr cds: A, C, D, DS, JCB, MC, V.

D ⌇ ⌇ ⌇ 🔥 SC

✔★★ **KING'S LODGE.** 2400 West Side Dr (37404), 4 mi NE at jct US 41, I-24 East Ridge, 4th Ave exit. 423/698-8944; FAX 423/698-8949; res: 800/251-7702. 138 rms, 2 story, 24 suites. S, D $40-$65; each addl $5; suites $60-$95; under 12 free. Crib free. Pet accepted, some restrictions. TV; cable (premium). Pool. Coffee in rms. Restaurant 7 am-11 pm. Rm serv. Bar 1 pm-3 am. Ck-out 11 am. Business servs avail. Refrigerators. Some balconies. Cr cds: A, C, D, DS, MC, V.

D ✔ ⌇ ⌇ 🔥 SC

★★ **LA QUINTA.** 7015 Shallowford Rd (37421), at I-75. 423/855-0011; FAX 423/855-0011, ext. 72. 132 rms, 2 story. May-Oct: S $59-$66; D $65-$85; each addl $10; suites $92-$125; under 18 free; higher rates special events; lower rates rest of yr. Crib free. Pet accepted, some restrictions. TV; cable (premium). Pool. Complimentary continental bkfst. Ck-out noon. Health club privileges. Some refrigerators; microwaves avail. Cr cds: A, C, D, DS, MC, V.

D ✔ ⌇ ⌇ 🔥 SC

★ **RED ROOF INN.** 7014 Shallowford Rd (37421), I-75 exit 5. 423/899-0143; FAX 423/899-8384. 112 rms, 2 story. June-July: S, D $43.99-$60.99; each addl $7; under 18 free; higher rates special events; lower rates rest of yr. Crib free. Pet accepted, some restrictions. TV; cable (premium). Complimentary coffee in lobby. Restaurant adj open 24 hrs. Ck-out noon. Cr cds: A, C, D, DS, MC, V.

D ✔ ⌇ 🔥

✔★ **SUPER 8.** 20 Birmingham Hwy (37419), I-24 exit 174. 423/821-8880. 74 rms, 3 story. Apr-Sept: S $42.88-$45.88; D $47.88-$55.88; each addl $5; under 12 free; lower rates rest of yr. Crib free. Pet accepted, some restrictions. TV; cable (premium). Complimentary coffee in lobby. Restaurant adj open 24 hrs. Ck-out 11 am. Coin lndry. Picnic tables. Cr cds: A, C, D, DS, MC, V.

D ✔ ⌇ 🔥 SC

Motor Hotel

★ ★ ★ **HOLIDAY INN CHATTANOOGA CHOO-CHOO.** *1400 Market St (37402), 8 blks S in Terminal Station.* 423/266-5000; FAX 423/265-4635. E-mail choochooh@aol.com; web choochoo.com. 360 rms, 48 train-car rms. S, D $79-$150; suites $150-$250. Crib free. TV; cable (premium), VCR avail. 3 pools, 1 indoor. Complimentary coffee in rms. Restaurant 7 am-10 pm. Rm serv 6:30 am-3 pm, 5 pm-midnight. Bars 11:30-1 am. Ck-out 11 am. Meeting rms. Bellhops. Concierge. Shopping arcade. Free airport transportation. Lighted tennis. Golf privileges. Exercise equipt. Bathrm phone, wet bar in suites. Some private patios, balconies. Turn-of-the-century atmosphere in restored 1909 train station; gaslights, formal gardens. Many old-style shops. Main lobby under original 85-ft freestanding dome. 1880 Chattanooga Choo-Choo engine. Cr cds: A, C, D, DS, JCB, MC, V.

🅳 🛍️ 🏋️ ➤ 🏃 🎿 🐾 🆂🅲

Hotels

★ ★ **CLARION.** *407 Chestnut St (37402), at 4th St; US 27 exit 1 C.* 423/756-5150; FAX 423/265-8708. E-mail clarion@cdc.net; web www.chattanoogaclarion.com. 205 rms, 12 story. S, D $79-$119; each addl $10; under 18 free. Crib $10. TV; cable. Pool. Coffee in rms. Restaurant 6:30 am-9:30 pm. Bar 2 pm-midnight; Sun to 10 pm. Ck-out 11 am. Meeting rms. Business center. Exercise equipt. Cr cds: A, C, D, DS, MC, V.

🅳 ➤ 🏃 🎿 🐾 🆂🅲 🏃

★ ★ ★ **MARRIOTT.** *2 Carter Plaza (37402), adj convention center.* 423/756-0002; FAX 423/266-2254. 343 rms, 16 story. S, D $65-$135; suites $150-$350; under 12 free; higher rates special events. Crib free. TV; cable, VCR avail. 2 pools, 1 indoor; whirlpool, poolside serv. Restaurant 6:30 am-11 pm. Bar; entertainment. Ck-out noon. Convention facilities. Business servs avail. Concierge. Shopping arcade. Garage parking. Exercise equipt; sauna. Game rm. Bathrm phones, refrigerators. Luxury level. Cr cds: A, C, D, DS, ER, MC, V.

🅳 ➤ 🏃 🎿 🐾 🆂🅲

★ ★ ★ **RADISSON READ HOUSE.** *827 Broad St (37402), M.L. King Blvd & Broad St.* 423/266-4121; FAX 423/267-6447. 238 rms, 10 story, 138 suites. S, D $108-$118; suites $118-$128; under 18 free. Crib free. TV; cable (premium). Pool. Restaurants 6:30 am-11 pm. Bar from 11 am. Ck-out noon. Meeting rms. Shopping arcade. Exercise equipt. Wet bars; some bathrm phones. Built to accommodate travelers on the Nashville/Chattanooga Railroad (1847). Cr cds: A, C, D, DS, ER, JCB, MC, V.

🅳 ➤ 🏃 🎿 🐾 🆂🅲

Inns

★ ★ ★ **ADAMS HILLBORNE.** *801 Vine St (37403).* 423/265-5000; res: 888/446-6569; FAX 423/265-5555. E-mail innjoy@worldnet.att.net; web innjoy.com. 10 air-cooled rms, 3 story. S, D $100-$275; each addl $25; under 4 free; wkly rates. Crib free. TV; cable (premium), VCR (movies). Complimentary full bkfst. Restaurant 6-10 pm. Rm serv. Ck-out 11 am, ck-in 4 pm. Business servs avail. In-rm modem link. Concierge serv. Gift shop. Exercise equipt. Some fireplaces. Mayor's mansion built in 1889; 16-ft coffered ceilings. Cr cds: A, D, MC, V.

🅳 🏃 🎿 🐾

★ ★ ★ **BLUFF VIEW.** *412 E 2nd St (37403).* 423/265-5033; FAX 423/757-0120. 16 rms in 3 bldgs, 2 story, 2 suites. S, D $100-$185; each addl $20; suites $200-$250. TV; cable. Complimentary full bkfst. Dining rm 11 am-10:30 pm. Ck-out noon, ck-in 3 pm. Balconies. Main house built 1928 on bluff overlooking river; antiques. Cr cds: A, DS, MC, V.

🎿 🐾

Restaurants

★ ★ **212 MARKET.** *212 Market St (37402), adj to Tennessee Aquarium.* 423/265-1212. E-mail rest212@chatt.com; web www.212market.com. Hrs: 11 am-3 pm, 5-9:30 pm; wkend hrs vary. Closed Jan 1, Dec 25. Res accepted. Bar. Wine list. Semi-a la carte: lunch $2.95-$10.50, dinner $9.75-$21.50. Sun brunch $6-$12. Child's meals. Specializes in fresh seafood, steak, rack of lamb. Own baking. Southwestern decor, original art. Cr cds: A, C, D, DS, MC, V.

🅳 🆂🅲 ➤

★ **COUNTRY PLACE.** *7320 Shallowford Rd (37421), I-75 exit 5.* 423/855-1392. Hrs: 6 am-9 pm. Closed Dec 25. Semi-a la carte: bkfst $2.79-$6.85, lunch, dinner $2.69-$8.75. Child's meals. Specializes in fried chicken, desserts. Salad bar. Dining rm features artwork and a miniature train. Cr cds: A, DS, MC, V.

🅳 🆂🅲 ➤

✔ ★ ★ **MT VERNON.** *1707 A Cummings Hwy (37409), 1½ mi SW on US 11, 41.* 423/266-6591. Hrs: 11 am-10 pm; Sat from 4:30 pm; early-bird dinner 4:30-6:30 pm. Closed Sun; also Dec 24-Jan 2. Serv bar. Semi-a la carte: lunch $4.25-$7.25, dinner $9.95-$13.95. Child's meals. Specializes in fresh seafood, vegetables, desserts. Family-owned for 43 yrs. Cr cds: A, DS, MC, V.

🅳 ➤

Unrated Dining Spot

VINE STREET MARKET. *414 Vine St.* 423/267-0162. Hrs: 10 am-4 pm; Fri, Sat 10 am-10 pm. Closed Sun; some hols. Serv bar. A la carte entrees: lunch $4-$8, dinner $11.50-$17.95. Child's meals. Specializes in desserts. Boxed lunches. Chef's choice daily. Menu recited. Cr cds: A, MC, V.

Cherokee National Forest (D-9 - E-7)

(See also Cleveland, Greeneville, Johnson City)

(NE, SE & SW of Johnson City via US 23, 321, TN 91; E of Cleveland on US 64)

Slashed by river gorges and creased by rugged mountains, this 630,000-acre forest lies in two separate strips along the Tennessee-North Carolina boundary, northeast and southwest of Great Smoky Mountains National Park (see). A region of thick forests, streams and waterfalls, the forest takes its name from the Native American tribe. There are more than 500 miles of hiking trails, including the Appalachian Trail. There are 29 campgrounds, 28 picnic areas, 8 swimming sites and 13 boating sites. Hunting for game, including wild boar, deer and turkey, is permitted under Tennessee game regulations. Fees may be charged at recreation sites. Contact Forest supervisor, PO Box 2010, Cleveland 37320; 423/476-9700.

Clarksville (C-4)

(See also Hopkinsville, KY)

Founded 1784 **Pop** 75,494 **Elev** 543 ft **Area code** 931

Information Clarksville/Montgomery County Tourist Commission, 312 Madison St, PO Box 883, 37041; 931/648-0001.

Clarksville, named for General George Rogers Clark, has achieved a balanced economy with many industries and heavy traffic in tobacco, grain and livestock. Clarksville has long been considered one of the top dark-fired tobacco markets in the world. Natural gas and low-cost TVA power have contributed to the town's industrial development. Clarksville is the home of Austin Peay State University.

What to See and Do

Beachhaven Vineyard & Winery. Tours of vineyard and winery; tasting room; picnic area. (Daily; closed Jan 1, Thanksgiving, Dec 25) I-24, exit 4. Phone 931/645-8867.   **Free.**

Clarksville-Montgomery County Museum. Built in 1898 as a US Post Office and Customs House, the museum houses changing history, science and art exhibits. (Daily exc Mon; closed some major hols) 200 S 2nd St. Phone 931/648-5780.   ¢¢

Dunbar Cave State Natural Area. This 110-acre park with small scenic lake was once a fashionable resort; the cave itself housed big band dances. The old bathhouse has been refurbished to serve as a museum and visitor center. Park (daily); cave (June-Aug, wkends, by res only). 5 mi SE via US 79, Dunbar Cave Rd exit. Phone 931/648-5526.   ¢

Fort Campbell Military Reservation. Home of the army's famed 101st Airborn Division (Air Assault). The post visitors center is just inside Gate 4; Don F. Pratt Museum is located in Wickham Hall. (Daily; closed Jan 1, Dec 25) TN 41A, in both TN & KY. Phone 502/798-3215.   **Free.**

Fort Donelson National Battlefield and Cemetery (see). 30 mi W on US 79.

Land Between The Lakes. Approx 31 mi E on US 79, Land Between The Lakes exit, then N. (See under KENTUCKY)

Port Royal State Historic Area. At the confluence of Sulphur Fork Creek and the Red River, Port Royal was one of the state's earliest communities and trading centers. A 300-ft covered bridge spans the river. (Daily) 5 mi E via TN 76, near Adams; follow signs. Phone 931/358-9696.

Annual Events

Old-Time Fiddlers Championship. Late Mar.

Walking Horse Show. Fairgrounds. Early June.

Motels

✔★ ★ **DAYS INN.** 1100 Connector Rd (TN 76) (37043), I-24 exit 11. 931/358-3194; FAX 931/358-9869. 84 rms, 2 story. S $36-$50; D $45-$60; each addl $6; under 16 free. Crib free. Pet accepted. TV; cable (premium). Pool. Complimentary continental bkfst. Restaurant adj 6 am-9 pm; wkends to 10 pm. Ck-out 11 am. Business servs avail. Microwaves avail. Cr cds: A, C, D, DS, MC, V.

D ✔ ≈ ≈ 🐾 SC

★ ★ **ECONO LODGE.** 201 Holiday Rd (37040), I-24 exit 4. 931/645-6300; FAX 931/645-5054. 103 rms, 2 story. S $38-$55; D $50-$69; each addl $6; under 12 free. Crib $6. TV; cable (premium), VCR avail (movies). Pool. Complimentary continental bkfst. Restaurant nearby. Ck-out 11 am. Coin lndry. Meeting rm. Business servs avail. In-rm modem link. Many microwaves; some refrigerators, whirlpools. Cr cds: A, C, D, DS, JCB, MC, V.

≈ ≈ 🐾 SC

★ ★ **QUALITY INN.** 803 N 2nd St (37040), 1½ mi NW on US 41A, 79. 931/645-9084; FAX 931/645-9084, ext. 340. 130 rms, 2 story. S $45-$61; D $55-$61; each addl $6; under 18 free. Crib free. Pet accepted, some restrictions. TV; cable (premium). Indoor pool; whirlpool. Sauna. Complimentary continental bkfst. Bar 5-11 pm. Ck-out noon. Coin lndry. Meeting rms. Business servs avail. Valet serv. Microwave in suites. Cr cds: A, C, D, DS, JCB, MC, V.

D ✔ ≈ ≈ 🐾 SC

Motor Hotels

★ ★ **HAMPTON INN.** 190 Holiday Rd (37040), I-24 exit 4. 931/552-2255; FAX 931/552-4871. 77 air-cooled rms, 2 story. S $51-$59;

D $59-$63; under 18 free. Crib free. TV; cable (premium). Pool; whirlpool. Complimentary continental bkfst. Restaurant nearby. Ck-out noon. Coin lndry. Meeting rm. Sundries. Exercise equipt. Some refrigerators, microwaves Cr cds: A, C, D, DS, MC, V.

D ≈ 🏋 ≈ 🐾 SC

★ ★ **RAMADA INN RIVERVIEW.** 50 College St (37040). 931/552-3331; FAX 931/647-5005. 154 rms, 7 story. S, D $54-$85; each addl $5; under 18 free. Crib free. Pet accepted, some restrictions. TV; cable (premium). Indoor pool. Restaurant 6 am-2 pm, 5-10 pm; Sat, Sun 7am-2 pm. Bar from 5 pm. Ck-out noon. Meeting rms. In-rm modem link. Microwaves in suites. Cr cds: A, C, D, DS, JCB, MC, V.

D ✔ ≈ ≈ 🐾 SC

✔★ ★ **TRAVELODGE.** 3075 Wilma Rudolph Blvd (37040), US 79 & I-24 exit 4. 931/645-1400; FAX 931/551-3917. E-mail Travel@Knight wave.com. 125 rms, 4 story. S, D $40-$50; under 18 free. Crib free. Pet accepted. TV; cable (premium). Heated pool; whirlpool. Complimentary full bkfst. Coffee in rms. Restaurant 6 am-9 pm. Rm serv. Bar 5:30 pm-midnight. Ck-out noon. Meeting rms. Business servs avail. Game rm. Microwaves avail. Cr cds: A, C, D, DS, MC, V.

D ✔ ≈ ≈ 🐾 SC

Cleveland (E-7)

(See also Chattanooga)

Pop 30,354 **Elev** 920 ft **Area code** 423

Cleveland is the location of the Superintendent's office of the Cherokee National Forest (see).

Motels

✔★ ★ **BAYMONT INN.** 107 Interstate Dr NW (37312). 423/339-1000; FAX 423/339-2760. 102 rms, 3 story, 14 suites. Apr-Sept: S, D, suites $45.75-$80.95; each addl $7; under 18 free; higher rates special events; lower rates rest of yr. Crib free. Pet accepted, some restrictions. TV; cable (premium). Pool. Complimentary continental bkfst. Complimentary coffee in rms. Restaurant adj open 24 hrs. Ck-out noon. Coin lndry. Meeting rm. Business servs avail. Health club privileges. Cr cds: A, C, D, DS, MC, V.

D ✔ ≈ ≈ 🐾 SC

★ ★ **HOLIDAY INN-NORTH.** 2400 Executive Park Dr (37312), jct TN 60 & I-75 exit 25. 423/472-1504; FAX 423/479-5962. 146 rms, 2 story. S $72-$80; D $70-$89; under 18 free; higher rates special events. Crib free. Pet accepted, some restrictions. TV; cable (premium). Pool. Restaurant 6 am-2 pm, 5-10 pm. Rm serv 7 am-9:30 pm. Ck-out noon. Meeting rms. Business servs avail. Sundries. Health club privileges. Cr cds: A, C, D, DS, JCB, MC, V.

D ✔ ≈ ≈ 🐾 SC

★ ★ **QUALITY INN CHALET.** 2595 Georgetown Rd (37311), jct TN 60 & I-75 exit 25. 423/476-8511. 97 rms, 2-3 story. No elvtr. May-Sept: S, D $56-$66; each addl $5; under 18 free; lower rates rest of yr. Crib $5. Pet accepted, some restrictions. TV; cable (premium). Pool; wading pool. Coffee in rms. Restaurant 11 am-10 pm. Ck-out noon. Coin lndry. Meeting rms. Some refrigerators; microwaves avail. Cr cds: A, C, D, DS, ER, MC, V.

D ✔ ≈ ≈ 🐾 SC

Restaurant

★ **ROBLYN'S STEAK HOUSE.** NW 25th St (37311), 2 blks E of I-75 exit 25. 423/476-8808. Hrs: 4-9 pm; Fri, Sat to 9:30 pm; Sun 11 am-2 pm. Closed major hols. Res accepted. Semi-a la carte: dinner

$5-$15. Sun buffet $6.49. Child's meals. Specializes in steak, seafood. Salad bar. Parking. Family-owned. Cr cds: A, C, D, DS, MC, V.

D SC ◻

Columbia (E-4)

(See also Franklin)

Settled 1807 **Pop** 28,583 **Elev** 637 ft **Area code** 931 **Zip** 38401
Information Maury County Convention & Visitors Bureau, #8 Public Square, 38401; 931/381-7176 or 888/852-1860.

James K. Polk, 11th president of the United States, spent his boyhood in Columbia and returned to open his first law office. The town is known for its many antebellum houses.

What to See and Do

Ancestral home of James K. Polk (1816). Built by Samuel Polk, father of the president, the Federal-style house is furnished with family possessions, including furniture and portraits used at the White House. Gardens link house to adjacent 1818 building owned by the president's sisters. Visitor center. (Daily; closed Jan 1, Thanksgiving, Dec 24-25) 301 W 7th St, US 412. Phone 931/388-2354. ¢¢

The Athenaeum (1835-37). Buildings of Moorish design were used as a girls' school after 1852; during the Civil War the rectory became headquarters of Union generals Negeley and Schofield. (Feb-Dec, daily exc Mon; fall tour Sept) 808 Athenaeum St. Phone 931/381-4822. ¢¢

Annual Events

Mule Day. Liar's contest, auction, parade, mule pull, square dance, bluegrass night, pioneer craft festival, knife and coin show. 1st wkend Apr.

National Tennessee Walking Horse Jubilee. Maury County Park. Contact the park, Experiment Station Lane; 931/388-0303. Late May-early June.

Maury County Fair. Maury County Park Fairgrounds. Phone 931/388-0303. Late Aug-early Sept.

Majestic Middle Tennessee Fall Tour. Phone 931/381-4822. Last wkend Sept.

Plantation Christmas Tour of Homes. 1st wkend Dec.

Motels

✔★ **DAYS INN.** *1504 Nashville Hwy (US 31N). 931/381-3297; FAX 931/381-8692.* 54 rms, 2 story. S, D $44-$55; each addl $4; suite $70; under 13 free; wkend rates. Crib free. TV; cable (premium), VCR avail. Pool. Complimentary continental bkfst. Restaurant nearby. Ck-out 11 am. Meeting rm. Business servs avail. Cr cds: A, C, D, DS, ER, MC, V.

D ≋ ⊠ 🔥 **SC**

★ **RAMADA INN.** *1208 Nashville Hwy, 2½ mi N on US 31. 931/388-2720; FAX 931/388-2360.* 155 rms, 2 story. S $42-$52; D $47-$57; each addl $5. Crib free. Pet accepted. TV; cable (premium), VCR avail. Pool. Restaurant 6 am-2 pm, 5-10 pm. Rm serv. Bar 4 pm-midnight. Ck-out noon. Meeting rms. Cr cds: A, C, D, DS, JCB, MC, V.

D 🐾 ≋ ⊠ 🔥 **SC**

Restaurants

★★ **THE OLE LAMPLIGHTER.** *1000 Riverside Dr. 931/381-3837.* Hrs: 4-10 pm; Sun to 9 pm. Closed some major hols; also 1st wk July. Res accepted. Bar. Semi-a la carte: dinner $8.95-$29.95. Child's

meals. Specializes in steak, seafood. Salad bar. Rustic log building at river. Cr cds: A, C, D, DS, MC, V.

D

✔★ **RANCH HOUSE.** *900 Riverside Dr. 931/381-2268.* Hrs: 4-8:30 pm. Closed Sun. Res accepted Mon-Thurs. Beer. Semi-a la carte: dinner $6.95-$15.95. Child's meals. Specializes in steak, fish. Overlooks river. Cr cds: A, C, D, DS, MC, V.

◻

Cookeville (D-6)

Settled 1854 **Pop** 21,744 **Elev** 1,118 ft **Area code** 931 **Zip** 38501 **E-mail** chamber@cookeville.com **Web** www.cookeville.com/chamber
Information Cookeville Area-Putnam County Chamber of Commerce, 302 S Jefferson Ave; 931/526-2211 or 800/264-5541

Cookeville, a cultural and industrial center for the upper Cumberland area, is the home of Tennessee Technological University.

What to See and Do

Burgess Falls State Natural Area. Scenic riverside trail (¾ mi) leads to an overlook of a 130-foot waterfall, considered one of the most beautiful in the state, located in a gorge on the Falling Water River. Fishing (Burgess Falls Lake & river below dam). Hiking trails. Picnicking (below dam). 8 mi S of I-40 exit 286 on TN 135. For information phone 931/432-5312.

Center Hill Dam and Lake. This 250-ft-high, 2,160-ft-long concrete and earth-fill dam controls flood waters of the Caney Fork River and provides electric power. The lake has a 415-mi shoreline. Swimming, waterskiing; fishing, hunting; boating. Picnicking at six recreation areas around reservoir. Camping (fee; hookups). Eight commercial docks. Some facilities closed Oct-mid-Apr. 25 mi W via I-40, TN 141. Phone 931/858-3125 or 615/548-4521. Also here is

Edgar Evins State Park. Approximately 6,000-acre park has boat launch facilities. Camping (dump station), cabins. Standard fees. Phone 931/858-2446 or -2114. Nearby is

Joe L. Evins Appalachian Center for Crafts. On 600 acres overlooking Center Hill Lake. Operated by Tennessee Technological University. Teaching programs in fiber, metal, wood, glass and clay. Exhibition galleries. (Daily; closed major hols) W on I-40, 6 mi S on TN 56. Phone 615/597-6801. **Free.**

Motels

✔★★ **ALPINE LODGE & SUITES.** *2021 E Spring St (38506), on US 70N at I-40 exit 290. 931/526-3333; res: 800/213-2016; FAX 931/528-9036.* 64 rms, 2 story, 24 suites. S $40-$44; D $48-$55; suites $60-$95; each addl $5; under 18 free. Crib free. Pet accepted; $5/day. TV; cable (premium), VCR avail (movies $2). Pool; wading pool. Complimentary continental bkfst. Restaurant 11 am-10 pm. Ck-out noon. Coin lndry. Business servs avail. In-rm modem link. Sundries. Refrigerators. Private patios, balconies. Picnic tables. Cr cds: A, C, D, DS, ER, JCB, MC, V.

D 🐾 ≋ ⊠ 🔥 **SC**

✔★ **BEST WESTERN THUNDERBIRD.** *900 S Jefferson Ave, ½ mi N of I-40 Sparta Rd exit 287. 931/526-7115.* 76 rms, 3 story. S $30-$45; D $35-$47; suites $60-$100; each addl $4; under 12 free. Crib $6. Pet accepted. TV; cable. Pool. Complimentary continental bkfst. Restaurant adj 6 am-midnight. Ck-out noon. Meeting rms. Business servs avail. Exercise equipt. Cr cds: A, C, D, DS, JCB, MC, V.

D 🐾 ≋ 🏋 ⊠ 🔥 **SC**

★★ **ECONO LODGE.** *1100 S Jefferson Ave, I-40 exit 287. 931/528-1040; res: 800/553-2666; FAX 931/528-5227.* 71 air-cooled rms, 2 story. May-Oct: S $39.95-$49.95; D $44.95-$54.95; each addl $5; suites

$59.95-$69.95; under 10 free; lower rates rest of yr. Crib $5. Pet accepted; $5. TV; cable (premium). Pool. Complimentary continental bkfst. Ck-out 11 am. Business servs avail. Many refrigerators. Cr cds: A, C, D, DS, ER, JCB, MC, V.

D ⚡ ≈ ✕ 🖊 SC

★ ★ EXECUTIVE INN. 897 S Jefferson Ave, at jct TN 136 & I-40, exit 287. 931/526-9521; FAX 931/528-2285; res: 800/826-2791. 83 rms, 2 story. S, D $35-$45; each addl $5. TV; cable (premium). Pool; wading pool. Continental bkfst. Restaurant 11 am-10 pm; Fri & Sat to 11 pm. Ck-out 11 am. Coin lndry. Meeting rm. Business servs avail. Cr cds: A, C, D, DS, MC, V.

D ≈ ✕ 🖊 SC

★ ★ RAMADA LIMITED SUITES. 1045 Interstate Dr. 931/372-0086; FAX 931/372-0030. Web www.tndirectory.com/crsuites. 60 rms, 3 story, 53 suites. S $54-$65; D $59-$70; each addl $5; suites $54-$70; under 18 free; higher rates special events. Crib free. TV; cable (premium). Indoor pool. Complimentary continental bkfst. Restaurant nearby. Ck-out 11 am. Coin lndry. Meeting rms. Business servs avail. In-rm modem link. Sundries. Exercise equipt. Refrigerators, minibars. Cr cds: A, D, DS, MC, V.

D ≈ ✕ 🖊 SC

Motor Hotel

★ ★ ★ HOLIDAY INN. 970 S Jefferson Ave, at jct I-40 & TN 136, exit 287. 931/526-7125. 200 rms, 2-3 story. S, D $67-$77; suites $127-$200; family rates. Crib avail. Pet accepted. TV; cable (premium). Indoor/outdoor pool; whirlpool. Restaurant 6 am-2 pm, 5-10 pm. Rm serv. Bar 4 pm-1 am. Ck-out noon. Meeting rms. Business center. In-rm modem link. Bellhops. Valet serv. Sundries. Exercise equipt. Game rm. Cr cds: A, C, D, DS, JCB, MC, V.

D ⚡ ≈ ✕ ✕ 🖊 SC 🛶

Restaurants

★ ★ NICK'S. 895 S Jefferson Ave, at jct I-40 & Sparta Hwy. 931/528-1434. Hrs: 11 am-2 pm, 5-10 pm; Fri to 10:30 pm; Sat 5-10:30 pm; Sun 11 am-2:30 pm. Continental menu. Bar. Semi-a la carte: lunch, dinner $5.95-$16.95. Specializes in char-broiled steak, seafood, ice cream pie. Parking. Cr cds: A, C, D, DS, MC, V.

D ✕

★ ★ SCARECROW COUNTRY INN. 644 Whitson Chapel Rd (38506). 931/526-3431. Hrs: 11 am-2 pm, 5-9:30 pm. Closed Sun, Mon; major hols. Res accepted. Setups. Semi-a la carte: lunch $4-$7.95, dinner $9.95-$17.50. Child's meals. Specialties: apple jack pork, hickory ham. Own desserts. Piano Tues-Sat. Parking. Built from logs of original log cabins and schoolhouse. Totally nonsmoking. Cr cds: A, DS, MC, V.

D

Covington (E-1)

(See also Memphis)

Pop 7,487 Elev 339 ft Area code 901 Zip 38019

What to See and Do

Fort Pillow State Historic Area. This archaeologically significant area consists of 1,646 acres on the Chickasaw Bluffs, overlooking Mississippi River. It contains substantial remains of a large fort, named for a confederate general, and five miles of earthworks. Fishing. Wooded trails (15 mi). Picnicking. Tent & primitive camping. Visitors center (Mon-Fri), nature exhibits. (Daily; closed Dec 25) Standard fees. 33 mi NW via US 51N & TN 87W. Phone 901/738-5581.

Crossville (D-7)

Pop 6,930 Elev 1,863 ft Area code 931 Zip 38555
Information Greater Cumberland County Chamber of Commerce, 108 S Main St, 38555; 931/484-8444.

More than 36,000 tons of multicolored quartzite are quarried in the Crossville area each year and sold for construction projects throughout the country. This Cumberland Plateau town also markets beef cattle, dairy products, strawberries, beans and potatoes. Hickory handles, charcoal, liquid smoke, rubber mats, office supplies, ceramic tile, exercise equipment, bus and truck mirrors, yarn and apparel are also produced locally.

What to See and Do

Cumberland County Playhouse. Indoor stage presentations by both professional and community actors. Picnic facilities, concession. 2 1/2 mi W on US 70S, overlooking Lake Holiday. For schedule, reservations and ticket prices phone 615/484-5000 or contact PO Box 484, 38557.

Cumberland General Store. Old-time country store. (Mid-Mar-Dec, daily; rest of yr, daily exc Sun; closed Jan 1, Thanksgiving, Dec 25) 4 mi S via US 127 in Homestead. Phone 615/484-8481.

Cumberland Mountain State Park. This 1,548-acre park, located along the Cumberland Plateau, is 1,820 feet above sea level. It stands on the largest remaining timberland plateau in America and has a 35-acre lake. Swimming pool, bathhouse, lifeguards; fishing; boating (rentals). Nature trails & programs, tennis. Picnicking, playground, concession, snack bar, dining room. Camping, tent & trailer sites, cabins. Standard fees. 4 mi S on US 127. Phone 615/484-6138.

Homesteads Tower Museum. The tower was built in 1937-1938 to house administrative offices of the Cumberland Homesteads, a New Deal-era project. A winding stairway leads to a lookout platform at the top of the octagonal stone tower. At the base of the tower is a museum with photos, documents and artifacts from the 1930s and 1940s. (Mar-Dec, daily; closed Easter, Labor Day, Thanksgiving). 4 mi S on US 127. Phone 615/456-9663.Museum ¢

Annual Event

Cumberland County Fair. Exhibits, horse, cattle and other animal shows, mule pulls, fiddlers' contest. Phone 615/484-6183. Late Aug.

Motel

✔ ★ DAYS INN. 105 Executive Dr. 931/484-9691; res: 800/626-9432. 61 rms, 2 story. Mid-May-Oct: S, D $50-$70; each addl $5; under 17 free; lower rates rest of yr. Crib free. Pet accepted, some restrictions. TV; cable (premium). Pool. Complimentary continental bkfst. Restaurant adj. Ck-out 11 am. Business servs avail. On river. Cr cds: A, C, D, DS, MC, V.

D ⚡ ≈ ✕ 🖊 SC

Motor Hotel

★ ★ HAMPTON INN. 3198 N Main St, I-40 exit 317. 931/456-9338; res: 800/426-7866; FAX 931/456-8758. 60 rms, 3 story. Apr-Oct: S, D $69-$89; under 18 free; family rates; higher rates special events; lower rates rest of yr. Crib free. TV; cable (premium). Complimentary continental bkfst. Complimentary coffee in rms. Restaurant adj open 24 hrs. Ck-out 11 am. Meeting rms. Business servs avail. In-rm modem link. Exercise equipt. Indoor pool; whirlpool. Cr cds: A, C, D, DS, JCB, MC, V.

D ≈ ✕ ✕ 🖊 SC

Resort

★ ★ ★ FAIRFIELD GLADE. (Fairfield Glade 38558) 10 mi N, 6 mi N of I-40 Peavine Rd (exit 322). 931/484-7521; FAX 931/484-3788. E-mail reservations@fairfieldglade.com; web www.fairfieldglade.com. 100 rms, 67 villas. Mar-Oct: S, D $100; villas $110-$150; golf package plan; lower rates rest of yr. Crib free. TV; cable (premium). Indoor/outdoor pool; wading pool. Playground. Supervised child's activities (June-Aug); ages 5-12. Restaurants 7 am-10 pm. Snack bar. Private club. Ck-out 10 am, ck-in 4 pm. Grocery. Meeting rms. Business servs avail. Sports dir. Indoor & lighted tennis, pro. 18-hole golf, greens fee $50, putting green, driving range. Miniature golf. Private beach. Boats, motors, dock. Entertainment. Lawn games. Rec rm. Exercise rm. Private patios, balconies. Picnic tables, grills. Cr cds: A, C, D, DS, MC, V.

Cumberland Gap National Historical Park

(see Kentucky)

Dickson (D-4)

(See also Hurricane Mills, Nashville)

Founded 1873 **Pop** 8,791 **Elev** 794 ft **Area code** 615 **Zip** 37055 **E-mail** chamber@dickson.net **Web** www.dickson.net/chamber
Information Chamber of Commerce, 119 US 70 E; 615/446-2349.

What to See and Do

Montgomery Bell State Resort Park. A 5,000-acre, wooded park with streams, brooks and three lakes in the Highland Rim. Replica of church on site where Cumberland Presbyterian Church was founded in 1810. Swimming, bathhouse; fishing; boating (rentals). Nature trails, backpacking; golf, tennis. Picnicking, playground, restaurant. Tent & trailer sites, lodging, cabins. Standard fees. 7 mi E on US 70. Phone 615/797-3101.

Annual Event

Old-Timers' Day Festival. Parades, entertainment and special events. 1st wkend May.

Dyersburg (D-2)

Pop 16,317 **Elev** 295 ft **Area code** 901 **Zip** 38024

Motels

✔★ ★ **COMFORT INN.** *815 Reelfoot Dr, I-155 exit 13. 901/285-6951; FAX 901/285-6956.* 82 rms, 2 story. Mar-Sept: S $55-$59; D $60-$65; each addl $6; under 18 free; lower rates rest of yr. Crib $6. TV; cable. Pool. Complimentary continental bkfst. Ck-out 11 am. Coin lndry. Meeting rms. Exercise equipt. Some refrigerators; microwaves avail. Cr cds: A, C, D, DS, JCB, MC, V.

★ ★ **HOLIDAY INN.** *US 51 Bypass, exit 13 on I-155. 901/285-8601; FAX 901/286-0494.* 106 rms, 2 story. S, D $59-$65; each addl $10; under 18 free. Crib free. TV; cable. Pool. Restaurant 6:30 am-2 pm, 5:30-10 pm. Rm serv. Ck-out noon. Meeting rms. Valet serv. Sundries. Cr cds: A, C, D, DS, JCB, MC, V.

Elizabethton (D-10)

(See also Johnson City)

Pop 11,931 **Elev** 1,530 ft **Area code** 423 **Zip** 37643
Information Elizabethton/Carter County Chamber of Commerce, 500 19E Bypass, PO Box 190, 37644; 423/547-3850 or 888/547-3852.

A monument on the lawn of Carter County Courthouse marks the spot where the Watauga Association was formed in 1772 by settlers in these hills. Isolated from the seaboard colonies, the pioneers were determined to organize for law and self-protection. Their constitution was the first to be adopted by independent Americans. Little is now known about this constitution except that it helped unite the people of eastern Tennessee to fight in the American Revolution.

What to See and Do

Roan Mountain State Park. The 2,104-acre park includes 6,285-ft Roan Mountain, one of the highest peaks in the eastern US. Atop mountain is 600-acre garden of rhododendron, in bloom late June (see ANNUAL EVENTS). Swimming pool; fishing. Nature trail. Cross-country skiing. Picnicking, playground, snack bar. Camping, cabins. Standard fees. 17 mi SE via US 19E, S on TN 143. Phone 423/772-3303 or -3314.

Sycamore Shoals State Historic Area. First colonial settlement west of the Blue Ridge Mountains has reconstructed fort consisting of five buildings and palisade walls; visitor center with museum and theater (daily). Tours of nearby Carter Mansion available by appt. Picnic sites. (See ANNUAL EVENTS) 1½ mi W on US 321. Phone 423/543-5808.   **Free.**

Watauga Dam and Lake. Earth and rock-fill TVA dam, 950 feet long and 331 feet high, impounds a 6,430-acre lake. Swimming, waterskiing; boating (docks). Camping, cabins. Visitor overlook (daily). 5 mi SE on US 19E, then 3 mi E on TN 67. Phone 423/542-2951.   **Free.**

Annual Events

Roan Mt Wild Flower Tours & Bird Walks. Roan Mountain State Park. May.

Covered Bridge Celebration. Elk Ave Bridge, downtown. Arts & crafts festival, parade, antique show, ice-cream eating contest. Area country music stars and local talent perform. 6 nights early June.

Rhododendron Festival. Roan Mountain State Park. Mid-late June.

Outdoor Drama. Sycamore Shoals State Historic Area. Depicts muster of Overmountain Men, who marched to King's Mountain, SC, and defeated the British. Phone 423/543-5808. Mid-July.

Overmountain Victory Trail Celebration. Reenactment in period costume of original 200-mi march. Late Sept.

Fort Donelson National Battlefield and Cemetery (C-3)

(See also Clarksville)

(1 mi W of Dover on US 79)

"Unconditional and immediate surrender!" demanded General Ulysses S. Grant when Confederate General Simon B. Buckner proposed a truce at Fort Donelson. Thus did Grant contribute to the long list of appropriate and pithy remarks for which American military men have become justly famous.

Nothing helped Grant so much during this four-day battle as weak generalship on the part of Confederate commanders John B. Floyd and Gideon J. Pillow. Although the Confederates repulsed an attack by Federal ironclad gunboats, the responsibility of surrendering the Confederate garrison of 15,000 was thrust upon Buckner on February 16, 1862. Grant's victory at Fort Donelson, coupled with the fall of Fort Henry 10 days earlier, opened the Tennessee and Cumberland rivers into the heart of the Confederacy. In Grant, the people had a new hero. His laconic surrender message stirred the imagination, and he was quickly dubbed "Unconditional Surrender" Grant.

The fort walls, outer defenses and river batteries still remain and are well-marked to give the story of the battle. A visitor center features a 10-minute slide program, museum and touch exhibits (daily; closed Dec 25). A six-mile self-guided auto tour includes a visit to the fort, the cemetery and the Dover Hotel, where General Buckner surrendered. The park is open year round, dawn-dusk. Contact Superintendent, PO Box 434, Dover 37058; 931/232-5706.   **Free.**

Franklin (D-5)

(See also Columbia, Nashville)

Founded 1799 **Pop** 20,098 **Elev** 648 ft **Area code** 615 **Zip** 37064
Information Williamson County Chamber of Commerce, City Hall, PO Box 156, 37065-0156; 615/794-1225.

Franklin is a favorite of Civil War buffs, who come to retrace the Battle of Franklin, a decisive clash that took place November 30, 1864. General John B. Hood, attempting to prevent two Union armies from uniting, outflanked the troops of General John Schofield. The Union troops, dug in around the Carter House, were discovered by Hood late in the afternoon. For five hours the battle raged. In the morning Hood found that the Schofield troops had escaped across the river to join forces with the Union army at Nashville. The Confederates suffered 6,252 casualties, including the loss of five generals at Carnton Plantation and a sixth general 10 days after the battle. The North suffered 2,326 casualties.

What to See and Do

Carnton Plantation and McGavock Confederate Cemetery. Federal house (1826) modified in the 1840s to reflect Greek-revival style. Built by an early mayor of Nashville, house was a social and political center. At the end of the Battle of Franklin, which was fought nearby, four Confederate generals lay dead on the back porch. The nation's largest private Confederate cemetery is adjacent. (Daily; closed most major hols) 1345 Carnton Lane, 1 mi SE off US 431 (Lewisburg Pike). Phone 615/794-0903.   **¢¢**

Carter House (1830). Served as the command post for the Union forces during the Battle of Franklin. Confederate museum has documents, uniforms, flags, guns, maps, Civil War prints. Guided tour of house and grounds, video presentation. (Daily; closed major hols) 1140 Columbia Ave, on US 31. Phone 615/791-1861.   **¢¢**

⭐ **Heritage Trail.** Scenic drive along highway from Brentwood through Franklin to Spring Hill, an area that was, in the mid-1800s, plantation country. Southern culture is reflected in the drive's many antebellum and Victorian houses; Williamson County was one of the richest areas in Tennessee by the time of the Civil War. N & S on US 31.

Historic District. Earliest buildings of Franklin, dating back to 1800; those along Main St are exceptional in their architectural designs and are part of a historic preservation project. Downtown area within 1st Ave S to 5th Ave S and N Margin St to S Margin St, centered around the Town Square and the Confederate Monument.

Annual Events

Heritage Foundation Town & Country Tour. Contact PO Box 723; 615/591-8500. 1st wkend May.

Carter House Christmas Candlelight Tour. Phone 615/791-1861. 1st wkend Dec.

Motels

🚭★ **BEST WESTERN FRANKLIN INN.** *1308 Murfreesboro Rd, TN 96 at I-65 exit 65. 615/790-0570; res: 800/251-3200; FAX 615/790-0512.* Web www.bestwestern.com/best.httm. 142 rms, 2 story. S, D $65-$75; each addl $5; under 12 free; higher rates: Fan Fair, special events. Crib free. Pet accepted, some restrictions. TV; cable (premium). Pool. Complimentary continental bkfst. Restaurant adj 6 am-11 pm. Ck-out noon. Meeting rms. Business servs avail. Cr cds: A, C, D, DS, MC, V.

🄳 ⛵ 🏊 ✈ 🔥 SC

★★ **HOLIDAY INN EXPRESS.** *1307 Murfreesboro Rd, TN 96 at I-65. 615/794-7591; FAX 615/794-1042.* 100 rms, 2 story. S $55-$64; D $60-$72; each addl $7; under 18 free; higher rates Fan Fair Week. Crib free. TV; cable (premium). Pool. Playground. Complimentary continental bkfst. Ck-out noon. Meeting rm. Cr cds: A, C, D, DS, JCB, MC, V.

🄳 🏊 ✈ 🔥 SC

Gallatin (D-5)

(See also Nashville)

Founded 1802 **Pop** 18,794 **Elev** 526 ft **Area code** 615 **Zip** 37066
Information Chamber of Commerce, 118 W Main, PO Box 26; 615/452-4000.

The county seat and market for tobacco and livestock, Gallatin is named for Albert Gallatin, Secretary of the Treasury under John Adams and Thomas Jefferson.

What to See and Do

Bledsoe Creek State Park. Waterskiing; fishing; boating (launch). Nature trails. Playground. Camping (hookups, dump station). Standard fees. 6 mi E on TN 25 to Ziegler Fort Rd, then 1½ mi S to Main Park Rd & the park entrance. Phone 615/452-3706.

Cragfont (1798). This late Georgian-style house was built for General James Winchester, Revolutionary War hero, by masons and carpenters brought from Maryland. It is named for the rocky bluff (with spring below) on which it stands. Galleried ballroom, weaving room, wine cellar; Federal period furnishings. Restored gardens. (Mid-Apr-early Nov, daily exc Mon) 5 mi E on TN 25, in Castalian Springs. Phone 615/452-7070.   **¢¢**

Trousdale Place. Two-story brick house built in early 1800s was residence of Governor William Trousdale; period furniture, military history library. 183 W Main St. Phone 615/452-5648 for schedule.   **¢¢**

Wynnewood (1828). Log inn, considered the oldest and largest log structure ever built in Tennessee, was originally constructed as a stagecoach stop and mineral springs resort; Andrew Jackson visited here many times. (Apr-Oct, daily; rest of yr, daily exc Sun; closed major hols) 7 mi E on TN 25, in Castalian Springs. Phone 615/452-5463.   **¢¢**

Annual Event

Sumner County Pilgrimage. Tour of historic houses. Contact Cragfont, 200 Cragfont Rd, Castalian Springs 37031; 615/452-7070. Last Sat Apr.

Motel

★★ **SHONEY'S INN.** *221 W Main St (TN 25). 615/452-5433; FAX 615/452-1665.* 86 rms, 2 story. S $36-$45; D $45-$55; each addl $6; under 19 free; higher rates Fanfare. Crib free. TV; cable. Pool. Complimentary coffee in lobby. Restaurant adj 6 am-midnight; Fri, Sat to 2 am. Ck-out noon. Meeting rms. Business servs avail. Cr cds: A, C, D, DS, ER, MC, V.

🄳 🏊 ✈ 🔥 SC

Hotel

★ ★ ★ **HOLIDAY INN.** *(615 E Main St, Hendersonville 37075) 2 mi E on US 31.* 615/824-0022; res: 800/465-4329; FAX 615/824-7977. 93 rms, 4 story. Apr-Dec: S, D $86-$96; suites $129-$139; under 18 free; lower rates rest of yr. Crib free. TV; cable (premium), VCR avail. Complimentary coffee in rms. Restaurant 6:30 am-10 pm. Bar 4-11 pm. Ck-out noon. Meeting rms. Business servs avail. In-rm modem link. Gift shop. Coin lndry. Exercise equipt. Pool. In-rm whirlpool, refrigerator, microwave in suites. Cr cds: A, C, D, DS, ER, JCB, MC, V.

D ⚲ ✈ ⊠ 🔥 SC

Gatlinburg (E-8)

(See also Pigeon Forge, Sevierville, Townsend)

Pop 3,417 **Elev** 1,289 ft **Area code** 423 **Zip** 37738 **Web** www.gatlinburg.com
Information Chamber of Commerce, 520 Parkway, PO Box 527; 423/430-4148 or 800/568-4748.

Gatlinburg has retained most of its mountain quaintness while turning its attention to tapping into the stream of tourists that flows through the town on its way into the Great Smoky Mountains National Park, the country's most visited national park. The city has accommodations for 40,000 guests and a $22-million convention center. At the foot of Mount LeConte and at the head of the Pigeon River, Gatlinburg is noted for its many shops that make and sell mountain handicrafts—brooms, candles, candies, pottery and furniture.

What to See and Do

Christus Gardens. Events from the life of Jesus portrayed in life-size dioramas; music and narration. Floral gardens in season. (Daily; closed Dec 25) 510 River Rd. Phone 423/436-5155. ¢¢¢

Craft shops. Along Main Street and E along US 321 on Glades Rd.

Great Smoky Mountains National Park (see).

Ober Gatlinburg Ski Resort. Double, 2 quad chairlifts; patrol, school, rentals; snowmaking; concession area, restaurant, bar. Longest run 5,000 ft; vertical drop 600 ft. (Dec-mid-Mar, daily) Also alpine slide, indoor ice-skating arena (daily; closed 2 wks Mar; fees); aerial tramway and sightseeing chairlift. Ski Mountain Rd, on Mt Harrison. Contact Ober Gatlinburg, Inc, 1001 Parkway; 423/436-5423 or 800/251-9202 (Dec-Mar). ¢¢¢¢¢

Scenic rides.

Gatlinburg Space Needle. Glass-enclosed elevator to observation deck for view of the Smokies. (Daily) Airport Rd. Phone 423/436-4629. ¢¢

Sky Lift. Double chairlift ride up Crockett Mountain to 2,300 ft. View of Smokies en route and from observation deck at summit; snack bar; gift shop. (Daily, weather permitting) 765 Parkway (US 441). Phone 423/436-4307. ¢¢¢

Sightseeing Chairlift-Ober Gatlinburg Ski Resort. Double chairlift operates to top of Mt Harrison. (Mar-Memorial Day, daily) Ski Mountain Rd, on Mt Harrison. ¢¢

Aerial Tramway-Ober Gatlinburg Ski Resort. Ten-min, two-mi tram ride to top of Mt Harrison. (Daily; closed 2 wks Mar) 1001 Parkway. Phone 423/436-5423. ¢¢¢

Annual Events

Spring Wild Flower Pilgrimage. Late Apr.

Scottish Festival and Games. Bagpipe marching bands, highland dancing, sheep dog demonstrations. 3rd wkend May.

Dulcimer Harp Festival. In Cosby, 20 mi NE on US 321 to TN 32S. Dulcimer convention; folk music; crafts demonstrations, storytelling, work-

shops. Participants from throughout the Appalachian region. For information contact PO Box 8, Cosby 37722; 423/487-5543. 2nd wkend June.

Craftsmen's Fairs. Craft demonstrations, folk music. Late July-early Aug; also mid-Oct.

Seasonal Events

Sweet Fanny Adams Theater. 461 Parkway. Professional theater presenting musical comedies, Gay 90s revue, old-time sing-along. Nightly exc Sun. Reservations advisable. Phone 423/436-4039. Late Apr-Nov.

Smoky Mountain Lights. Winter celebration including Yule log burnings, more than 2 million lights and other special events. Late Nov-Feb. Citywide.

Motels

★ **ALTO.** 404 Airport Rd. 423/436-5175; FAX 423/430-7342; res: 800/456-4336. 21 rms, 2 story. Late May-Oct: S, D $60-$70; each addl $6; under 16 free; lower rates rest of yr. Crib free. TV; cable (premium). Pool; wading pool. Playground. Restaurant adj 7 am-11 pm. Ck-out 11 am. Downhill ski 1 mi. Refrigerators. Picnic tables, grills. Cr cds: A, DS, MC, V.

⚲ ⚲ 🔥

★ ★ **BEST WESTERN CHALET INN.** 310 Cottage Dr, at River Rd. 423/436-5151; FAX 423/523-8363. 75 rms, 2 story, 1 kit. S, D $70-$89.50; kit. unit $90-$109.50; under 18 free. Crib free. TV; cable. Pool; wading pool. Complimentary continental bkfst Apr-Oct. Coffee in rms. Restaurant nearby. Ck-out 11 am. Business servs avail. Refrigerators. Sun deck. Many rms overlook Little Pigeon River. Cr cds: A, C, D, DS, MC, V.

🐾 ⚲ ⊠ 🔥 SC

★ ★ **BEST WESTERN CROSSROADS.** 440 Parkway, at jct US 441 & TN 321. 423/436-5661; res: 800/925-8889; FAX 423/436-6208. 78 rms, 2-4 story, 10 suites. May-Oct: S, D $49.50-$99.50; suites, kit. units $139.50-$150; lower rates rest of yr. Crib $6. TV; cable. Pool; wading pool. Ck-out 11 am. Coin lndry. Business servs avail. Downhill ski 2 mi. Some fireplaces. Covered patio. Cr cds: A, C, D, DS, MC, V.

D ⚲ ⚲ ⊠ 🔥 SC

✔ **BON AIR MOUNTAIN INN.** 950 Parkway. 423/436-4857; res: 800/848-4857. 74 rms, 3 story, 1 kit. chalet. Apr-Oct: S, D $43-$99; chalet $125-$175; higher rates special events; lower rates rest of yr. Crib free. Pet accepted. TV; cable. Pool. Restaurant nearby. Ck-out 11 am. Business servs avail. Downhill ski 1 mi. Refrigerators. Balconies. Cr cds: A, D, DS, MC, V.

D 🐾 ⚲ ⚲ ⊠ 🔥 SC

★ **BROOKSIDE RESORT.** 463 E Parkway, 3 blks E on US 321. 423/436-5611; FAX 423/436-0039; res: 800/251-9597. 216 rms in motel, cottages, 1-2 story, 30 kits. May-Nov: S $55-$110; D $70-$110; each addl $5; suites from $100; kit. units $55-$145; kit. cottages for 2-4, $60-$175; lower rates rest of yr. Crib free. TV; cable. Pool; wading pool, whirlpool. Playground. Restaurant opp 7 am-10 pm. Ck-out 11 am. Coin lndry. Meeting rm. Business servs avail. Downhill ski 6 mi. Lawn games. In-rm whirlpools, refrigerators, fireplaces. Picnic tables, grills. Spacious grounds. By mountain stream. Cr cds: A, C, D, MC, V.

D 🐾 ⚲ ⚲ 🔥

★ **CREEKSIDE.** 239 Sycamore Lane. 423/436-5977. 42 rms, 4 story, 1 kit. Apr-Nov: S $50-$75; D $58-$98; each addl $4; kit. unit $78-$88; lower rates rest of yr. Crib $5. TV; cable. Pool; wading pool. Coffee in lobby. Restaurant nearby. Ck-out 11 am. Refrigerators. Picnic tables, grills. Porches overlook stream. Cr cds: A, C, D, DS, MC, V.

D ⚲ ⊠ 🔥

✔ **EAST SIDE.** 315 E Parkway. 423/436-7569. 29 rms, 2-3 story. No elvtr. June-Oct: S $45-$60; D $45-$65; each addl $5; lower rates mid-Mar-May, Nov. Closed rest of yr. Crib $5. TV; cable. Pool; wading pool. Playground. Complimentary coffee in rms. Restaurant nearby. Ck-out 11 am. Refrigerators. Picnic tables, grills. Cr cds: DS, MC, V.

 ⚲ ⊠ 🔥 SC

★ **ECONO LODGE.** *405 Airport Rd.* 423/436-5836; *res:* 800/933-8670; *FAX* 423/523-8363. 33 rms. 1-4 persons $42-$89.50; suites $79.50-$129.50. Crib free. TV; cable (premium). Pool. Complimentary coffee in rms. Restaurant adj 6 am-10 pm. Ck-out 11 am. Business servs avail. Refrigerators. Cr cds: A, C, D, DS, MC, V.

★ ★ **GILLETTE.** *235 Airport Rd, opp convention center.* 423/436-5601; *FAX* 423/430-5772; *res:* 800/437-0815. 80 rms, 3 story, 1 kit. Late May-Oct: S, D $60-$75; each addl $10; kit. unit for 2-4, $85-$95; lower rates rest of yr. Crib $10. TV; cable. Pool. Complimentary coffee in rms. Restaurant nearby. Ck-out 11 am. Downhill ski 1 mi. Refrigerators. Balconies. Cr cds: A, C, D, DS, MC, V.

★ ★ **HAMPTON INN.** *967 Parkway.* 423/436-4878; *res:* 888/476-6597; *FAX* 423/436-4088. Web www.hampton-inn.com/gatlinburg. 96 rms, 4 story. S $67-$129; D $77-$129; each addl $5; under 18 free; golf plans; higher rates special events. Crib free. TV; cable (premium), VCR (movies). Heated pool; whirlpool. Complimentary continental bkfst. Restaurant adj 11 am-11 pm. Ck-out 11 am. Meeting rms. Business servs avail. Downhill ski ½ mi. Some refrigerators. Balconies. Cr cds: A, C, D, DS, JCB, MC, V.

★ ★ **JACK HUFF'S MOTOR LODGE.** *204 Cherokee Orchard Rd.* 423/436-5171; *res:* 800/322-1817. E-mail jhuffs_2@aol.com; web www.gatlinburg.com/jackhuffs. 60 rms, 3 story. June-Oct: S, D $68-$83; each addl $5; lower rates rest of yr. Crib free. TV; cable. Pool; wading pool, whirlpool. Complimentary coffee. Restaurant nearby. Ck-out 11 am. Business servs avail. Downhill ski 4 mi. Cr cds: DS, MC, V.

★ ★ **JOHNSON'S INN.** *242 Bishop Lane.* 423/436-4881; *FAX* 423/436-2582; *res:* 800/842-1930. E-mail info@johnsonsinn.com; web www.johnsonsinn.com. 80 rms, 1-4 story, 3 kits. June-Aug, Oct: S, D $59-$90; each addl $5; under 6 free; higher rates special events; lower rates rest of yr. TV; cable, VCR (movies). Pool; wading pool. Complimentary coffee. Restaurant nearby. Ck-out 11 am. Coin lndry. Business servs avail. Refrigerators, fireplaces. Cr cds: DS, MC, V.

★ ★ **LE CONTE VIEW.** *929 Parkway.* 423/436-5032; *FAX* 423/436-7973; *res:* 800/842-5767. 104 rms, 1-5 story. May-Oct: S, D $65-$105; each addl $7; suites $89-$141; under 18 free; fireplace units $14 addl; higher rates some hol wknds; lower rates rest of yr. Closed Dec 21-25. Crib $4. TV; cable. Indoor/outdoor pool; wading pool. Complimentary coffee in lobby. Restaurant nearby. Ck-out 11 am. Business servs avail. Downhill ski 1 mi. Refrigerators. Cr cds: A, C, D, DS, MC, V.

★ ★ **MIDTOWN LODGE.** *805 Parkway.* 423/436-5691; *FAX* 423/430-3602; *res:* 800/633-2446. 133 rms, 1-6 story, 13 kits. June-Oct: S, D $69.50-$99; suites $99.50-$129.50; kit cottages $99.50-$149.50; higher rates special events; lower rates rest of yr. Crib free. TV; cable. Pool; wading pool. Complimentary continental bkfst. Restaurant opp 7 am-11 pm. Ck-out 11 am. Business servs avail. Downhill ski 2 mi. Some refrigerators, fireplaces. Private patios, balconies. Cr cds: A, C, D, DS, MC, V.

★ ★ **OAK SQUARE.** *685 River Rd.* 423/436-7582; *FAX* 423/430-7230; *res:* 800/423-5182. 46 kit. suites, 4 story. Suites $55-$135; hol rates; ski plans; lower rates winter. Crib free. TV; cable. 2 pools, 1 indoor; whirlpool. Restaurant nearby. Ck-out 11 am. Meeting rm. Business servs avail. Downhill ski 1 mi. Fireplaces. Balconies. Opp river. Cr cds: MC, V.

✔★ ★ **QUALITY INN CONVENTION CENTER.** *938 Parkway.* 423/436-5607; *res:* 800/933-8674. 64 rms, 4 story. June-Oct: S, D $47-$95; under 18 free; higher rates hols, special events; lower rates rest of yr.

Crib $5. TV; cable. Pool; wading pool. Coffee in rms. Restaurant adj 7 am-11 pm. Ck-out 11 am. Meeting rm. Business servs avail. Coin lndry. Downhill ski 1 mi. Refrigerators. Private patios, balconies. Cr cds: A, C, D, DS, MC, V.

★ ★ **QUALITY INN SMOKYLAND.** *727 Parkway.* 423/436-5191; *res:* 800/933-8671. 40 rms, 2 story. Memorial Day wkend-mid-Nov: S, D $79-$104; lower rates rest of yr. Crib $6. TV; cable. Pool; wading pool. Complimentary coffee in rms. Restaurant adj. Ck-out 11 am. Downhill ski 3 mi. Refrigerators; some fireplaces. Cr cds: A, D, DS, MC, V.

★ ★ **RAMADA LIMITED.** *200 East Parkway (US 321).* 423/436-5043; *res:* 800/933-8679. 103 rms, 4 story. May-Oct: S, D up to 4 $84.50-$149.50; under 18 free; lower rates rest of yr. Crib $5. TV; cable. Pool; wading pool, whirlpool. Complimentary continental bkfst. Restaurant 7 am-2 pm. Ck-out 11 am. Coin lndry. Meeting rms. Business servs avail. Downhill ski 5 mi. Some fireplaces. Cr cds: A, D, DS, MC, V.

★ ★ **RIVER EDGE MOTOR LODGE.** *665 River Rd.* 423/436-9292; *FAX* 423/436-3943; *res:* 800/544-2764. 43 rms, 3 story. May-Oct: S, D $65-$135; each addl $5; higher rates: hols, Oct; lower rates rest of yr. Crib free. TV; cable. Pool; wading pool. Complimentary coffee in lobby. Restaurant nearby. Ck-out 11 am. Downhill ski 1 mi. Refrigerators; some fireplaces. Balconies. Cr cds: A, D, DS, MC, V.

★ ★ **RIVER TERRACE CREEKSIDE.** *125 LeConte Creek Dr.* 423/436-4865; *FAX* 423/436-4089; *res:* 800/473-8319. E-mail rivert@riverterrace.com. 69 units, 1-3 story. Mid-May-early Jan: S, D $62-$99; each addl $10; suites $99-$179; lower rates rest of yr. TV; cable (premium). Pool; wading pool. Complimentary continental bkfst. Restaurant adj 7 am-10 pm. Ck-out 11 am. Meeting rms. Business servs avail. Downhill ski 1 mi. Some in-rm whirlpools, fireplaces. Balconies. Cr cds: A, C, D, DS, MC, V.

✔★ **ROCKY TOP VILLAGE INN.** *311 Airport Rd.* 423/436-7826; *FAX* 423/436-7826; *res:* 800/553-7738. 89 rms, 3 story. No elvtr. June-Oct: S, D $45-$61; each addl $5; suites $91-$101; kit. cottages $125-$135; lower rates rest of yr. Crib free. TV; cable (premium). Pool; wading pool. Complimentary coffee in lobby. Restaurant adj 7 am-10 pm. Ck-out 11 am. Meeting rms. Business servs avail. Refrigerators. Picnic tables, grills. Cr cds: A, D, DS, MC, V.

★ ★ **ROCKY WATERS MOTOR INN.** *333 Parkway.* 423/436-7861; *FAX* 423/436-0241; *res:* 800/824-1111. E-mail rkywatrs@smoky-mtns.com; web www.smoky-mtns.com. 100 rms, 2-3 story. Early May-Oct: S, D $78-$83; each addl $5; lower rates rest of yr. Crib $2. TV; cable (premium), VCR (movies $3.50). 2 pools; wading pool, whirlpool. Coffee in lobby. Ck-out 11 am. Coin lndry. Meeting rm. Business servs avail. Downhill ski 2 mi. Refrigerators; some in-rm whirlpools, fireplaces. Private patios. Picnic tables. On river. Cr cds: A, C, D, DS, MC, V.

★ **RODEWAY INN.** *223 E Parkway, 1 blk E on US 321.* 423/436-5821; *FAX* 423/436-6876; *res:* 800/756-9669. 56 rms, 1-2 story. May-Oct: S, D $59-$89; each addl $5; suites $95-$135; lower rates rest of yr. Crib $5. TV; cable. Pool. Complimentary continental bkfst. Restaurant nearby. Ck-out 11 am. Downhill ski 5 mi. Refrigerators. Many balconies. Picnic tables. Cr cds: A, C, D, DS, MC, V.

★ **ROYAL TOWNHOUSE.** *937 Parkway, opp civic auditorium.* 423/436-5818; *FAX* 423/436-0411; *res:* 800/433-8792. 81 rms, 3 story. Late May-Nov: S, D $59.95-$89.95; each addl $5; under 17 free; lower rates rest of yr. Crib $5. TV; cable. Pool; wading pool. Complimentary coffee in rms. Restaurant nearby. Ck-out 11 am. Meeting rms. Business servs avail. Downhill ski 1 mi. Some refrigerators, fireplaces. Cr cds: C, D, DS, MC, V.

⊠ ≋ ⊠ 🐾 SC

★ ★ **TRAVELODGE.** *610 Airport Rd. 423/436-7851; res: 800/876-6888; FAX 423/430-3580.* 136 rms, 4 story, 15 suites. June-Oct: S, D $55-$88; each addl $6; suites $75-$150; under 17 free; higher rates hols; lower rates rest of yr. Crib free. TV; cable. 2 pools, 1 indoor; wading pool, whirlpool. Sauna. Coffee in rms. Restaurant 7 am-2 pm. Ck-out 11 am. Coin lndry. Meeting rms. Business servs avail. Downhill/x-country ski 4 mi. Game rm. Refrigerators. Balconies. Picnic tables. On river. Cr cds: A, C, D, DS; JCB, MC, V.

D 🐾 ⊠ ≋ ⊠ 🐾 SC

Motor Hotels

★ ★ **BENT CREEK RESORT.** *3919 E Parkway, 11 mi E on US 321. 423/436-2875; FAX 423/436-3257; res: 800/251-9336.* 108 rms, 3 story. No elvtr. Apr-Oct: S, D $99-$109; each addl $10; under 18 free; golf plans; lower rates rest of yr. Crib free. TV; cable (premium), VCR avail. Pool; wading pool. Playground. Restaurant 6:30 am-10 pm. Ck-out 11 am. Meeting rms. Business servs avail. 18-hole golf, greens fee $30, pro, putting green, driving range. Downhill ski 10½ mi. Health club privileges. Lawn games. Some refrigerators. Balconies. Cr cds: A, C, D, DS, MC, V.

D ⊠ 🏃 ≋ ⊠ 🐾 SC

✔★ ★ **DAYS INN GLENSTONE LODGE.** *504 Airport Rd. 423/436-9361; res: 800/362-9522; FAX 423/436-6951.* 217 rms, 5 story. S, D $39-$96; each addl $10; suites $85-$150; under 17 free. Crib free. TV; cable. 2 pools, 1 indoor; wading pool, whirlpool. Sauna. Playground. Restaurant 7 am-2 pm. Ck-out 11 am. Meeting rms. Business servs avail. In-rm modem link. Bellhops. Downhill/x-country ski 1 mi. Wet bar in suites. Picnic tables. On river. Cr cds: A, D, DS, MC, V.

D 🐾 ⊠ ≋ ⊠ 🐾 SC

✔★ ★ **GREYSTONE LODGE.** *559 Parkway. 423/436-5621; res: 800/451-9202; FAX 423/430-4471.* 257 rms, 2-5 story. June-Oct: S, D $69-$119; each addl $8; suites $99-$169; under 13 free; higher rates holidays; lower rates rest of yr. Crib free. TV; cable. Heated pool; wading pool. Complimentary continental bkfst. Ck-out 11 am. Coin lndry. Meeting rms. Business servs avail. Downhill ski 2 mi. Some fireplaces. Balconies. On river. Cr cds: A, C, D, DS, MC, V.

D 🐾 ⊠ ≋ ⊠ 🐾 SC

★ ★ **HOLIDAY INN SUNSPREE RESORT.** *520 Airport Rd. 423/436-9201; res: 800/435-9201; FAX 423/436-7974.* 402 rms, 2-8 story. May-Oct: S, D $69-$139; suites $150-$250; under 19 free; lower rates rest of yr. Crib free. Pet accepted. TV; cable (premium). 3 pools, 2 indoor; wading pool, whirlpools. Coffee in rms. Supervised child's activities (summer); ages 3-12. Restaurant 7 am-10 pm. Rm serv. Bar 5 pm-midnight. Ck-out 11 am. Coin lndry. Convention facilities. Business servs avail. Bellhops. Gift shop. Downhill ski 4 mi. Exercise equipt. Rec rm. Refrigerators. Picnic tables, grills. Cr cds: A, C, D, DS, JCB, MC, V.

D 🐾 🐾 ⊠ ≋ 🏃 ⊠ 🐾 SC

Hotels

★ ★ **EDGEWATER.** *402 River Rd. 423/436-4151; FAX 423/436-6947; res: 800/423-9582 (exc TN), 800/423-4532 (TN).* E-mail info@edgewater-hotel.com; web edgewater-hotel.com. 205 rms, 8 story. Apr-Oct: S, D $84-$129; each addl $5; suites $125-$175; under 16 free; lower rates rest of yr. Crib $5. TV; cable. Indoor/outdoor pool; whirlpool. Restaurant 7-11 am, 5-10 pm. Bar; entertainment. Ck-out 11 am. Meeting rms. Business servs avail. Downhill ski 1 mi. Some fireplaces. Balconies. On river. Cr cds: A, C, D, DS, MC, V.

D 🐾 🐾 ⊠ ≋ ⊠ 🐾 SC

★ ★ **PARK VISTA.** *705 Cherokee Orchard. 423/436-9211; FAX 423/436-5141; res: 800/421-7275 (exc TN).* E-mail prkvsta@parkvista. com; web www.parkvista.com. 312 rms, 15 story. S, D $59-$129; suites

$170-$400; under 17 free; higher rates special events. Crib free. TV; cable. Indoor pools; wading pool, whirlpool, poolside serv. Playground. Restaurant 6:30 am-2 pm, 5-10 pm. Rm serv 6:30 am-10:30 pm. Bar 4 pm-1 am. Ck-out 11 am. Coin lndry. Convention facilities. Business servs avail. Downhill ski 5 mi. Exercise equipt. Game rm. Balconies. Cr cds: A, C, D, DS, MC, V.

D 🐾 ⊠ ≋ 🏃 ⊠ 🐾 SC

Inns

★ ★ **BUCKHORN.** *2140 Tudor Mt Rd, left on Buckhorn Rd, right on Tudor Mt Rd; off US 321N. 423/436-4668; FAX 423/436-5009.* 12 rms, 2 story. S $95-$250; D $105-$250; each addl $25; wkly rates; higher rates Oct. Complimentary full bkfst. Restaurant (public by res), 7:30 pm sitting. Ck-out 11 am, ck-in 3 pm. Porch overlooks Mt LeConte. Cr cds: DS, MC, V.

D 🐾 ⊠ 🐾

✔★ ★ **BUTCHER HOUSE IN THE MOUNTAINS.** *1520 Garritt Ln. 423/436-9457; FAX 423/436-9884.* 5 rms, 1 with shower only, 3 story, 1 suite. No rm phones. Apr-Dec: S, D $89-$129; each addl $10; suite $89-$129; wkly rates; 2-day min wkends; higher rates hols (2-day min); lower rates rest of yr. Children over 12 yrs only. TV; cable (premium). Complimentary full bkfst. Ck-out 11 am, ck-in 3 pm. Balconies. Picnic tables. View of Smoky Mountains. Totally nonsmoking. Cr cds: A, MC, V.

⊠ 🐾

Restaurants

✔★ **BRASS LANTERN.** *710 Parkway. 423/436-4168.* Hrs: 11 am-10 pm. Bar 11 am-10 pm; Sat to 11 pm. Semi-a la carte: lunch, dinner $1.95-$14.95. Child's meals. Specializes in soup, ribs, chicken. Parking. Cr cds: A, C, D, DS, MC, V.

D SC 🍴

★ **HEIDELBERG.** *148 N Parkway. 423/430-3094.* Hrs: 11 am-11 pm. Res accepted. German, Swiss, Amer menu. Bar. Semi-a la carte: lunch $4.95-$13.95. A la carte entrees: dinner $8.95-$21.95. Child's meals. Specialties: sauerbraten, schnitzel, steak. German music. Parking. Cr cds: A, C, D, DS, MC, V.

D 🍴

★ ★ ★ **MAXWELL'S BEEF AND SEAFOOD.** *1103 Parkway. 423/436-3738.* Hrs: 4:30-10 pm; Fri, Sat 4-11 pm. Bar. Semi-a la carte: dinner $9.95-$36.95. Child's meals. Specializes in fresh seafood, prime rib, pasta. Parking. Cr cds: A, DS, MC, V.

D 🍴

★ ★ **OPEN HEARTH.** *1138 Parkway. 423/436-5648.* Hrs: 4-10 pm; Fri, Sat to 11 pm. Bar. Semi-a la carte: dinner $12.95-$39.95. Child's meals. Specializes in prime rib, steak, fresh seafood. Entertainment Fri, Sat. Parking. Family-owned. Cr cds: A, C, D, DS, MC, V.

D 🍴

✔★ ★ **PARK GRILL.** *1100 Parkway. 423/436-2300.* Hrs: 5-10 pm. Closed Dec 24. Bar. Semi-a la carte: dinner $8.95-$24.95. Child's meals. Specializes in trout, steak, vegetarian dishes. Parking. Located at entrance to Great Smoky Mountains National Park. Cr cds: A, C, D, DS, MC, V.

D SC 🍴

★ ★ **THE PEDDLER.** *820 River Rd. 423/436-5794.* Hrs: 5-10 pm; winter to 9 pm. Closed Dec 25. Bar. Semi-a la carte: dinner $13.95-$29.95. Child's meals. Specializes in steak. Salad bar. Own soups, desserts. Parking. Converted log cabin. Overlooks river. Cr cds: A, C, D, DS, MC, V.

D SC 🍴

Great Smoky Mountains National Park (E-8)

(See also Gatlinburg)

Web www.nps.gov/grsm

(44 mi SE of Knoxville via US 441)

The lofty peaks of the Appalachian Mountains stand tall and regal in this 800-square-mile area. They are products of a slow and powerful uplifting of ancient sediments that took place more than 200 million years ago. Red spruce, basswood, eastern hemlock, yellow birch, white ash, cucumber trees, silverbells, Fraser fir, tulip poplar, red maple and Fraser magnolias tower above hundreds of other species of flowering plants. Perhaps the most spectacular of these are the purple rhododendron, mountain laurel and flame azalea in bloom from early June to mid-July.

The moist, moderate climate has helped make this area a rich wilderness. From early spring to late fall the "coves" (open valleys surrounded by peaks) and forest floors are covered with a succession of flowers unmatched in the United States for colorful variety. Spring and summer bring heavy showers to the mountains, days that are warm, though 15°-20°F cooler than in the valleys below, and cool nights. Autumn is breathtaking as the deciduous trees change to almost every color in the spectrum. Winter brings snow, which is occasionally heavy, and fog over the mountains; while winter discourages many tourists, it can be a very good time to visit the park. (Some park roads, however, may be temporarily closed.)

A wonderful place to hike, half of the park is in North Carolina, while the other half is in Tennessee. The Appalachian Trail follows the state line for 70 miles along the high ridge of the park. The park preserves cabins, barns and mills of the mountain people, whose ancestors came years ago from England and Scotland. It is also a place to see the descendants of the Cherokee Indian Nation, whose ancestors hid in the mountains from the soldiers during the winter of 1838-1839 to avoid being driven over the "Trail of Tears" to Oklahoma. This is the tribe of Sequoya, a brilliant chief who invented a written alphabet for the Cherokee people.

Stop first at one of the three visitor centers: Oconaluftee (daily; closed Dec 25) in North Carolina, two miles north of Cherokee on Newfound Gap Road, designated US 441 outside of park or Sugarlands (daily; closed Dec 25) in Tennessee, two miles south of Gatlinburg and Cades Cove (daily; closed Dec 25) in Tennessee, 10 miles southwest of Townsend. Both have exhibits and information about the park. There are hundreds of miles of foot trails and bridle paths. Camping is popular; ask at any visitor center for locations, regulations. Developed campgrounds (inquire for fee) are available. Reservations may be made up to three months in advance by phoning 800/365-CAMP from mid-May-Oct for Elkmont, Cades Cove and Smokemont; reservations not taken for other sites.

The views from Newfound Gap and the observation platform at Clingmans Dome (closed winter), about seven miles southwest, are spectacular. Cades Cove, about 25 miles west of Sugarlands, is an outdoor museum reflecting the life of the original mountain people. It has log cabins and barns. Park naturalists conduct campfire programs and hikes during summer. There are also self-guided nature trails. LeConte Lodge, reached only on foot or horseback, is a concession within the park (late Mar-mid-Nov).

Fishing is permitted with a Tennessee or North Carolina state fishing license. Obtain regulations at visitor centers and campgrounds. The park is a wildlife sanctuary; any disturbance of plant or animal life is forbidden. Dogs and cats are not permitted on trails, but may be brought in if kept on leash or under other physical restrictive controls. Never feed, tease or frighten bears; always give them a wide berth, as they may inflict serious injury. Watch bears from a car with the windows closed. Park (daily). **Free.**

CCInc Auto Tape Tours, a 90-minute cassette, offers a mile-by-mile self-guided tour of the park. It provides information on history, points of interest and flora and fauna of the park. Available in Gatlinburg at motels and gift shops; in Cherokee, NC, at Raven Craft Shop on Main Street and at Log Cabin Trading Post, across from the cinema. Tapes also may be purchased directly from CCInc, PO Box 227, 2 Elbrook Dr, Allendale, NJ 07401; 201/236-1666. **¢¢¢¢**

For further information contact Superintendent, Great Smoky Mountains National Park, 107 Park Headquarters Rd, Gatlinburg 37738; phone 423/436-1200. Lodging is available in the park at LeConte Lodge, phone 423/429-5704.

Greeneville (D-9)

Settled 1783 **Pop** 13,532 **Elev** 1,531 ft **Area code** 423 **E-mail** gcp@greene.xtn.net **Web** greene.xtn.net/~gcp

Information Greene County Partnership, 115 Academy St, 37743; 423/638-4111.

Greeneville was the capital of the independent sovereign state of Franklin (1785-1788), formed by the rugged independent-minded Scotch-Irish settlers who seceded from North Carolina. A Greeneville tailor, Andrew Johnson, was elected to the Board of Aldermen in 1829 and went on to become president of the United States. Davy Crockett was born a few miles outside of town in 1786. Manufacturing, lumber, dairying and tobacco are most important today. A Ranger District office of the Cherokee National Forest is located in Greeneville.

What to See and Do

Andrew Johnson National Historic Site (see). College & Depot Sts.

Cherokee National Forest (see). 12 mi S on TN 70.

Davy Crockett Birthplace State Park. A 100-acre site overlooking Nolichuckey River serves as a memorial to Crockett—humorist, bear hunter, congressman and hero of the Alamo. Small monument marks birthplace; nearby is a replica of the log cabin in which Crockett was born in 1786. Swimming pool (fee). Picnicking. Camping (hook-ups). Museum and visitors center (Mon-Fri, or by appt). Park (daily). Standard fees. 3 mi E off US 11E. Phone 423/257-2167 or -2168.

Kinser Park. A 285-acre park surrounded by woodland, overlooking Nolichuckey River. Swimming pool (bathhouses, waterslide); boating (ramp). Nature trails; tennis courts; golf course; miniature golf, playing fields, go-cart track. Picnic facilities, playgrounds. Camping (fee; hookups). Fee for some activities. (Mid-Mar-Oct, daily) 6 mi S via TN 70S. Phone 423/639-5912. **Free.**

Motels

✔★ **CHARRAY INN.** *121 Serral Dr (37745). 423/638-1331; FAX 423/639-5289; res: 800/852-4682.* 36 rms, 2 story. S, D $44-$60; each addl $4; under 16 free. Crib free. TV; cable (premium), VCR avail. Coffee in rms. Restaurant 6-11 am; Sat 7-11:30 am. Ck-out 11 am. Meeting rms. Business servs avail. In-rm modem link. Airport transportation. Refrigerators. Cr cds: A, C, D, DS, MC, V.

⊠ 🐾 SC

★ **DAYS INN.** *935 E Andrew Johnson Hwy (37745). 423/639-2156; res: 800/329-7466.* 60 rms, 2 story. S, D $36-$120; each addl $6. Crib free. Pet accepted. TV; cable (premium). Complimentary continental bkfst. Restaurant nearby. Ck-out 11 am. Business servs avail. Cr cds: A, D, DS, MC, V.

🐾 ⊠ 🐾 SC

★★ **HOLIDAY INN.** *1790 E Andrew Johnson Hwy (37745). 423/639-4185; res: 888/557-5007; FAX 423/639-7280.* 90 rms, 2 story. S, D $53-$65; under 18 free; higher rates special events. Crib free. TV; cable (premium). Pool. Restaurant 7 am-2 pm, 6-10 pm. Rm serv. Bar. Ck-out noon. Meeting rms. Business servs avail. Cr cds: A, C, D, DS, JCB, MC, V.

D ⊠ 🏊 🐾 SC

Restaurant

★ ★ **AUGUSTINO'S.** *3465 E Andrew Johnson Hwy (37743). 423/639-1231.* Hrs: 11 am-2 pm, 5-10 pm; Sat from 5 pm; Sun brunch to 2 pm. Closed major hols. Italian menu. A la carte entrees: lunch $3.75-$9, dinner $5.45-$33. Sun brunch $4.50-$9. Child's meals. Specializes in fettucine, prime rib. Parking. Patio dining. Cr cds: A, DS, MC, V.

D 🔄

Harrogate (C-8)

Pop 2,657 **Elev** 1,300 ft **Area code** 423 **Zip** 37752

What to See and Do

Abraham Lincoln Museum. Collection, one of the largest of its type in the world, contains more than 25,000 pieces of Lincolniana and items related to Civil War. Research center. (Daily; closed Easter, Thanksgiving, Dec 25) S on Cumberland Gap Pkwy, US 25E, on the Lincoln Memorial University campus. Phone 423/869-6235. ¢

Cumberland Gap National Historical Park. 4 mi N on US 25E. (See under KENTUCKY)

Motor Hotel

★ ★ **RAMADA INN.** *(US 58, Cumberland Gap 37724)* 1/2 mi E on US 25E. *423/869-3631; FAX 423/869-5953.* 147 rms, 4 story. S $54; D $60; each addl $6; under 19 free. Crib free. Pet accepted, some restrictions; $25. TV; cable (premium), VCR avail. Pool. Playground. Restaurant 6:30 am-2 pm, 5:30-9:30 pm. Rm serv. Bar 5 pm-midnight; closed Sun. Ck-out noon. Coin lndry. Meeting rms. Valet serv. Sundries. Balconies. Cr cds: A, C, D, DS, MC, V.

D 🐾 🏊 ⛷ 🐾 SC

Hurricane Mills (D-3)

(See also Dickson)

Pop 40 (est) **Elev** 400 ft **Area code** 931 **Zip** 37078 **E-mail** hcchamber@waverly.net **Web** dogstar.waverly.net/hcchamber

Information Humphreys County Chamber of Commerce, 124 E Main St, PO Box 733, Waverly 37185; 931/296-4865.

What to See and Do

Loretta Lynn's Ranch. Tours of country music star's house, museum, Butcher Holler Home and simulated coal mine; Western and general stores. Swimming; fishing. Hiking; tennis. Camping. Special events including concerts, trail rides, campfires. (Mar-Dec) Fee for most activities. On TN 13. Phone 931/296-7700.

Nolan House. Restored, 12-room Victorian house (ca 1870); period furnishings; redoubt trail; dog-trot; family grave yard. Overnight stays avail. Tours (daily exc Sun). 8 mi N via TN 13 in Waverly. Phone 931/296-2511. ¢

Motels

✔★ ★ **BEST WESTERN.** *15542 TN 13S, on TN 13; I-40 exit 143. 931/296-4251; FAX 931/296-9104.* 89 rms, 2 story. May-Aug: S $50-$64; D $50-$70; each addl $4; under 12 free; higher rates special events; lower rates rest of yr. Crib $2. Pet accepted, some restrictions. TV; cable (premium), VCR avail (movies). Pool; whirlpool. Playground. Restaurant 6

am-9 pm. Ck-out 11 am. Coin lndry. Meeting rm. Some refrigerators; microwaves avail. Cr cds: A, C, D, DS, ER, MC, V.

D 🐾 🏊 ⛷ 🐾 SC

★ ★ **BUFFALO INN.** *15415 TN 13S, on TN 13N off I-40 exit 143. 931/296-7647; res: 800/841-5813; FAX 931/296-5488.* 78 rms, 2 story. S $40-$44; D $54-$64; each addl $5; higher rates special events. Crib free. Pet accepted. TV; cable (premium). Pool. Restaurant 6 am-10 pm. Ck-out noon. Meeting rm. Cr cds: A, C, D, DS, MC, V.

D 🐾 🏊 ⛷ 🐾 SC

Jackson (E-2)

Founded 1822 **Pop** 48,949 **Elev** 401 ft **Area code** 901

Information Jackson/Madison County Convention & Visitors Bureau, 400 S Highland, 38301; 901/425-8333 or 800/498-4748.

Railroading is both the tradition and past livelihood of Jackson, home and burial place of John Luther "Casey" Jones, hero of ballad and legend. Because many of General Andrew Jackson's soldiers and many of his wife's relatives settled here, the town was named in his honor. Today, Jackson is an industrial center of western Tennessee.

What to See and Do

Casey Jones Village. Complex of turn-of-the-century shops and buildings centered around the life of one of America's most famous railroad heroes. 5 mi NW at US 45 Bypass & I-40. **Free.** In the village are

Casey Jones Home and Railroad Museum. The original house of the high-rolling engineer who, on Apr 30, 1900, climbed into the cab of "Old 382" on the Illinois Central Railroad and took his "farewell trip to that promised land"—and a place in American folklore. On display are personal effects of Jones and railroad memorabilia, including railroad passes, timetables, bells and steam whistles; also steam locomotive of the type driven by Casey Jones and restored 1890s coach cars. (Daily; closed Easter, Thanksgiving, Dec 25) Phone 901/668-1222. ¢¢

Brooks Shaw & Son Old Country Store. Turn-of-the-century general store with more than 15,000 antiques on display; restaurant (see), ice-cream parlor, confectionery shop. (Daily; closed Easter, Thanksgiving, Dec 25) Phone 901/668-1223.

Chickasaw State Rustic Park. Park covering 11,215 acres features two lakes. Swimming; fishing; boating (rentals). Horseback riding. Picnicking, playground, recreation lodge. Tent & trailer sites, cabins. Standard fees. 16 mi SE on US 45, then 8 mi SW on TN 100. Phone 901/989-5141.

Cypress Grove Nature Park. Boardwalk more than 1 mi long winds through 165-acre cypress forest; observation tower, nature center, picnic shelter. (Daily) Approx 4 mi W on US 70W. Phone 901/425-8364. **Free.**

Pinson Mounds State Archaeological Area. Remains of ancient mounds of the Middle Woodland Mound period and more than 10 ceremonial and burial mounds of various sizes, including Sauls (72 ft high). Nature trail. Picnicking. Museum (Mar-Nov, daily; rest of yr, Mon-Fri); video programs. 9 mi S on US 45, then 2 1/2 mi E of Pinson on Ozier Rd. Phone 901/988-5614. **Free.**

Motels

✔★ ★ **BAYMONT INN.** *2370 N Highland Ave (38305), at I-40 exit 82A. 901/664-1800; FAX 901/664-5456.* 102 rms, 3 story. S $33.95-$41.95; D $41.95-$48.95; each addl $7; under 18 free. Crib free. TV; cable, VCR avail (movies). Pool. Coffee in rms. Complimentary continental bkfst. Restaurant adj 11 am-10 pm. Ck-out noon. Meeting rm. Business servs avail. Cr cds: A, C, D, DS, MC, V.

D 🏊 ⛷ 🐾 SC

★ ★ **BEST WESTERN OLD HICKORY INN.** 1849 US 45 Bypass (38305), 1/2 mi S of I-40, exit 80A. 901/668-4222; FAX 901/664-8536. 141 rms, 2 story. S $45-$52, D $49-$57; each addl $4; under 12 free. Crib $2. Pet accepted, some restrictions. TV; cable (premium). Pool; wading pool. Restaurant 6 am-10 pm. Rm serv. Bar 4 pm-1 am; entertainment exc Sun. Ck-out noon. Meeting rms. Business servs avail. Cr cds: A, C, D, DS, MC, V.

★ **CASEY JONES STATION INN.** 1943 US 45 Bypass (38305), I-40 exit 80A in Casey Jones Village. 901/668-3636; res: 800/628-2812. 53 rms, 2 story. May-Aug: S, D $49.95-$59.95; each addl $5; suites $109.95; under 18 free; lower rates rest of yr. Crib $5. TV; cable (premium). Pool. Complimentary coffee in lobby. Restaurant adj 6 am-10 pm. Ck-out 11 am. Meeting rm. Restored authentic cabooses and railroad cars converted to sleeping rms. Cr cds: A, C, D, DS, MC, V.

✔★ ★ **DAYS INN.** 1919 US 45 Bypass (38305). 901/668-3444; FAX 901/668-7778. 120 rms, 3 story. S $31-$36; D $37-$44; each addl $4; under 17 free. Crib free. TV; cable. Pool. Ck-out noon. Business servs avail. Cr cds: A, C, D, DS, MC, V.

★ **FAIRFIELD INN BY MARRIOTT.** 535 Wiley Parker Rd (38305), I-40 exit 80A. 901/668-1400. 105 rms, 3 story. Mar-Oct: S, D $46.95-$61.95; under 18 free; lower rates rest of yr. Crib free. TV; cable (premium). Heated pool. Complimentary continental bkfst. Restaurant adj 7 am-11 pm. Ck-out noon. Business servs avail. Cr cds: A, D, DS, MC, V.

★ ★ **HAMPTON INN.** 1890 US 45 Bypass (38305). 901/664-4312; FAX 901/664-7844. 120 rms, 2 story. S, D $61-$65; under 18 free. Crib free. TV; cable (premium). Pool. Complimentary continental bkfst. Restaurant adj 6 am-midnight. Meeting rm. Business servs avail. Health club privileges. Cr cds: A, C, D, DS, MC, V.

★ ★ **QUALITY INN.** 2262 N Highland Ave (38305), at jct US 45, I-40; exit 82A. 901/668-1066; FAX 901/660-6597. 88 rms, 2 story. May-Aug: S $38-$48; each addl $6; under 18 free; lower rates rest of yr. Crib $6. TV; cable (premium). Pool. Restaurant adj open 24 hrs. Ck-out noon. Coin lndry. Business servs avail. Microwaves avail. Cr cds: A, C, D, DS, JCB, MC, V.

Motor Hotels

★ ★ **COMFORT INN.** US 45 Bypass & I-40 (38305), exit 80A. 901/668-4100; FAX 901/664-6940. 205 rms, 4 story. S $59-$61; D $64-$69; suite $90; under 18 free. Crib free. TV; cable (premium). Pool; wading pool. Complimentary continental bkfst. Ck-out noon. Coin lndry. Meeting rms. Business servs avail. Sundries. Exercise equipt. Microwaves. Some patios, balconies. Cr cds: A, D, DS, JCB, MC, V.

★ ★ **HOLIDAY INN.** 541 Carriage House Dr (38305), I-40 exit 80A. 901/668-6000; FAX 901/668-9516. 135 air-cooled rms, 5 story, 54 suites. S, D $75-$125; each addl $6; suites $85-$175; under 19 free; higher rates special events. Crib free. TV; cable (premium). Indoor pool. Restaurant 6 am-9 pm. Rm serv. Bar. Ck-out noon. Meeting rms. Business servs avail. In-rm modem link. Bellhops. Beauty shop. Valet serv. Health club privileges. Game rm. Refrigerators. Balconies overlooking atrium. Cr cds: A, C, D, DS, JCB, MC, V.

★ ★ **SHERATON OLD ENGLISH INN.** 2267 N Highland Ave (38305), 3 mi N on US 45 at I-40 exit 82. 901/668-1571; FAX 901/664-8070. 103 rms, 2 story, 35 suites. S, D $79-$98; each addl $6; suites $89-$99; under 18 free; wknd plans. Crib free. TV; cable (premium), VCR

avail. Pool; poolside serv. Complimentary coffee in rms. Restaurant 6 am-10 pm. Bar; entertainment Sat. Ck-out noon. Valet serv. Health club privileges. Some refrigerators; bathrm phone in suites; microwaves avail. Some fireplaces, patios. English Tudor decor; antiques, paintings. Cr cds: A, C, D, DS, MC, V.

Restaurant

✔★ **OLD COUNTRY STORE.** Jct US 45 Bypass (38305), I-40, exit 80A, in Casey Jones Village. 901/668-1223. E-mail casey@aeneas.net; web caseyjonesvillage.com. Hrs: 6 am-10 pm. Closed Easter, Thanksgiving, Dec 25. Semi-a la carte: bkfst $1.49-$5.49, lunch, dinner $1.99-$9.99. Buffet: bkfst $5.49, lunch $5.99, dinner $6.99-$9.99. Specializes in Tennessee country ham, catfish, cobblers. Salad bar. Entertainment Fri, Sat. Parking. Turn-of-the-century decor. Family-owned. Cr cds: A, C, D, DS, MC, V.

Jamestown (D-7)

(See also Cookeville)

Pop 1,862 **Elev** 1,716 ft **Area code** 931 **Zip** 38556

Once a hunting ground for Davy Crockett and, later, Sergeant Alvin C. York, Jamestown was also the home of Cordell Hull, FDR's secretary of state.

What to See and Do

Big South Fork National River/Recreation Area. Approx 105,000 acres on Cumberland Plateau. Swimming pool; fishing, hunting; whitewater canoeing, rafting, kayaking. Nature trails, hiking, backpacking, bridle trails. Primitive & improved camping (yr-round; fee). Visitor center. 20 mi NE on TN 154, then TN 297. Phone 931/879-3625.

Historic Rugby. English colony founded in 1880s by author-statesman-social reformer Thomas Hughes. Highest priority was placed on beauty, culture, parks and recreational facilities. When it became difficult to make a living, the colony floundered. However, much has been preserved, and of the 17 original Victorian buildings remaining, 4 are open to the public. Hughes Public Library, unchanged since opening in 1882, contains unique 7,000-volume collection of Victorian era. Visitor center in Rugby Schoolhouse; guided walking tours (daily). (See ANNUAL EVENT) Also picnicking, hiking in surrounding river gorges on trails built by original colonists. Bookshop, traditional craft commissary, lodging in historic houses and cafe. 17 mi SE via TN 52. Phone 423/628-2441. Tours ¢¢

Pickett State Rustic Park. Park covering 14,000 acres in Cumberland Mountains; unusual rock formations, caves, natural bridges. Sand beach. Swimming; fishing; boating (rentals). Nature trails, backpacking. Picnicking, concession, recreation lodge. Camping, cabins. Standard fees. 2 mi N on US 127, then 11 mi NE on TN 154N. Phone 931/879-5821.

Annual Event

Rugby Pilgrimage. Tours of private historic houses in addition to buildings open regularly. Contact Historic Rugby, Inc, PO Box 8, Rugby 37733; 423/628-2441. 1st wknd Oct.

Jellico (C-8)

(See also Caryville)

Pop 2,447 **Elev** 982 ft **Area code** 423 **Zip** 37762

What to See and Do

Indian Mountain State Park. More than 200 acres. Swimming pool; fishing. Hiking trail. Picnicking, shelters; playgrounds. Camping. Standard fees. 3 mi off I-75, exit 160. Phone 423/784-7958.

Motel

✔★ **DAYS INN.** 1/4 mi S on US 25W at jct I-75 exit 160. 423/784-7281; FAX 423/784-4529. 126 rms, 2-3 story. No elvtr. S $39-$45; D $44-$55; each addl $5; under 18 free. Crib free. TV; cable (premium). Pool. Coffee in rms. Restaurant 6 am-9 pm. Ck-out 11 am. Cr cds: A, C, D, DS, JCB, MC, V.

D 🏊 🗙 🖍 SC

Johnson City (D-10)

(See also Elizabethton, Kingsport)

Settled 1782 **Pop** 49,381 **Elev** 1,692 ft **Area code** 423
Information Chamber of Commerce, 603 E Market St, PO Box 180, 37605; 423/461-8000.

Johnson City is a leading burley tobacco sales center, as well as a market and shipping point for Washington County's cattle, eggs and alfalfa. Chemicals, textiles, building materials, electronics and furniture are also produced in the town.

What to See and Do

Cherokee National Forest (see). E on US 321; S on US 23/19W.

East Tennessee State University (1911). (12,028 students) Campus has 63 buildings on 366 acres; Slocumb Galleries; Memorial Center (sports); James H. Quillen College of Medicine (1974). Tours of campus. Lake & Stout Sts. Phone 423/929-4112. Also on campus is

Carroll Reece Museum. Contemporary art and regional history exhibits; gallery tours; concert, film and lecture series. (Daily; closed major hols) Phone 423/929-4392. **Free.**

Hands On! Regional Museum. More than 20 "hands-on" exhibits designed for children of all ages. Traveling shows. (June-Aug, daily; rest of yr, daily exc Mon; closed major hols) 315 E Main St. Phone 423/434-4263. ¢¢

⭐ **Jonesborough.** Oldest town in Tennessee and the first capitol of the state of Franklin. 6 mi W off US 11 E.

Historic District. Four-by-six-block area through the heart of town, reflecting 200 yrs of history. Private residences, commercial and public buildings of federal, Greek-revival and Victorian styles; brick sidewalks, old-style lampposts, shops. Obtain walking tour brochures at Visitors Center, 117 Boone St; phone 423/753-5961.

Jonesborough History Museum. Exhibits highlight history of Jonesborough from pioneer days to early 20th century. (Daily; closed major hols) 117 Boone St, in Visitors Center. Phone 423/753-1015. ¢

Rocky Mount Historic Site & Overmountain Museum. Log house (ca 1770), territorial capitol under Governor William Blount from 1790 to 1792, is restored to original simplicity with much 18th-century furniture; log kitchen, slave cabin, barn, blacksmith shop, smokehouse. Costumed interpreters reenact a day in the life of typical pioneer family; tour (1 1/2 hrs) includes Cobb-Massengill house, kitchen and slave cabin, as well as self-guided tour through the adjacent Museum of Overmountain History. (Mar-Dec, daily; rest of yr, Mon-Fri; closed Thanksgiving, Dec 21-Jan 5) 4 mi NE on US 11E. Phone 423/538-7396. ¢¢

Tipton-Haynes Historic Site. Site of the 1788 "Battle of the Lost State of Franklin." Six original buildings and four reconstructions span American history from pre-colonial days through Civil War. Visitor center with museum display; gift shop. (Apr-Oct, daily; rest of yr, Mon-Fri) Special programs, events. 1 mi off I-181 exit 31, at S edge of town. Phone 423/926-3631. ¢¢

Whitewater rafting. Cherokee Adventures. Variety of guided whitewater rafting trips through the Nolichucky Canyon and along the Watauga and Russell Fork rivers. Mountain biking programs. (Mar-Oct) 17 mi S on US 19/23, exit 18, then 1 mi N on TN 81. Contact 2000 Jonesborough Rd, Erwin 37650; 423/743-7733 or 800/445-7238. ¢¢¢¢¢

Annual Events

Jonesborough Days. 6 mi W, in Jonesborough. Includes parade, art show, crafts, old-time games, traditional music, square dancing and clogging, food. July 4th wkend.

Appalachian Fair. N, just off I-181 in Gray at fairgrounds. Regional fair featuring livestock, agriculture and youth exhibits, antique display; entertainment. Phone 423/477-3211. 9 days late Aug.

National Storytelling Festival. 8 mi W in Jonesborough. Three-day gathering from across nation features some of the country's best storytellers. Phone 423/753-2171. 1st wkend Oct.

Christmas in Jonesborough. 6 mi W. Tours of historic houses, tree decoration, workshops, old-time holiday events. Dec.

Motels

★ **DAYS INN.** 2312 Brown's Mill Rd (37604). 423/282-2211; res: 800/329-7466; FAX 423/282-6111. 100 rms, 2 story. S $40-$45; D $45-$50; each addl $5; under 12 free; higher rates special events. Pet accepted. TV; cable. Pool. Complimentary continental bkfst. Ck-out 11 am. Coin lndry. Meeting rm. Business servs avail. Cr cds: A, D, DS, MC, V.

🖼 🏊 🗙 🖍 SC

★★ **FAIRFIELD INN BY MARRIOTT.** 207 E Mountcastle (37601). 423/282-3335; res: 800/828-2800. Web www.fairfieldinn.com. 132 rms, 3 story. S, D $39.95-$56.95; each addl $6-$9; under 18 free; higher rates special events. TV; cable (premium), VCR avail (movies). Pool. Complimentary continental bkfst. Complimentary coffee in lobby. Restaurant adj 11 am-10 pm. Ck-out noon. Business servs avail. In-rm modem link. Health club privileges. Cr cds: A, C, D, DS, MC, V.

D 🏊 🗙 🖍 SC

★★ **HAMPTON INN.** 508 State of Franklin Rd (37604). 423/929-8000; res: 800/426-7866; FAX 423/929-3336. 77 rms, 3 story. S $61-$66; D $66-$71; each addl $5; under 18 free; higher rates NASCAR races. Crib free. TV; cable (premium). Pool. Complimentary continental bkfst. Restaurant nearby. Ck-out noon. Meeting rms. Business servs avail. Health club privileges. Some refrigerators, minibars. Cr cds: A, D, DS, MC, V.

D 🏊 🗙 🖍 SC

✔★ **SUPER 8.** 108 Wesley St (37601). 423/282-8818. 60 rms, 3 story. No elvtr. S, D $36-$75; each addl $5; under 12 free; higher rates special events. Crib free. Pet accepted, some restrictions. TV; cable. Complimentary coffee. Restaurant adj open 24 hrs. Ck-out 11 am. Business servs avail. Coin lndry. Cr cds: A, C, D, DS, MC, V.

D 🖼 🏊 🗙 🖍 SC

Motor Hotels

★★★ **GARDEN PLAZA.** 211 Mockingbird Ln (37604). 423/929-2000; FAX 423/929-1783; res: 800/342-7336. E-mail gpjcfdmgr@cooperhotel.com. 186 rms, 5 story. S, D $85-$100; each addl $10; suites $125-$135; under 18 free; higher rates special events. Crib free. Pet accepted. TV; cable, VCR avail (movies). Indoor/outdoor pool; poolside serv. Restaurant 6:30 am-2 pm, 5-10 pm. Rm serv. Bar 5 pm-1 am. Ck-out noon. Meeting rms. Business center. Bellhops. Free airport transportation. Wet bar in suites. Luxury level. Cr cds: A, C, D, DS, MC, V.

D 🖼 🏊 🗙 🖍 SC 🏃

★ ★ **RAMADA INN.** *2406 N Roan St (37601). 423/282-2161; res: 800/272-6232; FAX 423/282-2488.* 197 rms, 2-4 story. S, D $59-$64; each addl $5; under 18 free; higher rates special events. Crib free. Pet accepted, some restrictions. Pool. Restaurant 6 am-2 pm, 5-10 pm. Rm serv. Bar 5 pm-1 am. Ck-out noon. Coin lndry. Business servs avail. Free airport transportation. Health club privileges. Cr cds: A, C, D, DS, ER, JCB, MC, V.

⊡ 🐾 ≋ ⛆ 🖎 SC

Hotel

★ ★ ★ **HOLIDAY INN.** *101 W Springbrook Dr (37604). 423/282-4611; res: 800/465-4329; FAX 423/283-4869.* 205 rms, 6 story. S, D $71-$85; each addl $6; suites $150-$325; under 18 free. Crib free. TV; cable (premium), VCR avail. Pool; poolside serv. Restaurant 6 am-10 pm. Bar 4:30 pm-1:30 am. Ck-out 11 am. Meeting rms. Business servs avail. In-rm modem link. Gift shop. Barber, beauty shop. Free airport transportation. Exercise equipt. Health club privileges. Cr cds: A, C, D, DS, MC, V.

⊡ ≋ 🏋 ⛆ 🖎 SC

Restaurants

★ **FIREHOUSE.** *627 W Walnut (37604). 423/929-7377.* E-mail tom@thefirehouse.com; web www.thefirehouse.com. Hrs: 11 am-10 pm; Fri, Sat to 10:30 pm. Closed Easter, Thanksgiving, Dec 24, 25. Semi-a la carte: lunch $6-$8, dinner $7-$15. Child's meals. Specializes in steak, ribs, barbecue beans. Own desserts. Parking. Converted fire hall (1930). Cr cds: A, MC, V.

⊡ 🍽

★ **MAKATO.** *3021 Oakland Ave (37601). 423/282-4441.* Hrs: 11 am-2 pm, 5-9 pm; Fri, Sat to 10 pm; Sun to 2:30 pm. Japanese menu. Bar. Complete meals: lunch $5.25-$11.43, dinner $7.35-$35. Child's meals. Specializes in seafood, steak. Sushi bar. Parking. Tableside cooking. Totally nonsmoking. Cr cds: A, D, DS, MC, V.

⊡

★ ★ **PARSON'S TABLE.** *(102 Woodrow Ave, Jonesborough 37659) W on US 11, 321. 423/753-8002.* Hrs: 11:30 am-2 pm, 5:30 pm-closing; Sun buffet to 2 pm. Closed Mon; Jan 1, Dec 24, 25. Res accepted. Continental menu. Semi-a la carte: lunch $6-$9, dinner $15-$25. Sun buffet $12.95. Child's meals. Own baking. Parking. In historic district in 1870s church with loft and parsonage. Victorian decor. Totally nonsmoking. Cr cds: A, DS, MC, V.

⊡

★ ★ **PEERLESS.** *2531 N Roan St (37601). 423/282-2351.* Hrs: 4-10:30 pm; Sat 4-11 pm. Closed Sun; major hols. Bar. A la carte entrees: dinner $8.95-$15.95. Specializes in fresh seafood, steak, chicken. Parking. Family-owned. Cr cds: A, C, D, DS, MC, V.

 ⊡ 🍽 ♥

Kingsport (C-9)

(See also Johnson City)

Settled 1761 **Pop** 36,365 **Elev** 1,208 ft **Area code** 423 **Web** kingsportchamber.org
Information Convention & Visitors Bureau, 151 E Main St, PO Box 1403, 37662; 423/392-8820 or 800/743-5282.

Located at a natural gateway to the Southwest, this area saw the passage of the Great Indian Warrior & Trader Path and Island Road (1761), the first road built in Tennessee. The trail later became the Great Stage Road and was used for 150 years, marking the beginning of Daniel Boone's Wilderness Road. Kingsport was a little town on the Holston River, but it was converted to a planned industrial city during World War I. The first council-

manager form of government in the state was installed in the town. The Eastman Chemical Company, the largest private employer in the state, is located in Kingsport.

What to See and Do

Bays Mountain Park. Plant and animal sanctuary covers 3,000 acres, 25 mi of trails; nature interpretive center, aviary, deer pen; otter, bobcat & wolf habitats; nature programs (summer, daily; rest of yr, wkends); ocean pool; planetarium (shows daily in summer; rest of yr, wkends). Exhibition gallery and library. Observation tower. 19th-century farmstead museum. Barge rides on 44-acre lake. Picnic tables. Park (daily). Fee for activities. 6 mi SE off TN 93. Phone 423/229-9447. Parking ¢¢

Boat Yard Park. On banks of the north and south forks of the Holston River. Historical complex includes Netherland Inn museum, picnic areas, playgrounds, boating, fishing; footpaths along river (2 mi). Fees for some activities. Phone 423/246-2010. **Free.**

Netherland Inn (1818). Large frame and stone structure on site of King's Boat Yard (1802) was a celebrated stop on the Great Stage Road and was operated for over 150 yrs as an inn and the town's entertainment center; it was especially popular from 1818 to 1841 and was visited by many prominent individuals, including Andrew Jackson, Andrew Johnson and James K. Polk. Now a museum with 18th- and 19th-century furnishings. Complex also includes wellhouse, flatboat, garden, log cabin (1773), children's museum, museum shop. Interpreters. (May-Sept, Sat-Mon; Apr & Oct, Sat, Sun) Phone 423/247-3211. ¢¢

Boone Dam and Lake. TVA dam, 160-ft-high and 1,640-ft-long, impounds a 33-mi-long lake with 130 mi of shoreline. Swimming; fishing; boating (marina). Picnicking. Overlook (daily). 12 mi SE via TN 36, TN 75. Phone 423/279-3500. **Free.**

Exchange Place. Restored 19th-century farm once served as a facility for exchanging horses and Virginia currency for Tennessee currency; crafts center; special events (fee). (May-Oct, wkends or by appt) 4812 Orebank Rd. Phone 423/288-6071. **Free.**

Fort Patrick Henry Dam and Lake. Companion to Boone Dam, this TVA dam, 95 ft high, 737 ft long, impounds a 10-mi-long lake. Swimming; fishing; boating. Overlook. (Daily) 4 mi S on TN 36. Phone 423/247-7891. **Free.** Along lakeshore is

Warriors' Path State Park. A 950-acre park with swimming pool, water slide, bathhouse; fishing; boating (marina, ramp, rentals). Nature, bridle trails; 18-hole golf, driving range, disc golf. Picnic grove, playground, concessions. Tent, trailer camping. Standard fees. 4 mi S on TN 36; I-81 exit 59. Phone 423/239-8531.

Annual Event

Kingsport Fun Fest. Citywide. More than 100 events including hot-air balloon races, sports events, entertainment. Phone 423/392-8800. Nine days late July.

Motels

★ ★ **COMFORT INN.** *100 Indian Center Court (37660), at TN 93 & US 11W. 423/378-4418; res: 800/328-5150; FAX 423/246-5249.* 122 rms, 2 story. S, D $50-$75; each addl $8; suites $70-$80; under 18 free. Crib free. Pet accepted; $8. TV; cable (premium). Pool; whirlpool. Sauna. Complimentary continental bkfst. Restaurant adj 11 am-10 pm. Ck-out noon. Coin lndry. Meeting rms. Business servs avail. Bellhops. Valet serv. Health club privileges. Some in-rm whirlpools. Cr cds: A, C, D, DS, ER, JCB, MC, V.

⊡ 🐾 ≋ ⛆ 🖎 SC

✔ ★ ★ **DAYS INN.** *805 Lynn Garden (37660). 423/246-7126; res: 800/329-7466; FAX 423/247-8785.* 65 rms, 2 story. June-Oct: S, D $40-$125; each addl $6; under 13 free; higher rates special events; lower rates rest of yr. Crib free. TV; cable (premium), VCR avail. Complimentary coffee in rms. Restaurant 6 am-8 pm. Ck-out 11 am. Meeting rms. Business servs avail. Coin lndry. Pool. Refrigerators; microwaves avail. Cr cds: A, C, D, DS, JCB, MC, V.

 ✔★ **ECONO LODGE.** *1704 E Stone Dr (37660).* 423/245-0286; res: 800/424-4777; FAX 423/245-2985. 52 rms, 2 story. S, D $37-$55; each addl $4; under 18 free. Pet accepted, some restrictions. TV; cable (premium). Complimentary continental bkfst. Restaurant adj open 24 hrs. Ck-out 11 am. Business servs avail. Cr cds: A, C, D, DS, MC, V.

★ ★ ★ **RAMADA INN.** *2005 La Masa Dr (37660).* 423/245-0271; res: 800/228-2828; FAX 423/245-7992. E-mail ramadainnkingsport@gal tex. com. 198 rms, 2 story. S, D $66-$150; each addl $6; under 18 free. Crib free. TV; cable (premium). Pool. Restaurant 6 am-2 pm, 5-10 pm; Sat, Sun from 7 am. Rm serv 7 am-10 pm. Bar 5 pm-midnight. Ck-out noon. Meeting rms. Business servs avail. Sundries. Free airport transportation. Lighted tennis. Health club privileges. Cr cds: A, C, D, DS, JCB, MC, V.

Hotel

★ ★ ★ **MARRIOTT'S MEADOW VIEW.** *1901 Meadow View Pkwy (37660), I-181 exit 52.* 423/578-6600; res: 800/820-5055; FAX 423/518-6630. 195 rms, 7 story. Jan-Nov: S, D $59-$139; each addl $10; under 5 free; wkend rates; golf plans; higher rates special events; lower rates rest of yr. Crib free. Velet parking $3. TV; cable (premium), VCR avail. Complimentary coffee in rms. Restaurant 6:30 am-10 pm. Bar. Ck-out 1 pm. Meeting rms. Business center. In-rm modem link. Gift shop. Coin lndry. Free airport transportation. Lighted tennis. 18-hole golf, greens fee $28-$32, pro, putting green, driving range. Exercise equipt. Heated pool; whirlpool, poolside serv. Some bathrm phones, balconies; refrigerators, microwaves avail. Cr cds: A, C, D, DS, JCB, MC, V.

Restaurant

★ ★ **SKOBY'S.** *1001 Konnarock Rd (37664).* 423/245-2761. Hrs: 5-10 pm; Fri, Sat 4:30-11 pm. Closed major hols. Res accepted Mon-Sat. Bar. A la carte entrees: dinner $7-$25. Child's meals. Specializes in steak, seafood. Salad bar. Own desserts. Parking. Dining areas with varied themes. Family-owned. Cr cds: A, C, D, DS, MC, V.

Knoxville (D-8)

Settled 1791 **Pop** 165,121 **Elev** 936 ft **Area code** 423 **Web** www.knoxville.org
Information Knox County Tourist Commission, 601 W Summitt Hill Dr, Suite 200B, Knoxville, TN, 37902-2011; 423/523-7263 or 800/727-8045.

First capital of Tennessee, Knoxville today is the manufacturing center for the east Tennessee Valley. In its early days, Knoxville was a frontier outpost on the edge of the Cherokee nation, last stop on the way west. Headquarters of the Tennessee Valley Authority, marketplace for tobacco and livestock, Knoxville is also a diversified industrial city, a product of power plant rather than plantation, and also of the atomic age rather than the Old South (Oak Ridge is only 22 miles away). It is a gracious city, with the University of Tennessee as a cultural center and dogwood-lined streets in its residential sections.

Founded by a Revolutionary War veteran from North Carolina, Knoxville, named after Secretary of War Henry Knox, quickly became a provisioning place for westward-bound wagons. It was known for its whiskey and wild times. East Tennessee had many Union sympathizers, and during the Civil War Knoxville was seized by the Confederates and became headquarters for an army of occupation. In 1863, Southern troops withdrew to Chattanooga, and a Union army moved in, only to be besieged by the Confederates. While the battle for Knoxville saw large sections of the city destroyed, the Confederate attack was rebuffed, and Knoxville remained in Union hands for the rest of the war.

The postwar years brought many former Union soldiers, skilled Northern workmen and investment capital to Knoxville. Within two decades its population more than tripled. During and since World War II it has enjoyed a similar period of industrial growth and commercial well-being. The University of Tennessee, Knoxville (1794) is located here.

What to See and Do

Beck Cultural Exchange Center-Museum of Black History and Culture. Research, preservation and display of the achievements of Knoxville's black citizens from the early 1800s. Gallery features changing exhibits of local and regional artists. (Tues-Sat; closed major hols) 1927 Dandridge Ave. Phone 423/524-8461. **Free.**

Confederate Memorial Hall. Antebellum mansion with Mediterranean-style gardens served as headquarters of Confederate General James Longstreet during siege of Knoxville. Maintained as a Confederate memorial, the 15-rm house is furnished with museum pieces, a collection of Southern and Civil War relics; library of Southern literature. (Tues-Fri) 3148 Kingston Pike SW. Phone 423/522-2371. ¢¢

Crescent Bend (Armstrong-Lockett House) and W. Perry Toms Memorial Gardens (1834). Collections of American and English furniture; English silver (1640-1820); extensive terraced gardens. (Mar-Dec, daily exc Mon) 2728 Kingston Pike. Phone 423/637-3163. ¢¢

AKIMA East Tennessee Discovery Center & AKIMA Planetarium. Science center with exhibits on life, energy, transportation, minerals, fossils; includes aquarium and planetarium. (Mon-Fri, also Sat afternoons; closed most hols) 516 N Beaman St, Chilhowee Park. Phone 423/594-1494. ¢¢

Governor William Blount Mansion (1792). House of William Blount, Governor of the Southwest Territory and signer of the US Constitution, was the center of political and social activity in the territory. Restored to period of late 1700s with period furnishings, Blount memorabilia; 18th-century garden. Tennessee's first state constitution was drafted in the governor's office behind the mansion. (Mar-Oct, daily exc Mon; rest of yr, Tues-Fri; closed major hols) 200 W Hill Ave. Phone 423/525-2375. ¢¢

James White's Fort. Original pioneer house (1786) built by founder and first settler of Knoxville; restored buildings include smokehouse, blacksmith shop, museum. (Mar-mid-Dec, daily exc Sun; Jan, Feb, Mon-Fri; closed major hols) 205 E Hill Ave. Phone 423/525-6514. ¢¢

Knoxville Museum of Art. Four galleries, gardens, great hall, ARTcade, exploratory gallery; collection of graphics. Changing exhibits. Gift shop. (Daily exc Mon; closed most hols) 1050 World's Fair Park Dr. Phone 423/525-6101. **Free.**

Knoxville Zoo. More than 1,000 animals, including big cats, gorillas, reptiles, elephants and marine animals; petting zoo. (Daily; closed Dec 25) E via I-40, Rutledge Pikes exit. Phone 423/637-5331. ¢¢¢

Marble Springs. Restored house of John Sevier, state's first governor (1796-1801, 1803-1809); original cabin and other restored buildings on 36 acres. (Daily exc Mon) Approx 6 mi S via US 441, TN 33, then W on TN 168. Phone 423/573-5508. ¢

McClung Historical Collection. More than 38,000 volumes of history and genealogy covering Tennessee and Southeastern US. (Daily; closed most hols) East Tennessee Historical Center, 314 W Clinch Ave. Phone 423/544-5744. **Free.**

Ramsey House (Swan Pond) (1797). First stone house in Knox County, built for Colonel Francis A. Ramsey, was social, religious, political center of early Tennessee. Restored gabled house with attached kitchen features ornamental cornices, keystone arches and period furnishings. (Apr-Oct, Tues-Sat & Sun afternoons; rest of yr, by appt) 6 mi NE, at 2614 Thorngrove Pike. Phone 423/546-0745. ¢¢

Sunsphere. Built for the 1982 World's Fair, this 266-ft tower has an observation deck that provides views of downtown and Smoky Mts. The Convention & Visitors Bureau Information Center is located here. 810 Clinch Ave. Phone 800/727-8045. **Free.**

University of Tennessee, Knoxville (1794). (27,018 students) W Cumberland Ave, US 11, 70. On campus are Frank H. McClung Museum (daily; closed major hols; phone 423/974-2144); Clarence Brown Theater on Andy Holt Dr; special collections, 1401 Cumberland Ave (Mon-Fri; phone 423/974-4480).

Annual Events

Dogwood Arts Festival. More than 150 events and activities throughout the community including arts & crafts exhibits and shows; over 80 public and private gardens on display; musical entertainment; parades; sporting events; more than 60 miles of marked dogwood trails for auto or free bus tours; special children's & sr citizen activities. Phone 423/637-4561. Mid-late Apr.

Tennessee Valley Fair. Chilhowee Park. Entertainment; livestock and agricultural shows; contests, exhibits, fireworks, carnival rides. Phone 423/637-5840. 10 days early-mid-Sept.

Seasonal Event

Artfest. Citywide celebration with children's activities; entertainment; changing exhibits, art shows; professional & community theatricals. Phone 423/523-7543. Aug-Oct.

Motels

✔★ ★ **BAYMONT INN.** *11341 Campbell Lakes Dr (37922), I-40/75 exit 373.* 423/671-1010; FAX 423/675-5039. 100 rms, 3 story. S, D $63.95-$99.95; each addl $7; under 18 free; lower rates rest of yr. Crib free. Pet accepted, some restrictions. TV; cable (premium), VCR avail. Pool. Complimentary continental bkfst. Complimentary coffee in rms. Restaurant adj 6 am-10 pm. Ck-out noon. Coin lndry. Meeting rms. Business servs avail. Exercise equipt; sauna. Some refrigerators; microwaves avail. Cr cds: A, C, D, DS, MC, V.

D ✔ ≈ ✗ ⇥ 🐾 SC

★ ★ **BEST WESTERN HIGHWAY HOST.** *118 Merchants Dr (37912), I-75N exit 108.* 423/688-3141; res: 800/826-4360; FAX 423/687-4645. Web www.travelbase.com/destination/knoxville/bestwest-highway. 213 rms, 6 story. S, D $59-$92; each addl $7; under 18 free; higher rates special events. Crib free. Pet accepted; $25 deposit. TV; cable (premium). Indoor pool; whirlpool. Complimentary coffee in rms. Restaurant open 24 hrs. Bar 11 am-midnight. Ck-out noon. Coin lndry. Gift shop. Meeting rms. Business servs avail. Valet serv. Game rm. Microwaves avail. Balconies. Cr cds: A, C, D, DS, ER, MC, V.

D ✔ ≈ ⇥ 🐾 SC

★ ★ **COMFORT INN.** *5334 Central Ave Pike (37912).* 423/688-1010; res: 800/228-5150; FAX 423/687-4235. 101 rms, 2 story. S $45-$70; D $55-$80; each addl $5; under 18 free. Crib $5. TV; cable (premium). Pool. Complimentary continental bkfst. Complimentary coffee in rms. Restaurant nearby. Ck-out noon. Business servs avail. Health club privileges. Cr cds: A, C, D, DS, MC, V.

≈ ⇥ 🐾 SC

★ ★ **COMFORT SUITES.** *811 Campbell Station Rd (37932).* 423/675-7585; res: 800/228-5150; FAX 423/675-4442. 59 rms, 2 story. Apr-Oct: suites $69-$109; under 18 free; higher rates special events; lower rates rest of yr. Crib free. TV; cable (premium). Complimentary continental bkfst. Complimentary coffee in rms. Ck-out noon. Business center. Sundries. Coin lndry. Exercise equipt. Indoor pool; whirlpool. Refrigerators, microwaves; some in-rm whirlpools. Cr cds: A, C, D, DS, JCB, MC, V.

D ≈ ✗ ⇥ 🐾 SC 🏃

★ ★ **COURTYARD BY MARRIOTT.** *216 Langley Pl (37922).* 423/539-0600; res: 800/321-2211; FAX 423/539-4488. 78 rms, 3 story. Apr-Oct: S, D $84-$104; each addl $10; under 12 free; higher rates Dogwood Arts Festival; lower rates rest of yr. Crib free. TV; cable (premium). Indoor pool. Complimentary coffee in rms. Restaurant 7-10 am. Ck-out noon. Meeting rms. Business servs avail. Sundries. Coin lndry.

Exercise equipt. Some in-rm whirlpools; refrigerator, microwave in suites. Some balconies. Cr cds: A, D, DS, MC, V.

D ≈ ✗ ⇥ 🐾 SC

✔★ ★ **DAYS INN.** *326 Lovell Rd (37922), I-40 exit 374.* 423/966-5801; res: 800/329-7466; FAX 423/966-1755. 120 rms, 2 story. S, D $43-$75; each addl $6; under 13 free; higher rates special events. Crib free. Pet accepted, some restrictions; $6. TV; cable (premium). Pool. Complimentary full bkfst. Restaurant adj 6 am-11 pm. Ck-out noon. Cr cds: A, C, D, DS, JCB, MC, V.

D ✔ ≈ ⇥ 🐾 SC

★ ★ **HAMPTON INN.** *119 Cedar Ln (37912), at I-75 & Merchants Rd.* 423/689-1011; res: 800/426-7866; FAX 423/689-7917. 130 rms, 3 story. May-Sept: S, D $60-$70; under 18 free; higher rates special events; lower rates rest of yr. Crib free. TV; cable (premium). Pool. Complimentary continental bkfst. Restaurant opp 6 am-10 pm. Ck-out 11 am. Business servs avail. Exercise equipt. Cr cds: A, C, D, DS, MC, V.

D ≈ ✗ ⇥ 🐾 SC

★ ★ **LA QUINTA MOTOR INN.** *258 Peters Rd N (37923).* 423/690-9777; FAX 423/531-8304. 130 rms, 3 story. S $60-$68; D $70-$78; each addl $10; under 18 free. Crib free. Pet accepted, some restrictions. TV; cable. Pool. Complimentary continental bkfst. Restaurant adj open 24 hrs. Ck-out noon. Coin lndry. Meeting rms. Business servs avail. Health club privileges. Microwaves avail. Cr cds: A, C, D, DS, MC, V.

D ✔ ≈ ⇥ 🐾 SC

✔★ ★ **RAMADA INN.** *323 Cedar Bluff Rd (37923).* 423/693-7330; FAX 423/693-7383. 178 rms, 2 story. S, D $52-$68; each addl $10; under 16 free; higher rates special events. Pet accepted, some restrictions. TV; cable (premium). Indoor pool. Restaurant 7 am-2 pm, 5-10 pm. Rm serv. Bar 5 pm-2:30 am; entertainment. Ck-out noon. Meeting rms. Business servs avail. Cr cds: A, C, D, DS, MC, V.

D ✔ ≈ ⇥ 🐾 SC

★ ★ **RAMADA SUITES LIMITED.** *5317 Pratt Rd (37912), I-75 exit 108.* 423/687-9922; res: 800/272-6232; FAX 423/687-1032. 58 suites, 4 story. May-Aug: S, D $69-$99; each addl $5; under 18 free; wknd rates; higher rates special events; lower rates rest of yr. Crib free. TV; cable (premium), VCR avail. Complimentary continental bkfst. Complimentary coffee in rms. Restaurant adj open 24 hrs. Ck-out noon. Meeting rms. Business center. In-rm modem link. Concierge. Sundries. Coin lndry. Exercise equipt. Indoor pool; whirlpool. Refrigerators, microwaves; some in-rm whirlpools. Cr cds: A, D, DS, JCB, MC, V.

D ≈ ✗ ⇥ 🐾 SC 🏃

★ **RED ROOF INN.** *5640 Merchants Center Blvd (37912), at I-75 exit 108.* 423/689-7100; res: 800/843-7663; FAX 423/689-7974. 84 rms, 2 story. S $31-$52; D $36-$64; each addl $7; higher rates special events. Crib free. Pet accepted, some restrictions. TV; cable (premium). Ck-out noon. Business servs avail. Health club privileges. Cr cds: A, C, D, DS, MC, V.

D ✔ ⇥ 🐾 SC

✔★ **RED ROOF INN-WEST.** *209 Advantage Place (37922), I-40/75 exit 378.* 423/691-1664; FAX 423/691-7210. Web www.red roof.com. 115 rms, 3 story. S, D $33.99-$69.99; each addl $9; under 18 free; higher rates: Dogwood Festival, special events; lower rates rest of yr. Crib free. TV; cable (premium). Complimentary coffee in lobby. Restaurant adj 6 am-10 pm. Ck-out noon. Business servs avail. Health club privileges. Cr cds: A, C, D, DS, MC, V.

D ⇥ 🐾 SC

★ **SUPER 8.** *6200 Paper Mill Rd (37919).* 423/584-8511; res: 800/800-8000. 139 rms, 2-3 story. No elvtr. S $44-$75; D $54-$95; each addl $5; under 18 free. Crib free. Pet accepted, some restrictions. TV; cable (premium). Pool; wading pool, whirlpool. Complimentary continental bkfst. Ck-out 11 am. Meeting rm. Business servs avail. Exercise equipt. Coin lndry. Cr cds: A, C, D, DS, JCB, MC, V.

D ⛵ ≈ 🏋 ⤫ 🔥 SC

Motor Hotels

★ ★ **BEST WESTERN LUXBURY.** *420 N Peters Rd (37922). 423/539-0058; res: 800/252-7748, ext. 7; FAX 423/539-4887.* 98 rms, 3 story, 23 suites. S, D $66-$72; each addl $6; suites $78-$125; under 18 free; wkend rates; higher rates special events. Crib free. TV; cable (premium). Pool. Complimentary continental bkfst. Coffee in rms. Restaurant nearby. Ck-out 11 am. Meeting rm. Business servs avail. Valet serv. Health club privileges. Bathrm phone, refrigerator, wet bar in suites. Cr cds: A, C, D, DS, MC, V.

D ≈ ⤫ 🔥 SC

✔★ **DAYS INN.** *1706 W Cumberland (37916), on Univ of TN campus. 423/521-5000.* 119 rms, 7 story. S, D $55-$65; each addl $5; under 12 free; higher rates special events. Crib free. Pet accepted; $15. TV; cable (premium). Ck-out 11 am. Complimentary continental bkfst. Meeting rms. Business servs avail. Cr cds: A, C, D, DS, JCB, MC, V.

D ⛵ ⤫ 🔥 SC

★ ★ **HOLIDAY INN.** *1315 Kirby Rd (37909), jct I-40 & I-75. 423/584-3911; FAX 423/588-0920.* 242 rms, 4 story. S, D $80-$119; under 18 free. Crib free. Pet accepted; $25. TV; cable (premium). Pool; whirlpool. Restaurant 6:30 am-10 pm. Rm serv. Bar 5 pm-1 am. Ck-out 11 am. Coin lndry. Meeting rms. Business servs avail. Free airport transportation. Health club privileges. Balconies. Picnic tables. Cr cds: A, C, D, DS, MC, V.

D ⛵ ≈ ⤫ 🔥 SC

★ ★ **HOWARD JOHNSON PLAZA.** *7621 Kingston Pike (37919). 423/693-8111; res: 800/446-4656; FAX 423/690-1031.* 162 rms, 4 story. S, D $58.50-$78.50; each addl $10; suites $100-$175; studio rms $65-$89.50; under 18 free. Crib free. Pet accepted, some restrictions; $10. TV; cable (premium). Pool. Restaurant 7 am-1 pm, 5-10 pm. Rm serv. Bar 4 pm-2 am; entertainment. Ck-out noon. Meeting rms. Business servs avail. Cr cds: A, C, D, DS, ER, JCB, MC, V.

D ⛵ ≈ ⤫ 🔥 SC

★ ★ **LA QUINTA INN.** *5634 Merchants Center Blvd (37912). 423/687-8989; res: 800/531-5900; FAX 423/687-9351.* 123 rms, 5 story. S, D $49-$75; each addl $5; higher rates special events. Crib free. Pet accepted. TV; cable (premium). Pool. Complimentary continental bkfst. Coffee in rms. Ck-out noon. Meeting rms. Health club privileges. Cr cds: A, C, D, DS, MC, V.

D ≈ ⤫ 🔥 SC

★ ★ **SIGNATURE INN-CEDAR BLUFF.** *209 Market Place Ln (37922). 423/531-7444; res: 800/822-5252.* Web www.signature-inns.com. 122 rms, 3 story. S, D $77-$80; under 17 free; higher rates special events. Crib free. TV; cable (premium). Pool. Complimentary continental bkfst. Restaurant nearby. Ck-out noon. Meeting rms. Business center. Valet serv. Exercise equipt. Health club privileges. Cr cds: A, D, DS, MC, V.

D ≈ 🏋 ⤫ 🔥 SC

★ ★ **WYNDHAM GARDEN HOTEL.** *208 Market Place Ln (37922). 423/531-1900; res: 800/996-3426; FAX 423/531-8807.* 137 rms, 2 story, 16 kit. suites. S, D $84-$119; each addl $10; kit. suites $99-$129; under 16 free. Crib free. TV; cable (premium). Pool; whirlpool. Restaurant 6:30 am-10 pm. Ck-out noon. Coin lndry. Meeting rms. Business servs avail. Exercise equipt. Refrigerator, wet bar in suites. Balconies. Grills. Cr cds: A, C, D, DS, MC, V.

D ≈ 🏋 ⤫ 🔥 SC

Hotels

★ ★ ★ **HILTON.** *501 Church Ave SW (37902). 423/523-2300; res: 800/445-8667; FAX 423/525-6532.* 317 rms, 18 story. S, D $99-$139; each addl $15; suites $230-$375; wkend rates; higher rates special events. Crib free. TV; cable (premium). VCR avail. Pool. Restaurant 6 am-10 pm. Rm serv. Bar 3-11 pm. Ck-out noon. Convention facilities. Business center. Exercise equipt; sauna. Gift shop. Free airport transportation. Some refrigerators. Cr cds: A, C, D, DS, MC, V.

D ≈ 🏋 ⤫ 🔥 SC ⬆

★ ★ ★ **HOLIDAY INN SELECT-DOWNTOWN.** *525 Henley St (37902), at Convention Center. 423/522-2800; res: 800/465-4329; FAX 423/523-0738.* 293 rms, 11 story. S, D $93-$180; each addl $10; suites $261-$400; under 18 free; wkend rates; higher rates special events. TV; cable (premium), VCR avail. Indoor pool; whirlpool. Restaurant 6:30 am-1:30 pm, 6-10 pm; Sat, Sun from 7 am. Bar 5 pm-midnight. Ck-out 11 am. Coin lndry. Convention facilities. Business center. In-rm modem link. Exercise equipt; sauna. Refrigerator in suites. Luxury level. Cr cds: A, C, D, DS, JCB, MC, V.

D ≈ 🏋 ⤫ 🔥 SC ⬆

★ ★ ★ **HYATT REGENCY.** *500 Hill Ave SE (37915). 423/637-1234; res: 800/223-1234; FAX 423/637-1193.* Web www.hyatt.com. 385 rms, 11 story. S, D $130-$160; each addl $25; suites $175-$425; under 18 free; wkend rates; higher rates special events. Crib free. Pet accepted, some restrictions; $25. TV; cable (premium), VCR avail. Pool; poolside serv. Playground. Restaurants 6:30 am-midnight. Bar 4 pm-1 am. Ck-out noon. Convention facilities. Business center. Beauty shop. Gift shop. Airport transportation. Exercise equipt; sauna. Many balconies. Contemporary decor; 8-story lobby with atrium. On hill above Tennessee River. Cr cds: A, C, D, DS, ER, JCB, MC, V.

D ⛵ ≈ 🏋 ⤫ 🔥 SC ⬆

★ ★ ★ **RADISSON.** *401 W Summit Hill Dr (37902). 423/522-2600; res: 800/333-3333; FAX 423/523-7200.* E-mail radknox@esper.com. 197 rms, 12 story. S $109-$119; D $119-$129; each addl $10; suites $175-$350; under 18 free; higher rates special events. Crib free. Pet accepted. TV; cable, VCR avail. Indoor pool. Restaurant 6 am-10 pm. Bar 4 pm-midnight. Ck-out noon. Meeting rms. Business servs avail. Gift shop. Exercise equipt. Microwaves avail. Cr cds: A, C, D, DS, ER, JCB, MC, V.

D ⛵ ≈ 🏋 ⤫ 🔥 SC

Restaurants

★ **BUTCHER SHOP.** *806 World Fair Park Dr (37902). 423/637-0204.* Hrs: 5-10 pm; Fri, Sat to 11 pm; Sun 4-10 pm. Closed major hols. Res accepted. Bar. Semi-a la carte: dinner $13-$23. Child's meals. Specializes in steak, seafood, chicken. Parking. Option to select steak and cook it; large, open charcoal grill. In park. Cr cds: A, C, D, DS, JCB, MC, V.

D ⤫

★ ★ **CALHOUNS.** *10020 Kingston Pike (37950). 423/673-3444.* Hrs: 11 am-10 pm; Sat to 11 pm; Sun to 9:30 pm. Closed Thanksgiving, Dec 25. Res accepted. Bar. Semi-a la carte: lunch $6.50-$10, dinner $9.95-$19. Child's meals. Specializes in baby back ribs, prime rib, hickory-smoked pork. Parking. Rustic decor; antiques, farm implements. Cr cds: A, C, D, DS, MC, V.

D ⤫ ♥

✔★ ★ **THE CHEF BISTRO.** *5003 Kingston Pike (37919). 423/584-1300.* Web user.icx.net./~thechef. Hrs: 11 am-2:30 pm, 6-10 pm; Mon to 2:30 pm. Closed Sun; major hols. Res accepted. French menu. Semi-a la carte: lunch $3.95-$10.95, dinner $12.95-$23.95. Specializes in veal, lamb, steak. Bistro decor. No cr cds accepted.

D

★ ★ **CHESAPEAKE'S.** *500 N Henley St (37902). 423/673-3433.* Hrs: 11 am-2:30 pm, 4:30-10 pm; Fri to 11 pm; Sat 4:30-11 pm; Sun

4:30-9:30 pm. Closed Jan 1, Thanksgiving, Dec 25. Res accepted. Bar. Semi-a la carte: lunch $5.95-$8.50, dinner $12.95-$24.95. Child's meals. Specializes in fresh seafood, Maine lobster. Parking. Outdoor dining. Cr cds: A, C, D, DS, MC, V.

D ⟋

✔★ ★ **CHINA INN.** *6450 Kingston Pike (37919). 423/588-7815.* Hrs: 11 am-3 pm, 4:30-10 pm; Fri, Sat to 10:30 pm; Sun 11 am-10 pm. Closed Thanksgiving, Dec 25. Chinese menu. Bar. Semi-a la carte: lunch $4.50-$8.50, dinner $6-$22. Parking. Cr cds: A, DS, MC, V.

D ⟋

★ ★ **THE CHOP HOUSE.** *9700 Kingston Pike (37922). 423/531-2467.* Web www.goldenpath.com/thechophouse. Hrs: 11 am-10 pm; Fri, Sat to 11 pm. Closed Thanksgiving, Dec 25. Bar. Semi-a la carte: lunch, dinner $4.49-$22.99. Child's meals. Specializes in pork chops, steak. Parking. Outdoor dining. Cr cds: A, D, DS, MC, V.

D ⟋

★ ★ **COPPER CELLAR.** *1807 Cumberland Ave (37916). 423/673-3411.* Hrs: 11 am-10:30 pm; Fri, Sat to 11:30 pm; Sun to 10 pm; Sun brunch to 2 pm. Closed Thanksgiving, Dec 25. Bar. A la carte entrees: lunch $4-$12, dinner $6.50-$26. Child's meals. Specializes in fresh seafood, prime rib. Parking. Cr cds: A, C, D, DS, MC, V.

D ⟋

★ ★ **COPPER CELLAR-CAPPUCCINO'S.** *7316 Kingston Pike (37919). 423/673-3422.* Hrs: 11 am-10 pm; Fri to 11 pm; Sat 5-11 pm; Sun 11 am-2 pm, 5-10 pm. Closed some major hols. Res accepted. Italian, Amer menu. Bar. Semi-a la carte: lunch $6.95-$12.95, dinner $9.95-$24.95. Sun brunch $11.95-$14.95. Specializes in prime beef, fresh seafood. Parking. Cr cds: A, C, D, DS, MC, V.

D ⟋

✔★ ★ **LITTON'S.** *2803 Essary Rd (37918). 423/688-0429.* Hrs: 11 am-9 pm; Fri, Sat to 10 pm. Closed Sun; most major hols. Semi-a la carte: lunch $5-$8, dinner $5-$15. Child's meals. Specializes in fresh seafood, steaks, desserts. Family-owned. Cr cds: A, D, MC, V.

D ⟋

✔★ ★ **MANDARIN HOUSE.** *314 J Merchants Dr (37912), I-75 N, exit 108. 423/689-4800.* Hrs: 11 am-9:30 pm; Fri, Sat to 10 pm. Res accepted. Chinese menu. Bar. Semi-a la carte: lunch $3.95-$5.25, dinner $7.95-$20. Buffet: lunch $5.25, dinner $7.95. Specializes in duck, seafood. Contemporary decor. Cr cds: A, C, D, DS, MC, V.

D SC ⟋

✔★ ★ **MANDARIN HOUSE.** *8111 Gleason Dr (37919). 423/694-0350.* Hrs: 11 am-9:30 pm; Fri, Sat to 10 pm. Res accepted. Chinese menu. Bar. Semi-a la carte: lunch $3.50-$5.25, dinner $5-$10. Specializes in buffet. Parking. Cr cds: A, C, D, DS, MC, V.

D SC ⟋

★ ★ **MICHAEL'S.** *7049 Kingston Pike (37919). 423/588-2455.* Hrs: 5-11 pm; Fri, Sat to midnight. Res accepted; required football wkends. Continental menu. Bar 4 pm-2:30 am. Semi-a la carte: dinner $8.95-$24.95. Child's meals. Specializes in beef, seafood. Valet parking. Atrium; brass, oak, beveled glass. Cr cds: A, C, D, DS, MC, V.

D SC ⟋

★ ★ **NAPLES.** *5500 Kingston Pike (37919). 423/584-5033.* Hrs: 11 am-2 pm, 5-10 pm; Fri to 11 pm; Sat 5-11 pm; Sun 5-10 pm. Closed July 4, Thanksgiving, Dec 24, 25. Res accepted. Italian menu. Bar. Semi-a la carte: lunch $5.99-$9.99. A la carte entrees: dinner $5.99-$15.95. Child's meals. Specializes in pasta, veal, seafood. Parking. Cr cds: A, C, D, DS, MC, V.

D SC ⟋ ♥

★ ★ **THE ORANGERY.** *5412 Kingston Pike (37919). 423/588-2964.* Hrs: 11:30 am-2:30 pm, 6-10 pm; Fri to 11 pm; Sat 6-11 pm. Closed Sun; most major hols. Res accepted. French, continental menu. Bar. 2

wine cellars. Semi-a la carte: lunch $5.95-$12.95, dinner $15-$30. Specialties: petite côtelettes d'agneau, boeuf Wellington, paella. Own baking. Pianist. Family-owned. European antiques, crystal chandeliers, and atrium; wine cellar dining area. Cr cds: A, C, D, MC, V.

D ⟋

★ ★ ★ **REGAS.** *318 N Gay St (37917), at Magnolia Ave. 423/637-9805.* Hrs: 11 am-10 pm; Sat 5-10 pm; early-bird dinner Mon-Sat 5-6:30 pm. Closed major hols. Continental menu. Bar. Wine list. Semi-a la carte: lunch $6-$17, dinner $13-$25. Child's meals. Specializes in clam chowder, prime rib, fresh seafood. Own baking. Entertainment Thurs-Sat. Dining rms individually decorated; fireplaces, original artwork. Family-owned. Cr cds: A, C, D, DS, MC, V.

D ⟋

★ ★ ★ **TUSCANY.** *5200 Kingston Pike (37919). 423/584-6755.* Hrs: 5-10 pm; Fri, Sat to 11 pm. Closed some major hols. Res accepted. Northern Italian, continental menu. Bar. Semi-a la carte: dinner $9-$23. Speciality: slow braised osso bucco, roast leg of lamb, veal. Parking. Intimate dining, trattoria-like atmosphere. Cr cds: A, C, D, DS, MC, V.

D ⟋

Unrated Dining Spot

APPLE CAKE TEA ROOM. *11312 Station W Dr (37922), exit 373. 423/966-7848.* Hrs: 11 am-2:30 pm. Closed Sun; major hols. A la carte entrees: lunch $2.25-$6. Child's meals. Specializes in salads, sandwiches, soups, desserts. Parking. Country antique decor. Fireplace, artwork. Totally nonsmoking. Cr cds: MC, V.

D ⟋

Lawrenceburg (E-4)

Founded 1815 **Pop** 10,412 **Elev** 890 ft **Area code** 931 **Zip** 38464

What to See and Do

David Crockett State Park. This 1,000-acre area is located on the banks of Shoal Creek, where Crockett once operated a gristmill. Swimming pool, wading pool, bathhouse; fishing; boating (rentals). Nature, bicycle trails; lighted tennis. Picnicking, playground, concessions; park restaurant doubles as a dinner theater in summer (reservations required). Tent, trailer sites. Visitors center housed in waterpowered gristmill (Memorial Day-Labor Day); amphitheater. Standard fees. W on US 64. Phone 931/762-9408.

Lebanon (D-5)

(See also Murfreesboro, Nashville)

Pop 15,208 **Elev** 531 ft **Area code** 615 **Zip** 37087

Information Lebanon/Wilson County Chamber of Commerce, 149 Public Square; 615/444-5503.

Tall red cedars thrive in this area as they did in the Biblical lands of Lebanon. Thus, the founding fathers named the city Lebanon. The dense cedar forest has been used for many industrial purposes including wood, paper and pencils. Since 1842, Lebanon has been the home of Cumberland University.

What to See and Do

Cedars of Lebanon State Park. Approx 831 acres within 9,000-acre state forest. Limestone cavern and sinks were reforested, in 1930s, with juniper. Swimming and wading pools. Hiking; game courts. Picnicking, playground, concession, recreation lodge. Tent & trailer sites, cabins. Nature center. Standard fees. 7 mi S on US 231, TN 10. Phone 615/443-2769.

Old Hickory Lake. Waterskiing; fishing; boating. 6 mi NW.

Motels

★ ★ **BEST WESTERN EXECUTIVE INN.** *631 S Cumberland St, I-40 exit 238. 615/444-0505; FAX 615/449-8516.* 125 rms, 2 story, 45 suites. May-Oct: S $45-$69; D $51-$69; each addl $5; suites $55-$89; under 12 free; lower rates rest of yr. Crib free. Pet accepted. TV; cable (premium). 2 pools, 1 indoor. Sauna. Restaurant adj 6 am-10:30 pm. Ck-out 11 am. Meeting rms. Business servs avail. Cr cds: A, C, D, DS, JCB, MC, V.

✔ ★ **DAYS INN.** *914 Murfreesboro Rd. 615/444-5635.* 52 rms, 2 story. May-Oct: S $32-$67; D $42-$70; each addl $5; under 18 free; higher rates special events; lower rates rest of yr. Crib free. Pet accepted; $5. TV; cable (premium). Pool. Complimentary continental bkfst. Restaurant nearby. Ck-out 11 am. Coin lndry. Business servs avail. Some refrigerators, microwaves. Cr cds: A, C, D, DS, ER, JCB, MC, V.

★ ★ **HAMPTON INN.** *704 S Cumberland, I-40 exit 238. 615/444-7400; FAX 615/449-7969.* Web www.hampton-inn.com. 83 rms, 2 story, 4 suites. S, D $55-$90; suites $105-$125; under 18 free; higher rates special events. Crib free. Pet accepted, some restrictions. TV; cable. Pool; whirlpool. Complimentary continental bkfst. Restaurant nearby. Ck-out 11 am. Lndry facilities avail. Meeting rms. Business servs avail. Exercise equipt; sauna. Cr cds: A, D, DS, MC, V.

★ **SHONEY'S INN.** *822 S Cumberland St. 615/449-5781; FAX 615/449-8201; res: 800/222-2222.* 111 rms, 3 story. Mid-June-mid-Aug: S, D $42-$62; each addl $6; under 18 free; lower rates rest of yr. Crib free. TV; cable. Indoor pool. Restaurant nearby. Ck-out noon. Meeting rms. Business servs avail. Some refrigerators. Cr cds: A, C, D, DS, MC, V.

Lenoir City (D-7)

(See also Knoxville, Sweetwater)

Founded 1890 **Pop** 6,147 **Elev** 798 ft **Area code** 423 **Zip** 37771 **Web** www.loudoncounty.org
Information Loudon County Chamber of Commerce, PO Box 909, Loudon 37774; 423/458-2067.

What to See and Do

Fort Loudoun Dam and Lake. This TVA dam, 4,190 ft long and 122 ft high, with a lock chamber to permit navigation of the river, transforms a 61-mi stretch of once unruly river into a placid lake extending to Knoxville. Fishing, boating on 14,600-acre lake. On US 11 at S end of city. Phone 423/986-3737. **Free.**

Tellico Dam and Lake. TVA dam on Little Tennessee River impounds 15,680-acre lake. Upper end of reservoir adjoins the Cherokee National Forest (see). Excellent fishing and boating with the Great Smoky Mountains as backdrop. Summer pool; boat access sites. Picnicking. Camping. Approx 3 mi S off US 321. Phone 423/986-3737.

Motels

✔ ★ **CROSS ROADS INN.** *1110 US 321N, at I-75 exit 81. 423/986-2011; FAX 423/986-6454; res: 800/526-4658.* 90 rms, 2 story. S

$31-$34; D $41-$45; under 12 free. TV; cable. Pool; wading pool. Ck-out 11 am. Business servs avail. Some refrigerators. Cr cds: A, D, MC, V.

★ **KING'S INN.** *1031 US 321N, 2 blks S of I-75 exit 81. 423/986-9091.* 50 rms, 2 story. S $29-$41; D $39-$45; each addl $5; under 18 free. Crib $5. TV; cable. Pool. Restaurant opp 10 am-10 pm. Ck-out 11 am. Refrigerators. Cr cds: A, DS, MC, V.

Inns

★ ★ ★ **THE MASON PLACE.** *(600 Commerce St, Loudon 37774) SW on I-75, exit 72 or 76, off US 11. 423/458-3921.* Web www.checkthenet.com/travel/mason.htm. 5 rms, shower only, 2 story. No rm phones. S, D $96-$120; higher rates: Univ of Tennessee football games, hols. Children over 14 yrs only. TV; VCR in sitting rm. Pool. Complimentary full bkfst; afternoon refreshments. Restaurants nearby. Ck-out 11 am, ck-in 3 pm. Lawn games. Restored plantation house (1865) furnished with period antiques. Fireplaces. No cr cds accepted.

★ ★ ★ **WHITESTONE COUNTRY INN.** *(1200 Paint Rock Rd, Kingston 37763) I-75 exit 72, 8 mi W on TN 72. 423/376-0113; res: 888/247-2464; FAX 423/376-4454.* E-mail moreinfo@whitestones.com; web www.whitestones.com. 11 rms, some with A/C, 2 story, 3 suites, 1 guest house. Rm phones in suites. S, D $85-$160; each addl $20; suites $125-$160; guest house $85-$125; under 12 free. Crib free. TV; VCR avail (movies). Complimentary full bkfst. Complimentary coffee in rms. Restaurant 8 am-8 pm. Ck-out 11 am, ck-in 3 pm. Business servs avail. In-rm modem link. Gift shop. Tennis privileges. Exercise equipt; sauna. Game rm. Rec rm. Lawn games. In-rm whirlpools, fireplaces; some refrigerators, microwaves. Many balconies. Picnic tables, grills. On lake. On 275 acres; surrounded by wildlife refuge. Totally nonsmoking. Cr cds: A, DS, MC, V.

Lewisburg (E-5)

(See also Shelbyville)

Settled 1837 **Pop** 9,879 **Elev** 734 ft **Area code** 931 **Zip** 37091 **E-mail** mcoco@tnweb.com
Information Marshall County Chamber of Commerce, 227 2nd Ave N; 931/359-3863.

Named for Meriwether Lewis, of the Lewis and Clark expedition, Lewisburg is largely linked to the dairy industry and is a trading and shipping center for the surrounding farms. Milk-processing plants are supplemented by factories producing air conditioners, furniture and pencils.

What to See and Do

Dairy Experiment Station. Operated cooperatively by the US Dept of Agriculture and the Univ of Tennessee on 615 acres. (Mon-Fri; wkends, by appt) 3 mi S on US 31A. Phone 931/270-2240. **Free.**

Henry Horton State Resort Park. Park covering 1,135 acres located on the estate of a former Tennessee governor is bordered by the scenic Duck River, a popular canoeing and fishing river. Facilities include swimming and wading pools. Clubhouse, golf course, lighted tennis; skeet & trap range. Picnicking, restaurant. Tent & trailer sites, cabins, resort inn. Standard fees. 11 mi NE of I-65, on US 31A. Phone 931/364-2222.

Tennessee Walking Horse Breeders & Exhibitors Association. All registrations, transfers and decisions concerning the walking horse breed are made at this world headquarters. Open to visitors, building contains a gallery of world champions. (Mon-Fri) 250 N Ellington Pkwy. Phone 931/359-1574. **Free.**

Manchester (E-5)

(See also Monteagle)

Pop 7,709 **Elev** 1,063 ft **Area code** 931 **Zip** 37355
Information Chamber of Commerce, 110 E Main St; 931/728-7635.

What to See and Do

Distillery tours.

Geo. A. Dickel Distillery. Distillery built in 1870 and re-created in 1959 produces and matures Tennessee sour mash "whisky." Country store. 30-45-min guided tours (Mon-Fri; closed major hols, Dec 24; also Friday before some hols) Approx 11 mi SW on TN 55 to Tullahoma, then N on US 41A, follow signs. Phone 931/857-3124.   **Free.**

Jack Daniel Distillery. Nation's oldest registered distillery. One-hour and 20-min guided tours include rustic grounds, limestone spring cave, old office. (Daily; closed Jan 1, Thanksgiving, Dec 25) 25 mi SW on TN 55, in Lynchburg. Phone 931/759-4221.   **Free.**

Normandy Lake. Completed in 1976, the dam is 2,734 ft high and impounds a 3,160-acre lake. Controlled releases provide a scenic floatway (28 mi) below the dam with public access points along the way. Summer pool; excellent spring and fall fishing. Picnicking. Camping. 8 mi W; 2 mi upstream from Normandy.

Old Stone Fort State Archaeological Park. Park covering 600 acres surrounds earthen remains of a more than 2,000 year old walled structure built along the bluffs of the Duck River. Fishing. Picnicking. playground. Camping. Museum. Standard fees. 1½ mi W off I-24, exit 110. Phone 931/723-5073.

Annual Event

Old Timer's Day. City Square. Parade, pet contest, entertainment, games, food. 1st Sat Oct.

Motels

★ ★ **AMBASSADOR INN & LUXURY SUITES.** *925 Interstate Dr, I-24 exit 110. 931/728-2200; FAX 931/728-8376; res: 800/237-9228.* 105 rms, 1-2 story. S from $45; each addl $5; suites $75-$100; under 12 free. Crib $5. TV; cable (premium), VCR avail. Pool. Complimentary continental bkfst. Restaurant adj 6 am-10 pm. Ck-out 11 am. Meeting rms. Exercise equipt. Refrigerators. Cr cds: A, C, D, DS, MC, V.

D 🏄 ✗ ⚡ 🐾 SC

★ ★ **HOLIDAY INN I-24.** *126 Expy Dr, I-24 exit 114. 931/728-9651; FAX 931/728-2208; res: 800/465-4329.* 141 rms, 2 story. S, D $61-$70; each addl $5; suites $72-$84; under 18 free. Crib free. Pet accepted. TV; cable (premium), VCR avail. Pool. Restaurant 6 am-2 pm, 5-10 pm. Rm serv. Bar 5 pm-midnight. Ck-out noon. Free guest lndry. Meeting rms. Business servs avail. In-rm modem link. Some refrigerators, microwaves. Cr cds: A, C, DS, JCB, MC, V.

D 🐾 ⚡ ⚡ 🐾 SC

✔★ **SUPER 8.** *2430 Hillsboro Hwy, 1 mi S on US 41 at I-24 exit 114. 931/728-9720.* 50 rms, 2 story. S $24-$36; D $31-$45; each addl $5; under 12 free; higher rates special events. Crib free. Pet accepted, some restrictions. TV; cable (premium). Pool. Complimentary continental bkfst. Ck-out 11 am. Cr cds: A, D, DS, MC, V.

D 🐾 ⚡ ⚡ 🐾 SC

Restaurant

★ **OAK FAMILY.** *947 Interstate Dr, I-24 exit 110. 931/728-5777.* Hrs: 11 am-10 pm; Sun buffet 11 am-9 pm. Closed July 4, Dec 24-25. Res accepted exc Sun. Semi-a la carte: lunch $4.69-$6.99, dinner $4.95-$12.95. Sun buffet $6.39-$7. Child's meals. Specializes in prime rib, lasagne. Salad bar. Cr cds: A, D, DS, MC, V.

D

Maryville (E-8)

(See also Knoxville, Townsend)

Founded 1795 **Pop** 19,208 **Elev** 989 ft **Area code** 423 **E-mail** chambcom@chamber.blount.tn.us **Web** chamber.blount.tn.us
Information Blount County Chamber of Commerce, 201 S Washington St, 37804; 423/983-2241 or 800/525-6843.

Maryville and its twin city, Alcoa, provide a scenic gateway to the Great Smoky Mountains National Park (see). The seat of Blount County, Maryville was once the home of Sam Houston, the only man in US history to serve as governor of two states; in 1807 he moved to this area from Virginia with his widowed mother and eight brothers.

What to See and Do

Maryville College (1819). (850 students) Liberal arts college. Twenty buildings represent architectural trends from 1869-1922. Fine Arts Center has plays, concerts, exhibits. Tours of campus. E side of town, main entrance on Lamar Alexander Pkwy (US 321). Phone 423/981-8000.

Sam Houston Schoolhouse (1794). Restored log building in which Sam Houston taught in 1812 at tuition rate of $8/term. Museum of Houston memorabilia in nearby visitor center. Picnicking. (Daily exc Mon; closed most major hols) 5 mi NE, off US 411 (follow signs), on Old Sam Houston School Rd. Phone 423/983-1550.   ¢

Motel

★ **PRINCESS MOTEL.** *2614 US 411S (37801), 2 mi S on US 129, 411. 423/982-2490.* 33 rms, 1-2 story. May-Oct: S $40-$50; D $50-$60; each addl $5; kit. units $210-$350/wk; under 12 free; higher rates special events; lower rates rest of yr. Crib $4. Pet accepted. TV; cable (premium). Pool. Restaurant adj open 24 hrs. Ck-out 11 am. Cr cds: A, C, D, DS, MC, V.

🐾 ⚡ ⚡ 🔥 SC

Inn

★ ★ ★ **BLACKBERRY FARM.** *(1471 W Millers Cove Rd, Walland 37886) 10 mi N on TN 321, first right after Foothills Pkwy. 423/984-8166; FAX 423/983-5708.* E-mail blkberryfrm@aol.com; web www.blackberry hotel.com. This English country house (1940) sits on 1,100 acres. 42 rms, 2 story. AP: S, D $395-$695; each addl $125. Children over 10 yrs only. TV in sitting rms; cable. Heated pool. Complimentary full bkfst. Dining rm 8-10:30 am, 6:30-8:30 pm. Ck-out noon, ck-in 4 pm. Business servs avail. Valet serv. Concierge serv. Tennis. Exercise rm. Game rm. Picnic tables. Cr cds: A, DS, MC, V.

D 🐾 ⚡ ⚡ ✗ 🐾 🔥

McMinnville (E-6)

Pop 11,194 **Elev** 976 ft **Area code** 931 **Zip** 37110 **E-mail** warrencotn@Blomand.net **Web** www.warrentn.com
Information McMinnville-Warren County Chamber of Commerce, 110 S Court Square, PO Box 574, 37111; 931/473-6611.

What to See and Do

Cumberland Caverns Park. Mined for saltpeter as long ago as the Civil War but not yet fully explored, the Cumberland Caverns offer a variety of underground formations and sights: old saltpeter mines; "Hall of the Mountain King" (600 ft across, 140 ft high); underground dining room; "God of the Mountain," a dramatization of the Creation with spectacular lighting (shown on every tour). Constant 56°F. Picnic area above ground. Tours (1¹/₂ hr). (May-Oct, daily) 7 mi SE, just off US 70S. Phone 931/668-4396. ¢¢¢

Fall Creek Falls State Resort Park. More than 16,000-acre park offers mountain scenery, 256-ft Fall Creek Falls and great fishing. Swimming pool; boating (rentals). Nature trails; backpacking, riding; 18-hole golf, sports facilities. Picnicking, concessions, restaurant, inn. Tent & trailer sites, cabins. Standard fees. 30 mi E via TN 30 to TN 284E, in Spencer. Phone 423/881-3241.

Rock Island State Rustic Park. Approx 850 acres, located on Center Hill Reservoir. Swimming; fishing; boating (ramp). Picnicking. Camping. Standard fees. 14 mi NE via US 70S. Phone 931/686-2471.

Motel

✔★ **SHONEY'S INN.** *508 Sunnyside Heights.* 931/473-4446. 61 rms, 3 story. S $42-$46; D $46; under 18 free. Crib free. Pet accepted, some restrictions. TV; cable (premium). Complimentary continental bkfst. Restaurant nearby. Ck-out noon. Meeting rms. Business servs avail. Pool. Some refrigerators, microwaves. Cr cds: A, C, D, DS, MC, V.

D ✒ ≈ ✕ ☠ SC

Inn

★ ★ **HISTORIC FALCON MANOR.** *2645 Faulkner Springs Rd.* 931/668-4444. E-mail falconmanor@falconmanor.com; web www.falcon manor.com. 5 rms, 1 with shower only, 2 story. No rm phones. S, D $105; each addl $10. Children over 11 yrs only. Premium cable TV in common rm; VCR. Complimentary full bkfst. Ck-out 11 am, ck-in 3 pm. Business servs avail. Gift shop. Lawn games. Microwaves avail. Fireplaces. Authentically restored Victorian mansion built in 1896. Totally nonsmoking. Cr cds: MC, V.

D ✕ ☠

Memphis (E-1)

Settled 1819 **Pop** 610,337 **Elev** 264 ft **Area code** 901 **Web** www.memphistravel.com
Information Convention & Visitors Bureau, 47 Union Ave, 38103; 901/543-5300.

Memphis, on the Mississippi, is an old town with a new face. It is both "old South" and modern metropolis. The city has towering office buildings, flashy expressways, a $60 million civic center—and historic Beale Street, where W.C. Handy helped give birth to the blues.

General James Winchester is credited with naming the city for the Egyptian city Memphis, which means "place of good abode." The Nile-like Mississippi, of course, was the inspiration. Winchester, Andrew Jackson and John Overton laid out the town on a land grant from North Carolina, selecting this site because of the high bluffs above the river and the natural harbor at the mouth of the Wolf River. The land deal was somewhat questionable, and General Jackson left under a barrage of criticism. River traffic quickly developed; stores, shops and sawmills appeared, and Memphis became one of the busiest and most boisterous ports in America.

For a short time, Memphis was the Confederate capital of the state, also serving as a military supply depot and stronghold for the Southern forces. In 1862, however, Northern troops seized the city after a river battle dominated by an armada of 30 Union ships and held it throughout the war.

Plagued by yellow fever epidemics, an impoverished Memphis made a slow postwar recovery. By 1892, however, the city was back on its feet, becoming the busiest inland cotton market and hardwood lumber center in the world.

Memphis dominates the flat, crop-rich, alluvial Mississippi Delta. It serves as hub of six railroads, port for millions of tons of river cargo annually and home of over 1,100 manufacturing plants in the Memphis area. In national competition it has been acclaimed as the Cleanest City, the Safest City and the Quietest City.

As much as one-third of the country's cotton crop is bought or sold in Memphis, known as the cotton center of the world, but the agricultural segment of the city's economy is highly diversified—corn, alfalfa, vegetables, soybeans, rice, livestock and even fish farming. Memphis has the largest medical center in the South and more than a dozen institutions of higher learning, including the University of Memphis and Rhodes College. A city with a civic ballet, a symphony orchestra, an opera company, a repertory theater, art galleries and College of Art, Memphis is also a major convention city and distribution center.

Throughout the world, Memphis has become associated with the legendary Elvis Presley. Graceland, Presley's home, and Meditation Gardens, site of his grave, have become a destination for thousands of visitors annually. Each August, memorial celebrations are held citywide in honor of the "king of rock and roll."

Transportation

Memphis Intl Airport: Information 901/922-8000; lost and found 901/922-8050; weather 901/544-0399.

Car Rental Agencies: See IMPORTANT TOLL-FREE NUMBERS.

Public Transportation: Memphis Area Transit Authority, phone 901/274-6282.

Rail Passenger Service: Amtrak 800/872-7245.

What to See and Do

★ **Beale St.** Part of a seven-block entertainment district, stretching east from the Mississippi River bluffs, with restaurants, shops, parks and theaters. Statue of W.C. Handy in Handy Park. Downtown, off Riverside Dr. Phone 901/526-0110. Also on Beale St is

W.C. Handy's Home. House where W.C. Handy wrote "Memphis Blues," "St Louis Blues" and other classic tunes. Collection of Handy memorabilia. 325 Beale St. Phone 901/527-2583 for schedule. ¢

Circuit Playhouse. Comedies, musicals and dramas. 1705 Poplar Ave. Phone 901/726-4656.

Crystal Shrine Grotto. Crystal cave made of natural rock, quartz, crystal and semi-precious stones carved out of a hillside by naturalistic artist Dionicio Rodriguez in the late 1930s. Also scenes by the artist depicting life of Jesus and Biblical characters. (Daily) 5668 Poplar Ave, in Memorial Park Cemetery. Phone 901/767-8930. **Free.**

Dixon Gallery and Gardens. Museum surrounded by 17 acres of formal and woodland gardens with a camellia house and garden statuary; exhibition galleries display American and Impressionist art, British portraits and landscapes, English antique furnishings, 18th-century German porcelain. (Daily exc Mon; closed some major hols) 4339 Park Ave. Phone 901/761-5250. ¢¢

Downtown Mall Trolley. Antique electric trolley loop runs up Main St and back in the Pinch Historic District providing transportation to hotels, Beale St and attractions such as Pyramid Arena and the National Civil Rights Museum. (Daily) For fees and schedule phone 901/577-2648.

★ **Graceland.** Elvis Presley home. Mansion tour includes main floor and lower level of house, trophy room, grounds, gravesite. Other attractions include Automobile Museum, Presley's jet airplanes. (Daily; mansion tour, Nov-Feb, daily exc Tues; closed Jan 1, Thanksgiving, Dec 25; res recommended) 3764 Elvis Presley Blvd. Contact PO Box 16508, 38186-0508; phone 901/332-3322 or 800/238-2000. ¢¢-¢¢¢¢

Gray Line bus tours. Contact 2050 Elvis Presley Blvd, 38106; 901/948-TOUR.

Hunt-Phelan Home. Restored antebellum house with original furniture, some dating back to early 1608. (Apr-Aug, daily; rest of yr, Thurs-Mon; closed Jan 1, Thanksgiving, Dec 24, 25) 533 Beale St. Phone 901/344-3166 or 800/350-9009. ¢¢¢

Libertyland. Educational/historical amusement park; carnival rides, live shows, costumed characters, games; shops; food. (Mid-June-late Aug, Wed-Sun; May-mid-June & late Aug-Labor Day, wkends only) E Parkway at Mid-South Fairgrounds. Phone 901/274-1776. Admission/8-ride ticket ¢¢¢-¢¢¢¢

Lichterman Nature Center. Wildlife sanctuary (65 acres) includes 12-acre lake, greenhouse and hospital for wild animals. Hiking trails (3 mi). Picnicking. (Daily exc Mon; closed Jan 1, Thanksgiving, Dec 24, 25) 1680 Lynnfield. Phone 901/767-7322. ¢

Meeman-Shelby Forest State Park. A 12,500-acre park with 2 lakes bordering the Mississippi River. Swimming pool; fishing; boating. Hiking and bridle trails. Camping, cabins. Nature center. Standard fees. 13 mi N via US 51, near Millington. Phone 901/876-5215.

Memphis Botanic Garden. Garden encompasses 96 acres; 20 formal gardens here include the Japanese Garden of Tranquility, the Rose Garden and the Wildflower Garden. (Daily; closed Jan 1, Thanksgiving, Dec 25) 750 Cherry Rd in Audubon Park. Phone 901/685-1566. ¢

Memphis Brooks Museum of Art. Paintings, drawings, sculpture, photographs, prints and decorative arts from Renaissance to present. Permanent and changing exhibits. Guided tours, lectures, films, performing arts series. (Daily exc Mon; closed Jan 1, Thanksgiving, Dec 25) In Overton Park, off Poplar Ave. Phone 901/722-3500. ¢¢

Memphis International Motorsports Park. Multi-use park features four tracks hosting a variety of racing events: drag, circle track, tractor pulls, motorcycle, go-cart and 4-wheeler. (Mar-Nov; daily) N on I-240, 5500 Taylor Forge Dr. For schedule phone 901/358-7223 or 901/353-6118. ¢¢¢¢

Memphis Pink Palace Museum and Planetarium. Exhibits focus on natural and cultural history of the mid-South. Many facets of the region, including insects, birds, mammals, geology, pioneer life, medical history, commerce and the Civil War, can be explored; also changing exhibits and IMAX Theater. (Daily; closed Jan 1, Thanksgiving, Dec 24, 25) Planetarium has shows weekends and in summer (fee). 3050 Central Ave. Phone 901/320-6320. ¢¢

Memphis Zoo & Aquarium. More than 2,800 animals in naturalistic habitats such as Cat Country, Primate Canyon, Animals of the Night and Once Upon a Farm. Tram, rides, cafe. (Daily; closed Thanksgiving, Dec 24, 25) Bounded by N Parkway, E Parkway & Poplar Ave. Phone 901/276-WILD. ¢¢¢

Mud Island. Fifty-acre island in the Mississippi is a unique park designed to showcase the character of the river. The River Walk is a five-block-long scale model of the Mississippi from Cairo, IL, to the Gulf of Mexico; the River Museum features 18 galleries that chronicle the development of river music, art, lore and history; also here are films, playground, river boat excursions, shops, restaurants, picnicking. Monorail to island at Front St exit off I-40. For fee information phone 901/576-7241. Also on island is

Memphis Belle. This B-17 bomber and her crew were the first to complete 25 missions over Nazi targets and return to the US during World War II. Named for the pilot's wartime sweetheart, the *Memphis Belle* was featured in a documentary by director William Wyler; film shown twice daily. Plane displayed under glass dome. 280 Mud Island Rd. ¢

★ **National Civil Rights Museum.** The nation's first civil rights museum honors the American civil rights movement and the people behind it, from colonial to present times. Exhibits, sound and light displays, audiovisuals and visitor participation programs; auditorium and courtyard. (Daily exc Tues; closed major hols) 450 Mulberry St, at the Lorraine Motel, site of the 1968 assassination of Dr. Martin Luther King, Jr. Phone 901/521-9699. ¢¢

National Ornamental Metal Museum. Architectural and decorative metalwork. (Daily exc Mon; closed major hols) 374 W California, on the river bluff. Phone 901/774-6380. ¢

Playhouse on the Square. Professional theater. 51 S Cooper, in Overton Sq. Phone 901/725-0776 or ticket office, 901/726-4656. ¢¢¢¢

Pyramid Arena. This 32-story, 22,500-seat stainless steel and concrete pyramid, overlooking the Mississippi River, is fashioned after the ancient Egyptian Great Pyramid of Cheops and is used as a multi-sports and entertainment arena. Tours (daily). Downtown Pinch Historic District, on the Wolf River at Auction St Bridge. Phone 901/521-9675. ¢¢

Rhodes College (1848). (1,400 students) On campus is the 140-ft-high Richard Halliburton Memorial Tower, with first editions of Halliburton's books; memorabilia. Clough-Hanson Gallery has changing art exhibits (Mon-Fri; closed hols). Tours of campus. 2000 N Parkway at University St. Phone 901/726-3000.

River cruises.

Delta Queen, Mississippi Queen and *American Queen* paddle wheelers offer 3- to 12-night cruises on the Mississippi, Ohio, Cumberland and Tennessee rivers. For details contact Delta Queen Steamboat Co, 30 Robin St Wharf, New Orleans, LA 70130-1890; 800/543-1949.

Memphis Queen. Sightseeing, dinner cruises aboard Mississippi riverboat. (Sightseeing, Mar-Dec, daily; dinner cruises, May-Sept, Wed-Sun) Foot of Monroe at Riverside Dr. Phone 901/527-5694. ¢¢¢-¢¢¢¢¢

★ **Sun Studio.** Legendary recording studio where Elvis Presley, Jerry Lee Lewis, Roy Orbison, Carl Perkins and Johnny Cash made their first recordings. (Daily; every ½ hr). (Daily; closed Jan 1, Thanksgiving, Dec 25) 706 Union Ave. Phone 901/521-0664. ¢¢

T.O. Fuller State Park. A 384-acre park where De Soto is believed to have crossed the Mississippi. Swimming pool, bathhouse. Golf. Picnicking, concessions. Campsites (hookups). Standard fees. 10 mi S on US 61, then 4 mi W on Mitchell Rd. Phone 901/543-7581. In the park is

Chucalissa Archaeological Museum. Archaeological project of University of Memphis at site of Native American village founded about A.D. 900 and abandoned circa 1500. Native houses and temple have been reconstructed; archaeological exhibits. Museum displays artifacts and dioramas; 15-minute slide program. (Daily; closed most hols; no admittance to village area after 4:30 pm) 1987 Indian Village Dr. Phone 901/785-3160. ¢¢

The Children's Museum of Memphis. Hands-on museum has created an interactive "kid-sized city" including a bank, grocery store and skyscraper, among others. Special workshops and exhibits. (Daily exc Mon; closed some major hols) 2525 Central Ave. Phone 901/458-2678. ¢¢

Victorian Village. Within 1 mi of downtown area, 600 block of Adams Ave. Eighteen landmark buildings, either preserved or restored, range in style from Gothic revival to neo-classical. The three houses open to the public are

Magevney House (1836). Restored house of pioneer schoolmaster Eugene Magevney. Oldest middle-class dwelling in the city, furnished with artifacts of the period. (Tues-Sat; closed Jan 1, Thanksgiving, Dec 24, 25) 198 Adams Ave. Phone 901/526-4464. **Donation.**

Woodruff-Fontaine House (1870). Restored and furnished Second Empire/Victorian mansion with antique textile/costume collection. Gift shop. (Daily; closed July 4, Thanksgiving, Dec 24, 25) 680 Adams Ave. Phone 901/526-1469. ¢¢

Mallory-Neely House (1852). Preserved Italianate mansion (25 rms) with original furnishings. (Daily exc Mon; closed Jan 1, Thanksgiving, Dec 24, 25) 652 Adams Ave. Phone 901/523-1484. ¢¢

Wild Water and Wheels. Wave-action pool, water slides, free-fall slides, children's pool and play area; arcade, sand volleyball courts, lockers, bathhouse. Picnic area, concessions, gift shop. (Memorial Day-Labor Day, daily; also wkends May) 6880 Whitten Bend Cove, off I-40E exit 14. Phone 901/382-9283. ¢¢¢¢

Annual Events

Zydeco Festival. Beale St. Cajun-Creole and zydeco blues bands entertain in Beale St clubs. Early Feb.

Beale Street Music Festival. Beale St. International roster of musicians returns to Memphis for a musical family reunion. Part of the Memphis in May festivities. Early May.

Memphis in May International Festival. Month-long community-wide celebration focuses on cultural and artistic heritage of Memphis while featuring a different nation each year. Major events occur weekends, but activities are held daily. Includes The Beale St Music Festival, World Championship Barbecue Cooking Contest and Sunset Symphony. Phone 901/525-4611. May.

Carnival Memphis. Features parade, exhibits, salute to industry, and the Cottonmaker's Jubilee. Phone 901/278-0243. 10 days early June.

Elvis Presley International Tribute Week. More than 30 events take place throughout the city in honor of Presley and his music. Phone 901/332-3322. Aug 8-16.

Labor Day Fest. Beale St. Memphis musicians perform blues, jazz, rhythm and blues, country and rock; at clubs and restaurants throughout the historic district. Phone 901/526-0110. Early Sept.

Mid-South Fair and Exposition. Mid-South Fairgrounds, E Parkway S & Southern Ave. Agricultural, commercial, industrial exhibits; midway rides and concerts. Largest rodeo east of the Mississippi. Phone 901/274-8800. Late Sept-early Oct.

Seasonal Events

Outdoor concerts. Raoul Wallenberg Overton Park Shell, said to be the true birthplace of rock 'n' roll; Elvis Presley gave one of his first live performances here. Concerts feature local blues, rock and jazz musicians; also theater, movies and dance presentations. For schedule phone 901/274-6046. Late Mar-early Nov.

Theatre Memphis. 630 Perkins Extended.Internationally acclaimed community theater. Phone 901/682-8323. Mainstage offers 6-play season Sept-June; Little Theatre features 4-play season July-May.

Additional Visitor Information

For further information contact the Convention & Visitors Bureau, 47 Union Ave, 38103; phone 901/543-5300. Tourists may also inquire at the TN St Welcome Center located at 119 N Riverside Dr, phone 901/543-5333.

City Neighborhoods

Many of the restaurants, unrated dining establishments and some lodgings listed under Memphis include neighborhoods as well as exact street addresses. Geographic descriptions of these areas are given, followed by a table of restaurants arranged by neighborhood.

Beale Street Area: Downtown area along seven blocks of Beale St from Riverside Dr on the west to Danny Thomas Blvd on the east.

Downtown: South of I-40, west of Danny Thomas Blvd (US 51), north of Calhoun Ave and east of the Mississippi River. **East of Downtown:** East of US 51.

Overton Square: South of Poplar Ave, west of Cooper St, north of Union Ave and east of McLean Blvd.

MEMPHIS RESTAURANTS BY NEIGHBORHOOD AREAS

(For full description, see alphabetical listings under Restaurants)

BEALE STREET AREA
Alfred's. 197 Beale St

DOWNTOWN
Automatic Slim's Tonga Club. 83 S Second St
Butcher Shop. 101 S Front St
Chez Philippe (Peabody Hotel). 149 Union Ave
Ciao Baby Cucina. 135 S Main St
Dux (Peabody Hotel). 149 Union Ave
Erika's. 52 S Second
The Pier. 100 Wagner Pl
Rendezvous. 52 S 2nd St

EAST OF DOWNTOWN
Aubergine. 5007 Black Rd
Benihana Of Tokyo. 912 Ridge Lake Blvd
Buckley's Fine Filet Grill. 5355 Poplar Ave
Buntyn. 3070 Southern Ave
Cooker Bar & Grille. 6120 Poplar Ave
Erling Jensen. 1044 S Yates Rd

Folk's Folly. 551 S Mendenhall Rd
Lulu Grille. 565 Erin Dr
Raji. 712 W Brookhaven Circle
Ronnie Grisanta & Sons. 2855 Poplar Ave
Saigon Le. 51 N Cleveland

OVERTON SQUARE
Anderton's. 1901 N Madison
India Palace. 1720 Poplar Ave
La Tourelle. 2146 Monroe Ave
Melos Taverna. 2021 Madison Ave
Paulette's. 2110 Madison Ave
The Public Eye. 17 S Cooper

Note: When a listing is located in a town that does not have its own city heading, it will appear under the city nearest to its location. In these cases, the address and town appear in parenthesis immediately following the name of the establishment.

Motels

★ ★ **COMFORT INN.** *2889 Austin Peay Hwy (38128), north of downtown.* 901/386-0033; FAX 901/386-0036. 83 rms, 20 kit. suites. S, D $49-$67; each addl $5; kit. suites $70-$130; under 16 free. TV; cable (premium). Indoor pool; whirlpool. Complimentary continental bkfst. Restaurant nearby. Ck-out noon. Meeting rms. Business servs avail. Cr cds: A, C, D, DS, ER, MC, V.

D ≈ 🏊 🐾 SC

★ ★ **COURTYARD BY MARRIOTT.** *6015 Park Ave (38119), east of downtown.* 901/761-0330; FAX 901/682-8422. 146 units, 3 story. S, D $86-$96; each addl $10; suites $102-$112; under 17 free. Crib free. TV; cable (premium), VCR avail. Heated pool; whirlpool. Complimentary coffee in rms. Restaurant 6:30-10 am. Bar 5-10 pm. Ck-out noon. Coin lndry. Meeting rms. Business servs avail. Valet serv. Sundries. Exercise equipt. Health club privileges. Refrigerator, microwaves avail. Cr cds: A, C, D, DS, MC, V.

D ≈ ✈ 🐾 SC

✔★ **HAMPTON INN.** *1180 Union Ave (38104), downtown.* 901/276-1175; FAX 901/276-4261. 126 rms, 4 story. S $56-$64; D $64-$70; under 18 free. Crib free. TV; cable (premium), avail. Pool. Complimentary continental bkfst. Restaurant nearby. Ck-out 11 am. Business servs avail. Sundries. Cr cds: A, C, D, DS, MC, V.

D ≈ 🏊 🐾 SC

✔★ **RED ROOF INN.** *6055 Shelby Oaks Dr (38134), I-40 exit 12, east of downtown.* 901/388-6111; FAX 901/388-6157. 108 rms, 2 story. S $43.99; D $51.99; each addl $8; under 18 free; higher rates special events. Crib free. Pet accepted, some restrictions. TV; cable (premium). Complimentary coffee in lobby. Restaurant adj open 24 hrs. Ck-out noon. Microwaves avail. Cr cds: A, C, D, DS, MC, V.

D 🐾 🏊 🐾

✔★ **RED ROOF INN SOUTH.** *3875 American Way (38118), east of downtown.* 901/363-2335; FAX 901/363-2822. 109 rms, 3 story. S $38.99-$54.99; D $41.99-$49.99; each addl $8; under 18 free. Pet accepted. TV; cable (premium). Complimentary coffee in lobby. Ck-out noon. Cr cds: A, C, D, DS, MC, V.

D 🐾 🏊 🐾

★ ★ **RESIDENCE INN BY MARRIOTT.** *6141 Poplar Pike (38119), east of downtown.* 901/685-9595; FAX 901/685-1636. 105 kit. suites, 4 story. Kit. suites $109-$154. Crib free. Pet accepted, some restrictions; $100-$200. TV; cable, (premium). Pool; whirlpool. Complimentary continental bkfst. Restaurant nearby. Ck-out noon. Coin lndry. Meeting rms. Business servs avail. Health club privileges. Microwaves. Private patios, balconies. Cr cds: A, C, D, DS, JCB, MC, V.

D 🐾 ≈ 🏊 🐾 SC

Motor Hotels

★ ★ **COMFORT INN-POPLAR EAST.** *5877 Poplar Ave (38119), east of downtown.* 901/767-6300; FAX 901/767-0098. 126 rms, 5 story. S, D $68-$79; each addl $6; under 18 free; higher rates special events. Crib free. Pet accepted, some restrictions, $20. TV; cable (premium). Pool. Complimentary continental bkfst. Rm serv. Ck-out noon. Meeting rms. Bellhops. Sundries. Free airport transportation. Exercise equipt. Cr cds: A, D, DS, MC, V.

D ⚓ ≈ ⨇ ⊠ 🐾 SC

★ ★ **COUNTRY SUITES BY CARLSON.** *4300 American Way (38118), east of downtown.* 901/366-9333; FAX 901/366-7835. 120 kit. suites, 3 story. Kit. suites $69-$99; under 16 free. Crib free. Pet accepted. TV; cable (premium). Pool; whirlpool. Complimentary continental bkfst. Complimentary coffee in rms. Restaurant adj open 24 hrs. Ck-out noon. Coin lndry. Meeting rms. Business servs avail. Valet serv. Sundries. Free airport transportation. Microwaves. Cr cds: A, C, D, DS, MC, V.

D ⚓ ≈ ⨇ ⊠ 🐾 SC

★ ★ **FRENCH QUARTER SUITES.** *2144 Madison Ave (38104), in Overton Square.* 901/728-4000; FAX 901/278-1262; res: 800/843-0353 (exc TN). 105 suites, 4 story. Suites $121-$190. Crib free. TV; cable (premium). Pool. Complimentary continental bkfst. Bar 5-11 pm; Fri, Sat to midnight; entertainment Wed-Sat. Ck-out noon. Meeting rms. Business servs avail. Free airport transportation. Exercise equipt. Some bathrm phones, refrigerators, in-rm whirlpools; microwave avail. Private patios, balconies. Interior atrium; New Orleans decor. Cr cds: A, C, D, DS, ER, JCB, MC, V.

D ≈ ⨇ ⊠ SC

★ ★ **RADISSON INN MEMPHIS AIRPORT.** *2411 Winchester Rd (38116), at Intl Airport, south of downtown.* 901/332-2370; res: 800/333-3333; FAX 901/398-4085. Web www.radisson.com. 211 rms, 3 story. S, D $99-$119; suites $125; under 12 free; wkend rates; higher rates special events. Crib free. TV; cable. Pool. Restaurant 6 am-2 pm, 5-10 pm. Rm serv. Bar 4 pm-midnight. Ck-out noon. Meeting rms. Business servs avail. Bellhops. Sundries. Free airport transportation. Exercise equipt. Lighted tennis. Cr cds: A, C, D, DS, ER, JCB, MC, V.

D ⚓ ≈ ⨇ ⨉ ⊠ 🐾 SC

★ ★ **RIDGEWAY INN.** *5679 Poplar Ave (38119), at I-240, east of downtown.* 901/766-4000; FAX 901/763-1857; res: 800/822-3360. 155 rms, 7 story. S, D $94-$129; each addl $15; suites $195-$295; under 12 free. Crib free. TV; cable (premium). Pool. Restaurant 6:30 am-11 pm; Fri, Sat to 1 am; Sun to 10 pm. Rm serv. Bar from 11 am; Fri, Sat to 1 am; Sun noon-10 pm. Ck-out noon. Meeting rm. Business servs avail. Free airport transportation. Exercise equipt. Health club privileges. Luxury level. Cr cds: A, C, D, DS, ER, MC, V.

D ≈ ⨇ ⊠ 🐾 SC

★ ★ **WILSON WORLD.** *2715 Cherry Rd (38118), east of downtown.* 901/366-0000; FAX 901/366-6361; res: 800/872-8366. 178 rms, 4 story, 90 suites. S, D $79-$85; each addl $6; suites $89-$99; under 18 free. Crib free. TV; cable (premium). Indoor pool. Restaurant 6 am-2 pm, 5:30-10 pm. Rm serv. Bar from 5 pm; pianist exc Sat, Sun. Ck-out noon. Meeting rms. Business servs avail. Bellhops. Gift shop. Barber, beauty shop. Free airport transportation. Refrigerators, wet bars. Balconies. Cr cds: A, D, DS, MC, V.

D ≈ ⨇ 🐾 SC

Hotels

★ ★ **ADAM'S MARK.** *939 Ridge Lake Blvd (38120), east of downtown.* 901/684-6664; FAX 901/762-7411. 408 rms, 27 story. S, D $119-$165; each addl $10; suites $250-$600; under 18 free; wkend rates. Crib free. TV; cable (premium). Pool. Restaurant 6:30 am-10 pm; Fri, Sat to 11 pm. Bar noon-1 am; Sun to midnight; entertainment. Ck-out noon.

Convention facilities. Business servs avail. Gift shop. Free airport transportation. Exercise equipt. Wet bar in suites. Cr cds: A, D, DS, MC, V.

D ≈ ⨇ ⊠ 🐾 SC

★ ★ ★ **CROWNE PLAZA.** *250 N Main (38103), downtown.* 901/527-7300; FAX 901/526-1561. Web www.crowneplaza.com. 402 rms, 18 story. S $125-$155; D $125-$175; each addl $10; suites $250-$400; under 18 free. Crib free. Pet accepted, some restrictions. Valet parking $10, garage $5. TV; cable (premium). Indoor pool; whirlpool. Restaurant 6 am-11 pm. Bar 11-2 am. Ck-out noon. Convention facilities. Business center. Concierge. Shopping arcade. Exercise equipt; sauna. Some refrigerators. Cr cds: A, C, D, DS, JCB, MC, V.

D ⚓ ≈ ⨇ ⊠ 🐾 SC ⛷

★ ★ ★ **EMBASSY SUITES.** *1022 S Shady Grove Rd (38120), east of downtown.* 901/684-1777; FAX 901/685-8185. 220 suites, 5 story. Suites $129-$149; under 12 free; wkend rates. Crib free. TV; cable (premium). Indoor pool; whirlpool. Complimentary full bkfst. Complimentary coffee in rms. Restaurant 11 am-10 pm. Bar to 11 pm. Ck-out noon. Coin lndry. Convention facilities. Business servs avail. In-rm modem link. Gift shop. Free airport transportation. Exercise equipt. Game rm. Refrigerators. Cr cds: A, C, D, DS, MC, V.

D ≈ ⨇ ⊠ 🐾 SC

★ ★ **FOUR POINTS BY SHERATON.** *2240 Democrat Rd (38132), near Intl Airport, south of downtown.* 901/332-1130; FAX 901/398-5206. 380 rms, 5 story. S $99-$114; D $109; each addl $10; suites $179-$450; under 18 free. Crib free. TV; cable. Pool; poolside serv. Restaurant 6 am-11 pm. Bars 3-11 pm. Fri, Sat to midnight, Sun 3:30-11 pm. Ck-out noon. Convention facilities. Business center. Free airport transportation. 2 lighted tennis courts. Exercise equipt; sauna. Wet bar in suites. Indoor courtyard. Cr cds: A, C, D, DS, ER, MC, V.

D ⚓ ≈ ⨇ ⨉ ⊠ 🐾 SC ⛷

★ ★ **HOLIDAY INN MIDTOWN MEDICAL CENTER.** *1837 Union Ave (38104), in Overton Square.* 901/278-4100; FAX 901/272-3810. 173 rms, 8 story. S, D $65-$70; suites $85-$154; under 18 free. Crib free. TV; cable. Pool. Restaurant 6 am-10 pm. Bar 5-11 pm. Ck-out noon. Meeting rms. Business servs avail. Free airport transportation. Health club privileges. Cr cds: A, C, D, DS, ER, JCB, MC, V.

D ≈ ⊠ 🐾 SC

★ ★ ★ **HOLIDAY INN SELECT.** *160 Union Ave (38103), at 2nd St, downtown.* 901/525-5491; FAX 901/525-5491, ext. 2399. 190 rms, 14 story. S, D $109-$129; each addl $10; suites $199; under 18 free. Crib free. TV; cable (premium). Pool. Restaurant 6 am-midnight. Rm serv. Bar 4 pm-midnight, Sat to 2 am. Ck-out 11 am. Meeting rms. Business center. In-rm modem link. Valet serv. Airport transportation. Exercise equipt. Wet bar in suites. Refrigerators. Cr cds: A, C, D, DS, ER, JCB, MC, V.

D ≈ ⨇ ⊠ 🐾 SC ⛷

★ ★ ★ **MARRIOTT.** *2625 Thousand Oaks Blvd (38118), southeast of downtown; I-240, exit 18.* 901/362-6200; FAX 901/360-8836. 320 rms, 12 story. S $79-$146; D $79-$161; suites $200-$350; under 18 free. Crib free. Pet accepted. TV; cable (premium). 2 pools, 1 indoor; whirlpool. Restaurant 6:30 am-11 pm; wkends from 7 am. Bars 11-2 am. Ck-out noon. Convention facilities. Business servs avail. In-rm modem link. Concierge. Free airport transportation. Exercise equipt; sauna. Some bathrm phones, refrigerators. Luxury level. Cr cds: A, C, D, DS, ER, JCB, MC, V.

D ⚓ ≈ ⨇ ⊠ 🐾 SC

★ ★ ★ **PEABODY.** *149 Union Ave (38103), downtown.* 901/529-4000; FAX 901/529-3600; res: 800/732-2639. This Italian Renaissance hostelry, opened in 1869, was rebuilt in 1925 and restored to its former opulence. An ornate travertine marble fountain is home to famed resident ducks, who waddle down from their penthouse apartment each morning and return each evening. 468 rms, 13 story. S $140-$295; D $160-$320; each addl $35; suites $285-$945; under 18 free. Crib free. TV; cable (premium), VCR avail. Heated pool; whirlpool. Restaurants 6:30 am-midnight (also see CHEZ PHILLIPE and DUX). Rm serv 24 hrs. Bar 11-2 am; entertainment. Ck-out 11 am. Convention facilities. Business center. In-rm modem link. Concierge. Shopping arcade. Barber, beauty shop. Extensive exercise rm; sauna, steam rm. Massage. Cr cds: A, C, D, DS, ER, JCB, MC, V.

D ⊠ ✗ ⊠ ⚲ SC ⚶

★ ★ **RADISSON.** *185 Union Ave (38103), downtown.* 901/528-1800; FAX 901/526-3226. 280 rms, 10 story. S, D $109-$119; each addl $10; suites $125-$245; under 18 free. Crib free. Garage/valet $5. TV; cable (premium). Pool; whirlpool. Restaurant 6-2 am. Bar 11 am-midnight. Ck-out noon. Convention facilities. Business servs avail. Gift shop. Exercise equipt; sauna. Near Beale St, Mud Island and Pyramid. Cr cds: A, C, D, DS, ER, JCB, MC, V.

D ⊠ ✗ ⊠ ⚲ SC

Restaurants

★ **ALFRED'S.** *197 Beale St (38103), in Beale St Area.* 901/525-3711. Hrs: 11-5 am. Bar. Semi-a la carte: lunch $3.95-$4.95, dinner $4.99-$14.99. Specializes in blackened catfish, barbecue ribs. Rock & Roll Tue-Sun. Parking. Outdoor dining. Cr cds: A, D, DS, MC, V.

D ⊒

★ ★ **ANDERTON'S.** *1901 N Madison (38104), in Overton Square.* 914/726-4010. Hrs: 11 am-10 pm; Sat 4-11 pm. Closed Sun; most major hols. Res accepted. Bar. Semi-a la carte: lunch $5.25-$16, dinner $9.75-$26.95. Child's meals. Specializes in seafood, steak, oyster bar. Parking. Family-owned. Cr cds: A, C, D, DS, MC, V.

D ⊒

★ ★ **AUBERGINE.** *5007 Black Rd (38117), east of downtown.* 901/767-7840. Hrs: 11:30 am-2 pm, 6-9:30 pm; Sat from 6 pm. Closed Sun, Mon; major hols. Res accepted. French menu. Serv bar. A la carte entrees: lunch $10, dinner $20-$25. Specialties: roasted breast of duck a la orange, roasted thigh of chicken with escargot, warm chocolate pyramid cake. Intimate dining. Totally nonsmoking. Cr cds: A, C, D, MC, V.

D

★ **AUTOMATIC SLIM'S TONGA CLUB.** *83 S Second St (38103), downtown.* 901/525-7948. Hrs: 11 am-2:30 pm, 5-10 pm; Fri to 11 pm; Sat 5-11 pm. Closed Sun; Jan 1, July 4, Dec 25. Res accepted. Jamaican menu. Bar. Semi-a la carte: lunch $4.75-$8.95, dinner $12.95-$21.95. Child's meals. Specialties: Argentinian-style churrasco, stacked tenderloin, hauchinango. Jazz Fri. Caribbean decor. Cr cds: A, MC, V.

D ⊒

★ ★ **BENIHANA OF TOKYO.** *912 Ridge Lake Blvd, east of downtown.* 901/683-7390. Hrs: 11:30 am-2 pm, 5-10 pm; Fri, Sat to 11 pm; Sun noon-2:30 pm, 5-10 pm; early-bird dinner 5-7 pm. Res accepted. Japanese menu. Bar 4:30-10 pm. Complete meals: lunch $5.75-$13.50, dinner $13-$28. Child's meals. Parking. Cr cds: A, C, D, DS, MC, V.

D ⊒

✔★ **BOSCOS PIZZA KITCHEN & BREWERY.** *(7615 W Farmington, Germantown 38138) E on US 72, at Poplar Ave, in Saddle Creek Shopping Plaza.* 901/756-7310. Hrs: 11 am-10:30 pm; Fri, Sat to 12:30 am. Closed Thanksgiving, Dec 25. Bar. Semi-a la carte: lunch $3.95-$8.95, dinner $4.95-$14.95. Specializes in wood-fired oven pizza, pasta. Own beer brewery. Parking. Outdoor dining. Contemporary decor. Cr cds: A, C, D, DS, MC, V.

D SC ⊒

★ **BUCKLEY'S FINE FILET GRILL.** *5355 Poplar Ave (38119), at Estate Dr, east of downtown.* 901/683-4538. Hrs: 4-9:30 pm; Fri, Sat to 10:30 pm. Closed Thanksgiving, Dec 24, 25. Bar. Semi-a la carte: dinner $8.99-$17.49. Specializes in filet steak, pasta. Parking. Artwork and hanging plants create a friendly atmosphere in this local favorite. Cr cds: A, D, DS, MC, V.

D ⊒

✔★ **BUNTYN.** *3070 Southern Ave (38111), east of downtown.* 901/458-8776. Hrs: 11 am-8 pm. Closed Sat, Sun; major hols. Semi-a la carte: lunch, dinner $3.50-$6.80. Child's meals. Specializes in meatloaf, chicken, beef tips. Own baking. Family-owned since 1920. Cr cds: MC, V.

D ⊒

★ ★ ★ **CHEZ PHILIPPE.** *(See Peabody Hotel)* 901/529-4188. Continental menu. Specialties: hushpuppies stuffed with shrimp provençale, roasted lamb rack. Hrs: 6-10 pm. Closed Sun; most major hols. Res accepted. Serv bar. Wine list. A la carte entrees: dinner $20-$30. Jacket. Elegant decor; high ceilings, silk drapes, large murals. Cr cds: A, C, D, DS, ER, JCB, MC, V.

D ⊒ ♥

★ ★ **CIAO BABY CUCINA.** *135 S Main St (38103), downtown.* 901/529-0560. Hrs: 11:30 am-10 pm; Fri to 11 pm; Sat 5-11 pm; Sun 5-9 pm. Closed most major hols. Res accepted. Mediterranean menu. Bar. Semi-a la carte: lunch $7-$11, dinner $11-$20. Lunch buffet $7.95. Child's meals. Specialties: farfalle with chicken and gorgonzola, roma tomato, grilled Atlantic halibut. Mediterranean decor; gourmet coffee shop adj. Cr cds: A, MC, V.

D ⊒

✔★ ★ **COOKER BAR & GRILLE.** *6120 Poplar Ave, east of downtown.* 901/685-2800. Hrs: 11 am-10:30 pm; Fri, Sat to 11:30 pm. Closed Thanksgiving, Dec 25. Bar. Semi-a la carte: lunch $2.95-$7.95, dinner $6.95-$14.95. Child's meals. Specializes in meat loaf, pot roast, pasta. Cr cds: A, D, DS, MC, V.

D ⊒ ♥

★ ★ ★ **DUX.** *(See Peabody Hotel)* 901/529-4199. Hrs: 6:30-10:30 am, 11:30 am-2:30 pm; 5:30-11 pm; Fri to midnight; Sat noon-2:30 pm, 5:30-midnight; Sun 6:30-11:30 am, 5:30 pm-midnight. Res accepted. Bar. Wine list. Semi-a la carte: bkfst $3.95-$13.95, lunch $6.95-$14.95, dinner $5.95-$28.95. Child's meals. Specializes in mesquite-grilled Black Angus steak and seafood. Own baking. Valet parking. Cr cds: A, C, D, DS, JCB, MC, V.

D ⊒ ♥

★ **ERIKA'S.** *52 S Second (38103), downtown.* 901/526-5522. Hrs: 11 am-2 pm; Fri, Sat 11 am-2 pm, 5:30-10 pm. Closed Sun; major hols. German menu. Beer. Semi-a la carte: lunch $4.95-$8.95, dinner $5-$11. Cr cds: A, C, D, DS, MC, V.

D ⊒

★ ★ ★ **ERLING JENSEN.** *1044 S Yates Rd (38119), east of downtown.* 901/763-3700. Hrs: 5-10 pm; Sun brunch 11:30 am-2 pm. Closed some major hols. Res accepted. French menu. Serv bar. Wine cellar. Semi-a la carte: dinner $25-$32. Sun brunch $24. Specializes in game, fresh seafood, veal. Elegant atmosphere. Totally nonsmoking. Cr cds: A, D, MC, V.

D

★ ★ **FOLK'S FOLLY.** *551 S Mendenhall Rd (38117), east of downtown.* 901/762-8200. Web www.memphistravel.com/folksfolly. Hrs: 6-11 pm; Sat from 5 pm; Sun 6-10 pm. Closed most major hols; also Jan 2. Res accepted. Bar. A la carte entrees: dinner $15.50-$36. Specializes in steak, seafood. Own desserts. Pianist Mon-Sat. Valet parking. Private, intimate dining. Cr cds: A, C, D, MC, V.

D ⊒

✔★ **INDIA PALACE.** *1720 Poplar Ave (38104), in Overton Square.* 901/278-1199. Hrs: 11 am-2:30 pm, 5-10 pm; Fri-Sun 11 am-3 pm, 5-10 pm. Closed Thanksgiving, Dec 25. Res accepted. Indian menu. Lunch buffet $5.95. Semi-a la carte: dinner $5.95-$10.95. Specialties: chicken Tikka massala, Palak paneer, Tandoori chicken. Own baking. Elephant and tiger murals; Indian decor. Cr cds: A, D, DS, MC, V.

D ⊒

★ ★ **LA TOURELLE.** *2146 Monroe Ave (38104), near Overton Square.* 901/726-5771. Hrs: 6-10 pm; Sun brunch 11 am-2 pm. Closed Jan

1, Thanksgiving, Dec 25. Res accepted. French menu. Wine cellar. A la carte entrees: dinner $21-$30. Complete meal: dinner $50. Specialties: rosemary-marinated rack of lamb, herb-coated veal chop, grilled mahi mahi. Own baking. Converted 1910 home; intimate dining. Totally non-smoking. Cr cds: MC, V.

★ ★ **LULU GRILLE.** *565 Erin Dr (38117), east of downtown. 901/763-3677.* E-mail eat@lulugrille.com; web www.lulugrille.com. Hrs: 11 am-10 pm; Fri, Sat to 11 pm. Closed Sun; most major hols. Res accepted. Bar. Semi-a la carte: lunch $5.95-$10.95, dinner $8.50-$22.95. Specializes in fresh seafood, pasta, game. Outdoor dining. Bistro atmosphere. Cr cds: A, C, D, DS, MC, V.

★ **MELOS TAVERNA.** *2021 Madison Ave (38104), in Overton Square. 901/725-1863.* Hrs: 4:30-10:30 pm. Closed Sun, Mon; July 4, Thanksgiving, Dec 25. Res accepted. Greek menu. Bar. Semi-a la carte: dinner $8.75-$21. Specializes in lamb, moussaka. Parking. Greek artwork. Cr cds: A, C, D, DS, MC, V.

★ ★ **PAULETTE'S.** *2110 Madison Ave (38104), in Overton Square. 901/726-5128.* Hrs: 11 am-10 pm; Fri, Sat to 11 pm; Sat, Sun brunch to 4 pm. Closed major hols. Res accepted. Continental menu. Bar. Semi-a la carte: lunch $6.95-$11.95, dinner $11.95-$21.95. Sat, Sun brunch $6.95-$12.95. Child's meals. Specialties: filet Paulette, grilled salmon, crabcakes. Pianist Fri-Sun. Parking. Cr cds: A, D, DS, MC, V.

★ ★ **THE PIER.** *100 Wagner Pl (38103), downtown. 901/526-7381.* Hrs: 5-9:30 pm; Fri, Sat to 10 pm. Closed most major hols. Super Bowl Sun. Res accepted. Semi-a la carte: dinner $11.95-$23.95. Special-izes in New England clam chowder, prime rib, fresh fish. On river; nautical decor. Cr cds: A, D, DS, MC, V.

★ **THE PUBLIC EYE.** *17 S Cooper (38104), in Overton Square. 901/726-4040.* Hrs: 11 am-10 pm; Fri, Sat to midnight; lunch buffet to 2 pm. Closed Jan 1, Dec 25. Bar. Semi-a la carte: lunch $4-$7, dinner $5-$20. Buffet: lunch $5.95. Child's meals. Specializes in barbecued pork, ribs. Parking. Cr cds: A, C, D, DS, MC, V.

★ ★ ★ **RAJI.** *712 W Brookhaven Circle, east of downtown. 901/685-8723.* French, Indian menu. Specialties: tandoori game hens with corn and cumin tomato sauce, grilled scallops and lobster in lentil pastry with ginger-flavored beurre blanc. Hrs: 7-11 pm. Closed Sun, Mon; most major hols. Res required. Bar. Wine list. Semi-a la carte: dinner $40. Several elegant dining rms in former residence. Totally nonsmoking. Cr cds: A, MC, V.

★ ★ **RONNIE GRISANTA & SONS.** *2855 Poplar Ave (38111), east of downtown. 901/323-0007.* Hrs: 5-11 pm. Closed Sun; major hols; also 1st wk July. Italian menu. Bar. Semi-a la carte: dinner $9.95-$25.95. Child's meals. Specialties: grilled porterhouse steak with truffles, grilled tuna in putenesca sauce, frutti di mare. Parking. Italian artwork. Cr cds: A, MC, V.

✔★ **SAIGON LE.** *51 N Cleveland (38104), east of downtown. 901/276-5326.* Hrs: 11 am-9:30 pm. Closed Sun; Thanksgiving, Dec 25. Res accepted. Chinese, Vietnamese menu. Semi-a la carte: lunch $3.45-$3.95, dinner $6.45-$8.75. Specialties: roasted wheat clute, Saigon egg roll, green shell mussels with French butter. Own baking. Casual dining. Cr cds: A, D, DS, MC, V.

Unrated Dining Spots

BUTCHER SHOP. *101 S Front St (38103), downtown. 901/521-0856.* Hrs: 5-10 pm; Fri, Sat to 11 pm. Closed Jan 1, Thanksgiv-ing, Dec 24, 25. Bar. Option to select and cook own steak. Served with salad, potato and bread $15-$21. Child's meals. Salad bar. Grill in dining room; 1907 building. Cr cds: A, D, DS, MC, V.

RENDEZVOUS. *52 S 2nd St, in Gen Washburn Alley, downtown. 901/523-2746.* Hrs: 4:30-11 pm; Fri from 11:30 am; Sat from 12:30 pm. Closed Sun, Mon; also 2 wks late July, 2 wks late Dec. Bar (beer). Semi-a la carte: lunch, dinner $3-$10. Specializes in barbecued ribs. In 1890 downtown building; memorabilia, many antiques, collectibles; jukebox. Cr cds: A, C, D, MC, V.

Monteagle (E-6)

(See also Manchester)

Pop 1,138 **Elev** 1,927 ft **Area code** 931 **Zip** 37356
Information Oliver's Smoke House Motor Lodge and Restaurant, US 64, US 41A, Box 579; 931/924-2091 or 800/489-2091.

A popular summer resort for more than a century, Monteagle is also famous for its Chautauqua Assembly, which has been held every summer since 1882.

What to See and Do

South Cumberland State Park. Extensive park system in southeastern Tennessee comprised of nine separate areas. Visitor Center is located east of Monteagle on US 41. Contact the Park Manager, Rte 1, Box 2196; 931/924-2980 or -2956. Within the system are

Carter State Natural Area. A 140-acre area that includes the Lost Cove Caves. 5 mi S of Sewanee on TN 56. **Free.**

Sewanee Natural Bridge. A 2-acre area that features a 25-ft sandstone arch overlooking Lost Cove. 2 mi S of Sewanee on TN 56. **Free.**

Foster Falls Small Wild Area. Foster Falls has the largest volume of water of any falls in the South Cumberland Recreation Area. Hiking. Picnicking. Camping (mid-Apr-mid-Oct). 7 mi S of Tracy City on US 41. **Free.**

Grundy Forest State Natural Area. Tracy City. Sycamore Falls, a 12-ft-high waterfall lying in the bottom of the Fiery Gizzard Gorge, and Chimney Rocks, a unique geological formation, are highlights of this 212-acre recreational area. The Fiery Gizzard Hiking Trail winds around moss-laden cliffs and mountain laurel to connect the forest with the Foster Falls Small Wild Area. Picnicking. **Free.**

Grundy Lakes State Park. An 81-acre site features the Lone Rock Coke Ovens. These ovens, operated in the late 1800s with convict labor, were used in making coke for the smelting of iron ore. Swimming. Hiking. Picnicking. Tracy City. **Free.**

Savage Gulf State Natural Area. Covering 11,500 acres, the area offers 70 miles of wilderness hiking trails, backcountry camping and rock climbing. The Savage Gulf cuts deep into the Cumberland Plateau and shelters virgin timber, rock cliffs, caves and many waterfalls. 27 mi NE, near Palmer on County 399E. **Free.**

Great Stone Door. An unique rock formation that is a 150-ft-high crevice at the crest of the Cumberland Plateau above Big Creek Gulf. Panoramic view of the area. Hiking. Picnicking. Near Bersheba Springs. **Free.**

University of the South (1857). (1,100 students) Campus covering 10,000 acres at an elevation of 2,000 ft features scenic mountain over-looks, hiking trails, waterfalls and caves; Gothic-revival architecture. On campus are duPont Library Collection of rare books and manuscripts (daily exc Sun); All Saints' Chapel; Leonidas Polk Carillon (concerts Sun). 4 mi SW via US 64, in Sewanee. For general information and details on free guided tours phone 931/598-1286.

Seasonal Events

Sewanee Summer Music Center Concerts. Guerry Hall, Univ of the South. 4-day festival concludes season. Phone 931/598-1225 or -1286. Wkends, late June-early Aug.

Monteagle Chautauqua Assembly. Concerts, lectures, academic courses, art classes. Phone 931/924-2268. Early July-late Aug.

Motel

✔★ ★ **BEST WESTERN-JIM OLIVER'S SMOKE HOUSE MO-TOR LODGE.** 850 Main St, I-24 exit 134. 931/924-2091; FAX 931/924-3175; res: 800/489-2091. Web www.thesmokehouse.com. 97 rms, 2 story. S $39-$69; D $49-$79; each addl $5; suites $75-$120; 1-2-bedrm cabins $99-$166; under 13 free. Crib $5. Pet accepted. TV; cable (premium). Pool. Playground. Restaurant 6 am-10 pm. Rm serv. Ck-out 11 am. Meeting rms. Business servs avail. Sundries. Tennis. Microwaves avail. Cr cds: A, DS, MC, V.

Inn

★ ★ **ADAMS EDGEWORTH INN.** Monteagle Assembly Grounds, I-24 exit 134. 931/924-4000; res: 877/352-9466; FAX 931/924-3236. E-mail innjoy@worldnet.att.net; web innjoy.com. 13 rms, 3 story, 1 suite. S, D $90-$145; each addl $25; suite $150-$185. Crib $25. TV in some rms, library. Complimentary full bkfst. Complimentary coffee in library. Ck-out 11 am, ck-in 4 pm. Antiques, art collection in 1896 building. On grounds of Monteagle Chatauqua Assembly. Cr cds: A, MC, V.

Morristown (D-9)

Settled 1783 **Pop** 21,385 **Elev** 1,350 ft **Area code** 423 **Zip** 37814
Information Chamber of Commerce, 825 W 1st North St, PO Box 9, 37815; 423/586-6382.

Bounded by Clinch Mountain and the Great Smoky Mountains, Morristown is a major manufacturing center. Davy Crockett lived in the town from 1794 to 1809.

What to See and Do

Cherokee Dam and Lake. TVA dam (6,760 ft long, 175 ft high) on Holston River. Fishing; boating. Visitor building & powerhouse tours (daily). 14 mi SW on US 11E to Jefferson City, then 5 mi N on TN 92. Phone 423/475-3136. **Free.**

Panther Creek State Park. More than 1,400 acres on Cherokee Lake. Swimming pool; fishing. Hiking trails. Picnic sites, playground. Campground. Visitors center. Standard fees. 4 mi S on US 11E, then 2 mi W on Panther Creek Rd. Phone 423/587-7046.

Rose Center. Historic building serves as a cultural center and includes a children's "touch" museum, historical classroom art gallery and historical museum. (Mon-Fri; closed some major hols) 442 W Second North St. Phone 423/581-4330. **Free.**

Motels

✔★ **DAYS INN.** 2512 E Andrew Johnson Hwy, I-81 exit 8. 423/587-2200; res: 800/329-7466; FAX 423/587-9752. 65 rms, 2 story. S $38-$48; D $42-$52; each addl $5; under 12 free; higher rates special events. Crib free. Pet accepted, some restrictions. TV; cable (premium). Complimentary continental bkfst. Restaurant nearby. Ck-out 11 am. Business servs avail. In-rm modem link. Some in-rm whirlpools, refrigerators. Cr cds: A, C, D, DS, MC, V.

★ ★ **HOLIDAY INN.** 3304 W Andrew Johnson Hwy. 423/581-8700; FAX 423/581-7128. 118 rms, 2 story. S, D $58-$84; each addl $6; under 18 free. Crib free. TV; cable. Pool. Restaurant 6 am-2 pm, 5-10 pm; Sun from 7 am. Rm serv. Ck-out noon. Meeting rms. Business servs avail. Sundries. Health club privileges. Cr cds: A, C, D, DS, JCB, MC, V.

★ ★ **RAMADA INN.** (37815). 6 mi S at I-81 & US 25E exit 8. 423/587-2400; res: 800/272-6232; FAX 423/581-7344. E-mail ramadam@ usit.net. 112 rms, 3 story. No elvtr. S, D $59-$94; each addl $5; higher rates special events. Crib free. Pet accepted. TV; cable. 2 pools; wading pool. Playground. Complimentary coffee in rms. Restaurant 6 am-2 pm, 5-9 pm. Rm serv. Ck-out noon. Meeting rms. Business servs avail. Exercise equipt. Private patios, balconies. Cr cds: A, C, D, DS, JCB, MC, V.

✔★ **SUPER 8.** 2430 E Andrew Johnson Hwy, I-81 exit 8. 423/586-8880; FAX 423/585-0654. 63 rms, 2 story. S $35-$40; D $39-$46; each addl $5; under 12 free; higher rates special events. Crib free. Pet accepted; $25. TV; cable (premium). Complimentary continental bkfst. Restaurant nearby. Ck-out 11 am. Meeting rms. Business servs avail. In-rm modem link. Health club privileges. Some in-rm whirlpools, refrigerators, microwaves. Cr cds: A, C, D, DS, MC, V.

Murfreesboro (D-5)

(See also Lebanon, Nashville)

Founded 1811 **Pop** 44,922 **Elev** 619 ft **Area code** 615
Information Rutherford County Chamber of Commerce, 501 Memorial Blvd, PO Box 864, 37133-0864; 615/893-6565.

Murfreesboro lies in the geographic center of Tennessee. Because of this strategic location, the town was almost named the state capital. The legislature did meet in Murfreesboro from 1819 to 1826, but it never returned after convening in Nashville. The area is rich in Civil War history and is known as the "antique center of the South." Rutherford County is also noted for its production of cattle and prize-winning Tennessee walking horses.

What to See and Do

Oaklands. This 19th-century mansion, an architectural blend of four different periods, was a social center before the Civil War and command headquarters for Union Colonel W.W. Duffield, who surrendered Murfreesboro to Confederate General Nathan Bedford Forrest at the house. Rooms restored and furnished with items appropriate to the Civil War period. Grounds landscaped in period style. (Daily exc Mon; closed major hols) 900 N Maney Ave, 2 mi N of I-24. Phone 615/893-0022. ¢¢

Stones River National Battlefield. Park covering approx 400 acres preserves the site of the Battle of Stones River (Dec 31, 1862-Jan 2, 1863), a bitter clash resulting in 10,000 Confederate and 13,000 Union casualties. The Confederates failed in this attempt to halt the Union advance on Chattanooga. The park includes the Hazen Monument (1863), one of the oldest memorials of the Civil War, and the National Cemetery, with 7,000 graves, tablets and markers. Self-guided tours; auto tape tour (1¼ hrs) at visitor center. Living history demonstrations, summer wkends. Visitor center has battlefield museum, films (daily). Battlefield and National Cemetery (daily; closed Dec 25). 3 mi from I-24 exit 78 on US 41/70S. Contact the Superintendent, 3501 Old Nashville Hwy, 37129; 615/893-9501. **Free.**

Annual Events

Street Festival & Folkfest. International dancers, arts & crafts. Early May.

Uncle Dave Macon Days. Old-time music, dance, arts & crafts; 615/893-2369. 2nd wkend July.

International Grand Championship Walking Horse Show. Early Aug.

Motels

✓★ ★ HAMPTON INN. 2230 Old Fort Pkwy (37129). 615/896-1172; FAX 615/895-4277. 119 rms, 2 story. S, D $59-$66; each addl $5; under 18 free. Crib free. Pet accepted, some restrictions. TV; cable, VCR avail. Pool. Complimentary continental bkfst. Restaurant adj open 24 hrs. Ck-out noon. Meeting rm. Business servs avail. Microwaves avail. Cr cds: A, C, D, DS, MC, V.

`D` `⚡` `≋` `⊠` `🐾` `SC`

★ ★ HOWARD JOHNSON. 2424 S Church St (37130), at jct US 231 & I-24. 615/896-5522; FAX 615/890-0024. 79 rms, 2 story. S $29.95-$69; D $34.95-$79; each addl $5; under 17 free; higher rates special events. Crib free. Pet accepted, some restrictions; $5. TV; cable (premium). Pool. Complimentary continental bkfst. Restaurant adj 11 am-8 pm. Ck-out 11 am. Coin lndry. Meeting rm. Business servs avail. Microwaves avail. Cr cds: A, C, D, DS, MC, V.

`D` `⚡` `≋` `⊠` `🐾` `SC`

★ ★ RAMADA LIMITED. 1855 S Church St (37130), I-24 exit 81. 615/896-5080. 80 rms, 2 story. Mar-Dec: S, D $39.95-$75; each addl $5; under 18 free; lower rates rest of yr. Crib free. Pet accepted. TV; cable (premium). Complimentary continental bkfst. Restaurant adj open 24 hrs. Ck-out noon. Meeting rms. Business servs avail. Sundries. Pool. Cr cds: A, C, D, DS, MC, V.

`D` `⚡` `≋` `⊠` `🐾` `SC`

★ ★ SHONEY'S INN. 1954 S Church St (37130). 615/896-6030; FAX 615/896-6037; res: 800/222-2222. 125 rms, 2 story. S, D $51-$57; each addl $6; under 18 free; higher rates special events. Crib free. TV; cable (premium). Pool. Complimentary coffee in lobby. Restaurant adj 6 am-11 pm. Ck-out noon. Meeting rms. Health club privileges. Some refrigerators. Cr cds: A, D, DS, MC, V.

`D` `≋` `⊠` `🐾` `SC`

Motor Hotels

★ ★ ★ GARDEN PLAZA. 1850 Old Fort Pkwy (37129). 615/895-5555; FAX 615/895-5555, ext. 165; res: 800/342-7336. 168 rms, 5 story. S, D $84-$94; each addl $10; suites $129; under 12 free. Crib free. Pet accepted, some restrictions. TV; cable (premium), VCR avail. Indoor/outdoor pool; whirlpool, poolside serv. Restaurant 6:30 am-11 pm. Rm serv. Bar 11 am-midnight. Ck-out noon. Meeting rms. Health club privileges. Refrigerators; some wet bars; microwaves avail. Cr cds: A, C, D, DS, MC, V.

`D` `⚡` `≋` `⊠` `🐾` `SC`

★ ★ HOLIDAY INN. 2227 Old Fort Pkwy (37129), at jct TN 96 & I-24. 615/896-2420; FAX 615/896-8738. 180 rms, 2-4 story. S, D $63-$75; higher rates special events. Crib free. Pet accepted. TV; cable (premium). Indoor/outdoor pool; whirlpool. Complimentary coffee in rms. Restaurant 6-11 am, 4:30-9 pm. Rm serv. Bar 4:30 pm-midnight. Ck-out noon. Coin lndry. Meeting rms. Business servs avail. Bellhops. Valet serv. Exercise equipt. Game rm. Cr cds: A, C, D, DS, JCB, MC, V.

`D` `⚡` `≋` `🏃` `⊠` `🐾` `SC`

★ ★ WINGATE INN. 165 Chaffin Pl (37129). 615/849-9000; res: 800/228-1000; FAX 615/849-9066. Web www.wingateinns.com. 86 rms, 4 story. S, D $65-$85; each addl $10; under 18 free; higher rates Fanfare. Crib free. TV; cable (premium). Complimentary continental bkfst. Complimentary coffee in rms. Restaurant adj 6 am-10 pm. Ck-out 11 am. Meeting rms. Business center. In-rm modem link. Sundries. Coin lndry. Exercise

equipt. Pool; whirlpool. Some refrigerators; in-rm whirlpool, minibar, wet bar in suites. Cr cds: A, D, DS, MC, V.

`D` `≋` `🏃` `⊠` `🐾` `SC` `🏃`

Restaurants

✓★ DEMOS' STEAK AND SPAGHETTI HOUSE. 1115 NW Broad St (37129). 615/895-3701. Hrs: 11 am-10 pm; wkends to 11 pm. Closed Thanksgiving, Dec 24, 25. Bar. Semi-a la carte: lunch $3.95-$6.95, dinner $5.95-$12.95. Child's meals. Specializes in steak, spaghetti, seafood. Parking. Contemporary decor; three dining areas. Cr cds: A, C, D, DS, MC, V.

`D` `🖵`

★ ★ PARTHENON MEDITERRANEAN. 1935 S Church St (37130). 615/895-2665. Hrs: 11 am-10 pm. Closed most major hols. Res accepted. Mediterranean menu. Bar. Semi-a la carte: lunch $5.95-$9.95, dinner $7.95-$21.95. Child's meals. Specialties: veal scalloysina Athena, filet Diana, lamb chops. Greek artwork. Cr cds: A, C, D, MC, V.

`D` `🖵`

✓★ SANTA FE STEAK CO. 127 SE Broad St. 615/890-3030. Hrs: 11 am-11 pm; Fri, Sat to midnight. Bar. Semi-a la carte: lunch $4.29-$6.99, dinner $5.49-$14.99. Child's meals. Specializes in steak, barbecue rib. Parking. Cr cds: A, C, D, DS, MC, V.

`D` `SC` `🖵`

Nashville (D-5)

(See also Franklin, Lebanon, Murfreesboro)

Settled 1779 **Pop** 488,374 **Elev** 440 ft **Area code** 615
Web nashville.musiccityusa.com/tour

Information Convention & Visitors Bureau, 161 4th Ave N, 37219; 615/259-4700.

Commercial center and capital city, Nashville's heritage is part Andrew Jackson's Hermitage and part Grand Ole Opry. It is often referred to as the "Athens of the South" because of its 16 colleges and universities, religious publishing firms and some 750 churches. To prove this point, it has the Parthenon, the only full-size replica of the Athenian architectural masterpiece.

The Nashville region's economy is diverse and the area has benefitted from low unemployment, consistent job growth and a broadening of the labor force. The city is a leader in publishing, finance and insurance, healthcare, music and entertainment, transportation technology, higher education and tourism.

In recent years, millions of dollars in investment capital have been used for new buildings and vast expansion programs. This redevelopment has given the lovely old capital a new and airy setting. Throughout this bustle of commerce and construction, Nashville retains an Old South quality, proud of its gracious homes and its old traditions.

These traditions stem back to the days when, in 1779, a band of pioneers built a log stockade on the west bank of the Cumberland River, naming it Fort Nashborough. The Cumberland Compact established a governing body of 12 judges at this wilderness village. By an act of the North Carolina legislature, the name was changed to Nashville. Nearly 50 years after Tennessee became a state, Nashville was made the permanent capital.

During the Civil War, the city was taken by Union troops in March 1862. In December 1864, a Confederate force under General John Bell Hood moved to the hills south of the city in an attempt to recapture it. However, two Union counterattacks virtually wiped out the Confederate army.

Just as the Cumberland Compact of May 1780 was an innovation in government, so was a new charter, which became effective in 1963, setting up Nashville and Davidson County under a single administration with a legislative body of 40 members.

Transportation

Nashville Intl Airport: Information 615/275-1675; lost and found 615/275-1675; weather 615/244-9393; cash machines, Main Terminal, entry level.

Car Rental Agencies: See IMPORTANT TOLL-FREE NUMBERS.

Public Transportation: Metro Transit Authority, phone 615/862-5950.

What to See and Do

Agricultural Museum. Former horse barn on historic estate. Oldest Agricultural Hall of Fame in US. Farm tools, equipment and household items of 19th and early 20th centuries. (Mon-Fri; closed state hols) Ellington Center, 6 mi S. Phone 615/360-0197. **Free.**

Belle Meade (1853). Mansion and outbuildings were once part of 5,300-acre working plantation. At turn of the century, Belle Meade was considered the greatest Thoroughbred breeding farm in the country. The 14-rm, Greek-revival mansion contains Empire and Victorian furnishings and heirloom showcase with racing trophies and mementos. Also on grounds are Dunham Station log cabin (1793) and the Carriage House (1890s), containing one of the South's largest carriage collections. (Daily; closed Jan 1, Thanksgiving, Dec 25) Harding Rd & Leake Ave, 7 mi SW. Phone 615/356-0501 or 800/270-3991. **¢¢¢**

Belmont Mansion. Built in the 1850s in the style of an Italian villa, this mansion, once considered one of the finest private residences in the US, has original marble statues, Venetian glass, gasoliers, mirrors and paintings in the 15 rms open to public; gardens feature large collection of 19th-century garden ornaments and cast iron gazebos. (June-Aug, daily; rest of yr, Tues-Sat; closed hols) 1900 Belmont Blvd, at Acklen Ave, on Belmont University campus. Phone 615/460-5459. **¢¢¢**

Car Collectors Hall of Fame. Antique car collection featuring cars of country music stars; post-World War I doctor's office; music parlor with rare musical instruments. (Daily; closed Jan 1, Thanksgiving, Dec 25) 1534 Demonbreun St. Phone 615/255-6804. **¢¢**

Cheatham Lake, Lock and Dam. Some recreation areas have swimming; fishing; boating (commercial docks). Camping (fee; electricity addl). Camping closed Nov-Mar. Fees for some areas. 30 mi NW on TN 12, near Ashland City. Phone 615/792-5697 or 615/254-3734.

Cheekwood-Nashville's Home of Art & Gardens. Cultural center on 55 acres includes museum with permanent collection of 19th- and 20th-century American art; Botanic Hall with atrium of tropical flora and changing plant exhibits; public greenhouses featuring orchids, camellias and plants from Central American cloud forests; and five major gardens specializing in dogwood, wildflowers, herbs, daffodils, roses and tulips. (Daily; closed some major hols) 8 mi SW on Forrest Park Dr, next to Percy Warner Park. Phone 615/356-8000. **¢¢**

Country Music Hall of Fame & Museum. Exhibits include Elvis Presley's Cadillac, films, costumes, musical instruments, memorabilia of country music notables. Participatory exhibits. (Daily; closed Jan 1, Thanksgiving, Dec 25) 4 Music Square E. Phone 615/256-1639. **¢¢¢** Also included is a visit to

　RCA Studio B. Studio where music greats recorded. Major renovation has updated the studio's equipment to current standards for session and demo recording.

Country Music Wax Museum and Shopping Mall. More than 60 wax figures; original stage costumes and memorabilia. Record, western wear, crafts and gift shops; restaurant, entertainment. (Daily; closed Thanksgiving, Dec 25) 118 16th Ave S. Phone 615/256-2490. **¢¢**

Cumberland Science Museum. Planetarium, live animal and science programs. (June-Aug, daily; rest of yr, daily exc Mon; closed most hols) 800 Fort Negley Blvd, near Greer Stadium. Phone 615/862-5160. **¢¢¢**

Fisk University (1866). (900 students) A National Historic District with Jubilee Hall, a historic landmark. Carl Van Vechten Art Gallery houses Stieglitz Collection of modern art. Aaron Douglas Gallery houses collection of African art. 17th Ave N. Phone 615/329-8500.

Fort Nashborough. Patterned after the pioneer fort established several blocks from this site in 1779, replica is smaller and has fewer cabins. Stockaded walls, exhibits of pioneer implements. (Daily exc Mon, weather permitting; closed major hols) 170 1st Ave N, at Church St, in N end of Riverfront Park. **Free.**

General Jackson. A 300-ft, 4-deck paddle wheel showboat on Cumberland River highlights a musical stage show in its Victorian Theater. Two-hr day cruises offer entertainment and optional food service; three-hr night cruises offer entertainment and dinner. (All yr; addl cruises in summer) For schedule and departure times, contact Customer Service, 2802 Opryland Dr, 37214; 615/889-6611. **¢¢¢¢**

Gray Line bus tours. Contact 2416 Music Valley Dr, Suite 102, 37214; 615/883-5555 or 800/251-1864.

J. Percy Priest Lake. Waterskiing; fishing; boating (ramps, commercial boat docks). Picnicking. Tent & trailer sites (fee). Visitor center near dam (Mon-Fri). Some areas closed Nov-Mar. 11 mi E off I-40. Phone 615/889-1975.

Museum of Beverage Containers and Advertising. More than 36,000 antique soda and beer cans form the largest collection of its kind. Also on display are thousands of period advertising pieces. (Daily; closed major hols) 15 mi N on I-65 to Millersville, 1055 Ridgecrest Dr. Phone 615/859-5236. **¢**

Museum of Tobacco Art & History. Houses exhibits tracing history of tobacco from Native Americans to present. On display are rare antique pipes, tobacco containers, snuffboxes, cigar-store figures; art, photographs. (Daily exc Sun; closed major hols) 800 Harrison St, at 8th Ave N. Phone 615/271-2349. **Free.**

Music Valley Wax Museum of the Stars. More than 50 lifelike wax figures of famous stars, dressed in authentic costumes. Also features Sidewalk of the Stars with hand and foot imprints of more than 250 stars. (Daily; closed Thanksgiving, Dec 25) 2515 McGavock Pike, NE via Briley Pkwy, exit 12. Phone 615/883-3612. **¢¢**

Nashville Toy Museum. Features unique displays of antique toys, including German and English bears from early 1900s, china dolls from 1850 and lead soldiers in battle dioramas. Train room contains more than 250 toy and model locomotives and two train layouts depicting Tennessee in the 1930s and Britain at the turn of the century. (Daily; closed Thanksgiving, Dec 25) 2613-B McGavock Pike. Phone 615/883-8870. **¢¢**

Old Hickory Lake. Several recreation areas around reservoir have swimming; fishing; boating (commercial docks). Hiking, archery. Picnicking. Tent & trailer sites (fee). (All yr; some areas closed Oct-Mar) 15 mi NE via US 31E, near Hendersonville. Phone 615/822-4846 or 615/847-2395.

★ **Opryland USA Theme Park.** A 120-acre entertainment showpark features American music from jazz and blues to pop, Broadway, country, gospel and rock 'n roll in live musical productions. Family thrill rides include the Screamin' Delta Demon, Wabash Cannonball and Hangman. Playgrounds; petting zoo; craft shops; restaurants. (Memorial Day-Labor Day, late Nov-Dec, Apr-Memorial Day, Labor Day-late Oct, wkends) 10 mi E on I-40, then 4 mi N on Briley Pkwy, exit 11. For information phone 615/889-6611. **¢¢¢¢¢** Opryland complex includes

　Grand Ole Opry. Live radio show featuring the best in country music is broadcast from the Grand Ole Opry House, the world's largest broadcast studio, which seats 4,400. The Opry has been broadcast weekends continuously since 1925. (Wkends all yr; also June-Aug, Tues matinees.) Reservations recommended. For information contact Opryland Customer Service, 2808 Opryland Dr, 37214; phone 615/889-6611. **¢¢¢¢¢**

　Grand Ole Opry Tours. One-hr, 3-hr and all-day bus tours include houses of country music stars, Music Row, recording studios, backstage visit to Grand Ole Opry House. Contact 2810 Opryland Dr, 37214; 615/889-9490. **¢¢¢¢¢**

　Opryland Museums. Located just outside Opryland Park, in the Plaza area, near the Grand Ole Opry House. **Minnie Pearl Museum** features 50 yrs of memorabilia; **Roy Acuff Museum** includes musical instruments; **Grand Ole Opry Museum** pays tribute to country stars with audio/visual and interactive devices. (Daily) **Free.**

Radnor Lake State Natural Area. A 1,100-acre environmental preserve with an 85-acre lake. Provides scenic, biological and geological areas for hiking and nature study. (Daily) 7 mi S on US 31, then 1 1/2 mi W on Otter Creek Rd. Phone 615/373-3467. **Free.**

Ryman Auditorium & Museum. Home of the Grand Ole Opry from 1943-1974. Tour includes a visit to the stage and displays and exhibits detailing the Ryman's unique and varied history. (Daily; closed Jan 1, Thanksgiving, Dec 25) 116 5th Ave N. Phone 615/254-1445. ¢¢

Sam Davis Home. Described as "the most beautiful shrine to a private soldier in the US," this stately house and 168-acre working farm have been preserved as a memorial to Sam Davis, Confederate scout caught behind Union lines and tried as a spy. Offered his life if he revealed the name of his informer, Davis chose to die on the gallows. His boyhood home is restored and furnished with many original pieces; grounds include kitchen, smokehouse, slave cabins and family cemetery where Davis is buried. (Daily; closed Jan 1, Thanksgiving, Dec 25) 20 mi S off I-24 in Smyrna, at 1399 Sam Davis Rd. Phone 615/459-2341. ¢¢

State Capitol (1845-1859). Greek-revival structure with 80-ft tower rising above the city; columns grace the ends and sides. Architect William Strickland died before the building was completed and was buried within its walls. Of special interest are the grand stairway, library, legislative chambers and murals in gubernatorial suite. (Mon-Fri; closed major hols) Charlotte Ave between Sixth & Seventh Aves. Phone 615/741-1621.

Tennessee State Museum. Exhibits on life in Tennessee from early man through the early 1900s. (Daily exc Mon; closed major hols) James K. Polk State Bldg, 5th Ave between Union & Deaderick Sts. Phone 615/741-2692. **Free.**

⭐ **The Hermitage** (1819; rebuilt after a fire in 1834). Greek-revival residence of President Andrew Jackson is furnished almost entirely with original family pieces, many of which were associated with Jackson's military career and years in the White House. Also on 660-acre estate are a garden with graves of Jackson and his wife, Rachel; two log cabins; a church; and visitor center and museum with biographical film on Jackson. (Daily; closed Thanksgiving, Dec 25, also 3rd wk Jan) 12 mi E off I-40 exit 221A, follow sign. Phone 615/889-2941. ¢¢¢ Included in fee is

⭐ **Tulip Grove** (1836). Greek-revival house of Andrew Jackson Donelson, Mrs. Jackson's nephew and President Jackson's private secretary. Interior has examples of 19th-century faux marbling.

The Parthenon. Replica of the Parthenon of Pericles' time was built in plaster for the Tennessee Centennial of 1897 and later reconstructed in concrete aggregate. As in the original, there is not a straight horizontal or vertical line and no two columns are placed the same distance apart. Houses 19th- and 20th-century artworks; changing art exhibits; replicas of Elgin Marbles; 42-foot statue of goddess Athena. (Apr-Sept, daily exc Mon; rest of yr, Tues-Sat; closed Jan 1, Dec 25) In Centennial Park, West End Ave & 25th Ave N. Phone 615/862-8431. ¢¢

The Upper Room Chapel and Museum. Chapel with polychrome wood carving of Leonardo da Vinci's "The Last Supper," said to be largest of its kind in world; also World Christian Fellowship Window. Museum contains various religious artifacts including seasonal displays of 100 nativity scenes and Ukranian eggs. (Mon-Fri; closed major hols) 1908 Grand Ave. Phone 615/340-7207. **Donation.**

Travellers Rest Historic House (1799). Restored Federal-style house of Judge John Overton. Maintained as a historical museum with period furniture, records, letters, the building reflects history and development of early Tennessee. Eleven-acre grounds with formal gardens, kitchen house, smokehouse. Gift shop. Allow at least 45 min for visit. (Tues-Sat, also Sun afternoons; closed Jan 1, Thanksgiving, Dec 25) I-65 exit 78, S on US 31 (Franklin Rd), follow signs. Phone 615/832-8197. ¢¢

Vanderbilt University (1873). (10,000 students) The 330-acre campus features 19th- and 20th-century architectural styles. The Fine Arts Gallery has a permanent collection supplemented by traveling exhibits. Blair School of Music offers regular concerts. West End Ave & 21st Ave S. For campus tours (all yr) phone 615/322-7771.

Annual Events

Running of the Iroquois Memorial Steeplechase. Old Hickory Blvd at entrance to Percy Warner Park. Natural amphitheater seats 100,000. Phone 615/322-7284. 2nd Sat May.

Music festivals. Nashville is host to many festivals, including Summer Lights in Music City (late May-early June), the International Country Music Fan Fair with its Grand Master Old-Time Fiddling Championship (early June), Gospel Music Week (Apr) and Franklin Jazz Festival (Aug).

Tennessee State Fair. Fairgrounds, Wedgewood Ave & Rains. Contact Box 40208-Melrose Station, 37204; 615/862-8980. Sept 11-20.

Longhorn Rodeo. Municipal Auditorium. Professional cowboys compete for world championship points. Phone 615/876-1016. 1 wkend mid-Nov.

A Country Christmas. Opryland Hotel. Offers events ranging from a musical stage show to an art, antique & craft show. Phone 615/871-7637.

Additional Visitor Information

The Nashville Convention and Visitors Bureau, 161 4th Ave N, 37219, has maps, brochures, lists of tour companies and calendar of events; phone 615/259-4700. Advance reservations are strongly advised for the summer season (mid-May-mid-Sept) and all weekends. The Visitor Information Center is located in the glass tower of the Nashville Arena at 501 Broadway; phone 615/259-4747.

City Neighborhoods

Many of the restaurants, unrated dining establishments and some lodgings listed under Nashville include neighborhoods as well as exact street addresses. Geographic descriptions of these areas are given, followed by a table of restaurants arranged by neighborhood.

Downtown: South of Harrison St, west of I-24/65, north of McGavock St and east of 12th Ave N. **South of Downtown:** South of McGavock St. **East of Downtown:** East of I-24/I-65. **West of Downtown:** West of I-40.

Music Row: Area includes 16th Ave S from West End Ave to Demonbreun St; Music Square E from South St to Demonbreun St; Music Square W from South St to Division St; and Division and Demonbreun Sts from 18th Ave S to I-40.

Opryland Area: South of McGavock Pike, west of Briley Pkwy (TN 155) and north and east of the Cumberland River.

NASHVILLE RESTAURANTS BY NEIGHBORHOOD AREAS

(For full description, see alphabetical listings under Restaurants)

DOWNTOWN
Arthur's (Union Station Hotel). 1001 Broadway
Capitol Grille (The Westin Hermitage Hotel). 231 6th Ave N
Casablanca. 1911 Broadway
Gerst Haus. 228 Woodland St
Goten 2. 209 10th Ave S
Mario's. 2005 Broadway
The Merchants. 401 Broadway
Mere Bulles. 152 2nd Ave N
Old Spaghetti Factory. 160 2nd Ave N
Pinnacle (Crowne Plaza Hotel). 623 Union St
Prime Cut Steakhouse. 170 2nd Ave N
Royal Thai. 204 Commerce St
Seanachie. 327 Broadway
Sole Mio. 94 Peabody St
Stock-Yard. 901 2nd Ave N
Towne House Tea Room & Restaurant. 165 8th Ave N
The Wild Boar. 2014 Broadway

NORTH OF DOWNTOWN
The Mad Platter. 1239 6th Ave N
Monell's Dining & Catering. 1235 6th Ave N
Sitar. 116 21st Ave N

SOUTH OF DOWNTOWN
Bluebird Cafe. 4104 Hillsboro Rd
Boscos. 1805 21st Ave S

Boundry. 911 20th Ave S
Loveless Cafe. 8400 TN 100
Midtown Cafe. 102 19th Ave S
Santa Fe Steak Co. 902 Murfreesboro Rd
Sunset Grill. 2001 A Belcourt Ave
The Trace. 2000 Belcourt Ave

EAST OF DOWNTOWN
101st Airborne. 1362 A Murfreesboro Rd
New Orleans Manor. 1400 Murfreesboro Rd

WEST OF DOWNTOWN
Belle Meade Brasserie. 101 Page Rd
F Scott's. 2210 Crestmoor Rd
Green Hills Grille. 2122 Hillsboro Dr
J Alexander's. 73 White Bridge Rd
Jimmy Kelly's. 217 Louise Ave
Ruth's Chris Steakhouse. 2100 West End Ave
Sperry's. 5109 Harding Rd
Tin Angel. 3201 West End Ave
Valentino's. 1907 West End Ave
Zola. 3001 W End Ave

OPRYLAND AREA
Cock Of The Walk. 2624 Music Valley Dr

Note: When a listing is located in a town that does not have its own city heading, it will appear under the city nearest to its location. In these cases, the address and town appear in parenthesis immediately following the name of the establishment.

Motels

★ ★ **BAYMONT INN.** 5612 Lenox Ave (37209), I-40 exit 204, west of downtown. 615/353-0700; res: 800/428-3438; FAX 615/352-0361. Web www.budgetel.com. 110 rms, 3 story. S $59.95-$71.95; D $59.95-$79.95; each addl $7; under 18 free; higher rates special events. Crib free. TV; cable (premium). Pool. Complimentary continental bkfst. Complimentary coffee in rms. Restaurant adj 6 am-11 pm. Ck-out noon. Meeting rms. Business servs avail. Sundries. Cr cds: A, C, D, DS, MC, V.

D ≋ ✕ 🔥 SC

✔★ ★ **BAYMONT INN-GOODLETTSVILLE.** (120 Cartwright Court, Goodlettsville 37072) 14 mi N on I-65, exit 97. 615/851-1891; FAX 615/851-4513. 100 rms, 3 story, 32 suites. Apr-Oct: S, D $45.95-$60.95; each addl $7; suites $95.95-$122.95; under 18 free; lower rates rest of yr. Crib free. Pet accepted, some restrictions. TV; cable (premium). Pool. Complimentary continental bkfst. Restaurant adj 6 am-10 pm. Ck-out noon. Meeting rm. Business servs avail. Valet serv. Sundries. Exercise equipt. Cr cds: A, C, D, DS, MC, V.

D ✔ ≋ ✕ 🔥 SC

★ ★ **CLUBHOUSE INN.** 2435 Atrium Way (37214), east of downtown. 615/883-0500; res: 800/258-2466; FAX 615/889-4827. 135 rms, 3 story, 17 suites. Apr-Oct: S, D $79-$104; each addl $10; suites $109-$129; under 16 free; wkend rates; higher rates special events; lower rates rest of yr. TV; cable (premium), VCR avail. Heated pool; whirlpool. Complimentary full bkfst. Ck-out noon. Coin lndry. Meeting rms. Business servs avail. Valet serv. Free airport transportation. Health club privileges. Refrigerator. Balconies. Cr cds: A, C, D, DS, MC, V.

D ≋ ✕ 🔥 SC

★ ★ **COMFORT INN-NORTH.** 2306 Brick Church Pike (37207), I-65 exit 87B, north of downtown. 615/226-9560; res: 800/288-5050. 95 rms, 4 story. S $42.95-$54.95; D $48.95-$59.95; each addl $5; under 16 free; higher rates special events. Crib free. TV; cable (premium). Pool. Complimentary continental bkfst. Restaurant adj open 24 hrs. Ck-out noon. Business servs avail. Cr cds: A, C, D, DS, MC, V.

D ≋ 🔥 SC

★ ★ ★ **COURTYARD BY MARRIOTT-AIRPORT.** 2508 Elm Hill Pike (37214), near International Airport, east of downtown. 615/883-9500; res: 800/321-2211; FAX 615/883-0172. 145 rms, 4 story. S, D $90-$120; wkend rates; higher rates special events. Crib free. TV; cable (premium), VCR

avail. Pool; whirlpool. Complimentary coffee in rms. Restaurant 6-10 am; wkend hrs vary. Bar 5-11 pm. Ck-out noon. Coin lndry. Meeting rms. Business servs avail. Valet serv. Sundries. Free airport transportation. Exercise equipt. Refrigerators avail. Some balconies. Cr cds: A, C, D, DS, MC, V.

D ≋ ✕ ✕ 🔥 SC

✔★ **DAYS INN.** (1009 TN 76, White House 37188) I-65 exit 108. 615/672-3746; res: 800/329-7466; FAX 615/672-0928. 100 rms, 2 story. June-Aug: S $35-$45; D $42-$60; each addl $5; under 12 free; higher rates Fanfare; lower rates rest of yr. Crib free. Pet accepted; $3. TV; cable (premium). Complimentary continental bkfst. Restaurant adj 6 am-10 pm. Ck-out 11 am. Business servs avail. Pool. Cr cds: A, C, D, DS, MC, V.

⇐ ≋ 🔥 SC

✔★ **DAYS INN RIVERGATE.** (809 Wren Rd, Goodlettsville 37072) 12 mi N on I-65, Rivergate exit 96. 615/859-1771; FAX 615/859-7512. 46 rms, 3 story. No elvtr. May-Aug: S, D $49.95-$95.95; each addl $5; under 12 free; higher rates special events; lower rates rest of yr. TV; cable (premium). Complimentary continental bkfst. Restaurant nearby. Ck-out 11 am. Business servs avail. Cr cds: A, D, DS, MC, V.

D 🔥 SC

★ ★ **ECONO LODGE OPRYLAND.** 2460 Music Valley Dr (37214), in Opryland Area. 615/889-0090; res: 800/553-2666; FAX 615/889-0086. 86 rms, 3 story. May-Oct: S, D $69.95-$74.95; each addl $10; under 18 free; higher rates special events; lower rates rest of yr. Crib free. Pet accepted, some restrictions. TV; cable (premium). Pool. Complimentary coffee in lobby. Restaurant nearby. Ck-out noon. Gift shop. Cr cds: A, C, D, DS, MC, V.

D ⇐ ≋ 🔥 SC

★ ★ **FAIRFIELD INN BY MARRIOTT.** 211 Music City Circle (37214), in Opryland area. 615/872-8939; res: 800/228-2800; FAX 615/872-7230. 109 rms, 3 story. May-Oct: S, D $83-$93; suites $129; under 18 free; higher rates Fanfare; lower rates rest of yr. Crib free. TV; cable (premium), VCR avail. Complimentary continental bkfst. Restaurant nearby. Ck-out noon. Meeting rm. Business servs avail. Free airport transportation. Exercise equipt. Indoor pool. Cr cds: A, C, D, DS, MC, V.

D ≋ ✕ 🔥 SC

✔★ **FIDDLERS INN.** 2410 Music Valley Dr (37214), in Opryland Area. 615/885-1440; FAX 615/883-6477. 202 rms, 2-3 story. Apr-Oct: S $49-$67; D $54-$72; each addl $5; under 18 free. Crib $5. TV; cable (premium). Pool. Restaurant adj 6:30 am-10 pm. Ck-out 11 am. Business servs avail. Gift shop. Cr cds: A, DS, MC, V.

D ≋ 🔥

✔★ ★ **HAMPTON INN.** (202 Northgate Circle, Goodlettsville 37072) 13 mi N on I-65, exit 97. 615/851-2828; FAX 615/851-2830. Web www.hampton-inn.com. 61 rms, 3 story. June-mid-Sept: S $69-$74; D $74-$79; under 18 free; higher rates Fanfare; lower rates rest of yr. Crib free. TV; cable (premium). Complimentary continental bkfst. Restaurant nearby. Ck-out noon. Meeting rms. Business servs avail. In-rm modem link. Health club privileges. Pool. Some in-rm whirlpools, refrigerators, microwaves, wet bars. Cr cds: A, D, DS, MC, V.

D ≋ 🔥 SC

★ ★ **HAMPTON INN.** 2350 Elm Hill Pike (37214), east of downtown. 615/871-0222; res: 800/426-7866; FAX 615/885-5325. Web www.hampton.com. 120 rms, 3 story. S, D $73-$89; each addl $10; under 18 free. Crib free. TV; cable (premium). Pool. Complimentary continental bkfst. Restaurant adj open 24 hrs. Ck-out 11 am. Meeting rm. Business servs avail. In-rm modem link. Near airport. Cr cds: A, C, D, DS, MC, V.

D ≋ 🔥 SC

★ ★ **HAMPTON INN.** 210 Crossings Place (37013), E on I-24, exit 60, east of downtown. 615/731-9911; res: 800/852-8789; FAX 615/731-9912. 86 rms, 4 story. S, D $70-$76; each addl $6; under 18 free; higher rates Fanfare. Crib $5. TV; cable (premium). Complimentary continental bkfst. Restaurant nearby. Ck-out noon. Meeting rms. Business servs avail. Free airport transportation. Exercise equipt. Health club privileges. Pool. Cr cds: A, C, D, DS, ER, MC, V.

D ⊠ ✕ ⊠ ⊠ SC

★ **HAMPTON INN-BRENTWOOD.** *(5630 Franklin Pike Circle, Brentwood 37027) S on I-65, exit 74B.* 615/373-2212; FAX 615/370-9832. 114 air-cooled rms, 5 story. S, D $79-$89; under 18 free. Crib free. TV; cable (premium). Complimentary continental bkfst. Restaurant adj 6 am-midnight. Ck-out noon. Meeting rms. Business servs avail. Sundries. Health club privileges. Some refrigerators. Cr cds: A, C, D, DS, MC, V.

D ⊠ ⊠ SC

★ **HOLIDAY INN EXPRESS.** *(909 Conference Dr, Goodlettsville 37072) 13 mi N on I-65, exit 97.* 615/851-6600; FAX 615/851-4723. 66 rms, 2 story. June-Aug: S, D $56-$120; each addl $5; under 12 free; lower rates rest of yr. Crib free. TV; cable. Complimentary continental bkfst. Restaurant nearby. Ck-out 11 am. Meeting rms. Pool. Some in-rm whirlpools. Cr cds: A, D, DS, JCB, MC, V.

D ⊠ ⊠ SC

★ **HOLIDAY INN EXPRESS.** *981 Murfreesboro Rd (37217), east of downtown.* 615/367-9150; res: 800/465-4329; FAX 615/361-4865. 210 rms, 2 story. S, D $65-$85; under 18 free; higher rates special events. Crib free. TV; cable (premium). Pool; whirlpool. Complimentary coffee in rms. Restaurant adj 11 am-11 pm; wkends to midnight. Ck-out noon. Coin lndry. Meeting rms. Business servs avail. Bellhops. Valet serv. Free airport transportation. Cr cds: A, D, DS, MC, V.

D ⊠ ✕ ⊠ ⊠ SC

★ **HOLIDAY INN EXPRESS.** *(354 Hester Ln, White House 37188) 20 mi N on I-65, exit 108.* 615/672-7200; res: 800/465-4329; FAX 615/672-7100. 54 rms, 2 story. Apr-Aug: S, D $50-$80; each addl $6; under 18 free; higher rates Fanfare; lower rates rest of yr. Crib free. Pet accepted; $5. TV; cable (premium). Complimentary continental bkfst. Restaurant nearby. Ck-out 11 am. Meeting rms. Business servs avail. In-rm modem link. Valet serv. Heated pool. Bathrm phones; some in-rm whirlpools, refrigerators, microwaves. Cr cds: A, C, D, DS, JCB, MC, V.

D ⊠ ⊠ ✕ ⊠ SC

★ **LA QUINTA.** *2001 Metrocenter Blvd (37228), north of downtown.* 615/259-2130; res: 800/687-6667; FAX 615/242-2650. Web www.laquinta.com. 120 rms, 2 story. S, D $67-$75; each addl $10; under 18 free. Crib free. TV; cable (premium). Pool. Complimentary continental bkfst. Restaurant adj 6 am-midnight. Ck-out noon. Business servs avail. Coin lndry. Cr cds: A, C, D, DS, MC, V.

D ⊠ ⊠ ⊠ SC

★★ **RAMADA INN & SUITES-SOUTH.** *2425 Atrium Way (37214), near International Airport, east of downtown.* 615/883-5201; res: 800/272-6232; FAX 615/883-5594. Web www.ramada.com/ramada.html. 120 suites, 3 story. S, D $83-129; under 18 free. Crib free. TV; cable (premium). Pool. Complimentary continental bkfst. Coffee in rms. Ck-out noon. Coin lndry. Meeting rms. Business servs avail. Valet serv. Free airport transportation. Refrigerators; microwaves avail. Cr cds: A, C, D, DS, JCB, MC, V.

D ⊠ ⊠ ✕ ⊠ ⊠ SC

★★ **RAMADA INN AIRPORT.** *709 Spence Lane (37217), southeast of downtown.* 615/361-0102; res: 800/288-2828; FAX 615/361-4765. 228 rms, 2 story. S, D $50-$75; each addl $8; under 12 free. Crib free. TV; cable (premium). Pool. Restaurant 6 am-2 pm, 5-9:30 pm. Rm serv. Bar 4 pm-2 am; entertainment. Ck-out noon. Bellhops. Sundries. Coin lndry. Meeting rms. Business servs avail. In-rm modem link. Airport transportation. Cr cds: A, C, D, DS, MC, V.

D ⊠ ✕ ⊠ ⊠ SC

★★ **RAMADA LIMITED AIRPORT-EAST.** *(5770 Old Hickory Blvd, Hermitage 37076) 6 mi E on I-40, exit 221B.* 615/889-8940; FAX 615/871-4444. Web www.rds2.com/motels/ramadsltd. 100 rms, 3 story.

June-Aug: S $35-$55; D $40-$70; each addl $6; under 18 free; higher rates special events; lower rates rest of yr. Crib free. Pet accepted, some restrictions; $5. TV; cable. Pool. Complimentary continental bkfst. Restaurant nearby. Ck-out noon. Business servs avail. Microwaves avail. Cr cds: A, C, D, DS, MC, V.

D ⚡ ⊠ ⊠ ⊠ SC

✔★ **RED ROOF INN.** *510 Claridge St (37214), I-40 exit 216, near International Airport, east of downtown.* 615/872-0735; FAX 615/871-4647. 120 rms, 3 story. Mar-Sept: S $39.99-$49.99; D $45.99-$55.99; each addl $6; under 17 free; higher rates special events; lower rates rest of yr. Crib avail. Pet accepted, some restrictions. TV; cable (premium). Complimentary coffee in lobby. Restaurant nearby. Ck-out 11 am. Free airport transportation. Cr cds: A, C, D, DS, MC, V.

D ⚡ ✕ ⊠ ⊠ SC

✔★ **RED ROOF INN-SOUTH.** *4271 Sidco Dr (37204), at jct I-65 & Harding Pl, south of downtown.* 615/832-0093; res: 800/843-7663; FAX 615/832-0097. 85 rms, 3 story. Mar-Sept: S $44.99-$69.99; D $46.99-$69.99; each addl $8; under 18 free; lower rates rest of yr. Crib free. Pet accepted. TV; cable. Complimentary coffee in lobby. Restaurant nearby. Ck-out 11 am. Business servs avail. Cr cds: A, C, D, DS, MC, V.

D ⚡ ⊠ ⊠ SC

★★★ **RESIDENCE INN BY MARRIOTT.** *2300 Elm Hill Pike (37214), near International Airport, east of downtown.* 615/889-8600; res: 800/321-3131; FAX 615/871-4970. Web www.residenceinn.com. 168 kit. suites, 2 story. Suites: 1-bedrm studio $109-$129; 2-bedrm penthouse $129-$159. Pet accepted; $150. TV; cable. Pool; whirlpool. Complimentary continental bkfst. Ck-out noon. Coin lndry. Meeting rms. Business servs avail. Refrigerators, microwaves; many fireplaces. Balconies. Cr cds: A, C, D, DS, JCB, MC, V.

D ⚡ ⊠ ⊠ ⊠ SC

★★ **SHONEY'S INN.** *1501 Demonbreun St (37203), in Music Row.* 615/255-9977; FAX 615/242-6127; res: 800/222-2222. 147 rms, 3 story. S $62-$72; D $72-$79; each addl $6; suites $109-$119; under 19 free; higher rates special events. Crib free. TV; cable (premium). Pool. Complimentary coffee in lobby. Restaurant adj 6 am-midnight. Ck-out noon. Meeting rms. Business servs avail. Cr cds: A, C, D, DS, ER, MC, V.

D ⊠ ⊠ ⊠ SC

★★ **SHONEY'S INN-NORTH.** *(100 Northcreek Blvd, Goodlettsville 37072) 13 mi N on I-65, exit 97.* 615/851-1067; FAX 615/851-6069; res: 800/222-2222. 111 rms, 3 story. S $55-$65; D $61-$71; each addl $6; under 18 free. Crib free. TV; cable (premium). Pool. Complimentary continental bkfst. Coffee in rms. Restaurant adj 6 am-11 pm; Fri, Sat to 1 am. Ck-out noon. Meeting rm. Business servs avail. In-rm modem link. Health club privileges. Refrigerators, microwaves avail. Cr cds: A, D, DS, ER, MC, V.

D ⊠ ⊠ ⊠ SC

★ **SUPER 8.** *412 Robertson Ave (37209), I-40 exit 204, west of downtown.* 615/356-0888. 68 rms, 3 story. June-July: S $57-$60; D $65.88-$70.88; each addl $5; suites $75-$80; under 12 free; higher rates special events; lower rates rest of yr. Crib free. Pet accepted. TV; cable (premium). Complimentary continental bkfst. Restaurant adj open 24 hrs. Ck-out 11 am. Business servs avail. Cr cds: A, C, D, DS, MC, V.

D ⚡ ⊠ ⊠ SC

✔★ **TRAVELERS REST INN.** *(107 Franklin Rd, Brentwood 37027) 1 blk W of I-65 exits 74B.* 615/373-3033; FAX 615/370-5709; res: 800/852-0618. 35 rms, 1-2 story, 2 kits. S $45-$52; D $52-$60; each addl $4; under 18 free. Crib $2. TV; cable (premium). Pool; wading pool. Complimentary continental bkfst. Complimentary coffee in rms. Restaurant nearby. Ck-out noon. Coin lndry. Business servs avail. Some refrigerators. Picnic table. Cr cds: A, C, D, DS, MC, V.

⊠ ⊠ ⊠ SC

Motor Hotels

★ ★ **AMERISUITES.** (202 Summit View Dr, Brentwood 37027) Approx 9 mi S on I-65, exit 74A. 615/661-9477; res: 800/833-1516; FAX 615/661-9936. Web www.travelbase.com/destination/nashville/ameri suites-brentwood. 126 kit. suites, 6 story. Mar-Oct: S, D $80-$150; each addl $10; under 18 free; higher rates special events; lower rates rest of yr. Crib free. Pet accepted, some restrictions; $10. TV; cable (premium), VCR (movies). Heated pool. Complimentary continental bkfst. Complimentary coffee in rms. Restaurant nearby. Ck-out noon. Meeting rms. Business center. Valet serv. Sundries. Coin lndry. Exercise equipt. Refrigerators, microwaves. Cr cds: A, C, D, DS, ER, JCB, MC, V.

★ ★ **AMERISUITES.** 220 Rudy's Circle (37214), in Opryland Area. 615/872-0422; res: 800/833-1516; FAX 615/872-9283. 125 suites, 5 story. S, D $120-$130; each addl $10; under 18 free; higher rates special events. Crib free. TV; cable (premium), VCR (movies). Pool. Complimentary continental bkfst. Complimentary coffee in rms. Restaurant nearby. Ck-out 11 am. Coin lndry. Meeting rms. Business center. Bellhops. Valet serv. Free airport transportation. Exercise equipt. Refrigerators. Cr cds: A, C, D, DS, MC, V.

★ **GUESTHOUSE INN & SUITES MEDCENTER.** 1909 Hayes St (37203), downtown. 615/329-1000; res: 800/777-4904. 108 rms, 7 story. Mar-Aug: S, D $64-$91; each addl $7; under 18 free; lower rates rest of yr. Crib free. TV; cable, VCR avail. Complimentary continental bkfst. Restaurant nearby. Ck-out noon. Coin lndry. Meeting rm. Business servs avail. Refrigerators, microwaves, wet bars. Cr cds: A, C, D, DS, MC, V.

★ ★ **HAMPTON INN AND SUITES.** 583 Donelson Pike (37214), near Nashville Intl Airport, east of downtown. 615/885-4242; res: 800/246-7866; FAX 615/885-6726. 111 rms, 7 story, 31 kit. suites. S, D $89-$129; kit. suites $119-$129; under 18 free; higher rates special events. Crib free. Parking. TV; cable (premium), VCR. Pool. Complimentary continental bkfst. Complimentary coffee in rms. Restaurant nearby. Ck-out noon. Meeting rms. Business servs avail. Gift shop. Free airport transportation. Exercise equipt. Some refrigerators. Cr cds: A, C, D, DS, MC, V.

★ ★ **HAMPTON INN-NORTH.** 2407 Brick Church Pike (37207), I-65 exit 87B, north of downtown. 615/226-3300; FAX 615/226-0170. 125 rms, 5 story. S, D $58-$73; under 18 free; higher rates special events. Crib free. TV; cable (premium). Pool. Restaurant nearby. Ck-out noon. Meeting rms. Business servs avail. Exercise equipt. Game rm. Cr cds: A, C, D, DS, MC, V.

★ ★ ★ **HILTON SUITES-BRENTWOOD.** (9000 Overlook Blvd, Brentwood 37027) S on I-65 exit 74B. 615/370-0111; res: 800/445-8667; FAX 615/370-0272. Web www.hilton.com. 203 suites, 4 story. S, D $125-$165; each addl $20; family rates. Crib free. Pet accepted, some restrictions. TV; cable (premium), VCR (movies $2). Indoor pool; whirlpool. Complimentary full bkfst. Coffee in rms. Restaurant 6-9:30 am, 11:30 am-1:30 pm, 5-10 pm; Sat, Sun 7-11 am, 5-10 pm. Rm serv from 5 pm. Bar 4 pm-midnight. Ck-out noon. Free guest lndry. Meeting rms. Business center. Gift shop. Exercise equipt. Rec rm. Refrigerators, microwaves, wet bars. Balconies. Cr cds: A, C, D, DS, ER, JCB, MC, V.

★ ★ ★ **HOLIDAY INN BRENTWOOD.** (760 Old Hickory Blvd, Brentwood 37027) I-65 exit 74A. 615/373-2600; FAX 615/377-3893. 248 rms, 8 story. S, D $79-$139; under 18 free; wkend rates. Crib free. TV; cable (premium). Pool; whirlpool. Complimentary coffee in rms. Restaurant 6:30 am-10 pm. Rm serv noon. Bar 4 pm-midnight. Ck-out noon. Coin lndry. Meeting rms. In-rm modem link. Bellhops. Sundries. Valet serv. 18-hole golf privileges. Exercise equipt; sauna. Cr cds: A, C, D, DS, JCB, MC, V.

★ ★ **HOLIDAY INN EXPRESS.** 1111 Airport Center Dr (37214), near International Airport, east of downtown. 615/883-1366; FAX 615/889-6867. 206 rms, 3 story. S, D $69-$99; each addl $8; under 18 free; higher rates special events. Crib free. TV; cable (premium). Pool. Complimentary continental bkfst. Restaurant nearby. Ck-out noon. Meeting rms. Business servs avail. Bellhops. Free airport transportation. Some balconies. Cr cds: A, C, D, DS, JCB, MC, V.

★ ★ **HOLIDAY INN EXPRESS-NORTH.** 2401 Brick Church Pike (37207), I-65 exit 87, north of downtown. 615/226-4600; FAX 615/228-6412. 172 rms, 5 story. Apr-Oct: S, D $55-$80; under 18 free; higher rates special events; lower rates rest of yr. Crib free. TV; cable (premium). Pool. Ck-out 11 am. Coin lndry. Meeting rms. Business servs avail. In-rm modem link. Exercise equipt; sauna. Cr cds: A, C, D, DS, JCB, MC, V.

★ ★ **HOLIDAY INN-THE CROSSINGS.** 201 Crossings Place (37013), E on I-24, exit 60, east of downtown. 615/731-2361; res: 888/683-8883; FAX 615/731-6828. E-mail ngt1@msn.com. 139 rms, 5 story. S, D $79-$89; each addl $7; under 18 free; higher rates special events. Crib free. Pet accepted, some restrictions. TV; cable (premium). Complimentary coffee in rms. Restaurant 6-10 am, 4:30-10 pm; Sat, Sun 7-11 am, 4:30-10 pm. Rm serv. Bar. Ck-out noon. Meeting rms. Business servs avail. In-rm modem link. Sundries. Free airport transportation. Exercise equipt. Health club privileges. Pool. Refrigerators avail. Cr cds: A, C, D, DS, MC, V.

★ ★ **SHONEY'S INN.** 2420 Music Valley Dr (37214), in Opryland Area. 615/885-4030; FAX 615/391-0632; res: 800/222-2222. E-mail shoneysnashville@travelbase.com. 185 rms, 5 story. June-Aug: S, D $115-$125; each addl $8; suites $139-$159; under 18 free; higher rates special events; lower rates rest of yr. TV; cable (premium). Indoor pool; whirlpool. Complimentary continental bkfst. Complimentary coffee in rms. Restaurant adj 6-11 am. Bar 4-11 pm. Ck-out 11 am. Meeting rms. Business servs avail. Valet serv. Sundries. Gift shop. Free garage parking. Free airport transportation. Cr cds: A, C, D, DS, MC, V.

✔ ★ **WILSON INN.** 600 Ermac Dr (37214), east of downtown. 615/889-4466; res: 800/945-7667; FAX 615/889-0484. 110 rms, 5 story. S, D $55-$85; each addl $7; suites $70-$87; under 19 free; higher rates special events. Crib free. Pet accepted. TV; cable (premium). Complimentary continental bkfst. Restaurant adj open 24 hrs. Ck-out noon. Meeting rms. Business servs avail. Free airport transportation. Refrigerators; wet bar in suites; microwaves avail. Cr cds: A, C, D, DS, JCB, MC, V.

Hotels

★ ★ **CLUBHOUSE INN CONFERENCE CENTER.** 920 Broadway (37203), downtown. 615/244-0150; FAX 615/244-0445. Web www.clubhouseinn.com. 285 rms, 8 story. S, D $94-$124; each addl $10; suites $114-$139; under 16 free. Crib free. TV. Pool. Complimentary bkfst buffet. Restaurant 5:30-8:30 pm. Ck-out noon. Convention facilities. Busines servs avail. Gift shop. Exercise equipt. Cr cds: A, C, D, DS, MC, V.

★ ★ **COURTYARD BY MARRIOTT.** 1901 West End Ave (37203), west of downtown. 615/327-9900; res: 800/321-2211; FAX 615/327-8127. 136 rms, 7 story. S, D $85-$95; suites $125-$135; under 18 free; higher rates special events. Crib free. TV; cable (premium). Complimentary coffee in rms. Restaurant 6:30 am-11 am. Bar 4-11 pm. Ck-out noon. Coin lndry. Meeting rms. Business servs avail. Exercise equipt. Refrigerator, microwave in suites. Balconies. Cr cds: A, C, D, DS, JCB, MC, V.

★ ★ ★ **CROWNE PLAZA.** *623 Union St (37219), opp capitol, downtown.* 615/259-2000; *res:* 800/447-9825; *FAX* 615/742-6056. Web www.crowneplaza.com. 473 rms, 28 story. S, D $154-$184; each addl $20; under 18 free; wkend rates. Crib free. Garage $10; valet parking $14. TV; cable (premium), VCR avail. Indoor pool. Restaurant 6 am-10 pm (also see PINNACLE). Rm serv to midnight. Bars 4 pm-midnight. Ck-out noon. Meeting rms. Business center. Concierge. Gift shop. Airport transportation. Exercise equipt. Luxury level. Cr cds: A, C, D, DS, ER, JCB, MC, V.

D 🏊 🏋 🍴 ✈ 🎿 🔥 SC 🛶

★ ★ ★ **DOUBLETREE.** *315 Fourth Ave N (37219), downtown.* 615/244-8200; *res:* 800/222-8733; *FAX* 615/747-4894. 338 rms, 9 story. S, D $139-$189; each addl $10; suites $250-$650; under 18 free; wkend rates. Crib free. Garage $12. TV; cable (premium), VCR avail. Indoor pool. Restaurant 6:30 am-10:30 pm. Bar 4 pm-1 am. Ck-out noon. Convention facilities. Business center. In-rm modem link. Gift shop. Exercise equipt. Wet bar in suites. Cr cds: A, C, D, DS, ER, MC, V.

D 🏊 🏋 🍴 🎿 🔥 SC 🛶

★ ★ ★ **DOUBLETREE GUEST SUITES.** *2424 Atrium Way (37214), near International Airport, east of downtown.* 615/889-8889; *FAX* 615/883-7779. 138 suites, 3 story. Mar-Oct: S, D $170-$210; each addl $10; under 18 free; lower rates rest of yr. Crib free. TV; cable (premium). Indoor/outdoor pool; poolside serv. Complimentary coffee in rms. Restaurant 6:30 am-11 pm. Bar 4-11 pm. Ck-out noon. Meeting rms. Business servs avail. In-rm modem link. Free airport transportation. Exercise equipt. Game rm. Refrigerators; microwaves avail. Some private patios, balconies. Cr cds: A, C, D, DS, MC, V.

D 🏊 🍴 🎿 🔥 SC

★ ★ ★ **EMBASSY SUITES.** *10 Century Blvd (37214), near International Airport, east of downtown.* 615/871-0033; *res:* 800/362-2779; *FAX* 615/883-9245. Web www.embassysuites.com. 296 suites, 9 story. Suites $129-$169; each addl $10; under 17 free; wkend plans. Crib free. Pet accepted, some restrictions. TV; cable (premium), VCR avail. Indoor pool; whirlpool. Complimentary full bkfst. Restaurant 6:30-9:30 am, 11 am-2 pm, 5-10 pm; Fri, Sat to 11 pm. Rm serv 11 am-11 pm. Bar 5 pm-midnight. Ck-out noon. Convention facilities. Business servs avail. Concierge. Gift shop. Free airport transportation. Exercise equipt; sauna. Game rm. Refrigerators, wet bars; microwaves avail. Atrium. Cr cds: A, C, D, DS, JCB, MC, V.

D 🐾 🏊 🏋 ✈ 🎿 🔥 SC

★ ★ **HOLIDAY INN SELECT-VANDERBILT.** *2613 West End Ave (37203), west of downtown.* 615/327-4707; *res:* 800/465-4329; *FAX* 615/327-8034. 300 rms, 14 story. May-Nov: S, D $130-$142; each addl $10; suites $150-$200; under 18 free; holiday rates; higher rates Fanfare, football games; lower rates rest of yr. Crib free. Pet accepted; deposit. TV; cable (premium), VCR avail. Complimentary coffee in rms. Restaurant 6 am-11 pm. Bar 2 pm-1 am; entertainment Fri, Sat. Ck-out noon. Meeting rms. Business center. In-rm modem link. Concierge. Gift shop. Coin lndry. Airport transportation. Exercise equipt. Pool. Balconies. Luxury level. Cr cds: A, C, D, DS, JCB, MC, V.

D 🐾 🏊 🏋 🍴 🎿 🔥 SC 🛶

★ ★ **HOWARD JOHNSON AIRPORT PLAZA.** *733 Briley Pkwy (37217), I-40 exit 215, east of downtown.* 615/361-5900; *res:* 800/446-4656; *FAX* 615/367-0339. 200 rms, 11 story. June-Oct: S, D $79-$89; each addl $10; under 18 free; lower rates rest of yr. Crib free. TV; cable (premium). Pool. Playground. Restaurant 6 am-10 pm. Bar 4 pm-midnight; entertainment. Ck-out noon. Meeting rms. Business center. Free airport transportation. Exercise equipt. Cr cds: A, C, D, DS, MC, V.

D 🏊 🏋 ✈ 🎿 🔥 SC 🛶

★ ★ ★ **LOEWS VANDERBILT PLAZA.** *2100 West End Ave (37203), downtown.* 615/320-1700; *res:* 800/336-3335; *FAX* 615/320-5019. Web www.loewshotel.com. 340 rms, 12 story. S $164-$214; D $184-$234; each addl $20; suites $450-$800; under 18 free. Crib free. Pet accepted. Garage $8; valet parking $12. TV; cable (premium), VCR avail. Restaurants 6:30 am-10 pm. Rm serv to midnight; Fri, Sat to 1 am. Bars 3 pm-1 am; entertainment exc Sun. Ck-out noon. Convention facilities. Business center. In-rm modem link. Concierge. Shopping arcade. Barber,

beauty shop. Exercise equipt. Minibars; microwaves avail. Luxury level. Cr cds: A, C, D, DS, JCB, MC, V.

D 🐾 🏋 🍴 🎿 🔥 SC 🛶

★ ★ ★ **MARRIOTT.** *600 Marriott Dr (37214), east of downtown.* 615/889-9300; *FAX* 615/889-9315. 399 rms, 18 story. S, D $145-$160; suites $200-$350; under 18 free; wkend plans. TV; cable (premium), VCR avail. Indoor/outdoor pool; whirlpool, poolside serv. Restaurant 6 am-10:30 pm. Bar 11-2 am. Ck-out noon. Lndry facilities. Convention facilities. Business center. In-rm modem link. Free parking. Free airport transportation. Lighted tennis. Exercise equipt; sauna. Picnic tables, grills. Near Percy Priest Lake. Luxury level. Cr cds: A, C, D, DS, ER, JCB, MC, V.

D 🎾 🏊 🍴 🎿 🔥 SC 🛶

★ ★ ★ **OPRYLAND HOTEL.** *2800 Opryland Dr (37214), 5 mi NE of jct I-40 & Briley Pkwy, in Opryland Area.* 615/889-1000; *FAX* 615/871-5728. Web www.country.com. 2,883 rms, 6 story. S, D $215-$255; each addl $15; suites $279-$1,100; under 12 free. Crib free. Valet parking $12. TV; cable (premium), VCR avail. Heated pools; wading pools, poolside serv, lifeguard. Restaurants 6:30-1 am. Rm serv 24 hrs. Bars 11-2 am; entertainment. Ck-out 11 am. Convention facilities. Business center. Shopping arcades. Barber, beauty shop. Airport transportation. 18-hole golf, greens fee $70-$85. Exercise equipt. Massage. Some refrigerators. Some balconies overlooking garden conservatory, cascades and delta. Showboat cruises avail. Cr cds: A, C, D, DS, JCB, MC, V.

D 🏌 🏊 🏋 🍴 🎿 🔥

★ ★ ★ **REGAL MAXWELL HOUSE.** *2025 Metrocenter Blvd (37228), north of downtown.* 615/259-4343; *res:* 800/457-4460; *FAX* 615/254-4918. Web www.regal-hotels.com/Nashville. 289 rms, 10 story. S $124-$172; D $139-$193; each addl $15; suites $195-$395; under 17 free; wkend plans. Crib free. Pet accepted, some restrictions. TV; cable (premium). Pool; whirlpool. Restaurants 6:30 am-10 pm. Bar 11 am-midnight. Ck-out noon. Convention facilities. Business servs avail. Gift shop. Lighted tennis. Exercise equipt; sauna, steam rm. Picnic tables. Luxury level. Cr cds: A, C, D, DS, JCB, MC, V.

D 🐾 🎾 🏊 🏋 🍴 🎿 🔥 SC

★ ★ ★ **RENAISSANCE.** *611 Commerce St (37203), downtown.* 615/255-8400; *FAX* 615/255-8202. Web www.renaissance.com. 673 rms, 25 story. S, D $124-$220; each addl $20; suites $275-$1100; under 18 free; wkend packages. Crib free. Garage $6; valet parking $12. TV; cable (premium), VCR avail. Indoor pool; whirlpool, poolside serv. Restaurant 6 am-10 pm; Fri, Sat to 11 pm. Rm serv 24 hrs. Bar 11-2 am. Ck-out noon. Convention facilities. Business center. Concierge. Exercise equipt; sauna. Some bathrm phones, refrigerators. Luxury level. Cr cds: A, C, D, DS, ER, JCB, MC, V.

D 🏊 🍴 🎿 🔥 SC 🛶

★ ★ ★ **SHERATON-MUSIC CITY.** *777 McGavock Pike (37214), near International Airport, east of downtown.* 615/885-2200; *res:* 800/325-3535; *FAX* 615/231-1134. Web www.tenn.com/sheraton. 412 rms, 4 story. S, D $159-$179; each addl $15; suites $150-$550; under 18 free; wkend rates. Pet accepted. TV; cable (premium), VCR avail. Indoor/outdoor pools; wading pool, whirlpool. Restaurants 6 am-11 pm. Bar 11-3 am; entertainment. Ck-out noon. Convention facilities. Business center. Concierge. Beauty shop. Gift shop. Free airport transportation. Lighted tennis. Golf privileges. Exercise rm; sauna. Bathrm phones; some refrigerators. Private balconies. On 23 landscaped acres on top of hill. Semiformal decor. Cr cds: A, C, D, DS, ER, JCB, MC, V.

D 🐾 🏌 🎾 🏊 🍴 🎿 🔥 SC 🛶

★ ★ ★ **UNION STATION.** *1001 Broadway (37203), downtown.* 615/726-1001; *res:* 800/331-2123; *FAX* 615/248-3554. Web www.grand heritage.com. 124 rms, 7 story, 13 suites. S, D $159-$250; each addl $20; suites $205-$305; under 17 free; wkend rates. Crib free. Pet accepted. Valet parking $10. TV; cable (premium), VCR avail. Coffee in rms. Restaurant 6:30 am-11 pm (also see ARTHUR'S). Bar 11 am-11 pm. Ck-out noon. Business center. Concierge. Valet parking. Health club privileges. In renovated historic train station (1897); stained-glass roof. Cr cds: A, C, D, DS, JCB, MC, V.

[D] [♿] [✕] [♨] [SC] [🚶]

★ ★ ★ **THE WESTIN HERMITAGE.** *231 6th Ave N (37219), downtown.* 615/244-3121; *res:* 800/251-1908; *FAX* 615/254-6909. 120 suites, 9 story. 1-bedrm suites $129-$189; 2-bedrm suites $250-$275; each addl $15; wkend rates. Valet parking $10. TV; cable (premium), VCR avail. Restaurant (see CAPITOL GRILLE). Bars 11 am-midnight. Ck-out noon. Meeting rms. Business center. Health club privileges. Bathrm phones, refrigerators, wet bars; microwaves avail. Hotel built in 1910 as a tribute to Beaux Arts Classicism; fully restored to original elegance. Cr cds: A, C, D, DS, JCB, MC, V.

[D] [✕] [♨] [🚶]

Restaurants

★ ★ **101ST AIRBORNE.** *1362 A Murfreesboro Rd (37217), east of downtown.* 615/361-4212. Hrs: 11 am-2:30 pm, 4:30-10 pm; Fri, Sat 5-11 pm; Sun 4:30-10 pm; Sun brunch 10 am-2:30 pm. Res accepted. Bar from 4 pm. Semi-a la carte: lunch $5.95-$10.95, dinner $9.95-$24.95. Sun brunch $16.95. Child's meals. Specializes in steak, seafood, prime rib. Entertainment Fri, Sat. Parking. House dramatizes a headquarters operation for the 101st Airborne Division; World War II memorabilia. Cr cds: A, D, DS, MC, V.

[D] [🪑]

★ ★ ★ **ARTHUR'S.** *(See Union Station Hotel)* 615/255-1494. Hrs: 5:30-10 pm; Fri, Sat to 11 pm; Sun to 9 pm. Closed major hols. Res accepted. Continental menu. Bar 5 pm-1 am. Wine cellar. Table d'hôte: dinner $55-$70. Specializes in seafood, lamb, flaming desserts. Own baking. Valet parking. Jacket. Menu changes wkly. In an Old World-style hotel converted from an 1897 train station. Cr cds: A, D, DS, MC, V.

[D] [🪑] [♥]

★ ★ **BELLE MEADE BRASSERIE.** *101 Page Rd (37205), west of downtown.* 615/356-5450. E-mail chefrobt@edge.net; web edge.net/~chefrobt. Hrs: 5-10 pm; Fri, Sat to 11 pm; early-bird dinner 5-7 pm. Closed Sun; some major hols. Res accepted. Bar. A la carte entrees: dinner $12-$24. Specializes in seafood, pasta, homemade desserts. Parking. Outdoor dining. Contemporary decor; original art. Cr cds: A, D, MC, V.

[D] [🪑]

★ **BLUEBIRD CAFE.** *4104 Hillsboro Rd (37215), south of downtown.* 615/383-1461. E-mail bluebirdcafe@aol.com; web www.bluebirdcafe.com; Hrs: from 5:30 pm; Sun from 6 pm. Closed some major hols. Res accepted. Bar. Semi-a la carte: dinner $4-$9. Specialties: Cajun catfish, chocolate chunk cheesecake. Parking. Popular performance club featuring songwriters and other entertainers. Cr cds: A, D, DS, MC, V.

[D]

✔★ **BOSCOS.** *1805 21st Ave S (37212), south of downtown.* 615/385-0050. E-mail nashville@boscos.com. Hrs: 11 am-11 pm; Fri, Sat to midnight; Sun brunch to 3 pm; hrs vary in Jan. Closed Thanksgiving, Dec 25. Res accepted. Mediterranean menu. Bar to 1 am; Fri, Sat to 2 am. Semi-a la carte: lunch $3.95-$12.95, dinner $3.95-$15.95. Sun brunch $3.95-$8.95. Child's meals. Specializes in wood-fired oven pizza, pasta, fresh fish. Brewery on site. Cr cds: A, D, MC, V.

[D] [🪑]

★ ★ **BOUNDRY.** *911 20th Ave S (37212), south of downtown.* 615/321-3043. E-mail boundry@bellsouth.net; web citysearch.com/nashville/boundry. Hrs: 5-11 pm; Fri, Sat to 1 am. Closed most major hols. Res accepted. Eclectic menu. Bar 4 pm-2:30 am. Semi-a la carte: dinner $9.95-$23.50. Specialties: planked trout, grilled Tennessee ostrich, lobster BLT pizza. Valet parking. Outdoor dining. Murals, artwork. Cr cds: A, C, D, DS, MC, V.

[D] [🪑]

★ ★ ★ **CAPITOL GRILLE.** *(See The Westin Hermitage Hotel)* 615/345-7116. Hrs: 6:30 am-2 pm, 5:30-10 pm; Sun brunch 11 am-2 pm. Res accepted. Bar 11 am-10 pm; Fri, Sat to 11 pm. Wine list. Semi-a la carte: bkfst $3.50-$9.95, lunch $5.95-$8.95, dinner $16.50-$24.95. Sun brunch $24.95. Specialties: sautéed red snapper, crème brûlée Napoleon, soft-shell crawfish. Valet parking. Russian paneling; marble columns. Cr cds: A, D, DS, MC, V.

[D]

★ ★ ★ **CASABLANCA.** *1911 Broadway (37208), downtown.* 615/327-8001. Hrs: from 5 pm. Closed Sun; most major hols. Res accepted. Continental menu. Bar. Wine cellar. A la carte entrees: $17-$25.50. Specialties: Moroccan spiced crab cakes, sautéed veal chops, Rick's bouillabaise. Piano Wed-Sat. Valet parking. Decor imitates the theme of the movie "Casablanca." Cr cds: A, C, D, DS, MC, V.

[D] [🪑]

✔★ **COCK OF THE WALK.** *2624 Music Valley Dr (37214), in Opryland Area.* 615/889-1930. Hrs: 5-9 pm; Fri, Sat to 10 pm. Closed Thanksgiving, Dec 24, 25; also Super Bowl Sun. Res accepted. Bar. Semi-a la carte: dinner $8.95-$12.50. Child's meals. Specializes in catfish, fried dill pickles, flipped cornbread. Parking. Split level dining in rustic atmosphere. Cr cds: A, D, DS, MC, V.

[D] [🪑]

★ ★ ★ **F SCOTT'S.** *2210 Crestmoor Rd (37215), west of downtown.* 615/269-5861. Hrs: 5:30-10 pm; Fri, Sat to 11 pm. Closed most major hols. Res accepted. Bar. Wine list. A la carte entrees: dinner $12.95-$24.95. Child's meals. Specializes in seafood, lamb. Entertainment. Valet parking. Art deco decor. Cr cds: A, C, D, DS, MC, V.

[D] [🪑]

✔★ **GERST HAUS.** *228 Woodland St (37213), downtown.* 615/256-9760. Hrs: 11 am-9 pm; Fri, Sat to 10 pm; Sun 4-9 pm. Closed Jan 1, Thanksgiving, Dec 25. Res accepted Mon-Fri. German, Amer menu. Bar. Semi-a la carte: lunch, dinner $6.95-$12.95. Specialties: Wienerschnitzel, pork loin, fresh oyster roll. German band Sat. Beer hall atmosphere. Bavarian decor; antiques. Family-owned. Cr cds: A, D, MC, V.

[D] [🪑]

✔★ **GOTEN 2.** *209 10th Ave S (37203), downtown.* 615/251-4855. Hrs: 11 am-midnight; Fri to 1 am; Sat 5 pm-1 am; Sun 5-10 pm. Closed Thanksgiving, Dec 25. Res accepted. Japanese menu. Bar. Semi-a la carte: lunch, dinner $3.50-$14.50. Specialties: sushi, tempura, bento box. Parking. Casual sushi bar in redeveloped historic building. Cr cds: A, D, DS, MC, V.

[D] [🪑]

✔★ ★ **GREEN HILLS GRILLE.** *2122 Hillsboro Dr (37215), west of downtown.* 615/383-6444. Hrs: 11 am-10 pm; Fri, Sat to midnight. Closed Thanksgiving, Dec 25. Bar to 11 pm; Fri, Sat to midnight. Semi-a la carte: lunch, dinner $5.95-$15.45. Child's meals. Specialties: lemon artichoke chicken, roasted chicken, barbecue ribs. Valet parking. Southwestern decor. Cr cds: A, C, D, DS, MC, V.

[D] [🪑]

✔★ ★ **J ALEXANDER'S.** *73 White Bridge Rd (37205), west of downtown.* 615/352-0981. Hrs: 11 am-10 pm; Fri, Sat to 11 pm. Closed Thanksgiving, Dec 25. Bar. Semi-a la carte: lunch, dinner $4.95-$17.95. Child's meals. Specializes in prime rib, fresh seafood, salads. Parking. Glass window permits diners to observe salad preparation area. Cr cds: A, D, DS, MC, V.

[D] [🪑]

★ ★ **JIMMY KELLY'S.** *217 Louise Ave (37203), west of downtown.* 615/329-4349. Hrs: 5 pm-midnight. Closed Sun; some major hols. Res accepted. Bar. Semi-a la carte: dinner $12.75-$28.75. Child's meals. Specializes in hand-cut aged beef. Valet parking. Outdoor dining. In renovated Victorian mansion (1911). Family-owned. Cr cds: A, D, MC, V.

[D] [🪑] [♥]

✔★ **LOVELESS CAFE.** *8400 TN 100 (37221), south of downtown.* 615/646-9700. E-mail nsh@aol.com; web www.citysearch.com /nas/lovelesscafe. Hrs: 8 am-2 pm, 5-9 pm; Sat, Sun 8 am-9 pm. Closed Jan 1, Thanksgiving, Dec 25. Res accepted. Semi-a la carte: bkfst $3.95-$9.95, lunch, dinner $5-$14.95. Child's meals. Specializes in scratch biscuits, fried chicken. Parking. Outdoor dining. Private dining in rms that were previously motel rms. Family-owned. Cr cds: A, MC, V.

D SC

★ **THE MAD PLATTER.** *1239 6th Ave N (37208), north of downtown.* 615/242-2563. Web www.madplatter.com. Hrs: 11 am-2 pm, 5:30-11 pm; Mon to 2 pm. Closed Sun; most major hols. Res required. Semi-a la carte: lunch $6.25-$11.95, dinner $18.50-$48. Specialties: rack of lamb moutarde, chocolate Elvis. Building more than 100 yrs old. Cr cds: A, D, DS, MC, V.

D

★ ★ **MARIO'S.** *2005 Broadway, downtown.* 615/327-3232. Hrs: 5:30-10:30 pm. Closed Sun; major hols. Res accepted. Northern Italian, continental menu. Bar. Wine cellars. A la carte entrees: dinner $18-$26. Specializes in pastas, fresh seafood, veal. Theater dining rm. Parking. Family-owned. Cr cds: A, C, D, DS, MC, V.

D

★ ★ **THE MERCHANTS.** *401 Broadway (37203), downtown.* 615/254-1892. Web www.themerchants.com. Hrs: 11 am-2:30 pm, 5-10 pm; Fri to 11 pm; Sat 5-11 pm; Sun 5-9 pm; Sun brunch 10:30 am-2:30 pm. Res accepted. Bar. Wine cellar. A la carte entrees: lunch $3.95-$10.95, dinner $9.95-$23.95; Sun brunch $5.95-$16.95. Specializes in fresh grilled meats and seafood. Own baking. Pianist. Valet parking. Outdoor dining. In historic building; original wood floors; dining on 3 levels. Cr cds: A, C, D, DS, MC, V.

D

★ ★ **MÉRE BULLES.** *152 2nd Ave N (37201), downtown.* 615/256-1946. Hrs: 5:30-10 pm; Fri, Sat to 11 pm; Sun brunch 11 am-3 pm. Closed Jan 1. Res accepted. Bar. Semi-a la carte: dinner $17.95-$32.95. Sun brunch $23.95. Specializes in pasta, seafood, steak. Entertainment. Local art on display. Cr cds: A, C, D, DS, MC, V.

D

★ ★ **MIDTOWN CAFE.** *102 19th Ave S (37203), south of downtown.* 615/320-7176. Hrs: 11 am-2:30 pm, 5-10 pm; Fri to 11 pm; Sat 5:30-11 pm; Sun 5-10 pm. Closed most major hols. Res accepted. Continental menu. Bar. Semi-a la carte: lunch $6.75-$10.95, dinner $11.25-$22.95. Child's meals. Specializes in fresh daily seafood. Valet parking. Intimate dining. Cr cds: A, DS, MC, V.

D

✔★ **MONELL'S DINING & CATERING.** *1235 6th Ave N (37208), Germantown, north of downtown.* 615/248-4747. Web www. citysearch.com/nas/monellsdining. Hrs: 11 am-2 pm; Fri 11 am-2 pm, 5-8:30 pm; Sat 8 am-1 pm, 5-8:30 pm; Sun 11 am-3 pm. Closed Mon; Dec 24 & 25. Semi-a la carte: bkfst, lunch $8-$10, dinner $10-$12. Specialties: skillet-fried chicken, sweet potato casserole, chocolate pecan pie. Parking. Family-style dining in 1870 historical home. Totally nonsmoking. Cr cds: MC, V.

D

★ ★ **NEW ORLEANS MANOR.** *1400 Murfreesboro Rd (37217), east of downtown.* 615/367-2777. Hrs: 5:30-9 pm. Closed Sun, Mon; Jan 1, Thanksgiving, Dec 24, 25. Res accepted. Serv bar. Buffet: dinner $31-$37. Child's meals. Specializes in seafood, lobster, prime rib. Salad bar. Parking. Scenic grounds; colonial-type mansion built in 1930. Cr cds: A, C, D, DS, MC, V.

D

✔★ **OLD SPAGHETTI FACTORY.** *160 2nd Ave N (37201), downtown.* 615/254-9010. Hrs: 11:30 am-2 pm, 5-10 pm; Fri to 11 pm; Sat noon-11 pm; Sun 4-10 pm. Closed Thanksgiving, Dec 24, 25. Bar. Semi-a la carte: lunch $3.25-$5.60. Complete meals: dinner $5-$10. Child's meals.

Specializes in spaghetti with a variety of sauces. In converted warehouse (1869); doorway arch from the Bank of London; antiques. Cr cds: A, D, DS, MC, V.

D

★ ★ **PINNACLE.** *(See Crowne Plaza Hotel)* 615/259-2000. Web www.crowneplaza.com. Hrs: 5-11 pm; Sun 5-9 pm. Res accepted. Continental menu. Wine. Semi-a la carte: dinner $19.95-$33.95. Specializes in steak, veal chops, peppered salmon steak. Valet parking. Revolving restaurant of 28th floor. Cr cds: A, C, D, DS, ER, JCB, MC, V.

D

★ ★ **PRIME CUT STEAKHOUSE.** *170 2nd Ave N (37201), downtown.* 615/242-3083. Hrs: 5-10 pm; Fri, Sat to 11 pm. Closed Thanksgiving, Dec 25. Res accepted. Bar from 4 pm. Semi-a la carte: dinner $15.95-$21.95. Child's meals. Specializes in steak, marinated chicken, fresh fish. Entertainment Fri, Sat. Outdoor dining. Option of cooking own steak. Cr cds: A, C, D, DS, MC, V.

D

✔★ **ROYAL THAI.** *204 Commerce St (37201), downtown.* 615/255-0821. Hrs: 11 am-3 pm, 5-10 pm; Fri to 11 pm; Sat 11 am-11 pm; Sun 4-10 pm. Closed Jan 1, Dec 25. Res accepted. Thai menu. Bar. Semi-a la carte: lunch $4.95-$6.95, dinner $6.95-$19.95. Specialties: pad kra pao, pla sam rod, pad Thai. Oriental decor. Family-owned. Cr cds: A, D, DS, MC, V.

D

★ ★ **RUTH'S CHRIS STEAKHOUSE.** *2100 West End Ave (37203), west of downtown.* 615/320-0163. Hrs: 5-10:30 pm; Sun to 9:30 pm. Closed major hols. Res accepted. Bar 4-10:30 pm. A la carte entrees: dinner $12.95-$28.95. Specialties: filet, porterhouse, Maine lobster. Valet parking. Cr cds: A, D, MC, V.

D

★ **SANTA FE STEAK CO.** *902 Murfreesboro Rd (37217), south of downtown.* 615/367-4448. Hrs: 11 am-11 pm; Fri, Sat to midnight. Closed Thanksgiving, Dec 25. Bar to 11 pm; Fri, Sat to 1 am. Semi-a la carte: lunch $4.49-$7.99, dinner $6.95-$14.99. Child's meals. Specializes in Southwestern cuisine, steak, chicken. Parking. Outdoor dining. Informal dining in three areas. Cr cds: A, D, DS, MC, V.

D

✔★ **SÉANACHIE.** *327 Broadway (37201), downtown.* 615/726-2006. Hrs: 11-1 am; Fri, Sat to 3 am; Sun noon-1 am; Sun brunch noon-3 pm. Closed Dec 25. Res accepted. Irish menu. Bar. Semi-a la carte: lunch, dinner $5.95-$14.95. Sun brunch $4.95-$14.95. Child's meals. Specialties: boxty, beef & Guinness pie, Irish stew. Celtic music Tues-Sun. Irish decor & atmosphere. Cr cds: A, C, D, DS, MC, V.

D

✔★ **SITAR.** *116 21st Ave N (37203), north of downtown.* 615/321-8889. Hrs: 11 am-2:30 pm, 5-10 pm; Sun noon-3 pm, 5-10 pm. Indian menu. Bar. Semi-a la carte: lunch $5.99-$7.99, dinner $6.95-$13.95. Buffet: lunch $5.99. Specialties: chicken tikka masala, lamb pasanda, karahai shrimp. Indian artwork. Cr cds: A, C, D, DS, MC, V.

D

★ ★ **SOLE MIO.** *94 Peabody St (37210), downtown.* 615/256-4013. Hrs: 11 am-9:30 pm; Fri, Sat to 11 pm; Sat, Sun brunch 11 am-3 pm. Closed Mon; most major hols. Res accepted. Bar. Semi-a la carte: lunch $7-$18. A la carte entrees: dinner $7-$23. Brunch $8.95-$12. Specialties: lasagne al forno, gnocchi sorrentino. Own pasta. Piano Fri, Sat. Parking. Outdoor dining. Cr cds: A, C, D, MC, V.

D

★ ★ **SPERRY'S.** *5109 Harding Rd (37205), west of downtown.* 615/353-0809. Hrs: 5-10 pm; Fri, Sat to 11 pm. Closed major hols. Continental menu. Bar to midnight. A la carte entrees: dinner $12.50-$28.50.

Specializes in fresh seafood, steak. Salad bar. Own desserts, soups, sauces. Parking. Nautical and hunting decor. Cr cds: A, C, D, MC, V.

★★ **STOCK-YARD.** *901 2nd Ave N (37201), downtown.* 615/255-6464. Web www.citysearch.com/stockyard. Hrs: 5-10 pm; Fri, Sat to 11 pm; Sun 5-9 pm. Closed Dec 25. Bars 4:30-11 pm. Semi-a la carte: dinner $15-$50. Child's meals. Specializes in charcoal-grilled steak, fresh seafood, grilled chicken breast. Entertainment. Parking. Cr cds: A, D, DS, MC, V.

★★ **SUNSET GRILL.** *2001 A Belcourt Ave (37212), south of downtown.* 615/386-3663. E-mail sunsetgrill@mindspring.com; web www.sunsetgrill.com. Hrs: 11-1:30 am; Sat from 4:45 pm; Sun 5-11 pm. Closed some major hols. Res accepted. Bar. Semi-a la carte: lunch $5-$10, dinner $6-$24. Child's meals. Specializes in fresh seafood, pasta, lamb. Valet Parking. Five dining areas include a glass-enclosed patio. Original artwork. Cr cds: A, C, D, DS, JCB, MC, V.

★ **TIN ANGEL.** *3201 West End Ave (37212), west of downtown.* 615/298-3444. Hrs: 11 am-11 pm; Fri to midnight; Sat 4:30 pm-midnight; Sun brunch 11 am-3 pm. Closed most major hols. Bar. A la carte entrees: lunch $7-$12, dinner $8-$17. Sun brunch $7-$12. Specialties: chicken quesadilla, Angel Louie spaghetti, meatloaf. Valet parking. In historical building. Cr cds: A, C, D, DS, MC, V.

★★ **THE TRACE.** *2000 Belcourt Ave (37212), south of downtown.* 615/385-2200. Hrs: 4 pm-2:30 am; Sun brunch 11 am-3 pm. Closed Jan 1, Dec 25. Continental menu. Bar. Semi-a la carte: dinner $9-$21. Sun brunch $6-$21. Specialties: lamb shank, tuna au poivre. Sun jazz. Valet parking. Outdoor dining. Cr cds: A, C, D, DS, MC, V.

★★★ **VALENTINO'S.** *1907 West End Ave (37203), west of downtown.* 615/327-0148. Hrs: 11 am-2 pm, 5-10 pm. Closed Sun; major hols. Res accepted. Northern Italian menu. Bar. Semi-a la carte: lunch $5.95-$10.95, dinner $9.95-$22.95. Specializes in chicken, seafood, pasta. Valet parking. Cr cds: A, C, D, DS, MC, V.

★★★ **THE WILD BOAR.** *2014 Broadway (37203), downtown.* 615/329-1313. Hrs: 6-10 pm; Fri to 10:30 pm; Sat 6-10:30 pm. Closed Sun; major hols. Res accepted. Contemporary French menu. Bar. Wine cellar. Semi-a la carte: dinner $22.95-$34.95. Specializes in fresh wild game, fresh seafood, souffles. Pianist Fri, Sat. Valet parking. European hunting lodge atmosphere; artwork, antiques. Cr cds: A, C, D, DS, MC, V.

★★ **ZOLA.** *3001 W End Ave (37203), west of downtown.* 615/320-7778. Hrs: 5:30-10 pm; Fri to 11 pm, Sat 5:30-11 pm. Closed most major hols. Res accepted. Semi-a la carte: dinner $10.50-$21.95. Specializes in fish, poultry, vegetarian entrees. Totally nonsmoking. Cr cds: A, DS, MC, V.

Unrated Dining Spot

TOWNE HOUSE TEA ROOM & RESTAURANT. *165 8th Ave N (37203), downtown.* 615/254-1277. Hrs: 8:30 am-2:30 pm. Closed Sat, Sun; major hols. Semi-a la carte: bkfst $3.95-$7.95, lunch $3.45-$7.50. Buffet: lunch $5.25. Salad bar. Own baking, soups. Historic 24-room mansion (1840's); fireplaces, oak floors, antiques, paintings. Cr cds: A, C, D, DS, MC, V.

Natchez Trace State Resort Park (D-3)

(40 mi NE of Jackson, off I-40)

Named for the pioneer trail that connected Nashville and Natchez, this 48,000-acre park is the largest recreation area in western Tennessee and the location of a pecan tree that is said to be the world's third largest. Four lakes provide swimming; fishing; boating (launch, rentals). Nature trails, backpacking. Picnicking, playground, recreation lodge. Tent & trailer sites, cabins, inn. Standard fees. Phone 901/968-8176.

Motels

✔★★ **BEST WESTERN CROSSROADS INN.** *(21045 TN 22N, Wildersville 38388) 8 mi W of park entrance, on TN 22 at I-40 exit 108.* 901/968-2532; FAX 901/968-2082. 40 rms. May-Oct: S $42-$50; D $48-$56; each addl $10; higher rates special events; lower rates rest of yr. Crib free. TV; cable (premium). Pool. Restaurant nearby. Ck-out 11 am. Cr cds: A, D, DS, MC, V.

★★ **PIN OAK LODGE.** *(567 Pin Oak Lodge Lane, Wildersville 38388)* 901/968-8176; FAX 901/968-6515. 20 rms, 2 story, 18 kit. cottages. Mar-Nov: S, D $56-$62; each addl $6; kit. cottages $65-$70; under 16 free; lower rates rest of yr. Crib free. TV in motel rms. Pool; wading pool. Playground. Restaurant 7 am-9 pm. Ck-out 11 am. Meeting rms. Lighted tennis. Rec rm. Dock. Balconies. Picnic tables, grills. On lake. State-owned; all facilities of park avail. Cr cds: A, DS, MC, V.

Oak Ridge (D-7)

(See also Knoxville)

Founded 1943 **Pop** 27,310 **Elev** 900 ft **Area code** 423 **Zip** 37830

Information Convention & Visitors Bureau, 302 S Tulane Ave; 423/482-7821 or 800/887-3429.

Oak Ridge was built during World War II to house "Manhattan Project" workers involved in the production of uranium 235 (the first atomic bomb's explosive element). Once one of the most secret places in the US, Oak Ridge is now host to thousands who come each year, drawn by the mysteries of nuclear energy. Built by the US government, Oak Ridge is known for scientific research and development. Although many of the installations are still classified, the city has not been restricted since March 1949.

What to See and Do

American Museum of Science and Energy. One of the world's largest energy exhibitions; fossil fuels, energy alternatives, resources and research. Hands-on exhibits, displays, models, films, games and live demonstrations. (Daily; closed Jan 1, Thanksgiving, Dec 25) 300 S Tulane Ave. Phone 423/576-3200. **Free.**

Bull Run Steam Plant. TVA-built with a 800-foot-high chimney, the plant has a roadside overlook. Visitor lobby and tours to powerhouse overlook (Mon-Fri). 5 mi SE, on shore of Melton Hill Reservoir. Phone 423/945-7200. **Free.**

Children's Museum of Oak Ridge. Hands-on exhibits and displays include the International Gallery, Discovery Lab, Waterworks, Playscape, Nature Walk, Pioneer Living and Oak Ridge history. Performances, exhibits, seminars, workshops. (Sept-May, daily; June-Aug, daily exc Sun; rest of yr, Mon-Fri; closed some hols). 461 W Outer Dr. Phone 423/482-1074. ¢¢

Frozen Head State Park. More than 12,000 acres in Cumberland Mountains. Trout fishing. Hiking trails (50 mi). Picnicking, playground. Primitive camping. Visitor center. Standard fees. Approx 18 mi NW on TN 62, then 4 mi N on Flat Fork Rd, follow signs. Phone 423/346-3318.

International Friendship Bell. Bell was designed to celebrate the dedication of Manhattan Project workers as a symbol of everlasting peace. (Daily) Bristol park, adj to Municipal building.   **Free.**

Melton Hill Dam and Lake. This TVA dam extends barge travel up the Clinch River to Clinton and provides electric power. Dam (103 ft high, 1,020 ft long) impounds 44-mile-long lake. Fishing; boating. Camping (fee). Visitor overlook. (Daily) 15 mi SW.   **Free.**

Oak Ridge Art Center. Permanent collection of original paintings, drawings and prints; temporary exhibits. (Daily; closed major hols) 201 Badger Ave. Phone 423/482-1441.   **Free.**

The Department of Energy's Graphite Reactor. The world's oldest nuclear reactor, the Graphite Reactor, was built during World War II as part of the "Manhattan Project." interpretive exhibits. ORNL visitor overlook with audiovisual presentation (daily). (Daily) 10 mi SW on Bethel Valley Rd. Phone 423/574-4160.   **Free.**

University of Tennessee Arboretum. Part of University of Tennessee Forestry Experimental Station. More than 1,000 species of trees, shrubs, flowering plants on 250 acres. Self-guided tours. (Mon-Fri) 901 Kerr Hollow Rd. Phone 423/483-3571.   **Free.**

Annual Event

Appalachian Music & Craft Festival. Children's Museum of Oak Ridge. Late Nov.

Motels

★ ★ **COMFORT INN.** 433 S Rutgers Ave. 423/481-8200; FAX 423/483-6142. 122 rms, 5 story, 26 suites. S, D $71-$81; each addl $7; suites $71-$91; under 18 free. Crib free. Pet accepted. TV; cable. Pool. Complimentary continental bkfst. Restaurant nearby. Ck-out noon. Coin lndry. Meeting rms. Business servs avail. Health club privileges. Refrigerator in suites. Cr cds: A, C, D, DS, ER, JCB, MC, V.

D ✔ ≈ ➘ ⚡ SC

✔★ **DAYS INN.** 206 S Illinois Ave. 423/483-5615; res: 800/329-7466. 80 rms, 2 story. S $43-$53; D $49-$59; each addl $3; under 12 free. Crib free. Pet accepted. TV; cable. Heated pool. Playground. Complimentary continental bkfst. Restaurant adj 6:30 am-midnight; Fri, Sat to 2 am. Ck-out 11 am. Meeting rms. Business servs avail. Refrigerators. Cr cds: A, C, D, DS, MC, V.

D ✔ ≈ ➘ ⚡ SC

★ ★ **HAMPTON INN.** 208 S Illinois. 423/482-7889; res: 800/426-7866; FAX 423/482-7493. 60 rms, 5 story. S, D $63-$89; each addl $7; under 18 free. Crib free. TV; cable (premium). Heated pool; whirlpool. Complimentary continental bkfst. Restaurant nearby. Ck-out 11 am. Coin lndry. Meeting rms. Business servs avail. In-rm modem link. Exercise equipt; sauna. Some refrigerators, microwaves. Cr cds: A, C, D, DS, MC, V.

D ≈ ✗ ⚡ SC

Motor Hotel

★ ★ ★ **GARDEN PLAZA HOTEL.** 215 S Illinois Ave. 423/481-2468; FAX 423/481-2474; res: 800/342-7336 (exc TN). 168 rms, 5 story. S, D $79-$99; each addl $7; suites $99-$115; under 18 free. Crib free. TV; cable (premium). Indoor/outdoor pool; whirlpool, poolside serv. Coffee in rms. Restaurant 6:30 am-2 pm, 5-10 pm. Rm serv. Bar. Ck-out noon. Meeting rms. Business center. Health club privileges. Refrigerator, wet bar in suites. Cr cds: A, C, D, DS, MC, V.

D ≈ ➘ ⚡ SC ⚒

Paris (D-3)

(See also Land Between The Lakes, KY)

Founded 1821 **Pop** 9,332 **Elev** 519 ft **Area code** 901 **Zip** 38242
Information Paris-Henry County Chamber of Commerce, PO Box 8; 901/642-3431 or 800/345-1103.

Only 14 miles from Kentucky Lake, Paris is a growing recreational center. It was named in honor of the Marquis de Lafayette, who was visiting in Nashville when the city was founded. The downtown area is lined with many buildings dating back to 1900.

What to See and Do

Nathan Bedford Forrest State Park. On the west bank of Kentucky Lake a monument marks the spot where, in 1864, Confederate General Forrest set up artillery. Undetected by Union forces, the hidden batteries detroyed both the Union base on the opposite shore and its protective warships on the Tennessee River. The area is now an 800-acre park offering fishing and canoe access to the lake. Nature trails & programs, backpacking. Picnicking, playground, concession. Camping, group lodge. View from Pilot Knob. Museum (Wed-Sun). Trace Creek Annex, located across Kentucky Lake, interprets a portion of the military history of the area. Standard fees. 21 mi S on US 641, E on US 70, then 8 mi N on US 191. Phone 901/584-6356.

Paris Landing State Park. An 840-acre park on Kentucky Lake with swimming beach, pools, waterskiing; boating (launch, rentals, marina). Golf, tennis courts. Picnicking, playground, concessions, lodging, restaurant. Camping. Standard fees. 16 mi NE on US 79. Phone 901/644-7359.

Annual Events

World's Biggest Fish Fry. Henry County Fairgrounds. Celebration includes rodeo, parade, contests, tournaments. Last full wk Apr.

Eiffel Tower Day & Hot Air Balloon Festival. Memorial Park. 2nd wkend Sept.

Motels

★ **BEST WESTERN TRAVELER'S INN.** 1297 E Wood St (US 79N). 901/642-8881. 98 rms, 2 story. S $40-$54; D $42-$57; each addl $4; under 12 free; wkly rates. Crib free. TV; cable. Pool. Complimentary continental bkfst. Restaurant adj 6 am-midnight. Private club; setups, beer. Ck-out noon. Meeting rms. Cr cds: A, C, D, DS, MC, V.

D ≈ ➘ ⚡ SC

✔★ **TERRACE WOODS LODGE.** 1190 N Market. 901/642-2642. 19 rms, 1-2 story. S $29-$31; D $33-$35; each addl $4; under 12 free. Crib $4. TV; cable. Complimentary coffee in lobby. Ck-out 11 am. Refrigerators, microwaves. Cr cds: A, C, D, DS, MC, V.

➘ ⚡

Restaurant

✔★ **PAULETTES.** 200 S Market St. 901/644-3777. Hrs: 11 am-8 pm. Closed Sun; most major hols. Res accepted. Semi-a la carte: lunch, dinner $1.95-$6.95. Child's meals. Specializes in sandwiches, quiche. Casual dining. Cr cds: MC, V.

Pigeon Forge (D-8)

(See also Gatlinburg, Sevierville)

Pop 3,027 **Elev** 1,031 ft **Area code** 423 **Zip** 37863 **Web** www.pigeon-forge.tn.us
Information Dept of Tourism, 2450 Parkway, PO Box 1390, 37868-1390; 423/453-8574 or 800/251-9100.

Located in the shadow of the Smokies, this resort town was named for the river on which it sits and the iron forge built in the early 1800s.

What to See and Do

Country music and comedy shows.

The Comedy Barn. 2775 Parkway. Phone 423/428-5222 for schedule. ¢¢¢¢

Memories Theatre. 2141 Parkway. Phone 423/428-7852 or 800/325-3078 for schedule. ¢¢¢¢

Smoky Mountain Jubilee. 2115 Parkway. Phone 423/428-1836 for schedule.

Country Tonite Theatre. (Mar-Dec, daily exc Mon) 2249 Parkway Blvd. Phone 423/453-2003 or 800/792-4308. ¢¢¢¢

Music Mansion Theatre. (Apr-Dec) 100 Music Rd. Phone 423/428-7469. ¢¢¢¢

Tennessee Music Theatre. (Mid-Apr-Oct) 2135 Parkway. Phone 423/428-5600 for schedule. ¢¢¢¢

Dollywood. Dolly Parton's entertainment park. More than 40 musical shows daily; over 30 rides and attractions and more than 70 shops and restaurants. 1 mi E on US 441, on Dollywood Lane. For schedule phone 423/428-9488. ¢¢¢¢

Flyaway. Vertical wind tunnel that simulates skydiving. Instructor assists participants in flight chamber and explains how to maneuver body to soar, turn and descend. Observation gallery (fee). (Mar-Nov, daily; winter schedule varies; closed Dec 25) 3106 Parkway. Phone 423/453-7777. ¢¢¢¢

Ogle's Water Park. An eight-acre water amusement park featuring Lazy River ride, giant wave pools, water slides and children's play area. Tube and locker rentals, dressing rooms, restaurants. (June-Aug, daily; May & Sept, wkends) 2530 Parkway. Phone 423/453-8741. ¢¢¢

Pigeon Forge Pottery. Visitors can watch craftspeople at work. (Daily; closed Jan 1, Dec 25) 2919 Middle Creek Rd. Phone 423/453-3883. **Free.**

Smoky Mountain Car Museum. More than 30 gas, electric and steam autos, including Hank Williams Jr's "Silver Dollar" car; James Bond's "007" Aston Martin; Al Capone's bulletproof Cadillac; the patrol car of Sheriff Buford Pusser from the movie *Walking Tall*; Elvis Presley's Mercedes. Historic gas pump globe display; *Burma Shave* signs. (May-Oct, daily) 2970 Parkway. Phone 423/453-3433. ¢¢

The Old Mill. Water-powered mill, in continuous operation since 1830, grinds cornmeal, grits, whole wheat, rye and buckwheat flours; dam falls are illuminated at night. Site (all yr); guided tours (Apr-Nov, daily exc Sun). 2944 Middle Creek Rd. Phone 423/453-4628. ¢¢

Motels

★ ★ **AMERICANA INN.** *2825 Parkway (US 441).* 423/428-0172. 170 rms, 4 story. S $40-$50; D $55-$75; higher rates hols, special events. Crib $10. TV. Heated pool; whirlpool. Restaurant 8 am-9 pm; closed Sun. Ck-out 11 am. Downhill ski 10 mi. Balconies. Cr cds: DS, MC, V.

D ✔ ≋ ⋈ 🔥

★ ★ **BAYMONT INN.** *2179 Parkway.* 423/428-7305; res: 800/896-2950; FAX 423/428-8977. 131 rms, 4 story. Apr-Dec: S, D $39.95-$99.95; suites $49.95-$109.95; higher rates special events; lower

rates rest of yr. Crib free. Pet accepted. TV; cable (premium), VCR avail (movies). Heated pool. Complimentary continental bkfst. Restaurant adj 11 am-11 pm. Ck-out noon. Coin lndry. Meeting rms. Business servs avail. Downhill ski 10 mi. Refrigerator, microwave in suites. Cr cds: A, C, D, DS, MC, V.

D ✔ ≋ ≋ ⋈ 🔥 SC

★ ★ **BEST WESTERN PLAZA INN.** *3755 Parkway (US 441)* (37868). 423/453-5538; res: 800/232-5656; FAX 423/453-2619. Web www.bwplazainn.com. 201 rms, 3-5 story. S, D $69-$129. Crib $6. TV; cable. Indoor/outdoor pool; whirlpool. Complimentary continental bkfst. Restaurant opp 7 am-9 pm. Ck-out 11 am. Meeting rm. Business servs avail. Downhill ski 6 mi. Sauna. Game rm. Some in-rm whirlpools, refrigerators, fireplaces. Cr cds: A, C, D, DS, MC, V.

D ≋ ≋ ⋈ 🔥 SC

★ ★ **BILMAR MOTOR INN.** *3786 Parkway, on US 441.* 423/453-5593; FAX 423/453-8953; res: 800/343-5610. 76 rms, 2-3 story. Late May-Labor Day, Oct: S, D $36-$85; each addl $5; lower rates Mar-mid-May, after Labor Day-Jan. Closed Jan-Feb. Crib $5. TV; cable. Heated pool. Complimentary continental bkfst. Coffee in rms. Restaurant nearby. Ck-out 11 am. Business servs avail. Some in-rm whirlpools, refrigerators. Cr cds: DS, MC, V.

D ≋ ⋈ 🔥 SC

✔ ★ **BRIARSTONE INN.** *3626 Parkway (US 441).* 423/453-3050; res: 800/523-3919. 57 rms, 3 story. No elvtr. July-Oct: S, D $32-$120; each addl $6; higher rates special events; lower rates rest of yr. TV; cable (premium). Pool; whirlpools. Coffee in rms. Restaurant adj 7 am-11 pm. Ck-out 11 am. Business servs avail. Refrigerators; some fireplaces. Cr cds: A, D, DS, MC, V.

D ≋ ⋈ 🔥 SC

★ ★ **CAPRI.** *4061 Parkway.* 423/453-7147; FAX 423/453-7157; res: 800/528-4555. 106 rms, 2 story. Apr-Dec: S $25-$105; D $25-$145; under 18 free; hols (2-day min); higher rates special events; lower rates rest of yr. Crib free. TV; cable (premium). Heated pool. Complimentary continental bkfst. Restaurant nearby. Ck-out 11 am. Meeting rms. Business servs avail. Downhill ski 5 mi. Many refrigerators. Cr cds: A, DS, MC, V.

D ≋ ≋ ⋈ 🔥

★ ★ **COLONIAL HOUSE.** *3545 Parkway (US 441).* 423/453-0717; FAX 423/453-8412; res: 800/662-5444. 63 rms, 3 story. Mar-Nov: S, D $29-$99; each addl $5; higher rates: hols, special events; lower rates rest of yr. Crib $5. TV; cable. Heated pool; wading pool. Complimentary continental bkfst. Ck-out 11 am. Downhill ski 7 mi. Some in-rm whirlpools, fireplaces. Some private patios, balconies. On river. Cr cds: A, DS, MC, V.

≋ ≋ ⋈ 🔥 SC

✔ ★ **CREEKSTONE INN.** *4034 River Rd.* 423/453-3557; res: 800/523-3919. 172 rms, 5 story. July-Oct: S $32-$114; D $38-$120; suites $68-$162; under 18 free; lower rates rest of yr. Crib $5. TV; cable. Pool. Restaurant nearby. Ck-out 11 am. Refrigerators. On Little Pigeon River. Cr cds: A, DS, MC, V.

D ✔ ≋ ⋈ 🔥 SC

★ ★ **DAYS INN.** *2760 Parkway, US 441.* 423/453-4707; res: 800/645-3079; FAX 423/428-7928. 144 rms, 3 story. May-Oct: S $68-$88; D $78-$98; each addl $5; under 17 free; higher rates: hols, special events; lower rates rest of yr. Crib free. TV; cable. Complimentary coffee in lobby. Restaurant adj 7 am-10 pm. Ck-out 11 am. Business servs avail. Downhill ski 7 mi. Cr cds: A, C, D, DS, MC, V.

D ≋ ≋ ⋈ 🔥 SC

★ **ECONO LODGE.** *2440 Parkway.* 423/428-1231; res: 800/632-6104; FAX 423/453-6879. 202 rms, 3 story. June-Oct: S, D $79-$89; under 18 free; higher rates: wkends, hols, special events; lower rates rest of yr. Crib free. TV. Pool; wading pool, whirlpool. Complimentary continental bkfst. Restaurant nearby. Ck-out 11 am. Meeting rm. Business servs avail. Downhill ski 10 mi. Picnic tables. View of river, mountains. Cr cds: A, C, D, DS, MC, V.

[D] [symbols] SC

★ **GREEN VALLEY.** *4109 Parkway (US 441).* 423/453-9091; FAX 423/453-9091, ext. 321; res: 800/892-1627. 50 rms, 3 story. No elvtr. May-Oct: S, D $48-$98; each addl $5; lower rates rest of yr. Crib $5. TV; cable (premium), VCR (movies $3). Heated pool. Ck-out 11 am. Downhill ski 7 mi. Refrigerators. Cr cds: MC, V.

[D] [symbols] SC

✓★★ **HOWARD JOHNSON.** *2826 Parkway.* 423/453-9151; res: 800/453-6008; FAX 423/453-4141. 145 rms, 3 story. May-Oct: S, D $38.80-$88.80; each addl $6; studio rms $36.80-$88.80; kit. units $74.80-$140; under 18 free; higher rates special events; lower rates rest of yr. Crib free. TV; cable (premium). Pool; wading pool. Restaurant 7 am-noon. Ck-out 11 am. Coin lndry. Business servs avail. Downhill ski 10 mi. Some in-rm whirlpools. Cr cds: A, C, D, DS, JCB, MC, V.

[D] [symbols] SC

★ **KNIGHTS INN.** *2162 Parkway (37868).* 423/428-3824; FAX 423/453-2564; res: 800/523-3919. 65 rms, 3 story. S, D $22-$102; under 18 free; higher rates: wkends, hols, special events. Crib $5. TV; cable (premium). Pool. Complimentary coffee in lobby. Restaurant opp 11 am-11 pm. Ck-out 11 am. Downhill ski 10 mi. Refrigerators. Cr cds: A, DS, MC, V.

[symbols] SC

✓★ **MAPLES MOTOR INN.** *2959 Parkway, 1/2 mi N on US 441.* 423/453-8883; res: 888/453-8883. 63 rms, 2 story. Mar-Dec: S $26-$85; D $36-$95; each addl $5; suites $79-$135; higher rates: some hols, special events. Closed rest of yr. Crib $5. TV; cable (premium). Pool. Complimentary coffee in lobby. Restaurant nearby. Ck-out 11 am. Some whirlpools, fireplaces. Picnic tables, grills. Cr cds: DS, MC, V.

[D] [symbols]

★★ **MCAFEE INN.** *3756 Parkway (US 441).* 423/453-3490; FAX 423/429-5432; res: 800/925-4443. 127 rms, 3 story. June-Aug, Oct: S, D $73-$98; higher rates: hols, special events; lower rates rest of yr. Crib $5. TV; cable (premium). Heated pool; wading pool, whirlpool. Complimentary continental bkfst. Coffee in rms. Restaurant adj 7 am-9 pm. Ck-out 11 am. Business servs avail. Downhill ski 5 mi. Refrigerators; some in-rm whirlpools, wet bars. Some balconies. Picnic tables. Cr cds: A, C, D, DS, MC, V.

[D] [symbols] SC

★ **MOUNTAIN BREEZE.** *2926 Parkway (US 441).* 423/453-2659; res: 888/453-2659. 71 rms. June-Oct: S, D $60-$95; kit. units $120; higher rates special events; lower rates rest of yr. Crib $4. TV; cable. Pool. Complimentary coffee in rms. Ck-out 11 am. Refrigerators, microwaves. Cr cds: DS, MC, V.

[D] [symbols] SC

✓★★ **NORMA DAN.** *3864 Parkway.* 423/453-2403; FAX 423/453-1948; res: 800/582-7866. 86 rms, 3 story. S $28-$78; D $34-$88; kit. cottage $85-$134; under 18 free; wkends, hols (2-3-day min); higher rates special events. Crib free. TV; cable (premium). Heated pool; wading pool, whirlpool. Complimentary coffee in lobby. Restaurant opp 7 am-10 pm. Ck-out 11 am. Coin lndry. Meeting rms. Business servs avail. Downhill ski 7 mi. Many refrigerators. Balconies. Picnic tables. Cr cds: A, C, D, DS, MC, V.

[D] [symbols]

★ **PARKVIEW.** *2806 Parkway (US 441).* 423/453-5051; res: 800/239-9116. 39 rms, 1-2 story. June-Oct: S, D $58-$90; higher rates some events; lower rates Mar-May, Nov-late Dec. Closed rest of yr. TV; cable. Heated pool. Complimentary coffee in lobby. Restaurant adj 7 am-10 pm. Ck-out 11 am. Cr cds: A, D, DS, MC, V.

[D] [symbols]

★★ **RAMADA INN.** *4010 Parkway (US 441) (37868).* 423/453-1823; FAX 423/453-2564; res: 800/523-3919. 123 rms, 3 story. No elvtr. Mid-May-Oct: S, D $29-$115; suites $49-$195; under 18 free; higher rates special events; lower rates rest of yr, under 18 free. TV; cable. Heated pool; whirlpool. Complimentary coffee in lobby. Restaurant nearby. Ck-out 11 am. Business servs avail. Downhill/x-country ski 7 mi. Refrigerators. Cr cds: A, D, DS, MC, V.

[D] [symbols]

★ **RIVER CHASE.** *3709 Parkway (US 441).* 423/428-1299; res: 888/754-3316; FAX 423/453-1678. 105 rms, 4 story. June-Oct: S, D $60-$95; each addl $5; higher rates hol wkends; lower rates rest of yr. Crib $10. TV. Heated pool. Restaurant opp 7 am-10 pm. Ck-out 11 am. Downhill ski 7 mi. Miniature golf. Some in-rm whirlpools. Cr cds: A, DS, MC, V.

[D] [symbols]

✓★ **RIVER PLACE INN.** *3223 Parkway (US 441).* 423/453-0801; res: 800/428-5590. 52 rms, 2 story. May-Oct: S, D $38.50-$88.50; each addl $5; under 12 free; higher rates special events; lower rates rest of yr. Closed Mid-Dec-mid-Mar. TV; cable. Pool. Restaurant adj 6 am-9 pm. Ck-out 11 am. Refrigerators. Balconies. Picnic tables, grills. On river. Cr cds: DS, MC, V.

[symbols]

✓★★ **RODEWAY INN/MOUNTAIN SKYS.** *4236 Parkway, on US 441.* 423/453-3530; FAX 423/423-2564. 116 rms, 2-3 story. No elvtr. May-Oct: S, D $26-$108; suite $62-$138; family rates; higher rates special events; lower rates rest of yr. TV; cable. Pool. Ck-out 11 am. Downhill ski 10 mi. Refrigerators. Cr cds: A, C, D, DS, MC, V.

[D] [symbols] SC

✓★ **TENNESSEE MOUNTAIN LODGE.** *3571 Parkway.* 423/453-4784; res: 800/446-1674. 50 rms, 3 story. May-Oct: S, D $28-$60; each addl $5; higher rates special events; lower rates rest of yr. Crib $2. TV; cable. Heated pool; wading pool. Restaurant adj 7 am-9:30 pm. Ck-out 11 am. Business servs avail. Downhill ski 6 mi. Refrigerators. On river. Cr cds: A, DS, MC, V.

[symbols]

★★ **VALLEY FORGE INN.** *2795 Parkway (US 441).* 423/453-7770; FAX 423/429-3816; res: 800/544-8740. 171 rms, 4 story. June-Aug, Oct: S, D $62.50-$92.50; suites $10-$50 addl; higher rates: wkends, hols, special events; lower rates rest of yr. Crib $4. TV; cable. 2 pools, 1 indoor; wading pool, whirlpool. Complimentary continental bkfst. Restaurant opp 6 am-9 pm. Ck-out 11 am. Coin lndry. Downhill ski 10 mi. Some in-rm whirlpools, refrigerators. Some balconies. On river. Cr cds: A, DS, MC, V.

[D] [symbols]

Motor Hotels

★★ **GRAND RESORT HOTEL AND CONVENTION CENTER.** *3171 Parkway (US 441).* 423/453-1000; FAX 423/428-3944; res: 800/362-1188. 425 rms, 5 story. May-Oct: S, D $70-$100; each addl $10; suites $80-$199; under 12 free; higher rates special events; lower rates rest of yr. Crib free. Pet accepted. TV; cable. Pool; whirlpool. Complimentary continental bkfst. Restaurant 7 am-9 pm. Rm serv. Ck-out 11 am. Convention facilities. Business servs avail. Gift shop. Downhill ski 7 mi. Some fireplaces. Cr cds: A, D, DS, MC, V.

[D] [symbols] SC

★★ **HEARTLANDER COUNTRY RESORT.** *2385 Parkway (US 441).* 423/453-4106; res: 800/843-6686; FAX 423/429-0159. 160 rms, 5 story. Late May-early Nov: S, D $59-$119; each addl $5; under 12 free; lower rates rest of yr. Crib free. Pet accepted. TV; cable. 2 pools, 1 indoor; whirlpool. Continental bkfst. Ck-out 11 am. Meeting rms. Business servs avail. Sundries. Game rm. Balconies. Cr cds: A, C, D, DS, MC, V.

[D] [symbols] SC

★★ **HOLIDAY INN.** *3230 Parkway, US 441.* 423/428-2700; res: 800/782-3119. E-mail hipftn@usit.net; web www.4lodging.com. 210 rms, 5 story, 10 suites. May-Oct: S, D $59-$129; suites $99-$199; under 18 free; higher rates special events; lower rates rest of yr. Crib free. TV. Indoor pool; whirlpool. Restaurant 7 am-10 pm. Ck-out 11 am. Coin lndry. Meeting rms. Business servs avail. In-rm modem link. Exercise equipt. Downhill ski 7 mi. Game rm. Some refrigerators. Cr cds: A, C, D, DS, JCB, MC, V.

D ⊠ ⊠ ⌘ ⌘ ⊠ SC

★ ★ RIVER'S LANDING RESORT. 4025 Parkway. 423/453-9081; res: 800/345-6799; FAX 423/428-3240. 181 rms, 2 story. May-mid-Nov: S, D $59-$125; each addl $9; golf package; higher rates: hols, football wkends, special events; lower rates rest of yr. Crib free. TV; cable. Indoor pool; wading pool, whirlpool. Playground. Ck-out 11 am. Meeting rms. Business servs avail. Downhill ski 10 mi. Cr cds: A, C, D, DS, MC, V.

D ⊠ ⊠ ⌘ ⊠ SC

★ ★ RIVERSIDE MOTOR LODGE. 3575 Parkway (US 441). 423/453-5555; res: 800/242-8366. Web www.pigeonforge.com. 56 kit. suites, 5 story. May-Oct: kit. suites $99-$150; each addl after 4, $5; under 16 free; lower rates rest of yr. TV; cable (premium). Indoor pool; whirlpool. Complimentary coffee in lobby. Restaurant nearby. Ck-out 11 am. Cr cds: A, DS, MC, V.

D ⊠ ⌘ ⊠

Inns

★ ★ DAY DREAMS COUNTRY INN. 2720 Colonial Dr. 423/428-0370; FAX 423/428-2622; res: 800/377-1469. E-mail day dreams@sprynet.com; web www.daydreamscountryinn.com. 6 rms, 2 story. No rm phones. S $69-$109; D $79-$119; each addl $15; under 2 free. Crib free. TV; cable (premium), VCR avail (free movies). Complimentary full bkfst; afternoon refreshments. Restaurants nearby. Ck-out 11 am, ck-in 3 pm. Downhill/x-country ski 10 mi. Antiques. Screened-in porches. Totally nonsmoking. Cr cds: DS, MC, V.

D ⌘ ⊠ ⌘ ⌘ SC

★ ★ HILTON'S BLUFF. 2654 Valley Heights Dr, US 321S S to Valley Heights Dr. 423/428-9765; res: 800/441-4188. 10 air-cooled rms, 2 story. No rm phones. Apr-Nov: S, D $79-$129; each addl $15-$20; wkly rates; lower rates rest of yr. TV. Complimentary full bkfst. Restaurant nearby. Ck-out 11 am, ck-in 3 pm. Meeting rm. Rec rm. Balconies. On hill with scenic mountain view; library, deck with rocking chairs. Totally nonsmoking. Cr cds: A, MC, V.

⊠ ⌘

Restaurants

✔★ APPLE TREE INN. 3215 Parkway (US 441) (37868). 423/453-4961. Hrs: 6:30 am-10 pm. Closed Jan-mid-Mar. Res accepted. Semi-a la carte: bkfst $1.50-$5.29, lunch $1.50-$6.95, dinner $4.25-$11; family style $9. Child's meals. Specializes in spoon bread. Soup, salad bar. Parking. Family-owned. Cr cds: A, MC, V.

D SC

★ OLD MILL. 2940 Middle Creek (37868). 423/429-3463. Hrs: 8 am-8:30 pm. Semi-a la carte: bkfst $5.25-$8.75, lunch $5.95-$8.95, dinner $9.99-$17.95. Child's meals. Specializes in prime rib, seafood, fried chicken. Parking. Art exhibits by local artists. Overlooks river. Totally nonsmoking. Cr cds: A, DS, MC, V.

D

✔★ TROTTER'S. 3716 Parkway (US 441). 423/453-3347. Hrs: 7 am-9 pm; Fri, Sat to 9:30 pm. Closed Jan-Mar. Semi-a la carte: bkfst $2-$7, lunch $2.25-$6.25, dinner $7.50-$11.95. Child's meals. Specializes in Southern cooking. Parking. Cr cds: DS, MC, V.

D ⊡

Savannah (E-3)

Pop 6,547 **Elev** 436 ft **Area code** 901 **Zip** 38372

What to See and Do

Pickwick Landing Dam, Lock and Lake. This TVA dam (113 ft high, 7,715 ft long) impounds a 53-mi-long lake with 496 miles of shoreline. Also a 1,000-ft-long navigation lock. Powerhouse visitor lobby. Navigation Museum at lock. (Daily) 14 mi S on TN 128. Phone 901/925-4346. **Free.** Adj is

Pickwick Landing State Resort Park. Approximately 1,400 acres adj to Pickwick Dam. Swimming pool, beach; fishing; boating (marina, launch, rentals). Nature trails; golf, tennis. Picnicking, playground, concession, cafe. Camping. Lodge (see). Standard fees. 15 mi S on TN 128 to TN 57. Phone 901/689-3129.

Shiloh National Military Park (see). 10 mi SW on TN 22.

Lodge

★ ★ PICKWICK LANDING. (, Pickwick Dam 38365) Just off TN 57, near Pickwick Dam, in state park. 901/689-3135; res: 800/250-8615; FAX 901/689-3606. 78 rms in 3-story lodge, 10 kit. cabins. Mar-Dec: S, D $58-$62; each addl $6; suites $175; kit. cabins (1-wk min) $540/wk; under 16 free; lower rates rest of yr. Crib free. TV; cable (premium). Pool; wading pool. Dining rm 7 am-8 pm. Ck-out 11 am. Meeting rms. Lighted tennis. 18-hole golf, pro, greens fee. Lawn games. Boat rentals. Lodge rms overlook lake; balconies. State-owned; all facilities of state park avail. Cr cds: A, MC, V.

D ⌘ ⌘ ⌘ ⌘ ⌘ SC

Sevierville (D-8)

(See also Gatlinburg, Pigeon Forge)

Founded 1795 **Pop** 7,178 **Elev** 903 ft **Area code** 423
Information Chamber of Commerce, 866 Winfield Dunn Pkwy, 37876; 423/453-6411.

Founded as part of the independent state of Franklin, this seat of Sevier County was named for John Sevier, who later became the first governor of Tennessee. Long a marketing center for a wide belt of farmland, Sevierville is only 16 miles from the Great Smoky Mountains National Park (see).

What to See and Do

Douglas Dam and Lake. This TVA dam (202 ft high, 1,705 ft long) on the French Broad River was built on a 24-hr work schedule during World War II to furnish power for national defense. It impounds a lake 43 mi long with 555 mi of shoreline. Swimming; fishing; boating. Camping. Overlook (daily). 11 mi NE off TN 66. Phone 423/453-3889. **Free.**

Forbidden Caverns. Natural chimneys, underground streams; stereophonic sound presentations. Temperature in cave is 58°F. (Apr-Nov, daily; closed Thanksgiving) 13 mi NE on US 411. Phone 423/453-5972. ¢¢¢

Smoky Mountain Deer Farm. Petting zoo includes deer, zebra, pygmy goats, llama. Pony rides and horseback riding (fee). (Daily; closed wk after Jan 1, Thanksgiving, Dec 25) 478 Happy Hollow Lane. Phone 423/428-3337. ¢¢

Motels

★ ★ COMFORT INN-MOUNTAIN VIEW SUITES. 860 Winfield Dunn Pkwy (37862). 423/428-5519; res: 800/441-0311; FAX 423/428-

6700. 95 air-cooled suites, 3 story. May-Oct: S, D $46-$159; each addl $5; under 18 free; golf plans; higher rates special events; lower rates rest of yr. Crib $7. TV; cable (premium). 2 pools, 1 indoor; wading pool, whirlpool. Complimentary continental bkfst. Complimentary coffee in rms. Restaurant nearby. Ck-out 11 am. Meeting rms. Business servs avail. Golf privileges. Downhill ski 16 mi. Refrigerators, wet bars. Balconies. Cr cds: A, C, D, DS, ER, MC, V.

D ✕ ⋈ ≋ ⋈ ⋈ SC

★★ **DAYS INN.** 1841 Parkway (37862). 423/428-3353; res: 800/590-4861; FAX 423/428-7613. 100 rms, 4 story. Apr-Oct: S $58-$88; D $78-$98; each addl $5; under 17 free; higher rates special events; lower rates rest of yr. Crib free. TV; cable. Heated pool. Complimentary continental bkfst. Restaurant nearby. Ck-out 11 am. Business servs avail. Downhill ski 10 mi. Some refrigerators. Cr cds: A, C, D, DS, MC, V.

D ≋ ≋ ≋ ⋈ SC

★★ **DAYS INN.** (3402 Winfield Dunn Hwy, Kodak 37764) I-40 exit 407. 423/933-4500; res: 800/304-3915; FAX 423/932-7996. 78 rms, 4 story. Apr-Oct: S, D $48-$88; each addl $5; under 17 free; higher rates special events; lower rates rest of yr. Crib free. TV; cable (premium). Complimentary continental bkfst. Restaurant opp 7 am-9 pm. Ck-out 11 am. Business servs avail. In-rm modem link. Heated pool. Some in-rm whirlpools. Balconies. Cr cds: A, C, D, DS, MC, V.

D ≋ ≋ ⋈ SC

★ **MIZE.** 804 Parkway (37862). 423/453-4684; FAX 423/453-0485; res: 800/239-9117. 42 rms, 1-2 story, 4 kits. May-Oct: S, D $38.50-$82.50; each addl $5; kit. units $45-$125; higher rates special events; lower rates rest of yr. TV; cable (premium). Pool. Complimentary coffee. Restaurant nearby. Ck-out 11 am. Business servs avail. Picnic tables, grill. Cr cds: A, D, DS, MC, V.

D ≋ ≋ ⋈

★ **OAK TREE LODGE.** 1620 Parkway (37862). 423/428-7500; FAX 423/429-8603; res: 800/637-7002. Web www.pigeonforge.com. 100 rms, 3 story, 22 suites. Mid-May-mid-Nov: S, D $59.50-$89.50; suites $79.50-$119.50; under 18 free; higher rates special events; lower rates rest of yr. Crib free. TV; cable. Heated pool. Complimentary continental bkfst. Complimentary coffee in rms. Restaurant nearby. Ck-out noon. Meeting rms. Business servs avail. Downhill/x-country ski 10 mi. Exercise equipt. Refrigerators. Balconies. Picnic tables, grills. Cr cds: A, D, DS, MC, V.

D ⋈ ✕ ≋ ✕ ⋈ ⋈ SC

★★ **QUALITY INN.** (37764). I-40 exit 407, at TN 66. 423/933-7378; res: 800/348-4652; FAX 423/933-9145. 78 rms, 3 story. May-Oct: S $58-$78; D $68-$98; each addl $5; under 17 free; higher rates: hols, car shows; lower rates rest of yr. TV; cable (premium). Indoor pool. Complimentary coffee in lobby. Restaurant adj 6 am-10 pm. Ck-out 11 am. Business servs avail. Downhill/x-country ski 20 mi. Balconies. Cr cds: A, C, D, DS, MC, V.

D ≋ ≋ ≋ ⋈ ⋈ SC

Inn

★★ **LITTLE GREENBRIER LODGE.** 3685 Lyon Springs Rd (37862). 423/429-2500; res: 800/277-8100. Web www.rodsguide.com/greenbrier.htm 10 rms, 8 with shower only, 2 share bath, 3 story. No rm phones. May-Dec: S $65; D $75-$110; lower rates rest of yr. Children over 12 yrs only. Cable TV in parlor. Complimentary full bkfst. Ck-out 11 am, ck-in 4 pm. Downhill ski 9 mi. Balconies. Antiques and Victorian decor in lodge built in 1939. Totally nonsmoking. Cr cds: DS, MC, V.

≋ ≋ ⋈ SC

Restaurants

✔★ **APPLEWOOD FARMHOUSE.** 240 Apple Valley Rd (37862). 423/428-1222. Hrs: 8 am-9 pm; Fri, Sat to 10 pm. Setups. Semi-a la carte: bkfst $4.25-$8.95, lunch $4.95-$7.95, dinner $11.95-$16.95. Child's meals. Specializes in apple fritters, country ham, fried chicken.

Parking. Grounds with gazebo, apple trees along river. Cr cds: A, D, DS, MC, V.

D ⋈

★★★ **FIVE OAKS BEEF AND SEAFOOD.** 1625 Parkway (37862). 423/453-5994. Hrs: 5-9 pm; Fri, Sat to 10 pm. Semi-a la carte: dinner $9.95-$26.95. Specializes in beef, seafood, flambé desserts. Parking. Restored private residence (1860). Totally nonsmoking. Cr cds: A, DS, MC, V.

D

Shelbyville (E-5)

Founded 1809 **Pop** 14,049 **Elev** 765 ft **Area code** 931 **Zip** 37160 **E-mail** bedford@edge.net **Web** www.shelbyvilletn.com

Information Shelbyville & Bedford County Chamber of Commerce, 100 N Cannon Blvd; 931/684-3482 or 888/662-2525.

Enshrined in the hearts and thoughts of every true citizen of Shelbyville is the Tennessee walking horse, that most noble of animals whose high-stepping dignity and high-level intelligence is annually celebrated here. There are 50 walking-horse farms and training stables within a 14-mile radius of town; obtain maps at the Chamber of Commerce.

Annual Events

Spring Fun Show. Celebration grounds. Amateur and professional-class walking horses compete. Phone 931/684-5915. 3 days late May.

Tennessee Walking Horse National Celebration. Outdoor arena at Celebration Grounds. More than 2,100 horses participate. Events conclude with crowning ceremonies for world grand champion walking horse. For tickets contact PO Box 1010, 37162; 931/684-5915. Late Aug.

Motels

★★ **BEST WESTERN CELEBRATION INN.** 724 Madison St. 931/684-2378; FAX 931/685-4936. 58 rms, 2 story. S $60; D $70; each addl $8; suites $80-$100; higher rates special events. Crib $3. TV; cable (premium), VCR avail. Indoor pool. Complimentary continental bkfst. Restaurant nearby. Ck-out noon. Coin lndry. Meeting rm. Exercise equipt. Cr cds: A, D, DS, MC, V.

D ≋ ✕ ≋ ⋈

★★ **SHELBYVILLE INN.** 317 N Cannon Blvd. 931/684-6050; res: 800/622-0466; FAX 931/684-2714. 72 rms, 2 story. S $44-$49; D $49-$55; each addl $6; under 18 free; higher rates special events. Crib free. Pet accepted, some restrictions. TV; cable (premium). Pool. Restaurant 6 am-2 pm, 5-9 pm. Ck-out noon. Meeting rms. Cr cds: A, C, D, DS, JCB, MC, V.

D ✔ ≋ ≋ ⋈ SC

Shiloh National Military Park (E-3)

(See also Savannah)

(10 mi SW of Savannah on TN 22)

Bitter, bloody Shiloh was the first major Civil War battle in the West and one of the fiercest in history. In two days, April 6 and 7, 1862, nearly 24,000 men were killed, wounded or missing. The South's failure to destroy Grant's army opened the way for the attack on and siege of Vicksburg, Mississippi (see). It was, however, a costly battle for the North as well.

General Grant's Army of the Tennessee, numbering almost 40,000, was camped near Pittsburg Landing and Shiloh Church, waiting for the Army of the Ohio under General Don Carlos Buell to attack the Confederates, who, they thought, were near Corinth, Mississippi, 20 miles south. But the brilliant Southern General Albert Sidney Johnston surprised Grant with an attack at dawn on April 6.

Although General Johnston was mortally wounded on the first day, the Southerners successfully pushed the Union Army back and nearly captured their supply base at Pittsburg Landing. On the second day, however, the Northerners, reinforced by the 17,918-man Army of the Ohio, counterattacked and forced the Confederates to retreat toward Corinth.

At Shiloh, one of the first tent field hospitals ever established helped save the lives of many Union and Confederate soldiers. Among the men who fought this dreadful battle were John Wesley Powell, who lost an arm, but later went down the Colorado River by boat and became head of the US Geological Survey, James A. Garfield, 20th president of the United States, Ambrose Bierce, famous satirist and short story writer, and Henry Morton Stanley, who later uttered the famous phrase, "Dr. Livingstone, I presume."

The park is open all year; closed Dec 25. Contact Superintendent, Rte 1, Box 9, Shiloh 38376; 901/689-5696. ¢

What to See and Do

Auto tour. Self-guided, 10-mi tour begins at the visitor center, where brochures can be obtained. Numbered markers indicate 14 points of interest.

National Cemetery. Buried here are about 3,800 soldiers, two-thirds of whom are unidentified. 10 acres on a bluff overlooking Pittsburg Landing and the Tennessee River.

Visitor Center. Museum exhibits and 23-mi historical film; bookstore opp. (Daily; closed Dec 25) 1 mi from park entrance, E off TN 22, near Pittsburg Landing.

Stones River National Battlefield

(see Murfreesboro)

Sweetwater (E-7)

(See also Lenoir City)

Pop 5,066 **Elev** 917 ft **Area code** 423 **Zip** 37874 **E-mail** mctourism@cococo.net **Web** www.monroecounty.com

Information Monroe County Chamber of Commerce Visitor Center, 4765 Hwy 68, Madisonville 37354; 423/442-9147 or 800/245-5428.

What to See and Do

Lost Sea. Glass-bottom boats explore the nation's largest underground lake (4½ acres) in the Lost Sea Caverns. Guided tours (1 hr). Temperature is constant at 58°F. (Daily; closed Dec 25) 6 mi SE on TN 68. Phone 423/337-6616. ¢¢¢

McMinn County Living Heritage Museum. The museum contains 26 exhibit areas with more than 6,000 items that reflect life in this region during the time span from the Cherokees to the Great Depression. (Mon-Fri, Sat & Sun afternoons; closed major hols) 522 W Madison Ave, 13 mi S on US 11, in Athens. Phone 423/745-0329. ¢¢

Motels

★ **BUDGET HOST.** *207 TN 68. 423/337-9357; FAX 423/337-7436.* 61 rms, 2 story. Mar-Nov: S $29.95-$39.95; D $33.95-$43.95; each

addl $7; under 10 free; wkly rates; higher rates football games; lower rates rest of yr. Crib $5. Pet accepted; $3. TV; cable (premium), VCR avail (movies). Complimentary coffee in lobby. Restaurant adj open 24 hrs. Ck-out 11 am. Coin lndry. Some refrigerators, microwaves. Cr cds: A, C, D, DS, MC, V.

★★ **COMFORT INN.** *803 S Main St, on US 11. 423/337-6646; FAX 423/337-5409.* 60 rms, 2 story. S $32-$55; D $36-$55; each addl $4; under 18 free. Crib $5. Pet accepted; $5. TV; cable. Pool; wading pool. Complimentary continental bkfst. Restaurant nearby. Ck-out 11 am. Business servs avail. Pond, picnic area. Cr cds: A, C, D, DS, ER, MC, V.

Restaurant

★★ **DINNER BELL.** *Oakland Rd & I-75, exit 62. 423/337-5825.* Hrs: 6 am-10 pm; Fri, Sat to 11 pm. Closed Dec 25. Res accepted. Semi-a la carte: bkfst $2.29-$4.79, lunch, dinner $1.69-$8.99. Buffet: bkfst $3.99, lunch $5.29, dinner $6.29. Child's meals. Specializes in southern cooking. Own cobblers. Salad bar. Parking. Gift shop. Family-owned. Cr cds: A, DS, MC, V.

Tennessee Valley Authority*

TVA projects are centered on and around the Tennessee River Valley, primarily in Tennessee, Kentucky and Alabama.

The new prosperity and immense industrial expansion of a large portion of the South is directly linked to the Tennessee Valley Authority, an independent corporate agency of the federal government created by an Act of Congress on May 18, 1933. More than 80,000 square miles in Tennessee, North Carolina, Virginia, Georgia, Alabama, Mississippi and Kentucky continue to benefit directly from its activities. In addition, the entire nation benefits indirectly from TVA research and development in a wide range of fields.

In 1933, most of the Tennessee Valley area was the scene of desperate poverty. Actually, it had never recovered from the Civil War. The depression that began in 1929 had struck another cruel blow. Senator George Norris of Nebraska, President Franklin D. Roosevelt and other national leaders knew that in a river valley of rich potential this was unnecessary and illogical. They proposed that the nation provide the tools the valley's people needed to build a new prosperity through proper use of the Tennessee River, its tributaries and its vast watershed.

Today, TVA dams and reservoirs regulate floodwaters on the Tennessee River and help reduce floods downstream on the Ohio and Mississippi rivers. They provide a year-round river channel for modern barges from the Ohio to Knoxville, making the river a busy waterway for industry. The same dams produce power for residents and industries. In the watershed area, TVA helps advance erosion control and vital farming and forestry improvements. It has eliminated malaria from the region by destroying mosquito breeding habitat. It operates a national environmental research center where many modern products of the US fertilizer industry are made.

This resource development effort has helped the people of the region strengthen their economy and build an unprecedented prosperity. Per capita income in the TVA area was only 45 percent of the national average in 1933. Today it stands at almost 80 percent of the national average.

Approximately eight million people live in the area served with TVA power. TVA power is distributed to local consumers through cooperatives owned by people of each area or by individual cities. Much of the original construction was financed by the federal government, and TVA has always earned appropriate income on this money. Today, TVA power facilities are financed with the agency's own power revenues and through bond and note sales. Meanwhile, TVA is repaying the original appropriations invested in its power system, plus dividends on that investment.

TVA operates 39 dams on the Tennessee River and its tributaries; of these, TVA owns 35. Coal-burning power plants, built mostly in the 1950s and 1960s, when power use exceeded the capacity of the dams, provide the primary souce of electricity today. Immense use by atomic and space installations was a main factor in requiring more power supply. Now the TVA system includes 11 coal-fired plants, one hydroelectric pumped-storage plant and two nuclear plants.

For visitors interested in recreation, TVA lakes provide more than 600,000 surface acres of water and 11,000 miles of shoreline. Along these reservoirs, there are more than 100 public parks, 450 access areas and 325 commercial recreation areas. The lakes provide excellent fishing for bass, walleye, crappie and other fish, with no closed season, and many other recreational opportunities. In the 1960s, TVA developed a 40-mile-long recreation and environmental-education area in western Kentucky and Tennessee, called Land Between The Lakes.

Visitors are welcome at TVA dams and steam plants. Public Safety Officers, who conduct tours, are on duty from 9 am-5 pm at the Raccoon Mountain facility. Golden Age and Golden Access Passports (see MAKING THE MOST OF YOUR TRIP) are honored at all TVA fee recreation areas.

Recreation maps of TVA lakes, with detailed routes to shoreline recreation areas, as well as navigation charts and maps for the major lakes, may be ordered by writing the TVA Map Sales Office, 1101 Market St, Chattanooga 37402. Specify the lake(s) of interest on each request. A free list of maps and their costs is available. Charts for mainstream lakes of the Tennessee River, showing navigation channels, water depth, buoys, lights, other navigation aids and recreation areas, are also available.

Limited material on the TVA and its diverse programs is available from the Technical Library, TVA, 400 W Summit Hill Dr, Knoxville 37902; 423/632-8000 or 423/632-2101.

Tiptonville (D-2)

Pop 2,149 **Elev** 301 ft **Area code** 901 **Zip** 38079
Information Northwest Tennessee Tourism, PO Box 963, Martin 38237; 901/587-4213.

What to See and Do

Reelfoot Lake. This 13,000-acre lake, 18 mi long and more than 2 mi wide, was created by the New Madrid earthquakes of 1811-1812. A bird and game refuge of unusual beauty, the lake has an untamed quality with vast expanses of lily pads and giant cypress trees growing from the water. More than 56 species of fish inhabit these waters, and 260 species of water and land fowl populate the area. Resorts around the lake provide boat rentals and guide services. 2 mi E on TN 21. On the S shore is

Reelfoot Lake State Park. Approximately 300 acres with a visitor center/museum exhibiting Native American artifacts, natural and cultural displays, earthquake simulator and specimens of local fauna (free). Fishing, duck hunting; boating (launch, rentals). Tennis courts. Picnicking, concession, restaurant, lodge (see). Tent & trailer sites. Boat excursions at park (May-Sept). Bald eagle tours (Dec-mid-Mar). Standard fees. 5 mi E on TN 21. Contact Superintendent, Rte 1, Box 296; 901/253-7756.

Lodge

★ **AIR PARK INN.** Rte 1, Box 2345, 8 mi N on TN 78, 3 mi E on TN 213. 901/253-7756; FAX 901/253-8940. 20 rms, 1-2 story. S, D $56; each addl $6; suites $75; under 16 free. Closed early Oct-Dec. TV; cable, VCR avail. Pool. Complimentary coffee in rms. Restaurant 7 am-8 pm. Ck-out 11 am. Meeting rms. Business servs avail. Tennis. Private patios.

3,500-ft landing strip. All facilities of Reelfoot Lake State Park avail; overlooks Reelfoot Lake. Cr cds: A, MC, V.

D ⚡ 🏃 ≋ 🔥 SC

Restaurant

✔★ **BOYETTE'S DINING ROOM.** 2½ mi E on TN 21. 901/253-7307. Hrs: 11 am-9 pm. Closed Thanksgiving, Dec 24, 25. Res accepted. Semi-a la carte: lunch $2.50-$11, dinner $3.50-$11. Child's meals. Specializes in catfish, country ham, fried chicken. Parking. On Reelfoot Lake. Family-owned. No cr cds accepted.

D

Townsend (E-8)

(See also Gatlinburg, Maryville)

Pop 329 **Elev** 1,036 ft **Area code** 423 **Zip** 37882 **E-mail** smokymvb@chamber.blount.tn.us **Web** chamber.blount.tn.us/smokymvb
Information Smoky Mountain Visitors Bureau, 7906 E Lamar Alexander Pkwy; 423/448-6134 or 800/525-6834.

What to See and Do

Cades Cove. 5 mi SE on TN 73, then 8 mi SW on unnumbered road in Great Smoky Mountains National Park (see).

Tuckaleechee Caverns. Cathedral-like main chamber is largest cavern room in eastern US; drapery formations, walkway over subterranean streams, flowstone falls; waterfalls tour. Temperature 58°F in caverns. Guided tours every 15-20 min (mid-Mar-mid-Nov, daily). 3 mi S, off US 321. Phone 423/448-2274. ¢¢¢

Motels

★★ **BEST WESTERN VALLEY VIEW LODGE.** 7726 Lamar Alexander Pkwy. 423/448-2237; res: 800/292-4844; FAX 423/448-9957. 91 rms, 2 story, 39 suites. May-Oct: S, D $49.50-$89.50; each addl $5; suites $64.50-$125.50; lower rates rest of yr. Crib $5. Pet accepted. TV; cable (premium). 3 pools, 1 indoor; whirlpools. Complimentary continental bkfst. Coffee in rms. Restaurant nearby. Ck-out 11 am. Meeting rms. Business servs avail. Lawn games. Refrigerators; some fireplaces; minibar in suites. Private patios, balconies. Covered picnic area, grill. Cr cds: A, C, D, DS, MC, V.

D 🐾 ≋ 🔥 SC

★★ **FAMILY INNS.** 7239 E Lamar Alexander Pkwy. 423/448-9100; FAX 423/448-6140; res: 800/332-8282. 39 rms, 2 story, 7 suites, 8 kits. May-Oct: S $46-$63; D $48-$85; each addl $5; suites $79-$139; kit. units $54-$99; under 18 free; higher rates hols; lower rates rest of yr. TV; cable. Heated pool. Complimentary continental bkfst. Restaurant nearby. Ck-out 11 am. Business servs avail. Refrigerator in suites. Picnic tables. On river. Cr cds: A, D, DS, MC, V.

D ⚡ ≋ 🔥 SC

✔★★ **HAMPTON INN.** 7824 E Lamar Alexander Pkwy. 423/448-9000; FAX 423/448-9524. E-mail hampton@esper.com. 54 rms, 2 story. Apr-Nov: S $39-$84; D $44-$89; under 18 free; higher rates special events; lower rates rest of yr. Crib free. TV; cable (premium). Pool. Complimentary continental bkfst. Coffee in rms. Ck-out 11 am. Business servs avail. Refrigerators. Cr cds: A, C, D, DS, MC, V.

D ≋ 🔥 SC

★★ **HIGHLAND MANOR.** 7766 E Lamar Alexander Pkwy. 423/448-2211; FAX 423/448-2312; res: 800/213-9462. Web www.highlandmanor.com. 50 rms, 2 story, 8 suites. May-Oct: S, D $49.50-$89.50; each addl $5; suites $59.50-$109.50; kit. units $89.50; family, wkly rates; golf plans; lower rates rest of yr. Crib $3. TV; cable (premium). Pool;

wading pool. Complimentary continental bkfst. Restaurant opp 7 am-11 pm. Ck-out 11 am. Meeting rms. Business servs avail. 18-hole golf privileges, greens fee $32, pro. Exercise equipt. Refrigerators. Balconies. Picnic tables. Opp river. Cr cds: A, C, D, DS, MC, V.

D ≈ ⅀ ⊠ ☒ SC

✔ ★ ★ **TALLEY-HO INN.** *8314 TN 73, 1/4 mi off US 321 on TN 73. 423/448-2465; FAX 423/448-3913; res: 800/448-2465.* E-mail talley hoinn@msn.com; web thesmokies/talley_ho. 46 rms, 2 story. June-Labor Day, Oct: S, D $42-$72; each addl $5; suites $79-$102; under 12 free; lower rates rest of yr. Crib $5. TV; cable. Heated pool; wading pool. Restaurant 7 am-9 pm. Ck-out 11 am. Meeting rm. Business servs avail. Tennis. Many refrigerators. Private patios, balconies. Cr cds: A, D, DS, MC, V.

D ⅀ ≈ ≈ ☒ SC

Inn

★ ★ **RICHMONT INN.** *220 Winterberry Lane, Old Tuckaleechee Rd to Laurel Valley. 423/448-6751; FAX 423/448-6480.* E-mail richmont inn@worldnet.att.com; web www.thesmokies.com/richmont_inn. 12 rms, 3 story. 1 suite. No rm phones. S, D $95-$200; each addl $35. Children over 12 yrs only. Complimentary full bkfst. Complimentary coffee in rms. Ck-out 10:30 am, ck-in 3 pm. Gift shop. Golf privileges. Exercise equipt. Lawn games. Built in style of Appalachian cantilever barn. Many antques. View of Rich Mountain. Totally nonsmoking. No cr cds accepted.

D ⅄ ⅀ ☒ ☒

Cottage Colony

★ **PIONEER CABINS & GUEST FARM.** *253 Boat Gunnel Rd (37882-0207). 423/448-6100; FAX 423/448-9652; res: 800/621-9751.* Web thesmokies.com/pioneer_cabins/. 7 kit. cabins, 1-2 story. (2-day min): cabins $97.50-$130; each addl $10; wkly rates. Crib free. TV; VCR. Restaurant nearby. Ck-out 11 am, ck-in 3 pm. Grocery 1/4 mi. Coin lndry. Hiking. Porches. Picnic tables, grills. On 47 private acres; fishing pond, petting farm. No cr cds accepted.

D ➳ ☒

Union City (D-2)

(See also Tiptonville)

Pop 10,513 **Elev** 337 ft **Area code** 901 **Zip** 38261

What to See and Do

Davy Crockett Cabin. Frontiersman's cabin is now a museum with period artifacts; grave of Crockett's mother is on grounds. (Memorial Day-Labor Day) 20 mi S on US 45W, in Rutherford. Phone 901/665-7166. ¢

Annual Event

Davy Crockett Days. Parade, arts & crafts. Phone 901/665-7253. Last wk Sept-first wk Oct.

Index

Establishment names are listed in alphabetical order followed by a symbol identfying their classification, and then city, state and page number. Establishments affiliated with a chain appear alphabetically under their chain name, followed by the state, city and page number. The symbols for classification are: [H] for hotel; [I] for inns; [M] for motels; [L] for lodges; [MH for motor hotels; [R] for restaurants; [RO for resorts, guest ranches, and cottage colonies; [U] for unrated dining spots.

Notes

Notes

M●bil
Travel
Guide

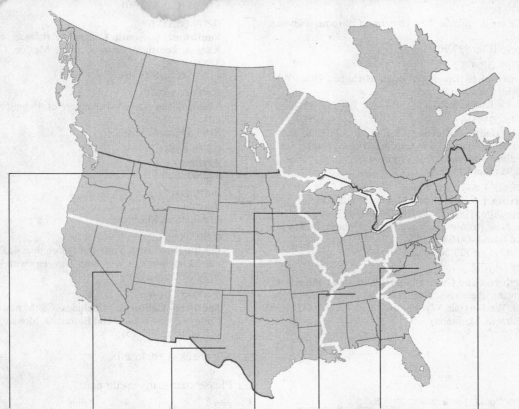

**Northwest &
Great Plains**

Idaho
Iowa
Minnesota
Montana
Nebraska
North Dakota
Oregon
South Dakota
Washington
Wyoming

Canada:
Alberta
British Columbia
Manitoba

**California
& the West**

Arizona
California
Nevada
Utah

**Southwest &
South Central**

Arkansas
Colorado
Kansas
Louisiana
Missouri
New Mexico
Oklahoma
Texas

**Great
Lakes**

Illinois
Indiana
Michigan
Ohio
Wisconsin

Canada:
Ontario

Southeast

Alabama
Florida
Georgia
Kentucky
Mississippi
Tennessee

Mid–Atlantic

Delaware
District of Columbia
Maryland
New Jersey
North Carolina
Pennsylvania
South Carolina
Virginia
West Virginia

Northeast

Connecticut
Maine
Massachusetts
New Hampshire
New York
Rhode Island
Vermont

Canada:
New Brunswick
Nova Scotia
Ontario
Prince Edward Island
Quebec

Mobil Travel Guide

Looking for the Mobil Guides . . . ?

**Call toll-free 800/533-6478 around the clock
or use the order form below.**

Please check the guides you would like to order:

☐ 0-679-00190-5
America's Best Hotels & Restaurants
$12.00 (Can $16.95)

☐ 0-679-00191-3
California and the West (Arizona, California, Nevada, Utah)
$16.95 (Can $23.50)

☐ 0-679-00194-8
Great Lakes (Illinois, Indiana, Michigan, Ohio, Wisconsin, Canada: Ontario)
$16.95 (Can $23.50)

☐ 0-679-00195-6
Mid-Atlantic (Delaware, District of Columbia, Maryland, New Jersey, North Carolina, Pennsylvania, South Carolina, Virginia, West Virginia)
$16.95 (Can $23.50)

☐ 0-679-00196-4
Northeast (Connecticut, Maine, Massachusetts, New Hampshire, New York, Rhode Island, Vermont, Canada: New Brunswick, Nova Scotia, Ontario, Prince Edward Island, Québec)
$16.95 (Can $23.50)

☐ 0-679-00198-0
Northwest and Great Plains (Idaho, Iowa, Minnesota, Montana, Nebraska, North Dakota, Oregon, South Dakota, Washington, Wyoming, Canada: Alberta, British Columbia, Manitoba)
$16.95 (Can $23.50)

☐ 0-679-00199-9
Southeast (Alabama, Florida, Georgia, Kentucky, Mississippi, Tennessee)
$16.95 (Can $23.50)

☐ 0-679-00200-6
Southwest & South Central (Arkansas, Colorado, Kansas, Louisiana, Missouri, New Mexico, Oklahoma, Texas)
$16.95 (Can $23.50)

☐ 0-679-00193-X
Major Cities (Detailed coverage of 45 major U.S. cities)
$18.95 (Can $26.50)

☐ 0-679-00241-3
Arizona
$12.00 (Can $16.95)

☐ 0-679-00192-1
Florida
$13.00 (Can $17.95)

☐ 0-679-00197-2
On the Road with Your Pet (More than 4,000 Mobil-rated Lodgings that Welcome Travelers with Pets)
$15.00 (Can $21.00)

☐ 0-679-00201-4
Southern California (Includes California south of Lompoc, with Tijuana and Ensenada, Mexico)
$13.00 (Can $17.95)

☐ My check is enclosed.

☐ Please charge my credit card

☐ VISA ☐ MasterCard ☐ American Express

Credit Card # _____

Expiration _____

Signature _____

Total cost of book(s) ordered $ _____

Shipping & Handling (please add $2 for first book, $.50 for each additional book) $ _____

Add applicable sales tax (In Canada and in CA, CT, FL, IL, NJ, NY, TN and WA.) $ _____

TOTAL AMOUNT ENCLOSED $ _____

Please ship the books checked above to:

Name _____

Address _____

City _____ State _____ Zip _____

Please mail this form to: Mobil Travel Guides, Random House, 400 Hahn Rd., Westminster, MD 21157